INN PLACES® 1995

Gay & lesbian and gay-friendly accommodations worldwide.

PUBLISHED BY	Ferrari International Publishing, Inc. PO Box 37887 Phoenix, AZ 85069 USA (602) 863-2408 Fax number available on request.
EDITOR & PUBLISHER	Marianne Ferrari

ISBN NUMBER	ISBN 0-942586-49-2

Printed in USA

MEMBER Australian Gay & Lesbian Travel Association & International Gay Travel Association

ON THE COVER

1995 Featured Inn
The White House Hotel
South Devon, England
see pages 2 and 89

ON THE COVER

1995 Featured Inn

The White House
At Chillington
South Devon, England

Fulfilling one's fondest images of what is picturesque, Devon, England is a bucolic land of impossibly green rolling hills, pastures where sheep wander in thick grass, and quiet villages which define the origins of the word "quaint."

In one such South Devon village, just a stone's throw from the sea, you can experience the tranquility of one of the most beautiful corners of coastal England by staying at *The White House Hotel*. In this august stone house with terraced gardens and an acre of manicured lawn, two English gentlemen, David and Michael, invite you to spend a few quiet days with good food and wine and personal, but unobtrusive service.

All rooms have ensuite bathrooms and color television. The bar, created from the old stone wall of the original house, is well stocked. David's much-praised cooking is featured in the Green Room restaurant, as is his extensive and carefully-chosen wine list.

CONTENTS

CONTENTS
Index by Country

HOW TO USE THIS GUIDE

How it is Organized

This book is organized into the following geographical areas: Africa, Asia, Europe, Pacific Region, Canada, Caribbean, Latin America and United States. Each area is organized alphabetically by country and, within each country, alphabetically by state (or province) and city, or just by city.

SAMPLE LISTING

Gay Orientation & Gender

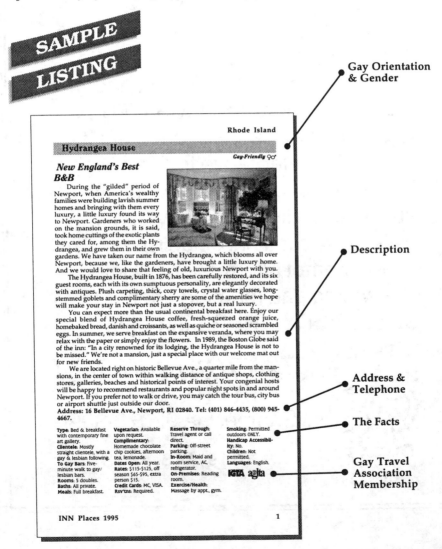

Rhode Island

Hydrangea House

Gay-Friendly ♀♂

New England's Best B&B

During the "gilded" period of Newport, when America's wealthy families were building lavish summer homes and bringing with them every luxury, a little luxury found its way to Newport. Gardeners who worked on the mansion grounds, it is said, took home cuttings of the exotic plants they cared for, among them the Hydrangea, and grew them in their own gardens. We have taken our name from the Hydrangea, which blooms all over Newport, because we, like the gardeners, have brought a little luxury home. And we would love to share that feeling of old, luxurious Newport with you.

The Hydrangea House, built in 1876, has been carefully restored, and its six guest rooms, each with its own sumptuous personality, are elegantly decorated with antiques. Plush carpeting, thick, cozy towels, crystal water glasses, long-stemmed goblets and complimentary sherry are some of the amenities we hope will make your stay in Newport not just a stopover, but a real luxury.

You can expect more than the usual continental breakfast here. Enjoy our special blend of Hydrangea House coffee, fresh-squeezed orange juice, homebaked bread, danish and croissants, as well as quiche or seasoned scrambled eggs. In summer, we serve breakfast on the expansive veranda, where you may relax with the paper or simply enjoy the flowers. In 1989, the Boston Globe said of the inn: "In a city renowned for its lodging, the Hydrangea House is not to be missed." We're not a mansion, just a special place with our welcome mat out for new friends.

We are located right on historic Bellevue Ave., a quarter mile from the mansions, in the center of town within walking distance of antique shops, clothing stores, galleries, beaches and historical points of interest. Your congenial hosts will be happy to recommend restaurants and popular night spots in and around Newport. If you prefer not to walk or drive, you may catch the tour bus, city bus or airport shuttle just outside our door.
Address: 16 Bellevue Ave., Newport, RI 02840. Tel: (401) 846-4435, (800) 945-4667.

Description

Address & Telephone

The Facts

Type: Bed & breakfast with contemporary fine art gallery.
Clientele: Mostly straight clientele, with a gay & lesbian following.
To Gay Bars: Five-minute walk to gay/lesbian bars.
Rooms: 5 doubles.
Baths: All private.
Meals: Full breakfast.

Vegetarian: Available upon request.
Complimentary: Homemade chocolate chip cookies, afternoon tea, lemonade.
Dates Open: All year.
Rates: $115-$125, off season $65-$95, extra person $15.
Credit Cards: MC, VISA.
Rsv'tns: Required.

Reserve Through: Travel agent or call direct.
Parking: Off-street parking.
In-Room: Maid and room service, AC, refrigerator.
On-Premises: Reading room.
Exercise/Health: Massage by appt., gym.

Smoking: Permitted outdoors ONLY.
Handicap Accessibility: No.
Children: Not permitted.
Languages: English.

IGTA aglta

Gay Travel Association Membership

INN Places 1995

1

Type of Accommodations

The American Hotel and Motel Association is in the process of establishing exact definitions for the various types of accommodations. B&B Homestead is now the official term for bed and breakfast in a private home. B&B Inn is a professional business providing accommodations to the public, even if the owner lives on the premises. Country Inn offers accommodations and a full-service restaurant accessible only by automobile.

INN Places® continues to honor the terminology chosen by each innkeeper, while encouraging adoption of these standardized definitions.

Gay Orientation & Gender

At the top right corner of each listing is the answer to the perennial first question, "How gay is it and is it for men or women?" The range of possible answers is given below. In describing clientele, these answers employ both words and the symbols for male ♂ and female ♀.

Men ♂	Gay male clientele
Women ♀	Female clientele
Gay/Lesbian ♂	Mostly gay men
Gay/Lesbian ♀	Mostly gay women
Gay/Lesbian ♀♂	Gay men & women about 50/50
Gay-Friendly ♀♂	Mostly straight (non-gay) clientele with a gay and lesbian following, or a place that welcomes gay & lesbian customers
Gay-Friendly ♀	Mostly straight (non-gay) clientele with a gay female following
Gay-Friendly ♂	Mostly straight (non-gay) clientele with a gay male following
Gay-Friendly 50/50	Half gay and half straight (Symbols indicate gay male ♂ or lesbian ♀ predominance)

Member AGLTA & IGTA

Many accommodations, as well as travel agents, now belong to one of two international gay and lesbian travel associations. AGLTA is the Australian Gay & Lesbian Travel Association. IGTA is the International Gay Travel Association. Membership in these organizations is indicated by the AGLTA or IGTA logo in the body of the listing or by the phrase "Member AGLTA/IGTA."

Description

A description of the inn's architecture, ambiance, decor, amenities and services helps you to decide which inn to choose. Information is frequently also given on local activities.

All the Facts

Up to 32 facts may be included in a given listing. Variations in the length of listings are determined by the amount of information supplied to us by each establishment.

How to Use This Guide

Type
Defines the kind of establishment (bed & breakfast, hotel, resort, etc.), and indicates whether a restaurant, bar or shops are on the premises.

Clientele
A more specific and detailed description than provided in the gay orientation & gender line.

Transportation
Tells you if airport/bus pickup is provided and if not, the best mode of transport is indicated.

To Gay Bars
The distance from your lodgings to the nearest gay or lesbian bar(s).

Rooms
The number and kind of rooms provided. A suite is an accommodation with more than one room. A cottage or cabin is an accommodation in a freestanding building. A bunkroom is a large room in which beds can be rented singly at a reduced rate. Bed sizes are also indicated.

Bathrooms
The actual number of private bathrooms and shared bathrooms. By comparing these to the total number of rooms, guests can anticipate both the potential availability of private baths and the number of people assigned to each shared bathroom.

Campsites
The number and kind of sites provided. Full RV hookups have both electric and sewer unless otherwise noted.

Meals
Describes meals included with room rate and those available at extra charge. Full breakfast includes meat, eggs and breads with coffee, tea, etc. Continental breakfast consists of breads & jams with coffee, tea, etc.

Vegetarian Food
Availability indicated.

Complimentary
Any complimentary foods, beverages or amenities.

Dates Open
Actual dates, if not open all year.

High Season
Annual season of high occupancy rate.

Rates
Range of rates, lowest to highest.

Discounts
Amounts and conditions.

Credit Cards
Lists cards accepted (MC=Master Card, Amex=American Express). Access is MC in Europe. Bancard is British.

Reservations
Tells if required and how far in advance.

Reserve Through
How to make reservations.

Minimum Stay
If required, indicates how long.

Parking
Availability and type.

In-Room
Facilities, such as TV, phone, air conditioning, etc., provided INSIDE your room.

On-Premises
Facilities not provided inside your room, but available on the premises.

Exercise/Health
Availability of facilities such as hot tub, gym, sauna, steam, massage, weights.

Swimming
Availability, type, location.

Sunbathing
Areas described.

Nudity
Indicates if permitted and where.

Smoking
Restrictions, if any, are noted and availability of non-smokers' rooms is indicated.

Pets
Restrictions described.

Handicap Access
Yes or no and limitations described.

Children
Preferences described.

Languages
All languages spoken by staff (first language listed is *always* the native language of the country).

Your host
Name(s) of innkeeper(s).

Staying at a B&B: *The Inn Things to Do*

By Chris Brandmeir, Innkeeper
The Inn at Swifts Bay, Lopez Island, Washington

If you've never stayed in a bed and breakfast inn before, here are a few thoughts to help in your planning. Many B&Bs are large homes converted to public inns because the house's charm, size, geographic location, or a combination of all three, make it suited to welcoming the traveling public. What you probably *won't* find are large wing additions, elevators, large check-in desks in the lobby, TV's and phones in each room, room service or a porter to carry your bags. However, the feel and comfort of the B&B or inn is maintained and often enhanced with niceties and amenities *not* found in institutional hotels or motels. Innkeepers encourage guests to take advantage of all the comforts and amenities provided.

Bed and breakfast inns provide private and very individually decorated quarters for their guests and usually common areas for the use of all guests at the inn. Innkeepers can be a great resource on the area you are visiting, and are available to assist you with whatever your particular needs might be, be it sightseeing tours or diet restrictions, since many B&Bs serve breakfast as part of the room rate. Any allergies (cats, dogs, goose down quilts) are very important items to mention in advance also.

Often, the inn's owner will be your personal host throughout your stay. As such, it is helpful to ask at the time you make your reservation if there are particular check-in and check-out times. Most B&B inns do not have 24-hour check-in staff, so, if your travels delay you, call to arrange check-in, if that is possible. Some inns have both shared baths and private baths, and rates vary accordingly. Some allow children, pets or smoking, however many do not. Most require advance reservations and have a cancellation policy.

Many people travel to B&Bs for their individuality, the opportunity to interact with fellow travelers, and for the more home-like feeling. Each bed and breakfast is different, depending on the character of each innkeeper, so policies are different. If you book a B&B through a travel agent, be sure to provide the agent with any special needs or requests and to have the agent provide you with the needed check-in and cancellation information, plus any special details you should know in advance.

Some B&Bs listed in *Inn Places* only accept gay men, lesbians, both, or are open to everyone, gay and straight, alike. The listing information will let you know this, and you can always ask the innkeeper, or ask him or her anything else, for that matter. They are there to make sure that your stay is as comfortable and pleasant as possible. Enjoy!

Chris Brandmeir and his partner, Robert Herrmann, operate the nationally-acclaimed **Inn at Swifts Bay** *on Lopez Island, Washington.*

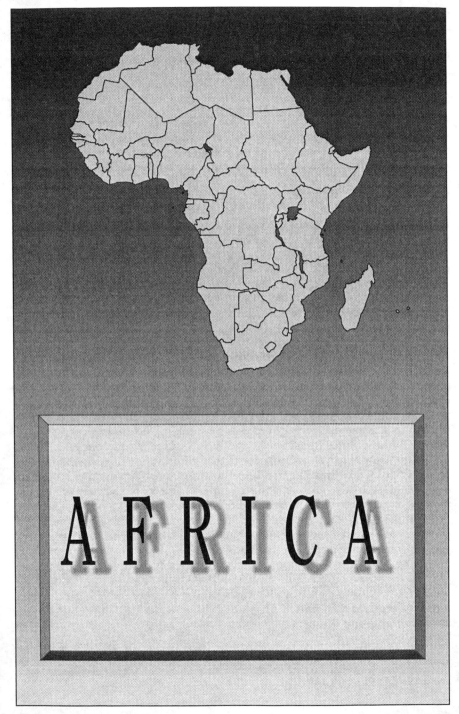

SOUTH AFRICA

JOHANNESBURG

Joel House

A Special Retreat in the Heart of the City

Joel House (AD 1912) is a delightful original Johannesburg home, restored to offer luxury accommodation in tranquil surroundings, right on the doorstep of all that matters in Johannesburg. Five individually-decorated en suite rooms (some with fireplaces) are served by an elegant drawing room, dining room, library, and a delightful English country garden. A splendid grand piano is provided for guests who enjoy playing, and personal service is of the highest degree. Tours of Johannesburg are also available on request. Welcome to a special retreat in the heart of the city!

Address: 61 Joel Rd nr Lily Rd, Berea 2198 Johannesburg South Africa. Tel: (27-11) 642-4426, Fax: (27-11) 642-5221.

Type: Full-service guesthouse with Rajah Room restaurant (formal dining).
Clientele: Mostly straight clientele with a gay & lesbian following.
Transportation: Airport bus or taxi. Free pick up from train station, R60 for airport pick up.
To Gay Bars: Gotham City 5 blks, Connections 7 blks. Champions, La Copa bistro 5-min drive.
Rooms: 5 rooms with twin, double, queen or king beds.
Bathrooms: All private.
Meals: Full breakfast with other meals available upon request.
Vegetarian: Available upon request.
Complimentary: Tea, coffee, juice, soda on arrival. Coffee, tea in library. Turn down sweets, chocolates.
Dates Open: All year.
High Season: September thru March.
Rates: R 170-190 per night singles, R 250-280 per night doubles, breakfast included.
Discounts: Group rate for entire house 15%.
Credit Cards: MC, VISA, Diners.
Rsv'tns: Required.
Reserve Through: Travel agent or call direct.
Parking: Free off-street secure parking limited to 5 automobiles.
In-Room: Ceiling fans, telephone, maid, room & laundry service. Oil radiators in winter.
On-Premises: TV lounge & meeting rooms. Glorious garden with fountain & pond for outdoor dining.
Exercise/Health: Walk our 2 German Pointer dogs. Private tennis courts nearby.
Swimming: 5 minutes to public swimming pool.
Sunbathing: In the garden.
Smoking: Permitted without restriction.
Pets: 2 cats & 2 dogs in residence, not necessary to bring your own.
Handicap Access: Yes. Only two steps to climb.
Children: Permitted over 14 years of age. Free if sharing with parents.
Languages: English, Afrikaans, some German, Zulu.
Your Host: Mark.

Africa continued next page

PIKETBERG

Noupoort Guest Farm

Gay-Friendly ♀♂

Noupoort Guest Farm is only 1-1/2 hours drive from Cape Town on the western slopes of the Piketberg mountains, a little known paradise set amongst spectacular rock formations. If you can appreciate crisp mountain air, scenic walks in unspoilt splendor, wholesome country fare, outdoor activity, star-filled skies, and an open hearth in the evenings, make *Noupoort Guest Farm* your country getaway. It is ideal for that relaxing break you deserve, whether you choose to be indulged and catered for, or simply prefer to self-cater in the privacy of your own country cottage.

Address: PO Box 101, Piketberg 7320 South Africa Tel: 0261-5754, Fax: 0261-5834.

Type: Guest farm with self-catering cottages.
Clientele: Mostly hetero clientele with a gay & lesbian following. Gay weekends are arranged.
Transportation: Car is best. Daily bus service from Cape Town to Piketberg. Nominal charge for pick up at Piketberg.
Rooms: 10 self-catering cottages with single or queen beds.
Bathrooms: All private.
Vegetarian: Available with prior notice.
Dates Open: All year.
Rates: From R130 per cottage per night.
Discounts: Group bookings.
Credit Cards: MC, VISA & Diners.
Rsv'tns: Required.
Reserve Through: Call direct.
Parking: Ample free off-street parking.
In-Room: Dining room, fireplace, kitchen, refrigerator, coffee/tea-making facilities & private braai.
On-Premises: Conference room with flipcharts, projector, VCR & monitor, TV lounge. BBQ & sun deck.
Exercise/Health: Sauna & basic work-out gym, Jacuzzi & weights.
Swimming: Pool on premises.
Sunbathing: At poolside, on patio & common sun decks.
Nudity: Permitted on special weekends.
Pets: Not permitted.
Children: No children under 12 years of age.
Languages: English, Afrikaans, Xhosa.
Your Host: Brent.

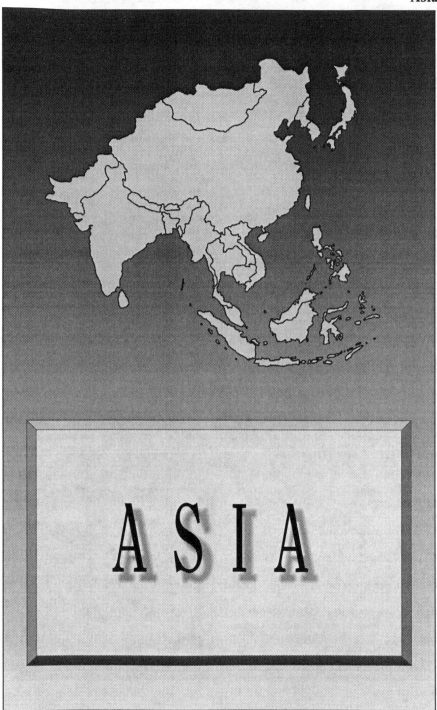

ASIA

THAILAND

BANGKOK

Aquarius, The

Men ♂

When you come to Bangkok, choose *The Aquarius*, the elegant accommodations that are traditionally Thai-West. Comfortable surroundings are enhanced by air conditioning, television and laundry service. Transport and tours are also provided. Our spacious gardens and extensive snack menu and bar provide comfortable, peaceful and beautiful surroundings for gay men in the heart of the world's most free and liberal city.

Address: 243 Hutayana, Soi Suanphlu, South Satorn Rd, Bangkok 10120 Thailand. Phone & Fax: (66-2) 286-0217 or (66-2) 286-2174.

Type: Thai house with restaurant & bar.
Clientele: Mostly men with women welcome, some hetero clientele.
Transportation: Pick up from airport 380 Baht, bus & train station 200 Baht.
To Gay Bars: 2 blocks or 10 min walk.
Rooms: 12 doubles.
Bathrooms: All private.
Vegetarian: Available upon request.

Dates Open: All year.
High Season: October 1-April 30.
Rates: 750 Baht.
Discounts: 5% for 7 days or more, 10% for 30 days or more.
Rsv'tns: Preferred.
Reserve Through: Call direct.
Parking: Limited off-street parking, some covered.
In-Room: AC, telephone, room & laundry service,

some rooms with color TV, ceiling fans, refrigerators.
On-Premises: TV lounge, laundry facilities, non-smokers lounge, large garden with seating.
Exercise/Health: Massage in house, 5 min walk to gym with weights, Jacuzzi, sauna, steam.
Swimming: 2 nearby pools; 5 min & 8 min walk.

Sunbathing: At poolside, on patio, private & common sun decks.
Smoking: Permitted, non-smoking areas & non-smoking rooms available.
Pets: Permitted with prior arrangement.
Handicap Access: Yes. Staff assistance available.
Children: Not permitted.
Languages: Thai, English.
Your Host: Vichai.

CHIANG MAI

Coffee Boy Cottages

Men ♂

The *Coffee Boy*, widely regarded as Thailand's leading gay bar, also provides luxury cottages individually designed in Lanna style and set in lush, tropical surroundings. The cottages are situated 1 km from the centre of the ancient city of Chiang Mai. The staff are able to recommend reputable, local tour operators and guides, travel agents, retail outlets and car, motorbike or bicycle rentals. The adjacent *Coffee Boy Bar*, a 70-year-old, traditional solid teak building set in lush, tropical gardens, where the new cottages have been built, is open daily from 8:30pm-1:00am, with a nightly Go-Go Boy Show and a spectacular cabaret show on Fri., Sat. and Sun. The ambiance of the bar is typically Thai, with quiet background music in a traditional setting. Over 50 charming

young men ensure that the guests' needs are fully cared for.

Chiang Mai, which means New City, was founded in 1926. The old city is surrounded by moats, and parts of the old wall still exist. Over 300 temples dominate the skyline. The city is accessible from all parts of Thailand by bus, train or air and has all the cultural advantages of Bangkok, but is small enough to explore on foot and has no traffic jams or air pollution. It is noted for its temperate climate, low humidity and cool nights. Numerous attractions, such as Hill Tribe villages, dot the surrounding area, and the Golden Triangle is a short distance away. Trekking in the hills is popular. Elephants are still widely used in the jungle. A highlight of your trip may be a visit to the Elephant Training Camp or an elephant safari. Thailand's highest peak is also nearby. The flora and fauna, spectacular waterfalls, hot geysers, ancient temples and archaeological sites will give an everlasting impression of Thailand's beauty.

Great restaurants offer a range of cuisines, including Thai, Chinese, Burmese, vegetarian and Western. After dinner, many visitors head for the Night Bazaar, where you can hone your bargaining skills. Chiang Mai has six gay men's bars, including our famous Coffee Boy Bar, so there is a remarkable choice of delightful, young men to entertain the visitor. There is also a large number of discos, at which gay people are very welcome.

Address: 248 Toong Hotel Rd, Chiang Mai 50000 Thailand. Tel: (66) 53 247021 (also fax), bar tel: (66) 53 244 458.

Type: Luxury cottages. **Clientele:** Men. **Transportation:** Free pick up from airport or train. **To Gay Bars:** Coffee Boy gay bar is adjacent, 5 other gay bars nearby. **Rooms:** 9 rooms & 4 luxury cottages. **Bathrooms:** All private baths with showers, basins, western-style toilets. **Meals:** Full American breakfast. **Complimentary:** Cold drinks, light snacks all day. **Dates Open:** All year. **High Season:** October-February. **Rates:** From 500-1000 Baht per night (US $20-$40). **Discounts:** 15% during off season. **Credit Cards:** MC & VISA. **Rsv'tns:** Preferred, with 30 day advance deposit. **Reserve Through:** Travel agent or call direct. **Parking:** Ample free off-street parking. **In-Room:** AC, sitting room, refrigerator, teak furniture & fittings reflecting North Thailand's architectural heritage in luxury cottages. AC, ceiling fans, refrigerator, maid & laundry service. **On-Premises:** Tropical gardens, water-lily pond, private entrance to Coffee Boy Bar. **Sunbathing:** On the patio. **Smoking:** No restrictions. **Languages:** Thai, English. **Your Host:** Narong.

PATTAYA

Le Cafe Royale Hotel

Gay/Lesbian ♂

An Oasis in the Mayhem of Pattaya's Nightlife

Le Cafe Royale Hotel is situated in the very heart of Pattaya's gay night life. The beach is just 100 metres from the hotel and Pattaya's premier gay beach is only a short taxi drive away. As a holiday center Pattaya has many avenues of entertainment to explore, from Go-Go bars, cabaret shows, discos and restaurants to sporting activities, beaches, islands and sightseeing tours.

Le Cafe Royale Hotel has recently been refurbished and decorated, offering guests comfortable, standard and superior rooms. All rooms have en suite shower rooms, air conditioning, mini bars and satellite TV with an in-house movie channel. We also offer 24-hour room service. Our piano bar and restaurant feature live piano music performed by resident and guest musicians.

Address: 325/102-5 Pattaya Land Soi 3, South Pattaya 20260 Thailand. Tel: (038) 423 515 or 428 303, Fax: (038) 424 579.

continued next page

Thailand

Type: Hotel with sidewalk cafe and bar.
Clientele: Mostly men with women welcome.
Transportation: Car is best. 2 hours from airport in Bangkok, 1,200 Bahts.
To Gay Bars: Piano bar on premises, close to 7 other gay bars (within 100 metres).

Rooms: 18 rooms & 2 suites with queen beds.
Bathrooms: All private toilet/showers.
Complimentary: Drink upon check-in.
Dates Open: All year.
Rates: Rooms from 600.00 Bahts/night.
Credit Cards: MC, VISA, Amex, Diners.
Rsv'tns: Required.

Reserve Through: Call direct.
Parking: Adequate, free on-street parking.
In-Room: Color TV, AC, maid, room, & laundry service, telephones, refrigerator, hot & cold water.
On-Premises: TV lounge.
Exercise/Health: Nearby gym, weights, sauna,

steam & massage.
Swimming: 10 minutes to gay beach.
Sunbathing: On beach.
Smoking: Permitted without restrictions.
Pets: Not permitted.
Handicap Access: No.
Children: Not permitted.
Languages: Thai, English, German, Dutch.

PHUKET

Home Sweet Home Guest House & Pow-Wow Pub and Restaurant

Gay/Lesbian ♂

Step Out of YOUR World and Into...OURS!

A place which defies description, *Home Sweet Home Guesthouse and Pow-Wow Pub & Restaurant* is a pub with live country, pop & Thai music; a restaurant with modestly priced, delectable Thai and European cuisine; an American Indian jewelry store, with authentic hand-made necklaces, bracelets and rings, right off the reservations; a museum with teak furnishings and Thai and Burmese antique artifacts, and it's a cozy, quaint, spacious guesthouse with eight colorfully and uniquely furnished suites and double rooms. Remember: Buddha, God and this "Good Fairy" have blessed this fantasyland. 10% off bill with this ad.
Address: 70/179-180 Paradise Complex, Moo 3, Ratuthit Rd, Patong Beach, Phuket 83150 Thailand. Tel: (6676) 340 756, Fax: (6676) 340 757.

Type: Guesthouse with restaurant, bar & American Indian jewelry store.
Clientele: Mostly men with women welcome in guesthouse. 50% gay & lesbian in bar & restaurant.
Transportation: Arrange for airport/bus pick up by staff. Van or taxi ($16 per car/van load) to Royal Paradise Hotel in Patong Beach.
To Gay Bars: All but 1 of more than 15 gay establishments are about a 1-minute walk.

Rooms: 3 rooms & 5 suites with king beds.
Bathrooms: 5 private shower/toilets & 3 private bath/shower/toilets.
Vegetarian: 75% of restaurant menu is Thai food. Many vegetarian dishes available.
Complimentary: Condoms on your pillow (US or European made).
Dates Open: All year.
High Season: November thru April.
Rates: Low season (May-Oct) $20-$32. High season (Nov-Apr) $32-$60.

Discounts: For stays over 1 week. 10% discount with this ad.
Credit Cards: MC & VISA.
Rsv'tns: Recommended during high season. Walk-ins accepted depending on availability.
Reserve Through: Call direct.
Parking: Ample off-street parking.
In-Room: Color TV, AC, refrigerator, telephone, room, maid & laundry service. VCR rental available.
On-Premises: TV lounge.

Video tape library in lobby.
Exercise/Health: Massage on request.
Swimming: 1 block to ocean.
Sunbathing: At the beach.
Smoking: Permitted.
Pets: Not permitted.
Handicap Access: No.
Children: Not permitted.
Languages: Thai, English.
Your Host: Chairat.

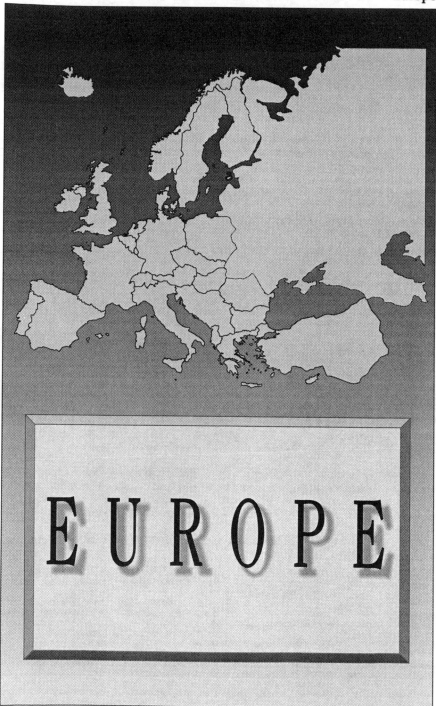

EUROPE

AUSTRIA

VIENNA

Hotel Urania

Gay/Lesbian ♀♂

Hotel Urania is conveniently situated in Vienna's city center, close to the city's many museums, shops, restaurants and cafés. Although a low-priced tourist hotel, amenities include private baths, telephone and radio in each room and either an expanded continental or full breakfast. The hotel also offers meeting rooms for groups up to 50 people, a television lounge, elevator and the restaurant, Pizzeria Esposito.

Address: Obere Weissgerberstrasse 7, 1030 Wien, Austria. Tel: (43) (1) 713 17 11, Fax: (43) (1) 713 56 94.

Type: Hotel with restaurant & bar
Clientele: Mostly gay & lesbian with some hetero clientele.
To Gay Bars: 5 blocks. 10-minute walk or 3-minute drive.

Rooms: 38 rooms with single or double beds.
Bathrooms: All private.
Meals: Expanded continental or full breakfast.
Dates Open: All year.
Rates: Double ATS 890, single ATS 340-650.

Credit Cards: VISA & Amex.
Rsv'tns: Required.
Parking: Free off-street parking.
In-Room: Telephone, room & maid service.
On-Premises: Meeting

rooms, TV lounge & bar.
Pets: Permitted.
Handicap Access: No.
Children: Not especially welcome.
Languages: German, some English.

BELGIUM

ANTWERP

Room With A View

Women ♀

Women now travel through an unbound Europe, meeting with each other by the merest chance. We thought it would be nice to lend chance a hand. *Room With A View* is a project offering bed and breakfast facilities in and around Antwerp, as an alternative to the usual hotel circuit. Please be sure to book at least one month in advance.

Address: c/o F Wouters, Vlaamse Kunstlaan 16, B-2020 Antwerpen Belgium. Tel: (32-3) 238 21 96.

Type: Bed & breakfast.
Clientele: Women only.
Transportation: Free pick up from airport, bus or train.
To Gay Bars: 10 mm to the city & several gay bars.
Rooms: 5 rooms with double beds.
Bathrooms: 3 en suite bath/toilets & 2 en suite shower/toilets.

Meals: Continental breakfast.
Vegetarian: Several vegetarian restaurants in town.
Complimentary: Tea & coffee.
Dates Open: All year.
High Season: July & August.
Rates: BF 750 all year.
Rsv'tns: Required.
Reserve Through: Call

direct.
Parking: Free on-street parking.
In-Room: Telephone, coffee & tea-making facilities & room service.
On-Premises: Meeting rooms.
Exercise/Health: Nearby gym & sauna.
Swimming: Nearby pool & river. 150km to ocean.
Sunbathing: At the

beach & nearby parks.
Smoking: Not permitted.
Pets: Not permitted.
Handicap Access: No.
Children: Welcome under 12 years old.
Languages: Dutch, French, English & a little Spanish.
Your Host: Françoise, Hilde, Lut & Nicole.

BRUGGE

Huize Heksentros Vrouwengasthof

A Woman's Oasis

Women ♀

Huize Heksentros is a women-only oasis for rest and relaxation. We are located just 1.5 km from the center of Brugge. Also known as the Venice of the north, Brugge is a picturesque medieval village. Other nearby cities of interest to visit are Oostende (20 km), Gent (40 km), Bruxelles (100 km) and Antwerp. There is a tandem bicycle available for our guests' use in exploring the small villages and enjoying the natural surroundings of our area.

Address: Leopold II laan 92, 8000 Brugge Belgium. Tel: (050) 330-602.

Type: Bed & breakfast. **Clientele:** Women only with some hetero clientele. **Transportation:** Car, train or bus. Free pick up from train, bus or ferry dock. **To Gay Bars:** 2 miles (15-minute walk). **Rooms:** 1 room with double beds. **Bathrooms:** Shared bath/shower/toilet, private WC & private sink. **Meals:** Expanded continental breakfast. **Vegetarian:** Always. **Complimentary:** Alcoholic & non-alcoholic drinks, tea & coffee. **Dates Open:** All year. **High Season:** Easter, Christmas, July & August. **Rates:** BF 800.00 per person per night (includes breakfast). **Discounts:** Please inquire. **Credit Cards:** Eurocard. **Rsv'tns:** Required by telephone. **Reserve Through:** Call direct. **Parking:** Limited on-street parking. **In-Room:** Kitchen, refrigerator, coffee & tea-making facilities & room service. **On-Premises:** Bicycles, videos. **Exercise/Health:** Massage. **Swimming:** At pool 1 km away, at seaside 12 km away. **Sunbathing:** On the beach or in our garden. **Nudity:** Permitted. **Smoking:** Permitted. **Pets:** Not permitted. **Handicap Access:** No. **Children:** Females permitted, males to age 12. **Languages:** Dutch, German, English, French.

CZECH REPUBLIC

PRAGUE

Prague Home Stay

Gay/Lesbian ♀♂

Prague Home Stay offers inexpensive rooms, not only at the above address, but even in a number of other rooms in the homes of our friends, members of Lambda Prague. Our own rooms provide quiet rest in a residential area, within easy 24-hour reach by tram of all parts of the city. The city, itself, is miraculous, with impressive architecture and historical monuments, hidden beauties and even ghosts. Your hosts will take the time to talk with guests and help them get to know this fascinating city.

Address: Pod Kotlárkou 14, 150 00 Prague 5 Czech Republic. Tel: (42 2) 527 388.

Type: Lodging & kitchen privileges in a private home. **Clientele:** Mostly gay & lesbian with some hetero clientele. **Transportation:** Metro B (Yellow Line) to station Andel, then 5 stops by trams No 4,7,9, stop Kotlárka. **To Gay Bars:** 20 minutes by municipal transport or car. **Rooms:** 1 single, 2 doubles with single beds & 1 suite with double bed. **Bathrooms:** 2 rooms share 1 bath. **Dates Open:** All year. **Rates:** USD $18-$30 per person (CZK 565-900). **Rsv'tns:** Required by telephone. **Reserve Through:** Call direct. **Minimum Stay:** 2 nights. **Parking:** Ample on-street parking. Room for 1 car on premises. Lot across the street. **In-Room:** Telephone upon request. **On-Premises:** Kitchen privileges for 2 rooms. **Sunbathing:** At the swimming pool. **Smoking:** Permitted. **Pets:** Not permitted. **Handicap Access:** No. **Children:** Not permitted. **Languages:** Czech, Slovak, English, German, Russian & Polish.

Villa David Hotel

Gay/Lesbian ♀♂

Villa David Hotel is a 1920's bourgeois house built on a slope next to a green hill area. The last owner was a pop singer. The house has been beautifully renovated with many modern features, including a terrace, a garden, a sauna and a restaurant and bar. The staff is friendly, and escort boys are available. All rooms have private baths, telephone, satellite TV and clock radio. The main tourist attractions of Prague can be easily reached by tram.

Address: Holubova 5, 150 00 Praha 5 Czech Republic. Phone & Fax: (42-2) 549820.

Type: Hotel with restaurant, sauna, bar & escorts. **Clientele:** Mostly gay & lesbian with some hetero clientele. **Transportation:** Tram #14 to the Laurová terminal, then 2-minute walk. **To Gay Bars:** On premises. **Rooms:** 6 suites with double beds, additional single beds available. **Bathrooms:** All en suite shower/toilets. **Meals:** Expanded continental breakfast. **Vegetarian:** Available upon request. **Dates Open:** All year. **Rates:** DM 50-DM 70 per person per night or CZK 850-1200. **Rsv'tns:** Recommended. **Reserve Through:** Reservations: call direct or Prague Home Stay (42 2 527388). **Parking:** Ample on-street parking. **In-Room:** Maid service, colour cable TV, telephone. **On-Premises:** Restaurant, bar, terrace & garden. **Exercise/Health:** Sauna. **Swimming:** 10-minute walk to municipal swimming pool. **Sunbathing:** In the garden. **Smoking:** Not permitted. **Pets:** Not permitted. **Handicap Access:** No. **Children:** Not permitted. **Languages:** Czech, German & English.

DENMARK

COPENHAGEN (KOBENHAVN)

Hotel Windsor

Gay-Friendly 50/50 ♀♂

Reasonable Accommodations Near the Central Station

Hotel Windsor offers centrally located and immaculately clean accommodations at prices reasonable for Denmark! You can walk to the gay bars and you can bring back friends, even to breakfast. Certain floors are designated for men only and have a somewhat bath house atmosphere. The hotel is accessed by a stairway, so be prepared to climb steps. We have cable TV in all rooms, and both telephone and fax service are in reception. Our staff is ready to help you with information about sightseeing, of which Tivoli Garden is the most spectacular example, with many restaurants, free shows, and an amusement park.

Address: Frederiksborggade 30, 1360 Kobenhavn K Denmark. Tel: 33 11 08 30, telefax: 33 11 63 87.

Type: Hotel with breakfast-only restaurant. **Clientele:** 75% gay & lesbian in summer, 50% in winter (2nd flr men only). **Transportation:** Airport bus to central station, then bus or taxi. **To Gay Bars:** 5-minute walk to men's bar, 10-minute walk to women's. **Rooms:** 10 singles, 10 doubles, 1 triple, 1 quad, 1 apartment. **Bathrooms:** 4 private, 1 shared bath per floor, sinks in room. **Meals:** Continental breakfast. **Vegetarian:** We can recommend vegetarian restaurant. **Dates Open:** All year. **High Season:** Mid May-early October. **Rates:** Single Dkr 325.00-400.00, double Dkr 450-600. **Credit Cards:** MC, VISA, Access, Eurocard. **Rsv'tns:** Required, especially in high season. **Reserve Through:** Call direct. **Parking:** Ample off-street pay parking, some free on-street after 6 PM. **In-Room:** Maid service, laundry service, cable color TV & refrigerator. **On-Premises:** TV lounge, public telephones. **Swimming:** Public pool nearby, nude beach accessible by train. **Sunbathing:** 2-minute walk to sunbathing area. **Nudity:** Permitted on men-only floor. **Smoking:** Permitted without restrictions. **Pets:** Not permitted. **Handicap Access:** No! Many stairs! **Children:** Permitted. **Languages:** Danish, English, Norwegian, Swedish, German, French, Italian. **Your Host:** John.

SKAGEN

Finns Pension

Gay/Lesbian ♀♂

Finns Pension is a beautiful old wood house decorated in the old style. It's a great place to stay for a holiday in this very special corner of Denmark, the most famous holiday place in the country. Enjoy the sun drenched beaches, lovely scenery, and outstanding local museums. The owner is gay and promotes a relaxed atmosphere for gay people.

Address: Ostre Strandvej 63, DK-9990 Skagen Denmark. Tel: (45) 98 45 01 55.

Type: Hotel with restaurant for guests.
Clientele: Mostly gay & lesbian with some hetero clientele.
Transportation: Car or train is best. Free pick up from train.
Rooms: 5 rooms with single or double beds.
Bathrooms: Sinks in rooms. Shared: 2 full baths, 1 shower & 1 WC.
Meals: Expanded continental breakfast.
Vegetarian: Available if ordered before arrival.
Dates Open: All year.
High Season: May 1-August 31.
Rates: High season: single Dkr 250-350, double Dkr 500-600. Low season: single Dkr 225-275, double Dkr 450-550.
Discounts: High season, 6% 3+ days, 12% 7+ days. Low season, 10% 3+ days, 15% 7+ days. Winter price includes all meals.
Credit Cards: MC, VISA, Eurocard, JGB.
Rsv'tns: Required.
Reserve Through: Call direct.
Parking: Limited free off-street parking.
In-Room: Radio & room service.
On-Premises: Garden, library, lounge, telephone, & laundry facilities.
Exercise/Health: Sauna & small weights.
Swimming: Public pool 1 km. Ocean beach nearby.
Sunbathing: At the beach or in the garden.
Nudity: Permitted at the beach.
Smoking: Permitted. No non-smoking rooms available.
Pets: Permitted.
Handicap Access: No. Stairs to rooms.
Children: Permitted, but maximum of 2.
Languages: Danish, English, German, Swedish.

We Appreciate Your Comments!

The editors of *INN Places*® actively seek your comments about accommodations you have tried.

Positive comments of interest may be included in the next issue, giving future readers the benefit of your experience. And it's a nice way of saying "thank you" to an innkeeper who extended you exceptional hospitality.

See the contents for the Reader Comment Form.

FRANCE

ALSACE

Espace Ballon d'Alsace

Gay-Friendly 50/50 ♀♂

Winter & Summer Sports in Rural France

Espace Ballon d'Alsace was built in 1973 with a modern architectural concept which takes maximum advantage of available sunlight and offers an exceptional setting for its 18th-century furniture.

From its unique position on top of the Ballon d'Alsace (1250 meters) there are panoramic views across the Vosges Mountains, the Black Forest and the Swiss Alps. In the pine forests surrounding the inn are numerous hiking trails and safe-bathing lakes. Tranquility reigns here in the heart of the southern Vosges, yet we are close to both Germany and Switzerland, just 80 km from Bale, 50 km from Mulhouse, and 25 km from Belfort.

The location is ideal for both summer and winter vacationing. Activities in the area include mountain biking, both Alpine and Nordic skiing, bobsledding, horseback riding and hang gliding. In this truly friendly inn, you will discover the delights of traditional home cooking and regional specialties, all carefully prepared by proprietor, Dominique Albert.

Address: La Musardière, 90200 Ballon d'Alsace France. Tel: 84 29 33 22, Fax: 84 23 96 40.

Type: Bed & breakfast guesthouse with restaurant & bar. Hotel (Auberge).
Clientele: 50% gay & lesbian & 50% straight clientele.
Transportation: Car, train or bus. Pick up from train.
To Gay Bars: 25 km to Belfort, 50 km to Mulhouse, 80 km to Bale.
Rooms: 15 rooms, dormitories, with single, double, queen, king &

bunk beds.
Bathrooms: 1 private bath/toilet, 5 private shower/toilets. Other share.
Meals: Continental breakfast & dinner.
Vegetarian: Available upon request.
Dates Open: All year.
Rates: FF 70-100 per person.
Discounts: Group discounts.
Credit Cards: MC, VISA & Eurocard.

Rsv'tns: Required.
Reserve Through: Travel agent or call direct.
Parking: Ample free off-street covered parking in front of Auberge, & garage.
In-Room: Color TV & maid service.
On-Premises: TV lounge, meeting rooms & terrace (panoramic, secluded).
Exercise/Health: Gym, mountain bikes, bobsled, skiing & walking (superb).

Swimming: 2 miles to lake.
Sunbathing: On the patio & in the garden.
Smoking: Permitted without restrictions.
Pets: Not permitted.
Handicap Access: Yes. 3 rooms.
Children: Welcome.
Languages: French, English & German.
Your Host: Dominique & Didier.

BAINS-LES-BAINS

Auberge Chez Dino

Gay-Friendly 50/50 ♀♂

Address: Hautmougey, Bains-les-Bains 88240 France. Tel: (29) 30 41 87.

Type: Hotel with restaurant.
Clientele: 50% gay & lesbian & 50% hetero clientele.
To Gay Bars: 30 km to Epinal.
Rooms: 7 apartments with kitchens.
Bathrooms: All private.

Dates Open: Closed January.
High Season: May-Sept.
Rates: 1 night, with breakfast, for 2 people FF 300. Weekly FF 1650.
Discounts: 10% in winter.
Credit Cards: MC, VISA, Amex, Carte Blanche & Eurocard.

Rsv'tns: Required 1 week in advance.
Reserve Through: Travel agent or call direct.
Parking: Ample off-street parking.
In-Room: Satellite color TV in German, French, English & Italian, kitchen.
Smoking: Permitted

without restrictions. Non-smoking rooms available.
Pets: Additional charge.
Handicap Access: Restaurant. Hotel not accessible.
Children: OK.
Languages: French, English, Spanish, German & Italian.

CANNES

Touring Hotel

Gay-Friendly ♀♂

Located in the heart of Cannes, the *Touring Hotel* is just five minutes from the sea and magnificent beaches of the Côte d'Azur. For your comfort, amenities include private baths, colour TV, direct dial telephones and minibar in every room. There is an elevator and TV lounge on the premises. Our reception staff is always on hand to offer you a warm welcome to our beautiful city.

Address: 11 rue Hoche, 06400 Cannes, France. Tel: 93 38 34 40, Fax: 93 38 73 34.

Type: Hotel.
Clientele: Mostly hetero with a gay & lesbian following.
Transportation: Take bus from airport.
To Gay Bars: 2 minutes.
Rooms: 24 doubles & 6 triples.
Bathrooms: All private.

Meals: Continental breakfast.
Complimentary: Minibars in rooms.
Dates Open: All year.
High Season: April-October.
Rates: Low season USD $50-$65. High season USD $55-$70.

Credit Cards: MC, VISA, Amex & Diners.
Rsv'tns: Required.
Reserve Through: Travel agent or call direct.
Parking: Limited off-street covered pay parking, 50,00 FF per day.
In-Room: Color TV, telephone, refrigerator, maid

& laundry service.
On-Premises: TV lounge.
Sunbathing: On the beach.
Pets: Permitted.
Handicap Access: Yes.
Children: Welcome.
Languages: French, English, German.
Your Host: Didier.

DOMME

La Dordogne Camping de Femmes

Women ♀

For those who have never seen the countryside of France, staying at *La Dordogne Camping de Femmes* is a special experience. In addition to the camaraderie with other women from many countries, you can bicycle or hike through the rolling, green countryside, or explore the fascinating caves and ancient castles nearby. Most accommodations consist of tent sites. There are also three caravans, which can be rented, and a bungalow tent, which is furnished, has a kitchen, etc., and accommodates two people. There are two bars on the premises, one for smokers and one for non-smokers. Wild womyn don't get the blues. They go to a women's campground for Dutch hospitality with a French accent.

Address: St.-Aubin de Nabirat, 24250 Domme France. Tel: (53) 28 50 28.

continued next page

France

Type: Campground.
Clientele: Women only.
Transportation: 8 km from railway station, taxis available.
To Gay Bars: 2 hrs by car to Toulouse.
Campsites: 20 tent sites, 4 electric, 3 caravans (campers), 2 toilets, 2 hot & 1 cold shower, laundry facilities, 2 bars, library.

Vegetarian: Always.
Complimentary: Snack bar on the campground.
Dates Open: May-Sept.
High Season: July & August.
Rates: FF 45.00 per day per woman for tent sites. Caravan with electric, FF 1050 per week for 2 persons.
Rsv'tns: Required.
Reserve Through: Call

direct.
Parking: Off-street private parking.
On-Premises: Meeting rooms, TV lounge, laundry facilities for guests.
Exercise/Health: Tennis, volleyball, pingpong hall, jeu de boule on the premises, nearby canoeing, riding, walking & bicycle trips.
Swimming: At pool on

premises.
Sunbathing: At poolside & tent sites.
Nudity: Topless only.
Smoking: Permitted outdoors & in one of the bars.
Pets: Permitted.
Children: Only girls over 14 years old.
Languages: Dutch, German, French, English.

MAULÉON D'ARMAGNAC

Association Amazones

Women ♀

The women of *Association Amazones* welcome you to their large country home in the Armagnac region of Southern France. Women from all over come here to experience the beauty and tranquility of this area. Activities are many and varied, including tennis, ping-pong, swimming in Lake Barbotan and touring the local countryside. We also get together with other women of the area. It is a scenic 1-1/2 hour drive to the seaside or to the Pyrenees Mountains.

Address: La Thébaïde, 32240 Mauléon d'Armagnac France. Tel: (62) 09 69 55.

Type: Guesthouse & disco with some camping.
Clientele: Women only.
Transportation: Car is best. Train & bus available.
To Gay Bars: 2 hours to Toulouse.
Rooms: 6 rooms with single & double beds.

Bathrooms: 1 shared bath/shower/toilet.
Campsites: Tent sites share indoor bathroom.
Meals: Full breakfast & dinner.
Vegetarian: Available at times.
Dates Open: July & August only.
Rates: Camping & meals

FF 115.00. Home & meals FF 135.00.
Rsv'tns: Required.
Reserve Through: Call direct.
Minimum Stay: 3 days.
Parking: Free on-road parking.
On-Premises: Color TV, telephone, laundry facility, kitchen & refrigerator.

Swimming: At lake 10 km away.
Nudity: Permitted.
Smoking: Permitted.
Pets: Permitted with prior permission.
Children: Not permitted.
Languages: French, English & Italian.

PARIS

Hotel Central Marais

Gay/Lesbian ♂

In the Middle of Everything

Hotel Central Marais is a small, exclusively gay hotel in the Marais, the aristocratic, historic quarter of central Paris. Surrounded by the principal gay bars and restaurants, it is only a 5-minute walk from Notre Dame, La Bastille and Les Halles. The hotel, built in the 17th century, has been carefully restored to enhance the charm of its old-world character, while providing modern conveniences. Accommodations consist of two double-bedded rooms per floor, with a bathroom off the short lobby between. A small, communal salon is available to guests on the first floor. Guests are substantially on their own, with guest services at a minimum. On the ground floor is the famous Belle Epoque bar, *Le Central*, a popular gay rendezvous. We speak English and French. A bientôt - Maurice

NOTE: *Hotel entry with intercom at 2, rue Ste. Croix de la Bretonnerie (corner building).*
Address: 33, rue Vieille-du-Temple (Enter: 2, rue Ste. Croix de la Bretonnerie), 75004 Paris France. Tel: (33) (1) 4887-5608, Fax: 4277-0627.

Type: Hotel above a popular men's bar.
Clientele: Mostly men with women welcome.
Transportation: From: CDG airport Bus Train (RER); Orly airport ORLY VAL (RER) to Chatelet Les Halles Sta, exit Centre Georges Pompidou.
To Gay Bars: On the premises or 12 gay bars within 10 minutes walk.

Rooms: 7 rooms with double beds.
Bathrooms: One shared bath per floor, private bath 5th floor (no lift).
Meals: Continental breakfast 35FF per day.
Dates Open: All year.
High Season: All year.
Rates: FF 400.00-480.00.
Credit Cards: MC, VISA & Eurocard.
Rsv'tns: Required.

Reserve Through: Call direct.
Parking: Parking is difficult. Parking garage under Hotel de Ville.
In-Room: Maid service & telephone.
On-Premises: TV lounge, meeting room & gay bar.
Exercise/Health: Gym, weights, Jacuzzi, sauna, steam & massage all available nearby.

Swimming: Pool nearby.
Sunbathing: By the river.
Smoking: Permitted.
Pets: Not permitted.
Handicap Access: No.
Children: Not permitted.
Languages: French & English.
IGTA

Hotel Louxor

Gay-Friendly 50/50 ♀♂

In a peaceful street, close to the northern and eastern railway stations and a few minutes from the main boulevards, department stores and entertainment centres of Paris, you will find the *Hotel Louxor,* a charming building, constructed at the turn of the century. You'll enjoy your intimate, individualized room and the quiet lounge where breakfast is served. You'll also appreciate the restful surroundings in the reading lounge. Here is a hotel which has not lost the human touch and where you will feel at home.
Address: 4 rue Taylor, Paris 75010, France. Tel: (33-1) 42 08 23 91, Fax: (33-1) 42 08 03 30.

continued next page

France

Type: Hotel.
Clientele: 50% gay & lesbian & 50% hetero clientele.
To Gay Bars: 6 blocks to gay bars or a 10-minute walk.
Rooms: 30 rooms with single or double beds.

Bathrooms: All private shower/toilets.
Meals: Breakfast.
Dates Open: All year except February.
Rates: Not reported for the current year.
Credit Cards: MC, VISA & Eurocard.

Rsv'tns: Required by fax with credit card number as guarantee.
Reserve Through: Travel agent or call direct.
Parking: Off-street parking.
In-Room: Color TV, direct-dial telephone, quiet lounge & reading lounge.

Smoking: Permitted without restrictions in the room. No public smoking sections.
Pets: Permitted.
Handicap Access: No.
Children: Permitted.
Languages: French & English.

Hotel des Batignolles

Gay-Friendly ♀♂

Hôtel des Batignolles is a modest and comfortable hotel where you can let go and relax when you return from a day of sightseeing in Paris. We're 10 minutes from Montmartre, Champs Elysees and the opera and convenient to the metro. The stations at Place de Clichy or Rome are a very short walk from here. On the way to the metro, you will pass many little restaurants and shops, so that any little errand will be easy to handle and you'll never run out of possibilities when choosing a restaurant.
Address: 26-28, rue des Batignolles, 75017 Paris France. Tel: (1) 43 87 70 40, Fax: 44 70 01 04.

Type: Hotel.
Clientele: Mostly straight clientele with a 20% gay & lesbian following.
Transportation: Roissybus to Opera 30 FF per person. Then taxi or metro or Bus 66 (runs till 9pm except Sun), get off Mairie 17 stop.
To Gay Bars: 2 blocks to

gay/lesbian bars.
Rooms: 35 doubles, 5 triples.
Bathrooms: All private.
Meals: Continental breakfast 25FF per person per day.
Dates Open: All year.
High Season: September-October.
Rates: Single or double

FF 310.00-350.00.
Credit Cards: MC, VISA, Amex, Diners, Access.
Rsv'tns: Required 15 days in advance.
Reserve Through: Call direct.
Parking: On-street parking.
In-Room: Color TV, telephone.
On-Premises: Garden.

Exercise/Health: 2 blocks to sauna.
Smoking: Permitted except in breakfast room.
Pets: Not permitted.
Handicap Access: No.
Children: Permitted.
Languages: French, English, Spanish, German, Arabic.

Private Paris Accommodations

Gay/Lesbian ♀♂

Your Home in Paris at a Reasonable Price

Rent a private, bright studio apartment in an 18th century building in the heart of St. Germain des Pres (around the corner from Place Furstemberg and two blocks from Cafe De Flor). The apartment has high-beamed ceilings, parquet floors, modern bath, kitchenette, king bed, convertible double bed sofa, telephone, and cable television in English. It is decorator-designed in a tasteful mix of modern and antique furnishings and accommodates up to four. There is weekly maid service. *Private Paris Accommodations* is the perfect alternative to hotels.
Address: Contact: NY B&B Reservation Center   Tel: In NY: (212) 977-3512, Outside NY: (516) 283-6785.

Type: Private apartment in St. Germain des Pres on Left Bank.
Clientele: Gay & lesbian.
Transportation: Metro or taxi.
To Gay Bars: Walking distance to many.
Rooms: 1 studio apart-

ment.
Bathrooms: Private shower/toilet.
Rates: US $115 for 2 people, US $130 for 3 people.
Credit Cards: Amex.
Rsv'tns: Required.
Reserve Through: Travel

agent or call direct.
Minimum Stay: 4 days.
Parking: On-street parking or parking in paid public garage.
In-Room: Color cable TV, telephone, kitchenette, refrigerator & weekly maid service.

Swimming: 10-minute walk to floating pool on the Seine.
Smoking: Permitted.
Pets: Inquire.
Handicap Access: No.
Children: Welcome.
Languages: French, English, Spanish, Italian.

SOUTHWEST FRANCE (RURAL)

Mondès

Women ♀

A Women's Inn in France's Armagnac Region

Combine the most beautiful countryside imaginable with the charm of historic French culture, the warm atmosphere of home, the camaraderie of summer camp and the feeling of land inhabited only by women and then you have *Mondès*.

A precious secret hidden amidst the hills of Gers in the Gascon region in the Southern French countryside between Toulouse and Bordeaux, *Mondès* is surrounded by bright yellow fields of sunflowers, whose beauty truly astonishes the first-time visitor. Grapevines and cornfields also fill the landscape, as well as light-brown stone and wood farmhouses over a hundred years old.

At *Mondès*, owners Dorothee and Monika immediately welcome you and make you feel at home and comfortable with their friendly hospitality. Women who enjoy a stay at *Mondès* have breakfast and dinner together outside in the warm sunshine while enjoying the view of a medieval chateau in the distance, which is like something out of a fairy tale. During the conversation around the table at mealtime, you can meet women from all parts of Europe, and the world, and hear German, English and French spoken. There is always much laughter and friendliness and sometimes guitar playing and singing.

Relax in the sun and swim in the beautiful natural lake surrounded by trees. Get a tan and float on an air mattress. Or, take a bicycle and ride around the sunny hills where Armagnac is produced. No matter what you do, you are certain to enjoy yourself in this incredibly romantic atmosphere filled with beauty and peace.
Address: Courrensan, 32330 Gondrin France. Phone & Fax: 6206 5905.

Type: Inn & campground.
Clientele: Women only.
Transportation: Car is best, train to Agen + bus to Gondrin. No charge for pick up from bus in Gondrin.
To Gay Bars: 150 km to Toulouse.
Rooms: 5 doubles.
Bathrooms: 1 bathroom with 2 showers shared.
Campsites: 20 tent sites with two toilets & 3 showers.

Meals: Full breakfast buffet & gourmet vegetarian dinners.
Vegetarian: Only.
Complimentary: Cocktails, wine, tea, coffee, juices, snacks.
Dates Open: All year.
High Season: July & August.
Rates: Per person per day: FF 165.00 breakfast & dinner, FF 30.00 camping, FF 130.00 camping, breakfast & dinner.
Discounts: Inquire.

Rsv'tns: Required.
Reserve Through: Call direct.
Minimum Stay: 3 days.
Parking: Adequate parking on own land.
On-Premises: Meeting rooms, laundry facilities, & living room with fireplace.
Exercise/Health: Bicycles, volleyball & swimming.
Swimming: In lake on private ground.
Sunbathing: Everywhere.

Nudity: Permitted around the lake.
Smoking: Permitted everywhere except in rooms.
Pets: Not permitted.
Handicap Access: No.
Children: Permitted. Males up to 8 years old.
Languages: French, German & English.

Roussa

Come and Fall in Love

Women ♀

Roussa is a 200-year-old renovated farmhouse with a beautiful, big garden, German-run, but international in atmosphere and clientele. You will find all holiday activities nearby, but no mass tourism. Come, and fall in love with the vineyards and the fields of sunflowers and corn which surround us. You'll enjoy discovering charming small towns and marketplaces and exploring musketeer-castles, medieval fortifications and Roman ruins. Terribly tempting dining specialties await you in Gascony, including famous wines. You can get in touch with a lesbian network through *Roussa,* making interesting contacts along the way. By the way, at *Roussa,* you can rent a beautiful conference room and organize, or participate in, group activities of all sorts. Ask for program. Gabriele, Monika and Chantal, with their pets (cats, hens, sheep), wish you a warm welcome.

Address: Courrensan, 32330 Gondrin France. Tel: 6206 58 96, Fax: 6264 45 34.

Type: Guesthouse & camping.
Clientele: Women only.
Transportation: Car recommended. Pick up from bus or train station.
Rooms: 7 rooms with single & double beds.
Bathrooms: 2 shared bath/shower/toilets & 3 shared WC.
Campsites: 10 tent sites.
Meals: Generous breakfast & vegetarian dinner.
Vegetarian: Always.
Complimentary: Cocktails, wine, tea, coffee, juices & snacks.
Dates Open: All year except November.
High Season: July-September.
Rates: Call for details.
Discounts: Call for details.
Rsv'tns: Call for reservations.
Reserve Through: Call direct.
Minimum Stay: 2 nights.
Parking: Adequate free off-street parking.
On-Premises: TV lounge, meeting rooms, laundry service.
Exercise/Health: Bicycles to rent on premises. Horseback riding & tennis nearby.
Swimming: Nearby pool & lake.
Sunbathing: In the garden.
Smoking: Permitted.
Pets: Dogs permitted, if they don't eat our cats.
Handicap Access: No.
Children: Welcome, boys only to age 10.
Languages: German, French & English.
Your Host: Gabriele, Monika & Chantal.

Saouis

Women ♀

Surrounded by vineyards, fields and woods, *Saouis* is situated 80 km from the Pyrenees and 120 km from the Atlantic Coast. For 7 years, women from many different countries have spent their holidays here in this beautiful, tranquil spot, spoiling themselves with the sun, fresh air and fine cuisine. The house has 5 double-rooms and plenty of space outdoors for tent camping. For women interested in outdoor activities, there is a small lake 5 km, and a paved tennis court 1 1/2 km, from the house. For women who have come without cars, transportation is available, for a fee, to the Pyrenees or the Atlantic Coast. It is also possible, without leaving the farm, to find quiet corners for peaceful solitude, sunbathing, reading and relaxing. If you appreciate good, healthy food, you will not be disappointed with the dishes we prepare! Reservations are required in advance.

Address: Cravencères, 32110 Nogaro France. Tel: 62 08 56 06.

Type: Guesthouse.
Clientele: Women only.
Transportation: Car is best. Pick up from bus in Manciet (near Mont-de-Marsan).
To Gay Bars: 150 km Toulouse Bagdam Cafe, & Bordeaux.
Rooms: 5 doubles.
Bathrooms: 2 shared hot showers & 2 WC's.
Campsites: 10 tent sites, 2 hot showers, 1 cold shower & 2 WC's.
Meals: Expanded continental breakfast and dinner.
Vegetarian: Mainly vegetarian meals.
Complimentary: Cocktails, "floc" (a regional specialty), & pousse rapier.
Dates Open: Mar-Oct.
High Season: Jul-Aug.
Rates: Rooms FF 170-FF 180, camping FF 130-150.
Rsv'tns: Recommended in July & August.
Reserve Through: Call direct.
Minimum Stay: 3 day minimum for rooms.
Parking: Adequate, free parking.
Swimming: At lake 5 km away. Swimming pool to be built in 1995.
Sunbathing: In the garden.
Nudity: Permitted.
Smoking: Permitted.
Pets: Permitted.
Handicap Access: Somewhat. 1 floor, but no wide walkways, etc.
Children: Permitted, but boys to age 10 only.
Languages: French, German, & English.
Your Host: Dagmar.

TOULOUSE

Auberge d'Enrose

Gay/Lesbian ♀♂

The Undiscovered Southwest France, Home of Armagnac & Fois Gras

Auberge d'Enrose, built in 1757, is an elegant stone farmhouse situated on a hilltop on nine acres of private woodland. In an informal country house atmosphere, there are five double bedrooms and two self-contained, self-catering apartments with private terraces. For guests requiring dinner, the menu usually includes regional specialties, such as fois gras, confit or magret de canard. We have an excellent wine list and a full range of spirits and liqueurs, including the celebrated Armagnac, for which Gascony is renowned. There is a large heated swimming pool and secluded sunbathing areas, as well as views of the Pyrenees. Local activities include golf, tennis and horseback riding. In the winter, skiing in the Pyrenees is just an hour away.

The house is 2km from the picturesque village of Solomiac and 1 km from Mauvezin, an ancient bastide with several restaurants, bars and a good selection of local shops. Gers, in the heart of Gascony, southwest France, is one of the least populated areas in this country, offering attractive scenery, considerable historical interest and the peace and calm of the countryside. Auch, 30km away and the capital of Gascony and birthplace of d'Artagnan, has a magnificent cathedral dating from the 11th century. Toulouse, 50km to the east, is built on the banks of the river Garonne and is the fourth largest city in France. Its city centre is very attractive, with many quaint, narrow streets, antique shops, numerous cafes, bars, restaurants and the largest Romanesque church in Europe, St. Sernin. The Spanish border is just over an hour away by car. The Mediterranean and Atlantic coasts can be reached in about two hours. There are many interesting day excursions, including Carcassonne, an ancient walled city, and Albi, the birthplace of Toulouse Lautrec, with its magnificent fortified cathedral.

Address: Solomiac, 32120 Mauvezin France. Tel: (33) 62 65 01 42, Fax: (33) 62 65 02 93.

Type: Farmhouse inn with restaurant & bar.
Clientele: Mostly gay & lesbian with some hetero clientele.
Transportation: Car is best. Free pick up from train.
To Gay Bars: 30 miles.
Rooms: 5 rooms & 2 apartments with double beds.
Bathrooms: All private.
Meals: Expanded continental breakfast.
Vegetarian: Available with advance notice.

Complimentary: Welcome cocktail on arrival & fruit in rooms. Tea & coffee in all rooms.
Dates Open: All year.
High Season: Jul& Aug..
Rates: 250-350 FF per night for 2 people. Apartment, 350-500 FF per night. 100 FF per night for extra person in apartment.
Discounts: 10% off for rooms & apartments if booked by the week.
Credit Cards: MC, VISA & Eurocard.

Rsv'tns: Normally required.
Reserve Through: Travel agent or call direct.
Parking: Ample free off-street parking.
In-Room: Colour TV & tea/coffee making facilities in rooms. Colour TV, linens, kitchen, refrigerator, cooker, and dishwasher in apartments.
On-Premises: TV lounge & laundry facilities.
Swimming: Large heated pool on premises.

Sunbathing: At poolside, on private & common sun decks and in secluded woodland areas.
Nudity: Permitted in woodlands & poolside if 100% gay clientele.
Smoking: Permitted.
Pets: Not permitted.
Handicap Access: No.
Children: Not permitted.
Languages: French & English.
Your Host: Richard & Peter.

IGTA

TOURS

Prieuré des Granges

Gay-Friendly ♀♂

Stay in a French Country Castle 1 Hour From Paris

The Loire Valley, where the French kings built their castles, is the best place to experience the history of France. *Prieuré des Granges* is an old mansion dating from the 17th and 19th centuries and surrounded by a garden full of aged trees and a swimming pool. All the large, southern-facing guest rooms overlook the garden, each one with its own bath (or shower) and private WC and each furnished with antiques.

We have taken great pleasure in arranging for our guests a most interesting stay in this region. We are only 15 minutes by car from the town of Tours, the true capital of the Loire Valley. In Savonnieres and Tours, you will find a variety of restaurants to choose from. Tennis, horseback riding, an 18-hole golf course, antique galleries, as well as tourist attractions, such as the museums of Tours and many castles, are all within easy reach.

Address: 37510 Savonnieres, Touraine, France   Tel: (47) 50 09 67, Fax: (47) 50 06 43.

Type: Bed & breakfast with antique shop.
Clientele: Mostly hetero with a gay & lesbian following.
Transportation: Car is best. Train to Tours, then taxi. T6V fast train, 55 minutes from Paris.
To Gay Bars: 6 miles or 15 minutes by car.
Rooms: 5 rooms, 1 with twin beds.
Bathrooms: 2 private bath/toilets & 3 private shower/toilets.

Meals: Continental breakfast. Addn'l charge for dinner (advance notice).
Vegetarian: Vegetarian restaurant in Tours.
Complimentary: All drinks at anytime.
Dates Open: Apr 1- Dec 31.
High Season: July-September.
Rates: 450 FF-500 FF for 2 people, breakfast included.
Discounts: 10% for

4 nights.
Rsv'tns: Required.
Reserve Through: Travel agent or call direct.
Parking: Free private parking on the property.
In-Room: Telephone.
On-Premises: Meeting rooms & TV lounge.
Exercise/Health: Tennis & horseback riding. Golf nearby.
Swimming: Pool on premises.
Sunbathing: At poolside.
Smoking: Permitted

without restrictions.
Pets: Permitted in the downstairs rooms.
Handicap Access: No.
Children: Welcomed if well-behaved.
Languages: French & English.
Your Host: Philippe, Serge & Xavier.

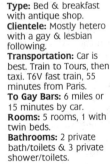

GERMANY

BERLIN

Arco Hotel Pension

Gay-Friendly 50/50 ♀♂'

Originally designed as a luxury flat in the Bismark era, the *Arco*, also called the *Petit Hotel,* has spacious, stately rooms, some with balconies overlooking Berlin's famous Kurfürstendamm, where people from around the world stroll past interesting shops or linger over aperitifs in the outdoor cafes. All rooms have telephones, all but a few have showers and sinks and some have full baths. Although our clientele is not all gay, our gay guests will feel quite at home.

Address: Kurfürstendamm 30, 10719 Berlin Germany. Tel: (030) 882 63 88, Fax: (030) 881 99 02.

Type: Hotel & pension. **Clientele:** 50% gay & lesbian & 50% straight. **Transportation:** Bus #109 from Tegel airport or Zoologischer Garten train station. Bus #119 from Tempelhof airport to Uhlandstrasse stop. **To Gay Bars:** 10-minute walk to gay/lesbian bars. **Rooms:** 20 rooms (18 doubles, 2 singles). **Bathrooms:** 6 private & 14 shared. **Meals:** Expanded continental breakfast. **Dates Open:** All year. **Rates:** Singles DM 68.00-135.00. Doubles DM 110.00-165.00. **Credit Cards:** MC, VISA, Amex, Diners Club. **Rsv'tns:** Preferred. **Reserve Through:** Call direct. **Parking:** Garage nearby. **In-Room:** Maid service, telephone, safe. **On-Premises:** Meeting rooms, public telephone & TV lounge. **Exercise:** Gym nearby. **Swimming:** Lake nearby. **Sunbathing:** At the lake or in the park. **Nudity:** Permitted at the lake and in the park. **Smoking:** Permitted without restrictions. **Pets:** Permitted. **Handicap Access:** No. **Children:** Permitted. **Languages:** German, English, Spanish, French, Italian & Portuguese. **Your Host:** Rolf, Jaques & Gerd.

Artemisia, Women Only Hotel

Women ♀

Artemisia, the hotel for women only, is located just minutes from the Kurfürstendamm, Berlin's most exciting avenue. Newly renovated and redecorated in soothing pastels, our hotel offers rooms with modern furniture, telephones and spacious, private bathrooms. *Artemisia's* special features also include a sun deck with an impressive view of Berlin.

At *Artemisia,* travelling women find complete comfort and convenience. If you come to Berlin, for business or pleasure, *Artemisia's* personal, woman-identified atmosphere will make your stay a memorable experience.

Address: Brandenburgischestrasse 18, D-10707 Berlin Germany. Tel: Current: (030) 87 89 05/87 63 73. From Jan '95: (030) 873 89 05/873 63 73, Fax: (030) 8618653.

Type: Hotel with bar. **Clientele:** Women only. **Transportation:** Taxi or U-bahn: Konstanzerstrasse, airport bus to Adenauerplatz. **To Gay Bars:** 10-minute drive to women's bars. **Rooms:** 7 rooms & 1 suite with single or double beds. **Bathrooms:** 1 private bath/toilet & 7 private shower/toilets. **Meals:** Lavish buffet-style breakfast with eggs, cereal, fruits, vegetables, yogurt, cheeses & meats, jams, etc. **Vegetarian:** Buffet breakfast has a variety of items to please everyone. **Complimentary:** Bar with room service. **Dates Open:** All year. **Rates:** Single 99.00-189.00 DM, double 169.00-260.00 DM. **Discounts:** On stays exceeding 1 week (7 nights). **Credit Cards:** MC, VISA, Amex, Eurocard & Diners. **Rsv'tns:** Recommended! **Reserve Through:** Call direct. **Parking:** Adequate free on-street parking. **In-Room:** Maid & laundry service, telephone, heat. In suite only: color cable TV. **On-Premises:** Meeting rooms, TV lounge, cocktail lounge, women's art displays. **Sunbathing:** On common sun deck. **Smoking:** Permitted without restriction except during breakfast (no smoking). **Pets:** Not permitted. **Handicap Access:** No. **Children:** Permitted, but males only up to 14 yrs. **Languages:** German, English, Italian & French.

Germany

Hotel Charlottenburger Hof

Gay-Friendly ♂

Hotel Charlottenburger Hof is located in Berlin's city center, just a 4-minute's walk from Kurfürstendamm, the city's most important avenue. The hotel is on the city train line's Charlottenburg stop, just 2 stops from the Zoological Garden main station. Several bus lines also stop in front of the hotel. Most of our guests are young tourists from Germany, Scandinavia, USA and France, who spend their holidays in Berlin. Our rooms are light, airy and modern, nearly all with newly-remodeled full baths, all newly-decorated in pleasant colors. All rooms have color cable TV, a safe without fee and a telephone. There is also laundry room for guests. Young Berlin artists regularly exhibit their paintings in our café-bistro, open round-the-clock. It is frequented by many students and artists offering endless possibilities for meeting people.

Address: Stuttgarter Platz 14, 10627 Berlin Germany. Tel: (49 30) 32 90 70, Fax: (49 30) 323 37 23.

Type: Hotel with small restaurant, newsstand & hair salon.	men's bar. **Rooms:** 45 rooms with single, double & king beds.	**High Season:** Summer. **Rates:** DM 90.00-DM 160.00.	**On-Premises:** TV lounge, laundry facilities, public telephones.
Clientele: Mostly straight clientele with a 40% gay male following, women welcome.	**Bathrooms:** 43 private shower/toilets, 2 private bath/toilets.	**Credit Cards:** None. **Rsv'tns:** Recommended. **Reserve Through:** Call direct.	**Smoking:** Permitted without restrictions. **Pets:** Not permitted. **Handicap Access:** No.
Transportation: Airport bus stops at hotel, or take taxi. Pick up from airport, bus or train.	**Meals:** Full breakfast, 5 DM extra. **Vegetarian:** Always available in restaurant.	**Parking:** Ample, free, on-street parking. **In-Room:** Maid service, color cable TV, telephone & safes.	**Children:** Permitted. **Languages:** German, English, Spanish, French, Italian.
To Gay Bars: Walk to	**Dates Open:** All year.		

Pension Niebuhr

Gay-Friendly 50/50 ♂

Willkommen, Bienvenue, Welcome

Pension Niebuhr follows an old Berlin tradition: You are accommodated in a house built in the beginning of this century, with converted former apartments, so you'll get a feeling of privacy. Rooms are typically spacious, with high ceilings. All have been newly furnished during the last 2 years and don't look like most hotel rooms. The interior is modern and decorated with paintings by young Berlin artists. 7 of the 12 rooms have private bathrooms, cable TV, telephone and clock/radio. The other 5 have sinks with hot water and a shared shower and toilet on the same floor. As a special free service, an extended breakfast is served in the room any time after 7am.

In the well-known district of Berlin-Charlottenburg, *Pension Niebuhr* is centrally-located, yet in a quiet neighborhood. Kurfürstendamm, the popular main street for shopping and strolling, is within a 3-minute walk. The S-Bahn-station Savignyplatz is about 200 meters from us. From there its just one station to Zoologischer Garten, the former main station of West Berlin. The surrounding area offers a wide choice of international restaurants with their typical cuisine, several little galleries, bars and antique shops. A VERY IMPORTANT NOTE: THIS IS A SAFE AREA.

Willi, the friendly host, is always glad to take the time to chat and share information about this great city.

Address: Niebuhrstr 74, 10629 Berlin, Germany. Tel: (030) 324 95 95, (030) 324 95 96, Fax: (030) 324 8021.

Type: Pension.
Clientele: 50% hetero with a gay male following.
Transportation: Bus (NR 109) from airport to Bleibtreustr, then -minute walk. From Zoo station, S-Bahn to Savignyplatz.
To Gay Bars: About 10 minutes by bus to gay bar area or 5 min walk to nearest bar.
Rooms: 12 rooms.
Bathrooms: 7 private showers/toilets, 5 rooms share.
Meals: Expanded continental breakfast.
Vegetarian: Vegetarian breakfast by request. Restaurants also offer vegetarian food.
Complimentary: Coffee, tea, juices, sparkling wine, coke & mineral water.
Dates Open: All year.
Rates: Single DM 95,00-DM 140,00. Double DM 125,00-DM 170,00.
Discounts: On stays exceeding 7 nights. Winter rates from Nov-Feb.
Credit Cards: MC, VISA, Amex & Eurocard.
Rsv'tns: Required.
Reserve Through: Call direct.
Parking: Limited free on-street parking. Empty spaces are hard to find.
In-Room: Color cable TV, telephone, maid & room service.
On-Premises: Fax machine.
Exercise/Health: Nearby gym, sauna & massage.
Swimming: Pool & lake 1 km away.
Sunbathing: At the park or lake.
Nudity: Permitted at the lake or partly common pool.
Smoking: Permitted without restrictions.
Pets: Permitted.
Handicap Access: No.
Children: Not especially welcome.
Languages: German & English.
Your Host: Willi.

Tom's House Berlin

Men ♂

You will appreciate the old-world charm of the spacious, individually furnished rooms in this grand turn-of-the-century Berlin apartment house. You will relax in our homelike atmosphere, and you will not believe the buffet breakfast we serve from 10:00 AM till 1:00 PM. You have your choice of yogurt, cereal, cheese, meat, smoked salmon, fruit salad, freshly baked German rolls, bread, eggs, marmalade, honey, jam, and sometimes even champagne! *Tom's House Berlin* is located in the gayest part of town. You can walk to a number of gay night spots, saving the expense of taxis or rental cars. Convenience is important, and our guests return year after year, because at *Tom's House Berlin* they always feel comfortable and at ease.
Address: Eisenacher Str. 10, D-10777 Berlin Germany. Tel: (030) 218 5544 or Fax: (4930) 213 4464.

Type: Bed & breakfast guesthouse predominantly for leather men.
Clientele: Men only.
Transportation: Taxi 20 minutes from Tegel, 10 minutes from Tempelhof, 30 minutes from Schönefeld airports.
To Gay Bars: Next door to men's bars.
Rooms: 8 rooms with single or double beds.
Bathrooms: All have sinks. 3 toilets & showers are shared by all.
Meals: Buffet breakfast: Eggs, cereal, yogurt, smoked salmon, meat, cheese, bread, rolls, orange juice, milk, jam, honey etc.
Complimentary: Free city map & boot jack in each room.
Dates Open: All year.
Rates: DM 130.00-DM 180.00.
Rsv'tns: Required, as early as possible.
Reserve Through: Call direct.
Parking: Adequate easy on-street parking & garage for off-street pay parking.
In-Room: Maid service. Some rooms have refrigerator.
On-Premises: TV lounge.
Exercise/Health: Nearby gym & sauna.
Swimming: In lake far away.
Sunbathing: In nearby public park.
Nudity: Permitted in public park.
Smoking: Permitted without restrictions.
Pets: Dogs only.
Handicap Access: No.
Children: Not permitted.
Languages: German, English & Danish.
Your Host: Christoph.

BRUNKEN/WESTERWALD

Lichtquelle, Frauenbildungsstätte

Women ♀

Lichtquelle, a women's seminar center, is a place for healing, meditation and therapy. Here women can find support on their journey of self-formation and self-discovery. When there are no seminars being held, women can come and make a single retreat. It is not possible to come for a holiday only.

Address: Hochstr. 11, 57539 Brunken Germany. Tel: (02742) 71587.

Type: Healing retreat.
Clientele: Women only.
Transportation: Car is best, pick up provided from train.
To Gay Bars: 15 miles (20 km).
Rooms: 2 dbl, 2 quads.

Bathrooms: 1 big shared bathroom.
Meals: Full board.
Vegetarian: Serve vegetarian food only (mainly macrobiotic).
Complimentary: Juices, mineral water.

Dates Open: All year.
Rates: DM 37.00-DM 40.00 per day.
Rsv'tns: Required.
Reserve Through: Please write for reservations.
Parking: Adequate, free off-street parking.

On-Premises: Meeting rooms.
Smoking: Not permitted.
Pets: Not permitted.
Handicap Access: No.
Children: Not permitted.
Languages: German, English, French.

BÜCKEN

Frauenferienhaus Altenbücken

Women ♀

For women who wish to learn and grow in the company of other like-minded women, *Frauenferienhaus Altenbücken* has established a country retreat and series of courses on a variety of subjects, including music and dance workshops and such subjects as Childhood Sexual Abuse and Undermining of Self-Esteem in Women's Lives. Here, you can participate in the courses, or just relax and get away from the bustle of daily life. For the more active, hiking, bicycling and swimming are available. Guests cooperate in food preparation and other tasks, and a memorable time is had by all.

Address: Schürmannsweg 25, 27333 Bücken Germany. Tel: (04251) 7899.

Type: Retreat with classes available.
Clientele: Women only.
Rooms: 2 singles, 4 doubles, 2 with 3 beds, 1 with 5 beds.
Bathrooms: 2 shared.
Meals: Groceries.
Vegetarian: Always.

Dates Open: All year.
Rates: DM 35.00 per woman per night.
Discounts: Group rates, children's rates.
Rsv'tns: Required.
Reserve Through: Call direct.
Parking: Free parking.

In-Room: Telephone, kitchen, refrigerator.
On-Premises: Meeting rooms.
Exercise/Health: Sauna nearby, bicycles on premises.
Swimming: Nearby.
Sunbathing: On the

lawn.
Smoking: Permitted in garden only.
Pets: Not permitted.
Children: Permitted, boys only to age 7.
Languages: German, English, French.

CHARLOTTENBERG

Frauenlandhaus

Women ♀

Address: Holzappeler Str 3, 56379 Charlottenberg Germany. Tel: (06439) 7531.

Type: Bed & breakfast guesthouse with workshops.
Clientele: Women only.
Transportation: Car or train. Pick up from train.
To Gay Bars: 50 miles to

Frankfurt, 60 miles to Cologne.
Rooms: 15 rooms with single or double beds.
Bathrooms: All shared.
Meals: Buffet breakfast, lunch, dinner.

Vegetarian: Always. Only vegetarian food.
Complimentary: Coffee & tea any time. No alcohol.
Dates Open: All year.
Rates: Not reported for

current year.
Discounts: Group rates, children's rates.
Rsv'tns: Required.
Reserve Through: Call direct.
Parking: Free parking.

In-Room: Coffee/tea-making facilities, kitchen, video tape library. **On-Premises:** Meeting rooms, telephone, piano. **Exercise/Health:** Sauna, massage, yoga, meditation. **Swimming:** Nearby lake. **Sunbathing:** On private sun decks or in the garden. **Nudity:** Permitted in the garden. **Smoking:** Permitted only in smoking room & in the garden. **Pets:** Not permitted. **Handicap Access:** No. **Children:** Permitted, boys to the age of 12. **Languages:** German, English & Italian.

DÜSSELDORF

Hotel Alt Graz

Gay-Friendly ♀♂

Hotel Alt Graz, located in the centre of town, is just a short walk to Central Station, several international restaurants, and plenty of shopping. A ten-minute walk from the hotel is the Altstadt, which is known as the longest bar in the world, with its hundreds of bars, discos, and restaurants.

Düsseldorf offers sightseers many attractions. Visit sea lions, piranhas, penguins and crocodiles at the Aqua Zoo, spend a day at the Kunsthalle art museum or the Goethe museum, or cheer on the ice hockey team, which has won five of the last six playoffs.

For your convenience, each rooms has a direct-dial telephone and cable TV. Our complimentary English breakfast will get you off to a good start each morning.

Please keep in mind that we are usually booked during every exhibition, so it is imperative that you make your reservations early.

Address: Klosterstrasse 132, 40211 Düsseldorf, Germany. Tel: (211) 36 40 28, Fax: (211) 36 95 77.

Type: Bed & breakfast hotel. **Clientele:** Mostly straight clientele with a gay/lesbian following. **To Gay Bars:** 5-minute walk to gay/lesbian bars. **Rooms:** 11 singles, 11 doubles & 2 triples with single & matrimonial beds. **Bathrooms:** 10 private, others share. **Meals:** Expanded continental breakfast. **Dates Open:** All year. **Rates:** DM 75-DM 135 single, DM 120-DM 215 double. **Credit Cards:** MC, VISA, Amex, Diners, Eurocard. **Rsv'tns:** Required. **Reserve Through:** Travel agent or call direct. **Parking:** On-street parking. **In-Room:** Telephone, color TV, maid service. **Smoking:** Permitted without restrictions. **Pets:** Not permitted. **Languages:** German, English.

EDERTAL-ANRAFF

Frauenbildungsstätte Edertal-Anraff

Women ♀

Women from all walks of life come to *Frauenbildungstätte Edertal-Anraff*, a retreat holding courses for women in a restful, rural atmosphere. While attending one of a variety of courses, women can experience the countryside through bicycling, walking, hiking, swimming, etc. Vegetarian meals are prepared in the farmhouse.

Address: Königsberger Str. 6, 34549 Anraff Germany. Tel: (05621) 3218.

Type: Retreat guest-house with restaurant & bar. Classes available. **Clientele:** Women only. **Transportation:** Car is best. Train to Bad Wildungen. Pick up from train or bus 5 DM. **Rooms:** 2 singles, 1 double, 3 triples, 1 quad & 1 apartment. **Bathrooms:** 4 shared bath/shower/toilets & 5 shared toilets. **Meals:** Groceries. **Vegetarian:** Always. **Dates Open:** All year. **Rates:** DM 20.00-DM 30.00 per woman per night. **Discounts:** For children & groups. **Rsv'tns:** Required. **Parking:** Free parking. **In-Room:** Color TV, video tape library, kitchen & refrigerator. **On-Premises:** Meeting rooms. **Exercise/Health:** Bicycles, canoe, kayak & horseback riding. **Swimming:** Nearby pool, river & lake. **Sunbathing:** On the lawn. **Smoking:** Not permitted. **Pets:** Permitted with prior reservation. **Handicap Access:** No. **Children:** Permitted, boys only to age 8. **Languages:** German, English & French.

HAMBURG

Künstler-Pension Sarah Petersen

Gay/Lesbian ♀♂

The Artist Pension

Located directly in the center of the beautiful seaport city of Hamburg, *Künstler-Pension Sarah Petersen* is keeping with the tradition of the famous European artist pensions of the twenties and thirties. Writers, actors, musicians, fashion designers and all people who like the special atmosphere of a small familiar hotel, are part of the good spirit our little guest house has to offer. Another reason to stay here is the rare early 19th century architecture and the creative furnishings. Our concept: A minimum of hotel and a maximum of private house interior. The *Künstler-Pension Sarah Petersen* is surrounded by museums, coffeehouses, small stores, restaurants and gay bars. A five-minute walk and you are at the big city lake Alster, with parks and open-air cafes.

Address: Lange Reihe 50, D-20099 Hamburg Germany. Phone & Fax: (040) 24 98 26.

Type: Guesthouse with small picturesque hotel bar.
Clientele: Good mix of gay men & women with 30% straight clientele.
Transportation: Airport bus to Hauptbahnhof.
To Gay Bars: 1/2 block or 4 minutes by foot.
Rooms: 6 rooms.
Bathrooms: 6 private sinks & 2 shared baths.

Meals: Expanded (meatless) continental breakfast.
Vegetarian: Breakfast. Several restaurants & coffeehouses nearby serve vegetarian food.
Complimentary: Tea, coffee, juices, beer, wine & champagne.
Dates Open: All year.
High Season: July, August, September.

Rates: Single DM 84.00, double DM 96.00.
Credit Cards: Eurocard.
Rsv'tns: Required with deposit.
Reserve Through: Call direct or write.
Parking: Free on-street parking, parking house around the corner.
In-Room: B&W & color TV, room service.
On-Premises: House bar

for guests & friends.
Swimming: 10-minute walk to indoor public pool.
Sunbathing: 5-minutes to Lake Alster.
Smoking: Permitted without restrictions.
Pets: Cats only.
Handicap Access: No.
Children: Permitted.
Languages: German & English.

NÜRNBERG

Hotel Zum Wal Fisch

Gay/Lesbian ♂

Home of the NLC Franken (Nürnberg Leather Club)

Hotel Zum Wal Fisch offers clean, plain rooms with warm and cold water in Nürnberg's old city. There is a WC and shower on every floor and a garden where guests can relax. A first-class breakfast buffet is available at DM 10. The gay bar on the premises is open daily from 17:00-01:00, using a separate entrance. The hotel, itself, is closed between 11:30 and 16:30.

Address: Jakobstr 19, 8500 Nürnberg 1 Germany. Tel: (0911) 225270.

Type: Hotel.
Clientele: Mostly men with women welcome.
To Gay Bars: Gay bar on premises.
Rooms: 15 rooms.
Bathrooms: WC &

shower on each floor. 9 private shower/WC.
Meals: Full breakfast buffet.
Dates Open: All year.
Rates: DM 50-DM 110. Extra charge for private

bath.
Reserve Through: Travel agent or call direct.
Parking: Limited on-street parking.
In-Room: Maid service.
Smoking: Permitted

without restrictions.
Pets: Small pets OK.
Handicap Access: No.
Children: Welcome.
Languages: German, English, Dutch & Italian.
Your Host: Heinz.

OBERNDORF

Fen Dyke Ranch

Women ♀

Fen Dyke Ranch, a women's education and holiday center, is located in a lovely rural setting. Managed by a group of women, *Fen Dyke Ranch* has been totally renovated and has space for a maximum of 9 women. The managers live in separate, private quarters. There is a horseback riding area behind the house, a genuine Finnish sauna, and an area for camping, sun-bathing and playing. There are also many interesting courses in western-style horseback riding, voice awareness, working with stained-glass and pottery, astrology, batik/painting, feminist philosophy, and self-awareness. Spare-time can be enjoyed by riding our own horses, taking a sauna, visiting the nearby forest with its petting zoo and park, or bathing in the lovely lakes nearby. Guests can also enjoy the Oste River, trips to Hamburg and Bremen and much more!

Address: Hasenfleet 4, 21787 Oberndorf/Oste Germany. Tel: (04772) 206.

Type: Guesthouse & campground.
Clientele: Women only.
Transportation: Car is best. Free pick up from the train in Wingst.
To Gay Bars: 90 km to Hamburg.
Rooms: 3 rooms with single or double beds.
Bathrooms: 1 shared toilet & 2 shared showers.
Campsites: 10 tent sites.

Toilet & kitchen facilities are in the house.
Vegetarian: Always available.
Dates Open: All year.
High Season: Christmas, New Year's Eve, Easter & July/August.
Rates: DM 25.00.
Discounts: On stays longer than 3 weeks.
Rsv'tns: Required.
Reserve Through: Call

direct.
Parking: Adequate free off-street parking.
On-Premises: Meeting room with color TV & piano.
Exercise/Health: Sauna.
Swimming: 1/2 hour drive to ocean beach. Ten minute drive to a lake.
Sunbathing: In the garden.

Nudity: Permitted in the garden & at the lake.
Smoking: Permitted in quads & passageway only.
Pets: Not permitted.
Handicap Access: No.
Children: Permitted, but no boys over 8 years old.
Languages: German, English & some French.

SCHÖLLNACH

Die Mühle (The Mill)

Gay/Lesbian ♂

By car, leave the Deggendorf/Passau autobahn at the Iggensbach exit. Schöllnach is 5 km. Call us from the marketplace, and we'll direct you to Englfing. Once there, you'll find *Die Mühle* set between two creeks, with an easygoing environment amid splendid scenery, away from the city noise. There are cozy rooms and a guest lounge, where we sometimes show movies. There is a shower & bath, sauna and solarium. Our frequent dances attract large crowds, including many locals.

Address: Englfing 16, 94508 Schöllnach Germany. Tel: (09903) 562.

Type: Inn.
Clientele: Mainly men, lesbians welcome.
Rooms: 13 doubles.
Bathrooms: Shared.
Campsites: Great space for camping. DM 5.00 per day.

Meals: Breakfast, lunch & dinner DM 60.00 per day. Breakfast only DM 9.50.
Dates Open: All year.
Rates: DM 60.00 per person.
Rsv'tns: Required 3 days

in advance.
Reserve Through: Call direct.
In-Room: Living room area, TV, bar, radio & record collection, books upon request.
Smoking: Permitted

without restrictions.
Pets: Permitted, please inquire.
Handicap Access: No.
Children: Not permitted.
Languages: German, English.

SIMMELSDORF

Hotel Sonnenhof

Men ♂

Fantastic Days and Hot Nights for Gay Men

Hotel Sonnenhof is the largest exclusively gay vacation and weekend getaway in Germany. Within our house and grounds, like-minded gay men relax in an uninhibited and discreet atmosphere. Nudism? No problem! In this clothing-optional environment, each person can enjoy the sun—dressed or undressed—as he pleases.

You'll find us north of Munich, about midway between Nürnberg and Bayreuth. The 3-story main house has common rooms where guests dine and socialize, a late-night disco bar, as well as a TV lounge with video and games. Guest rooms are well-furnished, some with private bath and balconies. Our 50-meter swimming pool is unequaled in the German gay scene. In winter, cross-country and downhill skiing are popular. Nearby castles and limestone caves make for interesting side trips at all times of the year. Canoeing, riding and tennis are also available.

Gay events held at *Hotel Sonnenhof* throughout the year include showtime with Miss Mara, a drag extravaganza, the election of Mr. Sonnenhof, and various drag and strip show events.

Address: Ittling 36, 91245 Simmelsdorf Germany. Tel: 09155/823.

Type: Hotel with disco/bar. **Clientele:** Men only. **Transportation:** Car is best. Pick up from train station. (Simmelsdorf free, Lanf/Peg DM 30,00.) **To Gay Bars:** 45 miles or a 40-minute drive. **Rooms:** 20 rooms & 1 apartment with single or double beds. **Bathrooms:** Private: 3 shower/toilet, 17 sink only. **Meals:** Buffet breakfast, dinner. **Complimentary:** Tea, coffee, cake, ice, cocktails & snacks. **Dates Open:** Closed in January. Call for details. **High Season:** May-September, December. **Rates:** Single DM 65,00 to DM 70,00. Double DM 130,00 to DM 170,00. **Discounts:** Varies per season. Please inquire. **Rsv'tns:** Required. **Reserve Through:** Call direct. **Minimum Stay:** Single day is DM 10,00 more per person. **Parking:** Free off-street parking. **On-Premises:** TV lounge & reading room. **Exercise/Health:** Sauna. Skiing nearby. **Swimming:** Pool on premises. **Sunbathing:** At poolside. **Nudity:** Permitted poolside. **Smoking:** Not permitted. **Pets:** Permitted. **Handicap Access:** No. **Children:** Not especially welcome. **Languages:** German, English.

TIEFENBACH

Frauenferienhaus Tiefenbach/Silbersee

Women ♀

Frauenferienhaus Tiefenbach combines a rural vacation retreat and conference center for women in the beautiful countryside of Germany near the border of the Czech Republic. The geography of the area makes it ideal for a variety of outdoor activities, from hiking and swimming in summer to skiing in the winter. We welcome lesbian and straight women who travel by themselves, in couples or in groups. Feminist psychodrama groups are possible.

Address: Hammer 22, 93464 Tiefenbach Germany. Tel: (09673) 499.

Type: Retreat with classes available. **Clientele:** Women only. **Transportation:** Car, train or bus. **Rooms:** 1 single, 4 doubles & 1 triple with single or double beds. **Bathrooms:** 1 en suite, 3 shared. **Vegetarian:** Available at extra cost. **Dates Open:** All year. **High Season:** December, January, July & August. **Rates:** DM 25.00 per woman per night. DM 55.00 per woman per night includes vegetarian meals. **Rsv'tns:** Required. **Reserve Through:** Call direct. **Parking:** Ample on-street parking. **On-Premises:** Meeting rooms & garden. **Exercise/Health:** Bicycles, horseback riding, nearby sauna & bath hall. **Swimming:** Lake on premises.

Sunbathing: On lake beach & on the lawn. **Smoking:** Not permitted. **Pets:** Not permitted. **Handicap Access:** Partially. **Children:** Not especially welcome. **Languages:** German, English.

WRIXUM/FÖHR

Kvindegard/Frauenhof

Women ♀

Located on the North Sea island Föhr, *Kvindegard,* a guest house for women only, lies in a quiet village just one km from the beach. We can accommodate up to 15 women in comfortable apartments. Guests can cook for themselves or enjoy the daily vegetarian supper menus prepared for them in the restaurant. The island and its sights can easily be explored by bicycle. Other activities to enjoy are riding, surfing and walking. It is also possible to walk across to other islands at low tide.

Address: Ohl Dörp 52, 2270 Wrixum, Island of Föhr Germany. Tel: (04681) 8935.

Type: Guest apartment with vegetarian dinner restaurant. **Clientele:** Women only. **Transportation:** Car to harbor, Dagebull, or train. Free pick up from ferry. **Rooms:** 5 apartments. **Bathrooms:** All with showers and toilets. **Vegetarian:** Available in vegetarian restaurant. **Dates Open:** All year.

High Season: From May until September. **Rates:** DM 60 for 2 people. DM 120 for 4 women in largest apartment. **Discounts:** Available for groups. **Rsv'tns:** Required. **Reserve Through:** Call direct. **Parking:** Adequate, free off-street parking. **In-Room:** Color TV, laundry service, kitchen, refrigerator. **On-Premises:** Meeting rooms, laundry facilities. **Exercise/Health:** Gym, weights, sauna, steam, massage, all within walking distance. **Swimming:** At nearby public pool or ocean beach 1 km. **Sunbathing:** On patio or nearby beach.

Nudity: Nude beach nearby. **Smoking:** Permitted. **Pets:** Permitted in 1 apartment only. **Handicap Access:** No. **Children:** All girls are permitted & boys up to 10 years old. **Languages:** German, English, Danish. **Your Host:** Susanne & Karin.

ZÜLPICH-LÖVENICH

Frauenbildungshaus e.V.

Women ♀

The *Frauenbildungs-und Ferienhaus Zülpich* is a very beautiful, rebuilt old farmhouse of wooden construction, with a large, quiet garden. This is a place for women to meet and to take various classes. The women stay for a week or weekend to learn together, live together, or do whatever together. Our classes include dancing, voice awareness, and introduction to healing methods such as Shiatsu, as well as computer courses. If there is room after course visitors have signed up, we take women who wish to stay for just a holiday, just to be lazy, go swimming in the nearby lake, take a bicycle ride, or visit the prehistoric places nearby and follow the traces of our ancestresses.

Address: Prälat-Franken-Str. 13, 53909 Zülpich-Lövenich Germany. Tel: (02252) 6577.

Type: Retreat with classes available. **Clientele:** Women only. **Transportation:** Car is best. **To Gay Bars:** 60 km or 30 minutes by car. **Rooms:** 1 apartment with single & double beds. **Bathrooms:** 1 private shower/toilet, 6 shared shower/toilets. **Meals:** Groceries. **Vegetarian:** Always. **Dates Open:** All year. **Rates:** DM 40.00-DM 50.00 per woman per night, food included. **Discounts:** Social discounts for the classes. (3 for each class possible.) **Rsv'tns:** Required. **Reserve Through:** Call direct. **Parking:** Adequate free on-street parking. **On-Premises:** Meeting rooms. **Exercise/Health:** Bicycles. **Swimming:** At nearby lake. **Sunbathing:** In the garden. **Nudity:** In the garden. **Smoking:** Not permitted in the house. **Pets:** Not permitted. **Handicap Access:** Yes. **Children:** Permitted. Boys allowed only to age 10. **Languages:** German & English.

GREECE

MYKONOS

Hotel Elysium

Gay/Lesbian ♀♂

The Most IN Island in the Mediterranean

You are captivated at first glance by the ever-changing patterns of blue and white on the walls, the narrow streets and the wonderful, sandy beaches, with waters in all shades of blue. Such intensive contrasts in colour, and such harmonious shapes, can be found on no other island. Mykonos is a place where sun, sea and entertainment come together in a superb, natural setting, to create the perfect atmosphere for your holiday. And, you'll find *Hotel Elysium* the perfect environment in which to enjoy it. It's the ultimate in glamour and luxury, with well-appointed rooms, excellent views of Mykonos Town, full restaurant and bar, swimming pool and gym.

Address: School of Fine Arts, Mykonos Town, Mykonos 84600 Greece. Tel: (289) 23952, 24210, 24684, Fax: (289) 23747.

Type: Hotel with restaurant & bar.
Clientele: Mostly gay with some straight clientele.
Transportation: Car is best, free hotel bus pick up from airport or port.
To Gay Bars: 2 minute walk.
Rooms: 43 rooms & 3 apartments with single, double or king beds.

Bathrooms: All private.
Meals: American buffet breakfast.
Complimentary: Juices.
Dates Open: April to November.
High Season: July 1 through September 15.
Rates: Doubles 16,000 drachmas to 31,000 drachmas, suites 22,000-45,000 drachmas, depending on season.

Discounts: 5% for stays of a week or more.
Credit Cards: VISA, Amex, Diners & Eurocard.
Rsv'tns: Required.
Reserve Through: Travel agent or call direct.
Parking: Free off-street parking.
In-Room: Color TV, telephone, refrigerator, maid & laundry service.
On-Premises: TV lounge,

meeting rooms.
Exercise/Health: Jacuzzi, sauna, gym, weights.
Swimming: Pool on premises, nearby ocean beach.
Sunbathing: At poolside.
Smoking: Permitted.
Pets: Permitted.
Children: Not permitted.
Languages: Greek, English, French, Italian & Spanish.

Mantours-Mykonos Holidays

Holidays for Body & Soul

Gay/Lesbian ♂

Formerly associated with the 15-year-old Mantours Berlin, Mantours USA is now a US-based hotel reservation system specializing in Europe's three top gay destinations of Greece's Mykonos and Spain's Ibiza and Sitges. Mantours also offers packages to most major European cities, such as Amsterdam, Copenhagen, Paris, Berlin, London, Athens, Madrid, Barcelona, Lisbon and Rome.

Mykonos accommodations include the following: The *Hotel Aegean* has fantastic harbor views, pool, bar, restaurant and gym; *Hotel Porto Mykonos* is a very comfortable bungalow hotel, a bit out of town and directly on the seaside, with all private baths and other amenities; *Hotel Leto*, in the center of Old Town, has rooms with private bath and balconies overlooking the sea; *Hotel Andromeda*, an easy walk from the bars, offers classy apartments in the town center, with gorgeous pool and in-room TV, private bath and kitchenette; *Hotel Vencia's* location outside of town offers a great view of Mykonos Town and provides rooms with private bath and balcony. The *Hotel Adonis* is a 32 room hotel with private baths. You can enjoy beautiful views of Mykonos from your private balcony. In Athens, the following hotels are available in classes A, B and C: *Andromeda* (Luxe), *Hotel Herodion* (A), *Hotel Amalia* (A), *King Minos* (A), *Electra Palace* (A), *Hotel Dorion Inn* (B), *Hotel Achilles* (C).
Address: Mantours USA, 4929 Wilshire Blvd #259, Los Angeles, CA 90010 Tel: (213) 930-1880 , (800) 798-4923, Fax: (213) 930-0194.

Villa Konstantin

A Peaceful Oasis Near the Heart of Mykonos

Gay/Lesbian ♀♂

Villa Konstantin is situated 700m from the town of Mykonos, offering panoramic sea views and peaceful tranquility just a ten-minute walk from the nightlife. All the stu-

VILLA KONSTANTIN MYKONOS GREECE

dios and apartments have large patios, wonderful sea views, private entrances, and accommodate from two to six people. *Villa Konstantin* is perfect for people who want to be somewhere quiet and beautiful yet near the pulse of the city. We look forward to meeting you.
Address: Mykonos 84600 Greece. Tel: (0289) 25824/26205, (0289) 23461, Fax: (0289) 26204.

Type: Studios & apartments.
Clientele: Mostly gay & lesbian with some straight clientele.
Transportation: Car is best, or Moto Bike. Free pick up from ferry dock.
To Gay Bars: A 10-minute walk or 2-minute drive.
Rooms: 5 rooms & 5 apartments with single

or double beds.
Bathrooms: All private shower/toilets.
Vegetarian: Available in town, a ten-minute walk.
Dates Open: April-October.
High Season: July, August, September.
Rates: 8,000 DR-35,000 DR.
Discounts: Large groups & stays of over 8 days.

Credit Cards: MC & VISA.
Rsv'tns: Required.
Reserve Through: Call direct.
Minimum Stay: 4 nights.
Parking: Limited free parking.
In-Room: Kitchen, refrigerator, coffee/tea-making facilities & maid service.
On-Premises: Laundry facilities & bar.
Swimming: Nearby pool

& ocean.
Sunbathing: On patio, private sun decks & at poolside.
Nudity: Permitted.
Pets: Permitted.
Handicap Access: No.
Children: Welcome.
Languages: Greek, English, Italian.
Your Host: Sharon.

IRELAND

CORK

Amazonia

Women ♀

The Welcome of Amazonia and Ireland Make an Unforgettable Vacation

From the hilltop windows of *Amazonia* you can look upon the beautiful, rolling, green hills of Ireland and the Atlantic Ocean. The beach is at the bottom of the hill and is very safe for swimming and sports. The walks to the nearby pubs afford marvelous views of the ocean rolling in along the rocky coastline. We have bikes, canoes, body boards, tennis racquets and golf clubs free for the guests' use and we can arrange horseback riding for you. Breakfast, which is either vegetarian or a full Irish fry, is served from 9:00 until 12:00 and you can eat as much or as little as you like! There is free tea and coffee all day. We prepare excellent vegetarian evening meals (optional) with lots of homemade wine and beer.

Address: Coast Road, Fountainstown, Myrtleville, Cork Ireland. Tel: (353-21) 831 115.

Type: Bed & breakfast guesthouse with campsites & small bar.
Clientele: Women only.
Transportation: Car or bus from Cork city. Pick up from arrival point in Cork city (airport, train, bus, ferry dock) £5.00.
To Gay Bars: 10 miles or 30 minutes by car.
Rooms: 3 rooms & 1 suite with single, double or queen beds.
Bathrooms: Private: 2 shower/toilets, 2 sinks. 1 shared bath/shower/ toilets.
Campsites: 3 tent sites with complete use of facilities & breakfast in the main house.
Meals: Full breakfast served until 12:00. Optional vegetarian evening meal, including homemade wine & beer, for £12 extra.
Vegetarian: As breakfast option or excellent evening meal.
Complimentary: Tea or coffee all day.
Dates Open: All year except Christmas.
High Season: May-Sept.
Rates: Rooms £12-£15, suite £22 per woman per day. Camping £5 per tent + £4 per woman (includes breakfast & use of house).
Discounts: 50% off for children.
Rsv'tns: Required during high season.
Reserve Through: Call direct.
Parking: Ample off-street free parking.
In-Room: B&W TV, coffee/tea-making facilities & room service.
On-Premises: TV lounge, library & laundry facilities.
Exercise/Health: Kayaks, bicycles, wind surfers & snorkeling equipment, other sports equipment free. Horseback riding arranged nearby.
Swimming: In nearby ocean or river.
Sunbathing: On the patio or in the garden.
Nudity: Permitted in the garden.
Smoking: Limited to garden & after dinner if necessary.
Pets: Permitted.
Handicap Access: Yes. Bungalow allows reasonable wheelchair access.
Children: Welcomed.
Languages: English, German, French & Italian.
Your Host: Penny & Aine.

Mont Bretia

Vacation in Ireland!

Gay/Lesbian ♀♂

Mont Bretia B&B nestles in the heart of the West Corks in a panoramic, unspoilt countryside. It's a great place to go bicycling (free!) and discover stone circles, castles and forts. Take walks by lake, forest or cliff in an area where natural harbours and pretty fishing villages dot a beautiful coastline. Regular boat service takes you to offshore islands. Here, too, you'll find probably the best pints of Guinness in Ireland. As West Cork is noted for its environmentally-conscious new residents, a wealth of holistic treatments are available in the area, as well as wholefood shops and cafes.

Address: Adrigole Skibbereen, West Cork Ireland. Tel: (028) 33 663

Type: Bed & breakfast.
Clientele: Mostly gay & lesbian with some hetero clientele.
Transportation: By car or we'll drop & collect from buses, no charge.
To Gay Bars: 50 miles.
Rooms: 4 rooms with single or double beds.
Bathrooms: 1 shared bath/shower/toilet & 1 shared toilet.

Meals: Full breakfast.
Vegetarian: Vegetarian meals £6-£12 Irish.
Complimentary: Tea & coffee.
Dates Open: All year.
High Season: June, July & August.
Rates: £13 Irish per person.
Rsv'tns: Required.
Reserve Through: Call direct.

Parking: Ample off-street parking.
In-Room: Bathrobes.
On-Premises: TV lounge, videos, books, sun lounges, outside tables & 1 acre garden.
Exercise/Health: Free bicycles.
Swimming: Nearby pool & ocean.
Sunbathing: In the garden & at the beach.

Smoking: Not permitted in bedrooms. Permitted in TV lounge & dining room.
Pets: Dogs only permitted.
Handicap Access: No.
Children: Welcomed if supervised.
Languages: Irish, English & some French & German.
Your Host: Lynn & Imelda.

DUBLIN

Frankies Guesthouse

Gay/Lesbian ♂

Established in 1989 in mews-style building over 100 years old, *Frankies* offers year-round accommodations exclusively for gays. Dublin has an expanding gay scene, which offers a variety of venues for those looking for adventure, and *Frankies* is located close to the bars, clubs and saunas. Travellers wishing to tour outside Dublin will find breathtaking scenery along the coast road, well worth the trip for those who enjoy the smell of the sea and a sense of freedom. You'll be glad you visited Ireland, a country renowned for its hospitality and friendliness.

Address: 8 Camden Place, Dublin 2 Ireland. Tel: Reservations: (01) 478 3087, Guestline: (01) 475 2182.

Type: Guesthouse.
Clientele: Mostly men with women welcome.
Transportation: Airport bus to city bus sta., taxi from bus sta. approx £3. Taxi from airport approx £10.
To Gay Bars: 8 minutes.
Rooms: 13 rooms with single or double beds.
Bathrooms: 5 en suite, 5 private sinks. Shared: 2 bath/shower/toilets,

1 WC.
Meals: Full Irish breakfast.
Vegetarian: Available on request.
Complimentary: Tea & coffee.
Dates Open: All year.
High Season: July, August, & September.
Rates: Singles from £15.00. Doubles from £30.00 + 12.5% V.A.T.
Discounts: On extended

stays.
Credit Cards: MC, VISA, Amex & Eurocard.
Rsv'tns: Required.
Reserve Through: Call direct.
Parking: Ample, free on-street parking.
In-Room: Color TV & maid service.
On-Premises: TV lounge.
Sunbathing: On the roof terrace.
Smoking: Permitted

without restrictions.
Pets: Not permitted. We have our own.
Handicap Access: Yes, some ground floor rooms.
Children: Not permitted.
Languages: English, Chinese & Malay.
Your Host: Joe & Frankie.

ITALY

FIRENZE (FLORENCE)

Morandi Alla Crocetta

Gay-Friendly ♀♂

The Special Feeling of a Genteel Tuscan Home

In the quiet, distinguished atmosphere of a former convent, *Morandi alla Crocetta* follows an ancient tradition of hospitality. Its location is close to every point of artistic and cultural interest, such as the Statue of David, the Archaeological Museum and the Academy of Fine Arts. This is a hotel for those seeking a small and comfortable place filled with character and charm, in the city-centre and yet away from the typical tourist establishments.

Address: Via Laura 50 Firenze 50121 Italy. Tel: (055) 2344747, Fax: (055) 2480954.

Type: Guesthouse.
Clientele: Mostly straight clientele with a gay & lesbian following.
Transportation: Taxi from airport US $15. From train station $7.00.
To Gay Bars: 2 blocks to gay/lesbian bars.
Rooms: 9 rooms with single & double rooms.
Bathrooms: All private.

Meals: Continental breakfast 18.000 Lire per person.
Dates Open: All year.
High Season: Easter, June-October.
Rates: 89.000 Lire-201.000 Lire.
Credit Cards: MC, VISA, Amex, Diners, Access, Eurocard.
Rsv'tns: Recommended.

Fax or phone O.K.
Reserve Through: Call direct.
Parking: Limited on-street parking.
In-Room: Maid & room service, color satellite TV, telephone, AC, mini-bar refrigerator & laundry service.
Exercise/Health: Nearby gym & weights.

Smoking: Permitted without restrictions.
Pets: Permitted if small and well-behaved.
Handicap Access: No.
Children: Permitted.
Languages: Italian, English, & limited French & German.

ISOLA D'ELBA

Casa Scala

Women ♀

Casa Scala is a small, old Italian house with two sun terraces, surrounded by a garden with trees and flowers, a perfect setting for relaxing when not participating in a workshop. Enjoy the beach which is 1 km away or visit the nearby small city and explore its cafes and shops or engage in a variety of activities such as tennis, diving, or boating.

Address: Loc. Filetto No 9, 57034 Marina di Campo, Isola d'Elba Italy. Tel: 0039-565-977777, Fax: 0039-565-977770.

Type: Cottage with workshops.
Clientele: Women only.
Transportation: Car is best or train from Florence to Elba, pick up from bus station Marina di Campo.
Rooms: 4 apartments with single beds.
Bathrooms: All shared.
Meals: Continental breakfast with workshop.

Dates Open: March-October.
High Season: July-August.
Rates: DM 1,000.00 for workshop for two weeks (includes accommodations & breakfast), or DM 30.00-DM 40.00 per night.
Credit Cards: Eurocheck.
Rsv'tns: Required.
Reserve Through: Call direct.
Minimum Stay: One

week in general. Single days for women from overseas.
Parking: Adequate free off-street parking.
In-Room: VCR, video tape library, kitchen, refrigerator, coffee & tea-making facilities.
On-Premises: Meeting rooms, garden.
Exercise/Health: Yoga.
Swimming: Nearby ocean beach.

Sunbathing: In the garden, on the beach.
Nudity: Permitted in the garden.
Smoking: Permitted.
Pets: Not permitted.
Handicap Access: No.
Children: Boys not permitted after 10 years of age.
Languages: German, Italian, English.
Your Host: Marianne & Elvira.

ROMA (ROME)

Hotel Scalinata di Spagna

Gay-Friendly ♀♂

Hotel Scalinata di Spagna has one of the best possible locations, full in the center of Rome and at the top of the famous Spanish Steps. At the foot of the steps is American Express's central office and in the surrounding streets, some of the most famous stores and finest restaurants in the world. Each room has private bath, air conditioning, telephone, security box, and a TV. Breakfast is served on the terrace overlooking all of Rome. Parking is nearby.

Address: Piazza Trinità dei Monti 17, 00187 Roma Italy. Tel: Bookings: (06) 679 3006 or (06) 699 40896, Fax: 699 40598.

Type: Bed & breakfast with roof garden.
Clientele: Mostly straight clientele with a gay/lesbian following.
Transportation: Taxi or Metro to Piazza di Spagna.
To Gay Bars: 5-minute walk to gay bar.
Rooms: 2 singles, 12 doubles, 3 triples.
Bathrooms: All private.
Meals: Expanded continental breakfast.
Complimentary: Tea, coffee, juices, candy on pillow.
Dates Open: All year.
High Season: June-October, except August.
Rates: LI 250,000-300,000.
Credit Cards: MC, VISA & Amex.
Rsv'tns: Required, two months in advance or at last moment.
Reserve Through: Call direct.
Parking: 30,000 Lire/day or on street.
In-Room: Mini bar, radio, AC, TV, maid, room, laundry service, telephone, safe deposit box.
On-Premises: TV lounge, public telephone.
Exercise/Health: Convenient to Borghese Garden for jogging. Steam, sauna, Jacuzzi, gym, 5 min away at Villa Borghese.
Swimming: Ocean beaches 20 miles by train.
Sunbathing: On beach or roof deck.
Smoking: Permitted without restrictions.
Pets: Permitted.
Handicap Access: Yes.
Children: Permitted.
Languages: Italian, English, Spanish, French, German.

TAORMINA

Hotel Villa Schuler

Gay-Friendly ♀♂

History & Tradition, Comfort & Romance

Family-owned *Villa Schuler* was converted from a Sicilian villa to a hotel in 1905. In recent years the hotel has been extensively refurbished, emphasizing its original elegance, charm and atmosphere. Superbly situated above the Ionian Sea, its unique location offers stupendous views of snow-capped Mount Etna and the Bay of Naxos. Its central position, next to the delightful Botanical Gardens and tennis courts, is just 2 minutes from Taormina's famous traffic-free  Corso Umberto. The ancient Greco-Roman theater and the cable-car to the beaches are just a 10-minutes' walk away.

The hotel is surrounded by its own extensive, shady, terraced gardens, where the fragrance of jasmine and bougainvillaea blossoms blend soothingly, enhancing the comfortable, romantic surroundings. Rooms are spacious, each with private bath/shower, WC, orthopaedic beds and mattresses, direct-dial telephone and

continued next page

Italy

electronic safe. Most have balcony/terrace or loggia and seaview. Other amenities include a roof terrace solarium, the palm terrace pavilion, dining and TV rooms (color satellite), small library, piano, 24-hour bar and room service, laundry, parking, garages and central heating. You have the choice of having breakfast served in your room, in the dining room or on the panoramic palm terrace overlooking the entire coastline. Tennis courts nearby. Regular shuttle-service to the beaches (May-Oct). Multilingual staff.

Address: Via Roma, 17 I-98039 Taormina/Sicily Italy. Tel: (39) 942-23481, Fax: (39) 942-23522.

Type: Bed & breakfast hotel & bar.
Clientele: Mainly hetero clientele with a gay & lesbian following.
Transportation: Airport bus to Taormina, or pick up from airport by arrangement Lire 85.000, taxi from train Lire 15.000.
To Gay Bars: 5-minute walk.
Rooms: 26 rooms, 1 suite & 4 apartments with single or double beds.

Bathrooms: Private: 8 bath/toilets, 15 shower/ toilets, 3 sinks. 1 shared bath.
Meals: Expanded continental breakfast.
Vegetarian: Restaurants nearby.
Dates Open: March to December.
High Season: Easter, August.
Rates: LIT 43.500-58.000 per person for B&B.
Credit Cards: MC, VISA, Amex & Eurocard.

Rsv'tns: Recommended, by FAX if possible, (39) 942-23522.
Reserve Through: Travel agent or call direct.
Parking: Adequate, free on-street parking, garage Lit. 11.000 per day.
In-Room: Maid & room service, telephone, safe, laundry service.
On-Premises: TV lounge, meeting rooms, laundry facilities, solarium, exotic garden, furnished terraces.

Exercise/Health: Nearby gym, weights, sauna & massage.
Swimming: At nearby ocean beach, shuttle service available.
Sunbathing: On the roof or at nearby beach.
Smoking: Permitted without restrictions.
Pets: Not permitted.
Handicap Access: No.
Children: Welcomed.
Languages: Italian, English, German, French, Spanish & Belgian.

NETHERLANDS

ALPHEN AAN DEN RIJN

Dakota Homestead

Gay/Lesbian ♀♂

Experience Holland's Green Heart

Dakota Homestead, our new Dutch Home, offers you a quiet, green place to relax but has the cultural events and nightlife of Amsterdam and other large cities close at hand. Our picturesque village nestles in the Green Heart of Holland, a typical Dutch polder landscape of large lakes, canals, windmills and farms, best explored on bicycle. This Green Heart lies in the middle of a circle formed by Amsterdam, The Hague, Rotterdam and Utrecht, all accessible by train or car in a half hour. Locally, we have the Avifauna ornithological park (with large tourboats), the Archeon archeological themepark, and one of Holland's rare golfcourses.

Address: Zuiderkeerkring 391, 2408 HT Alphen A/D Rijn The Netherlands. Tel: (01720) 74626, Fax: (01720) 71382.

Type: Bed & breakfast homestead.
Clientele: Mostly gay & lesbian with some hetero clientele.

Transportation: Car, train. Pick up from Leiden Hfl 15, Schiphol airport Hfl 30 (20-min). 20 min by train from Leiden,

Gouda, Utrecht.
To Gay Bars: 30-40 minutes to Leiden, Utrecht or Amsterdam.
Rooms: 1 room with

attic overflow for large parties. Single & double beds.
Bathrooms: 1 shared bath/shower, 1 shared

WC only.
Meals: Expanded continental breakfast.
Complimentary: Coffee, tea & water. Other drinks available at extra cost.
Dates Open: All year.
Rates: Hfl 50 for 1, Hfl 60 for 2, Hfl 10 for each

additional person.
Rsv'tns: Required.
Reserve Through: Call direct.
Parking: Adequate on-street residential parking.
In-Room: Color cable TV & room service.
On-Premises: Fax machine, laundry services.

Exercise/Health: Nearby gym.
Swimming: 3 pools, ocean & lake nearby.
Sunbathing: At the lake & beach.
Smoking: Permitted on patios or balcony. All sleeping rooms non-smoking.

Pets: Not permitted.
Handicap Access: No.
Children: Not especially welcome.
Languages: Dutch, English, German (one of us).
Your Host: Robert & Paul.

IGTA

AMSTERDAM

Amsterdam House BV

Gay-Friendly ♀♂

When you need a good accommodation in Amsterdam for you, your friends or your business associates, call *Amsterdam House*. We're close to the main railway station and other major transport intersections. All our 35 apartments and 6 houseboats are spacious and have luxuriously-furnished rooms, fully equipped kitchens, bathrooms, telephones, stereo and TV with CNN and a 24-hour movie channel. A fax, answering machine and photocopier are available on request, as is secretarial service. And of course, we provide linens, towels and maid service. Most of our apartments overlook the Amsterdam canals. Staying in one of *Amsterdam House's* apartments or houseboats, our guests have easy access, not only to Amsterdam International Airport, but to Amsterdam's business district and the complete range of amenities offered by this, one of Europe's greatest capitals. The unique experience of staying in a houseboat can make your stay in this, the Venice of the North, truly unforgettable and something special.
Address: Staalkade 4, 1011JN Amsterdam Netherlands. Tel: (31-20) 626 2577, Fax: (31-20) 626 2987, US: (305) 442-6580, (800) 770-2890, Fax: 446-2540.

Amsterdam House

Type: Apartment hotel.
Clientele: Mostly hetero with a gay & lesbian following.
Transportation: Free pick up with prior arrangement.
To Gay Bars: Some apartments are steps away & most are only 1 minute away.
Rooms: 35 apartments & 6 houseboats.
Bathrooms: All private.

Dates Open: All year.
High Season: June-September & New Year's Eve.
Rates: Hfl 95-425.
Discounts: For groups & long stays.
Credit Cards: MC, VISA, Amex & Diners.
Rsv'tns: Preferred.
Reserve Through: Travel agent or call direct.
Parking: Adequate on-street parking,

depending on traffic.
In-Room: Color TV, telephone, kitchen, refrigerator, maid & laundry service.
On-Premises: Meeting rooms & laundry facilities. Some houseboats have terraces.
Exercise/Health: Many exercise facilities in the neighborhood.
Sunbathing: At the beach.

Smoking: Permitted. Non-smoking rooms available.
Pets: Permitted.
Handicap Access: Some accommodations are accessible.
Children: Permitted.
Languages: Dutch, German, Spanish, English, French.
Your Host: Willemina & Cyril.

Anco

Men ♂

Under new management, since April, 1993, *Hotel Anco* still welcomes gay men from all over the world. Our building, dating from 1640, is between the famous leather district (Warmoesstraat) and the Red Light District, overlooking a canal. For guests in the hotel, it is possible to cruise and to make use of the nice patio. If you are sitting in the bar, you have a very nice view of a typical gay monument, "de Amsterdamse krul." Amenities include convenient late breakfast, personal attention and your own personal key, so you can do as you please.

Address: Oudezijds Voorburgwal 55, Amsterdam, The Netherlands. Tel: (20) 624 11 26, Fax: (20) 620 52 75.

Type: Hotel & bar for leathermen.
Clientele: Men only.
Transportation: Train from airport to central station, then taxi or 5-minute walk.
To Gay Bars: On premises, open from 10am-10pm. 2-minute walk to other gay bars.
Rooms: 12 rooms, 2 dormitories & 1 suite with private bath.
Bathrooms: Private: 14 sinks, 1 bath. Shared bath/shower/toilet on each floor.
Meals: Expanded continental breakfast.
Dates Open: All year.
High Season: June 1-October 31.
Rates: HFL 60.00-120.00. With private bath & TV Hfl 175.00.
Credit Cards: All cards accepted.
Rsv'tns: Required at least 4 weeks in advance in high season.
Reserve Through: Call direct.
Minimum Stay: 2 nights during high season.
In-Room: Maid service. One room has color cable TV.
On-Premises: Meeting room, gay bar.
Swimming: 20 miles to nude beach & lakeside Amsterdam.
Sunbathing: At the beach.
Nudity: Permitted on the floors & patio. 30-minute train ride to nude beach.
Smoking: Permitted without restrictions.
Pets: Permitted if clean.
Handicap Access: No.
Children: Not permitted.
Languages: Dutch, English, German, Italian & French.

Apart' Hotel Centre Apartments Amsterdam

Men ♂

The apartments and studios are new (some in restored old Amsterdam houses), spotlessly clean, attractively furnished and, for Amsterdam, palatial. Anybody who prefers the privacy afforded by self-catered accommodations, quiet and luxurious surroundings and enormous and comfortable double bed...all located just around the corner from Central Station and adjacent to Damrak, Dam-Square and Amsterdam's gay streets...all at less than luxury hotel prices—look no further! *Centre Apartments'* front door opens onto a pedestrian street, well-lit at night. Just in case anybody is worried for their safety in this ancient part of the city, there is a friendly police station in sight, a few steps away, where the pedestrian street joins Warmoesstraat. For self-catering supplies, there is a supermarket nearby.

Nearby Central Station is the starting point

Netherlands

for most city tram routes, canal boat excursions and coach and rail excursions to other parts of The Netherlands. Next door is the Museum Amstelkring, a 17th-century canal house with authentic period rooms and a secret Roman Catholic church in the attic. A short walk in either direction leads you to the famous Red Light District or the Royal Palace and Madame Tussaud's.

Address: Heintje Hoekssteeg 27, 1012 GR Amsterdam   The Netherlands. Tel: (020) 627 25 03, Fax: (020) 625 11 08.

Type: Luxury apartments & studios.
Clientele: Mostly gay men & gay leather men.
Transportation: Central Station (tram 1, 2, 4, 5, 9, 13, 16, 17, 24, 25) or taxi (tel 677 77 77).
To Gay Bars: Nearby.
Rooms: 14 fully-furnished apartments & studios. Apartments have single & double bed-rooms.
Bathrooms: Private.
Meals: Self catering.
Vegetarian: At nearby supermarkets.
Rates: In advance, per night: Apts F 175-195, studio F 145-165. F 50 standard service cost.
Rsv'tns: Required with deposit of F 450 (£150 or US $300) which is held until departure.
Reserve Through: Call direct
Minimum Stay: 3 nights.
Parking: No street parking. Use underground Victoria or de Bijenkorf parking areas.
In-Room: Radio, colour TV, kitchen, refrigerator & cooker. Some apart-ments have VCR, tape deck, or CD players.
Pets: Not permitted.
Handicap Access: No. Staircase to apartments, steps to studios.
Languages: Dutch, English, French, Italian, Portuguese, German & Spanish.

IGTA

Chico Guest House

Gay/Lesbian ♂

Address: Sint Willibrordusstraat 77, 1073 VA Amsterdam,   The Netherlands. Tel: (31-20) 675 4241.

Type: Guesthouse.
Clientele: Mostly men with women welcome.
To Gay Bars: 15 minutes walking, 3 minutes by tram.
Rooms: 3 rooms & 2 apartments with single & double beds.
Bathrooms: Rooms share baths on landing. Apartments have private baths.
Complimentary: Coffee & tea.
Dates Open: All year.
Rates: Hfl 40-Hfl 50 per person per night.
Rsv'tns: Required.
Reserve Through: Call direct.
Parking: Limited on-street parking.
In-Room: Clean towels daily, bed linen every 3-4 days.
Smoking: Permitted
without restrictions.
Pets: Not permitted.
Handicap Access: No.
Children: We prefer not.
Languages: Dutch, German, Indonesian & English.
Your Host: Ronald & Herman.

Freeland Hotel

Gay/Lesbian ♂

Freeland is centrally located, near the Leidseplein. There are garage parking facilities for your car. Go ahead and park it...you won't need it while you are in the city! The gayest streets in Amsterdam are a short walk away from your door, as are the most interesting tourist attractions. Bienvenue! Welcome!
Address: Marnixstraat 386, 1017 PL Amsterdam The Netherlands. Tel: (020) 622 75 11/627 75 78, Fax: 626 77 44.

Type: Hotel.
Clientele: Mostly men with women welcome.
Transportation: Trams 1, 2 and 5 from Central station.
To Gay Bars: Walking distance from gay/lesbian bars.
Rooms: Singles & doubles.
Bathrooms: Private all rooms.
Meals: Full Dutch breakfast.
Dates Open: All year.
Rates: Hfl 75.00-Hfl 95.00 single, Hfl 150.00-Hfl 175.00 double.
Credit Cards: MC, VISA & Amex.
Rsv'tns: Required.
Reserve Through: Call direct.
Parking: Pay for parking in nearby parking garage.
In-Room: Color cable TV & telephone.
On-Premises: TV lounge & meeting rooms.
Swimming: Ocean beach 20 kilometers, Zandvoort aan de zee.
Sunbathing: At the beach.
Pets: Small pets permitted.
Languages: Dutch, French, German, English & Spanish.

Greenwich Village Hotel

You Don't Need an Expensive Taxi

Gay-Friendly 50/50 ♀♂

Situated on the Kerkstraat, Amsterdam's gayest street, *Greenwich Village* places you right in the middle of what's happening. This is where you want to be: in the center of town within easy reach of nightlife, restaurants, museums and other attractions. The hotel has 2-, 3- and 4-person rooms with shower and bathroom and there is a café on the premises.

Address: 25 Kerkstraat, 1017 GA Amsterdam The Netherlands. Tel: (20) 626 9746 or Fax: (20) 625 4081.

Type: Apartment hotel with bar for residents, café downstairs. **Clientele:** 50% gay & lesbian & 50% straight clientele. **Transportation:** Tram 1, 2 & 5 from central station. **To Gay Bars:** Close to all gay/lesbian bars. **Rooms:** 10 rooms for 1-5 people. Guests receive their own front door key. **Bathrooms:** All private. **Meals:** Dutch breakfast. **Dates Open:** All year. **Rates:** Please inquire. **Reserve Through:** Call direct. **In-Room:** The larger rooms have sofas, tables & easy chairs. All rooms have refrigerators & colour TVs. **Nudity:** Short train ride to nude beach. **Smoking:** Permitted without restrictions. **Pets:** Not permitted. **Languages:** Dutch & English.

Hotel Aero

Gay/Lesbian ♂

Hotel Aero is conveniently located in the heart of Amsterdam. All rooms have been converted to satisfy modern tastes and are provided with every comfort and convenience. Most rooms have telephones and TV with VCR. Our Tavern de Pul, with its inviting Dutch atmosphere, is a place where everyone drops in and feels in his element.

Address: Kerkstraat 49, 1017 GB, Amsterdam-C, The Netherlands. Tel: (20) 622 77 28, Fax: 638 8531.

Type: Hotel with bar & gay-sex shop downstairs. **Clientele:** Mostly men with women welcome. **Transportation:** Taxi or trams or walking. **To Gay Bars:** All within walking distance & many on the same street. **Rooms:** 4 singles, 12 doubles. **Bathrooms:** 11 private, others shared. **Meals:** Full breakfast. **Dates Open:** All year. **Rates:** Hfl 130-Hfl 165. **Credit Cards:** MC, VISA, Amex, E-Card. **Rsv'tns:** Required two weeks in advance. **Reserve Through:** Call direct. **Parking:** Off- & on-street parking available. **In-Room:** Color TV, telephone & VCR in most rooms. **Swimming:** Ocean & lake beaches nearby. **Nudity:** 30-minute train ride to nude beach. **Smoking:** Permitted without restrictions. **Pets:** All permitted. **Handicap Access:** No. **Children:** Not permitted. **Languages:** Dutch, English, Spanish, French, German. **Your Host:** Pedro.

Hotel Orfeo

Men ♂

Orfeo is a mostly-male guesthouse in the centre of the city, two minutes walking distance from gay activities, museums, shopping mall, restaurants, and casino. All guests get their own keys and can come and go as they please. There is a fully-licensed bar on the hotel premises. Travellers from North or South America ALWAYS arrive in the early morning on the day after departure, and may wish to consider reserving a room from the previous day onwards, so that they can occupy their room immediately upon arrival. Reservations can be made by phone or mail. **Address: Leidsekruisstraat 14, 1017 RH Amsterdam (Centre) The Netherlands. Tel: (020) 623 1347, Confirmation only: Fax: 620 2348.**

Type: Bed & breakfast with bar. **Clientele:** 99% men. **Transportation:** From the airport take a taxi or train to Central Station. From Central Station take a taxi or tram no. 1, 2, or 5. **To Gay Bars:** 5-minute walk to gay & lesbian bars. **Rooms:** 3 singles, 11 doubles & 6 triples. **Bathrooms:** 6 private & 4 shared. **Meals:** Full breakfast.

Dates Open: All year.
High Season: April 1st-November 15th.
Rates: Hfl 72.50-195.00 with guaranteed reservation. NO refund on first night.
Credit Cards: All major credit cards.

Rsv'tns: Required in high season one month in advance.
Reserve Through: Call direct.
Minimum Stay: 4 nights in high season.
Parking: Covered off-street pay parking at

Prinsengracht.
In-Room: Personal safe, room and laundry service. Direct calling system.
On-Premises: TV Lounge, laundry facilities & public telephone.
Exercise/Health: Sauna.

Nudity: 30-minute train ride to nude beach.
Smoking: Permitted without restrictions.
Handicap Access: No.
Languages: Dutch, Spanish, French, German, Italian, Hebrew & English.
Your Host: Avi & Peter.

Hotel Sander

Gay/Lesbian ♀♂

This attractive 4-star hotel is situated only a block away from the Van Gogh Museum and the Concertgebouw (Concert Hall) and is just a ten-minute walk from the Kerkstraat gay area, a gay fitness centre and both the day and night saunas. *Hotel Sander* is also only a fifteen-minute walk from the most famous women's cafe in Amsterdam.

This 5-storey hotel has an elevator, so less athletic guests needn't worry about climbing the famous steep stairs of Amsterdam. The reception staff speaks English, German, French, Spanish, Italian and Portuguese and operates 24 hours a day, as does our fully licensed bar, *The Portal*. Guests can order snacks and refreshments at any time of the day or night. Room service is available from approximately 8:00-22:00, and a same day laundry and dry-cleaning service operates Monday through Friday.

All room rates include Dutch continental breakfast served in the spacious breakfast room adjacent to the bar area and ground floor reception. A large variety of side orders can be ordered from our breakfast staff.

In warm weather, patio doors open onto a flower-filled terrace and garden where guests can relax in an oasis of calm in the middle of a bustling city.

All guest rooms include colour cable TV, direct-dial telephone, radio, individual safe and en suite WC and shower. Some rooms also have bathtubs.

Hotel Sander is easy to reach from Schiphol Airport via the train to Station Zuid/WTC. From there, take either Bus 63 to Jacob Obrechtstraat (10 minutes), Tram 5 to the Concert Hall (10 minutes) or a taxi (approximately 15 guilders). From the Central Railway Station, take Tram 16 to Jacob Obrechtstraat (15 minutes).

Reservations can be make by phone, fax or mail. Ask about our special winter rates, including our offer of 1 night free on stays of 4 or more nights! This offer is valid from November 1st, 1994 to April 1st, 1995 (excluding Christmas and New Year). In the event that *Hotel Sander* is fully booked, our reception staff will be only too happy to suggest an alternative suitable accommodation.

Address: Jacob Obrechtstraat 69, 1071 KJ Amsterdam, The Netherlands.
Tel: (020) 6627574, Fax: (020) 6796067.

Type: Hotel with bar.
Clientele: Mostly gay & lesbian with some hetero clientele.
Transportation: To Jacob

Obrechtstraat: From Schiphol Airport, train to station Zuid then Bus 63; From Central Station, Tram 16.

To Gay Bars: 1 mile. A 10-minute walk or 5-minute drive.
Rooms: 20 rooms with single or double beds.

Bathrooms: All private.
Meals: Expanded continental breakfast.

continued next page

Netherlands

Vegetarian: Our bar serves some vegetarian snacks 24 hours a day. 5-minute walk to vegetarian restaurant.
Dates Open: All year.
High Season: 1 April-1 November, X-Mas-New Years.
Rates: Hi: single HFL 125-165, dble HFL 145-195, twin HFL 155-210. Low: single HFL 100-125, dble HFL 125-165, twin HFL 145-185.

Discounts: Winter: 1 night free on stays of 4 or more nights.
Credit Cards: MC, VISA, Amex, Diners & Eurocard.
Rsv'tns: Required.
Reserve Through: Call direct.
Parking: Adequate free on-street space. Pay parking covered garage HFL 17.50 (24hr).
In-Room: Color cable TV, telephone, coffee/tea-making facilities, room &

laundry service.
On-Premises: 24-hour bar & snack service.
Exercise/Health: Nearby gym, weights, Jacuzzi, sauna, steam & massage.
Swimming: Nearby pool, lake & ocean.
Sunbathing: At the beach.
Smoking: Permitted in bar, lounge & most rooms. Some non-smoking bedrooms available.

Pets: Not permitted.
Handicap Access: Yes. Elevator.
Children: Not especially welcome.
Languages: Dutch, English, German, French, Spanish, Italian & Portuguese.
Your Host: Frits & Michael.

IGTA

Hotel Wilhelmina

Gay-Friendly ♀♂

Hotel Wilhelmina is centrally located in the heart of Amsterdam's shopping and cultural centre, convenient to museums, the concert hall, Vondel Park, the World Trade Centre and the Central Station. Schiphol Amsterdam Airport is a 10-minute drive away. The hotel is recommended in the Michelin Hotel Guide, the Amsterdam Tourist Office, most European automobile clubs and airlines. The efficient management, inspired by great hospitality, will do all to enhance the pleasure and comfort of your stay. Breakfast is served in the hotel, and an enormous variety of restaurants can be found in the vicinity.

Address: Koninginne Weg 167-169, 1075 CN Amsterdam   The Netherlands. Tel: (020) 662 5467, Fax: (020) 679 2296, Telex: WILHL NL.

Type: Hotel.
Clientele: Mostly straight clientele with a gay & lesbian following.
Transportation: Trams 2 & 16 to Valeriusplein.
To Gay Bars: 1 km to Kerkstraat gay bars.
Rooms: 19 rooms with single or double beds.
Bathrooms: En suite: 14 shower/toilets, 5 sinks.

Shared: 3 showers, 3 WCs.
Meals: Full Dutch breakfast.
Vegetarian: Vegetarian breakfast. Vegetarian restaurants nearby.
Dates Open: All year.
High Season: March-November.
Rates: Dfl 75-Dfl 175.
Discounts: Please

inquire.
Credit Cards: Most major credit cards.
Rsv'tns: Required.
Reserve Through: Call direct.
Parking: Adequate free on-street parking.
In-Room: Maid, room & laundry service & color cable TV.
On-Premises: Private

dining rooms, TV lounge & bicycle storage.
Sunbathing: On the patio.
Smoking: Not permitted in dining room, lounge, toilets, or passageways.
Pets: Not permitted.
Handicap Access: No.
Children: Permitted.
Languages: Dutch, German & English.

ITC Hotel

Amsterdam is a unique and beguiling city. The famous canals, with their 16th-century houses and bridges, are in contrast to modern shopping streets and spacious parks. A few top attractions: The Rijksmuseum, The Van Gogh and Stedelijk museums (all close together), the Concertgebouw, Anne Frank House, the Zoo & Royal Palace. Amsterdam is the gay capital of Europe, therefore, the choice of night spots ranges from fashionable discos to levi or leather. You will find numerous bars, clubs, saunas, cinemas and bookstores, enough to fill everyone's needs 24 hours a day, 7 days a week, all year round. Don't forget your beach clothes in the summer. Zandvoort, 45 minutes away by train is the biggest gay nude beach area in Europe!

ITC HOTEL

Double/twin rooms with shower & toilet, triple available breakfast till noon - your own key bar - central location

Call Stewart
011-31-20-6230230 or write to
ITC Prinsengracht 1051
1017 JE Amsterdam
Holland

The *ITC Hotel* is the ideal base for your stay in Amsterdam. Situated on Prinsengracht, one of the main canals, it places you in the heart of Old Amsterdam. The moment you walk out the door, you are only a six-minute walk from Rembrandtplein and 8 minutes from Kerkstraat, the two main gay areas of Amsterdam. You will love the warm, friendly atmosphere and the welcome you receive at *ITC Hotel*. You will be glad to come "home" after an exciting day or night (or both, if you can manage) and relax in the lounge talking, drinking, watching TV with friends or other guests. The hotel bar is open till 12 midnight. The bedrooms, most with their own baths, are pleasantly furnished in a modern style. Other attractions are: a late breakfast, personal attention and your own front door key, so you can do as you please.

Address: Prinsengracht 1051, Amsterdam 1017 JE The Netherlands. Tel: (31 20) 623-0230, Fax: (20) 624-5846.

Type: Hotel with bar.
Clientele: Mostly men with women welcome.
Transportation: Tram from Central Station then Tram 4 to Prinsengracht.
To Gay Bars: 6-minute walk to men and women's bars.
Rooms: 15 rooms.
Bathrooms: 10 private & 1 shared.

Meals: Full breakfast buffet.
Dates Open: All year.
High Season: July-early October, Christmas, New Years, & Easter.
Rates: Singles Hfl 75.00-90.00, doubles Hfl 130.00-165.00, triples Hfl 215.00-220.00.
Credit Cards: MC, VISA, Access, Euro.

Rsv'tns: Advised at least 2 weeks in advance for weekends.
Reserve Through: Call direct.
Minimum Stay: 3 days weekends & holidays.
Parking: Garage nearby (fee).
In-Room: Color TV, telephone & radio.
On-Premises: TV lounge.

Swimming: 45 minutes by train to gay nude beach.
Smoking: Permitted without restrictions.
Pets: Permitted.
Handicap Access: No.
Children: Negotiable.
Languages: Dutch, English, French & German.

King Hotel

Gay-Friendly ♀♂

Housed in an authentic 17th-Century Amsterdam historic canal house overlooking one of Amsterdam's grand canals, *King Hotel* is an ideal location for either the tourist or business traveller who wants a high level of comfort for a low-level price. This 65-bed Royal Budget Hotel is right next to the Leidseplein in the center of Amsterdam, close to all attractions. The hotel is easily accessible from the central station or from the KLM City Centre airport bus stop at the Marriot Hotel.

Address: 85-86 Leidsekade, 1017 PN Amsterdam The Netherlands. Tel: (020) 624-9603. Fax: (020) 620-7277.

Type: Hotel.
Clientele: Mostly straight clientele with a gay & lesbian following.
Transportation: Tram 1, 2 & 5 to Leidseplein.
To Gay Bars: 4-min. walk to Kerkstraat gay area bars.
Rooms: 4 singles, 15 doubles, 4 triples, 2 quads.
Bathrooms: 6 shared baths.
Meals: Vegetarian or full

typical Dutch breakfast.
Vegetarian: Always available. Vegetarians especially welcome.
Dates Open: All year.
High Season: March-October.
Rates: Low season Hfl 55.00-Hfl 95.00. High season Hfl 70.00-Hfl 130.00. Extra bed Hfl 35.00.
Discounts: Please inquire.
Credit Cards: MC, VISA,

Access & Eurocard.
Reserve Through: Travel agent or call direct.
Parking: In front of hotel or at nearby garage.
In-Room: Wash basins, laundry, room & maid service.
On-Premises: Central heat & storage area for bicycles.
Swimming: 500 meters

to swimming.
Nudity: Short train ride to nude beach.
Smoking: Not permitted in dining room, toilets, or passageways.
Pets: Not permitted.
Handicap Access: No.
Children: Permitted.
Languages: Dutch, German, & English.

Liliane's Home; Guesthouse for Women Only

Women ♀

Small, Comfortable & Personal

Liliane's Home is located in a renovated manor in the stately Plantagebuurt and provides short- or extended-stay women-only lodging in the heart of Amsterdam. Public transportation access is excellent. Your room will be on one of two floors located directly above the owner's own home. This intimate arrangement ensures personal attention in a warm and comfortable environment. Common rooms include living room, kitchen and bath facilities.

This combination of central location and comfortable, intimate, personal service, provides all the necessary ingredients for a pleasant and successful visit to Amsterdam. Public transportation access is excellent. The bus, tram and metro all stop at the door, and transportation to and from Schiphol Airport is optimal. Downtown cultural centers, movies, galleries and a variety of nightlife are all within walking distance.

Address: Sarphatistraat 119, 1018 GB, Amsterdam, Netherlands. Tel & Fax: (020) 627 4006.

Type: Guesthouse.
Clientele: Women only.
Transportation: From Schiphol Airport, train to Central Station, then subway to Weesperplein or

tram 6, 7, 10. Pick up, Hfl 40.
To Gay Bars: 2 blocks or a 5-minute walk.
Rooms: 5 rooms with single or double beds.

Bathrooms: 2 private sinks only. Shared: 1 bathtub, 1 shower & 1 WC only.
Meals: Breakfast on weekends, Hfl 7,5 per

person.
Vegetarian: Vegetarian restaurants nearby.
Complimentary: Tea & coffee. Soft drinks & beer, Hfl 1,5.

Dates Open: All year.
Rates: Per room: Hfl 65 1 person, Hfl 110 2 people, Hfl 140 3 people.
Discounts: 5% for longer than 7 days.
Rsv'tns: Required.
Reserve Through: Call direct.

Minimum Stay: 2 days.
Parking: Limited on-street pay parking. Covered private parking, 1 car Hfl 25/day.
In-Room: Color cable TV, coffee/tea-making facilities, maid & laundry service.

On-Premises: Meeting rooms, garage, big living room & kitchen.
Exercise/Health: Massage. Nearby gym, weights, sauna, steam & massage.
Sunbathing: On the patio & balcony.

Smoking: Permitted in living room. Sleeping rooms are non-smoking!
Handicap Access: No.
Children: Not especially welcome.
Languages: Dutch, English & German.
Your Host: Liliane.

Maes B&B

Gay-Friendly 50/50 ♀♂

Maes B&B's recently-renovated turn-of-the-century home has quaint, comfortable guest rooms decorated in the style of that period, with the accent on cozy homelike ambiance. Awaken to fresh croissants, just part of the extended continental breakfast served in the privacy of your room. Our quiet street in the Concertgebouw area is near trams, the Concertgebouw, the Rijksmuseum, and the Van Gogh and the Stedelijk museums. Numerous restaurants and night spots are within walking distance, as is the Albert Cuyp street market and the trendy shopping street, PC Hooftstraat.

Address: Nicolaas Maesstraat 94A, 1071 RE Amsterdam The Netherlands. Tel: (3120) 679 4496, Fax: (3120) 679 5595.

Type: Bed & Breakfast.
Clientele: 50% gay & lesbian & 50% hetero clientele.
Transportation: Airport: train to Sta. Zuid/WTC, then tram #5 to Concertgebouw. Central Sta: tram #5 or #16 to Concertgebouw. Or taxi.
To Gay Bars: 20 minutes by foot.
Rooms: 3 rooms with single, double or king beds.

Bathrooms: 3 private sinks. Shared: 1 bath, 1 shower & 2 WCs.
Meals: Expanded continental breakfast.
Complimentary: Tea & coffee available from guest pantry all day.
Dates Open: All year.
Rates: Hfl 65.00-Hfl 120.00.
Rsv'tns: Required.
Reserve Through: Call direct.

Minimum Stay: 2 nights on weekends.
Parking: Limited free on-street parking. In 1995, parking meters will be installed.
On-Premises: Laundry facilities & guest pantry with refrigerator & coffee/tea-making facilities. Telephone & fax services.
Exercise/Health: Nearby gym, weights, Jacuzzi, sauna, steam & massage.

Swimming: In nearby North Sea & city swimming pools.
Sunbathing: On the beach or in the parks.
Nudity: Permitted at the beach & in some parks.
Smoking: Not permitted.
Pets: Not permitted.
Handicap Access: No.
Children: Welcome.
Languages: Dutch, English, some French & German.

Quentin, The

Gay-Friendly 50/50 ♀♂

Though this is not an entirely gay hotel, many lesbians and gay men treat it as their home-away-from-home. Many are visiting artists, musicians and performers. Many rooms have a picturesque view of the canal, with large windows to let the sun flood in. At *The Quentin,* decor is basic, but comfortable, and the rooms are cleaned daily. There is 24-hour service at the reception desk, where we provide tourist information, tour leaflets and guide books.

Address: Leidsekade 89, 1017 PN Amsterdam The Netherlands. Tel: (31-20) 626 21 87 or 627 44 08.   Fax: (31-20) 622 0121.

Type: Hotel with bar.
Clientele: 50% gay, lesbian & 50% hetero (good mix of men & women).
Transportation: From central station take Tram #1, 2 or 5, from airport KLM bus to centre (30 mins).
To Gay Bars: 5-minute walk to gay/lesbian bars.
Rooms: 15 rooms with single beds.

Bathrooms: All private.
Complimentary: House bar open 24 hours.
Dates Open: Feb 1st-Nov 30th, closed Dec-Jan.
High Season: Apr-Oct.
Rates: Singles approx. Hfl 75.00, doubles approx. Hfl 85.00, twin approx. Hfl 100.00. Large rooms Hfl 150.00.
Credit Cards: MC, VISA,

Amex & Diners.
Rsv'tns: Required.
Reserve Through: Call direct.
Parking: On-street pay parking, parking garage nearby.
In-Room: Maid service.
On-Premises: TV lounge, 24-hour house bar.
Swimming: 30 minutes to ocean beach, public

pool nearby.
Smoking: Permitted without restrictions.
Pets: Not permitted.
Handicap Access: No, steep stairs, no elevator.
Children: Not permitted.
Languages: Dutch, English, Spanish, French, German, Polish, Italian & Japanese.

Riverside Apartments

Gay-Friendly 50/50 ♀♀♂

Built in 1652 as a storehouse for grain, wheat, and other commodities, *Riverside Apartments* was recently renovated in the traditional Golden Age style, with wooden beams. It has magnificent canal views and has been luxuriously furnished to make you feel at home away from home. Each double apartment has a furnished lounge, a magnificent view, color TV, leather furniture, private kitchen with modern appliances, a bathroom, large separate bedroom and breakfast room. *Riverside Apartments* are located near everything, City Hall, the opera house, entertainment center, and a variety of excellent restaurants.

Address: Amstel 138, 1017 AD Amsterdam   Netherlands. Tel: (31 20) 627 9797, Fax: 627 9858.

Type: Apartments.
Clientele: 50% hetero & 50% gay/lesbian clientele.
Transportation: Tram 4 or 9 or taxi from Central Railway Sta, pick up on request for actual costs + 10%.
To Gay Bars: 1 block, 1 minute.
Rooms: 6 apartments with single, double, queen or king beds.
Bathrooms: All private bath/toilets.
Vegetarian: Two blocks away or catering.
Complimentary: Tea & coffee available in apartments.
Dates Open: All year.
High Season: Apr-Oct.
Rates: Hfl 150.00-Hfl 300.00 per day, Hfl 875.00-Hfl 1750.00 per wk & Hfl 3000.00-Hfl 5500.00 per month.
Discounts: 5% for cash.
Credit Cards: MC, VISA, Amex, Diners, Bancard, Eurocard.
Rsv'tns: Required.
Reserve Through: Call direct or fax.
Minimum Stay: One week.
Parking: Adequate off-street covered pay parking, limited on-street pay parking.
In-Room: Color cable TV, telephone, kitchen, refrigerator, coffee & tea-making facilities, maid & laundry service.
Exercise/Health: Nearby gym, weights, Jacuzzi, sauna, steam, massage.
Swimming: 30 min by train to ocean beach.
Sunbathing: On the beach.
Nudity: Northsea Beach & some Amsterdam areas (Sloterplas & Nieuwe Meer).
Smoking: Permitted without restrictions.
Pets: Permitted, if clean.
Handicap Access: No.
Children: Permitted if well-behaved.
Languages: Dutch, English, German, French.
Your Host: Geuje (Jerry).

Singel Suite, The Bed & Breakfast Suites

Gay-Friendly ♀♂

The *Singel Suite* is on the first floor of a classic Amsterdam *grachtenpand* house overlooking one of the prettiest canals in the heart of Amsterdam. The apartment has a separate living room, a bedroom, and a Jacuzzi-bath bathroom next to the patio. There is a minibar, telephone, fax, KTV and VCR with about 150 videos to choose from. Surrounded by culture, canals, and antique shops, the famous Spui, Rembrandtsplein, Leidseplein and the flowermarket are close by. We are also near the city's most well-known clubs & restaurants, among them the gay bars and discos of Reguliersdwarsstraat. Guests at *Singel Suite* will find something better than the average hotel. They will find luxury, privacy and comfort.

Address: Singel 420, 1016 AK Amsterdam, The Netherlands. Tel: (31-20) 625 8673, Fax: (31-20) 625 8097.

Type: Bed & breakfast apartment suite.
Clientele: We don't question our guests' orientation.
Transportation: Taxi from airport to Central Station, then tram 1, 2, or 5 (a 10-minute ride).
To Gay Bars: 1 block or a 2-minute walk.
Rooms: 1 apartment with king & extra bed.
Bathrooms: Private.
Meals: Expanded continental breakfast.
Vegetarian: Available nearby.
Complimentary: Cheese, sausages & a variety of appetizers in the minibar.
Dates Open: All year.
Rates: Hfl 245 for two persons.
Discounts: Weekly rates, 3 day weekend.
Credit Cards: MC, VISA, Amex, Diners & Eurocard.
Rsv'tns: Required.
Reserve Through: Call direct.
Minimum Stay: Depends on time of arrival. If in the morning, 2 days.
Parking: Limited on-street pay parking. Best to park in parking garage.
In-Room: Color cable TV, VCR, video tape library, telephone, refrigerator, limited kitchen, coffee/tea-making facilities & maid service.
On-Premises: Fax.
Exercise/Health: Jacuzzi on premises. Nearby gym, weights, Jacuzzi, sauna, steam & massage.
Swimming: Nearby pool. 30 minutes to ocean, 20 minutes to lake.
Sunbathing: On the patio & at the beach.
Nudity: 15-20 minutes to nude area.
Smoking: Permitted.
Pets: Small pets permitted with deposit.
Handicap Access: No.
Children: Welcome.
Languages: Dutch, French, English, German.
Your Host: Anthony & Jacqueline.

Sunhead of 1617

Gay/Lesbian ♀♂

The GENEROUS Dutch Treat!

Located in one of the oldest listed canal houses of rustic Amsterdam, this small and friendly bed-and-delicious-breakfast offers the best value for your money. Our very central, yet quiet, location is a five-minute walk from Central Station and virtually all the city's historical, cultural and gay amenities such as the Anne Frank House, the Homo monument, the Royal Palace, several historical churches and synagogues, the "Begijn" courtyard, the Theater museum and the Regulierdwarsstraat gay district. Our area is famous for its boutiques, good restaurants and cafés.

Upon arrival, guests are welcomed with a fresh fruit and wine basket. Each day, they are also served late afternoon delicacies, such as dim sum, sushi or cheese and paté, with our delectable house cocktail.

The third floor rooms overlook Amsterdam's loveliest canal and gabled roofs. Each room has vaulted ceilings, Japanese inspired decor, skylighting, modern toilet and shower, CTV, VCR, fridge, coffee/tea-making facilities, daily maid service and fresh flowers and plants galore! This 17th-century house has no elevator.

Full breakfast is served in the privacy of your own room from 8:00-10:30. Fruit juice and alcoholic beverages are available and dinner is served upon request. Other amenities include in-house pay phone, fax, IBM PC and video library. Guests also have access to the city center's best equipped gym with licensed trainer (US $10 per visit).

Address: Herengracht 152, 1016 BN Amsterdam, The Netherlands. Tel: (31-20) 626 1809, Fax: (31-20) 626-1823.

Type: Bed & breakfast.
Clientele: Mostly gay & lesbian with some hetero clientele.
Transportation: Pick up from airport Hfl 35.00. Pick up from train Hfl 10.00.
To Gay Bars: 4 blocks or a 5-minute walk.
Rooms: 2 rooms & 1 apartment with single or double beds.
Bathrooms: All private.
Meals: Full breakfast & afternoon snacks of dim sum or cheese and paté with wine.

Vegetarian: Available upon request. Many vegetarian restaurants & cafes nearby.
Complimentary: Welcome fruit basket & bottle of house wine. Mints on pillow, tea, coffee & cocktails.
Dates Open: All year.
High Season: July, August & December.
Rates: Hfl 110.00-Hfl 125.00 per room for 2. Special weekly rates.
Discounts: 10% discount for stays of a week or longer. 5% for cash.

Credit Cards: MC, VISA & Eurocard.
Rsv'tns: Advisable.
Reserve Through: Travel agent or call direct.
Minimum Stay: 2 days on weekends.
Parking: Adequate on-street pay parking. Free evenings & Sundays.
In-Room: Color cable TV, VCR, video tape library, telephone, ceiling fans, refrigerator, coffee/tea-making facilities, maid & laundry service.
On-Premises: Fax machine.

Exercise/Health: Nearby gym, weights, Jacuzzi, sauna, steam & massage.
Swimming: Nearby pool, ocean & lake.
Sunbathing: In the park.
Smoking: Not permitted in rooms.
Pets: Not permitted.
Handicap Access: No.
Children: Welcome.
Languages: Dutch, English, Tagalog, Cebuano, French & German.
Your Host: Carlos & Roelf-Jan.

Westend Hotel & Cosmo Bar

Gay/Lesbian ♂

Located on Kerkstraat, site of one of the heaviest concentrations of gay nightlife in Amsterdam, the *Westend* offers you comfortable rooms with shared showers, very centrally located to all gay bars and tourist attractions. Right downstairs from your room is an assortment of gay nightlife, interesting cafes, a gay video shop, even a night sauna.

Address: Kerkstraat 42, 1017 GM Amsterdam The Netherlands. Tel: (3120) 624 80 74, Fax: 622 99 97.

Type: Bed & breakfast with bar.
Clientele: Mostly men with women welcome.
Transportation: Train to Central Station, then taxi or tram line 1, 2 or 5.
To Gay Bars: Men's bars & sauna on the same & next block.
Rooms: 5 doubles also available for single use.
Bathrooms: 2 shared toilets & 2 shared showers.

Meals: Full breakfast served in the room between 11 and 12 AM at additional cost.
Dates Open: All year.
High Season: July, August, September.
Rates: Single Hfl 75.00. Room with double bed Hfl 100.00. Twin bedded room Hfl 120.00. Triple Hfl 150.00.
Credit Cards: MC, VISA, Amex & Eurocard.

Rsv'tns: Required 2 weeks in advance.
Reserve Through: Call direct.
Parking: Limited on-street parking with meters.
In-Room: Color TV upon request, maid service, telephone, refrigerator & coffee & tea-making facilities..
Sunbathing: On beach 1/2 hour away.

Nudity: 30-minute train ride to nude beach.
Smoking: Permitted without restrictions.
Pets: Small pets permitted.
Handicap Access: No.
Children: Not permitted.
Languages: Dutch, English, French & German.
Your Host: Herman.

BEEMTE-BROEKLAND

Jakonieshoeve

Gay-Friendly ♀♂

Our rustic farmhouse/pension is located between Apeldoorn and Vaassen on the Apeldoorns-Dierenskanaal. This area offers many possibilities, such as hiking trails, forests and interesting town markets. Our centrally-heated house has single, double and triple rooms and a sitting room with TV. Rooms on the first floor of *Jakonieshoeve* have running water. Shower and toilet are adjacent to the rooms. Linens and towels are on hand.

Address: Kanaal Noord 482, 7341 PH Beemte-Broekland Apeldoorn Netherlands. Tel: (05762) 1546.

Type: Guesthouse.
Clientele: Mostly hetero with 30% lesbian following.
Transportation: Pick up from train.
To Gay Bars: 10 min by car.
Rooms: 6 rooms with single beds.

Bathrooms: 1 shared.
Meals: Expanded continental breakfast.
Complimentary: Tea, coffee.
Dates Open: All year.
High Season: July & August.
Rates: Hfl 30.00 with breakfast all year.

Rsv'tns: Required.
Reserve Through: Call direct.
Parking: Ample free parking.
On-Premises: TV lounge, laundry facilities.
Swimming: In nearby lake.
Smoking: Permitted in

the living room only.
Pets: Not permitted.
Handicap Access: No.
Children: Permitted from 3 years & older.
Languages: English, French, German & Dutch.

DONKERBROEK

't Zijpad

Women ♀

't Zijpad, meaning the "she" or "side path," is a small-scale holiday resort for those seeking the peace of the countryside and contact with nature. We're in a charming and pastoral region of natural beauty on the edge of the Ontwijk estate woodlands, an area with many birds, protected plant species, deer and other wildlife

perfect for camping, bicycling and woodland walks. You need to be a Sherlock Holmes to find other tourists! The region affords opportunities for cultural sightseeing, as well. Quiet villages and historical towns, which preserve the old Frisian atmosphere, dot the countryside.

Accommodations are simple, practical and comfortable. The Garden House is a large room overlooking garden and woods and features a private shower. The Guest House is a detached summer house with sitting room, kitchen, colour TV and a sleeping loft. Bed & breakfast accommodations are in a small sitting room with bedroom upstairs. The camping area occupies 70 acres of woodland and walking paths and is exclusively for women, with room for six tents, each emplacement screened by wildflowers and bushes to ensure a degree of privacy. A table in a central area is for use by everyone. Those not traveling with camping equipment can rent tents, mattresses, storm lanterns and other necessities for a reasonable fee. Macrobiotic produce from our garden is also available. The locale offers a wide selection of restaurants to choose from.

Address: Balkweg 8, 8435 VP Donkerbroek Netherlands. Tel: (05168) 1752.

Type: Bed & breakfast guesthouse, campground.
Clientele: Mostly women with some men welcome.
Transportation: Charge for pick up from bus, train.
Rooms: 1 room, 1 apartment, 1 cottage & 1 cabin with single beds.
Bathrooms: All shared.
Campsites: 7 tent sites with cooling containers & cooking tiles. 2 covered dishwashing basins. Campers use guesthouse facilities.
Meals: Expanded continental breakfast for B & B only.
Complimentary: Tea, coffee, juices, homemade preserves.
Dates Open: All year.
High Season: April 1-October 15, Christmas, New Years, Easter, 1 week in February.
Rates: Rooms Hfl 160.00-Hfl 250.00 per week. B&B additional Hfl 27.50 per person per day. Camping Hfl 7.50 per night.
Rsv'tns: Required.
Reserve Through: Call direct.
Minimum Stay: Apt & cottage, 1 week, B&B, campground, 1 night.
Parking: Adequate, free off-street parking.
In-Room: Color TV, kitchen, refrigerator.
Swimming: Public pools in villages, river 50 m, lake 10 km.
Sunbathing: At campgrounds, terraces, in large garden & in woods.
Smoking: Permitted, but not in bedrooms.
Pets: Permitted by prior arrangement, female dogs only.
Children: Permitted, but no facilities, campground no males over 12.
Languages: Dutch, German, English, French & Frisian.

TERSCHELLING (WEST)

Pension Spitsbergen

Gay-Friendly 50/50 ♀♂

Our cozy, quiet *Pension Spitsbergen* is situated on a beautiful island surrounded by unspoiled nature, wide, clean beaches, dunes, woods and picturesque villages. We're in northern Holland, 7 minutes from the port of Terschelling W., one-and-a-half hours by boat from Harlingen (Friesland). Two of our pleasant rooms have harbor views. Nearby is the famous, 400-year-old lighthouse, which has the strongest lights in all Europe. The island has its own special character and is truly relaxing.

Address: Burgemeester Reedekerstraat 50, 8881 CB Terschelling West, The Netherlands. Tel: (05620) 3162. From 10-10-95: 0562-443162.

Type: Bed & breakfast guesthouse.
Clientele: 50% gay & lesbian & 50% hetero clientele.
Transportation: By ferry from Harlingen, then 7-minute walk to Pension.
To Gay Bars: Gay bars are located on the mainland.
Rooms: 4 rooms with double beds.
Bathrooms: Private & shared.
Meals: Full or continental breakfast.
Vegetarian: Only with breakfast. Vegetarian food nearby.
Complimentary: Specialities of the island.
Dates Open: Closed one month in winter.
High Season: Mid-July & August.
Rates: HFL 40-HFL 55 per person.
Discounts: 10% for stays of a week or more.
Rsv'tns: Required.
Reserve Through: Call direct.
Minimum Stay: 2 nights.
Parking: Best to leave car in Harlingen lots; car must be booked & is expensive!
In-Room: Maid service. 3 rooms with color TV.
On-Premises: Private dining room, public telephones.
Exercise/Health: Weights, sauna, massage, available nearby.
Swimming: Pool, lake & North Sea beach all nearby.
Sunbathing: At poolside, by lake or on beach. Beach is best.
Nudity: Permitted on the beach in quiet areas.
Smoking: Permitted except in bed.
Pets: Permitted.
Handicap Access: No.
Children: Permitted if 10 years or older.
Languages: Dutch, English, German.
Your Host: Hans.

UTRECHT

Utrecht Apartments

Men ♂

Address: Pauwstraat 1, 3512 TG Utrecht, The Netherlands. Tel: (030) 364 986, Fax: (030) 319 263.

Type: Apartments with videotheek & house with boys.
Clientele: Men only.
Transportation: From Central Station, bus to Centrum. 2nd stop Potterstraat. Oudegracht to #66, 1st street right Pauwstraat.
To Gay Bars: A few steps to 3 gay/lesbian bars & discos.
Rooms: 2 apartments with kitchens, single & double beds.
Bathrooms: All private.
Dates Open: All year.
Rates: Hfl 80-Hfl 240.
Rsv'tns: Required.
Reserve Through: Call direct.
Parking: Pay parking.
In-Room: Color cable TV, VCR, video tape library, telephone, kitchen, coffee & tea-making facilities.
Exercise/Health: Massage & whirlpool only with a boy of the house.
Sunbathing: On private sun decks.
Nudity: Permitted.
Smoking: Permitted without restrictions.
Pets: Permitted without restrictions.
Handicap Access: No.
Children: Not permitted.
Languages: Dutch, English, German.
Your Host: Rudi.

PORTUGAL

ALGARVE

Casa Amigos

An Intimate Guest House in the Algarve

Men ♂

The Algarve has a reputation for good weather, beautiful scenery and friendly locals. *Casa Amigos* offers a pleasant compromise between hectic cruising and do-nothing holidays, for, while we are situated among the scented orange and lemon groves of southern Portugal, we're 20 minutes' drive from a beach and interesting clubs. Our four double rooms have ensuite bathrooms and direct access to the pool. Take secluded walks by day or night. Gym, horseback riding scuba diving and daily excursions can be arranged, and massage is available in your room.

Address: Larga Vista, Foral, 8375 S.B. Messiness, Algarve Portugal. Tel: 351 82 56597.

Type: Bed & breakfast guesthouse with bar.
Clientele: Men only.
Transportation: Free pick up from Faro Airport or Tunes Railway Station.
To Gay Bars: 15-minute drive to bar.
Rooms: 3 rooms & 1 suite with single & double beds.
Bathrooms: All en suite.
Meals: Expanded continental breakfast. Evening meals & BBQ by arrangement.

Vegetarian: Available upon request.
Complimentary: Welcoming cocktail, tea & coffee in rooms.
Dates Open: All year.
High Season: May-October.
Rates: From £130-£175 per person per week. £50 extra for single occupancy.
Discounts: Large booking of 6-8.
Rsv'tns: Required.
Reserve Through: Call

direct.
Parking: Ample free off-street parking.
In-Room: Color TV & maid service.
On-Premises: Meeting rooms, TV lounge, poolside bar & food services.
Exercise/Health: Weights on premises. Nearby gym, weights, Jacuzzi, sauna & steam.
Swimming: Pool on premises. 15-minute drive to ocean.

Sunbathing: At poolside, on patio, roof & at the beach.
Nudity: Permitted at poolside & at gay beach (20-minute drive).
Smoking: Permitted.
Pets: Not permitted.
Handicap Access: 2 ground floor rooms.
Children: Not permitted under 18 years.
Languages: English, Portuguese & a little German.
Your Host: Roy & Paul.

Casa Marhaba

Gay/Lesbian ♂

"Marhaba" Means "Welcome"—We Mean to Make You Just That

Casa Marhaba is set on one acre in a pleasant rural area, 1 km from the nearest beach, 5 km from Carvoeiro and Lagoa, and 50 km west of Faro International Airport. All five of our double rooms have en suite bathrooms with showers. We serve a substantial continental breakfast on the poolside terrace and picnic lunches and pub-style snacks are available to order. Barbecue by the pool or enjoy the TV lounge with satellite TV and video facilities.

The Algarve region provides a perfect mix of contrasts: unspoiled countryside with miles of beaches; quaint and historical villages with lively towns and resorts; deep sea fishing and coastal boat trips; and great restaurants offering a wide range of cuisine. We will be delighted to recommend restaurants, beaches, and bars or help you with any other aspect of your holiday.

Address: Rua de Benagil, Alfanzina, 8400 Lagoa, Portugal. Tel/Fax: (0) 82 358720.

continued next page

Portugal

Type: Bed & breakfast guesthouse with bar.
Clientele: Mostly men with women welcome.
Transportation: Faro Airport, then rental car. Pick up can be arranged for a fee.
To Gay Bars: 10 miles or a 15-minute drive.
Rooms: 5 rooms with single or double beds.
Bathrooms: 5 private shower/toilets.

Meals: Expanded continental breakfast.
Vegetarian: Available upon advanced request. Vegetarian food nearby.
Complimentary: Welcome cocktail.
Dates Open: April thru October.
High Season: April thru October.
Rates: Single: £155 per week, £27 per night. Double: £190 per week,

£33 per night.
Rsv'tns: Required.
Reserve Through: Call direct.
Parking: Ample free off-street parking.
In-Room: Maid & laundry service.
On-Premises: TV lounge with satellite TV & video facilities.
Swimming: Pool on premises, ocean nearby.
Sunbathing: At poolside,

on patio & private sun decks.
Nudity: Permitted on special sun deck poolside.
Smoking: Permitted throughout.
Pets: Not permitted.
Handicap Access: No.
Children: Not especially welcome.
Languages: English & French.
Your Host: Tony & Sam.

Casa Pequena

Men ♂

All the Comforts of Home...

Situated in 1100 square metres of gardens on a hillside overlooking the village and beach of Praia da Luz, *Casa Pequena* is, first and foremost, our home. As such, you will find it comfortable and well-furnished with the usual amenities, including TV, video, audio equipment and a good library of books, all available to our guests. We have two guest rooms, each with adjacent bath/shower and we provide all linens, towels and beach towels. We also have a swimming pool, extensive terraces and sun-beds. If you want to explore, we can advise you where to visit and explain the eccentricities of gay nightlife in Portugal. You will have your own key so you can come and go as you please.

Address: Apartado 133, Praia da Luz, 8600 Lagos, Algarve Portugal. Tel & Fax: (351-82) 789068.

Type: Guesthouse with honour bar.
Clientele: Men only.
Transportation: Car is best. Pick up from airport, train, bus. 3,250 escudos from Faro airport. Free from Lagos.
To Gay Bars: 5 km or 10 minutes by car.
Rooms: 2 rooms with single or double bed.
Bathrooms: Private adjacent to room: 1 shower/toilet, 1 bath/shower/toilet.
Meals: Expanded continental breakfast. Other

meals can be provided at reasonable cost.
Vegetarian: Available upon request. Most restaurants have non-meat dishes.
Complimentary: Tea & coffee.
Dates Open: All year.
High Season: April/May-end of October.
Rates: 4000 escudos per night single. 6,500 escudos per night double.
Discounts: 10% if both rooms booked by same party.
Rsv'tns: Required.

Reserve Through: Call direct.
Minimum Stay: 3 nights minimum charge though you can stay for fewer nights.
Parking: Ample free off-street parking.
On-Premises: TV lounge. Entire house is available for guests.
Exercise/Health: Nearby hotel/sports centre with gym, weights, Jacuzzi, sauna, steam & massage.
Swimming: Pool on premises, ocean nearby.

Sunbathing: At poolside, on common sun decks & at nearby beaches (some nude).
Nudity: Permitted wherever guests feel comfortable.
Smoking: Permitted everywhere except in bedrooms.
Pets: Not permitted. 3 resident cats.
Handicap Access: No.
Children: Not especially welcome.
Languages: Portuguese, English, French.
Your Host: Jim & Geoff.

SPAIN

BALEARIC ISLANDS (IBIZA)

Casa Alexio

Men ♂

On top of a rise above the bay of Talamanca is placed the very private guesthouse called *Casa Alexio*, far away from any road noise, but only 3 minutes by car to town. From the breakfast terrace, one has a wonderful view over Ibiza Town, the harbor and the sea reaching to the neighboring island of Formentera. A pool with bar, terraces and a comfortable living room with cable TV add to your comfort. The beach is a five-minute walk.

Address: Barrio Ses Torres 16, 07819 Jesús, Ibiza Spain. Tel: (71) 31 42 49, Fax: 31 26 19.

Type: Guesthouse.
Clientele: Men only.
Transportation: Free pick up service or taxi from airport.
To Gay Bars: 1.7 miles or 3 minutes by car.
Rooms: 9 rooms with king beds.
Bathrooms: All private bathrooms.
Meals: Full German breakfast for additional charge.
Complimentary: Self-service bar at poolside.
Dates Open: All year.
High Season: April through October.
Rates: Double Pts 14,000.00 & single Pts 8,500.00.
Credit Cards: VISA, MC, Amex, Eurocard.
Rsv'tns: Required.
Reserve Through: Travel agent or call direct.
Parking: Free off-street parking.
In-Room: Satellite TV, AC, maid and laundry service.
On-Premises: TV lounge, meeting rooms, laundry facilities.
Exercise/Health: Whirlpool & sauna to be added.
Swimming: Pool, ocean beach next door.
Sunbathing: At poolside or on beach.
Nudity: Permitted at the pool. Nude beach nearby.
Smoking: Permitted without restrictions.
Pets: Not permitted.
Children: Not permitted.
Languages: Spanish, German & English.

Mantours-Ibiza Holidays

Holidays for Body & Soul

Gay/Lesbian ♂

Formerly associated with the 15-year-old Mantours Berlin, Mantours USA is now a US-based hotel reservation system specializing in Europe's top three destinations of Spain's Ibiza and Sitges and Greece's Mykonos. Mantours also offers packages to most major European cities, such as Amsterdam, Copenhagen, Paris, Berlin, London, Athens, Madrid, Barcelona, Lisbon and Rome.

Accommodations in Ibiza include a large variety of choices. *Delfin Verde* are spacious apartments near the harbor of Old Town Ibiza. Room amenities include large beds, air conditioning, telephone, TV, private bath, kitchenette and balcony with views.

Chateau Navila are luxury designer apartments with pool, garden, air conditioning and spectacular views. Their location is near the Old Town harbor, where

continued next page

you can walk to the bars and the action. *Tower De Cononico,* formerly a 14th-century castle, offers deluxe apartments with views of the harbor. It's only a 6-block walk to bars and clubs. *Mariano Apartments* are clean and very centrally located near bars and clubs. Each has living room, bedroom, private bath, telephone and thrice-weekly cleaning. *Edificio Plaza Apartments,* located opposite the Gay Garden Cafe, are centrally located one- and two-bedroom studios with kitchenette and balcony. *Ripoll Apartments* feature an elevator and convenient central location. Each has living room, bedroom, sofa bed, private bath, kitchenette, balcony and some views. *Hotel Don Quixote* is in Figueretas. Rooms have balcony and private bath. There is a roof terrace, pool and elevator, and the location is near both the beach and Old Town. *Cenit Apartments* are on a hill with spectacular views of Old Town. Studios have one bedroom with twin beds, private bath and balcony. The complex includes a bar and pool.

Address: Mantours USA, 4929 Wilshire Blvd #259, Los Angeles, CA 90010 Tel: (213) 930-1880 , (800) 798-4923, Fax: (213) 930-0194.

BALEARIC ISLANDS (MALLORCA)

Hotel Rosamar

Gay-Friendly ♀♂

The *Hotel Rosamar,* privately owned and recently refurbished, offers comfortable accommodation together with a friendly bar and a large, attractive garden terrace. All rooms have private bathrooms and terraces. It has a very easy, relaxed atmosphere. The hotel is situated in the midst of Palma's night life area with all the gay bars and discos situated on the same street and within walking distance of the hotel. There is also a small, interesting beach a ten-minute walk away. Mallorca is the largest of the Balearic Islands off the eastern coast of Spain. It is extremely beautiful with many changes of landscape and one of the most stunning beaches in Europe. Chopin, George Sand, Robert Graves, and now Michael Douglas are some of the people who have made their homes here.

Address: Avenida Joan Miro 74, 07015, Palma de Mallorca Spain. Tel: (3471) 732723 or Fax: (3471) 283828. In US:(407)994-3558, Fax:(407)994-3634.

Type: Hotel with bar.
Clientele: Mostly hetero with a gay & lesbian following.
Transportation: Taxi or airport bus to Plaza España, then taxi. Pick up from airport 2,500pta per trip. Hire car best for sightseeing.
To Gay Bars: All the present gay bars are located on the same street as the hotel.
Rooms: 40 rooms with single or double beds.
Bathrooms: All en suite.

Meals: Continental breakfast.
Vegetarian: 2 or 3 restaurants in Palma city 10 minutes away.
Dates Open: March 15th to January 6th.
High Season: July, August, September.
Rates: Per night per room: Double Pta 4,250.00-Pta 4,700.00, single Pta 2,700.00-Pta 3,000.00.
Credit Cards: MC, VISA & Eurocard.
Rsv'tns: Required.

Reserve Through: Travel agent or call direct.
Parking: Ample free off-street parking.
In-Room: Telephone, maid & laundry service, towels changed daily, most rooms with balconies.
On-Premises: Terrace, sun deck, meeting rooms & TV lounge.
Exercise/Health: Sauna 50 metres away.
Swimming: In the ocean.
Sunbathing: On common sun deck.

Nudity: Permitted on the sun deck at the discretion of other guests.
Smoking: Permitted.
Pets: Not permitted.
Handicap Access: No.
Children: Permitted only if WELL-controlled, otherwise NO!!!
Languages: Spanish, English, German, Italian, French.
Your Host: Bill & Basilio.

IGTA

SITGES

Hotel Romàntic i La Renaixença

Gay/Lesbian ♀♂

With the addition of two new motorways, Sitges is now just 20 to 30 minutes from central Barcelona. Because of this, Sitges in winter is rather alive, now, especially on weekends, as it is no longer only a tourist resort, but also a "district" of the big city, Barcelona. A stay in the *Hotel Romàntic or Hotel Renaixença* is a most refreshing alternative to the massified and depersonalized vacationing that seems to be more and more usual, these days. *The Romàntic* is ideally placed in the center of Sitges, a resort town with a long tradition, not only as a vacation spot, but also as a center for culture. From *The Romàntic,* you will find easy access, by foot, to the beach, promenade, museums, churches, bars, restaurants, nightspots, shops, etc. You will also be quite close to taxi, bus and trains, which can take you to places as diverse and interesting as the local waterpark (5 minutes by coach, gratis) and the city of Barcelona (45 minutes by train).

The hotel, itself, offers a little of both these worlds. Its spacious garden, at once elegant and casual, is open all day, with service for tea, coffee, snacks or drinks. Retreat from the world, if you wish, among the palms, trees, shrubbery and the two fountains in the garden. *The Romàntic* occupies three adjacent townhouses, which were built, circa 1880, as pleasure villas for wealthy families. During your stay, you can enjoy a kind of life that was once the privilege of the wealthy, and that nowadays would seem impossible to find. The rooms have been modernized with baths and comfortable beds, but they are also furnished with period furniture. Each room is different. All are well-kept and comfortable. Many rooms have terraces overlooking the garden. Several dining and sitting rooms occupy the first floor, including the bar,

with one of the most complete selections of drinks and refreshments in all of Spain. When you stay at *The Romàntic,* you are surrounded by art, sculptures, painting, drawings, lamps, ceramics and tiles, all impeccably kept. The atmosphere will remind you at once of a gentleman's club and of an Indian palace. Senyor Sobrer and his staff, headed by José Manuel, will always be at your disposal to make your stay in their hotel pleasant and problem-free. We think you'll agree that ours is a hotel that is unique in all of Spain. *Hotel Renaixença* has 16 rooms with private bath and WC, nicely decorated and at reasonable prices. There is also a tea room and bar service.

continued next page

Spain

**Address: Carrer de Sant Isidre 33, 08870 Sitges (Barcelona) (Catalunya) Spain.
Tel: (393) 894 8375, Fax: (393) 894 8167.**

Type: Bed & breakfast hotel with bar & solarium.
Clientele: Mostly gay & lesbian with some hetero clientele.
Transportation: From Barcelona aiport, train to Sants then train to Sitges. Taxi.
To Gay Bars: Centrally-located to all gay bars.
Rooms: 85 rooms with single or double beds.
Bathrooms: All private.

Meals: Continental breakfast, buffet breakfast.
Dates Open: La Renaixença all year. Hotel Romàntic all year.
High Season: May 15-October 15.
Rates: Pts 5,400-Pts 7,800 plus 6% VAT. (1994 season)
Credit Cards: VISA, Amex, Diners & Eurocard.
Rsv'tns: Required, but call-ins welcome.

Reserve Through: Call direct.
Minimum Stay: 1 day.
Parking: Off-street public pay parking.
In-Room: Telephone & maid service. Top rooms have ceiling fans.
On-Premises: Meeting rooms, TV lounge & solarium.
Swimming: Ocean beach and swimming pool nearby.
Sunbathing: On roof,

private & common sun decks.
Nudity: 1/2 hr walk to nudist beach.
Smoking: Permitted without restrictions.
Pets: Permitted.
Children: Welcome.
Languages: Catalan, Spanish, English, French & Italian.
Your Host: Gonçal.

Mantours-Sitges Holidays

Gay/Lesbian ♂

Holidays for Body & Soul

Formerly associated with the 15-year-old Mantours Berlin, Mantours USA is now a US-based hotel reservation system specializing in Europe's three top gay destinations of Spain's Sitges and Ibiza and Greece's Mykonos. Mantours also offers packages to most major European cities, such as Amsterdam, Copenhagen, Paris, Berlin, London, Athens, Madrid, Barcelona, Lisbon and Rome.

Accommodations in Sitges include the following: *Hotel Romantic* is a historic hotel in three adjacent 19th-century villas with deluxe garden, sun deck, lobby, bar, all located on a quiet street near the beach, shops and clubs; *Buena Ventura Apartments* are centrally located, modern studios with bedroom, bath, TV, kitchenette, radio, some with balcony, thrice-weekly maid service; *Hotel Sitges Park* is close to the action, and has its own bar and lounge, restaurant, garden with pool and rooms with private baths; *Mirador Apartments* have studios well-suited for students, with kitchenettes and baths and located in Sitges' old center near beach and nightlife; *Hotel Galeon* is a renovated 3-star hotel in Old Town with bar, restaurant, garden, pool and rooms with private bath and telephone; *Termes Apartments* include one bedroom and sofa bed, TV, kitchenette, balcony and thrice-weekly maid service.

Accommodations in Barcelona include *Hotel California,* whose rooms provide air conditioning, private baths, telephone and TV, kitchenette, VCR and twin beds. Amenities include bar, laundry, 24-hour room service, private car service, and ticket service for local shows.

In the Canary Islands, *Beach Boy Bungalows* is a resort for gay men only, located in the quiet campo area near the famed Yumbo Center in Playa Del Inglés. Each bungalow has all amenities, plus central pool, garden and bar.
**Address: Mantours USA, 4929 Wilshire Blvd #259, Los Angeles, CA 90010
Tel: (213) 930-1880 , (800) 798-4923, Fax: (213) 930-0194.**

TARRAGONA

MontyMar

Gay/Lesbian ♀

Get Close to Nature Without Giving Up Comfort

Miami Playa is a small settlement on the Mediterranean Sea coast. In this garden city, between the nearby mountains and the sea, and only 600 meters from the beach, you will find the Spanish-Moorish-style *MontyMar*. All rooms are on the ground floor with a little terrace facing our beautiful, quiet and peaceful patio with water-basin, fountain, plants and flowers. Here you can sunbathe, enjoy your drinks, or eat your meals. In addition to our dinners, you can find many

nearby restaurants with Spanish, French, and German specialities. We have about 4 km of sandy beach divided in 2 open beaches and about 8 small bays. You will also find our marvelous large nude beach 6 km to the south. None of our beaches are overcrowded, even in high season. For more mobility you can rent cars, bicycles, or motor-scooters, or take the train to the villages or towns (Barcelona, Tarragona, Tortosa) along the coast. Motor- and sailing-boat trips can be arranged for small groups. If you like nature but don't want to give up comfort, you will enjoy your vacation in our cherished surroundings at *MontyMar*.

Address: Av Principe De España, Apdo (Box) 113, E-43892 Miami Playa, Tarragona Spain. Tel: (0034) 77810530.

Type: Guesthouse.

Clientele: Mostly women with men welcome.

Transportation: Car is best. (Car rental at Barcelona airport.)

To Gay Bars: 17 km to Salou (25 min by car).

Rooms: 8 rooms.

Bathrooms: All private.

Meals: Full breakfast of eggs, yoghurt, cereals, meat, cheese, milk, orange juice, etc. Snacks & dinner at extra charge.

Vegetarian: Available upon request.

Complimentary: Welcome drink.

Dates Open: Apr 1 to Oct 15 (in May women only), Dec 15 to Jan 15 for women only.

High Season: July-August.

Rates: Pts 6,400.00-Pts 8,250.00 (approx $55-$75 USD) for double occupancy including breakfast & taxes.

Discounts: For groups of 10 or more people, upon request. 10% for individuals for stays of 11 or more days.

Rsv'tns: Accepted with prepayment for 3 nights.

Reserve Through: Call direct.

Parking: Adequate free off-street parking.

In-Room: Maid, room & laundry service.

On-Premises: Meeting rooms.

Swimming: 600 meters to ocean beach.

Sunbathing: On the patio, beach, private or common terraces.

Nudity: Nude beach

6 km away.

Smoking: Permitted without restrictions.

Pets: Permitted upon request with extra charge, US $2 daily.

Children: Welcome. May & Christmas when women only, permitted upon request.

Languages: Spanish, German, English, Hebrew.

Your Host: Ulla & Christel.

SWEDEN

BORLÄNGE

Kvinnohöjden, Feminist Study Center & Guesthome

Women ♀

Feminist Study Center and Retreat for ALL Women

Kvinnohöjden is a feminist study center and guesthome in rural Sweden. It is beautifully situated outside the small town of Borlänge, in Dalarna. The surrounding area of woodlands and bodies of water offers unlimited outdoor activities. Our several traditional buildings can house a total of 50 women. *Kvinnohöjden* is a meeting place for all women, young and old, heterosexuals and lesbians, women with or without children. Here, we meet without drugs and alcohol. Every woman is expected to participate in household activities.

Address: Storsund 90, 78194 Borlänge Sweden. Tel: (0243) 223707

Type: Guesthouse with bookstore.
Clientele: Women only.
Transportation: Pick up from airport, bus, train, 50 kronor round trip.
To Gay Bars: 2-1/2 hrs to Stockholm by train, 3 hrs by car.
Rooms: 22 rooms with bunk, single or double beds.
Bathrooms: Shared: 4 showers & 8 toilets. 7 private sinks.

Campsites: 3 tent sites. Tent rates same as room rates.
Meals: Full breakfast, lunch, & dinner.
Vegetarian: Only.
Complimentary: Free access to tea & coffee.
Dates Open: All year.
High Season: New Year, Midsummer (19-21 June), July.
Rates: Skr 165.00.
Discounts: Children's & membership rates.

Rsv'tns: Required, if possible.
Reserve Through: Call direct.
Parking: Adequate free parking.
On-Premises: Meeting rooms & TV lounge.
Exercise/Health: Sauna, table tennis, hiking, swimming, canoeing & bicycles.
Swimming: Nearby lake.
Sunbathing: On the lawn.

Nudity: Permitted by the house and lake.
Smoking: Permitted outdoors only.
Pets: Permitted, but special rooms must be reserved.
Handicap Access: No.
Children: Permitted, boys up to age 12.
Languages: Swedish & English.

SWITZERLAND

BASEL

White Horse Hotel

Gay-Friendly ♀♂'

The White Horse is a small hotel in the center of Basel. All our rooms have a shower, WC, television and telephone. Our rates include service, taxes and a Swiss breakfast buffet. We look forward to welcoming you at the *White Horse Hotel* the next time you visit Switzerland.

Address: Webergasse 23, CH-4005 Basel, Switzerland. Tel: (061) 691 57 57, Fax: (061) 691 57 25.

WHITE HORSE

Type: Hotel with a bar.
Clientele: Mostly straight clientele with a gay & lesbian following.
Transportation: Airport bus to central station, then taxi, or direct streetcar #8 to "Rheingasse."
To Gay Bars: 5-minute walk to gay/lesbian bar.
Rooms: 5 singles, 5 doubles (6 queen beds).
Bathrooms: All private showers & toilets.
Meals: Expanded continental breakfast.
Dates Open: All year.
High Season: Spring & autumn.
Rates: Single SF 95.00-125.00, double & queen SF 125.00-185.00.
Discounts: 10% to guests with a copy of Inn Places.
Credit Cards: VISA, Eurocard, Diners.
Rsv'tns: Required 2 wks in advance.
Reserve Through: Call direct.
Parking: Limited on-street parking.
In-Room: TV, telephone, alarm clock, color TV.
On-Premises: Public telephones, shoeshine machine.
Smoking: Permitted without restrictions.
Pets: Limited (1 dog or cat).
Handicap Access: No.
Children: Permitted.
Languages: German, French, English.

ZÜRICH

Rothus und Goldenes Schwert Hotel

Gay-Friendly 50/50 ♀♂'

The two hotels, *Rothus & Goldenes Schwert,* are under the same management and have the same reception desk. They are located in the heart of the old section of Zürich, where some buildings date back to the middle ages. It's just ten minutes walking to the railway station and the very center of town. On the premises, we have a restaurant and several bars offering everything from dancing to drag (travestie) shows. All rooms have telephones. *Rothus* is a one-star hotel and *Goldenes Schwert* is a two-star hotel.

Address: Marktgasse 14, CH-8001 Zürich, Switzerland. Tel: (41)(01) 252 15 30, 252 59 40 or Fax: 251 39 24.

Type: Hotel with restaurant, bar, disco, drag show and garden terrace.
Clientele: 50% gay/lesbian & 50% straight clientele.
Transportation: Airport shuttle SFr 16.00.
To Gay Bars: Gay bar on premises.
Rooms: 7 singles, 24 doubles, 3 triples,1 quad.
Bathrooms: All private.
Meals: Continental breakfast buffet.
Vegetarian: Available upon request.
Dates Open: All year.
High Season: June-Oct.
Rates: Rothus (WC/shower in corridor): Single SF 70.00, double SF 110. Goldenes Schwert: Single SF 110.00, double SF 150.00.
Credit Cards: VISA, Amex, Diners, Eurocard.
Rsv'tns: Required.
Reservations: Call direct.
In-Room: Maid service, telephone.
On-Premises: Meeting rooms, private dining rooms, TV lounge, laundry facilities, public telephones, & fax.
Swimming: River, lake, or nearby pool.
Smoking: Permitted without restrictions.
Pets: Permitted at SF 10.00 per day.
Handicap Access: No.
Children: Permitted, up to 12 yrs old free in same room.
Languages: German, French, Italian, English, & Spanish.
Your Host: Mr. Umberto.

UK (ENGLAND)

AVON *(SEE ALSO BATH)*

Barns, The

Gay-Friendly ♀♂

The Barns is a luxury country hotel providing both comfort and charm to those seeking a quiet break from routine. Though the building is quite secluded on 10 acres of woodland, we're close to the city's gay nightlife. Exceptional food is served in the candlelit woodland conservatory. Come and be spoilt. It's unique.

Address: Church Road, Abbotsleith, Bristol BS8 3QU UK (England). Tel: (01275) 372142.

Type: Luxury country hotel.
Clientele: Mostly hetero weekdays, more gay on weekends. Some exclusively gay weekends.
Rooms: 6 rooms in 2 converted barns.
Bathrooms: All private.

Meals: English pub nearby with excellent food.
Dates Open: All year.
Rates: £36.
Credit Cards: MC, VISA, Amex.
Rsv'tns: Recommended.
Reserve Through: Call

direct.
Parking: On-site uncovered free parking.
In-Room: Colour TV, tea/coffee-making facilities.
On-Premises: Conservatory overlooking woodlands.
Exercise/Health: Hiking.

Smoking: Permitted without restrictions.
Pets: Welcome.
Handicap Access: 1 room with rails in shower.
Languages: English & Spanish.
Your Host: Maddy & Richard.

BATH

Kennard Hotel, The

Gay-Friendly ♀♂

It's Lovely to Come Back to Excellent Accommodation

The Kennard Hotel is situated in a quiet Georgian street within a few minutes' level walking distance of the city centre. It is the ideal setting in which to enjoy the delights of this famous city. A building of historical importance, the hotel has been thoughtfully refurbished to provide modern comforts, with most rooms en-suite. Independent heating, colour television, direct-dial telephone, tea- and coffee-making facilities and sitting areas all add to your comfort. Bath is truly a city for all seasons. At *The Kennard,* we take great pleasure in helping our guests enjoy their visit to the City of Bath.

Address: 11 Henrietta Street, Bath, Avon BA2 6LL England. Tel: (01225) 310472, Fax: (01225) 460054.

Type: Bed & breakfast hotel.
Clientele: Mostly hetero with a gay & lesbian following.
To Gay Bars: 5-minute walk.
Rooms: 10 doubles &

2 singles.
Bathrooms: 10 private, others share.
Meals: Full English breakfast.
Vegetarian: Available upon request.
Complimentary: Coffee

& tea-making facilities in room.
Dates Open: All year.
Rates: £48-£58.
Credit Cards: MC, VISA, Amex & Diners.
Rsv'tns: Required.
Reserve Through: Call

direct.
Parking: On-street parking.
In-Room: Colour TV, direct dial phone, tea & coffee.
Children: Not permitted.
Languages: English.

BIRMINGHAM

Fountain Inn, The

Gay/Lesbian ♂

Built as a traditional Victorian public house, *The Fountain Inn* retains much of its original character. With guest accommodations having been totally refurbished to the highest standards in February, 1991 and redecorated in 1993, *The Fountain Inn* offers its guests a warm and welcoming stay. All rooms are en suite or have separate, private toilet and tea- and coffee-making facilities, telephone, central heating and colour TV with satellite movie channel and in-house video channel. Guest keys give 24-hour access.

The Fountain Inn's very popular, ground floor gay bar is only a 5 to 10-minute walk from the other gay bars and clubs, the main railway station and Birmingham's shopping and entertainment areas. Birmingham is known as the "Second City," (London being the first!) and is at the heart of the motorway network, with London approximately 1-1/2-hour's drive away and "Shakespeare country" only a half-hour's drive. Birmingham now boasts one of the largest conference centers, exhibition centers and international airports in Europe.

Address: 102 Wrentham St, Birmingham B5 6QL, West Midlands England. Tel: (021) 622 1452. In USA call (407) 994-3558, Fax: (407) 994-3634.

Type: Guesthouse inn with bar & pub food (available 12:00-14:00 weekdays).
Clientele: Mostly men with women welcome.
Transportation: Car, 5 min taxi ride from railway station (£2), taxi from Birmingham International Airport approx £12.
To Gay Bars: Five min walk to nearest bars & discos.

Rooms: 5 rooms with single or double beds.
Bathrooms: Private: 1 bath/toilet, 3 shower/toilet, 1 shower/wash basin & toilet.
Meals: Full breakfast.
Vegetarian: Available on request before arrival.
Complimentary: Tea/coffee making facilities & biscuits.
Dates Open: All year.
Rates: £25.00-£35.00 per night.

Discounts: 10% for 3 nights & over, if booked direct.
Credit Cards: MC, VISA & Amex.
Rsv'tns: Required.
Reserve Through: Travel agent or call direct.
Parking: Free off-street parking for 5 cars, on-street pay parking, free weekends.
In-Room: Color cable TV

with in-house, non-porn video channel, movie channel via satellite, telephone, coffee/tea-making facilities & maid service.
On-Premises: Meeting rooms.
Smoking: Permitted.
Pets: Not permitted.
Handicap Access: No.
Children: Not permitted.
Languages: English.
Your Host: Chris.

Oak Leaves Private Hotel

Men ♂

Oak Leaves Private Hotel is a small, friendly, seven-bedroom hotel situated two miles from Birmingham city center. Public transport as well as taxis are available for visiting local and nearby sights. The NEC and Birmingham International Airport are also close by. The hotel itself is set in a small forecourt of nine Georgian properties and is fully centrally heated and double glazed. All rooms now have running H/C. Accommodation and decor is of a high standard and a friendly welcome awaits all. We are ideally situated for access to all the Midlands, and trains from Birmingham link the whole country including N. Ireland and Europe, via various ports.

Address: 22 Gibson Dr, Handsworth Wood, Birmingham B20 3UB England. Tel: (021) 551 6510, Fax: (021) 551 0606, Visitors & guests: (021) 551-6732.

Type: Private hotel.
Clientele: Mostly men (women welcome).
Transportation: Taxi or bus from Edgbaston Street.

To Gay Bars: Close to all gay/lesbian bars.
Rooms: 7 rooms with single, double or king beds.
Bathrooms: 2 private

showers, 1 shared bath/shower/toilet & 1 shared WC.
Meals: Full English breakfast.
Vegetarian: 48-hour

notice required.
Complimentary: Tea, coffee, fruit juice on arrival.

continued next page

UK (England)

Dates Open: All year.
Rates: £23-£35 all year.
Discounts: Negotiable rates on longer stays.
Credit Cards: MC, VISA & Eurocard.
Rsv'tns: Required.
Reserve Through: Call direct.
Parking: Ample free off-street flood-lighted parking, not owned by hotel.
In-Room: Coffee/tea-making facilities, maid and laundry service.
On-Premises: TV lounge, laundry facilities for guests' use.
Exercise/Health: Gym, weights, sauna & steam at nearby health club.
Smoking: Permitted without restriction.
Pets: Permitted for a small fee.
Handicap Access: No.
Children: Not permitted.
Languages: English.

BLACKPOOL

Calton House

Gay/Lesbian ♀♂

Don't Delay...Book Today!

Calton House is an exclusively gay guesthouse situated a 10-minute walk from the centre of Blackpool and all gay bars and clubs. Shops, attractions and public transport are all a few-minutes walk away! Guests have their own keys and can come and go as they please. In fact, we like our guests to feel as if they are at home. We serve a full English breakfast and provide entertainment/buffets every bank holiday. Vegetarian meals are provided on request.

Address: 49 Egerton Road, Blackpool FY1 2NP England. Tel: (01253) 290 190, Fax: (01253) 751 052.

Type: Guesthouse.
Clientele: Exclusively gay & lesbian. Good mix of men & women.
Transportation: Train to Blackpool North Station, then a 3-minute walk.
To Gay Bars: 4 blocks or 1/2 mile. A 10-minute walk or 2-minute drive.
Rooms: 12 rooms with single, double or king beds.
Bathrooms: Private:
6 shower/toilet, 6 sink only. 2 shared bath/shower/toilet.
Meals: Full breakfast.
Vegetarian: Available if requested at time of booking.
Complimentary: Candy in rooms. Free buffets & drinks on bank holidays.
Dates Open: All year.
Rates: Per person per night: £11.00 standard room, £12.50 en suite,
£15.00 bank holidays.
Credit Cards: VISA & Diners.
Reserve Through: Call direct.
Parking: Ample on-street parking.
In-Room: Colour cable TV, VCR/video link, coffee/tea-making facilities, maid service & own key.
On-Premises: TV lounge.
Sunbathing: On the patio or at the beach.
Smoking: Permitted everywhere except the dining room.
Pets: Not permitted.
Handicap Access: No.
Children: Not especially welcome.
Languages: English, French, little Dutch, little German.
Your Host: Tony, Callum & Carl.

Derby Hotel

Gay-Friendly 50/50 ♀♂

Address: 2, Derby Rd, Blackpool FY1 2JF England. Tel: (01253) 23 708.

Type: Hotel with bar.
Clientele: 50% gay & lesbian & 50% hetero clientele.
To Gay Bars: 5 minutes.
Rooms: 11 rooms with single & double beds.
Bathrooms: Some en suite.
Meals: Full English breakfast. Dinner optional £4.00.
Complimentary: Concessions to Flamingo.
Rates: £14-£16.
Discounts: Early season.
Credit Cards: VISA, Access.
Parking: Easy parking on street.
In-Room: Tea & coffee-making facilities. Guests have own keys to outside door.
On-Premises: Patio.
Sunbathing: Sun lounge.
Smoking: Permitted.
Pets: Not permitted.
Handicap Access: No.
Children: OK over 3 years of age.
Languages: English.

Fairhaven Hotel

Gay/lesbian ♀♂

For comfortable lodgings and reasonable rates, visit us at *Fairhaven Hotel*, only 2 minutes from the gay pubs and clubs. All guests receive free concessionary passes to the Flamingo, Blackpool's gayest club.

Address: 42 Dickson Rd, Blackpool England. Tel: (01253) 24497.

Type: Hotel with licensed late bar.
Clientele: Gay & lesbian. Good mix of men & women.
To Gay Bars: 2 minutes

to bars & clubs.
Meals: Full breakfast.
Complimentary: Concessions to Flamingo club.
Dates Open: All year.
Rates: Not reported for

current issue.
Rsv'tns: Recommended.
Reserve Through: Call direct.
In-Room: Coffee & tea-making facilities.

On-Premises: TV lounge.
Pets: Not permitted.
Languages: English.

Highlands Hotel

Gay-Friendly 50/50 ♀♂

The *Highlands Hotel* is very much a home from home hotel. We are close to the bars, clubs, and shops, and a short walk to the ocean beach. All rooms are tastefully decorated with matching decor. We have a large disco bar with draught and bottle beer and a variety of food. Nothing at the *Highlands* is too much trouble. Our motto is: Arrive as guests, leave as friends!

Address: 46-54 High St, Blackpool, FY1 2BN England. Tel: (01253) 752 264, Fax: (0253) 23179.

Type: Hotel with restaurant & licensed residents' disco bar.
Clientele: 50% gay & lesbian & 50% straight clientele.
Transportation: Car, bus, train, taxi.
To Gay Bars: 5 minute walk to Flamingo. 8 minutes to other gay bars.
Rooms: 32 rooms, 18 suites & 1 apartment

with single, double & bunk beds.
Bathrooms: Private: 18 shower/toilets, 14 sinks. Shared: 4 showers, 5 WCs.
Meals: Full English breakfast & 4-course evening meal.
Vegetarian: Available upon request.
Complimentary: Tea & coffee in all rooms. Concession to Flamingo.

Dates Open: All year.
High Season: Jul-Nov 14.
Rates: £9.00-£25.50.
Credit Cards: VISA & Access.
Rsv'tns: Required.
Reserve Through: Call direct.
Parking: Adequate on-street parking.
In-Room: Color TV, coffee/tea-making facilities & maid service.

On-Premises: TV lounge.
Exercise/Health: Massage.
Swimming: Nearby pool & ocean beach.
Sunbathing: On the patio & at the beach.
Smoking: Permitted.
Pets: Small animals welcome.
Children: Permitted.
Languages: English.
Your Host: Mike & Olga.

Kingston Private Hotel

Gay-Friendly 50/50 ♀♂

Comfort and Quality Are Our Priority

At *Kingston Hotel,* you can relax in tasteful surroundings with a delightful home-away-from-home atmosphere. The resident proprietor gives every care and attention to service and cleanliness. A choice of menu is available, and the cozy bar is exceptionally well-stocked. All bedrooms have comfortable beds with duvets, modern furnishings, individually-controlled heating and hot and cold water. Towels and soap are available on request. Our high standard of catering is all home-cooked and prepared on the premises. A large choice of breakfast is included in the set price. The optional evening meal is a five-course meal with a choice of menu. Our aim is to live up to our motto, "Comfort and quality are our priority."

Address: 12 Cocker St, Blackpool NS Lancs FY1 1SF England. Tel: (01253) 24929.

continued next page

UK (England)

Type: Hotel with bar & hairdressing facilities. **Clientele:** 50% gay & lesbian & 50% hetero. **Transportation:** Car, bus, railway. Blackpool & Manchester airports not too far. **To Gay Bars:** 5 min to all gay places. **Rooms:** 1 single, 2 twin, 5 doubles, 3 quads. **Bathrooms:** 2 private showers, 2 shared showers, 3 shared toilets. **Meals:** Choice of breakfast. **Vegetarian:** Available upon request. **Complimentary:** Concessionary pass to Flamingo, tea, coffee, biscuits, nibbles on bar. **Dates Open:** All year. **High Season:** Easter to 1st week in Nov, especially last wk in Aug to 1st wk in Nov. **Rates:** From £12.00. **Discounts:** For bookings of 3 or more days. **Rsv'tns:** Advisable in high season, but not always necessary. **Reserve Through:** Travel agent or call direct. **Minimum Stay:** On Bank Holidays & Illumination weekends. **Parking:** Limited time on-street parking, local pub (charge), public car parks. **In-Room:** Maid service, room key with late pass keys. **On-Premises:** TV lounge, lending library, ironing facilities. **Swimming:** At nearby pool or ocean beach. **Sunbathing:** On patio or nearby beach. **Smoking:** Permitted. **Pets:** Small dogs only in guest rooms only with prior arrangement. **Handicap Access:** Welcome, but no wheelchair facilities or lifts. **Children:** Permitted in small quantities & prior arrangement. **Languages:** English. **Your Host:** Ann.

Primrose Hotel, The

Gay-Friendly 50/50 ♀♂

The Warmest Welcome in Town

Primrose Hotel is ideally situated close to North Station, a 5-minute walk from the town centre, promenade and theatres. The hotel is run by resident proprietors, whose main concern is your comfort and enjoyment. No effort is spared to make your holiday a happy one. Rooms feature modern furniture, comfortable beds, tea-making facilities, shaver and power point. Our lounge bar has McEwans on draught. You will find this charming, small hotel spotlessly clean. Nothing is too much trouble to ensure that your stay is a happy one. Just relax, you are in good hands and nobody does it better!

Address: 16 Lord St, Blackpool, Lancashire FY1 2BD England. Tel: (01253) 22488.

Type: Hotel with bar. **Clientele:** 50% straight & 50% gay/lesbian with some exclusively gay wknds including New Year, Easter. **Transportation:** Rail or motor car or coach. **To Gay Bars:** 2-minute walk to gay/lesbian bars. **Rooms:** 6 doubles, 2 triples, 1 quad, 1 twin. **Bathrooms:** 2 shared, 2 private. **Meals:** Continental breakfast or full English breakfast. **Vegetarian:** Upon request. **Complimentary:** Concessionary pass to the Flamingo night club, tea, coffee. **Dates Open:** All year. **High Season:** September 2nd-November 5th. **Rates:** Singles, £13.00-£18.00, doubles, £22.00-£36.00. **Discounts:** For senior citizens, stays over 3 nights, weekly stays. **Rsv'tns:** Advisable. **Reserve Through:** Write for information. **Parking:** Limited free on-street parking, 2-minute walk to car park. **In-Room:** Maid, room & laundry service, tea/coffee making facilities, late keys. **On-Premises:** TV lounge, masseur. **Exercise/Health:** Weights, Massage. **Swimming:** Excellent indoor pool nearby, ocean beach. **Sunbathing:** On the beach. **Smoking:** Permitted without restrictions. **Pets:** Small dogs only permitted in owner's room. **Handicap Access:** No, we have no ground-floor rooms. **Children:** Over 5 years preferred. **Languages:** English, limited French. **Your Host:** Barry & Chris.

Sunnyside House

Men ♂

Address: 27 Vance Road, Blackpool FY1 4QD England. Tel: (01253) 23 752.

Type: Bed & breakfast. **Clientele:** Men only. **To Gay Bars:** Short walk to Basil's, 501, Flamingo & Funny Girls. **Rooms:** 8 rooms. **Bathrooms:** Shared. **Meals:** Full English breakfast. **Complimentary:** Tea & coffee. **Dates Open:** All year. **Rates:** £10.00-£12.00. **Parking:** On-street parking. Large pay car park nearby. **In-Room:** TV, tea & coffee-making facilities. **On-Premises:** TV lounge. **Swimming:** A few minutes to the ocean. **Smoking:** Permitted without restrictions. **Pets:** Permitted by arrangement. **Handicap Access:** No. **Children:** Not especially welcome. **Languages:** English.

Tremadoc Guest House

Gay/Lesbian ♀♂

Tremadoc is a large, comfortable licensed guesthouse overlooking the sea and located only minutes from the town centre, North Station, North Pier, Gynn Square and the Promenade and five minutes from pubs and clubs. Rooms have hot and cold water, shaver points and colour TV. Front door and bedroom keys are supplied on arrival. There is a bar for guests, and a colour TV lounge for guests' use. Guests receive a concessionary pass to the Flamingo, a popular gay club. Breakfast is included, with evening meal optional. Singles are always welcome.

Address: 127-129 Dickson Rd, North Shore, Blackpool FY1 2EU England. Tel: (01253) 24 001.

Type: Guesthouse.
Clientele: Good mix of gay men & women.
Transportation: Bus or train from London or Manchester to Blackpool, then taxi.
To Gay Bars: 5 minutes to gay bars.
Rooms: 9 rooms with single, double & bunk beds.
Bathrooms: 1 shower room & 3 toilets.

Meals: Full English breakfast. Optional evening meal £4.00.
Vegetarian: Available upon request.
Complimentary: Free pass to Flamingo.
Dates Open: All year.
High Season: September through beginning of November.
Rates: High season £15.00. Low season £11.00.

Discounts: Winter specials available on request.
Rsv'tns: Required for Illumination weekends.
Reserve Through: Call direct. 24 hour answering service.
Parking: Ample free on-street parking.
In-Room: Tea-making facilities.
On-Premises: Colour TV lounge.

Exercise/Health: All available in nearby big hotel.
Swimming: Ocean beach across the road.
Sunbathing: On beach.
Smoking: Permitted without restrictions.
Pets: Not permitted.
Handicap Access: No.
Languages: English.

BOURNEMOUTH

Bondi

Gay/Lesbian ♀♂

Bondi of Bournemouth offers comfortable bed and breakfast rooms with colour TV, tea and coffee facilities. We're three minutes from the Queens Hotel Pub, the Triangle Club, the sea front and shopping. Guests receive concessionary passes to Triangle, The Cabaret Club and Bolts nightclubs. See you soon!

Address: 43 St Michael's Rd, Bournemouth BH2 5DP England. Tel: (01202) 554893.

Clientele: Gay & lesbian. Comfortable mix of men & women.
To Gay Bars: 3 minutes.
Rooms: 7 rooms.
Bathrooms: 3 shared.
Meals: Full English breakfast included. Inexpensive bar snacks till 10pm.
Complimentary: Coffee,

tea, & concessions to Triangle, Bolts, The Cabaret Club.
Dates Open: All year.
High Season: Jul-Aug.
Rates: £11.00 winter, £15.00 summer.
Discounts: Call for specials.
Rsv'tns: Required.
Reserve Through: Call

direct.
Parking: Ample on-street parking.
In-Room: Color satellite TV & tea/coffee making facilities.
On-Premises: Residents' lounge.
Swimming: 3 minutes to the sea front.
Smoking: Permitted

without restrictions.
Pets: Permitted.
Handicap Access: No.
Children: 10 years & up.
Languages: English, a little Spanish.
Your Host: Colin & Malcolm.

Double Four Hotel

Gay-Friendly 50/50 ♀♂

Only three minutes from the Triangle Club and an easy walk from the Queens Pub, *Double Four Hotel* offers comfortable lodgings to gay visitors. All rooms have colour TV with 24-hour movie channel and tea- and coffee-making facilities. Rooms with private showers and full en suite are available. Our guests get concessionary rates at local gay nightclubs and a free drink at the Queens! For reservations, call Richard or Lourens.

Address: 44/46 St Michael's Road, Bournemouth, Dorset BH2 5DY England. Tel: (01202) 555950.

Type: Hotel with restaurant and bar.
Clientele: 50% gay & lesbian & 50% hetero clientele.
Transportation: Car is best, coach & train service from London & Heathrow Airport.
To Gay Bars: 3 minutes.
Rooms: 11 rooms with single & double beds.
Bathrooms: 4 en suite, 5 private showers, 2 shared showers, 3 shared toilets.

Meals: Full English breakfast.
Vegetarian: Available upon request.
Complimentary: Tea & coffee, concessionary passes to gay night clubs.
Dates Open: All year.
High Season: July to September.
Rates: Summer £15.00 to £25.00, winter £13.00 to £20.00.
Discounts: On 7 night bookings.

Credit Cards: MC, VISA, Access, Amex & Diners.
Rsv'tns: Recommended, but not always necessary.
Reserve Through: Travel agent or call direct.
Parking: Adequate on-street parking, low cost parking lot nearby.
In-Room: Color TV, 24 hr movie channel, tea & coffee-making facilities, ceiling fans, maid service.
On-Premises: TV lounge & residents bar.
Swimming: 10 min walk

to pool & beach.
Sunbathing: At the beach.
Nudity: Nude beach 5 miles.
Smoking: Permitted in all rooms.
Pets: Permitted without restrictions.
Handicap Access: No.
Children: From 14 years.
Languages: English, Dutch, some German & French.
Your Host: Richard & Lourens.

Leicester Grange

Men ♂

Quality Accommodation Close to the Sea

Relax in the stylish comfort of *Leicester Grange*, a 1920's residence set high in an acre of grounds within the prestigious area of Branksome Park. The property enjoys a superb setting amidst mature trees, while being only some 5 minutes by car from the centre of Bournemouth town with its clubs and pub. The local beach is only a tree lined walk away and the unspoiled beach of Shell Bay at Studland can be reached via the ferry across the entrance to Poole Harbour, the second largest natural harbour in the world. Your stay in this relaxing residence will leave you refreshed and ready to enjoy the superb local countryside. The New Forest is within easy reach and there are a number of historic local houses to view.

Address: Bournemouth/Poole Tel: (01202) 760278.

Type: Bed & breakfast in a large, private house.
Clientele: Men only.
Transportation: Best to have own car. Good local taxi service.
To Gay Bars: 5 minutes by car to town center.
Rooms: 3 rooms with double beds.
Bathrooms: 2 en suite & 1 shared.
Meals: Good continental breakfast.
Complimentary: Tea or

coffee when you arrive. Water & mints each day in room.
Dates Open: All year except Christmas week. Phone to confirm.
High Season: July, August, & September.
Rates: En suite, £20.00-£25.00 per person per night. Shared bath, £15.00-£18.00 per person per night.
Discounts: Each 7th consecutive night at no

charge.
Credit Cards: MC, VISA.
Rsv'tns: Required. Can be made by telephone with credit card.
Reserve Through: Call direct.
Minimum Stay: Required bank holidays only.
Parking: Ample parking at top of the drive.
In-Room: Color TV.
Swimming: Public pool 10 minutes by car. Beach 5 minutes by car or 15

minute walk.
Sunbathing: On part of the grounds or at the beach.
Nudity: Permitted at the beach with care. Ask for details.
Smoking: Permitted.
Pets: Not permitted.
Handicap Access: No. Too many steps.
Children: Not permitted.
Languages: English.

Norwich House

Gay/Lesbian ♂

Our detached property on a quiet no-thru road assures you a comfortable and relaxing sojourn while enjoying our central heating, hot/cold water, your own keys, and no restrictions. Two gay clubs are 300 yards down the street, and guests receive a free pass to one of them. All rooms at *Norwich House* are tasteful and have color TV and tea & coffee makers. Full English breakfast is included.

Address: 30 Norwich Ave, Bournemouth BH2 5TH England. Tel: (01202) 553 985.

Type: Guesthouse.
Clientele: Exclusively gay/lesbian, 75% men with women very welcome.
Transportation: Coach direct from Heathrow Airport to Bournemouth Stn., then taxi.
To Gay Bars: 5-minute walk to gay clubs.
Rooms: 2 singles, 1 double, & 2 triples.
Bathrooms: 1 room has private shower, others share baths.
Meals: Full English Breakfast. Evening meal optional for £6.00.
Vegetarian: By prior arrangement.
Complimentary: Tea & coffee in room.
Dates Open: All year.
High Season: June through September.
Rates: £13.00-£18.00.
Discounts: Special spring rate.
Credit Cards: VISA, Access.
Rsv'tns: Recommended in high season.
Reserve Through: Call direct.
Parking: Adequate free parking on premises.
In-Room: Room service, colour TV, video tape library, coffee & tea-making facilities.
On-Premises: TV lounge & public telephone.
Swimming: 10-minute walk to pool or ocean beach.
Sunbathing: On beach.
Nudity: Nude beach at Studland Bay, 5 miles.
Smoking: Permitted, but not at mealtime.
Pets: Not permitted.
Handicap Access: No.
Children: Age limit 12 yrs.
Languages: English.
Your Host: Keith & Gordon

Orchard Hotel, The

Gay/Lesbian ♀♂

The Orchard is Bournemouth's longest established, year-round, exclusively gay hotel for men and women. A visit will show you why! We provide clean, comfortable and tasteful surroundings combined with a high standard of service at competitive rates. Ours is a 10-bedroom hotel with the Victorian Conservatory Lounge overlooking the garden. The sea is 4 minutes' walk, whilst the gay pub is 10 minutes away. There is a ferry to a nearby gay beach. We have a full residents' license, so drinks are available all day. We serve a delicious evening meal family style. It's a pleasant way to meet other guests and a good time is had by all.

Address: 15 Alumdale Rd, Alum Chine, Bournemouth BH4 8HX England. Tel: (01202) 767 767.

Type: Hotel with full residents' liquor license.
Clientele: Good mix of gay men & women.
Transportation: Free pick up from Bournemouth train or bus.
To Gay Bars: Free car service to clubs, or 10-minute walk to gay/lesbian clubs.
Rooms: 3 singles, 5 doubles & 2 triples.
Bathrooms: 6 private, 4 share.
Meals: Full English breakfast.
Vegetarian: Always available.
Complimentary: Tea & coffee & sandwiches throughout the day.
Dates Open: All year.
High Season: March-September.
Rates: £16.50-£18.00 per person.
Discounts: Winter 4th consecutive night free.
Credit Cards: VISA, ACCESS.
Rsv'tns: Not required, but advisable.
Reserve Through: Call direct.
Parking: Ample free on-street parking.
In-Room: Maid service, room service, laundry service, color TV.
On-Premises: Meeting rooms, TV lounge, public telephones, & cocktail lounge overlooking garden.
Swimming: 3-minute walk to ocean beach, ferry to gay beach 5 min. by car.
Sunbathing: On beach, in enclosed private garden.
Smoking: Permitted without restrictions.
Pets: Permitted.
Handicap Access: No.
Children: Not permitted.
Languages: English, Welsh, French.

BRIGHTON

Alpha Lodge Private Hotel

Gay/Lesbian ♂

THE Gay Hotel for Single People

As Brighton's longest established exclusively gay hotel (since 1980), *Alpha Lodge* welcomes gay men and women year round. We are situated in a pleasant Regency square, overlooking the Victorian Palace Pier, a few yards from the beach and most gay clubs. Local gay saunas and nude bathing beaches are nearby. Our well-appointed, intimate hotel, originally built in the early 1800's, is run by Derrick and Charles, both of whom are actively gay. It is run as a continuous house party.

Five rooms have double beds, each with its own private shower. The remainder, with single beds, are both with and without private showers. All rooms have colour TV, radio, intercom and hot drink facilities, and, of course, self-controlled central heating. There are adequate public showers, toilets, a bathroom and a cosy lounge with an open fire and colour TV. Our full English breakfast is renowned. The Steine Room Suite, consists of Turkish Bath, rest area with an open fire and colour TV, shower area, hair dryer, toilet and lockers. Towels and wraps are provided, and the facility is free to residents Wednesday, Friday and Saturday for 1-1/2 hours in early evening.

All guests have front door keys, and there are no petty restrictions. Friends may be brought in at all times. There is a safe for valuables (free). Everything is geared to make one's stay comfortable and relaxing. A full fire certificate has been issued. A map of Gay Brighton, a privilege card for entry to the gay clubs, and a welcoming drink upon arrival are all provided as part of the basic charge for the room. We are not licensed, but alcoholic drinks may be brought into the hotel, where ice and mixers are available 24 hours a day. We look forward to your joining us.

Address: 19 New Steine, Brighton, E Sussex BN2 1PD England. Tel: (01273) 609 632, Fax: (01273) 690 264.

Type: Guesthouse with a steam-room suite.
Clientele: Mostly men with women welcome. Exclusively gay.
Transportation: Take taxi or No. 7 minibus from the station.
To Gay Bars: 2-minute walk to gay & lesbian bars.
Rooms: 10 rooms with single & double beds.
Bathrooms: 1 shared bath, 8 showers (2 shared) & 4 shared toilets.
Meals: Full English breakfast. Cold soft drinks at low cost 24 hours.

Vegetarian: Available with overnight notice.
Complimentary: Coffee, tea, soft drink on arrival. Unlimited hot drinks in the rooms.
Dates Open: All year. Closed in December for vacation.
High Season: May-September.
Rates: Low season: £20.00-£38.00 per room; high season: £22.00-£42.00.
Discounts: 7th night free to all & 10% to members of gay groups.
Credit Cards: MC, VISA, Amex & Eurocard.

Rsv'tns: Recommended in summer 10 days in advance.
Reserve Through: Travel agent or call direct.
Minimum Stay: One night. Longer stays on bank holidays.
Parking: Free & pay parking on the street at or near the hotel.
In-Room: Color TV, beverage-making facilities, radio & intercom in all rooms. Room service for continental breakfast.
On-Premises: TV lounge, public telephone, meeting rooms & refrigerator for cold sodas.

Exercise/Health: Steam room (free on Wed., Fri. and Sat. evenings).
Swimming: Pool, ocean beach nearby.
Sunbathing: On the beach.
Nudity: 10-minute walk to public nudist beach.
Smoking: Permitted without restrictions.
Pets: Not permitted.
Handicap Access: No.
Children: Not permitted.
Languages: English.
Your Host: Derrick & Charles.

Ashley Court Guest House

Gay/Lesbian ♀♂

Breakfast on the terrace, then take an ambling stroll to the beach. When evening comes, it's still just a 2-minute walk to Brighton's main gay pub and club, making *Ashley Court* ideally located to all that Brighton has to offer. All rooms have colour TV and tea- and coffee-making facilities, not to mention private showers. After the hustle of London, you'll find Brighton the place to relax and renew.

Address: 33 Montpelier Rd, Brighton BN1 2LQ England. Tel: (01273) 739916.

Type: B&B guesthouse.
Clientele: Mostly gay & lesbian with some hetero clientele.
To Gay Bars: 2 minutes.
Rooms: 3 singles, 3 doubles & 2 triples.
Bathrooms: Private sinks & showers in all rooms, 3 shared toilets.
Meals: Full breakfast.
Vegetarian: Available

upon request.
Complimentary: Coffee & tea.
Dates Open: All year.
Rates: £15-£30 per night.
Discounts: Seventh night free.
Credit Cards: VISA.
Rsv'tns: Required.
Reserve Through: Travel agent or call direct.
Parking: Adequate on-

street restricted parking. Free non-controlled parking nearby.
In-Room: Colour TV, coffee making facilities & room service.
On-Premises: Laundry facilities.
Swimming: At nearby ocean.
Sunbathing: At the beach.

Nudity: Permitted at the Marina & Shoreham Beach.
Smoking: Permitted. Non-smoking rooms available.
Pets: Permitted.
Handicap Access: No.
Children: Permitted.
Languages: English.

Avalon House

Gay/Lesbian ♀♂

Brighton's "In" Place

Since Bob and Mike opened *Avalon House* in 1989, it has become internationally recognised as one of the friendliest guesthouses. More and more guests return time and again to enjoy their warm hospitality.

Cosy, old-world charm coupled with cleanliness, comfortable beds and elegant yet substantial breakfasts are hallmarks of the *Avalon* experience. Guests receive house and room keys on arrival for unrestricted access and their visitors are welcome. Guests also receive *Avalon's* own gay guide to Brighton, plus concession passes to clubs. All rooms have colour TV with satellite channels and guests my also select in-house movies, by arrangement. There are unlimited refreshment trays with drinks and biscuits in all bedrooms. *Avalon* is fully centrally heated.

Located in the heart of the gay community, which is the largest outside London, we are minutes from superb restaurants, shops, historical and leisure attractions. Brighton is also an ideal base from which to explore the beauty and history of the region.

Let Bob and Mike welcome you to *Avalon,* where all major cards are accepted.

Address: 7 Upper Rock Gardens, Brighton, BN2 1QE England. Tel: (01273) 692344, Fax: (01273) 692344.

Type: Bed & breakfast guesthouse.
Clientele: Mostly gay & lesbian with some hetero clientele. Leather guys particularly welcome.
Transportation: Taxi from local rail sta. Difficult parking. Cabs, public trans. good, reasonably priced. 40 min from Gatwick Airport.
To Gay Bars: 5-minute walk to most bars/clubs,

including super new leather bar open weekends.
Rooms: 8 rooms.
Bathrooms: En suite: 1 bath/shower/toilet, 3 shower/sink, 4 sinks. Others share.
Meals: Full breakfast.
Vegetarian: Always available.
Complimentary: Tea, coffee, chocolate, & biscuits in all guest rooms.
Dates Open: All year,

with special full board, houseparty-style Christmas package.
High Season: June to mid October.
Rates: £15.00-£30.00 per person per night.
Discounts: 1 free night for each period of 7 consecutive booked nights.
Credit Cards: MC, VISA, Access, Amex & Diners.
Rsv'tns: Required most wknds & Jun-Sept. Non-returnable deposit of

50% or full cost for 1 night.
Reserve Through: Call direct.
Minimum Stay: 2 nights on high season weekends, 3 on English bank holiday weekends.
Parking: 2 hr limited voucher parking our street. Nearby unrestricted street parking
In-Room: Colour & satel-

continued next page

UK (England)

lite TV, in-house video movies, coffee & tea-making facilities & maid service.
On-Premises: Ironing facilities & hair dryers. Owners safe available to secure valuables.

Exercise/Health: 3 gay male saunas & several well-equipped health centers/gyms within easy reach.
Swimming: 2 nearby pools & ocean beach.
Sunbathing: On the

beach.
Nudity: Nearby official & unofficial nudist beaches, some gay, some mixed.
Smoking: Permitted throughout the guesthouse.
Pets: Permitted by prior

arrangement with Bob & Mike.
Handicap Access: 2 street level rooms.
Children: By prior arrangement, age 10 years or older.
Languages: English.

Barrington's Private Hotel

Gay-Friendly 50/50 ♀♂

Luxury rooms and a full English breakfast enhance your stay at *Barrington's Private Hotel*. We are located opposite the Royal Pavilion and two minutes from *Revenge* nightclub and ocean beach.

Address: 76 Grand Parade, Brighton BN2 2JA England. Tel: (01273) 604 182.

Type: Hotel with licensed lounge bar.
Clientele: 50% gay & lesbian & 50% hetero clientele.
Rooms: Luxury rooms with double & twin beds.
Bathrooms: Private

showers, shared baths.
Meals: Full English breakfast.
High Season: June-September.
Rates: £16-£20 per person.
Reserve Through: Call direct.

Parking: Free parking behind hotel
In-Room: Remote control colour TV, radios & intercom.
Swimming: 2-minute walk to ocean.
Smoking: Permitted.
Pets: Small pets

permitted.
Handicap Access: No.
Children: Permitted over 5 years of age.
Languages: English.
Your Host: Barry.

Catnaps Private Guest House

Gay/Lesbian ♂

Catnaps is situated close to the sea, about 8 minutes' walk from the Royal Pavilion, unique to Brighton and actually the historical reason for the growth of the town in the 18th-19th centuries. We aim for a family atmosphere and we like guests to feel welcome. All rooms have hot and cold water and are centrally heated. Showers and toilets are in a separate area of the house and are easily reached from the bedrooms. Guests have their own keys to the house.

Address: 21 Atlingworth St, Brighton, E Sussex BN2 1PL England. Tel: (01273) 685 193.

Type: Guesthouse.
Clientele: Mostly men with women welcome.
Transportation: Taxi or bus from station.
To Gay Bars: 5-minute walk to gay & lesbian bars.
Rooms: 7 rooms.
Bathrooms: Shared baths & toilets. 2 rooms have private showers, all have sinks.
Meals: Full English breakfast.

Complimentary: Tea & coffee upon arrival.
Dates Open: All year.
High Season: June-August.
Rates: Single £17.00 for 1 night. Double £35.00 for a night with shower, £33.00 without shower.
Discounts: On longer stays.
Credit Cards: MC, VISA, Amex, Eurocard (5% service charge on all cards).
Rsv'tns: Preferred.

Reserve Through: Call direct.
Parking: Adequate free on-street parking.
In-Room: Tea or coffee delivered to room.
On-Premises: TV lounge & public telephone.
Swimming: Pool & ocean beach are nearby.
Sunbathing: On the beach.
Nudity: 5-minute walk to nude beach.
Smoking: Permitted

without restrictions.
Pets: Permitted with prior arrangement. Owner responsible for pets.
Handicap Access: No.
Children: Not normally, but open to requests.
Languages: English, limited French.
Your Host: Malcolm & Charlie.

Coward's Guest House

Men ♂

Coward's Guest House is a small, newly-refurbished guest house close to the sea and to all the amenities of Brighton and environs. All rooms are fitted with en-suite bath or shower.

Address: 12 Upper Rock Gardens, Brighton BN2 1QE England. Tel: (01273) 692677.

Type: Guesthouse.
Clientele: Mainly men with women welcome.
Transportation: Brighton Station, then taxi.
To Gay Bars: 7 gay bars & 5 gay clubs within 5 min walk.
Rooms: 2 singles, 4 doubles & 2 triples with single & double beds.

Bathrooms: 4 en suite. All rooms have showers.
Meals: Full English or vegetarian breakfast.
Vegetarian: Anytime.
Complimentary: Tea & coffee in all rooms.
Dates Open: All year.
High Season: April thru October.
Rates: Summer: double

£38.00-£45.00, single £24.00-£26.00. Winter: double £34.00-£42.00, single £21.00-£23.00.
Credit Cards: VISA, Access.
Rsv'tns: Required.
Reserve Through: Call direct.
Parking: Free on-street parking.

In-Room: Color TV.
Swimming: At nearby sea.
Sunbathing: On the beach.
Smoking: Permitted.
Pets: Not permitted.
Handicap Access: No.
Children: Not permitted.
Languages: English.
Your Host: Gerry & Cyril.

Hudsons Guest House

Gay/Lesbian ♀♂

Hudsons is an early 19th century gentleman's residence, which has been skillfully converted to an exclusively gay guest house. Concealed behind louvered doors in each room, are shower and washbasin, wardrobes and tea- and coffee-making facilities. All rooms also have colour TV, and some have sofas. Also of high standard is the decor, which was coordinated by Next Interiors. Devonshire Place is a quiet road in the middle of Brighton's gay village, so clubs and bars are only a five-minute walk from our door. Also nearby are the Royal Pavilion, the sea, beaches, the pier and the town centre. *Hudsons* is the only gay hotel inspected by, and whose standards are approved by, the Tourist Authority. The quality and warmth of *Hudsons* has established it in the fine tradition of English hospitality. We promise to do our best to make sure you go away wishing the next visit were tomorrow.

Address: 22 Devonshire Place, Brighton, E Sussex BN2 1QA England. Tel: (01273) 683 642 or Fax: 696 088.

Type: Guesthouse.
Clientele: Good mix of gay men & women.
Transportation: Train to Brighton Station then taxi or No. 7 bus.
To Gay Bars: Within easy walking distance (2 mins) of all gay bars.
Rooms: 9 rooms with single, queen or king beds.
Bathrooms: All have private showers, 1 has shower/toilet en suite.
Meals: Proper English breakfast in dining room with homemade preserves.

Vegetarian: Just ask, one of us is vegetarian! Superb vegetarian restaurants nearby.
Complimentary: Tea, coffee, sherry, juice, biscuits & free Brighton map at check-in, concessions to clubs.
Dates Open: All year.
Rates: Single £20.00-£28.00, double £32.00-£45.00 (includes breakfast for two).
Discounts: Mid-week, extended stay, and for Equity members.
Credit Cards: MC, VISA & Amex.

Rsv'tns: A good idea, but not always necessary.
Reserve Through: Travel agent or call direct.
Minimum Stay: Bank holidays or weekends.
Parking: On-street parking nearby.
In-Room: Washbasins, private shower, tea-making facilities, colour TV, central heating, telephone, laundry service, maid service.
On-Premises: Guests lounge.
Exercise/Health: Nearby gym, weights, Jacuzzi, sauna, steam, massage.

Swimming: At nearby ocean beach & pool.
Sunbathing: Patio and nearby beach.
Nudity: Permitted at nearby beach (10 mins).
Smoking: Permitted without restrictions.
Pets: Not permitted.
Handicap Access: No.
Children: Not permitted.
Languages: English, some French, German.
Your Host: Frank & Graham.

IGTA

Portland House Hotel

Gay-Friendly 50/50 ♀♂

The *Portland House* is a Grade 2 listed Regency building in Brighton's premier seafront square close to main attractions, such as Brighton Pavilion, theatres, shopping, entertainment, antique shops and the famous historic Lanes. Our informal, easy-going hotel and comfortable, unpretentious environment make folks feel relaxed. Choose standard, superior or four-poster rooms, all of which have en-suite facilities, direct-dial telephone, tea/coffee making facilities, radio alarm clock and hairdryer. Continental or full English breakfast is served in the dining room or in your room. Room or bar service is available for light snacks. Evening dinner, to order, features mainly English, French and vegetarian cuisines.

Address: 55-56 Regency Square, Brighton, East Sussex BN1 2FF England. Tel: (01273) 820464, Fax: (01273) 746036.

Type: Hotel with bar. **Clientele:** 50% gay & lesbian & 50% hetero clientele. **Transportation:** Pick up from train. **To Gay Bars:** 2 min walk. **Rooms:** 10 singles, 14 doubles. **Bathrooms:** All en suite. **Meals:** Full English or continental breakfast. **Vegetarian:** Available upon request. **Complimentary:** Tea & coffee-making facilities in room. **Dates Open:** All year except last 2 weeks of December and all of January. **Rates:** £20.00-£55.00 per person per night, includes breakfast. **Discounts:** 10% for weekly rentals. **Credit Cards:** MC, VISA, Amex, Diners. **Rsv'tns:** Required sometimes. **Reserve Through:** Travel agent or call direct. **Parking:** Adequate on-street pay parking. **In-Room:** Color TV, direct dial phones, tea & coffee-making facilities, alarm clock radio, hairdryer, maid & room service. **On-Premises:** Meeting rooms. **Swimming:** At nearby ocean beach. **Sunbathing:** On the beach. **Nudity:** Permitted near marina. **Smoking:** Permitted everywhere except the dining room. **Pets:** Permitted. **Handicap Access:** 5 steps to front door, lift to all floors. **Children:** Permitted. **Languages:** English.

Shalimar Hotel

Gay/Lesbian ♂

Undisputedly: Brighton's Most Centrally-Located Hotel for Clubs and Bars

Shalimar has been under the personal supervision of your Irish hosts, Kevin and Lawrence, since 1983. All rooms are tastefully decorated and have color TV, vanity units and shaving points. Front rooms have sea views. Deluxe rooms have full bath, fridge and a private balcony overlooking the sea and pier. An excellently-cooked breakfast is included. A free map gives you the locations of gay bars and clubs, and a privilege pass for entry to clubs is also provided. We now have a full residents' bar, the Backroom Bar, which is proving very popular and is a fun place to meet other guests. Send for our brochure. You will not be disappointed.

Address: 23 Broad St, Marine Parade, Brighton, Sussex BN2 1TJ England. Tel: (01273) 605316.

Type: Hotel with backroom resident's bar. **Clientele:** Mostly men with women welcome. **Transportation:** Car, taxi or bus. Nearest airport London Gatwick, then 1/2 hour by train to Brighton. **To Gay Bars:** 2 minutes by foot. **Rooms:** 10 rooms with single, double or queen beds. **Bathrooms:** 5 private & 3 private showers only. Shared: 1 full bath, 1 WC. **Meals:** Full breakfast. **Vegetarian:** Available upon request. **Complimentary:** Tea, coffee in rooms, glass of wine on presentation of INN Places. **Dates Open:** All year. **High Season:** April through October. **Rates:** £30-£50 for two people. **Discounts:** 10% on stays of 1 week or longer. **Credit Cards:** MC, VISA, Amex, Diners, Eurocard & Travellers Cheques. **Rsv'tns:** Preferred. **Reserve Through:** Travel agent or call direct. **Minimum Stay:** 3 days during bank holidays only. **Parking:** Adequate on-street parking. **In-Room:** Colour TV, telephone, coffee & tea-making facilities & room service. Deluxe rooms with refrigerators. **On-Premises:** Backroom bar, fun bar. **Exercise/Health:** Nearby gym, weights, Jacuzzi, sauna, steam, massage.

Swimming: Nearby pool. 2 minutes to the beach. Sunbathing: On beach. Nudity: 10 minutes to nude beach. Smoking: Permitted except in dining room, non-smokers' rooms available. Pets: Not permitted. Handicap Access: No. Children: Not permitted. Languages: English. Your Host: Kevin & Lawrence.

Sinclairs Guest House

Exclusively Gay

Gay/Lesbian ♂

Sinclairs is a historically listed building located within minutes of the major Brighton gay area, the famous Regency Pavilion and the sea. All bedrooms have color TV, alarm clock radios, free tea- and coffee-making facilities and central heating. Some have refrigerators and en-suite facilities. A full English breakfast is served till late in the morning, and a continental one till midday. Sinclairs is exclusively gay and provides a detailed, up-to-date map of the gay area. The garden is available in summer for relaxing in the sun.

Address: 23 Upper Rock Gardens, Brighton BN2 1QE England. Tel: (01273) 600 006 and (0831) 248 361.

Type: Bed & breakfast guest house. Clientele: Mostly men with women welcome. Transportation: Train to Brighton station, then taxi. To Gay Bars: 5-minute walk to nearest gay bar or club. Rooms: 5 rooms & 1 suite with single or double beds.

Bathrooms: 3 en suite, 3 sinks only, 1 shared WC, & 2 shared bath/shower/toilet. Meals: Full breakfast. Vegetarian: Upon request with no extra charge. Complimentary: Tea & coffee in room. Dates Open: All year. High Season: July-Sep.t Rates: £15.00-£20.00 per person.

Credit Cards: MC, VISA & Eurocard. Rsv'tns: Preferred. Reserve Through: Call direct. Parking: Adequate on-street parking. In-Room: Color TV, fridge, hair dryer, clock radios, coffee/tea-making facilities. On-Premises: Lounge.

Swimming: Ocean beach. Sunbathing: On beach & in garden. Nudity: Permitted on the public beach. Smoking: Permitted without restrictions. Pets: Not permitted. Handicap Access: No. Children: Not permitted. Languages: English, Spanish, French, German, Italian, Portuguese.

CORNWALL

Glencree Private Hotel

Gay-Friendly 50/50 ♀♂

You'll Agree "Glencree" is "The Place" to be

Glencree is a fine Victorian granite house, established as a private hotel since 1946. It has a wealth of character and a comfortable, friendly atmosphere. Nine well-appointed rooms are tastefully decorated. All have tea- and coffee-making facilities and colour TV, and most have full en suite facilities or sea views. We're conveniently located on level ground in a quiet road just off the seafront and overlooking the bowling greens, tennis courts and the sea beyond. The main shopping center is a short walk away, as is the main line rail station. You are assured of a warm welcome and personal service, with real home cooking. Penzance is ideally situated, if you wish to tour picturesque fishing villages, beaches and coves. There are plenty of golf courses, also horse riding, windsurfing, etc., for the more energetic.

Address: 2 Mennaye Rd Penzance, Cornwall TR18 4NG England. Tel/Fax: (01736) 62026. In US call (407) 994-3558, Fax: (407) 994-3634.

Type: Guesthouse with drink license. Clientele: 50% gay & lesbian & 50% hetero. Transportation: Train, Mainline Station 1/2 mile,

coach station 1/2 mile. To Gay Bars: 20 miles to gay pub/club. Rooms: 9 rooms & 1 apartment (sleeps 4) with single, double or

queen beds. Bathrooms: 6 private, 2 shared toilets & 1 shared bathroom. Meals: Full breakfast. Vegetarian: Available

upon request. Complimentary: Tea & coffee in room. Dates Open: Feb-Oct.

Continued next page

INN Places 1995

UK (England)

High Season: July & August.
Rates: Summer £14-£21, winter £12-£18 (per person).
Discounts: Weekly rates, 7th day free.
Credit Cards: VISA, Amex.
Rsv'tns: Advisable in the summer, walk-ins welcome.
Reserve Through: Travel agent or call direct.
Minimum Stay: 3 nights advance booking July/Aug only.
Parking: Ample free on-street parking.
In-Room: Color TV, coffee/tea-making facilities, room service, laundry service & maid service.
On-Premises: TV lounge & pay phone.
Exercise/Health: Nearby facilities.
Swimming: Nearby pool & ocean beach. (10-minute walk).
Sunbathing: At poolside, the beach or in the park.
Nudity: Permitted at some beaches. Please ask.
Smoking: Permitted in TV lounge. Non-smoking dining room, sleeping rooms available.
Pets: Well-behaved pets welcomed.
Handicap Access: No.
Children: Welcomed over 5 years old.
Languages: English & limited Spanish.
Your Host: Michael & David.

Rosehill in the Fern

Gay/Lesbian ♀♂

Cornwall is a beautiful, rural part of England, with fabulous beaches, cliffs and a warm climate (by British standards!). *Rosehill in the Fern* is about 10 miles from Truro, the small city which is the main town in Cornwall, with its magnificent cathedral built out of Cornish granite. We are also about 10 miles from the village of Perranporth, where there is a thriving gay club. The spectacular north Cornish coast, with its golden beach and breathtaking cliffs, is only five minutes by car. Our house is a very attractive eighteenth-century country house set in two acres of garden and woodland. The property is secluded but conveniently located for all that Cornwall has to offer, and is ideal for either a quiet "get away from it all" break, or a more energetic touring holiday (vacation).

The interior of the house is quietly and tastefully decorated and furnished, the emphasis being on country-house-style comfort, where guests are able to enjoy privacy or each other's company by choice. We have a large drawing room and dining room. Each bedroom is spacious and comfortably furnished with double or twin bed. Our two principal rooms have access through French windows to their own private patio with room to sit outside. The en suite bathrooms are appointed to a very high standard with bath, shower, wash basin and W.C. Guests are given a front door key and are encouraged to come and go as they wish. We aim to provide a high standard of comfort and good home cooking in order to ensure that our guests feel welcome and at home.

Address: Roseworthy, Camborne, Cornwall TR14 0DU England. Tel: (01209) 712 573.

Type: Guesthouse (private hotel).
Clientele: Mainly gay & lesbian with some hetero clientele.
Transportation: Car is best. Pick up airport, train, bus or ferry dock.
To Gay Bars: 10 miles to Perranporth.
Rooms: 3 rooms with single or double beds.
Bathrooms: All private.
Meals: Full English breakfast with three-course evening meals by arrangement for £12.50.
Vegetarian: We cater to special dietary needs with advance notice.
Dates Open: All year.
High Season: April-September.
Rates: £25.00 per person per night in high season, £20.00 during off season.
Discounts: Weekly and fortnightly rates.
Credit Cards: MC, VISA & Eurocard.
Rsv'tns: Greatly appreciated.
Reserve Through: Call direct.
Parking: Ample free off-street parking.
In-Room: Color TV, coffee & tea-making facilities.
On-Premises: TV lounge & meeting rooms.
Exercise/Health: Nearby gymnasium and leisure centre.
Swimming: At nearby full-sized heated pool or ocean.
Sunbathing: On the patio, lawn & at the beach.
Smoking: Permitted in public rooms, discouraged in sleeping rooms.
Pets: Dogs welcome by arrangement.
Handicap Access: Not equipped for severe disabilities.
Children: Not permitted.
Languages: English.
Your Host: Barry & Andy.

Ryn Anneth

Gay/Lesbian ♀♂

Join Us for Tea in an English Garden

Ryn Anneth is a small, exclusively gay, very friendly guesthouse in a quiet cul-de-sac close to beaches and the town centre. We have a reputation for cleanliness, cozy comfort and a sociable atmosphere. St. Ives is arguably the most beautiful town in Cornwall, and Cornwall one of the most beautiful counties in England. Nearby attractions range from prehistoric sites to modern theme parks and the new St. Ives Tate modern art gallery which opened in 1993.

Address: Southfield Place, St Ives, Cornwall TR26 1RE England. Tel: (01736) 793 247.

Type: Bed & breakfast.
Clientele: Exclusively gay & lesbian.
Transportation: Taxi or short walk from railway station.
To Gay Bars: Occasional gay/lesbian venues at various locations.
Rooms: 1 single, 3 doubles, & space for an extra person.
Bathrooms: 2 private sink/washbasins, 2 shared facilities.
Meals: Full breakfast.
Vegetarian: An hour's notice or pot luck. Vegetarian cafes in town.
Complimentary: Tea, coffee, soft drinks. A glass or two of homemade wine for all brave & sociable guests.
Dates Open: All year.
High Season: June through September.
Rates: £15-£18.
Rsv'tns: Preferable during high season.
Reserve Through: Call direct.
Parking: Ample, free on-street parking & nearby cheap carpark.
In-Room: Color TV, laundry service for long stay guests & just shout for tea/coffee.
On-Premises: Large lounge meeting room. TV if necessary, but considered a waste of time with so much beautiful Cornwall around you.
Exercise/Health: Available nearby.
Swimming: At ocean beach nearby & other hotel pools open to the public.
Sunbathing: On the patio, in the garden or on nearby beaches.
Smoking: Not permitted in dining room before meals.
Pets: Permitted if in strict control. No elephants please.
Handicap Access: No, St. Ives is very hilly.
Children: No, we are exclusively gay, and no children are gay.
Languages: English & occasionally BAD.

Woodbine Villa

Gay/Lesbian ♂

Woodbine Villa is a grade II listed 18th century former farmhouse in the centre of the pretty Georgian village of Grampound. The house is furnished with antiques. Your spacious bedroom may have a Victorian brass bed, mahogany half-tester, or even a genuine regency four-poster. Our British breakfast is substantial. The grill includes Cornish hogs pudding, even Kedgeree, if you fancy it! Quality fresh-cooked evening meals can be provided. I'll even throw in a complimentary decanter of wine (not literally). The sauna & gym will be open some nights for both guests and non-residents. All in all, spectacular scenery, fine beaches, pleasant weather, verdant countryside, pleasant walks and masses of historic houses, gardens and interesting places to visit make Cornwall a must on any trip to the U.K. I hope to welcome you as a house guest and I intend to offer true Cornish hospitality and would wish to make your stay with me both pleasant and memorable.

Address: Fore St, Grampound, near Truro, Cornwall TR2 4QP England. Tel: (01726) 882-005.

continued next page

UK (England)

Type: Bed & breakfast in a private home with sauna & gym open to guests & non-residents.
Clientele: Mostly men with women welcome.
Transportation: Coaches from Victoria Stn. & Heathrow to Grampound stop 200 yrds from house, but car is best.
To Gay Bars: 15-40 miles.
Rooms: 4 rooms with double or king beds.
Bathrooms: 1 shared shower, 1 shared bath/ shower/toilet & 1 shared toilet.
Meals: Full English breakfast.
Vegetarian: Available with 24 hour notice for evening meal. 2 restaurants in village.
Complimentary: Coffee, or choice of teas.
Dates Open: All year.
High Season: May through October.
Rates: £18.00-£22.00 for singles, £34.00-£40.00 for doubles. Rates may change for 1995.
Discounts: 10% to Bears Club members, anyone making a return visit, P.W.A.
Rsv'tns: Advisable.
Reserve Through: Call direct.
Minimum Stay: Additional charge for 1-night stays.
Parking: Free, limited off-street parking, free on-street parking.
In-Room: Maid service.
On-Premises: TV, VCR, log fireplace in drawing room.
Exercise/Health: Gym, weights & sauna.
Swimming: A few miles to sea beaches.
Sunbathing: On beach, patio or in garden.
Nudity: 5 miles to nude beach.
Smoking: Permitted outdoors.
Pets: Not permitted.
Handicap Access: No.
Children: Not permitted.
Languages: English, limited French.
Your Host: Mike.

COTSWOLDS

Crestow House

Gay-Friendly ♀♂

English Victorian Stone Country House in a Picturesque Cotswold Village

Crestow House was built in 1870 out of Cotswold sandstone by a local wool merchant. The generously-sized rooms and 12 foot ceilings speak of the affluence this region once knew. Stow is on the Fosse Way, the old wool route built at the time of the Roman occupation. The concluding battles of the English Civil War took place in the fields outside Stow. The town still preserves its Mediaeval stocks and has one of the oldest pubs in Britain. The wool trade has since given way to the antiques business, with Stow having about 20 antique dealers. There is also a twice-yearly horse trading fair (mid May and October) where gypsies from England and Ireland trade their ponies. The area is filled with castles and stately homes with formal, world-renowned gardens and is also known for its high quality food. We would be glad to recommend some of our fine local restaurants or cook for you if you let us know in the morning that you would like to eat with us that evening. Stow is about a 2-hour drive from London (1-1/4-hour train ride from Paddington Station), 20 minutes north of Oxford and 15 minutes south of Stratford-on-Avon, home of the Royal Shakespeare Company.

Crestow House is three-storied with a large conservatory, living room, dining room, large country breakfast room and back veranda, with some of the best views and sunsets in Britain. The house has a large walled back garden with heated swimming pool. The middle floor consists of four double bedrooms with en suite bathroom/toilets, antique furnishings, English country decor and modern double beds. The floor-to-ceiling windows make the best of the beautiful countryside that surrounds the house. The owners live on the upper floor.

Address: Stow-on-the-Wold, Gloucestershire, GL54 1JY England. Tel: (44) 451 832 129.

Type: Bed & breakfast country manor house.
Clientele: Mostly hetero with a gay & lesbian following.
Transportation: Car is best. Train service available from London's Paddington Station to Moreton-In-Marsh.
To Gay Bars: 15 miles or 35 minutes by car.
Rooms: 4 rooms with double or king (2 twin)

beds.
Bathrooms: All en suite.
Meals: Expanded continental breakfast.
Vegetarian: Available upon prior request. 5-minute walk to restaurant.
Complimentary: Tea or coffee on arrival, predinner sherry.
Dates Open: All year except Jan.
High Season: June-Sept.

Rates: £25-£34 per person British sterling.
Discounts: For 2 nights or longer.
Rsv'tns: Preferred.
Reserve Through: Call direct.
Parking: Free off-street parking.
In-Room: Color TV, laundry service.
On-Premises: Laundry facilities. Can send/receive fax.

Swimming: Pool on premises.
Sunbathing: At poolside.
Smoking: Not permitted.
Pets: Not permitted.
Handicap Access: No.
Children: Not especially welcome.
Languages: English, Spanish, Italian & German.
Your Host: Frank & Jorge.

IGTA

DERBYSHIRE

Hodgkinson's Hotel & Restaurant

Gay-Friendly 50/50 ♀♂

Hodgkinson's Hotel and Restaurant, built over 200 years ago, was purchased in run-down condition by Malcolm and Nigel and has been undergoing renovations ever since. Current restoration projects include the 1/4-acre of terraced gardens, affording fine views of the valley. The main project, however, is the opening of the caves which have been used as cellars until recent times. They form part of the labyrinth which runs through the hillside, supposedly dating back to Roman times. Malcolm's hairdressing salon, Redken-appointed, is now well-established, used by the local community & hotel guests.

Address: South Parade, Matlock Bath, Derbyshire DE4 3NR England. Tel: (01629) 582 170.

Type: Hotel and hairdressing salon.
Clientele: 50% gay & lesbian & 50% hetero clientele.
Transportation: Car is best, free pick up from train.
To Gay Bars: 3/4 hour to Derby, Nottingham, Sheffield.
Rooms: 6 doubles.
Bathrooms: All private

shower & toilet en suite.
Meals: Full breakfast.
Vegetarian: Available to order.
Complimentary: Tea & coffee in rooms.
Dates Open: All year.
Rates: £45.00-£80.00 double, £30.00 single.
Discounts: For special breaks & 2-night weekends.
Credit Cards: MC, VISA,

Amex, Access.
Rsv'tns: Recommended.
Reserve Through: Call direct.
Parking: Adequate off-street parking.
In-Room: Color TV, telephone, room & laundry service.
On-Premises: Meeting rooms.
Exercise/Health: Sauna.
Swimming: 2 miles to

pool.
Smoking: Permitted without restrictions.
Pets: Permitted, but not in dining room.
Handicap Access: No.
Children: Permitted.
Languages: English.
Your Host: Malcolm & Nigel.

We Appreciate Your Comments!

Positive comments of interest may be included in the next issue, giving future readers the benefit of your experience. And it's a nice way of saying "thank you" to an innkeeper who extended you exceptional hospitality.

See the contents for the Reader Comment Form.

DEVON *(SEE ALSO TORQUAY)*

Kildare Guest House

Gay-Friendly 50/50 ♀♂

The Kildare is a large, airy Edwardian house, having style and elegance, standing on a corner site a few minutes' walk from the city centre and rail station. There is a spacious dining room, a comfortable lounge with colour TV and a rooftop terrace with glorious views across Central Park. Rooms have showers, colour TV, tea and coffee makers. Your own keys give you freedom to come and go as you please. Full English breakfast is served.

Address: 82 North Rd East, Plymouth, England. Tel: (01752) 229 375.

Type: Guesthouse.
Clientele: 50% gay & lesbian & 50% hetero clientele.
To Gay Bars: Minutes to gay bars, 100 yds to gay club.
Rooms: 1 single, 3 doubles, 2 triples & 1 quad.

Bathrooms: All private.
Meals: Full English breakfast.
Dates Open: All year.
Rates: £15.00-£28.00.
Discounts: Weekly rates.
Rsv'tns: Required. Deposit of £7.00.
Reserve Through: Call direct.

Parking: Ample on-street parking.
In-Room: Private key, shower, colour TV, maid service, tea & coffee makers.
On-Premises: Spacious dining room, TV lounge with colour TV.
Sunbathing: On rooftop sun terrace.
Nudity: Permitted on roof terrace.
Smoking: Permitted except for dining room.
Pets: Not permitted.
Handicap Access: No.
Children: Not permitted.
Languages: English.
Your Host: John.

Tor Down House

Gay/Lesbian ♀♂

Tor Down House is a 16th century thatched traditional Devon longhouse in the heart of Dartmoor National Park. The interior contains a wealth of old-world charm. Old oak beams abound, and there is a great granite inglenook fireplace in both the residents' lounge and the dining room. Both contain authentic bread ovens. Each comfortable guest room has its own private bathroom facilities, colour TV, tea/coffee tray and four-poster bed. The 5 acres of garden has a multitude of flowering shrubs and trees, a water garden, lawns, and several secluded seating areas offering peace and tranquility. Belstone is a village of outstanding beauty and is surrounded by delightful riverside walks. The castled town of Okehampton lies just three miles west of the village.

Address: Belstone, Okehampton, Devon EX20 1QY England. Tel: (0837) 840 731.

Type: Bed & breakfast guesthouse.
Clientele: Gay & lesbian. Good mix of men & women.
Transportation: Car is best. Pick up from Exeter rail station or airport if required, £2.50 each way.
To Gay Bars: Exeter 25 mins by car.
Rooms: 3 doubles.

Bathrooms: All en suite.
Meals: Full breakfast. Evening meals Fri & Sat.
Vegetarian: Available upon request.
Complimentary: Tea, coffee, sherry & chock.
Dates Open: All year.
Rates: Mon-Thur £48.00, Fri-Sat £50.00, double room, £30 single.
Credit Cards: VISA & Bancard.

Rsv'tns: Required.
Reserve Through: Call direct.
Parking: Ample free off-street parking.
In-Room: Colour TV, four-poster beds, maid & room service.
On-Premises: Meeting rooms, TV lounge.
Exercise/Health: Horseback riding, cycle rental.
Swimming: 5 min to river, 1 hr drive to ocean beach.
Sunbathing: In the garden.
Smoking: Permitted in the lounge only.
Pets: Not permitted.
Handicap Access: No.
Children: Not permitted.
Languages: English.

White House Hotel

Gay-Friendly ♀♂

The *White House* is a lovely Grade II listed building with great aesthetic and architectural appeal. Set in an acre of lawned and terraced gardens on the edge of a South Devon village, the house has a unique atmosphere reminiscent of an altogether quieter and less hurried age.

Now think of South Devon: imagine a land of thatched cottages, cream teas, green fields, secret byways, where the climate is kind and where, for centuries, travellers have sought peace and quiet. Our special part of this beautiful and historic corner of England is called the South Hams, a name derived from the old English word "Hamme", meaning an enclosed or sheltered place.

To the west of us are Kingsbridge and the Salcombe Estuary, famous for its sailing. To the north are Totnes and the wild expanses of Dartmoor. To the east is picturesque Dartmouth, and sweeping 'round us to the south is the spectacular South Hams coastline with its rugged cliffs, sandy beaches and quiet coves, most of it protected by the National Trust.

Returning from a day spent out and about, guests can relax over a drink in the Normandy Bar Lounge, a cosy room in the oldest part of the house. Doctor Smalley's Drawing Room, from which French doors open onto the terrace and garden, offers elegant and comfortable surroundings in which to chat over the day's happenings.

The Green Room Restaurant is a delightful venue for sampling David's delicious food cooked on the kitchen range. We take advantage of the best fresh local produce and are always happy to cater for individual tastes.

All our bedrooms are en suite and each is individual in its furnishings and character. Books and pictures abound, the garden beckons and cocktails await you on the terrace.

Address: Chillington, Kingsbridge, South Devon TQ7 2JX England. Tel: (01548) 580580, Fax: 581124.

Type: Hotel with restaurant.
Clientele: Mainly hetero clientele with gay/lesbian following.
Transportation: Car is best. Pick up from train approx £17.
To Gay Bars: 25 mi to Plymouth & 18 via ferry to Torquay.
Rooms: 7 rooms with single or double beds.
Bathrooms: 4 private bath/toilets, 3 private shower/toilets.
Meals: Full breakfast. 4-course dinner available.

Vegetarian: Available upon advance notice.
Complimentary: Tea, coffee on arrival, beverage trays in all bedrooms.
Dates Open: April until after Christmas.
High Season: May, June, July, August, September.
Rates: Low season: £32.00-£49.00 per person. High season: £35.00-£53.00 per person.
Discounts: 10% for 2 or more nights on Dinner Room & Breakfast inclusive terms.

Credit Cards: MC & VISA.
Rsv'tns: Required.
Reserve Through: Call direct.
Minimum Stay: 2 nights on weekends.
Parking: Adequate, free off-street parking.
In-Room: Color TV, telephone, video tape library, coffee/tea-making facilities, room & maid service.
On-Premises: TV lounge & laundry facilities.
Swimming: Ocean beach 2 miles away.
Sunbathing: At beach or

in garden.
Nudity: Permitted at nudist beach 6 miles away.
Smoking: Permitted in bar lounge & bedrooms.
Pets: Dogs permitted by prior arrangement. Not allowed in public rooms.
Handicap Access: No.
Children: Permitted over 5 years of age.
Languages: English, French, & German.
Your Host: David & Michael.

DORSET *(SEE ALSO BOURNEMOUTH)*

Eagle House

Women ♀

Eagle House, built circa 1720, is a women-only guest house, centrally located in a quiet, picturesque lane near shops, cinema, etc. Stroll through gardens and along the sea front. Our area is renown as a magnificent walking district and is famous for the fossils that have been discovered here. Our guests have complete freedom to enjoy the area with activities such as riding, golf, swimming, sailing, windsurfing and walking along the sandy beaches. We have a sauna and spa for residents and a 1/3-acre garden for dog-lovers. At *Eagle House* we allow you maximum freedom to enjoy your holidays and minimum service. When our restaurant is not open, there are many places nearby for early or late breakfast.

Address: Sherborne Lane, Lyme Regis, Dorset DT7 3NY England. Tel: (01297) 442616.

Type: Guesthouse with restaurant in summer.
Clientele: Women only except for July & August.
Transportation: Car, coach, or train from London/Waterloo to Axminster 2 hrs 40 min, bus or taxi from station.
To Gay Bars: 27 miles to Exeter or Taunton.
Rooms: 6 doubles, 1 triple, 1 quad, 1 self-contained apartment, & 1 self-contained cottage with en suite bath.
Bathrooms: 1 en suite, 2 shared & a shared sauna, shower, whirlpool & spa.
Vegetarian: At our restaurant in summer.
Complimentary: Tea & coffee facilities on each floor.
Dates Open: All year.
High Season: Mid July to the end of 1st week in September.
Rates: Off-season £8.00 per night. July, August, Bank holidays £10.00 & add'l £1.00 for 1-night stay or double used as single.
Rsv'tns: Required.
Reserve Through: Call direct.
Parking: Limited pay parking.
In-Room: 4 with color TV. Refrigerator on 2 floors & kitchen on top floor. Cottage has refrigerator & TV.
On-Premises: 1/3 acre garden.
Exercise/Health: 5-person sauna/jet whirlpool/spa complex in building.
Swimming: At nearby (less than 5 min walk) ocean beach.
Sunbathing: At the nearby beach or in the garden.
Nudity: Permitted in the garden or at the beach.
Smoking: Permitted.
Pets: Permitted, inquire for restrictions.
Handicap Access: Ground floor room, use restaurant water closet.
Children: Permitted if teenage.
Languages: English, French, some Spanish, Italian, Danish.

HASTINGS

Sherwood Guesthouse

Gay-Friendly ♀♂

Watch the Ships Plying the English Channel

Sherwood is a Victorian seafront guesthouse with antique furnishings and wonderful views. Some rooms have sea views, the sea being the English Channel. Guests can watch giant tankers or fishing boats plying the waters. Breakfast is served in the dining room/conservatory, a glassed-in sun room with greenery and a view of a wild garden overlooked by a tall cliff and inhabited by badgers, foxes and an interesting variety of wild birds. Opposite the guesthouse is a bowling green and putting green. We are 15 minutes from the site of the Battle of Hastings and about 25 minutes from Rye, home of Paul McCartney. Hastings Old Town has many interesting antique shops, tea rooms and book shops.

Address: 15 Grosvenor Crescent, St Leonard's-on-Sea, Hastings, E Sussex, England. Tel: (44-424) 433 331.

Type: Guesthouse 1 hour from the Channel Tunnel or Brighton. **Clientele:** Mostly hetero with a 30% gay & lesbian following. Gay-owned. **Transportation:** 5 minutes to RR station. Free pick up from train. **To Gay Bars:** 5 minutes by car to Hastings. **Rooms:** 11 rooms with single, double or bunk beds. **Bathrooms:** 2 private & 2 shared. **Dates Open:** Closed 3 weeks around Xmas. **High Season:** July & August. **Rates:** Low season £15-£18. High season £18-£21. **Discounts:** For larger groups in 1 room. **Credit Cards:** VISA & Amex. **Rsv'tns:** Required. **Reserve Through:** Call direct. **Parking:** Ample free on-street parking. **In-Room:** Color TV (some with remote), coffee/tea-making facilities, intercom service & morning call for breakfast. **On-Premises:** TV lounge. **Swimming:** 3-minute walk to ocean beach. **Sunbathing:** On the patio & at the beach. **Smoking:** Not permitted in lounge or dining room. **Pets:** Dogs permitted. **Handicap Access:** No. **Children:** Welcome 5 years or older. **Languages:** English. **Your Host:** Eric & Derrick.

HEREFORD & WORCESTER

Riverside Hotel

Gay-Friendly ♂

Off the beaten track near Evesham is a small, family-run country house offering blissful accommodations with panoramic views of the river Avon and the Vale of Evesham. *Riverside Hotel* has individually-designed bedrooms, all with en-suite bathroom and a full, English breakfast included. Special dinner, bed and breakfast rate available.

Address: The Parks, Offenham Road, Evesham, Worcestershire WR11 5JP England. Tel: (01386) 446200, Fax: (01386) 40021.

Type: Inn with restaurant. **Clientele:** Mostly straight with a gay male following. **Transportation:** Car. **To Gay Bars:** 15 miles or 20 minutes by car. **Rooms:** Rooms & 7 suites with single or double beds. **Bathrooms:** All private. **Meals:** Full breakfast. **Vegetarian:** Available by arrangement. **Complimentary:** Tea, coffee & mineral water. **Dates Open:** All year. **Rates:** £60.00-£80.00. **Credit Cards:** MC, VISA, Eurocard & Switch. **Rsv'tns:** Required. **Reserve Through:** Travel agent or call direct. **Parking:** Ample free parking. **In-Room:** Color TV, telephone, coffee & tea-making facilities, maid & room service. **On-Premises:** Panoramic views. **Swimming:** Nearby pool & river. **Sunbathing:** On the patio. **Smoking:** Permitted everywhere except restaurant. **Pets:** Not permitted. **Handicap Access:** No. **Children:** Welcome. **Languages:** English.

LONDON

A Luxury Soho Studio By Clone Zone

Gay/Lesbian ♂

This modern accommodation is equipped with a high standard of amenities including a fully fitted kitchen, bathroom with bath and shower and a spacious lounge area.

One of the most appealing aspects of *A Luxury Soho Studio* is its central location, two floors above, but completely separate from, the busy Clone Zone shop, where our staff will be happy to advise about the London gay scene with its many pubs and clubs such as Heaven and Gay Discos, two of the largest in Europe.

Situated in the very heart of London's gay and lesbian village, *A Luxury Soho Studio* is also near the capitol's principal tourist attractions: Buckingham Palace, the National Art Gallery, the Houses of Parliament, the Tower of London, the Westend Theatreland, Chinatown, shopping and cafes. History, culture and fun are just a short walk, tube (subway) or taxi ride. Freedom Cars, a lesbian and gay cab company, is next door to us. In May, the Soho Pink Weekend Carnival and the Pink Angel Festival, two outrageous lesbian and gay parades, take place. June is the month of the internationally famous U.K. Lesbian and Gay Pride Weekend which attracts over 200,000 people from around the globe.

At any time of the year there is just too much to see and do in a single visit. We're sure you'll want to come back again and again.

Clone Zone is one of the world's largest and most respected chains of gay and lesbian retailing stores and is located throughout the U.K. These trendsetting stores have a large and original range of fashion, leather and rubberwear, along with books, magazines, toys, videos, greeting cards and much more.

Address: 64, Old Compton St, Soho, London, W1 England. Tel: Reservations: (171) 287 3530.

Type: Self-contained apartment.
Clientele: Mostly men with women welcome.
Transportation: Heathrow Airport tube to Leicester Square tube, then taxi or 1/4 mile walk.
To Gay Bars: Short walk to all gay venues.
Rooms: 1 apartment

with king bed & double sofa bed. Sleeps up to 4.
Bathrooms: Private bath/ toilet/shower.
Vegetarian: Available nearby.
Dates Open: All year.
High Season: June-September.
Rates: From £60 to £100 per night.
Discounts: 10% for

E.C.M.C., M.S.C & Bears Club.
Credit Cards: MC, VISA, Amex, Diners & Eurocard.
Rsv'tns: Required.
Reserve Through: Call direct.
Parking: Ample pay parking.
In-Room: Color TV, AC, telephone, kitchen, refrigerator, coffee & tea-

making facilities.
Exercise/Health: Nearby gym, weights, Jacuzzi, sauna, steam & massage.
Pets: Not permitted.
Handicap Access: No.
Children: Not especially welcome.
Languages: English.

Bromptons Guesthouse

Men ♂

Bromptons Guesthouse is conveniently located in Earl's Court, the centre of Gay London. We are within easy reach of London's airports, and with our central location, to all the major tourist spots and nightlife.

The guesthouse is personally run by Peter and Jeremy, and all our rooms are spacious, clean and decorated to a high standard. All our rooms have colour TV, direct-dial telephones, coffee/tea-making facilities, iron/ironing board and a hairdryer. Each room (including single occupancy) has a double bed. Maps and magazines of London's gay areas are provided in each room and Peter and Jeremy will be pleased to provide help and information to make your stay as fun as possible.

Bromptons is busy throughout the year because London is an all-year tourist city, and we recommend an early reservation. London is a city full of history, with the world's best theatre and great shopping. The ever-growing gay scene is lively and fun and bigger than that of any other European capital.

Come and join us for a vacation. In London there is always plenty to do and see throughout the year.

Address: PO Box 629, London SW5 9XF England. Tel: (171) 373 6559, Fax: (171) 370 3923.

Type: Guesthouse.
Clientele: Men only.
Transportation: From Heathrow: tube to Earl's Court. From Gatwick: Express train to Victoria, then tube to Earl's Court.
To Gay Bars: 250 yards.
Rooms: 10 (for single or double occupancy).
Bathrooms: 5 private, others share.
Dates Open: All year.
Rates: £45.00-£75.00.
Discounts: 10% for cash payment. Weekly rate, pay for 6 nights.
Credit Cards: MC, VISA, Amex.
Rsv'tns: Required.
Reserve Through: Call direct.
Parking: Off-street parking (but not recommended in Central London).
In-Room: Daily maid service, TV, phones, coffee & tea-making facilities, irons & hairdryers.
Exercise/Health: Nearby gym.
Sunbathing: At Hyde Park.
Smoking: Permitted without restrictions.
Pets: Not permitted.
Handicap Access: No.
Children: Not permitted.
Languages: English & Hebrew.
Your Host: Peter & Jeremy.

IGTA

Guys American Style Homestay

Gay/Lesbian ♀♂

For super value bed and breakfast accommodations in London, visit *Guys American Style Homestay,* only 15 minutes from Victoria/West End and the heart of London's gay life. All our rooms are tastefully decorated in traditional English country style and all rooms have wash basins, tea/coffee-making facilities and are all fully centrally heated. We are situated in southwest London, near two cinemas, gay sauna & clubs, ice rink, gym, swimming pool, parks and restaurants. Many of our guests make return visits and our vast experience will help you maximise your precious time spent with us in London.

Address: 38 Baldry Gardens, Streatham, London SW16 3DJ England. Tel: (181) 679 7269.

Type: Guesthouse.
Clientele: Mostly gay & lesbian with some hetero clientele.
Transportation: Gatwick/Heathrow 30 mins by car or 15 mins from Victoria to Streatham Common Br.
To Gay Bars: 5 min walk to Friday's, other gay bars 20 mins by taxi.
Rooms: 4 rooms with single or double beds.
Bathrooms: 2 shared baths with showers.
Meals: Full breakfast.
Vegetarian: Available upon request.
Complimentary: Tea & coffee in rooms.
Dates Open: All year.
Rates: Single £25.00, double £36.00.
Discounts: 10% for 5 or more days.
Credit Cards: MC, VISA.
Rsv'tns: Required.
Reserve Through: Call direct.
Minimum Stay: 2 nights.
Parking: Ample off-street & on-street parking.
In-Room: Color TV, tea/coffee-making facilities, public telephone, laundry service.
Exercise/Health: Gay sauna 15 min walk.
Swimming: 10 min walk to pool.
Smoking: Permitted, but state smoker when booking.
Pets: Not permitted.
Handicap Access: No.
Children: Not permitted.
Languages: English.

Manor House Hotel

Gay/Lesbian ♂

The *Manor House Hotel* is a private guesthouse, ideally situated for those visitors to London on a budget. The hotel rooms are tastefully decorated and furnished in the style of a Victorian home. The house is a very cosy venue for both gay men and women. Groups up to 16 can be catered for. All rooms have cable color TV, and tea, coffee and chocolate is available for guests. The house is minutes away from our local station, Hither Green. This is a B.R. line and links up with the underground system at London Bridge. Hither Green to the West End of London's theatres, pubs, bars and clubs is approximately 20 minutes. The *Manor House* is a very peaceful spot, an alternative way to stay in and explore London and beyond.

Holiday Apartments London provides one of the most convenient and economic ways of staying in the capital. Economy and luxury apartments, which sleep from two to five people, start at U.S. $90 per apartment per day. Booking payments can be made by U.S. $ cheques, VISA, Access, MasterCard and travellers cheques.

Address: 53 Manor Park, London SE13 5RA England. Tel: (181) 318 5590 , Fax: (181) 244 4196. In USA: (800) 71-ROYAL, Fax: (407) 994-3634.

Type: Private guesthouse with dining facilities. Holiday apartments available.
Clientele: Mostly men with women welcome.
Transportation: Airport transfers available. 20 mins from centre of London Charing Cross Sta by B.R. train. Taxi can be arranged.
To Gay Bars: 5 to 10 min.
Rooms: 4 singles, 4 doubles, 1 triple.

Bathrooms: 2 doubles en suite, 3 shared.
Meals: Buffet continental breakfast.
Vegetarian: Available upon request.
Complimentary: Coffee, tea, chocolate.
Dates Open: All year.
High Season: June-September.
Rates: Singles £28.00, twins & doubles from £35.00 & en suite £40.00-50.00.

Discounts: Weekly rates, long stays, group bookings.
Credit Cards: VISA, Access.
Rsv'tns: Recommended.
Reserve Through: Call direct.
Parking: Ample free off-street parking.
In-Room: Color TV/ video, tea/coffee making facilities.
On-Premises: Dinner parties available, beautiful

gardens.
Sunbathing: On private sun decks.
Smoking: Non-smoking rooms available.
Pets: Permitted if previously requested.
Handicap Access: Wheelchair access limited.
Children: Permitted.
Languages: English.
Your Host: John & Ian.

New York Hotel, The

Gay/Lesbian ♀♂

The New York Hotel is London's newest and most luxurious gay hotel, situated in the heart of London's gay scene. It is just a 3 minute walk from the Earls Court Underground Station, (Warwick Rd exit), and is ideally located for the many local gay bars, clubs, shops and activities in the Earls Court area. Our staff are always available to offer advice and directions. The hotel offers its visitors a unique and friendly atmosphere with many facilities, including a relaxed luxury lounge, beautiful private rear garden, new enlarged French restaurant and licensed bar facilities. We also have a new Jacuzzi and sauna to which hotel guests are given 24 hour access.

Our hotel offers the very best in accommodations, with 14 spacious and well decorated single, double, or twin rooms. All have 24 hour room service, en suite bathrooms equipped with high powered showers and hairdryers, colour TV, direct dial telephones, coffee-making facilities, trouser press and iron. A laundry service is available on request. *The New York Hotel* is proud to offer you the best and most luxurious gay accommodation in London. If you are looking for a wonderful time in London, then *The New York Hotel* is for you!

Address: 32 Philbeach Gardens, Earls Court, London SW5 9EB England. Tel: (171) 244 6884, Fax: (171) 370 4961.

Type: Hotel & restaurant.
Clientele: Good mix of gay men & women.
Transportation: Tube, taxi.
To Gay Bars: 2 blocks or 3-5 min walk to several.
Rooms: 5 singles, 9 doubles.
Bathrooms: 13 private, 2 shared.
Meals: Expanded continental breakfast.
Vegetarian: If someone requests a vegetarian meal, no problem for dinners.
Complimentary: Tea & coffee, biscuits & snacks in room.
Dates Open: All year.
High Season: May-Dec.
Rates: £45.00-£75.00.
Credit Cards: MC, VISA, Amex, Access, Eurocard.
Rsv'tns: Required.
Reserve Through: Call direct.
Minimum Stay: Required on holiday weekends.
Parking: Paid parking up the street for £10 a day (24 hr access).
In-Room: Color cable TV with remote, telephone, maid & room service.
On-Premises: TV lounge.
Exercise/Health: Jacuzzi & sauna with shower area.
Swimming: Nearby pool.
Sunbathing: Hotel garden or 1 hr on train to beach at Brighton.
Smoking: Permitted, non-smoking rooms available.
Pets: Not permitted.
Handicap Access: Yes, 1 room.
Children: Not permitted.
Languages: English, Spanish, French, Welsh, German.
Your Host: Dennis.

No. 7 Guesthouse

Gay/Lesbian ♂

London's Best Gay Guesthouse...Getting Better...

Number Seven is an exclusively lesbian and gay guesthouse and home to two gay guys, John and Paul.

Gay-owned and -run, the house, built during the reign of Queen Victoria, is set back from the road in a quiet tree-lined avenue, yet just a 5-minute walk from The Fridge, voted "London's Best Gay Club," and within easy reach of all the bars and clubs. *No. 7* is 15 minutes from the Houses of Parliament, Buckingham Palace, The Tower of London, the City of London's financial district, and the West End with all its shops, theatres, and fine restaurants. *No. 7* is extremely well located for public transport throughout the day and night, with its good connections to rail, tube (underground), bus and night-bus.

No. 7 opened in February, 1992 and we have consistently improved the facilities offered to our lesbian and gay guests. The house is tastefully furnished and decorated, including the Garden Bedroom with its stripped pine flooring, original Victorian fireplace, sky-blue decor, and French windows opening onto the walled garden. *No. 7* offers en suite facilities in all bedrooms with shower, wash basin and toilet. Some rooms also have a bathtub, including the Honeymoon Suite with its own corner-bath and bidet. All bedrooms benefit from ceiling fans and have remote colour TV, cable and video link, as well as tea and coffee-making facilities, hair dryer, and pine beds and furnishings throughout. A laundry service is available, and iron and board on request. All bedrooms have direct-dial telephones. Fax and photocopy available upon request.

Full English breakfast is available every morning in the conservatory over-

looking the garden, and is included in the price of your room. Try our over-easy eggs with British bacon, sausage, tomatoes/beans, mushrooms, and for a flavour of the good 'ol U.S....hash browns; if you like a Caribbean flavour add some plantain, or for the taste of real England how about some black pudding? If you can't manage all that, try our continental or vegetarian menu. There's fresh fruit, yoghurt, and of course, as much tea or coffee as you can drink.

No. 7 is just a two-minute walk from Brockwell Park, with its many outdoor leisure facilities; this is also the venue for the annual Gay Pride Festival.

Business or vacation, a warm welcome awaits you on your next visit to London.

Address: 7 Josephine Ave London SW2 2JU England. Tel: (44-181) 674 1880, Fax: (44-181) 671 6032.

Type: Bed & breakfast guesthouse.
Clientele: Mostly men with women welcome.
Transportation: Main line train, tube, bus, car, or taxi from London airports, intercity train stns; pick ups cost petrol plus time.
To Gay Bars: 4 min walk or 4 min by tube to a variety of gay & lesbian bars & clubs.
Rooms: 5 rooms with single, double or queen beds.
Bathrooms: 2 en suite bath/shower/toilets & 4 en suite shower/toilets.

Meals: Expanded continental breakfast, continental breakfast, buffet breakfast or full breakfast.
Vegetarian: Vegetarian breakfast always available. Good local vegetarian restaurants.
Complimentary: Tea & coffee on arrival & in rooms.
Dates Open: All year.
Rates: £35-£75.
Credit Cards: MC, VISA.
Rsv'tns: Required. Preferred credit card booking.
Reserve Through: Call direct.
Minimum Stay: 1 night.

Parking: Ample easy off-street free parking in front of Guesthouse.
In-Room: Clock/radio, remote CTV w/video & satellite link, direct-dial telephone, ceiling fans, tea/coffee-making facilities, Bahama fans, hair dryer, maid & laundry service. Iron & ironing board upon request.
On-Premises: Pay phone, dining room with maps & guides, conservatory, private walled garden, photo copier, FAX machine, message service.
Exercise/Health: Weights, rowing

machine, situp bench available upon request. Recreation Centre nearby.
Swimming: 2 pools 1/2 mile away.
Sunbathing: In front & back gardens.
Smoking: Permitted without restrictions in bedrooms.
Pets: Not permitted.
Handicap Access: No. 3 steps to front door, no wide doorways.
Children: Not permitted.
Languages: English, British Sign Language.

IGTA

One-Sixty (160) Regents Park Road

The Best Bed and Breakfast in London

Gay/Lesbian ♀♂

Chris welcomes you to his comfortable and elegant Victorian home. *160 Regents Park Road,* with just two bedrooms, is a friendly alternative to London's larger gay hotels: Offering a relaxed base for your sightseeing, trips to the theatre and ventures into the city's varied gay night life. The townhouse is on three floors (many stairs, no lift!) leading finally to an impressive roof garden. The style throughout is an eclectic mix of antiques, prints and draw-

ings, with many ultra-modern fittings. The larger bedroom, with book-lined walls, wooden floor and Oriental carpet, is reminiscent of a gentleman's library. A stunningly modern shower room adjoins and includes a toilet, washbasin and a really powerful shower. The smaller room is airy and light, with its own washbasin and use of the sumptuous bathroom on the floor below. Both rooms have remote-controlled color TV, bathrobes, hairdryer and telephones with itemised billing. Your breakfast choice is so "full," it may leave you feeling that way! Only the best ingredients are used, such as quality jams, breads and pastries, free-range eggs and bacon.

Our area is one of the most charming and celebrated corners of London, with a "village" atmosphere that has attracted millionaires and the famous. The range of shopping and eating could hardly be bettered, including stores of every necessity and a choice of over a dozen restaurants. From Primrose Hill, itself, there are wonderful views over London and close by are the open spaces of Hampstead Heath and Regents Park. From our Underground station, Chalk Farm, Piccadilly Circus is just 15 minutes away. In fact, *160 Regents Park Road* is the ideal compromise, close to the city centre, but without its noise and hassle. With all my experience and knowledge of what London has to offer, I hope you will share your time with me.
Address: Primrose Hill, London NW1 8XN England. Tel: 171 586-5266.

continued next page

UK (England)

Type: Bed & breakfast.
Clientele: Mostly gay & lesbian with occasional hetero clientele.
Transportation: Subway, car or taxi. From airports subway is Chalk Farm station.
To Gay Bars: 10 min to gay pubs & cafés in Camden Town & Hampstead.
Rooms: 2 rooms with double or queen bed.
Bathrooms: 1 en suite shower/toilet, 1 shared bath/shower/toilet.
Meals: Extensive English breakfast menu.
Vegetarian: Available with minimum notice. Vegetarian restaurant in neighborhood.
Complimentary: Tea, coffee, juices, & chilled water.
Dates Open: All year except Dec 15-Jan 1.
Rates: Small double, £45.00 for 1, £60.00 for 2 or large double, £75.00 for 2.
Discounts: For periods longer than 7 nights.
Credit Cards: MC, VISA & Eurocard.
Rsv'tns: Required.
Reserve Through: Travel agent or call direct.
Minimum Stay: 2 nights.
Parking: Adequate on-street parking.
In-Room: Color TV, maid service & telephone.
On-Premises: Dining room for daytime tea, coffee; roof terrace in summer; glazed dome for winter sitting; laundry facilities.
Swimming: At nearby covered public pools.
Sunbathing: On the roof.
Smoking: Permitted, but not encouraged.
Pets: Not permitted.
Handicap Access: No.
Children: Inquire.
Languages: English, French & Italian.
Your Host: Chris.

Philbeach Hotel

Gay/Lesbian ♂

London's Largest and Gayest Hotel

The Philbeach Hotel is London's largest, busiest and longest-established gay hotel with renowned fun on the top floor! Situated in a quiet, tree-lined crescent in the heart of Earls Court's gay village, it has 40 rooms. Most share, some have private bathrooms. There is an intimate bar, and the Wilde About Oscar garden restaurant serves French/International cuisine. We're close to bars and clubs and very close to the underground with direct links to West End theatres and all London airports. 24-hour reception/reservation facilities.

Address: 30-31 Philbeach Gardens, Earls Court, London SW5 9EB England. Tel: (171) 373 1244 or 373 4544, Fax: (171) 244 0149.

Type: Hotel with bar & restaurant.
Clientele: Mostly men with women welcome.
Transportation: Underground to Earl's Court Station (Picadilly or District Line) take Warwick Rd exit.
To Gay Bars: 1 block or 400 yards. A 3-min walk.
Rooms: 40 rooms with single or double beds.
Bathrooms: Private: 10 bath/toilets, 26 sinks. Shared: 4 showers, 4 toilets.
Meals: Expanded continental breakfast.
Vegetarian: Available in restaurant.
Dates Open: All year.
Rates: £25-£65 per room per night.
Discounts: 1 night free on 7-night stay.
Credit Cards: MC, VISA, Amex, Diners & Eurocard.
Rsv'tns: Required, especially for weekends.
Reserve Through: Travel agent or call direct.
Parking: Ample on-street parking.
In-Room: Color TV, maid service.
On-Premises: Meeting rooms & TV lounge.
Swimming: Nearby pool.
Sunbathing: In the private garden.
Nudity: Permitted in the garden.
Smoking: Permitted. Non-smoking rooms available.
Pets: Not permitted.
Handicap Access: No.
Children: Not permitted.
Languages: English, French, Thai.
Your Host: Tom.

Redcliffe Hotel

Gay/Lesbian ♂

For outstanding accommodation close to the Earls Court area, choose the *Redcliffe Hotel*. We provide super en suite rooms, all fabulously appointed throughout, with remote control TVs and direct-dial phones, and we serve an extensive continental breakfast. The renowned Manhattans Nightclub disco cabaret bar is on the premises, with bar facilities and lounge open 18 hours a day. Public transport from our door will take you to the very heart of London-Picadilly Circus and the vast gay scene in just ten minutes. The *Redcliffe* provides London's best highly affordable accommodation in the heart of London and has had the same experienced team of dedicated staff and management for some years.

Address: 268 Fulham Rd, London SW10 9EW England. Tel: (171) 823-3494, Fax: (171) 351-2467.

Type: Hotel with cabaret & disco.
Clientele: Mostly men with women welcome.
Transportation: Heathrow Airport-subway to Earl's Court, taxi to hotel; Gatwick Airport-30 min train ride to Victoria, taxi to hotel.
To Gay Bars: On premises or 7-minute walk to gay bars.

Rooms: 16 doubles, 4 mini-suites.
Bathrooms: All private.
Meals: Extensive continental breakfast. We aim to please.
Complimentary: Coffee, tea.
Dates Open: All year.
High Season: June-September.
Rates: £49.00-£59.00.
Discounts: For longer

stays.
Credit Cards: MC, VISA, Amex, Eurocard.
Rsv'tns: Suggested, weekends essential.
Reserve Through: Travel agent or call direct.
Parking: Limited parking.
In-Room: Color TV with remote, direct-dial telephone, tea/coffeemaking facilities, irons & hairdryer.

On-Premises: Same day laundry service, day long bar available, plus breakfast/TV lounge.
Smoking: Permitted except at breakfast.
Pets: Not permitted.
Handicap Access: No, but bar is accessible.
Children: Not permitted.
Languages: English, French.
Your Host: Bill & Murray.

MANCHESTER

Pat's Korner House

Gay-Friendly ♀♂

Our large, detached Victorian is cheerfully furnished and homey. Food is home-cooked and service is friendly. Formerly for men-only, *Pat's Korner House* is now gay-friendly with gays and lesbians most welcome. We're 1-1/2 miles from Manchester's center and can give you information about local gay nightlife.
Address: 37 Russell Rd, Whalley Range, Manchester M16 England. Tel: (061) 881 0029.

Type: Bed & breakfast.
Rooms: 6 doubles, 3 singles.
Bathrooms: Private: 2 bathrooms. Shared: 2 full bathrooms, 5 showers, 5 toilets.
Meals: Full English break-

fast.
Dates Open: All year.
Rates: £15 per person per night.
Discounts: On longer stays.
Rsv'tns: Required.
Reserve Through: Call di-

rect or travel agent for stays of more than 1 night.
Parking: Free off-street parking.
In-Room: TV available upon request.
On-Premises: TV lounge.
Smoking: Permitted

without restrictions.
Pets: Not keen on pets.
Handicap Access: Not very good, but we'd do our utmost to facilitate.
Children: Permitted.
Languages: English.
Your Host: Pat.

Rembrandt Hotel

Gay/Lesbian ♂

Rembrandt, City Centre Manchester Right at the Heart of Things

Rembrandt Hotel is situated in the heart of Manchester's gay village and provides comfortable rooms at very reasonable prices.

Downstairs from your bedroom is your own gay pub, where you can meet new friends. Just yards away, you'll find a varied selection of gay bars, restaurants, shops and nightclubs. With more direct flights than ever from the States to Manchester, *Rembrandt* is an ideal place to start your European holiday.
Address: 33 Sackville St, Manchester M1 3LZ England. Tel: (061) 236-1311.

Type: B&B hotel with 2 bars & restaurant.
Clientele: Mostly men with women most welcome.
Transportation: Train to Piccadilly, then taxi.
To Gay Bars: On premises. Others nearby.
Rooms: 2 singles & 4 doubles.

Bathrooms: 1 shared.
Meals: Full English breakfast.
Complimentary: Fruit in room.
Dates Open: All year.
Rates: Please inquire.
Credit Cards: AMEX, Access, Diners.
Rsv'tns: Recommended, especially weekends.

Reserve Through: Travel agent or call direct.
Parking: Pay parking nearby. On-street metres.
In-Room: Colour TV, teamaking facilities, & clock radio.
On-Premises: 2 bars & 1 restaurant.
Smoking: Permitted in all

areas.
Handicap Access: Many stairs, but we help handicapped guests.
Children: Not especially welcome.
Languages: English, Italian.

NEW FOREST/HAMPSHIRE

Japonica House

Women ♀

Japonica House is a detached house standing in an acre and a half of beautiful gardens in the picturesque village of Burley in the heart of New Forest, where donkeys and ponies roam freely. This unspoilt typical English village consists mainly of gift shops, craft fairs, wonderful cream teas, and a wonderful pub with a history of smuggling. There are also summer cricket matches on the village green, horse riding, and wagon rides.

Address: 1 Chapel Lane, Burley, Hampshire BH24 4DJ England. Tel: (0425) 403389.

Type: Bed & breakfast.
Clientele: Women only.
Transportation: Car is best, free pick up from train.
To Gay Bars: 30 min drive.
Rooms: 2 rooms with double beds.
Bathrooms: 1 shared.

Meals: Expanded continental or full breakfast.
Vegetarian: Available upon request.
Complimentary: Tea, coffee.
Dates Open: All year.
Rates: £10-£15 per person per night.
Rsv'tns: Required.

Reserve Through: Call direct.
Parking: Ample free off-street parking.
In-Room: Color TV, coffee & tea-making facilities.
Swimming: 6 miles to pool, 10 miles to ocean beach.

Sunbathing: In secluded gardens.
Smoking: Permitted.
Pets: Not permitted.
Handicap Access: No.
Children: Girls over 3, boys over 3 & under 13.
Languages: English.

NEWCASTLE-UPON-TYNE

Cheviot View Guest House

Gay/Lesbian ♂

One of England's Most Highly Recommended Gay Guest Houses

Cheviot View Guest House offers exceptional standards of service and comfort. Indulge yourself in luxury! Linden, of *APN Magazine* called it "...the best gay guest house I've ever stayed in..." *Northern Scene* called it "One of the best gay hotels in England." Here, you can enjoy Newcastle's sparkling and exciting nightlife, explore the coast and the magnificence of Northumbria. Our brochure gives details of champagne weekends, midweek breaks, mini-breaks and holidays.

Address: 194 Station Rd, Wallsend, Newcastle, NE28 8RD England. Phone & Fax: (091) 2620125.

Type: Guesthouse with bar.
Clientele: Mostly men with women welcome.
Transportation: Car or metro is best.
To Gay Bars: 3 miles or 10 minutes by car or metro.
Rooms: 5 rooms with single, double or king beds.
Bathrooms: Private: 1 bath/toilet, 1 shower/toilet. Shared: 1 bath/

shower/toilet.
Meals: Full English breakfast.
Vegetarian: Available at breakfast.
Complimentary: Tea, coffee, biscuits & orange juice in rooms. Mints on pillows.
Dates Open: All year.
Rates: £17.00-£25.00.
Discounts: For 5 or 7 nights stay.
Credit Cards: Amex.
Rsv'tns: Recommended.

Reserve Through: Call direct.
Parking: Ample free off-street parking.
In-Room: Exceptional standards of service & comfort. Color TV, coffee/tea-making facilities & room service.
On-Premises: TV lounge, solarium, private dining facilities, pay phone & laundry facilities.
Swimming: Nearby pool & ocean beach.

Sunbathing: At the beach.
Smoking: Permitted in designated areas. All rooms are non-smoking.
Pets: Small dogs permitted.
Handicap Access: No.
Children: Permitted.
Languages: English & French.
Your Host: Colin.

Stratford Lodge

Gay/Lesbian ♀♂

Situated in a tree lined crescent, *Stratford Lodge* is a mid-Victorian property only minutes from the amenities of the City Centre. Throughout its refurbishment, every effort has been made to retain its original features and character and to present them in a tasteful and comfortable light. We provide quality accommodations, contemporary and antique furnishings, easy parking and a friendly atmosphere exclusively for gay and lesbian guests. Our double rooms are of comfortable proportions and our master bedroom includes a Victorian fireplace and king-sized four poster bed. All rooms have colour satellite TV, and a tea and coffee tray. Continental breakfast is served in your room.

Address: 8 Stratford Grove Terrace, Heaton, Newcastle upon Tyne NE6 5BA England. Tel: (091) 265 6395, Mobile: 0831 879182.

Type: Bed & breakfast. **Clientele:** Gay & lesbian. Good mix of men & women **Transportation:** Metro from airport, then taxi, or taxi from British Rail Station. **To Gay Bars:** 1 mile or a 20-minute walk or 5-minute drive. **Rooms:** 5 rooms with single, double or king bed. **Bathrooms:** 1 bathroom per floor. **Meals:** Expanded continental breakfast. **Vegetarian:** Vegetarian continental breakfast available. Vegetarian restaurants in city. **Complimentary:** Tea & coffee tray in each room. Free entry into local gay clubs. **Dates Open:** All year. **Rates:** £17.00-£45.00. **Discounts:** Special business rates available & student discounts. **Rsv'tns:** Required. **Reserve Through:** Call direct. **Parking:** Ample on-street parking. **In-Room:** Color satellite TV, tea/coffee making facilities & laundry service. **On-Premises:** TV lounge with satellite TV. **Exercise/Health:** Traditional Swedish massage, Aromatherapy massage, solarium & sauna. Nearby gym, weights, Jacuzzi & steam. **Swimming:** Nearby pool & ocean. **Sunbathing:** On patio & beach. **Nudity:** Permitted in sauna. **Smoking:** Permitted except for sauna area. **Pets:** Not permitted. **Children:** Not especially welcome. **Languages:** English. **Your Host:** David & John.

NORFOLK

Old Case, The

Gay/Lesbian ♂

Set in a peaceful wooded countryside, *The Old Case* is an old timber-framed cottage with exposed beams and open fires. The vegetables, eggs and milk we use are from our small holding. When you visit our home, you are treated as a guest, not a customer, and your tranquillity is guaranteed. Visit the Suffolk coast (Benjamin Britten), the historic abbey at Bury St Edmunds, the gleaming spires of Cambridge, the "island" cathedral at Ely, or the ancient city and regional capital of Norwich, all within an hour's drive. Or, just take a walk down the lane to the windmill!

Address: Fen Rd Blo'Norton, Diss, Norfolk, IP22 2JH England. Tel: (01379) 898 025.

Type: Bed & breakfast with optional evening meal. **Clientele:** Mostly men with women welcome. **Transportation:** Car. Pick up from train £3.50. **To Gay Bars:** 17 miles or a 30-minute drive. **Rooms:** 2 rooms with double beds. **Bathrooms:** 1 shared bath/shower/toilet & 1 shared WC only. **Meals:** Full breakfast. Evening meals offered for additional cost. Home produced organic food. **Vegetarian:** Available upon request. **Complimentary:** Afternoon tea & coffee. **Dates Open:** All year except Christmas. **High Season:** July & August. **Rates:** £14 per person. **Discounts:** 10% on full week & special weekends occasionally. **Rsv'tns:** Required. **Reserve Through:** Call direct. **Parking:** Ample free off-street parking. Not suitable for disabled/ wheelchairs. **On-Premises:** Lounge with open fire, no TV. Gardens. **Swimming:** Nearby pool. 30 miles to coast. **Smoking:** Permitted in garden only. **Pets:** Permitted, but please check beforehand. **Handicap Access:** No. **Children:** Please inquire. **Languages:** English. **Your Host:** Geoffrey & John.

Warham Old Post Office Cottage

Gay-Friendly ♀♂

Warham Old Post Office Cottage offers a perfect setting for a quiet break in the country. It has many exposed beams and other period features, as well as home comforts. All rooms have wash basins, wardrobes, and tea/coffee making facilities. The common lounge has an inglenook fireplace, comfortable seating, and a colour TV. The village pub, Three Horseshoes, is adjacent to the cottage. Home cooking is the speciality for lunches and evening meals. Beaches and many attractions are nearby.

Address: c/o Three Horseshoes Free House In Warham near Wells-next-the-Sea, Norfolk NR23 1NL England. Tel: (01328) 710 547, Fakenham.

Type: Bed & breakfast inn with restaurant & bar.
Clientele: Mainly straight with some gay & lesbian clientele.
Transportation: Car is best.
To Gay Bars: In Norich, 1 hr by car.
Rooms: 2 singles, 3 doubles.
Bathrooms: 1 private,

1 shared, 1 W.C.
Meals: Full breakfast.
Vegetarian: Available at all times.
Complimentary: Tea & coffee in rooms.
Dates Open: All year.
High Season: Easter-September.
Rates: Low season £17.00-£19.00 per person, high season £19.00-£21.00.

Discounts: Inquire.
Rsv'tns: Not always required.
Reserve Through: Call direct.
Parking: Ample free off-street parking.
In-Room: Laundry service.
On-Premises: TV lounge, meeting rooms.
Swimming: At nearby ocean beach.

Sunbathing: At nearby ocean beach.
Smoking: Permitted in public rooms only, all bedrooms are non-smoking.
Pets: Permitted by prior arrangement.
Handicap Access: 1 downstairs suite, not wheelchair suitable.
Children: Not permitted.
Languages: English.

NOTTINGHAMSHIRE

Bathley Guest House

Gay/Lesbian ♂

Bathley Guest House is an exclusively gay bed & breakfast two minutes from the city's gay life. Conveniences include late keys and no restrictions, tea making facilities in all rooms, weekly rates on request. Concessions for admission to gay bars and sauna are available to our guests. Special midweek breaks are also available and women are welcome.

Address: 101 Bathley St, Trent Bridge, Nottingham NG2 2EE England. Tel: (0115) 9862 463.

Type: B & B guesthouse with bar for residents.
Clientele: Mostly men with women welcome.
To Gay Bars: 2 minutes from gay bars.
Rooms: 8 rooms with single & double beds.
Bathrooms: 2 shared.

Meals: Full English breakfast.
Complimentary: Concessions to local gay clubs & gay & lesbian sauna.
Dates Open: All year.
Rates: Single £17.00, double £28.50, twin rooms £29.50.

Discounts: Special midweek rates.
Reserve Through: Travel agent or call direct.
Parking: Ample free on-street parking.
In-Room: Tea/coffee making facilities.
On-Premises: TV lounge.

Smoking: Permitted only in lounge.
Pets: Welcome.
Handicap Access: No.
Children: Gay parents with children welcome.
Languages: English.
Your Host: Keith & Jeff.

Central Hotel

Gay-Friendly ♂

Central Hotel lives up to its name, being just 30 minutes from Nottingham, Derby, Sheffield and Robin Hood Centre. We're located 3 miles from the junction of highways 28 and M1. Bed and breakfast rooms have en-suite bathroom and colour TV, late keys and no restrictions.

Address: 1 Station Road, Sutton in Ashfield, Notts NG17 5FF England. Tel: (0623) 552373, Fax: (0623) 441306.

Type: Hotel with restaurant & licensed bar.
Clientele: Mainly straight with a 10% gay male following.
Transportation: Pick up from public transportation by prior arrangement.
To Gay Bars: 30 minutes by car to Sheffield, Derby, Nottingham.
Rooms: 17 rooms with twin & double beds.
Bathrooms: 15 private & 1 shared.
Meals: Full English breakfast.
Vegetarian: Always available.
Complimentary: Tea, coffee, biscuits in room.
Dates Open: All year.
Rates: £18.00-£45.00.
Credit Cards: MC, VISA, Access.
Rsv'tns: Preferred.
Reserve Through: Travel agent or call direct.
Parking: Adequate, free off-street parking.
In-Room: Color satellite TV, room service, laundry service & trouser press.
Exercise/Health: Massage available.
Smoking: Permitted without restrictions.
Pets: Not permitted.
Handicap Access: No special facilities.
Children: Permitted.
Languages: English.

SOMERSET

Bales Mead

Gay-Friendly 50/50 ♀♂

Bales Mead is a small, elegant Edwardian country house, offering superb, luxurious accommodation in an outstanding setting. The peaceful location has magnificent panoramic views of both the sea and the rolling countryside of Exmoor. All three double bedrooms are exquisitely furnished, offering every modern comfort and facility. Breakfast is served in the elegant dining room or *al fresco* in the summer, weather permitting. *Bales Mead* provides an excellent base for walking or touring Exmoor and the North Devon Coast.

Address: West Porlock, Somerset TA24 8NX England. Tel: (01643) 862565.

Type: Country house bed & breakfast.
Clientele: 50% gay & lesbian & 50% hetero clientele.
Transportation: Car is best, train from London to Taunton then bus to Porlock is possible.
To Gay Bars: 1-1/2 hours.
Rooms: 3 doubles.
Bathrooms: 1 shared bathroom & 2 shared toilets.
Meals: Expanded continental or full breakfast.
Vegetarian: Always available.
Complimentary: Tea, coffee & hot chocolate making facilities, mineral water, mints & toffees.
Dates Open: All year except Xmas & New Years.
High Season: May-October.
Rates: £22.00 per person per night B&B. Single occupancy of double room, £28.00 per person per night B&B.
Rsv'tns: Recommended.
Reserve Through: Call direct.
Parking: Parking available for 6 cars in private drive in front of house.
In-Room: Color TV, radio alarm clocks, hairdryers, & tea & coffee makers.
On-Premises: Central heating & log fire in winter. Lounge & dining room for breakfast. Private gardens available for sitting & relaxing.
Swimming: Nearby pool & ocean beach.
Sunbathing: At the beach.
Smoking: Not permitted.
Pets: Not permitted.
Handicap Access: No.
Children: Not permitted.
Languages: English, French, Spanish & German.
Your Host: Stephen & Peter.

SUSSEX

Fairlight Hotel

Gay-Friendly ♀♂

Fairlight Hotel welcomes you to Eastbourne. We have an excellent location near the center of town and close to clubs, pubs, and the sea. All rooms have private baths, colour TV, and tea/coffee making facilities. Enjoy our large garden or relax in the bar and games room.

Address: 41 Silverdale Rd, Eastbourne, East Sussex BN20 7AT England. Tel: (01323) 721 770.

Type: Hotel with licensed bar.
Clientele: Mostly hetero clientele with up to 30% gay & lesbian clientele.
Transportation: Short cab ride from railway station.
To Gay Bars: 10-minute walk to gay pub.
Rooms: 12 rooms with double & twin beds.

Bathrooms: All private.
Meals: Full English breakfast. Optional for 4-course evening meal £6.50.
Vegetarian: On request with notice.
Dates Open: All year.
High Season: June, July, September.
Rates: Off-season £15.00-£17.00, in-season

£17.50-£19.50.
Credit Cards: VISA & Access. Not for use on 1-night stays.
Rsv'tns: Required.
Reserve Through: Call direct.
Parking: On-street parking, usually ample.
In-Room: Colour TV & tea/coffee making facilities.

On-Premises: Games room.
Swimming: 2-minute walk to ocean.
Smoking: Not permitted in the dining room.
Pets: Dogs only permitted. Please phone ahead.
Handicap Access: No.
Children: Permitted.
Languages: English.

TORQUAY

Cliff House Hotel

Gay/Lesbian ♀♂

Alone in Its Excellence

Originally a millionaire's home, *Cliff House*, celebrating its 21st year, is an exclusive, luxury hotel with secluded garden at sea's edge. Here one can view the sea from the terrace that fronts the comfortable bar lounge. This gracious house has the elegance of a bygone age with the advantages of modern amenities. All bedrooms have a bathroom en suite. Full central heating warms us in early and late months, which are so delightful in this beautiful part of the country. There are ample parking facilities. Old friends meet, and new found friends are made. No one ever wants to leave.

Address: St. Marks Rd, Meadfoot Beach, Torquay TQ1 2EH England. Tel: (01803) 294 656, Fax: 211 983.

Type: Hotel with restaurant & bar.
Clientele: Good mix of gay men & women.
Transportation: Train or bus from London. Pick up from train.
To Gay Bars: A 5-minute walk or 2-minute drive.
Rooms: 16 rooms with single or double beds.
Bathrooms: All private bath/toilets.
Meals: Full English breakfast.

Vegetarian: With prior arrangement.
Complimentary: Tea & coffee in room.
Dates Open: All year.
High Season: Easter, June-October and Christmas.
Rates: £19.50-£26.00. Accounts subject to V.A.T.
Discounts: Party discounts.
Credit Cards: MC, VISA, Access & Switch.

Rsv'tns: Required during high season.
Reserve Through: Call direct.
Parking: Ample on- and off-street parking.
In-Room: Color TV, coffee & tea-making facilities & room service.
On-Premises: TV lounge, bar & public telephone.
Exercise/Health: Steam room, Jacuzzi, massage and gym.
Swimming: Ocean beach.

Sunbathing: On the beach, sun deck or in the secluded garden.
Nudity: Permitted in the secluded garden.
Smoking: Permitted without restrictions.
Pets: Dogs are permitted, but not in public rooms.
Handicap Access: Yes, 2 rooms.
Children: Not permitted.
Languages: English.

Melba House Hotel

Melba, The Toast of Torquay

Gay/Lesbian ♀♂

Melba House is situated on level ground approximately 300 metres from the beach overlooking Walnut Park. Town centre shops are about a 5-minute walk, while Torre Abbey Gardens and the Riviera Centre, with their many leisure activities, are about a 2-minute walk.

We have a comfortable residents lounge, a sun terrace and the attractive accommodations are decorated and furnished with every regard to the comfort of our guests. *Melba House* has no family rooms and is not suitable for young children. We look forward to the pleasure of your company.

Address: 62 Bampfylde Rd, Torquay, TQ2 5AY England. Tel: (01803) 213167.

Type: Bed & breakfast hotel.
Clientele: Mostly gay & lesbian with some hetero clientele.
Transportation: Car is best, especially for sightseeing, or train from Paddington Stn. London. Free pick up from train or bus.
To Gay Bars: 1/2 mile. 10-minute walk or 3-minute drive.
Rooms: 6 rooms with single or double beds.
Bathrooms: 6 private shower/toilets.
Meals: Full English breakfast.
Vegetarian: Available with 24hr notice. Also available nearby.
Complimentary: Tea & coffee.
Dates Open: All year.
High Season: July & August.
Rates: £16.00-£20.00 including tax.
Discounts: 10% on stays of 7 or more days.
Credit Cards: MC, VISA, Diners & Eurocard.
Rsv'tns: Required.
Reserve Through: Call direct.
Minimum Stay: 2 nights during high season.
Parking: Ample free off-street parking.
In-Room: Color TV, VCR, video tape library, telephone, coffee/ tea-making facilities & maid service.
On-Premises: TV lounge.
Exercise/Health: Nearby gym, weights, Jacuzzi/ spa, sauna, steam & massage. Sports field directly opposite.
Swimming: Nearby pool & ocean.
Sunbathing: On patio, common sun decks & at the beach.
Nudity: 2 miles to nude beach.
Smoking: Permitted except in dining room.
Pets: Not permitted.
Handicap Access: No.
Children: Not especially welcome.
Languages: English.
Your Host: Derek & David.

Red Squirrel Lodge

Gay-Friendly ♀♂

The English Tourist Board Rated Us Three Crowns!

A superb Victorian villa, *Red Squirrel Lodge* is in a quiet, peaceful area surrounded by spacious gardens. We are located near shops, buses and railway station, yet are only 200 yards from Torquay's finest beach. It is most beautifully furnished and has been established as a distinctive hotel for many years. You will be welcomed by resident proprietors John and David. A courtesy car from the bus and railway station is available.

Address: Chelston Rd Torquay, TQ2 6PU England. Tel & Fax: (01803) 605496.

Type: Hotel with bar.
Clientele: Mainly hetero clientele with a 20% gay & lesbian following.
Transportation: Car is best, or train from London Paddington Stn. Free pick up from bus or train.
To Gay Bars: 5 minutes by car.
Rooms: 14 rooms with single, double & queen beds.
Bathrooms: All private.
Meals: Full English breakfast. Optional dinner extra charge.
Vegetarian: Available with 24 hour notice.
Complimentary: Tea & coffee-making facilities in rooms. Tea, coffee, & soft drink upon arrival.
Dates Open: All year.
Rates: £20.00 per person/night minimum, £30.00 per person/night max in high season.
Discounts: For 2 or more nights in low season.
Credit Cards: MC, VISA & Amex.
Rsv'tns: Required with deposit.
Reserve Through: UK travel agent or call direct.
Minimum Stay: 3 nights high season (July-Aug).
Parking: Adequate, free off-street parking.
In-Room: Color TV & maid service.
On-Premises: TV lounge, pay phone, & separate bar for residents & friends.
Exercise/Health: Sport & leisure center 1/2 mile with gym, sauna, & Jacuzzi.
Swimming: At pool
1/2 mile away or ocean 250 yards.
Sunbathing: In extensive gardens.
Nudity: Permitted on nude beach 3 miles away.
Smoking: Permitted except in dining room.
Pets: Permitted except in dining room, bar & lounge.
Handicap Access: Yes. 3 ground floor rooms.
Children: Not permitted.
Languages: English.
Your Host: John & David.

UK (England)

Summerland House

Gay/Lesbian ♀♂

Summerland House is a small family hotel five minutes' walk from the harbour, beaches and town centre. All bedrooms have private showers and are well-furnished with colour TV, radio clock and tea making facilities. A comfortable dining room, separate TV lounge and a lounge bar are also for the use of guests. Our home-cooked meals are served with a smile. Your hosts do their utmost to ensure a happy stay in Torquay and to put you at ease the moment you arrive.

Address: 42 Warren Rd, Torquay, South Devon TQ2 5TL England. Tel: (01803) 297 120.

Type: Small, family hotel with full residential liquor license.
Clientele: Mostly gay in winter. Gay & straight clientele in summer.
To Gay Bars: 3-10 minute walk to gay/lesbian bars.
Rooms: 9 doubles.
Bathrooms: All rooms have showers & sinks. 1 WC on each landing.

Meals: Full English breakfast. Optional dinner at extra charge.
Vegetarian: Available with 24 hrs. notice.
Complimentary: Tea & coffee on arrival.
Dates Open: All year.
High Season: Summer.
Rates: £15.00-£23.00.
Rsv'tns: Recommended.
Reserve Through: Call direct.

Parking: Adequate on-street parking.
In-Room: Maid service, color TV, tea & coffee-making facilities.
On-Premises: TV lounge & public telephone.
Swimming: 5-minute walk downhill to ocean beach.
Sunbathing: On ocean beach.
Nudity: Permitted on

nude beach nearby.
Smoking: Permitted without restrictions.
Pets: Dogs are permitted.
Handicap Access: No.
Children: Permitted.
Languages: English, some French.
Your Host: Roger & Chris.

WARWICKSHIRE

Ellesmere House

Gay/Lesbian ♂

A Friendly Welcome to the Heart of England

Ellesmere House is an elegant, early Victorian town residence with spacious rooms furnished in antiques. It has been modernized to a high standard of comfortable accommodation and is situated in a quiet, tree-lined avenue within walking distance of all the facilities of this attractive town. Shakespeare's Stratford, The Castles at Warwick and Kenilworth are all within easy reach.

Address: 36 Binswood Ave Leamington Spa, Warwickshire CV32 5SQ England. Tel: (01926) 424-618.

Type: Bed & breakfast homestay.
Clientele: Mostly men with women welcome.
Transportation: Own vehicle is best, but train, bus OK.
To Gay Bars: Warwick gay bar 3 miles.

Rooms: 3 rooms with single or double beds.
Bathrooms: 2 private bath/toilets & 1 private shower/toilet.
Meals: Full English breakfast.
Dates Open: All year.
Rates: £28.00-£40.00.

Rsv'tns: Required.
Reserve Through: Call direct.
Parking: Adequate, free on-street parking.
In-Room: Color TV.
Sunbathing: In garden.
Smoking: Not encouraged.

Pets: Not permitted.
Handicap Access: No.
Children: Not permitted.
Languages: English, Spanish, limited French, Italian.
Your Host: Francisco & Colin.

YORKSHIRE

Bull Lodge

Gay-Friendly ♀♂

Bull Lodge is a modern, detached residence on a quiet side street, 3/4 mile from the city centre and close to the University and Barbican Leisure Centre. We're on a bus route and have private, enclosed parking. Single, twin, or double bedrooms are available. Twins and doubles can be with or without private shower and toilet. All rooms have tea & coffee facilities, colour TV, clock-radio, and direct-dial telephones. A full-choice English breakfast is served, evening meals can be ordered, and snacks and drinks are available.

York can be busy all year, so booking ahead is always a good idea. In the winter, weekends are usually busy, and June through October is busy almost every day. Allow at least two days to enjoy this beautiful city and it's many sights and attractions. York is also an excellent base to explore the surrounding countryside, the moors and the dales, or visit Castle Howard of **"Brideshead Revisited"** fame, only 15 miles away. If you're touring the U.K., relax for a few days here, between the busy cities of Edinburgh and London.

Address: 37 Bull Lane, Lawrence St, York YO1 3EN England. Tel: (01904) 415522.

Type: Guesthouse.
Clientele: Mostly straight clientele with a gay/lesbian following.
Transportation: Convenient direct bus from train/bus stations. Pick up by prior arrangement on minimum 2 night advance bookings.
To Gay Bars: 1 mile.
Rooms: 1 single, 6 doubles, 1 twin.
Bathrooms: 3 private, 2 shared. Ground floor with private suitable for disabled.
Meals: Full English breakfast. Evening meal additional charge (low season only).
Complimentary: Tea & coffee.
Dates Open: End January to mid-December.
High Season: June thru October.
Rates: 1995: summer £16.00-£19.00; winter £14.00-£16.00.
Discounts: 5% for more than 4 nights, also off-season rates.
Rsv'tns: Recommended for weekends & summer period.
Reserve Through: Travel agent or call direct.
Minimum Stay: Advance bookings min 2 nights.
Parking: Private enclosed parking.
In-Room: Color TV, Tea/coffee makers, radio alarm clocks, hot & cold water, maid service, telephone.
On-Premises: Non-smoking TV lounge with books & games.
Swimming: 10-minute walk to Barbican pool & leisure centre.
Smoking: Permitted except in lounge & dining room.
Pets: Permitted.
Handicap Access: Yes, ground floor en suite double room.
Children: Permitted.
Languages: English.
Your Host: Roy & Dennis.

Interludes

Little "Scene," But Great Scenery

Gay-Friendly 50/50 ♀♂

Interludes is an elegant Georgian townhouse with sea views, peacefully situated in a conservation area, yet close to beach, town centre, theatres, castle, etc. The hotel is licensed, and, because of our connections with the Stephen Joseph Theatre (artistic director Alan Ayckbourn), has a theatrical theme. The bedrooms are well equipped. *Interludes* is informal, friendly and most relaxing. Scarborough is an attractive resort, and is an ideal centre for exploring the nearby North Yorkshire Moors National Park and the historical towns of York and Whitby.

Address: 32 Princess St Scarborough, North Yorkshire YO11 1QR England. Tel: (01723) 360513 or Fax: (01723) 368597.

Type: Hotel.
Clientele: 50% gay & lesbian & 50% hetero.
Transportation: Car, bus or train (direct rail link to Manchester Airport).
Rooms: 5 rooms with twin, king, canopy & four poster beds.
Bathrooms: 4 en suite, 1 with sink & adjacent shower & toilet.
Meals: Full breakfast with 4 course dinner available at additional cost.
Vegetarian: Available with prior notification.
Complimentary: Tea, coffee, chocolate, juice, etc.

continued next page

UK (England)

Dates Open: All year.
High Season: July-September.
Rates: Low £44.00 per room, mid £48.00 per room, high £52.00 per room.
Discounts: Single occupancy, 5% to 15% groups of 7 or more, special package with Stephen Joseph Theatre. 10% for 7 or more days.
Credit Cards: MC, VISA.
Rsv'tns: Wise to confirm availability.
Reserve Through: Call direct.
Minimum Stay: Required public holiday weekends.
Parking: Adequate free on-street parking, limited during high season.
In-Room: Color TV, coffee & tea-making facilities & maid service.
On-Premises: Laundry facilities.
Swimming: Nearby pool & ocean beach.
Sunbathing: On the patio, at the beach.
Smoking: Permitted in lounge & outside. Non-smoking rooms available.
Pets: Not permitted.
Handicap Access: No.
Children: Not permitted.
Languages: English.
Your Host: Bob & Ian.

Pauleda House Hotel

Gay-Friendly ♂

Pauleda House Hotel is a small, comfortable family-run hotel, situated less than one mile from York's beautiful Minister and city centre. York is a comparatively small place and other than the abundance of stately homes, abbeys, etc. on the outskirts, the historical attractions are all within walking distance of each other. Our building itself is a fine example of the Victorian style. We are very close to the picturesque village green which gives a feeling of rural tranquillity while being only a 10-minute walk to the city centre. The River Ouse is close by, this being an alternative pleasant walk into the city.

Address: 123 Clifton, York YO3-6BL England. Tel: (01904) 634745, Fax 621327.

Type: Hotel with restaurant & bar.
Clientele: Mainly hetero clientele with a gay male following.
Transportation: By car, taxi from railway or bus station approx £2.40.
To Gay Bars: Less than one mile from York Arms & White Horse.
Rooms: 12 rooms with single, double or queen beds.
Bathrooms: All private shower/toilets.
Meals: Continental, expanded continental, or full breakfast.
Vegetarian: Available upon prior request.
Complimentary: Tea & coffee, free wine during special winter breaks.
Dates Open: All year.
High Season: April-Oct.
Rates: Rooms £16.00-£30.00 per person per night.
Credit Cards: MC, VISA, Access, Connect, Switch, Diners, Eurocard & Delta.
Rsv'tns: Required but walk-ins welcome.
Reserve Through: Call direct.
Parking: Ample free on-street & off-street parking. Private lot.
In-Room: Satellite color TV, telephone, maid service, radio/alarm, hairdryer, shoe cleaning, sewing kits, tissues.
On-Premises: Meeting rooms, ironing facilities, lounge, bar, dining room.
Swimming: At local swimming pools or river yards away.
Smoking: Permitted except in dining room.
Pets: Not permitted.
Handicap Access: No.
Children: Not permitted.
Languages: English.

Sun Hotel

Gay/Lesbian ♀♂

The Sun Hotel is a former coaching inn situated close to Bradford's historic city centre. Well-appointed accommodations are decorated in traditional style with pine furniture, colour TV and tea and coffee makers. Traditional English breakfast is included, and evening meals are by arrangement. Facilities include a popular public bar, which serves food, a beer garden and licensed function rooms. The hotel is close to many historic sites as well as modern tourist attractions.

Address: 124 Sunbridge Rd, Bradford, W Yorkshire BD1 2ND England. Tel: (01274) 737722.

Type: Hotel with gay & lesbian pub.
Clientele: Good mix of gay men & women.
To Gay Bars: Bar on premises. 2-minute walk to nightclub.
Rooms: 5 doubles.
Bathrooms: Shared. Planning en suite facilities.
Meals: Traditional English breakfast included. Paid lunch & snacks at bar.
Dates Open: All year.
Rates: £15.00 per person.
Discounts: Special weekend breaks available.
Rsv'tns: Helpful but not required.
Reserve Through: Call direct.
Parking: Free off-street parking.
In-Room: Colour TV, tea/coffee making facilities, & twin or double beds.
On-Premises: Public bar, beer garden, & function rooms.
Swimming: Close to Lake District.
Smoking: Permitted without restrictions.
Pets: Permitted with advance request.
Handicap Access: No.
Children: No problem, not usual.
Languages: English & German.

UK (SCOTLAND)

AVIEMORE

Auchendean Lodge Hotel

Gay-Friendly ♀♂

We are more a home than a hotel. So, come and relax in the Scottish Highlands in our Edwardian hunting lodge. *Auchendean Lodge* is an elegant, comfortable country hotel furnished with antiques and fine paintings. When you stay here, plan on enjoying interesting, award-winning food, good wines and malt whiskies, spectacular views of Spey and the Cairngorm Mountains, walking, fishing, golfing and skiing. Our hotel is set in a magnificent garden on the edge of 200 acres of mature forest. Call Ian or Eric for a brochure. Although our clientele is not exclusively gay, you will be warmly welcomed. **READER'S COMMENT: The Scottish dinners were superb. The hosts were very friendly and welcomed us warmly. The other guests, while not gay, were friendly and very nice. I would recommend this hotel without reservation, but plan on TWO nights. One night will make you want another."**—*Richard H., St. Louis, MO*

Address: Dulnain Bridge, Nr Grantown-on-Spey, Inverness-Shire PH26 3LU Scotland. Tel: (0479) 851 347.

Type: Inn with restaurant.
Clientele: Mostly hetero with a gay & lesbian following.
Transportation: Car is best.
To Gay Bars: 2 hrs by car.
Rooms: 8 rooms with single, double or queen beds.
Bathrooms: Private: 5 bath/- or shower/toilets, 3 sinks. Shared: 1 shower & 2 WC.

Meals: Full breakfast with dinner optional at £23.50.
Vegetarian: Available with advance notice.
Complimentary: Tea, coffee, biscuits.
Dates Open: All year.
High Season: Easter thru early October, Xmas & New Year.
Rates: B&B, summer £21.50-£39.00, winter £17.00-£31.00; B&B + dinner, summer £44.00-£62.50, winter

£39.50-£54.50.
Discounts: 10% for 3 days or more on dinner, bed & breakfast rates.
Credit Cards: MC, VISA, Amex, Diners.
Rsv'tns: Recommended.
Reserve Through: Call direct.
Parking: Ample free off-street parking.
In-Room: Color TV, coffee & tea-making facilities, room & laundry service.
Exercise/Health: Walk-

ing, fishing, golfing, skiing.
Swimming: Nearby pool, river, lake.
Sunbathing: In adjacent woods.
Smoking: Permitted in bedrooms & 1 lounge.
Pets: Permitted. Large gardens & woods attached to premises.
Handicap Access: Yes, restaurant. Flight of steps to bedrooms.
Children: Permitted.
Languages: English, French.

We Appreciate Your Comments!

Positive comments of interest may be included in the next issue, giving future readers the benefit of your experience. And it's a nice way of saying "thank you" to an innkeeper who extended you exceptional hospitality.

See the contents for the Reader Comment Form.

AYR

Roseland Guest House

Gay-Friendly ♀♂

Ayr, a seaside resort on Scotland's west coast, is situated 3 miles from Alloway, the birthplace of Scotland's national poet, Robert Burns. Long miles of golden sand, superb sports and recreational facilities and family entertainments have helped make Ayr one of Britain's premier coastal resorts. The area is renowned for its golf courses, where you can follow in the footsteps of the golfing greats. Royal Troon, 10 miles north, is the venue for the 1997 British Open. Ayr Racecourse annually hosts the Scottish Grand National (April) and the Scottish Gold Cup (Sept). The town annually hosts Scotland's premier Flower Show in August. History abounds in the area, where the coastline is dotted with dramatic castles perched on clifftops, including Culzean Castle, the area's top tourist attraction, which houses the flat given by the British to President Eisenhower for his lifetime use. *Roseland Guest House*, which offers a quiet, peaceful haven, is virtually in the town centre, which has a large variety of shops and entertainment. There are several restaurants in town, which offer local fare, and numerous others offering international cuisine. It's a great location for a quiet, restful holiday within easy travelling distance of Glasgow (45 mins), your direct point of entry to the country, and Scotland's capital, Edinburgh (1hr 45 mins). Your host, Ron, looks forward to welcoming you to *Roseland*.

Address: 15 Charlotte Street, Ayr KA7 1DZ Scotland. Tel: (01292) 283435.

Type: Bed & breakfast.
Clientele: Mostly hetero with gay & lesbian following.
Transportation: Car or train from Glasgow Airport to Ayr then taxi.
To Gay Bars: One hour by car or train to Glasgow.
Rooms: 4 rooms & 1 suite with single & double beds.
Bathrooms: 5 private sinks, 1 shared shower & 1 shared toilet.
Meals: Full breakfast.
Vegetarian: Five-minute walk to vegetarian restaurant.
Complimentary: Tea, coffee & biscuits in room.
Dates Open: All year.
High Season: July-August.
Rates: £15.00-£25.00 per person B&B. Self-catering, telephone for quote.
Discounts: 10% for 7 or more nights.
Rsv'tns: Preferred.
Reserve Through: Call direct.
Parking: Ample on-street pay parking.
In-Room: Color TV, coffee & tea-making facilities, maid service.
On-Premises: Communal lounge.
Swimming: Five min walk to pool, 2 min walk to beach.
Sunbathing: At nearby beach.
Smoking: Permitted everywhere.
Pets: Not permitted.
Handicap Access: No.
Children: Not especially welcome.
Languages: English.
Your Host: Ron.

EDINBURGH

Amaryllis Guest House, The

Gay/Lesbian ♀♂

The Amaryllis is a small guest house in the center of Edinburgh, 10 minutes from Princes St. and Edinburgh's gay bars, clubs, shops and restaurants. Owned by lesbians, it offers bed and breakfast accommodation to lesbians and gays, as well as to straight tourists. All rooms have TV and tea- and coffee-making facilities. Early and late trays are available for people who need to be up early or wish to stay in bed later!

Address: 5 Upper Gilmore Pl, Edinburgh, EH3 9NW Scotland. Tel: (031) 229 4669.

Type: Guesthouse.
Clientele: Mainly gay & lesbian with some hetero clientele.
To Gay Bars: 15 minute walk.
Rooms: 3 singles, 6 doubles, & 1 triple.
Bathrooms: 7 with private WC. 3 shared baths.

Meals: Full breakfast. Early or late trays are always available.
Vegetarian: Available on request.
Complimentary: Tea & coffee.
Dates Open: All year.
High Season: June-October.

Rates: £13-£17 per person.
Reserve Through: Call direct.
Parking: Adequate on-steet parking at night. Limited on-street parking by day.
In-Room: TV, coffee & tea-making facilities.

On-Premises: TV lounge.
Smoking: Permitted in all rooms.
Pets: Permitted.
Handicap Access: Yes. Ground floor.
Children: Permitted.
Languages: English.

Armadillo Guest House, The

Gay/Lesbian ♀♂

The Armadillo Guest House is highly commended by the Tourist Board of Scotland. It is newly refurbished throughout to an excellent standard and provides a friendly, warm atmosphere. We have maps and full information on gay and happy life here in Scotland. Come and join in the fun of "Tartan Kilt" country, only at *The Armadillo*.

Address: 12 Gilmore Place, Edinburgh, EH3 9NQ UK (Scotland). Tel: (031) 229 6457.

Type: Guesthouse.
Clientele: Mostly gay & lesbian with some hetero clientele.
Transportation: Bus, taxi.
To Gay Bars: A 20-minute walk or 5-minute drive.
Rooms: 6 rooms with single or double beds.

Bathrooms: Shared: 3 bath/shower/toilets, 3 WCs, 3 showers & 1 bathtub.
Meals: Full breakfast.
Vegetarian: Always available to guests.
Complimentary: Tea, coffee & set-up service.
Dates Open: All year.
High Season: July

through October.
Rates: Double/twin £15-£20. Single £16-£26.
Discounts: For longer stays.
Rsv'tns: Required.
Reserve Through: Call direct.
Parking: Limited off-street & on-street parking.

In-Room: Color TV, telephone, coffee/tea-making facilities, room, maid & laundry service.
On-Premises: Laundry facilities.
Pets: Permitted.
Handicap Access: No.
Languages: English.

Linden Hotel

Gay-Friendly 50/50 ♀♂

The *Linden Hotel* is Scotland's only gay hotel, located in the center of Edinburgh, close to the gay bars and nightclubs. The hotel is owned and operated by the Philbeach Hotel of London, an exclusively gay hotel. *The Linden* has an intimate atmosphere and an easygoing, relaxing atmosphere which is sure to make guests relax and enjoy themselves!

Address: 9-13 Nelson St, Edinburgh EH3 6LF Scotland. Tel: (031) 557-4344, Fax: (041) 556-7881.

Type: Hotel with bar & a Thai & European restaurant.
Clientele: 50% gay & lesbian & 50% straight clientele.
Transportation: Bus or taxi.
To Gay Bars: 5 minutes.
Rooms: 18 rooms with single or double beds.
Bathrooms: Private: 6 shower/toilets, 8 showers, 4 washbasins only.
Meals: Expanded conti-

nental breakfast.
Vegetarian: Available at lunch & dinner.
Complimentary: Tea & coffee in room.
Dates Open: All year.
High Season: July-August.
Rates: Single £32.00-£39.00, double £40.00-£55.00, triple £75.00.
Credit Cards: VISA, Amex, Access, Diners, JCB.
Rsv'tns: Required a

week in advance during high season.
Reserve Through: Travel agent or call direct.
Parking: Ample on-street parking & garage space for 1 car.
In-Room: Maid, room & laundry service, colour TV, telephone.
On-Premises: Meeting rooms, private dining rooms, TV lounge, public telephones.
Swimming: At nearby

ocean beach.
Sunbathing: In garden.
Nudity: Permitted in garden.
Smoking: Permitted without restrictions.
Pets: Permitted without restrictions.
Handicap Access: Yes. One ground floor bedroom.
Children: Not permitted.
Languages: English, French, Thai.
Your Host: Tony.

Mansfield House

Gay/Lesbian ♀♂

Mansfield House is elegantly furnished with many antiques and is considered to be THE place to stay in Edinburgh. It is centrally located and is near the local gay clubs, bars, discos, restaurants and shops.

Address: 57 Dublin St, Edinburgh, EH3 6NL Scotland (UK). Tel: (44-31) 556 7980.

Type: Guesthouse.
Clientele: Good mix of gays & lesbians.
Rooms: 5 rooms with double beds.
Bathrooms: 1 en suite with shower, bidet. Four rooms share 1 toilet & shower.

Meals: Continental breakfast available at breakfast bar.
Complimentary: Tea, coffee & biscuits in room.
Dates Open: All year.
High Season: June-Sept.
Rates: £25-£35. En suite:

£35-£55.
Rsv'tns: Required.
Reserve Through: Travel agent or call direct.
Parking: Limited off-street parking.
In-Room: Color TV, maid service, & ceiling fans in most rooms.

On-Premises: Public pay phone.
Smoking: Permitted.
Pets: Not permitted.
Handicap Access: No.
Children: Not permitted.
Languages: English.

UK (WALES)

AMMANFORD (DYFED)

Apple Cottage

Gay/Lesbian ♀

Apple Cottage, situated in an area of outstanding natural beauty, is an over-200-year-old, semi-detached, self-contained, stone cottage. The living area of this clean and cozy 1-bedroom accommodation, has an exposed painted stone wall with an open fire range, color television and fitted wool carpet and rugs. The fully-equipped kitchen includes an electric cooker and small fridge. Patio doors lead to a small, furnished patio area which overlooks a large, enclosed garden. The upstairs bedroom is furnished with antiques and has a velux window for extra light. From the front of the cottage are views of a wide grazing common with the Black Mountain as a backdrop. It is 2 miles to the Brecon Beacons National Park, about 10 miles to the Vale of Neath, known for magnificent and abundant waterfalls and 13 miles to Swansea City.

Address: 35 New Rd, Gwaun-Cae-Gurwen, Ammanford, Dyfed SA18 1UN Wales. Tel: (01269) 824072.

Type: Self-contained stone cottage.
Clientele: Mostly women with men welcome.
Rooms: 1 bedroom with 1 double & 1 single bed.
Bathrooms: Private shower/toilet with pine wash stand.
Dates Open: All year.

High Season: Jun 11-Sep 24, Easter, Christmas & New Year.
Rates: High season: £120-£130 per week. Off-season £100 per week. £20 per night.
Rsv'tns: Required, with deposit. Balance paid immediately on arrival.

Reserve Through: Call direct.
Parking: Off-street parking.
In-Room: Fully-equipped kitchen, color TV, open fire range, oil central heat, hot water, linens, thermostatically-controlled shower.

On-Premises: Large enclosed garden.
Exercise/Health: Horse riding, water sports, climbing, walking & swimming.
Languages: English.

CARDIFF

Courtfield Hotel

Gay-Friendly ♀♂

The Courtfield is a tastefully-decorated hotel close to Cardiff Castle and the city centre. Our setting is a wide and tree-lined avenue with stately homes and buildings. Our hotel, restaurant and bar have a mixed clientele. Gay bars are just 10 minutes away. Guests have their own keys.

Address: 101 Cathedral Rd, Cardiff, CF1 9PH Wales. Phone & Fax: (0222) 227-701.

Type: Hotel with restaurant & bar.
Clientele: Mostly straight clientele with a gay & lesbian following.
Transportation: Cardiff (Wales) airport, then taxi to city.
To Gay Bars: 10 minutes to gay bars.
Rooms: 16 rooms with single & double beds.
Bathrooms: 4 private shower/toilets. Shared: 2 bath/shower/toilet, 1 WC.
Meals: Full Welsh breakfast.
Vegetarian: Vegetarians catered for.
Complimentary: Tea & coffee facilities in rooms.
Dates Open: All year.
Rates: Single £25.00-£35.00, double £35.00-£50.00.
Discounts: 10% on long-term stays.
Credit Cards: MC, VISA, Amex, Access, Diners, Eurocard.
Rsv'tns: Required 1 week in advance.
Reserve Through: Travel agent or call direct.
Parking: On-street parking.
In-Room: Maid & room service, color TV, telephone, tea making facilities & clock radio.
On-Premises: Meeting rooms.
Swimming: Pool nearby.
Smoking: Permitted without restrictions.
Pets: Permitted by prior arrangement.
Handicap Access: No.
Children: Permitted.
Languages: English, Dutch, German & French.

GWYNEDD

Dewis Cyfarfod

Women ♀

Women's Guesthouse with Art Courses

Dewis Cyfarfod is a small, friendly, licensed women's guesthouse offering a warm welcome and a high standard of service. The house is set in an elevated position on five acres of woodland overlooking the River Dee in the Snowdonia National Park three miles from Bala and the largest natural lake in Wales. There are excellent facilities locally for many outdoor sports with equipment for hire and tuition available. Art tuition and residential courses in drawing, painting and sculpture are available at *Dewis Cyfarfod.*

Address: Llandderfel nr Bala, Gwynedd LL23 7DR Wales. Tel: 06783 243.

Type: Licensed guesthouse with art courses.
Clientele: Women only.
Transportation: Car is best.
To Gay Bars: 40 miles.
Rooms: 2 rooms with single beds.
Bathrooms: 2 ensuite shower/toilet.
Meals: Full breakfast.
Vegetarian: With prior notice.
Complimentary: Tea & coffee.
Dates Open: All year.
Rates: £16-£18.
Rsv'tns: Required.
Reserve Through: Call direct.
Parking: Ample free off-street parking.
In-Room: TV, tea & coffee-making facilities.
On-Premises: Small bar lounge.
Exercise/Health: Nearby weights, sauna & massage.
Swimming: 3 miles to swimming pool & lake.
Sunbathing: Anywhere on our 5 acres.
Smoking: Permitted anywhere. One non-smoking sleeping room.
Pets: Not permitted.
Handicap Access: Partially. Ground-floor rooms.
Children: Not especially welcome.
Languages: English, French, Spanish, German.

PACIFIC REGION

AUSTRALIA

NEW SOUTH WALES

BERRY

Tara Country Retreat

Gay/Lesbian ♀♂

Australia's Most Popular Country Gay Guest House

At *Tara Country Retreat* we especially welcome overseas guests, and are happy to take them on a tour of the surrounding tourist spots and koala and kangaroo parks. *Tara* is a convenient stop-off for travel between Sydney, Canberra and Melbourne. Facilities include swimming pool, spa, game room, TV and video. We can arrange for tennis, canoeing and guided bushwalks. *Tara* is only 9km from historic Berry, famous for fine restaurants and antique shops. It's 15 minutes from Seven Mile Beach and adjoins the nature reserve and rainforests of the Kangaroo Valley.

Address: 219 Wattamolla Rd. Berry, NSW 2535 Australia. Tel: (61) 44 641472, Fax: (61) 44 642265.

Type: Guesthouse & campground with restaurant, bar & a variety of village shops.
Clientele: Good mix of gay men & women.
Transportation: Car is best. Free pick up from train or bus, AUD $75 for pick up from airport.
To Gay Bars: Nearest bars are in Sydney, Canberra, or Wollongong. 50 miles or 1 hour.
Rooms: 6 rooms with single or queen beds.
Bathrooms: 2 shared showers & 2 shared WCs.
Campsites: 10 tent sites with use of guest house facilities. 2 RV parking sites.
Meals: Full country breakfast, other meals at extra charge.
Vegetarian: Available upon request.
Complimentary: Tea & coffee, wine with meals.
Dates Open: All year.
High Season: December & January.
Rates: AUD $50-AUD $120, campsites AUD $10.
Discounts: For mid-week stays.
Credit Cards: MC, VISA, Amex, Bancard.
Rsv'tns: Recommended.
Reserve Through: Travel agent or call direct.
Parking: Ample free off-street parking.
In-Room: Coffee & tea-making facilities.
On-Premises: TV lounge, meeting rooms & laundry facilities.
Exercise/Health: Jacuzzi, weights, massage, gym.
Swimming: Pool on premises, nearby swimming holes & river. 15-minute drive to ocean.
Sunbathing: At pool or riverside, on ocean beach.
Nudity: Permitted in pool area & Jacuzzi at discretion of other guests.
Smoking: Permitted without restrictions.
Pets: Dogs & cats permitted.
Handicap Access: Yes.
Children: No.
Languages: English.

IGTA aglta

BLUE MOUNTAINS

Bygone Beautys Cottages

From Pure Relaxation to Total Indulgence,

Gay-Friendly ♀♂

Bygone Beautys has a selection of fully self-contained cottages and holiday houses from which to choose when you stay in the Blue Mountains. For romantic couples, we have modest cottages, or for extra special occasions ask us about our Chalet with its triple spa and Joan Crawford 4-spray shower! For a few days away with family and friends, we have holiday houses which accommodate 6 to 20 people in comfort and style. No matter which property you choose, you will enjoy comfort, spaciousness, and an atmosphere of indulgence and relaxation.

All our accommodations are fully self-contained and have a lounge, fully-equipped kitchen, colour TV and all comforts. We also provide linens, feather quilts, towels, and the ingredients for a country breakfast of eggs, bacon, fresh oranges for squeezing (juicer provided) and a selection of fresh fruit. All your other provisions can be obtained from the local townships of Wentworth Falls or Leura. Alternatively, there are many excellent restaurants to choose from. All you have to do is come and enjoy yourselves.

At our Bygone Beautys Tea Rooms, guests are provided with a complimentary Devonshire Tea which can be enjoyed anytime during their stay.

Address: 20-22 Grose St, Leura, NSW 2780 Australia. Tel: (047) 84 3117, (047) 84 3108, Fax: (047) 58 7257.

Type: Bed & breakfast cottages with restaurant & bric-a-brac/craft shop. **Clientele:** Mostly hetero clientele with a gay & lesbian following. **Transportation:** Car or train, then taxi. **To Gay Bars:** 55 km, an hour by car. **Rooms:** 4 cottages with double, queen or king beds. **Bathrooms:** All private.

Meals: Full breakfast. **Vegetarian:** Available upon request. **Complimentary:** Chilled champagne upon arrival. Tea, milk, coffee & Devonshire tea. **Dates Open:** All year. **High Season:** June-Sept. **Rates:** Per person per night: AUD $57.50 (mid-week) to AUD $77.50 (weekends). **Discounts:** For children &

extended periods of stay. **Credit Cards:** Bancard. **Rsv'tns:** Required. **Reserve Through:** Call direct. **Minimum Stay:** Required. **Parking:** Ample free off-street parking. **In-Room:** Color TV, VCR, kitchen, refrigerator, coffee/tea-making facilities & laundry service. **Exercise/Health:** Jacuzzi

in one cottage only. **Sunbathing:** At beach. **Smoking:** Permitted in all areas. **Pets:** Not permitted. **Handicap Access:** Yes. **Children:** Older children welcome. **Languages:** Australian only.

Cleopatra Country Guesthouse

Gay-Friendly ♀♂

Cleopatra Country Guesthouse is a National Trust Classified house, opened in 1984, surrounded by an award-winning garden of one hectare. The *Guesthouse* has five beautiful guest rooms and a 36 seat restaurant, serving French Provincial food, which food critics regard as one of the best in Australia. Guests are offered total seclusion, sensational food, a tennis court, open fires and central heating, antique furniture, the best of linens and laces, and an atmosphere of great charm. All this is set in a mountain garden less than two hours' drive from Sydney.

Address: Cleopatra Street, Blackheath, NSW, Australia. Tel: (047) 878 456, Fax: (047) 876 092.

Type: Guesthouse with restaurant. **Clientele:** Mostly hetero clientele with a gay & lesbian following.

Transportation: Car is best. Train available from Sydney. Cheap taxi from local train station. **Rooms:** 4 rooms & 1

apartment with single, queen or double beds. **Bathrooms:** 3 private bath/toilets & 1 shared bath/shower/toilet.

Meals: Expanded continental breakfast, lunch & dinner. **Vegetarian:** Available upon prior request. Fish

always on the menu.
Complimentary: Tea & coffee.
Dates Open: Usually all year. Sometimes closed a few weeks around Jan-Feb.
High Season: Winter-Spring (July thru October).
Rates: AUD $150-$250

per person per day.
Discounts: 10% for stays over 3 days.
Credit Cards: MC, VISA, Amex & Bancard.
Rsv'tns: Required.
Reserve Through: Travel agent or call direct.
Parking: Ample off-street parking.

In-Room: Color TV, VCR & maid service.
Exercise/Health: Massage.
Swimming: Nearby pool.
Sunbathing: In the garden.
Smoking: Permitted in sitting room if it doesn't disturb other guests.

Pets: Not permitted.
Handicap Access: No.
Children: Not especially welcome.
Languages: English & French.
Your Host: Trish & Dany.

Trillium

Women ♀

Trillium, a women-only retreat in the Blue Mountains, offers a bed and breakfast with cosy rooms and log fires located on picturesque acres only 1-1/2 hours from Sydney. A beautiful Koori women's healing waterhole and falls are just a short bush walk from our retreat.

Address: 71 Seventh Ave, North Katoomba, NSW 2780 Australia. Tel: (047) 826 372.

Type: Bed & breakfast.
Clientele: Women only.
Transportation: Car is best. Pick up from train.
To Gay Bars: No gay bars in the area.
Rooms: 3 rooms with double beds.
Bathrooms: 2 shared shower/toilets.
Campsites: 6 tent sites.

Meals: Expanded continental breakfast.
Complimentary: Tea & coffee facilities in main room.
Dates Open: All year.
High Season: Winter.
Rates: AUD $45 per person per night.
Rsv'tns: Required.
Reserve Through: Call

direct.
Parking: Ample off-street parking.
On-Premises: TV lounge with colour TV & video tape library.
Swimming: Waterfall & swimming hole a 40-minute bush walk from house.
Sunbathing: On the lawn.

Nudity: Permitted throughout the grounds.
Smoking: Permitted outside on deck.
Pets: Not permitted.
Handicap Access: Yes.
Children: Welcome.
Languages: English & Australian.
Your Host: Natalie & Helen.

COFFS HARBOUR

Santa Fe Luxury Bed & Breakfast

Gay-Friendly 50/50 ♀♂

Santa Fe is not only the romance of Santa Fe, but the irresistible appeal of its lifestyle...a casual elegance.

Tucked away in a secluded valley just 10 minutes north of Coffs Harbour and only 2 minutes from beautiful Sapphire Beach, discover this unique peaceful retreat set in 5 acres of subtropical gardens, waterfalls and natural bushland. Take a stroll through the gardens, feed the Koi fish or relax around the large salt water pool that is set in terraced lawns and gardens. Enjoy a log fire, the adobe BBQ area and healthy breakfasts served on the deck.

Address: The Mountain Way, Coffs Harbour, NSW 2450 Australia Tel: (066) 537 700, Fax: (066) 537 050.

Type: Bed & breakfast.
Clientele: 50% gay & lesbian & 50% straight .
Transportation: Free pick up from airport & train.
Rooms: 3 rooms with single, queen or king beds.
Bathrooms: 3 private shower/toilets.
Meals: Full breakfast.
Vegetarian: Available

upon request.
Complimentary: Tea & coffee.
Dates Open: All year.
High Season: Nov-Feb.
Rates: Winter (May-Sept) AUD $95. Summer (Oct-Apr) AUD $115-$125.
Credit Cards: MC, VISA & Bancard.
Rsv'tns: Required.
Reserve Through: Call direct.

Parking: Ample free off-street parking.
In-Room: Color TV, VCR, video tape library, ceiling fans, coffee/tea-making facilities & room service.
On-Premises: TV lounge & laundry facilities.
Swimming: Pool & spa jet on premises. Nearby ocean, 5 minutes to gay beach.
Sunbathing: At poolside,

on common & private sun decks & at beach.
Smoking: Permitted outside only.
Pets: Not permitted.
Handicap Access: No.
Children: Not especially welcome.
Languages: English.
Your Host: Sharon, Ben & Alan.

MUDGEE

Parkview Guest House

Gay-Friendly ♀♂

Mudgee – Land of Wine, Honey and History

Built in 1859, *Parkview Guest House* exudes both charm and history with its eleven foot ceilings, wide verandah, beautiful fireplaces, superb woodwork and elegant hallways. The five guest rooms have private facilities, period furnishings and a small kitchen.

Most of Mudgee's fine shops, restaurants, coffee lounges and arts and crafts shops are within easy walking distance. The *Parkview's* central location makes it an excellent base from which to explore the nearby wineries, the historic towns of Gulgong, Hill End, Sofala and Hargraves, and take day trips to the Western Plains Zoo or Wellington Caves. For the truly active, Lake Windamere, south of Mudgee, is ideal for windsurfing, water skiing and boating.

Address: Cnr Douro & Market Sts, Mudgee, NSW 2850 Australia. Tel: (063) 72 4477.

Type: Guesthouse.
Clientele: Mostly straight clientele with a gay & lesbian following.
Transportation: Car is best. Also air & rail.
To Gay Bars: 3 hours to Sydney.
Rooms: 5 rooms with single or double beds.
Bathrooms: All private.
Meals: Full breakfast.

Complimentary: Tea, coffee, biscuits (cookies) & chocolates.
Dates Open: All year.
High Season: March to December.
Rates: AUD $60-$90.
Discounts: 10% to Sydney Gay & Lesbian Mardi Gras members.
Credit Cards: MC, VISA, Amex & Australian

Bankcard.
Rsv'tns: Required, but not necessary mid-week.
Parking: Adequate free off-street parking.
In-Room: Ceiling fans, kitchen, coffee/tea-making facilities & laundry service.
On-Premises: Laundry facilities.
Exercise/Health: Nearby

gym.
Swimming: Nearby pool.
Smoking: Permitted outside on verandah.
Pets: Permitted by arrangement.
Handicap Access: No.
Children: Welcome.
Languages: English.
Your Host: Paul

NORTHERN NEW SOUTH WALES

A Slice of Heaven Rural Retreat for Women

Women ♀

Spend a Few Days in Heaven!

A Slice of Heaven Rural Retreat for Women is a 12 acre permaculture paradise, peaceful, secluded and strategically situated on the Pacific Highway near Murwillumbah in Northern NSW. We offer bed and breakfast either in-house or in separate private accommodation. Gourmet dinners and lunches are available upon request. Facilities include a saltwater billabong-style pool and spa, tennis court, pool table, mini gym, large bath and bush walks. Tariffs are $70 per double and $50 per single. If you want to be pampered then our place is for you. For reservations call Carly on (066) 779276.

Address: Lot 3 Pacific Highway, Stokers Siding, Northern NSW 2484 Australia. Tel: (066) 779 276.

Type: Rural retreat B&B.
Clientele: Women only.
Transportation: Car is best. Free pick up for railway (Murwillumbah, NSW) or air (Coolangatta Airport/Gold Coast QLD).
To Gay Bars: 30 minutes by car.

Rooms: 2 rooms, 1 suite & 1 cottage with single or double beds.
Bathrooms: 2 private bath/toilets & 2 private shower/toilets.
Meals: Expanded continental breakfast.
Vegetarian: Readily

available upon request.
Complimentary: Tea, coffee, pre dinner drinks & liqueur coffee with other meals.
Dates Open: All year.
Rates: AUD $50 per single, AUD $70 per double.

Discounts: Stay 7 nights, pay for 6.
Rsv'tns: Required.
Reserve Through: Call direct.
Parking: Ample free off-street parking.
In-Room: Color TV, ceiling fans, refrigerator,

coffee & tea-making facilities.
On-Premises: TV lounge, meeting rooms & games room with VCR & video tape library.
Exercise/Health: Gym,

Jacuzzi, massage, tennis court, pool table & bush walks.
Swimming: Pool on premises.
Sunbathing: At poolside, on patio & common sun

decks.
Smoking: Permitted on verandahs & outside.
Pets: Not permitted.
Handicap Access: Yes.
Children: Not especially welcome.

Languages: English.
Your Host: Carly & Fae.

River Oaks B&B c/o Bill Schreurs

Gay/Lesbian ♂

Stay Gay in Byron Bay

Located 2-1/4 hours South of Brisbane and 1-1/4 hours from the Gold Coast is *River Oaks*. Accommodations range from budget to luxury and include continental breakfast. Evenings are very relaxing, beginning with the evening meal when you may dine either privately in your room, or with your hosts Bill and Bernard. Meals are prepared with fresh vegetables and herbs. The guesthouse is surrounded by five acres of rainforest and is near Tallow Beach and Kings Beach (a gay paradise). Day tours are available to the rainforest and national parks. A bus, which stops right next door, takes you to Byron Bay, a small, laid-back town only 3.5 km away. Byron Bay offers a relaxed atmosphere, beautiful beaches, no large developments and a variety of restaurants.
Address: 53-59 Broken Head Rd, Byron Bay, NSW 2481 Australia. Tel: (066) 85 86 79.

Type: B&B with restaurant.
Clientele: Mostly men with women welcome.
Transportation: Fly to Coolangatta, bus to Byron Bay. Free pick up from bus or train.
Rooms: 1 room, 2 suites & 1 cottage with double, queen or bunk beds.
Bathrooms: Private & shared.
Meals: Continental breakfast. Dinners available on request from

AUD $12 for a 3 course dinner.
Vegetarian: Available at all times. Many restaurants in town.
Complimentary: Tea & coffee.
Dates Open: All year.
High Season: December, January, Easter.
Rates: AUD $15-$85 low season. AUD $25-$105 high season.
Credit Cards: MC, VISA & Bancard.
Rsv'tns: Recommended.

Reserve Through: Travel agent or call direct.
Parking: Ample free off-street parking.
In-Room: Color TV, VCR, video tape library, ceiling fans, refrigerator, coffee/tea-making facilities, room & maid service.
On-Premises: TV lounge, meeting rooms, fax & laundry facilities.
Exercise/Health: Nearby gym, Jacuzzi & massage.
Swimming: Ocean on premises.

Sunbathing: On the beach.
Nudity: Permitted in our forest.
Smoking: Permitted in all rooms.
Pets: Not permitted.
Handicap Access: No.
Children: Not especially welcome.
Languages: English.
Your Host: Bill.

Wheel Resort, The

Gay-Friendly ♀

Our Entire Environment is Wheelchair-Accessible!

The Wheel Resort is a bush retreat with a small group of luxury self-contained cabins designed by an award-winning architect and located on 6-1/2 acres of rainforest. Our entire environment is wheelchair accessible. Cabins have private bush views, and screened verandas. They are furnished with linen, microwave ovens, stoves, and TVs. Good quality beds assure sleeping comfort. The swimming pool is gas or solar heated to 30 degrees celsius all year. Most guests who stay at *The Wheel Resort* return for the privacy and quiet. Birdwatchers and nature lovers are very happy here.
Address: 39-51 Broken Head Rd, Byron Bay, NSW 2481 Australia. Tel: (066) 856 139, Fax: 858 754.

continued next page

Type: Cabins with recreation area.
Clientele: Mainly straight clientele with a lesbian following.
Transportation: Car is best, taxi available. Pick up from airport, bus, train, cost depends on mileage.
To Gay Bars: 1-1/2 hrs.
Rooms: 3 2-bdrm cabins sleeping 5-6 people, 3 1-bdroom cabins sleeping 1-3 people.
Bathrooms: All private.
Campsites: 4 tent sites with 1 toilet & shower,

cooking facilities & BBQ.
Meals: Can be arranged.
Complimentary: Tea & coffee in cabins.
Dates Open: All year.
High Season: Oct-Jan.
Rates: AUD $430-AUD $870 per week, AUD $75-AUD $180 per day.
Discounts: 5% discount for wheelchair customers depending on season.
Credit Cards: VISA, Bancard & Amex.
Rsv'tns: Required, but cabins also available on nightly basis.
Reserve Through: Travel

agent or call direct.
Minimum Stay: Required during holiday season.
Parking: Ample free off-street parking.
In-Room: Color TV, ceiling fans, kitchen, refrigerator, coffee & tea-making facilities.
On-Premises: Outdoor meeting area, laundry facilities.
Exercise/Health: Massage, spa with hoist.
Swimming: Pool on premises, nearby ocean beach, river, lake.
Sunbathing: At poolside

& on beach.
Nudity: Permitted at night in pool & anytime in spa.
Smoking: Permitted.
Pets: Dogs permitted with fee.
Handicap Access: Yes, totally wheelchair accessible.
Children: Permitted.
Languages: Australian English.
Your Host: Philippa & Jeanette.

SYDNEY

Barracks, The

Men ♂

If you want to stay only five minutes' walk from the gay bars of Oxford St., *The Barracks* is for you. Our renovated Victorian has six stylishly furnished guest bedrooms, and a large TV lounge with current reading material. Four rooms have either balconies or direct access to the courtyard. One of these has stunning city views, another has a private bathroom. Breakfast is served from 7:00 a.m. till noon, for the convenience of late risers. We run a clean, uncluttered guesthouse, which you will find a pleasant and comfortable base from which to discover Sydney.
Address: 164 B Bourke St, Darlinghurst, Sydney 2010 Australia. Tel: (02) 360-5823 or Fax: (02) 332-2769.

Type: Bed & breakfast guesthouse.
Clientele: Men only.
Transportation: Taxi to & from airport A$12-A$15.
To Gay Bars: Three blocks or a 5-minute walk.
Rooms: 6 rooms with single or queen beds.
Bathrooms: 1 private shower/toilet, 5 sinks. Shared: 3 showers, 1 bath, 1 toilet.

Meals: Continental breakfast.
Complimentary: Coffee, tea, fruit juice & fruit.
Dates Open: All year.
Rates: AUD $55-AUD $95.
Discounts: Seventh night free except Mardi Gras weekend.
Credit Cards: MC, VISA, Amex & Bancard.
Rsv'tns: Required.
Reserve Through: Travel agent or call direct.
Parking: Adequate off-

street parking.
In-Room: Ceiling fans & maid service.
On-Premises: TV lounge, laundry facilities, BBQ & private courtyard.
Exercise/Health: Nearby gym, sauna, weights, steam & massage.
Swimming: 5-minute walk to pool. Ocean beach 8 kms, harbor beach 3 kms.
Sunbathing: At the beach, on patio & private

sun decks.
Nudity: Permitted in the courtyard.
Smoking: Permitted in most of the house. Non-smoking rooms available.
Pets: Not permitted.
Handicap Access: Not wheelchair accessible.
Children: Not permitted.
Languages: English.

Governors On Fitzroy

Gay/Lesbian ♀♂

For Business or Pleasure, the Inn Place!

Governors On Fitzroy Bed & Breakfast Guest House will be your home in Sydney, whether you are travelling for pleasure or for business. Our quiet cul-de-sac is conveniently located in Fitzroy St., Surry Hills, half a mile from the centre of Sydney.

Governors On Fitzroy was established in 1987, with the refurbishment of a terrace-style house built in 1863. The original Victorian features have been restored, creating the ambiance of a bygone period combined with the comforts of today. Each of the six individually-decorated guest rooms has a special feel. Four rooms have queen-sized beds, two have doubles. Each room has a vanity basin, and there are two shared bathrooms in the house. The tariff includes a full, American-style cooked breakfast served in the dining room. Breakfast, here, is a time to share the tales of travelling and to gain information on the city's "must do's." Complimentary coffee and tea are available 24 hours. A lounge and TV rooms with piano, a private garden with spa and sun deck, telephone and fax are available for guests' use.

Restaurants and coffee shops abound within walking distance, the range including many ethnic varieties. Your hosts are always ready with suggestions and directions to the restaurant of your choice. Sydney beaches are an important part of the local lifestyle, and *Governors On Fitzroy* has easy access, by bus, to many ocean and harbour beaches. World-famous Bondi Beach is only twenty minutes by public transport. Many others are equally convenient.

Transportation from the airport to the inn can be by taxicab or airport bus. Both are inexpensive, the taxi being more convenient, as the closest bus stop is four blocks away. Your hosts, Tom and Phillip, both live on the property and are able to provide any traveller with information and tips on enjoying Sydney and making the most of your stay in Australia.

Address: 64 Fitzroy St, Surry Hills, NSW 2010 Australia. Tel: (02) 331 4652, Fax: (02) 361-5094.

Type: Bed & breakfast.
Clientele: Good mix of gays & lesbians.
Transportation: Taxi from airport approximately AUD $15.
To Gay Bars: 2 blocks to men's/women's bars.
Rooms: 6 rooms with double & queen beds.
Bathrooms: 5 private sinks, 2 shared bath/ shower/toilets & 2 shared toilets.

Meals: Full breakfast.
Vegetarian: Upon request.
Complimentary: Coffee, tea available 24 hours.
Dates Open: All year.
High Season: February-March, during Gay & Lesbian Mardi Gras.
Rates: Single AUD $75, double AUD $95.
Credit Cards: MC, VISA, Amex.
Rsv'tns: Recommended.

Reserve Through: Call direct.
Parking: Limited on-street parking.
In-Room: Maid service.
On-Premises: Meeting rooms, telephone, TV lounge.
Exercise/Health: Spa on premises. Nearby gym, sauna & massage.
Swimming: 20-min drive to ocean.
Sunbathing: On common

sun decks or ocean beach.
Nudity: Permitted in spa area.
Smoking: Permitted, but not in bedrooms.
Pets: Not permitted.
Handicap Access: No.
Children: Not permitted.
Languages: English.

IGTA agsla

Kirketon Hotel

Gay-Friendly ♀○♂

The Kirketon, with licensed cocktail bar and restaurant, is in a very central position, a few minutes from Rushcutters Bay, ten minutes from the Opera House, Showground Cricket Ground, Bondi Beach and Randwick Racecourse. It offers convenient, around-the-corner proximity to the vibrant life of Kings Cross, and is right on a bus route to the city, the beaches and the airport. Sydney's beaches are a 20-minute drive from the hotel. Tea- and coffee-making facilities are provided in each room.

Address: 229-231 Darlinghurst Rd, Kings Cross 2010, Sydney, NSW Australia. Tel: (02) 360 4333 or Fax: (02) 360 4333.

Type: Bed & breakfast hotel with restaurant.
Clientele: Mostly straight clientele with a gay & lesbian following.
Transportation: Airport bus to door AUD $5.00.
To Gay Bars: 5-min. walk to gay bars.
Rooms: 63 rooms with single, bunk or double beds.
Bathrooms: Private: 18 baths, 45 sink only. Shared: 12 baths, 6 toilet only.

Meals: Continental breakfast.
Vegetarian: Available at restaurant.
Complimentary: Tea & coffee.
Dates Open: All year.
Rates: AUD $38.50-$105.
Discounts: Weekly rates, airline & travel agents.
Credit Cards: MC, VISA, Amex, Diners, Bankcard & Eurocard.
Rsv'tns: Required. Walk-ins OK if space available.
Reserve Through: Fax to

360 4333. Travel agent or call direct.
Parking: On-street parking at rear of building, covered pay parking 3 blocks away.
In-Room: Color TV, telephone, refrigerator & coffee/tea-making facilities.
On-Premises: Small meeting room.
Exercise/Health: 2 blocks to city gym & Oxford Gym.
Swimming: Nearby pool

& beach or Bondi Beach 20 minutes by train.
Sunbathing: At the beach.
Nudity: Lady Jane (nude) Beach is nearby.
Smoking: Permitted without restrictions.
Pets: Not permitted.
Handicap Access: Yes, from rear of building.
Children: Welcomed.
Languages: English, French & German.

Medina on Crown

Gay-friendly ♀○♂

Your Oasis of Luxury in the Middle of the City

The new five-star *Medina on Crown* is an ideal alternative for business executives, offering a range of competitively-priced one- and two-bedroom apartments in the heart of Sydney. Developed with an emphasis on the needs of business people, the *Medina on Crown's* executive apartments provide comfortable

Medina
EXECUTIVE APARTMENTS

and spacious settings in which to relax and wind down.

Each apartment includes fully-equipped kitchen and laundry facilities, and also provides direct-dial STD/ISD telephone, fax and a full range of business services. Many apartments offer wonderful views of the city and all feature ensuite bathrooms in each bedroom, enabling business people to share an apartment and cut costs. Women executives will appreciate the benefits of inviting business associates and friends to their apartment without the awkwardness of having guests in their bedroom. They may also dine in the privacy of their apartments, thus avoiding any problems caused by dining out alone.

The *Medina on Crown's* valet service can order in grocery and liquor supplies and will also pre-order food and beverages prior to guests' arrival. A charge-back facility enables guests to dine at any of 13 restaurants in the vicinity, and a complimentary shuttle service provides transport to various parts of the city. Our full residential conference facilities cater for groups up to 130 people and are specially designed for meetings, training seminars, fashion shows, product launches and exhibitions, and cocktail parties. We also provide standard conferencing equipment with added requirements, including secretarial, typing, fax and photocopying, available on request. Facilities also include a large outdoor pool and barbeque area, as well as a fully-equipped gym with spa, sauna and a rooftop tennis court. **Address: 359 Crown St, Surry Hills, Sydney, NSW 2010 Australia. Tel: (02) 360 6666, Fax: (02) 361 5965.**

Type: Five-star serviced apartments with restaurant.
Clientele: Mostly hetero with a gay & lesbian following.
Transportation: Taxi (AUD $30), or airport bus to Wynyard then taxi.
To Gay Bars: One block or 10-minute walk.
Rooms: 84 apartments with single, double or queen beds.

Bathrooms: All private.
Vegetarian: Available in restaurant on premises.
Dates Open: All year.
High Season: Sydney Gay Mardi Gras (Jan/Feb).
Credit Cards: MC, VISA, Amex & Diners.
Rsv'tns: Required.
Reserve Through: Travel agent or call direct.
Parking: Ample free underground parking with security.

In-Room: Telephone, color TV, VCR, AC, kitchen with microwave, refrigerator, coffee & tea-making facilities, maid & laundry service.
On-Premises: Meeting rooms, business services.
Exercise/Health: Gym, weights, Jacuzzi, sauna, massage, tennis, beauty/massage/health parlor.
Swimming: Pool on premises.

Sunbathing: Poolside and on rooftop tennis court.
Smoking: Permitted without restriction. Non-smoking rooms available.
Pets: Not permitted.
Handicap Access: Yes.
Children: Welcomed.
Languages: English, Chinese, Malay.
Your Host: Sue.

a💧lta

Observatory Hotel, The

Gay-Friendly ♀♂

Five-Star Luxury Tailored to the Individual

Part of the distinctive collection of Orient-Express Hotels, *The Observatory* is Sydney's most personal hotel, providing every conceivable luxury in the style of a period Australian home. Its 100 luxurious guest rooms feature CD's, video and marble bathrooms. The private Drawing Room, Globe Bar, restaurants and Health and Leisure Club offer a relaxed atmosphere ideal for both business and pleasure. Located just minutes from the CBD, *The Observatory* has also established a fine reputation as a conference venue. **Address: 89-113 Kent St, Sydney, NSW 2000 Australia. Tel: (02) 256 2222, Fax: (02) 256 2233.**

Type: Hotel with restaurant, bar, gift shop & health & leisure club.
Clientele: Mostly straight clientele with a gay & lesbian following.
Transportation: Bus, taxi or train. Pick up from airport in limousine, one way AUD $45 (domestic)-AUD $55 (international).
To Gay Bars: 30-minute walk or 10-minute drive.
Rooms: 75 rooms, 21 suites & 4 handicap-accessible rooms with single, double, queen or king beds.
Bathrooms: All private

full baths.
Vegetarian: Available upon request. 10 minutes to vegetarian restaurants.
Complimentary: Mineral water upon turndown.
Dates Open: All year.
High Season: Feb-Mar, Oct-Nov.
Rates: From AUD $265.
Discounts: Corporate & contract rates negotiable with Director of Sales.
Credit Cards: MC, VISA, Amex, Diners, Bancard & JCB.
Rsv'tns: Required.
Reserve Through: Travel

agent or call direct.
Parking: Limited covered parking, AUD $15 per day per car.
In-Room: Color cable TV, VCR, video tape library (concierge), AC, telephone, refrigerator, room, maid & laundry service. Coffee/tea-making facilities in suites.
On-Premises: Meeting rooms & secretarial services.
Exercise/Health: Gym, weights, Jacuzzi, sauna, steam, massage & flotation tank on premises. Nearby health club.

Swimming: Pool on New South WalesNew South Walespremises. Pool & ocean nearby.
Sunbathing: On private sun decks & at the beach.
Smoking: Permitted except in 1 restaurant & on non-smoking floor.
Pets: Not permitted.
Handicap Access: Yes.
Children: Welcome.
Languages: English, French, basic Japanese & Italian.
Your Host: Patrick & Marianne.

IGTA a💧lta

Sullivans Hotel

Gay-Friendly ♀♂

Do Sydney, Stay Sullivans

Sullivans is a small, stylish hotel with a delightful garden courtyard and an intimate atmosphere. It is close to all the major attractions and excellent shops and restaurants.

Address: 21 Oxford St, Paddington, Sydney NSW 2021 Australia. Tel: (61-2) 361 0222, Fax: (61-2) 360 3735.

Type: Hotel with restaurant.
Clientele: Mostly hetero with a gay & lesbian following.
Transportation: Airport bus or taxi to door.
To Gay Bars: 1 block or a 2-minute walk.
Rooms: 66 rooms with single or queen beds.
Bathrooms: All private.
Vegetarian: Healthy vegetarian breakfast & several vegetarian restaurants nearby.
Complimentary: Evening chocolates, tea & coffee in room.
Dates Open: All year.
High Season: Summer and Mardi Gras (early March).
Rates: AUD $75-$85 per room all year.
Discounts: Weekly discounts, 10%.
Credit Cards: MC, VISA, Amex, Diners, Bancard & Eurocard.
Reserve Through: Travel agent or call direct.
Minimum Stay: 5 nights during Mardi Gras.

Parking: Ample free covered parking with security controlled access.
In-Room: Colour TV, video tape library, AC, telephone, tea/coffee-making facilities, refrigerator, maid & laundry service.
On-Premises: TV lounge, meeting rooms, laundry facilities, typing, fax & photocopying.
Exercise/Health: Bicycles. Nearby gym, weights, Jacuzzi, sauna, steam & massage.

Swimming: Pool on premises. Ocean nearby.
Sunbathing: At poolside.
Smoking: Permitted in rooms. Non-smoking rooms available.
Pets: Not permitted.
Handicap Access: No.
Children: Welcome. Family rooms available.
Languages: English, American, Greek, Japanese & Polish.
Your Host: Gavan & Annie.

QUEENSLAND

BRISBANE

Allender Apartments

Gay-Friendly ♀♂

Allender is a beautifully appointed apartment block in a safe area close to the downtown centre, venues, clubs, pubs, restaurants, shops, and taxis. Each spacious and clean apartment is tastefully furnished with ultra-modern decor, fully-equipped separate kitchens, self-controlled heat and air, huge full-length mirrored wardrobes, direct dial phones, television, and security door intercom. Washing and drying facilities are also available. As a small, owner-operated establishment, we provide individual attention to your needs, as well as current tourist information.

Address: 3 Moreton St, New Farm, Brisbane, QLD Australia. Tel: (07) 358 5832.

Type: Apartments.
Clientele: Mostly hetero with a gay & lesbian following.
Transportation: Airport shuttle to downtown transit centre, then taxi, or taxi direct from airport (14km).
To Gay Bars: 1 mile, a 15-minute walk or 3-minute drive.
Rooms: 6 self-contained apartments with single, double or queen beds.
Bathrooms: All private.
Dates Open: All year.
High Season: Jan, Apr, Sep.
Rates: AUD $45-$50 single or double occupancy.
Credit Cards: MC & VISA.
Rsv'tns: Preferred.
Reserve Through: Travel agent or call direct.

Minimum Stay: 3 day advance minimum or 1 or 2 days subject to availability.
Parking: Ample on-street parking.
In-Room: Color TV, AC, telephone, security door intercom, kitchen, refrigerator, coffee/tea-making facilities & maid service.
On-Premises: Laundry facilities.

Swimming: Nearby pool.
Sunbathing: At poolside.
Smoking: Permitted in rooms.
Pets: Not permitted.
Handicap Access: No.
Children: Children stay occasionally.
Languages: English.

Edward Lodge

Men ♂

Brisbane's Finest All-Male Guesthouse

Edward Lodge was built in the 1920's in a tudor style. The rooms are all large, comfortably furnished and serviced each day. The lounge/breakfast room opens on to the courtyard where a generous complimentary continental breakfast is served until midday. Amenities also include 24-hour tea/coffee-making facilities and a spa.

Edward Lodge, located in the cosmopolitan Brisbane suburb of New Farm, is close to gay venues, cafes and restaurants, and a range of shopping, transportation and entertainment facilities. A stay at **Edward Lodge** is a relaxing and friendly experience.
Address: 75 Sydney St, New Farm, Brisbane 4005 Australia. Tel: (61 7) 254 1078.

Type: Bed & breakfast guesthouse.
Clientele: Men only.
Transportation: Bus, ferry or taxi.
To Gay Bars: 2 km.
Rooms: 8 rooms with twin or queen beds.
Bathrooms: 4 private shower/toilets & 2 shared bath/shower/toilets.

Meals: Expanded continental breakfast.
Complimentary: Tea, coffee & juices.
Dates Open: All year.
High Season: Mid year.
Rates: AUD $50-AUD $60.
Discounts: 10% for groups & organizations.
Credit Cards: MC, VISA & Bancard.
Rsv'tns: Recommended.

Reserve Through: Travel agent or call direct.
Parking: Ample on-street parking.
In-Room: Telephone, ceiling fans & laundry service.
On-Premises: TV lounge.
Exercise/Health: Weights, Jacuzzi & sauna. Nearby gym.
Swimming: Nearby pool.

Nudity: Permitted in Jacuzzi & sauna.
Smoking: Non-smoking rooms available.
Pets: Not permitted.
Handicap Access: No.
Children: Not permitted.
Languages: English.
Your Host: Gary & Grant.

CAIRNS

Be Bee's Tropical Resort

Gay/Lesbian ♀♂

Australia's Gateway to the Tropics

Be Bee's Tropical Resort, located 5 minutes from the heart of Cairns City and all the gay venues and attractions in the region, provides a broad range of accommodation choices suiting any traveller's needs. The resort provides an extensive tour booking and rental car service, a la carte dining and personalised service in a relaxed tropical garden environment. Relaxing on enticing golden sand beaches, walking through lush tropical rainforests, snorkelling over the wonders of the Great Barrier Reef or riding the white water rapids is only the start of a memorable holiday in one of the most diverse and beautiful regions of the world.
Address: PO Box 120, Edge Hill, Cairns, F.N. QLD 4870 Australia. Tel: (61) (70) 321-677 or Fax: 536681.

Type: Mini-resort motel with a la carte restaurant.
Clientele: Good mix of gay men and women.
Transportation: Free pickup from airport, bus, ferry, train.
To Gay Bars: 4 km or 7 min. by car to gay bar open Wed, Fri & Sat.
Rooms: 10 rooms, 4 suites & 9 apartments with double beds.
Bathrooms: 4 private shower/toilets, 10 shared

bath/shower/toilets.
Meals: Continental breakfast.
Vegetarian: Available by request.
Complimentary: Tea & coffee.
Dates Open: All year.
Rates: Single AUD $55-$130, double $65-$130.
Credit Cards: MC, VISA, Amex.
Rsv'tns: Advisable.
Reserve Through: Travel agent or call direct.
Parking: Ample off-street

parking, some covered.
In-Room: Color TV, video tape library, AC, telephone, ceiling fans, kitchen, refrigerator, coffee/tea-making facilities, room, maid & laundry services.
On-Premises: A la carte restaurant, laundry, tour bookings.
Exercise/Health: Jacuzzi, massage available. Nearby gym.
Swimming: Pool on premises, ocean beach

nearby.
Sunbathing: At poolside or on nearby beach.
Nudity: Permitted in the Jacuzzi.
Smoking: No rules for smoking.
Pets: Not permitted.
Handicap Access: No.
Children: Not permitted.
Languages: English
Your Host: Jeff & Cheynne.

IGTA **aglta**

Turtle Cove Resort Cairns

Gay/Lesbian ♀♂

Come Out of Your Shell at Turtle Cove

Quite simply, *Turtle Cove* is the world's only totally gay resort with its own completely gay beach. It also happens to be the biggest and best gay resort in Australia. We are situated just 30 minutes north of Cairns, the tropical city at the gateway to some of the greatest natural wonders of the world, not the least of which is the Great Barrier Reef. Upon arrival at Cairns International Airport, we'll whisk you in one of our courtesy coaches along the spectacular Coral Sea coast road north to the resort. Your beachfront or garden unit, which will be serviced daily, will have queen-sized and single bed, en suite bathroom,

air-conditioning, ceiling fan, TV, in-house video, ISD phone, radio, refrigerator, coffee- and tea-making facilities. The resort is all yours, including our massive pool, sun deck, Jacuzzi, beach terrace, resort shop, restaurant and cocktail bar. All this, plus our own totally private 1/4-mile-long beach.

Your complimentary tropical continental breakfast buffet can be supplemented by a cooked breakfast. Lunch snacks are served on the beach terrace. After pre-dinner cocktails, a sumptuous a la carte dinner is served. On Saturday nights, after dinner we'll take you to the gay nightclub for a rage. Late brunch on Sunday allows you to sleep in. In the evening, we'll surprise you with a BBQ on the terrace. Visiting the Great Barrier Reef, the world heritage Daintree Rainforest, Cape Tribulation and the Kuranda railway are all musts. *Turtle Cove Resort* runs its own all-gay trips to the Daintree by bus and to the Barrier Reef on a private chartered yacht, a couple times a week. Day trips can be arranged at the resort and depart from our front door. *Turtle Cove* hire cars are available, too. Any visit to *Turtle Cove* will seem much too short after you have had a chance to sample local attractions, meet the local men and women and enjoy our excellent facilities. All this, and your own secluded all-gay beach, where you can swim safely year-round in the warm Coral Sea.

Address: Captain Cook Hwy, PO Box 158, Smithfield Cairns, Far North Queensland 4878 Australia. Tel: 61 70 591 800, Fax: 61 70 591 969.

Type: Beachfront resort with restaurant, bar & resort shop.
Clientele: Good mix of men & women.
Transportation: Bus from airport our front door. Free pick up from airport, RR or bus station, city hotel.
To Gay Bars: 35 minutes to Cairns gay bar. Bus

from resort Sat nights.
Rooms: 26 rooms with single, double or queen beds.
Bathrooms: All rooms have private showers & toilets.
Meals: Tropical & continental buffet breakfast.
Vegetarian: Available in our restaurant.
Complimentary: Tea &

coffee in rooms, airport transfers, welcome drink on arrival.
Dates Open: All year.
Rates: AUD $84-AUD $130. AUD $15 per night for 2nd person.
Discounts: To IGTA members & travel & tour agents.
Credit Cards: MC, VISA, Amex, Diners, Bancard.

Rsv'tns: Required.
Reserve Through: Travel agent or call direct.
Parking: Ample free off-street covered parking.
In-Room: Colour TV, AC, refrigerator, telephone, ceiling fans, coffee/tea-making facilities, room & maid service. Rooms serviced daily. In-house video, video tape library.

On-Premises: Meeting rooms, private dining rooms & laundry facilities.
Exercise/Health: Jacuzzi, massage, beach equipment, volleyball, gym & weights.

Swimming: Pool, beachfront & river swimming hole on premises.
Sunbathing: At poolside, on our patio, common sun decks & on the beach.
Nudity: Permitted

poolside & on the beach.
Smoking: Permitted without restrictions.
Pets: Not permitted.
Handicap Access: Yes. All single story with minimal steps.
Children: Not permitted.

Languages: English, Dutch, German & French.
Your Host: Bert & Michael.

IGTA **agita**

Witchencroft (write: Jenny Maclean)

Women ♀

Welcome to *Witchencroft,* a landscaped 5 acre organic farm, in a forested valley only an hour from Cairns. It is an ideal base for exploring the coast and its hinterland, the Great Barrier Reef and World Heritage tropical rainforest. Relax and enjoy a country lifestyle in the midst of a wide range of things to do and see. The guesthouse has 2 private double rooms overlooking bush gardens and providing you with modern kitchen and ensuite facilities. *Witchencroft* also offers four-wheel drive trips and bush walks that are well off the tourist track. Vegetarian meals are available on request.

Address: PO Box 685 Atherton 4883, Australia. Tel: (070) 91-2683.

Type: Guesthouse on a 5-acre organic farm.
Clientele: Women only.
Transportation: Free pickup from Atherton, bus from Cairns daily, best to hire car.
To Gay Bars: 90 kms to Cairns.
Rooms: 2 apartments with double beds.
Bathrooms: All private shower/toilets.
Campsites: Tent sites.

Meals: Self-cater or enjoy our vegetarian cuisine.
Vegetarian: Strictly vegetarian.
Complimentary: Tea, coffee & milk.
Dates Open: All year.
High Season: July, August.
Rates: Single AUD $30, double AUD $50.
Discounts: Garden work exchange.
Rsv'tns: Required.

Reserve Through: Call direct.
Minimum Stay: Two nights.
Parking: Ample parking.
In-Room: Color TV, ceiling fans, kitchen, refrigerator, coffee & tea-making facilities.
Exercise/Health: Bushwalks.
Swimming: 10 minutes to rivers & lakes.
Sunbathing: In the

garden.
Nudity: Permitted.
Smoking: Permitted outdoors.
Pets: Permitted with restrictions because of resident livestock.
Handicap Access: Yes.
Children: Permitted.
Languages: English.

NOOSA

Noosa Cove

Gay/Lesbian ♂

The Gay Beach Resort Capital of Australia

You'll be met at the airport or terminal by our Mercedes Benz, then whisked to *Noosa Cove,* a resort set in the most sought-after location in Noosa near Australia's best beach. Our location overlooking Noosa's fabulous national park, provides access to many natural coves and beaches, including the famous gay naturist beach, Alexandria Bay. Guests can indulge in physical activities, such as bushwalking, surfing, windsurfing, waterskiing, boating, fishing, sailing and swimming, or just enjoy sun-baking by the private pool. Apartments in a sub-tropical garden and pool setting have two bedrooms, sunny balcony, kitchen and colour TV with remote in the main bedroom. The gay nightclub and restaurant are situated 2 minutes' walk from your apartment.

Address: 82 Upper Hastings St, Noosa, Queensland 4567 Australia. Tel: (074) 492668.

Type: Holiday apartments & guesthouse.

Clientele: Mostly men with women welcome.

Transportation: Pick up from airport & bus.

continued next page

Queensland

To Gay Bars: 1 block or 400 yards. 3 minutes by foot or 1 minute by car.
Rooms: 3 spacious, fully self-contained apartments & 1-bedroom studio unit with queen beds.
Bathrooms: All private.
Vegetarian: At 43 beachside restaurants within a 3-minute walk.
Complimentary: Tea & coffee.
Dates Open: All year.

High Season: 1st 2 weeks of January & school & public holidays.
Rates: High season, AUD $70- $100 per night. Low season AUD $40-$65 per night. Guesthouse AUD $35 per night.
Credit Cards: VISA, Amex & Bancard.
Rsv'tns: Recommended.
Reserve Through: Travel agent or call direct.
Parking: Ample free off-street covered parking.

In-Room: Color TV, VCR, telephone, ceiling fans, coffee & tea-making facilities, kitchen, refrigerator & laundry service.
Exercise/Health: Gym & weights on premises. Nearby gym, weights, Jacuzzi/spa, sauna & massage.
Swimming: Pool in apartment complex. Nearby ocean & river.
Sunbathing: At poolside,

on private sun decks, or at the beach.
Nudity: Permitted at poolside or at the beach.
Smoking: Permitted.
Pets: Not permitted.
Handicap Access: 1 apartment on ground level.
Children: Not permitted.
Languages: English.
Your Host: Alan & Michael.

SOUTH AUSTRALIA

ADELAIDE

City Apartments

Gay-Friendly ♀♂

Your home away from home, *City Apartments,* provides downtown and suburban locations with a range of standards: Economy, Executive, Superior. Most apartments are townhouses offering very private and independent living. Local gay information is provided on request.

Address: 70 Glen Osmond Rd (office), Parkside, SA 5063 Australia. Tel: Toll-free: (008) 888-501, Fax: (618) 272-7371.

Type: Serviced townhouse & apartments.
Clientele: Mainly hetero clientele with a gay & lesbian following.
Transportation: Taxi (only 15 minutes).
To Gay Bars: 5 blocks, 1/2 mile. A 15-minute walk or 5-minute drive.
Rooms: 40 apartments with single or queen beds.
Bathrooms: All private bath/shower/toilet.
Meals: Continental

breakfast your 1st morning.
Vegetarian: Freely available.
Complimentary: Tea & coffee.
Dates Open: All year.
Rates: Economy AUD $70-$85, Executive AUD $90-$123, Superior AUD $145-$165.
Discounts: 5% 7 nights, 15% 30 nights, 20% 60 nights.
Credit Cards: MC, VISA, Amex, Diners, Bancard.
Rsv'tns: Preferred, 1 wk

in advance.
Reserve Through: Travel agent or call direct.
Minimum Stay: 3 nights.
Parking: Ample free covered parking.
In-Room: Color TV, telephone, AC, kitchen, refrigerator, dishwasher, microwave, private laundry facilities.
On-Premises: TV lounge, laundry facilities for guests.
Exercise/Health: Nearby gym, weights, Jacuzzi, sauna, steam &

massage.
Swimming: Pool is 10 min away, ocean beach is 20 min away.
Sunbathing: Apartments have private courtyards.
Nudity: 1 hour to nude beach.
Smoking: Permitted without restrictions.
Pets: Not permitted.
Handicap Access: No.
Children: Welcome.
Languages: English.
Your Host: Brian.

aglta

Greenways Apartments

Gay-Friendly ♀♂

Adelaide, our state capital, features traditional stone architecture and wide encircling parklands. This elegant city is situated near one of the world's most famous winegrowing districts and is host to the Australian Formula One Grand Prix. These features, combined with the picturesque backdrop of the Adelaide Hills, give Adelaide an atmosphere found nowhere else in Australia. South Australia was the first Australian state to legalize homosexuality. *Greenways* provides excellent, comparatively cheap accommodations in fully furnished, self-contained private apartments. It is situated near city center and gay venues. Hosts are gay-friendly and are willing to assist with local information and they especially welcome international travelers.

Address: 45 King William Rd, North Adelaide, SA 5006 Australia Tel: (08) 267 5903, Fax: (08) 267 1790.

Type: Holiday apartments.
Clientele: Mostly straight clientele with a gay & lesbian following.
Transportation: Taxi best from airport, bus or train station.
To Gay Bars: 1 mile to gay/lesbian bars.
Rooms: 24 apartments with single or double beds.

Bathrooms: All private.
Dates Open: All year.
Rates: 1-bdrm AUD $63, 2-bdrm AUD $90 & up, 3-bdrm AUD $130 & up.
Discounts: AUD $5/night on stays of 7 days or longer.
Credit Cards: MC, VISA, Bancard, Diners.
Rsv'tns: Required 1 month in advance.
Reserve Through: Travel

agent or call direct.
Minimum Stay: 3 days.
Parking: Ample free off-street parking.
In-Room: Telephone, kitchenette, refrigerator, weekly maid service, AC/heat, color TV.
On-Premises: Coin-operated laundry facilities.
Exercise/Health: Public gym, spa & sauna 3/4 mi.
Swimming: Public pool

3/4 mile, ocean 15 miles.
Sunbathing: At public pool, on ocean beach (nude beach 1 hour).
Smoking: Permitted without restrictions.
Pets: Not permitted.
Handicap Access: No.
Children: Permitted.
Languages: English, Dutch, Japanese.

Rochdale Accommodation

Gay/Lesbian ♀♂

Adelaide's only accommodation provider for gay men and women, *Rochdale* is a private, traditional bed and breakfast modelled on the small family-run B&B's of Ireland and the United Kingdom. The residence is a typical late '20's Adelaide residence, with spacious, well-appointed rooms and an air of understated elegance. Wood panelling is used extensively throughout the formal living areas and open fires warm the study, lounge and one of the guest rooms. The gardens provide areas suited to quiet, seclude relaxing, reading and alfresco dining. We are within strolling distance of shopping and restaurants, conveniently located for easy access to the city and Adelaide Hills and serviced with public transport.

Address: 349 Glen Osmond Rd, Glen Osmond, SA 5064 Australia. Tel: (08) 379 7498, Fax: (08) 379 2483.

Type: Bed & breakfast.
Clientele: Mostly gay & lesbian with some hetero clientele.
Transportation: Car or public transport from city centre. Free pick up (by arrangement only) from airport, bus or train.
To Gay Bars: 7 minutes by car.
Rooms: 3 rooms with queen or double beds.
Bathrooms: 2 private shower/toilets, 1 shared bath/shower/toilet.

Meals: Full breakfast. 3 course gourmet dinner & luncheon picnic hamper available at additional cost with prior arrangement.
Vegetarian: Avialable with prior arrangement.
Complimentary: Morning or afternoon tea upon arrival, tea & coffee, Port in rooms.
Dates Open: All year.
Rates: AUD $45 single, AUD $75 double, dinner B&B AUD $150 minimum

2 persons.
Credit Cards: MC, VISA, Amex, Diners & Australian Bancard.
Rsv'tns: Required.
Reserve Through: Travel agent or call direct.
Parking: Limited free off-street parking.
On-Premises: TV lounge, meeting rooms.
Exercise/Health: Nearby gym, weights, Jacuzzi, sauna, steam & massage.
Swimming: Nearby pool

& ocean.
Sunbathing: On the patio.
Smoking: Permitted outside only.
Pets: Not permitted.
Handicap Access: One bathroom is accessible.
Children: Adult-oriented accommodation.
Languages: English.
Your Host: Peter & Brian.

agta

VICTORIA

DAYLESFORD

Balconies, The

Gay/Lesbian ♀♂

Relax on the Balconies and Enjoy the View of Beautiful Lake Daylesford

Go for a peaceful stroll in the 3 acres of garden and feed the pet ducks. Relax by the beautiful log fire and be spoilt with freshly-brewed coffee and gourmet cakes. Stroll around Lake Daylesford, take a dip in the indoor heated pool or challenge another guest to a game of pool. *The Balconies* is in the heart of the mineral springs and central goldfields and Daylesford is Australia's largest gay-populated country town.

Address: 35 Perrins St, Daylesford 3460 Victoria Australia. Phone & Fax: (053) 481 322.

Type: Bed & breakfast with in-house dinner.
Clientele: Good mix of gays & lesbians.
Transportation: Car, train & bus. Free pick up from train & bus.
To Gay Bars: 3 blocks or a 10-minute walk to Friday-night only gay bar.
Rooms: 5 rooms with single or queen beds.
Bathrooms: 2 private shower/toilets. Others share.
Meals: Expanded conti-

nental breakfast.
Vegetarian: Can be arranged.
Complimentary: Tea, coffee & cake.
Dates Open: All year.
Rates: AUD $75-$125.
Discounts: Mid-week Sun to Thur. Full price 1st night & half price for each following night.
Credit Cards: MC, VISA & Bancard.
Rsv'tns: Required.
Reserve Through: Travel agent or call direct.

Parking: Free off-street parking.
In-Room: Coffee & tea-making facilities.
On-Premises: TV lounge, video library & laundry facilities.
Exercise/Health: Jacuzzi on premises, nearby massage.
Swimming: Heated indoor pool on premises. Nearby pool, river & lake.
Sunbathing: On the patio.
Nudity: Permitted in indoor pool room.

Smoking: Permitted in games room or on balconies. All bedrooms are non-smoking.
Pets: Not permitted.
Handicap Access: Yes.
Children: Not especially welcome.
Languages: English, Greek, Italian & French.
Your Host: Geof & Theo.

aglta

Villa Vita

Gay/Lesbian ♀

The Original Kingston Inn

Villa Vita is a lovingly restored Australian gold rush inn, set in the internationally renowned "gay" tourist centre of Victoria. Nestled in 2 acres of heritage garden, *Villa Vita* offers the peace and tranquillity of the inspirational Central Highlands area that abounds with mineral springs, forests, wildlife and historic gold rush towns and hamlets.

Our inn, with it's "Provençal" ambience, is close to Daylesford. This historic town is the home of many wonderful attractions, among them, galleries, antique markets, spa and health complexes, lakes, mountains and bush and deep rivers.

At *Villa Vita* you will enjoy the warmth of sophisticated country hospitality, the wonderful cooking of your hosts, Jan and Maggie, and their special indulgences designed to give you a holiday to remember.

From the sunset-light library to the tropical lushness of the conservatory with

its steaming hot tub, you will find your home away from home at *Villa Vita*.
TO OPEN 1995

Address: Main Road, Kingston, Victoria Australia Tel: (053) 483 642.

Type: Bed & breakfast.
Clientele: Mostly women with men welcome.
Transportation: Car from Melbourne or Tullamarine Int'l Airport. Free pick up from airport, train or bus.
To Gay Bars: 10 miles.
Rooms: 3 rooms & 1 cottage with queen beds.
Bathrooms: All private shower/toilets.
Meals: Buffet breakfast.
Vegetarian: Special dietary needs catered to. Health food stores in

nearby Daylesford.
Complimentary: Champagne in room on arrival.
Dates Open: All year.
Rates: AUD $75-$110 per double per night.
Discounts: Concession card holders, HIV+ women & extended stays (3 or more nights).
Credit Cards: VISA.
Rsv'tns: Required.
Reserve Through: Call direct.
Minimum Stay: 2 nights.
Parking: Ample off-street parking.

On-Premises: Meeting rooms, TV lounge, VCR, video tape library & laundry facilities.
Exercise/Health: Jacuzzi & massage on premises. Nearby gym, weights, Jacuzzi, sauna & massage.
Swimming: Nearby pool, river & lake.
Sunbathing: On private sun decks & patio.
Nudity: Permitted in the conservatory, by negotiation with other guests.
Smoking: Permitted in

lounge or dining area by negotiation with other guests.
Pets: Permitted. Outside Pet'O'Tel service on premises.
Handicap Access: No.
Children: Welcome by negotiation. Periods set aside for HIV+ guests with children.
Languages: English, French. (Japanese & German by negotiation).
Your Host: Jan & Maggie.

MELBOURNE

Cosmopolitan Motor Inn

Gay-Friendly ♀♂

St Kilda Beach is a lively 24-hour tourist precinct with a vibrant nightlife, street cafes, Melbourne's biggest fun park, craft markets, continental cake shops, and a sheltered sandy swimming beach with beachside eating facilities - all this and only 10 minutes from downtown Melbourne by the city's famous trams. The *Cosmopolitan Motor Inn* offers superb accommodation in a friendly, relaxed atmosphere. We are totally committed to hospitality of the highest standard and offer modern, spacious, standard-through-luxury suites with every amenity possible. From the moment of your reservation to your departure, we are there to ensure your stay at the *Cosmopolitan* is most enjoyable and memorable.

Address: 4-6 Carlisle St, St. Kilda, Victoria 3182 Australia. Tel: (03) 534-0781, Fax: (03) 534-8262.

Type: Hotel with restaurant, bar, & conference functions.
Clientele: Mainly straight with 20% gay/lesbian following.
Transportation: Taxi or bus from airport, Melbourne's famous trams from City Centre.
To Gay Bars: Many choices nearby.
Rooms: 10 singles, 30 doubles, 28 triples, 6 quads, 9 apartments.
Bathrooms: All private.
Vegetarian: At all times.

Complimentary: Tea & coffee & complimentary drink or entree in restaurant with each dinner order.
Dates Open: All year.
Rates: AUD $75-AUD $105.
Discounts: 10% for more than 7 days.
Credit Cards: MC, VISA, Amex, Diners, Bancard.
Rsv'tns: Required.
Reserve Through: Travel agent or call direct.
Parking: Ample free off-street covered parking.

In-Room: Color TV, AC, telephone, kitchen, refrigerator, maid, room & laundry service.
On-Premises: Meeting rooms, laundry facilities for guests, restaurant & cocktail bar, business services such as photocopying, facsimile, typing, & 24-hr reception.
Exercise/Health: Nearby gym, massage & steam available to guests, Jacuzzi available in room.
Swimming: Across the road at St. Kilda Beach.

Sunbathing: At the beach.
Smoking: Permitted everywhere except in designated non-smoking suites.
Pets: Not permitted.
Handicap Access: Yes.
Children: Permitted under parental control.
Languages: English & Dutch.

Fitzroy Stables

Gay/Lesbian ♀

Fitzroy Stables is a converted 19th-century brick stable in a courtyard setting in historic Fitzroy, 2km from the centre of Melbourne. We are just off Brunswick Street, well known for its street cafes, bars, restaurants, night clubs, galleries and Bohemian lifestyle.

The *Stables* is a fully self-contained and fully furnished apartment with accommodation consisting of lounge/dining room with lofty ceiling, exposed beams and open fire, modern kitchen and bathroom and mezzanine bedroom.

Relax in an enchanting, rustic environment just a minute from one of Melbourne's most famous tourist streets.

Address: 124 Victoria St, Fitzroy, Melbourne, Victoria 3065 Australia. Tel: (03) 415 1507.

Type: Fully furnished apartment.
Clientele: Mostly women with men welcome.
Transportation: Airport bus or city. Tram, taxi or walk to Fitzroy.
To Gay Bars: 6 blocks or 1 mile. A 5-minute walk or 2-minute drive.
Rooms: 1 apartment with double bed.
Bathrooms: 1 private shower/toilet.
Vegetarian: Vegetarian restaurants one block.
Complimentary: Fruit, herbal tea, tea, coffee, milk, orange juice & homemade muesli.
Dates Open: All year.
Rates: AUD $80 per double per night.
Discounts: Stay 6 nights, get 7th night free.
Rsv'tns: Required.
Reserve Through: Call direct.
Parking: Limited on-street parking.
In-Room: Color TV, ceiling fans, telephone, kitchen, refrigerator, coffee & tea-making facilities.
Exercise/Health: Nearby gym, weights, Jacuzzi, sauna, steam & massage.
Swimming: Nearby pool & river. 1 hour to ocean.
Nudity: 1 hour to nude beach.
Smoking: Permitted in courtyard garden.
Pets: Not permitted.
Handicap Access: No.
Children: Not especially welcome.
Languages: English.

agta

Laird O'Cockpen Hotel

Men ♂

Enjoy the Ambience

Stay at the *Laird* and enjoy top class accommodation in house or at our annex, Norwood. Built in 1888, just 3km from the C.B.D. (city centre), the hotel reflects the charm of Melbourne. All our rooms are serviced daily and our friendly staff are here to make you feel at home. *The Laird* music/video bar is the most popular gay mens' bar, perfect for socializing. Saturday nights we host "Bootscoot" and BBQ. Nuggets bar is home to the leather scene, with two clubs meeting weekly. Included in our low tariff is free entry to Club 80, Australia's most famous gay mens' club, and Peel dance bar is just a short walk away. You have all the facilities of a great city at your doorstep.

Address: 149 Gipps St, Collingwood 3067, Melbourne, Victoria Australia. Tel: (03) 417 2832, Fax: (03) 416 0474.

Type: Hotel with bar & beer garden.
Clientele: Men only.
Transportation: Taxi from the airport.
To Gay Bars: Men's bar on premises. Others one block away.
Rooms: 9 rooms with double or queen beds.
Bathrooms: Shared: 2 bath/showers, 1 shower & 3 toilets.
Meals: Continental breakfast.
Vegetarian: Vegetarian cafés & restaurants nearby.
Complimentary: Tea, coffee & juice.
Dates Open: All year.
Rates: AUD $55 per room.
Discounts: Weekly rate
AUD $330, for 7-night consecutive stay.
Credit Cards: MC, VISA, Amex, Diners Club, Bankcard.
Rsv'tns: Required.
Reserve Through: Call direct.
Parking: Adequate on-street parking.
On-Premises: TV lounge, laundry facilities, public
telephone, 2 bars with pool table, pinball, video games, beer garden.
Smoking: Permitted without restrictions.
Pets: Not permitted.
Handicap Access: No.
Children: Not permitted.
Languages: English.

Melbourne Guesthouse, The

Men ♂

Melbourne's Most Stylish and Comfortable Gay Accommodation

The Melbourne Guesthouse is 10 minutes via tram from the city, an ideal location for tourists or businessmen seeking stylish gay accommodation. Enjoy superbly appointed, centrally-heated rooms, a large living and dining area overlooking a landscaped garden, a fully appointed kitchen, luxurious bathrooms, full laundry facilities, telephone, off-street parking and BBQ facilities. Other amenities include TV, video and stereo. Continental breakfast, fresh fruit, tea and coffee are available 24 hours. We are close to gay venues in Prahran and St. Kilda and to Chapel Street shopping, cafes and restaurants.

Address: 26 Crimea St, St Kilda, Victoria 3182 Australia. Tel: (03) 510 4707.

Type: Guesthouse.
Clientele: Men only.
Transportation: Taxi from airport or airport bus to Spencer St Station, then taxi.
To Gay Bars: 1.5 km. A 20-minute walk or 5-minute drive.
Rooms: 6 rooms with double or queen beds.
Bathrooms: Private: 1 shower/toilet, 1 sink.

Shared: 1 tub, 2 showers, 2 WCs.
Meals: Continental breakfast.
Complimentary: Tea, coffee, fruit juice, biscuits. Cup-a-soups in winter.
Dates Open: All year.
High Season: December-March.
Rates: AUD $55-$75.
Credit Cards: MC, VISA & Bancard.

Rsv'tns: Required.
Reserve Through: Travel agent or call direct.
Parking: Adequate free off-street parking (3 vehicle spaces).
In-Room: Refrigerator & maid service.
On-Premises: TV lounge, telephone & laundry facilities.
Swimming: Nearby pool & Port Phillip Bay.

Sunbathing: On garden lawn or at the beach.
Smoking: Permitted outside only.
Pets: Not permitted.
Handicap Access: No.
Children: Not especially welcome.
Languages: English.
Your Host: Garry & Lindsay.

One Sixty-Three Drummond Street

Gay/Lesbian ♂

163 Drummond Street is a magnificent Victorian mansion, authentically renovated, retaining all its original features including marble fireplaces, tiled entrance hall with Persian runners and winding cedar staircase. A 19th-century elegance together with 20th-century comforts and amenities distinguishes this guesthouse. The atmosphere is warm; one where friends, newcomers and their guests can relax in the communal living and dining areas furnished with antiques and artwork. We are committed to informality with 24 hour access to all facilities.

163 is located two minutes away from Melbourne's famous Italian restaurant Mecca, Lygon Street, the theaters, Chinatown and the central business center. We overlook the majestic gardens and The Exhibition Building.

Address: 163 Drummond Street, Carlton, Melbourne 3053 Australia Tel: (61-3) 663 3081.

Type: Guesthouse.
Clientele: Mostly men with women welcome.
Transportation: Taxi from airport.
To Gay Bars: A 20-minute walk or 5-minute drive.
Rooms: 7 rooms with single, double or queen beds.
Bathrooms: 4 private sinks only. 2 shared bath/shower/toilets, 1 shared WC only.
Meals: Expanded conti-

nental breakfast, tea or coffee is 24 hours, self-service.
Vegetarian: 5-minute walk to a vegetarian restaurant.
Complimentary: Beverages, self-service 24 hours in dining room. Confectionery, biscuits & fruit.
Dates Open: All year.
High Season: Summer & autumn.
Rates: AUD $35-$60.
Discounts: Weekly rates.

Credit Cards: MC, VISA & Bancard.
Rsv'tns: Required.
Reserve Through: Call direct.
Parking: Adequate on-street parking. 2-minute walk to 24hr covered car park.
In-Room: Color TV, ceiling fans & maid service.
On-Premises: TV lounge & laundry facilities.
Exercise/Health: Nearby gym, weights, Jacuzzi, sauna, steam &

massage.
Swimming: Nearby pool.
Sunbathing: On the patio.
Smoking: Permitted in designated areas (not TV lounge). Non-smoking rooms available.
Pets: Not permitted.
Handicap Access: No.
Children: Not especially welcome.
Languages: English.
Your Host: Ian.

NEWBURY

Blue Mount B&B

Gay-Friendly 50/50 ♀♂

Our B&B, *Blue Mount*, with queen-sized bed, en suite, TV and video library, nestles in a private cottage garden. Secluded amidst the beauty of the Central Highlands, and surrounded by tranquil views, it is close to Blackwood, Daylesford, Mineral Spas, good food, horseriding, wineries and more! It is 75 minutes from GPO Melbourne, Victoria. A lovely place to explore, or relax and do nothing!!

Address: Kearneys Rd Newbury (Trentham), Victoria 3458 Australia Tel: (054) 241 296.

Type: Bed & breakfast cottage with nearby shops.
Clientele: 50% gay & lesbian & 50% hetero.
Transportation: Car is best, but train & bus available from Melbourne & Ballarat.
To Gay Bars: 10 miles or a 20-minute drive to bar in Daylesford.
Rooms: 1 room & 1 cottage with queen beds.
Bathrooms: 2 private bath/toilets & 2 privated

shower/toilets.
Meals: Full breakfast. Other meals on request & availability.
Vegetarian: Available on premises & nearby.
Complimentary: Chocolates & cakes upon arrival. Tea (Ceylon, decaf, herbal), coffee, cheese, biscuits & fruits.
Dates Open: All year.
High Season: Winter (Mar-Aug).
Rates: AUD $75-$90 for double.

Discounts: Weekend packages (2 or more nights). $75 per night per double.
Rsv'tns: Required, depending on time of year.
Reserve Through: Travel agent or call direct.
Parking: Ample free off-street parking.
In-Room: Color TV, VCR, coffee/tea-making facilities, kitchenette, refrigerator & laundry service.
Exercise/Health: Nearby gym, weights, Jacuzzi,

sauna & massage.
Swimming: Nearby pool, river & lake.
Sunbathing: In the private garden.
Smoking: Permitted, but prefer guests to smoke outside the rooms.
Pets: Not permitted.
Handicap Access: Cottage accessible. Steps to B&B cause difficulties for wheelchairs.
Children: Welcome.
Languages: English.
Your Host: Kerry & Clive.

WARRNAMBOOL

Woodfield Cottage

Gay/Lesbian ♀

Experience the Alternative Bed and Breakfast

Woodfield Cottage offers relaxing, comfortable accommodation in a quiet rural setting. Only minutes from Warrnambool, we are ideally located for you to explore the district's many attractions such as Grampians Port Dairy, the Great Ocean Road and Shipwreck Coast. We serve hearty, country-style breakfasts and provide other meals by arrangement.

Address: Towerhill Road, Bushfield via Warrnambool, Victoria 3281 Australia. Tel: (018) 528 167.

Type: Bed & breakfast.
Clientele: Mostly women with men welcome.
Transportation: Car is best. Free pick up from train.
To Gay Bars: 3-hour drive to Melbourne.
Rooms: 3 rooms with double beds.
Bathrooms: Shared bath/shower/toilet.
Meals: Full breakfast.
Vegetarian: Available

upon request. Vegetarian food nearby.
Complimentary: Tea & coffee, mints on pillow, morning & afternoon teas.
Dates Open: All year.
Rates: AUD $40 per single, AUD $75 per double.
Credit Cards: VISA & Bancard.
Rsv'tns: Required.
Reserve Through: Call

direct.
Parking: Free off-street parking.
In-Room: Coffee & tea-making facilities.
On-Premises: TV lounge & laundry facilities.
Exercise/Health: Nearby gym, weights, Jacuzzi, sauna & massage.
Swimming: Nearby pool, ocean & river.
Sunbathing: On the patio & at the beach.

Smoking: Permitted outside only.
Pets: Not permitted.
Handicap Access: Yes. Wheelchair accessible.
Children: Not especially welcome.
Languages: English only.
Your Host: Linda & Irene.

WESTERN AUSTRALIA

PERTH

Court Hotel

Gay/Lesbian ♀♂

Come Sleep With Us

The *Court Hotel* is centrally situated to city shopping, transport, and all gay venues. It also has a gay bar on the premises. Built in 1880, the hotel combines a friendly atmosphere with old world charm.

Address: 50 Beaufort St, Perth WA 6000 Australia. Tel: (09) 328 5292, Fax: (09) 227 1570.

Type: Hotel with restaurant & bar.
Clientele: Mostly gay & lesbian with some hetero clientele.
Transportation: Train, airport bus, or taxi.
To Gay Bars: Gay bar on premises. 5 minute walk to all other gay venues.
Rooms: 10 singles & 10 doubles.
Bathrooms: 2 private, others share.
Vegetarian: Good vegetarian restaurant nearby.
Complimentary: Tea & coffee.
Dates Open: All year.
High Season: Dec-May.
Rates: AUD $30-$50.
Discounts: 10% off stays of more than 1 week.
Reserve Through: Call direct.
Parking: Limited free off-street parking.
On-Premises: TV lounge, meeting rooms & laundry facilities.
Exercise/Health: Sauna & gym nearby.
Swimming: River & pool 5 min. 20 min to ocean.
Sunbathing: On the roof, common sun decks, & nearby beach.
Smoking: Permitted without restrictions.
Pets: Not permitted.
Handicap Access: No.
Children: Not permitted.
Languages: English.

Penny's By The Sea

Gay/Lesbian ♀♂

Five minutes from the Indian Ocean and not far from the Karri Forests, is *Penny's By the Sea,* a bed and breakfast with friendly atmosphere and a host who is very knowledgeable about this interesting area. Lodgings are clean and comfortable, and breakfast is made from fresh, local produce. Join us in Western Australia on the Sunset Coast.

Address: PO Box 208, Scarborough, Sunset Coast, WA 6019 Australia. Tel: (09) 341-1411, Fax: (09) 245-1073, Mobile: (018) 1969 30.

Type: Bed & breakfast guesthouse.
Clientele: Good mix of gays & lesbians.
Transportation: Car or taxi.
Rooms: 2 rooms, 1 suite & 1 apartment with single, double or queen beds.
Bathrooms: 1 shared bath/shower/toilet & 1 shared shower.
Meals: Continental breakfast, bowl of fresh fruit.
Vegetarian: Restaurant within walking distance.
Complimentary: Mints on pillows, fresh fruit.
Dates Open: All year.
High Season: November-April.
Rates: Daily rates $40-$100. Rates negotiable.
Discounts: Seasonal rates.
Credit Cards: MC, VISA & Bancard.
Rsv'tns: Required.
Reserve Through: Call direct.
Minimum Stay: 2 nights.
Parking: Adequate off-street parking.
In-Room: Color TV, VCR, videos, telephone, kitchen, refrigerator, coffee & tea-making facilities & room service.
On-Premises: TV lounge & laundry facilities.
Exercise/Health: VictoriaVictoriaNearby gym, weights, Jacuzzi, sauna, steam & massage.
Swimming: Nearby pool & ocean.
Sunbathing: On the beach.
Nudity: Permitted.
Smoking: Permitted in lounge. Non-smoking rooms available.
Pets: Not permitted.
Handicap Access: No.
Children: Not especially welcomed.
Languages: English.

aglta

Swanbourne Guest House

Gay/Lesbian ♂

This four-star RAC-rated private residence, ten minutes outside central Perth, is set in lush gardens overlooking trees and Australian flora. A rear patio offers privacy for nude sunbathing. Golf, tennis and swimming pool are within walking distance. On our complimentary bikes, you can make the gay beach in 10 minutes. Claremont's yuppie, cosmopolitan atmosphere, restaurants, bars and shops, all top class, are also close by. The *Swanbourne's* cool, Mediterranean interior and large, exquisitely-appointed rooms make it a perfect haven from stressful, hectic city living, whilst offering all the amenities and activities a cosmopolitan city has to offer.

Address: 5 Myera St Swanbourne, Perth WA 6010 Australia. Tel: (09) 383 1981, mobile (018) 902 107.

Type: Bed & breakfast guesthouse.
Clientele: Mostly gay men with gay women welcome.
Transportation: Airport bus to Perth, then taxi. Free pick up from train or bus.
To Gay Bars: 4 miles or 10 minutes by car.
Rooms: 4 rooms, 1 suite, & 1 apartment with single, double, queen beds or king.
Bathrooms: 3 private. Shared: 2 bathtubs, 2 showers & 1 full bath.

Meals: Continental breakfast with fresh fruit when in season.
Vegetarian: Vegetarian food nearby.
Complimentary: Tea, coffee, mints on pillows & fresh flowers daily.
Dates Open: All year.
High Season: Nov-Apr.
Rates: AUD $55-AUD $75.
Discounts: One day free for weekly stays.
Credit Cards: MC, VISA & Bancard.
Rsv'tns: Required.
Reserve Through: Call direct.

Minimum Stay: 2 nights.
Parking: Ample free off-street covered parking.
In-Room: Color TV, VCR, video tape library, telephone, ceiling fans, kitchen, refrigerator, coffee & tea-making facilities, room & laundry service.
On-Premises: Meeting rooms, TV lounge, laundry facilities, courtyard with BBQ & free bicycles. Cars for hire.
Exercise/Health: Gym, weights on premises. Nearby Jacuzzi, sauna,

steam & massage.
Swimming: Nearby pool, ocean, river, lake & beach.
Sunbathing: On private & common sun decks, patio, lawn or at beach.
Nudity: Permitted on back patio.
Smoking: Permitted outside.
Pets: Not permitted.
Handicap Access: No.
Children: Not especially welcome.
Languages: English.

Treefern Retreat

Men ♂

Undoubtedly Perth's Finest, Setting the Standard for Others to Follow

Treefern Retreat is Perth's only exclusively gay premiere guesthouse. We would like you to feel at home, relax and enjoy yourselves while on holiday. With this in mind, we offer you great friendly hospitality in warm, private, cozy and spacious surroundings. Enjoy our generous breakfast, cool off in the secluded pool, soak those sore muscles in the Jacuzzi under the stars and relax in a sub-tropical setting with tea and scones. Enjoy your sumptuous dinner, cooked by your host, a highly qualified chef. Treat yourself to our homey, hospitable establishment at *Treefern Retreat*.

Address: 24 Ashton Rise, Woodvale, WA 6026 Australia. Phone & Fax: (09) 309 2982.

Type: Bed & breakfast guesthouse with dining room.
Clientele: Men only.
Transportation: Train or bus. Free airport transfers.
To Gay Bars: 20 km.
Rooms: 3 rooms with queen beds.
Bathrooms: 1 shower/bath/toilet.
Meals: Full breakfast. Optional 4-5 course sumptuous dinner AUD $20.

Complimentary: Tea, coffee, afternoon scones, bottle of champagne.
Dates Open: All year.
High Season: Nov to Apr.
Rates: Summer AUD $45(s)-$60(d). Winter (specials available) from AUD $30(s)-$50(d).
Discounts: 7 nights for the price of 6.
Rsv'tns: Required.
Reserve Through: Travel agent or call direct.

Parking: Adequate free off-street parking.
In-Room: Room service.
On-Premises: TV lounge, extensive video library, meeting room, private dining room & laundry facilities.
Exercise/Health: Weights & Jacuzzi. Free use of squash, tennis racquets & golf clubs at nearby facility.
Swimming: Pool on pre-

mises, 4 km to gay beach.
Sunbathing: At poolside, Jacuzzi & on patio.
Smoking: Permitted outside. Non-smoking sleeping room available.
Pets: Not permitted.
Handicap Access: No.
Children: Not especially welcome.
Languages: English.
Your Host: Lloyd.

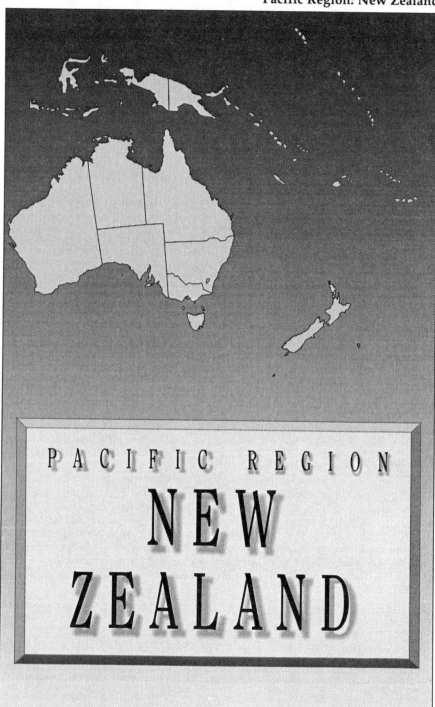

NORTH ISLAND

AUCKLAND

Aspen Lodge

Gay-Friendly ♀♂

Pink on the Outside, Warm & Inviting on the Inside

Aspen Lodge is a bed & breakfast hotel, offering you comfortable, quiet accommodation in a friendly, homey atmosphere. The central downtown location puts you within a 5-minute walk of City Centre, restaurants, bus depots, railway station, ferry terminal, and airport bus service. In addition to providing guests with a good, healthy breakfast, beverage-making facilities, laundry facilities, and a TV lounge, we can arrange rental cars, campervans, and sightseeing tours.
Address: 62 Emily Place Auckland, North Island New Zealand. Tel: (09) 379-6698, Fax: 3777-625.

Type: Bed & breakfast.
Clientele: Mostly straight clientele with a gay & lesbian following.
Transportation: Supershuttle from airport to door NZ $9 per person. Pick up from train, bus, central city locations.
To Gay Bars: 5-minute walk to gay bar.
Rooms: 14 singles, 6 doubles & 6 twins.
Bathrooms: 5 shared showers & 6 shared toilets.
Meals: Continental breakfast.
Vegetarian: 5-minute walk.
Complimentary: Tea & coffee.
Dates Open: All year.
High Season: November-May.
Rates: Single NZ $45, twin NZ $65.
Discounts: Winter, June through Oct. Yearly win-ter specials available.
Credit Cards: MC, VISA, Amex, Diners & JBC.
Rsv'tns: Required, especially in high season.
Reserve Through: Travel agent or call direct.
Parking: Limited on-street pay parking. 1st come, first served.
In-Room: Maid & laundry service.
On-Premises: TV lounge, laundry facilities, public telephones.
Exercise/Health: 5 min to nearby gym, weights, sauna, steam, massage.
Swimming: 5 min to nearby pool.
Sunbathing: On the patio.
Smoking: Permitted in public areas, rooms are non-smoking.
Pets: Not permitted.
Handicap Access: No.
Children: Permitted.
Languages: English.

Bavaria Bed & Breakfast Hotel

Gay-Friendly ♀♂

Friendly First-Class Service

Bavaria Bed & Breakfast Hotel is a small hotel in a serene, residential environment on the western slopes of Mount Eden, 3 km from the city centre. We have spacious bedrooms, all with private facilities, some with balcony. The TV/Guest Lounge opens onto a private sun deck and a delightful European breakfast is served in the sunny breakfast area, overlooking our private gardens. Restaurants, bus stop, bank and shops are within walking distance. For the more energetic, a beautiful scenic walk leads up to Mt. Eden's summit, an extinct volcano.
Address: 83 Valley Rd, Mount Eden, Auckland, New Zealand. Tel: (09) 6389 641, Fax: (09) 6389 665.

Type: Bed & breakfast.
Clientele: Mostly hetero with a gay & lesbian following.
Transportation: Airport shuttle.
Rooms: 4 singles, 7 doubles.
Bathrooms: All private.
Meals: Expanded European breakfast.
Vegetarian: We are very flexible & can provide Swiss-style breakfast, too.
Complimentary: Coffee, tea & cookies throughout the day.
Dates Open: All year.
High Season: October to April.
Rates: Single NZ $59, double NZ $89.
Credit Cards: MC, VISA, Amex, Bancard.
Rsv'tns: Suggested.
Reserve Through: Travel agent or call direct.
Parking: Ample off-street parking.
In-Room: Room service, some suites have balconies.
On-Premises: TV lounge & guest dining room.
Swimming: Pool within walking distance.
Sunbathing: On private sun deck.
Smoking: Not permitted.
Pets: Not permitted.
Handicap Access: No.
Children: Permitted.
Languages: English, German.

Dryden Lodge

Gay-Friendly 50/50 ♀♂

Dryden Lodge is a centrally-located hotel with a restaurant, gymnasium, game room, and modern accommodations. The owner is a New Zealand leatherman and very involved in the Auckland gay community.

Address: 27-31 Dryden St, Auckland, New Zealand. Tel: (09) 3780 892, Fax: 3781 282.

Type: Hotel with restaurant, gymnasium, game room, & laundry.
Clientele: 50% gay & lesbian & 50% hetero clientele.
Transportation: Free pick up from airport, bus, & train.
To Gay Bars: 5 min drive.
Rooms: 23 singles, 18 doubles, 2 triples, 2 quads.
Bathrooms: 6 private, 6 shared baths.

Meals: Continental breakfast.
Complimentary: Tea & coffee.
Dates Open: All year.
High Season: January-April.
Rates: Singles NZ $39, doubles NZ $59, rooms with private bathrooms NZ $69.
Discounts: 20% for more than a week.
Credit Cards: MC, VISA, Amex, Diners, Bancard.

Rsv'tns: Required.
Reserve Through: Travel agent or call direct.
Parking: Ample free off-street parking.
In-Room: Color TV, radio, telephone, room & laundry service, male maid service.
On-Premises: Meeting rooms, TV lounge, laundry facilities for guests, spacious grounds.
Exercise/Health: Gym with weights on pre-

mises.
Sunbathing: On the roof, private sun decks, in the gardens.
Smoking: Permitted, non-smoking rooms available.
Pets: Not permitted.
Handicap Access: Yes.
Children: Not encouraged.
Languages: English.
Your Host: Peter & Brett.

Remuera House

Gay-Friendly 50/50 ♀♂

For connoisseurs of olde-worlde character, *Remuera House*, built in 1901, is worth a stay and is full of interesting memorabilia. The dining room, for instance, features paintings, antiques and collectibles. Compare my price including a breakfast of cereals, bacon and eggs. Situated in an exclusive area, *Remuera House* is within walking distance to buses, shops, restaurants, take-outs and an extinct volcano. Larger than Britain, New Zealand is a motoring country. As a local history author, I can help you plan your vacation. Inexpensive hire cars can be arranged and there is easy access to and from the airport.

Address: 500 Remuera Rd, Remuera, Auckland, North Island New Zealand. Tel: (09) 524-7794.

Type: Bed & breakfast guesthouse.
Clientele: 50% gay & lesbian & 50% straight clientele.
Transportation: Airport shuttle buses to door, or bus from station.
To Gay Bars: 10 minutes by car or 15 minutes by bus to gay/lesbian bars.
Rooms: 9 rooms with single or double beds.
Bathrooms: 3 shared

showers & 3 shared toilets.
Meals: Continental and traditional cooked breakfast.
Complimentary: Tea & coffee making facilities in TV lounge.
Dates Open: All year.
High Season: November-May.
Rates: NZ $39-NZ $58.
Discounts: 10% on stays of 7 days or more.

Credit Cards: MC, VISA & Amex.
Rsv'tns: Required.
Reserve Through: Travel agent or call direct.
Parking: Free, safe off-street parking.
On-Premises: Character dining room, TV lounge, phone, laundry facilities, own front door key.
Swimming: 10 minutes to gay beach.
Sunbathing: On gay

beach.
Nudity: Three nude beaches in Auckland.
Smoking: Not permitted in dining room.
Pets: Not permitted.
Handicap Access: No.
Children: Permitted, but limited.
Languages: English. Linguist avail eves & wknds. French, Russian, Greek, Japanese & German.

BAY OF ISLANDS

ULU Estate

Men ♂

The Uninhibited "Inn Place" For Men...Naturally!

Located on the beautiful rugged Northland Pacific Coast, 20 miles south of Russell in historic Bay of Islands, **ULU Estate** is 41 acres (16.5ha) of remote, private, indigenous forest and streams, with modern farmhouse, offering economical, informal, farm-style accommodation for MEN. Double bedrooms and shared bunkrooms share all facilities. Toilets and showers are separate. Enjoy total seclusion, permitting an uninhibited lifestyle, clothing-optional to unrestricted nudity. Bush walk, hike, swim at the beaches, the plungepool, or sunbathe au-naturel, gregariously on extensive sun decks or privately. Polynesian/Oriental design and decor permits friendly unobtrusive mingling and socialising.

Address: RD 4 Hikurangi, Northland 0251 New Zealand. Tel & Fax: (09) 433-6552.

Type: Guesthouse.
Clientele: Men only.
Transportation: Car only. Helipad.
To Gay Bars: 4-1/2 hours or 200 miles. None locally. Bring your own liquor.
Rooms: 3 rooms & 2 bunkrooms with single, double or bunk beds.
Bathrooms: 2 shared showers & 2 shared toilets.
Meals: Continental breakfast, lunch, dinner & take out lunch for day trippers, beach or bush.
Vegetarian: Available by arrangement with advance notification.
Complimentary: Tea, coffee, fruit drinks & home baking.
Dates Open: All year.
High Season: October through May.
Rates: NZ $75.00 per person per day, all inclusive.
Discounts: 20% for 3 nights or more.
Credit Cards: VISA & Amex.
Rsv'tns: Preferred. Every effort for same day by telephone.
Reserve Through: Call direct.
Parking: Ample free off-street parking. Full 24-hour security.
On-Premises: TV lounge, recreation room & laundry facilities.
Exercise/Health: Triple-gym exerciser. Massage by appointment.
Swimming: River & plunge pool on premises, ocean beaches nearby.
Sunbathing: At poolside, on common & private sun decks, beach, or anywhere on estate.
Nudity: Permitted everywhere. Unrestricted.
Smoking: Rooms smoke free. Permitted outdoors on decks, open areas only. Not in bush
Pets: Not permitted.
Handicap Access: Yes. Ground level & ramp to upstairs level.
Children: Not permitted.
Languages: English.
Your Host: Peter & Bruce.

FEATHERSTON

Petra Kiriwai Farm

Women ♀

Kiriwai Farm is a small, cozy guesthouse on 350 acres of land, and provides panoramic views of the lake, ocean and mountain valleys. From this home base guests can enjoy hiking, biking, canoeing, kayaking and horseriding.
Address: RD 3, Featherston, New Zealand. Tel: 06 3077899.

Type: Guest house.
Clientele: Women only.
Transportation: Bus or train from Wellington. Pick up from Wellington airport (1 hr) NZ $50.
To Gay Bars: 100 km.
Rooms: 2 rooms with single or double bed.
Bathrooms: 1 private shower/toilet, 1 shared bath/shower/toilet.
Meals: Full breakfast, lunch & dinner.
Vegetarian: Mostly lacto vegetarian.
Dates Open: All year.
High Season: Dec-Feb.
Rates: NZ $50.
Discounts: Workshare 3 hr per day NZ $25.
Rsv'tns: Required.
Reserve Through: Call direct.
Minimum Stay: 3 days.
Parking: Adequate free parking.
On-Premises: Meeting rooms & laundry facilities.
Swimming: Nearby river, lake & ocean beach.
Nudity: Permitted in private garden.
Smoking: Not permitted in rooms.
Pets: Not permitted.
Handicap Access: No.
Children: Not especially welcome.
Languages: English, German.

MANGAKINO

Leiden Cottage

Men ♂

More Than Just a Discovery, it's Pure Magic

Mangakino is situated on the banks of Lake Maraetai, in the centre of the North Island, offering the visitor peace and tranquility. Here you can make *Leiden Cottage* your base and tour to Taupo (52Km) or visit Waitomo Caves (99Km) and Rotorua (67Km). *Leiden Cottage* offers you that pure magic of relaxation, and that's what makes Mangakino unique. It has a Maori Culture Centre, lake edge and bush walks, sunshine in summer, and snow skiing only 1-1/2 hours away. *Leiden Cottage* is also the home of Neimor Kennels, breeder of Miniature Dachshunds, and of aviaries housing the native parakeet, the Kakariki.

Address: 132 Rangatira Dr, Mangakino New Zealand. Tel: (07) 882-8212.

Type: Bed & breakfast homestay.
Clientele: Men only.
Transportation: Car is best.
Rooms: 2 rooms with single or double beds.
Bathrooms: Shared showers.
Meals: Continental breakfast & dinner.

Vegetarian: Available by arrangement.
Complimentary: Tea, coffee, juices, mints on pillow.
Dates Open: All year.
Rates: B&B NZ $15 per person, B&B & dinner NZ $25 per person.
Rsv'tns: Preferred.
Reserve Through: Travel

agent or call direct.
Parking: Adequate, free off-street parking.
In-Room: Maid service, coffee/tea-making facilities.
On-Premises: TV lounge, laundry facilities.
Exercise/Health: Massage.
Swimming: 5 minutes to lake, 3/4 hour to thermal

pools.
Sunbathing: In backyard.
Nudity: Permitted in backyard & inside.
Smoking: Permitted on deck. No smoking in bedrooms.
Pets: Inquire.
Handicap Access: No.
Children: Not permitted.
Languages: English.

SOUTH ISLAND

CHRISTCHURCH

Frauenreisehaus (The Homestead)

Women ♀

Frauenreisehaus (The Homestead) is the only women's backpackers hostel in New Zealand. A very spacious, 2-story, 100-year-old house built of double brick and concrete exterior, it is warm in the winter and cool in the summer (late January through early May). There is accommodation for 36 people in 4 double bed/single rooms, 2 twin bed rooms and 5 bunk rooms. There is plenty of common room in our TV lounge/library, with books and magazines in English, Japanese and German, a video

continued next page

and HBO (Sky TV, as we call it here), as well as a large games room with a pool table and board games.

Two large, airy, sunny kitchens are fully-equipped and stocked with crockery, glasses, cutlery, cooking utensils and free herbs and spices. The crockery is fine German china and the glasses crystal, a welcome change from the plastic and tin utensils most backpackers use. The beautiful dining room has French doors opening onto a small garden with fish pond and waterfall.

The bedrooms are spacious and clean. Linen, duvets, pillows, local telephone calls, washing facilities and bicycles are provided free. There are four shower and toilet areas and plenty of hot water. We do not limit the number of showers as many hostels do.

Guests can expect a very warm welcome. We greet each person, show her around the house and introduce her to other guests to make her feel at home. Our rates are almost the cheapest in the country, even though we provide the highest standard of accommodation that we can.

Only minutes from the city centre and information centre, we also provide information about our local area and the South Island of New Zealand. Christchurch is a beautiful garden city, with much to interest the traveller. For excitement, bungee jump, parachute dive or paraglide. For culture, enjoy free plays and concerts. There is stunning scenery, winter skiing, and an hour away are hot pools and whale watching.

Address: 272 Barbadoes St, Christchurch, New Zealand. Tel: (64-3) 366 2585.

Type: Backpackers hostel.
Clientele: Women only. Mostly hetero with a gay female following.
Transportation: Courtesy transport from train, bus or within the city. Within 6-minutes walk of the "Square" central city.
To Gay Bars: 5 blocks or a 10-minute walk.
Rooms: 4 double bed/single rooms, 2 twin bed rooms & 5 bunk rooms

(4 with 4 beds, 1 with 6 beds).
Bathrooms: 4 shared bath/shower/toilets.
Campsites: 3 tent sites.
Vegetarian: Good vegetarian food can be bought only 3 blocks away.
Complimentary: Tea, coffee & hot chocolate.
Dates Open: All year.
High Season: November until May.
Rates: Bunk rooms NZ

$12, twin rooms NZ $15, single rooms NZ $18.
Discounts: NZ $1 upon presentation of VIP card.
Rsv'tns: Required.
Reserve Through: Call direct.
Parking: Adequate free off-street parking.
On-Premises: TV lounge, game room, dining room, outdoor dining area & laundry facilities.
Swimming: Nearby pool, ocean & river.

Sunbathing: At the beach.
Smoking: Smoking permitted in cold weather in the game room.
Pets: Not permitted.
Handicap Access: No.
Children: Not especially welcome.
Languages: English. Usually German & Japanese.
Your Host: Sandra.

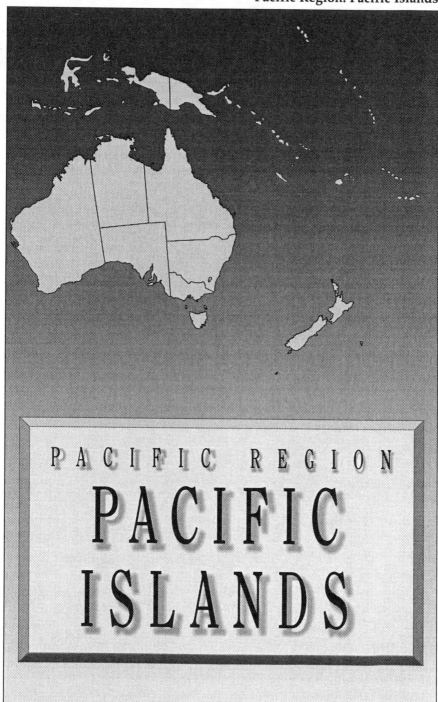

PACIFIC REGION

PACIFIC ISLANDS

FR. POLYNESIA/TAHITI

MOOREA ISLAND

Residence Linareva

Gay-Friendly 50/50 ♀♂

Just What you Need!

Here, at the foot of lush, green hills, on the shores of a lagoon, we have created an environment of tropical ease for gay, lesbian and other visitors from far away. Each of the typical Tahitian grass bungalows at *Residence Linareva* has its own character. Special care has been taken in decorating them with traditional crafts. Also enjoy the most exquisite French cuisine in the unique surroundings of our floating pub-restaurant and over-water terrasse. Charmingly converted from a former inter-island trading boat, this small, but delightful, floating restaurant specializes in fresh local seafood with a definite European flair and provides a romantic setting for cocktails at sunset.

Address: PO Box 1, Haapiti, Moorea, French Polynesia. Tel/Fax: (689) 56 15 35.

Type: Residence with floating bar-restaurant.
Clientele: 50% gay & lesbian & 50% hetero clientele.
Transportation: From Moorea airport, taxi or rental car. From dock, bus or rental car. Rental cars & scooters available.
To Gay Bars: A 5-minute drive.
Rooms: 3 rooms, 1 suite & 1 bungalow with king beds.
Bathrooms: All private shower & toilet.
Dates Open: All year.
Rates: 7,200-15,600 Pacific Francs.
Discounts: 20% for stays of at least 7 nights.
Credit Cards: MC & VISA.
Rsv'tns: Required.
Reserve Through: Travel agent or call direct.
Parking: Free parking.
In-Room: Color TV, ceiling fans, kitchen, refrigerator, coffee/tea-making facilities & maid service.
Exercise/Health: Bicycles, outrigger canoes, masks, snorkels.
Swimming: At deep water spot at end of pier or at nearby sand beaches.
Sunbathing: On private sun decks & beach.
Nudity: Permitted in garden & on raft.
Pets: Not permitted.
Handicap Access: No.
Children: Not especially welcome.
Languages: French, English & Italian.

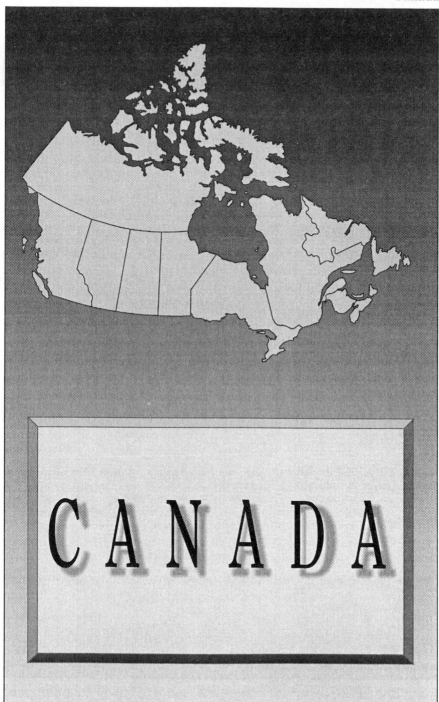

BRITISH COLUMBIA

SALT SPRING ISLAND

Blue Ewe

Gay/Lesbian ♀♂

The Super Natural Blue Ewe

The *Blue Ewe* is a private retreat on over 5 acres of secluded quiet with ponds, forested paths and ocean and mountain views. Wildlife shares the place with farm and domestic animals and friendly people. Canada's Super Natural Gulf Islands, and adjacent US San Juan Islands, offer peace, quiet and close-to-nature activities. Car ferry service from Washington State, Vancouver and Victoria is fast and frequent. Walkers and cyclists are guaranteed priority service and we pick up at the dock. Lots of artists and artisans offer unique things in not-too-close-by shops.
Address: 1207 Beddis Rd, Salt Spring Island, BC V8K 2C8 Canada. Tel: (604) 537-9344

Type: Bed & breakfast.
Clientele: Mostly gay & lesbian with some straight clientele.
Transportation: Car is best. Pick up from ferry docks & sea plane dock.
To Gay Bars: 30 miles or a 90-minute drive.
Rooms: 4 rooms & 1 cottage with single, queen or king beds.
Bathrooms: 2 private shower/toilets, 2 shared bath/shower/toilets.

Meals: Full breakfast.
Vegetarian: Always available on the premises & at nearby establishments.
Complimentary: Fridge space available.
Dates Open: All year.
High Season: Easter to Thanksgiving.
Rates: CDN $65-$95.
Discounts: 10% on 3 or more days, 1 day free on 7-day stay. CDN $15 off all rates for single occupancy.

Credit Cards: MC & VISA.
Rsv'tns: Recommended
Reserve Through: Travel agent or call direct.
Parking: Adequate free off-street parking.
On-Premises: Meeting rooms.
Exercise/Health: Jacuzzi, sauna, massage & trails. Nearby gym, weights, massage & track.
Swimming: Nearby pool, ocean & lake.
Sunbathing: On private

& common sun decks & in forest glens.
Nudity: Permitted in hot tub, sauna, on decks & in private wooded glens.
Smoking: Permitted outside only.
Pets: Permitted by prior arrangement.
Handicap Access: No.
Children: OK if accompanied by parent (under 1, over 5 to 12). Others prior arrangement.
Languages: English.

Green Rose

Gay-Friendly 50/50 ♀♂

Green Rose Farm & Guest House is a wonderfully restored 1916 Salt Spring Island farmhouse, set amidst 17 acres of field, orchards and forest. Guest rooms evoke the mood of old summer homes somewhere near the sea. Guests enjoy crisp, uncluttered spaces and, in the morning, a memorable breakfast inspired by the season. *Green Rose* is approximately 1-1/2 miles north of Ganges, the largest village on Salt Spring. The nearest ferry terminal is four miles away at Long Harbour. Fulford and Vesuvius terminals are also easily accessible. Nearby, are boat, kayak and bicycle rentals.
Address: 346 Robinson Rd, Salt Spring Island, BC V8K 1P7 Canada. Tel: (604) 537-9927

Type: Bed & breakfast guesthouse.
Clientele: 50% gay & lesbian & 50% straight ..
Transportation: Ferry from Vancouver or Victoria.
Rooms: 3 rooms with queen beds.
Bathrooms: 1 private bath/toilet & 2 private

shower/toilet.
Meals: Full breakfast.
Vegetarian: Available by arrangement.
Complimentary: Sherry in room.
Dates Open: All year.
High Season: June-Sept.r.
Rates: CDN $95.
Credit Cards: MC & VISA.
Rsv'tns: Recommended,

although not always necessary.
Reserve Through: Call direct.
Minimum Stay: 2 nights on holiday weekends (Canadian).
Parking: Ample off-street parking.
On-Premises: Living room with fireplace for

guests' use.
Swimming: Nearby lake.
Smoking: Permitted outside only.
Pets: Not permitted.
Handicap Access: No.
Children: Not especially welcome.
Languages: English.

Summerhill Guest House

Gay-Friendly 50/50 ♀♂

Capture the Magic and Romance of Island Living

Join us at *Summerhill,* our waterfront guesthouse in the heart of Canada's magnificent Gulf Islands. Beautifully-appointed guest rooms overlook either ocean or rolling meadows. Swim at the nearby beaches. Hike extraordinary Mount Maxwell. Explore numerous walking and cycling trails. Sail, canoe or kayak the coastline. Watch for whales, deer and eagles. Browse the shops and galleries in the village. In summer, escape with a book to a sun-drenched deck. In winter, relax by the fire in the tranquil sitting room.   Connections from Vancouver and Seattle.
Address: 209 Chu-An Drive, Salt Spring Island, BC V8K 1H9 Canada. Tel: (604) 537-2727 , Fax: (604) 537-4301.

Type: Bed & breakfast.
Clientele: 50% gay & lesbian & 50% straight. .
Transportation: Ferry (walk-on or with car) or float plane. Free pick up from ferry dock or float plane dock.
To Gay Bars: 1-1/2 hours by ferry.
Rooms: 3 rooms with single or queen beds.
Bathrooms: 1 private

shower/toilet & 2 private bath/toilet/showers.
Meals: Full breakfast.
Vegetarian: Available upon request. Vegetarian food & restaurant nearby.
Complimentary: Welcoming wine, beer, coffee, tea, juice. Room snacks.
Dates Open: All year.
High Season: May-Sept..
Rates: CDN $70-$90.

Credit Cards: MC & VISA.
Rsv'tns: Recommended.
Reserve Through: Call direct.
Parking: Ample free off-street parking.
On-Premises: Sitting & dining rooms, fireplace & guest refrigerator.
Exercise/Health: Nearby gym, weights & massage.
Swimming: Nearby ocean & lake.

Sunbathing: On the roof, common sun decks & at the beach.
Nudity: Permitted at discretion of other guests.
Smoking: Permitted outside.
Pets: Not permitted.
Handicap Access: No.
Children: Not especially welcome.
Languages: English.
Your Host: Michael & Paul.

TOFINO

West Wind Guest House, The

Gay/Lesbian ♀♂

The West Wind is a private cottage situated on two acres of wooded privacy. Enjoy our West Coast ambiance, feather beds, goose-down duvets, antique furnishings and gourmet kitchen. It's an ideal retreat for up to six people. In this area of pounding surf and windswept shores, you can go whale watching, surfing and fishing and enjoy the beauty of endless beaches and the ancient rainforest. Experience serenity, seclusion and solitude. Visit the artists' community of Tofino, which has fine restaurants, grocery stores and pubs. Enjoy a fine West Coast experience in any season while capturing the splendor and wilderness of Clayoquot Sound.

Address: 1321 Pacific Rim Hwy, Tofino, BC V0R 2Z0 Canada. Tel: (604) 725-2224

Type: Private cottage.
Clientele: Good mix of gays & lesbians.
Transportation: Car is best. Complimentary aiport or bus pick up/drop off.
To Gay Bars: 4-1/2 hours to Victoria.
Rooms: 1 cottage.
Bathrooms: Private bath.
Meals: Continental starter breakfast provided first day.
Complimentary: Coffee,

teas, fruit basket.
Dates Open: All year.
High Season: June to Oct.
Rates: Winter CDN $95 dbl, summer CDN $125 dbl.
Discounts: On extended stays in low season.
Credit Cards: VISA, Amex.
Rsv'tns: Required.
Reserve Through: Travel agent or call direct.
Minimum Stay: 2 nights.
Parking: Private covered parking.

In-Room: VCR, video tape library, kitchen, refrigerator, coffee/ tea-making facilities & laundry service.
On-Premises: Telephone, video library, laundry facilities & bicycles.
Exercise/Health: Hot tub, hiking, cycling, beachcombing, kayaking, canoeing & golfing.
Swimming: 5 minute-walk to ocean.

Sunbathing: On private sun decks, private garden & at the beach.
Nudity: Clothing optional with discretion. Nude sunbathing in private garden.
Smoking: Permitted on outdoor deck areas only.
Pets: Sorry, not permitted.
Handicap Access: No.
Children: Permitted.
Languages: English & Spanish.

VANCOUVER

Albion Guest House, The,

A Country Retreat in The City

Gay/Lesbian ♀♂

Imagine yourself in a beautiful sitting room with freshly-cut flowers, relaxing in front of a fireplace, sipping your complimentary aperitif. This is a typical scene at *The Albion Guest House*, a turn-of-the-century character home on a quiet, tree-lined residential street in the city. The inn's peaceful ambiance, immediately apparent from the playful statuettes which greet you as you arrive, fosters a warm feeling for all who visit. *Twist*, a Seattle gay newspaper, has commented that the innkeepers are "soft-spoken, generous and accommodating," and that their "personal flair for service and detail is seen in their individual decorations of the guest rooms." The inn's restful rooms are bright, spacious and individually decorated, all with comfortable iron beds covered with thick feather mattresses, fine cotton linens and down-filled duvets. Guests experience a sumptuous breakfast in the formal dining room, which has been whimsically hand-painted by a local artist, or in the sunny courtyard. Breakfast can include home-baked breads, pastries, omelettes, "Eggs on a Cloud," old fashioned oatmeal or an array of fresh fruits, juices and other healthful goodies.

Later, you may want to take advantage of the free bicycle rentals to explore Vancouver on your own. Chinatown and Gastown are just a few minutes away, as well as the expo "Skytrain." It's just three minutes' walk to popular restaurants, Starbuck's coffee shop, delicatessens, parks, theatre and shopping. Vancouver's gambling casinos, Queen Elizabeth Theatre and Van Dusen Gardens are also nearby. Area attractions include boating, parasailing, windsurfing and nude sunbathing at Wreck Beach. A health club is nearby. It's a 30-minute drive to the famous Capilano Suspension Bridge or Grouse Mountain, a major ski area with a panoramic view of Vancouver. The airport is just 15 minutes away. After a long day you can soak in the 6-person hot tub! Theme weekends include wommin-only, family & kids and leather weekend.

Address: 592 West Nineteenth Ave, Vancouver, BC V5Z 1W6 Canada. Tel: (604) 873-2287 or Fax: (604) 879-5682.

Type: Bed & breakfast guesthouse.
Clientele: Gay & lesbian, good mix of men & women.
Transportation: Car, taxi, shuttle or bus. 1 block to public transportation.
To Gay Bars: 1 minute by car.
Rooms: 4 rooms with queen beds.
Bathrooms: Private: 2 bath/toilet, 1 shower toilet. 1 shared bath/shower/toilet.
Meals: Full breakfast. Lunch if prearranged.
Vegetarian: If prearranged. Vegetarian restaurant 1 block away.
Complimentary: Sherry, wine, coffee, beverages on request & chocolates on pillows. Local calls.
Dates Open: All year.
High Season: June-October.
Rates: CDN $75-$120.
Discounts: Negotiable for extended stays.
Credit Cards: MC, VISA & Amex.
Rsv'tns: Recommended.
Reserve Through: Call direct.
Minimum Stay: Required.
Parking: Ample free covered parking. On-street parking is easy to find also.
In-Room: Color TV, telephone & video tape library. Some rooms have VCR's.
On-Premises: Complimentary bicycle/luggage storage, fireplace, refrigerator & fresh spring water.
Exercise/Health: Nearby fitness facility. Close to baths.
Swimming: Nearby in-

continued on page 150

British Columbia

door & outdoor pools & ocean beach.
Sunbathing: On common sun decks & patio.

Smoking: In designated areas only. Non-smoking establishment.
Pets: Not permitted.

Handicap Access: No.
Children: Permitted, especially on kids weekend.

Languages: English & French.

Colibri Bed & Breakfast

Calm in the City Centre

Gay/Lesbian ⚥

In the heart of the gay West End of beautiful Vancouver is *Colibri*. With unpretentious calm and a warm welcome, you'll find your home here while you discover the city, or yourself. Shop till you drop or take time for your inner self. *Colibri* is just blocks to scenic beaches, hectares of forest, and kilometres of oceanside promenade. Come, be yourself with us. A European-style bed and breakfast for those who value a sense of home while on the road.

Address: 1101 Thurlow St, Vancouver, BC V6E 1W9 Canada. Tel: (604) 689-5100 , Fax: (604) 682-3925.

Type: Bed & breakfast.
Clientele: Mostly gay & lesbian with some hetero clientele.
Transportation: Airport bus to Century Plaza, then walk 1 block west.
To Gay Bars: 2 blocks.
Rooms: 5 rooms with single, double, queen or king beds.
Bathrooms: 2 shared bath/shower/toilets.
Meals: Full breakfast.
Vegetarian: By arrangement on arrival. Restaurants nearby

(1-1/2 blocks).
Complimentary: Tea or coffee on arrival. In summer fresh Belgian chocolates on pillows at turn-down.
Dates Open: All year.
High Season: June-October.
Rates: Jun-Oct CDN $85-$120. Nov-May CDN $55-$80.
Discounts: Over 5 days stay, 10% off.
Credit Cards: MC, VISA & Amex.
Rsv'tns: Highly recom-

mended.
Reserve Through: Call direct.
Minimum Stay: 2 days in high season.
Parking: Adequate off-street & on-street parking. 2 locked garages.
In-Room: Maid & laundry service.
Exercise/Health: Nearby gym, weights, Jacuzzi, sauna, steam & massage.
Swimming: At Olympic-sized heated indoor pool 4 blocks away or nearby ocean.

Sunbathing: On common sun decks & at beach.
Nudity: Nude beach 20 minutes by bus.
Smoking: Permitted on front & back decks & on room balconies.
Pets: Not permitted.
Handicap Access: Regretably not.
Children: Permitted over age 10 with prior arrangement & permission of parents.
Languages: English & French.

Columbia Cottage Guest House

Gay-Friendly 50/50 ⚥

A Tranquil Oasis in the City with Fabulous Gourmet Breakfasts

On a tree-lined street, featuring an English country garden with a cascading waterfall flowing into the fish pond covered with waterlilies, *Columbia Cottage* offers peace and tranquility. Our resident chef tempts you with fine food - perhaps a Spanish Frittata with crab, English scones, fresh orange juice, or those wonderful BC berries with crême-Anglaise. We're a five-minute drive to gay clubs downtown or to Q.E. Park for a

romatic evening stroll to watch the sunset. Vancouver offers many attractions, so plan to stay a few days for complete satisfaction.

Address: 205 West 14th Ave, Vancouver, BC Canada. Tel: (604) 874-5327 , Fax: (604) 879-4547.

Type: Bed & breakfast.
Clientele: 50% gay & lesbian & 50% hetero clientele.
Transportation: Car or cab. 15 minutes from international airport.
To Gay Bars: 5-minute drive to Vancouver's gay clubs.
Rooms: 4 double rooms & 1 garden suite with single, double, queen or king beds.
Bathrooms: All private.
Meals: Full gourmet breakfast.
Vegetarian: Available, as well as other special diets, if requested at time of booking.
Complimentary: Robes, slippers, chocolates, cookies, coffee, tea, sherry & local calls.
Dates Open: All year.
High Season: May-October.
Rates: Summer CDN $80-$150, winter CDN $65-$110.
Discounts: For extended stays, business traveler.
Credit Cards: MC & VISA.
Rsv'tns: Recommended.
Reserve Through: Call direct.
Parking: Ample free parking.
In-Room: Maid & laundry service, telephone, refrigerator, kitchen, coffee/tea-making facilities.
On-Premises: Private dining room, enclosed garden.
Exercise/Health: Nearby gym, massage.
Swimming: 5 minutes from most beaches. Walk to nearby pool.
Sunbathing: On the patio, at the beach.
Nudity: 15-minute drive to nude beaches.
Smoking: Permitted outside only.
Pets: Not permitted.
Handicap Access: No.
Children: Permitted over 8 years old.
Languages: English.
Your Host: Gillian & Richard.

Nelson House

Simply Superlative!

Nelson House is a large, 1907 Edwardian on a quiet, residential street, only minutes' walk from the business district, shopping, entertainment, Stanley Park and the beaches. Glowing fireplaces and the wagging tail of a Springer Spaniel ensure a warm welcome. Eurostyle, the four guestrooms have private washbasins and share two baths. Each room has a distinctive decor, but the Studio, with a Far Eastern ambiance, its own fireplace, deck, kitchen and Jacuzzi ensuite, is especially appealing. For all types of travellers, we have all sorts of breakfasts. Early risers receive a light buffet, while from 9:00-10:30 a.m., a wholesome farmer's plate is served. Visit awhile. Your hosts are travellers, too.

Address: 977 Broughton St, Vancouver, BC V6G 2A4 Canada. Tel: (604) 684-9793

Type: Bed & breakfast.
Clientele: Mostly gay & lesbian with some hetero clientele.
Transportation: By car or airport bus to Sheraton Landmark Hotel, walk or taxi remaining 2 blocks.
To Gay Bars: Four blocks.
Rooms: 4 rooms & 1 suite with double or queen beds.
Bathrooms: 2 shared, 1 private with Jacuzzi. All guest rooms have wash basin.
Meals: Full breakfast.
Vegetarian: Available upon request, prior notice appreciated. Plenty of veggies nearby.
Complimentary: 2 kitchenettes stocked with tea & coffee.
Dates Open: All year.
High Season: June through September.
Rates: Low season CDN $58-$98, high season CDN $68-$140.
Discounts: Available by week in low season.
Credit Cards: MC & VISA.
Rsv'tns: Required.
Reserve Through: Travel agent or call direct.
Minimum Stay: 2 nights on holiday weekends only.
Parking: Ample free off-street parking.
In-Room: Maid service, some rooms with kitchens, some refrigerators. Studio has cable colour TV.
On-Premises: TV lounge, VCR, stereo, house telephone, complimentary storage of bicycles & bags.
Exercise/Health: Massage. Nearby gym, weights, Jacuzzi, sauana, steam & massage.
Swimming: Five- to ten-minute walk to ocean beach.
Sunbathing: On beach or private sun decks.
Nudity: Directions available to excellent clothing-optional beaches.
Smoking: Permitted on front porch or in garden.
Pets: Not permitted.
Handicap Access: No.
Children: Permitted by prior arrangement, 12 or older only.
Languages: English & French.
Your Host: David, O'Neal & Dorothy.

Rural Roots Bed and Breakfast

Gay/Lesbian ♂

Discover Your Roots at Rural Roots Bed and Breakfast

Rural Roots is a heather farm, one hour's drive from Vancouver, Canada. Enjoy an award-winning home on ten parklike acres that include gardens, an orchard and a small forest. Stroll the cow trails that wind through rolling pastures dotted with giant cedar, fir and maple trees. Relax in the hot tub, breakfast in a Victorian con-

servatory, lounge on the sun decks, or participate in farm activity. Explore the many recreational opportunities of the Fraser Valley. This unique setting provides guests with a chance to enjoy rural life at its best.

Address: 4939 Ross Road RR#18, Mt. Lehman, BC V4X 1Z3 Canada. Tel: (604) 856-2380 , Fax: (604) 857-2380.

Type: Bed & breakfast. **Clientele:** Mostly men with women welcome. **Transportation:** Car is best. **To Gay Bars:** 33 miles or an hour drive to Vancouver gay bars. **Rooms:** 3 rooms with single, double or queen beds. **Bathrooms:** 1 private bath/toilet, 2 shared shower/toilets. **Meals:** Full breakfast. **Vegetarian:** Available upon request. Vegetarian restaurants nearby. **Complimentary:** Tea, coffee & soft drinks. **Dates Open:** All year. **Rates:** CDN $40-$65. **Rsv'tns:** Required. **Reserve Through:** Call direct. **Parking:** Ample free parking. **In-Room:** Color TV. **On-Premises:** TV lounge. **Exercise/Health:** Jacuzzi. Recreation centre 20 minutes away. **Swimming:** Pool at recreation centre, 60 minutes to ocean. **Sunbathing:** On common sun decks. **Nudity:** Permitted in hot tub area. **Smoking:** Permitted outdoors only. **Pets:** Permitted. Kenneled at night. **Handicap Access:** No. **Children:** Not especially welcome. **Languages:** English, French & Spanish. **Your Host:** Jim & Len.

West End Guest House

Gay-Friendly ♀♂

Vancouver's PINK Victorian

In Vancouver's most gay-friendly neighbourhood, The West End, this historical Victorian home, appointed with antiques, period pieces and tshatshkas from the past, shares with our guests the charm and graciousness of a bygone era. You'll enjoy *West End Guest House's* attention to detail, our desire to meet your needs and answer your questions and our professional approach to bed and breakfast. Amenities, such as com-

plimentary parking, lending bikes, full breakfasts, sherry service and turndown

service, complement the decor and intimate privacy of the guest bedrooms.
Address: 1362 Haro St, Vancouver, BC V6E 1G2 Canada. Tel: (604) 681-2889 , Fax: 688-8812.

Type: Bed & breakfast guesthouse.
Clientele: Mostly hetero clientele with a gay & lesbian following.
Transportation: Car, taxi for 2 persons or Airport bus to Sheraton Landmark Hotel, then walk one block.
To Gay Bars: 4 blocks to gay/lesbian bars.
Rooms: 9 rooms with double or queen beds.
Bathrooms: 7 private, others share.

Meals: Full breakfast.
Vegetarian: Available upon request.
Complimentary: Coffee or tea all day, sherry service, turn-down tarts at bedtime.
Dates Open: All year.
High Season: May-October.
Rates: CDN $85-$195.
Discounts: Long term (5 days) Nov-March.
Credit Cards: MC, VISA, Amex, Discover.
Rsv'tns: Required.

Reserve Through: Call direct.
Minimum Stay: May apply. Winter weekends, 2 nights (Fri-Sat or Sat-Sun).
Parking: Adequate off-street parking.
In-Room: Telephone, remote color TV, maid service, queen beds, ceiling fans, room service.
On-Premises: Guest lounge, dining room, sun deck, meeting rooms.
Exercise/Health: Complimentary bikes for riding,

Stanley Park nearby for jogging.
Swimming: Nearby pool, ocean & sea water pool.
Sunbathing: On ocean beach.
Smoking: Not permitted.
Pets: Not permitted.
Handicap Access: No.
Children: Permitted, but more adult-oriented.
Languages: English, French.

VICTORIA

Camellia House Bed & Breakfast

Gay/Lesbian ♀♂

A warm welcome awaits you in our 1913 heritage home. At *Camellia House,* you can step back from the pressures of everyday life and give yourself up to the relaxation and charm of an old-fashioned B&B experience. Expect cheerful hospitality and attention to your comfort. Enjoy a quiet time or conversation with new friends on the veranda or sun deck, or perhaps an evening in front of a roaring fire. For significant occasions, enhance your experience with our *Celebrations Package.* Two-night *Island Escape Packages* include your choice of relaxation treatments.
Address: 1994 Leighton Rd, Victoria, BC V8R 1N6 Canada. Tel: (604) 370-2816.

Type: Bed & breakfast.
Clientele: Mostly gay & lesbian with some hetero clientele.
Transportation: Complimentary car or complimentary pick up from downtown ferry, seaplane, bus terminals.
To Gay Bars: 8 min by car to gay & lesbian bars.
Rooms: 3 rooms with double or queen beds.
Bathrooms: 1 private bath/toilet & 1 shared bath/shower/toilet.

Meals: Gourmet breakfast.
Vegetarian: Lacto-ovo vegetarian always available.
Complimentary: Tea, coffee, cookies & Belgian chocolates.
Dates Open: All year.
High Season: May through September.
Rates: CDN $69-$89 for two, CDN $59-$79 for one.
Discounts: 7th consecutive night free. Frequent sleeper discounts for re-

turn guests.
Credit Cards: MC & VISA.
Rsv'tns: Recommended & preferred.
Reserve Through: Travel agent or call direct.
Minimum Stay: 2 nights on holiday weekends.
Parking: Ample free on-street parking.
In-Room: Coffee & tea-making facilities.
On-Premises: TV lounge, laundry facilities, verandah, sun deck, garden & fireplace.
Exercise/Health: Health

& recreation centre & bicycle rental 1 block. Massage, reflexology & aromatherapy with advance notice.
Swimming: Pool 1 block, ocean beach 5-min drive.
Sunbathing: At ocean beach.
Smoking: Permitted outdoors.
Pets: Not permitted.
Handicap Access: No.
Children: Not permitted.
Languages: English, some Japanese & Spanish.

Lavender Link

Gay/Lesbian ♀♂

Link Up with Love and Laughter

Enjoy comfort in a 1912 tastefully renovated character home, only minutes from the Inner Harbour and downtown and two blocks from the ocean. Accommodations at *Lavender Link* consist of one room with private bath and entrance and one room with fireplace and shared bath. Relax in the TV lounge or outside on our 4-person swing. Enjoy coffee and muffins in the morning or, with additional charge, have a full breakfast. Vegetarian cuisine available.
Address: 136 Medana St, Victoria, BC V8V 2H5 Canada. Tel: (604) 380-7098.

Type: Guesthouse
Clientele: Gay, lesbian & gay-friendly clientele.
Transportation: Car is best.
To Gay Bars: 6 blocks or 3/4 mile. A 15-minute walk or 5-minute drive.
Rooms: 2 rooms with double or queen beds.
Bathrooms: 1 private bath/toilet/shower & 1 shared shower/toilet.
Meals: Continental breakfast. Full breakfast available for extra charge.
Vegetarian: Available upon request.

Complimentary: Coffee, mints on pillow, fruit bowl.
Dates Open: All year.
High Season: May thru September.
Rates: Double occupancy: CDN $60-$65, CDN $15 per extra person, summer CDN $65-$75 (May-Sept).
Discounts: Weekly rates available. Monthly rates in off season.
Rsv'tns: Required at most times.
Reserve Through: Call direct.
Parking: Adequate free

on-street parking.
In-Room: Coffee & tea-making facilities, maid service.
On-Premises: TV lounge, 4-person swing, picnic table, occasional use of phone.
Exercise/Health: Nearby YWCA or drive to recreation centres.
Swimming: Nearby pool. 3 miles to ocean, 45-minutes to lake, 1 hour to river.
Sunbathing: On patio or nearby beach (5-minute walk).
Nudity: Permitted in the

lounge area.
Smoking: Permitted outside only. Both rooms non-smoking.
Pets: 1 dog only & must not stay alone in room for a long period of time.
Handicap Access: Yes. 1 bedroom with private bath.
Children: Welcome. Single bed available for $15 extra.
Languages: English, some German, Yiddish, Hebrew & beginners Spanish.
Your Host: Gloro & Pearl.

Oak Bay Guest House

Gay-Friendly ♀♂

At this classic inn, established since 1922, we have your comfort and pleasure at heart. Guests at *Oak Bay Guest House* enjoy the peaceful location, scenic walks a block from the ocean, and the beautiful gardens that surround. All eleven rooms have private bathrooms. There are two sitting rooms decorated with antiques, a library and log fireplace. We are frequently complimented on our home-cooked breakfast. Golf, village shopping, fine dining and a city bus tour are accessible from our location, just minutes from downtown. Come, and enjoy.
Address: 1052 Newport Ave, Victoria, BC V8S 5E3 Canada. Tel: (604) 598-3812.

Type: Inn.
Clientele: Mostly straight clientele with a gay & lesbian following.
Transportation: Car is best. Bus stop right outside.
To Gay Bars: 2 miles or 10 mins by car.
Rooms: 11 rooms with single or queen beds.
Bathrooms: All private

bath/toilets.
Meals: Full breakfast.
Vegetarian: Available upon request.
Complimentary: Tea & coffee.
Dates Open: Feb-Dec inclusive.
High Season: Jun-Oct.
Rates: CDN $69-$110 winter, CDN $89-$150 summer.

Credit Cards: MC & VISA.
Rsv'tns: Required.
Reserve Through: Call direct.
Parking: Ample free off-street & on-street parking.
In-Room: Coffee & tea-making facilities.
On-Premises: TV lounge.
Swimming: Nearby pool, lake & ocean beach.

Sunbathing: On the beach.
Smoking: Permitted in sun room. All rooms non-smoking.
Pets: Not permitted.
Handicap Access: No.
Children: Not permitted.
Languages: English.

Ocean Wilderness

Gay-Friendly ♀♂

An Elegant Jewel in A Wilderness Setting

Ocean Wilderness has 9 guest rooms on five forested acres of oceanfront with breathtaking view of forests, the Straits of Juan de Fuca and the Olympic Mts. Large, beautifully decorated rooms with private baths and bed canopies are in the new wing. A silver service of coffee is delivered to your door as a gentle wake-up call. Home baking makes breakfast a special treat. Dinner can be arranged. The hot tub, in a Japanese gazebo, is popular with weary vacationers. Book your time for a private soak. Several rooms have private soak tubs for two, overlooking the ocean. **Address: 109 West Coast Rd RR#2, Sooke, BC V0S 1N0 Canada. Tel: (604) 646-2116.**

Type: Bed & breakfast inn with gift shop.
Clientele: Mostly straight with gay/lesbian following.
Transportation: Car is best.
To Gay Bars: 30 miles.
Rooms: 9 rooms with single, queen or king beds.
Bathrooms: All private.
Meals: Full breakfast.
Vegetarian: Available with prior notification or upon arrival.

Complimentary: Wake up coffee to your door on silver service.
Dates Open: All year.
High Season: May-October.
Rates: Summer (June 1/Oct 1) CDN $85-$170, winter (Oct 1/May 30) CDN $65-$140.
Discounts: Winter rates + 3 nights for the price of 2.
Credit Cards: MC, VISA.
Rsv'tns: Required in season.

Reserve Through: Travel agent or call direct.
Parking: Off-street parking.
In-Room: Room service, telephone, bar refrigerator, maid service.
On-Premises: Beach, wilderness, wildlife, hot tub for private soak in gazebo overlooking ocean.
Exercise/Health: Hot tub, massage by appointment.
Swimming: Ocean beach & river.

Sunbathing: On beach, patio, private sun decks.
Nudity: Permitted on private sun decks.
Smoking: Permitted outdoors only, all rooms non-smoking.
Pets: Permitted by prior arrangement.
Handicap Access: Yes, 1 room.
Children: Permitted occasionally, please inquire. Must be adult oriented.
Languages: English.

Weekender Bed & Breakfast, The

Gay/Lesbian ♀♂

A Seaside Bed & Breakfast

Weekender Bed & Breakfast is located just steps from the ocean, along Victoria's scenic drive. Our location is but a short distance from Beacon Hill Park, Cook Street Village, Fairfield Shopping Plaza, local restaurants, nightlife and most tourist attractions. The inn's spacious, bright rooms all have private baths. The deluxe suite has ocean views and a private sun deck. **Address: 10 Eberts St, Victoria, BC V8S 5L6 Canada. Tel: (604) 389-1688.**

Type: Bed & Breakfast.
Clientele: Mostly gay & lesbian with some hetero clientele.
Transportation: Car is best. Taxi from city centre, about $7.50. Free pick up from bus & Clipper Catamaran foot passenger terminal.
To Gay Bars: 2 miles or 30 minutes by foot, 5 minutes by car.
Rooms: 3 rooms with queen beds.

Bathrooms: 3 private bath/toilets.
Meals: Expanded continental breakfast.
Vegetarian: Always available.
Complimentary: Complimentary beverage on check-in. Fresh fruit always available.
Dates Open: Weekends October to May. Full time June to September.
High Season: Mid-May to end of September.

Rates: High season CDN $79-95. Low season CDN $69-$79.
Discounts: 7th consecutive night free.
Credit Cards: MC & VISA.
Rsv'tns: Recommended & preferred.
Reserve Through: Call direct.
Minimum Stay: 2 nights on holiday weekends & special events days.
Parking: Ample on-street parking.

In-Room: Maid service.
Exercise/Health: Massage. Nearby YMCA & YWCA.
Sunbathing: On private sun decks.
Smoking: Permitted outdoors only.
Pets: Not permitted.
Handicap Access: No.
Children: Not especially welcomed.
Languages: English.
Your Host: Michael.

WEST KOOTENAYS

Beach House, The

Gay-Friendly 50/50 ♀♂

A Tranquil Mountain Guest Retreat Minutes from Natural Hot Springs

Sister to Vancouver's *Columbia Cottage*, *The Beach House* is beautifully renovated and has outstanding views, delicious breakfasts and gracious hospitality. Explore the private beach and, as you take in the serene beauty of the Kootenays, plan your activities such as guided hiking, horseback excursions, cycling or fishing. Work out in our private gym or do nothing at all! To finish off the day, relax in the underground cave hot springs a few minutes away. Full board weekly rates available. Appropriate for adults seeking a rejuvenating getaway. Heterosexual friendly. **Address: PO Box 1375 Kaslo, BC V0G 1M0 Canada. Tel: (604) 353-7676 , Fax: (604) 879-4547.**

Type: Guesthouse retreat.
Clientele: 50% gay & lesbian & 50% straight clientele.
Transportation: Car. 1 hour from Castlegar Airport.
To Gay Bars: 40-minute drive to Nelson.
Rooms: 4 rooms with double or queen beds.
Bathrooms: 1 private shower/toilet & 2 private bath/toilet/showers.

Meals: Full gourmet breakfast. Lunch & dinner upon request.
Vegetarian: Available, as well as other special diets, if requested at time of booking.
Complimentary: Coffee, tea & cookies.
Dates Open: All year.
High Season: June-September.
Rates: Summer CDN $65-$95. Winter CDN $40-$65.
Discounts: On extended

stays.
Credit Cards: VISA.
Rsv'tns: Recommended.
Reserve Through: Call direct.
Parking: Ample free parking.
In-Room: Maid service.
Exercise/Health: Gym & weights on premises. Massage & natural hot springs nearby.
Swimming: Lake with private beach on premises. Nearby pool &

lake.
Sunbathing: On common sun decks & private beach.
Smoking: Permitted outside.
Pets: Not permitted.
Handicap Access: No.
Children: Not especially welcome.
Languages: English, French.
Your Host: Michael & Gillian.

WHISTLER MOUNTAIN

Coast Mountain Lodge

Gay/Lesbian ♀♂

Coast Mountain Lodge is a unique bed and breakfast guest chalet in Whistler, North America's premier ski resort. Whether you come for the skiing (some of the best on the continent), or to hike, bike, sightsee or golf, there is no better place to explore the magic of this year-round resort than from *Coast Mountain Lodge*. You will feel at home relaxing in front of the fireplace, soaking in the hot tub or retiring to one of the spacious guest rooms, all offering extremely comfortable beds, down duvets and breathtaking views of the surrounding mountains. **Address: 7406 Ambassador Crescent, Box 1370, Whistler, BC V0N 1B0 Canada. Tel: (604) 932-2890 , Fax: (604) 938-1250.**

Type: Bed & breakfast.
Clientele: Mostly gay & lesbian with some straight clientele.
Transportation: Car is best. Excellent bus service direct from Vancouver Int'l Airport.
To Gay Bars: 75 miles to Vancouver.
Rooms: 3 rooms with

queen or king beds.
Bathrooms: 1 private bath/toilet, 1 shared bath/shower/toilet & 1 shared WC.
Meals: Full breakfast.
Vegetarian: Vegetarian restaurant nearby.
Complimentary: Apres ski refreshments, hot chocolate, coffee, tea &

cakes.
Dates Open: All year.
High Season: December-March.
Rates: Summer CDN $50-$100. Winter CDN $100-$150.
Discounts: $25 per night on stays of 3 or more nights during winter.
Credit Cards: VISA.

Rsv'tns: Recommended.
Reserve Through: Call direct.
Minimum Stay: 2 nights on weekends.
Parking: Ample free off-street parking.
In-Room: Color cable TV & maid service.
Exercise/Health: Nearby gym, weights, Jacuzzi,

massage.
Swimming: At nearby pool & lake.
Sunbathing: On private & common sun decks & beach.
Nudity: Permitted in hot tub at discretion of guests.
Smoking: Outside only.
Pets: Not permitted.
Handicap Access: No.
Children: Not permitted.
Languages: English.
IGTA

ONTARIO

HAMILTON

Cedars Tent & Trailer Park

Gay/Lesbian ♀♂

Cedars Tent & Trailer Park is the only mixed campground in Ontario. We've been in business for ten years, building and improving each year. Come visit us on our 130 green Ontario acres.

Address: PO Box 195, Millgrove, ON L0R 1V0 Canada. Tel: (905) 659-7342 or 659-3655.

Type: Campground with rental trailers, clubhouse, restaurant & bar.
Clientele: Good mix of gay men & women.
Transportation: Car is best.
To Gay Bars: 5 miles to gay bars.
Bathrooms: Shower & toilet building plus outhouses throughout.
Campsites: 600 campsites with shared shower facilities.
Dates Open: April 1st through October 15th.
Rates: CDN $12.50 per person per day.
Reserve Through: Call direct.
Parking: Ample free parking.
On-Premises: Clubhouse with dance floor & game rooms.
Exercise/Health: Recreational area.
Swimming: Pool.
Sunbathing: At poolside.
Smoking: Permitted without restrictions.
Pets: Permitted. Must be on a leash.
Handicap Access: Yes.
Children: Welcome. Children under 12 free, parent responsible.
Languages: English & French.

OTTAWA/HULL

Rideau View Inn

Gay-Friendly 50/50 ♀♂

Victorian Elegance in the Heart of Ottawa

Rideau View Inn is a large Edwardian home built in 1907 with seven elegant guest rooms. It is located in the center of the city on a residential street just steps from fine restaurants, shopping, Parliament Hill and public transport. We offer a gourmet breakfast in our gracious dining room from 7:30-9:00am. Our guests are encouraged to relax in front of the fireplace in the living room, enjoy a leisurely stroll beside the Rideau Canal or a game of tennis in nearby public courts.

Address: 177 Frank St, Ottawa, ON K2P 0X4 Canada. Tel: (613) 236-9309 or (800) 268-2082, Fax: (613) 237-6842.

Type: Bed & breakfast.
Clientele: 50% gay & lesbian & 50% hetero clientele.
Transportation: Taxi.
To Gay Bars: 10-minute walk to gay/lesbian bars.
Rooms: 7 rooms with single, double or queen beds.
Bathrooms: 2 private bath/toilets & 4 shared bath/shower/toilets.
Meals: Full breakfast.
Vegetarian: Available with 1 days notice.
Complimentary: Tea & coffee.
Dates Open: All year.
Rates: Rooms CDN $58-$75.
Discounts: 15% discount on bookings of 7 days or more.
Credit Cards: MC, VISA, Amex & Enroute.
Rsv'tns: Required 1 week in advance.
Reserve Through: Travel agent or call direct.
Minimum Stay: On holiday weekends only.
Parking: Adequate free on- & off-street parking.
In-Room: AC & telephone.
On-Premises: TV lounge.
Sunbathing: On common sun decks.
Smoking: Smoke-free home.
Pets: Not permitted.
Handicap Access: No.
Children: Permitted.
Languages: English, French.
Your Host: George.

Starr Easton Hall

The Perfect Country Retreat

Gay-Friendly ♀♂

Starr Easton Hall, with all of its early Victorian charm, entertains guests as though they were at home. The four guest rooms are individually decorated and furnished with antiques. Guests may also use our upper foyer, music room and library. Individual dining rooms are refurnished appropriate to the era, creating an atmosphere of earlier, less rushed days. And

menus prepared with creative flair by our chef will appease the gourmet's palate. Great care has gone into the reconstruction of formal English gardens. Nestled amongst the century-old maples are unique flower and vegetable gardens that will delight one and all. Our goal is to be the friendliest place you'll ever find in which to relax and celebrate life's special moments.

Address: PO Box 215, RR #3, Jasper, ON K0G 1G0 Canada. Tel: (613) 283-7497.

Type: Inn with restaurant, bar & gift shop, 1 hour from Ottawa.
Clientele: Mostly straight clientele with a gay & lesbian following.
Transportation: Car is best. CDN $10-$20 for pick up from airport, bus or train.
To Gay Bars: 1 hour by car.
Rooms: 5 rooms with twin, double & king beds.
Bathrooms: 2 private &

2 shared.
Meals: Full breakfast.
Vegetarian: Available with prior arrangements.
Complimentary: Tea, coffee, chocolates, mints on pillows.
Dates Open: All year.
High Season: May-October, December-January.
Rates: CDN $50-$75.
Credit Cards: MC & VISA.
Rsv'tns: Appreciated.
Reserve Through: Call direct.
Parking: Ample free off-

street parking.
In-Room: Color TV, maid, laundry & room service.
On-Premises: TV lounge, private dining rooms, beautifully furnished lounge, quiet library, music room & laundry facilities.
Swimming: Pool on premises.
Sunbathing: At poolside & anywhere in 10-acre garden.
Smoking: Not permitted on 2nd floor or in bed-

rooms.
Pets: Not permitted except in exceptional circumstances.
Handicap Access: Yes. Wheelchair ramp to 1st floor.
Children: Permitted by special arrangements.
Languages: English, French, German & Czech.
Your Host: Arthur & Colleen.

Stonehouse, The

Country Tranquility

Gay/Lesbian ♀♂

The Stonehouse is a beautifully-restored 140-year-old Georgian stone house on 25 acres of rolling pastureland 1/2 hour from downtown Ottawa. The density of the 2-1/2-foot-thick walls, which insulate both summer and winter, is revealed by window sills of equal depth. The inside of the house is completely restored and includes quiet reading areas and rustic room settings. A 10-foot hedge provides complete privacy. Special weekend rates include meals.

Address: 2605 Yorks Corners Rd, Edwards, ON K0A 1V0 Canada. Tel: (613) 821-3822.

Type: Bed & breakfast.
Clientele: Mostly gay & lesbian, friendly to family friends.
Transportation: Car is best.
To Gay Bars: 30 minutes

by car to gay/lesbian bars.
Rooms: 3 rooms with twin, double or king bed.
Bathrooms: 2 shared bath/shower/toilets.
Meals: Continental

breakfast, full meals on weekends at extra charge.
Vegetarian: Available with prior arrangement.
Complimentary: Welcome cocktails, tea &

coffee anytime.
Dates Open: All year.
High Season: June-August, November-February.
Rates: CDN $55-$75.
Credit Cards: MC, VISA.

Rsv'tns: Appreciated.
Reserve Through: Call direct.
Parking: Ample, free off-street parking.
On-Premises: Relaxing lounge with fireplace, quiet reading & music

room, laundry facilities, kitchen during non-meal hrs.
Swimming: Old rock quarry nearby.
Sunbathing: On very large, private lawn & garden areas.

Nudity: Permitted if no one else objects.
Smoking: Not permitted on 2nd floor or in bedrooms.
Pets: Not permitted, special circumstances considered.

Handicap Access: No.
Children: Permitted by special arrangement.
Languages: English, limited French.
Your Host: David & Dick.

STRATFORD

Burnside

Gay-Friendly 50/50 ♀♂

Burnside is an ancestral, turn-of-the-century home featuring many family heirlooms and antiques, redecorated in light, airy colors. Our host is a horticultural instructor and an authority on local and Canadian geneology. Relax amid flowers and herbs in the gardens overlooking Lake Victoria. We are a mere 12 minutes' walk from the Stratford, Avon and Tom Patterson theatres and a short walk from interesting shops and good restaurants. Nearby is the Avon Trail, part of a network of trails enabling one to walk from London, Ontario to Niagara Falls.
Address: 139 William St, Stratford, ON N5A 4X9 Canada. Tel: (519) 271-7076.

Type: Bed & breakfast.
Clientele: 50% gay & lesbian & 50% hetero.
Transportation: Car is best. Free pick up from train & bus station. Use Stratford Airporter from airport to our front door.
To Gay Bars: 5-minute walk to gay/lesbian bar (Down the Street Bar & Cafe).
Rooms: 4 rooms with single, double or king beds.
Bathrooms: Shared: 1 full bath, 2 bathtubs, 2

showers & 1 toilet only.
Meals: Full or expanded continental breakfast.
Vegetarian: Cater to special diets.
Complimentary: Ice provided.
Dates Open: All year.
High Season: July & August.
Rates: Student CDN $25, single CDN $40, twin & double CDN $60, king CDN $70.
Discounts: For stays of over 2 nights.
Credit Cards: MC.

Rsv'tns: Required.
Reserve Through: Call direct.
Minimum Stay: 2 nights on July & August weekends.
Parking: Adequate free off-street parking.
In-Room: Central AC/ heat, refrigerator.
On-Premises: Private dining room, TV lounge with color cable TV, VCR & limited video tape library, & spacious gardens.
Exercise/Health: Whirl-

pool tub & massage.
Swimming: Lions Club pool 1/2 block, YMCA pool 3 blocks.
Sunbathing: At Grand Bend Beach & Shakespeare Conservation Park.
Smoking: Permitted outside.
Pets: Not permitted.
Handicap Access: No.
Children: Permitted but not encouraged.
Languages: English, limited French.
Your Host: Les.

Maples of Stratford, The

Gay-Friendly 50/50 ♀♂

The Maples of Stratford is a large Victorian home, built in 1905. It has been restored to reflect early century grace and charm, with a modern touch for your comfort and staying pleasure. We offer single through triple accommodations with central air conditioning and private or semi-private baths. The complimentary continental breakfast may include homemade breads, muffins or pastries, tea, coffee, juice, fruit salad and yogurt. We are just three blocks from the center of town and within walking distance of all theatres.
Address: 220 Church St, Stratford, ON N5A 2R6 Canada. Tel: (519) 273-0810.

Type: Bed & breakfast.
Clientele: 50% gay & lesbian & 50% straight clientele.
Rooms: 1 single, 2 doubles & 2 triples.
Bathrooms: 1 private & 2 shared.

Meals: Continental breakfast.
Dates Open: All year.
High Season: June thru Sept.
Rates: CDN $50-$95.
Credit Cards: VISA.
Rsv'tns: Required.

Reserve Through: Call direct.
Minimum Stay: Required during high season.
Parking: Ample free off-street parking.
In-Room: Maid service.
Smoking: Permitted out-

side only.
Pets: Not permitted.
Handicap Access: No.
Children: Not permitted.
Languages: English.

TORONTO

Burken Guest House

Gay-Friendly ♀♂

Toronto is one of the world's most exciting cities, and guests at *Burken Guest House* have the advantage of staying in a gracious home in a beautiful residential area adjacent to downtown. Eight tastefully-appointed rooms are furnished with period pieces and equipped with telephone, washbasin and ceiling fan. There is one bathroom on each floor. The breakfast room, with deck and access to the garden, is on the second floor. Our European atmosphere and friendly service will make your visit a most enjoyable one.

Address: 322 Palmerston Blvd, Toronto, ON M6G 2N6 Canada. Tel: (416) 920-7842, Fax: (416) 960-9529.

Type: Guesthouse.
Clientele: Mostly straight clientele with a gay/lesbian following.
To Gay Bars: 10 minutes by car, streetcar 15 minutes to gay/lesbian bars.
Rooms: 8 rooms with single or double beds.
Bathrooms: 2 shared bath/shower/toilet & 1 shared toilet only.
Meals: Continental breakfast included.
Dates Open: All year.
High Season: May through October.
Rates: Singles CDN $45-$55, doubles CDN $60-65.
Credit Cards: VISA & MC.
Rsv'tns: Required.
Reserve Through: Travel agent or call direct.
Parking: Limited free off-street parking.
In-Room: Maid service, telephone & ceiling fans.
On-Premises: TV lounge.
Smoking: Non-smoking establishment.
Pets: Not permitted.
Handicap Access: No.
Children: Permitted.
Languages: English, French & German.
IGTA

Catnaps 1892 Downtown Guesthouse

Gay/Lesbian ♀♂

Toronto's Purrfect Place to Be

Stay at *Catnaps* and enjoy personal, friendly attention. Our newly-renovated century home right downtown is the oldest Toronto gay and lesbian guesthouse. Each room has a different personality, and all are cozy and comfortable. We're close to 24-hour public transportation, and guests have use of kitchen and laundry facilities. Relax in a casual, informal atmosphere just steps from all Toronto has to offer...theatre, nightlife, shopping, world-famous tourist attractions. Next time you're passing through, stay with us and help us celebrate 15 years.

Address: 246 Sherbourne St, Toronto, ON M5A 2S1 Canada. Tel: (416) 968-2323 , Reservations: (800) 205-3694, Fax: (416) 413-0485.

Type: Bed & breakfast guesthouse.
Clientele: Good mix of gay men & women.
Transportation: Airport shuttle service from $30. Bus & train pick up from $5.
To Gay Bars: 2 blocks or 1/4 mile. 5 minutes by foot.
Rooms: 9 rooms & 1 suite with single, double or queen beds.
Bathrooms: 1 private toilet only, 2 shared bath/shower/toilets.
Meals: Expanded continental breakfast with fresh-baked goods.
Vegetarian: Readily available.
Complimentary: Coffee & tea all day.
Dates Open: All year.
High Season: May through September (Victoria Day through Labour Day).
Rates: Rooms CDN $40-$65.
Discounts: Coupons sent to our mailing list. Off-season weekly & monthly rates.
Credit Cards: MC & VISA.
Rsv'tns: Recommended.
Reserve Through: Travel agent or call direct.
Minimum Stay: 2 nights on holiday weekends.
Parking: Adequate off-street parking, CDN $5 per night.
In-Room: Color cable TV, AC, clock radios, ceiling fans & maid service.
On-Premises: Laundry facilities, kitchen, tourist information & guided tours.
Exercise/Health: Gym, weights, sauna, steam, massage & Jacuzzi nearby.
Swimming: Lake Ontario (Toronto Islands), YMCA & other clubs nearby.
Sunbathing: On beach at Toronto Islands and on house sun decks (private & common).
Nudity: Permitted on private sun deck only.
Smoking: Permitted in guest rooms, kitchen, garden & decks.
Pets: Small pets permitted by prior arrangement.
Handicap Access: No.
Children: Welcomed, some restrictions. Reservations required.
Languages: English, French & German.

Divine Lake Resort

Gay/Lesbian ♀♂

The Alternative Vacation Paradise In Canada

Divine Lake Resort is a gay heaven in Muskoka amid 86 acres of lovely nature 2 hours north of Toronto. Cottages and chalets with fireplaces and kitchenettes are available. There are two lounges, a bar, a restaurant, heated pool, hot tub, Finnish sauna, tennis court, table-tennis, pool table, TV-video room, and conference rooms. Outdoor activities include boating, windsurfing, fishing, hiking on breathtaking trails, cross-country skiing, and motorboat tours. Stay with us at *Divine Lake Resort,* the alternative vacation paradise in Canada.

Tel: (705) 385-1212 , Fax: (705) 385-1283. Information & reservations: (800) 263-6600.

Type: Resort with restaurant, bar, shops.
Clientele: 60% men, 40% women & some straight clientele.
Transportation: Free pick up from Port Sydney bus station & Huntsville train station.
To Gay Bars: On premises.
Rooms: 10 cottages, 9 chalets.
Bathrooms: All private.
Meals: Full breakfast, dinner.

Vegetarian: Available on request when booking.
Complimentary: Juices, tea & coffee.
Dates Open: All year.
High Season: June thru October.
Rates: CDN $89-$118 per person per night. Cottage for 2, CDN $690 per week without meals.
Discounts: Special packages available.
Credit Cards: MC, VISA & Amex.

Rsv'tns: Required.
Reserve Through: Travel agent or call direct.
Parking: Ample free parking.
In-Room: Fireplace, some color TV's, kitchen, refrigerator, maid service.
On-Premises: Meeting rooms, TV lounge, laundry facilities for guests.
Exercise/Health: Jacuzzi, sauna, gym, tennis court.
Swimming: Heated pool on premises, lake.

Sunbathing: Poolside, on sun deck, at the beach.
Smoking: In designated dining room area, lounge; non-smoking rooms available.
Pets: Not permitted.
Handicap Access: Yes, bathroom.
Children: Permitted on special occasions.
Languages: French, English & German.

IGTA

Hotel Selby

Gay/Lesbian ♀♂

For A Weekend Away, Toronto's Always A Great Choice

Hotel Selby offers a friendly, comfortable atmosphere not found at other establishments. We are currently the community's only AAA-approved hotel with restaurant and bar. *The Selby* was built in 1882 as the home of the Gooderhams, a prominent Canadian family of the Hiram Walker, Gooderham and Worts distillery. Later, it was the original site of a prestigious private girl's school, Branksome Hall. Today, the hotel is one of Toronto's landmark buildings of architectural and historical importance. Many of the 67 rooms have 15-foot ceilings, with original mouldings, wood-carved doorways and fireplace mantels. The main staircase has original stained glass windows. The chandelier in the lobby is from the Chrysler mansion in Gross Point, Michigan. Renovations in the hotel are ongoing, and a restaurant has recently opened. Present expansion includes an enlargement of the courtyard to accommodate a sunbathing area. *continued next page*

HOTEL SELBY
592 Sherbourne Street, Toronto, Ontario
For Reservations Call 1-800-387-4788

Hotel owner Rick Stenhouse says, "One of the most common remarks on our comment cards is on the friendliness of the staff."

Guests are invited to use the facilities of the Bloor Valley Health Club, a minute's walk from the hotel, at a nominal charge. This health club rivals any 5-star hotel club and 80% of the membership is from the community. In our new, fully-equipped common kitchenette for guests, there are microwave ovens, toasters, a refrigerator, and free, freshly-brewed coffee and tea available 24 hours a day. Coin laundry also available. Ernest Hemingway lived at the hotel during his time as a writer for the Toronto Daily Star in the early 1920's. The original Hemingway Suite, which overlooks the courtyard, has a working fireplace and an attached solarium. *Hotel Selby* is located in downtown Toronto, and is minutes away from many of Toronto's main tourist attractions.

Address: 592 Sherbourne St, Toronto, ON M4X 1L4 Canada. Tel: (416) 921-3142 , Fax: 923-3177 or (800) 387-4788.

Type: Hotel.
Clientele: Mostly gay & lesbian with some straight clientele.
Transportation: Airport limo or bus to downtown then taxi or subway.
To Gay Bars: 2 men's bars on premises, others 3 blocks.
Rooms: 67 rooms with double beds.
Bathrooms: 55 private bath/toilets & 2 shared bath/shower/toilets.

Meals: Continental breakfast.
Complimentary: Hot chocolate (winter), iced tea (summer).
Dates Open: All year.
High Season: May through October.
Rates: Summer: CDN $59.95-$79.95, suites CDN $75-$95; winter: CDN $49.95-$69.95, suites CDN $85-$125.
Discounts: AAA, students, seniors, all with valid ID. Weekly rates.

Credit Cards: MC, VISA & Amex.
Rsv'tns: Recommended.
Reserve Through: Travel agent or call direct.
Parking: Limited free parking, ample pay parking.
In-Room: Color cable TV & AC.
On-Premises: Vending machines & ice machine. Coin laundry.
Exercise/Health: Health club membership privileges: gym, weights,

Jacuzzi, sauna, massage, aerobics.
Swimming: Pool across the street.
Sunbathing: In courtyard.
Smoking: Permitted in rooms.
Pets: Permitted with prior arrangement.
Handicap Access: No.
Children: Children under 12 are free.
Languages: English, French, Greek, Spanish & Italian.

QUÉBEC

MONTRÉAL

Au Bon Vivant Guest House

Gay/Lesbian ♂

A Fine Home for the Discerning Traveller

Welcome to the *Au Bon Vivant Guest House*. Ideally located in the gay village, we are steps from the Metro, Latin Quarter, clubs, restaurants, and Lafontaine Park. We are also adjacent to gay-friendly Plateau Mount-Royal and within easy access to tourist attractions. Our three guest rooms share a bath and common living room. The colour scheme, Persian carpets and antiques were specifically chosen to create a calming, warm and inviting atmosphere. Our motto, "A fine home for the discerning traveller," hopefully describes the ambience we have created. We sincerely hope your stay with us is enjoyable and that you visit us again.

Address: 1648 Amherst, Montréal, Québec H2L 3L5 Canada. Tel: (514) 525-7744 , Fax (514) 525-2874.

Type: Bed & breakfast guesthouse
Clientele: Mostly men with women welcome.
Transportation: Airport bus to Berri terminal.
To Gay Bars: 1 block.
Rooms: 3 rooms with single, double or queen beds.
Bathrooms: 1 shared bath/shower/toilet.
Meals: Buffet breakfast.
Vegetarian: Available

upon request.
Complimentary: Tea, coffee & juice.
Dates Open: All year.
High Season: May-Oct.
Rates: High CDN $50-$80. Low CDN $40-$70.
Discounts: 10%-15% for stays of 7 or more days during low season.
Credit Cards: MC, VISA & Amex.
Rsv'tns: Required.
Reserve Through: Travel

agent or call direct.
Parking: Adequate off-street parking.
In-Room: Ceiling fans.
On-Premises: TV lounge & laundry facilities.
Exercise/Health: Nearby gym, weights, Jacuzzi, sauna, steam & massage.
Swimming: Nearby pool.
Sunbathing: On common sun decks.
Smoking: Permitted in

lounge area.
Pets: Not permitted.
Handicap Access: No.
Children: Not especially welcome.
Languages: French, English & some Spanish.
Your Host: Marcel & Derek.

IGTA

Auberge Encore

Gay-Friendly 50/50 ♀♂

Ideally located in downtown Montréal, *Auberge Encore* is the perfect location for your vacation in French Canada. Two apartments of contemporary design await you in a newly-renovated greystone townhouse. One block away, we invite you to walk along *The Main* and discover its trendy bistros, haute couture boutiques, thriving nightclubs, shops and galleries. We are also within walking distance of Place des Arts, major museums, Mt. Royal Park, Old Montréal and the underground city. Come, and enjoy "la joie de vivre à Montréal!"
Address: 53 Milton, Montréal, Québec H2X 1V2 Canada. Tel: (514) 287-9596 or Fax: 489-3148.

Type: Bed & breakfast apartments.
Clientele: 50% gay & lesbian & 50% hetero clientele.
Transportation: Car or taxi from Dorval airport or from Canadian National Station.
To Gay Bars: 5 blocks. A 10-minute walk or 5-minute drive.
Rooms: 1 bedroom & 1 apartment with queen beds.
Bathrooms: 1 private

bath/toilet & 1 private shower/toilet.
Meals: Full breakfast.
Vegetarian: Vegetarian restaurant 1 block away.
Complimentary: Perrier & homemade truffles upon arrival.
Dates Open: All year.
High Season: Summer.
Rates: CDN $100-$125.
Credit Cards: VISA.
Rsv'tns: Required.
Reserve Through: Travel agent or call direct.
Minimum Stay: 2 nights

on weekends, 4 nights on holidays.
Parking: Limited pay parking. Must reserve at time of booking.
In-Room: Color cable TV, VCR, AC, telephone, ceiling fans, kitchen, refrigerator, coffee/tea-making facilities & maid service.
On-Premises: Common lounge.
Exercise/Health: Nearby gym, weights, Jacuzzi, sauna, steam &

massage.
Swimming: Nearby pool & lake.
Sunbathing: On private sun decks.
Smoking: Permitted on balconies & patio.
Pets: Permitted.
Handicap Access: No.
Children: Welcome.
Languages: English & French.
Your Host: Richard & Duane.

Aux Berges

Canada's Finest All Male Hotel

Men ♂

From the time *Aux Berges* was founded in 1967, it has acquired an atmosphere which is relatively unique among establishments having a constant flow of guests. The fact that they are from various countries and backgrounds certainly helps to make their stay with us a most pleasant and memorable experience. We regard ourselves as a large family, and would gladly welcome you to join us. Our staff are always ready to help you with any problems you might have during your stay in Montréal.

Address: 1070 rue Mackay, Montréal, PQ H3G 2H1 Canada. Tel: (514) 938-9393 or (800) 668-6253.

Type: Hotel.
Clientele: Men only.
Transportation: Airport bus to Sheraton Center Hotel, then 5-minute walk, or taxi directly from airport CDN $25.
To Gay Bars: 1 block to gay bar.
Rooms: 49 rooms with double beds.
Bathrooms: 29 private baths, 20 sinks. Shared: 12 showers, 3 baths, 4 toilets.
Meals: Continental breakfast.
Dates Open: All year.
High Season: May-October.
Rates: CDN $65-$90.
Discounts: On 7-day stay, 2 days free (good Nov-Mar.).
Credit Cards: MC, VISA, Amex, Diners Club, En Route & Discover.
Rsv'tns: Recommended.
Reserve Through: Travel agent or call direct.
Parking: Adequate on- & off-street parking.
In-Room: Color TV with video, AC, telephone, laundry & maid service.
On-Premises: Kitchen facilities, 2 TV lounges & snack bar.
Exercise/Health: Sauna.
Swimming: Pool & lake nearby.
Sunbathing: On private sun deck & terrace.
Nudity: Permitted on the sun deck, terrace & sauna area.
Smoking: Permitted without restrictions.
Pets: Small pets permitted.
Handicap Access: No.
Children: Not permitted.
Languages: French, English, German & Spanish.
Your Host: Serge & Christian.

Château Cherrier B & B

Gay/Lesbian ♀♂

Château Cherrier is a magnificent Tudor building decorated throughout with authentic period furniture. Large original oils of the same period adorn the sitting room and entry. Our strategic location near the gay village, restaurants, boutiques and nightlife, is further enhanced by a private parking lot, a rarity in the area. Leo and Jacques invite you to experience Montréal.

Address: 550 rue Cherrier Montréal, QC H2L 1H3 Canada. Tel: (514) 844-0055 , (800) 816-0055, Fax: (514) 844-8438.

Type: Bed & breakfast in a private home.
Clientele: Mainly gay/lesbian with some hetero clientele.
Transportation: Taxi from airport 20 minutes.
To Gay Bars: 4 blks to rue Ste-Catherine gay bars.
Rooms: 8 rooms with double & twin beds.
Bathrooms: 1 private bath/toilet/shower, 2 shared showers, & 4 shared toilets.
Meals: Full breakfast prepared by Chef Leo.

Complimentary: Ice cubes.
Dates Open: April 1-November 30.
Rates: CDN $50-$75.
Credit Cards: MC, VISA, Amex.

Rsv'tns: Required.
Reserve Through: Travel agent or call direct.
Minimum Stay: 3 nights long weekends or grand event.
Parking: Free private

valet parking.
In-Room: AC, fan and maid service.
On-Premises: 2 living rooms, laundry service on long stays, shared refrigerator, safety box.

Swimming: In pool one block away.
Smoking: Permitted in lounge only, not in rooms.
Languages: French, English, a little Spanish.

La Conciergerie Guest House

Gay/Lesbian ♂

Your Resort in the City!

La Conciergerie is Montréal's premier guest house. Since our opening in 1985, we have gained an ever-growing popularity among travelers from Canada, the United States, Europe and Australia. A beautiful Victorian home, built in 1885, offers a total of 17 rooms, eight with shared bath and nine with private bath. All of the rooms are furnished with comfortable queen-sized beds and duvet comforters. The rooms are

air-conditioned for your comfort. A complimentary European breakfast, consisting of coffee, orange juice, bagels, croissants, English muffins, home-baked breads, fresh fruit, jams, etc., is offered to be enjoyed either in the breakfast room or on one of the outdoor terraces. In summer, you can take advantage of our private rooftop sun deck to work on your tan. All year round, there is a warm Jacuzzi to relax in. For reasons of safety, we do not allow smoking in any of the bedrooms. There is a full kitchen available for those with special diets, or just special desires!

The house is centrally located in Montréal, within walking distance of most major points of interest, including downtown shopping, charming Old Montréal, the cafe terrasses of rue St.-Denis (as well as its trendy boutiques), the busy main street Ste.-Catherine, Place des Arts, Palais des Congres and the East Village, with its many gay shops, restaurants, and those notorious bars. The Metro (subway) is just two blocks away, and we have maps and guide books to help you find your way around town. We can offer suggestions on where to shop and dine. There is plenty of on-street parking for those who drive, and the airport taxi rate is CDN $24.00.

Address: 1019 rue St.-Hubert, Montréal, PQ H2L 3Y3 Canada. Tel: (514) 289-9297 or Fax: 289-0845.

Type: Bed & breakfast.
Clientele: Mostly men with women welcome.
Transportation: Airport bus to Voyageur Bus Station. Then walk, or taxi directly for CDN $24. Take a cab if arriving by train.
To Gay Bars: 2 blocks to men's & women's bars.
Rooms: 17 rooms with queen beds.
Bathrooms: 9 private. Shared: 1 bathtub, 2 showers, 2 toilets, 1 full bath.
Meals: Expanded conti-

nental breakfast.
Vegetarian: Bring your own. Vegetarian restaurants nearby.
Dates Open: All year.
High Season: April-December.
Rates: High season CDN $52-$118, low season CDN $39-$98.
Discounts: On 7-day stays in off-season.
Credit Cards: MC, VISA, Amex & Diners.
Rsv'tns: Recommended.
Reserve Through: Call direct.

Minimum Stay: 3 nights on long weekends.
Parking: Ample free on-street parking.
In-Room: Maid service & AC.
On-Premises: Meeting rooms, TV lounge, public telephone, central AC/heat, laundry facilities, private terrace, gardens, & kitchen privileges.
Exercise/Health: Jacuzzi on premises. Massage by appointment only. Gym nearby.
Swimming: At nearby

pool.
Sunbathing: On common sun deck & roof.
Nudity: Permitted on roof & Jacuzzi.
Smoking: Permitted, except in bedrooms.
Pets: Permitted with prior notice.
Handicap Access: No.
Children: Not permitted.
Languages: French & English.

IGTA

La Douillette

Women ♀

Love to Travel, but Hate to Leave Home & Cat? Borrow Mine!

La Douillette is a private home with small garden, purring cat and wonderful cuisine. The house, furnished with antiques, conveys a feeling of tranquility. Each room is supplied with local maps and information about current events, to help you enjoy this great city of Montréal to the fullest. I will also be pleased to advise you in any way that will help you enjoy your stay. In summer, relax and enjoy a home-cooked breakfast in our flower garden. Bienvenue à toutes! *Micheline*
Address: 7235 de Lorimier St, Montréal, PQ H2E 2N9 Canada. Tel: (514) 376-2183.

Type: Bed & breakfast. **Clientele:** Women only. **Transportation:** Pickup from airport when possible, CDN $15.00. Bus from airport to Bonaventure Subway Stn, then to Iberville Stn. **To Gay Bars:** 15 minutes by car or metro. **Rooms:** 3 rooms with double or queen beds. **Bathrooms:** 1 shared bath/shower/toilet. **Meals:** Full breakfast. **Vegetarian:** Available at all times. **Complimentary:** Juices, tea & coffee. **Dates Open:** All year. **High Season:** Spring, summer & autumn. **Rates:** CDN $40-$60. **Discounts:** 10% for stays of more than 4 days. **Rsv'tns:** Recommended. **Reserve Through:** Call direct. **Parking:** Ample on-street parking. **In-Room:** Ceiling fans. **On-Premises:** TV lounge. **Swimming:** At free nearby pool or river. **Smoking:** Permitted with some restrictions. **Pets:** Not permitted. **Handicap Access:** No. **Children:** Permitted with restrictions. **Languages:** French, English, Spanish & German.

Le Chasseur Guest House

Gay/Lesbian ♂

Le Chasseur Guest House is a charming European bed and breakfast, centrally located in Montréal. Gay bars, restaurants, Old Montréal, the Latin Quarter and trendy boutiques are all nearby. Our staff will provide a wealth of information and will spare no expense to make your stay easy-going and relaxing. *Le Chasseur,* a step in the right direction. The bed and breakfast "recommended by friends for friends."
Address: 1567 rue St.-Andre, Montréal, PQ H2L 3T5 Canada. Tel: (514) 521-2238, Fax: (514) 843-5005.

Type: Guest house. **Clientele:** Mostly men with women welcome. **Transportation:** Airport bus to Terminus Voyageur, then 1 block walking. **To Gay Bars:** Right in the center of Montreal's gay area. **Rooms:** 8 rooms. **Bathrooms:** 2 private, others share. **Meals:** Expanded continental breakfast. **Vegetarian:** 2 blocks to vegetarian restaurant & store. **Dates Open:** All year. **High Season:** Mid-May thru mid-October. **Rates:** Low season CDN $30-$65. High season CDN $40-$75. **Discounts:** Packages on request, lower rates for 3 or more nights, no discounts on American/Canadian holidays. **Credit Cards:** MC, VISA. **Rsv'tns:** Required with credit card or money order. **Reserve Through:** Travel agent or call direct. **Minimum Stay:** 2 nights on long weekends. **Parking:** Ample on-street parking. **In-Room:** Clock radio, two rooms have refrigerators. **On-Premises:** We arrange for city guides. Bicycles are available, individual keys. **Exercise/Health:** 1/2 block to gym. **Smoking:** Permitted without restrictions. **Pets:** Permitted with prior arrangement. **Handicap Access:** No. **Languages:** French, English, limited Spanish.

Le St. Christophe Bed & Breakfast

Men ♂

French Country Charm in the Heart of the Gay Village

Upon my arrival, I was warmly greeted by my hosts Simon and Stephen, then led to one of their very charming rooms. The library, done in English style furnishings with a fireplace, a wall of bookshelves filled with plenty of reading material and a fine collection of art pottery; one of many throughout the house. After catching my breath from my trip, I left my room to enter a world very unique, even for Montreal. There is always something to discover at the *St. Christophe*. A very large living room with all the warmth and charm of a country inn. With a working fireplace to sit in front of or a corner to relax in and listen to music, watch TV or a video. Off in another corner a very inviting four man Jacuzzi. As Simon continued my tour I was led to the dining room where the tables were beautifully set for tomorrow's breakfast. I would find out that breakfast would be a highlight at the *St. Christophe*. I could expect eggs Benedict, omelets filled with a variety of sumptuous fillings, or French toast, the likes of which I've never experienced. I was told breakfast is served from 9:00 to 11:00 am but it is not uncommon for guests to linger until noon. Next, we were off to the breakfast deck set up like an outdoor cafe; very French. The deck is next to a small flower garden where Stephen also grows herbs and vegetables, which are served at breakfast. Then onto another floor where there is a very private sun deck and clothing is optional. I registered, and Stephen brought me up-to-date on what was happening in Montreal so that I could begin my adventure. *From the travel journal of a guest and now dear friend.*

Address: 1597 St.-Christophe, Montréal, PQ H2L 3W7 Canada. Tel: (514) 527-7836.

Type: Bed & breakfast guesthouse with full breakfast.
Clientele: Men only.
Transportation: Airport bus to Voyageur bus station. Walk one block. Take metro to Berri if arriving by train.
To Gay Bars: 1 block.
Rooms: 5 rooms with single or double beds.
Bathrooms: 2 private shower/toilet, 1 private

sink. 2 shared full baths.
Meals: Full breakfast.
Vegetarian: Available by pre-arrangement.
Complimentary: Fruits, coffee & tea.
Dates Open: All year.
High Season: Easter through Thanksgiving.
Rates: CDN $50-$69.
Discounts: On 7-day stays in off season.
Credit Cards: MC & VISA.
Rsv'tns: Required.

Reserve Through: Call direct.
Minimum Stay: 3 nights on long weekends.
Parking: Ample, free on-street parking.
In-Room: Color TV, maid, ceiling fans, room & laundry service.
On-Premises: TV lounge, private dining room, laundry facilities, fireplace, video tapes.
Exercise/Health: Jacuzzi.

Swimming: Nearby pool.
Sunbathing: On private sun decks.
Nudity: Permitted.
Smoking: Permitted without restrictions.
Pets: Permitted with prior notice.
Handicap Access: No.
Children: Not permitted.
Languages: French & English.
Your Host: Simon & Stephen.

Pension Vallières

We Welcome You to Montréal!

Gay/Lesbian ♀♂

We extend a warm welcome to guests at *Pension Vallières,* our cozy, quiet home in Montréal. The house is decorated in an "Art Deco" style and we offer two choices of accommodation. We have a bedroom with queen-sized bed, as well as a fully-equipped studio with a private entrance. Amenities in the studio include kitchenette, private bath, pool table, color cable TV and a stereo. You may choose from a variety of hearty breakfasts, which, if you like, we will serve in your room. To help make the most of your stay in Montréal, your hostess, Lucille, is available to take you on a sightseeing tour of this beautiful city.

Address: 6562, Delorimier St, Montréal, Québec H2G 2P6 Canada. Tel: (514) 729-9552.

Type: Bed & breakfast.
Clientele: Mostly gay & lesbian with some hetero clientele.
Transportation: Pick up from airport, train (CDN $8-$25), bus. #18 bus from airport to Bonaventure Subway Sta, then to Beaubien Station
To Gay Bars: 10 minutes by Métro.
Rooms: 1 room & 1 bachelor studio (private bath) with double or queen bed.
Bathrooms: 1 private bath/shower/toilet & 1 shared bath/shower/toilet.
Meals: Full breakfast.
Vegetarian: 5-minute walk to vegetarian food store.
Complimentary: Tea, herbal tea, coffee & juice.
Dates Open: All year.
High Season: Spring, summer, autumn.
Rates: CDN $40-$45 for 1 person, CDN $10-$15 for each extra person.
Discounts: 10% for stays of over 7 days.
Rsv'tns: Required.
Reserve Through: Call direct.
Parking: Ample on-street parking.
In-Room: Color cable TV, ceiling fan, coffee/tea-making facilities, kitchen, refrigerator, room & maid service.
On-Premises: Pool table, stereo & laundry facilities.
Sunbathing: Beach on Notre Dame islands.
Smoking: Permitted without restriction.
Pets: Not permitted.
Handicap Access: No.
Children: Permitted.
Languages: French & English.
Your Host: Lucille.

QUÉBEC

Le Coureur des Bois

Gay/Lesbian ♀♂

Le Coureur des Bois is located in a historic stone house typical of the early French Canadian period. Newly renovated, the interior of the house is modern. Seven guest rooms, each with its own character, are simply furnished with emphasis on cleanliness and comfort. None of our rooms have private bath, but with 3 full baths to 7 rooms, we've yet to have anyone complain. Fresh fruit, croissants, rolls, muffins, cheeses, cereals and coffee make up the continental breakfast.

What distinguishes us from the competition is our unique location within the walled city and the famous *Coureur des Bois* hospitality.

Address: 15 rue Ste.-Ursule, Québec, PQ G1R 4C7 Canada. Tel: (418) 692-1117.

Type: Guesthouse.
Clientele: Good mix of gay men & women.
Transportation: Taxi from airport or train.
To Gay Bars: 6-minute walk to gay/lesbian bars.
Rooms: 7 rooms with double or queen beds.
Bathrooms: 3 shared.
Meals: Our continental breakfast is a hearty combination of crois-sants, muffins, sweet breads, fruit dishes, cereals & assorted beverages.
Vegetarian: Available with advance notice.
Dates Open: All year.
High Season: April-November.
Rates: CDN $42-$92.
Credit Cards: MC, VISA, Amex & Diners.
Rsv'tns: Recommended.

Reserve Through: Travel agent or call direct.
Parking: 4-minute walk to underground parking for CDN $9 per day.
In-Room: Maid service.
On-Premises: TV lounge, outdoor terrace, & fridge in lounge.
Swimming: River & lake 15 minutes by car.
Sunbathing: On the terrace.

Smoking: Permitted, but not in bedrooms.
Pets: Permitted by prior arrangement.
Handicap Access: No.
Children: Not permitted.
Languages: French & English.
Your Host: Jean Paul & Mark.

Caribbean

BAHAMAS

NASSAU

Orchard Garden Apartment Hotel

Gay-Friendly ♀♂

Peaceful Seclusion in a Tropical Garden Setting

The *Orchard Garden Apartment Hotel* consists of cottages and studio apartments grouped around a swimming pool situated amidst a fully-enclosed, two-acre tropical garden of flowering vines, shrubs and century-old silk cotton trees. Cottages and apartments are fully-equipped with cutlery, crockery and cooking utensils. Beaches, tennis and squash courts, restaurants, bars and a discotheque are nearby. For your convenience, the central administration-reception area is staffed 24 hours. We invite you to the *Orchard* and undertake to do our best to make your stay in Nassau one that you would like to repeat.

Address: Village Rd, PO Box N1514, Nassau, Bahamas. Tel: (809) 393-1297 or Fax: (809) 394-3562.

Type: Cottage & apartment colony with Tree Frog Bar.
Clientele: Mostly hetero clientele with a gay & lesbian following.
Transportation: Taxi.
To Gay Bars: 8 miles or a 10-minute drive.
Rooms: 4 rooms, 11 apartments & 13 cottages with single, double & queen beds.
Bathrooms: All private bath/toilets.

Vegetarian: Available in adjacent Tamarind Hill restaurant.
Dates Open: All year.
High Season: Dec 15-Apr 21.
Rates: Summer (Apr 22-Dec 14) $55-$75. Winter (Dec 15-Apr 21) $65-$90.
Discounts: Military, travel agents, airlines, AAA. Advance reservations necessary along with prepayment.
Credit Cards: MC, VISA &

Amex.
Rsv'tns: Required.
Reserve Through: Travel agent or call direct.
Parking: Ample free off-street parking.
In-Room: Color cable TV, AC, ceiling fans, kitchen, refrigerator, coffee/tea-making facilities & maid service.
On-Premises: TV lounge in bar, fax service available.
Exercise/Health: Nearby full-service gym.

Swimming: Pool on premises, ocean nearby.
Sunbathing: At poolside, on patio & private sun decks.
Smoking: Permitted everywhere.
Pets: Permitted by arrangement.
Handicap Access: Yes.
Children: Welcome.
Languages: English & Spanish.
Your Host: Louis & Geoff.

BRITISH WEST INDIES

ANGUILLA

La Petite Maison d'Amour

Gay-Friendly ♀♂

A Place You Share with Someone You Love

La Petite Maison d'Amour is a romantic, intimate, private one-bedroom home at the water's edge with views overlooking four islands. This sensuous, unique, West Indian designer hideaway offers views from every room, fully-equipped kitchen and alfresco dining. The bedroom, with queen-sized bed and private patio, has an adjoining bath with a glass-block shower. A secluded beach with great snorkeling is a three-minute walk along the shore. Picnic basket, TV, tape & CD player, telescope, books, snorkels, masks and beach equipment are just a few of the extras. **Address: PO Box 232, Anguilla, British West Indies. Tel: (809) 497-3282.**

Type: Villa.
Clientele: Mostly hetero clientele with gays & lesbians welcome.
Transportation: Car or jeep is best. We arrange car/jeep rental and your taxi from the airport.
Rooms: One villa with queen bed.
Bathrooms: Private.
Meals: Will arrange to have refrigerator stocked.
Dates Open: All year.
High Season: Dec 15-Apr 15.
Rates: US $800-$1200 per week plus tax includes maid, no service charge.
Rsv'tns: Required.
Reserve Through: Call direct.
Minimum Stay: 1 week.
Parking: Ample free off-street parking.
In-Room: Color TV, telephone, ceiling fans, telescope, CD cassette player, games, books, kitchen & maid service.
On-Premises: Maid will do your laundry.
Swimming: 3 minutes to secluded beach.
Sunbathing: On two porches or the beach.
Smoking: Non-smokers preferred. Smoking permitted outdoors.
Pets: Permitted, but not recommended due to long distance travel.
Handicap Access: No.
Children: Not especially welcome.
Languages: English, some French.

BARBADOS

Roman Beach Apts

Gay-Friendly ♀♂

Basic Accommodations & Privacy on a Pink-White Sand Beach

If you're looking for the privacy and freedom you find when you don't stay in a big hotel...if you don't require all the amenities of the more commercial properties...if you want to taste of the local flavor of Barbados...you'll enjoy staying with us at *Roman Beach Apartments*. Our accommodations are basic, with serviceable furnishings and fans instead of air conditioning. All apartments have private baths and kitchens, so you can do your own cooking, or sample the many little restaurants of Oistintown. There simply is NO place on Barbados that you could call gay, so most of our clientele is straight. Our management, however, is gay-friendly and gays and lesbians are most welcome here. Ask manager Fran for information on how to make the most of your stay on the island. Our beach is beautiful. Its pink-white sand is rock free. The sea is placid here, though a surfing beach is only five minutes away. Nearby, you can find para-sailing, scuba diving, snorkeling and boat excursions. A local company offers horseback tours of the inland hills. **Address: Oistintown Christ Church, Barbados, West Indies Tel: (809) 428-7635 , (809) 428-2510, Fax: (809) 428-1057.**

Type: Apartments & youth hostel-style accommodations.
Clientele: Mostly straight clientele with a gay/lesbian following.
Transportation: Taxi from aiport U.S. $11.
To Gay Bars: No gay bars on Barbados. Gay-friendly bar in Bridgetown 6 miles.

Rooms: 10 apartments with kitchens. 2-3 person sleeping rooms with kitchen privileges.
Bathrooms: All private.
Dates Open: All year.
High Season: December 15th-April 15th.
Rates: Apartments US $35-$50 summer & US $45-$60 winter.
Credit Cards: None.

Rsv'tns: Recommended.
Reserve Through: Travel agent or call direct.
Minimum Stay: 3 days.
Parking: Adequate free off-street parking.
In-Room: Maid service, kitchen, & fans.
On-Premises: Public telephone.
Swimming: Ocean beach.
Sunbathing: On beach or

in gardens.
Smoking: Permitted without restrictions.
Handicap Access: 3 apartments accessible.
Children: Permitted.
Languages: English & Bajan.
Your Host: Fran.

JAMAICA

Hotel Mocking Bird Hill

Gay-Friendly ♀♂

Where Your Heart Will Sing & Your Soul Will Fly

Imagine yourself basking luxuriantly on the terrace, enjoying a peaceful setting with personalized service. While sipping your complimentary cocktail, watch the sun set behind the Blue Mountains. Enjoy fine dining in a tropical ambiance overlooking the lights of Port Antonio. We serve homemade Caribbean cuisine, using only fresh local produce.

Simple European elegance is combined with the charm and hospitality of the Caribbean. Airy, spacious rooms with original art provide a relaxed, gracious atmosphere. We offer tips and information to help you discover the natural beauty of Portland, Jamaica's most unspoiled parish.

You will appreciate the difference that is *Mocking Bird Hill*. Come, share our secret.

Address: PO Box 254, Port Antonio, Jamaica West Indies. Tel: (809) 993-3370 , (809) 993-7134, Fax: (809) 993-7133.

Type: Hotel with restaurant & bar. Gallery & studio to be opened.
Clientele: Mostly straight clientele with a gay & lesbian following.
Transportation: From Kingston: car rental or taxi. From Montego Bay: Inland flight to Port Antonio airport with free transfer to hotel.
Rooms: 10 rooms with single, queen or king beds.
Bathrooms: 7 en suite shower/toilets, 3 en suite bath/toilet/showers.

Meals: Additional charge for meals.
Vegetarian: Meals included in menu.
Complimentary: Welcome cocktail. Fruit & fresh flowers in room.
Dates Open: All year.
High Season: Dec 15-Apr 30.
Rates: Winter US $110 per room, summer US $95 per room.
Discounts: Group rates (10 or more people), long stays, repeat guests, travel industry. Call/fax for off-season specials.

Credit Cards: MC, VISA, Eurocard.
Rsv'tns: Recommeded. Walk-ins welcome.
Reserve Through: Travel agent or call/fax direct.
Parking: Ample free off-street parking.
In-Room: Ceiling fans, safe & laundry service.
On-Premises: TV lounge, telephone, babysitters, special tours & hikes arranged. Art classes & use of studio.
Exercise/Health: Walking/jogging trail. Massage with prior appointment.

Swimming: Pool & ocean.
Sunbathing: At poolside, beach or in the garden.
Smoking: Permitted. Non-smoking rooms available.
Pets: Not permitted.
Handicap Access: Yes. Limited, with no special facilities.
Children: Welcome, but not encouraged.
Languages: English, German & French.
Your Host: Barbara & Shireen.

Lighthouse Park

Rustic, Peaceful Caribbean Ambiance

Gay-Friendly ♀♂

Lighthouse Park is situated on 1-1/2 acres of seaside cliff property. We take pride in ensuring a relaxed, rustic, yet comfortable and hospitable atmosphere. Cabanas, A-frame cottages, a lovely stone villa and camping sites provide varied accommodations. All units are set amongst tropical foliage and flowers. Snorkeling and swimming are excellent, and there are clothing-optional areas. Local transport, both to town and to white sand beaches, is easy and bike rentals are available.

Address: PO Box 3, Negril, Jamaica, West Indies. Tel: (809) 957-4490.

Type: Seaside cabanas, a stone house & tent spaces.
Clientele: Mostly straight clientele with a gay/lesbian following.
Transportation: Airport bus US $25 per person 1 way, private taxi US $60. 1-1/2 hour (approx 45 min) scenic drive.
To Gay Bars: No gay bars in Jamaica.
Rooms: 10 doubles.
Bathrooms: 3 private, others share.
Campsites: Tent sites

(bring your own tents).
Vegetarian: Fresh fruit & vegetables available in town. Vegetarian plate available at most restaurants.
Dates Open: All year.
High Season: Dec 15th-May 1st.
Rates: Low season US $15-$105, high season US $20-$175 & 12-1/2% tax.
Discounts: 10% on stays of 14 days or longer.
Credit Cards: MC, VISA & Amex.

Rsv'tns: Required with 3-day deposit (certified check or money order).
Reserve Through: Travel agent or call direct.
Minimum Stay: 3 days during high season.
Parking: Adequate off-street security parking.
In-Room: Stone house has kitchen privileges & maid service. A communal kitchen is available.
Exercise/Health: Snorkeling on premises.
Swimming: Deep-sea

swimming off cliff on premises. 4 miles to white sandy beach.
Sunbathing: On beach or common sun decks.
Nudity: Permitted in sea-access areas & on sun decks.
Handicap Access: No.
Children: Not recommended under 12 years.
Languages: English.
Your Host: Sharon.

Seagrape Villas

Home Away From Home With Your Own Cook & Maid

♀♂

Rent a whole house for a Caribbean escape. Enjoy daily adventures, as you explore Jamaica's beaches, its history, sights, activities and landmarks. *Seagrape Villas* are 3 lovely houses right on the sea. Each has 4 bedrooms, 4 baths, a private pool and its own cook and maid. For two guests or groups up to 24, *Seagrape Villas* offer privacy and the opportunity to get to know the island and its people firsthand. Plan your own

delectable menu and shop with the cook, discovering local produce and cuisine. Rent a car to go to different places each day, exploring this friendly island.

Address: Ocho Rios, Jamaica West Indies. Tel: (800) 637-3608 or (312) 693-6884.

Type: 3 four-bedroom villas with cook & maid.
Clientele: Everyone welcome.
Transportation: Car is best.
Rooms: 3 villas, each with 4 bedrooms and single beds.
Bathrooms: A private bath for each bedroom.

Vegetarian: Always available.
Dates Open: All year.
High Season: December-April (Xmas-Easter).
Rates: $2500 per villa per week high season, $1800 low season.
Discounts: Available. Call for details.
Rsv'tns: Required.

Reserve Through: Travel agent or call direct.
Minimum Stay: 1 week.
Parking: Ample off-street parking.
In-Room: AC, ceiling fans, laundry service & maid service.
Swimming: Pool & ocean on premises.
Sunbathing: At poolside.

Nudity: Permitted poolside.
Smoking: Permitted anywhere.
Pets: Permitted.
Handicap Access: Yes, but not specially equipped.
Children: Children welcomed.
Languages: English.

DOMINICAN REPUBLIC

CABARETE

Purple Paradise

Women ♀

Magic at the Rainbow's End

Enjoy tranquility on an endless sandy beach. Chill out in the Jacuzzi and slide into the pool nestled in a lush garden. Savor scrumptious meals. Engage in quiet conversation in spacious, comfortable common areas, or simply admire the magnificent sea view. Visit our mountains and magical caves. Venture to nearby Cabarete for handmade gifts by local artisans. Do everything...or do nothing. At *Purple Paradise,* the choice is yours.

Address: Mail: Lindsay Rose, EPS D#148, PO Box 02-5548, Miami, FL 33102 Tel: (809) 571-0637 , Fax: (809) 571-0691/3346.

Type: Guesthouse with bar, restaurant & art shop.
Clientele: Women only.
Transportation: Taxi from airport direct to guesthouse.
Rooms: 5 rooms with single or double beds.
Bathrooms: All private shower/toilets.
Vegetarian: Served daily & vegetarian food nearby.
Complimentary: Welcome drink.

Dates Open: Nov-May, July-Sept.
High Season: December-March.
Rates: Weekly (7 nights): Summer USD $275-$335, winter USD $385-$445.
Discounts: If individual client refers/books 5 rooms, they get 1 room for a week free.
Rsv'tns: Required.
Reserve Through: Call direct.
Parking: Adequate free off-street parking.

In-Room: Maid service.
On-Premises: Indoor & outdoor lounge areas.
Exercise/Health: Jacuzzi on premises. Nearby gym, weights, massage, tennis, golf, windsurfing, scuba, snorkeling, mountain bikes, riding.
Swimming: Pool & ocean on premises. Nearby ocean & river.
Sunbathing: At poolside, on roof, patio, common & private sun decks & at the beach.

Nudity: Permitted in the pool.
Smoking: As the villa is "open air," smoking is permitted.
Pets: Not permitted.
Handicap Access: No.
Children: Not especially welcome.
Languages: Spanish, English, Dutch, German, French & Italian.
Your Host: Lindsay.

DUTCH WEST INDIES

SABA

Captain's Quarters

Gay-Friendly ♀♂

The Unspoiled Queen of the Caribbean

Rainforest: Orchids, tree frogs, crested hummingbirds. *Hiking:* Stunning views, tidal pools, mountain trails. *Scuba:* Sea turtles, pinnacles, hot springs, snorkeling. *History:* Pirates, sea captains, Saba lace.

Captain's Quarters is a 14-room Victorian guesthouse set in a tropical paradise, a short 10-minute flight from St Maarten. Saba offers spectacular scuba, hiking and relaxation in a storybook setting of Dutch "Gingerbread Villages" that date from the 1850s. Originally settled by pirates and sea captains as a safe haven for their families, "The Rock" was accessible only by footpaths and thousands of steps, until "The Road That Couldn't Be Built" was handcrafted in the 1950s. Saba will remind you of "Switzerland with Palm Trees." World-class scuba diving combines with well-marked hiking trails, a pristine rainforest and spectacular views at every turn to make Saba an unforgettable destination. Ecotourism is supported by the Saba Marine Park and the Saba Conservation Foundation.

For over 30 years, *Captain's Quarters* has hosted royalty, celebrities and adventurous travelers from throughout the world. Built around a sea captain's mansion (circa 1850), rooms feature antique and 4-poster beds (many with elegant canopies). Balconies and patios offer stunning views of the Caribbean and Mt. Scenery. Enjoy our garden dining pavilion, cliffside pool/bar and some of the friendliest people in the Caribbean. Convenient to all diving, trails, village shopping and the 1,064 steps to Mt. Scenery's Rainforest.

Little nightlife, less cruising — this is the perfect romantic getaway. **Note:** Saba has no beaches. All swimming is from rocks, boats, tidal pools and hotel swimming pools. However, since you have to fly through St. Maarten anyway, spend a few days there and enjoy some of the best beaches in the world. And if you're vacationing on St. Maarten, St. Barths, or Anguilla, remember, we're only minutes away. Come visit for a few days.

Address: Windwardside, Saba, Netherlands Antilles. Tel: (5994) 62201, Fax: (5994) 62377, In USA: (212) 289-6031, Fax: 289-1931.

Type: Hotel with restaurant & bar.
Clientele: Mostly straight clientele with a gay & lesbian following.
Transportation: 10-minute flight from St. Maarten, then short taxi ride (about $8) to hotel. Airport transfer included in package rates.
To Gay Bars: None. All bars on island are friendly.
Rooms: 14 rooms with single, double or queen beds.
Bathrooms: All private shower/toilet.
Meals: Full American breakfast.
Vegetarian: Available upon request.
Complimentary: Welcome drink.
Dates Open: All year.
High Season: Feb, Mar, Apr.
Rates: Summer $95-$125, extra person $35. Winter $95-$150, extra person $35.
Discounts: For stays of 3 or more nights, group packages. Off-season discounts for groups.
Credit Cards: VISA, MC & Discover.
Rsv'tns: Required. Walk-ins based on availability.
Reserve Through: Travel agent or call direct.
Parking: Ample free off-street parking.
In-Room: Balcony & maid service. Some rooms with AC, color cable TV, ceiling fans, refrigerator.
On-Premises: Meeting rooms & TV lounge.
Exercise/Health: Nearby gym.
Swimming: Pool on premises. Nearby ocean.
Sunbathing: At poolside.
Smoking: Permitted.
Pets: Permitted with advance approval.
Handicap Access: No.
Children: Welcome.
Languages: English, Dutch, Papiamento & Spanish.

IGTA

FRENCH WEST INDIES

ST BARTHELEMY

Hostellerie des Trois Forces

Gay-Friendly ♀♂

More than a regular vacation in the Caribbean, *Hostellerie des Trois Forces*, established by a French chef, offers you a warmhearted experience. Authentic peacefulness is the soul of our establishment. Eight private cottages, some with private bath, have handmade wooden furnishings designed to complement the different zodiac signs. The handhewn, mountaintop restaurant offers French and Creole and vegetarian specialities, a wood fire grill and a rolling flambé dessert cart. The restaurant has been reviewed from 1987 through July 1994 by publications such as *GQ, Vogue, NY Times, Los Angeles Times, Conde Nast,* and *Caribbean Travel and Life.*

Address: Vitet 97133, St. Barthelemy, FWI   **Tel: Direct:** (590) 276-125, **Fax:** (590) 278-138.

Type: Inn with French & Creole & vegetarian restaurant & bar.
Clientele: Mostly straight clientele with a gay & lesbian following.
Transportation: Taxi or rental car (we can reserve your car).
To Gay Bars: No gay bars on the island.
Rooms: 8 cottages, with four under construction.
Bathrooms: All private.
Meals: Continental breakfast, full breakfast available by special order.
Vegetarian: Food is love. We make French Creole vegetarian.
Dates Open: All year.
High Season: December through March.
Rates: US $75-$170.
Credit Cards: MC, VISA, Amex.
Rsv'tns: Required in high season, penalty for no-shows, cancellations.
Reserve Through: Travel agent or call or fax direct.
Parking: Adequate, free, off-street parking.
In-Room: Maid, room & laundry service, AC and every room has petit frigidaire.
Exercise/Health: Massage with polarity, yoga, astrological readings available.
Swimming: Pool on premises, ocean beach nearby.
Sunbathing: At poolside, on beach.
Nudity: Women can go topless by the pool. St. Barth has a nude beach.
Smoking: Permitted without restrictions.
Pets: Not permitted.
Handicap Access: No.
Children: Permitted.
Languages: English, French, German, some Spanish.

PUERTO RICO

SAN JUAN

Atlantic Beach Hotel

Gay/Lesbian ♂

By the sea, in the center of Condado is the best of all worlds! *The Atlantic Beach Hotel* is located in the tourist area, directly on the beach and has a very large bar and restaurant overlooking the beach. There are many restaurants and nightspots in the area. It is about 10 minutes to the historic old section of the city and 20 minutes to the airport.

Address: Calle Vendig #1, Condado San Juan, PR 00907. Tel: (809) 721-6900, Fax: (809) 721-6917.

Type: Hotel with restaurant & bar.
Clientele: Mostly men with women welcome.
Transportation: Taxi is best.
To Gay Bars: 3-4 blocks.
Rooms: 37 rooms with single or double beds.
Bathrooms: 27 private shower/toilets, other share.
Meals: Continental breakfast on the sun deck.
Vegetarian: Available upon request & vegetarian restaurant within 3 min walking distance.
Complimentary: Coffee, tea, cocoa & muffins every morning on the sun deck.
Dates Open: All year.
High Season: Dec 15-Apr 14.
Rates: Winter $75-$140, summer $60-$115.
Discounts: 10% to airline employees.
Credit Cards: MC, VISA, Amex, Diners & Discover.
Rsv'tns: Required.
Reserve Through: Travel agent or call direct.
Parking: Limited free off-street parking.
In-Room: Maid service, AC, color TV, telephone.
On-Premises: Laundry facilities.
Exercise/Health: Jacuzzi.
Swimming: Hotel overlooks ocean beach.
Sunbathing: On private sun deck, beach.
Smoking: Permitted.
Pets: Not permitted.
Handicap Access: Yes. Some areas have ramps, bathroom facilities.
Children: Not permitted.
Languages: Spanish, English, French.
IGTA

Embassy Guest House-Condado

Gay/Lesbian ♀♂

Welcome to the *Embassy Guest House-Condado* in the center of Condado, only steps to the beach in San Juan. Awaken to aqua-colored waters off Condado Beach. Relax under a coco palm. Dine at Panaché, our beachfront restaurant and bar. Or, enjoy nearby water and jet skiing, scuba diving, fishing, tennis, golf etc. The San Juan night, with casinos, discos, and shows, is nearby, as is shopping in Old San Juan. The *Embassy* staff helps you enjoy your stay, so come see why Puerto Rico is called the *"Shining Star of the Caribbean."*

Address: 1126 Calle Seaview-Condado, San Juan, PR 00907. Tel: (809) 725-8284, Fax: (809) 725-2400.

Type: Guesthouse with restaurant & bar on the beach.
Clientele: Mainly gay/lesbian with some straight clientele.
Transportation: Taxi or limo from airport, approx $15. 15 min drive.
To Gay Bars: On premises, others 4 blocks away.
Rooms: 1 suite, 7 doubles, 7 quads.
Bathrooms: All private.
Vegetarian: Upon request in "Panache Restaurant."
Complimentary: Coffee, tea.
Dates Open: All year.
High Season: December 1st through May 1st.
Rates: $50-$135 Dec 15 to Apr 30, $45-$85 May 1 to Dec 14.
Discounts: 10% on weekly stays during off-season.
Credit Cards: MC, VISA & Amex.
Rsv'tns: Recommended.
Reserve Through: Travel agent or call direct.
Minimum Stay: 2 days on holidays & in season.
Parking: Ample, free on-street parking.
In-Room: Maid & room service, color TV, AC, ceiling fans, refrigerators & coffee-makers.
On-Premises: Restaurant, bar, TV lounge & public telephones.
Swimming: Ocean beach.
Sunbathing: On beach or sun decks.
Smoking: Permitted without restrictions.
Pets: Not permitted.
Handicap Access: Yes.
Children: Permitted, no infants, please.
Languages: Spanish, English, French.
IGTA

Ocean Park Beach Inn

Gay/Lesbian ♀♂

Tropical Gardens by the Ocean

In July, 1993, *3 Elena Guesthouse* became home for two world travelers. Now refurbished, the new name is *Ocean Park Beach Inn*. Vacationers seeking a Caribbean retreat in a tropical setting of mature palms, lush foliage and multicolored blossoms, plus the convenience of Condado's casinos, restaurants and gay bars, will find a gentle way of life here. Ten airy, spacious rooms, redesigned with unique art and collectibles, all with private entrances, surround a luxuriant courtyard and rattan bar/veranda. Spectacular sun decks offer panoramic views of the turquoise sea, white sand beach, beautiful, tanned bodies and pastel city skyline in this year-round paradise.

Address: Calle Elena No 3, Ocean Park, San Juan, PR 00911. Phone or Fax: (809) 728-7418. (800) 292-9208.

Type: Bed & breakfast inn with bar & cafe.
Clientele: Good mix of gays & lesbians.
Transportation: Taxi, bus or rental car from airport. Car rental arranged through desk.
To Gay Bars: 5-minute walk.
Rooms: 10 rooms with double or queen beds.
Bathrooms: All private.
Meals: Tropical continental breakfast.
Vegetarian: At breakfast & lunch. Several restaurants in neighborhood.
Complimentary: Welcome cocktail, tea, coffee, chilled spring water & ice.
Dates Open: All year.
High Season: December 15-April 15.
Rates: High: $60-$105 daily, $360-$630 weekly. Low: $40-$75 daily, $200-$375 weekly.
Discounts: Weekly rates all year, travel industry personnel.
Credit Cards: MC & VISA.
Rsv'tns: Recommended.
Reserve Through: Travel agent or call direct.
Parking: Adequate free on-street parking.
In-Room: AC, ceiling fans, refrigerator & maid service. Some with kitchenette.
On-Premises: TV lounge & Fax. Beach towels, chairs & equipment provided.
Exercise/Health: Bikes & water sports. Full service gym nearby, massage by appointment.
Swimming: Ocean on premises. Gay beach at Ocean Park.
Sunbathing: On the patio, private & common sun decks & at gay beach.
Smoking: Permitted in designated rooms & outdoor areas. Non-smoking rooms available.
Pets: Permitted with special arrangements.
Handicap Access: Yes. Limited.
Children: Permitted.
Languages: English, Spanish.

Ocean Walk Guest House

Gay/Lesbian ♀♂

Where Europe Meets the Caribbean

Formerly a series of Spanish-style homes located directly on the best part of San Juan's beach, *Ocean Walk* is now a very casual resort complex with 40 comfortable rooms in a beautiful courtyard setting, with pool, bar and grill. On the large, elevated sun deck, you can enjoy a piña colada, while the sun sets, in a spectacular display of colors, on the horizon. After midnight, all is

continued next page

quiet, and you will hear only the gentle pounding of the surf. Yet, the fast-paced nightlife and the casinos are within walking distance.

Address: Calle Atlantic No 1, Ocean Park, San Juan 00911 Puerto Rico. Tel: (809) 728-0855 or (800) 468-0615, Fax: (809) 728-6434.

Type: Guesthouse with restaurant & bar.
Clientele: Mainly gay & lesbian with some hetero clientele.
Transportation: Taxi or rental car from San Juan Int'l Airport approx $10.
To Gay Bars: 10 min walk or short taxi ride.
Rooms: 37 rooms & 3 apartments with single, double & king beds.
Bathrooms: 34 private shower/toilets. 6 rooms

share bath/shower/toilet.
Meals: Continental breakfast.
Vegetarian: Available upon request.
Dates Open: All year.
High Season: Dec 15-Apr 15.
Rates: US $35-$80 in summer. US $50-$120 in winter.
Discounts: 10% airline discounts, weekly rates for minimum 2 weeks.
Credit Cards: MC, VISA,

Amex, Discover & Eurocard.
Rsv'tns: Recommended.
Reserve Through: Travel agent or call direct.
Parking: Adequate on-street parking.
In-Room: Color cable TV, AC, ceiling fans & maid service.
Swimming: At pool on premises or ocean beach.
Sunbathing: At poolside, on beach & common sun

decks.
Smoking: Permitted.
Pets: Special permission required.
Handicap Access: Yes. Limited & with assistance.
Children: Welcomed.
Languages: English, Spanish, French & German.

IGTA

VIEQUES ISLAND

New Dawn's Caribbean Retreat & Guest House

Gay/Lesbian ♀

Best of All Worlds...

Enjoy both mountain rest AND beach life on this unspoiled Caribbean island of Vieques. Its location on 5 acres of Pilon hillside, dotted with hibiscus, bougainvillaeas & grazing horses makes *New Dawn's Caribbean Retreat & Guest House* a complete environment of natural beauty. The main house is flower-covered and built for outdoor living with spacious decks. There are also a women's bunkhouse and tent sites. *New Dawn* was designed for people who like to go barefoot & who don't need all the comforts of home, but seek a truly relaxed, peaceful atmosphere.

Address: PO Box 1512, Bo Pilon, Rt 995, Vieques, PR 00765. Tel: (809) 741-0495.

Type: Guesthouse & campground retreat with restaurant & bar.
Clientele: Mostly women with men welcome.
Transportation: Rent a car or call on arrival for $5 pick up from airport or ferry dock.
To Gay Bars: San Juan gay/lesbian bars 2 hrs away on main island of Puerto Rico.
Rooms: 6 rooms & bunkhouse which sleeps six. Single, bunk & queen beds.
Bathrooms: Share 1 toilet indoors, 6 showers & 2 toilets outdoors.
Campsites: 4 wooden platform tent sites (tents not included), outside showers, bath house with 2 toilets,

volleyball, horseshoes, snorkeling gear, horses, bicycles.
Meals: Optional with extra charge.
Vegetarian: Available upon request.
Complimentary: Coffee & tea.
Dates Open: All year. Prefer May-Dec 14 rentals.
High Season: Dec-Apr.
Rates: Rooms $35-$45, camping $10 a person, bunkhouse $15 a person, May-Dec weekly, 6 bdrm guesthouse $1000 per week.
Discounts: May 16-Dec 14 reduced private weekly rental for entire retreat.
Rsv'tns: Required 1 mo in advance May thru

Dec, strongly suggested Jan thru Apr. Deposit required.
Reserve Through: Travel agent or call direct (leave message!).
Minimum Stay: 1 week from May 16-Dec 14.
Parking: Ample free off-street parking.
In-Room: Guesthouse only: telephone, laundry service, kitchen, refrigerator, ceiling fans, TV & VCR.
On-Premises: Meeting rooms, laundry facilities, bike rentals, boogie boards, snorkeling gear.
Exercise/Health: Bikes, windsurfing, volleyball, horseshoes, croquet, & horseback riding. Massage available.
Swimming: Ocean beach.

Sunbathing: On beach, private & common sun decks, patio or roof, tent sites.
Nudity: Permitted in campsites at discretion of campers.
Smoking: Permitted outside, not in dorm or sleeping areas.
Pets: Permitted with prior arrangement (CALL FIRST). We have our own animals to care for.
Handicap Access: Yes, special WC. Limited to 1st fl of guest house, bunkhouse, camping.
Children: Permitted. Children under 2 years free.
Languages: Spanish & English.
Your Host: Gail & Dail.

VIRGIN ISLANDS

COOPER ISLAND

Cooper Island Beach Club

Gay-Friendly ♀♂

A Casual Caribbean Beachfront Resort

Cooper Island Beach Club is on a 1 1/2-mile by 1/2-mile island, where there are no roads, nightclubs, malls or fast food outlets. Your principal activities will be sunning, swimming, snorkeling, reading, writing and enjoying relaxing meals. Our beachfront restaurant and bar offers dramatic sunset views. Sheltered from the sun, you can enjoy a cool drink with the Caribbean Sea lapping the sand only a few feet away. Our rooms, too, are on the beach, with open-plan living room, kitchen, balcony, bathroom and a shower that is almost outdoors!

Address: Cooper Island, British VI, USA Office: PO Box 512, Turners Falls, MA 01376. Tel: (800) 542-4624 (USA office), Fax: (413) 863-3662.

Type: Beach resort with restaurant, bar, & scuba dive shop.
Clientele: Mainly straight with gay & lesbian following.
Transportation: Pick up from ferry dock, no charge on scheduled trips.
Rooms: 4 rooms with queen beds.

Bathrooms: All private shower/toilets.
Vegetarian: Available for lunch & dinner with prior notice.
Dates Open: All year.
High Season: December 15th to April 15th.
Rates: Per night for 2: US $75 summer (Apr 16-Dec 14); US $115 winter (Dec 15-Apr 15). Meal and/or

dive packages available.
Discounts: Weekly discounts available.
Credit Cards: MC, VISA, with 5% handling charge.
Rsv'tns: Required.
Reserve Through: Travel agent or call direct.
Parking: Boat moorings available.
In-Room: Ceiling fans, kitchen, refrigerator &

maid service.
Swimming: In the ocean.
Sunbathing: On the beach.
Pets: Not permitted.
Handicap Access: No.
Children: Permitted, preferably over 10 yrs old.
Languages: English.

ST CROIX

On The Beach Resort

Gay/Lesbian ♀♂

The Virgin Island's Only Gay-Owned Beachfront Resort!

Jerry Hulse, Travel Editor, *Los Angeles Times*, says *On The Beach Resort* is "located directly on one of the loveliest beaches in the Caribbean," a beautiful, white sandy swimming beach on the quiet side of St. Croix. A special place for special people, *On The Beach* provides attractive and immaculate accommodations, two beachfront patios, a fresh water pool, hot tub, a wonderful gourmet restaurant and a charming beachfront bar. Explore miles of unspoiled and secluded beaches, swim, snorkel, sail, bask in the warm Caribbean sun or spend romantic evenings viewing breathtaking sunsets. Let us share our paradise with you. The magic is back!

Address: PO Box 1908, Frederiksted, St. Croix, USVI 00841-1908. Tel: (809) 772-1205 or (800) 524-2018 (Toll-free reservations).

Type: Beachfront resort with restaurant & bar.
Clientele: Gay & lesbian, good mix of men & women.
Transportation: Taxi from airport $10 for 2.
To Gay Bars: Gay bar on premises. 2 gay-friendly bars in Frederiksted.
Rooms: 4 rooms, 4 suites & 6 apartments with queen & king beds.
Bathrooms: All have private shower & toilet.
Meals: All rates include continental breakfast.

Vegetarian: Available in restaurant.
Complimentary: Welcome cocktail.
Dates Open: All year.
High Season: December 15th thru April 15th.
Rates: Low-season $50-$110, high-season $105-$180.
Discounts: 10% for repeat guests, add'l 5% for over 14 nights in winter. Special summer package rates.
Credit Cards: MC, VISA, Amex, Diners & Discover.

Rsv'tns: Required.
Reserve Through: Travel agent or call direct.
Minimum Stay: Low-season 3 nights, high season 1 week.
Parking: Ample free off-street parking.
In-Room: AC, ceiling fans, coffee/tea-making facilities, kitchen, refrigerator & maid service.
On-Premises: TV lounge, gourmet restaurant & beachfront bar.
Exercise/Health: Jacuzzi & massage.

Swimming: Pool on premises or ocean beach.
Sunbathing: At poolside & on ocean beach or common sun decks.
Smoking: Permitted without restrictions.
Pets: Not permitted.
Handicap Access: No.
Children: Not permitted.
Languages: English, Spanish.
Your Host: Bill.

IGTA

Prince Street Inn, The

Gay-Friendly ♀♂

Sea, Sand and Sun on a Shoestring!

If you enjoy a friendly, casual, comfortable atmosphere combined with a convenient location and affordable rates, *The Prince Street Inn* might be just your ticket to paradise. Our location in the central historical district of Frederiksted puts you a short stroll away from beautiful beaches, duty-free shopping and a wide variety of restaurants. Our charming inn, which served as a Danish Lutheran parsonage over a century ago, has six rooms, each with a unique design and named after an old St. Croix estate.

Address: 402 Prince St, Frederiksted, St Croix 00840 US Virgin Islands Tel: (809) 772-9550 or (800) 771-9550.

Type: Inn.	**Vegetarian:** Available nearby.	**Rsv'tns:** Preferred.	**Swimming:** At nearby ocean beach.
Clientele: Mainly straight clientele with a gay & lesbian following.	**Dates Open:** All year.	**Reserve Through:** Travel agent or call direct.	**Sunbathing:** On the beach.
Transportation: Taxi from airport.	**High Season:** December 15-April 15.	**Minimum Stay:** 2 nights.	**Smoking:** Permitted.
To Gay Bars: One mile.	**Rates:** Dec 15-Apr 15, $42-$85, Apr 16-Dec 14, $39-$70.	**Parking:** Ample free on-street & limited free off-street parking.	**Pets:** Not permitted.
Rooms: 5 suites & 1 cottage with single or king beds.	**Discounts:** 10% to airline & military personnel, 10% for stay of 2 or more weeks.	**In-Room:** Maid service, ceiling fans, coffee/tea-making facilities, kitchen & refrigerator. B/W TV & AC on request.	**Handicap Access:** No.
Bathrooms: All private bath/toilets.			**Children:** Permitted.
			Languages: English.
			Your Host: Paul & Charlotte.

ST THOMAS

Blackbeard's Castle

Gay-Friendly 50/50 ♀♂

The tower at *Blackbeard's Castle,* built in 1697 to scan the Caribbean for pirates and enemy ships is a national historic site. It provides a spectacular backdrop for the oversized fresh water pool and terrace. The views are exceptional! Spacious and quiet guest rooms provide all the expected amenities. It is an intimate inn whose owner-manager team offers all the personal touches that make a vacation memorable. Accolades include: *VOGUE:* "...remarkable view...an excellent restaurant." *AMEX:* "A first-class hotel and restaurant." *PRACTICAL GOURMET:* "...best restaurant on St. Thomas."

Address: PO Box 6041, St Thomas, USVI 00804. Tel: (809) 776-1234 , (800) 344-5771, Fax: (809) 776-4321.

Type: Hotel with restaurant, bar, & piano lounge with live jazz 8pm-midnight.	**Meals:** Continental breakfast.	agent or call direct.	**Sunbathing:** At poolside.
Clientele: 50% gay & lesbian & 50% straight clientele.	**Vegetarian:** Available upon request.	**Minimum Stay:** 3 days during high season.	**Smoking:** Permitted without restrictions.
Transportation: Taxi is best from airport.	**Complimentary:** Welcome cocktail.	**Parking:** Free adequate off-street parking.	**Pets:** Not permitted.
To Gay Bars: 5-minute drive to gay/lesbian bars.	**Dates Open:** All year.	**In-Room:** Cable color TV, AC, direct dial telephones, safes, daily maid service & kitchens in apartment suites.	**Handicap Access:** No.
Rooms: 12 doubles, 4 junior suites, & 4 apartment suites.	**High Season:** December 15th-April 30th.		**Children:** Permitted, over 16.
Bathrooms: All private.	**Rates:** Summer $75-$145. Winter $110-$190.	**On-Premises:** Gardens.	**Languages:** English, Portuguese, Spanish, German & French.
	Credit Cards: MC, VISA, Amex, Discover & Diners.	**Exercise/Health:** Massage by appointment.	
	Rsv'tns: Required.	**Swimming:** In the over-sized pool.	IGTA
	Reserve Through: Travel		

Secret Harbour Beach Resort

Gay-Friendly ♀♂

Suite Secret, Suite Experience

It's peaceful at *Secret Harbour Beach Resort,* where spacious studio, one- and two-bedroom suites overlook the palm-lined, crescent-shaped Caribbean beach. Swimmers find our waters buoyant and tranquil and snorkelers needn't venture far to find an abundance of undersea life. Other amenities include a full-service, 5-star PADI dive shop (with its own dive boat), the fitness center, tennis courts, car rental service and a duty and tax free boutique. Try the tempting dishes and tropical drinks at our seaside restaurants and beachside bar. Our Tamarind Restaurant and bar, for evening dining, lies within 30 feet of the gentle breaking waves. Guest comments include *"It was paradise..."* and *"...all we wished for and more."*

Address: 6280 Estate Nazareth, St Thomas 00802 USVI. Tel: (800) 524-2250 , (809) 775-6550, Fax: (809) 775-1501.

Type: Resort with restaurants, dive shop & tax-free, duty-free boutique.
Clientele: Mostly hetero clientele with a gay & lesbian following.
Transportation: Air to St. Thomas, then taxi to resort, approx $10-$12.
To Gay Bars: 4 miles or 20 minutes by car.
Rooms: 60 suites with single, queen or king beds.
Bathrooms: All private.
Meals: Continental breakfast.

Vegetarian: 2 very accommodating restaurants, with varied menus, on the premises.
Complimentary: VI rum in room upon arrival, managers welcome party each week.
Dates Open: All year.
High Season: Mid Dec-mid April.
Rates: Low $179-$309, high $265-$480.
Discounts: Groups. Call for value-season specials.
Credit Cards: MC, VISA, Amex & Discover.
Rsv'tns: Required.

Reserve Through: Travel agent or call direct.
Minimum Stay: Thanksgiving 4 nights, Christmas-New Years 7 nights.
Parking: Ample free off-street parking.
In-Room: Color cable TV, AC, ceiling fans, telephone, kitchen, refrigerator, coffee & tea-making facilities, & maid service.
On-Premises: Meeting rooms.
Exercise/Health: Gym with fitness equipment,

Jacuzzi & massage.
Swimming: Freshwater pool & ocean beach on premises.
Sunbathing: At poolside, on patio or terrace & on the beach.
Smoking: Permitted in restaurant & bars. Non-smoking rooms available.
Pets: Not permitted.
Handicap Access: No.
Children: Welcome holidays. Otherwise, mostly an adult resort.
Languages: English, some Spanish & Creole, French, Italian.

BELIZE

AMBERGRIS CAYE

Mata Rocks Resort

Gay-Friendly ♀♂

Belize It!

Swaying palm trees surround this unique beachfront resort on a pristine, white sandy beach. *Mata Rocks Resort* is a peaceful place to soak up the sunshine, while enjoying the beautiful, blue Caribbean water. Nine suites are in a two-story structure constructed of native hardwood, stucco and tile. They are cheerful and comfortable, with private bath, kitchenette, microwaves, ceiling fans and daily maid service. Dive and snorkel at our front door on the world's second-largest barrier reef.

Address: San Pedro Town, Ambergris Caye, Belize, Central America. Tel: (800) 288-8646, (501) 26 2336, Fax: (501) 26 2349.

Type: Oceanfront resort with bar.
Clientele: Mostly hetero with a gay & lesbian following.
Transportation: Taxi.
Rooms: 9 suites with double, queen or king beds.
Bathrooms: All private shower/toilets.

Vegetarian: Available nearby.
Dates Open: All year.
High Season: December thru April.
Rates: USD $85-125.
Discounts: Groups of 5 rooms or more.
Credit Cards: MC, VISA.
Rsv'tns: Required.
Reserve Through: Travel agent or call direct.
Minimum Stay: Required seasonally/holidays.
In-Room: AC, ceiling fans, kitchen, refrigerator, coffee & tea-making facilities, maid & laundry service.
Swimming: Ocean on premises.
Sunbathing: On private beach.

& common sun decks & beach.
Smoking: Permitted.
Pets: Not permitted.
Handicap Access: No.
Children: Children welcomed.
Languages: English, Spanish.

COSTA RICA

QUEPOS-MANUEL ANTONIO

Hotel Casa Blanca de Manuel Antonio S.A.

Gay/Lesbian ♀♂

Admittedly, our Hotel is Definitely NOT the Main Attraction Here...

...because we are within 15 minute's walking distance to Playita, the one and only gay beach in the whole country. Our small guesthouse is on a hillside overlooking the beaches. A steady ocean wind makes your stay comfortable and our private atmosphere makes you feel at home. Relax in our tropical garden, 2 pools, or on the sun deck.

If you like action, we can arrange beach or mountain horseback riding, boat trips into the mangroves, guided tours to Manuel Antonio National Park, multi-day excursions to untouched tropical islands, and any number of water adventures. Nearby Quepos provides ample nightlife with discos and casinos.

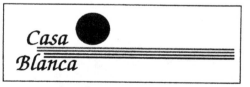

HOTEL CASA BLANCA DE ML. ANT. S.A.

Address: Apdo 194 6350 Quepos-Manuel Antonio, Costa Rica.
Phone & Fax: (506) 777-0253.

Type: Hotel guesthouse.
Clientele: Mostly gay & lesbian with some hetero clientele.
Transportation: Pick up provided by Sansa (400 Colones per person), TravelAir ($4 dollars per person) & Directo (free).
To Gay Bars: 175 km to San Jose (4-hr drive). Local bars mixed, especially in high season.
Rooms: 4 rooms, 2 suites & 4 apartments with single, double or king beds.
Bathrooms: All private.
Meals: Breakfast at additional charge of $5 plus tax.
Vegetarian: Available upon request on premises & at nearby restaurants.
Complimentary: Tea & coffee.
Dates Open: All year.
High Season: November-April.
Rates: USD, tax not included. Double: Low $35-high $60. Suite: Low $90-high $140. Apts: Low $40-high $70. $10 per extra bed.
Discounts: 15% for airlines.
Credit Cards: VISA, MC, Amex & Eurocard.
Rsv'tns: Required.
Reserve Through: Travel agent or call direct.
Parking: Adequate free off-street parking. Guarded private parking lot.
In-Room: All with ceiling fans & laundry service. Suites with kitchenette. Apartments with kitchenette, refrigerator & panoramic views.
On-Premises: Refrigerators & freezers outside of rooms. Laundry facilities, phone, tropical garden, flight & hotel reservation services.
Exercise/Health: Massage upon request. Gym, weights & massage in downtown Quepos.
Swimming: Pool on premises, gay beach within walking distance. Nearby pool & river.
Sunbathing: At poolside, in the garden, on common sun decks & at the beach.
Nudity: Permitted poolside, in the pool, in the garden & on the sun deck.
Smoking: Permitted without restrictions.
Pets: Permitted. Must have entered country legally & have all the paperwork.
Handicap Access: Yes. No stairs for suites, 4 rooms, garden & poolside.
Children: Not especially welcome.
Languages: Management: Spanish, English & German. Cleaning staff: Spanish, little English.
Your Host: Harald & Raimer.

IGTA

SAN JOSE

Hotel Colours, The Guest Residence San Jose

Gay/Lesbian ♀♂

Experience Not Just A Place, but A State of Mind.

Colours, the premier guesthouse of Costa Rica, is of Spanish-style architecture and located in San Jose, the capital city. Our location is conveniently set in an exclusive residential district a few minutes from the new Plaza Mayor mall, the US Embassy and several neighborhood parks. From here, it's just a 10-minute ride to central San José and only a block to pharmacies, grocery store, liquor store, bars, restaurants and a weekly farmers' market.

EXPERIENCE...

Colours
Destinations

YOUR DOORWAY TO OUR WORLD

If you are a first-time visitor, you may wish to be met and escorted directly to the *Residence* (a complimentary service with reservations of seven nights or more). Upon arrival and settling in, an orientation is offered, covering currency exchange, what's where in the neighborhood, massage, city access for shopping, sightseeing, restaurants and nightlife. Our multi-lingual staff members advise guests of guided day excursions to attractions outside San José, such as volcanos, biological reserves, rainforests, island/beach boat cruises, whitewater river rafting, bungee jumping and others.

From the main balcony of the poolside house, you look out over the enclosed garden and pool area, with a view in the distance of the mountain ranges surrounding the city. Take some time for sunning beside the solar-heated pool and have your complimentary tropical breakfast there or in the dining room. Join us at poolside again at cocktail hour, as we gather to meet and mingle with other guests and their friends. Our facility features various types of guest rooms to suit your taste and personal budget. All ten rooms are furnished with varied bed sizes, Bahamian paddle fans, clock radios and security safes. Telephones are soon to be installed. Also on the property are three large social rooms, one of which features English-speaking cable television. Whether your goal is to relax and unwind, adventure out and explore this tropical country, or both, *Colours* is a carefree place for it ALL to happen.

Speak to our friendly reservations staff about our other distinctive lodgings — *Colours, The Guest Mansion* in romantic Key West, and *Colours, The Mantell Guest Inn* in exciting South Miami Beach. **Address: c/o Colours Destinations Intl, PO Box 190738, Miami Beach, FL 33119-0738. Tel: (800) ARRIVAL (277-4825) or (305) 532-9341. Local San Jose (506) 232-3504.**

Type: Hotel guesthouse.
Clientele: Gay & lesbian. Good mix of men & women.
Transportation: Taxi from airport or inquire about airport transfers.
To Gay Bars: 10 minutes to gay bars.

Rooms: 10 rooms with single, double, queen or king beds.
Bathrooms: Private & shared.
Meals: Expanded continental breakfast or full breakfast. Other meals may be arranged.

Complimentary: Evening happy hour & turndown mints.
Dates Open: All year.
High Season: December through May.
Rates: US $59-$109.
Discounts: On extended stays, prepayments, for

single occupancy, inquire for others.
Credit Cards: All major credit cards.
Rsv'tns: Suggested.
Reserve Through: Travel agent or call direct.
Minimum Stay: On some holidays.

Parking: Ample, free, on-street parking.
In-Room: Maid & laundry service, ceiling fans & security safes.
On-Premises: TV lounge,

meeting rooms & guest refrigerator.
Exercise/Health: Full health club facilities & massage nearby.
Swimming: Pool on

premises.
Sunbathing: At poolside.
Nudity: Permitted poolside.
Smoking: Permitted, except in TV lounge.

Pets: Not permitted.
Handicap Access: No.
Children: Not permitted.
Languages: Spanish, English, limited French, German & Italian.

Joluva Guesthouse

Gay/Lesbian ♂

Stay at the Right Place...At the Right Price!

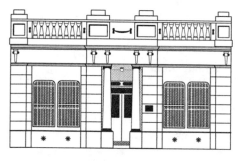

The friendliness of our all-gay, bilingual (Spanish and English) crew at *Joluva Guesthouse*, creates a relaxing and welcoming atmosphere. Our rates are friendly, too, and include a continental breakfast with tropical fruits. Our rooms are clean and spacious and have beds with luxury orthopedic mattresses. We're always ready to assist you with vacation plans, arranging tours or trips, or local information. One day small group tours (4-6 persons) in an air-conditioned van are offered exclusively for our guests. All gay activities and cultural attractions are within walking distance.

Address: Calle 3B, AVS 9 y 11 #936, San Jose, Costa Rica. Tel/Fax: (506) 223 7961. USA reservations & info, Toll Free No: (800) 298-2418.

Type: Bed & breakfast.
Clientele: Mostly men, and women welcome.
Transportation: Bus or taxi from airport or pick up for extra fee of approx $12.
To Gay Bars: 2 blocks or 10 minutes by foot.
Rooms: 8 rooms with single or double beds.
Bathrooms: 6 private, 1 shared.
Meals: Continental breakfast with tropical

fruits.
Vegetarian: We can direct you to vegetarian establishments.
Complimentary: Coffee all day.
Dates Open: All year.
High Season: September-May.
Rates: $20-$35 for single occupancy.
Discounts: 10% 7 nights stay, 15% for 14 nights or more.
Credit Cards: MC & VISA.

Rsv'tns: Required.
Reserve Through: Call direct: Costa Rica (506) 223 7961. US: (800) 298-2418.
Parking: Limited on-street parking or guarded pay lots which we strongly recommend.
In-Room: Color cable TV.
On-Premises: VCR available at $7.50 for 24 hours. Includes all selections from our video library.

Sunbathing: At the beach, which is reached by bus.
Smoking: Permitted but strongly discouraged.
Pets: Not permitted.
Handicap Access: No special provisions. Please inquire.
Children: Not especially welcomed.
Languages: English, Spanish & Polish.
Your Host: Jose, Greg & Peter.

MEXICO

GUADALAJARA

Ray and Bis Bed and Breakfast Guesthouse

Gay/Lesbian ♀♂

Ray and Bis Guesthouse is a privately-owned and -managed accommodation located in a quiet, safe, private residential area 20 minutes from downtown Guadalajara. The second largest city in Mexico, Guadalajara is a beautiful modern and colonial city with a variety of cultural events, excellent shopping, fine dining and year-round warm weather. We are five hours by car from Puerto Vallarta and four hours from Manzanillo.

At *Ray and Bis* guests can enjoy a home-like atmosphere and are pampered by Filipino-American-Mexican hospitality. In Mexico, we say *mi casa es su casa* and we mean it.

Address: 4063 Galaxia, Col. Lomas Altas, Guadalajara, Jalisco 45120 Mexico. Tel: (52-3) 813 08 42.

Type: Bed & breakfast guesthouse.
Clientele: Mostly gay & lesbian with some straight clientele.
Transportation: Free pick up & drop off to & from airport. Excellent bus & taxi service to downtown.
To Gay Bars: 15-20 minutes by cab (USD $5).
Rooms: 2 doubles & 1 single.

Bathrooms: Private & shared.
Meals: Complete breakfast in garden or in formal dining room.
Vegetarian: Available upon request.
Complimentary: Bottled water, fresh juice, coffee, tea & refreshments.
Dates Open: All year.
High Season: October to late April.
Rates: Double with private

bath & breakfast, $50. Double/single with shared bath & breakfast, $40.
Credit Cards: MC & VISA.
Rsv'tns: Required. Necessary for airport pick up.
Reserve Through: Call direct.
Parking: Ample off-street & on-street parking.
In-Room: Color TV & maid service.
On-Premises: Private garden, outdoor BBQ,

kitchen & refrigerator privileges.
Sunbathing: In the garden.
Nudity: Permitted in garden.
Smoking: Permitted without restrictions.
Pets: Not permitted.
Handicap Access: No.
Children: Not permitted.
Languages: Spanish, English & Tagalog.
Your Host: Raymond & Bismarck.

PUERTO VALLARTA

Casa Panoramica

Gay/Lesbian ♀♂

Dramatically-situated on a hillside, *Casa Panoramica* is a 24-room villa on 5 levels with spectacular and breathtaking views of the Bahia de Banderas and the town below. While remaining convenient to both beach and downtown, the villa's lofty vantage point catches the cool cross breezes from the mountains. Four separate dining areas, two bars, 2 large terraces for swimming and dining and a small terrace with BBQ provide a variety of relaxing

environments. The villa accommodates eight people comfortably, with complete housekeeping services provided.

Address: Apdo. Postal 114, Puerto Vallarta, JAL. 48300 Mexico. Tel: (800) 745-7805 or Fax: (310) 396-7855 CA USA, or call 52 322 23656 direct.

Type: Bed & breakfast in a private 7 bedroom villa.
Clientele: 80% gay & lesbian & 20% hetero clientele.
Transportation: Airport combi vans.
To Gay Bars: 6-12 blocks to gay bars.
Rooms: 7 rooms with double, queen & king beds.
Bathrooms: All private.
Meals: Full breakfast.
Vegetarian: Upon request.
Complimentary: Coffee, tea.
Dates Open: All year.
High Season: November thru May.
Rates: $85-$95 Nov-May, $65-$75 June-Oct.
Discounts: On stays over two weeks.
Credit Cards: MC, VISA.
Rsv'tns: Recommended 30 days in advance.
Reserve Through: Travel agent or call direct.
Minimum Stay: During Christmas.
Parking: Adequate, free, off-street parking.
In-Room: Maid & laundry service, ceiling fans.
On-Premises: Laundry facilities.
Exercise/Health: 5 blocks to new fully-equipped gym.
Swimming: Pool on premises, ocean beach 3 blocks.
Sunbathing: At poolside, on patio, common sun decks or beach.
Smoking: Permitted without restrictions.
Pets: Not permitted.
Handicap Access: Not accessible.
Children: Ages 6 and up permitted.
Languages: Spanish, English.

IGTA

Mission San Francisco

Gay-Friendly ♀♂

Your Private Casa Overlooking the Bay

Allow yourself to experience the extraordinary *Mission San Francisco* and its panoramic bay view. From your private luxurious home, you'll view the bay, tropical hillsides, margarita sunsets, nighttime city lights and palm studded village. Relax under the dome of the master bedroom suite or sun yourself on the very private rooftop terrace. *Mission San Francisco* is in the heart of the village, within walking distance of the gay beach, Mexican bazaar, supermarket, bars and restaurants. Included are 3 bedrooms and 2 baths, with additional rooms available. Weekly and monthly rates.
Tel: (916) 933-0370

Type: Two rental homes.
Clientele: Mostly hetero with a gay & lesbian following.
Transportation: Airport taxi to home approximately $5.
To Gay Bars: 6 blocks or a 10-minute walk.
Rooms: 1 3-bedroom, 2 bath home & 1 5-bedroom, 4 bath home with single, double & king beds.
Bathrooms: Private bath/ toilets.
Complimentary: Refrigerator stocked with beer & soft drinks upon arrival.
Dates Open: All year.
Rates: $295-$495 per week.
Discounts: 4th week free.
Rsv'tns: Required.
Reserve Through: Call direct.
Minimum Stay: Rates are by the week.
Parking: Ample on-street parking.
In-Room: Completely furnished homes with ceiling fans, color cable TV & full kitchens.
Exercise/Health: Nearby gym.
Swimming: 6 block walk to gay beach.
Sunbathing: On private sun decks or nearby beach.
Smoking: Permitted.
Pets: Not permitted.
Handicap Access: No.
Children: Welcome.
Languages: Spanish, English.
Your Host: Mike & Phil.

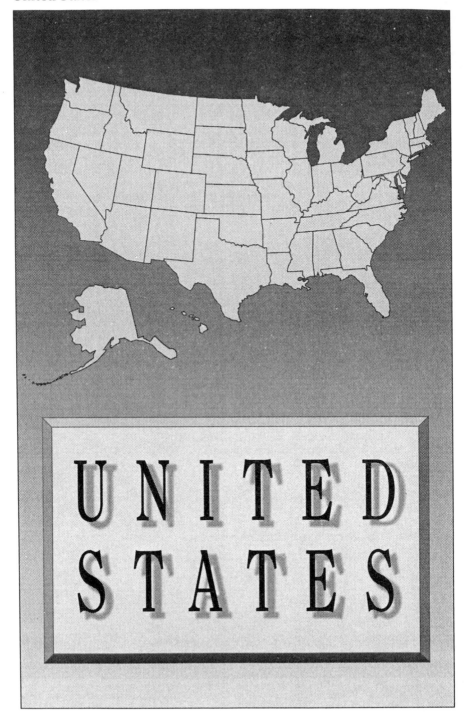

ALASKA

ANCHORAGE

Arctic Feather B&B

Gay/Lesbian ♀♂

Share the Warm Alaskan Energy

Arctic Feather Bed & Breakfast is conveniently located in a quiet residential neighborhood within easy walking distance of downtown. Many restaurants, the Anchorage Historical Museum, shopping and two gay bars are a five- to ten-minute walk. The Train Depot is several blocks away. Here you can catch the Alaska Railroad to Mt. McKinley, the tallest mountain in North America at 20,320 feet. Ship Creek river is adjacent to the train station and provides an opportunity to watch king salmon swim upstream to spawn.

Arctic Feather B&B has three guest rooms with queen-sized beds. One has a private bath and the other two share a bath. A large sun deck overlooks Cook Inlet and provides a view of Mt. McKinley. Guests have free access to bikes and can take advantage of the extensive scenic bike trails throughout the city. Anchorage is located on the edge of the Cook Inlet, with the Chugach mountains in the background, and is home to half of the total Alaskan population of 200,000.

While visiting Alaska, definitely plan on traveling outside Anchorage to enjoy the unspoiled wilderness, streams, lakes and mountain scenery. Having been a resident of Anchorage for the past 20 years, I will be glad to assist with suggestions on how to make your visit to our beautiful state a memorable one. A must is Portage Glacier, about 45 miles south. I can also offer ideas on horseback riding, rafting, fishing and sightseeing. I highly recommend a day trip to Prince William Sound and can steer you to the only licensed lesbian ship captain in Alaska with her own charter boat. Alaska is a very young state. Come and share the vibrant energy!

Address: 211 W Cook, Anchorage, AK 99501. Tel: (907) 277-3862.

Type: Bed & breakfast.
Clientele: Mostly gay & lesbian with some straight clientele.
Transportation: Taxi or rental car.
To Gay Bars: 15-minute walk or 3-minute drive to Blue Moon & Raven.
Rooms: 3 rooms with queen beds.

Bathrooms: 1 private bath/toilet, 2 shared bath/shower/toilet.
Meals: Continental breakfast.
Vegetarian: Available.
Complimentary: Tea & coffee.
Dates Open: All year.
High Season: Summer (June-September).

Rates: Summer $75-$85, winter $55.
Rsv'tns: Required.
Reserve Through: Travel agent or call direct.
Parking: Ample free off-street parking.
In-Room: Telephone.
On-Premises: Laundry facilities.
Exercise/Health: Bikes.

Swimming: Pool nearby.
Smoking: Permitted outside only. All rooms non-smoking.
Pets: Not permitted.
Handicap Access: No.
Children: Permitted.
Languages: English.

Aurora Winds, An Exceptional B&B Resort

Gay/Lesbian ♀♂

Aurora Winds, a 5200-square-foot home on nearly 2 acres, easily exceeds the standards expected by today's discriminating traveler. On the hillside above Anchorage, *Aurora Winds* enjoys privacy and seclusion year-round and provides guests with all the amenities that seasoned travelers have come to expect. Our location is less than 12 minutes from downtown Anchorage and the airport, 3 minutes from an 18-hole golf course, the zoo, horseback riding, tennis courts, snow machining and challenger-level cross-country and downhill skiing.

Address: 7501 Upper O'Malley, Anchorage, AK 99516. Tel: (907) 346-2533.

Type: Bed & breakfast.
Clientele: Good mix of gay men & women with some straight clientele.
Transportation: Car is best & advised. Pick up available with prior arrangement.
To Gay Bars: Approximately 15 minutes.
Rooms: 5 suites with queen beds.
Bathrooms: All private.
Meals: Expanded continental breakfast or full breakfast available.
Vegetarian: Available

with advance notice.
Complimentary: Coffee, tea, sodas, mineral waters, & evening night cap.
Dates Open: All year.
High Season: May 15-September 15.
Rates: Winter $65-$105 & summer $85-$125.
Discounts: For longer stays. Inquire for others.
Credit Cards: MC, VISA & Amex.
Rsv'tns: Recommended, especially during high season.

Reserve Through: Travel agent or call direct.
Parking: Ample free off-street parking.
In-Room: Telephone & color TV.
On-Premises: Meeting rooms, billiards room, TV lounge, theatre room, laundry facilities, & kitchen privileges.
Exercise/Health: Exercise room, free weights & 8-person Jacuzzi.
Swimming: 3 minutes to year-round Olympic indoor pool.

Sunbathing: On the common sun deck.
Nudity: Permitted in the hot tub.
Smoking: In designated areas only. All sleeping & common areas are non-smoking.
Pets: Permitted, on approval.
Handicap Access: Partial.
Children: Permitted on approval only.
Languages: English. Emergency Translator Available.
Your Host: Bill & James

Cliffside Bed & Breakfast

Women ♀

Soar With the Eagles

Alaska, spectacular at any season! Enjoy your loft hideaway at the edge of Chester Creek Greenbelt in the heart of Anchorage. It's just steps to trails for cross-country skiing, rollerblading, biking or strolling. Half an hour away is the famed Alyeska ski area. It's five hours to majestic Denali. Visit a glacier, go kayaking, windsurfing, whalewatching or hike the Chugach National Forest trails, all nearby. Or arrange for a guided motor-home trip. *Cliffside Bed & Breakfast* has three guest rooms with double beds, private baths, an all-women clientele and gourmet breakfasts.

Address: 2039 Cliffside Dr, Anchorage, AK 99501. Tel: (907) 274-0646.

Type: Bed & breakfast.
Clientele: Women only.
Transportation: Car is best. Pick up from airport available with advance notice.
To Gay Bars: 5 miles or 10 minutes by car.
Rooms: 3 rooms with double beds.
Bathrooms: 3 private bath/toilets.
Meals: Full breakfast. Box lunch available with advance notice.

Vegetarian: Available upon request.
Dates Open: All year.
High Season: Fur Rendezvous in February, summer (June, July, August).
Rates: $50-$80.
Discounts: 15% for 4 or more days.
Rsv'tns: Suggested.
Reserve Through: Call direct.
Minimum Stay: 2 days during holidays.

Parking: Ample free on-street parking.
In-Room: Color TV, VCR, video tape library, telephone.
On-Premises: TV lounge & laundry facilities.
Exercise/Health: Nearby gym with indoor track, weights, nautilus, Jacuzzi, sauna, steam, massage, etc.
Swimming: Pool nearby.
Sunbathing: On private sun decks or patio.

Nudity: Permitted on private deck.
Smoking: All rooms are non-smoking.
Pets: Restricted. Ask management when booking.
Handicap Access: No.
Children: Not especially welcomed.
Languages: English.

FAIRBANKS

Alta's Bed and Breakfast

Gay/Lesbian ♀♂

Stay in a log home in a wilderness setting, only twenty miles from the center of downtown Fairbanks. At *Alta's Bed & Breakfast*, amenities include screened outdoor hot tub with Jacuzzi, kennels, wooded motorhome and tent sites, and TV lounge. Available activities include sport fishing, snowmobiling, cross-country skiing, hiking, dog sled demonstrations, and watching the northern lights. *Alta's* is also within a mile of the Annual Alaska Women's Festival, held every July 4th weekend. For concert information contact Louise Barnes, (907) 479-0618.

Address: PO Box 82290, Fairbanks, AK 99708. Tel: (907) 457-0246.

Type: Bed & breakfast with tent sites.
Clientele: Mostly gay & lesbian with some straight clientele.
Transportation: Free pick up from airport, train & bus can be arranged.
To Gay Bars: 358 miles to Anchorage. Fairbanks, Fri & Sat late evenings at the Palace Saloon.
Rooms: 3 rooms with single, double & king beds.
Bathrooms: 1 private

shower/toilet & 1 shared bath/shower/toilet.
Campsites: 2 RV parking only & 4 tent sites with no toilet facilities.
Meals: Full breakfast.
Vegetarian: Available upon request.
Complimentary: Soda, coffee, tea & juices.
Dates Open: All year.
Rates: $50-$75.
Credit Cards: MC & VISA through B&B referral service.

Rsv'tns: Required.
Reserve Through: Travel agent or call direct.
Parking: Ample free parking. Heated garage for rental cars in winter.
In-Room: Maid service upon request.
On-Premises: TV lounge, laundry facilities & solarium dining room.
Exercise/Health: Jacuzzi, cross-country skiing, dog sledding, snowmobiling.
Sunbathing: On common

sun decks.
Nudity: Clothing optional on the sun deck & in the hot tub.
Smoking: Permitted outside only. All rooms are non-smoking.
Pets: Permitted. We have kennels & indoor space.
Handicap Access: No.
Children: Permitted.
Languages: English & Spanish.
Your Host: Pete.

KENAI

Moose Haven Lodge

For the Rest of Your Life

Gay-Friendly ♀♂

Escape the noise and stress of everyday living at *Moose Haven*, remote and private, and so quiet, you can hear the birds sing! Our cozy, tastefully-decorated rooms offer you the perfect place to relax, read a book, watch Alaskan videos, or just sunbathe on the deck. Our home is just minutes away from the world-famous Kenai River and excellent king salmon fishing. Hiking trails, sightseeing in Old Town Kenai and fine dining in Kenai's many restaurants are nearby. We provide evening meals family-style for an additional charge. We also have reservation-only dinners for the general public and cater private parties.

Address: Box 8597 Nikiski, AK 99635. Tel: (907) 776-8535, same number for Fax.

Type: Bed & breakfast motel.
Clientele: Mostly straight clientele with a small gay & lesbian following.
Transportation: Easy to find by car. Free transportation to & from the Kenai Airport.
To Gay Bars: 184 miles to Anchorage.
Rooms: 8 rooms with single, double, queen or king beds. 4 rooms can serve as 2-room suites.

Bathrooms: 2 rooms & 2 suites with private baths. 1 shared full bath.
Meals: Full breakfast. Full dinner for $15 per person. Menu includes wine, salad, entree, vegetable, homemade bread & dessert.
Vegetarian: Available upon request.
Complimentary: Beer, wine & soft drinks.
Dates Open: All year.
High Season: May-

September.
Rates: $60-$85.
Rsv'tns: Required.
Reserve Through: Travel agent or call direct.
Parking: Ample free parking.
In-Room: Color & black & white TV, video tape library, telephone, laundry, maid & room service. VCR available upon request.
On-Premises: TV lounge & laundry facilities.

Exercise/Health: Sauna.
Sunbathing: On private & common sun decks.
Smoking: Permitted on decks. All rooms are non-smoking.
Pets: Permitted. Are to be restrained at all times.
Handicap Access: Yes. Nurse on staff, wheelchair available.
Children: Welcome.
Languages: English.
Your Host: Roxanne & Les.

ARIZONA

FLAGSTAFF NOTE: Area Code changes to (520) Spring 1995

Hotel Monte Vista

Gay-Friendly ♀♂

Experience Yesteryear

Located on what was once the well-known Route 66, the *Monte Vista Hotel* has been a social and business center for Flagstaff since its inception in 1927. Today the hotel has been restored to its original splendor with antique reproductions, ceiling fans, brass, and plush carpeting. The renovation has created a unique atmosphere designed to make your stay a pleasant one. Notables including Clark Gable, John Wayne, Walter Brennan, Jane Russell, Spencer Tracey, Carol Lombard and Gary Cooper have, in years gone by, enjoyed the ambiance and comforts of Flagstaff's finest full service hotel.

Address: 100 North San Francisco St, Flagstaff, AZ 86001. Tel: (602) 779-6971, (800) 545-3068, Fax: (602) 779-2904. (Area code becomes 520 Spring 1995).

Type: Hotel with restaurant, bar, English Pub, and shops.
Clientele: Mostly straight clientele with a gay & lesbian following.
Transportation: Car is best. Free pick up from train. 2 blocks from Amtrac, 1 mile from Greyhound & 3 miles from airport.
To Gay Bars: 2 blocks.

Rooms: 52 rooms with single, double, queen, king or bunk beds.
Bathrooms: All private.
Vegetarian: Available in the hotel coffeeshop.
Dates Open: All year.
High Season: May-October.
Rates: High season $27-$120. Low season $25-$110.
Credit Cards: MC, VISA,
Amex & Discover.
Rsv'tns: Required, if possible. Walk-ins are welcome.
Reserve Through: Travel agent or call direct.
Parking: Adequate free off-street & on-street parking. We have our own lot.
In-Room: Color cable TV, telephone, ceiling fans & maid service.

On-Premises: Fax, copier & laundry facilities.
Swimming: Nearby pool.
Sunbathing: On the roof.
Smoking: Permitted inside some of the rooms. Non-smoking rooms are available.
Pets: Not permitted.
Handicap Access: No.
Children: Welcome.
Languages: English.
Your Host: Jimmy.

PHOENIX

Arizona Sunburst Inn

Men ♂

"A Man's Resort" in the Heart of Phoenix

The *Arizona Sunburst Inn* provides a unique setting in the Valley of the Sun that is totally private, yet in the heart of the city. Only blocks away from the gay bars and the only all-male, clothing-optional resort in Phoenix, we offer spacious rooms with queen-sized beds, cable TV, some private baths and some shared baths. A private suite with kitchen and private entrance is also available. A tropical-garden-like yard is complete with patios, a large pool and a hot tub.

Address: 6245 N 12th Place, Phoenix, AZ 85014. Tel: (602) 274-1474 or (800) 974-1474.

Type: Bed & breakfast resort.
Clientele: Men only.
Transportation: $10 for pick up from airport.
To Gay Bars: 6 blocks.
Rooms: Seven rooms & 1 suite with queen beds.
Bathrooms: Private & shared.
Meals: Expanded continental breakfast.
Dates Open: All year.
High Season: Oct to May.
Rates: $55-$125.
Credit Cards: MC, VISA, Amex.
Rsv'tns: Required.
Reserve Through: Travel agent or call direct.
Parking: Ample off-street & on-street parking.
In-Room: Color cable TV, AC, coffee/tea-making facilities & maid service.
On-Premises: Kitchen.
Exercise/Health: Hot tub & massage on premises. Nearby gym, weights, sauna & steam.
Swimming: Pool on premises.
Sunbathing: On the patio
area around the pool.
Nudity: Clothing optional.
Smoking: Permitted on patio. No smoking in rooms.
Pets: Not permitted.
Handicap Access: Yes.
Children: Not especially welcome.
Languages: English.
Your Host: Bill & Wayne.

Arrowzona Private Casita

Desert Casita on a Golf Course

Gay/Lesbian ♀♂

Stay in a casual, sophisticated casita with southwestern decor, queen bed, private bath, color cable TV/video and private telephone with free local calls. French doors open from the bedroom to a petite private patio. At *Arrowzona Private Casita,* you'll savor a delicious breakfast on the deck/patio overlooking the 11th green of an Arnold Palmer-designed championship golf course. Enjoy free use of facilities at the adjacent country club, including a $2 million health club, Olympic pool, lighted tennis courts, 2 golf courses and award-winning dining room.

Address: PO Box 11253, Glendale (Phoenix), AZ 85318-1253. Tel: (602) 561-0335, Fax: (602) 561-2300.

Type: Private mini resort bed & breakfast homestay.
Clientele: Gay & lesbian, good mix of men & women.
Transportation: Discounted self-drive autos available by prior reservation. Pick up from airport, train. Super Shuttle approx. $14.
To Gay Bars: 15-minute drive to gay/lesbian bars.
Rooms: 2 rooms with queen beds.
Bathrooms: All private.
Meals: Full breakfast, choice of menu, except summer season. Ex-

panded continental in summer.
Vegetarian: Please request at time of reservation.
Complimentary: Mixers for cocktails, welcome cocktail on arrival, tea, coffee, afternoon munchies, turndown service
Dates Open: All year.
High Season: November-April.
Rates: From $49-$122.
Discounts: Extended stays. Call for details.
Credit Cards: MC, VISA, Amex.
Rsv'tns: Required, MINIMUM 24 hours in

advance. Prefer more than 24 hours in advance if possible.
Reserve Through: Travel agent or call direct.
Minimum Stay: On certain holiday weekends.
Parking: Ample, free off-street parking.
In-Room: Color cable TV, VCR, AC, phones, ceiling fans, refrigerator, coffee/tea-making facilities, room, maid & laundry service.
On-Premises: Central AC, laundry facilities, bicycles.
Exercise/Health: Country club privileges including health club with gym, weights,

sauna, tennis & golf adjacent to facility.
Swimming: Pool on premises. Heated Olympic & lap pool at adjacent country club.
Sunbathing: At poolside, on patio, or on private sun decks.
Nudity: Permitted on private patio.
Smoking: Permitted outside with consideration to others, non-smokers' rooms avail.
Pets: Not permitted.
Handicap Access: Yes.
Children: Discouraged.
Languages: English, Spanish, French, German.

Larry's B & B

A Gay Place to Stay

Gay/Lesbian ♂

At *Larry's B & B,* our large private home offers three guest rooms, with shared bath or private bath, living and family rooms, all at economical rates. Guests enjoy the beauty of Phoenix's weather in the privacy of our pool area, surrounded by walls and tropical vegetation. We are near both golf and tennis facilities. Full breakfast is included, lunch and dinner are available by arrangement. Pickup at Sky Harbor Airport is $10.00.

Address: 502 W Claremont Ave, Phoenix, AZ 85013-2974. Tel: (602) 249-2974.

Type: A true bed & breakfast in our home.
Clientele: Mostly gay men with women welcome. Some straight clientele such as relatives or friends.
Transportation: Pick up from bus, airport or train for $10.
To Gay Bars: 5 minutes to gay/lesbian bars.
Rooms: 3 rooms with queen or king beds.
Bathrooms: 1 private bath/toilet, 1 shared full

bath.
Meals: Full breakfast, lunch & dinner by arrangement.
Vegetarian: Upon request.
Complimentary: Tea, coffee & soft drinks. Wine or hard drinks with meals.
Dates Open: All year.
High Season: January through April.
Rates: Singles $45-$50 daily, $250-$300 weekly. Doubles $50-$65 daily,

$300-$400 weekly.
Discounts: $5 off 2nd to 6th day per room on daily rate.
Rsv'tns: Preferred.
Reserve Through: Call direct.
Parking: Ample free off-street parking.
In-Room: Telephone, color TV & ceiling fans.
On-Premises: Central AC/heat, TV lounge, laundry facilities & use of refrigerators.
Exercise/Health: Jacuzzi.

Swimming: Pool, not heated in winter.
Sunbathing: At poolside, on patio & common sun decks.
Nudity: Permitted in backyard, please inquire.
Smoking: Permitted without restrictions.
Pets: Permitted.
Handicap Access: Yes.
Children: Permitted.
Languages: English, limited Japanese, Spanish.

Arizona

SEDONA NOTE: Area Code changes to (520) Spring 1995

A CasaLea

Gay-Friendly 50/50 ♀♂

Coming in Summer 1995: An Extraordinary Visit to Red Rock Country

Whether you're ready to rough it, or prefer to pamper yourself, the opportunities are here Amble the Red Rock Country trails or wander into nearby shops and galleries for a special experience.

Then come back to *A CasaLea Country Inn* and be a lounge lizard on your own deck or patio. Tote a towel to our courtyard hot tub before your soothing massage. Go around the corner to Sedona Health Spa to exercise or swim (be our guest!). From our sunken kiva to our lofty rooms, from the homeyness of hearthside dining to the refinement of the upstairs parlor, we provide the ambiance. You provide the romance. Hundreds of museum-quality artifacts imbue our home with the spirits of thousands of years of Native Americans, pioneers, cowboys, Orientals and even Mexican Caballeros. There's something interesting to look at around every corner, in every nook...almost everywhere.

Our Arizona buffet breakfasts feature hearty dishes prepared by local people. Original territorial cuisine ranges from chuckwagon chow to high falutin' foods. 'Nuff said. Your hosts, Lea and Vincent, represent such diverse living experiences as those of clayworker, educator, fisherman, writer, gardener, grandmother, uncle, historian, outdoor enthusiast, body worker, backstage and front stage artist and more. Stories are swapped with a sprinkling of humor. Come visit us for the fresh smell of Sedona's red earth after a summer thunderstorm, for the richness of reds, oranges and yellows of our fall colors, for the brief moments of soft snow, for a magnificent array of springtime beauty. It's all here! The reflections of Sedona's past and present await you at *A CasaLea*. **OPENING IN SUMMER, 1995.**
Address: PO Box 552, Sedona, AZ 86339. Tel: (602) 282-2833.

Type: Bed and breakfast with Southwest gift shop.
Clientele: 50% gay & lesbian & 50% straight clientele.
Transportation: Car is best. Free pick up from Sedona airport.
To Gay Bars: Two hours to Phoenix gay & lesbian bars.
Rooms: 8 rooms & 2 suites with single, queen or king beds.
Bathrooms: 11 private bath/toilets.
Meals: Full breakfast or Arizona buffet breakfast. Dinners served Fri, Sat &

Sun.
Vegetarian: Both meat and meatless dishes always available.
Complimentary: Tea, coffee, juices & goodies basket in room.
Dates Open: All year.
High Season: March-May & September-November.
Rates: $119-$229 plus tax & gratuity.
Discounts: Percentage discount for extended stay.
Credit Cards: Please inquire.
Rsv'tns: Required on certain holidays &

weekends.
Reserve Through: Call direct.
Minimum Stay: Required.
Parking: Ample free off-street parking.
In-Room: Color cable TV, AC, telephone, ceiling fans, refrigerator, wet bar, fireplace, room & maid service.
On-Premises: Meeting rooms & laundry facilities.
Exercise/Health: Sauna & massage on premises. Guests may use our membership at nearby

Sedona Health Spa.
Swimming: Oak Creek & pool nearby.
Sunbathing: On private sun decks, patio or in the garden.
Smoking: Permitted outdoors. All rooms are non-smoking.
Pets: Not permitted.
Handicap Access: Limited handicap-accessible. Please inquire.
Children: Welcomed 12 years or older.
Languages: English.

Cozy Cactus

Gay-Friendly ♀♂

Overlooking the valley between Sedona's red rock cliffs and one of John Wayne's favorite movie locations, Wild Horse Mesa, we invite you to share the sunsets from our patio, as they play across the nearby red cliffs. *Cozy Cactus* is a ranch-style home, comfortably furnished with family heirlooms and theatrical memorabilia from our professional careers. Each guest room has large windows and private bath. Each pair of bedrooms share a sitting room with fireplace and small kitchen, perfect for two couples traveling together.

Address: 80 Canyon Circle Dr, Sedona, AZ 86351. Tel: (602) 284-0082, (800) 788-2082.

Type: Bed & breakfast.
Clientele: Mostly straight clientele with a gay & lesbian following.
Transportation: Car is best.
To Gay Bars: 120 miles to Phoenix.
Rooms: 5 rooms with single, queen or king beds.
Bathrooms: All private bath/toilets.
Meals: Full breakfast.

Vegetarian: Available.
Complimentary: Refreshments available in the afternoon.
Dates Open: All year.
High Season: March-May, September-November.
Rates: $80-$95 for 2 people.
Discounts: Special weekly rates. AAA & Senior discount 10%.
Credit Cards: MC, VISA, Amex & Discover.

Rsv'tns: Recommended.
Reserve Through: Travel agent or call direct.
Parking: Ample free off-street parking.
In-Room: AC, refrigerator, & maid service. Fireplace in sitting area.
On-Premises: TV lounge & laundry facilities.
Exercise/Health: 3 major golf courses in town.
Swimming: 10 minutes to community pool. 15

minutes to swimming hole at Slide Rock.
Sunbathing: On the patio.
Smoking: Permitted on patios only.
Pets: Not permitted.
Handicap Access: Yes.
Children: Welcome.
Languages: English, Italian & ASL.

Paradise Ranch

Women ♀

If you are looking for a quiet place to relax from your daily routine or are interested in bringing someone special to a beautiful retreat, *Paradise Ranch* offers a Bed & Breakfast for women who want to experience the beauty of Sedona in a safe environment. Fill your lungs with our perfect clean air and bubble your cares away in the privacy of our hot tub, surrounded by beautiful trees and clear blue sky. Get in touch with your soul in our sweat lodge. Let yourself be pampered at *Paradise Ranch*, the area that the Yavapi Indians called the home of the Great Mother.

Address: 135 Kachina Dr, Sedona, AZ 86336. Tel: (602) 282-9769.

Type: Bed & breakfast & cottage.
Clientele: Women only.
Transportation: Car is best.
Rooms: 1 room & 1 cottage with double & queen bed.
Bathrooms: 1 private, 1 shared.
Meals: Full breakfast with room & continental

breakfast at guesthouse.
Vegetarian: Available if notified in advance.
Complimentary: Tea & coffee.
Dates Open: All year.
Rates: $85 to $125 per night.
Rsv'tns: Required.
Reserve Through: Call direct.
Parking: Ample free

parking.
In-Room: Color TV, evap cooler, kitchen, refrigerator, laundry service.
On-Premises: Meeting rooms.
Exercise/Health: Jacuzzi, massage, sweat lodge, life readings, life force transfusions, crystal healings.
Swimming: Creek.

Sunbathing: On patio.
Nudity: Permitted in Jacuzzi & while sunbathing.
Smoking: Not permitted.
Pets: Not permitted.
Handicap Access: No.
Children: Not permitted.
Languages: English, some German, some Spanish.

TUCSON NOTE: Area Code changes to (520) Spring 1995

Casa Alegre Bed & Breakfast Inn

Gay-Friendly ♀♂

Warmth & Happiness of a Bygone Era

Our distinguished, 1915 craftsman-style bungalow is just minutes from the University of Arizona and downtown Tucson. At *Casa Alegre*, each guest room has private bath and its decor reflects an aspect of Tucson's history, such as the mining industry or the Indian Nation. The Arizona sitting room opens onto the inn's serene patio and pool area, and is equipped with TV/VCR. A scrumptious full breakfast is served in the sun room, formal dining room or outside on the patio. Shopping, dining and entertainment are all within walking distance.

Address: 316 East Speedway Blvd, Tucson, AZ 85705. Tel: (602) 628-1800, Fax: (602) 792-1880.

Type: Bed & breakfast.
Clientele: Mostly straight with a gay & lesbian following.
Transportation: Car is best. Shuttle service from airport $15 maximum.
To Gay Bars: 3 blocks.
Rooms: 4 rooms with queen or king beds.
Bathrooms: All private bath/toilets.
Meals: Full breakfast.
Vegetarian: Available upon request.
Complimentary: Cool soft drinks & snacks by pool in summer, tea & goodies in front of fireplace in winter.
Dates Open: All year.
High Season: September 1 through May 31.
Rates: Summer $55-$70, rest of year $75-$95.
Discounts: 10% senior, corporate, week or longer stays.
Credit Cards: MC, VISA, Discover.
Rsv'tns: Preferred.
Reserve Through: Travel agent or call direct.
Parking: Ample free on-street & off-street covered parking.
In-Room: AC, ceiling fans, maid service.
On-Premises: Meeting rooms, TV lounge & guests' refrigerator on covered patio.
Exercise/Health: Spa on premises. Nearby gym, weights, sauna, steam & massage.
Swimming: Pool on premises.
Sunbathing: At poolside or on patio.
Nudity: Permitted in pool & patio area with discretion.
Smoking: Permitted outside only.
Pets: No facilities available for pets.
Handicap Access: No.
Children: Permitted under close supervision of parents because of antiques & pool.
Languages: English.

Casa Tierra Adobe Bed & Breakfast Inn

The Quintessential Desert Experience

Gay-Friendly ♀♂

Casa Tierra is located on five acres of beautiful Sonoran desert, fifteen miles west of Tucson and minutes from well-known attractions. This area is famous for its unique Saguaro cacti, spectacular mountain views and brilliant sunsets. Our rustic adobe home with vaulted brick ceilings, interior arched courtyard and Mexican furnishings, recalls haciendas found in old Mexico. Each guest room has a private bath, queen-sized bed, microwave oven, small refrigerator, private entrance and a patio overlooking the desert landscape. After a day of sightseeing, hiking or birding, enjoy the Jacuzzi or just relax with us in the quiet of the desert.

Address: 11155 West Calle Pima, Tucson, AZ 85743. Tel: (602) 578-3058.

Type: Bed & Breakfast inn.	**Meals:** Full breakfast.	**Rsv'tns:** Suggested.	**Sunbathing:** On the patio.
Clientele: Mostly straight with a gay & lesbian following.	**Vegetarian:** Always. **Complimentary:** Tea & coffee self-serve bar, fruit in room.	**Reserve Through:** Call direct. **Minimum Stay:** Two nights or $10 extra.	**Nudity:** Permitted in the Jacuzzi with discretion.
Transportation: Car is necessary.	**Dates Open:** Sept 1- May 31.	**Parking:** Ample free off-street parking.	**Smoking:** Permitted on outside private patios only.
To Gay Bars: 15 miles or 25 minutes.	**High Season:** Feb, Mar, Apr & holidays.	**In-Room:** Telephone, ceiling fans, evaporative	**Pets:** Not permitted. **Handicap Access:** No.
Rooms: 3 rooms with queen beds.	**Rates:** $75-$85. $10 extra for single night stay, $10	coolers, microwave & refrigerator.	**Children:** Welcomed, age 3 and older.
Bathrooms: 2 private bath/shower/toilet & 1 private shower/toilet.	for a third person. **Discounts:** 10% for 7 or more days.	**Exercise/Health:** Jacuzzi. Massage by appointment.	**Languages:** English & small amounts of Spanish. **Your Host:** Karen & Lyle.

Catalina Park Inn

Gay-Friendly 50/50 ♀♂

A Step Forward in Service, A Step Back in Time...

Overlooking Catalina Park, this historic residence is beautifully detailed throughout in Mexican mahogany and affords you an environment of understated elegance. Our guest rooms are handsomely furnished with antiques and some have private porches.

A sumptuous continental breakfast is delivered to your room or you may enjoy it in our lush Mediterranean garden. We are superbly located in Tucson's West University Historic District, just blocks from

continued next page

Fourth Avenue's eclectic shops, restaurants and nightlife. *Catalina Park Inn* offers a high level of comfort and friendly service.
Address: 309 E 1st St, Tucson, AZ 85705. Tel: (602) 792-4541, Fax: (602) 792-0838, Reservations: (USA only) (800) 792-4885.

Type: Bed & breakfast inn.
Clientele: 50% gay & lesbian & 50% straight clientele.
Transportation: Car is best, but shuttle services from airport are available for about $15.
To Gay Bars: 4 blocks. A 10-minute walk or 2-minute drive.
Rooms: 1 room, 1 suite & 1 cottage with double or queen beds.
Bathrooms: 3 private bath/toilet/showers.
Meals: Expanded continental breakfast.
Vegetarian: Many of the restaurants on Fourth Ave (just a few blocks away) offer vegetarian entrees. Organic market nearby.
Complimentary: Coffee & tea at all times from the Butler's Pantry.
Dates Open: All year.
High Season: Aug 15 thru May 15.
Rates: Low season (summer) $67.50-$97.50. High season (winter, fall) $90-$130.
Discounts: 10% for stays of a week or longer.
Credit Cards: MC & VISA.
Rsv'tns: Preferred.
Reserve Through: Travel agent or call direct.
Minimum Stay: Required during some periods.
Parking: Ample free on-street parking.
In-Room: Color TV, AC, telephone, fresh flowers, alarm clock radio, robes, hairdryers, newspaper, iron & board, full length mirror & maid service.
On-Premises: Meeting rooms for small groups, fax, large living room with fireplace & intimate study/parlor.
Exercise/Health: Massage available by arrangement. Nearby gym & weights.
Swimming: Nearby pool.
Sunbathing: In private patio & garden.
Smoking: Limited to outside areas: porches, garden, balconies.
Pets: Not permitted.
Handicap Access: No.
Children: Welcome over 10 years old.
Languages: English.
Your Host: Paul & Mark.

Hotel Congress

Gay-Friendly ♀♂

Where Summer Spends the Winter, Since 1919

This proud landmark has stood since the early days of the Southern Pacific Railroad. Renovation of the *Hotel Congress* in the late eighties revived its quiet elegance, leading the renaissance of Tucson's Arts District. The hotel's convenient location is near the convention center, shops and galleries, the city's new transit center, and just a mile from the university campus. The Cup Cafe serves breakfast, lunch and dinner with a southwestern flair. The Club Congress night spot features dancing with both live bands and disc jockeys.
Address: 311 E Congress, Tucson, AZ 85701. Tel: (602) 622-8848 or (800) 722-8848.

Type: Hotel with cafe, bar, disco, hair salon & specialty clothing shops.
Clientele: Mainly straight with a gay & lesbian following.
Transportation: 50 m from Amtrak & Greyhound stations, 10 miles from airport, bus or van.
To Gay Bars: 8 blocks. Wed night is gay night at Club Congress on the premises.
Rooms: 40 rooms with single, double or bunk beds.
Bathrooms: All rooms have private baths. Dorm rooms share.
Vegetarian: Cafe serves many vegetarian dishes.
Dates Open: All year.
High Season: January, February, March.
Rates: Summer $35-$45, winter $39-$50, rucksackers members $11 plus tax, non-members $14 plus tax.
Discounts: 10% senior citizens & U of A referrals, 20% Rucksackers.
Credit Cards: MC, VISA & Amex.
Rsv'tns: Required at peak times.
Reserve Through: Travel agent or call direct.
Parking: Adequate free off-street parking.
In-Room: Telephone & maid service. Most rooms with ceiling fans.
On-Premises: TV lounge. Meeting rooms can be arranged.
Exercise/Health: Nearby gym.
Swimming: Nearby pool.
Smoking: Permitted in rooms, bar & nightclub. Smoking section in cafe.
Pets: Well-behaved pets permitted with deposit.
Handicap Access: No. 2nd floor rooms accessible only by stairs.
Children: Welcomed & enjoyed, but no special facilities.
Languages: English & Spanish.

Montecito House

Mom, I'm Home!

Gay-Friendly ♀

Experience the friendly, relaxed atmosphere of *Montecito House*, my home, not a business. My B & B is a hobby, a way to meet people from around the world. Discussions at breakfast over fresh grapefruit juice from the tree in my yard are usual. Many guests meet here once and establish friendships that grow each year. Returning guests often mention the feeling of coming home again.

Address: PO Box 42352, Tucson, AZ 85733. Tel: (602) 795-7592.

Type: Bed & breakfast.
Clientele: 50% straight clientele with a gay female following.
Transportation: Car is best, pick up from airport, bus $10.
To Gay Bars: 3 miles.
Rooms: 2 rooms with double beds.
Bathrooms: 1 private bath/toilet & 1 shared bath/shower/toilet.
Campsites: RV parking with electric only, share

inside bathroom.
Meals: Continental breakfast.
Vegetarian: Available upon prior arrangement.
Complimentary: Tea, soda, coffee, juices, fresh fruit, nuts, crackers.
Dates Open: All year.
High Season: February.
Rates: $30 single, $35 double.
Discounts: On weekly rates with reservation.
Rsv'tns: Recommended.

Reserve Through: Call direct.
Parking: Ample, free off-street & on-street parking.
In-Room: Color TV, AC, telephone, maid service.
On-Premises: TV lounge, pinball, laundry facilities, use of kitchen if pre-arranged.
Exercise/Health: Nearby Jacuzzi/spa, massage.
Swimming: Nearby pool.
Sunbathing: At poolside or on patio.

Nudity: Permitted in the house with consent of other guests.
Smoking: Permitted on outside front porch only.
Pets: Not permitted, cat & dog in residence.
Handicap Access: Semi-1 level, but baths not WC accessible.
Children: Not encouraged, but call to discuss.
Languages: English.
Your Host: Fran.

Natural B&B Homestay

Natural Health and a Free Foot Massage

Gay/Lesbian ♀♂

Those preferring an inn where special attention is paid to decor and amenities may consider my home's environment much too spartan and not be happy here. At *Natural B&B Homestay*, the word natural is true in ALL senses of the word: The emphasis is on maintaining a natural, non-toxic, non-chemical environment, rather than embellishing the meals and furnishings. Use of aerosol spray deodorants, perfume and cologne is not permitted inside the house. Guests visiting my home are expected to remove their shoes when indoors. Primarily natural foods are served, for instance, guests can choose between soy milk and cow's milk at breakfast. There is NO central air conditioning: My home is water cooled, and only one bedroom has a window air conditioner. Nudity is accepted and encouraged. Nude guests may wander freely, both on the patio and in the living room. The innkeeper provides professional therapeutic body massage in addition to the complimentary foot massage.

Address: 3150 E Presidio Rd, Tucson, AZ 85716. Tel: (602) 881-4582, Fax: (602) 326-1385.

Type: Bed & breakfast with professional massage.
Clientele: Mostly gay & lesbian with some straight clientele.
Transportation: Airport "stagecoach" or car.
To Gay Bars: 8 blocks. A 15-minute walk or 5-minute drive.
Rooms: 3 rooms with single or double bed.
Bathrooms: Private: 1 shower/toilet, 1 bath/shower/toilet. 1 shared

shower.
Meals: Full breakfast.
Vegetarian: By prior arrangement for other meals. Vegetarian food nearby.
Complimentary: Cold pure filtered water, tea & candy.
Dates Open: All year.
High Season: Jan-May.
Rates: Summer $45-$55. Winter $55-$65.
Credit Cards: None.
Rsv'tns: Required.

Reserve Through: Call direct.
Parking: Ample on-street parking.
In-Room: Ceiling fans, telephone, room & laundry service.
On-Premises: TV lounge, meeting rooms, word processing, fax & laundry facilities.
Exercise/Health: Massage on premises. Nearby gym, weights, Jacuzzi, sauna & steam.

Swimming: Nearby pool.
Sunbathing: On patio & private sun decks.
Nudity: Permitted in the house & on patio at discretion of other guests.
Smoking: Permitted outside on the patio. All rooms are non-smoking.
Pets: Not permitted.
Handicap Access: No.
Children: Welcome.
Languages: English, Greek, German, Spanish.
Your Host: Marc.

SunCatcher, The

Gay-Friendly 50/50 ♀♂

A Desert Retreat

The guest rooms at *The SunCatcher* bear homage to four of the world's great hotels: The Connaught in London; The Regent in Hong Kong; The Oriental in Bangkok; and The Four Seasons in Chicago. Each of these four rooms is furnished in the style of its namesake. The bright and spacious living room and dining room are decorated in a warm and traditional manner. The focal points are the large copper-hooded fireplace and the mirrored mesquite wood bar. We provide all the desired amenities, from luxurious bath soaps and fine linens to the convenience of a video player in every room. Located at the eastern edge of Tucson, *The SunCatcher* offers uncompromising views of both the Catalina and Rincon Mountains. Our location has the best of both worlds. We are far enough from town that the quiet can be heard, yet we are close to major roadways. Certainly, our 4 acres of rolling hills and cactus will provide the greatest degree of privacy.

You have your choice of a delicious cold breakfast with fresh fruit and cereal, a specially prepared hot breakfast, or both. After a morning swim in our private pool, activities could include hiking in the nearby Saguaro National Monument, a game of tennis at our athletic club, or simply sitting in the Jacuzzi. Our garden porch is a wonderful spot to spend part of the day with a good novel. *The SunCatcher* is devoted to the comfort and convenience of our guests. We follow Southwestern tradition, offering hospitality, luxury and congeniality. You'll come to expect special treatment.

Address: 105 N Avenida Javalina, Tucson, AZ 85748. Tel: (602) 885-0883, (800) 835-8012, Fax: (602) 290-8821.

Type: Bed & breakfast.
Clientele: 50% gay & lesbian & 50% straight clientele.
Transportation: Car is best, no pick up service.
To Gay Bars: Twenty minutes to gay bar district.
Rooms: 4 rooms with queen beds.
Bathrooms: 4 private bath/toilets.
Meals: Full breakfast, poolside snacks & hors d'oeuvres.
Vegetarian: Available upon advance request.

Complimentary: Soft drinks, juices, bottled water, newspaper & fresh flowers in guest rooms.
Dates Open: All year.
High Season: Sept 15-May 15.
Rates: Summer $80-$100, winter $140-$165.
Credit Cards: MC, VISA, Amex, Discover & Diners.
Rsv'tns: Required.
Reserve Through: Travel agent or call direct.
Minimum Stay: Two nights.
Parking: Ample, free,

covered parking in five-car garage.
In-Room: Color TV, VCR, AC, telephone, hair dryers, scales, alarm clocks, maid service, robes, fresh flowers, complimentary newspaper.
On-Premises: Large living room with fireplace for conversations, garden porch for reading, video & reading libraries.
Exercise/Health: Jacuzzi, massage with reservation, private health club & tennis club.
Swimming: Pool on

premises.
Sunbathing: At poolside & on roof.
Nudity: Permitted on roof sun deck.
Smoking: Permitted outdoors only.
Pets: Not permitted.
Handicap Access: Yes, wide doors, ground level rooms.
Children: Permitted with advance notice only.
Languages: English & Spanish.
Your Host: Dave & Keith.

Tortuga Roja Bed & Breakfast

Gay/Lesbian ♀♂

Come, Share Our Mountain Views

Tortuga Roja Bed & Breakfast, is a 4-acre cozy retreat at the base of the Santa Catalinas, whose windows look out on an open landscape of natural high-desert vegetation. A bicycle and running path along the Rillito River right behind our house can be followed for four miles on either side. Our location is close to upscale shopping and dining and numerous hiking trails. It's an easy drive to the university, local bars and most tourist attractions. Some of our accommodations have fireplaces and kitchens.

Address: 2800 E River Rd, Tucson, AZ 85718. Tel: (602) 577-6822, (800) 467-6822. NOTE: March '95 area code changes to (520) 577-6822.

Type: Bed & breakfast.
Clientele: Good mix of gays & lesbians.
Transportation: Car is best. Free pick up from airport, bus & train.
To Gay Bars: 10-minute drive.
Rooms: 2 rooms & 1 cottage with queen beds.
Bathrooms: All private.
Meals: Expanded continental breakfast.

Dates Open: All year.
High Season: December-May.
Rates: In season $55-$85, off season $45-$75.
Discounts: For weekly & monthly stays.
Rsv'tns: Preferred.
Reserve Through: Travel agent or call direct.
Minimum Stay: $10 per person surcharge for 1-night stays.

Parking: Ample free off-street parking.
In-Room: Color TV, VCR, AC, ceiling fan, radio & telephone. Cottage has kitchen.
On-Premises: Laundry facilities & kitchen privileges.
Swimming: Pool & hot tub on premises.
Sunbathing: At poolside & on the patio.

Nudity: Permitted poolside & in hot tub.
Smoking: Permitted outdoors only.
Pets: Not permitted.
Handicap Access: Limited. Not wheelchair accessible.
Children: Permitted in guest cottage only.
Languages: English.

IGTA

ARKANSAS

EUREKA SPRINGS

Arbour Glen Victorian Inn, The

Gay-Friendly 50/50 ♀♂

Make Your Lodging Part of Your Vacation

The Arbour Glen, circa 1896, sits on a hillside overlooking the Eureka Springs historical district. Our tree-covered hollow is the perfect picturesque setting for relaxation and enjoyment and is home to hummingbirds, deer, and rare birds. *The Arbour Glen* has been completely restored with comfort in mind but retains its old world charm and elegance. Each guest room is decorated with antiques, handmade quilts, brass and iron bedsteads, and fresh flowers. We serve a full gourmet breakfast, with china, silver and fanciful linen, on the veranda overlooking the hollow. Our guests enjoy sipping coffee, while watching the deer and the birds. Though only steps away from downtown shops and restaurants, our location provides a secluded setting, very private and relaxing and comfortable. Spacious, shady verandas with swings overlook the rock and flower garden, complete with fish pond and fountain. There is a nearby nature trail for walking. Accommodations have hardwood floors with hand-hooked area rugs, extensive soundproofing for privacy, clawfoot tubs, deluxe, in-bath, brass-trimmed Jacuzzis for two, color cable TV with remote and VCR, all hidden in armoires. The house has heirloom antiques throughout and queen-sized Victorian beds. At Christmas, we feature a Victorian Christmas display.

Eureka Springs is a real Victorian village, nestled in the Ozark Mountains of Arkansas. The narrow, winding streets, hand-cut limestone walls and hillside parks and homes take advantage of the natural Ozark Mountain setting. One can discover shops and galleries filled with unique items not found anywhere else, many of which are lovingly and patiently handcrafted. Your stay here will definitely be an unforgettable experience.

Address: 7 Lema, Eureka Springs, AR 72632. Tel: (501) 253-9010, (800) 515-GLEN(4536).

Type: Bed & breakfast.
Clientele: 50% gay & lesbian & 50% straight clientele.
Transportation: Car is best. Pick up from airport.
To Gay Bars: 5 blocks. An 8-minute walk or 3-minute drive.

Rooms: 3 suites with double or queen beds.
Bathrooms: All private.
Meals: Full gourmet breakfast.
Vegetarian: Available with prior notification.
Complimentary: Mints, tea, coffee, soft drinks & afternoon desserts.

Dates Open: All year.
High Season: April through October.
Rates: Low season $65-$95, high season $75-$125.
Discounts: On reservations for more than 3 nights. Honeymoon packages available.

Credit Cards: MC & VISA to hold reservations.
Rsv'tns: Required.
Reserve Through: Call direct.
Minimum Stay: 2 nights on weekends, 3 nights on holiday & festival weekends.
Parking: Ample free off-

street parking.
In-Room: Color cable TV, VCR, AC, ceiling fans, refrigerator, coffee/ tea-making facilities, Jacuzzis

for two & maid service.
On-Premises: Nature trail.
Exercise/Health: Jacuzzi & nature trail.
Swimming: In nearby

river & lake.
Sunbathing: On the premises or at nearby lakes.
Smoking: Permitted outside on verandas only.

Pets: Not permitted.
Handicap Access: No.
Children: Not especially welcome.
Languages: English.

Cedarberry B & B Inn

Gay-Friendly 50/50 ♀♂

Voted #1 by Those Who Count Most–Our Guests!

Cedarberry Cottage is perhaps one of Eureka Springs' most unique bed and breakfast inns. This quaint little inn is famous for its abundant gourmet breakfasts, spacious suites and relaxed, home-like atmosphere. Its storybook appeal has captured the heart of many a traveler, and made it one of Eureka's most photographed fairy tale cottages, as well as a favorite for local home tours.

Our suites, featuring private baths, blend antique furnishings with modern conveniences. *The Garden Suite,* for two, features a private living room and gingerbread porch overlooking our English country garden. Our large upstairs *Hideaway Suite* accommodates two to four and features a spacious Victorian bath with clawfoot tub. The *Hideaway Suite* is ultra-private, making it ideal for honeymooners. For anniversaries, honeymoons or any special, intimate weekend, try our *Moods and Magic Suite.* This lovely room is appointed in rich Victorian colors, and features French doors, stained glass windows and an inviting jacuzzi for two.

At breakfast time, create your own morning atmosphere by choosing breakfast in the sunroom, on the deck, or privately on your own porch. Your delicious breakfast is served at a leisurely pace and at a time most convenient to you. House favorites include herb quiche, ham and cheese souffle and German-style apple pancakes. These wonderful specialties are always accompanied by an assortment of unique breads, hot muffins, pastry and fresh fruit. Many of our guests skip lunch!! At *Cedarberry Cottage,* our guests are pampered with fresh flowers from our garden, limited kitchen privileges and early-morning coffee on arising. Off-street parking and our trolley stop location add further to the carefree nature of your stay.
Address: 3 King's Hwy, Eureka Springs, AR 72632. Tel: (501) 253-6115 or (800) 590-2424.

Type: Bed & breakfast.
Clientele: 50% gay & lesbian & 50% straight clientele.
Transportation: Car is best. 1 hour from Fayetteville Airport.
To Gay Bars: 1/2 mile to gay/lesbian bar.
Rooms: Two 1-bedroom suites, one with Jacuzzi for two; one 2-bedroom suite with Jacuzzi for two. Double or queen beds.

Bathrooms: All private.
Meals: Full breakfast.
Vegetarian: Available with advance notice at time of reservation.
Complimentary: Tea, coffee, juice, ice.
Dates Open: All year.
High Season: March-December.
Rates: $69-$89 double occ., add'l person $20.
Discounts: 3 days or more & on Mon-Thur.
Credit Cards: MC, VISA &

Discover.
Rsv'tns: Advisable.
Reserve Through: Travel agent or call direct.
Minimum Stay: On holidays & special event weekends.
Parking: Ample off-street parking.
In-Room: Color cable TV, AC, ceiling fans & coffee & tea-making facilities.
On-Premises: Telephone access, limited kitchen privileges.

Exercise/Health: Some rooms with Jacuzzi.
Swimming: 10-minute drive to lake, river.
Sunbathing: At lake or river.
Smoking: Permitted, except in bedrooms.
Pets: Not permitted.
Handicap Access: No.
Children: Permitted if over 15 years of age.
Languages: English, Spanish.
Your Host: Rick & Jim.

Cliff Cottage and The Place Next Door, A Bed & Breakfast Inn

Gay-Friendly 50/50 ♀♂

For Lovers and Best Friends...

Cliff Cottage (1892), Historic Downtown's most photographed Victorian gingerbread "Painted Lady", and *The Place Next Door* (1994), an authentic Victorian replica, are ideally located on a little hill just 17 steps up from Main Street. Decorated with heirlooms, Victorian furnishings and art collected from world travels, the suites in *Cliff Cottage* and the guest rooms *Next Door* feature Jacuzzis, stocked refrigerators, and a charming old-world ambiance. An elf delivers a gourmet Silver-tray breakfast to private porches or balcony decks. Relax in front of the fireplace, visit the Wine Cave or take a romantic sunset cruise aboard the Inn's pontoon boat on Beaver Lake.

Address: 42 Armstrong St, Eureka Springs, AR. Tel: (800) 799-7409, (501) 253-7409.

Type: Bed & breakfast cottage & inn.
Clientele: 50% gay & lesbian & 50% straight clientele.
Transportation: Car is best. Air to Fayetteville, AR, Tulsa, OK or Springfield, MO & drive through the Ozarks.
To Gay Bars: All within minutes walking.
Rooms: 2 rooms & 2 suites with queen or king beds.
Bathrooms: All private.
Meals: Full gourmet

breakfast in rooms or in Inn dining room. Some luncheons, dinners.
Vegetarian: Available upon request.
Complimentary: Champagne, coffee, tea, juices, sodas, chocolates. Afternoon sherry/evening brandy at the Inn.
Dates Open: All year.
High Season: May-October & December.
Rates: $90-$135.
Discounts: Low season & weeknight discounts.
Credit Cards: MC, VISA.

Rsv'tns: Recommended, will take walk-ins.
Reserve Through: Call direct or travel agents.
Minimum Stay: 2 nights on holidays or special events, with a Saturday.
Parking: Ample off-street parking.
In-Room: Color cable TV, AC, ceiling fans, refrigerator, coffee-maker, maid & room service. Some VCRs.
Exercise/Health: Jacuzzis. Guest privileges available for recreation

facilities at nearby Holiday Island Resort. Pool, golf, tennis.
Sunbathing: 3 lakes & 2 rivers within a 20-minute drive.
Smoking: Permitted on deck or in garden only.
Pets: Not permitted.
Handicap Access: No.
Children: Over 12 welcome.
Languages: English, French, Spanish & German.
Your Host: Sandra.

Greenwood Hollow Ridge

Gay/Lesbian ♀♂

It's Gay in the Ozarks!

Greenwood Hollow Ridge is a country home located on 5 heavily-wooded acres in Eureka Springs, the little Switzerland of the Ozarks. We are the only EXCLUSIVE lodging in the area, a live-and-let-live community that charms every visitor. The entire downtown shopping district is listed on the National Register of Historic Places. Popular attractions include the Passion Play, arts & crafts fairs, music festivals, the Vintage Train Ride and watersports. Our guests have country club privileges for golf and tennis. Come and be gentled in the privacy of our quiet, country setting in the woods.

Address: Rte 4, Box 155, Eureka Springs, AR 72632. Tel: (501) 253-5283.

Type: Bed & breakfast.
Clientele: Exclusively

gay! Good mix of gay men & women.

Transportation: Car is a must! Free pickup from

airport.
To Gay Bars: 2 miles to

gay/lesbian bar.
Rooms: 3 rooms & 1 apartment with single, double & king beds.
Bathrooms: 1 private bath/toilet, 1 private shower/toilet, shared full bath.
Campsites: RV parking only.
Meals: Full breakfast.

Vegetarian: Available on request.
Complimentary: Welcome wine.
Dates Open: All year.
High Season: May through October.
Rates: Summer $45-$60, winter $35-$45.
Rsv'tns: Encouraged.
Reserve Through: Travel

agent or call direct.
Parking: 5 acres of parking.
In-Room: Color TV, ceiling fans, AC & kitchen.
On-Premises: Meeting rooms.
Exercise/Health: Jacuzzi & exercycle.
Swimming: 15-minute drive to lake.

Sunbathing: On patio or private sun deck.
Nudity: Permitted at spa.
Pets: Small pets OK.
Handicap Access: Yes, ramps.
Children: Not welcomed.
Languages: English & Spanish.

Pond Mountain Lodge & Resort

Get the Peak Experience...

Gay-Friendly ♀♂

Mountain breezes, panoramic views, and thoughtful hospitality await at historic Eureka Springs' *Pond Mountain Lodge & Resort*. Both a bed & breakfast and resort, casually elegant *Pond Mountain* is located just two miles south of Eureka Springs at the county's highest elevation. Guests can enjoy fishing ponds, swimming pool, and horseback riding. Jacuzzi suites, TV/VCRs, billiards room, refrigerators, microwaves, gourmet coffee service, complimentary champagne, hearty breakfasts each morning, warm and unintrusive hosting, and the serenity and beauty of 150 acres of mountain wonder make this the ideal respite.

Address: Rt 1 Box 50, Eureka Springs, AR 72632. Tel: (501) 253-5877 Reservations only: (800) 583-8043.

Type: B&B resort with riding stables.
Clientele: Mostly straight clientele with a gay & lesbian following.
Transportation: Car is best.
Rooms: 2 rooms & 4 suites with single, double, queen or king beds.
Bathrooms: All private.
Meals: Full breakfast & served buffet breakfast.
Vegetarian: Breakfast on request. Several excellent restaurants nearby.
Complimentary: Champagne, non-alcoholic sparkling cider, popcorn.

Gourmet coffee, candy in room. Winter: sherry.
Dates Open: All year.
High Season: Apr 15-Nov 5.
Rates: High season $75-$125. Winter $60-$112. Rates for 2, $7.50 per additional person.
Discounts: 10% on stays of more than 3 days, rental of more than 3 units, or "family" AARP. 5% AARP.
Credit Cards: MC, VISA.
Rsv'tns: Recommended for weekends for Jacuzzi suites.
Reserve Through: Travel agent or call direct.

Minimum Stay: 2 nights for special events (6 weekends per year).
Parking: Ample free off-street parking.
In-Room: Color TV, VCR, video tape library, AC, coffee/tea-making facilities, refrigerator, kichen & maid service. Some ceiling fans. Telephone in guest house.
On-Premises: Meeting room.
Exercise/Health: Jacuzzi in suites, massage by appointment. Hiking on 150 acres, fishing in private ponds. Horseback riding

add'l fee.
Swimming: Pool on premises. Nearby river & lake.
Sunbathing: At poolside & on common sun decks.
Smoking: Permitted on outside covered verandah only. All rooms non-smoking.
Pets: Not permitted.
Children: Welcome. Separate building has family units which accommodate children.
Languages: English.
Your Host: Judy.

We Appreciate Your Comments!

Positive comments of interest may be included in the next issue, giving future readers the benefit of your experience. And it's a nice way of saying "thank you" to an innkeeper who extended you exceptional hospitality.

See the contents for the Reader Comment Form.

CALIFORNIA

ANAHEIM (ORANGE COUNTY)

Country Comfort Bed & Breakfast

Gay/Lesbian. ♀♂

Country Comfort, City Sights!

Gay and lesbian travelers to the Orange County area will find themselves right at home here! We are only 7 miles from Disneyland and the Anaheim Convention Center, 5 miles from the *new* Anaheim Pond and the Anaheim Stadium, all of them on the same street leading to our B&B! Beaches are within 20 miles and you'll enjoy our solar-heated pool and Jacuzzi, too. Other nearby attractions include Knott's Berry Farm, the Orange County Performing Arts Center, the Los Angeles Theater District, Universal Studios, Magic Mountain, the Queen Mary, Catalina, Sea World, San Diego Zoo and the Wild Animal Park. In case you are looking for a few "wild animals" of a different sort, dance or dine at 11 local gay and lesbian clubs and bars!

We offer guests country-style hospitality in a quiet residential neighborhood in Orange. Our home is noted for its unique glass architecture looking out onto the Orange Hills. Private rooms are decorated for your comfort and pleasure, including bathrobes, TV, telephone, rocking chair, antiques and ceiling fan. The *Blue Room* has a private atrium entrance, perfect for relaxing by yourself or with a friend. Everyone is welcome to relax in the family room with super-screen TV, VCR and laser-disks. For the person with special needs, the home is handicap-accessible with adaptive equipment available on prior notice. Bicycles are available for a closer look at the locale, in addition to exercise equipment for the fitness buff.

Breakfast is bountiful, tailored to satisfy your individual needs. Our stuffed French toast has a reputation all its own, served country style. Early birds can enjoy their juice and cappuccino by the pool.

It's *your* holiday! We invite you to spend your time with us...in *Country Comfort.* **Address: 5104 E Valencia Drive, Orange, CA 92669. Tel: (714) 532-2802 or Fax: 997-1921.**

Type: Bed & breakfast. **Clientele:** Gay & lesbian, good mix of men & women. **Transportation:** Car is best. We pick up from Disneyland Hotel, airport shuttle stop or Anaheim Amtrack station. **To Gay Bars:** 10 miles by car. **Rooms:** 3 rooms with trundle, queen or king bed. **Bathrooms:** 2 private bath/toilets & 1 private shower/toilet. **Meals:** Full breakfast. **Vegetarian:** Upon request, many local restaurants. **Complimentary:** Tea, coffee, soft drinks, wine, beer. **Dates Open:** All year. **Rates:** $55-$65. **Discounts:** For extended stays (over 5 days). **Credit Cards:** None. **Rsv'tns:** Recommended 1-2 weeks in advance. Occasional last-minute rooms available. Call first. **Reserve Through:** Travel agent or call direct. **Minimum Stay:** Prefer 2 nights. **Parking:** Ample free on-street parking. **In-Room:** Color TV, telephone, ceiling fans, maid service. **On-Premises:** TV lounge, laundry facilities. Copier, fax, computer rental. **Exercise/Health:** Jacuzzi, treadmill, exercise bike, mini-trampoline. Nearby

gym, massage.
Swimming: Pool on premises, ocean is within 15 miles.
Sunbathing: At poolside, on common sun decks,

patio or nearby beach.
Smoking: Permitted outdoors on patio, atrium & sun deck.
Pets: Not permitted.
Handicap Access: Yes,

bath equip. available with prior arrangement.
Children: Permitted when the stay is private (no other booked guests).
Languages: English,

Signing.
Your Host: Joanne & Geri.

BERKELEY

Elmwood House B&B

Gay-Friendly ♀♂'

Our home was built in 1902, as the residence for University of California Latin Professor Wm. Augustus Merrill and his family. *Elmwood House* is a brown-shingled, redwood-trimmed epitome of the Berkeley Bay Tradition of turn-of-the-century architecture. We're conveniently located between the fashionable Elmwood shopping district and the U. of C., Berkeley campus. Dining, shopping and entertainment areas of this college town are nearby. Excellent public transit to San Francisco and adjoining Bay Area sights are at your doorstep. Enjoy your visit in the style of Old Berkeley!

Address: 2609 College Avenue, Berkeley, CA 94704-3406. Tel: (510) 540-5123 Phone & Fax.

Type: Bed & breakfast.
Clientele: Mainly straight with gay/lesbian following.
Transportation: Shuttle bus, public transit or car are best.
To Gay Bars: About 1 mile.
Rooms: 4 rooms with double & queen beds.
Bathrooms: 2 private & 1 shared.

Meals: Continental breakfast.
Vegetarian: Available at nearby restaurants.
Dates Open: All year.
High Season: Last two weeks of May.
Rates: $50-$100 plus tax.
Discounts: 10% for stays of 7 or more days.
Credit Cards: MC, VISA, Amex.
Rsv'tns: Required.

Reserve Through: Call direct.
Minimum Stay: One-night service charge.
Parking: Adequate free on-street & off-street parking.
In-Room: Maid service, telephone.
On-Premises: TV lounge, meeting rooms.
Swimming: 15 min walk to pool, 20 min drive to

lake, 1 hr drive to beach.
Smoking: 100% non-smoking.
Pets: Not permitted. We have 2 resident cats.
Handicap Access: No.
Children: Not encouraged.
Languages: English, some French & a little German.

IGTA

When in Town

BIG BEAR LAKE AREA

Beary Merry Mansion

Your Private Hideaway That's Not Too Far Away!

Gay/Lesbian ♀

Just under two hours from LA and Orange Counties, awaits your *private* home in Big Bear Lake, **Beary Merry Mansion**. Your stress level will melt like spring snow when you settle in to this cozy country charmer! Great for parties of four, PERFECT for parties of two! Winter and spring offer fabulous snow skiing at any of the three major resorts nearby. Summer and fall feature fishing and lake sports. Specialty shops are open year-round. Enjoy a refreshing change from hotel and B&B vacations. Come "up the hill" to your *private* home in the mountains.

Address: Big Bear Lake, CA. Tel: (800) 288-6805.

Type: Private cabin.
Clientele: Mostly women with men welcome.
Transportation: Car is best. However, there is a small craft airport with taxi service.
To Gay Bars: 1 hour down the mountain to San Bernardino.
Rooms: 2-bedroom cabin with full kitchen, living room & bath. Master has 1 queen bed. Other room has 2 twin beds.
Bathrooms: Private bath.
Dates Open: All year.
High Season: Winter ski season.
Rates: Winter $100-$165 per night. Summer/spring $85-$95 per night.
Discounts: Monday thru Thursday (excluding holidays), 15% discount on daily rates.
Rsv'tns: Required without exceptions.
Reserve Through: Call direct.
Minimum Stay: 2 nights. 3 nights on holidays.
Parking: Adequate free off-street parking.
In-Room: Color TV, VCR, microwave oven, kitchen & refrigerator.
Swimming: At nearby Big Bear Lake.
Sunbathing: On private sun deck.
Smoking: Not permitted.
Pets: Not permitted.
Handicap Access: No.
Children: Not permitted.
Languages: English.

Smoketree Lodge

Gay-Friendly ♀♂

Smoketree Lodge was originally built in the late 40's and early 50's and was frequented by movie stars over the years. All of our rooms have been recently upgraded. Our location in the San Bernardino Mountains is on three acres close to Big Bear Lake and a national forest. The main lodge house has five suites with bath and fireplace. There are also 25 cabins for two or for up to eight people. We are close to the village. You can walk to shopping and restaurants. Skiing, mountain biking, hiking and boating are only a few minutes away.

Address: 40210 Big Bear Blvd, PO Box 2801, Big Bear Lake, CA 92315. Tel: (909) 866-2415 or (800) 352-8581.

Type: Bed & breakfast & cabins in Big Bear ski resort area.
Clientele: Mostly straight with 10% gay & lesbian following.
Transportation: Car is best. Free pick up from Big Bear Airport.
To Gay Bars: San Bernardino, 1 hour & 30 minutes.
Rooms: 5 suites & 25 cabins.
Bathrooms: All private.
Meals: Continental breakfast in the B&B.
Complimentary: Coffee, tea, hot chocolate in room.
Dates Open: All year.
Rates: Low season $39-$185, High season $59-$220.
Credit Cards: MC, VISA, Amex & Discover.
Rsv'tns: Suggested.
Reserve Through: Travel agent or call direct.
Minimum Stay: Required in high season.
Parking: Ample free off-street parking.
In-Room: Color TV, telephone, maid service. Cabins have kitchens.
Exercise/Health: 2 Jacuzzis & massage.

Swimming: 2 heated pools on premises, 5 minutes to lake.
Sunbathing: At poolside.

Smoking: No smoking in office & B&B.
Pets: Small pets, $10 per night. May not be left un-

attended.
Handicap Access: No.
Children: Permitted.
Languages: English.

Your Host: Joseph & Russell.

CLEARLAKE AREA

Sea Breeze Resort

Gay-Friendly ♀♂

Glistening Water, Tree-Covered Mountains, Clear Blue Skies

Sea Breeze is a lakefront resort on California's largest natural lake. Enjoy swimming, boating and fishing just steps away from your tastefully-decorated, impeccably clean cottage with fully-equipped kitchen. You'll feel at home amid our beautifully landscaped grounds, and picturesque lake and mountain views. Exclusively for our guests are a covered lighted pier, boat slips/mooring, launching ramp, beach, swim float, picnic tables, chaise lounges and Weber barbecues. For those seeking more arduous activities, boat and jet ski rentals, parasailing, glider rides and top name entertainment are a short distance away.

Address: 9595 Harbor Dr, (Mail: PO Box 653), Glenhaven, CA 95443. Tel: (707) 998-3327.

Type: Resort & cottages.
Clientele: Mostly straight clientele with a gay & lesbian following.
Transportation: Car is best.
Rooms: 6 cottages with full kitchens, 1 room with refrigerator. Single, double, queen or king beds.
Bathrooms: All private bath/toilet/showers.
Campsites: 3 RV parking only sites. 3 with elec-

tric, sewer & water. No separate shower/toilet facilities.
Vegetarian: Available at nearby restaurants.
Complimentary: Coffee, tea, hot cocoa & ice.
Dates Open: Apr 1st through Oct 31st.
High Season: June through September.
Rates: $50-$75.
Credit Cards: MC, VISA.
Reserve Through: Call

direct.
Minimum Stay: 3 night minimum on holidays.
Parking: Ample free off-street parking. Ample parking for boat trailers on site
In-Room: Color cable TV, AC, ceiling fans, coffee/tea-making facilities, kitchen & refrigerator.
On-Premises: Laundry facilities.
Swimming: Lake on

premises.
Sunbathing: At the beach & on the lawns.
Smoking: Permitted without restrictions.
Pets: Not permitted.
Handicap Access: No.
Children: Well-disciplined children welcome.
Languages: English.
Your Host: Phil & Steve.

IDYLLWILD

Fern Village Chalets

Truly a Squirrel's Playground

Gay-Friendly ♀♂

Tucked away in a quiet glen on the banks of Strawberry Creek, Fern Village Chalets offer accommodations for the discriminating visitor. Our private, streamside chalets have treetop decks. Spacious motel rooms are also available. Guests enjoy watching birds and squirrels feeding in the early morning. Outdoor activities abound in the area. Come up and enjoy the fresh, clean mile-high air of Idyllwild today. It's one of southern California's most beautiful mountain resorts.

Address: 54821 N Circle Dr, PO Box 886, Idyllwild, CA 92549. Tel: (909) 659-2869

Type: Motel
Clientele: Mostly straight clientele with a gay & lesbian following.
Transportation: Car is the only way.
To Gay Bars: 50 miles or 1 hr, 15 min to Palm

Springs.
Rooms: 5 rooms & 4 chalets with double or king beds.
Bathrooms: 4 private bath/toilets & 5 private shower/toilets.
Vegetarian: Available at

nearby restaurants.
Complimentary: Tea & coffee.
Dates Open: All year.
High Season: June through September.
Rates: $45-$70
Discounts: For stays of 3

nights or longer.
Credit Cards: MC & VISA.
Rsv'tns: Required.
Reserve Through: Call direct.
Minimum Stay: 2 nights on weekends.

continued next page

INN Places 1995

213

California

Parking: Ample free off-street, covered parking.
In-Room: Color cable TV on request, ceiling fans & kitchen.
Swimming: At nearby public pool.
Smoking: Permitted, rooms are very smoke-free.
Pets: Permitted with restrictions: attended, kept off furniture, may not chase cats or squirrels.
Handicap Access: Yes, motel rooms, but not baths.
Children: Permitted.
Languages: English.
Your Host: Kathy & Dora.

LAGUNA BEACH

Casa Laguna Bed & Breakfast Inn

Gay-Friendly ♀♂

Sun, Sand & Sea

Casa Laguna is a unique, 21-room country inn on a terraced hillside, overlooking the Pacific Ocean. Its towering palms hover over meandering paths and flower-splashed patios, swimming pool, aviary and fountains, making this intimate, mission-style inn a visual delight. Many rooms and suites have sweeping views. A cottage, set on its own, has private garden, sun decks and ocean views. The mission house, itself, has two bedrooms and two fireplaces. Laguna Beach, combines art, seaside casualness and colorful landscapes for an ideal retreat.

Address: 2510 South Coast Hwy, Laguna Beach, CA 92651. Tel: (714) 494-2996, (800) 233-0449, Fax: 494-5009.

Type: Bed & breakfast inn.
Clientele: Mostly straight clientele with a gay & lesbian following.
Transportation: Car is best. Jitney service from Orange County Airport, about $20.
To Gay Bars: One mile to nearest one. There are others in Laguna Beach.
Rooms: 15 rooms, 4 suites & 2 Cottages. Single, double or king beds.
Bathrooms: All private shower/toilets.

Meals: Expanded continental breakfast.
Vegetarian: Fruit, cereals & breads available at breakfast.
Complimentary: Wine, cheese, snacks, tea & coffee are served each afternoon in the library.
Dates Open: All year.
High Season: July until Labor Day.
Rates: Winter $79-$175, summer $90-$250.
Discounts: Winter & mid-week discounts.
Credit Cards: MC, VISA, Amex, Diners, Bancard, Eurocard & Discover.
Rsv'tns: Required, but walk-ins accepted.
Reserve Through: Travel agent or call direct.
Minimum Stay: Only on national holidays.
Parking: Ample free off-street parking.
In-Room: Color cable TV, telephone, ceiling fans & maid service. Some rooms with refrigerators. Kitchens in the 4 suites & 2 private homes.
On-Premises: Meeting rooms & TV lounge/library.

Swimming: Pool.
Sunbathing: At poolside, on the patio & common sun decks.
Smoking: Permitted. Non-smoking rooms available.
Pets: Small pets permitted with prior arrangements.
Handicap Access: No.
Children: Permitted, but must be attended by an adult at all times.
Languages: English, Spanish.

Coast Inn

Gay/Lesbian ♂

The *Coast Inn* is the oldest and most popular gay resort in America, providing year-round fun right on the Pacific Ocean, with the world's most beautiful beaches. All rooms have color TV, phones, private baths, and a sunning deck overlooking the private bathing beach. We are also home to **Hunky's Bar & Grill** and the world famous **Boom Boom Room**, with dancing to the hottest and latest music til 2 am. We are 2 minutes from the West Street gay beach and 15 minutes from San Onofre nude beach. Dana Point Harbor is only five miles away and provides some of the finest surfing, windsurfing, sailing, fishing, snorkling, and scuba diving in Southern California. Disneyland is 30 miles away. Laguna Beach itself has a lot of fine shopping and dining and is home of The Pageant of the Masters.

Address: 1401 S Coast Hwy, Laguna Beach, CA 92651. Tel: (714) 494-7588 or (800) 653-2697.

Type: Resort hotel with restaurant, disco, Hunky's Bar & Grill, & Boom Boom Room.
Clientele: Mostly men with women welcome.
Transportation: Rental car from LAX or San Diego Airport or John Wayne Airport, 12 mi north.
To Gay Bars: World famous Boom Boom Room on the premises. 3 other bars in walking distance.
Rooms: 23 rooms
Bathrooms: Each room has a private bath & sunning deck.
Vegetarian: We have a full menu in the restaurant with some vegetarian food available.
Dates Open: All year.
Rates: $60-$160.
Discounts: Stay 6 days & get the 7th day free.
Credit Cards: MC, VISA, Amex, Diners, Discover.
Rsv'tns: Required.
Reserve Through: Travel agent or call direct.
Minimum Stay: On weekends.
Parking: Limited free off-street parking.
In-Room: Color cable TV, telephone, maid service, & room service.
Swimming: In the ocean
on the premises.
Sunbathing: On the beach & private & common sun decks.
Nudity: Permitted at San Onofre State Park.
Smoking: Permitted everywhere.
Pets: Permitted. Deposit required.
Handicap Access: No.
Children: Not permitted.
Languages: English.

LAKE TAHOE AREA

Bavarian House

Gay/Lesbian ♀♂

The Bavarian House is a gay and lesbian retreat in the Sierra Nevada Mountains, just four blocks from the ski lift at Heavenly Valley and one mile from the Tahoe casino nightlife. Each of our guestrooms is furnished in a rustic decor, with king-sized bed, TV/VCR and private bath. Couples and groups especially enjoy the separate three-bedroom, two-bath chalet. Guests congregate before the large, river-rock fireplace in the greatroom for wine, cheese and good conversation. A reading lounge with game tables and piano occupies the loft overlooking the greatroom, and is a good place to spend some quiet time. For outside fun, take in the sunsets and the clean, pine-scented air from either of the two large decks.

The Bavarian House

Travelers visit Lake Tahoe for more than Alpine skiing. In addition to the nineteen ski resorts, there are snowmobiling, horse-drawn sleigh rides, hiking, biking, horseback riding, tennis, golf, water sports on the lake, sightseeing, casinos, shows, outlet shopping, historic sites and many fine restaurants, all located amid the most beautiful scenery in the world.

Address: PO Box 624507, Lake Tahoe, CA 96154. Tel: (800) 431-4411, (916) 544-4411.

Type: Bed & breakfast guesthouse.
Clientele: Good mix of gays & lesbians.
Transportation: Shuttle or rental car from Reno airport (1 hr), or taxi from South Lake Tahoe Airport (15-min drive).
To Gay Bars: 10 minutes by car.
Rooms: 3 rooms with king beds.

Bathrooms: All private bath/toilets.
Meals: Continental breakfast Mon thru Fri with full breakfast on Sat and Sun.
Vegetarian: Available with advance notice.
Complimentary: Wine & cheese upon arrival. Set-ups, coffee, tea & juices.
Dates Open: All year.
Rates: $75-$95.

Discounts: For stays of one week or more.
Rsv'tns: Required.
Reserve Through: Call direct.
Minimum Stay: Two days.
Parking: Adequate free off-street parking.
In-Room: Color cable TV, VCR, video tape library & maid service.
Swimming: At nearby

lake.
Sunbathing: On common sun decks or nearby beach.
Nudity: 30-minute drive to nude beach.
Smoking: Permitted outside.
Pets: Not permitted.
Handicap Access: Not wheelchair accessible.
Children: Not permitted.
Languages: English.

Holly's Place

A Special Vacation Place for Women

Women ♀

What do you call a place where you can get away from it all, smell the fresh pine air, be with friends or alone, where you can cook your own meals or go out on the town? It's called *Holly's Place* at beautiful Lake Tahoe! Our place is 3 blocks from the beach, close to all shopping, 2 miles from the casinos, and close to all hiking and bicycling trails. In the winter, the skiing is great! We're only 2 miles from Heavenly Valley and close to many other downhill ski areas. Smowmobiling, snowboarding and x-country trails are also in the vicinity.

So, whether you are looking for relaxation, entertainment, fun in the snow or the summer sun, there is something for everyone in every season.

Our main desire is to provide a place where women can be themselves in an environment that is safe, supportive, relaxed, and most of all, fun! Our grounds are situated in a woodsy 3 acres close to downtown. For privacy, we've surrounded the property with 110 cords of split firewood stacked 7 feet high. Many guests have called *Holly's* "a wonderful oasis in the middle of South Lake Tahoe."

We want women to feel at home. Our cozy, clean cabins and rooms are decorated in rustic elegance. Our accommodations allow for privacy as well as group interaction. So if this is something you're looking for, we think you'll enjoy our place. This is a special place for all open and accepting women to vacation or celebrate special occassions. We also welcome children and well-behaved, non-aggressive, loving dogs. They will love it here as much as their moms. Almost everyone comes back time and time again, so we invite you to come to *Holly's* and find out for yourself.

Address: PO Box 13197, South Lake Tahoe, CA 96151. Tel: (916) 544-7040.

Type: Vacation place for women with guesthouse & cottages.
Clientele: Women only.
Transportation: Car is best.
To Gay Bars: 2-1/2 miles or an 8-minute drive.
Rooms: 3 rooms & 8 cabins with double or queen beds.
Bathrooms: 9 private bath/toilet/showers & 1 shared bath/toilet/shower.
Meals: Continental breakfast.
Complimentary: Tea & coffee in rooms & cabins.
Dates Open: All year.
High Season: Major holidays, Jan thru March, June thru September.
Rates: $85-$195.
Discounts: Cabins only: off-season 20% off midweek, 7th night free. In season, 8th night free.
Rsv'tns: Required.
Reserve Through: Call direct.
Minimum Stay: Yes.
Parking: Ample off-street parking.
In-Room: Cabins: Color TV, VCR, video tape library, ceiling fans, kitchen, refrigerator, coffee/tea-making facilities & fireplaces.
On-Premises: TV lounge, laundry facilities & free bike rentals.
Exercise/Health: Hot tub. Nearby gym, weights, sauna, steam & massage.
Swimming: Lake, pool nearby.
Sunbathing: On private & common sun decks, lawn and nearby lakeside beach.
Nudity: Permitted in hot tub only.
Smoking: Permitted outside only. All cabins & rooms are non-smoking.
Pets: Well-behaved dogs with prior approval only.
Handicap Access: No.
Children: Boys under 12, girls any age permitted.
Languages: English.

IGTA

Inn Essence

Gay/Lesbian ♀♂

A Special Place for You!

Nestled in the mountains at Lake Tahoe, amidst the world famous ski resorts and casinos, is *Inn Essence*. Gourmet chef for the stars and interior designer, Patrick Finn opens his home to you. The beautifully appointed rooms are just waiting to pamper you. Enjoy an aromatherapy spa, massage, facial or workout after a day of hiking, skiing, snowmobiling, swimming, sunbathing and more. Then snuggle in by the fire or enjoy an exciting show at the casinos. *Inn Essence* will truly be "a special place for you"! (Other homes available for groups.)

Address: 865 Lake Tahoe Blvd, South Lake Tahoe, CA 96150. Tel: (916) 577-0339, (916) 577-0118, (800) 57 TAHOE.

Type: Bed & breakfast with bookstore & gift shop.
Clientele: Mostly gay & lesbian with some straight clientele.
Transportation: Car or plane. Free pick up from bus or Reno airport.
To Gay Bars: 9 miles.
Rooms: 3 rooms with double or queen beds.
Bathrooms: 2 shared bath/shower toilets.
Meals: Full gourmet breakfast & breakfast in bed. Lunch, dinner & ca-tering available.
Vegetarian: Always available.
Complimentary: Tea, coffee, espresso, morning newspapers, gourmet treats, mints on pillow & turndown service.
Dates Open: All year.
Rates: $65-$125.
Discounts: Available for extended stays & for groups.
Rsv'tns: Recommended. Walk-ins welcome.
Reserve Through: Travel agent or call direct.
Minimum Stay: Holidays.
Parking: Ample free off-street & on-street parking.
In-Room: Color cable TV, VCR, video tape library, telephone, coffee/tea-making facilities, maid, room & laundry service.
On-Premises: TV lounge, laundry facilities, fax, copier, typewriter, an-swering machine, adding machine, office supplies.
Exercise/Health: Jacuzzi, gym, weights & massage on premises.
Swimming: Pool on pre-mises. River & lake nearby.
Sunbathing: At poolside, on common sun decks or at the beach.
Nudity: Permitted at gay nude beach.
Smoking: Permitted in smoking areas. Non-smoking rooms available.
Pets: Not permitted.
Handicap Access: Yes.
Children: Welcome.
Languages: English.
Your Host: Patrick.

Lakeside B 'n B Tahoe

Gay/Lesbian ♀♂

Romantic, Inexpensive, Right on the Water!

Lakeside B 'n B Tahoe, a private home smack-dab on the water, has antiques, plants and magnificent views of Lake Tahoe and mountains from all three guest rooms. There are steam room, Jacuzzi, grand piano, fireplace, library, lakeside deck and parklike grounds. Fresh baked bread and gargantuan gourmet break-fasts are served from a printed, personalized menu with many choices. Fabulous skiing in winter, swimming and boating in summer and 24-hour Nevada gaming action are minutes away. On the quiet north shore of Lake Tahoe, I'm 4 hours from San Francisco and 45 minutes from Reno.

Address: Box 1756, Crystal Bay, NV 89402. Tel: (702) 831-8281

Type: Bed & breakfast.
Clientele: Gay & lesbian, good mix of men & women.
Transportation: Car is best. Carry chains in winter.
To Gay Bars: About 1/2 hr drive to Faces in South Lake Tahoe or 45 min to Reno bars.
Rooms: 3 rooms with single or queen beds.
Bathrooms: 1 private & 1 shared.
Meals: Full breakfast from printed menu with many choices, daily gourmet special & fresh-baked bread.
Vegetarian: Available whenever a guest wants it.
Complimentary: Wine, coffee, other goodies, breakfast in bed if de-sired.
Dates Open: All year.
High Season: Dec-Apr (skiing season) & Jul-Sept.
Rates: $45.95-$99.95.
Discounts: 7th day free on weekly stays.
Rsv'tns: Required.
Reserve Through: Call direct.
Minimum Stay: $15 premium for one-night stays.
Parking: Ample free off-street parking.
In-Room: Color cable TV, VCR & video tape library.
On-Premises: Library, gi-ant screen TV, fireplace, grand piano, many musi-cal instruments, laundry facilities & lakeside deck with dramatic views of Lake Tahoe.
Exercise/Health: Steam room, Jacuzzi not always available to all. Swim-ming, boating, skiing, horseback riding, hiking,

nearby health club **Swimming:** Lake in back-yard, 1 minute walk down steep garden path. **Sunbathing:** At lakeside,	on private & common sun decks. Nude beach nearby. **Nudity:** Permitted. **Smoking:** Outside only.	**Pets:** Permitted, but have to get along with my dog, cats, rabbit & iguana. **Handicap Access:** No.	Steep steps & steep access to lake. **Children:** Welcomed. **Languages:** English, some French & Spanish.

SierraWood Guest House

Gay/Lesbian ♀♂

The Privacy is a Luxury in Itself

SierraWood is a romantic, cozy chalet in the woods, where you've dreamed of taking a special friend for an exciting vacation together or getting away by yourself for relaxation and renewal. Here, beside a rippling stream, we're surrounded by U.S. Forest preserve. For those who want to

balance the peace and privacy of the wooded chalet, the glittering allure of Lake Tahoe's gaming casinos, superstar entertainers, clubs, restaurants and nightlife is only a few miles away. In summer, you can charter *SierraWood's* own 25-foot *Lancer* for an exciting day on the waters of Lake Tahoe. Your hosts will serve cocktails and lunch, while you soak in the sun and the sights. On another day, try hiking through flowering meadows to the pristine alpine lakes nearby. The winter delight is downhill and cross-country skiing at one of three major ski resorts.

The chalet is an inviting, 5-bedroom, 3-bath home whose rustic architecture incorporates open-beam cathedral ceilings, pine paneling and both a rock fireplace and an antique potbelly stove. There are bay windows and floor-to-ceiling windows, plus an outdoor redwood hot tub with a view of the river, white fir and aspen woods. Our convivial cocktail hour begins with a soak in the hot tub. Then we join in the warm glow of a sumptuous dining table, sparkling with candlelight, Waterford crystal and the laughter and good conversation of happy company. A healthy breakfast is also included in the daily fare.

Address: PO Box 11194, Tahoe Paradise, CA 96155-0194. Tel: (916) 577-6073

Type: Bed & breakfast guesthouse with dinner included.
Clientele: Good mix of gay men & women.
Transportation: Car is best. Free pick up from airport & bus.
To Gay Bars: 12 miles to gay/lesbian bar & the casinos.
Rooms: 4 rooms with double, queen or king beds.
Bathrooms: 2 private sinks only & 2 shared

bath/shower/toilet.
Meals: Full breakfast & dinner.
Vegetarian: Available with 3 days' notice.
Complimentary: BYOB, set-ups provided, tea & coffee, beverages, mints on pillow, wine with dinner.
Dates Open: All year.
Rates: Single $70, double $110. Holidays $80-$130.
Rsv'tns: Preferred 2 days in advance.
Reserve Through: Travel

agent or call direct.
Minimum Stay: 2 days on holidays.
Parking: Ample free parking.
In-Room: Telephone, VCR, maid, room & laundry service.
On-Premises: Fireplace, lounge with color TV, laundry facilities.
Exercise/Health: Weights & hot tub with Jacuzzi.
Swimming: River on premises, lake nearby, nude

beach 45 min.
Sunbathing: On beach or common sun decks.
Nudity: On decks & in hot tub.
Smoking: Permitted without restrictions.
Pets: Small pets permitted, if housebroken.
Handicap Access: No.
Children: Not permitted.
Languages: English.
Your Host: David & LeRoy.

LEGGETT

Bell Glen B&B In The Redwoods & Eel River Redwoods Hostel

Gay-Friendly ♀

Bell Glen B&B is six romantic, beautifully-appointed cottages with four-poster beds, honeymoon tubs, private Jacuzzi and fireplace. *Eel River Redwoods Hostel* is a world-class hostel with small dorms. Both sit amid 10 lovely acres of trees along the banks of swimmer-friendly Eel River. There's a beautiful swimming hole, a 24-hour sauna, a British-style pub, hiking trails and nearby state parks. We have six free self-guided "eco-trips" with insider tips on touring the Avenue of the Giants or taking trees-and-seas tours to black sand beaches or the Lost Coast. Come stay with us. We're a wonderful find.

Address: 70400 Old Redwood Hwy 101, Leggett, CA, 95585. Tel: (707) 925-6425.

Type: Bed & breakfast resort plus European-style youth hostel.
Clientele: Mostly straight clientele with a lesbian following.
Transportation: Car is best. Greyhound or Amtrak. Free pick up from small airport or Amtrak stop at Garberville.
Rooms: 11 doubles, 1 triple, 8 quads & up.
Bathrooms: B&B has all private baths.
Meals: Expanded continental breakfast in B&B

only.
Vegetarian: Available upon request at the B&B.
Complimentary: Wine, hot chocolate, marshmallows, tea & mints in the B&B.
Dates Open: B&B open Apr 15-Nov 15. Hostel open all year.
High Season: Memorial Day-Labor Day.
Rates: B&B: $95-$145 for 1 or 2 people, off-season $75-$120. Hostel: $14 per person.
Discounts: B&B has package deals & off-

season specials and 10% for AAA members.
Credit Cards: MC, VISA, Discover & ATM cards.
Rsv'tns: Advisable.
Reserve Through: B&B: travel agent or call direct. Hostel: call direct.
Parking: Ample free parking.
In-Room: Refrigerator, maid service in B&B.
On-Premises: Kitchen, phone, VCR, laundry facilities & pub.
Exercise/Health: Jacuzzi, sauna, ping pong, basketball, horseshoes &

free bikes.
Swimming: River on premises.
Sunbathing: Riverside.
Nudity: Permitted at river, in sauna & Jacuzzi.
Smoking: Permitted outside only.
Pets: Not permitted.
Handicap Access: Yes. Some rooms accessible.
Children: Permitted.
Languages: English, Spanish.
Your Host: Gene.

LOS ANGELES

Comfort 10 Motel

Gay/Lesbian ♀♂

Address: 1615 N Western Ave, Hollywood, CA 90027. Tel: (213) 962-9700.

Type: Motel.
Clientele: Mostly gay & lesbian with some straight clientele.
Transportation: Car is best.
To Gay Bars: 1 block or 1/2 mile.
Rooms: 40 rooms with queen or king bed.

Bathrooms: All private shower/toilets.
Dates Open: All year.
Rates: $35-$45 plus tax.
Credit Cards: MC, VISA, Amex & Discover.
Rsv'tns: Required.
Reserve Through: Travel agent or call direct.
Parking: Ample free

parking.
In-Room: Color TV, VCR, free adult & gay movies, HBO, ESPN, CNN, AC, telephone, kitchen, refrigerator, maid & laundry service.
On-Premises: Laundry facilities.
Swimming: Pool on

premises.
Sunbathing: At poolside.
Pets: Not permitted.
Handicap Access: No.
Children: Welcome.
Languages: English, Spanish.

Grove Guest House, The

Gay/Lesbian ♀♂

Where Comfort is its Own Reward

Whether you are here for West Hollywood adventure, Hollywood excitement, or Los Angeles culture, stay with us at *The Grove Guest House*. You'll enjoy your own spacious and luxurious one bedroom home in a quiet historical district, very near all the fun that Southern California has to offer. You may walk to nearby clubs and shops, or relax by the glamorous black bottom pool and spa amidst lush tropical landscaping. With a full kitchen, VCR, cable TV with four movie channels, gas barbeque and delicious privacy, you may never want to leave!

Address: 1325 N Orange Grove Ave, Los Angeles (West Hollywood), CA 90046. Tel: (213) 876-7778, Fax: (213) 876-3170.

Type: Guesthouse.
Clientele: Mostly gay & lesbian with some hetero clientele.
Transportation: Car is best.
To Gay Bars: 1 block. A 5-minute walk or 2-minute drive.
Rooms: 1 cottage with single, double & queen beds.
Bathrooms: Private shower/toilet.
Meals: Continental

breakfast.
Vegetarian: Lots of vegetarian food nearby.
Complimentary: Kitchen is well stocked with a range of food & goodies.
Dates Open: All year.
Rates: $100 per day for 2 people. Additional people & selected dates slightly higher.
Rsv'tns: Required.
Reserve Through: Travel agent or call direct.
Parking: Ample free

parking.
In-Room: Color cable TV, VCR, video tape library, AC, ceiling fans, phone, kitchen, refrigerator, coffee & tea-making facilities.
Exercise/Health: Jacuzzi on premises. Nearby gym, weights, jacuzzi, sauna, steam & massage.
Swimming: Pool on premises. Nearby pool & ocean.

Sunbathing: At poolside.
Nudity: Permitted by pool & spa.
Smoking: Permitted without restriction.
Pets: Not permitted.
Handicap Access: No.
Children: Not especially welcome.
Languages: English, French.
Your Host: Oliver.

Holloway Motel

Gay/Lesbian ♀♂

The Holloway is a 22-unit motel centrally located in West Hollywood. This Southern California-style wooden stucco structure has traditional furnishings, very reasonable rates, and a warm, friendly feeling. Each room has color cable TV, air conditioning, phone, shower, toilet, and maid service. *The Holloway* is adjacent to restaurants and close to several gay and lesbian bars. A nearby gym offers discounts to *Holloway* guests. We are also near Hollywood, Beverly Hills, and Sunset Strip, and under 30 minutes from most major Southern California attractions.

Address: 8465 Santa Monica Blvd, West Hollywood, CA 90069. Tel: (213) 654-2454.

Type: Motel.
Clientele: Mostly gay & lesbian with some straight clientele.
Transportation: Car, taxi or LAX super shuttle.
To Gay Bars: 4 blocks.
Rooms: 20 rooms & 2 suites with single or queen beds.
Bathrooms: Each room has its own shower &

toilet.
Vegetarian: Available nearby.
Dates Open: All year.
Rates: $55 per night including tax, Sun-Thurs; $65, Fri-Sat. For studios add $10-$15 per night. Higher on holidays.
Discounts: Available for advance payment & extended stay.

Credit Cards: MC & VISA.
Rsv'tns: Recommended.
Reserve Through: Call direct.
Parking: Adequate free off-street covered parking.
In-Room: Color cable TV, AC, telephone, maid & room service.
Exercise/Health: Gym down the street offering

dicounts to Holloway guests.
Smoking: Permitted. Non-smoking rooms available.
Pets: Not permitted.
Handicap Access: No.
Children: Permitted.
Languages: English & Spanish.

Le Montrose Suite Hotel De Gran Luxe

Gay-Friendly ♂

Indulge Yourself...Stay With Us at Le Montrose

Le montrose
SUITE HOTEL DE GRAN LUXE

Nestled in a quiet, residential area two blocks from the world-famous Sunset Strip, *Le Montrose* is a most pleasant alternative, offering 120 charming suites, friendly, personalized service and attention to details with the special grace of a European-style hotel. Each suite includes sunken living room, cozy fireplace, refrigerator, color TV with VCR and twice-daily maid service. If you need to be in constant touch with your office, you'll value the state-of-the-art, multi-line telephone with dataport, fax capability and voice mail services in each suite. Most suites at *Le Montrose* include a kitchenette, and many offer private balconies with a breath-taking city view.

You can enjoy suite service dining in your suite or on the rooftop terrace, with a panoramic view of the west side. Superb dining indoors is available at the intimate Library Restaurant. Relax in the heated pool and spa, or catch a game of tennis on the lighted court. Both are located on the rooftop. Complimentary bicycles are available for exploring the surrounding West Hollywood area. Among the many attractions within a 7-mile radius of the hotel are Universal Studios, Mann's Chinese Theater, Pacific Design Center, Rodeo Drive, Cedars Sinai Medical Center and the Beverly Center. Ask about the Salon Room, which has 1,300 square feet of function space for small meetings or receptions. Other hotel services include valet laundry service, on-property laundry facilities, underground valet parking, in suite movies with Nintendo, currency exchange, full concierge and business services and a new, state-of-the-art fitness center.

Address: 900 Hammond St, West Hollywood, CA 90069. Tel: (310) 855-1115 or (800) 776-0666, Fax: 657-9192.

Type: Hotel with restaurant.
Clientele: Mostly straight clientele with a gay male following.
Transportation: Car is best.
To Gay Bars: 2 blocks or a 10-minute walk.
Rooms: 120 suites. 13 1-bedroom & 60 executive suites with kitchens. 36 junior suites with refrigerator (no kitchen). Double, queen or king beds.
Bathrooms: All private.
Vegetarian: Available upon request of guest.

Complimentary: Welcome fresh fruit. Departure, cookies & milk.
Dates Open: All year.
Rates: $165-$250.
Discounts: 35% discount if you ask for Ferrari Rate.
Credit Cards: MC, VISA, Amex, Diners & others.
Rsv'tns: Required. Call (800) 776-0666.
Reserve Through: Travel agent or call direct.
Parking: Ample covered pay parking.
In-Room: Color cable TV, VCR, premier movies &

Nintendo, AC, telephones (3 per suite), fireplaces, kitchen, refrigerator, coffee/tea-makers, room & laundry service, and maid service twice daily.
On-Premises: Meeting rooms & laundry facilities.
Exercise/Health: Full service fitness center. Free tennis & free bicycles for guest use. Rooftop terrace with Jacuzzi.
Swimming: Heated pool on premises. 10 miles to beaches.
Sunbathing: At poolside

or on the roof.
Smoking: Permitted. Non-smoking rooms are available.
Pets: Permitted with deposit.
Handicap Access: Yes.
Children: Permitted.
Languages: English, Spanish, French, German, Japanese, Chinese & Romanian.

IGTA

Le Parc Hotel

Gay-Friendly ♀♂

Be Who You Want To Be at Le Parc Hotel!

For those who prefer their luxury hotel to be more of a refuge from LA's fast lane than a tribute to it, we suggest *Le Parc Hotel*. Gracefully set in one of West Hollywood's most peaceful residential neighborhoods, you'll feel like you are miles away from the action, when in reality you are conveniently right in the middle of it. *Le Parc Hotel* offers elegant

Le Parc
suite hôtel de luxe

seclusion within walking distance of the bars, restaurants, sports clubs and businesses that make West Hollywood a world renowned gay destination. Whether traveling for business (Pacific Design Center, The Beverly Center, Melrose's art galleries or antique shops) or pleasure (Revolver, Mickys, Rage, Trunks...) your destination is just a short walk away.

Our 150 luxury suites provide a living room with fireplace, balcony, kitchenette, video cassette player, multi-line phones, walk-in closets and complimentary cable TV. As a truly full-service hotel, we offer morning and evening maid service, room service, free morning newspaper, and Cafe Le Parc, a private restaurant exclusively for guests of the hotel.

Casual and comfortable, with the feeling of an exclusive country club, *Le Parc* is a haven when your hectic day is over. While West Hollywood's best gyms, The Athletic Club and The Sports Connection are just around the corner, the hotel has its own facilities exclusively for guests' use, including a well-equipped gym and sauna, as well as a rooftop pool, jacuzzi and tennis court. *Le Parc Hotel* not only requests, but repects your business and community, and is committed to giving back to the gay and lesbian community via philanthropic endeavors. From the private guests-only restaurant, to the hotel's meeting and banquet rooms to the friendly service and amenities...*Le Parc Hotel* specializes in the fine art of casual elegance.

Address: 733 N. West Knoll Dr., West Hollywood, CA 90069. Tel: (310) 855-8888, Reservations USA only: (800) 578-4837, Fax: (310) 659-7812.

Type: Hotel with restaurant and bar.
Clientele: Mostly straight clientele with a gay and lesbian following.
Transportation: Car is best.
To Gay Bars: Three blocks.
Rooms: 150 suites with single, double & king beds.
Bathrooms: All private.
Vegetarian: Two restaurants & health food store nearby
Complimentary: Welcome fresh fruit basket.
Dates Open: All year.
Rates: Standard suite $165.00; Deluxe suite $185.00; One-bedroom suite $235.00.
Credit Cards: MC, VISA, Amex, Diners.
Rsv'tns: Required.
Reserve Through: Travel agent or call direct.
Parking: Adequate covered off-street pay parking (either valet or self-park).
In-Room: Color cable TV, AC, telephone, kitchen, refrigerator, coffee & tea-making facilities, maid, room, & laundry service.
On-Premises: Meeting rooms, laundry facilities.
Exercise/Health: Gym, weights, Jacuzzi, sauna, massage.
Swimming: Pool on premises.
Smoking: Permitted, non-smoking rooms available.
Pets: Permitted in standard suites only with $50 fee.
Handicap Access: Yes.
Children: Permitted.
Languages: English, Spanish, Arabic, French.
IGTA

Malibu Beach Inn

Gay-Friendly ♀♂'

Pier Out Your Window

The *Malibu Beach Inn* is a new, 47-room, oceanfront hotel *on the beach* at Malibu Pier in the heart of Malibu, California. This tiny coastal strip is a famous destination for tourists and sightseers and a getaway resource for the entire Los Angeles metropolitan area. Rooms on three levels each have a private oceanfront balcony with a sweeping view that includes Malibu Pier, world-famous Surfrider Beach, Malibu Colony and

the Pacific coastline from Point Dume to Palos Verdes. All rooms feature an honor bar stocked with snacks and beverages, a wet bar, remote TV, VCR and a safe. Most come complete with a cozy fireplace and some have Jacuzzis. A complimentary California continental breakfast is served. Small meeting facilities are available. Both business- and recreation-minded guests will find warmth, comfort and beauty here.

The *Malibu Beach Inn* enjoys a unique position in Malibu as the first beachfront hotel in nearly forty years. The inn is a thirty-five-minute drive from Los Angeles Int'l Airport, Hollywood, downtown LA and Beverly Hills, and is within easy driving distance of most of southern California's major attractions. Many of our guests will prefer to stay right here in Malibu, where fresh ocean breezes drive away city air and one can enjoy an ocean full of water sports, swimming snorkeling, surfing, wind surfing or sunning on wide, sandy beaches. Other popular pastimes include restaurant hopping, famous people watching, shopping, golf, horseback riding, deep sea fishing or tranquil walks along the shore at sunset. And don't forget to include a visit to the fabulous J. Paul Getty Museum. For year-round relaxation, recreation and hospitality, *The Malibu Beach Inn* delivers.

Address: 22878 Pacific Coast Hwy, Malibu, CA 90265. Tel: (310) 456-6444, Fax: 456-1499, (800) 4-MALIBU or Canada: (800) 255-1007.

Type: Hotel with gift shop.
Clientele: Mostly straight with a gay & lesbian following.
Transportation: Car is best. Pick up from airport $45.
To Gay Bars: 8 miles to Santa Monica & 25 miles to West Hollywood.
Rooms: 44 rooms & 3 suites.
Bathrooms: All private.

Meals: Expanded continental breakfast.
Complimentary: Tea, coffee, & mints.
Dates Open: All year.
High Season: April-November.
Rates: $125-$290.
Credit Cards: MC, VISA, Amex, Diners, & Bancard.
Rsv'tns: Required.
Reserve Through: Travel agent or call direct.
Minimum Stay: 2 nights

on weekends.
Parking: Limited free off-street covered parking.
In-Room: Color TV, AC, telephone, refrigerator, maid, room & laundry service.
On-Premises: Meeting rooms.
Exercise/Health: Gym, sauna, weights, steam, Jacuzzi & massage.
Swimming: Ocean beach on premises.

Sunbathing: On the beach or private sun decks.
Smoking: Permitted. Non-smoking rooms available.
Pets: Not permitted.
Handicap Access: Yes.
Children: Welcomed.
Languages: English, Spanish, & German.

INN Places 1995

Mondrian Hotel

Gay-Friendly ♀♂

Soaring Above the Ordinary

A multi-million-dollar modern art collection graces the walls and environs of *The Mondrian Hotel*, where each striking suite is an original, providing every convenience expected from a hotel in a class by itself. Huge windows frame spectacular panoramic views of West Hollywood, the Hollywood Hills, Beverly Hills or Century City from every suite. Each suite is abundant in luxury and space, with gracious marble

bathrooms and bright contemporary furniture. Remote-control television, full service cable, multi-line conference telephone, fully-stocked cocktail cabinet, plush terry cloth robe and complimentary newspaper delivered each morning are some of the essentials provided. When you're ready to venture out, some alluring diversions are outside your door. The hotel is located on the world-famous Sunset Strip, next door to the House of Blues and across the street from the Comedy Store. It's an easy walk to clubs and restaurants on Santa Monica Blvd., as well as to Sunset Plaza, which features shops such as Armani Exchange, Nicole Miller and Kenneth Cole. Minutes from the hotel are award-winning theatre performances, fashionable shopping boutiques, live music and concerts, trendy dance clubs, world-class restaurants, innovative art galleries and captivating museums. With proximity to the Pacific Design Center and the creative arenas of Beverly Hills and Hollywood, the *Mondrian* is in the heart and soul of Southern California.

After a busy day, dive into the outdoor pool or work out in the fully-equipped fitness center, with sauna, steam and whirlpool. Or savor the essence of California cuisine at *Cafe Mondrian*. Outstanding new jazz talent can be heard in the Mondrian Lounge. Popular lesbian dances are held seasonally and attract women from throughout the area. In the summer months, the Boogie Woogie Bar serves refreshing cocktails on the pool terrace.

Address: 8440 Sunset Blvd, West Hollywood, CA 90069. Tel: (213) 650-8999, Fax: 650-5215, Reservations: (800) 525-8029.

Type: Luxury hotel with restaurant, jazz bar, fitness center & gift shop.
Clientele: Mainly straight clientele with a gay & lesbian following.
Transportation: Car or Super Shuttle.
To Gay Bars: 3 blocks, a 10-minute walk or a 5-minute drive.
Rooms: 224 suites with single, queen or king beds.

Bathrooms: All private.
Dates Open: All year.
High Season: March, September.
Rates: $115-$375.
Credit Cards: MC, VISA, Amex, Diners, Bancard, Discover, JVC.
Rsv'tns: Required.
Reserve Through: Travel agent or call direct.
Parking: Adequate pay parking, $14 per day.
In-Room: Color cable TV,

AC, telephone, kitchen, refrigerator, coffee & tea-making facilities, maid, room & laundry service.
On-Premises: Meeting rooms, business services.
Exercise/Health: Fully-equipped fitness center with sauna, steam, whirl-pool, massage.
Swimming: Pool on premises.
Sunbathing: At poolside.
Smoking: Permitted in

bar & lounge. Non-smoking suites available.
Pets: Permitted with $100 refundable deposit.
Children: Welcomed.
Languages: English, Italian, Arabic, Spanish, German.

IGTA

Saharan Motor Hotel

Gay-Friendly ♂

The Saharan Motor Hotel is conveniently located in the heart of Hollywood. We're surrounded by famous restaurants, night clubs, theaters and shopping centers, not to mention many of the most popular gay night spots. Minutes from downtown LA, Universal Studios, Dodger Stadium, the Hollywood Bowl, the Chinese Theater and the Farmers' Market, the *Saharan* is equally convenient for both the business and the vacation traveler.

Address: 7212 Sunset Blvd, Los Angeles, CA 90046. Tel: (213) 874-6700 or Fax: (213) 874-5163.

Type: Motel.
Clientele: Mostly straight clientele with a gay male following.
Transportation: Super shuttle from LAX.
To Gay Bars: 4 blocks to men's bars.
Rooms: 54 rooms & 8 suites with double, queen or king beds.

Bathrooms: All private.
Complimentary: Coffee all day.
Dates Open: All year.
High Season: May-September.
Rates: Summer $40-$75, rest of year $36-$70.
Credit Cards: MC, VISA, Amex & Diners.
Rsv'tns: Recommended.

Reserve Through: Travel agent or call direct.
Parking: Adequate free parking.
In-Room: Maid service, satellite color TV, telephones & AC.
Swimming: Pool on premises or 20 minutes to ocean beach.
Sunbathing: At poolside

or on beach.
Smoking: Permitted without restrictions.
Pets: Not permitted.
Handicap Access: No.
Children: Permitted.
Languages: English, Spanish, Japanese & Chinese.

MARINA DEL REY

Mansion Inn, The

Gay-Friendly ♀♂

The Mansion Inn is a charming, European-style inn with a bed and breakfast ambiance. Completely remodeled, it's very clean and well maintained and has a relaxing environment with a friendly, unpretentious staff. The great location is within walking distance of Venice Beach and close to many attractions. Enjoy the beach during the day, local gay bars in the evening, or motor 20 minutes to West Hollywood night spots. Many restaurants are also within walking distance. If you like small, intimate places to stay, come visit *The Mansion Inn.* We would love to see you.

Address: 327 Washington Blvd, Marina del Rey, CA 90291. Tel: (310) 821-2557, (800) 828-0688, Fax: (310) 827-0289.

Type: Bed & breakfast inn with courtyard cafe.
Clientele: Mostly straight clientele with a 30% gay & lesbian following.
Transportation: Shuttle from LAX $8 per person, taxi from LAX $16.
To Gay Bars: 20 min walk or 5-10 min drive.

25 min drive to West Hollywood.
Rooms: 26 with 1 queen bed, 6 with 2 queen beds, 6 with 2 twin beds, 5 loft suites with queen bed upstairs, queen sleeper sofa downstairs.
Bathrooms: All private.
Meals: Expanded conti-

nental breakfast with bagels, English Muffins, sweet rolls, cold cereals, fruit, juices, coffee, teas.
Dates Open: All year.
High Season: June 1 through September 30.
Rates: $69-$125 USD.
Discounts: AAA, seniors, mid week specials,

Quests Memberships, some other discount memberships & corporate rates.
Credit Cards: MC, VISA, Amex, Diners, Discover, En Route.
Rsv'tns: Required.
Reserve Through: Travel agent or call direct.

Parking: Adequate free off-street covered parking.
In-Room: Color TV, AC, telephone, refrigerator, maid service, laundry service.

On-Premises: Courtyard patio & cafe.
Exercise/Health: 5 min drive to Golds Gym & World Gym.
Swimming: 1 block to ocean beach.

Sunbathing: On the beach.
Smoking: Permitted. Some non-smoking rooms available.
Pets: Not permitted.
Handicap Access: Yes.

Elevator, wide hallways, many equipped baths.
Children: Permitted. Under 12 stay free with existing bedding.
Languages: English, Spanish.

MENDOCINO COUNTY

Sallie & Eileen's Place

Women ♀

Sallie & Eileen's Place offers a safe and comfortable place for women near Mendocino, state parks, beaches, hiking, biking, horseback riding, river canoeing and a large women's community. The A-frame is a studio with fireplace and rockers, double bed and a large private bathroom with sunken tub. The cabin has lots of windows, and is wonderful in the rain. It also has a private yard and deck, a woodburning stove, and a loft bedroom with queen bed.
Address: Box 409, Mendocino, CA 95460. Tel: (707) 937-2028

Type: Studio cottage and a guesthouse.
Clientele: Women only.
Transportation: Car.
To Gay Bars: 3 1/2 hours by car.
Rooms: 2 cottages with double or queen beds.
Bathrooms: All private bath/toilets.
Complimentary: Mints, special blend of coffee, regular & decaf.
Dates Open: All year.
High Season: Spring

break, summer & Christmas.
Rates: A-frame $65, cabin $80 for 1-2, $15 each add'l woman, plus county tax.
Discounts: Weekly rates, mid-week specials during fall & winter.
Rsv'tns: Required.
Reserve Through: Call direct.
Minimum Stay: 2 nights, 3-4 on holiday weekends.

Parking: Ample free off-street parking.
In-Room: Kitchen, refrigerator & coffee/tea-makers. Fireplace in A-frame. Ceiling fans in cabin.
Exercise/Health: Hot tub $5 a day per person.
Swimming: 3 miles to ocean and river beaches.
Sunbathing: A-frame has private sun deck. Cabin has sun deck and its own yard.

Nudity: Permitted anywhere on the land.
Smoking: Not permitted in A-frame, permitted in cabin.
Pets: Dogs in cabin only, $5 per day per dog.
Handicap Access: No.
Children: Permitted in cabin only. $10 to age 12. No boy children over 10.
Languages: English, Spanish & French.
Your Host: Sallie & Eileen.

NAPA VALLEY

La Residence

...An Undiscovered Gem...

Gay-Friendly ♀♂

Just north of Napa where the vineyards begin, *La Residence* spans two acres of heritage oaks and redwoods. It's a smashing property, which has grown from a bed and breakfast into the valley's most elegant, yet relaxed, luxury inn. The inn's 20 rooms are divided between two buildings, The Mansion, and Cabernet Hall, a structure in the style of a French barn. Both stand at each end of the property, framing the lovely gardens, pool and spa. The Mansion is an excellent example of late 18th century Revival architecture and is entirely furnished in period antiques. Most of the generous rooms are complemented by exquisite armoires, sitting areas, designer fabrics, superb quality linens, fireplaces and double French doors opening onto verandas or patios. As guests pull into *La Res,* as it is fondly nicknamed, they drive past the inn's mini vineyard and fountain-graced entry.

Enjoy a full service breakfast, accompanied by piano and seasonal fire, in a beautiful dining room with French doors on two sides. A casual wine hour hosted by the innkeepers is served outdoors at sunset or by the fire in cooler weather.

This *"...relatively undiscovered...exquisite wallflower"* (**The San Francisco Examiner**) provides an excellent base from which to explore the largely under-reported Carneros region of Napa Valley, with its quiet rolling hills, meandering roads that are perfect for sightseeing or bicycling, and some very prestigious wineries that are extremely convenient to *La Residence.*

Bed & Breakfast Guide California notes that *"La Residence offers the best of both worlds - stylish yet casual accommodations"* and **Country Inns of California by Jacqueline Killeen** calls it *...one of the valley's loveliest country inns."* Although it may be an undiscovered gem in one of America's most popular travel destinations, *La Residence* is simply the best choice for the discriminating traveler.

Address: 4066 St Helena Highway, Napa Valley, CA . Tel: (707) 253-0337, Fax: (707) 253-0382.

Type: Inn.
Clientele: Mostly straight clientele with a gay & lesbian following.
Transportation: Car is best. Pick up by arrangement.
Rooms: 16 rooms & 4 suites with queen beds. Day beds for children or extra guests.
Bathrooms: Private: 10 shower/toilets, 8 full baths. 2 shared full baths.
Meals: Full breakfast.
Vegetarian: Available

with 1 day's notice.
Complimentary: Wine & hors d'oeuvres at sunset.
Dates Open: All year.
High Season: May thru November.
Rates: $100-$235 all year.
Discounts: Corporate rates for business travelers.
Credit Cards: MC, VISA, Amex & Diners.
Rsv'tns: Recommended.
Reserve Through: Travel agent or call direct.
Minimum Stay: 2 nights

on weekends & holidays.
Parking: Ample free, secure & safe, off-street parking.
In-Room: AC, telephone & maid service. Hairdryers, CD players in suites. Color TV available, room service available.
On-Premises: Conference center & fax. Honor bar in lobby.
Exercise/Health: Jacuzzi & massage on premises. Nearby health facilities, bicycling, horseback riding

& hot air ballooning.
Swimming: Heated pool on premises, lake nearby.
Sunbathing: At poolside or on the patio.
Smoking: Not permitted.
Pets: Not permitted.
Handicap Access: Yes.
Children: Well-behaved children very welcome. Crib available.
Languages: English, Dutch, German & French.
Your Host: David & Craig.

Willow Retreat

Gay-Friendly ♀♂

Secluded on forty acres in the hills behind Napa and Sonoma Valleys, *Willow* is the perfect retreat for those seeking escape from hectic city life. Swim and sun by the pool, play tennis on a hillside court surrounded by vineyards, bike, jog or walk on forest trails and country roads, stroll our grounds and treat yourself to just-picked blackberries, apples, walnuts, figs and plums. Tour the area's wineries, take a mud and mineral bath in Calistoga, try an early-morning hot air balloon ride or a glider plane ride, or picnic and ride horseback nearby.

Address: 6517 Dry Creek Rd, Napa Valley, CA 94558. Tel: (707) 944-8173

Type: Retreat facility for group events or individuals. **Clientele:** Everyone welcome. Sexual preference is unimportant. **Transportation:** Car is best. Pick up from bus can be arranged. Airport limo to Napa or Sonoma from SF or Oakland airports. **To Gay Bars:** 1-1/2 hr to San Francisco bars. 1 hr to Russian River bars. **Rooms:** 12 rooms with single, queen or king beds. **Bathrooms:** 10 private baths/toilets & 2 shared. **Meals:** Continental breakfast. **Vegetarian:** Always available. **Dates Open:** All year. **High Season:** May-October. **Rates:** Single $55-$75. Double $80-$110. Triple $115-$140. Quad $135-$165. **Discounts:** 10% on 4 days or more. Group rates. **Credit Cards:** MC & VISA. **Rsv'tns:** Required. **Reserve Through:** Call direct. **Minimum Stay:** Two nights on weekends April through October. **Parking:** Ample free off-street parking. **In-Room:** Self-controlled electric heat & community kitchen. **On-Premises:** Living room, dining room, community style kitchen, & public phone. **Exercise/Health:** Sauna, massage & hot tub. **Swimming:** Pool on premises. **Sunbathing:** At poolside. **Nudity:** Permitted in pool & hot tub areas only. **Smoking:** Permitted in designated outside areas. **Pets:** Not permitted. **Handicap Access:** Yes. **Children:** Permitted. **Languages:** English.

PALM SPRINGS & CATHEDRAL CITY

Alexander Resort

Men ♂

Chill Out in Beautiful Palm Springs

Epitomizing the serenity of the casual Palm Springs lifestyle is *Alexander Resort.* Its spacious, mist-cooled grounds have fountain, pool, spa and a fabulous mountain view. Guests enjoy hospitality that is both gracious and friendly. Rooms are furnished in desert hues, with direct-dial phones, refrigerators and remote color TV with adult videos. Use our bikes to explore many bike paths or enjoy Village Fest every Thursday evening nearby. Complimentary breakfast and light lunch are served at poolside daily, with Saturday cocktails and parties on major holidays.

Address: 598 Grenfall Rd, Palm Springs, CA 92264. Tel: (619) 327-6911 or (800) 448-6197.

Type: Garden court guesthouse. **Clientele:** Men only. **Transportation:** Car is best but bus & cabs are available. Free pick up from airport or bus. **To Gay Bars:** 2-minute drive to gay bars. 15 minutes to clubs. **Rooms:** 3 rooms, 3 studios with kitchens & 2 deluxe studios with kitchens & private patios. Twin or king beds. **Bathrooms:** 6 private bath/toilets & 2 private shower/toilets. **Meals:** Expanded continental breakfast & light lunch. **Vegetarian:** Available on request. **Complimentary:** Fruit & in room coffee & tea. Iced tea poolside. Saturday night get togethers w/wine or Margaritas. **Dates Open:** All year. **High Season:** December-June. **Rates:** $79-$99 all year. Specials off season (3rd night free, etc). **Discounts:** 10% for 7 days, 15% for 14 days & 20% for 30 days. More for longer stays and off season. **Credit Cards:** MC, VISA, Discover & Amex. **Rsv'tns:** Strongly recommended! **Reserve Through:** Travel agent or call direct. **Minimum Stay:** 2 nights on weekends in season. Longer for holiday periods. **Parking:** Ample free off-street parking. **In-Room:** Maid service, color TV, male video channel, VCR, telephone,

continued next page

AC/heat, kitchen, refrigerator, shower massage & coffee/tea service.
On-Premises: Laundry facilities, gas BBQ, & video library.
Exercise/Health: Jacuzzi, bicycles & cool mist outside cooling. Masseurs available for extra charge. Large gym nearby.
Swimming: In the pool.
Sunbathing: At poolside or on the patio.
Nudity: Permitted in all outside areas.
Smoking: Permitted without restrictions.
Pets: Not permitted.
Handicap Access: All facilities are at ground level.
Children: Not permitted.
Languages: English.

IGTA

Atrium/Vista Grande/Mirage

If You Don't Stay at the Mirage, You'll Wish You Had!

Men ♂

Palm Springs's unique new exotic male playground, *Atrium/Vista Grande/Mirage*, is set in a multi-level tropical environment. Some of the giant, contoured boulders, on which you can sunbathe nude or watch the night stars, weigh over 20,000 pounds. Individual limestone paths lead to rooms overlooking the waterfall grotto with its ring of fire. Both pools, the Jacuzzi and the atrium have outdoor mist systems. Our gym, fire pit, bar, large natural stone BBQ, botanical gardens, open-beam ceilings and private patios are worth the trip.
Address: 574 Warm Sands Dr, Palm Springs, CA 92264. Tel: (619) 322-2404 or (800) 669-1069. Fax: (619) 320-1667.

Type: Private male resort.
Clientele: Men only.
Transportation: Free pick up from the airport & bus.
To Gay Bars: Close to gay bars & restaurants.
Bathrooms: All private.
Complimentary: Coffee maker, fresh coffee, tea, cream, & sugar.
Dates Open: All year.
High Season: All year.
Rates: $79-$165.
Discounts: Airline personnel.
Credit Cards: All credit cards.
Rsv'tns: Recommended.
Reserve Through: Travel agent or call direct.
Minimum Stay: 2 days on weekends.
Parking: Adequate, free, off-street parking.
In-Room: Color TV, VCR, laundry & maid service, AC, telephone, & kitchen.
On-Premises: Laundry facilities (free).
Exercise/Health: 2 Jacuzzis & micro-cool outdoor mist.
Swimming: 2 pools on premises.
Sunbathing: At poolside or on the sun decks.
Nudity: Permitted everywhere.
Smoking: Permitted without restrictions.
Pets: Not permitted.
Handicap Access: No.
Children: Not permitted.
Languages: English, German, Dutch, limited French.
Your Host: Bob & Peter.

IGTA

Avanti Resort Hotel

Men. ♂

Hot Days, Hot Nights, Hot Men!!!

Avanti is a secluded resort at the foot of the San Jacinto Mountains and set in an environment of lush gardens, with large heated pool and spa, and an outdoor Kool Mist system. Fully-equipped kitchens, VCRs and microwaves are just a few of the many amenities offered. The resort is within walking distance of downtown Palm Springs, where guests can explore Palm Canyon Drive, a panoply of shops, restaurants and galleries, theatres and many gay establishments. Please join us for a memorable vacation.
Address: 715 San Lorenzo Rd, Palm Springs, CA 92264. Tel: (619) 325-9723 or (800) 572-2779.

Type: Hotel.
Clientele: Men only.
Transportation: Car is best, free pick up from airport, bus.
To Gay Bars: 3 blocks or a 5-minute walk.
Rooms: 5 rooms & 9

suites with queen or king beds.
Bathrooms: All private bath/toilets.
Meals: Continental breakfast served daily.
Vegetarian: 10-minute walk.
Complimentary: Coffee, iced tea & popcorn.
Dates Open: All year.
High Season: October to June.

Rates: $39-$110 per night per room.
Discounts: Stay 7 night for reduced rate.
Credit Cards: MC, VISA, Amex & Discover.
Rsv'tns: Required or recommended.
Reserve Through: Travel agent or call direct.
Minimum Stay: 2 days on weekends, 3 days on holidays.

Parking: Adequate off-street parking.
In-Room: Color cable TV, VCR, video tape library, AC, telephone, ceiling fans, kitchen, refrigerator, coffee & tea-making facilities, maid service.
Exercise/Health: Gold's Gym 3 miles, local gym 4 blocks.
Swimming: Heated pool.
Sunbathing: At poolside,

on patio.
Nudity: Permitted everywhere.
Pets: Not permitted.
Handicap Access: Mostly.
Children: Not permitted.
Languages: English.

IGTA

Camp Palm Springs Hotel

Men ♂

Join us at *Camp Palm Springs Hotel*, located adjacent to downtown, in wind-free south Palm Springs. The resort offers 20 rooms and suites facing a central courtyard with oversized pool and 16-man Jacuzzi. The eight designer rooms and suites offer eight unique, luxurious decors and extensive amenities while the Upper Deck rooms offer comfortable surroundings at very affordable prices. KoolFog makes every day pleasant around the pool area, which is fully secured for nude sunbathing and the freedom to be yourself throughout the facility.

Address: 722 San Lorenzo Rd, Palm Springs, CA 92264. Tel: (800) 793-0063, (619) 322-CAMP, Fax: (619) 322-5699.

Type: Hotel.
Clientele: Men only.
Transportation: Car is best, minutes from Palm Springs Airport.
To Gay Bars: 5 minutes to bars & gay restaurants. 10-12 minutes by foot.
Rooms: 17 rooms, 2 suites & 1 apartment with full, queen or king beds.
Bathrooms: All private.
Meals: Expanded California breakfast & lite lunch.
Vegetarian: 5 minutes away by auto.
Complimentary: Sun-Downer cocktail hour on

Saturdays.
Dates Open: All year.
High Season: February 1-May 31.
Rates: Summer from $49-$239, season $49-$249, high season $59-$299.
Discounts: For extended stays.
Credit Cards: MC, VISA, Amex.
Rsv'tns: Recommended.
Reserve Through: Travel agent or call direct.
Minimum Stay: 2 days on weekend, longer for certain holidays.
Parking: Ample off-street parking.
In-Room: Color cable TV,

VCR, AC, telephone, ceiling fans, refrigerator & maid service. Some kitchenettes & full kitchens.
On-Premises: TV lounge, meeting rooms & laundry facilities.
Exercise/Health: Jacuzzi.
Swimming: Pool on premises.
Sunbathing: At poolside, on patio, common & private sun decks.
Nudity: Permitted everywhere.

Smoking: Permitted without restrictions.
Pets: Permitted with restrictions & based on availability.
Handicap Access: No.
Children: Not especially welcome.
Languages: English.

IGTA

Canyon Club Hotel

Palm Springs Just Got a Lot Bigger!

Men ♂

The *Canyon Boy's Club* offers 32 recently-renovated, comfortable rooms, all with AC, TVs, phones and some with complete kitchens and private patios. Other amenities include a large swimming pool, the largest Jacuzzi of any gay resort, a dry sauna, steam room, cozy fireplace and continental breakfast. Enjoy the large, open, private, sunny, clothing-optional courtyard and outdoor misting system. The atmosphere is quiet, friendly and relaxed and we are within easy walking distance to the shops and restaurants of Palm Canyon. Rates from $49-$69.

Address: 960 N Palm Canyon Dr, Palm Springs, CA 92262. Tel: (619) 322-4367 or (800) 295-2582, Fax: (619) 322-4024.

Type: Hotel.
Clientele: Men only.
Transportation: Car is best, 1mile from airport.
To Gay Bars: 10 blocks or 1 mile. 20-minute walk or 5-minute drive.
Rooms: 32 rooms with double, queen or king beds.
Bathrooms: 30 private bath/toilet/shower, 2 private shower/toilet.

Meals: Continental breakfast.
Dates Open: All year.
High Season: Spring & Fall.
Rates: $49-$69.
Credit Cards: MC, VISA, Amex & Discover.
Rsv'tns: Recommended.
Reserve Through: Call direct.
Minimum Stay: Most weekends & holidays.
Parking: Ample free off-street parking.

In-Room: Color cable TV, AC, telephone, coffee/tea-making facilities, refrigerators & maid service. Some have full kitchens & private patios. Two in-house video channels.
On-Premises: Lobby with fireplace.
Exercise/Health: Jacuzzi, dry sauna & steam.

Nearby gym.
Swimming: Large pool on premises.
Sunbathing: At poolside & on the patio.
Nudity: Clothing optional everywhere except lobby.
Smoking: Permitted. No non-smoking rooms.
Pets: Not permitted.
Handicap Access: No.
Children: Not welcome.
Languages: English.

Columns Resort

Cool Relaxation in the Desert Sun

Men ♂

The *Columns* provides a relaxing, comfortable setting to enjoy in solitude or with new friends. Our newly-decorated rooms surround a large, heated pool and spa, in a tropical courtyard. Clothing is optional at all times, and our Cool Mist and air conditioning ensure your total comfort while you enjoy our mountain views. Each spacious room includes a kitchen and dining area, coffee maker, private bath, phone, color cable TV,

VCR and firm, queen-sized bed. Our large tape collection is available at your leisure. We pride ourselves on our tranquil, sharing environment and cleanliness. Come, relax with us.

Address: 537 Grenfall Rd, Palm Springs, CA 92264. Tel: (619) 325-0655, (800) 798-0655.

Type: Private resort hotel.
Clientele: Men only.
Transportation: Car is best. Free pick up from airport, train or bus with prior arrangement.
To Gay Bars: 3-4 blocks to men's bars.
Rooms: 7 studios with queen beds & kitchens.
Bathrooms: All private

shower/toilets.
Meals: Expanded continental breakfast provided daily.
Complimentary: Coffee/cream/sugar in rooms. Soft drinks, iced tea, lemonade & snacks available. Icebreakers 1/2x wk
Dates Open: All year.
High Season: Jan-Jun.

Rates: $55-$85.
Discounts: 10% on 6 days & to repeat guests. 1 day free for 7 or more nights.
Credit Cards: MC, VISA, Amex, Discover.
Rsv'tns: Highly recommended!
Reserve Through: Travel agent or call direct.
Minimum Stay: 2 nights

on weekends, longer on some holidays.
Parking: Ample, free, off-street parking.
In-Room: Maid service, AC, remote color cable TV & VCR, kitchen, refrigerator, coffee/tea-making facilities, telephone, ceiling fans, video tape library.
On-Premises: Laundry

facilities, barbeque, bicycles, fax/copier, modem, lap counter at pool. **Exercise/Health:** Jacuzzi, bicycles, micro-cool out-

door mist, add'l charge for massage. Gym passes available. **Swimming:** Pool on premises.

Sunbathing: At poolside. **Nudity:** Permitted inside compound. **Smoking:** Permitted without restrictions.

Pets: Not permitted. **Handicap Access:** No. **Children:** Not permitted. **Languages:** English. **Your Host:** Jack & Blaine.

Desert Palms Inn

Where the Gay go to Play

Gay/Lesbian ♂

The scene was set when Hollywood filmed "Palm Springs Weekend" here some 26 years ago. The Inn proved so successful, it has hardly changed since. Weekends will find the patio surrounding the key-hole shaped pool at *Desert Palms Inn* towel-to-towel with sunbathing bodies. We host about half a dozen annual special-event parties and dancing. Each of our beautifully furnished rooms has color cable TV, direct dial phones, air conditioning and a patio or balcony overlooking bright flowers and broad-leafed palms. Your "Palm Springs weekend" begins here.

Address: 67-580 E Palm Canyon Dr, Palm Springs, CA 92234. Tel: (800) 483-6029, (619) 324-3000, Fax: (619) 324-5706.

Type: Inn with restaurant, bar & gift shop. **Clientele:** Mostly men with women welcome. **Transportation:** Taxi is best. **To Gay Bars:** 5-minute drive to men's/women's bars. **Rooms:** 30 rooms with double or queen beds.

Bathrooms: All private. **Dates Open:** All year. **High Season:** Nov-June. **Rates:** Summer $45-$50, winter $45-$89. **Credit Cards:** MC, VISA, Amex. **Rsv'tns:** Required for weekends 2-3 weeks in advance. **Reserve Through:** Travel

agent or call direct. **Minimum Stay:** 2 days on holiday weekends. **Parking:** Adequate free off-street parking. **In-Room:** Color TV, AC, direct dial telephone & maid service. **On-Premises:** Public telephone, gift shop, copy machine, fax transmittals

& receiving. **Exercise/Health:** Jacuzzi. **Swimming:** Pool. **Sunbathing:** At poolside. **Smoking:** Permitted without restrictions. **Pets:** Not permitted. **Handicap Access:** No. **Children:** Not permitted. **Languages:** English, Spanish.

Desert Paradise Hotel

An Ambiance of Style & Sophistication

Men ♂

Lush garden settings and majestic mountain views create the mood at *Desert Paradise Hotel*. Our attention to detail and dedication to service afford each guest a truly memorable experience. Stylish accommodations include private bath, telephone, color TV, VCR, air conditioning and kitchens. Elegant grounds, a poolside mix of music and laughter, and proximity to the excitement of Palm Springs combine to meet your every expectation. This is a gentleman's resort of the highest caliber, representing the best the desert has to offer!

Address: 615 Warm Sands Dr, Palm Springs, CA 92264. Tel: (619) 320-5650, outside CA: (800) 342-7635, Fax: (619) 320-0273.

Type: Hotel. **Clientele:** Men only. **Transportation:** Car or taxi. 5 minute taxi ride to hotel. **To Gay Bars:** 5 minutes by car to bars. **Rooms:** 9 rooms & 2 apartments with queen or king beds. **Bathrooms:** All private shower/toilets. **Meals:** Fresh fruit expanded continental breakfast. **Vegetarian:** Available

upon request. **Complimentary:** Beverages available with breakfast. **Dates Open:** All year. **High Season:** Oct-Jun. **Rates:** $95-$165, subject to change. **Discounts:** Weekly rates, please inquire. **Credit Cards:** All major cards including MC, VISA, Amex, Diners & Discover. **Rsv'tns:** Preferable to assure availability. **Reserve Through:** Travel

agent or call direct. **Minimum Stay:** 2 nights on weekends, longer on some holidays. **Parking:** Ample free off-street parking. **In-Room:** Color cable TV, VCR, film library, AC, maid service, telephone, kitchen, refrigerator. **On-Premises:** Laundry facility for guests, large poolside patio area, lush garden settings. **Exercise/Health:** Spa, nearby gym.

Swimming: Pool on premises. **Sunbathing:** At poolside. **Nudity:** Permitted poolside. **Smoking:** Permitted except in lobby. **Pets:** Small pets permitted with restrictions. Inquire first. **Handicap Access:** Yes. **Children:** Not expecially welcomed. **Languages:** English. **Your Host:** Greg.

El Mirasol Villas

Experience Our Style, Discover Our Magic....

Men ♂

Our style and our magic are why so many guests return time after time, year after year to *El Mirasol Villas*. Have your complimentary breakfast and lunch al fresco. Relax all day in the private and peaceful tropically-landscaped grounds beside either of our two pools or the spa. Enjoy the magnificent view of the Santa Rosa Mountains and Mount San Jacinto while soaking up the inimitable Palm Springs climate. The new owner-host is refurbishing the accommodations and enhancing the beauty of the grounds and will provide you the finest in service and experience in Palm Springs.

Address: 525 Warm Sands Dr, Palm Springs, CA 92264. Tel: (619) 327-5913, (800) 327-2985, Fax: (619) 325-8931.

Type: Resort hotel.
Clientele: Men only.
Transportation: Drive, or fly into Palm Springs Regional Airport. Free pick up from airport.
To Gay Bars: A 10-minute drive.
Rooms: 6 suites & 9 cottages.
Bathrooms: All private.
Meals: Continental breakfast & lunch.
Vegetarian: Available by arrangement at time of reservation.
Complimentary: Sodas & juices all day. Wine & beer at lunch.
Dates Open: All year.
Rates: $85-$210.
Credit Cards: All major credit cards.
Reserve Through: Travel agent or call direct.
Parking: Ample, free off-street parking.
In-Room: Color cable TV, VCR, video tape library, AC, telephone, kitchen, refrigerator & maid service.
On-Premises: Laundry facilities, fax & copier.
Exercise/Health: Jacuzzi on premises. Nearby gym, sauna, steam & massage.
Swimming: Two pools on premises.
Sunbathing: Poolside, on private sun decks or patio.
Nudity: Permitted around 1 of the pools.
Smoking: Permitted.
Pets: Not permitted.
Children: Not permitted.
Languages: English & French.
Your Host: John.

Hacienda en Sueño

Men ♂

Hacienda en Sueño is reserved for the private, exclusive intimacy of those whose breeding and culture enable them to relax in only the cleanest and finest of environments. Up to 14 guests enjoy the luxury of *two* large, heated swimming pools. The poolside apartments range in decor from colorful to traditional to strikingly handsome contemporary. Bedrooms have king-sized beds, combination down and feather pillows and remote-controlled lighting. All rooms have well-equipped kitchens, and guests are encouraged to pick from our vegetable and herb gardens.

Address: 586 Warm Sands Dr, Palm Springs, CA 92264. Tel: (619) 327-8111, (800) 359-2007.

Type: Hotel.
Clientele: Men only.
Transportation: Free pick up from the airport.
To Gay Bars: 10 minutes' drive to gay bars.
Rooms: 7 1-bedroom apartments.
Bathrooms: All private.
Meals: Expanded continental breakfast.
Complimentary: Coffee & tea.
Dates Open: All year.
Rates: $59-$165.
Credit Cards: All major credit cards.
Rsv'tns: Required.
Reserve Through: Travel agent or call direct.
Parking: Ample off-street parking, some covered.
In-Room: Maid & laundry service, color cable TV, AC, telephone (free local calls), ceiling fans, kitchen & refrigerator.
On-Premises: VCR, remote lighting & laundry facilities.
Exercise/Health: Jacuzzi. Free use of Gold's Gym & Oasis. Workout gear provided.
Swimming: Two pools on premises.
Sunbathing: At poolside or on private & common sun decks.
Nudity: Permitted.
Smoking: Permitted without restrictions.
Pets: Permitted. Please inquire.
Handicap Access: Yes.
Children: Not permitted.
Languages: English, Spanish, German, & Polish.

IGTA

Harlow Club Hotels Palm Springs, CA

Gay/Lesbian ♂

Now Choose From Three Deluxe Resorts Committed to Excellence

The Harlow El Alameda

Bougainvillaea tumbles off the red-tiled roofs of the classic Spanish hacienda and bungalows. Gardenias and jasmine perfume charmed patios. Stone pathways wind through the enchanting tropical gardens. *The Harlow El Alameda* is, by day, a sunny paradise...by night a magically-lit oasis. Often compared to the best-loved small luxury hotels of Europe, *The Harlow El Alameda* is located in the center of fashionable downtown Palm Springs. Designer-award suites and rooms are spacious, most with working fireplaces, all with magnificent bathrooms, central air conditioning, VCR and refrigerator. Other facilities of this enchanting hotel include a fountain courtyard, garden pavilion and a superb library of feature films.

The Abbey West

The Abbey West occupies an acre of walled grounds nestled in the secluded celebrity enclave of Las Palmas. *The Abbey West* is an art deco gem, a landmark fantasy in black and white. Whether it's cocktails fireside or sunning poolside, you'll bask in the glamour of this romantic, enchanting retreat. All suites range from 400-600 square feet, have private patios and galley kitchens. All accommodations include phone, cable TV, VCR, air conditioning and heating with individual room controls.

Enjoy designer-appointed splendor in an area commanding the most magnificent views. *The Abbey West...* tastefully decadent.

The Casablanca

The tradition continues with *The Casablanca*. Look for the Fall, 1994 opening of the third of the the Harlow Club Hotels Palm Springs, CA. *The Casablanca* will feature a full-service restaurant. **Address: Palm Springs, CA. Tel: (800) 223-4073, (619) 325-0229, (619) 323-3977, Fax: (619) 322-8534.**

Type: Hotels.
Clientele: Mostly men with women welcome.
Transportation: Taxi, bus.
To Gay Bars: From a 2-minute walk to a 5-minute drive.
Rooms: 15 doubles, 1 suite (sleeps 4).
Bathrooms: All private baths.
Meals: Expanded continental breakfast, 2-course lunch with wine, beer (included in

rates).
Vegetarian: Complimentary, upon request.
Complimentary: Soft drinks, iced tea, mineral water at poolside all day, snacks, mints in rooms.
Dates Open: All year.
High Season: December through May.
Rates: $135-$295 all year.
Discounts: Call for weekly rates.
Credit Cards: MC, VISA & Amex.

Rsv'tns: Required.
Reserve Through: Travel agent or call direct.
Minimum Stay: 2 nights on weekends, 3-4 on holiday weekends.
Parking: Ample free parking.
In-Room: Private telephone, maid service, color cable TV, VCR, AC, refrigerator, hairdryer, snack basket.
Exercise/Health: Complete gym, Jacuzzi.
Swimming: Lap pool set

in tropical gardens for both hotels.
Sunbathing: At poolside, on private patio or sun deck.
Nudity: Permitted on private sun deck. Be discreet.
Smoking: No smoking in lobby.
Pets: Not permitted.
Children: No.
Languages: English.

California

Inn Exile

Men ♂

Where Being Gay Is a Way of Life

Close your eyes and fantasize about a place where the open air calls you to the sparkling pool in the desert sun. Breathe in the dramatic view of towering mountains, while being refreshed by our outdoor mist cooling system. At *Inn Exile,* clothing is always optional. All paths lead to the Gangway, where everyone gathers for breakfast and luncheon. Later, Happy Hour is a great time to be with new friends...all complimentary, of course. There's no need to miss your workout...our gymnasium is here for you.

Address: 960 Camino Parocela, Palm Springs, CA 92262. Tel: (619) 327-6413 or (800) 962-0186, Fax: (619) 320-5745.

Type: Resort.
Clientele: Men only.
Transportation: Car is best.
To Gay Bars: Three minutes by car, a 10 minute-walk.
Rooms: 4 rooms & 5 suites with king beds.
Bathrooms: 9 private full baths.
Meals: Expanded Continental breakfast, lunch.

Complimentary: Happy Hour.
Dates Open: All year.
Rates: $83-$114.
Discounts: For 7 nights or more.
Credit Cards: MC, VISA, Amex, Discover, Diners, Carte Blanche.
Rsv'tns: Required.
Reserve Through: Travel agent or call direct.
Minimum Stay: Required

at times. Please inquire.
Parking: Adequate, free off-street and on-street parking.
In-Room: Color TV, VCR, video tape library, AC, houseman service, telephone & refrigerator.
On-Premises: TV lounge.
Exercise/Health: Gym, weights & Jacuzzi.
Swimming: Pool on premises.

Sunbathing: At poolside.
Nudity: Permitted.
Smoking: Permitted without restriction.
Pets: Not permitted.
Children: Not permitted.
Languages: English.
Your Host: John & Carter.

IGTA

InnTrigue

Men ♂

The *InnTrigue* has acquired an adjoining hotel, enabling us to offer new options for accommodations. In addition to our original 8-room intimate and secluded hotel, we have a 20-room "annex" with heated pool, spa, spacious grounds, and 2-bedroom studios and suites. Rest assured, we will continue to extend the same courtesy and personal attention as always. Come relax around either of our sparkling pools and spas with spectacular mountain views in the heart of Palm Springs. Enjoy a touch of Southern hospitality in the two worlds of the *InnTrigue.*

Address: 526 Warm Sands Dr, Palm Springs, CA 92264. Tel: (619) 323-7505 or (800) 798-8781.

Type: Private male resort.
Clientele: Men only.
Transportation: Car is best. Free pick up from the airport or bus station.
To Gay Bars: Within walking distance of gay bars & restaurants.
Rooms: 28 rooms.
Bathrooms: All private.
Meals: Continental breakfast & happy hour.
Complimentary: Coffee,

tea & evening cocktails. Occasional cookouts, large cocktail parties & holiday dinners.
Dates Open: All year.
Rates: $65-$135.
Discounts: For extended stays. Please inquire.
Credit Cards: All major credit cards.
Rsv'tns: Recommended.
Reserve Through: Travel agent or call direct.
Minimum Stay: 2 nights on weekends.

Parking: Adequate free off-street parking.
In-Room: Color cable TV, VCR, male video tape library, AC, phone, kitchen, refrigerator, coffee/tea-makers & maid service.
On-Premises: Laundry facilities, cool-mist system, security access gate.
Exercise/Health: Jacuzzi, pool table & table tennis. Complimentary Gold's Gym day passes, mas-

sage by appt. & bicycles.
Swimming: 2 pools on premises.
Sunbathing: At poolside & on patios.
Nudity: Permitted everywhere.
Smoking: Permitted without restrictions.
Pets: Not permitted.
Handicap Access: Yes.
Children: Not permitted.
Languages: English.

Inntimate

Inntimate By Name and By Nature

Men ♂

Inntimate is intimate. Here you are treated like a personal guest at a friend's home. There are four personalized poolside studios adjoining serene, secluded grounds where you can relax in a home-like atmosphere. Each spacious studio has a king-sized bed, seating area, telephone, TV, and its own kitchen. The grounds provide privacy for natural sunbathing and offer mountain views for miles as well as a bar & a barbie. Enjoy intimate Aussie hospitality with perfect accommodations at the *Inntimate*.

Address: 556 Warm Sands Dr, Palm Springs, CA 92264. Tel: (619) 778-8334 or (800) 695-3846.

Type: Private resort hotel. **Clientele:** Men only. **Transportation:** No charge for pick up from airport or bus. **To Gay Bars:** Walking distance to gay bars & restaurants. **Rooms:** 4 studios with king beds. **Bathrooms:** All private. **Meals:** Kevin's kitchen kit provided in fridge until you can visit the market & stock your own kitchen. **Vegetarian:** Ten-minute walk to vegetarian restaurant/store. **Complimentary:** Fresh coffee & coffeemaker in rooms. **Dates Open:** All year. **Rates:** $69-$100 for one or two people. **Discounts:** For extended stay upon application. **Credit Cards:** MC, VISA, Discover. **Rsv'tns:** Advisable.

Reserve Through: Travel agent or call direct. **Minimum Stay:** Required at times. Please inquire. **Parking:** Adequate free off-street parking. **In-Room:** Color cable TV, AC, evaporative coolers, ceiling fans, telephone, kitchen, refrigerator, coffee & tea-maker & maid service. **Exercise/Health:** Massage by appointment. Gym passes available.

Swimming: Pool on premises. **Sunbathing:** At poolside or on private sun decks. **Nudity:** Permitted anywhere within the resort. **Smoking:** Permitted. **Pets:** Not permitted. **Handicap Access:** No. **Children:** Not permitted. **Languages:** English, Aussie style. **Your Host:** Kevin.

Triangle Inn

Everything, Except Ordinary!

Men ♂

Finally, a secluded men's resort that will exceed your expectations. As you pass through the gate of our sun-drenched tropical gardens, you are drawn to the sparkling pool and relaxing Jacuzzi and many other enjoyable recreations. At the *Triangle Inn,* you can select from our deluxe studios and 1- or 2-bedroom suites. Our rooms include remote TV and VCR, stereo with CD and tape player and private telephones. All rooms have central air conditioning with in-room thermostats. The junior suite and the 1- and 2-bedroom suites  come with fully-equipped kitchens. The studios offer a kitchenette. Uncompromising accommodations at affordable prices are what make the *Triangle Inn* so enticing.

Start your day off with a complimentary poolside buffet breakfast and an opportunity to meet other guests. Then relax by the pool (swimsuits optional), soak up some sun, take a stroll through downtown Palm Springs or explore the desert landscape on bikes. We're just a short 1-block walk from an Indian canyon and an exciting hike up the San Jacinto Mountains. As evening nears, get together with

continued next page

new-found friends to sample the myriad restaurants Palm Springs has to offer, or just put together your own barbecue. Conveniently located at the south end of Palm Springs, the Triangle Inn is a 5-minute drive to local nightspots where friendly locals mix freely with visitors to the Coachella Valley. No matter what time of year you visit, there is always something for you in Palm Springs. In short, the condition of the *Triangle Inn* is impeccable, the attitude casual, and the hospitality friendly. So whether you are planning to spend a couple of days or a week, you will feel welcome and at home at the finest men's resort in Palm Springs. See for yourself why the *Triangle Inn* is everything...except ordinary! Color brochure available upon request.

Address: 555 San Lorenzo, Palm Springs, CA 92264. Tel: (619) 322-7993, (800) 732-7555

Type: Inn.
Clientele: Men only.
Transportation: Free pick up from Palm Springs airport.
To Gay Bars: 5- to 10-minute drive to all gay bars.
Rooms: 3 rooms & 6 suites with queen or king beds.
Bathrooms: All private bath/toilets.
Meals: Expanded continental breakfast.

Dates Open: All year.
High Season: October 1-July 4.
Rates: $104-$219. Inquire for summer value rates.
Discounts: Inquire.
Credit Cards: MC, VISA & Amex.
Rsv'tns: Required.
Reserve Through: Travel agent or call direct.
Minimum Stay: 2 nights on weekends. Inquire for holiday periods.
Parking: Ample free off-

street parking.
In-Room: AC, maid service, telephone, stereo, CD, color TV, VCR, kitchen & refrigerator.
On-Premises: Video tape library.
Exercise/Health: Jacuzzi, massage by appointment & bicycles.
Swimming: Pool on premises.
Sunbathing: At poolside with micro-cool outdoor cooling system.

Nudity: Permitted at poolside.
Smoking: Permitted without restrictions.
Pets: Not permitted.
Handicap Access: Inquire.
Children: Not permitted.
Languages: English.
Your Host: Kevin & Matthew.

IGTA

We Appreciate Your Comments!

The editors of *INN Places*® actively seek your comments about accommodations you have tried.

Positive comments of interest may be included in the next issue, giving future readers the benefit of your experience. And it's a nice way of saying "thank you" to an innkeeper who extended you exceptional hospitality.

See the contents for the Reader Comment Form.

Versailles, The

Men. ♂

The Villa at Old Palm Springs

"Veni, vidi, vici..." said Julius Caesar as he gazed upon Rome, circa 400 B.C.

Under new management, they came, they saw, they conquered and have converted an old 1940's motel into *The Versailles,* The Villa at Old Palm Springs. Every vista is a jewel to behold. The fountains, the lushness of the foliage and the elegance of the rooms bring to mind an ancient villa lost in time. Each room is beautifully appointed with luxurious bed linens and a media center with an oversized TV, VCR, laser disc and CD stereo. The poolside courtyard's intimate setting is dreamlike with cool mist; a gracious, secluded retreat that is perfect for both couples and singles.

For the busy executive who must keep in touch with civilization, a fax, photo copy services, computer modem capability telephones and Fed-Ex are available. An extensive library of movies on laser discs are available for viewing in the privacy of your own suite or with new friends in the Forum Room.

Arrangements for unique day excursions, as well as dinner and theatre reservations, can be made by your concierge.

Address: 288 Camino Monte Vista, Palm Springs, CA 92262. Tel: (619) 320-2888, (800) 694-2888, Fax: (619) 323-1890.

Type: Deluxe men's hotel.
Clientele: Men.
Transportation: Car is best. Free pick up from airport.
To Gay Bars: About 1 mile.
Rooms: 16 rooms with queen or king beds.
Bathrooms: All private.
Meals: Continental breakfast.

Complimentary: Snacks in room. Pop & juice poolside.
Dates Open: All year.
High Season: Jan-Apr.
Rates: $100-$250.
Credit Cards: MC, VISA, Amex & Discover.
Rsv'tns: Required.
Reserve Through: Travel agent or call direct.
Parking: Ample free off-street & on-street

parking.
In-Room: Color cable TV, VCR, video tape library, AC telephone, kitchen, refrigerator, coffee/tea-making facilities & maid service.
On-Premises: Meeting rooms, TV lounge, fax, photocopier & laundry facilities.
Exercise/Health: Jacuzzi on premises.

Swimming: Pool on premises.
Sunbathing: At poolside.
Nudity: Permitted poolside.
Smoking: Permitted.
Pets: Not permitted.
Handicap Access: Yes.
Children: Not especially welcome.
Languages: English.

Villa, The

Gay/Lesbian ♂

Palm Springs is fast becoming the number one gay destination in the U.S., and *The Villa* is its largest, finest gay resort. Though a popular gathering spot, *The Villa* offers uncrowded luxury on 2-1/2 acres of lushly-planted grounds. You can lunch on the patio, lounge in the Poolside Bar, enjoy an espresso or wander off to a quiet corner beneath the over 70 palms on the property. Our 45 rooms, originally built by Elizabeth Arden, have been lovingly restored.

Address: 67-670 Carey Rd, Cathedral City, CA 92234.
Tel: (619) 328-7211. Reservations (800) VILLA OK, Fax: (619) 321-1463.

Type: Resort with pool bar & restaurant.
Clientele: Mostly men with women welcome.
Transportation: Car, cab.
To Gay Bars: 1/2 mile by car to men's bars.
Rooms: 45 rooms with double or queen beds.
Bathrooms: All private.
Meals: Continental breakfast.
Dates Open: All year.
High Season: Jan-Jul 4th.

Rates: Off season $54.95-$80.95, in season $59.95-$97.95, holidays $99.95-$107.95.
Discounts: Off season: 1 night free on 2-night stay. In season: Tue, Wed, Thurs free with 2 prior nights stay.
Credit Cards: MC, VISA, Amex.
Rsv'tns: Recommended.
Reserve Through: Travel agent or call direct.

Minimum Stay: 2-4 days on holidays.
Parking: Ample off-street parking.
In-Room: Separate entrances, remote control color TV/radio, direct-dial phone, maid services, refrigerators, microwaves, pullman kitchen & AC.
On-Premises: Meeting room, fireplace lounge, public telephone.
Exercise/Health: Sauna,

Jacuzzi, massage.
Swimming: Pool on site.
Sunbathing: At poolside or on lawn.
Smoking: Permitted. Non-smoking rooms available.
Pets: Not permitted.
Handicap Access: No.
Children: Not permitted.
Languages: English, limited Spanish.

IGTA

Whispering Palms Resort

Gay/Lesbian ♂

Perfect Getaway for Lovers & Just the Right Getaway for Singles

Welcome to tropical, romantic *Whispering Palms* resort. A friendly host escorts you to your spacious, theme-decorated suite with stereo TV, VCR and free adult videos. Outdoor misting cools the entire compound and drifts over you while you sunbathe. The gated and enclosed compound invites nude sunbathing and swimming. At night, tiki torches, soft music, twinkling lights, the murmur of the fountain, star-filled skies and the secluded Jacuzzi turn *Whispering Palms* into a magical wonderland. Come...live your fantasy at this oasis.

Whispering Palms
A PRIVATE RESORT
545 Warm Sands Drive
Palm Springs, California 92264
(619) 320-1300 or
1-800-699-WARM

Address: 545 Warm Sands Dr, Palm Springs, CA 92264. Tel: (800) 669-9276, (619) 320-1300, Fax: (619) 320-7535.

Type: Hotel.
Clientele: Mostly men
with women welcome.
Transportation: Hotel
limousine will pick up guests at airport or bus
station, no charge.
To Gay Bars: 10 blocks or

1/4 mile. 10 minutes by foot, 3 minutes by car.
Rooms: 2 rooms, 6 suites & 4 apartments with queen or king beds.
Bathrooms: All private.
Meals: Expanded continental breakfast.
Vegetarian: 10-minute walk to vegetarian store & restaurant.
Complimentary: Coffeemakers, coffee & tea in rooms.
Dates Open: All year.
High Season: February

through June.
Rates: Low season $35-$77, high season $65-$155.
Discounts: Midweek, weekly and monthly.
Credit Cards: MC, VISA, Amex, Diners, Bancard, Eurocard & Discover.
Rsv'tns: Preferred.
Reserve Through: Travel agent or call direct.
Minimum Stay: 2 nights on weekends.
Parking: Ample, free off-street parking.

In-Room: Color cable TV, VCR, video tape library, AC, ceiling fans, telephone, kitchen, refrigerator, coffee & tea-making facilities & maid service.
On-Premises: Exciting video library.
Exercise/Health: Jacuzzi-type spa, free bicycles, massage by appointment. Passes to Gold's Gym.
Swimming: Pool.
Sunbathing: At poolside

or on common sun decks.
Nudity: Permitted anywhere within hotel compound.
Smoking: Permitted without restrictions.
Pets: Permitted with prior arrangement.
Handicap Access: No.
Children: Not especially welcome.
Languages: English, Spanish.

KGTA

RUSSIAN RIVER

Applewood, formerly The Estate Inn

Gay-Friendly ♀♂

Applewood, An Estate Inn

The beauty of the redwoods, apple trees and vineyards...the relaxing pool and Jacuzzi...the stylish rooms with European down comforters...the pleasure of sitting by the fire or reading in the solarium...the marvelous food in a firelit dining room...your willing hosts and two tail-wagging dogs... all await your arrival at this contemporary Eden.

Once a mission-style retreat in the redwoods, *Applewood* has been transformed into an elegant country inn and restaurant that has become the darling of food critics and editors steering their readers to romantic getaways. Rave reviews have appeared in local papers and magazines, as well as regional and national magazines.

Jeff Cox of the **Santa Rosa Press Democrat,** says, "...*I've found a spot...where peace and quiet hang motionless under the boughs of the redwoods, and where the relaxed sensibility of a former time seems captured in the graceful lines of a building's architecture. And, while you're enjoying all this, you're also being served marvelous food.*" **Elle Magazine, January 1993** reports that *Applewood* is "...*a sumptuous romantic retreat*" that "*has been lovingly attended to by its two owners, who indulge guests with good food, books, and company.*"

And a **Pacific Northwest, October 1993** writer states, "*My room was almost decadently comfortable, tucked away in a quiet downstairs nook beside a redwood grove...*" with a "...*personal parlor....*"

Let *Applewood* be your great place to unwind and relax. Drive down country lanes. Picnic or taste wine at boutique wineries. Raft or canoe on the Russian River. Take a short drive to the coast to kick up a little sand on the beach. Or just languish in bed with a mimosa and someone special.

Address: 13555 Hwy 116, Guerneville, CA 95446. Tel: (707) 869-9093.

Type: Inn with restaurant serving 4-course dinners.

Clientele: Mostly straight clientele with a gay & lesbian following.

Transportation: Car is best. Free pick up from Santa Rosa airport.

To Gay Bars: 5-min drive to men's/women's bars.
continued next page

California

Rooms: 10 rooms & 6 suites with queen beds. **Bathrooms:** All private. **Meals:** Full breakfast included, dinner offered Tuesdays thru Saturdays. **Vegetarian:** Upon request with 1 day notice. **Complimentary:** Chocolates on pillows, coffee and tea all day. Suites with wine & soft drinks in refrigerator. **Dates Open:** All year.

High Season: Apr-Nov. **Rates:** Doubles $115-$225. **Credit Cards:** MC, VISA, Amex, Discover. **Rsv'tns:** Recommended. Essential for dinner. **Reserve Through:** Travel agent or call direct. **Minimum Stay:** 1 night midweek, 2 nights on weekends, 3 nights on holiday weekends. **Parking:** Ample, free off-street parking.

In-Room: Color TV, phone & maid service. Suites also have stocked refrigerator, hair dryer, VCR & video tape library & Jacuzzi baths. **On-Premises:** Meeting rooms, private dining rooms, public telephone, laundry facilities & fax. **Exercise/Health:** Jacuzzi, massage. Jacuzzi baths in suites. **Swimming:** Heated pool

on premises, river nearby. 10 minutes to ocean. **Sunbathing:** At poolside & on private verandas with suites. **Smoking:** Not permitted. **Pets:** Not permitted. **Handicap Access:** Yes, ramps, wide doors, grab bars. **Children:** Not permitted. **Languages:** English. **Your Host:** Darryl & Jim.

Bob & Jacques' Cottage

The Ultimate in Privacy

Gay/Lesbian ♂

Bob & Jacques' Cottage is situated on 7 beautiful, private acres in the heart of California's wine country, only 10 minutes from Guerneville's active nightlife and 5 minutes from the gay beach at the Russian River. Enjoy a hot tub under the stars, have a bottle of local wine on the porch overlooking the vineyards, or lounge by the beautiful new pool. The cottage has a full bath and kitchen, its own driveway and a sleeping loft with fantastic views, color TV, stereo and sun deck.

Address: 6471 Old Trenton Road, Forestville, CA 95436. Tel: (707) 575-1033.

Type: Cottage. **Clientele:** Mostly men with women welcome. **Transportation:** Car is best. **To Gay Bars:** 8 miles to all the bars. **Rooms:** 1 cottage with 2 queen beds. **Bathrooms:** Private bath/toilet/shower. **Complimentary:** Coffee & coffee-maker in cot-

tage. **Dates Open:** All year. **High Season:** Last weekend in May (women's weekend) to end of Oct. **Rates:** $90-$125. **Discounts:** Weekly rates available. **Rsv'tns:** Required. **Reserve Through:** Travel agent or call direct. **Minimum Stay:** 2 nights on weekends.

Parking: Ample, free off-street parking. **In-Room:** Color TV, VCR, video tape library, laundry service, telephone, kitchen, refrigerator, coffee & tea-making facilities. **On-Premises:** Sun deck. **Exercise/Health:** Jacuzzi on premises. Nearby gym, massage. **Swimming:** Pool on pre-

mises. River with gay beach 2 miles, or lake 35 miles away. **Sunbathing:** At poolside or on private sun deck. **Nudity:** Permitted. **Smoking:** Permitted. **Pets:** Permitted. **Handicap Access:** No. **Children:** Permitted. **Languages:** English. **Your Host:** Bob & Jacques.

Fern Grove Inn

Wineries, Vineyards and Towering Redwoods

Gay-Friendly 50/50 ♀♂

Located in Sonoma County's wine country, *Fern Grove Inn* is surrounded by premium wineries, towering redwoods, and the scenic Russian River and is ten minutes from the Sonoma Coast. Our spacious, private and romantic villas and cottage suites have fireplaces perfect for cool nights, private baths, refrigerator and TV, some with VCR. Breakfast features our renowned home-baked pastries and muf-  fins. Swim or lounge by our pool, lazily canoe the river, visit wineries. Your hosts invite you to sample our unparalleled hospitality and enjoy this true vacation paradise.

Address: 16650 River Rd, Guernewood Park, CA 95446. Tel: (707) 869-9083 or (800) 347-9083.

Type: Bed & breakfast with cottages.
Clientele: 50% gay & lesbian & 50% straight.
Transportation: Car is best or SFO Airport Express Bus to Santa Rosa & local bus to Guerneville.
To Gay Bars: 1 block to men's or women's bars, dancing.
Rooms: 2 villas, 9 suites & 6 studio cottages with queen beds.
Bathrooms: All private.

Meals: Expanded continental breakfast.
Vegetarian: Nearby restaurants.
Complimentary: Coffee & tea all day. Juice or sherry in the afternoon.
Dates Open: All year.
High Season: Apr-Oct.
Rates: $79-$159.
Discounts: Inquire about mid-week or off-season.
Credit Cards: MC, VISA, Amex, Diners, Discover.
Rsv'tns: Recommended.
Reserve Through: Travel

agent or call direct.
Minimum Stay: 2 nights most weekends. 3 nights holiday weekends.
Parking: Ample off-street parking.
In-Room: Color TV, refrigerator, & maid service.
On-Premises: Common room, guest telephone, & library.
Exercise/Health: Golf, tennis, horseback riding, jogging, hiking, canoeing, enzyme baths, & health

club all nearby.
Swimming: Pool on premises. 12 miles to ocean beach. River across the highway.
Sunbathing: At poolside or on river or ocean beaches.
Smoking: Permitted except in common rooms.
Pets: Not permitted.
Handicap Access: No.
Children: Permitted, but not encouraged.
Languages: English & some Spanish.

Fifes Resort

Come, Have It All!

Gay/Lesbian ♀♂

Get away and feel free at *Fifes,* the largest gay and lesbian resort in the country! Explore 15 beautiful acres of redwoods, rose gardens, meadows and a private beach on the Russian River. Cuddle up in one of 50 cozy country cabins or camp out under the stars. Enjoy poolside or fireside dining, the main bar, the large screen TV lounge and a full-service gym. Two-step in the Bunkhouse, the new C&W dance bar, or rent a canoe and head down the river. Whatever your pleasure, you can do it all and have it all at *Fifes,* the total gay resort!

Address: 16467 River Rd, Guerneville, CA 95446. Tel: (707) 869-0656, in CA: (800) 7-FIFES-1, Fax: (707) 869-0658.

Type: Cabins & campground with restaurant, bar & C&W dancing.
Clientele: Mostly gay & lesbian with some straight clientele.
Transportation: Car is best. Bus available.
To Gay Bars: Gay bars on the premises.
Rooms: 50 rooms with queen beds.
Bathrooms: All private.
Campsites: Over 60 tent sites with picnic tables on the Russian River. 1 restroom area with

showers.
Vegetarian: Limited vegetarian menu at restaurant.
Complimentary: Coffee.
Dates Open: All year.
High Season: May through October.
Rates: Rooms $50-$130, suites $65-$130, cottages $150-$215, campsites from $15 (holidays $18 per person).
Discounts: Travel agents 50% off with IATA number.
Credit Cards: MC, VISA,

Amex.
Rsv'tns: Required holidays, major event weekends. Suggested at other times.
Reserve Through: Travel agent or call direct.
Minimum Stay: High season: 2 nights weekends, 3 nights holiday weekends.
Parking: Adequate off-street parking.
In-Room: Maid service.
On-Premises: TV lounge & meeting rooms.
Exercise/Health: Full

service gym with weights on premises.
Swimming: Pool & river on premises.
Sunbathing: At poolside, on beach, in meadows & campground.
Smoking: Permitted in bar, pool area & rooms.
Pets: Not permitted.
Handicap Access: Limited access.
Children: Adult resort.
Languages: English.

IGTA

Golden Apple Ranch

Gay-Friendly 50/50 ♀♂

Golden Apple Ranch, gateway to the Russian River wine country, is a secluded retreat built among the towering redwoods and overlooking Bodega Bay. The lodge gallery and great room invite guests to read, relax, paint or dream the day away...while the private suites offer total seclusion. From the ranch, one can arrange to be chauffered through the wine country in our Classic Silver Cloud Rolls Royce or our luxury Continental convertible. Your host, John Stillion, is known for his gracious hospitality in seeing to guest's individual needs. We hope you can join us this season.

The Golden Apple Ranch

Occidental, California

Address: 17575 Fitzpatrick Lane, Occidental, CA 95465. Tel: (707) 874-3756, (800) 874-3756, Fax: (707) 874-1670.

Type: Art gallery lodge overlooking magnificent redwood groves.
Clientele: 50% gay & lesbian & 50% straight clientele.
Transportation: By car. Deluxe ground transportation available upon request.
To Gay Bars: 12 miles or 20 minutes.
Rooms: 5 suites.
Bathrooms: All private.
Meals: Continental breakfast 8-11 am. Lunch & dinner available upon request.

Vegetarian: Full vegetarian lunch & dinner available upon request.
Complimentary: Champagne, wine, or tea on arrival. Sherry or hot tea in the evening.
Dates Open: All year.
High Season: April-December.
Rates: $95-$145.
Discounts: Guests staying 3 or more nights will receive a 20% discount on lodging.
Rsv'tns: Required.
Reserve Through: Travel agent or call direct.

Parking: Ample parking in motor court & grounds.
In-Room: Telephone & maid service. Satellite color TV available in most suites.
On-Premises: Meeting rooms, TV lounge, weddings & celebrations.
Exercise/Health: Personalized massage available upon request. Internationally renowned osmosis baths in nearby Freestone.
Swimming: Public beaches 5 miles.

Sunbathing: On the roof or in the grassy meadow below the lodge.
Nudity: Permitted on the roof, grassy meadow, and public nude beach 10 miles away.
Smoking: Permitted on private decks, terraces & motor court.
Pets: Most welcome with prior arrangement.
Handicap Access: Yes.
Children: Most welcome with prior arrangement.
Languages: English & Spanish.
Your Host: John.

We Appreciate Your Comments!

Positive comments of interest may be included in the next issue, giving future readers the benefit of your experience. And it's a nice way of saying "thank you" to an innkeeper who extended you exceptional hospitality.

See the contents for the Reader Comment Form.

Highland Dell Inn

Gay-Friendly 50/50 ♀♂

Exceptional Service In a Spectacular Setting

The landmark *Highland Dell Inn,* with its vista of the Russian River, captures the serenity of a more gentle era. Rich, stained glass windows, a gigantic lobby fireplace, heirloom antiques and a collection of historical photos set the tone for arriving guests. The large pool is under the redwoods. The area offers canoeing, swimming, fishing, backpacking, nature trails, horseback riding, cross-country cycling, enzyme baths, and even hot-air ballooning. One of our guests comments, *"The warmth of your hospitality, the charm of this beautiful B&B, delicious food, the view...a perfect getaway. Lady (dog) certainly lives up to her name."*

Address: 21050 River Blvd, Box 370, Monte Rio, CA 95462-0370. Tel: (707) 865-1759 or (800) 767-1759.

Type: Bed & breakfast inn with dance CW social club.
Clientele: 50% gay & lesbian & 50% straight clientele. Sometimes more gay & lesbian than straight.

Transportation: Car is best.
To Gay Bars: 5-minute drive to most gay venues.
Rooms: 8 rooms & 2 suites with queen or king beds.
Bathrooms: 8 private baths, 2 private sinks. 1 shared shower & 1 shared toilet.
Meals: Full breakfast with dinners available Saturday nights during season.
Vegetarian: Available upon request.
Complimentary: Tea & coffee. Candies throughout. Chocolate truffles in room.
Dates Open: Open all year except for Dec 1-Dec 20.
High Season: May-October.
Rates: Summer $70-$255 & winter $49-$225.
Discounts: Inquire.
Credit Cards: MC, VISA, Amex, Discover & JCB.
Rsv'tns: Required.
Reserve Through: Travel agent or call direct.
Minimum Stay: 2 nights on weekends. 3 nights some holidays.
Parking: Ample, free off-street parking.
In-Room: Maid service, video tape library & telephone. Suites with color TV/VCR.
On-Premises: TV lounge & meeting rooms.
Exercise/Health: Nearby gym, massage, mineral & enzyme baths.
Swimming: Seasonal pool on premises. 6 miles to ocean beach & river nearby.
Sunbathing: At poolside or on the beach.
Smoking: Permitted in sun room only. All rooms are non-smoking.
Pets: Pets up to 35 pounds with pet deposit in 1st floor rooms only.
Handicap Access: No.
Children: Not especially welcome.
Languages: English.
Your Host: Glenn & Anthony.

Highlands Resort

Gay/Lesbian ♀♂

Highlands Resort is a country retreat on 4 wooded acres. You can plan your day while soaking in the outdoor hot tub, swim and sun at the pool or barbecue a meal with friends. Challenge another group to Trivial Pursuit, read a book or curl up in front of the fireplace. This is a place for relaxing. The resort feels like a mountaintop, yet is only a short walk to fine restaurants, shops, nightclubs.

Address: PO Box 346, 14000 Woodland Dr, Guerneville, CA 95446. Tel: (707) 869-0333.

Type: Inn & campground.
Clientele: Good mix of gay men & women.
Transportation: Car is best. Free pick up from bus.
To Gay Bars: 2 blocks to men's/women's bars. A 5-minute walk or 2-minute drive.
Rooms: 10 rooms, 1 suite & 6 cottages with double, queen or king beds.
Bathrooms: 10 private, others share.
Campsites: 30 tent sites with 3 showers & 2 restrooms.
Meals: Continental breakfast on holidays & special events.
Dates Open: All year.
High Season: Apr-Oct.
Rates: Summer $40-$118, winter $40-$78.
Credit Cards: MC, VISA, Amex & Discover.
Rsv'tns: Recommended.
Reserve Through: Travel agent or call direct.
Minimum Stay: 2 nights over weekends.
Parking: Ample free parking.
In-Room: Maid service, 2 kitchens.
On-Premises: TV lounge.
Exercise/Health: Hot tub.
Swimming: Pool on premises.
Sunbathing: At poolside or on the patio.
Nudity: Permitted around pool & hot tub.
Smoking: Permitted around pool & hot tub.
Pets: Not permitted.
Handicap Access: No.
Children: Not especially welcome.
Languages: English.

House of a Thousand Flowers

Gay-Friendly 50/50 ♀♂

Designed so that each room has its own spectacular view of the forest and the valley below, *The House of a Thousand Flowers* sits high on a bluff overlooking the Russian River. It is surrounded by sunny decks, intimate gardens, and walkways. There are two comfortably furnished guest rooms with private entrances, a shared bath, and an enclosed spa on the deck. There is a fireplace in the living room and an extensive book, music, and movie library for the guests. There are many activities, sunny beaches, quaint inns, and fine restaurants nearby.

Address: 11 Mosswood Circle, Cazadero, CA 95421. Tel: (707) 632-5571.

Type: Bed & breakfast.
Clientele: 50% gay & lesbian & 50% straight clientele.
Transportation: Pick up from airport in Santa Rosa, pick up from bus $10.
To Gay Bars: 9 miles or 10 minutes by car.
Rooms: 2 rooms with queen beds.
Bathrooms: 1 shared
bath/shower/toilet.
Meals: Full breakfast.
Vegetarian: Always available.
Complimentary: After-noon wine, after dinner liqueur.
Dates Open: All year.
High Season: July-Sept.
Rates: One rate, $85-$90 per couple, $60 single.
Credit Cards: MC, VISA.
Rsv'tns: Required.
Reserve Through: Call direct.
Parking: Free parking.
On-Premises: TV lounge, meeting rooms, laundry facilities.
Exercise/Health: Jacuzzi, massage.
Swimming: At nearby river & ocean beach.
Sunbathing: At beach &
common sun decks.
Nudity: Permitted on common sun deck by appointment only.
Smoking: Permitted in designated areas, non-smoking rooms available.
Pets: Not permitted.
Handicap Access: No.
Children: Not permitted.
Languages: English.
Your Host: Dave & Bob.

Huckleberry Springs

Gay-Friendly 50/50 ♀♂

Huckleberry Springs is five deluxe cottages on 56 wooded acres. Each cottage is unique. All have queen-sized beds, private baths, skylights and wood stoves. Breakfast and dinner are served in the main lodge, and there are private tables for two in the solarium or on the large deck. Guest sunbathe on the pool decks or on the landscaped hillside. The spacious lodge offers places to watch videos, listen to music, socialize or relax with a book or friend. Canoeing, hiking, bicycling, golf, tennis, wineries and the ocean are nearby.

Address: PO Box 400, Monte Rio, CA 95462. Tel: (707) 865-2683, (800) 822-2683.

Type: Cottages & B&B on 56 acres one mile from the river.
Clientele: 50% gay & lesbian & 50% straight clientele.
Transportation: Rental car is best.
To Gay Bars: 6 miles.
Rooms: 5 cottages with queen beds
Bathrooms: All private.
Meals: Full breakfast & dinner.
Vegetarian: With advance notice upon reservation.
Complimentary: Tea, coffee & spring water.
Dates Open: March 2-December 14.
High Season: May through September.
Rates: $145-$190. Full breakfast & dinner included in rate on weekends.
Credit Cards: MC, VISA & Amex.
Rsv'tns: Required.
Reserve Through: Travel agent or call direct.
Minimum Stay: 2 days.
Parking: Ample free parking.
In-Room: Ceiling fans, hairdryers, refrigerator & coffee & tea-making facilities.
On-Premises: Catering, kitchen with advance request, meeting rooms & TV lounge.
Exercise/Health: Jacuzzi, massage by appointment.
Swimming: Pool on premises, river nearby.
Sunbathing: Poolside, private & common sun decks, at nearby ocean, riverside beaches.
Nudity: Permitted in the hot tub.
Smoking: Permitted outdoors only.
Pets: Not permitted.
Handicap Access: Only the lodge.
Children: Not permitted.
Languages: English & Spanish.

IGTA

Mountain Lodge Resort

Gay-Friendly 50/50 ♀♂

Discover *Mountain Lodge Resort,* one of the Russian River's best-kept secrets. Explore the possibilities! Peaceful gardens and secluded decks nestle into the artfully-landscaped grounds. The pool and hot tubs overlook the Russian River. Gay bars of the area are a short distance away.

Address: PO Box 169, 16350 1st St, Guerneville, CA 95446. Phone/Fax: (707) 869-3722.

Type: Condo-style ground level units.
Clientele: 50% gay & lesbian & 50% straight clientele.
Transportation: Car is best from San Francisco.
To Gay Bars: 2-minute walk to gay & lesbian bars.
Rooms: 3 apartments with queen beds.
Bathrooms: All private.
Dates Open: All year. Weekly/monthly rentals based on availability.
High Season: May through September.
Rates: Summer $50-$125. Winter $40-$95. Based on double occupancy.
Discounts: For stays of three nights or more Sunday-Thursday or for a week or more.
Credit Cards: MC, VISA & Amex.
Reserve Through: Travel agent or call direct.
Minimum Stay: On holiday weekends.
Parking: Ample off-street parking. Gated security, key access only.
In-Room: Color cable TV, kitchen, refrigerator, coffee & tea-making facilities & maid service.
On-Premises: Laundry facilities.
Exercise/Health: Jacuzzi. Steam in one resort room.
Swimming: Pool & river on premises.
Sunbathing: At poolside, on the beach, or on private & common sun decks.
Nudity: Permitted in spas after dark with discretion.
Smoking: Permitted without restrictions.
Pets: Not permitted.
Children: Permitted. Small children at pool between 3 & 6 pm only.
Languages: English.

North Forty Resort

Gay/Lesbian ♀♂

The *North Forty* is nestled in the heart of the Guerneville Russian River recreational area, 90 minutes north of the Golden Gate, approximately 15 miles from the Pacific Ocean. Headquarter your vacation stay here. Enjoy seclusion, privacy, and peaceful ambiance in a cabin in your own *North Forty* redwood grove.

Address: PO Box 2414, Guerneville, CA 95446. Tel: (707) 869-9695, (800) 367-8936.

Type: Cottages with full kitchens.
Clientele: Mostly gay & lesbian with some straight clientele.
Transportation: Car is best.
To Gay Bars: Across the street from Fifes. 3 blocks to Rainbow Cattle Co.
Rooms: Two 2-bedroom cottages & eight 1-bedroom cottages.
Bathrooms: All private.
Vegetarian: At nearby restaurants.
Dates Open: All year.
High Season: May thru October.
Rates: Summer $45-$100. Winter $45-$65.
Discounts: Weekly rates. Mid-week, weekend specials. Discounts to Inn Places readers. Inquire.
Credit Cards: MC, VISA, Amex, & Discover.
Rsv'tns: Recommended.
Reserve Through: Call direct.
Minimum Stay: Holiday & special event weekends.
Parking: Private on-grounds parking. 5 cabins have car ports.
In-Room: Color TV, kitchen, refrigerator, coffee maker & coffee.
Exercise/Health: Bike rental shop nearby.
Swimming: 5-minute walk to public beach.
Sunbathing: On our lawn & picnic area or at the beach.
Smoking: Permitted. Non-smoking cabins available.
Pets: Permitted by prior arrangement only.
Handicap Access: Yes. 1 cabin wheelchair accessible.
Children: Permitted.
Languages: English, Spanish & German.
Your Host: Larry.

Paradise Cove

A Unique Place to Stay on the Russian River

Gay/Lesbian ♀♂

Paradise Cove is a luxurious, unique, adult resort where service and comfort are top priorities. All cabins have private baths, sundecks and fireplaces. The grounds were carefully planned to highlight seasonal changes in this northern California forest and wine country. From the spectacular burst of color in our rhododendron dell to cascading vines of Burmese honeysuckle, passion flower, palms and lilies of the Nile, there is even a hint of the tropics.

Address: 14711 Armstrong Woods Rd, Guerneville, CA 95446. Tel: (707) 869-2706 or (800) 880-2706.

Type: Resort.
Clientele: Good mix of gay men & women.
Transportation: Car.
To Gay Bars: 1 mile to men's/women's bars.
Rooms: 15 rooms with queen beds, fireplaces & sun decks.
Bathrooms: All private shower/toilets.
Meals: Coffee, tea, breakfast cakes on weekends, holidays.
Dates Open: All year.
High Season: May-September.
Rates: Off-season $50-$105, in-season $65-$135.
Discounts: Weekly rates & off-season packages may apply.
Credit Cards: MC, VISA, Amex & Discover.
Rsv'tns: Recommended.
Reserve Through: Call direct.
Minimum Stay: On holiday & special-event weekends.
Parking: Adequate free off-street parking.
In-Room: Wet bars, some have color cable TV.
On-Premises: Public telephones.
Exercise/Health: Hydrotherapy spa.
Swimming: In heated pool, nearby river 1 mi, ocean 15 mi.
Sunbathing: At poolside, on private sun decks.
Nudity: Permitted on private sun decks.
Smoking: Permitted without restrictions.
Pets: Not permitted.
Handicap Access: No.
Children: Discouraged.
Languages: English.

Rio Villa Beach Resort

Gay-Friendly 50/50 ♀♂

Rio Villa is a cluster of resort cabins, units and suites surrounded by spacious decks, abundant gardens and lush lawns, sheltered by the redwoods. Decor reflects the warmth of old-world charm. Newly-remodeled rooms have kitchens, private baths, sofas, king and queen beds, color TV, outdoor BBQs and private sun decks. A stroll through the old-fashioned herb and flower gardens along the river leaves one refreshed and grateful. Weekends, a buffet breakfast of homemade coffee cakes, muffins, fresh fruit, juices and coffee is served on the redwood patio.

Address: 20292 Hwy 116, Monte Rio, CA 95462. Tel: (707) 865-1143 or Fax: 865-0115.

Type: Beach resort.
Clientele: 50% gay & lesbian & 50% straight clientele.
Transportation: Car is best.
To Gay Bars: 10 minutes to men's/women's bars.
Rooms: 10 rooms, 2 suites & 2 cottage with double, queen & king beds.
Bathrooms: Private: 12 shower/toilets, 1 full bath & 1 sink. 1 shared shower.
Meals: Continental breakfast on weekends.
Complimentary: Tea & coffee in all kitchen units.
Dates Open: All year.
High Season: May-September.
Rates: High season $65-$150. Low season $57.50-$150.
Discounts: Multiple-day packages available. Off-season bargains.
Credit Cards: MC, VISA, Amex & Discover.
Rsv'tns: Preferred.
Reserve Through: Call direct.
Minimum Stay: High season weekends & holidays.
Parking: Ample, free, off-street parking.
In-Room: Color cable TV, kitchen, refrigerator & maid service.
Exercise/Health: Nearby Jacuzzi & massage.
Swimming: River on the premises, ocean beach nearby.
Sunbathing: On beach, private & common sun decks & patio.
Smoking: Permitted.
Pets: Not permitted.
Children: Permitted but not encouraged.
Languages: English.

Schoolhouse Canyon Park

Gay-Friendly 50/50 ♀♂

Camp at *Schoolhouse Canyon Park* under the beautiful redwoods on a 200 acre natural preserve and an existing homestead dating from the early 1850's. Swim, hike, sunbathe on the river beach, fish or just relax and enjoy the outdoor setting. It is located four miles east of Guerneville on River Road or take Interstate 101 north of Santa Rosa to River Road exit and go 12-1/2 miles west to the park. **Address: 12600 River Rd, Guerneville, CA 95446. Tel: (707) 869-2311.**

Type: Campsites, RV and trailer parking.
Clientele: 50% gay & lesbian (good mix of gays & lesbians) & 50% straight clientele.
To Gay Bars: 4-miles drive to gay/lesbian bars in Russian River.
Campsites: 50 sites & restrooms with showers & flush toilets.

Dates Open: 1st weekend in May through end of September.
High Season: May through September.
Rates: $20 per couple, add'l $5/person, plus tax.
Credit Cards: None.
Rsv'tns: Recommended.
Reserve Through: Call direct.
Minimum Stay: 3 nights

on holidays.
On-Premises: Fireplace on each campsite.
Exercise/Health: Hiking nearby.
Swimming: In the river.
Sunbathing: On river beach.
Nudity: Permitted in secluded areas.
Smoking: Permitted without restrictions.

Pets: Permitted on leash and properly cared for.
Handicap Access: No.
Children: Permitted in family section.
Languages: English, Spanish.
Your Host: John & Vernie.

Villa Messina

Gay-Friendly 50/50 ♀♂

A Landmark Bed and Breakfast Inn

Villa Messina, an imposing villa with panoramic views, is located high on a knoll surrounded by lush gardens and its own redwood forest. Elegant high ceilinged rooms are graced with heirloom antiques, artworks and objets d'art. Guest accommodations include goose-down comforters, bathrobes, TV with VCR, fresh flowers, spa tubs, fireplaces and private baths. Take in panoramic 360 degree views from vineyards to the geysers. Enjoy unsurpassed comfort and hospitality just 20 minutes from downtown Guerneville, yet a world away. **Address: 316 Burgundy Rd, Healdsburg, CA 95448. Tel: (707) 433-6655, Fax: (707) 433-4515.**

Type: Bed & breakfast.
Clientele: 50% gay & lesbian & 50% straight clientele.
Transportation: Car is best.
To Gay Bars: 20 minutes.
Rooms: 4 rooms & 1 suite with queen & king beds.
Bathrooms: 4 private bath/toilets & 1 private

bath/toilet/shower.
Meals: Full breakfast.
Vegetarian: Available upon request.
Complimentary: Tea, coffee & set-up service.
Dates Open: All year.
Rates: $130-$250 for 1 or 2 persons. Extra person $20.
Credit Cards: MC, VISA, Amex, Diners, Discover &

Carte Blanche.
Rsv'tns: Required.
Reserve Through: Call direct.
Parking: Adequate free parking.
In-Room: Color cable TV, VCR, AC & telephone.
On-Premises: Small conference rooms, living room & dining room.
Swimming: Nearby

ocean, river & lake.
Sunbathing: On common sun decks & patio.
Smoking: Permitted outside with safety precautions.
Pets: Not permitted.
Handicap Access: No.
Children: Not especially welcome.
Languages: English.

Village Inn

Gay-Friendly 50/50 ♀♂

In the towering redwoods 4 miles west of Guerneville, *The Village Inn* is secluded enough for a solitary retreat, yet central enough for all manner of outdoor sports. Nearby, are wineries, hot springs and the coast, only 9 miles away. Accommodations vary from rooms to apartments, some with private baths. The lobby, with seating for cozy conversations, and the deck are popular gathering spots, where you can enjoy cocktails served in the downstairs bar. Our restaurant's continental menu takes advantage of fresh and seasonal items.

Address: PO Box 850, Monte Rio, CA 95462. Tel: (707) 865-2304

Type: Hotel inn with restaurant & bar.
Clientele: 50% gay & lesbian & 50% straight clientele.
Transportation: Car is best.
To Gay Bars: 4 miles to men's/women's bars.
Rooms: 10 rooms & 8 suites with single, double or queen beds.
Bathrooms: Private: 3 bath/toilet, 9 shower/toilet, 4 sinks. 6 shared baths.
Meals: Continental breakfast.
Vegetarian: Available.
Complimentary: Coffee & muffins in the morning.
Dates Open: All year.
High Season: July-Sept.
Rates: Summer $30-$125 & winter $25-$110.
Discounts: 3 nights & 7 nights rates.
Credit Cards: MC, VISA, Amex & Discover.
Rsv'tns: Recommended for weekends.
Reserve Through: Call direct.
Minimum Stay: 2 nights on weekends in the summer.
Parking: Adequate free off- & on-street parking.
In-Room: Maid service, refrigerator, kitchenettes & coffee/tea-makers. Some have color or color cable TV.
On-Premises: Pay phone, common room with piano, dining terrace.
Swimming: In the nearby Russian River.
Sunbathing: On private decks & in beach area.
Smoking: Permitted in rooms only.
Pets: Not permitted.
Handicap Access: Yes, call & inquire.
Children: Permitted in some rooms.
Languages: English.

Willows, The

Gay/Lesbian ♀♂

Where Tourists are Treated Just Like Home Folk!

The Willows guesthouse offers a country home vacation on five spectacular acres overlooking the Russian River. In the main lodge, there are thirteen private, cozy bedrooms, some with fireplaces and color TVs, all with direct-dial telephones. Nine bedrooms have private baths. In the spacious living room, you will enjoy a large stone fireplace, extensive library and grand piano. A sun deck with hot tub and sauna extends the length of the lodge. On the

THE **Willows**

A GUESTHOUSE ON THE RUSSIAN RIVER
15905 RIVER ROAD • P.O. BOX 465
GUERNEVILLE, CA 95446 • (707) 869-2824

rambling, well-tended property, ideal for tent camping, you'll find quiet, wooded seclusion and sunny, landscaped lawns, which slope down to the private dock on

the river. Use of the canoes is provided at no additional charge. Guests at *The Willows* are served a complimentary breakfast of fresh fruit, pastries, juice and coffee, and are welcome to make use of the community kitchen and outdoor barbecues. Many excellent restaurants are a short walk away. At *The Willows*, you'll find a relaxed, and intimate and friendly atmosphere, where you can get away from it all, yet be in the heart of the maddening fun on the Russian River.

Address: PO Box 465, 15905 River Rd, Guerneville, CA 95446. Tel: (707) 869-2824, (800) 953-2828.

Type: Riverfront guesthouse inn with tent camping.
Clientele: Good mix of gay men & women.
Transportation: Car is best.
To Gay Bars: 2 blocks (1/4 mi). 10-minute walk or 1-minute drive.
Rooms: 13 rooms with queen beds.
Bathrooms: 9 private, 4 shared.
Campsites: Can accommodate 120 tent campers. RV access, no hook-ups. Full toilet & shower facilities, 4 showers for men, 2 showers for women, 2 toilets for each.
Meals: Expanded continental breakfast.
Vegetarian: At nearby restaurants.
Complimentary: Tea & coffee served all day.
Dates Open: All year.
High Season: May thru September.
Rates: Rooms $59-$119, special weekday rates.
Credit Cards: MC, VISA, Amex & Discover.
Rsv'tns: Required.
Reserve Through: Travel agent or call direct.
Minimum Stay: 2 nights on weekends (rooms only during peak season).
Parking: Ample free on- & off-street parking.
In-Room: Color cable TV, some VCR's, video tape library, telephone, ceiling fans, maid service.
On-Premises: Large community kitchen. Private dock with canoes & paddleboat on river.
Exercise/Health: Hot tub, sauna & massage. Gym in town.
Swimming: In the river.
Sunbathing: On the beach or common sun deck, 5 acres of park-like grounds.
Nudity: Permitted in designated areas.
Smoking: Permitted outside the lodge. All rooms non-smoking.
Pets: Not permitted.
Handicap Access: No.
Children: Not permitted.
Languages: English.

SACRAMENTO

Hartley House Inn

Gay-Friendly 50/50 ♀♂

Opening Doors to a New Standard of Excellence

Come stay at our stunning turn-of-the-century mansion, surrounded by the majestic elm trees and stately homes of historic Boulevard Park in midtown Sacramento. We have exquisitely appointed rooms and are located near the State Capitol, Old Sacramento, the Sacramento Community Convention Center, and fine restaurants and coffee cafes. We even have a cookie jar filled with freshly-baked cookies! At *Hartley House Inn*, we are committed to providing our guests with elegance, warmth and attention to detail. These are the qualities that bring our guests back time and time again.

Address: 700 Twenty-Second St, Sacramento, CA 95816-4012. Tel: (916) 447-7829, Fax: 447-1820.

Type: Bed & breakfast.
Clientele: 50% gay & lesbian & 50% straight clientele.
Transportation: Car is best, airporter to door approx $15.
To Gay Bars: 5 blocks to gay/lesbian bars.
Rooms: 5 rooms with double or queen beds.
Bathrooms: All private.
Meals: Full breakfast.
Vegetarian: Always available.
Complimentary: Cookies, beverages, turndown service with mints on pillow.
Dates Open: All year.
High Season: Spring through fall.
Rates: $79-$135.
Discounts: Corporate & government discounts available.
Credit Cards: MC, VISA, Amex, Discover, Carte Blanche, Diners & ATM cards.
Rsv'tns: Recommended.
Reserve Through: Travel agent or call direct.
Minimum Stay: On holiday weekends only.
Parking: Ample, free on- & off-street parking.
In-Room: Maid, room & laundry service, color cable TV, AC, ceiling fans & telephone (no charge for local calls).
On-Premises: Meeting room, dining room, library & fax facilities.
Exercise/Health: Massage on premises with appointment. Discount at nearby local health club.
Swimming: In lake, river or nearby pool.
Sunbathing: On beach or patio.
Smoking: Permitted outdoors.
Pets: Not permitted.
Handicap Access: No.
Children: Permitted if older and by prior arrangement.
Languages: English & Spanish.
Your Host: Randy.

Rancho Cicada

Gay/Lesbian ♂

Experience the Old Swimming Hole & Get Back to Nature

Rancho Cicada Retreat is located on a beautiful, isolated and private stretch of the Cosumnes River, in the Gold Country of the Sierra foothills, about 50 miles east of Sacramento. Peacocks stroll through rock gardens and lawns in our natural riverside setting. It's a perfect place for clothing-optional activities, such as swimming, sunbathing, hot tubbing, croquet, volleyball or floating on an air mattress. There is also good fishing, and nature hikes are led by a naturalist. The retreat is not listed in any telephone directory, and is only discreetly advertised. **Guest comment:** *"Rancho Cicada is a terrific alternative to the B&B circuit." —Ernie, SF CA*

Address: PO Box 225, Plymouth, CA 95669. Tel: (209) 245-4841

Type: Camping retreat with campground & cabins.
Clientele: Mostly men with women welcome.
Transportation: Car is best.
To Gay Bars: One hour by car.
Rooms: 2 cabins with single, double or queen beds.
Bathrooms: 2 private in cabins, shared at campsites.
Campsites: 22 tents on platforms. Tents equipped with queen, double or single mat-

tress. Hot showers, wash basins & flush toilets in separate men/women facilities.
Meals: Catering provided for private groups.
Vegetarian: When private group rents entire facility, caterer will prepare vegetarian dishes.
Complimentary: Coffee available in cabins.
Dates Open: Cabins, all year. Tents, May 1-Oct 1.
High Season: June, July & August.
Rates: Tents $70-$90 per person for entire weekend. Cabins $200 for

entire weekend, $350 per week.
Rsv'tns: Required.
Reserve Through: Call direct.
Minimum Stay: On weekends.
Parking: Ample free parking.
In-Room: Color TV, VCR, ceiling fans, refrigerator & coffee/tea-making facilities in cabins only.
On-Premises: Fully-furnished kitchen with refrigerator & large adjustable BBQ. 900 sq. ft. deck for meetings & dancing.

Exercise/Health: 2 Jacuzzis
Swimming: River with several swimming holes within walking distance.
Sunbathing: On private cabin sun decks, on common sun decks & large lawn.
Nudity: This is a clothing-optional retreat.
Smoking: Permitted in designated areas. Non-smoking rooms available.
Pets: Not permitted.
Handicap Access: No.
Children: Not permitted.
Languages: English.
Your Host: David & Mark.

ST HELENA

Ink House Bed & Breakfast, The

Gay-Friendly ♀♂

"Manly, Yes, But I Liked it, Too"

In the old days, when residents of nearby San Francisco needed an escape, they boarded a ferry across a bridgeless bay and made a day-long journey on horseback or buggy over rural hills and through pristine countryside to find peace and rejuvenating rest in nearby Napa Valley. Only an hour's drive and some sixty miles away, Napa Valley is worlds apart. Here, amidst lush, rolling hills,

rows of manicured vineyards, hillsides, rock palisades, beautiful lakes and meandering streams, you'll find the *Ink House Bed & Breakfast.*

Built in 1884 by Theron H. Ink, this landmark home is the image of country living. Whether in the spacious formal parlors or high in the rooftop observatory, with its magnificent 360-degree panoramic vista, your hosts provide inviting comfort and warm hospitality that is unsurpassed. Decorated throughout with fine antiques, *Ink House* has four guest rooms with vineyard views, queen-sized beds and private baths, differing only in size. Complimentary sherry, brandy, sweets and Calistoga mineral waters are included. Our elaborate full or expanded continental breakfast caused one guest to write, "If this is a continental breakfast, then Fred and Ginger are dancing on the table! "After breakfast, you might want to borrow one of the inn's bicycles to tour the valley, or let your host arrange for chauffered tours in festive and beautifully-restored 1947 Packard convertible limousines. Ernie, past director of the San Francisco Gay Men's Chorus and the Honolulu Symphony and Opera choruses, provides visiting guests with the kind of care and respect for privacy that he expects for himself. Peruse the guestbook, and read what others have had to say. The *Ink House* is "...one of those finds." To everyone, the *Ink House* says, "Welcome! E komo mai. The house is yours." **Address: 1575 St. Helena Hwy at Whitehall Ln, St. Helena, CA 94574. Tel: (707) 963-3890 or (800) 553-4343.**

Type: Bed & breakfast.
Clientele: Mostly straight with a gay & lesbian following.
Transportation: Car is best. Round trip pick up from bus-airport to destination direct: from Yountville, $10 each, from Napa, $15 each.
To Gay Bars: 45 minutes to Russian River, Vallejo, 1 hr 20 min to San Francisco.
Rooms: 4 rooms with queen beds.
Bathrooms: 4 private.
Meals: Full breakfast & expanded continental breakfast interchanged daily.
Complimentary: Sherry, brandy, Calistoga mineral water, juices & sweets.
Dates Open: All year.
High Season: April-October.
Rates: $95-$165.
Credit Cards: MC & Visa.
Rsv'tns: Recommended.

Reserve Through: Travel agent or call direct.
Minimum Stay: Weekends, 2 nights. April through October & Dec 15-Jan 15.
Parking: Ample, free off-street parking.
In-Room: Color TV with VCR, video tape library, AC, telephone & maid service.
On-Premises: Professional size pool table & large barn conference/

meeting facility.
Exercise/Health: Bicycles.
Swimming: At nearby lake.
Sunbathing: In the yard.
Smoking: Permitted outdoors only.
Pets: Not permitted.
Handicap Access: No.
Children: Not expecially welcomed.
Languages: English & Spanish.
Your Host: Ernie & Jim.

SAN DIEGO

Balboa Park Inn

More Than You'll Pay For...

Gay/Lesbian ♀♂

Balboa Park Inn is a collection of 26 distinctive, immaculate and beautifully appointed suites, located in the heart of San Diego's gay community. We're just footsteps (1-1/2 blocks) from Balboa Park and the world famous San Diego Zoo. Nearby are the numerous cafes, shops, restaurants and nightclubs of Hillcrest, the city's gayest area of town. A short drive will find you at the Pacific's doorstep, including Black's Beach, a favorite spot for nude sunbathing. Rent a car to see the sights, or use our comprehensive public transportation system. We're just minutes from the airport, train station and bus terminal downtown, and only 20 miles from Tijuana, Mexico, the world's most visited city.

The *Balboa Park Inn* is your affordable, "family"-oriented destination in San Diego. Stay with us. We promise that you'll always get more than you paid for!
Address: 3402 Park Blvd, San Diego, CA 92103. Tel: (619) 298-0823, (800) 938-8181, Fax: (619) 294-8070.

Type: Bed & breakfast inn.
Clientele: Good mix of gay men & women, with some straight clientele.
Transportation: Car is best or taxi from airport.
To Gay Bars: 6 blocks to men's, 3 blocks to women's bar. A 15-minute walk or 5-minute drive.
Rooms: 19 suites & 7 rooms with single, queen or king beds.
Bathrooms: All private.

Meals: Expanded continental breakfast.
Complimentary: Coffee, tea or hot chocolate in suite.
Dates Open: All year.
High Season: Summer.
Rates: $80-$190 plus tax.
Discounts: For established business accounts.
Credit Cards: MC, VISA, AMEX, Diner's, Carte Blanche, Discover.
Rsv'tns: Required 3-4 wks. ahead in summer.
Reserve Through: Travel

agent or call direct.
Minimum Stay: 3 days on holiday weekends.
Parking: Ample, free, on-street parking.
In-Room: Color cable TV, VCR, telephone, AC, kitchen, refrigerator, coffee/tea-making facilities, ceiling fans, room, laundry & maid service.
On-Premises: Maids do laundry.
Swimming: Pool nearby, 10-15-min drive to ocean beach, 30-min drive to

Black's Beach.
Sunbathing: On private and common sun decks.
Smoking: Permitted without restrictions.
Pets: Not permitted.
Handicap Access: Yes, one room.
Children: Permitted.
Languages: English, Spanish.

IGTA

Beach Place, The

Gay/Lesbian ♂

Minutes from downtown, Hillcrest and most tourist attractions, the ocean beach section of San Diego retains the charm of a small town. No high-rise hotels block the view or prevent access to the beach. At *The Beach Place,* you enjoy the privacy of your own apartment with deck, small garden, full kitchen with microwave, bedroom with queen bed and living room with color TV and adult films. The central courtyard has a gazebo with a huge hot tub, as well as a patio for sunbathing.

Address: 2158 Sunset Cliffs Blvd, San Diego, CA 92107. Tel: (619) 225-0746

Type: Guesthouse.
Clientele: Mostly men with women welcome.
Transportation: Car is best.
To Gay Bars: 10-minute drive to numerous bars in Hillcrest, Pacific Beach & Point Loma.
Rooms: 4 suites with queen beds.
Bathrooms: All private.
Complimentary: Tea, coffee, sugar, salt, pepper & utensils.
Dates Open: All year.
Rates: $75 per night or $375 per week for 2 people. $15 per night per additional guest.
Discounts: Weeknight rates for single, subject to availability.
Rsv'tns: Required.
Reserve Through: Travel agent or call direct.
Minimum Stay: 2 days.
Parking: Adequate off-street covered parking.
In-Room: Kitchen with microwave & refrigerator, color cable TV, ceiling fans & maid service.
On-Premises: Gas barbeque available in the courtyard.
Exercise/Health: Jacuzzi.
Swimming: 4 blocks to ocean beach.
Sunbathing: On the patio & private sun decks.
Nudity: Permitted on sun decks.
Pets: Sometimes with prior arrangement.
Children: Permitted at times with prior arrangement.
Languages: English

IGTA

Dmitri's Guesthouse

Gay/Lesbian ♂

Overlooking downtown in one of San Diego's historic turn-of-the-century neighborhoods, *Dmitri's* is minutes from the convention center, Gaslamp entertainment area, Horton Plaza shopping, Balboa Park, our famous zoo, the Old Globe Theatre, the Aerospace Museum, Old Town, the bays and beaches, and just blocks from the stops for bright red trolleys that go to Tijuana, Mexico. A variety of accommodations with private baths include continental breakfast served at poolside.

Address: 931 21st St, San Diego, CA 92102. Tel: (619) 238-5547

Type: Guest house.
Clientele: Mostly men with women welcome.
Transportation: Pick up from airport, bus or train, $6.
To Gay Bars: 6 blocks to gay/lesbian bars.
Rooms: 5 doubles with queen beds, or 1-2 double beds.
Bathrooms: 3 private, 2 shared.
Meals: Continental breakfast.
Complimentary: Tea & coffee.
Dates Open: All year.
High Season: July-September.
Rates: 2 people $45-$75, $15 per extra person.
Discounts: Weekly rates available.
Credit Cards: MC, VISA.
Rsv'tns: Required.
Reserve Through: Travel agent or call direct.
Minimum Stay: 2 nights on weekends.
Parking: Adequate free on-street parking.
In-Room: Maid service, color TV, kitchen.
On-Premises: Telephone, TV lounge.
Exercise/Health: Hot tub.
Swimming: Pool.
Sunbathing: At poolside or on common sundecks.
Nudity: Permitted.
Smoking: Permitted outdoors.
Pets: Not permitted.
Handicap Access: No.
Children: Not permitted.
Languages: English, limited Spanish.

Hillcrest Inn, The

Gay/Lesbian ♀♂

Good Value In the Heart of Gay Hillcrest

The Hillcrest Inn is one of San Diego's newer hotels, a 45-room establishment in the midst of the city's favorite restaurant, bar and shopping neighborhood. Each room is tastefully decorated and has private bath and telephone. The building has security gates and a beautiful new Jacuzzi and sunning patio. The downtown business district and the harbor are directly to the south. Balboa Park, with its zoo, museums, galleries and restaurants, is immediately to the east. Mission Bay, Sea World and Pacific beaches are a short drive to the north.

Address: 3754 5th Ave. San Diego, CA 92103. Tel: (619) 293-7078, (800) 258-2280.

Type: Hotel.
Clientele: Mostly gay & lesbian, with some straight clientele.
Transportation: Auto, city bus or taxi.
To Gay Bars: 6 bars within a 2 block radius.
Rooms: 45 rooms with twin, double, queen & king beds.
Bathrooms: All private bath/shower/toilets.

Dates Open: All year.
Rates: $49-$55.
Discounts: Week long reservations, pay for 5 nights, get 2 free.
Credit Cards: MC, VISA, Amex, Diners & Bancard.
Rsv'tns: Recommended.
Reserve Through: Travel agent or call direct.
Parking: Limited, free off-street parking & adjacent pay lot.

In-Room: Color TV, telephone, ceiling fans, maid service, kitchen & refrigerator.
On-Premises: Laundry facilities, snack machines, tour desk.
Exercise/Health: Jacuzzi.
Swimming: Ocean beach 15 min by car.
Sunbathing: On private sunning patio.
Smoking: Permitted

without restrictions.
Pets: Not permitted.
Handicap Access: Yes, ramps & special bathroom facilities.
Children: Not permitted.
Languages: English, some Spanish, French & German.
Your Host: Roger.

IGTA

Keating House

Gay-Friendly 50/50 ♀♂

This Is No Addam's Family Victorian!

Keating House is a bright, sunny bed and breakfast overflowing with light, color and flowering plants. Over 100 years old, it has retained the charm and glamour of the turn-of-the-century. But this is no museum! We're a take-your-shoes-off relax-and-stay-awhile kind of place. Touring "America's finest city" can be exhausting, but not when you start and end your day with us. Have the time of your life, then, we'll return you to your world refreshed, relaxed and rejuvenated.

Address: 2331 Second Ave, San Diego, CA 92101. Tel: (619) 239-8585, (800) 995-8644.

Type: Bed & breakfast inn.
Clientele: 50% gay & lesbian & 50% straight clientele.
Transportation: Bus, taxi, or car.
To Gay Bars: Short drive or cab ride to men's & women's clubs.
Rooms: 8 rooms with double or queen beds.
Bathrooms: 2 private

bath/toilets & 3 shared bath/showers.
Meals: Full, sumptuous breakfast served every morning.
Complimentary: Beverages.
Dates Open: All year.
Rates: Rooms $50-$85 per night. Third person $25.
Discounts: 10% for 5 days or more.

Credit Cards: MC, VISA, Amex & Discover.
Rsv'tns: Required.
Reserve Through: Travel agent or call direct.
Minimum Stay: 2 nights on holidays & Valentine's weekend.
Parking: Unlimited, free on-street parking.
On-Premises: Large front porch. 2 lush sun & shade gardens.

Swimming: 10 minutes to ocean beaches. 15 minutes to Coronado Island.
Sunbathing: In the sun garden.
Smoking: Permitted outside only.
Pets: Not permitted.
Handicap Access: No.
Children: Permitted.
Languages: English, French, limited Spanish.

SAN FRANCISCO

Alamo Square Bed & Breakfast Inn

Fine Service...Gracious Surroundings

Gay-Friendly ♀♂

A complex of two Victorian mansions, an 1895 Queen Anne and an 1896 Tudor Revival, is today the *Alamo Square Inn*, a unique and gracious bed and breakfast in San Francisco's largest historical district. A variety of accommodations are available, from cozy guest rooms to the luxurious Oriental-influenced suites overlooking the sweeping San Francisco skyline. Take breakfast in the filtered sunlight of our morning room, in the solarium or in the atrium.

Address: 719 Scott St, San Francisco, CA 94117. Tel: (415) 922-2055, (800) 345-9888, Fax: (415) 931-1304.

Type: Inn.
Clientele: Mostly straight clientele with a gay & lesbian following.
Transportation: Airport shuttle $11 per person or taxi $25.
To Gay Bars: 10-minute walk to Castro St. gay & lesbian bars.
Rooms: 9 rooms, 3 suites & 1 apartment with single, queen or king beds.
Bathrooms: 13 private bath/toilets.
Meals: Full breakfast.
Vegetarian: Upon request.
Complimentary: Cocktail set-ups, coffee, tea, sherry & wine.
Dates Open: All year.
High Season: July-September.
Rates: $85-$275.
Discounts: 10% off for 7 or more days.
Credit Cards: MC, VISA, Amex, Diners Club.
Rsv'tns: Required.
Reserve Through: Travel agent or call direct.
Minimum Stay: 2 nights on weekend bookings.
Parking: Free off-street parking for up to 14 cars.
In-Room: Maid, room & laundry service & telephone. Some have refrigerators & TV.
On-Premises: Laundry facilities & meeting rooms.
Exercise/Health: Private Jacuzzi in one suite. Massage by appointment. Tennis courts in the park across the street.
Sunbathing: On common sun decks.
Smoking: Permitted outside.
Pets: Not permitted.
Handicap Access: No.
Children: Permitted.
Languages: English, French, German, Italian.

Anna's Three Bears

Your Escape in San Francisco

Gay-Friendly 50/50 ♀♂

World travelers of the Edwardian Golden Age maintained a "pied-a-terre" in their favorite city. In today's hustle and bustle, *Anna's Three Bears* could be yours. A magnificently restored 100-year-old Edwardian, the *Bears* is an adventure in days gone by when elegance, graciousness and thoughtfulness were a way of life.

More than just a place to stay, the proprietors of *Anna's Three Bears* have created the ultimate retreat. Entirely furnished with antiques gathered from around the world, each suite has a stunning view of downtown San Francisco and the Bay, spacious living and dining rooms, fully-stocked kitchens, fireplaces, lavish linens, and handmade quilts. Each and

Photograph by John Sutton ©1993

continued next page

every bed is a marvelous example of old-world craftsmanship.

Located on a quiet residential street in historic Buena Vista Gardens, we are just a few steps from world renowned restaurants and bars, as well as the excitement of the Castro. The house invokes an atmosphere that is perfect for that magical romantic getaway for two or a magical adventure with friends. Imagine hosting a candlelit dinner surrounded by historical elegance, then retiring to an evening together in front of a roaring fire as you marvel at the spectacular night view which lies before you.

Anna's Three Bears is one of the most charming and unusual inns you'll ever find. Come and experience San Francisco in grand style and indulge yourself in a way you could never imagine.

Address: 114 Divisadero St, San Francisco, CA 94117. Tel: (800) 428-8559, (415) 255-3167, Fax: (415) 552-2959.

Type: Bed & breakfast.
Clientele: 50% gay & lesbian & 50% straight clientele.
Transportation: Car. Public transport is 1 & 2 blocks away.
To Gay Bars: 4 blocks or an 8-minute walk to The Castro.
Rooms: 3 suites with single, double, queen or king beds.
Bathrooms: All private.
Meals: Continental

breakfast.
Vegetarian: Several very good vegetarian restaurants nearby.
Complimentary: Kitchen stocked with tea, coffee, fruit, muffins, bread, milk, juices, etc.
Dates Open: All year.
High Season: August, September & December.
Rates: $200-$250 double daily, $25 per additional person. $1000-$1400 double weekly, $100 per

additional person.
Credit Cards: MC, VISA, Amex.
Rsv'tns: Recommended.
Reserve Through: Travel agent or call direct.
Minimum Stay: 2 nights on weekends.
Parking: Adequate on-street parking. Short term permit available.
In-Room: Color cable TV, telephone, refrigerator, stocked kitchen, coffee & tea-making facilities &

maid service.
On-Premises: Private living & dining rooms.
Smoking: Smoking permitted on back decks only.
Pets: Not permitted.
Handicap Access: Yes, ground floor apartment. Not handicap-equipped.
Children: Not especially welcome.
Languages: English.
Your Host: Michael.

Beck's Motor Lodge

Gay-Friendly 50/50 ♀♂

If you've searched for a hotel with moderately-priced, comfortable accommodations in a picturesque neighborhood setting, discover *Beck's Motor Lodge* on world-famous Market St. In the midst of the Castro area and convenient to everything, it is surrounded by tree-lined streets, quaint shops and Victorian homes. It's easy to relax with special touches like in-room fresh coffee service, refrigerators, parking, color TV/Showtime and our private sun deck with lovely views of the city. Our staff is friendly and accommodating.

Address: 2222 Market St, San Francisco, CA 94114. Tel: (415) 621-8212, (800) 227-4360, Fax: (415) 241-0435.

Type: Motel.
Clientele: 50% gay & lesbian & 50% straight clientele.
Transportation: Airport shuttles.
To Gay Bars: 1 block.
Rooms: 57 rooms with queen or king beds.
Bathrooms: All private.
Vegetarian: Amazing Grace is 1 block away.
Complimentary: Coffee in room.

Dates Open: All year.
High Season: May through October.
Rates: Summer $71-95, winter $62-$85.
Discounts: Senior citizen & AAA 10%.
Credit Cards: VISA, MC, Amex, Diners & Discover.
Rsv'tns: Required.
Reserve Through: Travel agent or call direct.
Parking: Adequate free off-street parking.

In-Room: Color cable TV (Showtime), telephone, refrigerator, maid service & coffee & tea-making facilities. 10 rooms have AC.
On-Premises: Laundry facilities for guests.
Exercise/Health: Gym & weights nearby.
Swimming: 3-1/2 miles to ocean beach.
Sunbathing: On common sun decks.

Smoking: Permitted in all rooms.
Pets: Not permitted.
Handicap Access: No ramps, but doors are wide.
Children: Welcomed.
Languages: English, Spanish, French & Tagalog.
Your Host: Irene.

Black Stallion Inn

Men ♂

Located in the heart of the Castro, the *Black Stallion Inn* provides a quiet and relaxing atmosphere for those visiting San Francisco. This renovated Victorian flat is on the itinerary of many tours of the area. Guests can make themselves at home in front of the wood-burning stove in the common room or on the spacious sun deck. There is a modern, shared kitchen for lunches and evening meals. The inn is located a block-and-a-half from gay bars and has its own private party nightly, except Monday, which guests may attend for a small donation.

Address: 635 Castro St, San Francisco, CA 94114. Tel: (415) 863-0131

Type: Bed & breakfast.
Clientele: Men only.
Transportation: Door-to-door airport shuttle to B&B, approximately $8-$12 each. Taxi not over $35 including tip.
To Gay Bars: 1-1/2 blocks to countless gay bars.
Rooms: 8 rooms.
Bathrooms: Shared: 3 baths & 2 half baths.
Meals: Expanded continental breakfast.
Vegetarian: Available upon request.
Complimentary: Coffee,

tea, & juice available all day.
Dates Open: All year.
High Season: June-Oct..
Rates: Single $80-$95, double $95-$110.
Discounts: Off-season & weekday specials. *Inn Places* discount & gift bonus.
Credit Cards: MC, VISA, Amex & Discover.
Rsv'tns: Highly recommended.
Reserve Through: Travel agent or call direct.
Minimum Stay: On weekends, holidays &

special events.
Parking: On-street pay & free. 1 garage space or 1 secured space $10 night.
In-Room: Maid service. Guests share telephone & answering service.
On-Premises: Kitchen with fireplace, large sun deck, laundry facilities, private social club. TV in social club available during non-operating hours.
Exercise/Health: Limited weights & workout bench on sun deck. Within 3 blocks of 3 full service gay gyms.

Swimming: Nearby pool & ocean.
Sunbathing: On common sun decks & at the beach. 2-3 miles to gay beach, nudist beach.
Nudity: Permitted anywhere inside the inn & on the deck with discretion.
Smoking: Permitted if smokers are considerate.
Pets: Not permitted.
Handicap Access: No.
Children: Not especially welcome.
Languages: English.
Your Host: James.

Bock's Bed & Breakfast

In Operation Since 1980

Gay/Lesbian ♀♂

Bock's is a lovely 1906 Edwardian residence in the Parnassus Heights area of San Francisco with beautiful views of the city. Golden Gate Park is two blocks away and public transportation is nearby. Host, Laura Bock, has restored the original virgin redwood walls of the dining and entry rooms as well as the mahogany inlaid oak floors of the latter. The latest renovation project was completed with the addition of a new bathroom & the restoration of two original pocket doors on the main floor. Laura's enthusiasm and touring tips about her native city are enjoyed by an international clientele.

Address: 1448 Willard St, San Francisco, CA 94117. Tel: (415) 664-6842, Fax: (415) 664-1109.

Type: Bed & breakfast.
Clientele: Mostly gay & lesbian with some straight clientele.
Transportation: From airport take one of the van shuttles outside the 2nd level.
To Gay Bars: 1 mile to gay/lesbian bars.
Rooms: 3 rooms with single, double or queen beds.
Bathrooms: 1 private shower/toilet, 1 private sink, others share full

bath.
Meals: Expanded continental breakfast.
Vegetarian: I can accommodate special needs & there is vegetarian food nearby.
Complimentary: Coffee, tea, hot chocolate service in rooms. Small, shared guest refrigerator.
Dates Open: All year.
High Season: May through October.
Rates: $40-$75 plus tax, $10 each add'l person.

Discounts: 10% discount for stays of a week or more.
Credit Cards: None.
Rsv'tns: Recommended.
Reserve Through: Call direct.
Minimum Stay: 2 nights.
Parking: On-street parking. Inexpensive lot 2 blocks away.
In-Room: Color or B&W TV, telephone, electric hot pot, radios, coffee/tea-making facilities.
On-Premises: Laundry fa-

cilities, guest refrigerator.
Swimming: Pool nearby, ocean beach 3 miles away.
Sunbathing: On private or common sun decks.
Smoking: Non-smokers only.
Pets: Not permitted.
Handicap Access: No.
Children: Permitted.
Languages: English, smattering of French.
Your Host: Laura

IGTA

Carl Street Unicorn House

Gay/Lesbian ♀

Carl Street Unicorn House is a small Victorian house located near San Francisco's Golden Gate Park within walking distance of great restaurants and cafes, the aquarium, museums, and a variety of interesting shops. There is a collection of over 200 ethnic dolls, many pieces of artwork and antiques befitting a Victorian home. Your host resides on the top floor, while guests occupy the ground floor. A very special dog, called Shayna, is a resident.

Address: 156 Carl St, San Francisco, CA 94117. Tel: (415) 753-5194

Type: Bed & breakfast.
Clientele: Mostly women with men welcome, some straight clientele.
Transportation: Airport shuttle van to door.
To Gay Bars: 5-10 minutes' drive to gay/lesbian bars.
Rooms: 2 rooms with double beds.

Bathrooms: 1 shared bath/shower/toilet.
Meals: Expanded continental breakfast.
Vegetarian: Restaurant & deli nearby.
Complimentary: Tea & coffee.
Dates Open: All year.
High Season: Summer.
Rates: $40-$50, $5 extra

for 1 night stay.
Discounts: 10% on stays of 7 days or more.
Rsv'tns: Required.
Reserve Through: Call direct.
Minimum Stay: Required on weekends.
Parking: On-street parking.
On-Premises: TV lounge.

Swimming: 5 min drive to pool.
Sunbathing: On the patio.
Smoking: Not permitted.
Handicap Access: No.
Children: Permitted if over 10 years.
Languages: English.

Chateau Tivoli

Gay-Friendly 50/50 ♀♂

The Greatest Painted Lady In the World

Chateau Tivoli is an authentic period restoration of a Victorian mansion built in 1892. The book *Painted Ladies Revisited* calls it "...the greatest Painted Lady in the world." Fully licensed as a hotel Bed & Breakfast, and as a location for receptions and special events, the residence features nine guest bedrooms and five and one half bathrooms. The building exterior has become a San Francisco landmark, painted in twenty-two different colors and shades, and highlighted with brilliant gold leafing. The roof is multi-colored slate tile, mounted in a special diamond pattern and surrounded by  fabulous iron grill work. The interior is resplendent with hardwood floors, stately columns and numerous stained glass windows. There are four woodburning fireplaces. The walls and ceilings in bedrooms and hallways are covered in Bradbury & Bradbury wallpaper and accented by gold leaf and various faux treatments.

The mansion has been so faithfully restored that guests experience the sensation of a timetravel journey back to San Francisco's romantic golden age of opulence. Here, they are surrounded by genuine antiques and art from the estates of Cornelius Vanderbilt, Charles de Gaulle, J. Paul Getty, the Countess of Richelieu and the famous San Francisco madame, Sally Stanford. Spacious and grand, the rooms and suites feature elegant canopy beds and marble baths, balconies and views, fireplaces and stained glass, towers and turrets, each facet contributing to the atmosphere that makes *Chateau Tivoli* a truly unforgettable experience.

Address: 1057 Steiner St, San Francisco, CA 94115. Tel: (415) 776-5462, (800) 228-1647, Fax: (415) 776-0505.

Type: Bed & breakfast.
Clientele: 50% gay & lesbian & 50% straight clientele.
Transportation: Airport bus to downtown, then taxi.
To Gay Bars: Ten minutes to gay & lesbian bars.
Rooms: 5 doubles, 3 suites (one with 2 bedrooms) & 1 apartment.
Bathrooms: Five private, others share with only one other room.
Meals: Expanded continental breakfast Mon-Fri, full champagne breakfast Sat & Sun.
Complimentary: Wine, coffee, tea, herb tea, juice, etc.
Dates Open: All year.
High Season: March-October.
Rates: $80-$200.
Discounts: For 4 or more days.
Credit Cards: MC, VISA & Amex.
Rsv'tns: Required.
Reserve Through: Travel agent or call direct.
Minimum Stay: None.
Parking: Ample, on-street parking in residential neighborhood.
In-Room: Maid service, telephone.
On-Premises: Meeting rooms, private dining rooms, laundry facilities.
Sunbathing: On patio.
Smoking: Limited to porches, balconies and patio.
Pets: Not permitted.
Handicap Access: Yes, call ahead.
Children: Valuable antiques in all areas. Parents must take full responsibility.
Languages: English.
Your Host: Rodney, Willard & Melissa.

Essex Hotel, The

Gay-Friendly ♀♂

The Essex Hotel, totally renovated in recent years, is centrally located and within walking distance of all major points, including Cable Car line, Union Square, Chinatown, theaters and many fine restaurants. Polk Street is only a block away and gay men's bars are two blocks away. The Airporter shuttle to our front door is only $9. The hotel has a European atmosphere, pleasant, comfortable double rooms with high-quality furnishings, color TV, maid service, and direct dial phones. Most rooms have private baths.

Address: 684 Ellis St, San Francisco, CA 94109. Tel: (415) 474-4664 or (800) 453-7739. In CA (800) 443-7739.

Type: Hotel.
Clientele: Mostly straight clientele with a gay & lesbian following.
Transportation: Airporter shuttle $9.00.
To Gay Bars: 2 blocks to men's bars.
Rooms: 100 rooms with single or queen beds.

Bathrooms: 50 private bath/toilets, others share. 50 private sinks.
Complimentary: Coffee.
Dates Open: All year.
Rates: $39-$69 winter, $49-$79 summer.
Discounts: 10% to holders of Inn Places, subject to room availability.

Credit Cards: MC, VISA & Amex.
Rsv'tns: Suggested.
Reserve Through: Travel agent or call direct.
Parking: Adequate on-street pay parking.
In-Room: Color TV, direct dial phone, maid service.
On-Premises: Public tele-

phone, central AC/heat.
Smoking: Permitted without restrictions.
Pets: Not permitted.
Handicap Access: No.
Children: Permitted.
Languages: English, French, German.

IGTA

We Appreciate Your Comments!

The editors of **INN Places**® actively seek your comments about accommodations you have tried.

Positive comments of interest may be included in the next issue, giving future readers the benefit of your experience. And it's a nice way of saying "thank you" to an innkeeper who extended you exceptional hospitality.

See the contents for the Reader Comment Form.

Hotel Triton

Gay-Friendly ♀♂

A Hit Hotel on the Bay

Upon entering the lobby of the *Hotel Triton*, guests immediately know they have entered a unique and exciting place. Each handcrafted lamp and table is a fine work of art. The walls are murals and the columns are gold leaf. *The Triton* gives a new definition to the word "style." Guest rooms and suites are like no others in San Francisco. Adorned in hand-painted wall finishes, they have lavish comforters, fully-stocked honor bars and amenities too numerous to mention. In the tradition of all

that is exciting and new, *The Triton* has invited celebrity designers to "do their thing." The results: Take a walk on the wild side with Joe Boxer, or indulge your romantic fantasies with Suzan Briganti. These everchanging suites simply have to be experienced.

Located just blocks from the financial district, the hotel is ideal for business travelers, whether for extended stays, board meetings or receptions and think tanks. Our "Creative Zone," with its state-of-the-art services and equipment, is a richly-appointed meeting room, complete with outdoor terrace. *The Triton* provides fax, copy and secretarial services and a helpful professional staff to assist with any special requests. When it's time for a break from the frantic pace of business, spend an hour or so working out in the mezzanine level exercise room. *The Triton* is home to two exciting restaurants. *Aioli* is a romantic and mysterious setting showcasing contemporary artwork and serving Mediterranean cuisine for lunch and dinner seven days a week. *Cafe de la Presse* is the ultimate international meeting place. Visitors congregate here to browse newspapers from around the world and have a coffee or a quick bite.

Address: 342 Grant Avenue, San Francisco, CA 94108. Tel: (415) 394-0500, (800) 433-6611, Fax: (415) 394-0555.

Type: Hotel with restaurant and bar.
Clientele: Mostly straight clientele with a gay & lesbian following.
Transportation: Car is best. Airport shuttle $10.00. Limousine from airport: shared $9.00, private $50.00.
To Gay Bars: 1/2 block or a two-minute walk.
Rooms: 133 rooms, 7 suites with double, queen and king beds.
Bathrooms: All private.
Vegetarian: Vegetarian restaurants within walking distance.
Complimentary: Morning coffee service and evening wine service.
Dates Open: All year.
High Season: August-October.
Rates: Winter/spring: $99.00-$139.00. Summer/fall: $119.00-$169.00.
Discounts: "Out in Style" package: Sun-Thurs $109.00, Fri-Sat $129.00.
Credit Cards: MC, VISA, Amex, Diners, Bancard, Discover.
Rsv'tns: Required.
Reserve Through: Travel agent or call direct.
Parking: Ample pay parking (24hr valet parking with unlimited in/out services).
In-Room: Color cable TV, AC, telephone, refrigerator, room, maid & laundry service. Some rooms with VCR, coffee & tea-making facilities.
On-Premises: Meeting rooms & business center.
Exercise/Health: Gym, weights. Jacuzzi, sauna, steam, massage nearby.
Swimming: Nearby pool & ocean.
Smoking: Permitted in lobby & smoking rooms. Non-smoking rooms available.
Pets: Not permitted.
Handicap Access: Yes.
Children: Not especially welcomed.
Languages: English, French, German, Chinese (Mandarin & Cantonese), Russian.
Your Host: Jan, Peter, Jane & Kirsten.

Inn On Castro

Gay/Lesbian ♀♂

The innkeepers invite you into a colorful and comfortable environment filled with modern art and exotic plants. All rooms vary in size and have private baths. Our most expensive accommodation is the patio suite with sun deck. The *Inn On Castro's* location is unique, just 100 yards north of the intersection of Market and Castro, where you are in a quiet neighborhood, yet only a stone's throw away from the Castro Theater, plus dozens of bars, restaurants and shops. With the *Underground* almost virtually adjacent to the *Inn*, big-name store shopping and cable car, etc. are just a few minutes away. There is literally something for everyone.

Address: 321 Castro St, San Francisco, CA 94114. Tel: (415) 861-0321.

Type: Bed & breakfast.
Clientele: Good mix of gay men & women.
Transportation: Supershuttle from airport approx $11 per person.
To Gay Bars: Less than 1-minute walk to men's/women's bars.
Rooms: 6 rooms & 2 suites with double, queen or king beds.
Bathrooms: All private.
Meals: Full breakfast.
Vegetarian: Available with advance notice.
Complimentary: Afternoon wine, brandy night cap, tea, coffee, juices.
Dates Open: All year.
High Season: May-October.
Rates: Rooms $75-$145.
Credit Cards: MC, VISA, Amex.
Rsv'tns: Recommended 1 month in advance.
Reserve Through: Call direct.
Minimum Stay: 2 days on weekends, 3 on holidays, 4 days Folsom Fair, Castro Fair & Gay Lib days.
Parking: Adequate parking.
In-Room: Color TV on request, telephone, maid service, refrigerator.
On-Premises: Lounge & dining room.
Exercise/Health: Gym, weights, jacuzzi, sauna, steam & massage across the street.
Swimming: Nearby pool.
Sunbathing: On private sun decks.
Smoking: Permitted on patio, front porch, rear deck.
Pets: Not permitted.
Handicap Access: Patio suite is handicap-accessible.
Children: Permitted but not encouraged.
Languages: English, French, German & Dutch.

Inn San Francisco, The

Gay-Friendly ♀♂

Distinctly San Franciscan Warmth & Hospitality

Feel the years slip away, as you step through the massive, wooden doors of the *Inn San Francisco.* Each of the guest rooms is individually decorated with antique furnishings, fresh flowers, marble sinks, polished brass fixtures and exquisite finishing touches. All are extraordinarily beautiful and the feeling of classic, old-world elegance and grandeur is carried throughout. In the garden, under the shade of an old fig tree, an enchanting gazebo shelters the inviting hot tub.

Address: 943 S Van Ness Ave, San Francisco, CA 94110. Tel: (415) 641-0188, (800) 359-0913, Fax: (415) 641-1701.

Type: Bed & breakfast inn.
Clientele: Mostly straight clientele with a gay & lesbian following.
Transportation: Yellow Airport Shuttle $9 person.
To Gay Bars: 8 blocks to men's, 5 blocks to women's bars.
Rooms: 16 rooms, 5 suites & 1 apartment with single, double or queen beds.
Bathrooms: 17 private bath/shower/toilets, 5 share.
Meals: Buffet breakfast.

Vegetarian: Our breakfast includes a huge array of fresh fruits, granola, homemade breads or muffins & a cheese plate.
Complimentary: Coffee, tea, sherry complimentary in parlor, truffles in room.
Dates Open: All year.
Rates: Rooms $75-$195.
Discounts: Stays of 1 week or longer.
Credit Cards: VISA, MC, Amex, Diners, Carte Blanche, Discover.
Rsv'tns: Required.

Reserve Through: Travel agent or call direct.
Minimum Stay: Weekends, particularly on holidays, require a 2 night stay, but we are flexible. Call.
Parking: Several covered garages w/electric door openers, parking $10/ night.
In-Room: Maid & laundry service, color TV, telephone, refrigerator.
On-Premises: Laundry facilities.
Exercise/Health: Redwood hot tub in tropical

gazebo.
Sunbathing: On private & common sun decks, patios & on rooftop.
Smoking: Not permitted in parlor.
Pets: Not permitted.
Handicap Access: No.
Children: Permitted.
Languages: English, Spanish, Chinese, limited French.
Your Host: Marty & Jane.

King George Hotel

Gay-Friendly ♀♂

Charm, Warmth & Tradition in San Francisco

Just one block from the cable cars and San Francisco's famous shopping and dining district, Union Square, *The King George Hotel* is a charming English-style hotel, very gay-friendly and well-informed about gay venues and events. All the rooms in this hotel are first class. It's a great home base for visitors desiring both value and convenience. The hotel is just ten minutes from the Castro district, 15 minutes from Fisherman's Wharf and under an hour and a half from the Russian River, making it ideal for both business and leisure travel.

Address: 334 Mason St, San Francisco, CA 94102. Tel: (800) 288-6005, (415) 781-5050, Fax: 391-6976.

Type: Hotel.
Clientele: Mostly straight clientele with a gay & lesbian following.
Transportation: Pick up from airport $9 per person each way. Shuttle from SFO airport, Coliseum BART to Powell St Sta. from Oakland.
To Gay Bars: 5 blocks or 1/2 mile. 5-minute walk or 10 minutes by car, including parking.
Rooms: 140 rooms & 2 suites with single, twin, queen or king beds.
Bathrooms: All private

bath/toilets.
Vegetarian: Tea room menu includes meatless tea sandwiches & pastries.
Dates Open: All year.
High Season: April 1-November 14.
Rates: $102 single, $112 double. Call 800# for year-round special rates.
Discounts: Special packages, holiday specials & membership in IGTA.
Credit Cards: MC, VISA, Amex, Diners, Eurocard & Discover.
Rsv'tns: Required, but

walk-ins taken on a space-available basis.
Reserve Through: Travel agent or call direct.
Parking: Ample covered off-street pay parking. $15.50 daily with in-out privileges.
In-Room: Color TV, telephone, room, maid & laundry service.
On-Premises: Meeting rooms. Fax, secretarial services, photocopying, concierge, same-day laundry/valet.
Exercise/Health: Nearby gym, weights, Jacuzzi,

sauna, steam & massage.
Swimming: Nearby pool.
Smoking: No rooms designated as non-smoking.
Pets: Not permitted.
Handicap Access: Yes. Race-style wheelchairs, deaf phone kit.
Children: Welcome. Rollaway beds, cribs, concierge services of things to do with kids.
Languages: English, French, Spanish, German, Tagalog, Japanese & Dutch.

Langtry Inn

Perfect for that Victorian Affair

Gay/Lesbian ♀

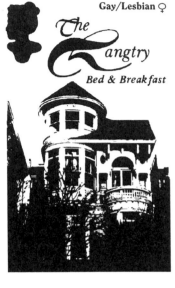

Described by a reviewer as the "best place in the world for women to stay," *The Langtry* provides the elegance you deserve in a beautifully restored 1894 Queen Anne-style Victorian, where your room is exquisitely appointed with period antiques and fresh flowers. After a gourmet breakfast, stroll through our neighborhood historical district, ride a cable car or walk on the beach. Later, dine by candlelight in your own room or relax in our hot tub or participate in special events held in our parlor.

Address: 637 Steiner, San Francisco, CA 94117. Tel: (415) 863-0538.

Type: Bed & breakfast.
Clientele: Mostly women with men welcome.
Transportation: Super Shuttle from S.F. airport is $9.00.
To Gay Bars: 3 blocks to nearest gay bar. 10-minute walk or 3-minute drive to Castro bars.
Rooms: 4 rooms & 1 suite with queen beds.
Bathrooms: 2 private bath/toilets & 1 shared bath/shower/toilet.
Meals: Full breakfast.
Vegetarian: Breakfast.
Complimentary: Brandy, sherry, tea, coffee, wine & soda.
Dates Open: All year.

High Season: May-August.
Rates: High season $75-$130, suite $175.
Discounts: For week stays and any mid-week night off-season.
Credit Cards: MC & VISA with 5% surcharge.
Rsv'tns: Recommended.
Reserve Through: Travel agent or call direct.
Minimum Stay: Holiday & seminar weekends min. of 2 nights.
Parking: Adequate free on-street parking.
In-Room: Private phone lines, coffee & tea-making facilities, maid service, TV on request.

Color cable TV in suite.
On-Premises: Meeting rooms, TV lounge, VCR, private dining room, laundry facilities, central heat.
Exercise/Health: Hot tub & massage, tennis court across the street.
Sunbathing: On common sun deck.
Nudity: Permitted in hot tub.

Smoking: Non-smokers' & smokers' rooms available.
Pets: Not permitted.
Handicap Access: No.
Children: Not permitted.
Languages: English, Russian, German & Dutch.
Your Host: Alla.

IGTA

Leland Hotel

Gay/Lesbian ♂

For Pacific hospitality in San Francisco, visit The *Leland Hotel,* located in the lively and entertaining Polk Street District. Some of the city's most exciting gay life is up the street, down the street, across the street. We offer sunny and spacious European-style rooms with either private or shared baths and also comfortable studio apartments. Our rooms are affordable, comfortable and within easy walking distance of the Theater District, the symphony and opera houses, Nob Hill, Chinatown, the cable cars and many other San Francisco attractions. An abundance of fine restaurants, boutiques and bars are at our doorstep, as well as local public transportation. Whether you're coming to San Francisco for business or pleasure, the *Leland* is one of the most convenient, affordable, and friendly places to stay.

Address: 1315 Polk St, San Francisco, CA 94109. Tel: (415) 441-5141 or (800) 258-4458.

Type: Hotel.
Clientele: Mostly men with women welcome.
Transportation: Shuttle from airport to hotel.
To Gay Bars: Gay bar on premises, others are on the same street.
Rooms: 12 studio apartments, 96 rooms.
Bathrooms: 72 private, 36 rooms share.
Dates Open: All year.
High Season: Summer months.
Rates: Daily $25-$58.
Discounts: On stays of 1 week or longer.
Credit Cards: MC, VISA, Amex & Discover.
Rsv'tns: Recommended during summer months.
Reserve Through: Travel agent or call direct.

Parking: Adequate on-street parking & pay lot across the street.
In-Room: Maid service, color TV, telephone, studios have private baths, kitchens.
On-Premises: Large lobby, 24-hour front desk.
Exercise/Health: Nearby health clubs.
Smoking: Permitted without restrictions.
Pets: Not permitted.
Handicap Access: Yes.
Children: Not recommended.
Languages: English, German.
Your Host: Bruce.

IGTA

Lemon Tree Homestays

Even Teddy Bears Get to Snooze....

Gay/Lesbian ♂

At *Lemon Tree Homestays,* we offer a quiet and comfortable guest room overlooking our garden, and a healthy continental breakfast. You may enjoy our Mediterranean-style home with its sunny and inviting interior. Our garden is filled with herbs and flowers and features a fragrant Meyer lemon tree. Meditate, relax or sun yourself in our bit of heaven within the city.

Close to many points of interest, the Castro and excellent public transportation, our home and garden are ideal places to unwind after a busy day of sightseeing.

Address: PO Box 460424 San Francisco, CA 94146. Tel: (415) 861-4045

Type: Private home with guest room.
Clientele: Mostly men with women welcome.
Transportation: Shuttle from airport or public transportation to downtown SF. Muni train to Church St Station, then walk 2 blocks.
To Gay Bars: 2 blocks.
Rooms: 1 room with queen bed.
Bathrooms: Shared bath. Available for private use for additional nightly fee.

Meals: Continental breakfast.
Vegetarian: Our food is low fat, low cholesterol. Special dietary needs accommodated. 2 blocks to vegetarian restaurant.
Dates Open: All year.
Rates: $50-$75.
Discounts: 10% for stays of 10 or more days.
Rsv'tns: Written reservation forms w/deposit required. Send for brochure/form.
Reserve Through: Call

direct.
Minimum Stay: 2 nights.
Parking: Restricted on-street parking.
In-Room: Local sightseeing information & transit maps.
On-Premises: TV & stereo in living room, house phone for local calls, garden areas. Some space in family refrigerator.
Exercise/Health: Nearby gym, weights, Jacuzzi, sauna, steam & massage.
Swimming: Pool at Cen-

tral YMCA. 20-minute transit ride to ocean.
Sunbathing: On the patio or in the garden.
Smoking: Permitted in garden only. Non-smoking sleeping room.
Pets: Not permitted.
Handicap Access: No.
Children: Not welcome.
Languages: English, some Spanish & German.
Your Host: David & Peter

Metro Hotel, The

Gay-Friendly 50/50 ♀♂

A Great Discovery

A small, affordable Victorian hotel with 23 rooms on two floors, the *Metro Hotel* is situated in a historic district of San Francisco, near Golden Gate Park. We have completely new interiors with private baths in each room. Great food is available at La Dolce Vita Cafe. Make your stay in San Francisco a memorable event with our quiet rooms, English garden, patio and friendly atmosphere. Our convenient location is only 10 minutes by bus from downtown San Francisco, and 8 blocks from the Castro District.

Address: 319 Divisadero St, San Francisco, CA 94117. Tel: (415) 861-5364, Fax: (415) 863-1970.

Type: Hotel.
Clientele: 50% gay & lesbian & 50% straight clientele.
Transportation: Car or airport shuttle.
To Gay Bars: 8 blocks to men's bars.
Rooms: 23 rooms with suites, double or queen beds.
Bathrooms: All private.
Vegetarian: Available at restaurant.
Dates Open: All year.
High Season: Summer.
Rates: $45-$89.
Discounts: Call to see what is available at the time.
Credit Cards: MC, VISA, Amex, Discover.
Reserve Through: Travel agent or call direct.
Parking: Free parking 6pm-9am.
In-Room: Cable color TV, telephone, maid service.
Sunbathing: On patio.
Smoking: Permitted.
Pets: Not permitted.
Handicap Access: No.
Children: Permitted.
Languages: English.
Your Host: Pam & Jim.

Oceanview Farms Bed & Breakfast

Gay/Lesbian ♂

Country Living on the Pacific Coast

Oceanview Farms Bed & Breakfast is a working horse breeding farm 50 minutes from San Francisco's Castro District and 45 minutes from Santa Cruz's boardwalk. From our decks, look out over the mares and foals to the Pacific Ocean. Walk to sand beaches and rocky tide pools. Herds of harbor seals lounge on the rocks and, in spring, grey whales migrate past the farm. State parks with magnificent California redwood trees are nearby. San Gregorio nude beach is 15 minutes away and there are several nude beaches toward Santa Cruz.

Address: 515 Bean Hollow Rd, Box 538, Pescadero, CA 94060. Tel: (415) 879-0698, Fax: (415) 879-0478.

Type: Bed & breakfast.
Clientele: Mostly men with women welcome.
Transportation: Car is best.
To Gay Bars: 40 miles.
Rooms: 2 rooms with queen beds.
Bathrooms: All private.
Meals: Full breakfast & big country breakfast.
Vegetarian: Request with reservation.
Complimentary: Tea & coffee, mints on pillows, various in-room amenities.
Dates Open: All year.
Rates: $75 double, $65 single.
Rsv'tns: Required.
Reserve Through: Travel agent or call direct.
Minimum Stay: 2 days on weekends.
Parking: Ample free off-street parking.
In-Room: Maid service.
On-Premises: Laundry facilities.
Exercise/Health: Nearby sauna.
Swimming: Nearby ocean.
Sunbathing: On common sun decks or at the beach.
Nudity: Permitted with discretion.
Smoking: Permitted outside on decks.
Pets: Not permitted.
Handicap Access: No.
Children: Not especially welcome.
Languages: English.
Your Host: Mike & Cliff.

Pension San Francisco Tourist Hotel

Gay-Friendly 50/50 ♀♂

Pension San Francisco is a European-style hotel centrally-located six blocks from Castro, 2 from Polk and 3 from Folsom Street. We're convenient to public transportation and affordable and fun for guests who want to explore a variety of San Francisco delights. We welcome you to a tradition of hospitality one expects to find in San Francisco, with attractive, multi-national, multi-lingual and friendly gay concierges, who consistently provide personalized attention to every comfort.

Address: 1668 Market St, San Francisco, CA 94102. Tel: (415) 864-1271, Fax: 861-8116, (800) 886-1271.

Type: Hotel with bar & restaurant.
Clientele: 50% gay & lesbian & 50% straight clientele.
Transportation: Airport shuttle $9.
To Gay Bars: 3 blocks to men's bars. 6 blocks to women's.
Rooms: 8 singles & 28 doubles.

Bathrooms: All shared baths with vanity sink in each room.
Dates Open: All year.
Rates: $42-$55.
Discounts: 10% for INN Places readers reserving direct.
Credit Cards: MC, VISA, & Amex.
Rsv'tns: Required.
Reserve Through: Call

direct.
Minimum Stay: On some holiday weekends.
Parking: Ample, off-street pay parking. Free on-street parking.
In-Room: Room & maid service.
Exercise/Health: Gym, Jacuzzi, sauna & steam all close by.
Swimming: Pool nearby.

Smoking: Non-smoking rooms available.
Pets: Permitted upon approval.
Children: Permitted.
Languages: English, Spanish, French, Italian & Mandarin.
Your Host: Andy.

Phoenix, The

Gay-Friendly ♀♂

The Phoenix has been featured in magazines and on TV for its unique artistic retreat ambiance. With more than 300 pieces of original art gracing the grounds, *The Phoenix* features a famous mural at the bottom of its swimming pool and a 70 ft tall mural on its western wall. The hotel attracts a hip celebrity clientele (John F. Kennedy Jr., k.d. lang, and Sinead O'Connor) and its restaurant is world-famous for its Caribbean cuisine and poolside dining. *The Phoenix* is a festive one acre resort in the middle of the city.

Address: 601 Eddy St, San Francisco, CA 94109. Tel: (415) 776-1380 or FAX: (415) 885-3109.

Type: Hotel with restaurant & bar.
Clientele: Mostly straight clientele with a gay/lesbian following.
To Gay Bars: 1-6 blocks to men's bars.
Rooms: 11 singles, 30 doubles, & 3 suites.
Bathrooms: All private.

Meals: Continental breakfast.
Vegetarian: Available in restaurant.
Dates Open: All year.
Rates: Singles & doubles $69-$99. Suites $110-$135.
Discounts: Winter rates.
Credit Cards: MC, VISA,

Amex, & Diners.
Reserve Through: Travel agent or call direct.
Parking: Ample, free off-street parking.
In-Room: Color TV, maid, room & laundry service & telephone.
On-Premises: Meeting rooms & sculpture garden.

Swimming: Pool on premises.
Sunbathing: At poolside.
Languages: English, Spanish, French & German.

IGTA

Renoir Hotel

Gay-Friendly ♀♂

San Francisco's Newest First Class Downtown Hotel

The *Renoir Hotel* is a newly-reno-vated historical landmark building, just three blocks from Folsom Street, Polk Street, and three subway stations from the Castro. It is the best bargain in downtown San Francisco, providing charming European ambiance with classical music throughout. The ornate interior includes an original Renard in the reception area and Renoir prints placed tastefully throughout the hotel. The Renoir Restaurant and cocktail lounge serves breakfast, lunch and dinner. Both the lobby cafe and restaurant provide room service. *Inn Places* discount to $59 available most dates (or pick up coupon at Visitors Center). **Address: 45 McAllister St, San Francisco, CA 94102. Tel: (415) 626-5200 or (800) 576-3388.**

Type: Hotel with restaurant, bar, espresso bar & gift shop.
Clientele: Mostly straight with a gay & lesbian following.
Transportation: BART subway from Oakland airport to Civic Center Station. Shuttle van from SF Airport to hotel.
To Gay Bars: 2 blocks. About 10 gay bars within 5 blocks.
Rooms: 123 rooms & 3 suites with twin, double, queen & king beds.
Bathrooms: All private.
Vegetarian: Vegetarian items on restaurant &

cafe menus.
Dates Open: All year.
High Season: May 15-Nov 15.
Rates: High season $79-$150, low season $49-$99.
Discounts: 10% AAA, Corporate rate $64, Senior rate $59, rate with discount coupon from Visitors Center $59.
Credit Cards: All major credit cards.
Rsv'tns: Required.
Reserve Through: Travel agent or call direct.
Minimum Stay: Gay Day Parade weekends & some sold-out periods,

for last minute reservations.
Parking: Ample off-street pay parking & valet parking. Lot $8 day, valet $24 day.
In-Room: Color TV, telephone, maid, room & laundry service.
On-Premises: Meeting rooms. Executive level offers modem hookups for computers.
Exercise/Health: YMCA 1 block from hotel with 7 floors of facilities. Non-member admission $13 per day.
Swimming: At nearby YMCA pool.

Nudity: 7 miles to nude beaches.
Smoking: Permitted in half the rooms & the bar. Non-smoking rooms available.
Pets: Not permitted.
Handicap Access: Yes. 3 handicap rooms. Ramp provided upon request.
Children: Welcome.
Languages: English, German, French, Russian, Spanish/Portuguese, Cantonese/Mandarin/Tagalog
Your Host: Steve.

San Francisco Cottage

Gay/Lesbian ♀♂

The Perfect San Francisco Experience

San Francisco Cottage offers a lovely cottage and an elegant studio apartment in the rear garden of a San Francisco Edwardian home. Our superb location is on a quiet, residential street, yet it is just a five-minute stroll to Castro Street shops, bars, cafes and restaurants. Public transportation is close and convenient. The studio apartment has a complete kitchen, a living room area, with sofa, love seat and tables, a dining area with black lacquer table and chairs, queen-sized bed, and a bathroom with shower and charming claw tub. This unit has elegant, contemporary decor in grey with blue, green and lavender accents. The living room area opens onto a flowered garden patio through a paneled sliding- glass door.

The cottage is decorated in Santa Fe-style colors and furniture and has a living room, queen-sized bed, modern kitchen and dining table and chairs. French doors open onto a redwood deck and fabulous terraced garden. This loft-like cottage has tons of light and charm. Both units are equipped with telephone, cable TV, VCR and stereo. Laundry and barbecue facilities are also available. Enjoy the moderate climate of "Everybody's Favorite City" by having morning coffee or afternoon cocktails on either the garden patio or the redwood deck and terraced garden, both of which are accessible from each unit. These two units are very special and romantic and available for the perfect San Francisco experience.

Address: 224 Douglass St, San Francisco, CA 94114. Tel: (415) 861-3220, Fax: (415) 626-2633.

Type: Self-catering cottage & studio apartment.
Clientele: Gay & lesbian.
Transportation: Shuttle buses or taxi from airport. Best way downtown is metro.
To Gay Bars: 3 short blocks to gay bars.
Rooms: 1 cottage & 1 apartment with queen beds.

Bathrooms: Both private.
Complimentary: Tea & coffee set-up in rooms.
Dates Open: All year.
High Season: March through October.
Rates: $95-$115 per night, $600-$725 per week.
Discounts: Weekly & monthly rates.
Credit Cards: MC & VISA.

Rsv'tns: Required.
Reserve Through: Travel agent or call direct.
Minimum Stay: 2 nights.
Parking: Ample on-street parking.
In-Room: Color cable TV, VCR, stereo, telephone, kitchen & refrigerator.
On-Premises: Laundry facilities.
Exercise/Health:

5-minute walk to gay gym.
Sunbathing: On private sun deck & patio.
Pets: Not permitted.
Handicap Access: No.
Languages: English.

IGTA

Victorian Hotel

Gay-Friendly 50/50 ♀♂

In a premiere downtown location, the 165 room, full service, landmark 1913 *Victorian Hotel* is adjacent to the San Francisco Shopping Center (90 shops) and the Muni/Bart underground, with a 10-minute access to the Castro. It is just steps away from Powell Street Cable Car, Moscone Convention Center and withing walking distance of SOMA gay nightclubs, Folsom Street bars and Polk Street. Our highly-regarded Market Roastery restaurant and bar offers superb food and service. We provide a warm, friendly staff plus value and location for budget-minded travelers.

Address: 54 Fourth St, San Francisco, CA 94103. Tel: (415) 986-4400, (800) 227-3804.

Type: Hotel with restaurant & bar.
Clientele: 50% gay & lesbian & 50% straight clientele.
Transportation: Airport shuttle direct to hotel (30 minutes).
To Gay Bars: Several bars within 2 blocks. Castro Street within minutes by underground.
Rooms: 160 rooms & 3 suites with single, double or queen beds.
Bathrooms: Private: 100

full baths, 65 sinks only. Others share.
Meals: Continental breakfast.
Vegetarian: Available upon request. Many menu items are vegetarian.
Dates Open: All year.
High Season: July, August, September.
Rates: With private bath: summer $69-$109, low season $49-$89.
Discounts: Senior & corporate 10%.

Credit Cards: MC, VISA & Amex.
Rsv'tns: Preferred.
Reserve Through: Travel agent or call direct.
Parking: Off-street covered pay parking, $10 per day extra.
In-Room: Color TV, telephone, room & maid service.
Smoking: Smoking permitted. Non-smoking rooms available.

Pets: Not permitted.
Handicap Access: Yes. Elevator, street level, easy access.
Children: Not refused, but we have no facilities for children.
Languages: English & Spanish.
Your Host: Alan & Rali.

IGTA

Villa, The

Gay/Lesbian ♀♂

This Is San Francisco

What makes San Francisco a great place to live? The spectacular views, and *The Villa* has them. Many people call ours the greatest view of the city, not only because of how beautiful the skyline is, day or night, but of how close you are to it. When *The Villa* is your home, you live just minutes from the financial and shopping districts of downtown San Francisco, while uniquely removed from the city's hectic pace.

And of course, there is the nightlife, which may be San Francisco's most enduring attribute.

Address: 379 Collingwood, San Francisco, CA . Tel: (415) 282-1367, (800) 358-0123, Fax: (415) 821-3995.

Type: Guesthouse.
Clientele: Good mix of gays & lesbians.
Transportation: Easily accessible by car, or shuttle from airport.
To Gay Bars: 3 blocks or a 5-minute walk.
Rooms: 4 rooms, 3 suites & 4 apartments with single, double, queen or king beds.
Bathrooms: Rooms: private & shared. Apartments have private

baths.
Vegetarian: Restaurants nearby.
Dates Open: All year.
High Season: Summer & Fall.
Rates: Weekly from $400-$800. Monthly rates available.
Discounts: Please inquire.
Credit Cards: MC, VISA & Amex.
Rsv'tns: Recommended.
Reserve Through: Call

direct.
Minimum Stay: One week.
Parking: Free off-street & on-street parking.
In-Room: Color cable TV, VCR, telephone, kitchen, refrigerator & maid service.
On-Premises: TV lounge, laundry facilities & shared kitchen on each floor.
Swimming: Pool on premises, ocean nearby.

Sunbathing: At poolside & on common sun decks.
Smoking: Permitted inside the rooms. Non-smoking rooms available upon request.
Pets: Not permitted.
Handicap Access: Yes.
Children: Permitted, but not especially welcome.
Languages: English & Spanish.

IGTA

Western Exposure

Come Home to Your Own Community

Gay/Lesbian ♀♂

Through *Western Exposure,* local lesbians and gay men invite you to vacation in their homes. Enjoy breakfasts, gay events, resources, fun. You can network, meet friends in the community and make connections. Accommodations are available throughout San Francisco, Berkeley and Oakland. All host homes are visited and approved prior to your arrival.

Address: PO Box 2116 Berkeley, CA 94702. Tel: (510) 869-4395, Fax: (510) 254-0265.

Type: Bed & breakfast.
Clientele: Good mix of gays & lesbians.
Transportation: Airport shuttle to SF or East Bay homes ($9-$16). Pick up generally not provided.
To Gay Bars: Depends on location.
Rooms: 15 rooms & 2 suites with singles or doubles.
Bathrooms: 3 private bath/toilets, others share.

Meals: Continental breakfast.
Vegetarian: Always available.
Complimentary: Depends on host arrangement.
Dates Open: All year.
High Season: Summer.
Rates: $35-$65 1 person per night. 2nd person, add 20%.
Discounts: 10% off for 2 week stay, 20% for 3 week stay & 30% for 4+ week stay.

Rsv'tns: Required.
Reserve Through: Travel agent or call direct.
Parking: On-street parking. Varies per location.
In-Room: Varies per location.
On-Premises: Laundry facilities. Other amenities vary per location.
Exercise/Health: Varies per location.
Swimming: Varies per location.
Sunbathing: Poolside

(1 location). Patios, backyards.
Smoking: Permitted outside of homes only. Non-smoking rooms available.
Pets: Not permitted.
Handicap Access: We will try to provide accessible homes as requested.
Children: Welcome, depending on location.
Languages: English & French.

We Appreciate Your Comments!

Positive comments of interest may be included in the next issue, giving future readers the benefit of your experience. And it's a nice way of saying "thank you" to an innkeeper who extended you exceptional hospitality.

See the contents for the Reader Comment Form.

Willows, The

Your Haven Within The Castro

Gay/Lesbian ♂

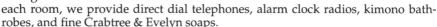

Housed in a 1904 Edwardian, *The Willows* derives its name from the handcrafted bentwood willow furnishings which grace each room. Complementing these unique pieces are antique dressers and armoires, plantation shutters, cozy comforters and fine English wallpaper borders. Each of our eleven guest bedrooms also has the country freshness of flowers, potted plants and dried floral arrangements. As an added comfort to each room, we provide direct dial telephones, alarm clock radios, kimono bathrobes, and fine Crabtree & Evelyn soaps.

The Willows is noted for its homey atmosphere and personal, friendly service. In the morning, wake up to a newspaper at your door followed by the pampered touch of breakfast served in bed. To help you plan your day's activities, our innkeepers are always available with helpful suggestions and directions. The sitting room welcomes guests to gather in the evening for cheese and conversation. Upon returning to the Inn at night, guests will appreciate the touch of a turned-down bed softly illuminated by the warmth of a glowing table lamp and a port nightcap, our classic finish to another day at *The Willows*. At the crossroads to the city's efficient transportation system, each of San Francisco's unique neighborhoods, attractions and convention sites are easily accessible. Dotting our neighborhood are a wide range of fine restaurants, specialty and second hand shops, gyms, bars and a vintage '30s movie palace.

Address: 710 14th St, San Francisco, CA 94114. Tel: (415) 431-4770, Fax: (415) 431-5295.

Type: Bed & breakfast inn.
Clientele: Mostly men with women welcome.
Transportation: Airport shuttle to the inn $10.
To Gay Bars: 1/2 block to men's bar, 3 to women's.
Rooms: 10 rooms & 1 suite with single or queen beds.
Bathrooms: Shared : 4 water closets, & 4 showers. Sinks in all rooms.

Meals: Expanded continental breakfast.
Vegetarian: Vegetarian-only restaurant (Amazing Grace) 1/2 block away.
Complimentary: Sherry nightcap with chocolate truffle.
Dates Open: All year.
High Season: June 15th-November 15th.
Rates: $56-$125.
Credit Cards: MC, VISA & Discover.

Rsv'tns: Recommended 2 weeks in advance.
Reserve Through: Call direct.
Minimum Stay: 2 nights on weekends.
Parking: Adequate on-street, limited off-street pay parking.
In-Room: TV on request, direct dial telephone, alarm clock radios, maid & room service, refrigerator in some rooms.

On-Premises: TV lounge area, refrigerator in pantry.
Exercise/Health: Co-ed & women's gyms 1 block.
Swimming: Nearby pool & ocean.
Smoking: Permitted without restrictions.
Pets: Not permitted.
Handicap Access: No.
Children: Not permitted.
Languages: English, German.

SANTA BARBARA

Glenborough Inn

Have Breakfast in Bed in a Romantic B&B

Gay-Friendly ♀♂

You step into the past, where life was quieter and the pace relaxed. Your room is fresh, immaculate, old-fashioned, with plants, fresh flowers and antiques. You might meet others around the fireplace, or in the gardens for hors d'oeuvres, or indulge yourself in the enclosed garden hot tub for private use. Pamper yourself with a gourmet breakfast delivered to your room. Leave your car, and take the shuttle to the beach or around town. The *Glenborough Inn* is Santa Barbara's most romantic gay-owned, gay-friendly B&B.

Address: 1327 Bath St, Santa Barbara, CA 93101. Tel: (805) 966-0589 or (800) 962-0589, Fax: 564-2369.

Type: Bed & breakfast inn.
Clientele: Mostly straight clientele with a gay/lesbian following.
Transportation: Taxi from airport or train station.
To Gay Bars: 5 minutes by car to gay bars.
Rooms: 8 rooms & 3 suites with queen beds.
Bathrooms: 5 private & 3 shared full baths.
Meals: Full gourmet breakfast.
Vegetarian: No meat is served at the inn. Spe-

cial diets accommodated with advance notice.
Complimentary: Evening refreshments & hors d'oeuvres, hot drinks & cookies nightly.
Dates Open: All year.
High Season: June-Oct.
Rates: $80-$175.
Discounts: Midweek corporate rates for guests on business.
Credit Cards: MC, VISA, Amex, Diners & Discover.
Rsv'tns: Recommended (not usually needed midweek).

Reserve Through: Travel agent for Mon-Thurs stays or call direct.
Minimum Stay: 2 nights on weekends & 3 nights for 3-day holidays.
Parking: Ample free off- and on-street parking.
In-Room: Telephones & maid service.
On-Premises: Parlour, gardens, guest refrigerator, bicycles & fax.
Exercise/Health: Outdoor enclosed (garden) Jacuzzi on sign-up basis.
Swimming: At nearby

ocean beach.
Sunbathing: In gardens & at nearby beach.
Nudity: Nude beach nearby.
Smoking: ALL rooms are non-smoking; smoking permitted in gardens & patios.
Pets: Not permitted.
Handicap Access: No.
Children: Not especially welcomed.
Languages: English, Spanish & sign language.
Your Host: Michael, Steve & Ken.

Ivanhoe Inn

Gay-Friendly ♀♂

This lovely Victorian house, surrounded by a white picket fence entwined with colorful flowers, is now the *Ivanhoe Inn*. Accommodations, including comfortable suites and a separate cottage, are individually decorated. Each morning, a picnic basket will appear outside your door with a continental breakfast in it. Each suite has a kitchen, so you may make your own coffee, then eat in the privacy of your room, or on the sunny patio or garden. The Santa Barbara area is renowned for its wineries and fine restaurants. The beach is just a few blocks from our door.

Address: 1406 Castillo St, Santa Barbara, CA 93101. Tel: (805) 963-8832

Type: Bed & breakfast & separate cottage.
Clientele: Mostly straight clientele with a gay/lesbian following.
Transportation: Taxi or airport limo. Pick up from train.
To Gay Bars: Close to gay/lesbian bars.
Rooms: 1 room, 3 suites & 1 2-bdrm cottage with queen or king beds.
Bathrooms: Private: 1 shower/toilet, 2 bath/toilet/showers. 2 shared

full baths.
Meals: Expanded continental breakfast.
Complimentary: Wine & cheese on arrival. Crackers, coffee, tea, hot chocolate, wine & condiments in room.
Dates Open: All year.
High Season: April through September.
Rates: $57-$195, $20 per extra person.
Discounts: On extended stays. 40% off Sun thru Thur except holidays and

special days.
Credit Cards: MC, VISA, Amex & Diners.
Rsv'tns: Preferred.
Reserve Through: Travel agent or call direct.
Minimum Stay: 2 nights on weekends.
Parking: Ample off-street & on-street parking.
In-Room: Color cable TV, ceiling fans, kitchen, refrigerator, coffee/tea-making facilities, maid service.
On-Premises: Laundry facilities.

Exercise/Health: Complimentary bikes.
Swimming: 14 blocks to ocean beach.
Sunbathing: On beach.
Nudity: Nude beach nearby.
Smoking: Not permitted except on patios.
Pets: Permitted in cottage & downstairs rooms.
Handicap Access: No.
Children: Permitted.
Languages: English, limited Spanish.
Your Host: Mary & Roy.

SONOMA

Sonoma Chalet B&B

A Wine Country Getaway

Gay-Friendly ♀♂

One of the first bed and breakfast inns established in Sonoma, our Swiss-style farmhouse and country cottages are situated on three acres, blocks from Sonoma's historic square. Relax in *Sonoma Chalet's* uniquely decorated rooms with fireplace or wood-burning stove, antiques, quilts and collectibles. Cross a wooden bridge to the popular fairy-tale-like Honeymoon Cottage. Complimentary bicycles are available for the more ambitious, or simply relax in the outdoor Jacuzzi. Enjoy a delightful continental breakfast served in our kitchen or on the deck overlooking a 200-acre ranch.

Address: 18935 Fifth St West, Sonoma, CA 95476. Tel: (707) 938-3129, (800) 938-3129.

Type: Bed & breakfast.
Clientele: Mostly straight clientele with gays & lesbians welcome.
Transportation: Car is best.
To Gay Bars: 1-hour drive to San Francisco & Russian River resorts.
Rooms: 2 rooms, 1 suite & 3 cottages with double or queen beds.

Bathrooms: 4 private & 1 shared.
Meals: Expanded continental breakfast.
Complimentary: Tea & coffee. Sherry in room.
Dates Open: All year.
High Season: April-October.
Rates: $75-$135.
Credit Cards: MC, VISA & Amex.

Rsv'tns: Required.
Reserve Through: Travel agent or call direct.
Minimum Stay: 2 nights on weekends & holidays during high season.
Parking: Ample free parking.
In-Room: Ceiling fans, refrigerator, coffee & tea-making facilities.
Exercise/Health: Free

use of bicycles, Jacuzzi on premises. Nearby gym, weights & massage.
Smoking: Permitted outside only.
Pets: Not permitted.
Handicap Access: No.
Children: By prior arrangement.
Languages: English.
Your Host: Joe.

Starwae Inn

A Creative Haven in the Country

Gay-Friendly ♀♂

Behind a lush hedge of lilacs, two miles south of Sonoma, is a retreat for artists, art lovers, and people who love both life and the country. *Starwae Inn* offers cottages creatively rejuvenated by local artists Janice Crow and John Curry from buildings that once housed their pottery works. Each cottage is unique and intimate, with original art and a growing collection of hand-crafted furnishings. Wonderfully unpretentious, *Starwae Inn* emphasizes renewal and creature comforts like cotton robes, plump duvets, complimentary coffee and fruit in your room. Come visit and rediscover the true meaning of re-creation.

Address: 21490 Broadway (Hwy 12), Sonoma, CA . Tel: (707) 938-1374, (800) 793-4792, Fax: (707) 935-1159.

Type: B&B cottage.
Clientele: Mostly straight clientele with a gay & lesbian following.
Transportation: Car is best. Sonoma has door-to-door transportation from San Francisco airport.
To Gay Bars: One hour to San Francisco, one hour to Russian River resorts.
Rooms: Two cottages (3 suites, 1 room). Can be rented as entire cottage

or separately, with queen bed (double futon beds in suites).
Bathrooms: All private.
Meals: Expanded continental breakfast.
Vegetarian: Health food store two miles, fresh vegetable store three miles away.
Complimentary: Tea, gourmet coffee, fruit juice.
Dates Open: All year.
High Season: May-October.

Rates: $90.00-130.00.
Discounts: Weekly & monthly rates November-March.
Credit Cards: MC, VISA.
Rsv'tns: Required.
Reserve Through: Travel agent or call direct.
Minimum Stay: Required.
Parking: Ample free off-street parking.
In-Room: AC, refrigerator, kitchen, coffee & tea-making facilities, maid service.

On-Premises: Meeting rooms, fax.
Exercise/Health: Nearby Jacuzzi, sauna, steam, massage.
Sunbathing: On private patio.
Smoking: Permitted outside only.
Pets: Not permitted.
Handicap Access: No.
Languages: English.
Your Host: Janice & John.

COLORADO

ASPEN

Hotel Aspen

Gay-Friendly ♀♂

Best Way to Stay in Aspen

This striking, contemporary forty-five room hotel on Main Street has large, beautifully-appointed rooms with king or queen beds, wet bars, cable TV, air conditioning, in-room safes, refrigerators, and private baths. Most rooms open onto terraces or balconies and some have private Jacuzzis. Guests relax year-round under beautiful mountain skies on our patio courtyard with its heated swimming pool and two Jacuzzis. In the lounge, take in in-

credible panoramic views while enjoying a complimentary mountain breakfast or afternoon wine and cheese in the lounge.

Hotel Aspen is the perfect home base from which to enjoy what the spirited town of Aspen has to offer. In winter, there is world class skiing. Summer sports include golf, tennis, swimming, hiking, biking, river rafting and trout fishing. For the culturally-minded, there are daily concerts, dance and theater. And whatever the season, there are numerous shops, galleries and restaurants.

From the moment you arrive, our professional staff caters to your needs, ensuring a vacation that goes beyond expectation. *Hotel Aspen* is centrally located, just a short stroll from everything, and is convenient to free publthic transportation. The airport is only three miles from town and the city of Denver is a scenic 3-1/2 hour drive from Aspen.

Address: 110 W Main St, Aspen, CO 81611. Tel: (800) 527-7369, Fax: (303) 920-1379.

Type: Hotel with breakfast & meeting room.
Clientele: Mainly straight with a gay & lesbian following.
Transportation: Car. City provides shuttle transport from airport. Amtrak from Denver to Glenwood Springs.
To Gay Bars: About 3 blocks.
Rooms: 40 rooms & 5 suites with double, queen or king beds.
Bathrooms: All private.
Meals: Expanded continental buffet breakfast. We call it a Mountain Breakfast.

Vegetarian: At almost all restaurants. Best in Aspen, Explore Booksellers & Coffeehouse, is only 2 blocks away.
Complimentary: Apres-ski receptions in season.
Dates Open: All year.
High Season: Ski season: Xmas thru New Years, 2nd wk of Feb thru 3rd wk of Mar. July 4th.
Rates: Summer, $59-160 per night; winter $69-$295 per night.
Discounts: Inquire. Mention *Inn Places* for an instant 10% discount.
Credit Cards: MC, VISA, Amex, Diners & Discover.

Rsv'tns: Strongly suggested.
Reserve Through: Travel agent or call direct.
Minimum Stay: At certain times. Inquire.
Parking: Ample free off-street & on-street parking.
In-Room: Cable color TV, AC, telephone, refrigerator, coffee/tea-maker & maid service. 4 rooms with Jacuzzi.
On-Premises: Meeting rooms, valet service, & helpful front desk staff.
Exercise/Health: Gym & outside Jacuzzi. Day passes available at the

Aspen Athletic Club.
Swimming: On premises large outdoor heated pool. 25 miles to Reudi Reservoir.
Sunbathing: At poolside or on private sun decks.
Smoking: Permitted in rooms, but not in common areas.
Pets: Not permitted.
Handicap Access: Yes. All 1st floor rooms.
Children: Permitted.
Languages: English, Spanish, German, French & Australian.

CARBONDALE

Starbuck's Ranch

Women ♀

In the Heart of the Rockies

Close to Aspen, yet nestled in the quiet Cattle Creek valley, *Starbuck's Ranch* provides the perfect combination of natural beauty, vacation activities and relaxing comforts. With horses and a riding ring, private trout stream and restful gazebo, hiking trails and mountain views, hostesses Janet and Becky give you the best of Colorado's gorgeous western slope. Stay in a beautiful contemporary ranch house with vaulted ceiling, or have a private cabin with a deck overlooking Cattle Creek. Breakfast is served in the sunroom. Enjoy a fire in the winter or a hot tub anytime.

Address: 3390 County Rd 113, Carbondale, CO 81623. Tel: (303) 945-5208

Type: Bed & breakfast.
Clientele: Women only.
Transportation: Car, train or plane.
To Gay Bars: 170 miles.
Rooms: 2 rooms & 1 1-bedroom cabin.
Bathrooms: Rooms: private toilets, shared shower. Cabin: private shower.
Meals: Enjoy breakfast in the sunroom.
Vegetarian: Available upon request.

Complimentary: Tea, coffee, soft drinks. Cheese, crackers, wine & beer in gazebo.
Dates Open: All year.
High Season: Ski season, Xmas thru New Years, 4th of July.
Rates: Summer $40-$85 per night. Winter $50-$95 per night.
Discounts: 7th night free with 1-week stay.
Rsv'tns: Required.
Reserve Through: Call

direct.
Parking: Ample free off-the-road parking.
In-Room: Phone, refrigerator, ceiling fans & maid service. color TV/VCR on request, with movie library. Color TV, refrigerator, stove, microwave in cabin.
On-Premises: River rock fireplace in living room, gazebo by creek, sunroom, deck, stocked fishing holes.

Exercise/Health: Hot tub, fishing.
Sunbathing: By the hot tub or by the gazebo and creek.
Pets: Permitted if responsibly maintained.
Handicap Access: No.
Children: Permitted if responsibly maintained.
Languages: English.
Your Host: Janet & Becky.

COLORADO SPRINGS

Pikes Peak Paradise B & B

Gay-Friendly 50/50 ♀♂

We're So Happy, You Might Even Say We're...Gay!

If you take: a Southern mansion and hospitality, an unexcelled view of Pikes Peak...mix with: romantic atmosphere and privacy, a fireplace, queen bed and fresh sheets, gourmet breakfast...add: friendly hosts eager to make you feel at home, a pinch of good conversation...fold in: a basketful of dreams yet-to-be, a plentiful supply of "glad-to-be-gay..." shake and bake with enjoyment, it yields a large bundle of unforgettable moments and memories at *Pikes Peak Paradise*.

Address: PO Box 5760, Woodland Park, CO 80866. Tel: (800) 354-0989 or Fax: (719) 687-9008.

Type: Bed & breakfast.
Clientele: 50% gay & lesbian & 50% straight clientele.
Transportation: Car.
To Gay Bars: 25 minutes to Colorado Springs gay/ lesbian bars.
Rooms: 5 rooms with queen beds.
Bathrooms: 3 private bath/toilets & 2 private shower/toilets.
Meals: Full gourmet breakfast. Breakfast in bed available.

Vegetarian: Available upon request.
Complimentary: Tea, coffee, soft drinks, pea- nuts, crackers & cheese, & mints on pillows.
Dates Open: All year.
High Season: May- October.
Rates: $85-$150.
Discounts: $15 off per night for gays/lesbians if specified in making reservations.
Credit Cards: MC, VISA, Amex, & Discover.

Rsv'tns: Requested.
Reserve Through: Travel agent or call direct.
Parking: Ample free off- street parking.
In-Room: Ceiling fans, re- frigerator, fireplace, hot tub.
On-Premises: Public tele- phones & living room with piano.
Exercise/Health: Mas- sage $50/hour. Jacuzzi.
Swimming: 10 miles to public pool.
Sunbathing: On patio. Deluxe room has private

deck.
Nudity: Permitted on pri- vate deck & in hot tub.
Smoking: Permitted out- doors.
Pets: Toy breed dogs & declawed cats by prior arrangement.
Handicap Access: Yes, 1 deluxe room with Jacuzzi tub.
Children: Permitted if over 12 yrs.
Languages: English.
Your Host: Tim, Martin & Priscilla.

CREEDE

Old Firehouse No. 1, Inc., The

Gay-Friendly ♀♂

Built in 1892, *The Old Firehouse B&B* was home for years to the Creede volun- teer fire department. Located on Main Street, this historic building was completely renovated in 1992. Four spacious Victorian bedrooms with private baths and a li- brary sitting room are on the second floor, while the main floor features a Victorian Ice Cream Parlour. Once a rich mining town, Creede, the only town in Mineral County, offers visitors a fascinating selection of galleries, shops, restaurants and a mining museum, as well as some of Colorado's most spectacular scenery.

Address: Main Street (PO Box 603), Creede, CO 81130. Tel: (719) 658-0212

Type: Victorian B&B with Victorian Ice Cream Parlour.
Clientele: Mostly straight clientele, lesbian & gay community welcome.
Transportation: Car (Rte 149). Private plane to Creede Airport. Arrange- ments made for free pick up from airport.
To Gay Bars: 200 miles.
Rooms: 4 rooms with queen beds. 1 room with twin & Hollywood beds.

Bathrooms: All private. Suite: private with 2 people, shared with 4.
Meals: Full breakfast.
Vegetarian: Always available.
Complimentary: Coffee, teas & ice for rooms.
Dates Open: All year, ex- cept March (we close for renovations).
High Season: June through September.
Rates: Room: single $60, double $70. Suite for 4

$110. $20 per additional person (rollaway & breakfast).
Credit Cards: VISA, MC, Discover.
Rsv'tns: Recommended.
Reserve Through: Call direct.
Parking: Ample free, safe on- & off-street parking.
In-Room: Maid service.
On-Premises: Library lounge, kitchenette.
Exercise/Health: Won- derful walks everywhere.

Sunbathing: On smoking porch on back of building.
Smoking: Not in rooms. Permitted in Ice Cream Parlour & on smoking porch only.
Pets: Not permitted.
Handicap Access: Ice Cream Parlour only. Rooms on 2nd floor, no elevator.
Children: Permitted when well-behaved.
Languages: English & Spanish.
Your Host: Jessie.

INN Places 1995

DENVER

Mile Hi Bed/Breakfast

Home Away From Home

Gay/Lesbian ♂

Mile Hi Bed/Breakfast offers contemporary lodging at reasonable rates, with king or twin beds, balcony, semi-private bath, color cable TV, VCR, air-conditioning, phone, breakfast, a library, video selections, laundry facilities, massage, and discount coupons. *Mile Hi* is in a lovely, centrally-located, contemporized 1910 Victorian home. It is only three blocks to buses. Clubs, bars, and eateries are nearby. Your hosts will be glad to assist you with information about places to go and things to do. Please kick off your shoes, relax, and enjoy our home, while you're away from yours! *Please Note: We may move. Please inquire for updated information.* **Address: Denver, CO 80220-1127. Tel: (303) 329-7827 or (800) 513-7827.**

Type: In home stay in private home.
Clientele: Mostly men with women welcome.
Transportation: Taxi $12.
To Gay Bars: 6 blocks.
Rooms: 2 rooms with twin or king beds.
Bathrooms: 2 shared bath/shower/toilet.
Meals: Expanded continental breakfast. Dinners available with advance notice.
Vegetarian: Available with advance notice.
Complimentary: Set-up service, tea, coffee.
Dates Open: All year.
Rates: $39-$49, subject to change.
Discounts: 7th night free with week's stay.
Rsv'tns: Preferred.
Reserve Through: Travel agent or call direct.
Parking: Ample on-street parking.
In-Room: Color cable TV, VCR, video tape library, telephone & refrigerator.
On-Premises: Laundry facilities.
Exercise/Health: Massage on premises.
Sunbathing: On the patio.
Smoking: Permitted outside only.
Pets: Permitted, please inquire.
Handicap Access: No.
Children: Not permitted.
Languages: English.
Your Host: Bob & Tony.

P.T. Barnum Estate & The Annex

Gay/Lesbian ♀♂

P.T. Barnum Estate consists of the main house with 14 rooms that include two parlors, a solarium with a Tiffany stained glass window, a country kitchen and pantry, numerous balconies and porches. We're located near downtown Denver's business area, Mile Hi Stadium, the Colorado Convention Center, major hotels, restaurants and drinking establishments, gay bars and male bath houses. There is very convenient access to Interstate 25, 6th Avenue and the ski areas of the Rocky Mountains to the west. Thirty

miles west of Denver, there is limited gambling in Central City, Colorado.

The grounds of the estate abound with roses, flowers, hollyhocks, petunias and hanging baskets. Outbuildings include The Doll House, The Chicken Coop, The Carriage House, and the Livery Stable. The house is chock full of antiques and accent pieces of furniture and other items of interest to make this a truly different and unusual bed and breakfast experience. Enjoy the ambiance and nostalgia of yesteryear by staying with Bart and Herb at the *P.T. Barnum Estate* in beautiful Denver. Our guests comments: Great! Wonderful! Fantastic! We'll be back! Terrific location! We'll tell our friends! Had a great time! So unusual—nothing like it! Bart & Herb, you guys are OK!!!!! Want to come back, stay at the *P.T. Barnum Estate* and go skiing in the winter!

The Annex is located in the gay Capitol Hill area and features spectacular views of downtown Denver, the State Capitol, Rocky Mountains and Pikes Peak. *The Annex* is loaded with amenities and is within walking distance of downtown Denver and numerous gay bars.

Address: 360 King St, Denver, CO 80219. Tel: (303) 830-6758

Type: Bed & breakfast.
Clientele: Mostly gay & lesbian with some straight clientele.
Transportation: Taxi.
To Gay Bars: 12 blocks to gay/lesbian bars.
Rooms: 2 doubles.
Bathrooms: 1 private &

1 shared.
Meals: Expanded continental breakfast.
Dates Open: All year.
Rates: $40-$65 per night.
Discounts: Weekly or group rates.
Rsv'tns: Recommended.
Reserve Through: Travel

agent or call direct.
Parking: Adequate on-street parking in a safe neighborhood.
On-Premises: TV, telephones with free local calls.
Smoking: Permitted on balconies.

Pets: Not permitted.
Handicap Access: No. Stairs to all rooms & facilities.
Children: Not permitted.
Languages: English, some German & Japanese.
Your Host: Bart & Herb.

Victoria Oaks Inn

Gay/Lesbian ⚥

The warmth and hospitality of *Victoria Oaks Inn* is apparent the moment you enter this historical, restored 1896 mansion. Elegant, original oak woodwork, tile fireplaces and dramatic hanging staircase replete with ornate brass chandelier, set the mood for a delightful visit. The nine guest rooms are finished with stylish, restored antiques from the turn-of-the-century and have panoramic views through leaded glass windows and soft colors throughout. The individual character and appointments

of *Victoria Oaks Inn* are designed for your personal comforts in your home-away-from-home. Whether your visit is for business or pleasure, *Victoria Oaks* is conveniently located near Denver's bustling business and financial district, numerous shopping areas and varied tourist attractions.

The mansion is quietly nestled blocks from many of Denver's finest restaurants and close to major traffic arteries, providing quick access for any excursion. The historic Capitol Hill district offers special attractions, including the Unsinkable Molly Brown House, Botanic Gardens and the domed State Capitol Building. Within walking distance are the city park, the zoo, the Museum of Natural History and Imax Theatre. As a home you'd love to come home to, whether for a night or for the week, *Victoria Oaks* stands proudly apart. As a small inn, we offer personalized services not often available at larger hotels. Begin each morning with an inspiring continental breakfast, including freshly-squeezed orange juice, blended coffee and teas and a choice of fresh pastries, croissants, bagels and fresh fruits with the morning paper. Start your evening with a complimentary glass of wine from our wine cellar.

Address: 1575 Race St, Denver, CO 80206. Tel: (303) 355-1818, (800) 662-OAKS(6257).

Type: Bed & breakfast.
Clientele: Mostly gay &

lesbian with some straight clientele.

Transportation: Taxi.
To Gay Bars: 4 blks to

gay/lesbian bars.
continued next page

Colorado

Rooms: 9 doubles. **Bathrooms:** 1 private, others share. **Meals:** Expanded continental breakfast. **Complimentary:** Tea, coffee, juices, beer, wine & sodas. **Dates Open:** All year. **High Season:** June-

August. **Rates:** $45-$85. **Discounts:** Weekly and group rates. **Credit Cards:** MC, VISA, Amex, Diners & Discover. **Rsv'tns:** Recommended 2 weeks in advance. **Reserve Through:** Travel agent or call direct.

Parking: Adequate free off-street parking. **In-Room:** Maid & laundry service & telephone. **On-Premises:** Meeting rooms, private dining rooms, TV lounge & laundry facilities. **Sunbathing:** In the backyard.

Smoking: Permitted without restrictions. **Pets:** Not permitted. **Handicap Access:** No. **Children:** Permitted if well-behaved. **Languages:** English. **Your Host:** Clyde.

KEYSTONE

Tanrydoon

Gay/Lesbian ♀♂

Tanrydoon: A Place for All Seasons

Tanrydoon is located at 9100 feet in the heart of the Colorado Rockies amidst the year-round world-class resorts of Keystone, Breckenridge, Copper Mountain and Vail. Our three-story contemporary Victorian home backs up against a private golf course. It features 1300 square feet of outside decks for sunning and relaxing with magnificent views of the mountains. Our guests may choose from two different accommodations, the Deluxe and the Luxury Suite. Our Deluxe accommodation includes your private room with its queen-sized bed, remote color TV, and private bath. It's warm, very comfortable and the least expensive of our accommodations. Our Luxury Suite is a luxuriously-decorated king-sized room with a king-sized bed, remote color TV, remote stereo VCR, stereo system, a two-person whirlpool bath and luxury bathroom featuring double sinks and a two-person, double-headed massage shower. This suite comes with an adjoining reading den and can easily accommodate small parties of up to 4 people. It's perfect for that "special" occasion.

During your stay with us, you'll begin each day with a delicious home-cooked breakfast prepared by your hosts. Then enjoy the hiking, biking, sailing, rafting, fishing, ice skating, snowmobiling, skiing or any of the many other activities our beautiful and historical area has to offer. In the evening, dine at one of our county's many excellent affordable restaurants. Afterward, return to *Tanrydoon*, a cozy fire, a glass of wine and new friends. We know you'll find a "season" perfect for you with us. We're *Tanrydoon* and that means "your home away from home." Come and meet us. Summer, winter, spring or fall.

Address: 463 Vail Circle, Dillon, CO 80435. Tel: (303) 468-1956.

Type: Bed & breakfast. **Clientele:** Good mix of gay men & women. **Transportation:** Use rental car or airport shuttle. **Rooms:** 1 room & 1 suite. **Bathrooms:** All private bath/toilets.

Meals: Full breakfast for all. **Vegetarian:** Request when placing reservation. **Complimentary:** Soft drinks, coffee, tea, juices, wine & beer. **Dates Open:** All year. **High Season:** November 15th-April 15th.

Rates: Low season $50-$80. High season $60-$95. Group rates available. **Discounts:** One free night on a 7-night reservation. **Credit Cards:** MC & VISA. **Rsv'tns:** Recommended. **Reserve Through:** Travel

agent or call direct. **Minimum Stay:** Holidays only. **Parking:** Ample free off-street parking. **In-Room:** Color TV, limited maid service. The luxury suite has a Jacuzzi & VCR. **On-Premises:** TV lounge.

Exercise/Health: Jacuzzi in luxury suite.
Sunbathing: On common sun deck.
Smoking: Permitted with consideration to others.
Pets: Not permitted.
Handicap Access: No.
Languages: English.
Your Host: Rich.

CONNECTICUT

MYSTIC

Adams House, The

Gay-Friendly ♀♂

"Quaint & Cozy...Friendly...Beautiful...& Relaxing"

Adams House is a 1790's-era house on a full acre of lush greenery and flower gardens, offering a homey colonial atmosphere featuring old fashioned fireplaces in the dining room and two bedrooms. Guests can choose between the main house and the *Adams Carriage House,* a self-contained building just far enough away to ensure total privacy. Breakfast is a delicious medley of fresh fruit, homemade muffins and coffeecakes with fabulous coffee. Guests' comments: "Quaint, cozy, fun, relaxing." "A perfect getaway." "Friendly, beautiful." "A blessing."
Address: 382 Cow Hill Rd, Mystic, CT 06355. Tel: (203) 572-9551.

Type: Bed & Breakfast.
Clientele: Mostly straight clientele with gays & lesbians welcome.
Transportation: Plane to Groton, taxi, train or ferry to New London, then taxi. Free pick up (usually) from Mystic train station.
To Gay Bars: 9 miles to New London.
Rooms: 6 rooms with queen beds & 1 suite with double & queen beds.
Bathrooms: 8 private.
Meals: Expanded continental breakfast & Saturday wine/cheese party 5pm-7pm.
Vegetarian: Always available.
Complimentary: Hot or iced tea on arrival or request.
Dates Open: All year.
High Season: Memorial Day to Labor Day.
Rates: $95-$175. Off-season rates available.
Discounts: Sun-Thur nights, 3rd night half price. November through April negotiable.
Credit Cards: MC, VISA, Amex & Discover.
Rsv'tns: Recommended for weekends & Jun-Sep.
Reserve Through: Call direct.
Minimum Stay: 2 nights on weekends & holidays.
Parking: Ample free off-street parking.
In-Room: AC & maid service. Carriage House has color cable TV, VCR & refrigerator.
On-Premises: TV lounge.
Exercise/Health: Sauna in Carriage House.
Swimming: 20-30 minutes by car to several beaches, 1 nude.
Sunbathing: On the lawn or at the beaches.
Nudity: At nude beach.
Smoking: Permitted in yard only.
Pets: Not permitted.
Handicap Access: Carriage House accessible, 2 steps.
Children: Welcome in Carriage House.
Languages: English.
Your Host: Mary Lou & Greg.

DELAWARE

MILTON

Honeysuckle

Women ♀

A Haven for Women Near the Sea

Come to *Honeysuckle* and enjoy the easygoing atmosphere at our popular Victorian inn and adjoining houses, Wisteria and Larkspur, near the Delaware beaches. Women feel at home in the comfortable spaces that our houses provide. Our sauna and outdoor hot tub are year-round favorites. In summer, stroll our porches, decks and gardens to the large in-ground pool with privacy fencing. Snuggle by the fireside in winter. VCRs, stereos, games, a canoe and our library of women's books and music will keep you busy between trips to the beaches, restaurants and outlet malls.

Address: 330 Union St, Milton, DE 19968. Tel: (302) 684-3284

Type: Inn & 2 adjoining houses.
Clientele: Women only.
Transportation: Car is best.
To Gay Bars: 12 miles to Rehoboth gay/lesbian bars.
Rooms: 3 rooms & 2 private rental houses with double or queen beds. Each private house accommodates up to 4 people.
Bathrooms: 1 private bath/whirlpool tub. Others shared. Outdoor shower by pool.
Meals: Full breakfast at inn only.
Vegetarian: Upon request.
Complimentary: Coffee and teas.
Dates Open: All year.
High Season: Summer (June through September).
Rates: $80-$150.
Discounts: 10% for 7 days or more.
Credit Cards: MC & VISA.
Rsv'tns: Required.
Reserve Through: Call direct.
Minimum Stay: On holiday weekends only.
Parking: Ample free off-street parking.
In-Room: Inn: self-controlled AC/heat & one room with whirlpool in bath. Houses: AC/heat & one bathroom has whirlpool/massage.
On-Premises: TV lounge & kitchens.
Exercise/Health: Weights, sauna, outdoor hot tub & whirlpool in private baths. Massage available.
Swimming: Pool on premises.
Sunbathing: At poolside or on the beaches.
Nudity: Permitted poolside.
Smoking: Permitted outdoors.
Pets: Not permitted, excellent kennel nearby.
Handicap Access: 1 house available with 1st floor bedroom/bath.
Children: Not permitted.
Languages: English.

REHOBOTH BEACH

Guest Rooms at Rehoboth & Southside Suites

Take a Memory Home
Gay/Lesbian ♀♂

Guest Rooms & Southside Suites are two newly-decorated Victorian houses. The *Guest Rooms* is a distinctive 5-bedroom cottage with a spacious outer deck. Each room features period furniture, from Victorian to Art Deco, which may be purchased. The *Southside Suites* are located one block from the beaches and have a tropical atmosphere. Spoil yourself on our front verandah while enjoying the ocean breezes. Both accommodations include off-street parking, continental breakfast, color cable TV and workout room with hot tub.

Address: 45 Baltimore Ave & 44 Delaware Ave, Rehoboth Beach, DE 19971. Tel: (302) 227-8355

Type: Bed & breakfast guesthouses.
Clientele: Good mix of gays & lesbians.
Transportation: Free pick up from bus & ferry dock. Bus stops 1 block away. Ferry is 10 minutes away.
To Gay Bars: 5 houses from the Blue Moon.
Rooms: 9 doubles & 3 apartments.
Bathrooms: 3 private, others share.

Meals: Expanded continental breakfast.
Complimentary: Set-up service, coffee.
Dates Open: All year.
High Season: May 31 (Memorial Day) thru Sept 1 (Labor Day).
Rates: Summer $95-$165, fall/spring $75-$125, winter $60-$100.
Discounts: Discount with free dinner at a restaurant during off-season.

Credit Cards: MC, VISA, Amex & Discover.
Rsv'tns: Required.
Reserve Through: Call direct.
Minimum Stay: Required.
Parking: Off-street parking.
In-Room: Color TV, AC, refrigerator & maid service.
On-Premises: Meeting rooms.
Exercise/Health:

Weights & Jacuzzi on premises.
Swimming: 1 block to ocean.
Sunbathing: On private sun decks or at the beach.
Smoking: Both houses are non-smoking.
Pets: Not permitted.
Handicap Access: No.
Children: Not permitted.
Languages: English.

Mallard Guest Houses, The

Rehoboth's newest Quaze!
Gay/Lesbian ♀♂

The Mallard Guest Houses provide comfortable accommodations in this quaint Atlantic seashore community nestled just south of Delaware Bay. We have bicycles available so that you can enjoy a warm afternoon riding along the beach or visiting our town's many attractions. Enjoy the best of Rehoboth, while staying at the best in Rehoboth.

Address: 67 Lake Ave, Rehoboth Beach, DE 19971. Tel: (302) 226-3448

Type: Guesthouses. Three locations in Rehoboth.
Clientele: Gay & lesbian. Good mix of men & women.
Transportation: Car is best.
To Gay Bars: 1/2 block.
Rooms: 20 rooms.
Bathrooms: 9 private & others share.
Meals: Continental

breakfast.
Complimentary: Coffee & tea.
Dates Open: All year.
High Season: Memorial Day-Labor Day.
Rates: $45-$120.
Credit Cards: MC, VISA.
Rsv'tns: Required.
Reserve Through: Travel agent or call direct.
Parking: Adequate off-street parking.

On-Premises: TV lounge.
Exercise/Health: Bicycles. Hot tub planned.
Swimming: 2 blocks to ocean beach.
Sunbathing: On private sun decks & at beach.
Smoking: Permitted in

designated areas. All rooms are non-smoking.
Pets: Not permitted.
Handicap Access: Not fully accessible.
Languages: English.

IGTA

Rams Head Inn

Men ♂

Friendly and inviting, *The Rams Head Inn* is uniquely surrounded by fields and forests, not crowds and traffic, yet it's close to the beach, bars, restaurants and shops. Enjoy breakfast in the light-drenched screened breakfast room, relax by the pool with sunning patio, soak in the hot tub, tone up in the full-sized gym with a 10-person sauna, mingle during our hospitality hour with select bar specials, or just relax and read in the library. Each guest room has a queen-sized bed, cable TV, VCR, refrigerator, hairdryer and central air conditioning.
Address: RD 2 Box 509, Rehoboth Beach, DE 19971-9702. Tel: (302) 226-9171.

Type: Bed & breakfast.
Clientele: Men only.
Transportation: Car is best. Pick up at Salisbury/Wicomico airport.
To Gay Bars: 2 miles to gay/lesbian bar.
Rooms: 1 economy room, 3 deluxe rooms & 3 superior rooms, all with queen beds.
Bathrooms: 6 private shower/toilets & 1 shared tub/shower.
Meals: Expanded continental breakfast.
Complimentary: Full service bar between 2pm-4pm.
Dates Open: April-October.
High Season: Memorial Day-Labor Day.
Rates: In season $90-$130. Call for off-season rates.
Credit Cards: MC, VISA & Discover.
Rsv'tns: Required.
Reserve Through: Call direct.
Minimum Stay: 2 days in season, 3 days on holidays.
Parking: Ample, free off-street parking.
In-Room: Maid service, color cable TV, VCR, video tape library, refrigerator & hairdryer.
On-Premises: Full service bar, fireplace & library.
Exercise/Health: Full gym with sauna, Jacuzzi & hot tub.
Swimming: Heated pool on premises, ocean beach 3 miles.
Sunbathing: At poolside & on the beach.
Nudity: Permitted poolside & in spa & sauna area.
Smoking: Permitted without restriction.
Pets: No permitted.
Handicap Access: No.
Children: Not permitted.
Languages: English.
Your Host: Jim & Carl.

Rehoboth Guest House

Gay/Lesbian ♀♂

The *Rehoboth Guest House* is a charming Victorian beach house 1-1/2 blocks from the beach. You can feel at home in one of our 12 airy, white-washed rooms with large windows and painted floors. Relax over continental breakfast in the sun room or rock on the flower-lined front porch. Enjoy one of our sun decks or bask on nearby gay beaches. Also enjoy enclosed outdoor cedar showers, Saturday evening wine and cheese get-togethers, or explore the nearby shops, restaurants and bars. Whether you are taking a long vacation or grabbing a weekend, you will always feel relaxed and welcome at the *Rehoboth Guest House.*
Address: 40 Maryland Ave, Rehoboth, DE 19971. Tel: (302) 227-4117.

Type: Bed & breakfast guesthouse.
Clientele: Mostly gay & lesbian with some hetero clientele.
Transportation: Car is best or "beach bus" to/from Washington, DC.
To Gay Bars: 1 block.
Rooms: 12 rooms & 1 apartment that sleeps 4. Single or double beds.
Bathrooms: 4 shared baths, 2 shared half baths, 1 private half bath.
Meals: Continental breakfast.
Complimentary: Wine & cheese in backyard or living room on Sat eves.
Dates Open: All year.
High Season: May-October.
Rates: Sept 16-May 15, $45-$55; May 16-Sept 15, $55-$90; Apartment $125-$150.
Discounts: Special rates for Sun-Thur stays.
Credit Cards: MC, VISA.
Rsv'tns: Required.
Reserve Through: Travel agent or call direct.
Minimum Stay: 2 nights weekends, holiday weekends 3 nights.
Parking: Some rooms with free off-street parking, limited free on-street parking.
In-Room: AC, some rooms with ceiling fans.
On-Premises: 2 sun decks, front porch with rockers, 2 picnic tables in backyard, 2 outdoor, enclosed showers/dressing rooms with hot water.
Exercise/Health: Gym a few blocks away on boardwalk.
Swimming: 1-1/2 blocks to beach, short walk to gay beaches.
Sunbathing: On common sun decks or at the beach.
Smoking: Permitted without restrictions. Prefer that guests smoke on porch or decks.
Pets: Not permitted.
Handicap Access: No.
Children: Not permitted.
Languages: English.

Renegade Resort

Gay/Lesbian ♂

The *Renegade Resort* has 28 rooms, a restaurant, bar and a visitor information center. The *Renegade* is near the beach and also has a swimming pool on the premises. Enjoy our high-tech dance club, hi-energy bar, 2nd level mezzanine balcony, new light show and high-powered sound system for your dancing pleasure. The *Renegade* is the best place in Rehoboth to catch live track acts and has both the best in exotic male dancers and video lounge and comedy club entertainment. There are different Theme Parties every weekend. The pool is open daily to the public. Each summer the *Renegade* serves as host to the Rehoboth Gay Pride festival. Treat yourself.

Address: Rte 1, Box 11, 4274 Hwy 1, Rehoboth Beach, DE 19971. Tel: (302) 227-1222, (302) 227-4713, Fax: (302) 227-4281.

Type: Motel with restaurant, dance bar & visitor information center.
Clientele: Mostly men with women welcome.
To Gay Bars: Gay/lesbian bar on premises.
Rooms: 28 doubles.
Bathrooms: All private.
Meals: Continental breakfast.

Dates Open: All year.
High Season: Memorial Day-Labor Day.
Rates: Call for rates.
Discounts: On weekly stays or longer.
Credit Cards: VISA & MC.
Rsv'tns: Required in high season.
Reserve Through: Call direct.

Minimum Stay: 3 nights on Memorial & Labor Day weekends.
Parking: Ample free off-street parking.
In-Room: Color TV, AC, maid service & telephone.
Swimming: Public pool on premises or ocean beach (1 mile).
Sunbathing: At poolside

or on ocean beach.
Smoking: Permitted without restrictions.
Pets: Small pets permitted with a $25 deposit.
Handicap Access: Yes.
Children: Permitted in motel. Not permitted in the bar or pool area.
Languages: English.
Your Host: Wayne.

Silver Lake

"Gem of the Delaware Shore"

Gay/Lesbian ♀♂

There is nothing quite like *Silver Lake*, the "gem of the Delaware shore", as described by *The Washington Post*. Located in a tranquil setting in the midst of a waterfowl preserve on Rehoboth Beach's most scenic drive, this beautiful home offers its guests much more than a conventional bed and breakfast. It is also the resort's closest

guesthouse to gay Poodle Beach, and is just a short walk to the best restaurants, shops and clubs.

The spectacular lake and ocean view from the main house's sprawling columned veranda along with a beautifully landscaped garden provide an inviting introduction to *Silver Lake*. Inside, the reception room reflects cool, clean comfort. The off-white walls serve as a crisp backdrop for the beautiful view, contemporary furnishings and original art on display throughout the house.

All the bedrooms at *Silver Lake* have private tiled baths with full-sized tubs and showers, cable TV and central air conditioning. Some of the rooms have

continued next page

panoramas of the lake and ocean beyond, while others look out on the numerous varieties of pine and evergreen surrounding the property.

Guests may enjoy breakfast quietly in their rooms, on the veranda or patio, or in the second floor sunroom with its comfortable antique rattan furniture and original pine paneling. Here, too, the lake and dunes are on full display. Breakfast includes muffins baked daily, an assortment of fresh fruit, juice, tea, coffee, along daily newspapers.

Behind the main house is the Carriage House with its very private, large two-bedroom apartments. Each has a private entrance, living room and dining area, complete kitchen and queen beds in the bedrooms.

Silver Lake is about quality of life. Whether for a weekend or extended vacation, guests enjoy an ambience of comfort and relaxation in the midst of nature at its best.

Address: 133 Silver Lake Dr, Rehoboth Beach, DE 19971. Tel: (302) 226-2115, (800) 842-2115.

Type: Bed & breakfast guesthouse.
Clientele: Gay & lesbian. Good mix of men & women.
Transportation: Car is best.
To Gay Bars: Walking distance.
Rooms: 11 rooms & 2 two-bedroom apartments with double, queen or king beds.
Bathrooms: All private.
Meals: Expanded continental breakfast.

Complimentary: Tea, coffee, juices & fruit.
Dates Open: All year.
High Season: Summer.
Rates: In season $80-$150, off season from $50.
Discounts: For longer stays.
Credit Cards: MC, VISA & Amex.
Rsv'tns: Required.
Reserve Through: Call direct.
Minimum Stay: 2 nights on summer weekends.

Parking: Ample, free off-street parking.
In-Room: Color cable TV, AC, maid service, kitchens in apartments.
On-Premises: Meeting rooms, kitchenette, sun room, lounge, BBQ grills, beach chairs & towels, outdoor shower, lake front lawn & gardens. Business services.
Exercise/Health: On jogging & biking course. Gym nearby.
Swimming: 5-minute

walk to gay ocean beach.
Sunbathing: On the beach.
Smoking: Permitted.
Pets: Permitted in apartments only.
Handicap Access: Yes, call for details.
Children: Not permitted except by prior arrangement.
Languages: English.
Your Host: Joe & Mark

DISTRICT OF COLUMBIA

WASHINGTON

Brenton, The

Gay/Lesbian ♂

Dating from 1891, *The Brenton* is located in the Dupont Circle neighborhood, 12 blocks north of the White House. Rooms are spacious and well-appointed, with antiques, art and Oriental carpets on handsome wood floors. The rooms are air conditioned, have direct-dial phones and most have ceiling fans. In the European tradition, the baths are shared, and the ultra-firm beds have colorful linens and feather pillows. The cozy front parlor welcomes you to relax with new friends and the staff encourages questions about local sights, activities and dining. Make yourself at home, and enjoy Washington as the locals do.

Address: 1708 16th St NW, Washington, DC 20009. Tel: (202) 332-5550 or (800) 673-9042.

Type: Guesthouse.
Clientele: Mostly men with women welcome.
Transportation: Metro to Dupont Circle, then short walk.
To Gay Bars: 2 blocks to gay bar.
Rooms: 8 rooms with single, double, queen or king beds.
Bathrooms: 3 shared bath/shower/toilets, 1 shared toilet.
Meals: Expanded continental breakfast.
Complimentary: Cocktail hour in evening, coffee, tea, always.
Dates Open: All year.
High Season: March through October.
Rates: $69-$99.
Credit Cards: MC, VISA, Amex & Discover.
Rsv'tns: Recommended.
Reserve Through: Travel agent or call direct.
Parking: Limited on-street pay parking.
In-Room: Maid service, telephone, AC, ceiling fans.
On-Premises: Dining rooms, TV lounge.
Exercise/Health: Nearby gym.
Smoking: Permitted without restrictions.
Pets: Not permitted.
Handicap Access: No.
Children: Not permitted.
Languages: English.
Your Host: Bob.

IGTA

Capitol Hill Guest House

Gay-Friendly 50/50 ♀♂

Capitol Hill Guest House is a Victorian row house with original woodwork and appointments, ideally located in the historic Capitol Hill district. Formerly home to congressional pages, the house has ten moderately-priced rooms with the flavor of a bygone era. We're a short walk from the Capitol and the mall, close to the Eastern Market and fine restaurants. Whether for business or pleasure, the convenience and charm of our house will make your stay comfortable and fun.

Address: 101 Fifth St NE, Washington, DC 20002. Tel: (202) 547-1050.

Type: Bed & breakfast guest house.
Clientele: 50% gay & lesbian & 50% straight clientele. Gay owned & operated.
Transportation: Taxi from airport, metro from Union Station.
To Gay Bars: 6-7 blocks to men's or women's bars.
Rooms: 10 rooms with single, double or queen beds.
Bathrooms: 3 shared bath/shower/toilets.
Meals: Continental breakfast.
Vegetarian: Available at nearby restaurants.
Complimentary: Sherry in living room.
Dates Open: All year.
High Season: Spring & fall.
Rates: $45-$85.
Discounts: For senior citizens.
Credit Cards: VISA, MC, Amex (with surcharge), Discover.
Rsv'tns: Recommended.
Reserve Through: Travel agent or call direct.
Parking: Adequate, free, on-street parking, permits provided.
In-Room: B&W TV for fee.
On-Premises: Refrigerator in the hall.
Swimming: 6 blocks to indoor public pool.
Smoking: Permitted on porch or in backyard.
Pets: Not permitted.
Handicap Access: No.
Children: Permitted, if over 8 years.
Languages: English, American Sign Language.
Your Host: Mark.

Embassy Inn

Gay-Friendly ♀♂

The Embassy Inn is a charming, gay-friendly B&B on historical 16th St. We offer a relaxing, friendly atmosphere and convenience to metro stops, restaurants, grocery store and nightlife. You'll enjoy personalized service, continental breakfast, and evening sherry, as you relax in the warm lobby with a great selection of books and magazines. Our staff is always happy to help with dining suggestions, tourist information or directions. The inn is a great value and is easily accessible to all of Washington's sights. The neighborhood is quaint and offers something for everyone.

Address: 1627 16th St, Washington, DC. **Tel:** (202) 234-7800 or (800) 423-9111, **Fax:** (202) 234-3309.

Type: Hotel inn.
Clientele: Mostly straight clientele with a gay & lesbian following.
Transportation: Taxi from airport. Metro Red line from Union Station to Dupont Circle, then 4-1/2 blocks to inn.
To Gay Bars: 2 blocks to men's bar, 5 blocks to Dupont Circle gay & lesbian bars.
Rooms: 38 rooms with single & double beds.
Bathrooms: All private shower/toilets.
Meals: Expanded continental breakfast.
Complimentary: Evening sherry year-round, coffee/tea 24 hours.
Dates Open: All year.
High Season: April, May & September.
Rates: High season $69-$99, low season $50-$79.
Discounts: On extended stays, weekend rates, government (business) travel, based on availability.
Credit Cards: MC, VISA, Amex, Carte Blanche & Diner's.
Rsv'tns: Preferred.
Reserve Through: Travel agent or call direct.
Parking:]Limited on-street parking, 24-hr pay garage 8 blocks away.
In-Room: Telephone, color TV, AC, maid service.
On-Premises: Dry cleaning service & TV lounge.
Smoking: Not permitted in main lobby. Non-smoking rooms available.
Pets: Not permitted.
Handicap Access: No.
Children: Permitted.
Languages: English, German & Spanish.

Guest House, The

Gay/Lesbian ♀♂

Come to the Mountains 2-1/2 Hours from Washington, DC

Our *Guest House* sits high above the Lost River Valley at the edge of a national forest. Extensive views and absolute privacy provide our guests the peace and quiet they deserve. In our main lodge, guests tend to gather around the immense native stone fireplace. Another living room is surrounded by windows with views of the mountains and valley. There are wraparound porches at treetop level. Ladderback rockers are everywhere. After arrival, soak away your city tensions in our indoor hot tub. By morning, you'll be in a mountain frame of mind. Breakfasts are served family-style, with fresh fruit, yogurt and traditional country fare.

The house holds thirteen spacious rooms with private baths, central air conditioning and a heated pool. Such outdoor activities as white water rafting, rock climbing, hiking, horseback riding, canoeing and fishing are all available in the

area. The one-million-acre George Washington National Forest is adjacent to the property. Rockcliff Lake and Lost River State park are nearby.
Address: Settlers Valley Way, Lost River, WV 26811. Tel: (304) 897-5707, Fax: 897-5707.

Type: Bed & breakfast guesthouse.
Clientele: Mostly gay & lesbian with some straight clientele.
Transportation: Car is best.
To Gay Bars: 2-1/2 hours to Washington, DC, or Richmond, VA, gay bars.
Rooms: 13 rooms & 1 cottage with single, double or queen beds.
Bathrooms: All private shower/toilets.

Meals: Full breakfast. Group dinners arranged with prior notice.
Vegetarian: Available.
Complimentary: Tea, coffee, juices, wine & beer.
Dates Open: All year.
High Season: April through November.
Rates: $65-$85.
Discounts: For senior citizens, AARP.
Credit Cards: MC, VISA & Diners.

Rsv'tns: Suggested.
Reserve Through: Call direct.
Parking: Ample free off-street parking.
In-Room: AC, ceiling fans, telephone & maid service.
On-Premises: Private dining rooms, TV lounge, meeting rooms. Main house has kitchen, 2 large living rooms with fireplaces. 3000 sq ft lodge open to guests.

Exercise/Health: Indoor hot tub. Outdoor Jacuzzi.
Swimming: Pool on premises. River & lake nearby.
Sunbathing: At poolside.
Smoking: Permitted without restrictions.
Pets: Not permitted.
Handicap Access: No.
Children: Not permitted.
Languages: English & French.
Your Host: Bob & Bill.

Kalorama Guest House at Kalorama Park

Gay-Friendly ♀♂

The Kalorama Guest House is the place to call home when you are in D.C. We are located on a quiet, tree-lined street, only a short walk from two of Washington's most trendy neighborhoods, Dupont Circle and Adams Morgan. You'll be near a potpourri of bars, ethnic restaurants, nightspots, antique shops and the underground metro. After staying in a bedroom decorated tastefully with Victorian antiques and enjoying a continental breakfast, an evening aperitif and our nationally-known hospitality, we're sure you'll make our house your home whenever you visit Washington. If you prefer a smaller, more intimate guest house, please inquire abour our other property, *Kalorama Guest House at Woodley Park.*
Address: 1854 Mintwood Pl NW, Washington, DC 20009. Tel: (202) 667-6369.

Type: Bed & breakfast.
Clientele: Gay-friendly establishment. Mostly straight clientele with a gay & lesbian following.
Transportation: Taxi or subway are best.
To Gay Bars: 4 blocks to men's bars at Dupont Circle.
Rooms: 29 rooms & 2 suites with double or queen beds.
Bathrooms: 12 private, 19 rooms share (2-3 rooms per bath).

Meals: Continental breakfast.
Complimentary: Sherry in parlor (afternoon aperitif), lemonade in summer.
Dates Open: All year.
High Season: Mar-Jun & Sep-Oct.
Rates: Rooms $50-$95, suites $80-$115.
Discounts: AAA.
Credit Cards: MC, VISA, Amex, Diners.
Reserve Through: Travel agent or call direct.

Minimum Stay: 2 nights required occasionally.
Parking: Pay parking off-street and free on-street parking.
In-Room: AC, maid & laundry service. Some rooms with ceiling fans.
On-Premises: Meeting rooms, TV lounge, guest fridge, laundry facilities.
Exercise/Health: Gym with weights nearby.
Swimming: In nearby pool.
Sunbathing: On land-

scaped backyard.
Smoking: Discouraged in breakfast room. Non-smoking rooms available.
Pets: Not permitted.
Handicap Access: No.
Children: Prefer those over 10 years old.
Languages: English.
Your Host: Tammi & Rick.

IGTA

Take along the Expert

Ferrari's Places of Interest™ contains articles contributed by gay and lesbian journalists on the scene, giving insight into gay and lesbian communities worldwide. With its accompanying directory, it's the perfect vacation planner.

Little White House, The

Gay/Lesbian ♀♂

Country Comfort...City Convenience

Amid majestic oak trees on the east end of "America's Main Street," *The Little White House* offers spacious rooms with queen-sized beds and panoramic views of the Capitol Dome and the Washington Monument. A screened porch overlooking the large yard is perfect for relaxing after a hard day of business or sightseeing. The formal parlor and sitting room are available for small meetings or receptions. City buses, stopping a block away, offer direct service to the subway, the Capitol, the Smithsonian Museum and the "other" White House.

Address: 2909 Pennsylvania Ave SE, Washington, DC 20020. Tel: (202) 583-4074.

Type: Bed & breakfast.
Clientele: Gay & lesbian.
Transportation: Easy access by car to airport & interstates. On city bus lines, 1/2 mile to subway.
To Gay Bars: 1-1/2 miles to Capitol Hill gay & lesbian bars.
Rooms: 4 rooms with single, double or queen beds.
Bathrooms: 2 shared

bath/shower/toilets & 1 shared toilet.
Meals: Expanded continental breakfast.
Vegetarian: Available upon request with at least 48 hours notice.
Dates Open: All year.
Rates: $69.
Discounts: IGTA members.
Credit Cards: MC, VISA & Amex.

Rsv'tns: Required.
Reserve Through: Travel agent or call direct.
Minimum Stay: 2 nights on weekends & holidays.
Parking: Ample free off-street parking.
In-Room: AC, ceiling fans, coffee & tea-making facilities & maid service.
On-Premises: TV lounge with VCR & movie collec-

tion, meeting rooms, extensive library.
Smoking: Permitted on porches only. All rooms are non-smoking.
Pets: Not permitted.
Handicap Access: No.
Children: Not especially welcomed.
Languages: English.
Your Host: Larry & Bill.

IGTA

Windsor Inn

Gay-Friendly ♀♂

A Relaxing Oasis in Washington

A relaxed atmosphere and personalized service typify *The Windsor Inn*, a charming art deco-style bed and breakfast on historical 16th Street, convenient to the metro and a variety of restaurants. We're happy to help with dining suggestions, tourist information, etc. Rooms are comfortable and pleasantly decorated. Our nine suites have beautiful ceiling borders and a basket of special soaps and shampoo, extra-thick towels and small refrigerators. The *Windsor* is also close to nightlife and sights. We are a friendly alternative to the larger convention hotels.

Address: 1842 16th St NW, Washington, DC 20009. Tel: (202) 667-0300, (800) 423-9111, Fax: (202) 667-4503.

Type: Hotel inn.
Clientele: Mostly straight clientele with a gay & lesbian following.
Transportation: Taxi from airport. From Union Station take metro red

line to Dupont Circle, then walk 5-1/2 blocks.
To Gay Bars: 3 blocks to men's bars & 5 blocks to gay & lesbian bars.
Rooms: 44 rooms & 2 suites with single, double

or queen beds.
Bathrooms: All private.
Meals: Expanded continental breakfast & evening sherry.
Complimentary: Sherry in lobby all year, coffee

& tea 24 hours.
Dates Open: All year.
High Season: April, May & September.
Rates: High season $69-$150, low season $50-$99.

Discounts: On extended stays, govt. ID, weekend rates (space-available). **Credit Cards:** MC, VISA, Amex, Diners, Carte Blanche. **Rsv'tns:** Preferred.

Reserve Through: Travel agent or call direct. **Parking:** On-street parking, some limitations. **In-Room:** Maid service, telephone, color TV, AC, refrigerator in 2 suites &

7 rooms. Laundry service. **On-Premises:** Small conference room, same-day laundry service, dry cleaning. **Smoking:** Lobby non-smoking. Non-smoking

rooms available. **Pets:** Not permitted. **Handicap Access:** No. **Children:** Permitted. **Languages:** English, limited Spanish & French.

Wm. Lewis House, The

Gay/Lesbian ♀♂

Built just after the turn of the century in 1904, this classically inspired house has been painstakingly restored to it's original grandeur. *The Wm. Lewis House* is a warm and charming reflection of the quality of a bygone era. Relax in the gilded parlor or richly paneled dining room in front of one of four working fireplaces. The spacious rooms are appointed with family heirlooms and antique carpets. This convenient location is close to the nightlife, theatres, and restaurants of Dupont Circle, 17th St., Adams Morgan and U St., and not far from the Mall. Three different Metro lines are within walking distance.

**Address: 1309 R St NW, Washington, DC .
Tel: (202) 667-4019 or (202) 462-7574.**

Type: Bed & breakfast. **Clientele:** Good mix of gays & lesbians. **Transportation:** Metro to U St or Dupont Circle, then a short walk. **To Gay Bars:** 4 blocks. A 5-minute walk. **Rooms:** 4 rooms & 1 apartment with double beds. **Bathrooms:** 2 shared bath/shower/toilets. 1 shared WC/toilet. **Meals:** Continental

breakfast. **Vegetarian:** Many vegetarian restaurants nearby. **Complimentary:** Coffee, tea & snacks. **Dates Open:** All year. **Rates:** $65-$85. Apartment $120. **Discounts:** On extended stays. **Credit Cards:** MC & VISA. **Rsv'tns:** Required. **Reserve Through:** Call direct.

Parking: Adequate on-street parking. Permits provided. **In-Room:** Ceiling fans, telephone & maid service. **On-Premises:** Laundry facilities. **Exercise/Health:** Nearby gym. **Swimming:** Nearby pool. **Sunbathing:** In nearby

parks. **Smoking:** Permitted in garden only. **Pets:** Not permitted. **Handicap Access:** No. **Children:** Welcome if over 8 years. Must be supervised. **Languages:** English. **Your Host:** Theron & Dave.

FLORIDA

AMELIA ISLAND

Amelia Island Williams House

Gay-Friendly ♀♂

An Historic Bed & Breakfast with a Heritage of Elegance

This elegant Antebellum mansion was built in the grand style in 1856 by a wealthy Boston banker. As the town's most historic home, featuring some of the most outstanding architectural details in Fernandina, it is the perfect setting for the owner's extensive Oriental art and antique collection. The four superb guest suites include a regal anniversary suite, with original Napoleonic antiques, for that "special occasion." Breakfast is served in the opulent red and gold dining room.

From your base at *Amelia Island Williams House,* enjoy 13 miles of unspoiled beaches, horseback riding, golf, tennis, fishing and shopping in restored historic downtown. See the back cover for two full-color photos of the inn.

Address: 103 S 9th St, Amelia Island, FL 32034. Tel: (904) 277-2328.

Type: Bed & Breakfast.
Clientele: Mainly straight clientele with a gay & lesbian following.
Transportation: Car. 30 minutes from Jacksonville International Airport.
To Gay Bars: 45-minute drive.
Rooms: 4 rooms with king or queen beds.
Bathrooms: All private.
Meals: Expanded continental breakfast.

Vegetarian: No meat served at breakfast. Will cook for dairy allergies.
Complimentary: Wine & cheese in afternoon.
Dates Open: All year.
High Season: Summer.
Rates: $95-$135 per night.
Credit Cards: MC & VISA.
Rsv'tns: Required.
Reserve Through: Travel agent or call direct.
Minimum Stay: Required

during special events weekends.
Parking: Ample off-street & on-street parking.
In-Room: Color cable TV, video tape library, VCR, AC, ceiling fans & maid service.
Exercise/Health: Massage on call.
Swimming: Nearby ocean.
Sunbathing: At the beach.

Smoking: Not permitted in house. Permitted on porch & in courtyard only.
Pets: Not permitted. Pet boarding service available at vet's or in private home.
Handicap Access: No.
Children: Not especially welcome. 12 years & up OK.
Languages: English.

BOCA RATON

Floresta Historic Bed & Breakfast

Gay/Lesbian ♀♂

Floresta is a historic home built in 1923 in the Spanish-Mediterranean tradition. Located in a very safe, residential neighborhood, it's a great area for touring by bike (bikes are available to our guests with a deposit) or by foot.

Our guests occupy a very private, detached guest house. Lush landscaping and our own citrus trees surround the private pool. If you prefer, there is a gay beach just 1-1/2 miles away. *Floresta* is just 5 minutes to the beach by car or 15 minutes by bike. Boca Raton is 20 minutes away from West Palm Beach and less than an hour from South Beach/Miami.

Address: 755 Alamanda St, Boca Raton, FL 33486. Tel: (407) 391-1451.

Type: Bed & breakfast guesthouse.
Clientele: Gay & lesbian. Good mix of men &

women.
Transportation: Car is best. 30 min from Palm Beach by shuttle bus,

1 hr from Miami.
To Gay Bars: One mile or 5 minutes by car, 20 minutes by foot.

Rooms: 2 rooms & 1 cottage with queen beds.
Bathrooms: All private.
Meals: Continental

breakfast.
Complimentary: Fresh orange & grapefruit when trees are in bloom.
Dates Open: All year.
High Season: From Christmas to Easter.
Rates: $55-$125 year-round.
Discounts: Available,

please inquire.
Rsv'tns: Preferred.
Reserve Through: Call direct.
Parking: Ample free off-street parking.
In-Room: Color cable TV, VCR & ceiling fans.
On-Premises: TV lounge & laundry facilities.

Exercise/Health: Bikes available with deposit.
Swimming: Pool on premises. Nearby ocean, lake & Intracoastal Waterway.
Sunbathing: At poolside or on patio.
Nudity: Permitted poolside.

Smoking: Permitted outdoors only.
Pets: Call ahead.
Handicap Access: No.
Children: Call ahead.
Languages: English.
Your Host: Wayne & Paul.

DAYTONA BEACH

Buccaneer Motel

Gay/Lesbian ♀♂

Here on Daytona's famous Atlantic Avenue, *Buccaneer Motel* is situated across the street from 23 miles of beach. Each room is decorated with mementos from the innkeepers' buccaneering days. Guests in our second-level rooms have the added advantage of waking to an incredible view of the Atlantic Ocean sunrise. Within a few blocks, there is a vast array of fine dining, shopping plazas, fast food and evening entertainment. Rental bikes are available for use on the many nearby trails. Fishing, boating and other water activities are all available close by. **Address: 2301 N Atlantic Ave, Daytona Beach, FL 32118. Tel: (904) 253-9678 or (800) 972-6056.**

Type: Small motel.
Clientele: Mostly gay & lesbian with some straight clientele.
Transportation: Car is best. Call ahead for free transport from & to airport, bus, or train. Taxi service locally.
To Gay Bars: 1-3/4 mi to 2 mi.
Rooms: 8 rooms, 7 suites, 4 apartments & 1 cottage with double, queen or king beds.
Bathrooms: All private.
Vegetarian: Numerous restaurants & grocery stores within walking

distance.
Complimentary: Coffee & tea in the lobby in morning.
Dates Open: All year.
High Season: Feb, March 'til mid April & Memorial Day through Labor Day.
Rates: $25-$55 low season. $45-$120 high season.
Discounts: Multi-night, 10% or $5 off per night except weekend only or holiday stays.
Credit Cards: MC, VISA, Discover & Eurocard.
Rsv'tns: Recommended.
Reserve Through: Travel

agent or call direct.
Minimum Stay: 6 nights for Daytona 500 in Feb, Bike Week in Mar, 4 nights for July 4th.
Parking: Ample free parking.
In-Room: Color cable TV, AC, telephones, maid service, ceiling fans, kitchen, refrigerator & room safes.
On-Premises: Laundry facilities & BBQ grill.
Exercise/Health: Bicycles to rent.
Swimming: Pool on premises. Nearby ocean beach & river. Natural

springs 30 mi.
Sunbathing: At poolside, on common sun decks, the patio or on the beach.
Smoking: Permitted without restrictions.
Pets: Small house pets welcome. Guests must pick up after pets.
Handicap Access: No, bathroom doors too narrow.
Children: Permitted.
Languages: English.
Your Host: Larry.

IGTA

Villa, The

Gay/Lesbian ♀♂

Live Like Royalty

Live like royalty in our national-register historical 17 room Spanish mansion, designed and constructed in 1929 by the finest craftsmen. A circular drive provides access to the mansion's entrance. The interior is richly detailed, particularly the public areas, and continues the Spanish style theme of the exterior. This mansion is one of the finest examples of Spanish Colonial Revival architecture in Volusia County, rivaling mansions in Miami and Palm Beach. Our guests appreciate the privacy provided by the secluded, walled garden, complete with swimming pool, private sun deck and elegant public areas. Stay in guest rooms named for nobility. The King Juan Carlos, Queen Isabella, Marco Polo, and Christopher Columbus Rooms are decorated with fine period antiques. Most rooms have a large balcony overlooking the pool and gardens. *The Villa*, located on over two acres of land, is within walking distance of Daytona's famous beach, restaurants, shopping and nightlife.

Address: 801 N Peninsula Dr, Daytona Beach, FL 32118. Tel: (904) 248-2020 or Fax: (904) 248-2020.

Type: Bed & breakfast.
Clientele: Mainly gay & lesbian with some straight clientele.
Transportation: Car or taxi. Pick up from airport or train can be arranged.
To Gay Bars: 12 blocks.
Rooms: 4 rooms with queen or king beds.
Bathrooms: All private.
Meals: Expanded continental breakfast & continental breakfast.
Complimentary: Tea, coffee & soft drinks.
Dates Open: All year.
High Season: Feb, Mar, Apr.
Rates: Off season $65-$135, in season $85-$185.
Discounts: Last night free on weekly stay.
Credit Cards: MC & VISA.
Rsv'tns: Required in most cases.
Reserve Through: Travel agent or call direct.
Minimum Stay: Required during peak season & special events.
Parking: Ample free off-street parking.
In-Room: Maid service, color TV, AC & ceiling fans.
On-Premises: TV lounge, use of refrigerator.
Exercise/Health: Nearby gym, weights & tanning salons.
Swimming: Pool on premises, 4 blocks to ocean beach.
Sunbathing: At poolside, on roof, private & common sun decks.
Nudity: Permitted on pool deck.
Smoking: Permitted outside only.
Pets: Not permitted.
Handicap Access: No.
Children: Not permitted.
Languages: English.

IGTA

ENGLEWOOD

Surf and Sand Apartments

Gay-Friendly 50/50 ♀♂

Walk Out the Door Into the Gulf of Mexico

Enjoy your dream vacation by the week, month or season at *Surf and Sand*, located on Manasota Key, just 30 miles from both Sarasota and Ft. Myers. We offer you the beautiful Gulf of Mexico right outside your front door, the gently rolling surf, a wide sandy beach and picturesque sunsets every evening. All of the apartments are completely furnished and have color TV, air conditioning and ceiling fans. **Address: 1120 Shoreview Dr, Manasota Key, Englewood, FL 34224. Reservations: (813) 697-7707 or (813) 474-5878.**

Type: Beachfront apartments.
Clientele: 50% gay & lesbian & 50% straight clientele.
Transportation: Car is best.
To Gay Bars: 30 miles.
Rooms: Apartments with single & king beds.
Bathrooms: All private

bath/toilets.
Dates Open: All year.
High Season: January thru April.
Rates: Jan-May $1500-$1600 per month. Summer $500 and up per month.
Rsv'tns: Required.
Reserve Through: Call direct.

Minimum Stay: 1 week.
Parking: Ample off-street parking.
In-Room: Color TV, AC, ceiling fans, kitchen, refrigerator, coffee & tea-making facilities.
Swimming: Ocean on premises.
Sunbathing: On the patio & at the beach.

Smoking: Permitted.
Pets: Small animals permitted.
Handicap Access: No.
Children: Allowed, but not especially welcome.
Languages: English.
Your Host: Cleo.

FT LAUDERDALE

Admiral's Court

Gay-Friendly 50/50 ♀♂

Guys Love it Here!!! Girls Love it Here!!!

Admiral's Court, a *Superior Small Lodging*, is located in the safe, exclusive Las Olas area, near the beach and nightlife. Enjoy luxury at reasonable rates in our tropical garden paradise set beside a picturesque canal. Since 1980, your hosts, Marc and Harry, have lovingly cared for this well-run, clean, quiet establishment. Relax on a lounge by one of our two pools or in your room with comfy king-sized bed, remote color cable TV, central AC, overhead paddle fan, refrigerator and private bath. Efficiencies and suites have full, separate kitchens. **Address: 21 Hendrick's Isle, Ft Lauderdale, FL 33301. Tel: (305) 462-5072, (800) 248-6669, Fax: (305) 763-8863.**

Type: Motel.
Clientele: Usually 75% gay & lesbian clientele.
Transportation: Taxi or auto is best transportation.
To Gay Bars: Six blocks to Cathode Ray on Las Olas Blvd.
Rooms: 11 rooms, 7 suites & 15 efficiencies with full kitchens. King beds.
Bathrooms: All private baths.
Dates Open: All year.

High Season: December 15th through Easter.
Rates: Summer $35-$95, fall $50-$100, winter $65-$130.
Discounts: Weekly rates, plus summer special: every 4th week free.
Credit Cards: MC, VISA, Amex, Discover.
Rsv'tns: Required.
Reserve Through: Travel agent or call direct.
Minimum Stay: None.
Parking: Adequate free off-street parking.

In-Room: Color cable TV, AC, telephone, maid service (in-season), kitchen (in efficiencies) & refrigerators (in all rooms).
On-Premises: Fishing from our dock, laundry facilities & BBQ area. Tropical gardens feature hybrid Hibiscus & Bougainvillaea.
Exercise/Health: Nearby gym, weights, sauna & steam.
Swimming: 2 pools, one heated, & ocean beach.

Sunbathing: On common sun deck, patio, beach, at poolside, or on our 225-foot dock.
Smoking: Permitted without restrictions.
Pets: Permitted with pet fee.
Handicap Access: No.
Children: Not especially welcome.
Languages: English, Spanish.
Your Host: Marc & Harry.
IGTA

King Henry Arms

Gay/Lesbian ♂

The Best Is Yet to Come: YOU!

King Henry Arms, with its friendly, home-like atmosphere and squeaky-clean accommodations, is just the place for that romantic getaway. Spend your days relaxing amidst the tropical foliage by our pool, or at the ocean beach, just 300 feet away. Enjoy your evenings at the many restaurants and clubs, before returning to the quiet comfort of your accommodations. Truly a jewel by the sea.

Address: 543 Breakers Ave, Ft. Lauderdale, FL 33304-4129. Tel: (305) 561-0039 or (800) 205-KING (5464).

Type: Motel.
Clientele: Mostly men with women welcome.
Transportation: Car or taxi from Ft. Lauderdale airport.
To Gay Bars: 2 miles to gay/lesbian bars.
Rooms: 4 rooms, 6 suites & 2 apartments with single, double or king beds.
Bathrooms: All private bath/toilet/showers.
Meals: Continental breakfast.

Vegetarian: Restaurants & stores nearby.
Dates Open: All year.
High Season: Winter months.
Rates: Spring thru fall $43-$57, winter $70-$90.
Discounts: 5% on 8-30 nights, 10% on 31-60 nights and 15% on 61 nights or more, plus summer specials.
Credit Cards: MC, VISA, Amex & Discover.
Rsv'tns: Prefer 1 month in advance, earlier in

season.
Reserve Through: Travel agent or call direct.
Minimum Stay: 7 nights in high season.
Parking: Adequate free off-street parking.
In-Room: Maid service, color cable TV, telephone, AC & refrigerators. Apartments & suites have kitchens.
On-Premises: Laundry facilities.
Exercise/Health: Gym nearby.

Swimming: Pool on premises, ocean beach nearby.
Sunbathing: At poolside, on beach or patio.
Smoking: Permitted without restrictions.
Pets: Not permitted.
Handicap Access: No.
Children: Not especially welcomed.
Languages: English.
Your Host: Don & Roy.

IGTA

Palms on Las Olas, The

Men ♂

Fort Lauderdale's Finest Guest Suites

Affordable luxury in classic fifties style await at *The Palms on Las Olas*. Spacious accommodations, ranging from simple hotel rooms to grand one-bedroom suites, include AC, remote control cable TV, telephones and, in season, a full continental breakfast. We're in the heart of "chic" Las Olas Boulevard, one mile from the beach, and close to shops, restaurants and bars. This is the most central, safe location available. Relax by the pool, or take a water taxi from our private dock and explore the canals and waterways of Old Fort Lauderdale.

Address: 1760 E Las Olas Blvd, Ft. Lauderdale, FL 33301. Tel: (305) 462-4178, (800) 550-POLO, Fax: (305) 463-8544.

Type: Guesthouse motel.
Clientele: Gay men only.
Transportation: Car is best.
To Gay Bars: 5 blocks or 1/2 mile. An 8-minute walk or 2-minute drive.
Rooms: 2 rooms, 5 suites, 1 cottage & 6 efficiencies with single, queen or king beds.
Bathrooms: All private.
Meals: Expanded continental breakfast, high

season only.
Dates Open: All year.
High Season: Dec-Apr.
Rates: Summer $55-$85, winter $75-$125.
Credit Cards: MC, VISA, Amex.
Rsv'tns: Requested.
Reserve Through: Travel agent or call direct.
Minimum Stay: 3 days during high season.
Parking: Ample free off-street parking.

In-Room: Color cable TV, AC, telephones, coffee/tea-making facilities, maid, room & laundry service. Efficiencies & apartments with full kitchens.
On-Premises: Laundry facilities & fax.
Exercise/Health: Nearby gym.
Swimming: Heated pool on premises, ocean nearby.

Sunbathing: At poolside & on common sun decks.
Nudity: Permitted poolside.
Smoking: Permitted.
Pets: Not permitted.
Handicap Access: No.
Children: Not especially welcome.
Languages: English.

IGTA

Royal Palms Resort, The

Five-Star Luxury Beneath Towering Palms

Men ♂

Welcome to the award-winning *Royal Palms Resort,* Fort Lauderdale's only 5-star accommodation for gay men. Come and experience our tropical paradise for that special vacation, where atmosphere, attention to detail and service are unequaled. At *The Royal Palms,* nestled beneath towering palms, all accommodations surround the secluded tropical garden, pool and sun deck, where a complimentary breakfast is served. We are within minutes of shops, bars and restaurants and two blocks from the the main Fort Lauderdale beach.

The Royal Palms was chosen as one of the top five gay accommodations in the United States by *Out & About Newsletter, July 1994,* and the city of Fort Lauderdale has awarded us "Hotel of the Year."

Address: 2901 Terramar St, Ft Lauderdale, FL 33304. Tel: (305) 564-6444 or Fax: (305) 564-6443.

Type: Hotel with bar.
Clientele: Men only.
Transportation: Car is best, but taxi service very good.
To Gay Bars: 3 miles (10 min drive).
Rooms: 10 rooms, 4 suites & 4 apartments with queen beds.
Bathrooms: All private.
Meals: Expanded continental breakfast.
Dates Open: All year.

High Season: Mid-December–May.
Rates: Summer $90-$130, winter $120-$180.
Credit Cards: MC, VISA & Amex.
Rsv'tns: Strongly recommended.
Reserve Through: Travel agent or call direct.
Minimum Stay: 3 days in high season.
Parking: Ample free off-street parking.

In-Room: Color cable TV, VCR, video tape library, AC, ceiling fans, telephone, kitchen, refrigerator, coffee/tea-making facilities & maid service.
Exercise/Health: Nearby gym, weights, Jacuzzi & sauna.
Swimming: Pool on premises, nearby ocean beach.
Sunbathing: At poolside,

on beach, patio, private sun decks.
Nudity: Permitted.
Smoking: Permitted.
Pets: Not permitted.
Children: Not permitted.
Languages: English, Spanish & French.
Your Host: Richard & Craig.

IGTA

JASPER

Swan Lake Bed & Breakfast

Gay/Lesbian ♂

Swan Lake Bed & Breakfast is located 15 miles south of the Georgia border near the Swanee River. It is 1.6 miles off Route 75 at exit 85, and 10 miles from Route 10. With 78.6 acres of private, wooded land, we have plenty of trails for hiking and horseback riding. In addition to human inhabitants, the land is populated by many breeds of swans, other waterfowl, pheasants, peacocks, sheep and goats. Most of the food served at the B&B is raised or grown on the premises.

Address: PO Box 1623, Jasper, FL 32052. Tel: (904) 792-2771

Type: Bed & breakfast.
Clientele: Mostly men with women welcome.
Transportation: Car is best. Free pick up from Jacksonville airport.
To Gay Bars: 38 miles to gay bar in Valdosta, GA.

Rooms: 1 single & 3 doubles.
Bathrooms: Shared.
Meals: Full breakfast.
Vegetarian: Always available.
Complimentary: Cocktails, beer, sodas & fruit juice.

Dates Open: All year.
Rates: Single $25, double $35.
Credit Cards: VISA.
Rsv'tns: Required.
Reserve Through: Call direct.
Parking: Ample free off-

street parking.
In-Room: Color TV, maid & laundry service.
On-Premises: TV lounge & laundry facilities.
Exercise/Health: Jacuzzi on premises.

continued next page

Swimming: Pool on premises.
Sunbathing: On common

sun decks & at poolside.
Nudity: Permitted.
Smoking: Permitted

without restrictions.
Pets: Permitted.
Handicap Access: No.

Children: Not permitted.
Languages: English.
Your Host: Jim & Jim.

KEY WEST

Big Ruby's Guesthouse

Gay/Lesbian ♂

On our quiet little lane, in peace and privacy, our three guesthouses, each in traditional historic design, stand secluded behind a tall fence. Inside *Big Ruby's*, luxury touches are everywhere. Immaculate rooms have sumptuous beds with four king-sized pillows and superthick bath sheets. Awaiting you outside are a beautiful lagoon pool, spacious decks and lounge areas in a tropical garden. Full breakfast is served at poolside. Evenings, we gather by the pool for wine and the easy companionability of good conversation. You'll never feel so welcome, so comfortable, so at home.

Address: 409 Appelrouth Lane, Key West, FL 33040-6534. Tel: (305) 296-2323 or (800) 477-7829.

Type: Guesthouse.
Clientele: Mostly men with women welcome.
Transportation: Fly to Key West, 15 min by cab (less than $12) to guesthouse.
To Gay Bars: Less than 1/2 block.
Rooms: 17 rooms with queen or king beds.
Bathrooms: Private: 12 shower/toilet, 3 full baths. 2 shared full baths.
Meals: Full breakfast every morning. Dinners on Christmas, New Year & Thanksgiving.

Complimentary: Wine each evening from 6pm-8pm except Sunday.
Dates Open: All year.
High Season: December 21-April 30.
Rates: Winter $110-$195, summer $69-$127.
Discounts: 10% on stays of 7 days or more between 5/1-12/20, excluding holidays.
Credit Cards: MC, VISA, Amex, Discover, Diners Club & Carte Blanche.
Rsv'tns: Recommended.
Reserve Through: Travel agent or call direct.

Minimum Stay: On holidays.
Parking: Limited off-street parking.
In-Room: Maid service, color cable TV, AC, Bahama fan, refrigerator, 4 king size pillows, huge, thick towels, laundry service, video library. Some rooms with VCR.
On-Premises: TV lounge, public telephone.
Exercise/Health: Rainforest (outdoor tropical shower). Nearby gym & massage.
Swimming: Pool, nearby

ocean beach.
Sunbathing: At poolside, on private or common sun decks, ocean beach.
Nudity: Permitted poolside & in sunning yard.
Smoking: Permitted without restrictions. 2 non-smoking rooms available.
Pets: Not permitted.
Handicap Access: Yes.
Children: Not permitted.
Languages: English.
Your Host: George & Frank.

IGTA

Blue Parrot Inn

Gay/Lesbian ♀♂

Major renovations completed in 1989 enhanced the 1884 charm displayed by this historical wooden conch-style guesthouse. *Blue Parrot Inn* is located in the quiet uptown Old Town area close to bars, restaurants, galleries and the newest shops. Enjoy our complimentary continental breakfast in a secluded tropical setting at poolside each morning. We welcome guests both gay and straight...adults only, please.

Address: 916 Elizabeth St, Key West, FL 33040. Tel: (305) 296-0033 or (800) 231-BIRD (2473).

Type: Guesthouse.
Clientele: Good mix of gay men & women with some straight clientele.
Transportation: Short taxi ride from airport.
To Gay Bars: 4-5 blocks to men's/women's bars.
Rooms: 10 rooms & 2 apartments with double or queen beds.
Bathrooms: All private.
Meals: Expanded conti-

nental breakfast.
Dates Open: All year.
High Season: Feb-Mar.
Rates: Summer $55-$95. Winter $95-$140.
Credit Cards: MC, VISA, Amex, Discover.
Rsv'tns: Recommended. 1-night deposit is refundable 2 wks before arrival, less 10% handling fee.
Reserve Through: Travel agent or call direct.

Minimum Stay: 3 days on holidays & peak periods.
Parking: Adequate on-street parking.
In-Room: Maid service, AC, color cable TV, refrigerator & ceiling fans.
Exercise/Health: Nearby gym, massage.
Swimming: Pool on premises. Ocean beach nearby.
Sunbathing: At poolside or

on common sun decks.
Nudity: Permitted on upper sun deck.
Smoking: Permitted without restrictions.
Pets: Not permitted.
Handicap Access: No.
Children: Not permitted.
Languages: English.

IGTA

Brass Key Guesthouse

The Only Thing Missing is You!

Gay/Lesbian ♂

Key West's premier gay and lesbian guesthouse offers attentive service and luxury accommodations in a traditional Conch-style setting of wide verandas, louvered plantation shutters and ceiling fans. Expansive sun decks, a sparkling heated pool and a whirlpool spa glisten within *The Brass Key's* private, hedged compound featuring flowering hibiscus, bouganvillaea, jasmine and seven varieties of exotic palms.

Located on a quiet street in the heart of Old Town's finest neighborhood, *The Brass Key* is surrounded by restored homes, galleries, restaurants and shops and is just minutes from the nightlife of world-famous Duval Street. The harborfront is but two blocks away, offering casual waterside restaurants and salty bars, as well as gay sailing excursions and seaplane adventures.

The fourteen guest rooms and one-bedroom suite at *The Brass Key* are light and airy, featuring handcrafted furniture and traditional antiques, tropical fabrics and local artworks. Each offers king/queen bed, air-conditioning, telephone, cable TV, hair dryer, Caswell-Massey toiletries, refrigerator and nightly turndown.

While the amenities and service of *The Brass Key* are first-class, the atmosphere is always friendly and laid-back: guests enjoy morning conversation during the breakfast buffet; later, many spend the day relaxing together in the sun chaises surrounding the pool. For the energetic, *The Brass Key* often arranges group charters for an afternoon snorkel cruise or sunset champagne sail. The evening's cocktail hour provides a further chance to share the day's exploits (and the previous night's misdeeds) and to finalize dinner and club plans.

The Brass Key has been featured by *The Advocate, Conde Nast Traveler,* Joy Williams' *The Florida Keys,* and was recently awarded *Out & About's* highest rating ("Four Stars - Highly Recommended"). Join us soon and let our staff and guests welcome you to the native warmth and exotic verve of the Caribbean.

Address: 412 Frances St, Key West, FL 33040. Tel: (305) 296-4719, (800) 932-9119, Fax: (305) 296-1994.

Type: Bed & breakfast guesthouse.
Clientele: Mostly men with women welcome.
Transportation: Airport pick up $6.
To Gay Bars: 5-7 blocks to gay & lesbian bars.
Rooms: 14 rooms & 1 suite with queen or king beds.
Bathrooms: All private.
Meals: Expanded continental breakfast.
Complimentary: Afternoon cocktails.

Dates Open: All year.
High Season: Mid-December–mid-April.
Rates: Summer, $75-$140. Winter, $130-$215.
Credit Cards: MC, VISA & Amex.
Rsv'tns: Highly recommended.
Reserve Through: Travel agent or call direct.
Minimum Stay: Required holidays, special events.
Parking: Ample free on-street parking.
In-Room: AC, ceiling

fans, telephone (free local calls), color cable TV with remote, hair dryer, refrigerator, maid & turndown service.
On-Premises: Spacious living room with breakfast area.
Exercise/Health: Whirlpool spa on premises & gym nearby. Bicycles at guesthouse.
Swimming: Heated pool on premises. Ocean beach half mile.
Sunbathing: At poolside

or on sun decks.
Nudity: Permitted on rooftop sun deck.
Smoking: Permitted. Non-smoking rooms available.
Pets: Not permitted.
Handicap Access: Yes. Wheelchair ramp. 1 unit designed for physically challenged.
Children: Not permitted!
Languages: English.

IGTA

Chelsea House

A Welcome as Generous as Our Lush, Tropical Gardens

Chelsea House is a uniquely open, restored 19th-century, two-story home with 15 guestrooms and two-bedroom suites. Suites have full kitchen, living room, hardwood floors and two private balconies. Our acre of land, two blocks from Duval Street, has extensive, tropical gardens, pool with clothing-optional sun deck, and on-property parking. We provide a thorough orientation for guests and are always around to lend friendly advice. Experience the unique ambiance of this historic Old Town, adult-only home and the special attention to individual needs from an informed, experienced staff. Gay-owned and -operated.

Address: 707 Truman Ave, Key West, FL 33040. Tel: (305) 296-2211, USA & Canada: (800) 845-8859, Fax: (305) 296-4822.

Type: Guesthouse.
Clientele: 50% gay & lesbian & 50% straight clientele.
Transportation: Fly to Key West International. $16 per person round trip for airport pick up.
To Gay Bars: 2 blocks.
Rooms: 13 rooms & two 2-bedroom suites with double, queen or king beds.
Bathrooms: All private.
Meals: Expanded continental breakfast buffet.
Vegetarian: Available nearby.
Complimentary: Cuban coffee & iced tea all day. Chocolates at nightly turndown.
Dates Open: All year.
High Season: December 15-April 17.
Rates: Summer $75-$165, winter $115-$260, spring $95-$190.
Discounts: 10% for 7 or more days in summer.
Credit Cards: MC, VISA, Discover, Bancard & Eurocard.
Rsv'tns: Preferred.
Reserve Through: Travel agent or call direct.
Minimum Stay: On holidays & special events.
Parking: Adequate free off-street parking.
In-Room: Color cable TV, AC, ceiling fans, telephone, safe, hair dryer, refrigerator, coffee/tea-making facilities & maid service.
Exercise/Health: Nearby full-service health facility & water sports.
Swimming: Pool on premises, Gulf of Mexico nearby.
Sunbathing: At poolside or clothing optional sun deck above pool building.
Nudity: Permitted on clothing optional sun deck.
Smoking: Permitted.
Pets: Not permitted.
Handicap Access: Yes.
Children: Not permitted.
Languages: English, German, French, Russian, Spanish & Turkish.
Your Host: Robb, Gary & Jim.

Coconut Grove

Gay/Lesbian ♂

Enjoy unparalleled views of Old Town and the Gulf of Mexico from our rooftop decks at *Coconut Grove Guest House*. The widow's walk provides a private spot to tan, take in the ocean air or experience Key West's sunsets. Friendliest service and largest, best suites in town.

Address: 817 Fleming St, Key West, FL 33040. Tel: (305) 296-5107, (800) 262-6055.

Type: Guesthouse.
Clientele: Mostly men with women welcome.
Transportation: Taxi.
To Gay Bars: 3 blocks to men's/women's bars.
Rooms: 3 singles, 11 doubles, 1 suite, 4 1-bedroom apartments in annex across the street.
Bathrooms: 18 private, 2 shared.
Meals: Continental breakfast.
Dates Open: All year.
High Season: December 20th-April 15th.
Rates: High season, $79-$200. Low season, $55-$100.
Credit Cards: MC, VISA.
Reserve Through: Travel agent or call direct.
Minimum Stay: Required at certain times.
Parking: On-street parking.
In-Room: Maid service, color TV, kitchen, refrigerator & AC.
On-Premises: Meeting rooms, telephone.
Exercise/Health: Gym, weights.
Swimming: Pool, ocean beach.
Sunbathing: At poolside, on beach, common sun decks, or roof.
Nudity: Permitted at the pool & sun decks.
Smoking: Permitted without restrictions.
Pets: Not permitted.
Handicap Access: No.
Children: Not permitted.
Languages: English, French, Swedish.

IGTA

We Appreciate Your Comments!

The editors of **INN Places**® actively seek your comments about accommodations you have tried.

Positive comments of interest may be included in the next issue, giving future readers the benefit of your experience. And it's a nice way of saying "thank you" to an innkeeper who extended you exceptional hospitality.

See the contents for the Reader Comment Form.

Colours, The Guest Mansion Key West

Gay/Lesbian ♀♂

Experience Not Just a Place, but a State of Mind.

This rare and stately Victorian mansion in the center of Old Town Key West has undergone a contemporary conversion, yet retains its original architectural details, such as chandeliers, 14-foot ceilings and polished wood floors. Accommodations vary from simple sitting rooms to suites with multiple beds, cable TV, refrigerator, paddle fan, private baths, air conditioning, balconies with hammocks and even kitchenettes. Rooms are painted

EXPERIENCE...

Colours
Destinations

YOUR DOORWAY TO OUR WORLD

in true, historical colors and decorated with antiques and wicker throughout. Arrange for airport transfers (complimentary with a 7-night stay or more) and your fantasy begins with an informal tour of the island. Continental breakfast is served at poolside amidst palms, night-blooming jasmine and colorful flowers.

Sunbathe or stroll just a half block to the shops, amusements, art galleries, restaurants, outdoor cafes, bars and discos of Duval St. Wander north toward Old Mallory Square on the harbor of the Gulf of Mexico or south toward the Atlantic beaches and the southernmost point of the continental United States. Celebrate colourful sunsets by our pool with our complimentary island cocktails. Feel truly pampered each evening on finding your bed turned down, a mint on your pillow and fresh bath linen awaiting your return from Key West's nightlife, a late affair lasting till dawn.

Arrangements for day excursions of fishing, sailing, windsurfing, bicycling, snorkeling the coral reef, flying in a seaplane, as well as dinner and theatre reservations can be made through your hosts. Rent our bicycles to take an interesting tour of the island. Speak to our friendly reservations staff about our other distinctive lodgings—*Colours The Mantell Guest Inn* in exciting South Miami Beach, and *Hotel Colours The Guest Residence* in exotic San Jose, Costa Rica.

Address: 410 Fleming St, Key West, FL 33040. Tel: (305) 294-6977, Reservations: (800) ARRIVAL (277-4825) or (305) 532-9341, Fax: 534-0362.

Type: Guesthouse hotel.
Clientele: Mostly gay & lesbian with some straight clientele.
Transportation: Free pick up from airport or bus if staying 7 nights or more (otherwise $15 roundtrip per person).
To Gay Bars: 1-2 blocks to bars & discos.
Rooms: 7 rooms & 5 suites (2 with kitchens) with single, double, queen or king beds.
Bathrooms: 10 private & 2 shared.
Meals: Expanded conti-nental breakfast.
Complimentary: Sunset cocktails and impromptu parties. Movie library & turndown service with mints on pillows.
Dates Open: All year.
High Season: Winter.
Rates: Summer $54-$135 & winter $82-$185, double occupancy.
Discounts: For single occupancy, longer stays & prepayment. Inquire for other.
Credit Cards: MC, VISA, Amex & Discover.
Rsv'tns: Recommended.

Reserve Through: Travel agent or call direct.
Minimum Stay: On some holidays.
Parking: Limited on-street parking.
In-Room: Phone, refrigerators, AC, ceiling fans & maid service. Some have color cable TV & full kitchens.
On-Premises: TV lounge with video tape library.
Exercise/Health: Massage & full health club facilities nearby.
Swimming: Heated pool on premises. Only 4-10 blocks to ocean beaches.
Sunbathing: At poolside, on sun deck or ocean beach.
Nudity: Permitted at poolside.
Smoking: Permitted, but not in TV lounge.
Pets: Not permitted.
Handicap Access: No.
Children: Not permitted.
Languages: English, limited Spanish & French.

IGTA

Coral Tree Inn

Men ♂

Coral Tree Inn is a newly renovated resort in the heart of Old Town, across the street from The Oasis, our mother house. Ten suites open onto balconies, with multi-level sun decks cascading from the 3rd level down to the pool, courtyard and whirlpool under the trellis and the coral tree. Tastefully decorated rooms have AC, color cable TV, Bahama fans, refrigerators, hair dryers, coffee-makers, and robes to wear during your visit. Clothes are optional and complete concierge services are available in 4 languages. You will find our hospitality genuine and generous.

Address: 822 Fleming St, Key West, FL . Tel: (305) 296-2131 or (800) 362-7477.

Type: Guesthouse with beer & wine bar.
Clientele: Men only.
Transportation: Taxi from airport.
To Gay Bars: 3-1/2 blocks.
Rooms: 10 rooms with queen beds.
Bathrooms: All private.
Meals: Expanded continental breakfast.
Complimentary: Wine & hors d'oeuvres at sunset for an hour by the pool.
Dates Open: All year.
High Season: December 16-May 1.
Rates: Summer $110, winter $165.
Discounts: Airline flight service.
Credit Cards: MC, VISA & Amex.
Rsv'tns: Strongly advised.
Reserve Through: Travel agent or call direct.
Minimum Stay: Required on holidays & special events.
Parking: Limited free on-street parking. Car is not really needed.
In-Room: Color TV, AC, ceiling fans, refrigerator, maid service.
Exercise/Health: Jacuzzi & use of 2 Jacuzzis at The Oasis.
Swimming: Pool & nearby ocean beach. Use of 2 pools at The Oasis.
Sunbathing: At poolside or on common sun decks.
Nudity: Permitted in public areas.
Smoking: Permitted.
Pets: Not permitted.
Handicap Access: No.
Children: Not permitted.
Languages: English (even British), Russian, German, Spanish & Turkish.

Curry House

Key West's Premiere Guest House for Men

Men ♂

If you find many of your new friends speak with an intriguing accent, it's because the *Curry House* is internationally popular. With only nine rooms, getting to know your fellow guests happens naturally while lounging by our black lagoon pool or at our daily happy hour. As your hosts, we're wholeheartedly at your service. Your room will be immaculate, your bed as comfortable as any you've ever slept in. *Curry House* is a short 3-block stroll from Duval Street, Key West's lively mainstream.

Address: 806 Fleming St, Key West, FL 33040. Tel: (305) 294-6777 or (800) 633-7439.

Type: B&B guesthouse.
Clientele: Men only.
Transportation: Airport taxi, approx. $6.
To Gay Bars: 4 blocks to men's bars.
Rooms: 9 rooms with double & queen beds.
Bathrooms: 7 private.
Meals: Full breakfast.
Vegetarian: Available nearby.
Complimentary: Free cocktail hour from 4-6 PM.
Dates Open: All year.
High Season: January through May.
Rates: Summer $75-$95, winter $110-$140.
Credit Cards: MC, VISA, Amex.
Rsv'tns: Recommended during in-season (3-6 months in advance).
Reserve Through: Call direct or travel agent.
Minimum Stay: 3 nights in high season, 1 night on summer weekends.
Parking: Ample free on-street parking.
In-Room: Refrigerator, maid service, AC, ceiling fans.
On-Premises: Public telephone.
Exercise/Health: Jacuzzi.
Swimming: Pool or ocean beach.
Sunbathing: At poolside or on private or common sun decks.
Nudity: Permitted at poolside and on balconies.
Smoking: Permitted without restrictions.
Pets: Not permitted.
Handicap Access: No.
Children: Not permitted.
Languages: English.

IGTA

Cypress House

Men ♂

Cypress House is a luxury guest house for those who wish to reside in an atmosphere of style and comfort. A congenial staff awaits to show you to your spacious, air conditioned bedroom in a grand, 1887 Conch mansion. Whether you feel like partying and sleeping late, or rising early for a dip in our long pool, you'll enjoy the mind-soothing experience... sunny days, exciting nights!

Address: 601 Caroline St, Key West, FL 33040. Tel: (305) 294-6969 or (800) 525-2488, Fax: (305) 296-1174.

Type: Guesthouse.
Clientele: Men only.
Transportation: Taxi from airport.
To Gay Bars: 4 blocks to men's bars.
Rooms: 15 rooms & 2 suites with double, queen or king beds.
Bathrooms: 3 private bath/toilets, others share.
Meals: Expanded continental breakfast.

Complimentary: One hour cocktail hour daily.
Dates Open: All year.
High Season: December 20th-May 1.
Rates: Summer $59-$99, winter $100-$225.
Discounts: 7 nights or more 10% with cash payment or travelers checks.
Credit Cards: MC, VISA, Amex, Diners, Carte Blanche, Eurocard & Bancard.

Rsv'tns: Recommended 1-2 months in advance.
Reserve Through: Travel agent or call direct.
Minimum Stay: Required for some holidays and weekends.
Parking: Adequate on- and off-street parking.
In-Room: Self controlled AC/heat & maid service.
On-Premises: TV lounge & house telephone.
Swimming: 40-foot

heated pool or ocean beach.
Sunbathing: On beach, common sun decks or at poolside.
Nudity: Permitted on roof terrace.
Smoking: No cigars on premises.
Pets: Not permitted.
Handicap Access: Partially, call for details.
Children: Not permitted.
Languages: English.

Duval House

Gay-Friendly 50/50 ♀♂

A Traditional Inn in Paradise

Outside our front gate lie the galleries, sidewalk cafes and exciting nightlife of Duval Street. Yet, within the *Duval House* compound, seven historic Victorian houses are surrounded by magnificent tropical gardens. Relax under our century-old Banyan tree, swim in our romantic pool, enjoy a free buffet breakfast on a sunny deck. We pride ourselves on being friendly and open to all. Rooms feature wicker and antiques, with ceiling fans, Caribbean colors, and restful porches or balconies for you to enjoy the gentle island tradewinds.

Address: 815 Duval St, Key West, FL 33040. Tel: (305) 294-1666 or (800) 22-DUVAL.

Type: Inn.
Clientele: 50% gay &

lesbian & 50% straight clientele.

Transportation: Taxi from airport.

To Gay Bars: 1/2 block to men's & 3 blocks to

women's bars.
Rooms: 26 rooms & 3 suites with double or queen beds.
Bathrooms: 27 private shower/toilets & 2 shared showers.
Meals: Expanded continental breakfast.
Dates Open: All year.
High Season: December 22nd thru April 15th.

Rates: High season $120-$190, low season $85-$140.
Discounts: 10% weekly during off-season.
Credit Cards: MC, VISA, Amex, Discover & Diners.
Rsv'tns: Recommended.
Reserve Through: Travel agent or call direct.
Parking: Adequate off-street parking.

In-Room: AC, maid service, suites have kitchen & ceiling fans.
On-Premises: TV lounge.
Exercise/Health: Nearby gym, weights, sauna & steam.
Swimming: Pool on premises, ocean beach nearby.
Sunbathing: At poolside, private sun decks, or on

ocean beach.
Smoking: Permitted without restrictions.
Pets: Not permitted.
Handicap Access: No.
Children: Under 16 years discouraged.
Languages: English, German.

Eaton Lodge

Gay-Friendly ♀♂

A Traditional Inn

You're invited to enjoy the special comforts of *Eaton Lodge,* a Key West guesthouse with a proud tradition of welcoming travelers. Start your day with breakfast served in the garden or on your own quiet veranda. There's also an evening hospitality hour. Located just off Duval in the heart of Key West, *Eaton Lodge* is *the* guesthouse you will return to year after year.

Address: 511 Eaton St, Key West, FL 33040. Tel: (305) 292-2170, (800) 294-2170.

EATON LODGE

TRADITIONAL INN

Type: Guesthouse.
Clientele: Mostly straight clientele with a gay & lesbian following.
Transportation: Taxi from airport.
To Gay Bars: 2 blocks or a 5-minute walk.
Rooms: 14 rooms with single, double, queen or king beds.
Bathrooms: 14 private bath/toilets.

Meals: Expanded continental breakfast.
Complimentary: Evening cocktails.
Dates Open: All year.
High Season: Dec 15 to Easter.
Rates: $65-$90 summer, $125-$150 winter.
Credit Cards: MC, VISA & Amex.
Rsv'tns: Recommended.
Reserve Through: Travel

agent or call direct.
Minimum Stay: During holidays & special events.
Parking: Limited pay parking.
In-Room: Color cable TV, VCR, AC, ceiling fans, telephone, refrigerator & maid service.
Exercise/Health: Jacuzzi.
Swimming: Pool on premises. Ocean nearby.

Sunbathing: At poolside.
Smoking: All rooms are non-smoking with private decks where smoking is permitted.
Pets: Not permitted.
Handicap Access: Yes.
Children: Not especially welcome.
Languages: English.

Take along the Expert

Ferrari's Places of Interest™ contains articles contributed by gay and lesbian journalists on the scene, giving insight into gay and lesbian communities worldwide. With its accompanying directory, it's the perfect vacation planner.

Heron House

Feel Free...Feel Relaxed...Feel Welcomed

Gay-Friendly ♀♂

Amidst orchids, bougainvillaea, jasmine and palms, a secluded tropical garden fantasy awaits you, a warm and friendly place to relax and to dream, *Heron House*. Spacious sun decks surround a sparkling pool. Our light, airy and spacious rooms are a careful mix of old and new. A tropical flare with wicker, casual and comfortable. Luxurious marble bathroom vanities reflect an attention to detail.

Address: 512 Simonton St, Key West, FL 33040. Tel: (305) 294-9227, (800) 294-1644, Fax: (305) 294-5692.

Type: Guesthouse.
Clientele: Mostly straight clientele with a gay & lesbian following.
Transportation: Car or airport, then taxi.
To Gay Bars: 1 block to men's bars.
Rooms: 18 rooms with double, queen or king beds.
Bathrooms: All private bath/toilets.

Meals: Expanded continental breakfast.
Vegetarian: 1 block away.
Dates Open: All year.
High Season: December 1-May 31.
Rates: Winter $105-$195, summer $85-$155.
Credit Cards: MC, VISA, Amex & Diners.
Rsv'tns: Recommended.
Reserve Through: Travel agent or call direct.

Minimum Stay: During holidays and special events.
Parking: Ample on-street parking.
In-Room: Maid service, ceiling fans & AC. Some rooms have color TV, refrigerators & telephones.
On-Premises: House phone.
Swimming: Pool, ocean beach.

Sunbathing: At poolside, on roof or on private or common sun decks.
Nudity: Permitted.
Smoking: Permitted without restrictions.
Pets: Not permitted.
Handicap Access: Yes. Ramps.
Children: Not permitted.
Languages: English.

IGTA

Island House

More Than Just a Guest House!

Men ♂

Island House, Key West's largest exclusively male resort, is in a private, enclosed compound. The 34 guest units have A/C, ceiling fans, telephones, and room safes. Most have TV and refrigerator. Our cafe is open for breakfast, lunch and Sunday brunch. Our air conditioned gym has free weights, a Marcy workout center and shower/locker facilities. Enjoy the dry sauna, Jacuzzi, or the largest guesthouse pool in Key West. Clothing is optional throughout the compound. Our friendly staff are always available for assistance. Call us and "rediscover a man's resort."

Address: 1129 Fleming St, Key West, FL 33040. Tel: (305) 294-6284 or (800) 526-3559.

Type: Guest house with restaurant, bar, clothing, suntan, scuba shops.
Clientele: Men only.
Transportation: Taxi from airport approx. $5.
To Gay Bars: 8 blocks to men's bars.
Rooms: 24 doubles, 8 suites.
Bathrooms: 22 private, others share.
Complimentary: Coffee.
Dates Open: All year.
High Season: Christmas through Easter.

Rates: Rooms $65-$120, suites/efficiencies $90-$200.
Credit Cards: MC, VISA & Amex.
Rsv'tns: Recommended.
Reserve Through: Travel agent or call direct.
Minimum Stay: Varies according to season/holidays.
Parking: Limited off-street parking.
In-Room: Maid service, telephone, self-controlled AC, alarm clocks & safes.

Most have color TV & refrigerators.
On-Premises: TV lounge, laundry facilities, public telephones.
Exercise/Health: Hot tub, dry sauna. Small gym with daily/monthly memberships available.
Swimming: Large pool on premises.
Sunbathing: At poolside, on common sun decks.
Nudity: Permitted anywhere in compound.
Smoking: Not permitted

in sauna or gym.
Pets: Small pets permitted with a deposit, add'l fee may be required.
Handicap Access: Limited, add'l fee may be required.
Children: Not permitted.
Languages: English, Spanish, French, German.
Your Host: Jack & Jeff.

IGTA

Key Lodge Motel

Gay-Friendly ♀♂

Key Lodge is a little different. We're a motel located on Duval St. in the heart of Key West's Old Town. The environment is friendly and private, the company mixed. Our accommodations are first rate. We have individually decorated rooms, each with color TV, AC, refrigerator, phone, and ceiling fans, and a heated pool. *Key Lodge* is in one of Key West's best locations.

Address: 1004 Duval St, Key West, FL 33040. Tel: (305) 296-9915.

Type: Motel.
Clientele: Mostly straight clientele with a gay & lesbian following.
Transportation: Car is best. Taxi from airport, $6.
To Gay Bars: 3 blocks.
Rooms: 16 rooms & 6 suites with single, queen or king beds.

Bathrooms: All private.
Meals: Morning coffee.
Dates Open: All year.
High Season: Christmas.
Rates: Winter $130-$158. $68-$86 rest of year.
Credit Cards: MC, VISA, Amex & Discover.
Rsv'tns: Required.
Reserve Through: Travel

agent or call direct.
Minimum Stay: During holidays & special events.
Parking: Ample off-street parking.
In-Room: Color TV, AC, ceiling fans, telephone, refrigerator & maid service.

Swimming: Heated pool on premises.
Sunbathing: At poolside or at the beach.
Pets: Pets $10 per day.
Handicap Access: Yes.
Children: Permitted.
Languages: English.

Knowles House, The

Gay/Lesbian ♀♂

House & Gardens Tour Favorite, 1993

The Knowles House is a charming, restored 1880's Conch home in historic Olde Town Key West, just five blocks from Duval Street. We provide our bed and breakfast guests an intimate and romantic setting.

Address: 1004 Eaton St, Key West, FL 33040.   Tel: (305) 296-8132 or (800) 352-4414.

Type: Bed & breakfast guesthouse.
Clientele: Mostly gay & lesbian with some straight clientele.
Transportation: Car or taxi. $10 for pick up from airport.
To Gay Bars: 6 blocks.
Rooms: 5 rooms with double, queen or king beds.

Bathrooms: 2 private, others share.
Meals: Expanded continental breakfast.
Dates Open: All year.
High Season: Jan-May.
Rates: Summer $59-$99. Winter $79-$125.
Credit Cards: MC, VISA & Amex.
Rsv'tns: Recommended.
Reserve Through: Travel

agent or call direct.
Parking: Ample on- and off-street parking.
In-Room: AC, color cable TV with remote, ceiling fans & maid service.
On-Premises: Coffee/tea-making facilities & refrigerator.
Exercise/Health: Nearby gym & massage.
Swimming: Pool on

premises.
Sunbathing: Poolside & private or common sun decks.
Nudity: Permitted.
Smoking: Permitted on decks. Non-smoking rooms available.
Pets: Not permitted.
Languages: English.
Your Host: Steve, Scott & Paul.

Lighthouse Court

Men ♂

Lighthouse Court is Key West's largest, most private guest compound. A variety of restored conch houses connected by decking, nestled in lush tropical foliage, it combines the charm of days past with contemporary taste and design. Accommodations include rooms, apartments and even a private home. Rooms have air conditioning and/or Bahama fans, refrigerators, and many have kitchen facilities. Located one block from historic Duval Street, *Lighthouse Court* is a short stroll from shops, galleries, beaches, sailing & snorkeling as well as Key West's famous nite life.

Address: 902 Whitehead St, Key West, FL 33040. Tel: (305) 294-9588.

Type: Guesthouse with restaurant, bar & health

club.
Clientele: Men only.

Transportation: Taxi from airport.

To Gay Bars: 1 block to

continued next page

Florida

Duval St bars.
Rooms: 4 singles, 30 doubles, 4 suites & 4 efficiencies.
Bathrooms: 38 private & 4 shared.
Vegetarian: Breakfast & lunch.
Complimentary: Coffee.
Dates Open: All year.
High Season: Jan 20 thru Easter, Fantasy Fest-late October, New Years' Eve.
Rates: $50-$180.
Credit Cards: MC & VISA.
Rsv'tns: Preferred.
Reserve Through: Call direct.
Minimum Stay: Required on holidays.
Parking: Ample free on-street parking.
In-Room: Maid & room service, AC, ceiling fans, fridge, telephone, TV in suites.
On-Premises: Meeting rooms, TV lounge, beer-and-wine bar.
Exercise/Health: Jacuzzi, health club on premises, gym, weights, massage.
Swimming: Pool on premises, ocean beach nearby.
Sunbathing: At poolside, on roof, common sun decks, or on beach nearby.
Nudity: Permitted.
Smoking: Permitted without restrictions.
Pets: Not permitted.
Handicap Access: Inquire.
Children: Not permitted.
Languages: English, French.

Lime House Inn

Men ♂

An Island Within An Island

In the heart of historic Old Town Key West, *Lime House* is described as an island within an island. Though just steps from the waterfront, it's two blocks from Duval Street's shopping and nightlife. It's simply the most private and friendly guest house in Key West. Enjoy the lifestyle in this old conch mansion, lounging in the pool or hot tub. Most rooms have private bath and kitchenette. All rooms have telephone, air conditioning and cable TV. Come, stay with us. Let us be a part of your best vacation ever!
Address: 219 Elizabeth St, Key West, FL 33040. Tel: (305) 296-2978 or (800) 374-4242, Fax: (305) 294-5858.

Type: Guesthouse.
Clientele: Men only.
Transportation: Drive from Miami or fly to Key West & take a taxi or limo to Lime House.
To Gay Bars: 5 blocks to men's bars.
Rooms: 11 rooms with single, double, queen or king beds.
Bathrooms: 8 private & 3 shared.
Meals: Expanded continental breakfast.
Complimentary: Cocktail hour each evening except Sunday.
Dates Open: All year.
High Season: February-March.
Rates: Summer $65-$95, winter $98-$140.
Discounts: 10% for stays of 7 nights or longer during certain months. Please inquire.
Credit Cards: MC, VISA, Amex, Diners & Discover.
Rsv'tns: Highly recommended.
Reserve Through: Travel agent or call direct.
Minimum Stay: 2 nights on weekends. 3 nights on weekends Feb & Mar.
Parking: Ample, free on-street parking. 1 handicap spot on premises.
In-Room: Color cable TV, coffee/tea-making facilities, AC, telephone, ceiling fans, kitchen, refrigerator, maid & laundry service.
On-Premises: Fax.
Exercise/Health: Jacuzzi. Nearby gym, weights, sauna, steam & massage.
Swimming: Pool on premises, ocean beach 2 blocks.
Sunbathing: At poolside, on beach.
Nudity: Permitted anywhere on premises.
Smoking: Permitted.
Pets: Not permitted.
Handicap Access: Yes, 1 room.
Children: Not permitted.
Languages: English, German, French, Swiss, Flemish & Italian.
Your Host: Jim & Godfrey.

Mangrove House

Men ♂

Intimate and Friendly in the Key West Tradition

Mangrove House is an intimate and friendly guesthouse, exclusively for gay men, in the true Key West tradition. Located in the centre of historic Old Town Key West, less than 2 blocks from the heart of Duval Street, the fully-restored building is a charming "Eyebrow" house, one of only 81 remaining on the island. Both accommodations and grounds are comfortable and spacious. Clothing is optional around the beautiful 15 foot x 25 foot solar heated pool and hot tub. Complimentary breakfast is served poolside every morning.

Address: 623 Southard St, Key West, FL . Tel: (800) 294-1866, (305) 294-1866, Fax: (305) 294-8757.

Type: Guesthouse.
Clientele: Men only.
Transportation: Car, taxi from airport, walk from bus depot.
To Gay Bars: 2 blocks or a 3-minute walk.
Rooms: 2 rooms & 2 apartments with double or queen beds.
Bathrooms: 4 private bath/toilets.
Meals: Continental breakfast May-Nov, expanded continental breakfast Dec-Apr.

Complimentary: Refreshments in the afternoon.
Dates Open: All year.
High Season: December-April.
Rates: Low season $65-$105, high season $105-$150, Fantasy Fest $125-$195.
Discounts: 10% for stays of 7 or more nights except during Fantasy Fest.
Credit Cards: MC, VISA, Amex.
Rsv'tns: Highly recom-

mended.
Reserve Through: Travel agent or call direct.
Minimum Stay: 3 nights for holidays, 4 nights for Fantasy Fest.
Parking: Ample on-street parking on safe residential street.
In-Room: Color cable TV, AC, ceiling fans & maid service. Apartment has kitchen, refrigerator & coffee/tea-making facilities.
Exercise/Health: Jacuzzi & weights on premises.

Nearby gym, massage.
Swimming: Pool on premises. Nearby ocean.
Sunbathing: At poolside.
Nudity: Permitted in pool area.
Smoking: Permitted without restrictions.
Pets: Not permitted.
Handicap Access: No. 4 steps from street to rooms.
Children: Not especially welcome.
Languages: English, French, German & Italian.

Newton Street Station

Men ♂

Join Us in Our Corner of Paradise

Newton Street Station, formerly the home of the stationmaster of the Florida East Coast Railway, is an intimate guesthouse in a quiet, residential section of Old Town Key West. Rooms are individually-decorated and breakfast is served on the tropical sun deck. Lounge by the pool, nude, if you like, enjoy the tropical gardens, or workout on the exercise deck. Visit shops and galleries, or enjoy some of the finest water sports in the country. *Newton Street Station* is one of the friendliest, all-men's guesthouses in Key West, where our goal is to make you feel welcome.

Address: 1414 Newton St, Key West, FL 33040. Tel: (305) 294-4288 or (800) 248-2457, Fax: (305) 292-5062.

Type: Guesthouse.
Clientele: Men only.
Transportation: Inexpensive taxi ride from airport.
To Gay Bars: 5 minutes by car to men's bars.
Rooms: 6 rooms & 1 suite with double beds.
Bathrooms: 4 private, 2 shared & 1 half-bath.
Meals: Continental breakfast.
Dates Open: All year.
High Season: December

15th-April 30th.
Rates: Winter $80-$115, summer $55-$70.
Discounts: 10% for a week or more, or for members of nudist/naturist groups.
Credit Cards: MC, VISA & Amex.
Rsv'tns: Highly recommended.
Reserve Through: Travel agent or call direct.
Minimum Stay: During holidays & special

events.
Parking: Ample free on-street parking.
In-Room: Maid service, color cable TV's, AC, some ceiling fans.
On-Premises: TV lounge & free local phone calls.
Exercise/Health: Weights & bicycles
Swimming: Pool or nearby ocean.
Sunbathing: At poolside, on private & common sun decks, or patio.

Nudity: Permitted anywhere on premises.
Smoking: Permitted without restrictions.
Pets: Not permitted.
Handicap Access: No.
Children: Not permitted.
Languages: English, limited French & limited German.
Your Host: John.

IGTA

Oasis, A Guest House

Men ♂

Oasis, A Guesthouse is Key West's most elegant guesthouse, a magnificently restored 1895 mansion in the historic district, where you capture the true charm and excitement of this idyllic isle. Multi-level sun decks allow secluded sunbathing, plus breathtaking views of town and gulf. Tastefully-appointed rooms have AC, private bath, color TV, Bahama fans and robes to wear during your visit. We have two of the island's largest private pools. Our Jacuzzi, sun decks and pools open 24 hours a day, clothes optional. Share the tranquil beauty of our home and experience our genuine and generous hospitality.

Address: 823 Fleming Street, Key West, FL 33040. Tel: (305) 296-2131 or (800) 362-7477, Fax: (305) 296-5972.

Type: Guesthouse with beer & wine bar.
Clientele: Men only.
Transportation: Taxi from airport.
To Gay Bars: 4 blocks to men's/women's bars.
Rooms: 19 rooms with queen beds.
Bathrooms: 19 private bath/toilets.
Meals: Expanded continental breakfast.
Complimentary: Wine

party every evening with hors d'oeuvres by the main pool.
Dates Open: All year.
High Season: January-April.
Rates: Summer $75-$120, winter $95-$170.
Discounts: 10% airline travel agents.
Credit Cards: MC, VISA & Amex.
Rsv'tns: Preferred.
Reserve Through: Travel

agent or call direct.
Minimum Stay: During holidays & special events.
Parking: Plenty of on-street parking.
In-Room: Maid service, color TV, refrigerator, AC & ceiling fans.
Exercise/Health: Jacuzzi.
Swimming: 2 large pools on premises.
Sunbathing: At poolside, on beach or private sun

decks.
Nudity: Permitted.
Smoking: Permitted without restrictions.
Pets: Not permitted.
Handicap Access: No.
Children: Not permitted.
Languages: English, Spanish, German & Russian.

IGTA

Pilot House Guest House

Gay-Friendly 50/50 ♀♂

Home of Southernmost Hospitality

Pilot House is a grand two-story Victorian mansion built, circa 1900, by Julius Otto as his private home. Today the structure stands proud in the center of the Key West historical district known as Old Town. It boasts verandas and porches with hand-milled spindels and gingerbread trim. After the labored restoration in 1990, receiving the prestigious "Excellence Award for Preservation" by the Florida Keys Preservation Board, we opened the doors to the mansion as a guest residence. *Pilot House* is appointed with a careful blend of antiques and decorated with tropical furnishings, accommodating the discriminating tastes of experienced travelers. We

offer unique lodging accommodations with six guest rooms to choose from, all with private bath, color cable TV, phone, air conditioning and paddle fans.

When you reach your destination at our Southernmost City, you will appreciate our careful attention to detail. The guest rooms' original hardwood floors gleam with pride as they support the massive moldings stretching to the twelve-foot ceilings.

The home, known for its many luxurious fireplaces, still remains. We carefully chose the wallpapers and fabrics to complement the original character of the Otto house, and added our own touch of modern convenience with marbled baths and fully-equipped kitchens. Our staff is on hand to provide you with information to our palm-studded island that only a local can share with you.

Kayak the Keys with a wildlife expert, take a bicycle tour with a native, discover our tropical reef scuba diving with a pro, see our famous sunset aboard a schooner sailboat. After a full day of fun and sun, come back to our secluded spa and relax in our tropical garden and patio. A casual dinner in a popular eatery and the nightlife of the famous Duval Street is just a half block from our back door.

Address: 414 Simonton St, Key West, FL 33040. Tel: (800) 648-3780, (305) 294-3800, Fax: (305) 294-9298.

Type: Guesthouse.
Clientele: 50% gay & lesbian & 50% straight clientele.
Transportation: Taxi.
To Gay Bars: 2 blocks.
Rooms: 6 rooms & 6 suites with double or queen beds.
Bathrooms: All private.
Dates Open: All year.
High Season: January, February, March.
Rates: $135-$300 in sea-

son, $75-$175 off-season.
Discounts: 10% weekly.
Credit Cards: VISA, Amex, Diners Club, Carte Blanche, Discover, Eurocard.
Rsv'tns: Preferred.
Reserve Through: Travel agent or call direct.
Minimum Stay: 3 nights or more on holidays & special events.
Parking: Limited off-steet pay parking.

In-Room: Color cable TV, private line phone, AC, ceiling fans, queen beds, coffee/tea-making facilities, kitchens, refrigerator, maid service.
On-Premises: Botanical garden.
Exercise/Health: Jacuzzi, bike rack with nearby rentals.
Swimming: Pool on premises, 4 blocks to gulf.
Sunbathing: At poolside.

On sun deck for penthouse.
Smoking: Not permitted in rooms. Plenty of balcony & patio areas for smoking.
Pets: Not permitted.
Handicap Access: Yes.
Children: Not especially welcome.
Languages: English.

Pines of Key West

Gay/Lesbian ♂

The Best Vacation of Your Life!

The Pines, Key West's original exclusively gay guesthouse, offers the perfect combination of congenial atmosphere and relaxation. We are located only a few minutes' walk from Key West's finest beaches, bars, shops and restaurants. Join us for continental breakfast on the patio, then sun all day long by our large pool. Our spacious hot tub provides an ideal setting to meet new friends and adapt to Key West's casual island atmosphere. Come to *The Pines* and experience the best vacation of your life!

Address: 521 United St, Key West, FL 33040. Tel: (305) 296-7467 or (800) 282-PINE (7463).

Type: Guesthouse.
Clientele: Mostly men with women welcome.
Transportation: Car or taxi from airport.
To Gay Bars: All bars within walking distance.
Rooms: 14 rooms with double, queen or king beds.
Bathrooms: All private.
Meals: Continental breakfast.
Dates Open: All year.

High Season: December 15th-April 30th.
Rates: Summer $59-$79, winter $90-$120.
Discounts: Weekly rates during summer, approx. 10% off for stays of 7 or more days.
Credit Cards: MC, VISA, Amex, Discover & Diners.
Rsv'tns: Required.
Reserve Through: Travel agent or call direct.
Minimum Stay: Fantasy

Fest 6 days, summer holidays 3, Xmas/New Years 7.
Parking: Adequate, free off-street & on-street parking.
In-Room: Color cable TV, telephone, AC, maid service, refrigerator & ceiling fans.
Exercise/Health: Jacuzzi.
Swimming: Pool on premises, ocean beach 2 blocks.

Sunbathing: At poolside & 2nd floor sun deck.
Nudity: Permitted at poolside or on common sun deck.
Smoking: Permitted.
Pets: Not permitted.
Children: Not permitted.
Languages: English.

IGTA

Rainbow House

Women ♀

Welcome to Paradise!

Wake up and join us for a scrumptious breakfast buffet in our air conditioned glass pavilion. Let yourself go...sunbathe nude at poolside in a secure, secluded atmosphere. Go scuba diving, kayaking, parasailing. You can do it all in Key West! We'll book reservations for you for sailboats and snorkeling or sunset cruises. (Women-only cruises ARE available!) Join the womyn who have a memorable experience at the *Rainbow House*... Your dreams really do come true.

Address: 525 United St, Key West, FL 33040. Tel: (305) 292-1450, (800) 74-WOMYN (800 749-6696).

Type: Bed & breakfast guesthouse.
Clientele: Women only.
To Gay Bars: 5-minute walk to gay/lesbian bars.
Rooms: 15 rooms & 9 suites.
Meals: Expanded continental breakfast.
Open: All year.
High Season: January through April.
Rates: $69-$169.
Credit Cards: MC, VISA, Discover, Preferred, Amex.
Rsv'tns: Strongly recommended.
Reserve Through: Call direct or travel agent.
Minimum Stay: During holidays.
Parking: On-street parking.
In-Room: Maid service, color TV, phones, AC.
Kitchens available.
Exercise/Health: Jacuzzi.
Swimming: In pool or 1 block to ocean.
Sunbathing: At poolside, on private sun decks or on ocean beach.
Nudity: Permitted at poolside.
Pets: Not permitted.
Handicap Access: One unit available.
Children: Not permitted.

Languages: English.
Your Host: Marion.
IGTA

Sea Isle Resort

Gay/Lesbian ♂

Sea Isle is in the very heart of Old Town Key West, close to beaches, water sports of both the Gulf and the Atlantic and a short stroll from shops, restaurants, art galleries and nightspots. You'll be impressed with your guest room. It's comfortable, handsome and immaculate, with private bath, air conditioning and telephone. Stay in good shape using our Nautilus equipment and free weights. Swim in the pool, then stretch out on the poolside deck or the secluded clothing-optional sun deck.

Address: 915 Windsor Lane, Key West, FL 33040. Tel: (305) 294-5188 or (800) 995-4786, Fax: (305) 296-7143.

Type: Resort/compound.
Clientele: Mostly gay men, women welcome.
To Gay Bars: 3 blocks.
Rooms: 16 doubles, 6 quads & 2 suites.
Bathrooms: All private.
Meals: Continental breakfast.
Complimentary: Cocktail parties on weekends.
Dates Open: All year.
High Season: December through April.
Rates: For 2 people, summer $75-$90, suites $105, winter $110-$125, suites $150, extra person $20 per night.
Discounts: 7th night free during low season.
Credit Cards: MC, VISA, Amex & Discover.
Rsv'tns: Strongly suggested.
Reserve Through: Call direct.
Minimum Stay: On holidays.
Parking: Ample off-street parking.
In-Room: Color TV, telephone, AC & mini-refrigerator.
On-Premises: Large private courtyard.
Exercise/Health: Nautilus, free weights & hot tub.
Swimming: Large, climate-controlled pool on premises, ocean beach nearby.
Sunbathing: At poolside, on beach, on private sun decks.
Nudity: Permitted on upper sun deck.
Smoking: Permitted without restrictions.
Pets: $10.00 add'l charge per day for pets.
Handicap Access: With assistance.
Children: Not permitted.
Languages: English.
Your Host: Randy & Jim.
IGTA

Seascape

Gay-Friendly ♀♂

Seascape is ideally located in Old Town Key West betweeen Duval St. and the Hemingway House. Restored in recent years, the inn, circa 1889, features a tropical garden, pool-spa and sun decks. All rooms have private baths, air conditioning, color cable TV, bahama fans and queen-sized bed. It's a few steps to the finest eating and drinking establishments in town and just minutes to both the Atlantic Ocean and the Gulf of Mexico. In season, greet other guests at complimentary sunset wine hour. **"Sparkling"** *New York Times*

Address: 420 Olivia St, Key West, FL 33040. Tel: (305) 296-7776 (phone & fax).

Type: Guesthouse.
Clientele: Mostly straight with a gay & lesbian following.
To Gay Bars: 1-minute walk to men's/women's bars.
Rooms: 5 rooms with queen beds.
Bathrooms: All private shower/toilets.
Meals: Expanded continental breakfast.
Complimentary: Wine hour in season.
Dates Open: All year.
High Season: December 1 to April 30.
Rates: Winter $94-$114, summer $69-$89.
Credit Cards: MC, VISA, Amex & Discover.
Rsv'tns: Recommended.
Reserve Through: Call direct.
Minimum Stay: On some holidays.
Parking: Adequate on-street parking. Everything is within walking distance.
In-Room: Self-controlled AC, maid service, color cable TV & ceiling fan.
On-Premises: Public telephone, ice & pop machine.
Swimming: Pool-spa on premises or 2-minute walk to ocean.
Sunbathing: At poolside and on common sun decks.
Smoking: Permitted without restrictions.
Pets: Not permitted.
Handicap Access: No.
Children: Not permitted.
Languages: English.

Simonton Court Historic Inn & Cottages

Gay-Friendly 50/50 ♀♂

Once You Stay Here, You'll Always Come Back

Simonton Court is an elegant, yet relaxed retreat for body and soul in the heart of Old Town Key West, America's Caribbean island. A collection of gracefully restored Old Town Key West buildings, the property dates from the 1880's and Key West's cigar-making era. It is an *exceptionally* romantic, quiet resort setting for adults, perfectly situated less than a block from lively Duval Street and just three blocks from Key West's harbor and Mallory Square. All forms of en-

tertainment — unique shops, excellent restaurants, live theater and a bar for everyone's taste — are only a short walk away. America's only living coral reef makes for some of the finest diving, snorkeling, fishing and boating experiences anywhere in the world.

A lovely private garden compound, with hot tub and three separate pools, brick paths, tin roofs, French doors and lush foliage canopies create the ambiance for three levels of accommodation. An old cigar-makers' factory, now the Inn, and a building called the Manor House, offer charming rooms, each unique and each with either kitchenette or refrigerator. Cottages, with wood floors and wicker furniture, are ideal for 2-6 people, with 2-3 separate sleeping areas and private

continued next page

porches and/or decks. The Mansion, built in the Victorian era, is now the property's most elegant accommodation, offering an unsurpassed level of service. Some of the Mansion's suites have outdoor decks, and one has a most private widow's walk for sweeping panoramic views of the city and ocean, with an in-room Jacuzzi - *very* romantic! A few rooms can be combined into suites; two rooms in the Manor House form a private suite with a pool and deck for the exclusive use of the suite when combined.

The staff is friendly and helpful, but low-key, never intrusive. A luscious complimentary continental breakfast is served every morning and can be carried into one of many garden alcoves or porches.

Address: 320 Simonton St, Key West, FL 33040. Tel: (800) 944-2687, (305) 294-6386, Fax: 293-8446.

Type: Cottage Inn.
Clientele: 50% gay & lesbian & 50% straight clientele.
Transportation: Taxi or airport shuttle 10 minutes from airport.
To Gay Bars: 4 blocks to gay & lesbian bars.
Rooms: 2 rooms, 14 suites & 6 cottages with bunk, double, queen or king beds.
Bathrooms: All private shower/toilets.
Meals: Expanded continental breakfast.
Vegetarian: Vegetarian food available at several restaurants within 4 blocks.
Dates Open: All year.
High Season: Dec 15-May 1 & all national holidays.
Rates: In season $150-$350, mid season $130-$255, low season $110-$200.
Discounts: Airline.
Credit Cards: MC, VISA, Amex & Discover.
Rsv'tns: Recommended.
Reserve Through: Travel agent or call direct.
Minimum Stay: 2 days weekends, 5 days Christmas, New Years & Fantasy Fest.
Parking: Ample on-street or pay parking.
In-Room: Color cable TV, AC, telephone, ceiling fans, refrigerator, coffee & tea-making facilities & maid service. Most units with VCR, some with kitchens.
Exercise/Health: Hot tub.
Swimming: 3 pools, 2 heated. 3 blocks to beach.
Sunbathing: At poolside or on beach.
Smoking: Permitted without restrictions.
Pets: Not permitted.
Handicap Access: No.
Children: Not permitted.
Languages: English.
IGTA

Tropical Inn

Tropical Delight in the Heart of Old Town

Gay-Friendly ♀♂

Enjoy your vacation getaway at the *Tropical Inn*, our restored historical Conch house with large airy rooms, balconies overlooking Duval St. and tropical gardens. All rooms have private baths and air conditioning, many have large color televisions and private balconies. Our garden suites have their own private garden and spa. We're near the beaches and the bars in historic Old Key West.

Address: 812 Duval St, Key West, FL 33040. Tel: (305) 294-9977

Type: Guesthouse.
Clientele: Mostly straight clientele with a gay & lesbian following.
Transportation: By air, then take taxi.
To Gay Bars: 1/2 block to men's/women's bar. A 3-minute walk.
Rooms: 5 rooms & 2 suites with single, double or queen beds.
Bathrooms: All private bath/toilets.
Dates Open: All year.
High Season: October-May.
Rates: Summer $65-$98, high season $75-$139.
Credit Cards: MC, VISA, Discover, Diners & Amex.
Rsv'tns: Required.
Reserve Through: Call direct.
Minimum Stay: Suites in season, holidays & special events. 3 days on weekends.
Parking: Ample on-street parking.
In-Room: Maid service, color TV, & AC. Kitchen in garden suites.
On-Premises: Refrigerator.
Exercise/Health: Jacuzzi.
Swimming: Nearby ocean.
Sunbathing: On private sun decks, patio.
Smoking: No smoking in rooms.
Pets: Not permitted.
Handicap Access: No.
Children: Not especially welcome.
Languages: English.

Upper Echelons

Gay-Friendly ♀♂

Manor House in Margaritaville

Take this unique opportunity to bring your "chosen family" (house sleeps six) to *Upper Echelons,* and relax in the tropical, laid-back ambiance of Olde Town Key West, a long time mecca for writers, artists, treasure seekers and true individualists. Enjoy the comfortable luxury of a restored, historic, Neoclassical mansion with pool, verandas, gourmet kitchen, antiques—the works! Enjoy the nightlife, restaurants, sunsets, pier and friendly natives, all within blocks. Spend a week or the season. Reservations are a must.

Address: Key West, FL . Tel: (404) 642-1313

Type: Private home.
Clientele: Mostly straight clientele with a gay & lesbian following.
Transportation: Drive from Miami or take a taxi from Key West Airport.
To Gay Bars: 4 blocks or a 10-minute walk.
Rooms: 3 bedrooms with single, queen & king beds. Accommodates 6 people.
Bathrooms: Private & shared.
Vegetarian: Numerous restaurants, delis & market nearby.
Dates Open: All year.
High Season: Dec thru Mar.
Rates: $2,500 per week off-season. $3,500 per week in-season.
Rsv'tns: Required.
Minimum Stay: 1 week minimum.
Parking: On-street parking.
In-Room: Color cable TV, VCR, AC, telephone & ceiling fans.
Swimming: Pool on premises, ocean nearby.
Sunbathing: On the patio, at poolside or nearby beach (10-minute ride).
Pets: Not permitted.
Handicap Access: No.
Children: Welcome.
Languages: English.

MIAMI & SOUTH BEACH

Bayliss, The

Gay/Lesbian ♀♂

This gay-owned and -operated 1939 Art Deco gem features both hotel rooms and efficiency apartments, all with private baths, telephones, cable TV and fridges. Each has been restored with vintage colors, fabrics and furniture reflecting Miami Beach's heyday of the 30's and 40's. The beach, nightlife, shopping and dining are within a one-block radius of *The Bayliss.* There is no additional charge for telephone usage. Canadian dollar exchange is complimentary, as is our travelers check cashing service. Call direct for off-season and weekly rates.

Address: 504 14th St, Miami Beach, FL 33139. Tel: (305) 534-4763, Fax: (305) 534-9177.

Type: Hotel.
Clientele: Good mix of gays & lesbians.
To Gay Bars: 1/2 block.
Rooms: 9 rooms with queen beds.
Bathrooms: All private.
Complimentary: Condoms & gift packs in the room.
Dates Open: All year.
High Season: Nov-Apr.
Rates: Low season $60-$80, high season $90-$125.
Discounts: Weekly rates.
Credit Cards: MC & Visa.
Rsv'tns: Required with 1 night's deposit.
Reserve Through: Call or fax direct.
Minimum Stay: On some holiday weekends.
Parking: Limited free off-street parking.
In-Room: Color cable TV, AC, telephone, ceiling fans, maid, room & laundry service. VCR rentals available, video tape library. Some rooms with kitchens.
On-Premises: Laundry facilities.
Smoking: Permitted without restrictions.
Pets: Permitted with prior approval.
Handicap Access: With assistance.
Children: Not permitted.
Languages: English & Spanish.
Your Host: Wade & Gabriel.

Chelsea Hotel

Gay-Friendly ♀♂

For the best deal in town, come to the *Chelsea Hotel* in the beautiful Art Deco district of Miami Beach. Located just two blocks from the ocean, we are also just a short walk away from the Convention Center, international dining, and nightclubs. Room amenities include color TV, air conditioning, telephone, refrigerator and shower/bath. We also provide 24-hour security as well as sightseeing and tour information. The airport and downtown business area are only 20 minutes from the hotel. **Address: 944 Washington Ave, Miami Beach, FL 33139. Tel: (305) 534-4069, Fax: (305) 672-6712.**

Type: Hotel.
Clientele: Mostly straight clientele with a gay & lesbian following.
Transportation: Bus from airport. Pick up provided for $10.
Rooms: 43 rooms.
Bathrooms: All Private.
Vegetarian: Restaurants nearby.
Dates Open: All year.
High Season: October-March.
Rates: From $40 & up. Weekly rates available.
Discounts: Please inquire.
Credit Cards: MC, VISA, Amex & Eurocard.
Reserve Through: Call direct.
Parking: On-street & off-street pay parking.
In-Room: Color TV, AC, phones, refrigerator & maid service.
On-Premises: Coin laundry, 24-hour security.
Swimming: 2 blocks to ocean beach.
Sunbathing: At nearby beach.
Smoking: Permitted without restriction.
Pets: Not permitted.
Children: Some restrictions. Please inquire.
Languages: English, Spanish & German.

Colours, The Mantell Guest Inn

Gay/Lesbian ♀♂

Experience Not Just a Place, But a State of Mind

Another South Beach First: Colours, The Mantell Guest Inn

Miami Beach has earned its reputation as "the" new gay destination. A recent Human Rights Ordinance outlawing discrimination against gays and lesbians passed unanimously in the city, recognizing the vast contributions the gay community makes to the renaissance of this historic oceanfront resort. It's no surprise to find a Gay Business Guild, gay political activists, restaurants with drag waiters, clubs, hotels and hundreds of gay-friendly businesses.

EXPERIENCE...

Colours
Destinations

YOUR DOORWAY TO OUR WORLD

Consequently, South Beach, the almost forgotten resort district discovered by artists and gay entrepreneurs and saved from the wrecking ball by historic preservationists a decade ago, has become the hottest global vacation spot of the Gay 90's. The streets and beaches are once again crowded with tourists, film companies and international fashion photographers who have come to enjoy the magic that has long been Miami Beach. Renovated hotels and shops spill onto the avenues with restaurants, art galleries, designer clothing boutiques, modeling agencies and some of the world's hottest nightclubs. Now at the center of this gay mecca is *Colours, The Mantell Guest Inn.*

This historic art deco hotel was completely renovated in 1994 and sold as individual units. This new idea in gay travel certainly brightens the locations for travelers who want to go to a stunning resort with the comfort of a home. Experience ... the boardwalk, white sandy beaches, turquoise waters and warm ocean breezes within one block. Experience ... a refreshing late afternoon swim in our secluded tropical pool, under swaying palms and clear blue skies. Experience ... dancing till dawn at the hottest clubs or the culinary delights of South Beach's finest restaurants. Experience ... uniquely appointed rooms, with terraces, ocean views and kitchenettes available.

Speak to our friendly reservations staff about our other distinctive lodgings — *Colours, The Guest Mansion* in romantic Key West, and *Colours, The Guest Residence* in exotic San Jose, Costa Rica.

Address: 255 West 24th St, South Miami Beach, FL 33140. Tel: (305) 538-1821 Local. Reservations: (800) ARRIVAL, (305) 532-9341, Fax: (305) 534-0362.

Type: Hotel inn guesthouse.
Clientele: Mostly gay & lesbian with some straight clientele.
Transportation: Super shuttle from Miami Int'l Airport. Pick up from airport $20-$30 roundtrip per person.
To Gay Bars: 2 blocks or a 5-minute walk.
Rooms: 25+ studios with single, double or queen beds.
Bathrooms: All private bath/toilets.
Meals: Expanded conti-nental breakfast.
Complimentary: Evening happy hour, turndown mints.
Dates Open: All year.
High Season: November-May.
Rates: Summer (June-Oct) $49-$119.
Discounts: Single occupancy, length of stay, method of payment & prepayment.
Credit Cards: MC, VISA, Amex & Discover.
Rsv'tns: Required.
Reserve Through: Travel agent or call direct.
Minimum Stay: Required for certain events, holidays.
Parking: Adequate free on-street parking.
In-Room: Color TV, AC, telephone, kitchen, refrigerator, coffee/tea-making facilities & maid service. Some units with color cable TV & ceiling fans.
On-Premises: TV lounge, laundry facilities & fax.
Exercise/Health: Gym & weights on premises. Nearby Jacuzzi, sauna, steam & massage.
Swimming: Pool on premises, ocean nearby.
Sunbathing: At poolside, beach, on patio & common & private sun decks.
Nudity: Permitted at poolside.
Smoking: No smoking in TV lounge. Non-smoking rooms available.
Pets: Not permitted.
Handicap Access: Yes.
Children: Not especially welcome.
Languages: English, Spanish & French.

Island House

Men ♂

You'll Feel Right at Home and You'll Want to Come Again!

Your stay at the *Island House* is your ticket to a magical vacation of sun, sea breezes, dining, nightlife and romance. Staffed and dedicated to catering to your lifestyle, we offer the service and amenities you desire. You will be comfortable in our luxuriously furnished rooms, suites and villas, all with private baths, air conditioning, direct room phones, color cable TV and refrigerators or kitchenettes.

Relax! Enjoy our lushly landscaped tropical patio, sun deck and gardens. Take off your shoes, put your feet up, feel the warmth of the sun. Enjoy the feeling all over, "au naturel," if you like. Unwind in the Jacuzzi with your new friends. Come to the *Island House*, come awaken your senses!

There are now three Miami Beach/South Beach locations, all conveniently located to hot nightlife and beautiful gay/gay nude beaches.

Address: 3 beach locations, check in at 715 82nd St, Miami Beach, FL 33141. Tel: (305) 864-2422, (800) 382-2422, Fax: (305) 865-2220.

Type: Guesthouses.
Clientele: Men only.
Transportation: From airport: car, taxi, shuttle. Pick up from airport, $15 per person, $30 minimum. Call to arrange details.
To Gay Bars: 4 blocks or 1/2 mile. A 5-minute walk or drive.
Rooms: 12 rooms, 3 suites, 2 apartments & 1 cottage with double, queen or king beds.
Bathrooms: All private.
Meals: Expanded continental breakfast.
Vegetarian: 2 vegetarian restaurants conveniently located (10-minute drive), delivery available.
Complimentary: Coffee, tea, hot chocolate & orange juice.
Dates Open: All year.
High Season: Dec 1-Apr 30 & holidays.
Rates: Summer $45-$129. Winter $59-$149.
Discounts: Discounts for extended stays, subject to availability.
Credit Cards: MC, VISA, Amex & Discover.
Rsv'tns: Suggested. However, we will try to accommodate your last minute plans.
Parking: Ample free parking.
In-Room: Color cable TV, AC, kitchen, refrigerator, coffee/tea-making facilities, direct-dial phones, ceiling fans, laundry & maid service.
On-Premises: TV lounge, laundry facilities, fax & copier (in office, available

continued next page

for guest use).
Exercise/Health: Jacuzzi & massage on premises. Gym, weights, sauna & steam nearby.
Swimming: Ocean nearby.

Sunbathing: On the patio, common sun decks, or at the beach.
Nudity: Permitted on tropical sun patio/deck with Jacuzzi spa. 5 min to gay nude beach.

Smoking: Permitted in your room or on outside patio areas.
Pets: Permitted in certain rooms & suites by special prior arrangement.
Handicap Access: No.

Languages: English, Spanish, French & German.
Your Host: Richard.

IGTA

Jefferson House, The

Gay/Lesbian ♀♂

THE House on the Beach...

is *Jefferson House*, located in the midst of the historical Art Deco District of South Beach. Famous Miami Beach and exciting Ocean Drive are a few blocks from our door, as are the diverse restaurants and clubs of the area. All of our air conditioned rooms have private baths and queen-sized beds, and are tastefully appointed to add warmth and charm. Enjoy the friendly hospitality of a fine breakfast served on our deck overlooking a lovely tropical garden and pool. Come and experience the camaraderie that *The Jefferson House* has to offer.

Address: 1018 Jefferson Ave, Miami Beach, FL 33139. Tel: (305) 534-5247

Type: Bed & Breakfast.
Clientele: Mostly gay & lesbian with some straight clientele.
Transportation: Car, taxi, shuttle or bus.
To Gay Bars: 3 blocks. A 5-minute walk or 2-minute drive.
Rooms: 6 rooms & 1 suite with queen beds.
Bathrooms: All private shower/toilets.
Meals: Full breakfast.
Vegetarian: Available

upon request.
Complimentary: Set-up service.
Dates Open: All year.
High Season: Oct 15-Apr 30.
Rates: High season $85-$135, low season $65-$115.
Discounts: TAC 10%.
Credit Cards: MC, VISA & Amex.
Rsv'tns: Required.
Reserve Through: Travel agent or call direct.

Minimum Stay: Required on weekends.
Parking: Limited on-street parking.
In-Room: AC, radio & maid service, phones with free local calls.
On-Premises: TV lounge & laundry facilities. New Jet-Stream spa.
Exercise/Health: Nearby gym, weights, tennis, track & basketball. Special rates for guests.
Swimming: Pool on

premises, ocean nearby.
Sunbathing: On the patio or at the beach.
Smoking: Permitted anywhere.
Pets: Not permitted.
Handicap Access: No.
Children: Not especially welcome.
Languages: English, Spanish & a little German.
Your Host: Gerry.

IGTA

Normandy South

Men ♂

If Gauguin Had Stopped Here, He May Never Have Made it to Tahiti!

Standing on a palm-lined street in a quiet, safe, residential neighborhood close to the convention center, *Normandy South* is a Mediterranean revival home among similar architectural gems dating from Art Deco's heydey, the Roaring 20s. Within easy walking distance of South Beach's ever-expanding choice of gay clubs, trendy restaurants and chic (and funky!) shops, we welcome the sophisticated male traveler who demands a prime location, luxury and elegance without formality and stuffiness.

Guest accommodations are generous, each with a new marble and tile bath en suite, and are poshly furnished with queen- and king-sized beds, exciting, original art and colorful dhurries. In addition to three doubles and two suites (one with its own terrace) in the main house, there is a separate two-bedroom carriage house at the opposite end of the spectacular "Miami Vice" pool.

When not out dancing, shopping or cruising the gay beaches, guests are encouraged to lounge poolside, perfecting a no-tan-line tan, socialize in the Jacuzzi or work off those extra piña coladas in the 44-foot lap lane. For a change of pace, one can slip off to the shaded grotto and luxuriate in the hot tub beneath a thatched chickee, or snooze in the oversized hammock. As might be expected in this tropical hideaway, clothing is optional both inside and outside. Should one choose, a freshly-plucked hibiscus or jasmine tucked behind one's ear is raiment enough. What is not optional is smoking. Guests are strictly limited to non-smokers, no exceptions. Here, one is free to enjoy, without interference, the freshly-scented ocean breezes and fragrant blossoms that abound.

Address: Miami Beach, FL. Tel: (305) 674-1197, Fax: (305) 532-9771.

Type: Guesthouse.
Clientele: Men only.
Transportation: Super Shuttle or taxi direct from airport to guesthouse.
To Gay Bars: 10 minutes to Warsaw, Paragon, Westend, Hombre, Snap, Twist, Kremlin.
Rooms: 3 rooms, 2 suites & one 2-bedroom carriage house with queen or king beds.
Bathrooms: All private.
Meals: Tropical continen-

tal breakfast.
Dates Open: All year.
High Season: November through April.
Rates: Winter $90-$160, summer $70-$120.
Credit Cards: MC, VISA & Amex.
Rsv'tns: Recommended.
Reserve Through: Travel agent or call direct.
Minimum Stay: Varies with season & holiday.
Parking: Ample, free off-street parking.
In-Room: Full-range

cable TV, central air, maid & complimentary laundry service, refrigerator, VCR w/fun flics, ceiling fans.
Exercise/Health: Gym & Jacuzzi with massage by appointment.
Swimming: Heated pool w/lap lane on premises. Five minutes to gay beaches.
Sunbathing: At poolside, on private or common sun decks & at public beaches.

Nudity: Clothing optional inside, at poolside, on sun decks, in grotto, at nude beach.
Smoking: Completely, totally & absolutely non-smoking inside & outside.
Pets: Permitted with prior arrangement.
Handicap Access: No.
Children: Not permitted.
Your Host: Hank & Bruce.

IGTA

Shore Club Ocean Resort, The

Gay/Lesbian ♀♂

The Only Full Service Gay Resort in South Beach

The Shore Club Resort is a 226-room, newly-renovated resort with an Olympic-sized pool, poolside cabanas and poolboy service. The property boasts 5 bars and 2 restaurants for indoor-outdoor dining, plus 24-hour room service. There are two lobby retail shops, a full service hair salon, an oceanfront water sports concession, a beach club for weekend tea dances, and a 30 foot stage for concerts under the stars. There are also spa services, concierge services and oceanfront suites with large balconies.

Shore Club will not sacrifice service or style in any of its operations and offers only first class accommodations and service. The resort, just two blocks from the Miami Beach Convention Center, will cater to conventions as well as individuals. Groups of up to 150 people can be catered to and convention service professionals are available to assist with all meeting needs. The management is working with area clubs and attractions on a variety of promotional packages and discounts.

Address: 1901 Collins Ave, Miami Beach, FL 33139. Tel: (800) 327-8330, (305) 538-7811, Fax: (305) 531-1158, Office: (305) 534-3443.

Type: Full service resort with restaurants, bars & clothing shops.

Clientele: Mostly gay & lesbian with some straight clientele.

Transportation: Taxi from Miami International Airport.

To Gay Bars: On the premises.

continued next page

Florida

Rooms: 206 rooms & 10 suites with double or king beds.
Bathrooms: All private.
Meals: Special packages available upon request.
Vegetarian: Available upon request at all times in our main dining room.
Complimentary: Mints & "condomints" on pillows.
Dates Open: All year.
High Season: December thru April.
Rates: Standard room: low $69, high $79. 2-bdrm/3 bath oceanfront suite: low $275, high $315.
Discounts: Vary. Available during specially-packaged weekends.
Credit Cards: MC, VISA, Amex, Diners & Eurocard.
Rsv'tns: Required, but walk-ins welcome if rooms are available.
Reserve Through: Travel agents or call direct (800) 327-8330.
Parking: Adequate off-street parking.
In-Room: Color cable TV, AC, telephone, safe, mini bar, maid & room service.
On-Premises: Meeting rooms, fax, secretarial work, copies & laundry facilities.
Exercise/Health: Gym, Jacuzzi & massage on premises. Nearby gym.
Swimming: Olympic-sized pool & ocean on premises.
Sunbathing: At poolside, on private balconies & on the beach.
Smoking: Permitted. Non-smoking rooms available.
Pets: Not permitted.
Handicap Access: No.
Children: Welcome.
Languages: English, Spanish, German & Hebrew.
Your Host: Patrick, Gina, Michael & Wendy.

IGTA

Villa Paradiso Guesthouse

Gay/Lesbian ♀♂

A Breath of Fresh Air on South Beach

Where else in the 1990's but South Beach? Be in the heart of the Art Deco District at *Villa Paradiso Guesthouse.* You have your own studio or one-bedroom apartment overlooking a lush garden courtyard. Set in tropical colors, the newly-renovated apartments feature ceiling fans, hardwood floors, Art Deco furniture, French doors and complete kitchens. You are 1/2 block from the beach and 2 blocks from the gay beach. Eat and model-watch on world famous Ocean Drive, shop and party on Washington Avenue and, of course, lay your head to rest at *Villa Paradiso.*

Address: 1415 Collins Ave, Miami Beach, FL 33139. Tel: (305) 532-0616, Fax: (305) 667-0074.

Type: Guesthouse.
Clientele: Mostly gay & lesbian with some straight clientele.
Transportation: Taxi or Super Shuttle from airport.
To Gay Bars: 1/2 block to Warsaw, Orchid. 5-10 minutes to Twist, Kremlin, Paragon & Westend.
Rooms: 15 studios & 2 apartments with double or queen beds.
Bathrooms: All private bath/toilet/showers.
Dates Open: All year.
High Season: November-April.
Rates: High: night $75-$115, week $395-$650, month $1375-$1875. Low: night $55-$95, week $275-$475, month $825-$1375.
Credit Cards: MC, VISA & Amex.
Rsv'tns: Advised, but walk-ins welcome.
Reserve Through: Call direct.
Parking: On-street pay parking. 1 block to parking garage.
In-Room: Color TV, AC, ceiling fans, telephone, kitchen, refrigerator, coffee/tea-making facilities & maid service.
On-Premises: Laundry facilities.
Swimming: 1/2 block to ocean beach & 2 blocks to gay beach.
Sunbathing: At the beach.
Smoking: Permitted.
Pets: Not permitted.
Handicap Access: Yes, with assistance.
Languages: English, Spanish & French.
Your Host: Greg & Glenn.

ORLANDO

A Veranda B&B

Relive a Bygone Southern Era

Gay-Friendly 50/50 ♀♂

Welcome to the *Veranda*, located within the Lawsona Historical District in downtown Orlando. All of our suites have hardwood floors, private baths and are beautifully furnished with Oriental rugs, art and exceptional period pieces. Designer bed linens, feather pillows and goose down duvets are just a few of the many special touches that will make your stay as comfortable as possible. Each of our suites is complete with telephone intercom system, color cable television and your very own French door entrance to the wrap-around veranda. We are the ONLY licensed bed and breakfast in Orlando.

Address: 115 N Summerlin Ave, Orlando, FL 32801. Tel: (407) 849-0321

Type: Bed & breakfast cottages.
Clientele: 50% gay & lesbian & 50% straight clientele.
Transportation: We provide airport pick up. Shuttle service $18 each way.
To Gay Bars: 6 blocks.
Rooms: Rooms, suites and villas with double & king beds.
Bathrooms: All private.

Meals: Expanded continental breakfast.
Vegetarian: Nearby.
Complimentary: Wine, cocktail hour, turn-down mints.
Dates Open: All year.
Rates: $65-$140.
Discounts: Senior, weekly.
Credit Cards: MC, VISA, Amex.
Rsv'tns: Required.
Reserve Through: Travel agent or call direct.

Parking: Adequate off-street & on-street parking. In the heart of downtown.
In-Room: Color cable TV, video tape library, AC, telephone, kitchen, refrigerator, coffee/tea-making facilities, maid, room & laundry service.
On-Premises: Fax. Wedding courtyard for all sexual preferences.
Exercise/Health: Jacuzzi

& massage. Nearby gym, weights, Jacuzzi, sauna, steam.
Swimming: Nearby pool, ocean, river & lake.
Sunbathing: On the patio, veranda & private sun decks.
Smoking: Permitted.
Pets: Permitted.
Handicap Access: Yes.
Children: Welcome.
Languages: English.
Your Host: Blair.

Garden Cottage Bed & Breakfast

Gay/Lesbian ♀♂

Escape to a relaxed garden atmosphere in historical downtown Orlando. Located in a quiet, safe neighborhood, our renovated 1920's home has a cozy garden cottage adjacent to it. *Garden Cottage* is beautifully decorated with antiques, wicker, fine art, designer linens and accents. Sunbathe in the garden, stroll to famous Lake Eola and downtown to Church Street Station and marketplace, unique shops, galleries, restaurants, coffeehouses and nightclubs. Disney, MGM, Universal Studios, Hard Rock Cafe, Sea World, and more, are within 15-30 minutes by car. Beaches are a 45-minute drive away.

Address: 1309 E Washington St Orlando, FL 32801. Tel: (407) 894-5395, Fax: (407) 894-3809.

Type: Bed & breakfast.
Clientele: Mostly gay & lesbian with some straight clientele.
Transportation: Car or taxi from airport. $10 for airport pick up when available.
To Gay Bars: 10 blocks, 1-1/2 miles, a 10-minute walk or a 2-minute drive. Other bars 2-3 mi.
Rooms: 1 cottage with queen bed.
Bathrooms: Private shower/toilet.

Meals: Expanded continental breakfast.
Vegetarian: Vegetarian breakfast (bread, fruit, muffins, bagels, croissants) & 2 blocks to vegetarian restaurants.
Complimentary: Tea, coffee, cocoa & fruit juices in room at all times.
Dates Open: All year.
High Season: Spring break, Thanksgiving & Christmas.
Rates: $60-$75.
Discounts: 15% to NGLTF

(National Gay & Lesbian Task Force) members. Must show card!
Rsv'tns: Required.
Reserve Through: Call direct.
Parking: Ample off-street parking.
In-Room: Color cable TV, VCR, video tape library, AC, ceiling fans, telephone, kitchen, refrigerator, coffee & tea-making facilities, maid service & laundry service for towels & bed linens.

Exercise/Health: YMCA 2 blocks away with gym, weights, sauna & massage. Must pay!
Sunbathing: In courtyard.
Smoking: Permitted outside in the courtyard only. Room is non-smoking.
Pets: Not permitted.
Handicap Access: No.
Children: 1 child's rollaway bed available with extra charge.
Languages: English.

Parliament House Hotel

Gay/Lesbian ♂

Parliament House Hotel, the world's most famous all gay resort and entertainment complex, provides comfortable, modern motel-style rooms, restaurant, daytime bar, disco with live entertainment and even gay shops on the premises. Our location is very convenient to other gay night spots in Orlando, as well as to shopping, restaurants and theaters downtown. Welcome to Florida's premier gay resort!

Address: 410 N Orange Blossom Trail, Orlando, FL 32805. Tel: (407) 425-7571, Fax: (407) 425-5881.

Type: Motel with restaurant, bars, disco & shops.
Clientele: Mostly men with women welcome.
Transportation: Taxi.
To Gay Bars: 5 bars in the complex.
Rooms: 120 doubles.
Bathrooms: All private.
Vegetarian: Available in restaurant.
Dates Open: All year.
High Season: Winter.
Rates: $35-$80 plus tax.
Credit Cards: MC, VISA, Amex.
Rsv'tns: Suggested.
Reserve Through: Call direct.
Parking: Ample secured parking.
In-Room: Room & maid service, color TV, telephone, & AC.
On-Premises: Footlight Theater, 24 hour restaurant, lounge, laundry & shops.
Exercise/Health: Fitness center nearby & volleyball courts.
Swimming: Lake behind property. Pool on premises.
Sunbathing: At lakeside or poolside.
Smoking: Permitted without restrictions.
Pets: Permitted with deposit.
Handicap Access: Yes.
Children: Not permitted.
Languages: English.

ST AUGUSTINE

Pagoda

Women ♀

Pagoda, a residential cottage community of lesbians, includes the newly-renovated spiritual and cultural center, The Pagoda Temple of Love, available to all women for rest, retreat, recuperation and healing. We have been providing our non-profit, women-only retreat space for 17 years. Our 3-story house has been converted to multi-purpose use and includes a theater for concerts. The building is supported by donations, memberships and guests. Retreat expenses are tax deductible. Our kitchen is vegetarian and is available for our guests' use.

Address: 2854 Coastal Hwy, St Augustine, FL 32095-2308. Tel: (904) 824-2970

Type: Guest house in lesbian community with cultural center.
Clientele: Women only.
Transportation: Rental car is best, airport 1 hr away.
To Gay Bars: 15 miles or a 20-minute drive to Kahuna's at Crescent Beach.
Rooms: 5 rooms with double beds.
Bathrooms: 2 shared bath/shower/toilets.
Vegetarian: Kitchens are vegetarian. Veggie & health food stores in St. Augustine.
Dates Open: All year.
High Season: Mar-Sept weekends fill up fast.
Rates: $15 per night per woman.
Discounts: Monthly memberships available.
Rsv'tns: Required.
Reserve Through: Call direct.
Parking: Ample, free on-premises parking.
In-Room: AC.
On-Premises: Kitchen, library, TV lounge, house phone, meeting rooms, laundry facilities.
Exercise/Health: Jogging & swimming, massage.
Swimming: Pool on premises, nearby beach.
Sunbathing: At poolside & on the beach.
Nudity: Only in the pool.
Smoking: Permitted outdoors. Pool has smoking area.
Pets: Not permitted.
Handicap Access: Yes.
Children: Females only.
Languages: English.
Your Host: Paula.

Take along the Expert

Ferrari's Places of Interest™ contains articles contributed by gay and lesbian journalists on the scene, giving insight into gay and lesbian communities worldwide. With its accompanying directory, it's the perfect vacation planner.

ST PETERSBURG & CLEARWATER

Cape House

Gay/Lesbian ♀♂

Still The Suncoast's ONLY Inn on the Gulf

Relax in this completely restored Cape Cod house on the white sands of St. Petersburg Beach. *Cape House* is steps away from the azure waters of the Gulf of Mexico. It's a quiet respite from a hectic and hurried world. The house is furnished with antiques and imported items. All bedrooms have queen-sized beds and private baths. Guests enjoy the spacious deck with spa, the library/den, our social hour and the varied, homemade expanded continental breakfast each morning. Wet bar and TV available in den.

Address: 2800 Pass-A-Grille Way, St. Petersburg Beach, FL 33706. Tel: (813) 367-6971

Type: Bed & breakfast inn.
Clientele: Good mix of gay men & women.
Transportation: Rental car from airport is best, 2 airport shuttles available.
To Gay Bars: 5-minute walk to gay & lesbian bars.
Rooms: 3 rooms with queen beds.
Bathrooms: All private bath/toilets.

Meals: Expanded continental breakfast.
Vegetarian: Available upon request.
Complimentary: Wet bar has complimentary mixes & snacks at cocktail hour.
Dates Open: All year.
High Season: December-April.
Rates: $60.
Discounts: For 6 or more nights.

Rsv'tns: Required.
Reserve Through: Travel agent or call direct.
Minimum Stay: Required.
Parking: Ample, off-street parking.
In-Room: Central AC, radio, ceiling fans, maid service. TV in room upon request.
On-Premises: TV lounge, guest den with wet bar

& laundry facilities.
Exercise/Health: Spa.
Swimming: At Gulf beach.
Sunbathing: On the beach or deck.
Smoking: Permitted outside on deck or enclosed porch.
Pets: Not permitted.
Handicap Access: No.
Children: Not permitted.
Languages: English.

Garden Guest Houses

Gay/Lesbian ♂

Lush gardens and a gorgeous tropical pool surround *Garden Guest Houses*, an intimate retreat that's quiet and secluded, yet located in the heart of the Tampa Bay Area, just a few blocks to museums and restaurants. Walk or bike to bay beaches or take a short drive to gulf beaches. Comfortable beds, immaculate rooms, and thoughtful service make you feel welcomed and at home.

Address: 920 4th St South, St Petersburg, FL 33701. Tel: (813) 821-3665

Type: Bed & breakfast guesthouses in an enclosed compound.
Clientele: Mostly men with women welcome.
Transportation: Car is best.
To Gay Bars: Nine blocks to St. Pete bars, 30 min to Tampa bars.
Rooms: 5 suites, 1 apartment & 3 cottages with single, double, queen or king beds.

Bathrooms: All private.
Meals: Continental breakfast available on Sundays.
Dates Open: All year.
High Season: December 15 through April 15.
Rates: Winter $38-$110, summer $38-$55.
Discounts: Weekly, monthly & seasonal.
Credit Cards: MC & VISA.
Rsv'tns: Recommended.
Reserve Through: Travel

agent or call direct.
Parking: Ample free off-street parking.
In-Room: Color cable TV, video tape library, AC, maid & laundry service, ceiling fans, telephone, kitchen, refrigerator & coffee/tea-maker.
On-Premises: Laundry facilities, 2 outdoor BBQ's with tables & chairs.
Swimming: Tropical pool on premises, nearby bay

& gulf beaches.
Sunbathing: Poolside.
Nudity: In the pool & poolside.
Smoking: Permitted in rooms & common areas.
Pets: May be permitted, please inquire.
Handicap Access: No.
Children: Not permitted.
Languages: English.
Your Host: Michael.

Sea Oats by the Gulf

Gay-Friendly 50/50 ♀♂

Sea Oats, on lovely Treasure Island, is minutes from St. Petersburg, directly on the Gulf of Mexico. The hotel, with its traditional Key West charm, is modern with beautifully-appointed apartments, efficiencies and studios overlooking the Gulf. Rooms are individually climate controlled, have color cable TV and fully-equipped kitchenette with microwave. Other amenities include a private yard bordered by palm trees and an eight person Jacuzzi. John's Pass, where you can charter boats, go parasailing, take dinner cruises or enjoy many fine restaurants and shops, is one block away. We are AAA approved.

Address: 12625 Sunshine Lane, Treasure Island, FL 33706. Tel: (813) 367-7568, Fax: (813) 397-4157.

Type: Motel.
Clientele: 50% gay & lesbian & 50% straight clientele.
Transportation: Car is best. Limo from Tampa airport available. $10 each way (40 minute ride).
To Gay Bars: All within 5-20 minutes.
Rooms: 1 room & 10 apartments with double & queen beds.
Bathrooms: 7 private

shower/toilets & 4 private bath/toilet/showers.
Dates Open: All year.
High Season: Jan-May.
Rates: Low $35-$95, high $50-$110.
Discounts: 2 week or longer stay.
Credit Cards: MC & VISA.
Reserve Through: Call direct.
Minimum Stay: Required weekends only, Fri/Sat.
Parking: Adequate free

on-street parking.
In-Room: Color cable TV, AC, kitchen, refrigerator, coffee/tea-making facilities, maid & laundry service. Some with ceiling fans.
On-Premises: Laundry facilities.
Exercise/Health: Jacuzzi on premises. Nearby gym.
Swimming: Ocean on the premises & nearby.
Sunbathing: On the

patio, in the backyard or at the beach.
Nudity: Permitted in Jacuzzi area if you book it.
Smoking: Permitted.
Pets: Permitted. Extra flat $10 fee. Small dog, no cats.
Handicap Access: No.
Children: Welcome if well-behaved.
Languages: English.
Your Host: JoAnn & Christie.

SARASOTA

M-T-In Bed & Breakfast

Men ♂

Fun Here or Nearby–Quiet Solitude, if Wanted

M-T-In Bed & Breakfast is a lovely private home run by nice people, offering bargain accommodations to nice men in a quiet, relaxing atmosphere. The house has a dishwasher, disposal, ice maker and laundry, which guests may use. There are five color TVs, four VCRs, a piano, an organ, a guitar, a 10- by 20-foot nude deck, a 28- by 14- by 9-foot pool, large spa/hot tub, gay magazines galore, conversation, if desired, privacy, if not. We are close to theaters, arts, museums and gay bars and permit smoking.

Address: Sarasota, FL . Tel: (813) 927-1619.

Type: Bed & breakfast guesthouse.
Clientele: Men only.
Transportation: Car is necessary. Rental car from airport.
To Gay Bars: 3-5 miles or 6 & 10 minutes by car.
Rooms: 3 rooms with 2 queen & 1 king bed.
Bathrooms: All private baths.
Meals: Continental breakfast, kitchen & grill

privileges.
Vegetarian: Available nearby.
Complimentary: Wine or cocktail on arrival, set-ups available.
Dates Open: All year.
High Season: Dec 15-Apr 15.
Rates: Single $30, double $50.
Discounts: 7th day free.
Rsv'tns: Required, with 1st night's deposit.

Reserve Through: Call direct.
Parking: Ample free off-street parking.
In-Room: Color cable TV, AC, ceiling fans, VCR, video tape library, reading & visual material, maid & laundry service.
On-Premises: TV lounge, laundry facilities, guest refrigerator, deck, phone & lush gardens.
Exercise/Health: Spa.

Swimming: Solar heated pool on premises, nearby gulf beach.
Sunbathing: At poolside, on private & common sun decks.
Nudity: Permitted.
Smoking: Permitted.
Pets: Not permitted.
Handicap Access: No.
Children: Not permitted.
Languages: English.
Your Host: Ted & Marco.

TAMPA

Birdsong Bed and Breakfast

Experience the Natural Beauty of Florida Woodlands

Women ♀

Birdsong B&B offers a tranquil atmosphere on five wooded acres adjacent to a wildlife preserve and the Alafia River. Created especially for women, the spacious private room has its own entrance, kitchen and bath. Hawks, owls, towhees and whippoorwills call from the oak and pine woodland, providing inspiration for creative work, relaxation or romance. Horseback riding, canoeing, camping, swimming, hiking and bike trails are only minutes away. Secluded, yet centrally located, we are less than an hour to beaches, downtown Tampa, and Orlando attractions.

Address: Tampa, FL . Tel: (813) 654-8179

Type: Bed & breakfast.
Clientele: Women only.
Transportation: Car.
To Gay Bars: 35-minute drive to Tampa bars.
Rooms: 1 room with queen bed and kitchen.
Bathrooms: Private shower/toilet.
Meals: Expanded continental breakfast.
Complimentary: Fruit juices, coffee, tea, kitchen staples.
Dates Open: All year.
High Season: December-April.
Rates: $60.
Rsv'tns: Required.
Reserve Through: Call direct.
Minimum Stay: 2 nights on weekends.
Parking: Ample free off-street parking.
In-Room: Color TV, AC, ceiling fans, telephone, kitchen, refrigerator, coffee & tea-making facilities.
Exercise/Health: Massage & bikes. Nearby canoe & horse rentals, hiking trails.
Swimming: Nearby lake & Gulf of Mexico beaches.
Sunbathing: Anywhere.
Nudity: Permitted in certain areas.
Smoking: Permitted outside.
Pets: Not permitted.
Handicap Access: Limited. Call to inquire.
Children: Permitted on approval.
Languages: English.

Gram's Place B&B Guesthouse

Gay/Lesbian ♀♂

An Artists Retreat and a Music Lovers Paradise for All

Grams Place was named in honor of singer/songwriter Gram Parsons (1946-1973), who discovered Emmylou Harris and influenced the Rolling Stones, The Eagles, The Byrds, and thousands worldwide. Designed for those interested in music and the arts, it provides a relaxing, laid back, quiet atmosphere. Guests are encouraged to bring their favorite music, so they feel at home. Musicians, singers, actors, painters, and poets frequently stay and perform here, but all are welcomed. Music played upon request, VCR & CD rental available. There are skylights throughout the house, a fireplace and an outdoor tropical courtyard/pub with waterfall and Jacuzzi.

Address: 3109 N Ola Ave, Tampa, FL 33603. Tel/Fax:(813) 221-0596, Beeper: 292-1415, Res: (800) GRAMS PLACE (472-6775)

Type: Bed & breakfast cottage guesthouse with pub by Jacuzzi.
Clientele: Mostly gay, lesbian & bisexual with some straight clientele.
Transportation: We offer personal shuttle service, for half the price of cab fare, to bars, restaurants, airport, train & bus.
To Gay Bars: 1 mile or 2 minutes by car.
Rooms: 12 rooms. 2 with kitchenettes.
Bathrooms: 5 private, others share.
Meals: Expanded continental breakfast.
Complimentary: Coffee, tea, sodas, juices & lemonade.
Dates Open: All year. May be closed during July & August. Please inquire.
High Season: Dec-Apr.
Rates: $35-$100.
Discounts: Weekly & monthly rates.
Credit Cards: All major cards accepted by 800 reservation number.
Reserve Through: Travel agent or call direct.
Parking: Ample on- & off-street free parking in a well-lit area.
In-Room: Color HBO & cable TV, AC, ceiling fans, telephone & maid service.
On-Premises: TV lounge, laundry facilities, & kitchen privileges. Live music most Sundays.
Exercise/Health: Jacuzzi & outside shower/toilet facilities.
Swimming: Public pools nearby. 30 minutes to ocean beach.
Sunbathing: On the private sun deck by the Jacuzzi.
Nudity: Permitted if other guests do not mind.
Smoking: Prefer outside smoking, but not mandatory.
Pets: Permitted, with restrictions.
Handicap Access: No.
Children: Permitted over 5.
Languages: English.
Your Host: Mark.

WEST PALM BEACH

Hibiscus House B&B (formerly Palm West)

Tropical Elegance At Its Best
Gay-Lesbian ♀♂

Recapture early Florida at the *Hibiscus House B&B.* Originally built as the mayor's mansion, the house has seven guestrooms individually decorated with antiques, all with private baths and private terraces. The suite has a terrace, living room, bedroom and bath. The poolside cottage sleeps 6 and has a kitchen. Relax with a complimentary cocktail by the tropical pool or take our bikes and explore Palm Beach in leisurely fashion. Your hosts, Raleigh & Colin, are always accessible. Our clientele come as guests and leave as friends!

Address: 501 30th St, West Palm Beach, FL 33407. Tel: (407) 863-5633, (800) 203-4927.

Type: Bed & breakfast. **Clientele:** Mainly gay & lesbian with some straight clientele. **Transportation:** Pick up service available from airport, bus, train, port, rental car advised. **To Gay Bars:** 5 blocks to men's bars. **Rooms:** 5 rooms, 1 suite & 1 cottage with queen beds. **Bathrooms:** 2 private bath/toilets & 5 private shower/toilets. **Meals:** Full breakfast. **Vegetarian:** Available with advance notice. **Complimentary:** Cocktails, tea, coffee, soda, chocolates on pillow. **Dates Open:** All year. **High Season:** December through April. **Rates:** Low season $55-$120, high season $75-$150. **Discounts:** For long-term stays. **Credit Cards:** MC, VISA, Amex. **Rsv'tns:** Required. **Reserve Through:** Travel agent or call direct. **Parking:** Ample, free off-street parking. **In-Room:** Maid service, color TV, telephone, AC & ceiling fans. **On-Premises:** Laundry facilities & kitchen privileges. **Swimming:** In pool on premises or 15 minutes to ocean. **Sunbathing:** Poolside or patios & private sun decks. **Nudity:** Permitted with discretion. **Smoking:** Permitted with restrictions. **Pets:** Small pets permitted. **Handicap Access:** No. **Children:** Not permitted. **Languages:** English. **Your Host:** Raleigh & Colin.

West Palm Beach Bed & Breakfast

Gay/Lesbian ♀♂

West Palm Beach Bed & Breakfast, an enchanting house built in the 1930's, has private baths, AC, paddle fans, cable TV, all set in a private Key West-style compound. Your hosts have retained the charm of old-world Florida with white wicker furniture in a colorful Caribbean decor. Tan by the poolside or on private sun decks secluded by lush tropical foliage. Tour the area on complimentary bicycles, or just relax and kick off your sandals! We are centrally located, one block from the waterway, minutes to beaches or the town of Palm Beach. We look forward to making your stay an enjoyable and memorable one!

Address: 419 32nd St, Old Northwood Historic District, West Palm Beach, FL 33407-4809. Tel: (407) 848-4064 or (800) 736-4064. Fax: (407) 842-1688.

Type: Bed & breakfast guesthouse with cottage. **Clientele:** Good mix of gays & lesbians. **Transportation:** Complimentary pickup from airport, bus, train, Port of Palm Beach. Rental car advised. **To Gay Bars:** 6 blocks.. **Rooms:** 2 rooms & 1 cottage with queen beds. **Bathrooms:** 1 private bath/toilet & 2 private shower/toilets. **Meals:** Expanded Continental breakfast. **Vegetarian:** Available upon request. **Complimentary:** Iced tea & wine. **Dates Open:** All year. **High Season:** December-April. **Rates:** Summer $55-$95, winter $65-$115. **Discounts:** Weekly, midweek and off-season rates. **Credit Cards:** MC, VISA, Amex & Diners. **Rsv'tns:** Required. **Reserve Through:** Travel agent or call direct. **Minimum Stay:** 2 nights on holidays. **Parking:** Ample, free, well-lit, off-street parking & on-street parking. **In-Room:** Color cable TV, VCR, maid service, AC, ceiling fans, kitchen, refrigerator, coffee & tea-making facilities. **On-Premises:** TV lounge. **Exercise/Health:** Jogging trail by waterway, bicycle path (complimentary bicycles available), nearby public tennis & golf. **Swimming:** Pool on premises. Nearby ocean, including MacArthur Beach (gay). **Sunbathing:** At poolside, on patio & common sun decks & at the beaches. **Nudity:** Permitted on sun decks, in gardens, at poolside with consent of other guests. **Smoking:** Permitted outdoors, all rooms non-smoking. **Pets:** Not permitted. **Handicap Access:** No. **Children:** Not especially welcomed. **Languages:** English. **Your Host:** Dennis.

IGTA

GEORGIA

ATLANTA

Above The Clouds B&B

Women ♀

We'd like to share our 50-mile view of the Blue Ridge Mountains with people who enjoy the quiet and privacy of a mountain getaway. We call our place *Above the Clouds*. Our guests occupy a large suite with its own private entrance, deck and spa, a queen-sized bed and adjoining bath. There is a winery in town which guests can visit, and nearby, a restored gold mine and native crafts to browse and buy. You can hike the Appalachian Trail, go canoeing and horseback riding or, on a lazier day, enjoy a picnic in the woods.

Address: Rt 4 Box 250, Dahlonega, GA 30533. Tel: (706) 864-5211.

Type: Bed & breakfast.
Clientele: Women only.
Transportation: Car is best.
To Gay Bars: One hour by car to Atlanta bars.
Rooms: 1 suite with queen bed.
Bathrooms: Private bath/ toilet.
Meals: Full breakfast.
Vegetarian: Breakfast available with advance notice. Vegetarian restaurant in Dahlonega.
Complimentary: Soft drinks, coffee, tea & hot chocolate.
Dates Open: All year.
High Season: Labor Day through Thanksgiving.
Rates: $75 per night per couple.
Rsv'tns: Required with 50% deposit.
Reserve Through: Call direct.
Minimum Stay: 2 nights for holidays & special events.
Parking: Ample free off-street parking.
In-Room: Color TV, VCR, video tape library, AC, telephone, ceiling fan, refrigerator & coffee & tea-making facilities.
Exercise/Health: Jacuzzi.
Sunbathing: On private sun decks.
Nudity: Permitted in spa & on sun deck.
Smoking: Permitted outside.
Pets: Not permitted.
Handicap Access: No.
Children: Not especially welcomed.
Languages: English & some Spanish.
Your Host: Diane & Donna.

Ansley Inn

Experience Atlanta From the INN-SIDE...

Gay-Friendly ♀♂

Nestled in the heart of mid-town Atlanta, in historic Ansley Park, *Ansley Inn* offers exceptional residental living and beautiful conference and reception facilities in a turn-of-the-century English Tudor mansion. Previously home to Atlanta clothier and philanthropist, George Muse, and then an exclusive boarding house for young, single women, the house underwent a monumental 2-1/2 year refurbishing program after being purchased by the present owners in 1987. Massive fireplaces, crystal chandeliers, original impressionistic art, marble floors and period pieces from Chippendale, Queen Anne and Empire all create a magical ambiance you will remember long after your visit.

A stay at *Ansley Inn* enables you to have the best of both the old world and the new. Each uniquely decorated room is equipped with cable color TV, phone, wet

continued next page

bar, bath with Jacuzzi, climate control and ample closet space. Some of our rooms have fireplaces and many have four poster beds. Continental breakfast is served in the dining room and in the afternoon appetizers and set ups await you in the living room. We also offer the morning paper, catered lunch and dinner in your room, same day laundry and dry-cleaning, 24-hour concierge service, and health club privileges.

Ansley Inn is located in the middle of everything that makes Atlanta wonderful. We're just minutes from Downtown's Underground, a few short blocks from the theatre district, and we're surrounded by the greenery of five public parks. Our neighbors include High Museum, Woodruff Arts Center, and Atlanta Botanical Gardens. MARTA, Atlanta's award-winning subway system, is also within walking distance.

We consider it our pleasure as well as our responsibility to help you feel comfortable during your visit with us. Our concierge staff will be happy to assist you with dinner reservations, taxis, rental car arrangements, business information and services, or whatever else it takes to make things run smoothly for you.

Address: 253 15th St NE, Atlanta, GA 30309. Tel: (404) 872-9000, (800) 446-5416, Fax: (404) 892-2318.

Type: Inn.
Clientele: Mostly straight clientele with a gay & lesbian following.
Transportation: MARTA or taxi.
To Gay Bars: 6 blocks or 1/4 mile. A ten-minute walk or 5-minute drive.
Rooms: 13 rooms, 1 suite & 2 apartments with queen beds.
Bathrooms: All private.

Meals: Expanded continental breakfast.
Vegetarian: Available with 24hr notice.
Complimentary: Tea, coffee & set-up service.
Dates Open: All year.
Rates: $85-$450.
Discounts: 20% corporate.
Credit Cards: MC, VISA, Amex, Diners, Discover.
Reserve Through: Travel agent or call direct.

Parking: Ample, free off-street parking.
In-Room: Color cable TV, AC, telephone, ceiling fans, kitchen, refrigerator, maid, laundry & room service.
On-Premises: Meeting rooms. Business services available upon request.
Exercise/Health: Jacuzzi & massage. Nearby gym & massage.

Swimming: Pool on premises. Nearby river & lake.
Sunbathing: At poolside.
Smoking: Permitted with some restrictions in public space.
Pets: Permitted.
Handicap Access: Yes.
Children: Welcome.
Languages: English, limited Spanish.
Your Host: Tim.

Hidden Creek

Men to Mint Juleps

Men ♂

Hidden Creek, only fifteen minutes from exciting midtown Atlanta nightlife, offers a relaxing respite with its 2.5 acres of forest, spring fed creek and secluded garden hot tub. Inside, the imposing stone fireplace, oak pool table and picture windows overlooking the creek and garden, highlight a rich and uniquely designed interior. The private woodland setting provides a world that encourages freedom of spirit and expression, a comfortable place to meet people and make new friends, and an inviting home away from home. Member of Atlanta Convention & Visitors Bureau.

Address: 201 North Mill Rd, Atlanta, GA 30328. Tel: (404) 705-9545

Type: Bed & breakfast guesthouse.
Clientele: Men only.

Transportation: Car is best. Marta rail system, bus.
To Gay Bars: 15 minutes

by transportation. Easy to locate.
Rooms: 5 rooms with

queen beds.
Bathrooms: 3 private, 1 shared.

Meals: Full breakfast.
Complimentary: Hot & cold drinks, social hour, all male video library.
Dates Open: All year.
Rates: $65-$95, $20 each additional person.
Credit Cards: MC, VISA, Amex.
Rsv'tns: Required.
Reserve Through: Travel agent or call direct.
Minimum Stay: Required. Varies with different holidays or events.
Parking: Adequate off-street parking.
In-Room: Color cable TV, VCR, telephone, ceiling fans, AC & maid service.
On-Premises: Fireplace, oak pool table, wet bar, baby grand piano & laundry service.
Exercise/Health: Weight room, secluded garden hot tub & massage by appointment.
Swimming: Nearby pool.
Sunbathing: On common sun deck.
Nudity: Permitted in spa with discretion.
Smoking: Limited to exterior only.
Pets: Not permitted.
Handicap Access: No.
Children: Not permitted.
Languages: English.
Your Host: Scott & Tom.

IGTA

Our Home

Gay/Lesbian ♀♂

Azaleas, dogwood, magnolias and roses decorate our tranquil surroundings. Your own private entrance, and private parking area, lead to your private room and bath at *Our Home*. Newly renovated, the room features an entire wall graced by a leaded, stained-glass window. The grounds are interestingly landscaped and include a fish pond. Our location is just 20 minutes from downtown Atlanta via route 29, 15 minutes from Stone Mt. Park, and is easily accessible from Interstate 85, both north- and southbound, from Hwy 20, both east- and westbound and I-285 around Atlanta, Exit 29.

Address: 1451 Sanden Ferry Drive, Decatur (Atlanta), GA 30033. Tel: (404) 491-0248.

Type: Bed & breakfast.
Clientele: Good mix of gays & lesbians.
Transportation: Car is best.
To Gay Bars: 30 minutes by car to gay & lesbian bars.
Rooms: 1 room with 2 single beds & private entrance.
Bathrooms: 1 private shower/toilet.
Meals: Continental breakfast.
Vegetarian: Health food cafe 1/4 mile away.
Complimentary: Tea, coffee, juices, plus condoms in the room.
Dates Open: All year.
Rates: Single $60, double $65. May be higher when the Olympics are in town.
Discounts: Call directly to Our Home for discount.
Rsv'tns: Required.
Reserve Through: Travel agent or call direct.
Minimum Stay: 2 nights.
Parking: Ample free off-street parking and circular drive.
In-Room: AC, refrigerator.
On-Premises: 2 TV lounges (one non-smoking) with color TV, to interact with hosts, too.
Exercise/Health: Guest access with host to nearby gym.
Swimming: Guest access to nearby pool with host.
Sunbathing: On the patio.
Smoking: Not encouraged, but permitted in TV lounge.
Pets: Not permitted, 2 dogs on premises.
Handicap Access: No.
Children: Not especially welcomed.
Languages: English.

Upper Echelons

Glamour-Glamour

Gay/Lesbian ♀♂

For business or pleasure, come visit Atlanta, a brave and beautiful city, a city "too busy to hate." Come celebrate at *Upper Echelons,* a secure, serene, sophisticated, petite penthouse in the heart of downtown Atlanta. A dramatic and romantic condo with black lacquered kitchen, mirrored walls and all the amenities awaits the two of you.

Address: 215 Piedmont Ave NE, Atlanta, GA . Tel: (404) 642-1313.

Type: Luxuriously-furnished downtown petite penthouse.
Clientele: Men and women.
Transportation: Car is best.
To Gay Bars: 2 miles.
Rooms: One studio with kitchen.
Bathrooms: Private bath.
Vegetarian: Restaurants nearby.
Dates Open: All year.
Rates: $79 per night. 3 or more nights $69.
Discounts: Weekly & monthly rates available.
Rsv'tns: Required. Please, no calls after 10pm EST.
Reserve Through: Call direct.
Minimum Stay: 2 nights.
Parking: Secured parking spot at front door.
Swimming: Pool on premises.
Sunbathing: At poolside.
Smoking: Permitted.
Pets: Not permitted.
Languages: English.

HAWAII

HAWAII (BIG ISLAND)

Hale Kipa 'O Pele

Gay/Lesbian ♀♂

Romance Flows Where Lava Glows!

Hale Kipa 'O Pele bed and breakfast is named for the sacred spirit, Madame Pele, goddess of fire, ruler of Hawaii's volcanoes and protector of the forest. It is believed that Pele's spirit guards the property even today! Situated on the volcanic slopes of Mt. Hualalai, above the sunny southern Kona coast, the tropical estate and plantation-style home are distinctly unique. A majestic volcanic dome graces the entrance drive. The house surrounds an open-air atrium with lava rock waterfall, koi pond and a tiled walkway providing a private entrance to each room-suite.

The *Maile* is a corner room with spacious sitting area, private bath and intimate covered patio. The *Ginger* has a large walk-in closet, private bath with sunken tub and sliding glass doors that access the wooden deck and provide a view of the gardens. The expansive *Pele Bungalow* has a cozy bedroom, full bath, living room, mini-kitchen and a large private covered patio overlooking the fruit tree grove.

A covered wooden lanai wraps around the entire front of the home, providing full panoramic views of the lush landscape. Enjoy a buffet-style tropical continental breakfast at YOUR leisure on the lanai or in the dining room. After a day of activities, relax in the garden Jacuzzi or enjoy movies on the Pro-Logic Surround Sound(tm) system.

Hale Kipa 'O Pele is a close 5 miles to the beach and all activities. Guests can enjoy scuba diving, para-sailing, deep sea fishing, helicopter tours, or walk along the scenic shores and quaint village-style shops of old Kona Town.

We cater to both singles and couples seeking the true "ALOHA" spirit and a serene and romantic atmosphere that only a tropical-style bed and breakfast can offer! Our guests will be rejuventated by exotic Hawaii, and the enthusiasm of both hosts who truly cherish this small part of the world known as PARADISE!

Address: PO Box 5252, Kailua-Kona, HI 96745. Tel: (800) LAVAGLO, (808) 329-8676.

Type: Bed & breakfast & bungalow.
Clientele: Good mix of gays & lesbians.
Transportation: Rental car is best. Airport courtesy pick up for travel industry employees.
To Gay Bars: 6 miles.
Rooms: 2 suites & 1 bungalow with queen beds.
Bathrooms: All private bath/shower/toilets.
Meals: Tropical island-style continental breakfast.
Complimentary: Refreshments upon arrival, wine & cheese at sunset.
Dates Open: All year.
Rates: $65-$135 plus room & state taxes.
Discounts: 10% for 7 nights & for travel industry/airline employees.
Credit Cards: MC & VISA.
Rsv'tns: Required.
Reserve Through: Travel agent or call direct.
Minimum Stay: Usually 2 nights.
Parking: Adequate free off-street parking.
In-Room: Ceiling fans & maid service. Bungalow has mini-kitchen, cable TV & VCR.
On-Premises: TV lounge with theatre sound & video tape library. Expansive covered decks.
Exercise/Health: Jacuzzi on premises. Gym & racquetball nearby.
Swimming: Nearby ocean.
Sunbathing: On private & common sun decks, the lawn or at the beach.
Nudity: Permitted in the Jacuzzi & at nude beach.
Smoking: Permitted outside & on covered decks.
Pets: Not permitted.
Handicap Access: No.
Children: Not especially welcome.
Languages: English.

Hale Ohia Cottages

Volcano Magic Unleashed

Gay-Friendly 50/50 ♀♂

Our architecturally unique *Hale Ohia Cottages* and deluxe suites are just a mile from Hawaii Volcano National Park. Our setting is in a botanical garden developed over a period of sixty years. On the grounds, you can read under a wisteria-covered gazebo or soak in a heated, Japanese furo beneath the Sougi pines. The stars in Hawaii's night sky will enchant you. Both cottages and suites have private baths. One cottage has its own lava rock fireplace. Breakfast is brought to your room.

Address: PO Box 758, Volcano, HI 96785. Tel: (800) 455-3803 or (808) 967-7986, Fax: (808) 967-8610.

Type: Bed & breakfast & cottages.
Clientele: 50% gay & lesbian & 50% straight clientele.
Transportation: Car is best.
To Gay Bars: 26 miles.
Rooms: 3 suites & 2 cottages with single, double or queen beds.
Bathrooms: All private shower/toilets.

Meals: Continental breakfast.
Vegetarian: Vegetarian health food store nearby.
Complimentary: Tea & coffee.
Dates Open: All year.
High Season: Nov 15-Jan 15 & June 15-Sep 5.
Rates: $60-$95.
Discounts: Travel agents, ASU, Kamaaina. 2 or more nights.

Credit Cards: MC & VISA.
Rsv'tns: Required.
Reserve Through: Travel agent or call direct.
Parking: Ample free off-street covered parking.
In-Room: Kitchen, refrigerator, coffee/tea-maker, maid & laundry service.
On-Premises: Meeting rooms.
Exercise/Health: Steam, massage & heated

Japanese furo.
Swimming: In nearby ocean.
Sunbathing: In private sun area.
Smoking: Smoking permitted outside only.
Pets: Not permitted.
Handicap Access: Yes. One unit is barrier free.
Children: Welcomed over 6 years of age.
Languages: English.

Huliaule'a

Share the Spirit of Aloha at the Edge of Creation

Gay/Lesbian ♀♂

Aloha! Enter the magical world of *Huliaule'a* a unique and timeless Hawaiian bed and breakfast experience. Nestled on a hill on 22 secluded tropical acres is a warm and welcoming home overlooking verdant green rainforests and the enticing blue Pacific. Close by are black sand beaches, steam caves, warm springs and Volcano National Park. There is all this and so much more! *Inn Places editor's*

note: The following are quotes from readers' comments about **Huliaule'a***:* "This was paradise!!!...A real treasure hidden away." "...Superior to all we visited. Shawn was ... an excellent cook, and provided unsurpassed service...." "Wonderful host &

continued next page

home. Way back off of main road. Total silence. Great place to get away. Shawn is extremely accommodating to guests. He draws maps to incredible places for a true island experience."

Address: PO Box 1030, Pahoa, HI 96778. Tel: (808) 965-9175.

Type: Bed & breakfast.
Clientele: Mostly gay & lesbian with some straight clientele.
Transportation: Rental car is best. From Hilo Airport 30 minutes, from Kona 2 1/2 hours.
To Gay Bars: 10 minutes to gay-friendly restaurant in Pahoa. 2-1/2 hours to gay bar.
Rooms: 3 rooms with queen beds.
Bathrooms: 1 private bath/toilet/shower & 1 shared bath/toilet/shower.

Meals: Full breakfast. Dinner available at extra charge.
Vegetarian: Always available at breakfast & dinner.
Complimentary: Tea, coffee, juice & wine.
Dates Open: All year.
High Season: January thru March, June thru August.
Rates: $40-$75.
Discounts: 15% discounts on stays over 6 nights & to airline/travel employees.
Rsv'tns: 2 weeks in

advance preferred.
Reserve Through: Travel agent or call direct.
Minimum Stay: 2 nights.
Parking: Ample free off-street parking.
In-Room: Maid & laundry service upon request. One room with private entrance & deck.
On-Premises: TV/VCR (no TV reception), house phone, living room, dining room, 40-foot deck, & refrigerator for guest use.
Exercise/Health: 20-minute drive to massage,

acupuncture, warm springs & steam vents.
Swimming: Nearby ocean & warm springs.
Sunbathing: On the beach.
Nudity: At nearby nude beach.
Smoking: Permitted outside and on covered Lanai.
Pets: Not permitted.
Handicap Access: No.
Children: Welcomed over 8 years old.
Languages: English.
Your Host: Shawn & staff.

Kalani Honua By The Sea Retreat

Gay-Friendly 50/50 ♀♂

Kalani Honua - Heaven on Earth

Kalani Honua By The Sea is a Hawaiian country getaway with comfortable lodgings, delicious cuisine, optional health and educational programs, a 25-meter pool, spa, tennis, horses, nearby national parks and secluded beaches. Our area includes warm springs, natural steam baths and the spectacular Volcanoes National Park. Our coast is blessed with tropical forest and ocean breezes. Activities include swimming with friendly dolphins at Kehena black-sands beach and our annual gay/lesbian gatherings: Pacific Men, Gay Spirit and Haku Mele (Sister Voices).

Address: Box 4500-IP Kalapana Beach, HI 96778. Tel: (808) 965-7828, Reservations: (800) 800-6886.

Type: Retreat, conference center with restaurant & native gift shops.
Clientele: 50% gay & lesbian & 50% straight clientele.
Transportation: Rental car is best. Airport pick up $25.
To Gay Bars: 30 miles or a 45-minute drive.
Rooms: 35 rooms & 4 cottages with single, double, queen or king beds.
Bathrooms: 13 private & 27 shared.
Campsites: 20 tent sites

with convenient showers & restrooms.
Meals: Continental breakfast included with rooms.
Vegetarian: Always available.
Complimentary: Tea, coffee, juices.
Dates Open: All year.
Rates: Rooms $30-$75, cottages $85, bunkrooms & campsites $15-$28 per person.
Discounts: 10-20% to bonafide airline employees, senior citizens, island natives.
Credit Cards: MC, VISA,

Amex & Diners Club.
Rsv'tns: Preferred.
Reserve Through: Travel agent or call direct.
Parking: Ample, free off-street parking.
In-Room: Maid service. Some rooms have kitchens.
On-Premises: Meeting rooms, private dining rooms, TV lounge, laundry facilities, kitchens.
Exercise/Health: Weights, Jacuzzi, sauna, steam & massage.
Swimming: Pool on premises. Ocean beach, river & lake nearby.

Sunbathing: At poolside, on beach or on common sun decks.
Nudity: Permitted anytime on beach or after 7pm at pool & spa.
Smoking: Permitted outdoors.
Pets: Not permitted.
Handicap Access: Yes.
Children: Permitted. Families housed together to afford privacy for others.
Languages: English, Spanish, French, German & Japanese.
Your Host: Richard, Delton & Dottie.

R.B.R. Farms

Gay/Lesbian ♂

R.B.R. Farms is, to this day, a working macadamia nut and coffee plantation. The old plantation home has been totally renovated and a swimming pool added. The house is secluded, accessed only by an unimproved 3/4-mile-long drive. *R.B.R. Farms* is privately-owned and -managed, so it retains the personal touch and attention to detail that sets us apart among outstanding bed and breakfasts in the world. *R.B.R. Farms...* a place to come, to stay, to remember, to return.

Address: PO Box 930, Captain Cook, HI 96704. Tel: (800) 328-9212, Phone & Fax: (808) 328-9212.

Type: Bed & breakfast.
Clientele: Mostly men with women welcome.
Transportation: Rental car is best.
To Gay Bars: Kona has a gay bar.
Rooms: 4 rooms & 1 cottage with single, queen or king beds.
Bathrooms: 1 private bath/toilet, 4 shared bath/shower/toilets.
Meals: Full breakfast.

Vegetarian: Available upon request.
Complimentary: Soft drinks, iced tea daytimes at pool, mints on pillow.
Dates Open: All year.
Rates: $60-$175.
Credit Cards: MC, VISA.
Rsv'tns: Required.
Reserve Through: Travel agent or call direct.
Minimum Stay: Usually two nights.
Parking: Ample free

parking.
In-Room: Color cable TV, VCR, ceiling fans & maid service.
On-Premises: Public telephones.
Exercise/Health: Gym, weights, Jacuzzi & massage.
Swimming: Pool on premises, ocean beach nearby.
Sunbathing: At poolside, on common sun decks &

on the beach.
Nudity: Permitted at poolside & on private decks.
Smoking: Not permitted in rooms. Permitted on grounds & common areas.
Pets: Not permitted.
Handicap Access: No.
Children: Not permitted.
Languages: English.
Your Host: Bill.

IGTA

Samurai, The

Gay/Lesbian ♀♂

The Samurai is an authentic Samurai house imported from Japan and reconstructed in Captain Cook, Hawaii. As you are greeted by a trickling waterfall leading to koi ponds and temple grass in an intimate Japanese garden, your impression is that of entering a moment in Old Japan. You may choose a traditional tatami room or a western-style room with standard furnishings. The expansive rear lanai has a breathtaking view of the southern Kona coast.

Address: 82-5929 Mamalahoa Hwy, Captain Cook, HI 96704. Tel: (808) 328-9210.

Type: Bed & breakfast.
Clientele: Mostly gay/lesbian with some straight clientele.
Transportation: Rental cars are necessary on the big island.
To Gay Bars: 20 minutes.
Rooms: 3 doubles & 1 apartment.
Bathrooms: 2 private. 2 of the rooms share 1 bath.
Meals: Continental breakfast.
Complimentary: Tea, coffee, & juice.

Dates Open: All year.
High Season: Winter & late summer.
Rates: $45-$75 all year.
Discounts: On stays longer than a week.
Credit Cards: MC & VISA.
Rsv'tns: Required.
Reserve Through: Travel agent or call direct.
Parking: Free off-street parking.
In-Room: Color TV, VCR. 1 room has kitchen, 1 has fridge.
On-Premises: TV lounge,

meeting rooms, & laundry facilities.
Exercise/ Health: Hot tub.
Swimming: 15-minute drive to ocean beach.
Sunbathing: On private decks.
Nudity: Permitted on private decks. 30-minute drive to gay nude beach.
Smoking: Permitted on the lanais.

Pets: Not permitted.
Handicap Access: Accessibility to one room on the 1st floor.
Children: Permitted.
Languages: English & American Sign Language.
Your Host: Douglass.

Wood Valley B & B Inn

Gay/Lesbian ♀

Off the Tourist Track, But Close to Power Spots

Glimpse old Hawaii at our secluded plantation home on twelve acres of pasture and gardens near Volcano National Park and beaches of green or black sand. *Wood Valley Bed & Breakfast* serves a home-grown breakfast and Kona coffee each morning. Lomi Lomi massage is available, and you can relax in our outdoor hot tub or steam bath. Our clientele is mostly women, with men welcome.
Address: PO Box 37, Pahala, HI 96777. Tel: (808) 928-8212, (800) 854-6754, Fax: (808) 928-9400.

Type: Bed & breakfast with a farm atmosphere.
Clientele: Mostly women with men welcome.
Transportation: Rent a car and arrive in daylight hours. Car is essential.
To Gay Bars: 40-min flight to Honolulu gay bars.
Rooms: 1 single, 2 doubles.
Bathrooms: Unique outdoor bathing & indoor shared toilet.
Campsites: Tent sites, toilet & shower.
Meals: Full breakfast,
food options are limited, please call ahead. Kitchen privileges.
Vegetarian: All vegetarian cuisine.
Complimentary: Welcome to graze in orchard & garden.
Dates Open: All year.
High Season: November-March.
Rates: Single $36, double $56 with 9% transit accommodation tax.
Discounts: 11th day free. Work exchange avail-
able, please inquire.
Credit Cards: None.
Rsv'tns: Recommended, with deposit.
Reserve Through: Call direct.
Parking: Ample free off-street parking.
In-Room: Telephone.
On-Premises: Laundry facilities, shared lanai, kitchen, dining room & VCR with tapes of local interest.
Exercise/Health: Walking trails, steam bath,
massage available.
Swimming: Ocean beach is 15 miles away.
Sunbathing: On the beach, in the backyard.
Nudity: Clothing is optional.
Smoking: Permitted outdoors.
Pets: Not permitted.
Handicap Access: No.
Children: Permitted with prior arrangement.
Languages: English.

KAUAI

Anahola Beach Club

Gay/Lesbian ♀♂

Enjoy the Surroundings of Old Hawaii

Anahola Beach Club is a quaint island home set in tropical splendor with shoreline views, elegantly-landscaped grounds and acres of land to explore. Swaying palm trees, white, sandy beaches, swimming and fishing are outside your door. We are located 1 mile from Donkey Beach (nude), and 5 miles from Kapaa (restaurants, shopping centers and gay bar). If you can appreciate seclusion and privacy, let us show you a little Hawaiian hospitality and the personal service you deserve.
Address: PO Box 562, Anahola, HI 96703. Tel: (808) 822-6966 or (800) ANAHOLA (262-4652).

Type: Bed & breakfast guesthouse.
Clientele: Good mix of gay men & women.
Transportation: Rental car.
To Gay Bars: 5 miles or ten minutes by car.
Rooms: 3 rooms with queen beds.
Bathrooms: 1 private bath/toilet/shower. Other
share bath/shower/toilet.
Meals: Full breakfast.
Vegetarian: Available upon request.
Complimentary: Cocktails.
Dates Open: All year.
Rates: $60-$70 single, $75-$85 double.
Rsv'tns: Suggested.
Reserve Through: Travel agent or call direct.
Minimum Stay: None.
Parking: Ample free off-street parking.
In-Room: Maid, room & laundry service & ceiling fans.
On-Premises: TV lounge.
Swimming: Ocean beach on premises.
Sunbathing: On the beach or private sun decks.
Nudity: Permitted on private sun deck. 1 mile from gay beach.
Smoking: Permitted on the decks.
Pets: Not permitted.
Handicap Access: No.
Children: Not especially welcomed.
Languages: English.

IGTA

Garden Island Bed & Breakfast

Gay/Lesbian ♀♂

Experience Polynesian Paralysis!

Come and experience Polynesian paralysis at our home. After you have hiked Waimea Canyon, Alakai Swamp, the Kalalau trail of the Na Pali coast, and while you are bird watching, surfing, golfing, snorkeling and enjoying all the other activities convenient to *Garden Island B&B*, relax in the luxurious comfort of our home. We are located in the foothills above Poipu Beach and have sweeping ocean and mountain views. Awaken to the smell of fresh, homemade breads and enjoy local fruits and juices. We provide true "Aloha."

Address: 4379 Panui St, Kalaheo, Kauai, HI 96741. Tel: (808) 332-7971, (800) 558-5557, Fax: (808) 332-7739.

Type: Bed & breakfast.
Clientele: Mostly gay & lesbian with some straight clientele.
Transportation: Rental car (no public transportation).
To Gay Bars: 20 minutes by plane to Honolulu.
Rooms: 2 rooms & 2 suites with double, queen or king beds.
Bathrooms: 2 private & 2 shared bath/toilet/ showers.

Meals: Tropical continental breakfast.
Vegetarian: Available upon request.
Complimentary: Tea, coffee & set-up service.
Dates Open: All year.
Rates: $50-$85. $110 for 4 in king suite.
Discounts: 10% for stays of 7 or more days.
Rsv'tns: Suggested.
Reserve Through: Travel agent or call direct.
Minimum Stay: 3 nights.

$10 surcharge for 1 or 2 nights.
Parking: Ample free off-street parking.
In-Room: Color cable TV, telephone, ceiling fans, refrigerator & maid service.
On-Premises: TV lounge with 52" TV, fax, copier & laundry facilities.
Exercise/Health: Jacuzzi in king suite.
Swimming: Ocean nearby.

Sunbathing: On the beach.
Nudity: 45-minute drive to nude beach.
Smoking: Permitted in living room, lobby or outside. No smoking in rooms.
Pets: Not permitted.
Handicap Access: No.
Children: Welcome.
Languages: English.
Your Host: Don & Bob.

IGTA

Hale Kahawai Bed & Breakfast

Gay/Lesbian ♀♂

See Kauai Inn Style, Inn Taste, Inn Absolute Comfort!

Your host, Gary Gordon, invites you to this luxurious island home. Beautiful *Hale Kahawai* sits on the north bank overlooking the Wailua River gorge, traditionally one of the most sacred areas in all Hawaii. Along the river, are many of the revered archaelogical sites of Kauai's ancient royal capital, settlement of kings, queens and kahunas. Our location across Kuamoo Road from Opaeka's Falls is a short stroll from Poliahu Heiau, one of the largest of Kauai's sacred temples.

A serene, sensuous garden retreat surrounds the three guest rooms and one studio, with cable TV, bath and kitchenette, all with original art, romantic ceiling fans and queen or king SertaPerfect (TM) mattresses. Enjoy tropical breakfasts in the open-beamed dining lounge or outside on the lanai, overlooking the spacious bamboo-shaded sundeck, koi and waterlily pond, and exotic landscape composed of marbled turquoise sky, towering Mounts Waialeale and Kawaikini, sugarcane fields and mango forests. With 70% of Hawaii's beaches on Kauai, secluded and

continued next page

scenic sands are within minutes of *Hale Kahawai*. Besides sunworshipping, other outdoor activities abound, such as cruising through Wailua River State Park, helicopter tours, horseback riding, golf, snorkeling, hiking Kauai's trails, hidden interior or famous Na Pali Coast. Fine dining and shopping are close by.

Relax in the evenings in the garden hot tub, illuminated by Tiki torches, or share a movie with friends in the state-of-the-art screening room, featuring Dolby (TM) Surroundsound (TM) stereo and 100" screen laserdisc projection system. Many of the island's gay and lesbian community visit *Hale Kahawai* to enjoy vintage and recent releases from the expanding collection of over 1,000 discs. It's another way for *Hale Kahawai* to share Kauai Aloha by bringing together our guests and friends. Write, call or fax for brochure and photos. Come share Kauai Aloha!

Address: 185 Kahawai Place, Kapaa, HI 96746. Tel: (808) 822-1031 or Fax: 823-8220.

Type: Bed & breakfast.
Clientele: Mostly gay & lesbian with some straight clientele.
Transportation: Car rentals from airport.
To Gay Bars: Gay-friendly bar 5 miles away in Kapaa.
Rooms: 3 rooms & 1 apartment with queen or king beds.
Bathrooms: 2 private bath/toilets & 1 shared bath/shower/toilet.
Meals: Expanded continental breakfast.
Vegetarian: Available upon request.
Complimentary: Tea, coffee, juices, fruit, & sodas.
Dates Open: All year.
High Season: December through January.
Rates: Rooms $60-$85 & apartment $95, plus 10.17% tax.
Discounts: For stays of 7 nights & longer.
Credit Cards: MC, VISA.
Rsv'tns: Required.
Reserve Through: Travel agent or call direct.
Minimum Stay: 3 nights.
Parking: Adequate free off-street parking.
In-Room: Maid service & ceiling fans. Apartment has color cable TV, kitchen & refrigerator.
On-Premises: Meeting rooms, private dining room & TV lounge.
Exercise/Health: Jacuzzi, massage, Soloflex, Kauai Athletic Club.
Swimming: Ocean beach & Wailua river nearby.
Sunbathing: On common sun decks, ocean beach, in the garden & hot tub.
Nudity: Clothing-optional hot tub, nearby gay nude beach.
Smoking: Permitted on the lanai or in the garden only. No smoking in the house.
Pets: Not permitted.
Handicap Access: No.
Children: Not permitted.
Languages: English.

Kalihiwai Jungle Home

Be Tarzan or Jane in Our Jungle Home

Gay-Friendly 50/50 ♀♂

Waterfall, jungle and mountain views await you from this beautiful Northshore 2-bedroom vacation rental on the Garden Island of Kauai. *Kalihiwai* is two minutes from snorkeling and windsurfing, a 10-minute jungle walk to the beach and minutes from nude sunbathing on Secret Beach. An ideal place for a dream vacation is provided by this 1,100 sq. ft. rental situated on 1/2 acre of tropical splendor, all beautifully furnished, with glassed-in panoramic views from each room. Call Thomas, (808) 828-1626.

Address: PO Box 717, Kilauea, HI 96754. Phone & Fax: (808) 828-1626.

Type: Vacation rental.
Clientele: 50% gay & lesbian & 50% straight clientele.
Transportation: Car is best. Airport less than 1 mile from home.
To Gay Bars: 15 miles or a 30-minute drive.
Rooms: 2 rooms with queen or king beds.
Bathrooms: All private bath/toilet shower & outdoor shower at edge of jungle.
Vegetarian: Vegetarian health food restaurants nearby.
Complimentary: Papayas & bananas on arrival.
Dates Open: All year.
Rates: $95-$150 per day.
Discounts: For longer stays of 1-4 weeks & for a single person.
Rsv'tns: Required.
Reserve Through: Travel agent or call direct.
Minimum Stay: Required.
Parking: Adequate free parking on premises.
In-Room: Color TV, telephone, ceiling fans, private full kitchen, coffee/tea-making facilities, laundry service. Maid service extra.
On-Premises: Laundry facilities, fax & private phone.
Exercise/Health: Nearby gym, weights, Jacuzzi, sauna, steam, massage, facial.
Swimming: Nearby Olympic-sized lap pool, ocean, river & lake.
Sunbathing: On the patio & beach.
Nudity: Permitted on the patio & in outdoor area behind house.
Smoking: Permitted only outside in front of house.
Pets: Not permitted.
Handicap Access: Downstairs unit is easily accessible.
Children: Welcome.
Languages: English.
Your Host: Thomas.

Kauai Condo

Take Your Partner To Paradise!

Gay-Friendly ♀♂

Work magic on body and soul in our elegant hideaway on a small island in the Pacific. Located just steps from the ocean, our secluded ground floor condominium enjoys views of ocean, beach, pool and gardens. *Kauai Condo* is furnished in sandwashed rattan, fine upholstery, Asian accents, cut Berber carpet, Italian floor tile and an *exceptionally* equipped kitchen. Shopping and fine dining are a stroll from the resort. World famous beaches, Haena

(Bali Hai), Lumahai and Donkey Beach (nude), are a short drive.

Address: 1202 E Pike St Suite #1062-IP, Seattle, WA 98122-3934. Tel: (800) HI KAUAI (445-2824).

Type: Condo.
Clientele: Mostly straight clientele with a gay & lesbian following.
Transportation: Car is best.
To Gay Bars: 1 mile or 5 minutes by car.
Rooms: Condo with queen beds.
Bathrooms: Private.
Vegetarian: Available nearby.
Dates Open: All year.
High Season: Dec 16-Apr 15.
Rates: Low season $60-$95, high season $75-$110, plus applicable taxes.
Credit Cards: Checks only.
Rsv'tns: Required. Full payment 30 days prior to arrival.
Reserve Through: Travel agent or call direct.
Minimum Stay: 3 nights.
Parking: Ample free off-street parking.
In-Room: 2 color cable TVs, VCR, cable FM, cassette tape library, ceiling fans, kitchen & refrigerator. Maid service for extra charge.
On-Premises: Laundry facilities & BBQ.
Exercise/Health: Tennis, Jacuzzi.
Swimming: Pool on premises, ocean nearby.
Sunbathing: At poolside, on lanai, lawn & beach.
Pets: Not permitted.
Handicap Access: No.
Children: Not especially welcome.
Languages: English.

Mahina Kai

Relax and Renew Your Spirit at...

Gay/Lesbian ♀♂

Kauai's pre-eminent gay accommodation, *Mahina Kai*. This artist's home, a blue-tiled Asian-Pacific villa on two acres of secluded estate grounds on Anahola Bay, overlooks the ocean. The exotic and dramatic design provides a separate guest wing with several tropical decor bedrooms, lanais, a living room and a guest kitchenette. A tropical breakfast is served in the garden courtyard. Enjoy the lagoon pool and hot tub enclosed in a Japanese garden or join other guests in bicycling, snorkeling, hiking along the Na Pali coast trail or taking a helicopter tour or Zodiac boat trip.

Address: PO Box 699, Anahola, Kauai, HI 96703. Tel: (808) 822-9451 or (800) 290-0691.

Type: Bed & breakfast.
Clientele: Mostly gay & lesbian with some straight clientele.
Transportation: Car is best. Car rental at airport (no public transportation).
Rooms: 3 rooms & 1 2-bedroom apartment with double beds.
Bathrooms: 3 private bath/toilet/showers, 1 shared bath/toilet/shower.
Meals: Continental breakfast.
Vegetarian: Excellent vegetarian food neaby in Kapaa.
Complimentary: Tea, coffee & popcorn.
Dates Open: All year.
High Season: All year.
Rates: $95-$115.
Credit Cards: MC, VISA.
Rsv'tns: Required.
Reserve Through: Travel agent or call direct.
Minimum Stay: 3 nights.
Parking: Ample free off-street parking.
In-Room: Color TV, ceiling fans. Apartment has color cable TV, VCR, ceiling fans & refrigerator.
On-Premises: Coffee/tea-making facilities, meeting rooms, TV lounge, library & fax machine.
Exercise/Health: Spa.
Swimming: In our pool or at ocean beach across the road.
Sunbathing: At poolside, on beach, on private or common sun decks.
Nudity: Permitted on the grounds, 2 miles to nude gay beach.
Smoking: Permitted on lanai only. Rooms are non-smoking.
Pets: Not permitted.
Handicap Access: No.
Languages: English.

Māla Lani (Heavenly Garden) Guest House

Gay/Lesbian ♀♂

A Tropical Retreat that is Private, Relaxing and Friendly

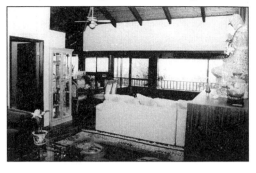

Write a ticket to your Aloha dreams with a visit to the Garden Isle, steeped in legend, unforgettable beauty and romance. Come experience refined country living on Sleeping Giant Mountain with spectacular mountain and pastoral views. *Mala Lani*, set in lush botanical gardens, offers all the comforts of home in self-contained, completely private, superbly-appointed Pacific Rim decor suites. Close to beaches, shopping and restaurants. Your hosts will welcome you into our home to share the Kauai we have come to know and love. Color brochure on request.

Address: 5711 Lokelani Rd, Kapaa, Kauai, HI 96746. Tel: (808) 832-0422, Fax: (808) 823-0420.

Type: Guesthouse.
Clientele: Mostly gay & lesbian with some straight clientele.
Transportation: Rental car from airport.
To Gay Bars: 10 minutes by car.
Rooms: 1 2-bedroom suite with queen bed & 2 extra-long twin beds. 1 1-bedroom suite with queen bed & queen sofa bed. 1 studio with queen bed.
Bathrooms: All private. Outdoor shower with hot water.

Complimentary: Bananas, papayas & avocados from the garden when in season. Color brochure.
Dates Open: All year.
Rates: 2-bedroom suite $195, 1 bedroom suite $125, studio $75. Rates for 2 people. $20 per add'l person per night. Tax extra.
Discounts: For stays of 7 or more nights.
Credit Cards: MC & VISA.
Rsv'tns: Required.
Reserve Through: Travel agent or call direct.

Minimum Stay: 3 nights. $20 surcharge for stays of 1 or 2 nights.
Parking: Ample off-street parking.
In-Room: Telephone, cable color TV, VCR, ceiling fans, refrigerator, microwave, coffeemaker. 2-bedroom has gourmet kitchen with dishwasher.
On-Premises: BBQ, lawn chaises, individual lanais or patios. XXX video library.
Exercise/Health: Soloflex, Jacuzzi. Nearby

full gym, massage arranged. State Mt. hiking trail near house.
Swimming: 10 minutes to ocean beaches.
Sunbathing: Chaise lounges in gardens.
Nudity: At Donkey Beach (15 minutes).
Smoking: Permitted outdoors only.
Pets: Not permitted.
Handicap Access: No.
Languages: English.

IGTA

Mohala Ke Ola B&B Retreat

Gay-Friendly ♀♂

Rejuvenate in Paradise.

Leave the cares and stresses of civilization behind. Enjoy a Hawaiian lomi-lomi massage or rejuvenate with one of the other body treatments available, including shiatsu, acupuncture and Reiki. Yoga and painting classes are also available.

Mohala Ke Ola B&B Retreat is situated high above the lush Wailua River Valley and is surrounded by magnificent mountain and waterfall views. It provides an ideal location from which to explore the island. We'll gladly share our insights on the best hikes, scenic lookouts, secret beaches, tropical gardens, helicopter and boat tours.

Address: 5663 Ohelo Rd, Kapaa, Kauai, HI 96746. Tel: (808) 823-6398.

Type: Bed & breakfast.
Clientele: Mostly straight clientele with a gay & lesbian following.
Transportation: Car is best. $10 for pick up from airport.
To Gay Bars: 5 miles or a 10-minute drive to Sideout.
Rooms: 2 rooms with queen beds. Overflow room & extra beds available.
Bathrooms: All private.

Meals: Continental breakfast.
Vegetarian: Local Thai & health food store deli.
Complimentary: Coffee & tea.
Dates Open: All year.
High Season: Nov-May.
Rates: Low $65-$80. High $75-$90.
Discounts: Weekly rate 15%.
Rsv'tns: Required.
Reserve Through: Travel agent or call direct.

Minimum Stay: Prefer 3 nights minimum.
Parking: Ample free off-street parking.
In-Room: Ceiling fans.
On-Premises: TV lounge, meeting rooms & laundry facilities.
Exercise/Health: Jacuzzi, massage, acupuncture, lomi lomi, shiatsu, Reiki on premises.
Swimming: Pool on premises. Ocean & river nearby.

Sunbathing: At poolside or on the beach.
Nudity: Permitted in hot tub & pool at discretion of other guests. 15 min to nude beach.
Smoking: Permitted outside only. This is a non-smoking environment.
Pets: Not permitted.
Handicap Access: No.
Children: Not especially welcome.
Languages: English, Japanese & German.

Ola Hou Guest Retreat

"Ola Hou" Means "To Revive"

Gay/Lesbian ♀♂

Tropical gardens create a meditative environment in this secluded, truly private estate, known as *Ola Hou Guest Retreat*. A two-bedroom apartment and one-bedroom cottage, decorated with a hint of Polynesia, have king or queen beds, color cable TV, VCR, CD system, telephone and laundry facilities. Swimming suits are optional around the large pool with spa and multi-level decks. Beach and snorkel gear, bikes, hiking equipment, maps and vacation guides are available. The Koi pond and water garden are filled with water lilies, brightly-colored Koi and other exotic fish. Our herb garden is available for your cooking enjoyment.

Address: 332 Aina Loli Place, Kapaa, Kauai, HI 96746. Tel: (800) 772-4567.

Type: Apartments & cottage.
Clientele: Mainly gay & lesbian with some straight clientele.
Transportation: Car is best.
To Gay Bars: 15 minutes by car to bar in Kapaa.
Rooms: One 2-bedroom apartment & a cottage with kitchens & queen beds.
Bathrooms: All private.

Dates Open: All year.
High Season: Winter & holidays.
Rates: Off-season: $100/night, $550/week plus tax. In season: $125/night, $625/week plus tax.
Credit Cards: MC, VISA.
Rsv'tns: Required.
Reserve Through: Call direct.
Minimum Stay: 3 nights.
Parking: Ample free off-

street & on-street parking.
In-Room: Cable color TV, VCR, video tape library, ceiling fans, telephone & kitchen.
On-Premises: Laundry facilities.
Exercise/Health: Jacuzzi, mountain bikes available. Tennis racquets, golf clubs & snorkeling equipment.
Swimming: Pool on premises, nearby beach only

9 minutes by car.
Sunbathing: On private & common sun decks & at nearby beach.
Nudity: Permitted, property fully enclosed.
Smoking: Permitted outside only.
Pets: Not allowed.
Handicap Access: No.
Children: Not permitted.
Languages: English.
Your Host: David & Joseph.

Pali Kai

"Mountain by the Sea"

Gay/Lesbian ♀♂

Kauai's spectacular North Shore surrounds you at *Pali Kai,* on a hilltop with views of mountains, valley and ocean. All bedrooms in this beautiful home have queen beds with private baths and each has a sweeping ocean view. There is a shared living room with cassette player, books and an island information guide. A hot tub and garden with barbecue overlook the ocean. A luxurious lawn and lush gardens surround the house and a scenic path leads to the Kalihiwai River and beach. Swimming and snorkeling beaches, hiking trails and rivers for kayaking are nearby. **Address: PO Box 450, Kilauea, Kauai, HI 96754. Tel: (808) 828-6691.**

Type: Bed & breakfast with panoramic views of mountains, Kalihiwai Valley & the ocean. **Clientele:** Gay & lesbian. Good mix of men & women. **Transportation:** Car is essential, rent at airport. **To Gay Bars:** 20 minutes by car.

Rooms: 3 rooms with ocean views, all queen beds. **Bathrooms:** All private. 1 with sink/toilet & private outdoor shower. **Meals:** Island-style breakfast. **Dates Open:** All year. **Rates:** $80-$105 singles. $90-$120 doubles.

Rsv'tns: Required. **Reserve Through:** Travel agent or call direct. **Minimum Stay:** 3 nights. **Parking:** Ample off-street parking. **In-Room:** Refrigerator, microwave, ceiling fan, coffee/tea-making facilities & maid service. **Exercise/Health:** Jogging

path to river & beach, hot tub available to all. **Swimming:** At nearby ocean beaches. **Sunbathing:** At beach & in front yard. **Nudity:** In hot tub & at some nearby beaches. **Smoking:** Permitted outdoors only. **Languages:** English.

Royal Drive Cottages

A Cozy Tropical Hideaway

Gay-Lesbian ♀♂

Looking for quiet and privacy? Up in the lush green hills of the Eden-like Wailua district, down a private road, you'll find the beautiful *Royal Drive* guest cottages. Each has a well-equipped kitchenette, private bath and you may choose between king-sized or twin beds. You look out upon a lush tropical garden, with exotic flowers and fruit trees for guests' picking in season. The temptation to settle under a tree in the garden and never move is strong.

Your host, Bob, lives between the cottages and is very available and happy to share his extensive knowledge of the islands. He will offer suggestions to help make your stay truly special, guiding you to off-the-tourist-path places and experiences.

The Wailua area is an excellent location, mid-way between the dramatic North Shore and the spectacular Waimea Canyon at the other end of the island. The cottages are a short 5- to 10-minute drive to beaches for surfing, swimming and snorkeling, to the Wailua River for kayaking and water skiing, and also to hiking, golf, shopping and a concentration of some of the best restaurants on the island.

From a guest book filled with unsolicited enthusiasm: "Kauai is full of beautiful secrets and your place is one of them."

Address: 147 Royal Drive, Wailua, Kauai, HI 96746. Tel: (808) 822-2321

Type: Cottages. **Clientele:** Mainly gay/lesbian with some straight clientele. **Transportation:** Car rental at airport. **To Gay Bars:** 10 min drive. **Rooms:** 2 cottages with twin or king beds. **Bathrooms:** All private. **Complimentary:** Tropical fruit trees for guests' picking in season. **Dates Open:** All year. **Rates:** Single $50-$70, double $80. **Discounts:** 10% for 1 week or more. **Credit Cards:** None. **Rsv'tns:** Required. **Reserve Through:** Travel agent or call direct. **Parking:** Ample free off-street parking. **In-Room:** Well-equipped kitchenette in each cottage. **On-Premises:** Laundry facilities. **Exercise/Health:** Jacuzzi. Nearby gym, massage & Kauai Athletic Club. **Swimming:** Ocean beach & river nearby, gay nude beach 15 minutes. **Sunbathing:** On common sun deck or lawn. **Nudity:** Permitted on common sun deck. **Smoking:** Permitted outdoors. **Pets:** Not permitted. **Handicap Access:** 3 stairs up to one cottage, 1 step to the other. **Children:** Not permitted. **Languages:** English.

MAUI

Anfora's Dreams

Gay-Friendly 50/50 ♀♂

Maui Condos With Your Lifestyle in Mind

Like a jewel piercing the Pacific Ocean, lush, tropical Maui and her magnificent volcanoes rise out of the sea to warmly caress your soul. *Anfora's Dreams,* with both one and two bedroom condos, are located in sunny Kihei. Both ocean and park are just across the road. Units are completely furnished in deluxe style, with total comfort in mind. Take a walk along the beach or a refreshing dip in the pool or Jacuzzi. Here, on Maui, you will learn the true meaning of "Maui No Ka Oi." Maui is the best!

Address: Attn: Dale Jones, PO Box 74030, Los Angeles, CA 90004. Tel: (213) 737-0731, Reservations or Fax: 737-2160.

Type: Condo. **Clientele:** 50% gay & lesbian & 50% straight clientele. **Transportation:** Car is best. **To Gay Bars:** 15 miles or 20 minutes by car. **Rooms:** 2 condos with queen beds. **Bathrooms:** All private bath/toilets. **Vegetarian:** Complete kitchens in condos. **Dates Open:** All year. **High Season:** November 15 through February 15. **Rates:** $50-$120. **Rsv'tns:** Required, but can do spot bookings on available basis. **Reserve Through:** Call direct. **Parking:** Ample free off-street parking. Assigned space with guest spaces available. **In-Room:** Color cable TV, telephone, kitchen, refrigerator, ceiling fans, coffee & tea-making facilities. Some with AC. **On-Premises:** Laundry facilities. 2-bedroom, 2-bath has washer/dryer in unit. **Exercise/Health:** Jacuzzi, nearby gym. **Swimming:** Pool on premises, ocean across the road. **Sunbathing:** At poolside, on patio & nearby beach. **Nudity:** Nude beach 10 minutes away. **Pets:** Not permitted on Maui. **Handicap Access:** Yes. Single only. **Children:** We welcome all guests with open arms. **Languages:** English.

Blair's Original Hana Plantation Houses

Serenity Defined

Gay-Friendly 50/50 ♀♂

Watch the sunrise from cliffs overlooking the rugged coastline. Bathe in secluded pools fed by mountain waterfalls, once known only to ancient Hawaiian kings. Hike through lush tropical jungles and fields of bamboo. Completely escape mainland tensions and enjoy a traditional Hawaiian vacation on 5 superbly landscaped acres on the remote, exclusive windward coast of Maui. This is serenity. This is Hana. These are the *Original Hana Plantation Houses.*

Address: PO Box 249, Hana, Maui, HI 96713. Tel: (808) 248-7868, (800) 228-HANA, Fax: (808) 248-7867.

Type: Guesthouses. 15 private homes (14 in Hana, 2 deluxe on Molokai).
Clientele: 50% gay & lesbian & 50% straight ..
Transportation: Car from Kahuli Airport, via Hana Hwy or fly directly into Hana.
To Gay Bars: 1.5 hours.
Rooms: 1 studio, 8 homes, 1 apt, 1 guesthouse, 2 deluxe homes on Molokai.
Bathrooms: All private.

Vegetarian: Health food cafe at our Botanical Gardens.
Complimentary: Bananas, avocados, citrus, passion fruit, coffee and coconuts from our plantation.
Dates Open: All year.
High Season: January-March, July-September.
Rates: $55-$185 plus tax.
Discounts: 10% for stays longer than 1 week.
Credit Cards: MC, VISA, Amex.

Rsv'tns: Required.
Reserve Through: Travel agent or call direct.
Minimum Stay: 2 nights.
Parking: Free off-street parking.
In-Room: Maid service, color TV, phone, kitchen, refrigerator, ceiling fans.
On-Premises: Laundry facilities.
Exercise/Health: Hot tub, small gym. Massage arranged.
Swimming: Natural

pools, waterfalls & ocean beach are nearby.
Sunbathing: On beach & on private sun decks.
Nudity: Permitted on private lanai. Clothing optional beach, pools nearby.
Smoking: Permitted outdoors.
Pets: Not permitted.
Handicap Access: No.
Children: Not permitted.
Languages: English.

IGTA

Camp Kula-Maui B&B

Where Happy Campers Play

Gay/Lesbian ♀♂

Pamper yourself in *Camp Kula's* big, bright, clean and comfortable Hawaiian home. *Camp Kula* is upcountry with panoramic views of the ocean, mountains and valley. We're centrally located to restaurants, or, bottom line: Our pots and pans are your pots and pans! Camp's friendly staff will happily direct you to (clothing-optional) beaches, secluded waterfalls, hiking trails, incredible snorkeling, swimming and windsurfing hot spots. Or sit by our campfire, rock in our Koa swing, or nap in the hammocks while the windchimes play. Come to camp and experience Maui's magic the native way.

Address: PO Box 111, Kula, Maui, HI 96790. Tel: (808) 878-2528 Phone & Fax.

Type: Bed & breakfast.
Clientele: Good mix of gay men & women.
Transportation: Rental car. No public transportation on Maui.
To Gay Bars: 45-min. drive to Lahaina, 20 min to Hamburger Mary's.
Rooms: 3 rooms with single, double or king beds.
Bathrooms: 2 shared bath/shower/toilets.
Meals: Continental breakfast with fresh island fruits, juices, Kona coffee and fresh baked goods.
Vegetarian: Upon request. Health food store nearby.

Complimentary: Refreshments upon arrival, tea/coffee anytime, wine at "happy camper" hour.
Dates Open: All year.
High Season: Dec 15th-Mar 31, Jun15th-Sept 15th.
Rates: Low season $42-$65, high season $50-$78.
Discounts: 10% for 8 or more nights.
Credit Cards: MC, VISA with 5% service charge.
Rsv'tns: Required with a bankcard guarantee. 30-day cancellation, 50% cancellation fee.
Reserve Through: Travel agent or call direct.

Minimum Stay: 3 nights.
Parking: Ample secured parking on property.
In-Room: Color TV, VCR. Complimentary skincare, bodycare & suncare.
On-Premises: Telephone, fax, color TV, private meeting lounge, spacious living & dining rooms and a huge party kitchen.
Exercise/Health: YMCA, Nautilus World, Powerhouse Gym & Valley Isle Fitness, all nearby.
Swimming: Ocean beach & waterfalls nearby.
Sunbathing: On patio, lawn, or beach.

Nudity: Permitted anywhere on our 7 private acres & at nearby beaches.
Smoking: Permitted outdoors.
Pets: No. We supply pets for you to love on our private grounds.
Handicap Access: Yes.
Children: Permitted if over 5 years.
Languages: English, limited Spanish.
Your Host: D.E. & "El Ray."

IGTA

Golden Bamboo Ranch

Tropical Splendor in a Garden Paradise

Gay-Friendly 50/50 ♀♂

This private, seven-acre estate is nestled on the lower slopes of upcountry Maui along the spectacular road to Hana. *Golden Bamboo Ranch* is centrally located to all of Maui's bounty— 10 minutes from Hookipa windsurfing beach, Twin Falls, with natural swimming pools, or the "cowboy" town of Makawao. We have just renovated a cottage and three plantation house suites, all with unobstructed, panoramic ocean views through horse pastures (we have horses) and forests on one side and a tropical garden and lily pond on the other.

Address: 1205 Kaupakalua Rd, Haiku, Maui, HI 96708. Phone & Fax: (808) 572-7824.

Type: Cottage & plantation house suites.
Clientele: 50% gay & lesbian & 50% straight clientele.
Transportation: Rental car is best.
To Gay Bars: 30 minutes to Hamburger Mary's in Wailuku.
Rooms: 3 suites & 1 cottage with single, queen or king beds.
Bathrooms: 4 private bath/toilet/showers.
Meals: Expanded continental breakfast left daily in accommodations.
Vegetarian: Available with prior notice. 15-minute drive to 2 vegetarian restaurants & 2 health food stores.
Dates Open: All year.
Rates: $60-$80.
Discounts: For seven or more days.
Credit Cards: MC, VISA & Amex.
Rsv'tns: Required.
Reserve Through: Travel agent or call direct.
Parking: Ample free off-street parking.
In-Room: Color TV, VCR, telephone, ceiling fans, kitchen, refrigerator, coffee/tea-making facilities & maid service.
On-Premises: Laundry facilities.
Exercise/Health: 5 minutes to Twin Falls hiking path to waterfalls & natural swimming pools.
Swimming: Nearby ocean & natural swimming pools.
Sunbathing: On the patio & at the beach.
Nudity: Permitted on patios & terraces. 30 minutes to super gay nude beach.
Smoking: Permitted on patios & terraces. Non-smoking rooms available.
Pets: Not permitted.
Handicap Access: Yes. Plantation house is ground level.
Children: Not especially welcome.
Languages: English, French & Spanish.
Your Host: Marty & Al.

IGTA

Hale Makaleka

Women ♀

Hale Makaleka, a bed and breakfast for women, is situated in a garden setting with a lanai that provides an ocean view. We have a large, light and airy room with private bath and private entrance overlooking the garden. Tropical breakfast is served on our upstairs deck from where whales can be seen during winter months. Relax at "home" in restful seclusion, chat with us about "mainland" happenings, stories of Maui, sightseeing, shopping, activities in the lesbian community, or explore. Resort activities, dining experiences or yellow sand beaches are within four miles.
Address: 535 Kupulau Dr, Kihei, HI 96753. Tel: (808) 879-2971.

Type: Bed & breakfast.
Clientele: Women only.
Transportation: Rental car.
To Gay Bars: 30 minutes to Hamburger Mary's in Wailuku.
Rooms: 1 double with private entrance.
Bathrooms: Private.
Meals: Full tropical breakfast.
Vegetarian: Available upon request.
Dates Open: All year.
Rates: $60 double, $55 single.
Rsv'tns: Required.
Reserve Through: Call direct.
Minimum Stay: 2 days.
Parking: Adequate, free off-street parking.
In-Room: Color TV.
On-Premises: Laundry facilities, refrigerator & telephone.
Exercise/Health: Nearby gym.
Swimming: One mile to ocean beach.
Sunbathing: In secluded garden, on nearby beach.
Nudity: Permitted in garden & at "Little Beach" 6 miles away.
Smoking: Permitted outside.
Pets: Not permitted.
Handicap Access: No.
Children: Not permitted.
Languages: English.
Your Host: Margaret & Jackie.

Halfway to Hana House

Gay-Friendly 50/50 ♀♂

Relax & Rejuvenate...Awaken Your Senses!

A truly delightful B&B with exquisite mountain and ocean views, *Halfway to Hana House* is peaceful and quiet. The clean, airy studio has a separate entrance and spacious private bath. Its mini-kitchen has a hotplate, microwave, toaster, coffeemaker and refrigerator. Your exotic tropical breakfast is served outdoors in a colorful, breezy setting of bamboo and palms overlooking the sea. Off the beaten path and on the way to Hana, the rural location and proximity to fresh water pools makes this hideaway a memorable one.
Address: PO Box 675, Haiku, Maui, HI 96708. Tel: (808) 572-1176, Fax: (808) 572-3609.

Type: Bed & breakfast with champagne, wine, beer available for purchase.
Clientele: 50% gay & lesbian & 50% straight clientele (1 studio ensures complete privacy).
Transportation: Car is best. No public transportation available.
To Gay Bars: 20 miles by car to Wailuku.
Rooms: 1 private studio suite with double bed.
Bathrooms: 1 private shower/toilet.
Meals: Expanded continental breakfast which includes homemade Hawaiian coconut pudding.
Vegetarian: All breakfasts.
Complimentary: Chocolate-covered macadamia nuts, herb teas.
Dates Open: All year.
High Season: December through April.
Rates: $50-$80.
Discounts: 10% for 7 or more days.
Rsv'tns: Recommended. Walk-ins welcome if space is available.
Reserve Through: Travel agent or call direct.
Minimum Stay: 3 nights.
Parking: Ample off-street parking area shaded by trees.
In-Room: Coffee & tea-making facilities, beach mats, shampoo, razors & toothpaste. Color TV available upon request.
On-Premises: Telephone, refrigerator, laundry facilities, covered patio with table & chairs.
Exercise/Health: Nordic track, trampoline, massage.
Swimming: Nearby fresh water pools, ocean beach 15 min away, lap pool 20 mi away.
Sunbathing: At the beach, on private patio & private grounds.
Nudity: Permitted on private patio & in secluded areas on private ground.
Smoking: This is a non-smoking environment.
Pets: Permitted if specific arrangements are made.
Handicap Access: No, pathways are gravel.
Children: Permitted over age of 10.
Languages: English, limited French & Japanese.

Huelo Point Flower Farm B&B

A Real Cliffhanger!

Gay-Friendly 50/50 ♀♂

For a romantic getaway, visit our private, glass-walled cottage, perched at the edge of a 300-foot cliff on a beautiful 2-acre oceanfront, gated estate on Maui's North Shore. *Huelo Point Flower Farm B&B* has spectacular views of Waipio Bay and Haleakala Crater and is close to streams and waterfalls. We also have a 60-foot swimming pool, with waterfall, and a hot tub. The stunning main house, which sleeps up to six, is also available for vacation rental. It's secluded and peaceful here, yet only 1/2 hour away from the airport.

Address: PO Box 1195, Paia, Maui, HI 96779. Tel: (808) 572-1850.

Type: Bed & breakfast & rental home.
Clientele: 50% gay & lesbian & 50% straight clientele.
Transportation: Rental car.
To Gay Bars: 35 minute drive.
Rooms: Main house for six with double, queen & king beds, plus cottage with queen bed.
Bathrooms: All private.
Meals: Expanded continental breakfast.

Vegetarian: Almost always available.
Complimentary: Tea & coffee.
Dates Open: All year.
Rates: $95 for cottage. $1500 per week for main house.
Discounts: Kama'aina discount 10%. Local residents weekly discounts 10%.
Rsv'tns: Required. Walk-ins welcome if space is available.
Reserve Through: Travel

agent or call direct.
Minimum Stay: 2 days.
Parking: Ample off-street parking on gated estate.
In-Room: Color TV, telephone, kitchen & refrigerator.
On-Premises: Laundry facilities.
Exercise/Health: Jacuzzi, massage, professional exercise bike, & rowing machine.
Swimming: Pool on premises. 20 min drive to ocean beach. 10 min

walk to waterfalls.
Sunbathing: At poolside & on the patio.
Nudity: Permitted.
Smoking: Permitted.
Pets: Permitted by request.
Handicap Access: Yes.
Children: Small children could be a problem because of 300 foot cliff.
Languages: English, French, & Russian.
Your Host: Guy & Doug.

Huelo Pt. Lookout B&B

Gay-Friendly 50/50 ♀♂

The Real Hawaii...It's Still There if You Know Where to Look

Where else could you sit and watch rainbows march to your doorstep and slip over your house? Or be able to hike to a 127-foot waterfall and swim in its pools? Come prepared to enjoy the unique peace and beauty as well as the drama and power of Maui's north shore...bananas, red gingers, papayas, a hot tub and shower under the stars. *Huelo Pt. Lookout B&B* is a private, 2 acre estate ideally located for you to explore the exquisite beauty of the real Hawaii.

Address: PO Box 117, Paia, HI 96779. Phone & Fax: (808) 573-0914.

Type: Bed & breakfast & cottage.
Clientele: 50% gay & lesbian & 50% straight clientele.
Transportation: Car is essential. There is no public transportation.
To Gay Bars: 40 minutes by car.

Rooms: 1 suite with king bed & queen foldout. 1 cottage with queen bed & queen futon.
Bathrooms: Private.
Meals: Expanded continental breakfast.
Vegetarian: Several wonderful vegetarian restaurants & grocery

stores available in Paia, a 30-minute drive.
Complimentary: Tea & coffee. We often provide special surprise snacks of fruit, nuts, bread or cookies.
Dates Open: All year.
Rates: Suite $95 per night. Cottage $125 per

night.
Discounts: Reduced rates for 1 week or longer.
Rsv'tns: Required. Standby sometimes available.
Reserve Through: Travel agent or call direct.

continued next page

Minimum Stay: 3 days.
Parking: Lots of free parking!
In-Room: Coffee/tea-making facilities, telephone, color TV. Suite: Kitchenette. Cottage: VCR, kitchen, microwave, washer/ dryer.
On-Premises: Laundry facilities. We own a video store, so guests have free reign!
Exercise/Health: Jacuzzi. Massage by arrangement. Nearby yoga classes, hiking, riding.

Swimming: Nearby ocean, waterfalls & pools.
Sunbathing: On private sun decks.
Nudity: Permitted in hot tub & on sun decks at discretion of other guests.

Smoking: Permitted outside only.
Pets: Permitted outside only.
Handicap Access: No.
Children: Not especially welcome.
Languages: English.
Your Host: Jeff & Sharyn.

Jack & Tom's Maui Condos

Gay-Friendly ♀♂

Tropical Sun, Sandy Beaches, Gentle Trade Winds...Maui No Ka Oi *(is the best)*

Explore the island, play a little tennis, relax by the pools or enjoy the sand and surf of the finest beaches on Maui, including the nude beach at Makena (only minutes away). At the end of your day, return to your private one- or two-bedroom condominium to freshen up for a night out. Or, if you prefer, prepare dinner in your own fully-equipped kitchen and enjoy a quiet evening at home. All units at *Jack & Tom's Maui Condos* are clean, comfortable and equipped to make you want to stay a lifetime.

Address: Margaret Norrie Realty, PO Box 365, Kihei, HI 96753. Tel: (800) 800-8608, (808) 874-1048, Fax: (808) 879-6932.

Type: Private condominiums within larger complexes.
Clientele: Mostly straight clientele with a gay & lesbian following.
Transportation: Car is a must on Maui. We can arrange car rental.
To Gay Bars: 12 miles or a 25-minute drive.

Rooms: 36 cottages with queen or king beds.
Bathrooms: All private.
High Season: December 15 to April 15.
Dates Open: All year.
Rates: Summer $35-$90, winter $45-$125.
Rsv'tns: Required.
Reserve Through: Travel agent or call direct.

Minimum Stay: 5 days.
Parking: Ample off-street parking.
In-Room: Color cable TV, AC, ceiling fans, telephone, kitchen & laundry facilities. Some units have VCRs, stereos.
Exercise/Health: Nearby gym.
Swimming: Pool on

premises. Ocean beach across the street.
Sunbathing: At poolside or on the beach.
Smoking: Permitted. Non-smoking units available.
Pets: Not permitted.
Handicap Access: Yes.
Languages: English.
Your Host: Jack & Tom.

Kailua Maui Gardens

Gay-Friendly 50/50 ♀♂

Stay With Us for a True Tropical Island Experience

Located in the picturesque village of Kailua, *Kailua Maui Gardens* is an undiscovered hideaway on the edge of Maui's vast rainforest. Enchanting pathways and bridges lead you through two acres of fabulous gardens, which surround our well-appointed accommodations, most with ocean views. The house has its own pool, spa and barbecue lanai area. Cottage guests can relax in the garden spa, where they will be surrounded by the lush gardens. Enjoy nearby waterfalls and natural swimming pools. It's an ideal setting for large groups, individuals and couples.

Address: SR Box 9 (Hana Hwy), Haiku, Maui, HI 96708. Tel: (800) 258-8588, (808) 572-9726.

Type: Cottage & house rental.
Clientele: 50% gay & lesbian & 50% straight clientele.
Transportation: Rental car is best, $30 for pickup from airport.
To Gay Bars: 40 minutes.
Rooms: 3 cottages, one 3-bdrm house & one 1-bdrm apartment with queen or king beds.
Bathrooms: All private bath/toilets.
Vegetarian: Chef & vegetarian food available with prior notice.
Complimentary: Fresh fruit, tea, coffee & tropical flowers from estate gardens.
Dates Open: All year.
High Season: June-Sept & Dec-March.

Rates: $55-$200 plus tax.
Discounts: For 7 days or longer.
Rsv'tns: Required.
Reserve Through: Travel agent or call direct.
Minimum Stay: 2 nights.
Parking: Ample, free off-street parking.
In-Room: Color TV, VCR, stereo/compact disc player, kitchen, telephone, ceiling fans.
On-Premises: Two outside BBQs, covered lanai for house & covered lanai at common area for cottages.
Exercise/Health: Private spa for house & garden spa for cottages.
Swimming: Pool with house, 8 miles to ocean,

1/4 mile to waterfall, natural pools.
Sunbathing: At poolside or on private patios.
Nudity: Permitted in pool area & around spas.
Smoking: Permitted outdoors.

Pets: Not permitted.
Handicap Access: Main house is accessible.
Children: Over 12 years permitted.
Languages: English.

IGTA

Waipio Bay Lookout

Travel Into Yesterday's Hawaii

Gay-Friendly 50/50 ♀♂

The north shore of Maui is the rugged, tropical Hawaii that you see in the ads and movies. Listen to the waves crash against the cliffs, as you rest and relax at this secluded, two-acre estate. *The Waipio Bay Lookout* sits high on a 300-foot cliff, overlooking Waipio Bay in magical Huelo, along the road to Hana. Our location offers spectacular ocean views from every room, a swimming pool, Jacuzzi, cliffside sun deck and private patios. We're close to natural pools and waterfalls, and only 30 minutes from the airport.

Address: PO Box 1095, Haiku, HI 96708. Tel: (808) 572-4530.

Type: Bed & breakfast.
Clientele: 50% gay & lesbian & 50% straight clientele.
Transportation: Car is best.
To Gay Bars: 30 minutes.
Rooms: 2 suites with queen beds.
Bathrooms: All private bath/toilets.

Meals: Expanded continental breakfast.
Vegetarian: Available.
Dates Open: All year.
Rates: $75-$85.
Discounts: 10% weekly.
Reserve Through: Travel agent or call direct.
Parking: Ample free off-street parking.

In-Room: Ceiling fans, kitchenette, refrigerator, coffee & tea-making facilities.
On-Premises: Laundry facilities.
Exercise/Health: Jacuzzi & massage.
Swimming: Pool on premises, natural pools & ocean nearby.

Sunbathing: At poolside.
Nudity: Permitted poolside.
Smoking: Not permitted.
Pets: Not permitted.
Handicap Access: No.
Children: Absolutely no children due to proximity of cliff.
Languages: English & Spanish.

OAHU & HONOLULU

Hotel Honolulu

Gay/Lesbian ♀♂

Although it is in the heart of Waikiki, *Hotel Honolulu* has been carefully designed to be different from any other in modern day Hawaii. We are trying to create an oasis in time to take our guests back to the quieter, more gentle and relaxed way of life in these beautiful islands. Large and small studios and suites each have a different theme. All have kitchens, baths and outside lanai. Enjoy the rooftop garden sun deck for relaxation and comfort. We are two blocks from the beach and next door to our best gay clubs and the nicest restaurants and shops in the famed Kuhio district.

Address: 376 Kaiolu St, Honolulu, HI 96815. Tel: (808) 926-2766, (800) 426-2766 (US/CAN), Fax: (808) 922-3326.

Type: Hotel.
Clientele: Good mix of gay men & women.
Transportation: Pre-arranged airport/Waikiki shuttle, or taxi. 1st class airport shuttle R/T is $25 with lei greeting.
To Gay Bars: The main gay bars are on our block.
Rooms: 15 rooms & 10 suites with king or queen beds.
Bathrooms: All private.

Complimentary: Coffee & tea.
Dates Open: All year.
High Season: November to March.
Rates: $69-$103.
Credit Cards: MC, VISA, Amex, Diners, Discover & JCB.
Rsv'tns: Preferred.
Reserve Through: Call direct or reserve through your travel agent.
Minimum Stay: 4 days from Dec 20 to Jan 6.

Parking: Adequate off-street, covered, pay parking. Least expensive on the island.
In-Room: Color TV, AC, ceiling fans, telephone, kitchen & refrigerator.
On-Premises: Laundry room & garden sun deck.
Exercise/Health: Massage on premises. Nearby gym & sauna.
Swimming: Ocean beach 2 blocks away.
Sunbathing: On beach &

common sun deck (lanai).
Smoking: Permitted without restrictions.
Pets: Small pets permitted.
Handicap Access: No. Only on the 1st floor.
Children: Permitted.
Languages: English, Spanish, French, German & Hawaiian.
Your Host: Richard & Darlene.

IGTA

The Mango House

Oahu's Only Gay & Lesbian B & B

Gay/Lesbian ♀

The Mango House, a delightful alternative to Waikiki hotels, has views of the ocean, Honolulu, Punchbowl Crater, and the harbor. From your breezy corner room, you'll see mango trees in the backyard. Wake to the aroma of baking bread, served with island juice, fresh fruit and Kona coffee. Explore Hanauma Bay, a snorkeler's paradise; Japanese temples; bamboo forests; waterfalls and hidden pools. Sun and swim at the island's best beaches. We supply beach gear, maps, cooler and ice. As one guest said, "Great food, great views, great advice, great location!"

Address: 2087 Iholena St, Honolulu, HI 96817. Tel: (808) 595-6682(Tel/Fax) or (800) 77-MANGO.

Type: Bed & breakfast.
Clientele: Mostly women with men welcome.
Transportation: Taxi from airport, $11, rental car is best.
To Gay Bars: 15 minutes to gay & lesbian bars.
Rooms: 2 rooms with queen or king beds.
Bathrooms: 1 private, 1 shared.
Meals: Aloha continental breakfast with homemade

bread & mango jam.
Vegetarian: We accommodate special diets.
Complimentary: Passion-orange fruit juice on arrival, cookie jar.
Dates Open: All year.
Rates: $60-$85, plus tax.
Discounts: $3/day for cash, 10% for 7 days.
Credit Cards: MC & VISA.
Rsv'tns: We accept short-notice reservations, but call first.

Reserve Through: Travel agent or call direct.
Minimum Stay: 3 days. For shorter stays call 5 days ahead.
Parking: Ample, on-street parking.
On-Premises: TV/VCR, laundry facilities, beach chairs, snorkeling, cooler & ice, beach towels, maps & killer brownies.
Exercise/Health: Ocean snorkeling, basketball

court across the street.
Swimming: Waikiki & Queen's Surf area 15-min. drive, Kailua (windsurfing) is 20 min.
Sunbathing: At ocean beach or on patio.
Nudity: OK, if guests don't mind the neighbors!
Smoking: Permitted outdoors.
Pets: No, we have a pet parakeet in the household.

Handicap Access: No, stairs. **Children:** Permitted, if over 10 years. **Languages:** English & limited Spanish. IGTA

Waikiki AA Studios
(Bed & Breakfast Honolulu & Statewide)

Gay-Friendly ♀♂

Waikiki AA Studios provides a choice of studios or bed & breakfast accommodations in private homes throughout the islands. We serve you better by discussing your needs on the phone, via our 800 number, and finding out what you like. We confirm availability by phone and ask you to confirm the accuracy of that confirmation in writing when you send us the necessary deposit and flight information. We're the largest B&B agency on the Islands. We also specialize in finding good rates on rental cars and inter-island flights. One call does it all. You'll be pleased with our efficient service.

Address: 3242 Kaohinani, Honolulu, HI 96817. Tel: (808) 595-7533 or (800) 288-4666, Fax: (808) 595-2030.

Type: Studios, hosted rentals & statewide bed & breakfast reservation service.
Clientele: Mostly straight clientele with a gay & lesbian following.
To Gay Bars: Some are near men's/women's bars.
Rooms: 9 studio apartments in Waikiki, 390 homestays & studios in other locations.
Bathrooms: All private in Waikiki, private & shared elsewhere.
Meals: Breakfast in homestays varies with host.
Dates Open: All year.
High Season: December 15th-Easter.
Rates: $40-$150.
Discounts: On weekly & monthly stays.
Credit Cards: MC, VISA.
Rsv'tns: Recommended.
Reserve Through: Travel agent or call direct.
Minimum Stay: 3 days.
Parking: Both free and pay parking.
In-Room: Studios have color TV, telephone, AC, kitchen.
On-Premises: Studios have laundry facilities.
Swimming: Studios have pool, ocean is 1-1/2 blocks away.
Sunbathing: At poolside, on beach.
Smoking: No restrictions in studios. 25% of homestays permit smoking.
Pets: Not permitted.
Handicap Access: Some locations are accessible.
Languages: English.

Waikiki Vacation Rentals

Gay-Friendly ♀♂

Waikiki Vacation Rentals offers you a range, from budget to deluxe, of fully-furnished condos with full kitchens, washer, dryer, phone and TV. You can reserve weekly, monthly and sometimes daily. Each has a view of city, ocean or mountains. All condos are within walking distance of "Old Waikiki" (gay bars, discos, baths and shops), and the ocean beach. Enjoy the privacy of your own condo apartment (just bring a toothbrush) while catching the nightlife of Waikiki. This is our 17th year in business!

Address: 1860 Ala Moana Blvd #108, Honolulu, HI 96815. Tel: (808) 946-9371 or (800) 543-5663, Fax: (808) 922-9418.

Type: Condominium rentals.
Clientele: Both straight & gay men & women.
Transportation: Airport shuttle, cab or rental car.
To Gay Bars: 1-3 blocks to men's & women's bars.
Rooms: 20 apartments with single, double, queen or king beds.
Bathrooms: All private.
Dates Open: All year.
High Season: Thanksgiving to Easter.
Rates: Low season $45-$135, high season $65-$175.
Discounts: For monthly stays, 10%-20%.
Credit Cards: MC, VISA, Amex, Diners, JCB.
Rsv'tns: 1-4 months in advance for high season.
Reserve Through: Travel agent or call direct.
Minimum Stay: 7 days
(some exceptions).
Parking: Free parking at condos. Fee at hotel/condo.
In-Room: Color TV, VCR, telephone, full kitchen, refrigerator, AC, washer, dryer.
On-Premises: Laundry facilities.
Exercise/Health: Jacuzzi, sauna, paddle tennis & tennis.
Swimming: Pool & ocean
beach.
Sunbathing: On beach & sun decks, at poolside or on roof.
Smoking: Non-smoking units available.
Pets: Not permitted.
Handicap Access: No. Bathrooms are regular design.
Children: Permitted.
Languages: English.

IDAHO

ASHTON

Fish Creek Accommodations

Gay/Lesbian ♀

West of the Teton Mountains, surrounded by Idaho's remote beauty, *Fish Creek Accommodations* provides clear skies, seclusion, and peacefulness for optimum relaxation. Yellowstone National Park and Jackson Hole, Wyoming, are easy scenic drives from here. Winter options include a 1-1/2 mile cross-country ski tour to your log cabin with cozy wood stove, unlimited cross-country skiing from your doorstep, and Alpine skiing a short distance away. In summer, fish at nearby places such as Henrys Fork of the Snake River. Hike, bike, or observe birds and wildlife. Come, experience the quiet.

Address: Warm River, PO Box 833, Ashton, ID 83420-0833. Tel: (208) 652-7566.

Type: Log cabin & loft. **Clientele:** Mostly women with men welcome. **Transportation:** Car. Nearest airports in Idaho Falls, ID & Jackson, WY. **Rooms:** 1 cabin & 2 loft rooms with double beds. **Bathrooms:** All private. **Complimentary:** Coffee & teas.

Dates Open: All year. **High Season:** Summer & ski season. **Rates:** Winter, $75-$105 per night. Summer, $60-$90 per night. **Discounts:** Weekly & monthly rates. **Rsv'tns:** Required. **Reserve Through:** Call direct.

Minimum Stay: 2 nights. **Parking:** Acres of free off-street parking, some covered. **In-Room:** Telephone, library of women's books, kitchen, refrigerator, coffee & tea-making facilities. **Swimming:** Nearby river & lake.

Sunbathing: On patio, private sun decks & 20 acres. **Smoking:** Smoking outside only. **Pets:** Permitted. Dogs must be leashed. **Handicap Access:** No. **Children:** Permitted, but not especially welcome. **Languages:** English.

ILLINOIS

CENTRAL ILLINOIS

Little House On The Prairie, The

Gay-Friendly ♀♂

Home of the Stars

The Little House On The Prairie is a Queen Anne Victorian homestead surrounded by acres of woodlands, gardens, swimming pool and pond. "It is a showpiece of a home, full of turn-of-the-century Victorian antiques, wooden parquet floors and theater memorabilia...and it is anything but little." (Mike Monson, *Champaign-Urbana News-Gazette*)

Guests at *The Little House On The Prairie* have included many stars who performed at the The Little Theatre On The Square in Sullivan druing the 60's, 70's and 80's. It is in the heart of Amish country, yet only 3 hours from Chicago and 2 hours from St. Louis.

Address: PO Box 525, Sullivan, IL 61951. Tel: (217) 728-4727.

Type: Bed & breakfast. **Clientele:** Mostly straight clientele with a gay & lesbian following. **Transportation:** Car is best.

To Gay Bars: 60 miles to Champaign, IL. **Rooms:** 4 rooms with single, double & queen beds. **Bathrooms:** 2 private

shower/toilets, 2 private bath/shower/toilets.
Meals: Full breakfast.
Vegetarian: Available if asked for in advance.
Complimentary: Wine, tea, cheese, crackers & fruit. Mints in room.
Dates Open: April 1 thru January 1.
High Season: June thru

August. Usually sold out in advance.
Rates: $55-$70.
Rsv'tns: Required.
Reserve Through: Call direct.
Parking: Ample free parking.
In-Room: AC, maid service & video tape library. 1 room with color TV &

VCR. Coffee/tea-making facilities available.
On-Premises: Meeting rooms & TV lounge.
Exercise/Health: Jacuzzi on premises. Nearby gym, weights, sauna & massage.
Swimming: Pool on premises. Nearby lake.
Sunbathing: At poolside.

Nudity: Permitted in the wooded area.
Smoking: Permitted in sun room & outdoor areas.
Pets: Not permitted.
Handicap Access: No.
Children: Not especially welcome.
Languages: English, French & Italian.
Your Host: Guy & Kirk.

CHICAGO

City Suites Hotel

Gay-Friendly ♀♂

The City Suites Hotel offers a touch of European style with comfortable and convenient accommodations at affordable rates. Located on Chicago's dynamic near north side, close to famous Halsted St., Wrigley Field and the eclectic Sheffield/Belmont area, we're in the heart of Chicago's gay community. Only steps from our door, you'll find the city's finest dining, shopping, theatres and exciting nightlife. The *City Suites* is truly Chicago's best value!

Address: 933 West Belmont, Chicago, IL 60657. Tel: (312) 404-3400, Fax: (312) 404-3405.

Type: Hotel.
Clientele: Mostly straight, with a gay & lesbian following.
Transportation: Taxi.
To Gay Bars: 1 block to gay/lesbian bar.
Rooms: 16 guest rooms & 29 suites.

Bathrooms: All private.
Dates Open: All year.
Rates: $79-$89.
Discounts: Group.
Credit Cards: MC, VISA, Amex & Discover.
Rsv'tns: Recommended.
Reserve Through: Travel agent or call direct.

Parking: Ample, off-street, pay parking.
In-Room: Maid service, telephone, AC & color cable TV.
On-Premises: Laundry facilities.
Swimming: Lake Michigan nearby.

Sunbathing: At the lake.
Smoking: No restrictions.
Pets: Not permitted.
Handicap Access: No.
Children: Permitted.
Languages: English.

IGTA

House of Two Urns, The

Gay-Friendly ♀♂

The House of Two Urns earned its name from the pair of concrete urns at the top of its roof and the repeated motif in the stained-glass windows. This charming two-flat, eclectically furnished with antiques and local art, is near downtown, the gallery district, art bars and alternative theater venues. It is very convenient to public transportation from O'Hare airport and to downtown, is close to the expressway, and has off-street parking. A side garden produces fruits and berries which seasonally grace the breakfast table and patio chairs offer a place to lounge and watch the lettuce grow in the garden.

Address: 1239 N Greenview Ave, Chicago, IL 60622-3318. Tel: (312) 235-1408.

continued next page

Illinois

Type: Bed & breakfast.
Clientele: Mainly straight with gay/lesbian following.
Transportation: Blue Line subway from O'Hare airport to Division is best or 2 blocks from expressway by car.
To Gay Bars: 28 blocks to Newtown, a 10-minute drive.
Rooms: 3 rooms with double beds.

Bathrooms: 2 shared.
Meals: Expanded continental breakfast.
Vegetarian: Always.
Complimentary: Coffee & soda.
Dates Open: All year.
High Season: Mar-Oct.
Rates: $45-$60 plus tax.
Discounts: For stays of 1 week or longer.
Credit Cards: MC, VISA, Amex.
Rsv'tns: Required.

Reserve Through: Call direct.
Minimum Stay: 2 nights.
Parking: Limited free off-street parking, 1 free reserved garage space available.
In-Room: AC, 2 rooms with ceiling fans.
On-Premises: TV lounge, telephone, refrigerator, 2 sitting rooms.
Swimming: 1 block to outdoor pool, 8 blocks to

enclosed pool.
Sunbathing: In the garden.
Smoking: Not permitted indoors.
Pets: Not permitted. Two cats rule already.
Handicap Access: No.
Children: Not permitted.
Languages: English, German, French & limited Spanish.

Lions Inn

Men ♂

Your Alternative Getaway to the Windy City

Lions Inn is a romantic bed and breakfast in a charming, three-story brownstone located in Chicago's historic Andersonville neighborhood. It's just minutes from Chicago's most celebrated gay nightclubs, restaurants and entertainment and a 20-minute cab or bus ride from downtown Chicago. The intimate accommodations feature a guest floor with two elegantly-trimmed bedrooms (one with woodburning fireplace), a sitting room with TV, VCR and stereo, an exclusive rooftop deck with Jacuzzi, and a private backyard with patio. The sitting room is

also where a complimentary continental breakfast awaits you each morning.
Address: 1473 W Catalpa, Chicago, IL 60640. Tel: (312) 769-3119.

Type: Bed & breakfast.
Clientele: Men only.
Transportation: Taxi is best or subway to Jefferson Park Station, then Foster St bus. $1.50 with transfer.
To Gay Bars: 6 block walk. Local transportation, 10 minutes to most of Chicago's bars.
Rooms: 2 rooms with queen beds.
Bathrooms: 1 shared bath/shower/toilet &

1 shared toilet only.
Meals: Expanded continental breakfast.
Vegetarian: A vegetarian would do OK with the expanded continental breakfast.
Dates Open: All year.
Rates: $55-$65 all year.
Discounts: 10% on 4 nights or more.
Credit Cards: MC & VISA.
Rsv'tns: Suggested, but not necessary if rooms are available.

Reserve Through: Call direct.
Minimum Stay: Two nights on weekends.
Parking: Adequate free on-street parking.
In-Room: Maid service, AC, ceiling fans. Kitchen available upon request.
On-Premises: Lounge with TV & stereo, rooftop deck & patio.
Exercise/Health: Jacuzzi on roof-top deck.
Swimming: 8 blocks to

lake, 1/2 hour to gay beach.
Sunbathing: On the roof & on private sun decks.
Nudity: Permitted on private roof sun deck & in Jacuzzi.
Smoking: Permitted on back porch.
Pets: Not permitted.
Handicap Access: No.
Children: Not permitted.
Languages: English.
Your Host: Jon.

Magnolia Place Bed & Breakfast

Gay/Lesbian ♀♀♂

True Southern Hospitality Provided by Yankees, Imagine!

You'll find *Magnolia Place Bed & Breakfast* in the more leisurely-paced Andersonville neighborhood, 15 minutes north of downtown and a few minutes from Lake Michigan beaches. This is Chicago's Swedish neighborhood, filled with beautiful, tree-lined streets, large homes and quaint shops. The guesthouse is a Victorian rowhouse, decorated in a traditional style, accented with country and prairie antiques. The large, comfortable rooms have natural light, brass beds, quilts and wicker furniture. There are hardwood floors, three fireplaces and a garden for warm weather enjoyment. **Address: 5353 N Magnolia, Chicago, IL 60640. Tel: (312) 334-6860.**

MAGNOLIA PLACE B&B

Type: Bed & breakfast.
Clientele: Gay & lesbian. Good mix of men & women.
Transportation: Rapid transit, airport shuttle or taxi to downtown, then northbound Howard B train (EL), exit at Berwyn stop.
To Gay Bars: 6 blocks to men's bars, 8 blocks to women's bars.
Rooms: 3 rooms with double or queen beds. Rollaway available.
Bathrooms: 1 shared bath/shower/toilet &

1 shared toilet only.
Meals: Expanded continental breakfast.
Vegetarian: Always available. Vegetarian restaurants nearby.
Complimentary: Chilled, filtered water & fresh fruit in room.
Dates Open: All year.
Rates: $60 single occupancy, $70 double occupancy.
Credit Cards: MC, VISA & Discover.
Rsv'tns: Required 72 hours in advance.
Reserve Through: Call

direct.
Minimum Stay: 2 nights.
Parking: Ample, free on-street parking.
In-Room: Self-controlled AC, ceiling fans & maid service.
On-Premises: TV lounge.
Swimming: 6 blocks to Lake Michigan beaches.
Sunbathing: On lake beach or short drive to Belmont Rocks gay beach.

Smoking: Non-smoking house. Permitted outdoors in the garden.
Pets: Not permitted; fluffy, friendly American Eskimo Spitz in residence.
Handicap Access: No.
Children: No children under age 12.
Languages: English.
Your Host: Steve & Mike.

We Appreciate Your Comments!

Positive comments of interest may be included in the next issue, giving future readers the benefit of your experience. And it's a nice way of saying "thank you" to an innkeeper who extended you exceptional hospitality.

See the contents for the Reader Comment Form.

Old Town Bed & Breakfast

Gay/Lesbian ♀♂

Old Town Bed & Breakfast is a modern townhouse with antiques and art, private walled garden and a woodburning fireplace located near the gay community, where most businesses are gay-owned and where there are many gay restaurants, bars and retail stores. The two guest rooms have an adjoining library and sitting room and a marble bath with steeping tub. Our quiet, residential location with on-street parking and great access to public transportation, is near Lake Michigan, Lincoln Park, the central business district and North Michigan Avenue shopping.
Address: 1451 N North Park Ave, Chicago, IL 60610-1226. Tel: (312) 440-9268.

Type: Bed & breakfast.
Clientele: Mostly gay & lesbian with some straight clientele.
Transportation: All transportation is best.
To Gay Bars: 2 blocks.
Rooms: 2 rooms with queen beds.
Bathrooms: 1 & 1/2 shared.
Meals: Expanded continental breakfast.
Vegetarian: Always available.
Complimentary: Tea, coffee & juice.
Dates Open: All year.

Rates: All rooms $75.
Discounts: Extended stays.
Credit Cards: MC, VISA, Amex.
Reserve Through: Travel agent or call direct.
Parking: Ample off-street parking.
In-Room: Color cable TV, video tape library, telephone & laundry service.
On-Premises: TV lounge with fireplace, meeting rooms.
Exercise/Health: Nearby gym.

Swimming: Nearby pool & lake.
Sunbathing: In enclosed private garden.
Nudity: Permitted upstairs.
Smoking: This is a non-smoking house. Smoking permitted in walled gar-

den.
Pets: Not permitted.
Handicap Access: No.
Children: Not permitted.
Languages: English, German, French, Italian & Spanish.
Your Host: Michael.

Park Brompton Hotel

Gay-Friendly ♀♂

English Elegance With the Flair of Chicago Style

In the tradition of fine, old English inns, the *Park Brompton Hotel* offers a romantic 19th-century atmosphere on Chicago's bustling North Side. Poster beds and tapestry furnishings lend a hint of Dickensian spirit to finely-appointed rooms. Steps away from the park and Lake Michigan, *Park Brompton* is located in

Chicago's largest gay district, where fine dining, shopping and theatres abound. Wrigley Field, Halsted Street, Lincoln Park Zoo and a beautiful lakefront are nearby, and it's a ten-minute ride to downtown.

Address: 528 W Brompton, Chicago, IL, 60657. Tel: (312) 404-3499 or Fax: 404-3495.

Type: Hotel.
Clientele: Mostly straight, with a gay & lesbian following.
Transportation: Taxi.
To Gay Bars: 1 block to gay/lesbian bars.
Rooms: 7 suites with kitchenettes, 25 single rooms.
Bathrooms: All private.
Dates Open: All year.
Rates: $75-$89.
Discounts: Group.
Credit Cards: MC, VISA, Amex & Discover.
Rsv'tns: Recommended.
Reserve Through: Travel agent or call direct.
Parking: Ample off-street pay parking.
In-Room: Maid service, telephone, AC & color cable TV.
On-Premises: Laundry facilities.
Swimming: Lake Michigan nearby.
Sunbathing: At the lake.
Smoking: No restrictions.
Pets: Not permitted.
Handicap Access: No.
Children: Permitted.
Languages: English.

Surf Hotel

Gay-Friendly ♀♂

On a quiet, tree-lined street in Lincoln Park, yet just 10 minutes from downtown Chicago, *The Surf Hotel* combines atmosphere with accessibility. We're steps away from Chicago's beautiful lakefront, the park, the zoo, the city's finest restaurants and Chicago's version of the Off-Broadway theatre district. Built in 1920, *The Surf* offers tastefully-appointed rooms and is a truly affordable alternative for discriminating guests who prefer personality and ambiance when choosing lodgings.

Address: 555 W Surf, Chicago, IL 60657. Tel: (312) 528-8400, Fax: (312) 528-8483.

Type: Hotel.
Clientele: Mainly straight with gay/lesbian following.
Transportation: Taxi is best.
To Gay Bars: One block.
Rooms: 14 singles, 18 doubles & 2 suites.
Bathrooms: All private.
Vegetarian: Available nearby.
Dates Open: All year.
Rates: $75-$89.
Discounts: Group.
Credit Cards: MC, VISA, Amex, Discover.
Rsv'tns: Recommended.
Reserve Through: Travel agent or call direct.
Parking: Ample, off-street pay parking.
In-Room: Color cable TV, AC, maid service. Limited room service.
On-Premises: Laundry facilities.
Exercise/Health: Discounted daily rates at nearby health club with gym & weights.
Swimming: At nearby Lake Michigan.
Sunbathing: At the lake.
Smoking: Permitted without restrictions.
Pets: Not permitted.
Handicap Access: No.
Children: Permitted.
Languages: English.

Villa Toscana Guest House

Gay/Lesbian ♀♂

A European-Style Guest House

Located in the beautiful East Lakeview neighborhood, *Villa Toscana* is in the heart of Chicago's nightclub and theater district and only steps from Lake Michigan's shoreline. Our gardens provide areas for relaxation, entertainment or private receptions. Make yourself comfortable near the wood-burning fire in the living room and enjoy a complete breakfast each morning in our dining room.

Address: 3447 N Halsted, Chicago, IL 60657-2414. Tel: (800) 404-2643, (312) 404-2643.

continued next page

Illinois

Type: Guesthouse.
Clientele: Mostly gay with some straight clientele.
Transportation: Subway.
To Gay Bars: Next door.
Rooms: 4 doubles & 1 triple.
Bathrooms: All shared.
Meals: Complete breakfast.

Complimentary: Sherry in room.
Dates Open: All year.
High Season: May-November.
Rates: $69 weekdays, $79 weekends.
Credit Cards: MC & VISA.
Rsv'tns: Required.
Reserve Through: Travel

agent or call direct.
Minimum Stay: Required.
Parking: Off-street parking available upon request.
In-Room: Color TV, AC & room service.
On-Premises: Meeting rooms.
Swimming: 2 blocks to

lake.
Sunbathing: On common sun decks.
Pets: Not permitted.
Handicap Access: No.
Languages: English, Italian & Spanish.

IGTA

INDIANA

MISHAWAKA

Kamm's Island Inn/Kamm's Island

Five Secluded Acres in the Gay Outdoors!

Gay/Lesbian ♀♂

Kamm's Island Inn is a secluded riverside lodging facility set in the 100 Center, the historic Kamm's Brewery Complex, which also houses movies, dining, specialty shops and Mind Readers bookstore. Spacious rooms and balconies overlooking our private island and the St. Joe River, create a tranquil, comfortable stay for our guests. Kitchenettes provide convenience for long-term stays. Guests can walk to Truman's, Indiana's largest gay and lesbian nightclub and piano bar. We can cater banquets and arrange special parties for gay and lesbian groups using our facilities.

Address: 700 Lincolnway W, Mishawaka, IN 46544. Tel: (219) 256-1501 or (800) 955-KAMM.

Type: Inn with restaurants, cafe, bar, disco, movie theatre, bistro & shops.
Clientele: Mostly gay & lesbian with some straight clientele.
Transportation: Car or taxi from airport or train station or pick up with advance notice for $5 per trip.
To Gay Bars: Bar on premises owned & operated by Truman's management.
Rooms: 27 rooms & 1 hospitality suite with conference room.

Double, queen or king beds.
Bathrooms: 28 private bath/toilets.
Meals: Continental breakfast.
Vegetarian: Small menu at on-site restaurant.
Complimentary: Brewed coffee & tea.
Dates Open: All year.
Rates: $37.50-$95.
Discounts: Weekly discounts available.
Credit Cards: MC, VISA, Amex & Discover.
Rsv'tns: Recommended.
Reserve Through: Travel agent or call direct.

Minimum Stay: Required on some Notre Dame football game weekends & other Notre Dame events.
Parking: Ample free off-street parking.
In-Room: AC, color cable TV, telephone, kitchen, refrigerator, coffee/tea-makers & maid & laundry services.
On-Premises: Meeting rooms & laundry facilities.
Exercise/Health: Jogging trails on Kamm's Island or take your canoe/kayak to East Races.

Swimming: River on premises. Planning for pool installation.
Sunbathing: On the island.
Smoking: Permitted. Non-smoking rooms available.
Pets: Small pets permitted. Some deposit may be required.
Handicap Access: Yes.
Children: Welcomed, under 12 stay free. Baby beds available.
Languages: English & some Spanish.

LOUISIANA

BATON ROUGE

Brentwood House

A Home Stay with Class

Gay/Lesbian ♂

Brentwood House is a 100-year-old home located in a safe residential neighborhood. The huge pecan trees in our 1-acre yard provide an enjoyable park-like setting. Each guest room offers unique decor and the hot tub and deck area offer a place for nude sun bathing. New Orleans and Acadiana are only an hour away. **Address: PO Box 40872, Baton Rouge, LA 70835-0872. Tel: (504) 924-4989, Fax: (504) 924-1738.**

Type: Home stay.
Clientele: Mostly men with some straight clientele, women welcome.
Transportation: Car or taxi. $10 for pick up from airport, bus or ferry dock.
To Gay Bars: 6 miles or a 15-minute drive.
Rooms: 2 rooms with king & full bed.
Bathrooms: Shared: 1 toilet/shower, 1 toilet/tub.

Meals: Expanded continental breakfast.
Vegetarian: Available upon prior request.
Complimentary: Sherry or soft drink on arrival. Coffee, soft drinks & fruit at all times.
Dates Open: All year.
High Season: LSU football season & Mardi Gras.
Rates: $69-$75.
Discounts: Coupons for discount on return visit.

Rsv'tns: Required.
Reserve Through: Travel agent or call direct.
Parking: Ample, free, well-lit off-street parking.
In-Room: Color TV & maid service.
On-Premises: TV lounge, meeting rooms, private dining room & laundry facilities.
Exercise/Health: Walking, jogging & running trails.

Sunbathing: On common sun decks.
Nudity: Permitted in the house, backyard & on the sun deck.
Smoking: Smoking permitted outside in covered smoking area only.
Pets: Not permitted.
Handicap Access: No.
Children: Not permitted.
Languages: English, some French.
Your Host: Tom.

NEW ORLEANS

A Private Garden

Gay/Lesbian ♀♂

Romantic Hideaway Near New Orleans' Garden District

There is *A Private Garden* in the historic Faubourg Lafayette. Here, your romantic hideaway can be a studio or a two-room apartment set in a secluded patio garden with a spa. Eighteenth-century decor is complemented by a private bath, cable TV, telephone and videos. Just a block away, catch the St. Charles streetcar line for an easy 10-minute ride to the French Quarter, or walk to some of the city's best restaurants. **Address: 1718 Philip St, New Orleans, LA 70113. Tel: (504) 523-1776.**

Type: Bed & breakfast.
Clientele: Good mix of gay men & women.

To Gay Bars: 1 mile or 10 minutes by car.
Rooms: 2 self-contained

apartments with single, double & queen beds.
Bathrooms: 2 private.

1 bath/shower/toilet & 1 shower/toilet.

continued next page

Louisiana

Meals: Expanded continental buffet breakfast. Dates Open: All year. Rates: $50-$65. Rsv'tns: Required. Reserve Through: Call direct. Parking: Ample on-street parking. In-Room: Color cable TV, VCR, video tape library, AC, ceiling fans, kitchen, refrigerator, coffee/tea maker, telephone, maid & laundry service. On-Premises: Laundry facilities. Exercise/Health: Jacuzzi. Swimming: Local pools available. Sunbathing: On the patio. Nudity: Permitted. Entire compound is private. Smoking: Permitted. Pets: Not permitted. Handicap Access: No. Children: Not especially welcomed. Languages: English.

Big D's Bed & Breakfast

Gay/Lesbian ♀♂

Big D's Bed & Breakfast is located in the historic Faubourg Marigny on the fringe of the French Quarter. The clean, comfortable rooms have color TV, AC, telephone, ceiling fans and coffee/tea-making facilities. There is one private and one shared bath. Other amenities include continental breakfast and complimentary drink card.

Address: 704 Franklin Ave, New Orleans, LA 70117. Tel: (504) 944-0216

Type: Bed & breakfast. Clientele: Gay & lesbian. Good mix of men & women. To Gay Bars: A 1-minute walk, 5-minute drive. Rooms: 2 rooms & 1 suite with double or king beds. Bathrooms: 1 private bath/toilet, 1 shared bath/shower/toilet. Meals: Continental breakfast. Vegetarian: Available. Complimentary: One free complimentary drink card. Tea, coffee & mints. Dates Open: All year. High Season: Summer, Mardi Gras & Jazz Fest. Rates: High season $75-$125, low season $35-$55. Discounts: Discount only during Mardi Gras & Jazz Fest. Credit Cards: MC, VISA, Bancard & Discover. Rsv'tns: Required. Parking: Ample, free on-street parking. In-Room: Color TV, AC, telephone, ceiling fan, coffee/tea-making facilities, kitchen, refrigerator & laundry service. On-Premises: TV lounge & laundry facilities. Smoking: Permitted in sleeping room, kitchen & lounge. Pets: Not permitted. Handicap Access: No. Children: Welcome. Languages: English. Your Host: Joyce.

Bourgoyne Guest House

Gay/Lesbian ♀♂

A Courtyard Retreat on Bourbon Street

The excitement of Bourbon Street, coupled with a courtyard retreat from the hullabaloo is what *Bourgoyne Guesthouse* offers visitors to the fabled French Quarter. Fine restaurants, museums, bars, discos...everything you'd want to see in the old section of the city is an easy walk from our central location. Guest accommodations range from cozy studios to spacious one- and two-bedroom suites of unusual style and elegance. All are furnished with antiques and all have private baths, kitchens, air conditioning and telephones.

Address: 839 rue Bourbon, New Orleans, LA 70116. Tel: (504) 524-3621 or (504) 525-3983.

Type: Guesthouse. Clientele: Mostly gay & lesbian with some straight clientele. Transportation: Taxi or airport shuttle. To Gay Bars: 1 block to men's bar, 7 blocks to women's bars. Rooms: 3 rooms & 2 suites. Bathrooms: All private. Dates Open: All year. Rates: $57-$130. Credit Cards: MC & VISA. Rsv'tns: Recommended. Reserve Through: Travel agent or call direct. Parking: Off-street pay parking nearby. In-Room: AC, color TV, telephones, complete kitchens, maid & laundry service. On-Premises: Meeting rooms, laundry facilities, kitchen. Sunbathing: On the patio. Smoking: Permitted without restrictions. Pets: Not permitted. Handicap Access: No. Children: Permitted. Languages: English & French.

Boys On Burgundy

Gay/Lesbian ♂

Boys on Burgundy is located in the heart of the French Quarter, only steps from the bars and famous New Orleans sights and restaurants. This spacious, quiet B&B with friendly, courteous hosts, offers reasonable rates, cable TV, unlimited local calls and large, comfortable rooms that make you feel at home. Everyone is invited to enjoy our large, well-landscaped patio. No standard institutional hotel stay here!

Address: 1030 Burgundy St, New Orleans, LA . Tel: (800) 487-8731.

Type: Bed & breakfast. **Clientele:** Mostly men with women welcome. **Transportation:** Airport shuttle service. **To Gay Bars:** 3 blocks. **Rooms:** 3 rooms with king beds. **Bathrooms:** 1 private bath/toilet, shared bath/shower/toilet. **Meals:** Continental breakfast.

Vegetarian: Available nearby. **Dates Open:** All year. **High Season:** September through May. **Rates:** Call for rates. **Credit Cards:** MC & VISA. **Rsv'tns:** Required. **Reserve Through:** Call direct. **Minimum Stay:** 2 nights, except for certain holidays.

Parking: Adequate on-street parking. **In-Room:** Color cable TV, AC, telephone, kitchen, refrigerator, coffee/tea-making facilities. **On-Premises:** Large, well-landscaped patio, kitchen privileges. **Exercise/Health:** Massage. Nearby gym, weights, spa, sauna, steam & massage.

Swimming: Nearby pool. **Sunbathing:** On the patio & at private clubs. **Smoking:** Permitted on the patio. **Pets:** Not permitted. **Handicap Access:** No. **Children:** Not especially welcome. **Languages:** English.

Bywater B&B

Gay/Lesbian ♀

Bywater B&B is a late Victorian "double shot-gun" cottage in the Bywater neighborhood, a short distance from Faubourg Marigny and the French Quarter and close to tourist attractions. Space for guests includes living room, library, dining room, kitchen and enclosed backyard patio. This is a women-owned and -operated B&B.

Address: 1026 Clouet St, New Orleans, LA . Tel: (301) 588-6850.

Type: Bed & breakfast. **Clientele:** Mostly women with men welcome. **Transportation:** Car is best or airport limo to a French Quarter hotel, then taxi. Taxi from AMTRAK station. **To Gay Bars:** 10 blocks or a 5-minute drive. **Rooms:** 4 rooms with single or double beds.

Bathrooms: 2 shared bath/shower/toilets. **Meals:** Continental breakfast. **Complimentary:** Coffee, tea, soft drinks & juices. **Dates Open:** All year. **Rates:** $50-$60. **Discounts:** Stays of more than two weeks. **Rsv'tns:** Required. **Reserve Through:** Call

direct. **Minimum Stay:** 2 nights on weekends, longer during Jazz Fest & Mardi Gras. **Parking:** Adequate on-street parking. **In-Room:** AC, ceiling fans & telephone. **On-Premises:** TV lounge, laundry facilities & use of kitchen.

Sunbathing: On the patio. **Smoking:** No smoking except on patio. **Pets:** Permitted. Inform us when making reservations. **Handicap Access:** No. **Children:** Welcome. **Languages:** English. **Your Host:** Betty-Carol, Marti & Joan.

Fourteen Twelve Thalia, A Bed and Breakfast

Gay/Lesbian ♀♂

Brant-lee and Terry wish to welcome you into their home, *Fourteen Twelve Thalia, A Bed & Breakfast.* Your spacious, bright and comfortable one-bedroom apartment in this renovated Victorian house has a king-sized bed, private bath, kitchen with microwave, a large living room with queen-sized sofa sleeper, access to laundry facilities, color cable TV and a private entrance. The patio is available for sunbathing and relaxing among the flowers. Our location in the lower Garden

continued next page

Louisiana

District is convenient to the French Quarter, downtown and the art and warehouse districts, the convention center and Super Dome.
Address: 1412 Thalia, New Orleans, LA 70130. Tel: (504) 522-0453.

Type: Bed & breakfast.
Clientele: Mostly gay & lesbian with some straight clientele.
Transportation: Car, streetcar or taxi.
To Gay Bars: 14 blocks to French Quarter bars. From 5-20 minutes by car, taxi or streetcar.
Rooms: Self-contained apartment with king bed, queen sleeper sofa & private entrance. For 2-4 people.
Bathrooms: Private.

Meals: Breakfast furnishings supplied for self-catering kitchen.
Vegetarian: Available with advance notice.
Complimentary: Tea, coffee, juices & fresh fruit.
Dates Open: All year.
High Season: Mardi Gras, Jazz Fest, Sugar Bowl/ New Years.
Rates: $75-$95 or $125-$175 during special events.
Discounts: For stays of

more than 3 nights.
Rsv'tns: Recommended.
Reserve Through: Call direct.
Minimum Stay: 2 nights. Mardi Gras 4 nights, other special events 3 nights.
Parking: Ample on-street parking.
In-Room: Color cable TV, AC, stereo, telephone, ceiling fans, kitchen & refrigerator. Washer/dryer available.
On-Premises: Laundry

facilities.
Sunbathing: On the patio.
Smoking: Not permitted in the apartment. Permitted on deck or patio.
Pets: Small pets that are crate trained.
Handicap Access: Yes. Low steps, wide doors, accessible bath.
Children: Welcomed but limited to 2.
Languages: English.

French Quarter B & B

Gay/Lesbian ♀♂

An 1822 Creole Cottage With a Friendly Cajun Host

French Quarter B & B is a private, 800 sq. ft. apartment, located a half-block from the French Quarter and within walking distance of all major attractions. The apartment, which sleeps up to six, has a large living room, bedroom, kitchen and bath. The kitchen is completely equipped, including a microwave and coffeemaker, plus iron and ironing

board. Temperatures are kept comfortable by ceiling fans, air conditioning and heat. In the summer guests can cool off in the beautiful, tropically landscaped swimming pool.
Address: 1132 Ursulines St, New Orleans, LA 70116. Tel: (504) 525-3390.

Type: Private apartment.
Clientele: Good mix of gay men & women.
Transportation: Taxi or airport limo.
To Gay Bars: 2 blocks.
Rooms: 1 apartment with queen bed.
Bathrooms: 1 private.
Meals: Expanded continental breakfast (food in refrigerator, you cook).
Vegetarian: Available.

Complimentary: Coffee, juice, tea & soft drinks.
Dates Open: All year.
High Season: October thru May, Jazz Fest, Mardi Gras & Sugar Bowl.
Rates: $65 for 1-2 people, $125 during special events.
Discounts: For 2 weeks or more.
Credit Cards: MC & VISA.
Rsv'tns: Required.

Reserve Through: Travel agent or call direct.
Minimum Stay: One night service charge ($90 instead of $65).
Parking: Adequate, free on-street parking.
In-Room: Color cable TV, AC, phones, laundry service, kitchen, refrigerator & ceiling fans.
Exercise/Health: Massage.

Swimming: Pool.
Sunbathing: At poolside.
Nudity: Permitted around pool at certain times.
Smoking: Permitted. No non-smoking rooms.
Pets: Not permitted.
Handicap Access: No.
Children: Not permitted.
Languages: English.

Lafitte Guest House

Gay/Lesbian ♀♂

The French Quarter's Premier Guest House For Over 40 Years

This elegant French manor house, meticulously restored to its original splendor and furnished in fine antiques and reproductions, has all the comforts of home, including air conditioning. Located in the quiet, residential section of famous Bourbon St., *Lafitte Guest House* is just steps from the French Quarter's attractions. Continental breakfast is served in your room, in our tropical courtyard or in our Victorian parlour.

Wine and hors d'oeuvres are served each evening at cocktail hour. Parking is available on the premises.

Address: 1003 Bourbon St, New Orleans, LA 70116. Tel: (504) 581-2678 or (800) 331-7971.

Type: Bed & breakfast guesthouse.
Clientele: Mostly gay & lesbian with some straight clientele.
Transportation: Limo from airport. Pick up from airport or train, $21 taxi, $31 limo (for 2).
To Gay Bars: 1 block or a 3-minute walk.
Rooms: 12 rooms, 2 suites & 2 apartments with double, queen or king beds.
Bathrooms: 7 private

bath/toilets & 7 private shower/toilets.
Meals: Continental breakfast.
Vegetarian: Vegetarian food nearby.
Complimentary: Wine & hors d'oeuvres.
Dates Open: All year.
High Season: Sept 1st-Dec 1st, Jan 1st-May 31st.
Rates: 1-bdrm $79-$165, 2-bdrm suite $210-$270.
Discounts: AAA 10%.
Credit Cards: MC, VISA, Amex & Discover.

Rsv'tns: Required with deposit.
Reserve Through: Travel agent or call direct.
Minimum Stay: 2 days on weekends. Inquire for special events.
Parking: Ample off-street parking.
In-Room: Color TV, AC, telephone & maid service. Some rooms have refrigerators & ceiling fans.
On-Premises: Victorian parlor & courtyard.

Exercise/Health: Nearby gym, weights, Jacuzzi/spa, sauna, steam & massage.
Swimming: Available at two of our off-premises townhouses.
Sunbathing: At poolside.
Smoking: Permitted without restrictions.
Pets: Not permitted.
Handicap Access: No.
Children: Permitted.
Languages: English, French & Spanish.

Macarty Park Guest House

A Tropical Paradise in the City

Gay/Lesbian ♀♂

Enjoy beautiful, small, private poolside cottages, spacious suites and rooms in this Eastlake Victorian home. Located in a national historical district, *Macarty Park* is just five minutes from the French Quarter. Step out of your room into lush, tropical gardens and jump into the sparkling pool. Enjoy the tranquility of the cool water on moonlit nights. Rooms are tastefully decorated in antique and contemporary furnishings,

and are impeccably clean, each with a private bath. All this for a fraction of what you would pay elsewhere!

continued next page

Louisiana

Address: 3820 Burgundy St, New Orleans, LA 70117-5708. **Tel:** (504) 943-4994 or (800) 521-2790.

Type: Bed & breakfast guesthouse with cottages. **Clientele:** Mostly gay & lesbian with some straight clientele. **Transportation:** Cab from airport. **To Gay Bars:** 10 blocks. **Rooms:** 5 rooms, 1 suite & 2 cottages with double, queen or king beds. **Bathrooms:** 6 private bath/toilet/showers & 2 private shower/toilets. **Meals:** Continental breakfast. **Complimentary:** Brewed coffee & tea. **Dates Open:** All year. **Rates:** $39-$105. **Credit Cards:** MC, VISA & Amex. **Rsv'tns:** Required with deposit. **Reserve Through:** Travel agent or call direct. **Minimum Stay:** 2 days on weekends. **Parking:** Ample free off-street parking. **In-Room:** Color TV, AC, telephone & maid service. Some accommodations have kitchen, refrigerator, ceiling fans, coffee & tea-making facilities. **Swimming:** Pool on premises. **Sunbathing:** At poolside, on common sun decks & on patio. **Nudity:** Permitted in the pool at night. **Smoking:** Permitted without restrictions. **Pets:** Not permitted. **Handicap Access:** No. **Children:** Not especially welcomed. **Languages:** English & French.

Mentone Bed & Breakfast

Gay/Lesbian ♀♂

Mentone Bed & Breakfast offers a suite in a Victorian home in the Faubourg Marigny district next to the historic French Quarter. The suite is furnished with antiques and Oriental rugs, has thirteen-foot ceilings, a sitting room, and a private entrance. The sound of the paddle wheels on the river and of the horse-drawn carriages in the street below lull guests to sleep in the evenings. Enjoy the solitude of our home and tropical garden, or venture five blocks into the heart of the Quarter for entertainment and nightlife.

Address: 1437 Pauger St, New Orleans, LA 70116. **Tel:** (504) 943-3019.

Type: Bed & breakfast. **Clientele:** Mostly gay & lesbian with some straight clientele. **Transportation:** Car is best. Shuttle or limo from airport at expense. **To Gay Bars:** 3-4 blocks. **Rooms:** 2 suites with single, double or queen beds. **Bathrooms:** All private shower/toilets. **Meals:** Expanded continental breakfast of pastries or bread, fruit bowl. **Complimentary:** Champagne, coffee, & tea. **Dates Open:** All year except Christmas. **High Season:** Sep 1-Jun 1. **Rates:** $75-$100 except for special events. **Discounts:** Reduction after 7-night stay. **Rsv'tns:** Preferred. **Reserve Through:** Call direct. **Minimum Stay:** On weekends and for special events. **Parking:** Adequate free on-street parking or limited off-street free parking. **In-Room:** Color TV, AC, ceiling fans, telephone, kitchenette, refrigerator & coffee & tea-making facilities. **Smoking:** On the balcony off the suite. Non-smoking rooms. **Pets:** Not permitted. **Handicap Access:** No. **Children:** Permitted on approval. **Languages:** English & limited French.

Parkview

Gay-Friendly 50/50 ♀♂

Parkview offers comfortable accommodations and cozy atmosphere in a quaint Creole cottage. Centrally-located, across from Washington Square and adjacent to the French Quarter, *Parkview* is surrounded by restaurants, bars, jazz clubs, theatres, and curio shops. Enjoy a private entrance through a lush patio to your private home-away-from-home at *Parkview*. Reasonable rates.

Address: 726 Frenchmen St, New Orleans, LA 70116. **Tel:** (504) 945-7875.

Type: Guesthouse. **Clientele:** 50% gay & lesbian & 50% straight. **Transportation:** Taxi. **To Gay Bars:** 5 minutes. **Rooms:** 2 apartments with queen & king beds. More units available in 1995. **Bathrooms:** All private. **Complimentary:** Coffee, orange juice. **Dates Open:** All year. **High Season:** New Years, Jazz Fest, Mardi Gras. **Rates:** Summer $60-$70. Fall, winter, spring $80-$90. Special events $100-$125. **Rsv'tns:** Required. **Reserve Through:** Call direct. **Minimum Stay:** 2 days. **Parking:** Limited on-street parking. **In-Room:** Color cable TV, AC, telephone, ceiling fans, kitchen, refrigerator, coffee & tea-making facilities. **Sunbathing:** On the patio. **Smoking:** Permitted. **Pets:** Not permitted. **Handicap Access:** No. **Children:** Not permitted. **Languages:** English.

Rober House

Gay/Lesbian ♀♂

Welcome to America's most fascinating city, whose unique personality was blended from many cultures. New Orleans offers you fun, music, excitement and delicious foods. Come, experience and capture the charm of the French Quarter at *Rober House.* Here, in a quiet, residential location, our one-bedroom, living, kitchen and full-bath condos are fully furnished and have all the amenities, plus courtyard and swimming pool, and can sleep up to 4 people. Great savings only minutes from fabulous restaurants and tourist attractions.

Address: 822 Ursulines St New Orleans, LA 70116-2422. Tel: (504) 529-4663 or 523-1246.

Type: Guesthouse.
Clientele: Mostly gay & lesbian with some straight clientele.
Transportation: Taxi from airport $21. Shuttle bus, $10 per person, stops across the street.
To Gay Bars: Two blocks to 1 bar & three blocks to 4 other bars, all in the same direction.
Rooms: Three apartments with queen bed & queen sofa bed. Each sleeps up to 4 people.
Bathrooms: All private.
Vegetarian: Health restaurant nearby.
Complimentary: Coffee.
Dates Open: All year.
High Season: Special events weeks & weekends.
Rates: July 1-Aug 31, $69-$89. Rest of year, $90-$125, except special events periods (call for rates).
Discounts: Weekly rates.
Rsv'tns: Required.
Reserve Through: Travel agent or call direct.
Minimum Stay: 3 days in summer & 2 days rest of year.
Parking: On-street parking & plenty of parking garages near Canal St.
In-Room: Color TV, AC, ceiling fans, telephone & kitchen with refrigerator.
Swimming: Pool.
Sunbathing: At poolside.
Nudity: Permitted poolside if no one else objects.
Smoking: Preferably outside the apartments.
Pets: Permitted except for snakes & other reptiles.
Handicap Access: 1 unit is accessible with help.
Children: Welcomed.
Languages: English, German & Danish.

Royal Barracks Guest House

Gay/Lesbian ♀♂

In a newly-renovated Victorian home located in a quiet, residential neighborhood, a charming French lady will offer you the hospitality of the historical French Quarter. Within a few blocks are 24-hour restaurants, bars and delicatessens. Rooms at *Royal Barracks* are individually decorated, have private entrances and have all modern conveniences. All open onto our high-walled, private patio with wet bar, refrigerator and ice maker. Our avid return customers, many of whom often book a year in advance, consider their accommodations here their own secluded, private hideaway.

Address: 717 Barracks St, New Orleans, LA 70116. Tel: (504) 529-7269, Fax: (504) 529-7298.

Type: Guesthouse.
Clientele: Mostly gay & lesbian with some straight clientele.
Transportation: $10 per person airport shuttle, taxi $20 flat fee.
To Gay Bars: 1/2 block to men's & 7 blocks to women's bars.
Rooms: 4 rooms & 1 suite with double & queen beds.
Bathrooms: All private.
Meals: Expanded continental breakfast.
Complimentary: Kenwood water, fruits, cookies, coffee & tea.
Dates Open: All year.
High Season: April (Jazz Fest) & February (Mardi Gras).
Rates: Jun 15-Sep 15, $55-$80. Winter, $65-$110.
Credit Cards: MC & VISA.
Rsv'tns: Required.
Reserve Through: Travel agent or call direct.
Parking: On-street parking.
In-Room: Color TV, telephone, ceiling fans, AC & maid service.
On-Premises: Ice machine & refrigerator in the courtyard.
Exercise/Health: Jacuzzi.
Smoking: Permitted without restrictions.
Pets: Not permitted.
Handicap Access: No.
Children: Permitted.
Languages: French, English & Spanish.
Your Host: Christine & John.

Ursuline Guesthouse

Gay/Lesbian ♀♂

Our guesthouse is located in the midst of the French Quarter, near restaurants, shops, museums and all that makes New Orleans famous. Constructed in the 18th century, *Ursuline Guest House* is today an historical structure enhanced with all the modern amenities desirable to the out-of-town guest. All rooms have modern bathrooms, air conditioning, color cable TV, carpeting or hardwood floors, are furnished with an eclectic blend of furniture, and open onto a serene, old French Quarter courtyard with wrought iron furniture and a hot tub. We are confident you will be pleased.

Address: 708 rue des Ursulines, New Orleans, LA 70116. Tel: (504) 525-8509, (800) 654-2351, Fax: (504) 525-8408.

Type: Guesthouse.
Clientele: Mostly gay & lesbian with some straight clientele.
Transportation: Airport shuttle $12. Taxi $22 for 1 or 2 people.
To Gay Bars: One block.
Rooms: 14 rooms with single, double & queen beds.
Bathrooms: All private.
Meals: Continental

breakfast.
Vegetarian: Vegetarian restaurant within walking distance.
Complimentary: Coffee. Wine in courtyard each evening.
Dates Open: All year.
High Season: Sept-May.
Rates: $60-$100. Higher on holidays & for special events.
Credit Cards: MC, VISA &

Amex.
Rsv'tns: Recommended.
Reserve Through: Call direct.
Minimum Stay: Two nights weekends & 3-5 days during special events & holidays.
Parking: Limited off-street parking $7/day.
In-Room: Color TV, AC, direct dial telephone & maid service.

Exercise/Health: Whirlpool in courtyard.
Smoking: Permitted without restrictions.
Pets: Permitted with restrictions.
Handicap Access: Yes.
Children: Not especially welcomed.
Languages: English.

MAINE

AUGUSTA

Maple Hill Farm B&B Inn

Gay-Friendly ♀♂

Get Away From It All, Yet Be Near It All...

On 62-acres just minutes from Augusta, *Maple Hill Farm* is the only B&B Inn in the Capitol area. Breakfast is hearty country fare, cooked to order from our menu. Guest rooms provide a variety of amenities, including private bath and a whirlpool for two! *Maple Hill Farm* provides an excellent "base camp" from which to explore Maine. Hike through fields and woods, enjoy the private swimming hole, or relax in front of the fireplace. The coast, lakes, mountains and Freeport shopping are all within an hour's drive. Hallowell, just 3 miles away, is the gay community for this area.

Address: Outlet Rd, RR1 Box 1145, Hallowell, ME 04347. Tel: (207) 622-2708, (800) 622-2708, Fax: (207) 622-0655.

Type: Bed & breakfast with gallery.
Clientele: Mostly straight clientele with a gay & lesbian following.
Transportation: Car is best. Rentals available at Portland or Augusta airports.
To Gay Bars: 5 miles to

P.J.'s in Augusta. 1 hour to Portland bars.
Rooms: 6 rooms & 1 suite with double or queen beds.
Bathrooms: Private: 3 shower/toilets, 1 full bath. 1 shared full bath.
Campsites: Rustic camping adjacent to small

spring-fed pond in woods. Very private.
Meals: Full breakfast cooked to order from menu.
Vegetarian: Cooked to order breakfast. Excellent vegetarian-oriented restaurant nearby.
Complimentary: Evening

tea or sherry, coffee. Mints in room.
Dates Open: All year.
High Season: July-October (summer & fall foliage).
Rates: Summer $45-$90. winter $40-$80.
Discounts: Government rates available.

Credit Cards: MC, VISA, Amex, Diners & Discover.
Rsv'tns: Recommended.
Reserve Through: Travel agent or call direct.
Minimum Stay: Required some peak summer & fall weekends.
Parking: Ample free off-street parking.
In-Room: AC, telephone & maid service. Some rooms with color TV. 1 room with Jacuzzi bath.
On-Premises: TV lounge, meeting rooms, fax machine.
Exercise/Health: Jacuzzi in 1 guest room. Nearby gym & massage.
Swimming: Swimming hole in the woods. 1 mile to lake.
Sunbathing: On common sun decks & at the swimming hole.
Nudity: Permitted at swimming hole.
Smoking: Permitted outside or on covered porch only, not inside building or rooms.
Pets: Not permitted.
Handicap Access: Yes. Ramp to 1st floor guest room & fully accessible bathroom.
Children: Well-behaved children over 8 are welcome. Younger children by permission only.
Languages: English, some French.
Your Host: Scott.

BAR HARBOR

Homestead

Gay/Lesbian ♀

Warm hospitality, exquisite antiques, hand-hewn beams and wide, pumpkin pine floorboards lend warmth to *Homestead*, a tastefully decorated New England country home built in 1860 and located at the gateway of Acadia Nat'l. Park. Protected by spreading chestnuts and maples, the house commands a view over 3-1/2 acres of fields and herb and flower gardens bounded by fir, spruce and birch. Colorful birds can be observed from the private deck. Nearby, are romantic beaches and opportunities for biking, canoeing, kayaking, cross-country skiing, etc.

Address: PO Box 508, Bar Harbor, ME 04609. Tel: (207) 288-9041.

Type: Bed & breakfast.
Clientele: Mostly women with men welcome.
Transportation: Auto or fly to Bangor or Trenton, then car. We will pick up from Trenton, no charge.
To Gay Bars: 1 hour to The Rage in Bangor.
Rooms: 3 rooms with double or queen beds.
Bathrooms: 1 shared bath/shower/toilet.
Meals: Expanded continental breakfast in summer, full breakfast rest of year.
Vegetarian: Available with prior notification.
Complimentary: Tea, coffee, juices.
Dates Open: All year.
High Season: Mid June-mid October.
Rates: $55-$75.
Discounts: Kitchen privileges for stays of 5 or more days.
Credit Cards: MC, VISA.
Rsv'tns: Recommended.
Reserve Through: Call direct.
Parking: Ample free off-street parking.
In-Room: Maid service.
On-Premises: TV lounge, laundry facilities, use of refrigerator, telephone, gardens, & deck for sunbathing.
Exercise/Health: Massage.
Swimming: Ocean beach or lake at Acadia National Park. Pool at Y or racquet club.
Sunbathing: On beach or sun decks.
Smoking: Permitted outside only. Non-smoking rooms available.
Pets: Not permitted.
Handicap Access: No.
Children: Welcome.
Languages: English.

Lindenwood Inn

A Quiet Place by the Harbor

Gay-Friendly ♀♂

Built at the turn of the century, *Lindenwood Inn* derives its name from the stately linden trees that still line the front lawn now, as they did then. Recently remodeled, each room is individually decorated and has a private bath. The inn is filled with an eclectic mix of art and furnishings gathered by the host in his travels. Many rooms feature harbor views from sun-drenched balconies. Relax and unwind in one of the inn's elegant sitting rooms, or on the large, shaded porch, while listening to the sounds of the harbor just a few steps away.

Address: Box 1328 Clark Point Rd, Southwest Harbor, ME 04679. Tel: (207) 244-5335.

Type: Inn.
Clientele: Mostly straight clientele with a gay & lesbian following.
Transportation: Car is best. Pick up from airport.
To Gay Bars: 40 miles or 1 hour by car.
Rooms: 6 rooms, 5 suites & 2 cottages with double or queen beds.
Bathrooms: Private: 9 bath/toilets & 2 shower/toilets & 2 housekeeping cottages.
Meals: Full breakfast.
Vegetarian: Available upon request.
Complimentary: Tea, coffee & set-up service.
Dates Open: All year.
High Season: July, August, September & October.

continued next page

Maine

Rates: Winter $35-$85, spring $45-$95, summer $75-$135, fall $65-$125. **Credit Cards:** MC, VISA, Amex. **Rsv'tns:** Suggested in the summer. **Reserve Through:** Call direct.

Minimum Stay: Summer only. **Parking:** Ample free off-street parking. **In-Room:** Ceiling fans & maid service. **On-Premises:** Meeting rooms, sitting rooms with fireplaces, balconies, guest kitchen & private access to water. **Exercise/Health:** Nearby gym, weights, Jacuzzi/spa, suana, steam & massage. **Swimming:** Nearby ocean, river & lake. **Sunbathing:** On private sun decks & nearby beach.

Nudity: Nude beach nearby. **Smoking:** Permitted on porches only. **Pets:** Not permitted. **Handicap Access:** No. **Children:** Not especially welcomed. **Languages:** English.

Manor House Inn

Bar Harbor's Historical Victorian Inn

Gay-Friendly ♀♂

The moment you step into the front entry, a romantic Victorian past becomes the present. Our elegant common rooms are decorated with antiques, Victorian wallcoverings, original maple floors and several working fireplaces. Our in-town location on tree-lined West St. lets you enjoy privacy, while staying within easy walking distance of Bar Harbor's fine shops, restaurants, whale watching, schooner rides, bike rentals, and even Bar Island. The spacious suites at *Manor House Inn* are graciously furnished, have working fireplaces, private baths, garden views and king-sized beds.

Address: 106 West St, Bar Harbor, ME . Tel: (207) 288-3759.

Type: Bed & breakfast. **Clientele:** Mostly straight clientele with a gay/lesbian following. **Transportation:** Car is best. **Rooms:** 7 rooms & 5 suites with queen or king beds. **Bathrooms:** All private bath/toilets. **Meals:** Full breakfast.

Complimentary: Tea, coffee, lemonade, iced tea & apple cider in season. **Dates Open:** May through October. **High Season:** July through October. **Rates:** Seasonal $85-150, off season $55-$100. **Credit Cards:** MC & VISA. **Rsv'tns:** Highly recommended as early as possible. **Reserve Through:** Call direct. **Minimum Stay:** 2 nights July & August & holiday weekends. **Parking:** Adequate on-street & off-street parking. **In-Room:** Maid service. Some rooms have fireplaces, cottages have kitchens & color cable TV. **On-Premises:** TV lounge, veranda & gardens. **Swimming:** Beaches at the ocean or nearby lakes. **Sunbathing:** On the beach. **Smoking:** Not permitted. **Pets:** Not permitted. **Children:** Permitted (12 years and up). **Languages:** English.

ELLSWORTH

Carriage House

Men ♂

Our Victorian home is in the hamlet of Ellsworth, Maine, near Bar Harbor and the gateway to Acadia National Park. It's a popular area for cross-country skiing, hiking, biking, canoeing and mountain climbing. Many also enjoy exploring the antique shops in the area. *Carriage House* contains a working greenhouse operated in conjunction with a florist's shop. In summer, we serve breakfast on our greenhouse patio from which guests can view a profusion of flowering and exotic plants.

Address: 64 Birch Ave, Ellsworth, ME 04605. Tel: (800) 669-5795 or (207) 667-3078, Fax: 667-3079.

Type: Bed & breakfast.	**Vegetarian:** Available	Carte Blanche.	beach & lake. Nude beach
Clientele: Men only.	with advance notice.	**Rsv'tns:** Required.	within 20 miles.
Transportation: Car is	**Complimentary:** Evening	**Reserve Through:** Call	**Sunbathing:** On beach.
best. Free pick up from	coffee & pastries.	direct.	**Smoking:** Permitted
airport.	**Dates Open:** All year.	**Parking:** Ample off-street	without restrictions.
To Gay Bars: 25 miles.	**High Season:** Summer.	parking.	**Pets:** Not permitted.
Rooms: 1 single & 3	**Rates:** Summer $35-$55.	**In-Room:** Color TV.	**Handicap Access:** No.
doubles.	Rest of year $25-$45.	**On-Premises:** Two sitting	**Children:** Not permitted.
Bathrooms: 2 shared.	**Credit Cards:** MC, VISA,	rooms.	**Languages:** English.
Meals: Full breakfast.	Amex, Diners, Discover &	**Swimming:** Nearby ocean	**Your Host:** Bob & Lonnie.

KENNEBUNK

Arundel Meadows Inn

Gay-Friendly ♀♂

A Relaxing Getaway With a Four-Star Breakfast!

Small and personal, this nineteenth-century farmhouse has rooms and suites decorated in art and antiques, with private bathrooms and summer air conditioning. Three rooms have working fireplaces and all have comfortable sitting areas for reading and relaxing. Nearby Kennebunkport has antiques, artists' studios and excellent restaurants. Golf, tennis, fishing and cross-country skiing are readily accessible. At *Arundel Meadows Inn,* guests enjoy spring picnic meadows, summer flower gardens, fall foliage and winter fires in the living room.

Address: PO Box 1129, Kennebunk, ME 04043-1129. Tel: (207) 985-3770.

Type: Bed & breakfast.	**Bathrooms:** All private.	**Discounts:** 10% on 5	**Swimming:** Ocean beach
Clientele: Mostly straight	**Meals:** Full breakfast.	nights or more.	is nearby.
clientele, with gays &	**Vegetarian:** Available	**Credit Cards:** MC & VISA.	**Sunbathing:** At the
lesbians welcome.	upon request.	**Rsv'tns:** Required.	beach, on the patio, 2
Transportation: Car is	**Complimentary:** After-	**Reserve Through:** Call	rooms with private sun
best.	noon tea.	direct.	decks.
To Gay Bars: 10 miles to	**Dates Open:** All year	**Minimum Stay:** 2 days on	**Nudity:** Not permitted.
Ogunquit, ME, 25 miles to	(subject to change).	weekends Memorial Day	**Smoking:** Not permitted.
Portland, ME gay bars.	**High Season:** Memorial	through Columbus Day.	**Pets:** Not permitted.
Rooms: Five rooms and	Day through Columbus	**Parking:** Adequate free	**Handicap Access:** Yes.
two suites with single,	Day.	off-street parking.	**Children:** Not permitted
double, queen and king	**Rates:** Summer $75-	**In-Room:** AC & maid ser-	under 12 years of age.
beds.	$110, winter $55-$85.	vice. Color TV in 3 rooms.	**Languages:** English.

LINCOLNVILLE BEACH

Sign of the Owl B & B

Gay/Lesbian ♀♂

Visit with us in our 1794 Maine farmhouse nine miles north of Camden's beautiful harbor. *Sign of the Owl* is convenient for day trips to Acadia Nat'l Park, Vinalhaven, Bar Harbor and Islesboro. A sandy public beach is but 2 miles from the house and a small private beach is a 10-minute walk through the woods. Many fine restaurants, gift and antique shops are nearby. The bathroom is shared, so please be considerate of other guests.

Address: RR 2, Box 85, Lincolnville Beach, ME 04849. Tel: (207) 338-4669.

Type: Bed & breakfast	car at Bangor airport.	**Bathrooms:** 1 shared	upon request.
with an antique shop.	**To Gay Bars:** Nearest	bath/shower/toilet &	**Dates Open:** All year.
Clientele: Mostly gay &	gay bars are in Portland,	1 shared shower/toilet.	**High Season:** July-
lesbian with some	a 2-hour drive.	**Meals:** Full gourmet	September.
straight clientele.	**Rooms:** 3 rooms with	breakfast.	
Transportation: Rent a	single or double beds.	**Vegetarian:** Available	*continued next page*

Maine

Rates: $35-$65. **Discounts:** Stay one week, 7th day free. **Credit Cards:** MC, VISA, Amex. **Rsv'tns:** Recommended. **Reserve Through:** Call direct.

Parking: Ample free off-street parking. **In-Room:** Maid service, color or B&W TV. **On-Premises:** Meeting rooms, central heat, TV lounge. **Exercise/Health:** Hiking,

swimming, bike trails. **Swimming:** 4-minute walk to ocean beach, 6 miles to lake. **Sunbathing:** On ocean beach, at lakeside, in backyard. **Smoking:** Permitted out-

side only. **Pets:** Permitted with prior arrangement. **Handicap Access:** No. **Children:** Not permitted. **Languages:** English. **Your Host:** John & Duncan.

NAPLES

Lamb's Mill Inn

Gay/Lesbian ♀♂

Ewe Hike, Ewe Bike, Ewe Ski, Ewe ZZzzz...

Lamb's Mill Inn is a small country inn nestled among the foothills of the White Mountains in the picturesque village of Naples. Surrounded by two of Maine's largest lakes, Sebago and Long Lake, Naples is the hub of summertime water ac-

tivities in this area. Winter brings cross-country and alpine skiers, snowmobilers and ice fishermen. The spectacular fall foliage invites hikers and bikers to hit the trails. In spring, canoeing the Saco River and nearby ponds is a popular pastime. The inn is a 19th-century farmhouse, newly renovated and abounding with country charm. Our six rooms offer a romantic atmosphere and feature private baths. You will awaken to the aroma of a full country breakfast served in our two gracious dining rooms. Enjoy the privacy and scenic beauty of twenty acres of field and woods, or a leisurely stroll to the charming village. Browse along the causeway and discover parasailing, aerial sightseeing, watercycling, windsurfing and tours on the Songo River Queen. Play golf and tennis, or visit the many country fairs and flea markets. Dine in gourmet restaurants, or sample local Yankee recipes in small cafes and diners. To end an exciting day, unwind in our hot tub. All this and more is yours at *Lamb's Mill Inn,* an inn for all seasons.

Address: Box 676, Lamb's Mill Rd, Naples, ME 04055. Tel: (207) 693-6253

Type: Bed & breakfast inn. **Clientele:** Good mix of gays & lesbians. **Transportation:** Car from Portland airport 25 miles away. **To Gay Bars:** 25 miles to Portland gay/lesbian bars. **Rooms:** 6 rooms with queen or king beds. **Bathrooms:** All private. **Meals:** Full breakfast, catered dinner for 4 available. **Vegetarian:** Owner is

vegetarian. **Complimentary:** Ice & munchies available in afternoon as well as tea & coffee. **Dates Open:** All year. **High Season:** Summer & for fall foliage. **Rates:** Summer, fall & winter $75-$85, spring $65-$75. **Discounts:** Sixth consecutive night free. 15% midweek (Mon-Thurs) for 3 night stay. **Credit Cards:** MC & VISA. **Rsv'tns:** Recommended.

Reserve Through: Travel agent or call direct. **Minimum Stay:** Two nights on weekends in high season. **Parking:** Ample free off-street parking. **In-Room:** Color cable TV, maid service, refrigerator. **On-Premises:** 2 private dining rooms, 2 TV lounges, stereo, BBQ's, 1 reading & game lounge. **Exercise/Health:** Jacuzzi, treadmill, canoeing, windsurfing, parasailing, boat rides, water cycling,

trails, downhill skiing, bicycling. **Swimming:** Town beach is at the bottom of our hill on Long Lake. **Sunbathing:** On patio, private sun decks or anywhere on 20 acres. **Smoking:** Permitted outside. **Pets:** Not permitted. **Handicap Access:** No. **Children:** Not permitted. **Languages:** English.

IGTA

OGUNQUIT

Beauport Inn and Antiques

Gay-Friendly 50/50 ♀♂

Comfortable Elegance

The *Beauport Inn* is a cozy, expanded cape-style home with an attached antique shop. Located on Shore Road on the trolley line, approximately halfway between town center and Perkins Cove, our inn provides a quiet location within easy walking distance to shops, restaurants, beach, Playhouse and the Marginal Way walking path.

Relax in our pine-panelled living room with piano and fireplace, our comfortable TV area or on our deck overlooking the gardens. Breakfast is served in the dining room or may be enjoyed on the deck.

Address: PO Box 1793, 102 Shore Rd, Ogunquit, ME 03907. Tel: (800) 646-8681, (207) 646-8680.

Type: Bed & breakfast with antique shop.
Clientele: 50% gay & lesbian & 50% straight clientele.
Transportation: Car is best.
To Gay Bars: 1/2 mile. A 10-minute walk or 3-minute drive.
Rooms: 4 rooms with twin or queen beds.
Bathrooms: All private.

Meals: Expanded continental breakfast.
Vegetarian: At nearby restaurants.
Dates Open: March 1st to December 15th.
High Season: July & August.
Rates: Summer, $85. Fall & spring, $60.
Discounts: 10% for weekly stays.
Credit Cards: MC, VISA &

Amex.
Rsv'tns: Required.
Reserve Through: Call direct.
Minimum Stay: Required.
Parking: Adequate free off-street parking.
In-Room: AC & maid service.
On-Premises: TV lounge.
Exercise/Health: Nearby gym, massage & golf.

Swimming: Nearby ocean.
Sunbathing: On common sun decks & at the beach.
Smoking: Permitted outside only. Entire house is non-smoking.
Pets: Not permitted.
Handicap Access: No.
Children: Not especially welcome.
Languages: English.

Heritage of Ogunquit

Gay/Lesbian ♀

Maine's Best B & B

Heritage of Ogunquit is a new Victorian reproduction in a quiet area which is just an eight-minute walk to the beach, cove and the fabulous Marginal Way floral footpath along the ocean's edge. *The Heritage* features a hot tub, giant cedar deck, sitting room with TV and VCR, refrigerator and microwave. Expanded continental breakfast is served overlooking perennial gardens and five acres of woods. Local 12-step information is always available to our guests. Lesbian-owned and -operated.

Address: PO Box 1295, Ogunquit, ME 03907. Tel: (207) 646-7787.

Type: Bed & breakfast.
Clientele: Mostly women with men welcome.
Transportation: Car. Pick up from airport in Portland, ME, $35 roundtrip, from bus in Portsmouth, NH, $25 roundtrip.
To Gay Bars: 5-minute walk.
Rooms: 4 rooms with queen beds. 1 room has additional single bed & 1 also has queen sleeper sofa.

Bathrooms: 2 private bath/toilets & 2 shared bath/shower/toilets.
Meals: Expanded continental breakfast.
Vegetarian: Nearby restaurant.
Dates Open: All year.
High Season: July & August.
Rates: $45-$75.
Discounts: Off-season special rate packages (including dinner) available.
Credit Cards: MC & VISA.

Rsv'tns: Recommended.
Reserve Through: Call direct.
Minimum Stay: 2 nights on weekends & 3 nights on holiday weekends.
Parking: Ample free off-street parking.
In-Room: Ceiling fans.
On-Premises: Common room with TV, VCR, refrigerator & microwave.
Exercise/Health: Hot tub & mini exercise area with treadmill & free

weights.
Swimming: Ocean nearby.
Sunbathing: On common sun decks & at the beach.
Smoking: Not permitted indoors.
Pets: Permitted on occassion. Call for details.
Handicap Access: No.
Children: Welcome.
Languages: English, limited German & Spanish.
Your Host: Rica.

INN at Two Village Square, THE

Gay/Lesbian ♀♂

Ogunquit, Maine—The Quiet Alternative

THE INN At Two Village Square, a spacious Victorian summer home, perches on a wooded hillside overlooking Ogunquit, yet is secluded amidst the trees of our five acres. Our heated pool and hot tub are surrounded by greenery on three sides, with a wall of glass doors providing ocean views. Public rooms are furnished in a light, summery style. Guest rooms are on three levels, some with ocean views, others looking into the treetops. We are gratified by the number of lesbian and gay guests who return to enjoy vacations, celebrate special occasions, renew friendships or make new acquaintances.

Address: 135 US Rte 1, PO Box 864, Ogunquit, ME 03907. Tel: (207) 646-5779.

Type: Bed & breakfast inn.
Clientele: Good mix of gays & lesbians.
Transportation: Car. Free pick up from airport or bus in Portsmouth NH. Check with us about train service beginning 1995.
To Gay Bars: 2-minute walk to gay & lesbian dance bar & piano bar.
Rooms: 18 rooms with double, queen or king beds.
Bathrooms: Private: 14 full baths, 3 sinks. Shared: 1 full bath, 2 toilets.
Meals: Expanded continental breakfast.
Complimentary: Tea/coffee in guest kitchen. In season: Tues pm BBQ; Sat nite get-acquainted party (also holidays).
Dates Open: April through October.
High Season: June 20th through September 7th.
Rates: In season $55-$125. Off season $35-$60. Spring & fall $45-$75.
Credit Cards: MC, VISA, Amex & Discover. Debit cards.
Rsv'tns: Strongly recommended in season.
Reserve Through: Call direct.
Minimum Stay: On holidays and in season. Short stays as space permits.
Parking: Ample free off-street parking.
In-Room: Color TV, AC, ceiling fans & maid service.
On-Premises: Common sitting rooms, TV lounge, public telephone, & piano. Shared guest kitchen with refrigerator for cold food preparation & serving.
Exercise/Health: Gym, hot tub & bicycles. Massage nearby.
Swimming: Heated pool on premises. Gay section of beach a short walk away.
Sunbathing: On poolside deck, sun deck, or nearby public beach.
Smoking: Not permitted in common rooms.
Pets: Not permitted (facilities for cats & dogs nearby).
Handicap Access: Minimal accessibility.
Children: Permitted with prior arrangement.
Languages: English.

Leisure Inn

Gay-Friendly 50/50 ♀♂

The Warm Feelings of Grandmother's House

Capture the feel of coastal village life in Ogunquit, a picturesque resort town by the sea. *Leisure Inn* is traditionally Maine, with uniquely-decorated guest rooms reflecting all the charm of old New England. In summer, there's plenty of fun in the sun, but have you ever known the sensation of walking the beach after the first snow of autumn? Everything in Ogunquit is within walking distance, from fine restaurants, to quaint and interesting shops. We're only a five-minute walk from the beach.

Address: 6 School St, PO Box 2113, Ogunquit, ME 03907. Tel: (207) 646-2737.

Type: Bed & breakfast guesthouse, cottages, apts.
Clientele: 50% gay & lesbian & 50% straight clientele.
Transportation: Car is best.
Rooms: 12 rooms, 3 apartments & 3 cottages with double & queen beds.
Bathrooms: 10 private & 3 shared. 2 rooms have sink/washbasin only.
Meals: Continental breakfast.
Dates Open: May-October.
Rates: $58-$82.

Credit Cards: MC, VISA.
Rsv'tns: Preferred (and advised for July & August).
Reserve Through: Call direct.

Minimum Stay: Two days on weekends, 3 on summer holiday weekends.
Parking: Ample, free off-street parking.

In-Room: Room service, most have color TV, AC, some kitchens.
On-Premises: Meeting rooms.
Swimming: Short walk

to ocean beach.
Sunbathing: At beach, on patio.
Pets: Not permitted.
Languages: English, French.

Ogunquit House

Gay-Friendly 50/50 ♀♂

Originally a schoolhouse in 1880, *Ogunquit House* is now a tastefully-restored bed and breakfast in a country setting at the edge of town. We offer a clean, comfortable, reasonably-priced vacation spot. Guest rooms are spacious, with both private and shared baths. Beach, restaurants, shops, movies and art galleries are all within walking distance. Ogunquit's trolley stops almost at your door to bring you to the Marginal Way, Perkins Cove and The Playhouse.

Address: 7 King's Hwy, Box 1883, Ogunquit, ME 03907. Tel: (207) 646-2967

Type: Bed & breakfast & cottages.
Clientele: 50% gay & lesbian & 50% straight clientele.
Transportation: Car is best.
To Gay Bars: 2 blocks to men's/women's bars.
Rooms: 6 rooms & 4 cottages with single, queen or king beds.
Bathrooms: 8 private, others share.

Meals: Continental breakfast.
Vegetarian: Three nearby restaurants offer vegetarian food.
Dates Open: March 15-January 2.
High Season: July through August.
Rates: $59-$135 summer, $45-$70 winter.
Credit Cards: MC, VISA, Discover.
Rsv'tns: Recommended.

Reserve Through: Call direct.
Minimum Stay: Summer 2 nights, holidays 3 nights.
Parking: Ample free off-street parking.
In-Room: Maid service, AC, some have kitchen & refrigerator and color cable TV.
On-Premises: TV lounge.
Swimming: 5-minute walk to ocean beach.

Sunbathing: On beach, patio, or private sun decks.
Smoking: Permitted without restrictions.
Pets: Permitted with restrictions in the cottages.
Handicap Access: No.
Children: Permitted in cottages, over 12 only in the inn.
Languages: English.

PEMBROKE

Yellow Birch Farm

Gay/Lesbian ♀

Yellow Birch Farm is a small working farm near wild, unspoiled Cobscook Bay, offering a tranquil environment in a beautiful, remote, nature lover's paradise. The area is of particular interest to birdwatchers. The small, comfortable two-room cottage has a full kitchen, woodstove, outdoor hot shower and private outhouse. The studio features a woodburning stove, skylights, private entrance and a full bath. We supply all linens. An expanded continental breakfast is served in the privacy of your cottage or studio.

Address: RR 1, Box 248-A, Pembroke, ME 04666. Tel: (207) 726-5807.

Type: B&B or weekly rental in a cottage or large studio.
Clientele: Mostly women with men welcome.
Transportation: Car is best.
To Gay Bars: 2-1/2 hours to Bangor.
Rooms: One cottage with bunk beds & queen futon & 1 large studio with double bed.
Bathrooms: 1 private

bath/toilet & 1 private outhouse & outdoor hot shower.
Meals: Expanded continental breakfast.
Vegetarian: Organically raised vegetables available from the farm.
Dates Open: Studio, all year. Cottage, Apr-Oct.
Rates: $45 double, $15 each additional person.
Discounts: Housekeeping basis. $250 wk double

occupancy, $50 per additional guest.
Rsv'tns: Required.
Reserve Through: Travel agent or call direct.
Parking: Ample free parking.
In-Room: Room service, telephone, kitchen, refrigerator, color TV & ceiling fans.
Swimming: Nearby lakes & ocean.
Sunbathing: On private

sun decks.
Nudity: Permitted anywhere.
Smoking: Permitted outside.
Pets: Not permitted.
Handicap Access: No.
Children: Permitted over 12 years old.
Languages: English & French.

INN Places 1995

SEBAGO LAKE REGION

Maine-ly For You

Home of Maine's Women's Music Festivals

Gay-Friendly 50/50 ♀

Maine-ly For You is a complete resort on 33 acres, with cottages and campsites along an 1800-foot waterfront beach equipped with dock and swimming float. The accent is on outdoor activities, such as water sports, hiking on trails, mountain climbing, exploring ice caves, canoeing, etc. We also have a softball field. Usually, the clientele is mixed, but twice a year, the entire place is reserved for 4-day women's music festivals with crafts, entertainment and workshops. Please check with us for details about these womens' festivals.

Address: RR2 Box 745, Harrison, ME 04040. Tel: (207) 583-6980.

Type: Lakeside cottages and campground.
Clientele: 50% gay & lesbian & 50% straight clientele. Women's festivals June & August.
Transportation: Car is best.
To Gay Bars: 45 min by car to Portland, 30 min to Lewiston.
Rooms: 20 rustic cottages.
Bathrooms: All private.
Campsites: 45 wooded sites, 20 waterfront sites, all with electric & water. Modern, clean restrooms with flush toilets & free showers, recreation room.
Dates Open: May 15-Oct 15th.
High Season: Late June to Labor Day.
Rates: Campsites: wooded $18, waterfront $25. Call for rates on cottages.
Rsv'tns: Recommended.
Reserve Through: Call direct.
Minimum Stay: 1 week for cottages.
Parking: Ample parking.
In-Room: Kitchen, refrigerator, some heat.
On-Premises: Meeting rooms, TV lounge, laundry facilities, recreation room, country store, boat rentals.
Exercise/Health: Swimming, boating, hiking, fishing, softball, basketball.
Swimming: In lake on premises.
Sunbathing: On the beach by the lake.
Smoking: No smoking in bath house, lodge, or recreation room.
Pets: Permitted, on leash with deposit.
Handicap Access: Partially, inquire.
Children: Permitted.
Languages: English.
Your Host: Rita.

TENANTS HARBOR

East Wind Inn

Gay-Friendly ♀♂

Perched on the harbor's edge of the St. George Peninsula on Penobscot Bay, *The East Wind Inn* offers a spectacular view of the ocean. It was lovingly restored in 1975, with polished brass fixtures and tasteful antiques. Guest rooms have harbor views and the spacious porches are perfect for rocking, reading and smelling the salt air. Visitors can walk or bike to beaches, tidal pools and berry picking or drive to museums, nightclubs, movies, plays and festivals. Winter sports enthusiasts can just step outside for cross-country skiing or snowshoeing, and downhill skiers only drive a short distance to the Camden Snow Bowl.

Address: PO Box 149, Tenants Harbor, ME 04860. Tel: (207) 372-6366.

Type: Bed & breakfast inn with restaurant.
Clientele: Mostly straight clientele with a gay/lesbian following.
Transportation: Car is best. Fly to Portland (85 mi), Bangor (70) or Rockland. Rent a car or take limo service.
To Gay Bars: 80 miles to nearest gay/lesbian bars.
Rooms: 22 doubles, 3 suites & 1 apartment with single or double beds.
Bathrooms: 12 private & 7 shared.
Meals: Continental breakfast.
Vegetarian: Available with 2 hrs notice.
Complimentary: Tea, coffee, & soft drinks.
Dates Open: All year.
High Season: July through October 15.
Rates: Single with shared bath $48. Double w shared bath $74, private $96, suite $110, & apartment $130.
Discounts: Lower rates Nov-April.
Credit Cards: MC, VISA, Amex.
Rsv'tns: Recommended.
Reserve Through: Travel agent or call direct.
Parking: Ample free off-street parking.
In-Room: Self-controlled AC/heat, direct dial phone, & maid service.
On-Premises: Meeting rooms for up to 50 people, theater style. Private dining rooms & TV lounge.
Exercise/Health: Nearby gym, weights, Jacuzzi, sauna, steam, massage.
Swimming: Nearby

ocean, pool, river & lake. **Sunbathing:** On beach or common sun deck.

Smoking: Permitted without restrictions. **Pets:** Not permitted ex-

cept by prior written agreement. **Handicap Access:** No.

Children: Permitted, if 12 years or older. **Languages:** English.

MARYLAND

ANNAPOLIS

William Page Inn

Gay-Friendly ♀♂

Built in 1908, this dark brown, cedar-shingle, wood-frame structure was the local Democratic party clubhouse for more than fifty years. Today, its wraparound porch, furnished with Adirondack chairs and striped canvas awnings, presents a distinctive appearance, especially in the historical district, where a fair number of the buildings are brick. *The William Page Inn* has a total of five distinctively-appointed guest rooms. Accommodations may include semi-private or private bath. The entire third floor is a spacious, light-filled room with dormer windows, each with window seat, skylight, sitting area with sofa bed, cable television and private bath with whirlpool tub and separate shower. The first-floor room with private bath and porch access is convenient for persons who might find stairs difficult. All accommodations include queen-sized bed, sitting areas, daily housekeeping, central heating and air-conditioning, full buffet breakfast each morning, and full-time professional staff. Off-street parking is available to our guests at no additional charge. *The William Page Inn* is in the Historical District of Annapolis, Maryland, fifty yards from the visitor's gate of the U.S. Naval Academy and two blocks from the downtown waterfront. Our bed and breakfast inn offers guests a handsomely renovated turn-of-the-century home with a feeling of quiet, hushed, elegance and Victorian splendor. The inn is carefully furnished in genuine antiques and period reproductions. In the entry foyer, an open stairway is flanked by crystal chandeliers and artwork. The common room has sitting areas and makings for a wet-bar set-up. *The William Page Inn* is a Mobil, AAA and Maryland Bed & Breakfast rated and approved establishment.

Address: 8 Martin St, Annapolis, MD 21401. Tel: (410) 626-1506 or (800) 364-4160. Fax: (410) 263-4841.

Type: Bed & breakfast. **Clientele:** Mainly straight with gay & lesbian following. **Transportation:** Car is best. Additional charge for pick up from airport, train or bus. **To Gay Bars:** 40 minutes to DC bars/Baltimore bars. **Rooms:** 4 rooms & 1 suite with queen beds. **Bathrooms:** 3 private bath/toilet/showers, 1 shared bath/shower/

toilet. **Meals:** Full breakfast. **Vegetarian:** Available upon request. **Complimentary:** Wet bar set up, complimentary sodas. **Dates Open:** All year. **High Season:** March-November. **Rates:** Winter $60-$110, summer $85-$150. **Discounts:** Mid week, stays of 5 or more days, winter rates. **Credit Cards:** MC, VISA.

Rsv'tns: Required, but walk-ins welcome. **Reserve Through:** Travel agent or call direct. **Minimum Stay:** For special events only. **Parking:** Limited free off-street parking. **In-Room:** AC, maid service. Color cable TV in suite. **On-Premises:** Meeting rooms. **Exercise/Health:** Jacuzzi en suite. **Swimming:** Nearby state

park beach, 2 hrs to ocean beach. **Sunbathing:** At nearby state park beach. **Smoking:** Permitted outdoors. **Pets:** Not permitted. **Handicap Access:** No. **Children:** Permitted if 12 yrs, or older. **Languages:** English. **Your Host:** Robert & Greg.

BALTIMORE

Mr. Mole Bed & Breakfast

Splendid Suites on Historic Bolton Hill

Gay-Friendly ♀♂

Mr. Mole has renovated his grand 1870 Baltimore row house on historic Bolton Hill, close to downtown, Inner Harbor, the Symphony and Antique Row, to provide gracious accommodations for discriminating guests. The comfortable, English-style decor, with 18th- and 19th-century antiques, adorns five spacious suites with private phones and full baths. Two suites offer a private sitting room and two bedrooms. Garage parking, with automatic door opener, is included, as is a hearty Dutch-style breakfast of homemade bread, cake, meat, cheese and fruit.

Address: 1601 Bolton St, Baltimore, MD 21217. Tel: (410) 728-1179 or Fax: 728-3379.

Type: Bed & breakfast. **Clientele:** Mostly straight clientele with a gay & lesbian following. **Transportation:** Car or taxi. **To Gay Bars:** 5 minutes by car to gay/lesbian bars. **Rooms:** 3 rooms & 2 suites with queen beds.

Bathrooms: All private bath/toilets. **Meals:** Expanded continental breakfast. **Complimentary:** Chocolates. **Dates Open:** All year. **High Season:** Mar-Nov. **Rates:** $75-$145. **Credit Cards:** MC, VISA,

Discover & Amex. **Rsv'tns:** Required. **Reserve Through:** Travel agent or call direct. **Minimum Stay:** 2 nights on weekends in high season. **Parking:** Free parking in garage with automatic opener.

In-Room: Maid service, AC, telephone & clock radio. **Smoking:** Permitted outdoors only. **Pets:** Not permitted. **Children:** Well-mannered children over 10 years permitted. **Languages:** English, French, German & Dutch.

CUMBERLAND

Red Lamp Post

Gay/Lesbian ♀♂

We would like to welcome you to *Red Lamp Post,* our living home. Become part of the environment and enjoy the company of your hosts Kery and Gary. Located just 3 miles from historic downtown Cumberland, we are near antique shops, the C&O Canal, the new Allegheny Central Railroad, Early American historic sites, scenic beauty, Rocky Gap State Park, Deep Creek Lake, winter sports, hiking and biking trails (bike rentals available). Enjoy homemade breakfast and snacks and refreshments in the evening.

Address: 849 Braddock Rd, Cumberland, MD 21502. Tel: (301) 777-3262.

Type: Bed & breakfast. **Clientele:** Mostly gay & lesbian with some straight clientele. **Transportation:** Car or free pick-up at train or airport from DC or Pittsburgh (commuter from Pittsburgh). **To Gay Bars:** 1-1/2 hours to Hagerstown, Altoona,

Morgantown bars. **Rooms:** 3 rooms with single or queen beds. **Bathrooms:** 1-1/2 shared. **Meals:** Full breakfast included, dinner available at additional cost. **Vegetarian:** Available on request. **Complimentary:** Refresh-

ments upon arrival. Cocktails. **Dates Open:** All year. **High Season:** Summer and fall. **Rates:** $55 single, $65 double. Inquire about specials. **Discounts:** Discount for 3 days or more. **Credit Cards:** MC & VISA.

Rsv'tns: Required. **Reserve Through:** Call direct. **Minimum Stay:** Required during special events in the area. **Parking:** Adequate free off-street parking. **In-Room:** AC, electric blanket & ceiling fans. **On-Premises:** Living room & TV lounge with fireplaces, sunroom or deck for breakfast. **Exercise/Health:** Spa, weights & rowing machine. **Swimming:** 10 minutes by car to lake. **Sunbathing:** On patio. **Smoking:** Permitted in designated areas. **Pets:** Not permitted. **Handicap Access:** No. **Children:** Not permitted. **Languages:** English. **Your Host:** Gary & Kery.

MASSACHUSETTS

AMHERST

Ivy House B&B

Gay-Friendly 50/50 ♀♂

Four Miles From Northampton's 10,000 Cuddling, Kissing Lesbians *National Enquirer*

Our colonial cape home, portions circa 1740, has been handsomely restored with distinctive interiors, exposed beams, fireplace, country kitchen and new baths. The patio and lovely landscaped grounds add to the atmosphere of this romantic setting. *Ivy House* is close to the Northampton scene, Cummington gay beach, and Vermont, just a block from U. Mass Fine Arts Center, and near the homes of Robert Frost and Emily Dickinson. The five colleges, Old Deerfield, Brimfield, and the Berkshires, are also convenient. Hosts John and Keith welcome both men and women.

Address: 1 Sunset Court, Amherst, MA 01002. **Tel:** (413) 549-7554.

Type: Bed & breakfast.
Clientele: 50% gay & lesbian & 50% straight clientele.
Transportation: Car is best. Pick up from Hartford-Springfield airport $25 per person, $5 from Amherst bus or train station.
To Gay Bars: 5 miles.
Rooms: 1 room with double bed & 1 room with twin beds.
Bathrooms: 2 shared.
Meals: Expanded continental breakfast.
Dates Open: All year.
High Season: Mid-May college graduations and fall foliage.
Rates: $50-$70 year-round.
Discounts: For midweek or more than 6 nights.
Credit Cards: MC, VISA.
Rsv'tns: Required.
Reserve Through: Travel agent or call direct.
Minimum Stay: 2 nights at peak periods.
Parking: Adequate free off-street parking.
On-Premises: Laundry facilities for guests.
Swimming: Nearby pool, river & lake.
Sunbathing: On the patio.
Smoking: Outside on porch only.
Pets: Not permitted.
Handicap Access: No.
Children: Not especially welcomed.
Languages: English, French & Spanish.
Your Host: Keith & John.

BOSTON

Chandler Inn

Gay-Friendly ♀♂

Location, Location, Location!

On the edge of historic Back Bay and the wonderfully eclectic South End, Boston's most exciting small hotel offers visitors myriad fringe benefits, great rates and a location just two blocks from the train and bus stations. *The Chandler Inn* is nestled within the diverse neighborhood of the South End. Here, you'll find a lively collection of restaurants, shops and a wide spectrum of social life. All of this is no more than a short walk from fashionable Newbury St., Copley Place, Theater district and the convention center.

Address: 26 Chandler St, Boston, MA 02116. Tel: (617) 482-3450 or (800) 842-3450.

Type: Bed & breakfast hotel with gay bar on premises.
Clientele: Mostly straight clientele with a gay & lesbian following.
Transportation: Taxi from airport $15. 2 block walk from Back Bay Amtrak/subway station.
To Gay Bars: Gay/lesbian bar inside building.
Rooms: 56 doubles.
Bathrooms: All private.
Meals: Continental breakfast.

Dates Open: All year.
High Season: April-November.
Rates: Singles $74-$84. Doubles $84-$94.
Discounts: AARP.
Credit Cards: All credit cards.
Rsv'tns: Required.
Reserve Through: Travel agent or call direct.
Parking: Limited on-street parking. Municipal lots 2 blocks away.
In-Room: Private direct-dial telephone, color TV

& AC.
Exercise/Health: Discount at Metropolitan Health Club 1 block away.
Sunbathing: On Boston's Esplanade, a ten minute walk from the hotel.
Smoking: Permitted

without restrictions.
Pets: Not permitted.
Handicap Access: No.
Children: Permitted.
Languages: English, Spanish, & French.

Four-Sixty-Three Beacon Street Guest House

Gay-Friendly 50/50 ♀♂

Boston's Best Slept Secret

Located in Boston's historic Back Bay, the *463 Beacon Street Guest House* offers a comfortable and affordable hotel alternative. Our turn-of-the-century brownstone-style building includes private baths, kitchenettes, cable TV, air conditioning and complimentary local phone service, Our warm, quiet, residential setting is near public transportation, the Prudential-Hynes Convention Center, colleges, restaurants, and is minutes away from downtown Boston and Cambridge. Discounted weekly rates and parking available.

Address: 463 Beacon St, Boston, MA 02115. Tel: (617) 536-1302.

Type: Guesthouse.
Clientele: 50% gay & lesbian & 50% straight clientele.

Transportation: Taxi, public transportation, airport shuttle bus.
To Gay Bars: Five min-

utes by car to gay bars.
Rooms: 20 rooms with double &

king beds.
Bathrooms: 16 private bath/toilets, 4 sink/washbasins only.
Meals: Meals not included.
Complimentary: Coffee, tea.
Dates Open: All year.

High Season: May-October.
Rates: $50-$80 per night.
Discounts: Discounts for weekly rates.
Credit Cards: MC, VISA, Amex.
Rsv'tns: Required.
Reserve Through: Travel

agent or call direct.
Parking: Limited off-street parking.
In-Room: Color cable TV, telephone, AC, kitchenette with refrigerator.
On-Premises: Laundry facilities.
Sunbathing: 1 unit with

private deck.
Smoking: Permitted with some restrictions.
Pets: Not permitted.
Handicap Access: No.
Children: Permitted.
Languages: English, French & Spanish.

Greater Boston Hospitality

An Uncommonly Civilized Way to Travel

Gay-Friendly ♀♂

Greater Boston Hospitality, offers superb accommodations in the Boston area in hundreds of friendly, private homes and inns, all of which are carefully screened for comfort, cleanliness and congeniality of hosts. Bed and breakfasts range from Federal to Colonial to Georgian, from cozy to luxury, from city to suburb to country. Neighborhoods throughout Boston are included. Many of our accommodations include parking. All include breakfast and knowledgeable, friendly hosts. Be it for business or pleasure, we'll help you to have a welcoming and wonderful time.

Address: PO Box 1142 Brookline, MA 02146. Tel: (617) 277-5430.

Type: Reservation service for Bed & breakfasts, guesthouses & inns.
Clientele: Mostly straight with a gay & lesbian following.
Transportation: Car, taxi or subway.
To Gay Bars: 10 blocks or 1/2 mile. 15 minutes by foot.
Rooms: 180 rooms & 10 suites with single, double, queen or king beds.
Bathrooms: 160 private.

Shared 10 bath/shower/toilets & 18 showers only.
Meals: Expanded continental breakfast, continental breakfast or full breakfast.
Vegetarian: Several vegetarian restaurants in the greater Boston area.
Complimentary: Many hosts offer cold and/or hot drinks, candy & flowers.
Dates Open: All year.
High Season: April 1-December 1.

Rates: $40-$130.
Discounts: Seventh day free.
Credit Cards: MC & VISA.
Rsv'tns: Required.
Reserve Through: Travel agent or call direct.
Parking: Adequate parking: free, pay, off- & on-street.
In-Room: Color cable TV, AC, telephone & maid service.
On-Premises: Libraries, pianos & decks.
Exercise/Health: Gym,

weights, sauna, steam & massage.
Swimming: Pools on premises & nearby pool, ocean & lake.
Sunbathing: On patios.
Smoking: Generally permitted outside only.
Pets: Not permitted.
Handicap Access: Some are.
Children: Not especially welcomed.
Languages: English.
Your Host: Kelly, Lauren & Jack.

Iris Bed & Breakfast

Convenient to Boston and Cape Cod

Women ♀

Unique to the suburban Boston area, *Iris* is a woman-owned and -operated private home bed and breakfast for women. Our home is warm, cheerful, and smoke-free, with large rooms. Continental breakfast includes homemade breads and muffins prepared by Vicki, a graduate of culinary arts school. Our two cats and one dog are friendly and entertaining. Our convenient location is only 15-30 minutes from downtown Boston, depending on traffic.

Address: PO Box 4188, Dedham, MA 02027. Tel: (617) 329-3514.

Type: Bed & breakfast.
Clientele: Women only.
Transportation: Car is best
To Gay Bars: 15-minute drive.
Rooms: 1 room with double bed.

Bathrooms: Shared bath.
Meals: Continental breakfast.
Dates Open: All year.
Rates: $55-$60 per night.
Rsv'tns: Required.
Reserve Through: Call direct.

Parking: Ample free on-street parking.
In-Room: AC.
Swimming: Pool at gay club 15 min by car, ocean beach 45 min by car.
Smoking: Iris is a non-

smoking bed & breakfast home.
Pets: Not permitted.
Handicap Access: No.
Children: Not permitted.
Languages: English.
Your Host: Vicki & Vici.

Oasis Guest House

Gay/Lesbian ♀♂

Devoted to Providing Fine Accommodations Since 1982

Oasis Guest House was one of the first gay bed and breakfasts to set a standard of quality in gay and lesbian accommodations, a standard we continue to honor today. From lobby to outdoor decks, the inn is handsomely and comfortably appointed with such amenities as private and shared baths, central AC, color TV and telephones in rooms. Complimentary coffee, juice and Danish are served each morning. Come evening, we provide cocktail set-ups (BYOB) and hors d'oeuvres. Experience an atmosphere that caters to your life-style and your budget.

Address: 22 Edgerly Rd, Boston, MA 02115. Tel: (617) 267-2262, Fax: (617) 267-1920.

Type: Bed & breakfast.
Clientele: Mainly gay/lesbian with some straight clientele.
Transportation: Taxi from airport $14 or subway to Hynes Convention Center/ICA.
To Gay Bars: 5-10 minutes' walk to gay/lesbian bars.
Rooms: 16 rooms.
Bathrooms: 10 private, 3-1/2 shared.
Meals: Continental breakfast.
Complimentary: Cocktail set-up service with hors d'oeuvres, evening snacks.
Dates Open: All year.
High Season: May-October.
Rates: $50-$78 per night plus tax.
Credit Cards: MC, VISA, Amex.
Rsv'tns: Recommended especially in-season.
Reserve Through: Travel agent or call direct.
Minimum Stay: On some weekends.
Parking: Limited off-street parking.
In-Room: Color TV, AC, direct dial telephone & maid service.
On-Premises: TV lounge & central AC, decks.
Sunbathing: On common sun decks.
Smoking: Permitted, with restrictions.
Pets: Not permitted.
Handicap Access: No.
Children: Not permitted.
Languages: English.
IGTA

Victorian Bed & Breakfast

Women ♀

TLC In Massive Doses

Our guests say: "Thanks for such friendly hospitality, helpful Boston hints and great food. You two are a delight!" "We feel like we've found a home in the big city." "The best place, the best hosts!" *Victorian Bed & Breakfast* offers elegant and comfortable accommodations just 5 minutes from Boston's Copley Place. All the tourist attractions of the city, plus gay and lesbian bars are nearby. We're sure you'll find your accommodations feel just like home...only better!

Tel: (617) 536-3285.

Type: Bed & breakfast.
Clientele: Women only.
Transportation: Car or taxi from airport, free pick up from train.
To Gay Bars: Close to all gay/lesbian bars.
Rooms: 1 room accommodates up to 4 women with king size bed & double couch.
Bathrooms: Private bath/toilet.
Meals: Full breakfast.
Vegetarian: Food to please all tastes and needs.
Complimentary: Soft drinks.
Dates Open: All year.
High Season: All year.
Rates: $50 for 1, $65 for 2, $75 for 3 & $85 for 4.
Rsv'tns: Required.
Reserve Through: Call direct.
Minimum Stay: 2 nights on weekends.
Parking: Free off-street parking.
In-Room: Large living room, easy chairs, black & white TV, AC, laundry done by hostess, if stay longer than 4 nights, maid service.
Smoking: Not permitted.
Pets: Not permitted.
Handicap Access: No.
Children: Not permitted.
Languages: English.
Your Host: Claire & Lois.

LENOX

Summer Hill Farm

Berkshire Arts and a Country Setting

Gay-Friendly ♀♂

Enjoy the beauty and culture of the Berkshires at *Summer Hill Farm,* a 200-year-old colonial farmhouse on a 20-acre horse farm. Rooms are pleasantly furnished with English family antiques; delicious country breakfasts are served family-style in the dining room or on the sunporch. A haybarn has been newly converted to a delightful, spacious, 2-room, all-season guest cottage. We're in the country, yet minutes from Tanglewood, Jacob's Pillow Dance, theatres, fine art galleries, restaurants and shops. Choose from a wide variety of outdoor activities. The countryside is beautiful in all seasons. Come for the fall colors or our winter wonderland.

Address: 950 East St, Lenox, MA 01240. Tel: (413) 442-2057.

Type: Bed & breakfast.
Clientele: Mostly straight clientele with a gay & lesbian following.
Transportation: Car is best. No charge for pick up from local bus.
Rooms: 6 rooms with single, double, queen or king beds.
Bathrooms: All private.
Meals: Full home-cooked breakfast. Continental breakfast in cottage.
Vegetarian: Available with special request.

Dates Open: All year.
High Season: Mid June-Labor Day & October.
Rates: Summer & October $60-$150. Winter & spring $50-$110.
Discounts: For groups & stays of a week or more, up to 20% discount; mid-week reductions.
Rsv'tns: Required.
Reserve Through: Call direct.
Minimum Stay: On July, August, October & holiday weekends.

Parking: Ample free off-street parking.
In-Room: Color cable TV, AC & maid service. Two rooms with fireplaces, 1 with refrigerator. Cottage: coffee/tea-making facilities, refrigerator, TV & AC.
Exercise/Health: Children's riding by arrangement. Nearby gym, sauna, massage, hiking, biking, canoeing, skiing, tennis, horse riding.
Swimming: 5 miles to lake.

Sunbathing: On private or common sun decks & on the lawns.
Smoking: Permitted on small sun porch & outdoors. No smoking indoors.
Pets: Not permitted.
Handicap Access: Yes. Cottage only.
Children: Infants, & children 5 & over. Must be well-behaved & closely supervised.
Languages: English.
Your Host: Michael & Sonya.

Walker House

A Most Harmonious Place to Visit

Gay-Friendly ♀♂

Walker House, is an 1804-era federal manor, furnished in antiques, on 3 acres of gardens and woods near the center of the picturesque village of Lenox. Rooms, decorated with a musical theme honoring composers, such as Beethoven and Mozart, have private baths, some with claw-foot tubs and fireplaces. Our library theatre features a large-screen video projection system. Walk to galleries, shops and good restaurants. Tanglewood, Jacob's Pillow and summer theatres are only a short drive.

Address: 74 Walker St, Lenox, MA 01240. Tel: (413) 637-1271.

Type: Bed & breakfast inn.
Clientele: Mainly straight with a gay & lesbian following.

Transportation: Car is best. 1 block from New York & Boston buses.
To Gay Bars: 35 miles to Albany & Northampton.

Rooms: 8 rooms with single, double, queen or king beds.
Bathrooms: All private.
Meals: Expanded conti-

nental breakfast.
Vegetarian: Breakfasts have no meat; other veg-

continued next page

etarian meals available at restaurants within walking distance.
Complimentary: Bottle of wine in room, afternoon tea each day.
Dates Open: All year.
High Season: July, August, October.
Rates: Summer $70-$170, Oct $70-$150, Sept & Nov-Jun $60-$120; lower rates midweek.

Discounts: 10% off for single persons in rooms depending on availability.
Rsv'tns: Advisable during busy periods.
Reserve Through: Call direct.
Minimum Stay: On holidays & summer weekends.
Parking: Ample free on- & off-street parking.
In-Room: AC, maid

service.
On-Premises: Meeting rooms, TV lounge, library theatre with large-screen video projection system.
Exercise/Health: Nearby gym, massage.
Swimming: Nearby river & lake.
Sunbathing: On the patio, lawns & garden, at the beach.
Smoking: Permitted on

veranda & other outdoor areas; non-smoking rooms available.
Pets: Permitted by prior approval at reservation time.
Handicap Access: Yes. 3 1st floor rooms accessible.
Children: 12 years of age & older welcome.
Languages: English, Spanish, French.

MARTHA'S VINEYARD

Captain Dexter House of Edgartown

Gay-Friendly ♀♂

Romantic guest rooms, each uniquely different, are distinctively decorated with fine furnishings to create the warmth and ambiance of an elegant private home. Each has its own bathroom. Several have working fireplaces and four-poster beds with white lace canopies. At *Captain Dexter House of Edgartown*, rooms are richly appointed with many amenities, to let you know how special you are to us. Fresh, home-baked breakfast breads are served in our elegant dining room or enchanting flower-filled garden. It's only a short stroll to the beach, shopping and dining.

Address: 35 Pease Point Way, PO Box 2798, Edgartown, MA 02539. Tel: (508) 627-7289.

Type: Bed & breakfast.
Clientele: Mostly straight clientele with a gay & lesbian following.
Transportation: Car to ferry or airport.
To Gay Bars: 1-1/2 hours to Boston's gay/lesbian bars.
Rooms: 11 rooms with double or queen beds.
Bathrooms: 5 private bath/toilets, 6 private shower/toilets.

Meals: Expanded continental breakfast.
Complimentary: Lemonade, sherry.
Dates Open: April through November.
High Season: Mid June through Labor Day.
Rates: Summer $110-$200, winter $65-$175.
Credit Cards: MC, VISA, Amex & Diners.
Reserve Through: Travel agent or call direct.

Minimum Stay: Required on high season weekends.
Parking: Ample off-street parking.
In-Room: Maid service, some rooms with AC or ceiling fans.
On-Premises: Meeting rooms, laundry facilities, refrigerator.
Exercise/Health: Nearby aerobics classes & gym.
Swimming: At nearby

ocean beach.
Sunbathing: In yards & at nearby ocean beach.
Nudity: Permitted on beach at Gay Head.
Smoking: Permitted in all rooms.
Pets: Not permitted.
Handicap Access: No. Prefer 12 years or older.
Children: Permitted.
Languages: English.

NORTHAMPTON

Tin Roof Bed & Breakfast

Gay/Lesbian ♀

Visit Lesbianville, USA

Tin Roof is a turn-of-the-century farmhouse in the scenic Connecticut River Valley, five minutes from Northampton.

Our peaceful backyard has panoramic views of the Berkshire Hills and gardens galore. Breakfast features home-baked muffins, fruit, yogurt, granola, juice and hot beverage of choice. There's color TV, a lesbian video library and a front porch with porch swing. Whether you're considering moving to the area or just visiting, your long-time resident hosts will give you lots of local information and acclimate you to the area. Friendly felines in residence.

Address: PO Box 296, Hadley, MA 01035. Tel: (413) 586-8665

Type: Bed & breakfast.
Clientele: A women's space where lesbian-friendly men are welcome.
Transportation: From Hartford airport, rent a car or take a bus to Northampton.
To Gay Bars: 10 minutes to gay/lesbian bars.
Rooms: 3 rooms with double beds.
Bathrooms: 1 shared bath/shower/toilet, 1 shared toilet.
Meals: Expanded continental breakfast.
Vegetarian: Upon request.
Dates Open: All year.
Rates: Single $55, $60 for two people.
Discounts: 7th night free.
Rsv'tns: Required.
Reserve Through: Call direct.
Minimum Stay: 2 nights on weekends & holidays.
Parking: Ample off-street parking.
On-Premises: Laundry facilities, TV in living room.
Exercise/Health: Nearby health club.
Swimming: In nearby river.
Sunbathing: In the garden.
Smoking: Permitted outside.
Pets: Not permitted.
Handicap Access: No.
Languages: English.
Your Host: Jane & Diane.

PROVINCETOWN

Ampersand Guesthouse

Gay/Lesbian ♂

   Ampersand Guesthouse is a fine example of mid-nineteenth century Greek Revival architecture located in the neighborly west end of Provincetown, just a short walk from town center. Each of the bedrooms is unique in its layout, creating a range of accommodations from suites of two to three rooms, to shared baths, to private baths. All are furnished in a careful blend of contemporary appointments and restored antiques, many original to the house. There is also a studio apartment that looks out on both the water and the yard.

   Continental breakfast is served daily in the large, gracious living room, a gathering place for guests throughout the day & evening. It has a fireplace seating arrangement, a gaming table and a dining area for relaxing and socializing. And guests have use of the yard as well as a second-story sun deck which commands a view of the harbor and Commercial Street. You may be looking for a quiet, restful time for meeting new friends, walking or sunbathing on the nearby beaches, and enjoying the singular views of nature around Provincetown. Or you may be seeking the bustle of a resort town famous for its shops, restaurants, and active social life. In either case, *Ampersand Guesthouse* provides a delightful home base both in season and off.

Address: 6 Cottage St, PO Box 832, Provincetown, MA 02657. Tel: (508) 487-0959.

continued next page

Type: Guesthouse.
Clientele: Mostly men with women welcome.
Transportation: Take taxi from the airport or walk from town center.
To Gay Bars: 6 blocks to men's bars.
Rooms: 12 rooms & 1 apartment with double or queen beds.

Bathrooms: 7 private bath/toilets & 2 shared bath/shower/toilets.
Meals: Continental breakfast.
Dates Open: All year.
High Season: Memorial Day-Labor Day week.
Rates: $49-$69 off season, $59-$111 high season.
Credit Cards: MC, VISA &

Amex.
Rsv'tns: Required.
Reserve Through: Call direct.
Minimum Stay: 5 nights in July & Aug, 2 nights on May, June & September weekends & off-season holidays.
Parking: Limited free off-street parking.

In-Room: Maid service.
On-Premises: TV lounge.
Swimming: Ocean beach nearby.
Sunbathing: Sun decks.
Smoking: Permitted without restrictions.
Pets: Not permitted.
Children: Not permitted.
Languages: English.
Your Host: Bob & Ken.

Angel's Landing

Gay/Lesbian ♀♂

Overlooking the Cape's most picturesque harbor, *Angel's Landing* is a perfect place to relax and enjoy your holiday in the gayest town in the Northeast. We are located in the center of Provincetown, near all local shops, restaurants and bars. The beaches are nearby, ideal for swimming and sunbathing. We extend a warm welcome to our guests and hope to see you soon in Provincetown.

Address: 353 Commercial St, Provincetown, MA 02657. Tel: (508) 487-1600.

Type: Vacation condo complex with coffee shop & sandwich shop.
Clientele: Mostly gay & lesbian with some straight clientele.
Transportation: Car, plane or bus.
To Gay Bars: 2 blocks to men's & women's bars.
Rooms: 16 apartments

with double beds.
Bathrooms: All private.
Dates Open: May 15-Oct 31. 3 units available all year.
High Season: May-September.
Rates: $475-$850 per week.
Rsv'tns: Required.
Reserve Through: Call

direct.
Minimum Stay: Required in season.
Parking: Not available on premises.
In-Room: Full kitchens. Some units have color TV.
Exercise/Health: Nearby gym.
Swimming: Ocean nearby.
Sunbathing: On beach,

patio, private or common sun decks.
Smoking: Permitted without restrictions.
Pets: Permitted with deposit.
Handicap Access: Some units accessible, but toilets not oversized.
Children: Permitted.
Languages: English.

Beaconlite Guest House

Gay/Lesbian ♀♂

A Provincetown Tradition Like No Other

Our reputation for comfort and service has grown by word-of-mouth of our guests. The *Beaconlite* has become their home away from home. Centrally located (but without the noise), our rooms, 3 with fireplaces, have private baths, ceiling fans, color

cable TV, and queen or double beds. The elegant "English Country House" charm of our spacious common rooms feature open fire, grand piano and antique furnishings. Continental breakfast is provided daily and free parking is available. Multi-level decks provide panoramic views of P'town and the Cape. We're open year-round.

Address: 12 Winthrop St, Provincetown, MA 02657. Tel: (508) 487-9603.

Type: Guesthouse.
Clientele: Mostly men in high season. Good mix of men & women at other times.

Transportation: Car or ferry, air from Boston. Free airport pick up provided if arranged.
To Gay Bars: 2 minutes'

walk to gay bar, 1/2 block to tea dance.
Rooms: 12 rooms, 3 suites & 1 apartment with double or queen

beds.
Bathrooms: 5 private bath/toilets & 11 private shower/toilets.
Meals: Continental

breakfast.
Vegetarian: Available in local restaurants.
Complimentary: Coffee & tea.
Dates Open: All year.
High Season: Mid June to mid September.
Rates: In-season $80-$150, off-season $55-$115.
Discounts: Off season, 5 plus days, 15% (Nov 1, 1994-May 15 1995).
Credit Cards: MC, VISA & Discover.
Rsv'tns: Required.
Reserve Through: Travel agent or call direct.
Minimum Stay: 5 to 7 days during high season.
Parking: Free off-street parking, 1 car per room.

In-Room: Color cable TV, VCR, AC, ceiling fans, refrigerator, laundry & maid serice.
On-Premises: TV lounge, laundry services & fax machine.
Exercise/Health: Nearby gym, weights & massage.
Swimming: Nearby pool & ocean.

Sunbathing: On private sun decks.
Smoking: Permitted in appointed bedrooms, not in common guest areas.
Pets: Not permitted.
Handicap Access: No.
Children: Not permitted.
Languages: English.
Your Host: Stephen, Trevor & Pat.

Boatslip Beach Club

Simply the Best for Over 25 Years!

Gay/Lesbian ♀♂

The *Boatslip Beach Club*, beginning its 28th season, is a 45-room contemporary resort on Provincetown Harbor. Thirty-three rooms have glass doors opening onto private balconies overlooking our fabulous deck, pool, private beach and the bay. All rooms have either queen or double beds, private baths and color cable TV. Off-street parking, morning coffee, admission to Tea Dance and sun cots are all complimentary. We offer a full-service restaurant, poolside grille and raw bar and evening entertainment. Call or write your hosts: *Peter Simpson and Jim Carlino* for further information....*YOU OWE IT TO YOURSELF!!!*.

Address: 161 Commercial St Box 393, Provincetown, MA 02657. Tel: (800) 451-SLIP (7547), (508) 487-1669, Fax: 487-6021.

Type: Hotel with restaurant, bar, disco, card & gift shop, & sportswear boutique.
Clientele: Gay & lesbian. Good mix of men & women.
Transportation: Car is best. Walk from ferry.
To Gay Bars: Bar on premises, good mix of men & women. Women's bar 2 blocks away.
Rooms: 30 rooms with double beds & 15 rooms with queen beds.

Bathrooms: All private bath/toilets.
Meals: Morning coffee.
Vegetarian: Available.
Dates Open: April thru October.
High Season: June 18th-September 7th.
Rates: Off season $70-$90. In season $110-$150.
Discounts: Group rates available. Call for information.
Credit Cards: MC & VISA.
Rsv'tns: Strongly recommended in season.

Reserve Through: Call direct.
Minimum Stay: Three nights by reservation, less if available.
Parking: Ample free covered off-street parking.
In-Room: Color cable TV, maid service, limited room service. Ceiling fans in some rooms.
On-Premises: Meeting rooms, public telephone, central heat, restaurant & bar.
Exercise/Health: Nearby

gym, weights & massage.
Swimming: Pool or ocean beach.
Sunbathing: On beach, private/common sun decks or poolside.
Smoking: Permitted without restrictions.
Pets: Not permitted.
Handicap Access: No.
Children: Permitted, but not recommended.
Languages: English.
Your Host: Peter & Jim

IGTA

Bradford Gardens

What A Wonderful Retreat From Life!

Gay/Lesbian ♀♂

At *Bradford Gardens* you can choose from beautiful, oversized rooms with hardwood floors, fireplaces and antiques or wonderful Cape Cod cottages with fireplaces, decks and fully equipped kitchens. Also available are two-bedroom, two-level townhouses with all the above amenities. We offer full gourmet breakfasts, spacious rose gardens and daily maid service. Only one block from the ocean and a five-minute walk to town, come pamper yourself in P-Town. You deserve it!

continued next page

Address: 178 Bradford St, Provincetown, MA 02657. Tel: (508) 487-1616, (800) 432-2334.

Type: Bed & breakfast & cottages.
Clientele: Mostly gay & lesbian with some straight clientele.
Transportation: Free pick up from airport, bus, ferry dock.
To Gay Bars: 10-minute walk to gay/lesbian bars.
Rooms: 8 doubles, 4 cottages, 5 townhouses.
Bathrooms: All private.
Meals: Full gourmet breakfast.
Vegetarian: Available upon request.
Complimentary: Mints on pillows.
Dates Open: All year.
High Season: July, August.
Rates: In season $110-$185, off-season $65-$155.
Discounts: Weekly, off-season & mid-week stays.
Credit Cards: MC, VISA, Amex.
Rsv'tns: Required.
Reserve Through: Travel agent or call direct.
Minimum Stay: 3 nights July & August.
Parking: Ample off-street free parking.
In-Room: Maid service, color TV, ceiling fans, kitchen.
On-Premises: Walkabout gardens, lawn swing.
Swimming: Ocean beach nearby.
Sunbathing: On beach, private sun decks or in garden.
Smoking: Permitted in rooms.
Pets: Permitted in cottages.
Handicap Access: No.
Children: Not permitted.
Languages: English, French.
Your Host: Susan & Melanie.

IGTA

Brass Key Guesthouse

Unique in Provincetown

Gay/Lesbian ♂

The Brass Key Guesthouse is renowned for providing gay and lesbian travelers with the finest in luxury accommodations, attentive service and meticulous housekeeping. In concert with numerous accolades from its guests and from travel writers of the gay media, *The Brass Key* is one of five gay-designated lodgings throughout the United States to receive *Out & About's* coveted Editor's Choice award.

Located on a quiet side street in the heart of town, ten guest rooms in a restored 1828 sea captain's home and two charming private cottages overlook the heated dip pool and landscaped courtyard. All accommodations offer traditional New England architecture enhanced by English and American Country antiques. Yet no two rooms are alike: each presents its own special warmth and personality with details such as a vaulted skylit ceiling, a teddy bear loft, a working fireplace, framed antique quilts or courtyard and harbor views.

Throughout the four seasons, *The Brass Key* presents a private and exclusive retreat. In the early Spring, flowering tulips, forsythia, azalea and rhododendron greet guests. From Memorial Day through September, the action shifts to the sun: while many guests enjoy the seashore beaches, others relax and socialize in the enclosed courtyard. In the Fall, as crisp nights complement the warm days of Indian summer, and later, throughout the quiet of Winter, a blazing fire in the hearth accords the perfect backdrop to savor a bottle of wine and ward off the outside chill.

Guests of *The Brass Key* are offered every amenity to ensure their year-round comfort: individually-controlled heating and air-conditioning, telephone, color cable televisions with VCR and videocassette library, refrigerator, hair dryer, Caswell-Massey bath toiletries; some deluxe rooms further feature fireplaces, king beds and oversized whirlpool baths.

The staff of *The Brass Key* looks forward to the pleasure of your company.
Address: 9 Court St, Provincetown, MA 02657. Tel: (508) 487-9005, (800) 842-9858, Fax: (508) 487-9020.

Type: Bed & breakfast guesthouse.
Clientele: Mostly men with women welcome.
Transportation: Ferry, auto, or plane from Boston. Provincetown airport taxi $5.
To Gay Bars: 2 blocks to gay & lesbian bars.
Rooms: 10 rooms & 2 cottages with double, queen or king beds.
Bathrooms: All private.
Meals: Expanded continental breakfast.

Complimentary: Afternoon cocktails.
Dates Open: All year.
High Season: Mid-June – mid-September.
Rates: In season $120-$205 & off season $50-$95.
Credit Cards: MC, VISA & Amex.
Rsv'tns: Highly recommended.
Reserve Through: Travel agent or call direct.
Minimum Stay: Required in season, during holi-

days & special events.
Parking: Ample free off-street parking.
In-Room: Color cable TV, VCR, video tape library, AC, telephone, ceiling fans, refrigerator. Laundry, maid & turndown service.
On-Premises: Spacious living room with breakfast area, wood-burning fireplace.
Exercise/Health: Whirlpool spa & nearby gym.
Swimming: Pool on the

premises; also nearby ocean beaches.
Sunbathing: Poolside courtyard & sun decks.
Smoking: Permitted. Non-smoking rooms available.
Pets: Not permitted.
Handicap Access: Yes. Wheelchair parking & ramp. 1 unit for the physically challenged.
Children: Not permitted.
Languages: English.

IGTA

Cape View Motel

Gay-Friendly 50/50 ♀♂

Cape View is on the highest bluff in North Truro, very much in the Provincetown area, but away from the bustle of downtown. Every unit has a panoramic view of the harbor and bay. Rooms are spacious and have color TV. Deluxe efficiencies have private balconies and telephone with free local calls. White sand beaches are nearby, or you can relax at our pool. We are eight minutes from Provincetown and its nightlife, galleries, museums and delightful shops and restaurants. Dune rides, whale watching helicopter excursions and fishing excursions can be arranged.

Address: Rte 6, PO Box 114, North Truro, MA 02652. Tel: (508) 487-0363, (800) 224-3232.

Type: Motel.
Clientele: 50% gay & lesbian & 50% straight clientele.
Transportation: Car is best. Provincetown Airport or Ferry, then taxi. Pick up from airport.
To Gay Bars: 8-minute drive.
Rooms: 32 rooms with 2 doubles or 1 king bed. 20 units have completely equipped kitchens.

Bathrooms: All private.
Meals: Morning coffee.
Complimentary: Free ice 24 hours.
Dates Open: Apr 15-Nov 1.
High Season: June 28-Sept 7 (Labor Day).
Rates: Off season $45-$59.90, in season $65-$89.90.
Discounts: 5% for weekly stays.
Credit Cards: MC, VISA &

Amex.
Rsv'tns: Highly suggested.
Reserve Through: Call direct.
Minimum Stay: 2 nights on weekends, more on certain holidays.
Parking: Ample free off-street parking.
In-Room: Color cable TV, AC, telephone, kitchen, refrigerator & maid service.

Swimming: Pool on premises, beaches nearby.
Sunbathing: At poolside, on the beach & on private sun decks.
Nudity: Permitted on private sun decks.
Smoking: Permitted everywhere.
Pets: Not permitted.
Handicap Access: No.
Children: Permitted.
Languages: English & French.

Take along the Expert

Ferrari's Places of Interest™ contains articles contributed by gay and lesbian journalists on the scene, giving insight into gay and lesbian communities worldwide. With its accompanying directory, it's the perfect vacation planner.

Captain's House

Gay/Lesbian ♂

The Captain's House is one of the oldest guest houses of Provincetown. Built more than a century ago, it represents the typical architecture and simple elegance of a bygone era. Though on busy Commercial St., we're located up a secluded little alley where there is an absence of noise and a lot of unexpected privacy. Our great little patio, loaded with flowers, provides a private setting for our cocktail bar, morning coffee, cook-outs or sun tanning. Our rooms are charming, immaculate and comfortable, with reasonable rates.

Address: 350-A Commercial St, Provincetown, MA 02657. Tel: Guest phone: (508) 487-9794, Reservations: (800) 457-8885.

Type: Guesthouse.
Clientele: Mostly men with women welcome.
Transportation: Taxi from airport 5 minutes. 2-minute walk from bus, ferry.
To Gay Bars: 5-10 minutes' walk to everything.
Rooms: 1 small single, 8 doubles & 2 rooms with 2 beds.
Bathrooms: 3 private &

2 shared. All rooms have sinks.
Meals: Continental breakfast.
Dates Open: All year.
High Season: Memorial Day-Labor Day.
Rates: $35-$80.
Discounts: By request on stays of 7 days or more.
Credit Cards: MC, VISA.
Rsv'tns: Necessary, as soon as possible.

Reserve Through: Call direct.
Minimum Stay: 5 days if weekend is desired.
Parking: Adequate free on-street parking.
In-Room: Color TV, maid service, refrigerator, & ceiling or window fans.
On-Premises: TV lounge, public telephone & central heat.
Swimming: Ocean beach

nearby.
Sunbathing: On beach or private patio.
Smoking: Permitted without restrictions.
Pets: Permitted with prior approval.
Handicap Access: No.
Children: Not permitted.
Languages: English, French.
Your Host: Jeff.

Carl's Guest House

Men ♂

Where Strangers Become Friends

Our house is decorated in the clean, simple manner most suited to a beach vacation. Friendly, decent guys come from around the world to enjoy sea, sun and sand. At *Carl's Guest House,* all guest rooms are private, clean, comfortable and fairly priced. You can kick off your shoes and relax in an inviting living room with stereo, cable TV and a selection of video tapes of all ratings. We have been catering to gay *gentlemen* since 1975.

Address: 68 Bradford St, Provincetown, MA 02657. Tel: (508) 487-1650 or (800) 348-CARL.

Type: Guesthouse.
Clientele: Men.
Transportation: $1 bus, $5 taxi from airport; short walk from bus stn & boat dock.
Rooms: 14 rooms with single, double or queen beds.
Bathrooms: 3 private, 11 rooms share.
Meals: Complimentary coffee, tea, soups and ice

in lounge service area.
Complimentary: Coffee, tea, etc.
Dates Open: All year.
High Season: June-September.
Rates: Summer $45-$85, other times $25-$50.
Discounts: For groups, gay business organizations during off season.
Credit Cards: MC & VISA.
Reserve Through: Call

direct.
Parking: Limited off-street & adequate on-street parking.
In-Room: Color TV, private sun decks, patios, room service, AC, fridge, ceiling fans & telephone.
On-Premises: TV lounge with color cable TV.
Exercise/Health: Nearby gym, weights.
Swimming: Ocean beach

nearby.
Sunbathing: On beach, private or common sun deck.
Nudity: Permitted on sun decks, in shower rooms.
Smoking: Smoking areas are limited and must be requested.
Pets: Not permitted.
Handicap Access: No.
Children: Not permitted.
Languages: English.

Chicago House, The

Gay/Lesbian ♀♂

When in P-Town, Think of Chicago... (House, That Is!)

Chicago House, surrounded by charming gardens, canopied porches, inviting decks and patios, offers guests ten attractive rooms, nearly all with private bath, and three apartments with kitchenettes. Guests return each year, to the two historical Cape Cod homes that make up *Chicago House,* for the delicious homemade muffins and cakes baked daily for continental breakfast. One of the oldest established P-Town guesthouses, we stay open all year, offering a roaring fire in the common room in winter. We're centrally located, but on a quiet side street.

Address: 6 Winslow St, Provincetown, MA 02657. Tel: (508) 487-0537 or (800) SEE-PTOWN (733-7869).

Type: Bed & breakfast guesthouse.	**Bathrooms:** Private: 1 bath/toilet, 8 shower/ toilets. Others share.	Amex. **Rsv'tns:** Suggested. **Reserve Through:** Call direct.	**Exercise/Health:** Gym & weights nearby. **Swimming:** Nearby pool & ocean beach.
Clientele: Good mix of gay men & women. **Transportation:** Car or boat from Boston. Free pick up from airport & ferry dock.	**Meals:** Continental breakfast. **Vegetarian:** Available in restaurants. **Complimentary:** Tea, coffee, mints on pillow.	**Minimum Stay:** During July & August. **Parking:** Adequate, free off-street parking. **In-Room:** Color TV, maid service, kitchen & refrig-	**Sunbathing:** On patio or nearby poolside & ocean beach. **Smoking:** Permitted. **Pets:** Permitted with advance notice & some
To Gay Bars: 1 block or 1 min walk. **Rooms:** 10 rooms, 1 apartment & 2 studio apartments with single, double, queen or king beds.	**Dates Open:** All year. **High Season:** July & August. **Rates:** Summer $49-175 & winter $20-115. **Credit Cards:** MC, VISA &	erator. **On-Premises:** TV lounge, meeting rooms, courtesy phone & guest refrigerator.	restrictions. **Handicap Access:** No. **Children:** Permitted off season. **Languages:** English.

Coat of Arms

Gay/Lesbian ♂

Coat of Arms is a vintage 1810 New England Colonial home which was converted to Victorian in 1886. It's located in central Provincetown at the tip of Cape Cod. Rooms are comfortable and cozy and, like many guest houses in Provincetown, have shared baths. Entertain your personal guests in the lounge, which has a large private bar where you can keep your own bottles. *Coat of Arms* is within strolling distance of fine restaurants, gift shops, theaters, artists' studios and gay bars and clubs.

Address: 7 Johnson St, Provincetown, MA 02657. Tel: (508) 487-0816.

Type: Guesthouse. **Clientele:** Mostly men with women welcome. **Transportation:** Taxi from airport 10 min or less, 5 min walk from ferry & bus.	showers. **Meals:** Coffee & pastries in the morning only. **Complimentary:** Ice, set-ups at bar. **Dates Open:** March 15 to November 1.	**Reserve Through:** Call direct. **Minimum Stay:** 4 days in summer, 7 for Carnival week, 4th of July, Labor Day. **Parking:** Limited free off-	100 yards. **Sunbathing:** On beach, patio or common sun decks. **Smoking:** Permitted without restrictions, non-smoking rooms available.
To Gay Bars: 1-2 minutes to bar. **Rooms:** 10 rooms with single or double beds. **Bathrooms:** 4 shared	**High Season:** June thru September. **Rates:** $45-$65 summer, $30-$50 off season. **Rsv'tns:** Recommended.	street parking. **In-Room:** Maid service, ceiling fans. **On-Premises:** TV lounge. **Swimming:** Ocean beach	**Pets:** Not permitted. **Handicap Access:** No. **Children:** Not permitted. **Languages:** English. **Your Host:** Skip & Arpina.

Courtland Guest House

Gay/Lesbian ♂

The Courtland Guest House is a restored captain's home of the Federal period, circa 1820-1840. The charm and ambience of another era prevails, while you enjoy all the modern amenities to which you are accustomed. In season, coffee, tea, juice and homemade muffins and breads are served in the common room, which overlooks the garden. It's a short walk to shops, galleries, restaurants and nightclubs. Free parking is available.

Address: 14 Court St, Provincetown, MA 02657. Tel: (508) 487-2292.

continued next page

Massachusetts

Type: Guesthouse.
Clientele: Mostly men with women welcome.
Transportation: Car, bus or boat.
To Gay Bars: 1 block to gay/lesbian bars.
Rooms: 7 rooms & 1 efficiency apartment with single, queen or king beds.
Bathrooms: 1 private shower/toilet, 2 shared bath/shower/toilet & 1 toilet only.
Meals: Continental breakfast.
Vegetarian: Restaurants within 2 blocks.
Dates Open: April-November.
High Season: June-September.
Rates: In-season $40-$90, off-season $25-$65.
Credit Cards: MC, VISA & Amex.
Rsv'tns: Suggested.
Reserve Through: Call direct.
Minimum Stay: Holidays 4 days, weekends 2 days.
Parking: Ample free off-street parking.
In-Room: Some rooms have color cable TV. 1 has AC.
On-Premises: Common lounge with bar, refrigerator & microwave.
Swimming: Ocean beach.
Sunbathing: On beach or in yard.
Smoking: Permitted without restrictions.
Pets: Not permitted.
Handicap Access: No.
Children: Not permitted.
Languages: English & limited German & French.

Dexter's Inn

Gay/Lesbian ♀♂

Come Out to Provincetown & Feel at Home With Us.

If you have not yet visited Provincetown, the experience of a lifetime awaits you. The sea, the sunsets, the people and *Dexter's Inn* are here for your pleasure After continental breakfast in our cozy common room or flower garden patio, you have but a two-minute walk to the ocean or great shops and restaurants. When your day

6 Conwell Street
Provincetown, MA 02657
(508) 487-1911

is done, your comfortable air conditioned room welcomes you. We invite you to relax and enjoy your time with us. Come out, come out wherever you are. You'll be glad you did!

Address: 6 Conwell St, Provincetown, MA 02657. Tel: (508) 487-1911.

Type: Bed & breakfast guesthouse.
Clientele: Good mix of gays & lesbians.
To Gay Bars: 5-minute walk.
Rooms: 15 rooms with double beds.
Bathrooms: 12 private shower/toilet & 1 shared bath/shower/toilet.
Meals: Expanded continental breakfast.
Dates Open: All year.
High Season: July & August.
Rates: $75-$85 summer, $50-$60 off season.
Discounts: Special off-season rates for long stays.
Credit Cards: MC & VISA.
Rsv'tns: Recommended.
Reserve Through: Call direct.
Minimum Stay: In high season, for summer weekends (May, June, September) and holidays.
Parking: Free ample parking.
In-Room: Maid service, color cable TV & AC. Some rooms with refrigerator & ceiling fans.
On-Premises: Sun deck, patio & TV lounge.
Swimming: Ocean beach nearby.
Sunbathing: On ocean beach or sun decks.
Smoking: Permitted on sun deck & in outdoor areas.
Pets: Not permitted.
Handicap Access: Limited.
Children: Not permitted.
Languages: English.

Dusty Miller Inn

Gay/Lesbian ♀

Guests Thrive On the Friendly, Easy Atmosphere!

Making guests feel at home is our specialty at *Dusty Miller*. The pleasant comfort of our porch rocking chairs seems to promote interesting conversations, and friendships are struck there. Our porch rockers also give you a great vantage point for peoplewatching. Expect to feel at ease and in the perfect mood to enjoy the fun of Provincetown. Our rooms are well-appointed and comfortable, and eight of them have refrigerators.

Address: 82 Bradford St, Provincetown, MA 02657. Tel: (508) 487-2213.

Type: Guesthouse.
Clientele: Mostly women with men welcome.
Transportation: Taxi. Free pick up from airport with at least one week prior arrangement.
To Gay Bars: Across the street.
Rooms: 13 rooms & 1 apartment with 1 single & 13 double beds.

Bathrooms: 10 private, others share.
Meals: Morning coffee or tea.
Dates Open: All year.
High Season: Memorial Day to Labor Day.
Rates: In season: $38 single, $68-$75 double, $110 apt. Off season: $27 single, $40-$50 double, $75 apartment.

Credit Cards: MC & VISA.
Rsv'tns: Required.
Reserve Through: Call direct.
Minimum Stay: Rooms: 2 nights in season (holidays 3 nights). Apts: 2 nights (in season 5 nights).
Parking: 1 space per room on premises or in private lot approximately

1 block away.
In-Room: Maid service. Ceiling fans, fans, or AC in all rooms. Color TV, refrigerators in 7 rooms & apartment. Other rooms have B&W TV & access to refrigerators & color TV.
On-Premises: BBQ grills, common room, & desk phone in office.

Swimming: Ocean beach nearby.
Sunbathing: On the beach or in the front yard.
Smoking: Permitted without restrictions.
Pets: Permitted in designated rooms.
Handicap Access: No.
Children: Permitted.
Languages: English.

Elephant Walk Inn

Elephant Walk "Unforgettable"

Gay/Lesbian ♀♂

Elephant Walk Inn was built as a private country home in 1917. The large mission-style house was converted to an inn some years later. Its proximity to the center of town and the then existing railroad made it a favorite stop for early Provincetown visitors.

The decor of the inn recalls the romantic feeling of an Edwardian house of the past. Many of the rooms are decorated with original paintings, prints and antiques. One room has a canopy bed, another a four-poster, while brass and enamel beds grace two others. Old captain's bureaus, antique tables and Oriental carpets are scattered about.

However, to this echo of the past have been added the modern conveniences of the present. Each guest room has its own private bath as well as a remote cable color TV, a small refrigerator, and a ceiling fan. Air-conditioning is also available as an option.

Continental breakfast is served each morning on the glass-enclosed front porch where guests can also find a varied supply of reading material. Some guests enjoy their coffee on the large second floor sun deck which is at the rear of the inn overlooking the landscaped garden. The deck, with its scattering of summer furniture, is a favorite gathering spot for guests to meet and to enjoy a drink after a day at the beach.

Free parking is provided on the premises. Although a car is not necessary for seeing Provincetown with its myriad shops, restaurants and clubs, it is convenient to have one for exploring and finding a secluded beach with windswept dunes. June and September are the perfect times to do that. The days are warm and bright and although everything is open, there are no crowds.

Please call or write for a free brochure.

Address: 156 Bradford St, Provincetown, MA 02657. Tel: (508) 487-2543 or (800) 889-WALK (9255).

Type: Bed & breakfast.
Clientele: Good mix of gay men & women.
Transportation: Pick up from airport, ferry or bus available.
To Gay Bars: 5-minute walk to men's, women's

bars.
Rooms: 8 rooms with double, queen or king beds.
Bathrooms: All private shower/toilets.
Meals: Continental breakfast.

Dates Open: April 15th-November 1st.
High Season: June 23rd-September 9th.
Rates: In season $82-$88, off season $42-$60.
Discounts: One night free on weekly stays Apr 15-

Jun 15, Sep 17-Oct 9.
Credit Cards: MC, VISA, Amex & Diners.
Rsv'tns: Required 4-8 wks in advance in high season.

continued next page

Reserve Through: Call direct.
Minimum Stay: 3 nights in season, more on weekends, holidays.
Parking: Ample free off-street parking.
In-Room: Maid service, color TV, refrigerator, ceiling fans, some with air-conditioning.
On-Premises: Lounge, sun deck.
Swimming: Ocean beach 1-1/2 blocks.
Sunbathing: On beach or common sun deck.
Smoking: Permitted without restrictions.
Pets: Not permitted.
Handicap Access: No.
Children: Not permitted.
Languages: English.
Your Host: Len.

Gabriel's

Come Close to Heaven

Gay/Lesbian ♀

Perhaps there really are small corners of this earth that come close to heaven. I've tried to make *Gabriel's* such a place. I've taken care with every aspect of this beautiful old home: to grace its French doors, porches and stairways with antiques and furnishings chosen one-by-one. Every room is different, each with its own special personality. And then I've added modern conveniences: cable TV, in-

Come close to heaven.

room phones, and fully-equipped kitchens. We offer computer, copy and fax services, a steam room, sauna, hot tubs and a gym. My staff and I have made every effort to provide all the amenities and individual service you could desire at *Gabriel's.*

This year we are delighted to announce that we've expanded. We have added a library and gorgeous skylit meeting space, *Sirens Workshop Center,* which is now available for workshops, conferences, special events and commitment ceremonies. Yoga classes are available daily. Our off-season weekend course themes include: body work, dream work, nature & ecology, relationships, sexuality, spirituality, health, healing, career/business, visual and performing arts. A brochure detailing *Sirens* events is available in September.

Please accept my personal invitation to stay with us and grow with us. We will do everything we can to make your visit perfect, coming as close as possible to heaven. *Gabriel Brooke, Innkeeper*

Address: 104 Bradford St, Provincetown, MA 02657. Tel: (508) 487-3232 or Fax: (508) 487-1605.

Type: Guesthouse & workshop center.
Clientele: Mostly women with men welcome.
Transportation: Free pick up from airport, bus or ferry dock.
To Gay Bars: 1 block.
Rooms: 10 room & 10 apartments with double or queen beds.
Bathrooms: 16 private baths. 4 shared baths.
Meals: Homemade breakfast.
Complimentary: Coffee, tea, juice, fruit, muffins, cereal, chocolates on pillow.
Dates Open: All year.
High Season: Memorial Day to Labor Day week.
Rates: Winter $50-$100, Border season $65-$120, high season $75-$150.
Discounts: Nov 1st-Apr 1st, 3rd night free with coupon, coupons for repeat guests.
Credit Cards: MC & VISA.
Rsv'tns: Recommended.
Reserve Through: Travel agent or call direct.
Minimum Stay: 2 nights in season & on weekends off season.
Parking: Reserved parking in a nearby lot for $3 per night.
In-Room: Cable TV, telephones, housekeeping service, fully equipped kitchens (in apartments). Some rooms with refrigerators, AC, ceiling fans & fireplaces.
On-Premises: TV lounge, conference room, library, games, common kitchen for light meals, two gardens.
Exercise/Health: Yoga classes, 2 outdoor hot tubs, sauna, steam room, exercise room, discounts on massage.
Swimming: Nearby ocean beach.
Sunbathing: On beach and common sun decks.
Nudity: Permitted on patio in our enclosed yard.
Smoking: Permitted with restrictions, smoke-free rooms available.
Pets: Usually not permitted, but sometimes we bend.
Handicap Access: No.
Children: Permitted.
Languages: English, French.

IGTA

Haven House

A One-of-A-Kind Guest House Compound

Gay/Lesbian ♂

An unusual and popular Key West-style guesthouse right in the heart of Provincetown, *Haven House* consists of four early nineteenth-century buildings surrounded by beautiful gardens and encircling a private solar-heated swimming pool. We offer a wide variety of guest rooms ranging from our poolside rooms with private bath, air-conditioning, television and refigerator, to our economic shared baths. All rooms are comfortable, extremely clean and reasonably priced. If you are looking for a friendly, casual and fun atmosphere, *Haven House* should be your Provincetown choice.

Address: 12 Carver St, Provincetown, MA 02657. Tel: (508) 487-3031, (800) 261-2450.

Type: Guesthouse.
Clientele: Mostly men with women welcome.
Transportation: Free airport pick up. Call on arrival.
To Gay Bars: Men's bar across the street. Others within walking distance.
Rooms: 27 rooms & 1 suite.
Bathrooms: 12 private. Other rooms share baths.
Meals: Continental breakfast.
Dates Open: All year.
High Season: Mid-June thru mid-September.
Rates: In season $40-$130. Off season $30-$75.
Credit Cards: MC, VISA, Amex & Discover.
Rsv'tns: Required.
Reserve Through: Travel agent or call direct.
Minimum Stay: 5 nights in season, unless there is an opening.
Parking: Adequate, free off-street parking. 1 car per room.
In-Room: Maid service.
On-Premises: Laundry facilities, gas BBQ, ice, & bike rack.
Exercise/Health: Nearby gym, weights.
Swimming: Pool on premises.
Sunbathing: At poolside or on private sun decks.
Nudity: Permitted by pool.
Smoking: Permitted without restrictions.
Pets: Permitted in one room only. Call to reserve.
Handicap Access: One room is somewhat accessible.
Children: No.
Languages: English.

IGTA

Heritage House

Having a Wonderful Time...Wish You Were Here!

Gay/Lesbian ♀♂

Our house, with thirteen rooms on three floors, a large common room, two verandas and views of Cape Cod Bay and the harbor, is next door to the Heritage Museum between Commercial Street and Bradford Street. Some of the best people watching in Provincetown is to be had from the upper and lower verandas of *Heritage House*. Shops, the bay beach and many fine restaurants are just a short walk from our door. Our fluffy towels, fresh and crisp linens, sparkling-clean bathrooms, delicious coffee, homemade muffins and a friendly,

comfortable atmosphere will help make your stay a pleasant one. We are committed to providing our guests with all these things and more. As your hosts, we'd like to help you enjoy the magic of Provincetown.

Address: 7 Center St, Provincetown, MA 02657. Tel: (508) 487-3692.

Type: Guesthouse.
Clientele: Mostly gay & lesbian with some straight clientele.
Transportation: Car or fly into Provincetown Airport from Boston's Logan Airport. Free pick up from airport & ferry wharf.
To Gay Bars: 5-minute walk to women's & men's bars.
Rooms: 13 rooms & 1 2-bedroom condo with single, double or king beds.
Bathrooms: 4 shared bath/shower/toilets. Condo with private bath.
Meals: Expanded continental breakfast.
Vegetarian: Breakfast is mostly vegetarian & restaurants featuring vegetarian selections are only a 5-minute walk.
Complimentary: Ice available. Refrigerator on each floor.
Dates Open: All year.

continued next page

Massachusetts

High Season: June through September & holiday weekends. **Rates:** In season $49-$115, off season $40-$100. **Discounts:** Off-season group rates available. **Credit Cards:** MC, VISA & Amex. **Rsv'tns:** Preferred. **Reserve Through:** Call direct. **Minimum Stay:** 2 nights for in-season weekends & 3 nights on holiday weekends. **Parking:** Limited free off-street & on-street parking. **In-Room:** Maid service. **On-Premises:** TV lounge with color cable TV & VCR. **Exercise/Health:** Gym, weights & massage nearby. **Swimming:** In nearby ocean. **Sunbathing:** At beach. **Smoking:** Permitted without restrictions. **Pets:** Not permitted. **Handicap Access:** No. **Children:** Not especially welcomed. **Languages:** English.

Lamplighter Inn & Cottage

Gay/Lesbian ♀♂

Lamplighter Inn is just a stroll from most beaches and the town center. Our antique sea captain's home is on one of Provincetown's highest hills, overlooking the bay, ocean and harbor and is within walking distance of all restaurants, shops, discos, bars and marinas. Our inn is immaculate and we strive to assure that your stay will always be remembered. Our must-see gardens include a watergarden, cacti, bonsai, rare shrubs and perennials. So, come relax and enjoy Provincetown at the *Lamplighter Inn.*

Address: 26 Bradford St, Provincetown, MA 02657. Tel: (508) 487-2529 or Fax: 487-0079.

Type: Bed & breakfast guesthouse inn & cottage. **Clientele:** Mostly gay/lesbian (summer) with some straight clientele (winter). **Transportation:** Car, bus. Ferry or Cape Air from Boston. Free pick up from airport, bus, ferry dock. **To Gay Bars:** 3 blocks or 1/8 mile. 5 minutes by foot or 1 minute by car. **Rooms:** 7 rooms, 2 suites & 1 cottage with double beds. **Bathrooms:** 8 private bath/shower/toilets, 2 shared bath/shower/toilets. **Meals:** Continental breakfast. **Vegetarian:** Available at local restaurants, delis & grocery stores. 5-minute walk to A&P. **Complimentary:** Ice. **Dates Open:** All year. **High Season:** June through October. **Rates:** Winter $40-$85, spring & fall $45-$95, summer $75-$140. **Discounts:** Off season specials & discounts on longer stays. **Credit Cards:** MC, VISA, Amex, Diners & Discover. **Rsv'tns:** Required in peak season & preferred for USA holidays. **Reserve Through:** Travel agent or call direct. **Minimum Stay:** Required during peak season, holidays & special events. **Parking:** Adequate, free off-street parking. **In-Room:** Color cable TV, AC, telephone, ceiling fans, maid service, kitchen, refrigerator. **On-Premises:** Roof-top deck, bike rack, patios & BBQ grill. **Exercise/Health:** Local gym nearby. Weights, massage. **Swimming:** At nearby pool, ocean, lake or bay. **Sunbathing:** On patio, common sun decks, roof deck or nearby beach. **Nudity:** Permitted on roof-top deck. **Smoking:** Permitted in some rooms & outside. Non-smoking rooms available. **Pets:** Not permitted. **Handicap Access:** No. **Children:** Not especially welcomed. **Languages:** English. **Your Host:** Michael & Joseph

Lotus Guest House

Gay/Lesbian ♀♂

Provincetown's Victorian-style *Lotus Guest House* offers spacious rooms with private or shared baths, a common deck and garden. There is also a large suite available with private front porch and bath. From the guest house, it is a short walk to your favorite restaurants, clubs and beaches and one block from bus and ferry service.

Address: 296 Commercial St, Provincetown, MA 02657. Tel: (508) 487-4644.

Type: Guesthouse with men's clothing shop. **Clientele:** Mostly gay/lesbian with some straight clientele. **Transportation:** Taxi from airport, Boston Ferry & bus lines 1/2 block. **To Gay Bars:** 1 block. **Rooms:** 12 rooms & 1 suite with double beds. **Bathrooms:** 3 private bath/toilets & 2 shared bath/shower/toilets. **Complimentary:** Morning coffee. **Dates Open:** May through October. **High Season:** July & August. **Rates:** In season $50-$95, off season $30-$70. **Discounts:** Call about weekly specials. **Credit Cards:** MC, VISA & Amex. **Rsv'tns:** Recommended. **Reserve Through:** Travel agent or call direct. **Minimum Stay:** 2 nights weekends, 3-7 nights holidays, call. **Parking:** Limited on-street parking, Municipal & private lots 1/2 block away.

In-Room: Maid service & ceiling fans.
On-Premises: Large com-mon deck, tables & chairs in garden.
Swimming: Ocean beach.
Sunbathing: On beach & patio.
Smoking: Permitted.
Pets: Not permitted.
Handicap Access: No.
Languages: English.

Normandy House

A Room With More Than Just A View

Gay/Lesbian ♂

Awaken each morning to a gentle sea breeze and sweeping ocean views of Provincetown harbor and Cape Cod Bay. Then, join us in our sun-drenched common room for continental breakfast. Rooms have TV, VCR and refrigerator, and most have air conditioning and ceiling fans. Furnishings range from contemporary to antiques. Shed the accumulated tensions of urban living by relaxing on the sun deck with panoramic views of the lower cape, or melt those frazzled nerves away in the hot tub! *Normandy House* is your haven by the sea.

Address: 184 Bradford St, Provincetown, MA 02657. Tel: (508) 487-1197 or (800) 487-1197.

Type: Guesthouse.
Clientele: Mostly men with women welcome.
Transportation: Free pickup from airport, dock and bus.
To Gay Bars: 10-minute walk to men's/women's bars.
Rooms: 8 rooms & 1 apartment with double or queen beds.
Bathrooms: 5 private & 2 shared.

Meals: Continental breakfast.
Complimentary: Ice & mixes.
Dates Open: All year.
High Season: Mid-June to mid-September.
Rates: High season $60-$125, low season $35-$65.
Credit Cards: MC, VISA.
Rsv'tns: Required.
Reserve Through: Call direct.

Minimum Stay: 4 nights on Memorial Day weekend, 7 nights on big holidays & Carnival.
Parking: Limited free off-street parking.
In-Room: Cable color TV, VCR, video tape library, AC, ceiling fans, telephone, kitchen, refrigerator & maid service.
On-Premises: Lovely common room w/sun porch, sun deck, Jacuzzi.

Exercise/Health: Jacuzzi.
Swimming: Nearby town beach & National Seashore beaches.
Sunbathing: On common sun deck, patio & at nearby beaches.
Smoking: Permitted. Non-smoking rooms available.
Pets: Not permitted.
Handicap Access: No.
Children: Not permitted.
Languages: English.

Ranch, The

Meanwhile, back

Men ♂

at *The Ranch,* a 22-room guesthouse in the center of Provincetown, guests tend toward the western and leather type, but not exclusively. The rooms are small, but clean, comfortable and attractively decorated. Rooms have names, such as Stud Stall, Bull Pen, Dale Evans Suite, etc., instead of numbers. A large common lounge has stereo, TV/VCR and a private bar with free ice and mix. There is free morning coffee, a sun deck and a courteous staff to answer all your questions.

Address: 198 Commercial St, Box 26, Provincetown, MA 02657. Tel: (508) 487-1542.

Type: Guesthouse with private bar.
Clientele: Men only.
Transportation: Plane, car, bus, ferry.
To Gay Bars: 1 block to all gay bars.
Rooms: 22 rooms with single, double or queen beds.
Bathrooms: 4 large

shared full baths with 2 showers & 2 sinks in each.
Meals: Continental breakfast.
Complimentary: Set-up service.
Dates Open: April 15-Sept 15.
High Season: June 15-Sept 15.

Rates: Off season $30-$40, in season $45-$60.
Rsv'tns: Required.
Reserve Through: Travel agent or call direct.
Parking: Limited on-street parking.
In-Room: Ceiling fans, maid service.
On-Premises: TV lounge.
Swimming: Nearby pool

& ocean beach.
Sunbathing: On common sun decks.
Smoking: Permitted.
Pets: Not permitted.
Handicap Access: No.
Children: Not permitted.
Languages: English.

Ravenwood Guestrooms & Apts

Gay/Lesbian ♀

Originally a sea captain's residence, *Ravenwood* now offers comfortable and inviting guestrooms and apartments to Provincetown visitors. Some rooms have ocean views, others feature decks or beamed ceilings. Guests relax in an enclosed backyard. Each accommodation has its own outside sitting or picnic area. We are centrally located, directly across the street from the harbor, near the beach and only a 10-minute stroll to the center of town. A year-round oceanfront one-bedroom condo and a Cape Cod cottage are also available for long weekends or by the week. **Address: 462 Commercial St, Provincetown, MA 02657. Tel: (508) 487-3203.**

Type: Guest room & year-round apartments, condo & year-round cottage.
Clientele: Women. Men permitted only if accompanied by their women friends.
Transportation: Plane, bus, ferry, car from Boston.
To Gay Bars: 5 blocks to men's/women's bars.
Rooms: 1 room, 3 apartments, 1 cottage & 1 oceanfront condo.
Bathrooms: All have private shower & toilet.
Vegetarian: Available at many nearby restaurants.
Complimentary: Mints on pillows, private catering of flowers, champagne, balloons, etc can be arranged.
Dates Open: All year.
High Season: Spring whale watching, fall foliage, winter holidays & July & August.
Rates: Summer $75-$125, winter $50-$110.
Discounts: Off season third consecutive night free.
Credit Cards: All major cards accepted for deposit only.

Rsv'tns: Recommended.
Reserve Through: Travel agent or call direct.
Minimum Stay: 3 nights holiday wknds, 7 nights July-Aug & Oct Women's Week. Inquire about shorter stays.
Parking: Ample off-street parking. 1 private spot per room. Other parking available
In-Room: Color cable TV, ceiling fans & refrigerators. Apts have kitchens.
On-Premises: Patio, BBQ, private fenced-in yards or private decks.
Exercise/Health: Gym & Jacuzzi 4 blks, massage available.
Swimming: At ocean beach.
Sunbathing: On ocean beach, private sun decks & in private garden.
Nudity: Permitted on private decks of apts.
Smoking: Permitted without restrictions. Non-smoking rooms available.
Pets: Not permitted.
Handicap Access: Studios are accessible.
Children: Permitted (age restrictions).
Languages: English.
Your Host: Valerie.

Richmond Inn, The

Gay/Lesbian ♂

The Richmond Inn, an 1870's renovated captain's home, is perfectly located in Provincetown's West End only one block from the beach. Savor the spectacular views of the bay from either of our sun decks or venture into the excitement of Commercial Street, only steps away. Charming and convenient, *The Richmond Inn* enjoys numerous repeat guests who consider it home when in Provincetown. **Address: No. 4 Conant St, Provincetown, MA 02657. Tel: (508) 487-9193.**

Type: Guesthouse.
Clientele: Mostly men with women welcome.
Transportation: Plane from Boston to P'town airport, taxi to inn. Boat 9:30am from Boston, walk to inn.
To Gay Bars: 1 block to nearest bar, 1 min walk to afternoon tea dance.
Rooms: 12 rooms with single or double beds.
Bathrooms: 2 private bath/toilets. Others share bath/shower/toilets.
Meals: Continental breakfast in season.
Vegetarian: Health food restaurants nearby.
Complimentary: Coffee & juices available in common room daily in season.
Dates Open: All year.
High Season: June 20-September 5.
Rates: High season $40-$90, low season $25-$50.
Credit Cards: MC, VISA, Amex.
Rsv'tns: Recommended.
Reserve Through: Call direct.
Minimum Stay: Major holidays during high season.
Parking: Adequate free off-street parking. 6 spaces available on first-come basis.
In-Room: Maid service.
On-Premises: TV lounge, guest refrigerator.
Exercise/Health: Gym approximately a 10-minute walk from Inn.
Swimming: 15 min walk to gay beach, 1/2 block to bay beach.
Sunbathing: On common sun decks & nearby beaches.
Smoking: Not permitted.
Pets: Not permitted.
Handicap Access: No.
Children: Not especially welcome.
Languages: English, Spanish.
Your Host: Kevin.

Roomers

Gay/Lesbian ♂

Provincetown...the name alone evokes thoughts of a quaint fishing village surrounded by beautiful beaches and untamed sand dunes, fine restaurants and a shopper's paradise. *Roomers Guest House* maintains the charms of the past, but has the crisp, clean, contemporary feel of today. Each room is decorated with quality antiques and has private bath, queen-sized bed, ceiling fan, TV and refrigerator. Cozy and intimate...that's *Roomers'* style.

Address: 8 Carver St, Provincetown, MA 02657. Tel: (508) 487-3532.

Type: Guesthouse.
Clientele: Mostly men with women welcome.
Transportation: Free pickup from airport or ferry.
To Gay Bars: Gay bar across the street, others 1-3 blocks.
Rooms: 9 rooms with twin or queen beds.

Bathrooms: All private.
Meals: Continental breakfast.
Dates Open: All year.
High Season: Memorial Day weekend, July, August & Labor Day weekend.
Rates: In-season $95-$125, off-season $50-$85.
Credit Cards: MC, VISA,

Amex.
Rsv'tns: Required.
Reserve Through: Call direct.
Minimum Stay: 5 days in-season.
Parking: Free off-street parking, 1 space per room.
In-Room: Refrigerator, maid service, color

cable TV.
On-Premises: 2 common rooms.
Sunbathing: In side yard.
Smoking: Permitted without restrictions.
Children: Not permitted.
Languages: English.
Your Host: Andrew & Gary.

Rose & Crown Guest House

Gay/Lesbian ♀♂

Where if It's Worth Doing, It's Worth Over-Doing

The Rose & Crown is a classic Georgian square rigger, built in the 1780's. A ship's figurehead greets visitors from her post above the paneled front door. During restoration, wide floorboards were uncovered and pegged posts and beams exposed. An appealing clutter of Victorian antiques and art fills every nook. The front yard is quite festive. Its water garden and multiple colors make it the most photographed house in town.

Address: 158 Commercial St, Provincetown, MA 02657. Tel: (508) 487-3332.

Type: Guesthouse.
Clientele: Good mix of gay men & women with some straight clientele.
Transportation: Pick up from airport.
To Gay Bars: Across the street from men's, 3 blocks to women's.
Rooms: 6 rooms, 1 apartment & 1 cottage with single, queen or king beds.
Bathrooms: 5 private,

3 shared.
Meals: Continental breakfast.
Dates Open: All year.
High Season: Memorial Day thru September.
Rates: Rooms $30-$90, cottages & apts. $65-$150.
Discounts: Varies. Please inquire.
Credit Cards: MC, VISA, Diners.
Rsv'tns: Required in

season.
Reserve Through: Travel agent or call direct.
Minimum Stay: On particular holidays.
Parking: Limited pay parking.
In-Room: Color TV, ceiling fans & maid service. Kitchen in apartments & cottage.
Exercise/Health: Nearby gym.
Swimming: Nearby

ocean beach & pool.
Smoking: Permitted in room & outside. Not permitted in common rooms.
Pets: Permitted only in cottage.
Handicap Access: No.
Children: Not especially welcome.
Languages: English.
Your Host: Sam.

Rose Acre

Women ♀

A Provincetown Classic

and women's house offering rooms, apartments and a cottage. Enjoy the unhurried atmosphere of a rambling old-fashioned Cape house. Tucked down a private drive, *Rose Acre* offers decks, gardens, parking and a yard, and is always open. Brochure available.

Address: 5 Center St, Provincetown, MA 02657. Tel: (508) 487-2347.

continued next page

Type: Apartments, cottage & guest rooms.
Clientele: Women only.
Transportation: From Boston: car, plane (Cape Air) or ferry boat, pick up from airport, bus, ferry dock.
To Gay Bars: 1 block to gay bars.
Rooms: 2 rooms, 4 apartments & 1 cottage with double beds.

Bathrooms: All private.
Complimentary: Coffee, tea.
Dates Open: All year.
High Season: June, July & August.
Rates: Apts. & cottage $70-$140, rooms $65-$70.
Discounts: Off-season on request.
Rsv'tns: Preferred.
Reserve Through: Call direct.

Minimum Stay: 5 nights in high season.
Parking: Adequate off-street parking.
In-Room: Color cable TV, coffee/tea-making facilities. All apartments have full kitchens, rooms have use of kitchen & refrigerator.
Exercise/Health: Nearby gym.

Swimming: Ocean beach nearby.
Sunbathing: On the beach, common sun deck & in private yard.
Smoking: Permitted except in sleeping rooms in house.
Pets: Not permitted.
Handicap Access: No.
Children: Not permitted.
Languages: English.

Sandpiper Beach House

Gay/Lesbian ♀♂

The *Sandpiper* is a beautiful thirteen-room turreted Victorian guesthouse on the beach next to the world famous Boatslip. All rooms have private baths and color cable television, and several boast glass doors and private balconies overlooking the harbor. Most have lovely bay views. Complimentary off-street parking and morning coffee are available. Meet other house guests or play the piano in the lovely living room. Use of our private beach and the Boatslip's pool, sun cots, and free admission to Tea Dance at the Boatslip are also included. We are open year 'round and off-season rates are available. Please call or write for further information.

Address: 165 Commercial St, PO Box 646, Provincetown, MA 02657. Tel: Outside MA: (800) 354-8628 or (508) 487-1928.

Type: Guesthouse.
Clientele: Gay & lesbian. Good mix of men & women.
Transportation: Car is best, or taxi from airport.
To Gay Bars: Next door to men's & 2 blocks to women's bar.
Rooms: 10 rooms with double beds & 3 with queens.
Bathrooms: All private shower/toilets.
Meals: Continental breakfast in season.

Complimentary: Mints on pillows.
Dates Open: All year.
High Season: June 18th-Sept 9th.
Rates: $55-$130.
Discounts: Off-season rates available.
Credit Cards: MC, VISA & Discover.
Rsv'tns: Required in season. Strongly recommended off season.
Reserve Through: Call direct.
Minimum Stay: 6 nights

in season. Varies off season.
Parking: Adequate free off-street parking.
In-Room: Cable color TV, ceiling fans & maid service. Most have AC. Some with refrigerators.
On-Premises: Common room with piano, large veranda & patio.
Exercise/Health: Nearby gym, weights & massage.
Swimming: Pool next door in season. Ocean

beach.
Sunbathing: At poolside, on beach, private sun decks or patio.
Smoking: Permitted with some restrictions.
Pets: Not permitted.
Handicap Access: Limited accessibility.
Children: Permitted, but not recommended.
Languages: English.
Your Host: Dale.

IGTA

Sea Drift Inn

Men ♂

Sea Drift is a complex of two guesthouses catering to gay men. We're within walking distance of all restaurants, shops and bars. We provide such amenities as extra beach towels, parking passes, aspirin, hygienically-correct showers and items you might forget to pack. Eighteen double rooms with European-style shared baths have daily maid service. A private bar has ice, mixers and limes, stereo, TV/VCR with movies. BBQ facilities for guests are outside, as are a sundeck and expanded garden and patio. We serve continental breakfast and occasionally host cocktail parties.

Address: 80 Bradford St, Provincetown, MA 02657. Tel: (508) 487-3686.

Type: Guesthouse.
Clientele: Men only.
Transportation: Free pick up from Provincetown Airport.
To Gay Bars: 1 block to men's bars.
Rooms: 18 rooms with single or double beds.
Bathrooms: 5 shared bath/shower/toilets.
Meals: Continental breakfast.
Complimentary: Set-up service, ice.
Dates Open: All year.
High Season: July & August.
Rates: $30-$70.
Discounts: 10% on each night after 7 days.
Credit Cards: MC, VISA & Discover.
Rsv'tns: Highly recommended.
Reserve Through: Call direct.
Minimum Stay: 2 nights on weekends & 5 on holidays.
Parking: Limited, free, off-street parking.
In-Room: Maid, room & laundry service.
On-Premises: TV lounge & outside deck.
Swimming: 2 blocks to ocean beach.
Sunbathing: On deck or beach.
Smoking: Permitted without restrictions.
Pets: Not permitted.
Handicap Access: No.
Children: Not permitted.
Languages: English.
Your Host: Bill & Dick.

ShireMax Inn

Gay/Lesbian ♂

The *ShireMax Inn*, named for our two Samoyed-Husky dogs, is in its 10th season, and is known as your home away from home with that extra added comfortableness and charm. We're in the quiet west end, blocks from all bars, restaurants and shops and a few steps from private beaches on the bay. The apartments are large one- and two-bedroom units with sun deck, private entrance, color TV, VCR and telephone. The main house consists of seven large individually-decorated rooms, each with plenty of space for entertaining. Three rooms have double beds, one has 2 double beds. All have private baths and color TV, and the 3 rooms upstairs share king/queen and double beds. Most of our guests prefer the common room for socializing, cocktails, watching a selection of over 600 movies or sitting on a huge roofed front porch watching all the interesting people going by. We have a large sun deck where breakfast is served, weather permitting, and a beautiful side garden.

We have plenty of parking, but once here, you won't need a car. We're ready to answer any questions on where to go, what to do or where to eat. The kitchen, including refrigerator, is always at your disposal, as are the laundry facilities for longer staying guests. There is a gas grill, perfect for an intimate dinner for two, available to everyone. Reservations are a must, far in advance for Memorial Day weekend, 4th of July weekend and especially during Carnival Week. I am an innkeeper who can say I am very proud of my type of guests. Many come in as new guests and leave as friends whom we look forward to seeing over and over again. While at the Inn, we tend to all your needs and provide many extra amenities not offered by any other establishments. It takes extra work, but the rewards are proportional to happy guests.

Address: 5 Tremont St, Provincetown, MA 02657. Tel: (508) 487-1233 or (508) 487-4621.

continued next page

Massachusetts

Type: Guesthouse inn.
Clientele: Mostly men with women welcome.
Transportation: Free pick up from ferry, bus or airport.
To Gay Bars: 4 blocks to men's & 5 blocks to women's bars.
Rooms: 7 rooms & 2 apartments with double, queen or king beds.
Bathrooms: 4 private shower/toilets & 1 shared shower/toilet.
Meals: Expanded continental breakfast & snack.

Complimentary: Tea & coffee or BYOB. Set-ups provided.
Dates Open: April 15-Nov 1 & New Years weekend.
High Season: June 25-Sept 10th, Memorial Day weekend & New Years Eve.
Rates: Rooms $30-$85, apartments $500-$750 weekly. (3rd & 4th person $10 extra per night.)
Discounts: Nov 1-Mem Day, 3rd night free or stay 1 week and pay for 5 nights.
Credit Cards: MC & VISA.

Rsv'tns: Recommended 2 months in advance, in season.
Reserve Through: Call direct.
Minimum Stay: 3 days in June, 5-7 in July & Aug.
Parking: Ample free off-street parking.
In-Room: Color TV & VCR in apts. Rooms have maid service & limited laundry service (small fee).
On-Premises: Kitchen, TV lounge, guest phone, laundry facilities, in-house movies, iron,

ironing board, beach chairs, umbrellas & blankets.
Swimming: Ocean beach 1/2 block.
Sunbathing: On the beach, private or common sun deck.
Nudity: Permitted on private apartment decks only.
Smoking: Permitted without restrictions.
Pets: Pets permitted with prior arrangement.
Handicap Access: Limited.
Children: Not permitted.
Languages: English.

Six Webster Place

A 1750's Bed & Breakfast

Gay/Lesbian ♀♂

Six Webster Place is a newly restored 1750's bed and breakfast located on a quiet lane in the heart of historic Provincetown. This historic home is an ideal year-round retreat for guests who seek a small and intimate colonial atmosphere in the spirit and style of Ye Old New England. The architecture, layout and amenities are of a grace and character of a bygone era, recently improved for modern convenience and comfort (yes, indoor plumbing was installed in 1986). In addition to our traditional guest rooms with working fireplaces and private baths, we now offer luxury apartments as well.

Address: 6 Webster Place, Provincetown, MA 02657. Tel: (508) 487-2266, (800) 6-WEBSTER.

Type: Bed & breakfast.
Clientele: Mostly gay & lesbian with some straight clientele.
Transportation: Free pickup from airport, bus, ferry.
To Gay Bars: 1 block to men's/women's bars.
Rooms: 7 rooms, 2 suites & 3 apartments with double, queen or king beds.
Bathrooms: Private.

6 shower/toilets, 2 full baths. 2 shared full baths.
Meals: Expanded continental breakfast.
Vegetarian: All vegetarian.
Dates Open: All year.
High Season: June-October.
Rates: Summer $50-$95, winter $35-$75.
Credit Cards: MC, VISA, Amex & Discover.

Rsv'tns: Recommended.
Reserve Through: Travel agent or call direct.
Minimum Stay: 5 days in July & August.
Parking: Free off-street parking (1 space per rental).
In-Room: Maid service, color TV/VCR, ceiling fans. Most rooms have fireplaces.
On-Premises: TV lounge.
Swimming: Ocean beach,

bay beach.
Sunbathing: On beach, common sun decks & patio.
Smoking: Permitted without restrictions.
Pets: Not permitted.
Handicap Access: Studio apartment is accessible.
Children: Permitted in off-season.
Languages: English.

IGTA

Swanberry Inn, The

Gay/Lesbian ♀♂

Leave the Real World Behind!

A century-old restored Victorian sea captain's house, the *Swanberry Inn* is ideally located on a quiet side street in central Provincetown. Here, just a block from the harbor beach, many of our rooms have pleasant water views. All ten guestrooms are furnished with brass beds and have been uniquely decorated. Our attentive staff keeps the house meticulously clean and is ready to assist you with ideas and recommendations of things to do, or to allow you to discover P'town on your own. Leave the real world behind!

Address: 8 Johnson St, Provincetown, MA. Tel: (800) 847-7926 or (508) 487-4242.

Type: Bed & breakfast. **Clientele:** Good mix of gays & lesbians. **Transportation:** Take ferry or fly from Boston. Cars are unnecessary. Pick up from airport. **To Gay Bars:** 5 minutes by foot to men's & women's bars. **Rooms:** 10 rooms with single, double or queen beds. 5 rooms with 1 shared bath are men-only.

Bathrooms: 5 private. 1 shared bath with 2 showers, 2 sinks & 1 toilet. **Meals:** Continental breakfast. **Complimentary:** Iced tea in afternoon, mints on pillows. **Dates Open:** All year. **High Season:** Mid June through Labor Day. **Rates:** Summer $60-$100, winter $40-$75. **Discounts:** Off-season

specials vary from 10%-50%. Call for information. **Credit Cards:** MC & VISA. **Rsv'tns:** Recommended. **Reserve Through:** Travel agent or call direct. **Minimum Stay:** Required in-season. **Parking:** Adequate free off-street parking. **In-Room:** Color cable TV, AC, ceiling fans & maid service. **On-Premises:** TV lounge. **Exercise/Health:** Nearby

gym. **Swimming:** At the beach, less than 100 yards. **Sunbathing:** At the beach or poolside at nearby resort complex. **Smoking:** Permitted with some restrictions. Common space is non-smoking. **Pets:** Not permitted. **Handicap Access:** No. **Children:** Not especially welcome. **Languages:** English.

Three Peaks

A Victorian Bed and Breakfast

Gay/Lesbian ♀♂

Three Peaks is an 1870's Victorian house in the quiet East End, a few moments' walk from the art galleries, shops, restaurants, bars and entertainment of central Provincetown. Town beaches are a short block away, while the National Seashore, Herring Cove and Race Point can be easily reached by bicycle or, in season, the town "Loop" bus, which stops a few feet from our door. Rooms and apartments have double beds, private baths and TV. Park your car in our private lot.

Address: 210 Bradford St, Provincetown, MA 02657. Tel: (800) 286-1715 or (508) 487-1717.

Type: Bed & breakfast. **Clientele:** Good mix of gays & lesbians. **Transportation:** Free pick up from airport, bus or ferry dock. **To Gay Bars:** 10 minutes by foot. **Rooms:** 3 rooms & 1 apartment with double beds.

Bathrooms: All private bath/toilets. **Meals:** Continental breakfast. **Dates Open:** All year. **High Season:** Memorial Day weekend through Labor Day weekend. **Rates:** In-season $80-$105, rest of year $50-$85.

Discounts: Mid-season & off-season specials. **Credit Cards:** MC & VISA. **Rsv'tns:** Recommended for high season. **Reserve Through:** Call direct. **Minimum Stay:** 2-3 nights. 4 nights for holidays & special events. **Parking:** Ample free off-

street parking. **In-Room:** Color cable TV & refrigerator. **On-Premises:** Common room/reading room, outdoor patio/deck, lawn sitting areas & bicycle racks. **Exercise/Health:** Nearby gym, tennis, bicycle

continued next page

rental & bicycle trails. **Swimming:** One block to bay beach. **Sunbathing:** On patio/deck & nearby beach. **Smoking:** Permitted outside only. **Pets:** Not permitted. **Handicap Access:** No. **Children:** Not especially welcome. **Languages:** English.

Trade Winds Inn

Gay/Lesbian ♂

Trade Winds Inn is one of the most friendly and gracious inns you'll find. Each room has a special charm, some with poster beds and antiques, others with brass beds or designer wicker furniture. The suite has vaulted ceilings and fridge. Most rooms have private baths, color TV and VCR. Meet other guests at our late-afternoon cocktail hour. We're conveniently located a few steps from Commercial St., with free parking.

Address: 12 Johnson St, Provincetown, MA 02657. Tel: (508) 487-0138, Fax: (508) 487-9484.

Comfortable, Attractive Rooms and Cottage. Centrally Located, Ample Parking. Open Year Round.

12 Johnson St., Provincetown, MA 02657
(508) 487-0138

Type: Guesthouse.
Clientele: Mostly men with women welcome.
Transportation: Use car, airport bus or ferry.
To Gay Bars: 3 blocks to men's or women's bars.
Rooms: 1 single, 14 doubles & 1 cottage.
Bathrooms: 11 private, 5 shared.
Meals: Continental breakfast.
Complimentary: Afternoon cocktail mixes provided, BYOB.
Dates Open: All year.
High Season: June 15th-September 15th. Memorial Day weekend.
Rates: Summer $40-$120, off-season $65.
Discounts: Off-season specials, please ask.
Credit Cards: MC, VISA & Amex.
Rsv'tns: Required.
Reserve Through: Travel agent or call direct.
Minimum Stay: 5 nights over weekends in high season.
Parking: Ample free off-street parking.
In-Room: Color TV, VCR, maid service & refrigerator.
On-Premises: TV lounge, public telephone, patio.
Exercise/Health: Exercise room on premises, whirlpool.
Swimming: Ocean beach within walking distance.
Sunbathing: On ocean beach or patio.
Smoking: Permitted without restrictions.
Pets: Not permitted.
Handicap Access: No.
Children: Not permitted.
Languages: English.
Your Host: Jim & Bruce.

Watermark Inn

Gay-Friendly 50/50 ♀♂

Located in Provincetown's quiet east end, we have created the ultimate vacation place. Outside, the *Watermark Inn* retains the charm of traditional New England architecture, but on the inside, you'll find ten magnificent, contemporary-styled suites. The inn is right on the beach, with more than 80 feet of private deck for lounging and sunning.

Address: 603 Commercial St, Provincetown, MA 02657. Tel: (508) 487-0165, Fax: (508) 487-2383.

Type: Inn.
Clientele: 50% gay & lesbian & 50% straight clientele.
Transportation: Car, ferry boat, plane or bus.
To Gay Bars: Walking distance to gay & lesbian bars.
Rooms: 10 suites with queen or king beds.
Bathrooms: All private.
Dates Open: All year.
High Season: Memorial Day-late October.
Rates: $65-$275.
Discounts: Weekly rates.
Credit Cards: MC, VISA & Amex.
Rsv'tns: Recommended.
Reserve Through: Call direct.
Minimum Stay: In summer and on holidays.
Parking: 1 off-street space per suite.
In-Room: Maid service, color TV, kitchen, telephone & refrigerator.
Exercise/Health: Nearby health club.
Swimming: Bay beach in front of inn.
Sunbathing: On beach or private sundecks.
Smoking: Permitted without restrictions.
Pets: Not permitted.
Handicap Access: Inquire.
Languages: English.

Watership Inn

Gay/Lesbian ♂

A home to ship captains in the seafaring days of the 1820's, *Watership Inn* is now a comfortable inn. Enjoy the fresh, salt air, clean skies and bright, Cape Cod sunshine. Walk the beaches or cycle the miles of trails through the dunes. *Watership Inn* is half a block from the harbor, right in the center of town, close to everything, yet on a quiet sidestreet. Current renovations at the inn will add a widow's walk on the highest roof. From here, guests will be able to see all of Provincetown and 20 miles in three directions.

Address: 7 Winthrop St, Provincetown, MA 02657. Tel: (508) 487-0094

Type: Bed & breakfast. **Clientele:** Mostly men with women welcome. **To Gay Bars:** 2 blocks to all gay bars. **Rooms:** 14 rooms & 1 apartment with double beds. **Bathrooms:** 14 private shower/toilet, others share.

Meals: Expanded continental breakfast. **Complimentary:** Ice & mixers. **Dates Open:** All year. **Rates:** Rooms $28-$92, apartment $60-$130 per night. **Credit Cards:** MC, VISA, Amex & Discover. **Rsv'tns:** Required.

Reserve Through: Call direct. May call through travel agent in winter. **Minimum Stay:** Required on some holiday weekends. **Parking:** Ample free parking. **In-Room:** Maid service, some color TVs, 1 ceiling fan.

Swimming: At nearby pool & ocean beach. **Sunbathing:** On private & common sun decks. **Smoking:** Permitted without restrictions. **Pets:** Not permitted. **Handicap Access:** No. **Children:** Not permitted. **Languages:** English.

West End Inn

Gay/Lesbian ♀♂

Opening in May, 1995

Located in the quiet West End, this 1850 Greek Revival house features various types of accommodation. These include private baths, shared baths, a suite with harbor views and private sun deck, and apartments. A ten-minute walk along a manicured, garden-lined waterfront gets you to the town center or the beach. At the *West End Inn* an expanded continental breakfast is served daily. In town, there are wa-

terside tea dances, discos and entertainment complexes and bars. Interesting activities include whalewatching and biking through the dunes.

Address: 44 Commercial St, Provincetown, MA 02657. Tel: (508) 487-9555, (800) 559-1220.

Type: Bed & breakfast & 2 fully-equipped apartments. **Clientele:** Mostly gay & lesbian with some straight clientele. **Transportation:** Free pickup from airport, bus or ferry. **To Gay Bars:** 10-minute walk to men's & women's bars. **Rooms:** 4 rooms, 1 suite & 2 fully-equipped apts

for 2-4 guests. Single, double, queen or king beds. **Bathrooms:** 4 private baths & 3 private sinks. 1 shared full bath. **Meals:** Expanded continental breakfast. **Dates Open:** May-October. **High Season:** Memorial Day weekend, mid-June-Labor Day. **Rates:** $45-$145.

Credit Cards: MC, VISA. **Rsv'tns:** Required. **Reserve Through:** Travel agent or call direct. **Minimum Stay:** 5 nights in season. **Parking:** Limited free parking. **In-Room:** Maid service. Rooms with private bath have refrigerators. TV/VCR in suite & apartments. **On-Premises:** TV lounge.

Swimming: Small ocean beach across the street, gay beach 15-min. walk. **Sunbathing:** On beach, private sun decks. **Smoking:** Not permitted at breakfast table. **Pets:** Not permitted. **Handicap Access:** No, 3 stairs. **Children:** Not permitted. **Languages:** English. **Your Host:** Warren.

Willows, The

More Than A Guesthouse

Gay/Lesbian ♀♂

The Willows is a unique guest complex in the peaceful west end, with privacy and parking on one of the largest parcels of land in Provincetown, nearly an acre. Sun umbrellas, tables and chairs are placed around the grounds, and breakfast is served on the front lawn. Rooms, suites and luxurious, fireplaced apartments all have private baths and daily housekeeping service. We're within easy walking distance of the beaches, the center of town, shops, restaurants, art galleries and the wharf, with its fishing fleet, sightseeing boats and whale watching excursions.

Address: 25 Tremont St, PO Box 937 Provincetown, MA 02657. Tel: (508) 487-0520

Type: Guest complex.
Clientele: Good mix of men & women.
Transportation: Car, bus, ferry from Boston, air from Boston or New York; free pick up from airport, bus, ferry dock.
To Gay Bars: 3-5 minute walk.
Rooms: 5 rooms, 4 suites, 7 apartments & 1 cottage with single, double or queen beds.
Bathrooms: All private.
Meals: Continental breakfast, home baked

muffins, loaf cakes & coffee bars during high season, weather permitting.
Dates Open: February 1- November 30.
High Season: June 17- September 8, Memorial Day weekend.
Rates: Summer $90- $150, spring/fall $55-$115, winter $55- $95.
Discounts: 10% for stays of 2 weeks or longer.
Credit Cards: MC & VISA.
Rsv'tns: Required.

Reserve Through: Call direct.
Minimum Stay: 5 nights Jul 4, Labor Day; 3 in season, Memorial Day; 2 for apts w/fireplaces (off-season)
Parking: Adequate, free off-street parking, 1 space per rental unit.
In-Room: Color cable TV, maid service, ceiling fans, kitchen, refrigerator.
On-Premises: Ice-making machine (excluding winter).
Exercise/Health: Nearby

gym with weights & massage.
Swimming: At nearby ocean or bay beach.
Sunbathing: On the grounds & at nearby ocean or bay beach.
Smoking: Permitted except in office.
Pets: Not permitted.
Handicap Access: No.
Children: Permitted at times, discouraged during summer, inquire.
Languages: English.
Your Host: Michael & Paul.

Windamar House

We Have A Way With Women

Gay/Lesbian ♀

Windamar is one of Provincetown's most beautiful, historical, seaside properties. It stands on half an acre with colorful English flower gardens and manicured lawns. This mini-estate is directly across from Cape Cod Bay in the quiet east end. From the moment you step into Windamar's elegant, two-story entrance hall and take the winding staircase to one of her fine guest rooms, you know that you are in a very special place. Every detail in this stately home, circa 1840, has been lovingly attended to. Each room has its own unique decor, tastefully wallpapered and filled with antiques and original artwork. The front rooms have water views and the others views of the gardens. No matter the location of your room, you have a pleasant view of a natural setting. One of the most popular accommodations is the dramatic studio room that features a cathedral ceiling, an entire wall of glass overlooking the gardens and an antique carved bed. The penthouse apartment has expansive water views, skylights, exposed beams and cathedral ceiling...a wonderful mix of old and new. The centrally-located common room offers guests a pleasant mingling space and use of refrigerator, microwave and cable TV with VCR. Continental breakfast features fresh-baked muffins and breads. It's only a 15-minute walk through the east end gallery district to the downtown area, just far enough away from the hustle-bustle, but close enough to enjoy the nightlife, restaurants, shops and galleries that Provincetown offers. Provincetown Tennis Club is a 3-minute walk. At low tide, guests can take a romantic stroll on the tidal flats directly across the street and view the town from a totally different vantage point. The clientele is mostly women, with men most welcome. In the off-season, the entire house can be booked for reunions, special events, small conferences or seminars.

Address: 568 Commercial St, Provincetown, MA 02657. Tel: (508) 487-0599

Type: Bed & breakfast guesthouse.	**Meals:** Continental breakfast.	direct.	Bay 300 feet directly across the street. Nearby
Clientele: Mostly women with men welcome. Some straight clientele off season.	**Vegetarian:** Provincetown has a lot available for vegetarians.	**Minimum Stay:** 5 nights on July 4th & Labor Day, 4 nights Memorial Day.	ocean beach.
		Parking: Ample free off-street parking. Full	**Sunbathing:** On Windamar's exceptional estate-like grounds or at
Transportation: Car or plane. Free pick up from	**Dates Open:** All year. **High Season:** June 15-	private lot at rear of the property.	the beach.
airport, bus or ferry dock.	September 15.	**In-Room:** Maid service.	**Smoking:** Permitted in common areas.
To Gay Bars: 20-minute leisurely walk.	**Rates:** Summer: rooms $60-$125; apts $750-$850	**On-Premises:** TV/VCR lounge, common room	**Pets:** Not permitted. **Handicap Access:** No.
Rooms: 6 room & 2 fully-equipped apart-	per week. Off season: rooms to $85; apts $85-	with refrigerator & mi- crowave.	**Children:** Not permitted. **Languages:** English &
ments with double or queen beds.	$110 per day. **Discounts:** Off season,	**Exercise/Health:** 3- minute walk to tennis	French. **Your Host:** Bette & Jan.
Bathrooms: 4 private shower/toilets. 4 rooms	long stays, or booking the whole house.	club. Massage can be ar- ranged.	**IGTA**
share 3 baths.	**Rsv'tns:** Required. **Reserve Through:** Call	**Swimming:** Cape Cod	

WILLIAMSTOWN

River Bend Farm

Peaceful, Welcoming, Romantic

Gay-Friendly 50/50 ♀♂

River Bend Farm is one of the loveliest places in New England, an authentic 1770 Georgian Colonial whose great, stone chimney contains five separate fireplaces. Big, antique beds, hand-woven spreads, soft, thick towels and crisp linens, turned back at night, set a tranquil tone of luxurious country comfort. Mouth-watering full breakfasts feature farm fresh granola, honey and jam and home-baked breads and muffins. Hiking, skiing, swimming, golf, Williamstown Theater Festival, Tanglewood and other Berkshire cultural attractions are nearby. **Address: 643 Simonds Rd, Williamstown, MA 01267. Tel: (413) 458-3121, (800) 418-2057.**

Type: Bed & breakfast.	**Transportation:** Car or	hours.	shared baths.
Clientele: 50% gay &	bus. Free pick up from	**Rooms:** 1 single & 4	**Meals:** Full breakfast.
lesbian & 50% straight	bus.	doubles.	Other meals by arrange-
clientele.	**To Gay Bars:** 1-1/2	**Bathrooms:** 2 large	ment.

continued next page

Massachusetts

Vegetarian: Available upon special request. **Complimentary:** Fresh apple cider or lemonade, depending on season. **Open:** All year. **High Season:** Sep-Oct. **Rates:** $70-$100, depending on the number of persons per room. **Credit Cards:** MC, VISA, Amex & Discover. **Rsv'tns:** Preferred & a good idea! **Reserve Through:** Call direct. **Minimum Stay:** On holiday & college weekends or October foliage weekends. **Parking:** Ample, free off-street parking. **Swimming:** Nearby pool. Naturally fed springs nearby (1/2 mile). **Sunbathing:** On lawn & hammocks. **Smoking:** Permitted outside on porch only. **Handicap Access:** No. **Pets:** Not permitted. **Children:** Permitted if well-behaved. **Languages:** English, Spanish & some French. **Your Host:** Jeff & Bob.

MICHIGAN

SAUGATUCK & DOUGLAS

Campit

Gay/Lesbian ♂

Where Friendly People Camp

When visiting Saugatuck, gay & lesbian campers can stay in an all gay-operated, all gay and lesbian campground located just 7 miles from Saugatuck's gay beach and 6 miles from the gay bars. *Campit* features all the usual amenities, such as mini-store with ice and soft drinks, modern bath and shower facilities and a game room. We're also near a supermarket, so it's easy to make a run for that one item you forgot to pack.

Address: 6635 118th Ave, Fennville, MI 49408. Tel: (616) 543-4335

Type: Campground. **Clientele:** Mostly men with women welcome. **Transportation:** Car is best. **To Gay Bars:** 10 minutes to men's/women's bars in Saugatuck. **Rooms:** 60 campsites. **Dates Open:** May 1st-Nov 1st. **Rates:** $10 per person, $3 per night for electric. **Discounts:** Group rates. **Rsv'tns:** Required on holiday weekends. **Reserve Through:** Call direct. **Minimum Stay:** 3 nights on holidays. **Parking:** Plenty of off-street parking. **On-Premises:** TV lounge & laundry facilities. **Exercise/Health:** Free weights. **Swimming:** At the lake in Saugatuck. **Pets:** Permitted, if on leashes. **Handicap Access:** No, steps up to restrooms. **Children:** Not permitted. **Languages:** English.

Deerpath Lodge

Women ♀

An Enchanting Retreat

Deerpath is a striking contemporary redwood lodge set on a dune overlooking the Kalamazoo River. The river and 45 wooded acres seclude this quiet women-only retreat from public access. Saugatuck, the infamous art colony and mecca of innovative shops and restaurants, is just 5 minutes by car, longer by boat. The lodge is close to Lake Michigan beaches, marina, golf, galleries, gay bars, excellent cross-country ski trails and great shopping. Saugatuck is a year-round tourist town. Winter Holiday & "Ski & Snuggle" packages are available.

Address: PO Box 849, Saugatuck, MI 49453. Tel: (616) 857-DEER(3337).

Type: Bed & breakfast guesthouse. **Clientele:** Women only. **Transportation:** Auto. Free pick up from bus. **To Gay Bars:** 6 miles. **Rooms:** 3 rooms with king beds. **Bathrooms:** 1 private shower/toilet & 2 private bath/shower/toilets. **Meals:** Full breakfast. **Vegetarian:** Available upon request.

Complimentary: Occasional cocktails. **Dates Open:** All year. **High Season:** June, July, August. **Rates:** $80-$90. **Discounts:** Early prepayment, group booking. **Rsv'tns:** Required. **Reserve Through:** Call direct. **Minimum Stay:** Required. **Parking:** Ample off-street

parking. **In-Room:** AC. 1 kitchenette with refrigerator & coffee/tea-making facilities. **On-Premises:** Meeting rooms. **Exercise/Health:** Jacuzzi, Nordic Track, Exercycle. Massage nearby. **Swimming:** Nearby lake. **Sunbathing:** Riverside or at the beach. **Nudity:** Nude beach

nearby. **Smoking:** Permitted outside. Non-smoking rooms available. **Pets:** Not permitted. **Handicap Access:** Yes. Main floor suite w/assistance. Bathroom not wheelchair accessible. **Children:** Welcome only if carefully supervised. **Languages:** English. **Your Host:** Linda & Dianne.

Douglas Dunes Resort

Gay/Lesbian ♀♂

Douglas Dunes Resort is located in the Saugatuck/Douglas area, along the Lake Michigan shoreline. Accommodations range from deluxe motel rooms and cottage suites to steam bath-style rooms. Guests can lounge at our large heated pool with bar service, dine at our award-winning *Cafe Sir Douglas,* dance the evening away in our disco, enjoy entertainment in the cabaret, or just relax in our bistro bar or garden deck. In winter, enjoy cross-country skiing or snowmobiling. **Address: 333 Blue Star Highway, Douglas, MI 49406. Tel: (616) 857-1401.**

Type: Motel with restaurant, bar & disco. **Clientele:** Good mix of gay men & women. **Transportation:** Car is best. Bus, Amtrak, airport in Grand Rapids. **To Gay Bars:** On premises. **Rooms:** 23 rooms, 23 steam bath-style rooms, 3 suites & 10 cottages with double or king beds.

Bathrooms: 36 private bath/toilets. Steam bath-style have showers, share baths. **Vegetarian:** Available upon request. **Dates Open:** All year. **High Season:** Summer. **Rates:** Winter $48, summer $25-$125. **Credit Cards:** MC, VISA, Amex, Diners & Discover. **Rsv'tns:** Required.

Reserve Through: Travel agent or call direct. **Minimum Stay:** Weekends package. **Parking:** Ample off-street parking. **In-Room:** Color TV, AC, telephone, ceiling fans, maid & room service. **On-Premises:** Meeting rooms, TV lounge. **Exercise/Health:** Nearby gym.

Swimming: Pool on premises, 1/2 mi to lake. **Sunbathing:** At poolside. **Smoking:** Permitted. **Pets:** Permitted with deposit & not left alone. **Handicap Access:** Yes. **Children:** Permitted. **Languages:** English.

IGTA

Kirby House, The

Gay/Lesbian ♀♂

A beautifully-restored 105-year-old Victorian manor on the state historical registry, *The Kirby House* is known for its comfortable elegance, warm hospitality and sumptuous breakfast/brunch buffets. Entirely furnished with turn-of-the-century antiques, the house becomes an adventure into days gone by. The establishment offers a beautiful, secluded pool, hot tub and sunning decks overlooking acres of woodland. *The Kirby House* is more than a place to stay, it's a place to linger.
Address: PO Box 1174, Saugatuck, MI 49453. Tel: (616) 857-2904.

continued next page

Michigan

Type: Bed & breakfast. **Clientele:** Mostly gay & lesbian with some straight clientele. **Transportation:** Car is best. Free pick up from Amtrak, bus and airport. **To Gay Bars:** 4 blocks to gay bars. **Rooms:** 8 rooms with single, double or queen beds. **Bathrooms:** 6 private & 2 share. **Meals:** Full breakfast buffet. **Vegetarian:** Available upon request. **Dates Open:** All year. **High Season:** June through October. **Rates:** $65-$85 per day wkdys & off-season wknds, $75-$100 per day summer weekends. **Discounts:** 10% on extended stays and vacation packages. Sun-Thurs package-5 nights for price of 4. **Credit Cards:** MC, VISA, Amex & Discover. **Rsv'tns:** Required. **Reserve Through:** Travel agent or call direct. **Minimum Stay:** 3 nights July & August wknds. 2 nights other wknds. **Parking:** Ample off-street parking. **In-Room:** Maid service & ceiling fans. **On-Premises:** Courtesy telephone, kitchen privileges, ice & gas BBQ. **Exercise/Health:** Bicycles, Jacuzzi & X-country skis. **Swimming:** Pool or lake. **Sunbathing:** At poolside, lakeside or on common sun decks. **Nudity:** 2 miles to nude beach. **Smoking:** Permitted in common areas. **Pets:** Permitted with restrictions. **Handicap Access:** No. **Children:** Permitted weekdays with prior arrangement. **Languages:** English. **Your Host:** Loren & Marsha.

Moore's Creek Inn

Where Friendships Are Formed

Gay/Lesbian ♀♂

Saugatuck is a quaint, little village 3 hours from Detroit and 2 1/2 from Chicago. It's known as a popular beach resort for gays and lesbians and as an artistic haven, and it has a large selection of specialty shops. *Moore's Creek Inn* is an old-fashioned farmhouse, over 100 years old. Rooms are decorated in different themes: The Erte Elegance room is filled with Erte prints. Walt's Woom has Disney paraphernalia. The Teddy Bear Den features small

and large stuffed bears. Two gathering rooms have grand piano, movie library and a 50-inch TV.

Address: 820 Holland St, Saugatuck, MI 49453. Tel: (616) 857-2411, (800) 838-5864.

Type: Bed & breakfast. **Clientele:** Mainly gay & lesbian with some straight clientele. **Transportation:** Car is best. Free pick up from airport. **To Gay Bars:** 3 miles or ten-minute drive. **Rooms:** 4 rooms with single or double beds. **Bathrooms:** 4 private shower/toilets. **Meals:** Full breakfast. **Vegetarian:** Cold or hot cereals, fruit & cheese. **Complimentary:** Tea, coffee, mixes for cocktails (no alcohol). Evening wine & cheese tasting. **Dates Open:** All year. **High Season:** May-September. **Rates:** Summer $75-$85, winter $65-$75. **Discounts:** Four or more days, 10% off, full occupancy party 10% off. **Credit Cards:** MC, VISA. **Rsv'tns:** Required. **Reserve Through:** Travel agent or call direct. **Minimum Stay:** 2 days in season. **Parking:** Ample off-street parking. **In-Room:** Ceiling fans. **On-Premises:** Meeting rooms, TV lounge. **Exercise/Health:** Massage at nearby salon. **Swimming:** At nearby lake. **Sunbathing:** On the beach. **Smoking:** Permitted in 1st floor gathering rooms only, not in bedrooms. **Pets:** Not permitted. **Handicap Access:** No. **Children:** Not encouraged. **Languages:** English. **Your Host:** Clif & Fred.

Take along the Expert

Ferrari's Places of Interest™ contains articles contributed by gay and lesbian journalists on the scene, giving insight into gay and lesbian communities worldwide. With its accompanying directory, it's the perfect vacation planner.

Newnham SunCatcher Inn

Gay/Lesbian ♀♂

Newnham SunCatcher Inn is on a secluded lot in the heart of Saugatuck's business district, close to shops, restaurants, recreation and the lake beaches. The turn-of-the-century home with wraparound porch, complete with gingerbread carvings, has been carefully restored to the grandeur of its day. Period furniture once again graces its 5 bedrooms. Behind the main house, a small cottage provides more private accommodations. Features are a large sun deck, hot tub and swimming pool.

Address: 131 Griffith Box 1106, Saugatuck, MI 49457. Tel: (616) 857-4249.

Type: Bed & breakfast.
Clientele: Mostly gay & lesbian with some straight clientele.
Transportation: Free pick up from airport, train.
To Gay Bars: 3-minute drive to gay/lesbian bars.
Rooms: 5 doubles, 1 cottage (cottage is a guest house with complete facilities & sleeps 6).
Bathrooms: 3 private, others share.

Meals: Full breakfast.
Complimentary: Tea, coffee, juices, mints on pillow.
Dates Open: All year.
High Season: May-October.
Rates: Rooms $65-$85 weekdays & off-season weekends, $75-$100 summer weekends, cottage call for prices.
Discounts: During off-season.
Credit Cards: MC, VISA.

Rsv'tns: Required.
Reserve Through: Call direct.
Minimum Stay: 2 nights on weekends.
Parking: Ample free off-street parking.
In-Room: Maid, room & laundry service, AC.
On-Premises: Common room, meeting room, TV lounge, telephone, kitchen available.
Exercise/Health: Jacuzzi.
Swimming: In-ground

heated swimming pool.
Sunbathing: At poolside or on private sun decks.
Nudity: 3 mi to nude beach.
Smoking: Permitted on outside deck only.
Pets: Not permitted.
Handicap Access: No.
Children: Permitted weekdays only.
Languages: English.

MINNESOTA

DULUTH

Stanford Inn

Gay-Friendly ♀♂

The *Stanford Inn* is an elegant Victorian home built in 1886. There is natural woodwork and hardwood floors throughout and the entrance is graced by a hand-carved oak staircase and an eight-foot stained glass window. The 4 bedrooms are all charmingly decorated with period antiques, the suite has a private bath, and all accommodations include complete gourmet breakfast and room service coffee. We are located two blocks from Leif Erickson Park, the Rose Garden, Lake Superior, and within walking distance of shops and restaurants.

Address: 1415 E Superior St, Duluth, MN 55805. Tel: (218) 724-3044.

Type: Bed & breakfast.
Clientele: Mainly straight clientele with a gay & lesbian following.
Transportation: Car is best.
Rooms: 3 rooms & 1 suite.
Bathrooms: 1 private & 2 shared.
Meals: Full gourmet breakfast & room service

coffee.
Vegetarian: Available upon request.
Complimentary: Coffee, tea, & juices.
Dates Open: All year.
High Season: May through Oct.
Rates: $65-$95.
Discounts: For weekdays (Sun-Thur), groups, also corporate rates.

Credit Cards: MC, VISA, Amex & Discover.
Rsv'tns: Required.
Reserve Through: Call direct.
Parking: Adequate off-street & on-street parking.
In-Room: Room service.
On-Premises: TV lounge.
Exercise/Health: Sauna.
Swimming: Lake 2

blocks. Creek 1 mile.
Sunbathing: On the beach.
Smoking: Permitted on the porch.
Pets: Not permitted.
Handicap Access: No.
Children: Permitted in the suite.
Languages: English.

HINCKLEY

Dakota Lodge

Gay-Friendly 50/50 ♀♂

Dakota Lodge, completely renovated in 1991, is comfort and elegance set on nine acres in beautiful east-central Minnesota. With a rustic exterior and a gracious interior, the lodge was designed for privacy and comfort. Bedrooms, individually decorated with antiques and comfortable furniture, have queen beds and private baths. Some rooms have whirlpools and fireplaces. *Dakota Lodge* offers a TV lounge, library, and a living room with fireplace. Tired of relaxing? We're near a Vegas-style casino, two state parks, a paved 37-mile bike trail, and great cross-country ski trails.

Address: Rt 3, Box 178, Hinckley, MN 55037. Tel: (612) 384-6052.

Type: Bed & breakfast.
Clientele: 50% gay & lesbian & 50% straight clientele.
Transportation: Car is best, no charge for bus pick up service.
To Gay Bars: 1-1/2 hrs to gay bars by car.
Rooms: 5 rooms with queen beds.
Bathrooms: All private.
Meals: Full breakfast.

Vegetarian: Available upon prior arrangement.
Complimentary: Tea, coffee, fruit juices.
Dates Open: All year.
Rates: $58-$110 double occupancy.
Discounts: Groups, 3 or more days.
Credit Cards: MC, VISA & Discover.
Rsv'tns: Required.
Reserve Through: Travel

agent or call direct.
Parking: Ample, free off-street parking.
In-Room: AC, antiques, 4 rooms with fireplaces, maid service. Some rooms with whirlpool.
On-Premises: TV lounge, living room with fireplace, piano, library.
Exercise/Health: Whirlpools in some rooms.
Swimming: At nearby

lake.
Smoking: Permitted in TV lounge & some guest rooms, non-smoking rooms available.
Pets: Not permitted.
Handicap Access: Common areas & 1 guest room fully accessible.
Children: OK with prior arrangement.
Languages: English.
Your Host: Mike & Tad.

KENYON

Dancing Winds Farm

Women ♀

Where the Relaxed & Unexpected are a "Whey" of Life!

Imagine a relaxed, country setting with goats frolicking in the pastures and women working in the cheese plant and on the farm. We are proud to be Minnesota's first Farmstead Goat Cheese Plant and purveyors of quality-tasting, award-winning, low-fat/low-sodium fresh cheeses.

You can watch us milking the goats, making the cheeses, or just kick back and enjoy the peaceful surroundings. Long walks, star-gazing, bicycling, canoeing, swimming, x-country skiing, snowshoeing or reading by the stone fireplace are what *Dancing Winds Farm* is all about!

Address: 6863 Co. #12 Blvd, Kenyon, MN . Tel: (507) 789-6606.

Type: Bed & breakfast, campground with licensed cheesery on farmstead.
Clientele: Women only.
Transportation: Car is best.
To Gay Bars: 60 miles to Minneapolis & 40 miles to Rochester gay/lesbian bars.
Rooms: 1 room & 1 suite with double, or queen beds.

Bathrooms: Private bath/shower/toilet & shared shower/toilet.
Campsites: 3 tent sites with shower & toilet available. Evening bonfires upon request.
Meals: Full breakfast, fresh goat's milk & cheeses. Specialty is goat cheese omelets & fresh biscuits!

Vegetarian: Available upon request.
Complimentary: Tea, coffee, juices.
Dates Open: All year.
High Season: Feb-Mar, summer months & early spring for kidding season.
Rates: Rooms (including breakfast) $50 for two, $25 for one. Campsites (two persons per site) $10, breakfast extra

charge.
Discounts: Work exchange available.
Credit Cards: MC, VISA.
Rsv'tns: Required at most times.
Reserve Through: Call direct.
Parking: Ample, free off-street parking.
In-Room: Heat and ceiling fans.
On-Premises: TV lounge,

VCR & fireplace. Laundry facilities at extra charge. **Exercise/Health:** Massage upon request. Gym & weights nearby.

Swimming: Pool, river & reservoir nearby. **Sunbathing:** Yard & patio. **Smoking:** Permitted outdoors only.

Pets: Permitted by previous permission ONLY. **Handicap Access:** 1st floor with help. Otherwise, no. Old farmhouse.

Children: Permitted by previous permission only. **Languages:** English, limited French. **Your Host:** Mary.

MINNEAPOLIS & ST PAUL

Abbotts Como Villa

Fit For a King, But Made For a Queen

Gay/Lesbian ♀♂

Abbotts Como Villa is one of two gay-owned bed and breakfasts in the Twin Cities area. Built in 1873, this 3,500 square foot home sits on a half-acre wooded yard. Inside, the parlor, with crystal chandeliers, velvet drapes and a grand piano, is yours to enjoy. Choose one of four guest rooms, furnished with antiques. Located one block from 450-acre Como Park with a free zoo, golf course, jogging trails, swimming pool and Lake Como. We are 15 minutes from the airport and Mall of America and a short drive to bars.

Address: 1371 W Nebraska Ave, St Paul, MN 55108. Tel: (612) 647-0471.

Type: Bed & breakfast. **Clientele:** Mostly gay & lesbian with some straight clientele. **Transportation:** Car is easier, but busline is nearby. **To Gay Bars:** 1-1/2 miles. **Rooms:** 4 rooms. **Bathrooms:** 1 room with private shower. 2 rooms share shower. **Meals:** Continental

breakfast Monday-Thursday, full breakfast on weekends. **Vegetarian:** Available upon request. **Complimentary:** Coffee, juice, tea, soda & cookies. **Dates Open:** All year. **Rates:** $65 weekdays, $70-$78 weekends. **Discounts:** On longer stays. **Credit Cards:** VISA, MC &

Discover. **Rsv'tns:** Required. **Reserve Through:** Travel agent or call direct. **Parking:** Ample free off-street parking in horseshoe driveway. **In-Room:** AC, maid & room service. Color TV & VCR available upon request. **On-Premises:** TV lounge, baby grand piano &

covered porches. **Exercise/Health:** Gym nearby. **Swimming:** 6 blocks to pool. **Smoking:** Permitted outside only. **Pets:** Not permitted. **Handicap Access:** No. **Children:** Not permitted. **Languages:** English. **Your Host:** Ron.

Brasie House

A Comfortable Retreat in a Great City!

Gay-Friendly 50/50 ♀♂

Brasie House is a 1913 vintage Craftsman house located in a great "walking" area of fine, old homes, interesting shops and some of the city's most popular restaurants and coffee houses. Downtown clubs, the Lakes, the Guthrie Theater and Walker Sculpture Garden are all close by. The decor, complete with resident cats, is a whimsical blend of turn-of-the-century, Oriental, traditional, contemporary, Victorian, antiques and eclectic tchotchkes. Breakfast, featuring fresh baked goods and homemade jams, can be served in the urban garden with brick patio or on the balcony overlooking the garden.

Address: 2321 Colfax Ave S, Minneapolis, MN 55405. Tel: (612) 377-5946.

continued next page

Minnesota

Type: Bed & breakfast.
Clientele: 50% gay & lesbian & 50% straight clientele.
Transportation: Taxi is best. Airport shuttle to Hyatt, then cab or #17 bus to Brasie House.
To Gay Bars: 3 miles or 15 minutes by car. 10 miles or 30 minutes to St Paul bars.
Rooms: 3 rooms with double or queen beds. 1 room with fireplace.
Bathrooms: 2 shared bath/shower/toilets.
Meals: Expanded veg-etarian continental breakfast.
Vegetarian: Several restaurants within 4 blocks of B&B.
Complimentary: Tea/coffee-making facilities & guest refrigerator.
Dates Open: All year.
High Season: May-October.
Rates: $49-$70.
Discounts: 7th night 1/2 price, frequent-stay discount & whole house rental discount.
Credit Cards: MC, VISA, Amex.

Rsv'tns: Required.
Reserve Through: Call direct or reserve through travel agent.
Minimum Stay: 2 days on weekends during high season.
Parking: Adequate free on-street parking, off-street available.
In-Room: AC & maid service. Fireplace in one room. Telephone by request.
On-Premises: TV lounge with VCR & classic movie collection.
Exercise/Health: Nearby gym, weights, sauna, Jacuzzi, steam & massage.
Swimming: At nearby river & lakes.
Sunbathing: On common sun deck or nearby beach.
Smoking: Not permitted.
Pets: Not permitted, cats in residence.
Handicap Access: No. Guest rooms are upstairs on 2nd floor.
Children: Not especially welcome.
Languages: English.

Country Guest House, The

Gay/Lesbian ♀

Country Comfort

We're located in the scenic St. Croix valley along the Minnesota/Wisconsin border, 30 minutes from St. Paul. The *Guest House* is secluded, nestled on a 20-acre hobby farm with some farm animals. On the property, leisurely stroll along groomed walking trails, take a row boat ride on the wildlife pond, sunbathe in the nude, or cross-country ski. Just minutes away, enjoy the old river towns, inner tube down the famous Apple River, downhill ski at several nearby resorts and visit Minneapolis/St Paul.

Address: 1673 38th St Somerset, WI 54025. Tel: (715) 247-3520.

Type: Guesthouse.
Clientele: Mostly women with men welcome.
Transportation: Car is best.
To Gay Bars: 30 minutes by car.
Rooms: 2-bedroom cottage with double beds.
Bathrooms: All private shower/toilets.
Complimentary: Coffee & tea.
Dates Open: All year.
Rates: $75 per night.
Discounts: On weekly stay.
Rsv'tns: Required.
Reserve Through: Call direct.
Minimum Stay: 2 nights on weekends & holidays.
Parking: Ample free parking.
In-Room: Stereo, telephone, kitchen, refrigerator, coffee/tea-making facilities.
Exercise/Health: Walking trails & row boat.
Sunbathing: Anywhere.
Nudity: Permitted anywhere on the property.
Smoking: Permitted without restrictions.
Pets: Not permitted.
Handicap Access: No.
Children: Not especially welcome.
Languages: English.
Your Host: Myra & Lynette.

Eagle Cove Bed and Breakfast

Gay/Lesbian ♀♂

One Hour From Mpls, 5 Hrs from Milwaukee, 7 Hrs From Chicago

Panoramic views of Lake Pepin, the widest spot on the Mississippi River, and the Rush River Valley become yours, as you climb the winding ridge road to *Eagle Cove*. At this scenic six-acre country getaway, guests enjoy relaxing by the fireplace, biking on nearby developed trails, antiquing in quaint river towns, walking on groomed trails among the wildlife, or cross-country skiing from the doorstep. Eagle sightings are best in early and late winter.

Address: Box 65, W 4387 120th Ave, Maiden Rock, WI 54750. Tel: (800) 467-0279, (715) 448-4302.

Type: Bed & breakfast.
Clientele: Mostly gay & lesbian with some straight clientele.
Transportation: Car is best. Pick up from airport in Minneapolis $40 per trip.
To Gay Bars: 65 miles or

a 75-minute drive.
Rooms: 4 rooms with double, queen or king beds.
Bathrooms: 2 shared baths, 2 rooms with private sink/vanity.
Meals: Expanded continental breakfast.
Vegetarian: Always no meat for expanded continental breakfast.
Dates Open: All year.

High Season: Memorial Day through October 31. October is most popular.
Rates: High season $40-$100.
Discounts: Free night with 6 room rentals. Group discounts.
Credit Cards: VISA.
Rsv'tns: Required.
Reserve Through: Call direct.
Minimum Stay: 2 night

minimum Sept/Oct weekends.
Parking: Ample free parking.
In-Room: Color TV, VCR, video tape library, AC, refrigerator & maid service.
On-Premises: Fireplace lounge.
Exercise/Health: Outdoor spa.
Sunbathing: On patio, common sun deck &

6 acre ridgetop.
Nudity: Permitted in spa at discretion of other guests.
Smoking: Permitted outdoors only.
Pets: Permitted with $50 deposit.
Handicap Access: Yes. All rooms wheelchair accessible.
Children: Adult retreat.
Languages: English.

MISSOURI

KANSAS CITY

Doanleigh Wallagh Inn

Gay-Friendly ♀♂

Doanleigh Wallagh Inn is a haven for people seeking the ultimate B&B experience. Guests are invited to use the first floor's two living rooms, two dining rooms and complimentary snack bar. Five guest rooms are on the second floor, with private bath, king or queen bed, and appointed with European and American antiques, cable TV and telephone. Some rooms have a porch or fireplace. Ed and Carolyn help guests find the right activities, restaurants, and shopping to make their Kansas City trip memorable. Enjoy the beauty that has been used for Hallmark cards and for Younkers and Jones store ads.

Address: 217 East 37th St, Kansas City, MO 64111. Tel: (816) 753-2667 or Fax: (816) 753-2408.

Type: Bed & breakfast.
Clientele: Mostly straight clientele with a gay & lesbian following.
Transportation: Car is best. Free pick up from train station with advance notice. Possible pick up from airport shuttle stops.
To Gay Bars: 2 blocks to nearest gay/lesbian bar. 5 minutes by foot or car to others.
Rooms: 5 rooms with queen or king beds.

Bathrooms: 1 private bath/toilet & 4 private shower/toilets.
Meals: Full breakfast.
Vegetarian: Upon advance notice.
Complimentary: Homemade cookies, fruit juices, soda & snacks.
Dates Open: All year.
High Season: December.
Rates: $80-$110.
Discounts: Long-term rates available.
Credit Cards: MC, VISA, Amex.

Rsv'tns: Required.
Reserve Through: Travel agent or call direct.
Minimum Stay: 2 nights some holiday weekends.
Parking: Ample free off-street parking.
In-Room: Maid service, color cable TV, telephone & AC.
On-Premises: Meeting rooms, TV lounge & laundry facilities. Fax, computer hookup on phones.
Exercise/Health: 5-minute

drive to Golds gym.
Sunbathing: In the backyard.
Smoking: Permitted in 1st floor living rooms. Sleeping rooms non-smoking.
Pets: Not permitted.
Handicap Access: No.
Children: Permitted, please inquire.
Languages: English, some French & Romanian.
Your Host: Ed & Carolyn.

Take along the Expert

Ferrari's Places of Interest™ contains articles contributed by gay and lesbian journalists on the scene, giving insight into gay and lesbian communities worldwide. With its accompanying directory, it's the perfect vacation planner.

ST LOUIS

Brewers House Bed & Breakfast

Gay/Lesbian ♀♂

Brewers House is a Civil War-vintage home, whose location amidst several breweries, is minutes from downtown and only blocks from bars, restaurants and shops. Some rooms feature fireplaces and unusual items. The hot tub in the intimate garden area offers total privacy. Enjoy a view of downtown from the deck. Visit the Soulard Market, a colorful open-air market established in 1790, or Anheuser-Busch, home of the world's largest brewery (free tours include the Clydesdales and beer tasting), or take a ride to the top of the Gateway Arch.

Address: 1829 Lami Street, St. Louis, MO 63104. Tel: (314) 771-1542.

Type: Bed & breakfast.
Clientele: Good mix of gays & lesbians.
Transportation: Car is best or cab from Transit Station. Free pick up from train.
To Gay Bars: 7 blocks or 1/2 mile. 15 minutes by foot, 5 minutes by car.
Rooms: 3 with double or king beds.

Bathrooms: 1 private bath/toilet, 1 private sink & 1 shared bath/shower/toilet.
Meals: Expanded continental breakfast.
Vegetarian: Available upon request. Restaurant nearby.
Complimentary: Coffee always available.
Dates Open: All year.

Rates: $50-$55.
Discounts: 7th day free.
Credit Cards: MC & VISA.
Rsv'tns: Recommended.
Reserve Through: Travel agent or call direct.
Parking: Ample parking.
In-Room: Color cable TV, AC, ceiling fans, maid service & laundry service.
On-Premises: TV lounge.
Exercise/Health: Jacuzzi.

Sunbathing: On common sun decks.
Nudity: Permitted in Jacuzzi in secluded garden.
Smoking: Permitted.
Pets: Permitted, but call ahead.
Handicap Access: No.
Children: Permitted.
Languages: English.

Napoleon's Retreat Guest House Bed & Breakfast

Gay-Friendly 50/50 ♀♂

Follow Napoleon...Retreat in Style!

Napoleon's Retreat, an elegantly-appointed second-empire townhouse dating to the 1880's, is in St. Louis's Lafayette Square, one of the nation's oldest historical districts. In our three spacious bedrooms, guests enjoy the elegant ambiance of antiques along with conveniences such as color TV's and telephones. From *Napoleon's Retreat,* one can visit St. Louis's restored Union Station shopping and entertainment complex, Busch Stadium and Brewery, the Gateway Arch and riverfront park, Cherokee St., Antique Row and the world-renowned Missouri Botanical Gardens, as well as enjoy excellent dining.

Address: 1815 Lafayette Ave, St Louis, MO 63104. Tel: (314) 772-6979.

Type: Bed & breakfast guesthouse.
Clientele: 50% gay & lesbian & 50% straight clientele.
Transportation: Car. From airport 20 minutes on Hwy 70.
To Gay Bars: 5 blocks or 1 mile. 20-minute walk or 5-minute drive.
Rooms: 2 rooms & 1 suite with double or queen beds.

Bathrooms: All private.
Meals: Full breakfast.
Vegetarian: Breakfast available with prior notification. Meals at nearby restaurants.
Complimentary: Beer, wine, tea, coffee & juices.
Dates Open: All year.
Rates: $65-$80.
Credit Cards: MC, VISA & Discover.
Rsv'tns: Required.

Reserve Through: Travel agent or call direct.
Parking: Ample on-street parking.
In-Room: Color cable TV, AC, ceiling fans, telephone, maid & room service.
On-Premises: Meeting rooms.
Exercise/Health: 2 miles to YMCA with gym, weights, Jacuzzi, sauna, steam & massage.

Swimming: Pool at YMCA.
Sunbathing: On the roof.
Smoking: Permitted outside only.
Pets: Not permitted.
Handicap Access: No.
Children: Welcomed.
Languages: English.
Your Host: Michael & Jeff.

St. Louis Guesthouse in Historic Soulard

Come Home to St. Louis

Gay/Lesbian ♂

The St. Louis Guesthouse, in historical Soulard, is tucked between downtown, Busch Stadium, the Anheuser Busch Brewery and the Farmers Market. A gay bar and restaurant are next door. Of the eight apartments in the building, two are available as guest suites. Each has large rooms, a private bath, wet bar with refrigerator and a private entrance opening onto a pleasant courtyard. If your visit to St. Louis is for business or pleasure, please consider *The St. Louis Guesthouse* your home away from home.

Address: 1032-38 Allen Ave, St Louis, MO 63104. Tel: (314) 773-1016.

ST. LOUIS

GUESTHOUSE

In Historic Soulard

St. Louis Mo.

Type: Guesthouse.
Clientele: Mostly men with women welcome.
Transportation: Car is best. Free pick up from airport, bus or train.
To Gay Bars: Next door.
Rooms: 2 suites with double beds.
Bathrooms: All private shower/toilets.
Complimentary: Coffee, tea & hot chocolate always available.
Dates Open: All year.
Rates: $50.
Discounts: Weekly rate.
Credit Cards: Amex & Discover.
Rsv'tns: Required.
Reserve Through: Call direct.
Parking: Ample free off-street & on-street parking.
In-Room: Color cable TV, VCR, closed circuit porn, ceiling fans, kitchen, refrigerator, coffee/tea-maker, telephone (free local calls), maid service & laundry service.
On-Premises: Laundry facilities & BBQ.
Exercise/Health: Non-sexual massage is $40 for 1 hour.
Sunbathing: On the patio.
Smoking: Permitted.
Pets: Not permitted.
Handicap Access: No.
Children: Not permitted.
Languages: English.

We Appreciate Your Comments!

The editors of **INN Places**® actively seek your comments about accommodations you have tried.

Positive comments of interest may be included in the next issue, giving future readers the benefit of your experience. And it's a nice way of saying "thank you" to an innkeeper who extended you exceptional hospitality.

See the contents for the Reader Comment Form.

NEVADA

For Lake Tahoe area listings, see Lake Tahoe Area California

LAS VEGAS

Las Vegas Private Bed & Breakfast

Gay/Lesbian ♂

Lucky You!

My home, *Las Vegas Private Bed & Breakfast,* features a unique, European décor with lots of amenities. Outside are tropical plants and trees around the pool area. Further back are the aviaries, with tropical birds and parrots. Las Vegas has 24-hour entertainment. Other activities: desert sightseeing, water sports on Lake Mead, private sailboats with catered dining, Grand Canyon tours in a private plane, Laughlin excursions, alpine mountain tours, winter skiing, and hiking to hot springs along the Colorado River.

Address: Las Vegas, NV . Tel: (702) 384-1129.

Type: Bed & breakfast.

Clientele: Mostly men with women welcome.
Transportation: Pick up from airport at minimal charge.
To Gay Bars: 5-block walk to gay bars.
Rooms: 2 rooms & 1 suite with queen or king beds.
Bathrooms: 2 shared full bathrooms, one with whirlpool. Outside hot/ cold shower.
Meals: Full breakfast & evening snack, other

meals by request.
Vegetarian: Available upon request.
Complimentary: Cocktail, etc.
Dates Open: All year.
High Season: Spring & late summer, holidays.
Rates: One person $59, double $49 per person, triple $12 add'l.
Discounts: 25% after 7-day stay.
Credit Cards: All major cards accepted.
Rsv'tns: Required.

Reserve Through: Travel agent or call direct.
Minimum Stay: Week-end 2 nights, Saturday arrival OK.
Parking: On-street parking.
In-Room: Color cable TV, VCR, AC, ceiling fans, room service & laundry service.
On-Premises: Meeting rooms, laundry facilities.
Exercise/Health: Jacuzzi & sauna.
Swimming: Pool on pre-

mises.
Sunbathing: At poolside or on the patio.
Nudity: Permitted without restrictions.
Smoking: Permitted outdoors in most areas.
Pets: Not permitted.
Handicap Access: No, not wheelchair accessible.
Children: Not permitted.
Languages: English, German, French, Danish, Swedish & Norwegian.

NEW HAMPSHIRE

ASHLAND

Country Options

Gay-Friendly 50/50 ♀♂

Our location in the foothills of the White Mountains makes *Country Options* an easily accessible getaway destination. We're just two hours from Boston and visitors are assured abundant natural beauty and diverse outdoor activities year-round. We are on the main street of a busy little village with shops, restaurants and a bike rental/repair shop nearby. The area offers a challenging golf course and unspoiled Squam Lake, where *On Golden Pond* was filmed. The inn offers a comfortable, relaxed atmosphere, antique decorations and newly-decorated common areas and bathrooms.

Address: 27-29 N Main St, Ashland, NH 03217. Tel: (603) 968-7958.

Type: Bed & breakfast.
Clientele: 50% gay & lesbian & 50% straight clientele.
Transportation: Car is best. We will pick up from bus station in Plymouth.
To Gay Bars: 1 hour to Manchester gay/lesbian bars.

Rooms: 5 rooms with double beds.
Bathrooms: 2 shared bath/shower/toilets.
Meals: Full breakfast.
Vegetarian: Upon request.
Dates Open: All year.
High Season: Fall foliage.
Rates: Singles $35, doubles $45-$50.

Rsv'tns: Recommended.
Reserve Through: Call direct.
Minimum Stay: 2 nights on holiday weekends.
Parking: Adequate free off-street parking.
In-Room: Self-controlled heat.
On-Premises: TV lounge.
Swimming: River, lake or

nearby indoor pool.
Sunbathing: On nearby beach or in small backyard area at the inn.
Smoking: Permitted outdoors.
Pets: Not permitted.
Handicap Access: No.
Children: Permitted, but infants not encouraged.
Languages: English.

BATH VILLAGE

Evergreen Bed and Breakfast

Gay/Lesbian ♂

Come OUT to the White Mtns. & Enjoy Our GAY-ONLY B&B!

Come, enjoy our hot tub room with stone walls, mirrored exercise area and BYOB pub. There's always lots to do, indoors or out. Browse for moose, hike, ski, tube the river, bike, antique, etc....etc. Set in a large, circa 1822 home, *Evergreen B&B* is comfortably furnished with an eclectic mix of antiques. Some guest rooms have working fireplaces. Our modest rates include a full breakfast and lots of gay country hospitality. "Spend a night, a week, or longer if you can. I guarantee you'll never want to leave..." *Lifestyles, Apr., '93.*

Address: Bath Village, NH 03740. Tel: (603) 747-3947.

Type: Bed & breakfast with BYOB bar.
Clientele: Mostly men with women welcome
Transportation: Car is best, can arrange pick up from bus.
To Gay Bars: 90 miles to Sherbrooke, Canada gay/lesbian bar, 3 hours to Montreal.
Rooms: 5 rooms with double beds, 2 with fireplaces.
Bathrooms: 2 shared, 1

private.
Meals: Full breakfast.
Vegetarian: Upon request.
Complimentary: Cocktail set-ups, coffee, teas.
Dates Open: All year.
High Season: Fall foliage & summer, February for skiers.
Rates: $40-$69.
Discounts: Weekly rates.
Rsv'tns: Recommended.
Reserve Through: Call direct.

Minimum Stay: 2 nights on holiday weekends.
Parking: Ample, free off-street parking.
In-Room: Maid service, ceiling fans.
On-Premises: Meeting rooms, TV lounge, music room & BYOB pub.
Exercise/Health: Hot tub & work-out bench on premises, full gym nearby.
Swimming: River & lake nearby.

Sunbathing: Private sunbathing area.
Nudity: Permitted in sunbathing & hot tub area.
Smoking: Permitted only on porch.
Pets: Not permitted.
Handicap Access: No.
Children: Not permitted.
Languages: English, limited Spanish, French, German.

BETHLEHEM

Highlands Inn, The

Women ♀

A Lesbian Paradise!

At the end of a half-mile driveway on 100 scenic mountain acres, *The Highlands Inn* sits majestically above beautiful mountain and valley views. A 200-year-old lovingly-restored farmhouse, the facilities have been operated as a country inn for over 100 years. Peace, privacy, total relaxation and warm New England hospitality await you.

100 Acres • Pool
Hot Tub • Trails

20 Charming Rooms
Peace & Privacy

The Highlands Inn

P.O. Box 118
Bethlehem, NH 03574
(603) 869-3978

A LESBIAN PARADISE

Fifteen miles of trails, for walking hand-in-hand or cross-country skiing in winter, grace the property. An enormous heated pool with sun deck is a gathering place for swimmers and sun-worshippers alike.

The 20 charming guest rooms are individually decorated with antiques and comfortable furniture and most have private baths. Spacious common areas include a large living room with fireplace and many sitting areas, a well-stocked library, an enormous sunny breakfast room, a TV/VCR area with an excellent gay/lesbian video collection, and a wicker-filled enclosed wrap-around porch. Our private hot tub/Jacuzzi is perfect after a day of cross-country skiing or hiking.

We're open year-round with special holiday celebrations, lesbian commitment ceremonies and special events.

The atmosphere of the inn is warm and friendly. We're large enough for plenty of mixing and mingling, but also large enough to get away by yourselves if that's your desire. Conveniently located, we're just 2-1/2 hours from Boston and the Maine coast, 4-1/2 hours from Provincetown and 3 hours from Montreal.

Come enjoy spectacular fall colors, super winter skiing, lush mountain springtime and all summer sports. We're here for you year-round—A Lesbian Paradise! Try to arrive before sunset as sunsets at the inn are spectacular.

Address: Box 118 (IP), Bethlehem, NH 03574. Tel: (603) 869-3978.

Type: Bed & breakfast inn.
Clientele: Women only. A Lesbian Paradise.
Transportation: Car is best. Closest major airport: Manchester, NH 1-1/2 hrs. Free pick up from bus.

To Gay Bars: 1-1/2 hours to gay/lesbian bars.
Rooms: 19 rooms & 1 cottage with double or queen beds.
Bathrooms: 14 private bath/toilets. Shared: 2 bath/shower/toilets, 1 toilet only.

Meals: Deluxe continental breakfast.
Vegetarian: Breakfasts don't include meat. Vegetarian options at most local restaurants.
Complimentary: Lemonade, cider, popcorn, pretzels, coffee & tea.

Dates Open: All year.
High Season: Summer, fall & winter weekends.
Rates: Rooms $55-$110.
Discounts: For longer stays varying seasonally (ex. 20% off 7-night stay year-round, except holidays).

Credit Cards: MC & VISA. **Rsv'tns:** Recommended. (Sign always says No Vacancy. Ignore it if driving by without reservations). **Reserve Through:** Call direct or travel agent. **Minimum Stay:** On in-season weekends 2 nights. Longer on holidays. **Parking:** Ample free parking. **In-Room:** Self-controlled heat & maid service. Some rooms have kitchens available & some have TVs/VCRs. Video tape library, refrigerator, coffee & tea-making facilties. **On-Premises:** TV lounge, VCRs, use of the farmhouse's full kitchen, library, piano, BBQ grills, stereo & boardgames. **Exercise/Health:** Hot tub, Jacuzzi & lawn games. Massage can be arranged. **Swimming:** Heated pool, nearby rivers & lakes. **Sunbathing:** On common sun deck or at poolside. **Smoking:** Permitted. Some areas & rooms are smoke-free. **Pets:** Permitted in certain rooms, with prior arrangement. **Handicap Access:** Yes. **Children:** Permitted with a gay parent. **Languages:** English.

IGTA

CENTRE HARBOR

Red Hill Inn

Gay-Friendly ♀♂

Quiet, Peaceful and Secluded, Yet Close to Everything...

The *Red Hill Inn* is a restored estate on sixty acres overlooking the White Mountains and Squam Lake. Two hours north of Boston, our 21 individually decorated guest rooms offer beautiful views of fields, woods or mountains. In the fall, the foliage is spectacular, as the trees in the Sandwich Range turn bright colors and the lakes turn a brilliant blue.

All of our rooms have private baths and telephones for your convenience, and are decorated with beautiful antiques. Many have fireplaces, and some also have romantic Jacuzzis so situated that you can see the fireplace while in them! Some suites have sitting rooms in addition to the bedroom and bath.

We're located in the heart of the Lakes Region, at about the center of New Hampshire. During the winter months, we have cross-country ski trails right outside the front door, and rent equipment for those who want to try it out! We're twenty minutes from downhill skiing as well. Swimming, boating, golf and tennis are all within a mile of us, and antique and craft shops are in every direction. And don't forget, there's no sales tax in NH!

The inn boasts a wonderful restaurant, where everything is made from scratch, and a small lounge where we have a fireplace and weekend entertainment. Chef Elmer Davis was featured in the May issue of *Yankee* magazine. He takes great pride in cooking the old fashioned way, with care.

We've been open since 1985 and are proud to have created a place where everyone feels at home. The inn is our home, and all are welcome. Our clientele is mixed, men and women, gay and straight. We hope that you will come to see the beautiful New Hampshire countryside and experience an authentic country inn! **Address: RFD #1, Box 99M, Centre Harbor, NH 03226. Tel: (603) 279-7001.**

Type: Inn with bar and restaurant, cross-country ski trails. **Clientele:** Mostly straight clientele with a gay/lesbian following. **Transportation:** Car is best. Free pick up from airport or bus. **To Gay Bars:** 90-minute drive to Manchester gay/ *continued next page*

lesbian bars.
Rooms: 17 rooms, 3 suites & 1 cottage with single, double, queen or king beds.
Bathrooms: All private.
Meals: Full breakfast.
Vegetarian: On our menu nightly.
Dates Open: All year.
High Season: Mid-June through November 1st.

Rates: $85-$145.
Discounts: For longer stays.
Credit Cards: MC, VISA, Amex, Diners, Carte Blanche & Discover.
Rsv'tns: Helpful.
Reserve Through: Travel agent or call direct.
Minimum Stay: 2 nights on weekends in season.
Parking: Ample free

parking.
In-Room: Telephone & maid service. 5 rooms have Jacuzzis & 13 have fireplaces.
On-Premises: Private dining rooms, meeting rooms, TV lounge, public telephone & central heat.
Exercise/Health: 5 rooms have Jacuzzis.

Swimming: At nearby lake.
Sunbathing: On beach.
Smoking: Permitted without restrictions.
Pets: Not permitted.
Handicap Access: No.
Children: Well-behaved only!
Languages: English.

IGTA

FRANCONIA

Bungay Jar

Gay-Friendly ♀

Built from an 18th century barn, *Bungay Jar* has six large guest rooms or suites with beautiful mountain or woodland views. Welcoming touches in your room are lavish linens, handmade quilts, ornate beds and comfortable chairs or a desk for reading and writing. Breakfast specialties include oatmeal pancakes with pure maple syrup, popovers and fresh fruit salads. Enjoy private balconies, lush gardens, waterlily pond and walks thru woods to a hidden stream without a neighbor in sight. Near all major White Mountains attractions, but off the beaten path.

Address: PO Box 15 Easton Valley Rd, Franconia, NH 03580. Tel: (603) 823-7775.

Type: Bed & breakfast.
Clientele: Mostly straight. Strong lesbian following, especially in winter, men always welcome.
Transportation: Car is best.
To Gay Bars: 15 min from Highland Inn.
Rooms: Cottage with 6 rooms, single, double, queen or king beds.
Bathrooms: Private: 2 bath/toilet, 2 shower/

toilet. 1 shared shower/ toilet/sink.
Meals: Full breakfast & afternoon tea & snacks.
Vegetarian: All breakfasts (meat served separately). Please inform us of dairy product intolerance.
Complimentary: Afternoon snack with tea.
Dates Open: All year.
High Season: July-October.
Rates: Winter $60-$100,

fall foliage $75-$120, summer $65-$105.
Discounts: Inquire.
Credit Cards: MC, VISA, Discover.
Rsv'tns: Advised.
Reserve Through: Call direct.
Minimum Stay: 2 nights weekends & holidays.
Parking: Ample, off-street parking (15 acres).
In-Room: Maid service.
On-Premises: Fireplace, common area, tele-

phone.
Exercise/Health: Sauna, hiking trails. Massage by appointment.
Swimming: At nearby pool, river, lake.
Nudity: Permitted in private, 2-person sauna.
Smoking: Not permitted.
Pets: Not permitted.
Handicap Access: No.
Children: Permitted over age 6.
Languages: English.

Horse & Hound Inn, The

Gay-Friendly ♂

Off the beaten path at the base of Franconia's Cannon Mountain and adjacent to White Mountains National Forest and the Franconia Notch State Park is one of New England's finest traditional inns. Visitors to the *Horse & Hound* are treated to a quiet, relaxed atmosphere of pine paneling, three cozy fireplaces and comfortable guest rooms. The area supports plenty of activities such as hiking, boating, cross-country skiing, antiquing, and sightseeing. There are also bluegrass festivals, chamber music concerts, craft demonstrations, and museums.

Address: 205 Wells Rd, Franconia, NH 03580. Tel: (603) 823-5501, (800) 450-5501.

Type: Bed & breakfast inn with restaurant & lounge.
Clientele: Mostly straight clientele with a gay male following.
Transportation: Car is best.
To Gay Bars: 1-1/2 hrs to Manchester, NH, 2-1/2 hrs to Boston, MA.
Rooms: 8 rooms & 2 suites with double, queen or king beds.
Bathrooms: Private: 7 bath/toilets, 1 shower/

toilet. 2 shared bath/shower/toilet.
Meals: Full breakfast & dinner with map.
Vegetarian: Always available.
Dates Open: Closed April/early May & November till Thanksgiving.
High Season: Fall foliage Sep 15-Oct 15 & ski time Dec 26-Mar 31.
Rates: Spring/summer $50-$110 & fall/winter $60-$120.
Discounts: AAA, seniors

with AARP. Mention *Inn Places* for 20% discount Sun-Thur, 10% Fri-Sat.
Credit Cards: MC, VISA, Amex, Diners & Discover.
Rsv'tns: Preferred.
Reserve Through: Travel agent or call direct.
Parking: Ample free off-street parking.
In-Room: Window fans & maid service.
On-Premises: TV lounge, VCR in lobby & laundry facilities.
Exercise/Health: Gym

with nautilus 12 miles.
Swimming: 1-1/2 mi to lake, $2.50 fee.
Sunbathing: On grassy backyard.
Smoking: Permitted except in dining room & lobby.
Pets: Permitted, $10 charge.
Handicap Access: No.
Children: Permitted, additional charge.
Languages: English.
Your Host: Bill & Jim.

HART'S LOCATION

Notchland Inn, The

Gay-Friendly ♀♂

A Magical Location... Naturally Secluded

Get away from it all, relax and rejuvenate at our comfortable 1862 granite mansion located on 400 acres in the midst of beautiful mountain vistas. *The Notchland Inn* rests atop a knoll at the base of Mount Bemis and looks out upon Mounts Hope and Crawford.

Within *The Notchland Inn,* experience the comforts and pleasures of attentive and friendly hospitality! Settle in to one of our seven guest rooms or four spacious suites, each individually appointed and all with woodburning fireplaces and private baths. The front parlor is a perfect place to sit by the fire and read or to visit with other guests. The music

continued next page

room draws guests to the piano, or to the stereo to listen to music they personally select. The sun room offers a great place to sip your coffee and read a novel or just enjoy the great views.

In the evening, *Notchland's* wonderful 5-course dinner is served in a romantic, fireplaced dining room looking out to the gazebo by our pond. Our Chef creates a new menu each day, her elegant flair respecting the traditional while exploring the excitement of international cuisines. Morning brings a bountiful country breakfast to fuel you for the adventures of the day.

Nature's wonders abound at *Notchland* and include 8,000 feet of Saco River frontage and two of the area's best swimming holes. The Davis Path hiking trail starts just across the road from the Inn. Other activities to enjoy are mountain biking, cross-country skiing, snowshoeing, fishing, or soaking in the wood-fired hot tub which sits in a gazebo by the pond. For animal lovers there's a Burnese Mountain Puppy, two Belgian draft horses, a miniature stallion and two llamas.

Nearby attractions include: Crawford Notch, ski areas, shopping at North Conway's antiques, arts & crafts, and factory outlet stores, and the Mount Washington Auto Road & Cog Railway.

Address: Hart's Location, NH 03812-9999. Tel: Reservations: (800) 866-6131 or (603) 374-6131, Fax: (603) 374-6168.

Type: Inn with restaurant.
Clientele: Mostly straight clientele with a gay & lesbian following.
Transportation: Car is best. Free pick up from bus.
To Gay Bars: 2 hours to Manchester, NH. 2+ hours to Portland, ME.
Rooms: 7 rooms & 4 suites with single, double, queen or king beds.
Bathrooms: 6 private shower/toilets & 5 private bath/shower/toilets.
Meals: Full breakfast & dinner.

Vegetarian: Available with advance notice (dinners by reservation, prepared to order). All dietary restrictions considered.
Complimentary: Chocolate, apples, fruit, coffee, tea, cider juices. Various treats at various times.
Dates Open: All year.
High Season: Foliage (Sep 15-Oct 20) & Christmas to New Year (Dec 23-Jan 1).
Rates: Per person per night MAP double occupancy: mid-week $73-$85, Fri-Sat $78-$90, Holiday & foliage $85-$105.

Discounts: 3, 4 & 5 night mid-week packages (per person per package, MAP, double occupancy) $180-$325.
Credit Cards: MC, VISA, Amex & Discover.
Rsv'tns: Subject to prior booking.
Reserve Through: Travel agent or call direct.
Minimum Stay: Required at times.
Parking: Ample free off-street parking.
In-Room: Maid service, some ceiling fans.
On-Premises: Meeting rooms.
Exercise/Health: Spa,

massage by appointment. Nearby gym, weights, Jacuzzi, sauna, steam, massage, skiing, sleigh & carriage rides.
Swimming: River on premises. Nearby pool, river & lake.
Sunbathing: On patio, lawns or at the beach.
Smoking: Non-smoking environment.
Pets: Not permitted.
Handicap Access: No.
Children: Mature children only. No TV. Many animals & outdoor activities.
Languages: English.
Your Host: Les & Ed.

NORTH CONWAY & CHOCORUA

Mt. Chocorua View House Bed & Breakfast

Gay-Friendly ♀♂

Mt. Chocorua View House is a beautifully-renovated 17-room home built 150 years ago in the quaint village of Chocorua. The open-beam ceilings and open staircase add charm to this century-and-a-half old home that has housed Emily Post, President Franklin Roosevelt and others. The woodburning Franklin fireplace, paddle fans and porches make you feel like you're in a home away from home. Centered in the White Mountains, you are minutes away from lakes for swimming and canoeing, mountains to ski or hike, shopping outlets or just plain relaxing.

Come and partake of the many activities nearby or just relax in the quiet, comfortable surroundings of yesteryear and discover the hospitality and serenity of Chocorua.

Address: Rte 16, PO Box 348 Chocorua, NH 03817-0348. Tel: (603) 323-8350.

Type: Bed & breakfast with breakfast & lunch restaurant.
Clientele: Mainly straight with some gay & lesbian clientele.
Transportation: Car is best. Bus stop about 2000 ft. Pick up from bus.
To Gay Bars: 1 hour to Manchester or Portsmouth, NH, or Portland & Ogunquit, ME.
Rooms: 6 rooms & 1 suite with single or double beds.
Bathrooms: 1 private full bath. Shared: 1 full bath, 1 shower/toilet, 1 toilet.
Meals: Expanded continental breakfast.
Vegetarian: Available.
Complimentary: Coffee, tea, juice, cokes, hot chocolate, & lemonade. Set-ups always available.
Dates Open: All year.
High Season: July to September. October/November for autumn foliage.
Rates: $55-$145, $10 per additional person. Autumn foilage season, $69-$145.
Credit Cards: MC, VISA, Amex, & Discover.
Rsv'tns: Requested for priority confirmation.
Reserve Through: Call direct.
Parking: Ample free parking.
In-Room: Ceiling fans.
On-Premises: TV lounge, guest living room, dining room, kitchen, & enclosed porch. Cable TV in living room.
Exercise/Health: Boating.
Swimming: Lake Chocorua & White Mt. State Park lake 2 miles, Silver Lake 3 miles.
Sunbathing: On common sun decks & lawn in back of inn.
Smoking: Permitted in designated areas.
Pets: Well-behaved pets permitted.
Handicap Access: No.
Children: Permitted.
Languages: English & German.
Your Host: Eric.

NEW JERSEY

ATLANTIC CITY

Ocean House

Men ♂

Let It All Hang Out at Our Oasis!

During its long history *Ocean House* has served both as a private home and as a convent. Since 1964, this 125-year-old house has been a guest house exclusively for men. It is located in the heart of Atlantic City, within easy walking distance of most casinos. The bars are just a few blocks away and the beach is right down the street. We extend a special welcome to men who are active in A.A. fellowship. Relax and enjoy a friendly, comfortable environment in the middle of this fast-paced casino city. We will do our utmost to make your stay an enjoyable one.

Address: 127 S Ocean Ave, Atlantic City, NJ 08401-7202. Tel: (609) 345-8203.

Type: Guest house.
Clientele: Men only.
Transportation: From Amtrak & the municipal bus terminal: jitney (mini bus) on Pacific Ave to South Carolina Ave. Walk back 1/2 block.
To Gay Bars: 2 blocks to men's bars.
Rooms: 15 rooms with single, double or queen beds.
Bathrooms: 1 private, 2 shared. All rooms have washing facilities.
Complimentary: Morning coffee.
Dates Open: All year.
High Season: Summer.
Rates: In season $28-$105, off season $28-$70.
Discounts: 7th consecutive night free in summer, 6th & 7th consecutive nights free off season.
Credit Cards: MC, VISA, plus 8% handling fee.
Rsv'tns: Advised at all times. Call or write for brochure.
Reserve Through: Call direct.
Minimum Stay: Reservations on summer weekends, 2 nights. Walk-ins no min.
Parking: Limited free off-street parking.
In-Room: Self-controlled AC.
On-Premises: Color TV lounge, VCR, video tape library, telephone, refrigerator, large enclosed porch.
Swimming: Ocean beach.
Sunbathing: On beach, enclosed porch or fire escape.
Nudity: Permitted anywhere on premises not visible from street.
Smoking: Permitted without restrictions.
Pets: Not permitted.
Handicap Access: No.
Children: Not permitted.
Languages: English.

PLAINFIELD

Pillars, The

Gay-Friendly 50/50 ♀♂

Sylvan Seclusion With Easy Access to Manhattan

The Pillars is a lovingly-restored Victorian/Georgian mansion. Relax by the Music Room fire, read a book from the living room library, play the organ, listen to the stereo, watch a video. Swedish breakfast at *The Pillars* is expanded continental, served at your convenience, but you may wish to cook your own in the huge kitchen. We have over 20 years' experience in the hospitality industry and are eager to offer a quality experience to our guests. Plainfield is a beautiful town with easy access to Manhattan by commuter train. It's a town where rainbow flags and windsocks can be seen on local houses and is fast becoming the "Gay Capital of New Jersey."

Address: 922 Central Ave, Plainfield, NJ 07060-2311. **Phone & Fax:** (908) 753-0922 or (800) 37-2REST.

Type: Bed & breakfast.
Clientele: 50% gay & lesbian & 50% straight clientele.
Transportation: Train or bus to Plainfield, car or taxi to house.
To Gay Bars: 1/2 mile. 8 miles to the famous "Den" at Rutgers University.
Rooms: 3 suites with twin or queen beds.
Bathrooms: All private bath/shower/toilets.
Campsites: Parking for self-contained RV with electric & water hookup.

Meals: Expanded continental breakfast.
Vegetarian: Facilities to prepare your own vegetarian meals.
Complimentary: Coffee, tea, mints on pillows & turn-down service. Beverages afternoon & evening.
Dates Open: All year.
Rates: $65-$105.
Discounts: Call for discounts.
Rsv'tns: Required.
Reserve Through: Travel agent or call direct.

Parking: Ample off-street parking.
In-Room: AC, coffee/tea-making facilities, maid & room service.
On-Premises: Meeting rooms, TV lounge, VCR, stereo, organ, laundry & kitchen facilities, library & fireplace.
Exercise/Health: Health clubs in the area.
Swimming: Outstanding gay nude beach at nearby Sandy Hook.
Sunbathing: In secluded backyard.

Smoking: Permitted only on the sun porch in inclement weather.
Pets: Well-behaved dogs permitted with prior arrangement. We have a Cairn Terrier.
Handicap Access: No.
Children: Welcome under 2 years old & over 12 years old. Crib, playpen & cots available.
Languages: English.
Your Host: Chuck & Tom.

IGTA

NEW MEXICO

ALBUQUERQUE

Casa Celina

Gay/Lesbian ♀♂

Where Beauty Surrounds,
Food Abounds and the Heart is Content

   Casa Celina, in Albuquerque's North Valley, is one mile from Old Town and within walking distance of the Nature Center Wildlife Preserve. Relax in our spacious living room with fireplace, the patio, or a hammock under the apple trees. Speak to us in English, Portuguese, Spanish or Italian and we'll answer in kind. Visit the Albuquerque Balloon Fiesta in October and Indian Pueblo dances in summer. In Old Town find unique jewelery shops and the Natural History Museum or travel to Santa Fe for art galleries, skiing and an array of exquisite restaurants.
Address: 3019 Rio Grande Blvd NW, Albuquerque, NM 87107. Tel: (505) 345-7307.

Type: Bed & breakfast. **Clientele:** Mostly gay & lesbian with some straight clientele. **Transportation:** Taxi. Pick up from airport $10. **To Gay Bars:** 6 miles or a 15-minute drive. **Rooms:** 2 rooms with single, queen or king beds. **Bathrooms:** 1 shared bath/shower/toilet & 1 shared toilet only.

Meals: Expanded continental breakfast. **Vegetarian:** By request (we are generally vegetarians). Vegetarian food nearby. **Complimentary:** Tea, coffee, fruit & cheese tray or happy hour munchies. **Dates Open:** All year. **High Season:** Summer, fall. **Rates:** Fall/summer $60-

$85. Winter $55-$60. **Rsv'tns:** Required. **Reserve Through:** Call direct. **Parking:** Ample off-street parking. **In-Room:** AC. **On-Premises:** TV lounge. Business services: copying, computer use, interpreting & translating Spanish, Portuguese, Italian or English. **Swimming:** Pool nearby.

Sunbathing: On the patio. **Smoking:** Not permitted anywhere inside or on the premises. **Pets:** Not permitted. **Handicap Access:** Yes. Ramps & access around toilet. Wide door on bedroom & bathroom. **Children:** Not especially welcome. **Languages:** English, Portuguese, Spanish & Italian.

Casitas at Old Town, The

A Glimpse of the Past Beneath a Sea of Sky

Gay/Lesbian ♀♂

   Enjoy the hospitable warmth and comfort of New Mexico's classic adobe dwellings on the secluded edge of Albuquerque's oldest historical area. *Casitas at Old Town* are early dwellings restored to modern comfort with fireplace, kitchen area, bedroom, bath and patio, all furnished with authentic New Mexico pieces. Stroll into the plaza of nearby Old Town with its adjacent museums, drive an hour to Santa Fe, or just relax in absolute privacy...with one foot in the park.
Address: 1604 Old Town Rd NW, Albuquerque, NM . Tel: (505) 843-7479.

Type: Suites with private entrances. **Clientele:** Mostly gay & lesbian with some straight clientele. **Transportation:** Car is best. **To Gay Bars:** A 15-minute drive to men's & women's bars. **Rooms:** 2 suites with double or queen bed.

Bathrooms: 2 private shower/toilets. **Vegetarian:** 1 block to vegetarian food. **Complimentary:** Tea & coffee makings in each suite. **Dates Open:** All year. **Rates:** $85 all year except 1st 2 weeks in October ($115). **Discounts:** On extended

stays. **Rsv'tns:** Preferred. **Reserve Through:** Travel agent or call direct. **Minimum Stay:** 2 days. **Parking:** Ample off-street parking. **In-Room:** AC, kitchen, refrigerator, coffee & tea-making facilities. **Exercise/Health:** Nearby gym.

Sunbathing: On patio. **Nudity:** Permitted on patios. **Smoking:** Not permitted. **Pets:** Not permitted. **Handicap Access:** No. **Children:** Not especially welcome. **Languages:** English, minimal Spanish.

Dave's B&B

Casual and Private for Gays and Leatherfolk

Gay/Lesbian ♂

Convenient to Old Town and downtown, 1 mile north of I-40, *Dave's B&B* is my home and is decorated with original art, including Indian kachinas, pottery and rugs. All advertising is directed solely to gays, lesbians and leatherfolk. The emphasis is on privacy and a casual, make-yourself-at-home style. My southwest adobe-style home is surrounded by six-foot privacy walls and patios with trees, fountain, hot tub and seating and sunning areas. Both rooms open directly onto patios. The larger room (master suite) has a fireplace, unique four-poster bed and a very large adjoining bath/dressing area.

Address: PO Box 27214, Albuquerque, NM 87125-7214. Tel: (505) 247-8312.

Type: Bed & Breakfast.
Clientele: Mostly gay men & leatherfolk with women welcome.
Transportation: Car is best.
To Gay Bars: Convenient to gay bars.
Rooms: 1 room & 1 suite with double or queen beds.
Bathrooms: All private.
Meals: Expanded continental breakfast.

Vegetarian: Always available.
Complimentary: Regular & decaf coffee & herbal tea.
Dates Open: All year.
High Season: May 15-Oct 15.
Rates: High season $70-$90. Off season $60-$75.
Credit Cards: MC & VISA.
Rsv'tns: Required, but check if passing through.
Reserve Through: Call

direct.
Parking: Ample garage parking plus RV space.
In-Room: Color TV, VCR, ceiling fans, telephone & maid service. One room with fireplace.
On-Premises: Living room with fireplace & piano, laundry facilities, kitchen privileges, PC & Fax.
Exercise/Health: Outdoor hot tub, weights &

rowing machine. Nearby gym.
Sunbathing: On the walled patio.
Nudity: Permitted on the rear patio & in the hot tub.
Smoking: Permitted.
Pets: Not permitted.
Handicap Access: Yes, ground floor.
Children: Not permitted.
Languages: English.
Your Host: Dave.

Hacienda Antigua Bed and Breakfast

Gay-Friendly ♀♂

Secluded, Serene and Romantic – A Perfect Retreat!

Walk through the massive carved gates of *Hacienda Antigua* and step back in time. The gentle courtyard with its big cottonwood tree and abundance of flowers is the heart of this 200-year-old adobe hacienda. In summer, relax on the peaceful portal or bask in the sun by the large swimming pool. In winter enjoy a crackling piñon fire in your own kiva fireplace. Enjoy the outdoor Jacuzzi year-round. Visitors linger, not wanting to leave the warm Southwestern hospitality, full breakfasts, and splendid rooms comfortably furnished with antiques.

Address: 6708 Tierra Dr NW, Albuquerque, NM . Tel: (505) 345-5399.

Type: Bed & Breakfast. **Clientele:** Mostly straight with gays & lesbians welcome. **Transportation:** Car is best. **To Gay Bars:** 5 miles. **Rooms:** 4 rooms & 1 suite with single, double, queen or king beds. **Bathrooms:** All private. **Meals:** Full breakfast.

Vegetarian: Served upon request. Our breakfasts are ample & we will accommodate any dietary request. **Complimentary:** Glass of wine. Chocolates in room. **Dates Open:** All year. **High Season:** Aug,-Oct. **Rates:** $85-$110. **Credit Cards:** MC & VISA.

Rsv'tns: Required. **Reserve Through:** Travel agent or call direct. **Parking:** Ample free off-street parking. **In-Room:** AC, ceiling fans & fireplaces. **On-Premises:** TV lounge. **Exercise/Health:** Jacuzzi on premises. Gym & weights nearby.

Swimming: Pool on premises. **Sunbathing:** At poolside or on the patio. **Smoking:** Permitted outside. **Pets:** Not permitted. **Handicap Access:** No. **Children:** Not especially welcome. **Languages:** English.

Hateful Missy & Granny Butch's Boudoir

A Rather Queer Bed & Breakfast

Gay/Lesbian ♀

Your Albuquerque dreams become reality at *Hateful Missy and Granny Butch's Boudoir,* just blocks from Old Town, the original Albuquerque settlement. Snuggled amid centuries-old adobes, shops, museums and points of gay/lesbian interest, this intimate bed and breakfast offers hominess not usually experienced while traveling. Sample Granny Butch's mean New Mexican cuisine. Thrill to Hateful Missy's seasonal organic produce. Swoon in your cozy chamber with bath, locking closet, cable TV and VCR. This is *not* a hotel. We're as friendly and comfortable as our name suggests. Remember: The gravy may be lumpy but the beds ain't. **Address: 728 Lulac NW, Albuquerque, NM . Tel: (800) 397-2482, (505) 243-7063.**

Type: Bed & breakfast with small in-house boutique featuring adult accessories. **Clientele:** Mostly women with men welcome. **Transportation:** Car is best. **To Gay Bars:** 2 miles. 3-4 minutes by car. **Rooms:** 2 rooms with queen beds. **Bathrooms:** Private & shared. **Meals:** Expanded continental breakfast. **Vegetarian:** Available

upon request. Vegetarian food nearby. **Complimentary:** Drinks, snacks available all day. Seasonal homegrown produce. **Dates Open:** All year. **High Season:** June thru ski season. **Rates:** $75-$150 double occupancy. **Rsv'tns:** Required. **Reserve Through:** Call direct. **Minimum Stay:** 2 nights for holiday seasons & special events (balloon

fiesta, State Fair, etc.). **Parking:** Ample free off-street & on-street parking. End of well-lit cul-de-sac. **In-Room:** Color cable TV, VCR, video tape library, ac, ceiling fans, telephone, room & maid service. Fresh flowers. **On-Premises:** Refrigerator, sun room & garden, water garden & laundry facilities. **Exercise/Health:** Nearby gym, weights, Jacuzzi, sauna, steam & massage.

Swimming: Nearby river, waterpark & many public pools. **Sunbathing:** In the garden. **Nudity:** Permitted in the house & garden. **Smoking:** Permitted outside only! All rooms non-smoking. **Pets:** Permitted. Arrangements made at time of reservations. **Handicap Access:** No. **Children:** No children, please. **Languages:** English. **Your Host:** Butch & Rita.

Rio Grande House

Gay-Friendly ♀♂

This landmark adobe residence, *Rio Grande House,* is located near historic Old Town, major museums and the Rio Grande nature center. Southwestern charm is reflected throughout with beamed ceilings, brick floors, Kiva fireplaces and museum-quality antiques. Collectibles from East Africa, Nepal, Pakistan and Yemen are used to decorate each room.

Address: 3100 Rio Grande Blvd NW, Albuquerque, NM 87107. Tel: (505) 345-0120.

Type: Bed & breakfast. **Clientele:** Mostly straight clientele with a gay & lesbian following. **Transportation:** Car is best. **To Gay Bars:** 15-min drive. **Rooms:** 5 rooms with double, queen or king

beds. **Bathrooms:** All private shower/toilets. **Meals:** Full breakfast. **Vegetarian:** Available upon request. **Dates Open:** All year. **High Season:** Jun to Oct.. **Rates:** $50-$95.

Rsv'tns: Required. **Reserve Through:** Call direct. **Parking:** Ample off-street parking. **In-Room:** Color TV, AC & telephone. **On-Premises:** Laundry facilities.

Sunbathing: On patio. **Smoking:** Permitted. Non-smoking rooms available. **Pets:** Not permitted. **Handicap Access:** No. **Children:** Not permitted. **Languages:** English.

W.E. Mauger Estate

Linda Ronstadt Slept Here!

Gay-Friendly 50/50 ♀♂

W.E. Mauger Estate is a wonderfully intimate, restored Queen Anne residence, whose high ceilings and rich brass appointments mark it singularly old-fashioned. We take great pride in offering comfortable Victorian accommodations for 20 souls in a style reminiscent of an era when graciousness, thoughtfulness and elegance were a way of life. Our 8 rooms have private baths with shower. The full breakfast includes fresh fruit and baked goods, juice, assorted egg dishes, and regional specialities. Walk to the convention center. We are rated 3-star by Mobil and 3-diamonds by AAA.

Address: 701 Roma Ave NW, Albuquerque, NM 87102. Tel: (505) 242-8755, Fax: (505) 842-8835.

Type: Bed & breakfast.
Clientele: 50% gay & lesbian & 50% straight clientele.
Transportation: Car is best or taxi.
To Gay Bars: 3 miles by car.
Rooms: 7 rooms & 1 suite with single, double, queen or king beds.
Bathrooms: All private baths with showers.

Meals: Full breakfast.
Vegetarian: Available if pre ordered.
Complimentary: Wine, cheese, juice, cookies, brownies, chips, fruit, candy & coffee.
Dates Open: All year.
High Season: Mar thru Oct.
Rates: $65-$115.
Discounts: Long stays, booking whole house.

Credit Cards: MC, VISA, Amex & Diners.
Rsv'tns: Required.
Reserve Through: Call direct.
Minimum Stay: 2 nights for special events.
Parking: Ample, free, off-street parking, private lot, will accept RV.
In-Room: Color TV, maid & room service, AC, ceiling fans, coffee/

tea-making facilities & refrigerator.
On-Premises: TV lounge, meeting rooms, catering for special occasions.
Swimming: Nearby river.
Sunbathing: On patio.
Smoking: Permitted in designated outside areas.
Pets: Call to inquire.
Handicap Access: No.
Children: Call to inquire.
Languages: English.

W.J. Marsh House Victorian B&B Inn, The

We Even Have A Ghost!

Gay-Friendly 50/50 ♀♂

The W.J. Marsh House Victorian Bed & Breakfast Inn, built in 1895, is on the National Register of Historical Places and is located in Albuquerque's old *Railroad Town* area. Six unique guest rooms, brimming with antiques, provide for those "siestas" so necessary at a 5,000 ft. elevation. Two female ghosts, dressed in turn-of-the-century gowns, are often seen in the Rose Room. We're five minutes from the airport, walking distance from UNM and the convention center downtown, and a few minutes drive from Old Town, the zoo and nature center, museums, the Indian Pueblo Cultural Center, and the world's longest, highest tramway.

Address: 301 Edith SE, Albuquerque, NM 87102. Tel: (505) 247-1001.

Type: Bed & breakfast inn with separate Victorian cottage.
Clientele: 50% gay & lesbian & 50% straight clientele.
Transportation: Car is best. Cab from airport less than $7 one way.
To Gay Bars: 2-3 miles from 2 gay bars & 8-12 blocks from lesbian bar.
Rooms: 6 rooms, 2 suites & 1 cottage with single, double or queen beds.
Bathrooms: 2 private toilets with shared shower & 2 shared bath/shower/

toilets.
Meals: Full gourmet breakfast in house. Full kitchen in cottage (breakfast not provided).
Vegetarian: Available with prior notice. Many vegetarian restaurants nearby.
Complimentary: Depends on time of year & mood of the Innkeeper. Alcohol is not provided.
Dates Open: All year.
High Season: First week of October (International Balloon Fiesta). Make reservations by May.

Rates: Single $49-$99, double $79-$109. Inquire for suites & cottage.
Discounts: Seniors 10%, over age 65. Stays of one week or more (for anyone).
Rsv'tns: Preferred. Walk-ins accepted IF space is available. Please do not call after 9pm.
Reserve Through: Call direct.
Minimum Stay: During Balloon Fiesta: 3 nights weekends, 2 nights during the week.
Parking: Ample free off-

street & on-street parking. Well-lit walkways to entrances.
In-Room: AC & maid service. Color cable TV, ceiling fans & kitchen in cottage. Laundry service on request.
On-Premises: Meeting rooms, laundry facilities & phone.
Exercise/Health: Self-guided walking tours. Nearby gym, Jacuzzi, sauna, steam & massage.
Swimming: Nearby pools, river & lakes.
Smoking: Not permitted

anywhere, not even on the grounds!
Pets: Not permitted.

Handicap Access: No.
Children: Permitted in cottage only. Permitted

in main house if 16 or older.
Languages: English,

Spanish, French & sometimes German.

ESPAÑOLA

Inn of La Mesilla, The

The Essence of Northern New Mexico

Gay-Friendly 50/50 ♀♂

The Inn of La Mesilla is a private residence bordering the Santa Clara Indian Reservation. The Hoemann's invite you to enjoy two private bedrooms, each with private bath. Our pueblo-style home has Mexican tile throughout. The Inn has a new hot tub with large, festive deck for sunning or enjoying views. The Inn is minutes from Chimayo, Puye Cliffs, Santa Fe, Taos and eight northern Indian pueblos. A full breakfast is served, and afternoon snacks are available from 5:00-6:00 pm. Two Springer Spaniels, Pork Chop and Te-Bone, reside in home.
Address: Rt 1, Box 368A, Española, NM 87532. Tel: (505) 753-5368.

Type: Bed & breakfast.
Clientele: 50% gay & lesbian & 50% straight clientele.
Transportation: Car is best.
To Gay Bars: 30 minutes to Santa Fe.
Rooms: 2 rooms with queen or king bed.
Bathrooms: All private bath/showers.
Meals: Full breakfast &

afternoon refreshments.
Vegetarian: Special veggie dishes for breakfast if requested in advance.
Complimentary: Afternoon snacks between 5pm-6pm.
Dates Open: All year.
Rates: $80 for 1 or 2 people. $90 for one night stays.
Rsv'tns: Required.

Reserve Through: Travel agent or call direct.
Minimum Stay: 2 nights.
Parking: Ample free parking.
In-Room: Color cable TV & ceiling fans.
On-Premises: TV lounge & use of refrigerator for sodas & such.
Exercise/Health: Hot tub on premises. Nearby gym, hot springs &

massage.
Sunbathing: On hot tub deck.
Smoking: Permitted outside only.
Pets: Not permitted. Kennel 5 minutes away.
Handicap Access: No.
Children: Not permitted.
Languages: English, some Spanish & a little German.

La Villita House

Gay-Friendly ♀♂

A Special Place in the Heart of Northern New Mexico!

Leave the city and beaten paths for an authentic adventure in rural Northern New Mexico. Located between Santa Fe and Taos, just off the Taos Hwy, *La Villita House*, adobe home of an artist and teacher, offers a private room, bath with Jacuzzi, alfalfa fields and ancient cottonwoods next to the Rio Grande River. *La Villita* is surrounded by pueblos, grand vistas and incomparable cuisine. Continental breakfast and coyote choir included! **Guest Comment:** *"We wanted to get the feel of rural New Mexico - and we got it!!"*
Address: PO Box 605, Alcalde, NM 87511. Tel: (505) 852-2887.

Type: In-home bed & breakfast with artist's studio.
Clientele: Mostly straight clientele with a gay & lesbian following.
Transportation: Car is best. $35 for airport pick up.
To Gay Bars: 35 miles to bars in Santa Fe.
Rooms: 2 rooms with single or queen beds.

Bathrooms: 1 private bath/toilet & 1 shared shower/toilet.
Meals: Continental breakfast.
Vegetarian: Available at restaurants in Española, 6 miles away.
Complimentary: Tea, coffee & soft drinks.
Dates Open: All year.
Rates: $30-$50.
Reserve Through: Call

direct.
Parking: Ample free off-street parking.
On-Premises: TV lounge with color TV & VCR, telephone, kitchen & refrigerator privileges, laundry facilities, covered picnic area.
Exercise/Health: Jacuzzi on premises. Nearby gym, weights & massage.
Swimming: At nearby

river.
Sunbathing: On the patio or by the river.
Smoking: Not permitted.
Pets: Not permitted.
Handicap Access: Yes.
Children: Not especially welcome.
Languages: English & a little Spanish.
Your Host: Jan.

RED RIVER

Valley Lodge Family Motel

Gay-Friendly ♀♂

Valley Lodge Family Motel offers you a choice of cabins or apartments with modern facilities. Amenities include color cable TV, fireplaces in some rooms, and kitchens furnished with basic utensils. The lodge is on Main Street within one block of excellent restaurants, gift shops, cozy lounges, rental shops, snowmobile tours and a trout stream. Our rivers and lakes are stocked weekly in the summer for the best trout fishing anywhere. Cross-country skiing is less than 4 miles away. Jeep tours to old ghost towns, gold mines and high country lakes are available. **Address: PO Box 304, Main St, Red River, NM 87558. Tel: (505) 754-2262, Reservations (800) 951-2262.**

Type: Motel in one of NM's best ski areas.
Clientele: 85% straight clientele with gays & lesbians welcome. (Gay-owned.)
Transportation: Car is best.
To Gay Bars: 2-1/2 hours to Santa Fe.
Rooms: 6 suites & 2 cabins with queen beds.
Bathrooms: All private.
Meals: Donut shop on premises.
Dates Open: Closed April & sometimes in early November.
High Season: Ski season (Thanksgiving till April) & summer.
Rates: Winter $46-$115. Summer $39-$96. Holiday rates slightly higher.
Discounts: In low season. Please inquire.
Credit Cards: MC & VISA.
Rsv'tns: Preferred.
Reserve Through: Travel agent or call direct.
Minimum Stay: 2 nights.
Parking: Ample off-street parking.
In-Room: Color cable TV & remote, telephone, kitchen, coffee/tea-mak-ing facilities & maid service.
On-Premises: Grills & picnic area in summer.
Smoking: Permitted.
Pets: Permitted in cabins only.
Handicap Access: No.
Children: Welcome.
Languages: English.
Your Host: Delores & Theresa.

RUIDOSO

Sierra Mesa Lodge

Gay-Friendly ♀♂

An Inn For Love

Sierra Mesa Lodge is a magnificently elegant and romantic bed and breakfast inn nestled into a wooded hillside and designed for your relaxation and privacy. Five charming guest rooms offer diverse decor, comforters, goosedown pillows, brass or four-poster beds, rockers, chaise lounges and private baths. Our full gourmet breakfast can be enjoyed in the privacy of your room or in the dining room. The spacious living room invites conversation and refreshments in front of the fireplace and the indoor hot tub spa offers relaxation at the end of a busy day of golf, horse racing, hiking, swimming, fishing, skiing, sledding or sight-seeing. **Address: PO Box 463, Ft Stanton Rd, Alto, NM 88312. Tel: (505) 336-4515.**

Type: Bed & breakfast inn.
Clientele: Mostly straight clientele with a gay & lesbian following.
Transportation: Car is best. Free pick up from local airport (private plane).
Rooms: 5 rooms with queen beds.
Bathrooms: All private.
Meals: Full gourmet breakfast.
Vegetarian: Upon request for breakfast.
Complimentary: Afternoon tea, coffee & pastries. Chocolates in rooms, various snacks in common room.
Dates Open: All year.
High Season: July, August, September & Thanksgiving through Easter.
Rates: $80-$90 per night.
Credit Cards: MC, VISA, Amex, Discover.
Rsv'tns: Required.
Reserve Through: Call direct.
Minimum Stay: 2 nights on weekends on holidays & in summer.
Parking: Ample free off-street parking.
In-Room: Ceiling fans & maid service.
On-Premises: Telephone.
Exercise/Health: Hot tub on premises. Nearby gym, massage.
Swimming: Nearby pool.
Sunbathing: On common sun decks, 3 acres of woods & meadows.
Nudity: Permitted in hot tub only. Only 1 couple at a time in hot tub.
Smoking: Not permitted.
Pets: Not permitted.
Handicap Access: No.
Children: Permitted 14 years & older.
Languages: English.
Your Host: Larry & Lila.

SANTA FE

Arius Compound

Experience Adobe Living

Gay-Friendly ♀♂

in your own authentic Santa Fe *Casita*, ideally located on Canyon Road, the heart of Santa Fe's historic East Side with charming shops, galleries and fine restaurants. Up a quiet lane, surrounded by high adobe walls filled with gardens, patios, fruit trees and our ever-hot redwood tub, each *Casita* has 1 or 2 bedrooms, fully-equipped kitchen, living room with corner Kiva fireplace (wood provided), private bath or shower, private patio and loads of Southwest style. Don't be a visitor. Live here, at *Arius Compound*, if only for a few days.

Address: PO Box 1111, 1018-1/2 Canyon Rd, Santa Fe, NM 87504. Tel: Out of Town: (800) 735-8453, Local: (505) 982-2621, Fax: (505) 989-8280.

Type: Cottages.
Clientele: Mostly straight clientele with a strong gay & lesbian following.
Transportation: Car is best.
Rooms: 3 cottages with single, double or queen beds.
Bathrooms: 2 private shower/toilets & 1 private bath/shower/toilet.
Dates Open: All year.
High Season: July-August.
Rates: Low $80, high $175.
Credit Cards: MC, VISA & Amex.
Rsv'tns: Not required, but usually sold out without reservations.
Reserve Through: Call direct.
Parking: Adequate off-street parking.
In-Room: Color cable TV, telephone, ceiling fans, kitchen, refrigerator, coffee & tea-making facilities.
Exercise/Health: Jacuzzi.
Swimming: Nearby pool.
Sunbathing: On private & common sun decks & patio.
Smoking: Permitted outside. Non-smoking rooms available.
Pets: Permitted. Check first.
Handicap Access: No.
Children: Welcome.
Languages: English.
Your Host: Len & Robbie.

Four Kachinas Inn Bed & Breakfast

Our Breakfasts Will Win Your Acclaim

Gay-Friendly ♀♂

On a quiet street, built around a private courtyard, *Four Kachinas Inn* is a short walk from the historic Santa Fe Plaza via the Old Santa Fe Trail. Rooms have private baths, private entrances and southwestern furnishings which include antique Navajo rugs, Hopi kachina dolls, handcrafted wooden furniture and saltillo tile floors. A continental-plus breakfast, prepared by our award-winning baker, is served in your room. Afternoon refreshments are served in the adobe guest lounge. **Guest Comments:** *"I was born in New Mexico, and this B&B felt like home....Great breakfasts here, too." -Felix, Berkeley, CA*

Address: 512 Webber St, Santa Fe, NM 87501. Tel: (505) 982-2550, (800) 397-2564.

Type: Bed & breakfast.
Clientele: Mostly straight clientele with gays & lesbians welcome.
Transportation: Car is best.
To Gay Bars: 5 blocks. A 15-minute walk or 5-minute drive.
Rooms: 5 rooms with single, queen or king beds.
Bathrooms: All private.
Meals: Expanded continental breakfast.
Complimentary: Tea, soft drinks & cookies every afternoon in guest lounge.
Dates Open: Feb 1st through Jan 1st.
High Season: May 1st through Oct 31st.
Rates: High season $98-$113. Low season $88-$98.
Credit Cards: MC & VISA.
Rsv'tns: Required.
Reserve Through: Call direct.

continued next page

New Mexico

Minimum Stay: 2 nights for low season weekends. 3-5 nights certain holidays & special events.
Parking: Adequate free off-street parking. RVs would need to park on street.
In-Room: Color cable TV, ceiling fans, telephone & maid service.
On-Premises: Guest lounge (no TV).
Exercise/Health: Nearby gym, weights, Jacuzzi, sauna, steam & massage.
Swimming: Nearby pool.
Sunbathing: On the patio.
Smoking: Permitted outside only. All rooms are non-smoking.
Pets: Not permitted.
Handicap Access: Yes. 1 room & guest lounge are wheelchair accessible.
Children: Not especially welcome.
Languages: English, Spanish, some French.
Your Host: Andrew & John.

Jamelos Properties

Gay/Lesbian ♀♂

Beautiful Casitas Near the Heart of Santa Fe

Jamelos Properties offers accommodations in various fully-furnished and very well-appointed private homes, which will accommodate up to six caring, friendly, responsible people. No smoking indoors, please. Proximity of these casitas to The Plaza (which is the geographical center of Santa Fe) is from four blocks to 1-1/2 miles. For further information and for reservations, call Joel or Sam (originators and former owners of the *Inn On Castro*) at (505) 988-3399, between 8am and 9pm, mountain time.
Tel: (505) 988-3399.

Type: Furnished casitas for rent.
Clientele: Gay & lesbian. Good mix of men & women.
Transportation: Car is best.
To Gay Bars: Short drive to gay bar in downtown Santa Fe.
Rooms: Choose double room or 1- or 2-BR house.
Bathrooms: All private.
Dates Open: All year.
High Season: Summer & ski season.
Rates: $125-$175 nightly, $750-$1050 weekly.
Rsv'tn: Required.
Reserve Through: Call direct.
Minimum Stay: 2 nights.
Parking: Adequate, free off-street parking.
In-Room: Telephone, refrigerator, color TV.
On-Premises: Fully-furnished homes.
Exercise/Health: Nearby gym, weights, Jacuzzi, sauna, steam & massage.
Swimming: Nearby pool.
Smoking: Non-smoking only.
Pets: Not permitted.
Handicap Access: One house is accessible.
Children: One child at a time per home.
Languages: English, Spanish, French, Italian.
IGTA

Open Sky B&B

Gay-Friendly 50/50 ♀♂

Spectacular Views and Gorgeous Sunsets

Open Sky B&B is a spacious and serene adobe, minutes south of Santa Fe off the historic Turquoise Trail. There are two north-facing guest rooms, with views of Santa Fe's lights and southwestern decor, which have private baths. There's a large living room with fireplace, a garden courtyard space and privacy to relax or take an enjoyable outdoor walk. Breakfast is served in the gallery, facing the garden courtyard. A third room has been added which includes a fireplace, sitting area and patio.
Address: Rt 2 Box 918, Turquoise Trail, Santa Fe, NM 87505. Tel: (505) 471-3475.

Type: Bed & breakfast.
Clientele: 50% gay & lesbian & 50% straight clientele.
Transportation: Car is best, shuttlejack from airport.
To Gay Bars: 16 miles.
Rooms: 3 rooms with queen or king beds.
Bathrooms: 2 private bath/toilet & 1 private shower/toilet.
Meals: Expanded continental breakfast.
Vegetarian: Available upon request.
Complimentary: Gourmet coffee, herbal teas, fresh flowers!
Dates Open: All year.
High Season: Summer & holidays.
Rates: $70-$110.
Discounts: 10% for over 7 nights or if one party books all rooms.
Rsv'tns: Preferred for guaranteed availability.
Reserve Through: Call direct.
Parking: Ample off-street SAFE parking.
In-Room: Color TV, telephone, refrigerator.
On-Premises: Large 600 sq. ft. living room with fireplace.
Exercise/Health: Jacuzzi, cross-country skiing, hiking, bicycling & massage.
Swimming: At nearby river & lake.
Sunbathing: On the patio.
Smoking: Permitted outside only. Entire B&B is smoke-free.
Pets: Not permitted inside.
Handicap Access: Yes.
Children: Permitted with restrictions.
Languages: English & German.

Triangle Inn-Santa Fe, The

Gay/Lesbian ♀♂

Santa Fe is one of the world's most desirable travel destinations, offering the traveler an extraordinary range of vacationing opportunities. The Inn is the perfect retreat from which to explore all that Northern New Mexico has to offer. This secluded, rustic compound provides private casitas, complete with fireplaces, kitchenettes, private decks and courtyards, plus a common garden compound with relaxing hot tub and sun deck. Breakfasts include the best home-baked muffins in New Mexico! Find the real Southwest at *The Triangle Inn-Santa Fe*.

Address: PO Box 3235, Santa Fe, NM 87501. Phone & Fax: (505) 455-3375.

Type: Inn.
Clientele: Good mix of gays & lesbians.
Transportation: Car is best.
To Gay Bars: 10 miles to gay/lesbian bars.
Rooms: 6 cottages with queen or king beds & kitchens.
Bathrooms: All private.
Meals: Expanded continental breakfast & fully-equipped kitchen.
Vegetarian: All breakfasts are vegetarian.

Complimentary: Gourmet coffee, herbal teas, juices, afternoon snacks & occasional afternoon cocktails.
Dates Open: All year.
High Season: Holidays & fiestas.
Rates: Low season $80-$120. High season $100-$140.
Discounts: On weekly stays.
Credit Cards: MC, VISA & Eurocard.
Rsv'tns: Recommended.

Reserve Through: Travel Agent or call direct.
Minimum Stay: 3 days during holidays & fiestas.
Parking: Ample, free, off-street covered parking.
In-Room: Color TV & VCR with video tape library, telephone, ceiling fans, kitchen, refrigerator, coffee/tea-making facilities & maid service.
Exercise/Health: Jacuzzi on premises. Nearby gym, weights, sauna,

steam & massage.
Swimming: Nearby pool.
Sunbathing: On private & common sun decks.
Smoking: Non-smoking rooms available.
Pets: Permitted with advance notice ($5 per day).
Handicap Access: No.
Children: Children of all ages welcome.
Languages: English & Spanish.
Your Host: Sarah & Karan.

TAOS

Ruby Slipper, The

Gay/Lesbian ♀♂

A Perfect Balance of Privacy & Personal Attention

At *The Ruby Slipper,* our guest rooms, individually decorated with handmade furniture, have private baths and fireplace or woodstove. Breakfast specialties include scrumptious breakfast burritos, omelettes and banana pancakes. Our lovely grounds are complete with an outdoor hot tub. A vacation in Taos might include hiking, horseback riding, world-class skiing, gallery viewing, shopping or visiting Taos Pueblo. *The Ruby Slipper* is Northern New Mexico's most popular and relaxing gay-friendly bed and breakfast. Come see what everybody's talking about!

Address: PO Box 2069, Taos, NM 87571. Tel: (505) 758-0613.

Type: Bed & breakfast.
Clientele: Mostly gay/lesbian with some straight clientele.
Transportation: Car is best. 2-1/2 hours from Albuquerque by car. Taxi

from bus stop to Ruby Slipper, $5.
To Gay Bars: 1-1/4 hours to Santa Fe gay & lesbian bars.
Rooms: 7 rooms with double, queen or king

beds.
Bathrooms: All private.
Meals: Full breakfast.

Vegetarian: Always.
Complimentary: In-room

continued next page

coffee-maker with fresh ground coffee & assorted teas.
Dates Open: All year.
High Season: Summer, holidays and ski season.
Rates: $74-$104 per night for two, $84-$114 for Xmas holidays.
Discounts: On weekly stays, if booked directly.

Credit Cards: MC, VISA, Amex, Discover.
Rsv'tns: Recommended.
Reserve Through: Travel agent or call direct.
Minimum Stay: 2-3 days on holidays.
Parking: Adequate free off-street parking.
In-Room: Maid service, some fireplaces, ceiling

fans, coffee & tea-making facilities.
On-Premises: Telephone, common room for guests, refrigerator stocked with items for purchase.
Exercise/Health: Hot tub on the premises, health club in town.
Swimming: 10 minutes to pool, 20 to Rio Grande.

Sunbathing: On hot tub deck or patio.
Nudity: Permitted in the hot tub.
Smoking: Permitted outdoors.
Pets: Not permitted.
Handicap Access: Yes, call for details.
Children: Permitted.
Languages: English.

NEW YORK

BUFFALO

Old Schoolhouse Guest House

Gay/Lesbian ♂

Approximately 180 years ago, *Old Schoolhouse Guest House* served as an actual schoolhouse for the local community. Now a personable guest house decorated in antiques, its country setting far from town, provides a quiet place to get away from it all. Enthusiasts will enjoy the owner's antique car collection, which includes a 1958 Buick Limited that once belonged to Lucille Ball.

Address: 1148 Townline Rd, Alden, NY 14004. Tel: (716) 683-6590.

Type: Guest house.
Clientele: Mostly men with women welcome.
Transportation: Chauffeured limousine for special events, taxi to and from airport and bars.
To Gay Bars: 20 minutes to Buffalo gay/lesbian bars.

Rooms: 4 doubles.
Bathrooms: 2 shared.
Meals: Continental breakfast, extra charge for full breakfast and dinner upon request.
Dates Open: All year.
Rates: End of Sept through Apr, $35-$45; May though Sept, $40-$60.

Discounts: For over 3 nights.
Rsv'tns: Required.
Reserve Through: Call direct.
Parking: Ample free off-street parking.
In-Room: Maid service on request, color TV.
Swimming: Pool on

premises.
Sunbathing: At poolside or on patio.
Smoking: Permitted without restriction.
Pets: Not permitted.
Handicap Access: No.
Children: Not permitted.
Languages: English.
Your Host: Tom & Bill.

CATSKILL MOUNTAINS

Bradstan Country Hotel

Gay-Friendly ♀♂

That Uptown Feeling in *Upstate* N.Y.

After a 21 month, painstaking renovation, *Bradstan Country Hotel* was awarded The First Sullivan County Board of Realtors Award for Architectural Excellence. In addition to our large comfortable rooms, the *Bradstan* also features a 70-foot private deck and a 60-foot front porch overlooking beautiful White Lake, where your favorite water activities are at your beck and call. At the end of the day, order up your favorite cocktail and enjoy the live cabaret entertainment in *Bradstan's* own piano bar lounge. All this just 2 hours from NYC. Ask us about hosting your special affair or meeting at our inn.

Address: Route 17B, PO Box 312, White Lake, NY 12786. Tel: (914) 583-4114.

Type: Bed & breakfast inn with cottages & bar.
Clientele: Mainly straight

clientele with a gay & lesbian following.
Transportation: Car is

best, no charge for pick up, prior arrangement required.

To Gay Bars: Piano bar on premises with mixed crowd.

Rooms: 2 rooms, 3 suites & 2 cottages with queen beds.
Bathrooms: All private.
Meals: Expanded continental breakfast.
Vegetarian: Our breakfast is acceptable for vegetarians.
Dates Open: Open weekends all year & 7 days a week from 4/1 to 8/31.
High Season: Memorial Day to Labor Day.

Rates: $95-$105 summer, $65-$75 winter.
Discounts: Discounts available to groups & stays of 5 nights or more.
Credit Cards: MC, VISA & Discover.
Rsv'tns: Recommended.
Reserve Through: Call direct.
Minimum Stay: 2 night minimum stay on week-ends from Memorial Day to 10/31.

Parking: Free adequate on-street & off-street parking.
In-Room: Maid service, ceiling fans; year round cottages have color cable TV & full kitchens.
On-Premises: Piano lounge, meeting rooms.
Swimming: At private lake.

Sunbathing: On sun deck or private lake front.
Smoking: Permitted.
Pets: Not permitted.
Handicap Access: No.
Children: Permitted with prior arrangement, over the age of 8.
Languages: English.
Your Host: Scott & Edward.

Stonewall Acres

Gay/Lesbian ♀♂

A Bit of Norman Rockwell Americana...Village Voice

Get away from it all just ninety miles from New York City in our cozy farmhouse and charming cottages full of collectibles. We have thirteen acres of lovely grounds with lawn and woods, flower gardens an in-ground Esther Williams pool and a private pond. The house has two double rooms and there are two cottages, one fully winterized. The New York Press says "*Stonewall Acres* is a pretty place, has a rejuvenating atmosphere and a congenial owner."
Address: PO Box 556, Rock Hill, NY 12775. Tel: (914) 791-9474 in NYC Metro area: (800) 336-4208.

Type: Guesthouse with 2 cottages, one fully winterized.
Clientele: Mostly gay/lesbian with some straight clientele.
Transportation: Car is best.
To Gay Bars: 25-minute drive to gay/lesbian bar.
Rooms: 2 rooms & 2 cottages with double beds.
Bathrooms: All private.
Meals: Full breakfast in main house.
Vegetarian: Available by prearrangement.
Complimentary: Tea, coffee.
Dates Open: All year.
High Season: July-August.
Rates: Weekends $59, cottages $60-$68, midweek discounts.
Discounts: Midweek and full week.
Credit Cards: Amex & Discover.
Rsv'tns: Preferred.
Reserve Through: Call direct.
Minimum Stay: 2 nights select weekends.
Parking: Ample off-street parking.
In-Room: Kitchens in the cottages, hot tub in deluxe double.
On-Premises: Picnic & BBQ area.
Exercise/Health: Fishing, rowing, walking trails on 13 acres, hot tub in deluxe double.
Swimming: Pool on premises.
Sunbathing: At poolside.
Smoking: Permitted in designated areas.
Pets: Permitted with prior arrangement.
Handicap Access: No.
Children: Permitted.
Languages: English.

COOPERSTOWN

Toad Hall

Gay-Friendly ♀♂

Toad Hall, circa 1824, is a large stone farmhouse restored to highlight its early American ambiance, featuring the original beehive bread oven. Large bedrooms have private baths tiled in slate. Downstairs, are eclectic furnishings and a wall mural depicting local history. In 1992, *Country Living Magazine* featured us in March, and *Country Inns Magazine* in December. *Toad Hall* is minutes from both the baseball and soccer halls of fame, the Glimmerglass Opera, the Fenimore House Folk Art Museum, the Farmer's Museum, the Corvette Museum and Lake Otsego.
Address: RD 1, Box 120, Fly Creek, NY 13337. Tel: (607) 547-5774.

Type: Bed & breakfast with custom furniture, folk art & gift shop.
Clientele: Mostly straight clientele with a gay & lesbian following.
Transportation: Car.
To Gay Bars: 30 minutes to Utica gay/lesbian bars.
Rooms: 3 rooms with queen beds.

continued next page

New York

Bathrooms: All private bath/toilets.
Meals: Full breakfast.
Vegetarian: Upon advance request.
Complimentary: Coffee, tea, upon request.
Dates Open: All year.
High Season: June through October.

Rates: $80.
Credit Cards: MC, VISA, Amex & Discover.
Rsv'tns: Required in summer.
Reserve Through: Travel agent or call direct.
Minimum Stay: Holiday weekends.
Parking: Ample off-street

parking.
In-Room: Color cable TV, AC & ceiling fans.
Exercise/Health: Nearby gym, weights, Jacuzzi, sauna, steam, massage, bowling, handball & nautilus.
Swimming: Six miles to lake.

Sunbathing: At lakeside or on sun deck.
Smoking: Not permitted.
Pets: Not permitted.
Handicap Access: No.
Children: Permitted 12 years & over.
Languages: English, limited Spanish.

CUBA

Rocking Duck Inn

Gay-Friendly ♀♂

Bucolic Bliss in Southwestern New York State

The *Rocking Duck Inn* is located on four landscaped acres in the heart of the Village of Cuba in the Southern Tier of New York State. Cuba is an untouched village, representing the way things used to be, a village green and gazebo, the circulating library, the South Street Historic District, and unique Victorian homes restored to their original glory. The Inn, built in 1852, is an Italianate brick Victorian home which retains many of its original details amid the mix of traditional and modern appointments brought by the innkeepers.

The Inn provides four comfortable non-smoking guest rooms, each including private bath with tub/shower. Two of the rooms have decorative fireplaces and seating areas with chaise lounges. Another is a less formal retreat which echoes the feel of an earlier America. The fourth reflects rural simplicity and is furnished in the early Mission taste. The common rooms include a large parlor with wood-burning fireplace and several intimate seating areas, the library, with a more club-like feel (this is the only inside designated smoking area), and the breakfast room with bay window overlooking the North Lawns, crystal chandelier, and individual tables for guests. A full breakfast is offered any time between 8:30 and 10:00am, or earlier or later with prior arrangement. The Inn is Triple A approved.

"Grandma's house" has a restaurant now! American heritage dining in an 1856 restoration offers every creature comfort from a tavern menu to an evening's entertainment! A showcase for the region's bounty: award-winning Cuba cheese, maple syrup, a unique bread, New York State wines—the best of the best! Your dining room—our dining room—bliss!

Here is a quick sketch of some of what you'll find in New York's Southern Tier...Alfred State College, Alfred University, Houghton College and St. Bonaventure University, state and local parks, Alpine and Nordic skiing areas, arts and crafts, antiques and county fairs, music and regional and traveling theatre, boating and fishing, ice and roller skating, golfing, cycling, tennis, autumn foliage, Cuba, Chautauqua and Rushford Lakes, scenic railroads and museums ranging from Indians, to oil, to glass, to Western art and ceramics. It's an easy drive to Niagara Falls, Corning Glass Center and Chautauqua Institute. We are located 4/10 of a mile south of exit 28 on Rte. 17, the Southern Tier Expressway. Watch for our sign on your left, and turn left on Medbury Avenue! Come enjoy the quiet ambiance of the *Rocking Duck*. We'll be looking for you!

Address: 28 Genesee Parkway, Cuba, NY 14727-1130. Tel: (716) 968-3335.

Type: Country bed & breakfast inn, restaurant & antique shop.
Clientele: Mainly straight clientele with a gay & lesbian following.
Transportation: Car is best. Air service to Buffalo or Rochester, rental cars available. 1-1/2 hours to Cuba.
To Gay Bars: Buffalo

1-1/2 hrs, Rochester
1-1/2 hrs, Jamestown
1 hr, Elmira 1-3/4 hrs.
Rooms: 4 rooms with twin or double beds.
Bathrooms: 3 private bath/toilets en suite & 1 private bath/toilet down the hall.
Meals: Full breakfast. Restaurant on premises.
Vegetarian: Available with prior arrangement.
Complimentary: Tea &

coffee, hospitality tray on arrival, mints.
Dates Open: All year.
High Season: Summer through Oct 31.
Rates: US $60-$75 plus 8% tax all year.
Discounts: AARP/Senior Citizen, AAA/CAA.
Credit Cards: MC, VISA, Amex, Optima, Diners Club, Carte Blanche.
Rsv'tns: Preferred.
Reserve Through: Travel

agent or call direct.
Parking: Ample free off-street lighted parking.
In-Room: Maid service. Telephone on request.
On-Premises: TV lounge & space for small meetings.
Swimming: Public lake beaches 25 min & 40 min, state park pool 40 min.
Sunbathing: On 4 acres of lawn.

Smoking: Permitted in library or outside only. All other rooms non-smoking.
Pets: Not permitted, but boarding facilities available locally with prior arrangement.
Handicap Access: No.
Children: Permitted 12 years or older.
Languages: English.
Your Host: Ted & David.

ELMIRA & CORNING

Rufus Tanner House

Gay-Friendly 50/50 ♀♂

"Peaceful," "A great time," and "Can we live here?" are some of the comments we've had from guests at our 1864 Greek Revival farmhouse. Wonderful antiques help retain the charm of the tastefully and comfortably updated interior. Find a spot on our 2-1/2 acres of lawn and garden to relax or hold your commitment ceremony, and a romantic dinner for 2 is always a possibility, followed by a dip in the outdoor hot tub.

Stay with us at *Rufus Tanner House* just 1 or 2 nights or enjoy one of our packages. See you soon!
Address: 60 Sagetown Rd, Pine City, NY 14871. Tel: (607) 732-0213.

Type: Bed & breakfast.
Clientele: 50% gay & lesbian & 50% straight clientele.
Transportation: Car is best. Free pick up from airport or bus.
To Gay Bars: 15 minutes to David in Elmira, 45 minutes to Common Ground in Ithaca.
Rooms: 4 rooms with doubles & 1 queen bed.
Bathrooms: All private & 1 with Jacuzzi.
Meals: Choice of breakfast.

Vegetarian: Available upon request.
Complimentary: Tea, juice, soda, chocolate on pillow.
Dates Open: All year.
High Season: May 1-November 1.
Rates: $40-$95 per night for two, $5 each extra guest.
Discounts: Special honeymoon & weekend packages & long term stays of 4 or more nights.
Credit Cards: MC & VISA.
Rsv'tns: Required.

Reserve Through: Travel agent or call direct.
Parking: Ample free off-street parking.
In-Room: Maid & room service.
On-Premises: Baby grand piano, CD's, color cable TV, VCR, small video tape library, telephone, refrigerator, laundry facilities for long term guests.
Exercise/Health: Weight machine, treadmill, running areas, outdoor hot tub. Jacuzzi in one room

& nearby full service fitness center.
Swimming: Nearby creek. 45 min to Cayuga & Seneca Lakes.
Sunbathing: On common sun decks.
Nudity: Permitted in hot tub.
Smoking: Not permitted.
Pets: Not permitted.
Handicap Access: No.
Children: Permitted if well-behaved.
Languages: English.
Your Host: Bill & John.

We Appreciate Your Comments!

Positive comments of interest may be included in the next issue, giving future readers the benefit of your experience. And it's a nice way of saying "thank you" to an innkeeper who extended you exceptional hospitality.

See the contents for the Reader Comment Form.

FIRE ISLAND

Belvedere

Men ♂

For magnificent terrace views over 100 miles of water, with superb sunsets, stay at *Belvedere*. Many of our rooms have terraces because this old mansion was built in the tradition of a Venetian palace, complete with towers, domes, statuary and fountains. There are also sun decks, a hot tub, a Roman swimming pool and an extensive gym. Though our rooms are not large, they have frescoed ceilings, antiques, Oriental rugs and crystal chandeliers. Most have private baths.

Address: Box 4026, Cherry Grove Fire Island, NY 11782. Tel: (516) 597-6448.

Type: Guesthouse and cottages.
Clientele: Men only.
Transportation: Car, Long Island RR or air.
To Gay Bars: 2 blocks or a 5-minute walk.
Rooms: 30 rooms, 5 suites & 30 cottages with single double & king beds.
Bathrooms: 20 private bath/toilets & 10 private sink/washbasins. Others share.

Meals: Continental breakfast weekends & holidays.
Complimentary: Coffee always available & cocktail parties on holiday weekends.
Dates Open: May 1st-Oct 15th.
Rates: Rooms $60-$100 weekdays, $225-$400 weekends.
Credit Cards: MC, VISA & Amex.
Rsv'tns: Required.

Reserve Through: Call direct.
Parking: Ample pay parking at ferry terminal on mainland.
In-Room: Refrigerator & ceiling fans. Some color TVs & VCRs.
On-Premises: TV lounge & coffee/tea-making facilities.
Exercise/Health: Gym, weights & Jacuzzi.
Swimming: Pool & 5 minutes to ocean beach.

Sunbathing: At poolside, beach, patio, roof, private and common sun decks.
Nudity: Permitted in all sunbathing areas.
Pets: Not permitted.
Handicap Access: Yes.
Children: Not permitted.
Languages: English & French.

IGTA

Carousel Guest House

Men ♂

Sun, Surf & Solace Far From the Manhattan Crowd

Fire Island is an island of contrasts. Here is the absence of autos, the presence of deer, the lull of the surf and the beat of the disco. Set in a garden among holly, cherry, pine, calendula, rose and zinnia, the *Carousel Guest House* offers a charming retreat near both the beach and Fire Island's gay night life.

Address: PO Box 4001, Cherry Grove Fire Island, NY 11782-0998. Tel: (516) 597-6612.

Type: Guesthouse.
Clientele: Mostly men.
Transportation: Sayville ferry to island, then 2-minute walk.
To Gay Bars: 1 minute to men's bars.
Rooms: 2 singles & 9

doubles.
Bathrooms: 3 shared & an outdoor shower.
Meals: Continental breakfast.
Dates Open: May-Oct.
Rates: $60-$175.
Credit Cards: MC, VISA &

Amex.
Rsv'tns: Highly recommended.
Reserve Through: Call direct.
Minimum Stay: 2 nights on weekends.
Swimming: Ocean beach

300 ft away.
Sunbathing: On beach or common sun decks.
Smoking: Permitted.
Pets: Not permitted.
Handicap Access: No.
Children: Not permitted.
Languages: English.

Cherry Grove Beach Hotel

Gay/Lesbian ♀♂

Cherry Grove Beach Hotel, Fire Island's largest gay resort, has been totally modernized so you can enjoy staying with us as much as you enjoy playing with us! Located in the heart of the Grove, the resort now offers sixty-four newly-renovated studio apartments with choice of standard or deluxe rooms, all with private baths and added security safeguards. Home of the Ice Palace entertainment complex, *Cherry Grove* offers live entertainment, a piano bar, dancing with NYC's top DJ's, drag shows, contests, movies and theme parties, as well as swimming, weightlifting, aerobics classes and vollyball games.
Address: PO Box 537, Sayville, NY 11782-0537. Tel: (516) 597-6600.

Type: Hotel with bar & disco.
Clientele: Good mix of gay men & women.
Transportation: Ferry.
To Gay Bars: Within 200 feet of 5 gay bars.
Rooms: 64 studio apartments with high rise sleep sofas for 2.
Bathrooms: All private.
Vegetarian: 3 restaurants have vegetarian alternatives.

Dates Open: May 1-November 1.
High Season: Memorial Day-Labor Day.
Rates: Off season $39-$135 & in season $65-$199.
Discounts: Group & midweek.
Credit Cards: MC, VISA, Amex & Discover.
Rsv'tns: Required.
Reserve Through: Call direct.

Minimum Stay: Two nights on weekends.
Parking: At ferry terminal on the other side.
In-Room: Color TV, AC, maid service, telephone, ceiling fans, kitchen & refrigerator.
Exercise/Health: Gym & weights.
Swimming: In the Olympic pool or at the nearby ocean beach.
Sunbathing: At poolside

or on the beach.
Nudity: Permitted on the beach.
Smoking: Permitted. Non-smoking rooms are available.
Pets: Not permitted.
Handicap Access: Yes. Rooms available.
Children: Not permitted.
Languages: English.
Your Host: Isaac.

Fire Island Pines

Gay/Lesbian ♀♂

Our redwood home is located near the ocean, a block from the dock, shopping and bars. Each room at *Fire Island Pines* is appointed with two beds and refrigerator. Relax on our two decks, or in our open-air, eight-person hot tub, which is fenced, for privacy.
Address: 9B Ocean Walk, PO Box 5314, Fire Island, NY 11782. Tel: (516) 597-6767 or (718) 424-3951.

Type: Bed & breakfast in a private home.
Clientele: Mostly gay & lesbian with some straight clientele.
Transportation: L.I. railroad to Sayville. Special taxi to ferry boat to the Pines. 1 block from ferry dock.
To Gay Bars: 1 block or a 3-minute walk to gay/lesbian bars.

Rooms: 4 rooms & 1 suite with single beds.
Bathrooms: 1 private bath/shower/toilet, 2 shared bath/shower/toilets.
Meals: Cooking privileges available.
Dates Open: Memorial day weekend till 2 weeks after Labor Day.
Rates: Rooms $200/ weekend per person,

2 room suite $800/ weekend for 4, higher on holidays, May-June.
Rsv'tns: Required.
Reserve Through: Travel agent or call direct.
Minimum Stay: 2 nights.
Parking: Ample mainland.
In-Room: Refrigerator.
On-Premises: Laundry facilities, $5 per load.
Exercise/Health: 8 per-

son Jacuzzi & weights.
Sunbathing: On the common sun decks & patio.
Nudity: Permitted in Jacuzzi area.
Pets: Not permitted.
Handicap Access: Yes, lower level of house.
Children: Not especially welcomed.
Languages: English, limited Spanish.

Take along the Expert

Ferrari's Places of Interest™ contains articles contributed by gay and lesbian journalists on the scene, giving insight into gay and lesbian communities worldwide. With its accompanying directory, it's the perfect vacation planner.

ITHACA

Pleasant Grove B & B

Ithaca and the Finger Lakes Wine Country

Gay-Friendly 60/40 ♀♂

Pleasant Grove is a comfortable country home from the 1930's above the west shore of Cayuga Lake in the Finger Lakes wine country. Panoramic views from the deck make afternoon tea and morning breakfast special times. Hike, birdwatch and cross-country ski in our fields and woods. Taughannock Falls State Park provides swimming and boating on Cayuga Lake. Four golf courses are minutes away. Wineries, antique shops and fine restaurants make a visit memorable. Both Cornell University and Ithaca College are fifteen minutes away.

Address: 1779 Trumansburg Rd (Rte 96), Jacksonville, NY 14854. Tel: (607) 387-5420 or (800) 398-3963.

Type: Bed & breakfast.
Clientele: 60% gay & lesbian & 40% straight clientele.
Transportation: Car.
To Gay Bars: 10 miles from gay/lesbian bar.
Rooms: 3 rooms with queen beds.
Bathrooms: 1 private, others share.
Meals: Full breakfast.

Vegetarian: Always available.
Complimentary: Afternoon, tea, coffee.
Dates Open: All year.
High Season: May-October.
Rates: $60-$75.
Rsv'tns: Preferred.
Reserve Through: Call direct.
Minimum Stay: During

major university & college weekends.
Parking: Ample, free off-street parking.
Exercise/Health: Cross-country skiing, hiking & birdwatching. Golf courses nearby.
Swimming: Cayuga Lake & streams nearby.
Sunbathing: Common sun decks.

Smoking: Not permitted in the house.
Pets: Not permitted.
Handicap Access: No.
Children: Permitted over 12 years old by prior arrangement.
Languages: English & German.
Your Host: James & Robert.

LAKE GEORGE

King Hendrick Motel

Escape to the Adirondacks!

Gay-Friendly ♀♂

King Hendrick Motel consists of cabins and deluxe efficiencies in a quiet, secluded location three miles south of the village. All guest quarters have air conditioning and color cable TV. There is a private back deck with a panoramic view of the hills, a picnic area in the woods, a pool, walking/bike trails to the lake and spectacular fall foliage. We are only 20 minutes from Saratoga Springs with its antiquing and factory outlet shopping. Other area attractions are whitewater rafting, horseback riding, hiking, the Saratoga Performing Arts Center, the mineral baths and wonderful amusement parks.

Address: Rte 9, Lake George, NY. Tel: (518) 792-0418.

Type: Motel, cabins & efficiencies.
Clientele: Mostly straight clientele with a gay/lesbian following.
Transportation: Car is

best.
To Gay Bars: 10 miles to gay/lesbian bar.
Rooms: 3 rooms, 8 apartments & 16 cottages with double beds.

Bathrooms: All private.
Meals: Continental breakfast.
Dates Open: All year.
High Season: Memorial Day through Labor Day,

fall foliage.
Rates: $45-$115.
Credit Cards: MC, VISA, Amex & Discover.
Rsv'tns: Required.
Reserve Through: Call

direct.
Parking: Ample free off-street parking.
In-Room: Color cable TV, AC, maid service & refrigerator.

On-Premises: Screen porch.
Exercise/Health: Nearby gym, sauna, steam, massage.
Swimming: Pool on

premises, 3 miles to lake.
Sunbathing: At poolside & on private & common sun decks.
Smoking: Permitted.
Pets: Permitted.

Children: Welcome.
Languages: English & Spanish.
Your Host: Barry.

LONG ISLAND

Cozy Cabins

Gay/Lesbian ♀♂

On the Montauk Hwy, near both Bridgehampton and East Hampton and less than a mile from ocean beaches, *Cozy Cabins* has been a Hampton landmark since the late 1940's. The cabins are nestled on 7 acres of heavily-wooded land, affording privacy and space rare to the modern Hampton scene. Recently renovated, the cabins are new from top to bottom, while maintaining their old look and rustic charm. They now boast cathedral ceilings, modern baths and kitchens, antique furnishings and a sun deck with Jacuzzi.

Address: Box 848, Montauk Hwy, Wainscott, East Hampton, NY 11975. Tel: (516) 537-1160.

Type: Motel & inn.
Clientele: Mainly gay/lesbian with some straight clientele.
To Gay Bars: Across the street to men's/women's bar.
Rooms: 20 cabins with kitchens. 1 single, 12 doubles, 7 triples.
Bathrooms: All private.
Dates Open: All year.

High Season: Memorial Day through Labor Day.
Rates: In-season $89-$125, off-season $69-$99.
Discounts: For groups.
Credit Cards: VISA & MC.
Rsv'tns: Required.
Reserve Through: Call direct.
Minimum Stay: 2 nights in summer.
Parking: Ample off-street

parking.
In-Room: Color cable TV, maid service, AC, ceiling fans & refrigerator. Some rooms have fireplaces.
On-Premises: Laundry facilities, pay phone, sun deck with 9 foot hot tub, BBQ area.
Exercise/Health: Jacuzzi.
Swimming: One mile to ocean beach.

Sunbathing: On ocean beach, patio, common sun decks & Jacuzzi area.
Smoking: Permitted without restrictions.
Pets: Permitted, please inquire.
Handicap Access: No.
Children: Not permitted.
Languages: English.
Your Host: Dennis.

One Thirty-Two North Main

The Hot Place to be COOL This Summer

Gay/Lesbian ♂

To make each guest feel like a personal friend visiting has been the primary objective at *One Thirty-Two North Main* for 23 summers. On two tranquil acres, just steps from quaint village shops and trendy restaurants, we offer fifteen accommodations in various locations, including the main house, the annex, the cottage and the cabana, and an unusually inviting large and secluded swimming pool surrounded by a "jungle" of trees. From *One Thirty-Two*, it's a 5-minute drive or bike ride to one of the world's most beautiful beaches.

Address: 132 N Main St, East Hampton, NY 11937. Tel: (516) 324-2246 or 324-9771.

Type: Mini-resort.
Clientele: Mostly men with women welcome.
Transportation: Car, train or bus. Short walk from Long Island RR station, Hampton Jitney & Hampton Express bus stops.
To Gay Bars: 4 miles to bar, disco & restaurant.
Rooms: 13 rooms, 1 apartment & 1 cottage with single, double or

queen beds.
Bathrooms: 5 private shower/toilets & 8 shared full baths.
Meals: Continental breakfast.
Dates Open: May-Sept.
High Season: All weekends from July 4th to Labor Day.
Rates: $65-$225.
Discounts: On stays including 5 weekdays.

Credit Cards: MC, VISA, Amex.
Rsv'tns: Required.
Reserve Through: Travel agent or call direct.
Minimum Stay: 2 nights on weekends in July & August.
Parking: Ample free off-street parking.
In-Room: Maid service, refrigerator, ceiling fans. Some accommodations

have AC.
On-Premises: TV lounge.
Exercise/Health: Nearby gym, weights, steam & massage.
Swimming: 20 ft by 50 ft pool on premises, 1 mile to ocean beach.
Sunbathing: At poolside, on patio or ocean beach.
Nudity: Permitted at poolside.

continued next page

Smoking: Permitted without restrictions. **Pets:** Permitted in annex or cabana. **Handicap Access:** Yes, very small step at back entrance. **Children:** Permitted in annex or cabana. **Languages:** English, Italian. **Your Host:** Tony

Sag Harbor Bed & Breakfast

Women ♀

Quaint Yet Compelling...

Indulge yourself in our romantic hideaway nestled in the woods of Sag Harbor, right in the middle of The Hamptons on Long Island. Relax in any one of *Sag Harbor Bed & Breakfast's* five lounging areas, indoors or out. Enjoy the ample skylights bathing every room in a rainbow of light. Stroll through our enchanting whaling village with its array of rustic shops, gourmet restaurants, and exclusive wharf. You can do practically everything...golf, tennis, sailing, hiking, biking, horseback riding...or virtually nothing...sipping wine by the fireplace or sunbathing on the secluded deck.

Address: Sag Harbor, NY . **Tel: (212) 505-7869 or (516) 725-5945 wknds.**

Type: Country home bed & breakfast. **Clientele:** Mostly women with gay men welcome. **Transportation:** Car is best, free pick up from airport, bus, ferry dock, train. **To Gay Bars:** 3 miles. **Rooms:** 3 rooms with double or queen beds. **Bathrooms:** All private bath/shower/toilets. **Meals:** Full country breakfast, other meals by request at additional charge. **Vegetarian:** Breakfast only. Vegetarian food nearby. **Complimentary:** Wine upon arrival. **Dates Open:** All year. **High Season:** Summers, holidays. **Rates:** $100-$125 per night in winter, $125-$150 per night in summer. **Discounts:** Seasonal summer rates, half & full shares also available in summer. **Rsv'tns:** Required. **Reserve Through:** Call direct. **Minimum Stay:** Required in summer, not in winter. **Parking:** Adequate free off-street parking. **In-Room:** Room service. **On-Premises:** Meeting rooms. **Exercise/Health:** Bicycles & other sports equipment. **Swimming:** Nearby ocean, lake, pond & bay. **Sunbathing:** On common sun deck. **Nudity:** Permitted on private deck overlooking nature reserve. **Smoking:** Permitted, non-smoking rooms available. **Pets:** Not permitted. **Handicap Access:** Yes, downstairs room. **Children:** Permitted. **Languages:** English, French, Spanish & Italian.

NEW YORK

A Bed & Breakfast Reservation Center in New York

Gay/Lesbian ♀♂

Perfect Accommodations in New York, Southampton or Paris

Having started out as the host of a Manhattan bed and breakfast, I know that potential guests appreciate getting a clear and honest description of the accommodations and of the surrounding neighborhood before they book. I know they appreciate dealing with a person who is not only interested in booking once, but looking down the road for repeat business.

A Bed & Breakfast Reservation Center in New York offers a wide variety of bed and breakfast accommodations in New York City at prices

ranging from $60 to $90 per night. Several are within a few blocks of major Midtown hotels and theatres. We also have private studios and apartments for people who wish to be on their own. Unhosted facilities start at $100 per night, some less. Apartments are also available by the month.

Our clients are not only tourists, but corporations who are trying to cut down on their corporate travel expenses. Our hosts are New Yorkers who make their guest rooms or apartments available for paying guests. Our hosted accommodations include continental breakfast.

All accommodations are personally inspected. I turn down an average of seven out of ten inquiries to join our center, although many have been doing bed and breakfast for years. I prefer to turn down a property, rather than to place someone in an accommodation that is not satisfactory.

We can suggest reasonably-priced airport pick up to facilitate getting into New York. Aside from finding the most appropriate accommodations for our guests, we try to enhance their stay in New York by assisting in every way possible.

Our main office is in the seaside resort of Southampton, on Long Island, where we also have available accommodations. And now, you can also call us for accommodations in Paris, France.

Address: PO Box 2646, Southampton, NY 11969-2646. Tel: In NY: (212) 977-3512, Outside NY: (516) 283-6785.

Type: Bed & breakfast & apartments.
Clientele: Mostly gay & lesbian with some hetero clientele.
Transportation: Taxi is best. Charge for pick up from public transportation stations.
To Gay Bars: Walking distance to most, depending on the accommodation.
Rooms: 25 rooms, 10 suites & 15 apartments.
Bathrooms: Most are private, but some are shared.
Meals: Continental breakfast at hosted accommodations.
Complimentary: Tea & coffee.
Dates Open: All year.
Rates: $60-$90 hosted or $100-$220 unhosted private apartments.
Credit Cards: Amex.
Rsv'tns: Required.
Reserve Through: Travel agent or call direct.
Minimum Stay: 2 days.
Parking: Variety of adequate parking conditions. On-street pay parking.
In-Room: Color TV, AC, ceiling fans, telephone, kitchen, & refrigerator.
On-Premises: Laundry facilities. Doorman & concierge service with secured buildings.
Sunbathing: On private sun decks when available.
Smoking: Permitted sometimes.
Pets: Permitted sometimes.
Handicap Access: Some are accessible.
Children: Permitted.
Languages: English, Spanish & French.

IGTA

A Greenwich Village Habitué

Your Perfect Home Away From Home

Gay-Friendly 50/50 ♀♂

A Greenwich Village Habitué has fully-appointed apartments available in an owner-occupied 1830's Federal brownstone in the historic West Village. Antique filled apartments come complete with living room, sleeping alcove, dining alcove, fully-equipped kitchen and full bath. The apartments overlook a formal English garden. They are perfect for both business or tourism and are only a short distance from the Convention Center.

As Quoted by Mimi Reed of Food and Wine Magazine, *November 1993*
"It was to our delight, an immaculate, graciously stocked and elegantly furnished apartment (with a mahogany sleigh bed) in a brownstone. It seemed a great bargain."
Address: West Village, NYC, NY . Tel: (212) 243-6495.

Type: Private, fully-equipped apartments.
Clientele: Sophisticated, well-traveled persons, some of whom are gay & lesbian.
Transportation: Taxi or Cary bus.
To Gay Bars: Walking distance to most gay & lesbian bars.
Rooms: 2 fully-appointed private apartments with double beds & queen sofa bed.
Bathrooms: Private.
Meals: Fixings provided for continental breakfast.
Vegetarian: Complete vegetarian/health food center nearby.
Dates Open: All year.
Rates: $117 plus taxes (single or double occupancy).
Rsv'tns: Advance reservation required.
Reserve Through: Call direct.
Minimum Stay: 3 nights.
Parking: Limited on-street pay parking.
In-Room: AC, color TV, telephone, answering machine, full kitchen, refrigerator, coffee & tea-making facilities. Daily maid service available for additional charge.
Exercise/Health: Nearby gym.
Smoking: Not permitted.
Pets: Well-behaved smaller pets permitted.
Handicap Access: No.
Children: Well-behaved older children permitted.
Languages: English, Spanish.
Your Host: Matthew & Lewis.

A Village Bed & Breakfast

Gay/Lesbian ♀♂

In a Manhattan brownstone, *A Village B&B* offers studio apartments with king-sized beds, fireplaces, Oriental rugs, high ceilings and large bathrooms for less than the price of a hotel room. Amenities include refrigerator, microwave, hair dryer, iron, ironing boards, and dishes. Our quiet and comfortable rooms are convenient to all the exciting Manhattan attractions. Whether your stay is a weekend or a week, please phone us first. We'll make you feel comfortable in New York City. As a bonus, we have access to theater tickets for as little as $10. Ask for details.
Address: 131 E 15th St #2N, New York, NY 10003. Tel: (800) 387-9117, (212) 387-9418.

Type: Private studio apartments.
Clientele: Gay & lesbian. Good mix of men & women.
Transportation: Taxi from Grand Central Stn.or Port Authority is about $5.
To Gay Bars: Walking distance.
Rooms: Private apartments and guest rooms.
Bathrooms: All private.
Vegetarian: 1 block to 24-hr deli with salad bar & hot food. Food may be brought to the apartment.
Complimentary: Coffee, tea always available.
Dates Open: All year.
Rates: $75-$95 single or double, includes tax.
Discounts: Stay 7 nights, 8th night free.
Rsv'tns: Required with one night's deposit. Please phone ahead. Frequently full.
Reserve Through: Travel agent or call direct.
Parking: On-street parking or secure garage 1/2 block away.
In-Room: Remote control color cable TV, refrigerator, microwave, coffee pot, & all the amenities.
Smoking: Permitted.
Pets: Small pets OK, but you must call ahead.
Handicap Access: No.
Children: Permitted, but you must call ahead.
Languages: English, Spanish, French, Italian.
Your Host: Jim & Jim.

Abode Bed & Breakfast, Ltd

Gay-Friendly ♀♂

Privacy & Luxury in a NYC Brownstone or Apartment

Have your heart set on staying in one of those delightful, old brownstones? Or how about a contemporary luxury apartment in the heart of Manhattan? *Abode* selects hosts with great care, and all homes are personally inspected to ensure the highest standards of cleanliness, attractiveness and hospitality. All the attractions of New York City—theatres, museums, galleries, restaurants, parks and shopping— are within easy reach. Select an

unhosted contemporary luxury apartment or a private apartment, with country inn ambiance, in an owner-occupied brownstone.

Address: PO Box 20022, New York, NY 10021. Tel: (212) 472-2000.

Type: Reservation service organization.
Clientele: Mostly straight clientele with a gay & lesbian following.
Transportation: Taxi.
To Gay Bars: Within a few blocks in most Manhattan neighborhoods.
Rooms: 200 apartments. Most have queen beds, some double, some king.
Bathrooms: All private.
Meals: Fixings for conti-

nental breakfast provided in most apartments.
Vegetarian: Nearby supermarkets.
Dates Open: All year.
Rates: $100-$300 per night.
Discounts: Special rates for extended stays of 1 month or longer.
Credit Cards: Amex.
Rsv'tns: Required.
Reserve Through: Call

direct.
Minimum Stay: Required.
Parking: Ample pay parking.
In-Room: Color/color cable TV, VCR, AC, telephone, answering machine, kitchen, refrigerator, coffee & tea-making facilities. Daily maid service can be arranged at guests' expense.

On-Premises: Laundry facilities at several apartments.
Smoking: We have smoking & non-smoking accommodations.
Pets: Not permitted.
Handicap Access: No.
Children: Over 12 years permitted in some apartments. Please inquire.
Languages: English.

Chelsea Mews Guesthouse

Gay/Lesbian ♂

Friendly, Private & Affordable

Ours is an old fashioned atmosphere, with Victorian garden. Guestrooms are furnished with antiques, and there is even an antique shop on the ground floor. You'll find the location of *Chelsea Mews* very convenient to all attractions, transportation and shopping. Advance reservations are advised.

Address: 344 W 15th St, New York, NY 10011. Tel: (212) 255-9174.

Type: Guesthouse.
Clientele: Mostly men with women welcome.
Transportation: Any city transportation.
To Gay Bars: 1-1/2 blocks.

Rooms: 8 rooms with single or double beds.
Bathrooms: 1 private bath/toilet, others share bath/shower/toilet.
Meals: Continental breakfast of coffee &

continued next page

fruit.
Dates Open: All year.
Rates: $65-$150.
Rsv'tns: Required.
Reserve Through: Call

direct.
Parking: Ample on-street pay parking.
In-Room: Color TV, AC, telephone, refrigerator,

coffee & tea-making facilities & maid service.
On-Premises: Garden.
Smoking: All rooms non-smoking.

Pets: Not permitted.
Handicap Access: No.
Children: Not especially welcomed.
Languages: English.

Colonial House Inn

Being Gay Is Only Part of Our Charm

Gay/Lesbian ♀♂

Colonial House is like a European hotel. The inn, on a quiet street in Chelsea, has 20 modern and impeccably clean rooms. All have TV, radio and air conditioning, sinks and direct-dial phone. Some rooms have private baths and fireplaces. Most have refrigerators. The roof sun deck and homemade muffins at breakfast round out the amenities, but the real attraction here is service, including a 24-hour concierge. If you have any trepidation about the Big Apple, this is the place to stay. *Out & About, December, 1992.*

Address: 318 W 22nd St, New York, NY 10011. Tel: (212) 243-9669, (800) 689-3779, Fax: (212) 633-1612.

Type: Bed & breakfast inn.
Clientele: Good mix of gays & lesbians.
Transportation: Airport bus to city, then taxi. Paid car service. Will provide pick up from airport.
To Gay Bars: 1/2 block to several men's, 10-min walk to women's bars.
Rooms: 20 rooms, doubles & triples.
Bathrooms: 12 shared baths & 8 private. All

rooms have washing facilities.
Meals: Continental breakfast. Fresh-baked homemade muffins, bagels, special house-blend coffee, assorted juices daily, fresh fruit & cereal.
Complimentary: Tea, coffee & mints.
Dates Open: All year.
Rates: $65-$99 daily, $420-$665 weekly.
Discounts: Special winter & weekly rates.

Rsv'tns: Recommended.
Reserve Through: Travel agent or call direct.
Parking: On-street parking or 1/2 block to off-street pay parking.
In-Room: Maid service, color TV, AC, direct dial phones, radios, alarm clocks, some with refrigerators or fireplaces.
On-Premises: TV lounge.
Exercise/Health: Weights on premises. Gym & massage nearby.

Sunbathing: On common sun deck or rooftop.
Nudity: Permitted on sun deck.
Smoking: Permitted in rooms.
Pets: Not permitted.
Handicap Access: No.
Children: Mature children permitted.
Languages: English, Spanish, Portuguese & Italian.

IGTA

East Village Bed & Breakfast

Women ♀

East Village Bed & Breakfast is situated in a tasteful second-floor apartment located in an urban, multi-cultural, multi-ethnic neighborhood close to shops, galleries and affordable restaurants. Greenwich Village, SoHo, Chinatown and other areas of interest are within easy reach. The kitchen comes complete with items for preparing your own continental breakfast. Otherwise, you are usually on your own in your own apartment.

Address: 244 E 7th St, New York, NY 10009. Tel: (212) 260-1865.

Type: Bed & breakfast.
Clientele: Women only.
Transportation: Airport bus to Grand Central Sta. or Port Authority in Manhattan. Then taxi or bus.
To Gay Bars: Twenty

minute bus ride or a little longer walk.
Rooms: 2 rooms with single or double bed.
Bathrooms: 1 shared bath/shower/toilet.
Meals: Self-service conti-

nental breakfast.
Vegetarian: Available if requested in advance.
Complimentary: Coffee, tea, juices & snacks.
Dates Open: All year.
Rates: $50-$75 per day

for 1 or 2 people.
Rsv'tns: Recommended.
Reserve Through: Call direct.
Minimum Stay: 2 nights on weekends.
Parking: Adequate free

on-street parking.
In-Room: AC & telephone.
On-Premises: Guests

may use kitchen, refrig-
erator & watch TV.
Smoking: Not permitted.

Pets: Usually permitted
but call in advance.
Handicap Access: No.

There are stairs.
Children: Permitted.
Languages: English.

Three Thirty-Three West 88th Associates

Gay/Lesbian ♀♂

Beautifully-Furnished Apartments in Manhattan

For visits to New York, consider these exceptional one-bedroom apartments, just restored, in an 1890's brownstone on the west side of Manhattan, directly across the park from the Metropolitan Museum of Art. From *333 West 88th's* advantageous location, it's an easy trip, via subway or bus, to the theater district, the World Trade Center and the ferry to the Statue of Liberty. You can walk to Lincoln Center. Riverside Park, whose handsome promenade overlooks the Hudson, is 200 feet from the door. Apartments are unhosted, giving guests maximum independence. Coffee and tea are provided, and nearby groceries are open 24 hours a day. **Address: 333 West 88th St, New York, NY 10024. Tel: (212) 724-9818.**

Type: Bed & breakfast.
Clientele: Mostly gay & lesbian with some straight clientele.
Transportation: Taxi from airports. #1 subway line to 86th St Station.
To Gay Bars: 8 blocks.
Rooms: Unhosted B&B

apartments & hosted B&B rooms.
Bathrooms: All private.
Complimentary: Coffee & tea set-up.
Dates Open: All year.
Rates: $450-$700 weekly.
Rsv'tns: Required.

Reserve Through: Call direct.
Minimum Stay: Required.
Parking: Limited free on-street parking. Nearby garages suggested.
In-Room: Color TV, AC, telephone, kitchen & re-

frigerator.
Smoking: Permitted.
Pets: Well-behaved animals permitted.
Handicap Access: No.
Children: Welcome.
Languages: English.
Your Host: Albert.

OTEGO

A Woodchuck's Hollow

Gay-Friendly 50/50 ♀♂

An Inexpensive Alternative to the Hotel Syndrome!

A Woodchuck's Hollow is very country! Besides seeing that occasional pesky woodchuck, in the summer you can see bluebirds, hummingbirds, turkey and deer. You can spend a quiet evening listening to the distant train whistle or kick back with an outdoor BBQ. In winter, hike or cross-country ski our 70 acres of farmland and hills. Although secluded, we are in an area of tourist attractions: 10 minutes from the Soccer Hall of Fame, 20 minutes from the Corvette Hall of Fame and 45 minutes from Cooperstown Baseball Hall of Fame. **Address: RD 2 Otsdawa Rd 60A-7, Otego, NY. Tel: (607) 988-2713.**

Type: One-bedroom efficiency.
Clientele: 50% gay & lesbian & 50% straight .
Transportation: Car. Pick up from airport & bus. Charge depends on the number of people.
To Gay Bars: 60 miles. 15 miles to gay-friendly bar.
Rooms: 1 apartment with single bed & queen sofa.
Bathrooms: Private shower/toilet.
Vegetarian: Nearby

store & restaurant.
Complimentary: Tea, coffee & pop. Stocked refrigerator, set-up service (food, alcohol) by request.
Dates Open: All year.
High Season: July 4th weekend, August.
Rates: $125 with 2-day minimum. $50 per day after minimum. $250 weekly.
Discounts: Extra friendly discount on 3rd day, $10 off.

Rsv'tns: Usually required.
Reserve Through: Call direct.
Minimum Stay: 2 days.
Parking: Ample free off-street covered parking.
In-Room: AC, kitchen, refrigerator, coffee/tea-making facilities & laundry service. Color cable TV, telephone & maid service upon request.
On-Premises: Laundry facilities.
Exercise/Health: Nearby

Jacuzzi.
Swimming: Stream on premises. Nearby river & lake.
Sunbathing: On grassy knoll.
Smoking: Permitted on porch. Non-smoking room available.
Pets: Not permitted.
Handicap Access: Yes. Call ahead.
Children: Does not matter.
Languages: English.
Your Host: Wendy.

SWAIN SKI AREA

Fairwise Llama Farm B&B

Gay-Friendly 50/50 ♀♂

Fairwise Llama Farm is a place for all seasons, with woods, valleys, meadows and the silence of the country. Built as a family farm in the 1850's, it has served as such ever since. Long ago, Indians camped here as they fished the Canaseraga Creek. Stroll our grounds and visit the many different types of farm animals, including llamas, miniature horses, sheep and goats. Also on the farm is a gift, craft and pet shop. Set in the valley of Canaseraga, *Fairwise Llama Farm* is two miles from the Swain ski slopes for downhill skiing, and minutes from Letchworth and Stonybrook state parks. On the farm you can enjoy crosscountry skiing, snowmobiling, hiking and fishing.

Address: 1320 Rt 70, Canaseraga, NY 14822. Tel: (607) 545-6247.

Type: B&B with gift shop.
Clientele: 50% gay & lesbian & 50% straight clientele.
Transportation: Car is best.
Rooms: 2 rooms with queen beds.

Bathrooms: 1 shared bath/shower/toilet, 1 shared toilet only.
Meals: Full breakfast.
Complimentary: Tea & coffee, mints on pillow.
Dates Open: All year.
Rates: $27.50 single, $50.00 double.

Rsv'tns: Required.
Parking: Ample free off-street parking.
In-Room: Ceiling fans, maid & room service.
On-Premises: TV lounge, laundry facilities.
Nudity: Permitted in the house.

Smoking: Permitted in living room.
Pets: Not permitted.
Handicap Access: No.
Children: Not at this time.
Languages: English.
Your Host: Phil & Thom.

WINDHAM

Point Lookout Mountain Inn

Gay-Friendly ♀♂

Come, Enjoy Our Point of View

Point Lookout Mountain Inn, high on a cliffside, overlooking a spectacular view encompassing 5 states, is the quintessential mountain lodge. Clean and comfortable guest rooms provide beautiful views. Our guests thoroughly enjoy the "Raid-the-Refrigerator" breakfast. The full-service restaurant features creative cuisine, emphasizing Mediterranean foods. The atmosphere is casual and comfortable, the staff is friendly and knowledgeable, the food is fabulous, the view is spectacular, and all this is waiting just for you. Come, enjoy our point of view.

Address: Rte 23 Box 33, East Windham, NY 12439. Tel: (518) 734-3381.

Type: Inn with restaurant, bar, fireplace lounge, variety of shops.
Clientele: Mostly straight clientele with a gay & lesbian following.
Transportation: Car is best. Free pick up from bus.
To Gay Bars: 30 miles to Albany or Woodstock gay/lesbian bars.
Rooms: 13 rooms with double or queen beds.
Bathrooms: All private.
Meals: "Raid-the-refrigerator" breakfast.
Vegetarian: Restaurant menu includes wide selection of vegetarian & vegan.
Dates Open: All year.
High Season: January through March. July through October.
Rates: $55-$125.
Discounts: Group rates, long-term discounts, ski packages, mid-week (non-holiday) 3rd night free.
Credit Cards: MC, VISA,

Amex, Diners & Discover.
Rsv'tns: Recommended 1 week in advance, 3 weeks for holiday weekends.
Reserve Through: Travel agent or call direct.
Minimum Stay: 2 nights on holiday weekends.
Parking: Ample, free off-

street parking.
In-Room: Color TV, ceiling fans & maid service.
On-Premises: Meeting rooms, TV lounge, private dining rooms, fireplace lounge, game room & picnic area.
Exercise/Health: Walking trails. 7 miles to ski

Windham, 4 miles to major NYS hiking trail system.
Swimming: River & lake nearby.
Sunbathing: On common sun decks, private trails, & in picnic area.
Smoking: Permitted.
Pets: Permitted if well-

behaved. $10 per day with $50 refundable deposit.
Handicap Access: Restaurant, yes. Inn, no.
Children: Permitted.
Languages: English & Italian.
Your Host: Rosemary & Mariana.

WOODSTOCK

River Run Bed & Breakfast

Gay-Friendly ♀♂

Our exquisite 1887 Queen Anne "cottage" is surrounded by the Catskill Forest Preserve, with its magnificent hiking trails, splended foliage and superb skiing. Our eclectic Victorian village features tennis, swimming, theatre, museum, antiques, a weekly country auction and a variety of restaurants. Rejuvenate on our delightful wraparound porch or in our book-filled parlor, complete with piano and fireplace. Step into the oak-floored dining room, bathed in the colors of the inn's signature stained-glass windows, and enjoy homemade breakfasts and refreshments. At *River Run,* all are welcome, and all are made comfortable.
Address: Main St, Fleischmanns, NY 12430. Tel: (914) 254-4884.

Type: Bed & Breakfast.
Clientele: Mostly straight clientele with a significant gay & lesbian following.
Transportation: Car is best. Trailways bus stops at our front door, direct from NYC.
To Gay Bars: 35 miles or a 50-minute drive to Clicks in Kingston.
Rooms: 7 rooms & 1 apartment with single, double, queen or king beds.
Bathrooms: Private: 3 shower/toilet, 3 bath/shower/toilet. 2 shared

full baths.
Meals: Full breakfast.
Vegetarian: Available upon request. Most diets accommodated.
Complimentary: Afternoon refreshments.
Dates Open: All year.
High Season: Memorial Day-Labor Day, Sep-Oct (foliage), Dec-Mar (skiing).
Rates: $45-$90.
Discounts: 10% for single & 4 or more night stays.
Credit Cards: MC, VISA.
Rsv'tns: Strongly recommended. Walk-ins accommodated if space is available.

Reserve Through: Travel agent or call direct.
Minimum Stay: 2 nights weekends, 3 nights holiday weekends.
Parking: Ample free on-street parking.
In-Room: Color & B/W TV, maid service. Kitchen in apartment.
On-Premises: TV lounge, VCR, tea-making facilities, fireplace & piano.
Exercise/Health: Massage. Nearby gym, Jacuzzi.
Swimming: Stream on premises. Nearby pool, river & lake.

Sunbathing: On private grounds & at nearby pool.
Smoking: Inn is non-smoking except for apartment accommodation.
Pets: Well-behaved, fully-trained, well-socialized pets permitted.
Handicap Access: Yes. Apartment is on ground level.
Children: Welcome. Rollaway, crib available.
Languages: English, French.
Your Host: Larry.

NORTH CAROLINA

ASHEVILLE

AppleWood Manor B&B

Gay-Friendly ♀

Two acres of trees and wildflower gardens form the backdrop for this fine, old turn-of-the-century colonial known as *AppleWood Manor*. Its spacious guest rooms, decorated with antiques and lace, have balconies, fireplaces and, of course, private baths. There is a parlor and a library in which to relax after the day's activities. For breakfast, we make fresh muffins, breads and entrees and serve them with specially-blended coffee and teas and seasonal fruit. The Botanical Gardens are only two blocks away and bikes are available for riding.

Address: 62 Cumberland Circle, Asheville, NC 28801. Tel: (704) 254-2244.

Type: Bed & breakfast.
Clientele: Mainly straight with gay female following.
Transportation: Car is best. Free pick up from airport
To Gay Bars: 7 minutes by car.
Rooms: 4 rooms & 1 cottage with queen beds.
Bathrooms: All private.
Meals: Full breakfast.
Vegetarian: Available

upon request.
Complimentary: Tea, cordial, chocolates, fresh flowers.
Dates Open: All year except Christmas Eve & Christmas Day.
High Season: Autumn.
Rates: $85-$115.
Credit Cards: MC & VISA.
Rsv'tns: Required, but walk-ins accepted if space is available.
Reserve Through: Travel

agent OK, but we prefer you call direct.
Minimum Stay: 2 nights on weekends & month of October.
Parking: Ample free off-street parking.
In-Room: AC, fireplace, balcony, ceiling fans.
Exercise/Health: Badminton, croquet, bicycles & guests have complimentary use of nearby fitness center with

weights, sauna & aerobics.
Sunbathing: On private sun decks.
Smoking: Not permitted.
Pets: Not permitted.
Handicap Access: No.
Children: Permitted 12 years of age & older.
Languages: English.
Your Host: Susan & Maryanne.

Bird's Nest Bed & Kitchen, The

Country Living in the City

Gay/Lesbian ♀

Seclusion and quiet are yours just a short walk from downtown Asheville, when you stay with us at *Bird's Nest Bed & Kitchen.* Our inn sits on top of a hill overlooking both the city and the beautiful Blue Ridge Mountains. The views are magnificent. Your accommodations have a private entrance, private bath, master bedroom with sunporch, fully-equipped kitchen, and guests also have their own private living room

and dining room on the second floor of our home. Boating, hiking, skiing and horseback riding are all available in the area.

Address: 41 Oak Park Rd, Asheville, NC 28801. Tel: (704) 252-2381.

Type: Guesthouse.
Clientele: Mostly women with men welcome.
Transportation: Car is best.
To Gay Bars: 1 mile.
Rooms: 1 apartment with double & queen bed.
Bathrooms: Private.
Vegetarian: There are 2 excellent vegetarian res-

taurants within 1 mile.
Complimentary: Coffee, tea, cereal & staples.
Dates Open: All year.
High Season: May-November.
Rates: $65 per night for 1 or 2 people.
Rsv'tns: Required.
Reserve Through: Call direct.
Minimum Stay: 2 nights

on weekends.
Parking: Ample off-street parking.
In-Room: Color TV, VCR, stereo, ceiling fans, telephone, kitchen, & refrigerator.
Exercise/Health: Gym, weights, Jacuzzi, sauna, steam, & massage all 1/2 mile away.
Swimming: Pool 1/2 mile

away.
Sunbathing: On private sun decks.
Smoking: Permitted outside.
Pets: Not permitted.
Handicap Access: No.
Children: Permitted on approval.
Languages: English & Spanish.
Your Host: Elizabeth.

Carolina Bed & Breakfast

Gay-Friendly ♀♂

Carolina Bed & Breakfast, a very comfortable 1900 Colonial Revival home, is located near downtown Asheville in the Montford Historic District. Five second-floor guest rooms are decorated in antiques and collectibles. All have private baths and air-conditioning and four have working fireplaces. There are two parlors and two porches for our guests to use and lovely gardens to stroll through. We are close to Biltmore House, the Blue Ridge Parkway, Great Smokey Mountains, regional crafts, excellent restaurants and shopping.

Address: 177 Cumberland Ave, Asheville, NC . Tel: (704) 254-3608.

Type: Bed & breakfast.
Clientele: Mostly straight clientele with a gay & lesbian following.
Transportation: Auto is best.
To Gay Bars: 1/2 mile. A 10-minute walk or 2-minute drive.
Rooms: 5 rooms with queen beds.
Bathrooms: 2 private bath/toilets & 3 private

shower/toilets.
Meals: Full breakfast.
Vegetarian: Available upon request. There is an excellent vegetarian restaurant downtown.
Complimentary: After-noon refreshments. Candy in guest rooms & public areas.
Dates Open: All year.
High Season: April-December.

Rates: $70-$90.
Credit Cards: MC, VISA & Discover.
Rsv'tns: Required.
Reserve Through: Travel agent or call direct.
Minimum Stay: 2 nights weekends & 3 nights on holiday weekends.
Parking: Ample off-street parking.
In-Room: AC & ceiling fans. Some rooms with

fireplaces.
Exercise/Health: Massage. Nearby gym, weights, Jacuzzi & massage.
Smoking: Limited to porches only.
Pets: Not permitted.
Handicap Access: No.
Children: Not especially welcome.
Languages: English.
Your Host: Sam & Karin.

Corner Oak Manor

Gay-Friendly ♀

Surrounded by trees, this lovely English Tudor home is located in a quiet residential neighborhood minutes from the famed Biltmore Estate and Gardens. *Corner Oak Manor* was decorated by an interior designer, whose contributions include an oval drop ceiling in the living room, beautiful bathrooms and window treatments and coordinated wall coverings. A living room fireplace, baby grand piano and an outdoor deck with hot tub are among the gracious amenities. Karen, a gourmet cook, enjoys surprising guests with creative breakfasts which include four-cheese herb quiche, blueberry-ricotta pancakes, and Italian country omelets.

Address: 53 Saint Dunstans Rd, Asheville, NC . Tel: (704) 253-3525.

Type: Bed & breakfast.
Clientele: Mostly straight clientele with a lesbian following.
Transportation: Car is

best.
To Gay Bars: 2 miles.
Rooms: 3 rooms & 1 cottage with queen beds.
Bathrooms: 1 private

shower/toilet & 3 private bath/toilet/showers.
Meals: Full breakfast.
Vegetarian: Available with 1 day's notice. Sev-

eral vegetarian restaurants nearby.
Complimentary: After-noon refreshments,

continued next page

INN Places 1995

chocolates in room.
Dates Open: All year.
High Season: April-December.
Rates: $85-$125 per night double occupancy.
Credit Cards: MC, VISA, Amex & Discover.
Rsv'tns: Required.

Reserve Through: Call direct.
Minimum Stay: 2 nights on weekends.
Parking: Ample off-street parking.
In-Room: AC & ceiling fans. Kitchen in cottage.
On-Premises: Telephone

& refrigerator.
Exercise/Health: Jacuzzi on premises. Gym & massage nearby.
Swimming: Nearby pool.
Smoking: Permitted outside only. All rooms are non-smoking.
Pets: Small pets permit-

ted in cottage.
Handicap Access: No.
Children: Welcome in cottage. 12 years old & younger.
Languages: English.
Your Host: Karen & Andy.

Inn on Montford, The

Gay-Friendly ♀♂

We Specialize in Stress Reduction

The Inn on Montford is a vintage 1900 Arts-and-Crafts interpretation of a gabled English cottage by Asheville's most famous architect. Generous, light-filled rooms, accented by our collection of antiques, porcelains and Oriental rugs, have fireplaces, and several bedrooms have Jacuzzis. The famous inn dog, Jeff Davis, has been joined by colleague Dolley Madison. A center for music and arts, Asheville is an undiscovered treasure for gay people, and our neighborhood is a center for alternative lifestyles.

Address: 296 Montford Ave, Asheville, NC 28801. Tel: (704) 254-9569, (800) 254-9569, Fax: (704) 254-9518.

Type: Bed & breakfast.
Clientele: Mostly straight clientele with a gay & lesbian following.
Transportation: Car is best.
To Gay Bars: 1 mile.
Rooms: 4 rooms with queen beds.
Bathrooms: All private bath/toilets.
Meals: Full breakfast.
Vegetarian: Available on request. Fruit, whole-

grain cereal, home-made bread always available.
Complimentary: Coffee, tea, soft drinks.
Dates Open: All year.
High Season: October, May, July, December.
Rates: $90-$120.
Credit Cards: MC, VISA, Amex & Discover.
Rsv'tns: Recommended.
Reserve Through: Travel agent or call direct.
Minimum Stay: In

October & on weekends.
Parking: Ample, free, off-street parking.
In-Room: AC & fireplaces.
Exercise/Health: Gym. Tennis court nearby.
Smoking: Permitted outdoors. All rooms are non-smoking.

Pets: Not permitted.
Handicap Access: No.
Children: Permitted as long as they obey house rules.
Languages: English & French.
Your Host: Owen & Ripley.

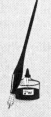

BAT CAVE

Old Mill B & B

Gay/Lesbian ♀♂

Come, be lulled to sleep on the banks of a rushing mountain stream in spectacular Hickory Nut Gorge. *Old Mill B&B* provides rustic comfort in rooms overlooking the river and hearty breakfasts of eggs benedict or soda-water pancakes with sausage and homemade apple sauce to fortify you for days of hiking, tubing, rafting, canoeing, tennis or golf. Shopping and dining are all close by, as is Asheville, Biltmore House, the Blue Ridge Parkway, Chimney Rock Park, Lake Lure, Flat Rock Playhouse, and the Carl Sandburg Home.

Address: Hwy 64/74/9, Box 252, Bat Cave, NC 28710. Tel: (704) 625-4256.

Type: Bed & breakfast with antique & gift shop.
Clientele: Mostly gay & lesbian with some straight clientele.
Transportation: Car is best.
To Gay Bars: 20 miles to Asheville gay/lesbian bars.
Rooms: 4 rooms.
Bathrooms: All private.
Meals: Full breakfast.

Complimentary: Drinks on arrival.
Dates Open: All year.
Rates: $55-$85.
Discounts: 10% for *INN Places* readers.
Credit Cards: MC, VISA, Amex, Discover.
Rsv'tns: Recommended.
Reserve Through: Travel agent or call direct.
Minimum Stay: 2 nights on weekends.

Parking: Ample free on-street parking.
In-Room: Maid service, ceiling fans, & sitting areas. 3 rooms have color TV.
On-Premises: TV lounge with VCR.
Exercise/Health: Soloflex & hot tub.
Swimming: River out back with tubing.
Sunbathing: Sun decks.

Smoking: Permitted without restrictions.
Pets: Permitted with restrictions.
Handicap Access: Limited accessibility.
Children: Please call.
Languages: English & limited Spanish.
Your Host: Walt.

BLOWING ROCK

Stone Pillar B & B

Gay-Friendly ♀♂

A Mountain Getaway For You & A Special Friend

Visit *Stone Pillar B&B* for a homey atmosphere in a friendly, scenic mountain community on the Blue Ridge Parkway. *Stone Pillar* provides easy access to quaint village antique, craft, and specialty shops, fine restaurants, summer theatre, hiking, cross-country ski trails, seven ski slopes and some of the most beautiful scenery in the Blue Ridge Mtns. Relax in the rock garden or in front of a warm fire. Your hosts, George and Ron, can help you plan a variety of activities and events to make your visit to Blowing Rock a memorable one.

Address: PO Box 1881, Pine St, Blowing Rock, NC 28605. Tel: (704) 295-4141.

Type: Bed & breakfast.
Clientele: Mostly straight clientele with a gay & lesbian following.
Transportation: Private auto is best.
To Gay Bars: 30 miles to Hickory, NC gay bars.
Rooms: 6 rooms with single, double or queen beds.
Bathrooms: All private.
Meals: Full breakfast.
Vegetarian: Available with 24 hrs notice.

Dates Open: All year.
High Season: Summer & fall foliage.
Rates: $50-$90 summer, $45-$80 winter.
Discounts: Stay 4 nights, 5th night free, 10% for group taking the entire house.
Credit Cards: MC & VISA.
Rsv'tns: Advisable 2 weeks ahead in peak season.
Reserve Through: Call direct.

Minimum Stay: 2 nights on weekends, high season, & holidays.
Parking: Ample, off-street parking.
In-Room: Alarms, radios, ceiling fans.
On-Premises: Living & dining areas with fireplace.
Exercise/Health: All degrees of hiking trails nearby, whitewater rafting.
Swimming: 2 blocks to

town pool.
Smoking: Permitted outdoors.
Pets: Not permitted.
Handicap Access: 1 room is handicap accessible.
Children: Not encouraged.
Languages: English.
Your Host: George & Ron.

North Carolina

CHAPEL HILL

Joan's Place, c/o M. Joan Stiven

Women ♀

Joan's Place is a B & B for women in my home, offering a rustic setting, secluded among trees, with a serene and picturesque environment. I have 2 bedrooms, one large with double bed, one smaller with double bed. There is a shared, full bath across the hall. Guests have access to my living room, with TV and stereo, ping-pong room downstairs, and large deck overlooking the trees. I am 2 miles south of Chapel Hill and UNC Campus, with easy access to Raleigh, Durham and Research Triangle Park.

Address: 1443 Poinsett Dr, Chapel Hill, NC 27514. Tel: (919) 942-5621.

Type: Bed & breakfast. **Clientele:** Women only. **Transportation:** Personal car only. **To Gay Bars:** About 8 miles to Durham gay bar. **Rooms:** 2 rooms with double beds. **Bathrooms:** 1 shared bath/shower/toilet.

Meals: Continental breakfast. **Vegetarian:** Available upon request. 2 vegetarian stores & vegetarian restaurants nearby. **Complimentary:** Tea, coffee & juices. **Dates Open:** All year. **High Season:** Spring,

summer and fall. **Rates:** $45-$48 per night. **Discounts:** Weekly rates. **Rsv'tns:** Preferred. **Reserve Through:** Call direct. **Parking:** Ample, free off-street parking. **In-Room:** AC & telephone.

On-Premises: TV lounge. **Smoking:** Permitted outdoors. **Pets:** Not permitted. **Handicap Access:** No. **Children:** Not permitted. **Languages:** English. **Your Host:** Joan.

HENDERSONVILLE

Stillwell House Bed & Breakfast

Gay-Friendly 50/50 ♀♂

Stillwell House was built in the 1920's with a European flavor. Located in the beautiful Blue Ridge mountains between Asheville and Lake Lure, it is within walking distance of downtown Hendersonville. The atmosphere at *Stillwell House* is low-key and we want you to feel right at home. It's a very quiet, relaxing and private place in which to spend your holiday. Hiking trails, golfing and observing the dramatic fall foliage are among the many activities available to our guests.

Address: 1300 Pinecrest Dr, Hendersonville, NC 28739. Tel: (704) 693-6475.

Type: Bed & breakfast. **Clientele:** 50% gay & lesbian and 50% straight clientele. **Transportation:** Car is best. **To Gay Bars:** 25 miles to Asheville NC. **Rooms:** 2 rooms with queen beds. **Bathrooms:** All private bath/toilet/shower. **Meals:** Expanded conti-

nental breakfast. **Vegetarian:** Not available. **Complimentary:** Tea, coffee, juice, milk, soft drinks. **Dates Open:** All year. **High Season:** May thru October. **Rates:** $55-$65. **Discounts:** 7th night free. **Credit Cards:** MC, VISA. **Rsv'tns:** Required.

Reserve Through: Call direct. **Minimum Stay:** Two days during high season. **Parking:** Ample off-street parking. **In-Room:** Color cable TV in one room, ceiling fans, AC, VCR, video tape library & maid service. **On-Premises:** TV lounge. **Exercise/Health:** Nearby gym, weights, Jacuzzi,

sauna. **Swimming:** YMCA pool & city pool. Lake Lure Beach in Lake Lure NC. **Sunbathing:** On the patio & at the beach. **Smoking:** Not permitted. **Pets:** Not permitted. **Handicap Access:** No. **Children:** Permitted if 12 years or older. **Languages:** English.

HOT SPRINGS

Duckett House Inn

The Babbling Brook Lulled Us to Sleep....

Gay-Friendly 50/50 ♀♂

Located on 4-1/2 acres with a large wooded area next to Spring Creek, *The Duckett House* is a turn-of-the century folk Victorian farm house. With its large wraparound porch and maple and dogwood trees, there are many spots to lie around and read or nap the afternoon away. For the more adventuresome, there are hiking trails, including the Appalachian Trail, or whitewater rafting on the scenic French Broad River. Nearby attractions include the Biltmore Estate and the Great Smokey Mtns National Park. Evenings, we offer fine vegetarian dinners and a cozy common room. Each room has a working fireplace with firewood happily supplied.

Address: on Hwy 209, PO Box 441, Hot Springs, NC 28743. Tel: (704) 622-7621.

Type: Bed & breakfast.
Clientele: 50% gay & lesbian & 50% straight clientele.
Transportation: Car is best. Pick up from airport $.75 per mile our car, $.65 per mile your car. Shuttle available for A.T. hikers.
To Gay Bars: 40 miles to Asheville, 63 miles to Knoxville.
Rooms: 6 rooms with double, queen or king beds.
Bathrooms: 2 shared.
Campsites: Tent sites.

Meals: Full breakfast with dinner available for additional fee.
Vegetarian: We serve lacto-ovo vegetarian meals with occasional seafood.
Complimentary: Tea & coffee.
Dates Open: All year.
High Season: May-July.
Rates: $43 singles, $60 doubles, $15 each additional person, includes full breakfast.
Discounts: Group rates 1 night 10%, 2 nights 15% when renting the

whole house.
Rsv'tns: Required, but walk-ins accepted if space is available.
Reserve Through: Call direct.
Parking: Ample free off-street parking, safe to leave vehicle if on over-night hike.
In-Room: Ceiling fans.
On-Premises: Laundry facilities available for small charge.
Exercise/Health: Nearby gym, weights, massage therapist. Hot mineral springs with no sulphur

smell 1/3 mi from Duckett House.
Swimming: In nearby creek.
Sunbathing: In private area near creek.
Nudity: Permitted. We are on 5 acres in private creek area.
Smoking: Permitted on the porch only.
Pets: Permitted with prior arrangements.
Handicap Access: Limited access.
Children: Not permitted under 12 years of age.
Languages: English.

WILMINGTON

Southern Heritage

A Truly Casual Beach Experience!

Gay/Lesbian ♀♂

Whether you're looking for a laid-back vacation, or you'd like to spend every waking moment on the go, Wilmington is the perfect getaway! With the beach ten minutes away and bars and restaurants, shopping, historic sites and more all downtown, there's something for everyone. Come stay with us at *Southern Heritage*, in the center of it all.

Address: 614 S 2nd St, Wilmington, NC 28401. Tel: (910) 251-9501.

Type: Guesthouse.
Clientele: Good mix of gay men & women.
Transportation: Car is best.
To Gay Bars: 5 blocks to gay bars. A 7-minute walk or 2-minute drive.
Rooms: 2 rooms with double or queen beds.
Bathrooms: 1 private bath/shower/toilet & 1 private shower/toilet.
Vegetarian: Downtown restaurants, Cafe Phoenix.
Complimentary: Coffee.
Dates Open: All year.
High Season: June-September.
Rates: $50.
Credit Cards: MC & VISA.
Rsv'tns: Required.
Reserve Through: Travel agent or call direct.
Minimum Stay: Required during high season.
Parking: Ample on-street parking.
In-Room: AC & ceiling fans.
On-Premises: TV, Kitchen, dining room, living room & balcony.
Exercise/Health: Gym, weights, Jacuzzi, sauna, steam & massage nearby.
Swimming: Nearby ocean.
Sunbathing: On the beach.
Smoking: Permitted, prefer outside on balcony.
Pets: Not permitted.
Children: Not especially welcome.
Languages: English.

WINSTON-SALEM

Wachovia Bed & Breakfast

Gay-Friendly ♀♂

Wachovia Bed & Breakfast is a European-style bed and breakfast in a cozy, tranquil setting with the convenience and attraction of a metropolitan area. The lovely rose-and-white Victorian cottage has a wrap-around porch, five bedrooms, a spacious dining room, a cozy parlour, and simple, refined furnishings. Guests can enjoy breakfast at their leisure and may eat in the dining room, in their room, or on the porch. Attractions within walking distance include the Stevens Center for performing arts, gourmet restaurants, antique and specialty shops, parks and several exercise facilities.

Address: 513 Wachovia St, Winston-Salem, NC 27101. Tel: (910) 777-0332.

Type: Bed & breakfast.
Clientele: Mostly straight clientele with a gay & lesbian following.
Transportation: Car. Free pick up from airport, train or bus.
To Gay Bars: 8 blocks.
Rooms: 5 rooms with single or double beds.
Bathrooms: 2 private shower/toilets, 3 private sinks. Others share.
Meals: Full breakfast.
Vegetarian: Available with advance notice or at nearby Rainbow Cafe.
Complimentary: Coffee, tea, soft drinks, wine & sherry.
Dates Open: All year.
Rates: $45-$65.
Credit Cards: MC & VISA.
Rsv'tns: Required but walk-ins welcome.
Reserve Through: Call direct.
Parking: Ample free off-street & on-street parking.
In-Room: AC, ceiling fans, maid service.
On-Premises: TV lounge & laundry facilities.
Exercise/Health: Nearby gym, weights, Jacuzzi, sauna, steam, massage.
Swimming: At a YMCA or YWCA.
Smoking: Not permitted.
Pets: Not permitted.
Handicap Access: No.
Children: Welcome.
Languages: English.
Your Host: Susan.

OHIO

CINCINNATI

Prospect Hill B & B

The Perfect Country Retreat in the City

Gay-Friendly 50/50 ♀♂

We invite you to join us at the *Prospect Hill Bed & Breakfast,* an elegantly-restored 1867 Italianate townhouse with spectacular views of downtown Cincinnati. The building is nestled into a wooded hillside in the Prospect Hill National Historical District, within a mile of most gay bars and restaurants. Your comfort is assured in our spacious rooms, tastefully decorated with period furnishings and amenities, such as sofas, views, bathrobes, ice buckets and wood-burning fireplaces. *"Thanks for making me feel like I was on vacation even though I was not."*

Address: 408 Boal St, Cincinnati, OH 45210. Tel: (513) 421-4408.

Type: Bed & breakfast.
Clientele: 50% straight & 50% gay & lesbian clientele.
Transportation: Car is best.
To Gay Bars: 8 blocks to gay/lesbian bar & restaurant.
Rooms: 3 rooms with double or queen beds.
Bathrooms: 1 private & 1 shared bath/shower/toilet.
Meals: Expanded continental & buffet

breakfast.
Vegetarian: Available upon request.
Complimentary: Mints on pillows, tea, coffee, soft drinks, cookies, fruit basket.
Dates Open: All year.
High Season: June-October.
Rates: Winter $79-$99, summer $79-$109.
Discounts: 10% for 1 week or more.
Credit Cards: MC, VISA, Amex, Discover.

Rsv'tns: Recommended.
Reserve Through: Call direct.
Minimum Stay: 2 nights on in-season weekends. Not required otherwise.
Parking: Ample, free off-street parking.
In-Room: Color TV, AC & maid service.
On-Premises: Woodburning fireplace, telephone, refrigerator, coffee/tea-maker, large side deck, shade trees.
Exercise/Health: Jacuzzi

on premises. Gym, weights, Jacuzzi, sauna, steam nearby.
Swimming: Nearby pool.
Sunbathing: On common sun decks.
Smoking: Permitted outside.
Pets: Not permitted.
Handicap Access: No.
Children: Permitted if 12 years or older.
Languages: English.
Your Host: Gary & Tony.

COLUMBUS

Five Fourty Two Bed & Breakfast

Get Away From It All in the Heart of the City

Gay/Lesbian ♀♂

Built during the German Village boom of the 1870's and renovated in the 1980's, *Five Fourty Two* offers the discriminating guest a true home-away-from-home. A working fireplace connects the parlor and bedroom of our luxury suite, which is accented with South Carolina watercolors and antique glassware. *Five Fourty Two* is close to all attractions in German Village, the largest privately-funded historical area in the US, with acres of century-old brick houses,

continued next page

streets and sidewalks, quaint local businesses and the finest restaurants in central Ohio.

Address: 542 Mohawk St, Columbus, OH 43206. Tel: (614) 621-1741.

Type: Bed & breakfast.
Clientele: Mostly gay & lesbian with some straight clientele.
Transportation: Car is best. Pick up from airport with prior notifcation, $10.
To Gay Bars: 1 mile or 5 minutes by car.
Rooms: 1 suite with queen bed.

Bathrooms: Private bath/ toilet.
Meals: Expanded continental breakfast.
Vegetarian: Special menus on request!
Complimentary: Tea, coffee, water, or soda on request.
Dates Open: All year.
Rates: $75-$95.
Rsv'tns: Required.

Reserve Through: Call direct.
Parking: Ample free on-street parking.
Temporary resident parking permit available.
In-Room: Color cable TV, VCR, video tape library, AC, telephone & fireplace.
On-Premises: Patio.
Sunbathing: On the

patio.
Smoking: Permitted on porch & patio. Rooms are non-smoking.
Pets: Not permitted. 2 cats on the premises.
Handicap Access: No.
Children: Not permitted.
Languages: English, Spanish, French & Anglo-Saxon.

OREGON

ASHLAND & MEDFORD

Country Willows Bed & Breakfast Inn

Gay-Friendly ♀♂

For a Special Vacation with a Special Someone

Country Willows is a restored 1890s farmhouse located against a rolling hillside on a lush five acres of farmland, surrounded by magnificent mountain ranges. We have four rooms, a living room and a den in the main house, a separate cottage, and three rooms in the renovated barn. Our premier Sunrise Suite has a fireplace and oversized 2-person bathtub. Full, two-course country breakfasts are served in the breakfast room. Enjoy numerous outdoor activities, as well as the Shakespeare Festival, Crater Lake, the Britt Musical Festival, and nearby, first-class restaurants. You are welcome at *Country Willows!*

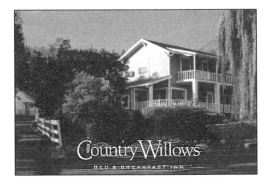

Address: 1313 Clay St, Ashland, OR 97520. Tel: (503) 488-1590, (800) WILLOWS, Fax: (503) 488-1611.

Type: Bed & breakfast inn.
Clientele: Mostly straight clientele with a gay & lesbian following.
Transportation: Car is best. Medford airport (15 mi) with service to/from SF & Portland, shuttle $8. Free pick up from Ashland airport.

To Gay Bars: 3 hours.
Rooms: 6 rooms & 2 suites with single, queen or king beds.
Bathrooms: All private.
Meals: Full breakfast.
Vegetarian: Breakfasts prepared so they are always acceptable to vegetarians. Vegetarian food nearby.

Complimentary: Coffee, tea, hot chocolate, spiced cider, fruit & cookies always available.
Dates Open: All year.
High Season: June 1-October 31.
Rates: $90-$165.
Discounts: 25% in off-season (Nov 1- May 1).
Credit Cards: MC & VISA.

Rsv'tns: Required.
Reserve Through: Travel agent or call direct.
Minimum Stay: On weekends during high season.
Parking: Ample free off-street parking.
In-Room: AC & maid service. Some rooms with ceiling fans, kitchen,

refrigerator, coffee/tea-making facilities.
On-Premises: TV lounge & laundry facilities.
Exercise/Health: Jacuzzi.

Swimming: Heated pool on premises, lake nearby.
Sunbathing: At poolside.
Smoking: Not permitted.

Pets: Not permitted. We can make arrangements for kennels.
Handicap Access: No.
Children: No children un-

der the age of 12.
Languages: English, some German. Japanese (in a pinch).
Your Host: Dan.

Will's Reste

Shakespeare's Neighbor

Gay/Lesbian ♀♂

Will's Reste, our small, intimate, friendly and well-located cottage, offers comfortable accommodations a few blocks from the Oregon Shakespeare Festival Theatres, Lithia Park and some of Oregon's finest restaurants. Set between the Siskiyou and Cascade Mountains, at 2000 feet, Ashland offers unsurpassed views, cross-country and downhill skiing, many internationally-known cultural events and almost every type of outdoor recreation. Enjoy the peace and serenity of Ashland, a welcome respite from today's frantic lifestyle. So park your car, forget it, and enjoy one of the West's favorite destinations.

Address: 298 Hargadine St, Ashland, OR 97520. Tel: (503) 482-4394.

Type: Traveller's accommodations.
Clientele: Mainly gay & lesbian with some straight clientele.
Transportation: Car is best, pick up from airport $10.
To Gay Bars: 3 blocks to gay bar.
Rooms: Self-contained guest house with double or queen beds.

Bathrooms: Private & shared.
Dates Open: All year.
High Season: July, August, September & ski season.
Rates: $60-$75.
Discounts: Weekly rates.
Rsv'tns: Recommended.
Reserve Through: Travel agent or call direct.
Parking: Adequate free on-street parking.

In-Room: Coffee/tea-making facilities, kitchen, refrigerator.
Exercise/Health: Hot tub and outdoor shower, nearby mineral baths & gym.
Swimming: Nearby pool and lake, river 30 miles.
Sunbathing: On patio or private sun decks.
Nudity: Permitted in hot tub at discretion of other

guests.
Smoking: Permitted outdoors only.
Pets: No, resident dog & cat.
Handicap Access: Please inquire.
Children: Please inquire.
Languages: English, limited French, Spanish.

Willow-Witt Ranch

Wake to Meadows Filled With Wildflowers

Gay/Lesbian ♀

Imagine...You wake under a down comforter and look out over an expanse of meadows filled with wildflowers and ringed by stately conifers and rock outcroppings. This is *Willow-Witt Ranch*. Sweet, clean air, exquisite quiet, total privacy, unlimited hiking, a dip in the pond, a hot tub under the stars and a gourmet breakfast. Fresh vegetables and flowers, eggs from our chickens, and fresh cheese from our goat milk. Attractions include rafting the Rogue or Klamath rivers, nearby lakes and Ashland's Shakespeare Festival, galleries, theaters and restaurants.

Address: 658 Shale City Rd, Ashland, OR 97520. Tel: (503) 776-1728 or Voice Mail: (503) 734-9522.

Type: Bed & breakfast.
Clientele: Mostly women with men welcome.

Transportation: Car is best.
To Gay Bars: 13 miles to

Ashland gay/lesbian mixed bar.
Rooms: 1 room with 2

double beds.
Bathrooms: 1 private.

continued next page

Oregon

Meals: Full breakfast.
Vegetarian: Always available. Extensive vegetarian menus at many Ashland retaurants.
Complimentary: Tea.
Dates Open: May 1 through October 31.
High Season: July, August.
Rates: $60-$120.
Discounts: 10% for weekly stay.
Rsv'tns: Advisable 1-2 weeks in advance.
Reserve Through: Call direct.
Parking: Ample free off-street parking.
In-Room: Private entry, sun deck, & maid service.
Exercise/Health: Hot-tub, massage, 440 acres for hiking & pond for swimming.
Swimming: Spring-fed pond on property. 20 minutes to public pool or numerous lakes.
Sunbathing: Anywhere on grounds.
Nudity: Permitted.
Smoking: Permitted on decks only. All rooms are non-smoking.
Pets: Permitted, with prior arrangement.
Handicap Access: Yes, prior arrangement necessary.
Children: Especially welcomed. Please join us for milking & feeding the animals.
Languages: English.
Your Host: Suzanne & Lanita.

BROOKINGS

Oceancrest House

Gay-Friendly ♀♂

A Pelican Bay Hideaway

Oceancrest House, on the beautiful Oregon coast 3.5 miles north of the California border, offers guests a very private and quiet place to relax. Your room, physically detached from our home, has a view that faces directly onto the beach. We enjoy pampering our guests with luxurious furnishings and delicious baked goodies. Watch the waves and the pelicans. Count the starfish. Walk on a secluded beach, or in the redwood forests close by. Fish in our famous rivers, or go whale-watching. Escape from the ordinary at *Oceancrest House.*

Address: 15510 Pedrioli Dr, Brookings, OR . Tel: (800) 769-9200 or Fax: (503) 469-8864 (shared).

Type: Bed & breakfast.
Clientele: Mostly straight clientele with a gay & lesbian following.
Transportation: Car is best, take Hwy 101. Pick up from Crescent City, CA airport $5 each trip.
To Gay Bars: 3 hours away in Medford.
Rooms: 1 very large room with queen bed.
Bathrooms: Private shower/toilet.
Meals: Expanded continental breakfast.
Vegetarian: All breakfast trays are vegetarian & vegetarian dishes available in most restaurants.
Complimentary: Juices, soda, bottled water, gourmet coffees, candies & fresh fruit.
Dates Open: All year.
High Season: May 31-Oct 31.
Rates: $89 year-round.
Discounts: 15% on 7-day week.
Credit Cards: MC, VISA, Discover.
Rsv'tns: Required.
Reserve Through: Travel agent or call direct.
Minimum Stay: 2 nights on summer weekends & 3-day holidays.
Parking: Ample free off-street parking.
In-Room: Color cable TV, VCR, video tape library, stereo with tapedeck/radio, refrigerator, microwave, coffee/tea-maker, guitar, games, books, binoculars & maid service.
Exercise/Health: Golf courses.
Swimming: Nearby pool, river & ocean.
Sunbathing: On private sun decks or at the beach.
Smoking: Permitted outside only.
Pets: Not permitted.
Handicap Access: No.
Children: Accepted if over 12 years old.
Languages: English & French.

We Appreciate Your Comments!

Positive comments of interest may be included in the next issue, giving future readers the benefit of your experience. And it's a nice way of saying "thank you" to an innkeeper who extended you exceptional hospitality.

See the contents for the Reader Comment Form.

South Coast Inn Bed & Breakfast

Gay-Friendly 50/50 ♀♂

Charm & Comfort on Oregon's Rugged, Unspoiled Southern Coast

Surrender yourself to turn-of-the-century hospitality. Enjoy coffee in front of the stone fireplace. Relax in the spa or sauna, or bask in the warmth of beautiful antiques. Wake up to a gourmet breakfast and a beautiful ocean view. *South Coast Inn* is centrally located in Brookings, on the southern Oregon coast. Built in 1917, and designed by Bernard Maybeck, the inn exhibits the grace and charm of a spacious craftsman-style home. Your hosts, Ken and Keith, extend a warm welcome.

Address: 516 Redwood St, Brookings, OR 97415. Tel: (800) 525-9273, (503) 469-5557, Fax: 469-6615.

Type: Bed & breakfast.
Clientele: 50% gay & lesbian & 50% straight clientele.
Transportation: Car is best.
Rooms: 4 rooms with queen beds.
Bathrooms: 1 private bath/toilet & 3 private shower/toilets.

Meals: Full breakfast.
Dates Open: All year.
High Season: Memorial Day through September.
Rates: $74-$94.
Discounts: 10% senior.
Credit Cards: MC, VISA, Amex & Discover.
Rsv'tns: Required.
Reserve Through: Travel agent or call direct.

Parking: Ample free off-street parking.
In-Room: Color/color cable TV & ceiling fans.
Exercise/Health: Indoor Jacuzzi & sauna.
Swimming: Nearby pool, river & ocean.
Sunbathing: On the patio, common sun decks & at the beach.

Smoking: Permitted outside only.
Pets: Not permitted.
Handicap Access: No.
Children: Welcomed if 12 or over.
Languages: English.
Your Host: Ken & Keith.

O'BRIEN

Mountain River Inn

Women ♀

Mountain River Inn is snuggled into 27 forested acres on a mountainside above the beautiful Illinois River. Our guests enjoy walking secluded woodland trails, exploring 1700 feet of private river access, and then relaxing in the spa or sauna. We serve an American-style breakfast, made with our own homegrown eggs and fresh-baked goodies. Vegetarian breakfast is also prepared. Our environment is drug- and alcohol-free. Women's retreats on such subjects as rebirthing, drumming and meditation are frequently held. Attend one of ours, or plan your own.

Address: PO Box 34, O'Brien, OR 97534. Tel: (503) 596-2392.

continued next page

Oregon

Type: Bed & breakfast & campground.
Clientele: Women only.
Transportation: Pick up from airport, inquire for fee.
To Gay Bars: 1-3/4 hours to Ashland gay-friendly bars.
Rooms: 3 doubles.
Bathrooms: 1 shared, shower downstairs, upstairs bath & outdoor shower house.
Campsites: Primitive campsites for 50, outdoor shower/toilet building.
Meals: Full breakfast in B&B.
Vegetarian: Available upon request.
Complimentary: Non-alcoholic drinks upon prior request.
Dates Open: February thru November.
High Season: Summer.
Rates: B&B $25-$50, camping $8 per night.
Discounts: On weekly stays
Rsv'tns: 2 weeks in advance advisable in summer.
Reserve Through: Call direct.
Parking: Ample off-street parking.
On-Premises: TV lounge with stereo.
Exercise/Health: Hot tub & sauna.
Swimming: At river or primitive swimming hole
20 minutes away.
Sunbathing: By the river, at swimming hole or on the sun deck.
Nudity: Permitted.
Smoking: Permitted outdoors.
Pets: Not permitted.
Handicap Access: No.
Children: Permitted with prior approval.
Languages: English, limited Spanish.

PORTLAND

A Tudor House Bed & Breakfast

Gay-Friendly ♀♂

A Tudor House B&B is located in a quiet, up-scale neighborhood of fine large homes. Only minutes by car from shopping centers, theatres, restaurants, parks, attractions and bus lines, it is also convenient to the Convention Center and airport. The main rooms in *Tudor House* are elegantly furnished with antiques and period pieces. The four guest rooms have private bath, cable TV and telephone and the Antique Suite is particularly

appealing to those wishing complete privacy. A nearby park provides public swimming pools, tennis courts and a running and cycling track.

Relocating? Inquire about our extended stay rates.

Address: 2321 NE 28th Ave, Portland, OR 97212. Tel: (503) 287-9476, Fax: (503) 287-7675.

Type: Bed & breakfast.
Clientele: Mostly straight clientele with a gay & lesbian following.
Transportation: Car or taxi is best.
To Gay Bars: 4 blocks. A 4-minute walk or 2-minute drive.
Rooms: 2 rooms, 1 suite & 1 apartment with single, double, queen or king beds.
Bathrooms: 2 private & 1 shared.
Meals: Full breakfast.
Vegetarian: Available upon request. Vegetarian food within 4 blocks.
Complimentary: Tea & coffee set-ups in rooms.
Dates Open: All year.
High Season: June thru Sept. Thanksgiving, Xmas & New Years.
Rates: $60-$95.
Discounts: Continuous extended stay from 1 week to a month or more. Discount increases with length of stay.
Credit Cards: MC, VISA, Amex & Discover.
Rsv'tns: Required.
Reserve Through: Call direct.
Parking: Ample free off-street & on-street parking.
In-Room: Color cable TV, VCR, video tape library, AC, ceiling fans, telephone, refrigerator, coffee & tea-making facilities. 1 suite with kitchen.
On-Premises: Computer & fax.
Exercise/Health: Nearby gym, weights, Jacuzzi, sauna, steam & massage.
Swimming: Nearby pool.
Sunbathing: On the patio.
Smoking: Limited smoking outside only.
Pets: Cats not permitted. Small dogs negotiable. No drop-in pets.
Children: Welcome.
Languages: English, some French.
Your Host: Milan.

MacMaster House

Location–FABULOUS!

Gay-Friendly ♀♂

This classic Colonial Revival house has high-vaulted ceilings, seven fireplaces, many European antiques and an eclectic art collection. Accommodations feature such amenities as queen beds, fireplaces, private baths and antiques. Walk from *MacMaster House* to Washington Park's jogging and hiking trails and tennis courts. The business and financial district, theaters and the art museum are nearby, as are the boutiques, pastry and wine shops, markets and art galleries of the avant-garde Nob Hill neighborhood.

Address: 1041 SW Vista Ave, Portland, OR 97205. Tel: (503) 223-7362.

Type: Bed & breakfast.
Clientele: Mostly straight clientele with a gay & lesbian following.
Transportation: Airport bus to Hilton Hotel, then taxi. Car is ok.
To Gay Bars: 15-20 minutes by foot.
Rooms: 7 rooms & 2 suites with double or queen beds.

Bathrooms: 2 private, others share.
Meals: Full breakfast.
Complimentary: Red & white wine, local ale, sodas & fruit juices in guest's refrigerator.
Dates Open: All year.
High Season: June-September.
Rates: $70-$115 plus lodging tax.

Credit Cards: MC, VISA, Amex & Discover.
Rsv'tns: Advisable.
Reserve Through: Call direct.
Parking: Limited on-street parking.
In-Room: Color TV & AC.
Exercise/Health: Facilities nearby.
Swimming: At nearby pool.

Sunbathing: On the beach.
Smoking: Permitted on veranda only.
Pets: Pet in residence.
Handicap Access: No, stairs.
Children: Not especially welcomed. Permitted over 13 years old.
Languages: English.

Mark Spencer Hotel, The

Gay-Friendly ♀♂

A rare find in downtown Portland, the 100 room *Mark Spencer,* with its neo-classic design and intimate lobby, conveys a feeling of warmth and comfort. Our guest quarters are designed to complement the needs of today's traveller with air-conditioning and cable television being standard features. Non-smoking rooms are also available. For business travellers, personal phones, executive work areas and rooms with fully-equipped kitchens add convenience to extended stays. Convenient to the financial district and near many restaurants and shops, we welcome you to experience the advantages of *The Mark Spencer Hotel.*

Address: 409 SW 11th Ave, Portland, OR 97205. Tel: (503) 224-3293 or (800) 548-3934 (US & Canada), Fax: (503) 223-7848.

Type: Hotel.
Clientele: Mostly straight clientele with a gay & lesbian following.
Transportation: Car is best. Airport shuttle drops off 4 blocks away. Then walk or take a taxi.
To Gay Bars: Across the street. Also 4 gay bars & 2 gay restaurants within one block.
Rooms: 55 rooms & 46 suites with single or queen beds.

Bathrooms: All private.
Complimentary: Tea & coffee.
Dates Open: All year.
Rates: $57-$88.
Discounts: 10% corporate rate. Some seasonal, but these are based on availability at time of reservation.
Credit Cards: MC, VISA, Amex, Diners & Discover.
Rsv'tns: Required.

Reserve Through: Travel agent or call direct.
Parking: Off-street pay parking, $8.
In-Room: Color cable TV, AC, telephone, kitchen, refrigerator, coffee/tea-making facilities, maid & laundry service.
On-Premises: Meeting rooms & laundry facilities.
Exercise/Health: Nearby gym, weights & Jacuzzi.

Sunbathing: On the roof.
Smoking: Permitted. Non-smoking rooms available.
Pets: Permitted with $200 deposit.
Handicap Access: No.
Children: Welcome, but we offer no special activities or programs.
Languages: English.

Sullivan's Gulch Bed and Breakfast

Gay/Lesbian ♀♂

Western Hospitality Celebrating Diversity

Sullivan's Gulch Bed & Breakfast, a lovely 1904 home, is in the charming, quiet area of NE Portland known as Sullivan's Gulch. We are near the famed Lloyd Center shopping mall and cinemas, the Convention Center and the Coliseum, two blocks from NE Broadway's shops, micro-breweries and restaurants, and minutes from downtown. We serve an expanded continental breakfast that celebrates our local bakeries and the natural abundance of the Pacific Northwest. Our three comfortable rooms have private bath, queen bed and ceiling fans. *We celebrate the diversity of all people.*

Address: 1744 NE Clackamas Street, Portland, OR 97232. Phone & Fax: (503) 331-1104 .

Type: Bed & breakfast.
Clientele: Mostly gay & lesbian with gay-friendly straight folk welcome.
Transportation: Car is best. Public transportation nearby. We offer free pick up service from all terminals.
To Gay Bars: 5 blocks.
Rooms: 3 rooms with queen beds.
Bathrooms: All private.

Meals: Expanded continental breakfast, special requests honored.
Vegetarian: Special requests honored.
Complimentary: Coffee & tea available all day.
Dates Open: All year.
High Season: Summer.
Rates: $70 plus tax, based on double occupancy.
Discounts: 5th night free.

Credit Cards: VISA, MC & Amex.
Rsv'tns: Required.
Reserve Through: Travel agent or call direct.
Parking: Adequate free off-street & on-street parking.
In-Room: Ceiling fans. Breakfast served in room upon request.
Exercise/Health: Gyms nearby.

Sunbathing: On common sun deck.
Smoking: Not permitted.
Pets: Resident dog. Well-behaved dogs permitted.
Handicap Access: No. Many steps.
Children: Not especially welcome.
Languages: English.
Your Host: Skip & Jack.

Washingtonia Inn

Gay/Lesbian ♀♂

Relax in the Scenic Splendor of the Pacific Northwest

The Washingtonia Inn stands at the entrance to the Columbia River Gorge, 25 minutes from downtown Portland, enjoying unique and dramatic views of the gorge and Mt. Hood. While at the inn, enjoy the scenic wonders of the Pacific Northwest. Walk to the top of Multonomah Falls, visit Mount St. Helens Volcanic Monument, or ski Mt. Hood year 'round. Guests can enjoy a gourmet meal prepared by the onsite catering company, take a sailing trip on the Columbia, or relax in a hammock by the perennial garden.

Address: 602 NW 18th Loop, Camas, WA 98607. Tel: (206) 834-7629.

Type: Bed & breakfast with sailing & full-service private catering.
Clientele: Mostly gay & lesbian with some straight clientele.
Transportation: Car from airport or train. Pick up from airport, bus or train, $10.
To Gay Bars: 15 minutes to Vancouver, WA or 20-25 minutes to downtown Portland.
Rooms: 3 rooms & 1 suite with queen or king beds.

Bathrooms: 1 private bath/toilet/shower & 2 shared bath/toilet/ showers.
Meals: Full breakfast.
Vegetarian: Available upon request.
Complimentary: Nightcap, afternoon tea or cocktails.
Dates Open: All year.
High Season: Summer & spring.
Rates: May 1-Oct 31, $60-$150. Nov 1-Apr 30, $55-$150.
Rsv'tns: Required.

Reserve Through: Travel agent or call direct.
Parking: Adequate free off-street parking.
In-Room: Color cable TV, VCR, ceiling fans, coffee/ tea-making facilities, maid, room & laundry service.
On-Premises: TV lounge, meeting rooms, private dining rooms, laundry facilities & computer office.
Exercise/Health: Massage & Nordic Track on premises. Nearby full-service health facilities.

Swimming: Nearby pool & river.
Sunbathing: On patio, private & common sun decks.
Nudity: Permitted at nude beach 20 minutes away.
Smoking: Not permitted.
Pets: Not permitted. Pet reservations may be made at a local kennel.
Children: Not especially welcome.
Languages: English, Spanish & Japanese.
Your Host: Denys & Jay.

ROGUE RIVER

Whispering Pines Bed & Breakfast/Retreat

Peace & Quiet & Country Comfort Gay/Lesbian ♀♂

Cradled in the Cascade foothills of Southern Oregon, just 15 minutes off Interstate 5, peace and solitude abound on the 32 acres of pine and pasture that make up *Whispering Pines Bed & Breakfast/Retreat*. In summer, swim in our pool, or enjoy river rafting, fishing, hiking, biking and nearby cultural activities such as the Oregon Shakespeare Festival and the Britt Music Festival. In winter, ski your cares away, then return to our steamy hot tub. Or just sit back, relax, and enjoy the quiet of our rural setting.

Address: 9188 W. Evans Creek Rd, Rogue River, OR 97537. Tel: (503) 582-1757 or (800) 788-1757.

Type: Bed & breakfast. **Clientele:** Mainly gay/lesbian with some straight clientele. **Transportation:** Car is best. Pick up from bus or Medford airport, fee or free depends on length of stay. Small charge for other trips. **To Gay Bars:** One hour to Ashland gay/mixed bar (Cook's Tavern). **Rooms:** 2 rooms with queen beds, 1 bunkhouse with 3 doubles (sleeps 6). **Bathrooms:** Rooms share 1 bath. Bunkhouse has shower & composting toilet. **Campsites:** RV's & camping available. **Meals:** Full country breakfast. **Vegetarian:** Available upon request. **Dates Open:** All year. **High Season:** May-October.

Rates: Rooms $55-$65 double occupancy. **Discounts:** 10% for 3 or more nights. **Rsv'tns:** Preferred. **Reserve Through:** Call direct. **Parking:** Ample, free off-street parking. **In-Room:** AC. **On-Premises:** TV lounge. **Exercise/Health:** Hot tub. **Swimming:** Pool on premises, river nearby. **Sunbathing:** At poolside or on private & common sun decks. **Nudity:** Permitted. **Smoking:** Permitted in a very limited outside location only. **Pets:** Not permitted. **Handicap Access:** No. **Children:** Permitted by special arrangement. **Languages:** English. **Your Host:** Lorna & Karen.

WALDPORT

Cliff House Bed & Breakfast

Pampered Elegance By the Sea Gay-Friendly ♀♂

Cliff House, a luxuriously restored older home with lots of history and a spectacular ocean view, allows you to escape to a peaceful atmosphere and refresh the spirit in a romantic setting amid shore pines. Eight miles of uninterrupted beach run in front of the house. Each room has plush bedding and is uniquely decorated with antiques, and has its own ocean or bay view, cedar bath, and balcony. Lounge in a hammock, play croquet, walk, or explore the beach. Northwest Best Places gives us 3 stars! Sailing, deep-sea fishing, whalewatching are some activities.

Address: Box 436, Yaquina John Pt, Adahi St, Waldport, OR 97394. Tel: (503) 563-2506.

Type: Bed & breakfast. **Clientele:** Mostly straight clientele with a gay/lesbian following. **Transportation:** Car is best. Will arrange for rental car or pick up from local airport or pick up from Waldport bus station. **To Gay Bars:** 1-3/4 hrs. to Eugene gay/lesbian bars. **Rooms:** 4 rooms & 1 suite with double, queen or king beds. **Bathrooms:** All private. **Meals:** Full breakfast. **Vegetarian:** Always available upon request. **Complimentary:** Afternoon tea & occasional aperitifs, goodies in room. **Dates Open:** March-October or by special reservation. **High Season:** July-September. **Rates:** $95-$225. **Credit Cards:** Accept MC & VISA to hold room. Prefer cash or check for payment. **Rsv'tns:** 7-day cancellation notice ($20 fee regardless). **Reserve Through:** Call direct. **Minimum Stay:** 2 days on weekends, holidays, longer in season.

continued next page

Oregon

Parking: Ample free parking.
In-Room: Color cable TV & VCR. 2 rooms have refrigerator.
On-Premises: Meeting room, VCR & TV, grand piano, game table, dining room, telephone, fireplace.
Exercise/Health: Massage, golf, horseback riding, croquet, 10-jet hot tub.
Swimming: Ocean beach, river & lake on premises.
Sunbathing: On the beach, balconies or common sun decks.
Nudity: Permitted in hot tub.
Smoking: Permitted outdoors.
Pets: Not permitted, but kennel nearby.
Handicap Access: Yes.
Children: Not permitted.
Languages: English, Spanish.
Your Host: Gabrielle.

YACHATS

Oregon House, The

See the Coast From Our Point of View

Gay-Friendly ♀♂

High on a cliff above the Pacific Ocean, *Oregon House* is like no other property on the Oregon coast. Surrounding the complex are 3 1/2 acres of forest, lawn and wooded trails, a creek crossed by arched wooden bridges, a lighted trail down the cliff to the beach. The beach is ideal for bonfires and picnics, tidepooling, mussel gathering, kite flying and collecting sand dollars. Lodgings, decorated in country inn style, are sited across the property. Five have fireplaces, three have Jacuzzi tubs, one has a private hot tub and fireplace, nine have kitchens and all have private baths.

Address: 94288 Hwy 101, Yachats, OR 97498. Tel: (503) 547-3329.

Type: Inn with small gift shop.
Clientele: Mostly straight with a gay & lesbian following.
Transportation: Car is best.
To Gay Bars: 1-1/2 hrs or 80 miles to Eugene.
Rooms: 2 rooms, 7 suites & 1 cottage with single, queen or king beds.
Bathrooms: All private bath/toilets.
Dates Open: All year.
High Season: May 15-October 15, every weekend, holiday & school break.
Rates: High season $45-$100 plus tax, low season $30-$85 plus tax.
Credit Cards: MC, VISA, Diners & Discover.
Rsv'tns: Recommended.
Reserve Through: Call direct.
Minimum Stay: 3 nights
July, August & some holidays & 2 night weekends some holidays & high season.
Parking: Adequate free off-street parking.
In-Room: Ceiling fans, kitchen, refrigerator & coffee/tea-making facilities.
On-Premises: Telephone.
Exercise/Health: Jacuzzi in 3 rooms, hot tub in 1 room.
Swimming: Ocean beach for the hardy.
Sunbathing: On the beach, patio & private sun decks.
Smoking: Permitted outside only.
Pets: Not permitted.
Handicap Access: One room.
Children: Permitted if well-behaved.
Languages: English.
Your Host: Bob & Joyce.

See Vue

Lodging Where the Mountains Meet the Sea

Gay-Friendly 50/50 ♀♂

A coastal landmark since 1945, the *See Vue*, with its spectacular ocean view, is nestled between the breathtaking Coast Mountains and the everchanging Pacific Ocean. Room motifs of the ten units range from the quaint Granny's Rooms to the northwest American Indian Salish Room. Fireplaces, antiques and flourishing indoor plants contribute to the homey and restful serenity. There is easy access to miles of hiking trails, tidepools, Heceta Head Lighthouse, Sea Lion Caves, restaurants and coastal shopping.

Address: 95590 Hwy 101, Yachats, OR 97498. Tel: (503) 547-3227.

Type: Motel.
Clientele: 50% gay & lesbian & 50% straight clientele
Transportation: Car is best.
To Gay Bars: 1-1/2 hours gay bars in Eugene, OR.
Rooms: 6 rooms, 4 suites & 1 cottage with single or double beds.
Bathrooms: All private.
Dates Open: All year.
High Season: June 1st-September 30th.
Rates: Summer $40-$60, winter $30-$50.
Credit Cards: MC & VISA.
Rsv'tns: Recommended at least 3 weeks in advance.
Reserve Through: Call direct.
Minimum Stay: On

rooms with kitchen or fireplace, 2 nights on weekends or in high season.
Parking: Ample off-street parking.

In-Room: Color TV, maid service on request, kitchen.
On-Premises: Massage.
Swimming: In the ocean, if you are brave (cold

water!).
Sunbathing: On ocean beach.
Smoking: Permitted with restrictions; some non-smoking rooms.

Pets: Permitted if not left unattended.
Handicap Access: No.
Children: Permitted.
Languages: English, French.

Yachats Inn

Gay-Friendly ♀♂

The *Yachats Inn* is on a spectacular stretch of the Oregon Coast. The sandy beach at low tide is wonderful for beachcombing and rocks provide tide pools for exploration. We are an older, 1940's motel. Every room has its own personality. South rooms have a spectacular view of the coast and a spouting horn at high tide. North rooms have an ocean/bay view. Upstairs rooms feature a glassed-in sun porch filled with flowers. There is easy access to the beach, plenty of hiking trails nearby, and Yachats has several fine restaurants and small gift shops.

Address: PO Box 307, Yachats, OR 97498. Tel: (503) 547-3456.

Type: Motel inn.
Clientele: Mostly straight clientele with a gay & lesbian following.
Transportation: Car is best.
To Gay Bars: 1-1/2 hrs to Eugene.
Rooms: 20 rooms & 1 suite with single, double or queen beds.
Bathrooms: All private.
Vegetarian: There are a number of restaurants in town which serve vegetarian meals.
Complimentary: Coffee all day.

Dates Open: All year.
High Season: May 15-Sep 30.
Rates: $40-$81, double occupancy.
Discounts: 6 nights with 7th free during winter season.
Credit Cards: MC, VISA, Amex & Discover.
Rsv'tns: Recommended for suites & during summer.
Reserve Through: Travel agent or call direct.
Minimum Stay: Required for suites, 2 nights on weekends.

Parking: Adequate free off-street parking.
In-Room: Color cable TV, maid service. Some rooms with fireplace/kitchens, refrigerators, and utensils.
On-Premises: Recreation lounge with large stone fireplace, piano, kitchen, meeting room; books, puzzles, games. Free coffee starting about 7:30 am.
Swimming: Indoor, heated, 8 ft deep swimming pool.
Sunbathing: Lots of

places throughout manicured grounds.
Smoking: Permitted without restrictions. Be courteous to others.
Pets: Permitted if well-behaved, housebroken. $3 night each pet.
Handicap Access: Wheelchair accessible. Not barrier free.
Children: Permitted & welcomed.
Languages: English, some German, Spanish & Swedish.

We Appreciate Your Comments!

The editors of *INN Places*® actively seek your comments about accommodations you have tried.

Positive comments of interest may be included in the next issue, giving future readers the benefit of your experience. And it's a nice way of saying "thank you" to an innkeeper who extended you exceptional hospitality.

See the contents for the Reader Comment Form.

PENNSYLVANIA

KUTZTOWN

Grim's Manor

Gay/Lesbian ♀♂

The 200-year-old *Grim's Manor* site, at the edge of Pennsylvania Dutch country, includes a historic stone farmhouse on five secluded acres of land. Step back in time, experiencing the history of this home and its period decor, while enjoying all modern comforts. The property includes a huge restored barn, complete with hex signs. The manor is near the city of Reading, antique shops, Doe Mountain skiing, Hawk Mountain birdwatching, the Clove Hill Winery, Crystal Cave, Dorney Park and Wildwater Kingdom.

Address: 10 Kern Road, Kutztown, PA 19530. Tel: (610) 683-7089.

Type: Bed & breakfast. **Clientele:** Mostly gay & lesbian with some straight clientele. **Transportation:** Car is best, free pick up from Allentown or Reading Airport or Bieber Tours Inc in Kutztown. **To Gay Bars:** 1/2 hr to Reading/Allentown, PA, 1-1/2 hrs to Philadelphia, 2 hrs to NYC. **Rooms:** 4 rooms with queen beds. **Bathrooms:** All private shower/toilets. **Meals:** Full breakfast, served all-you-can-eat homestyle. **Vegetarian:** Available upon request. **Complimentary:** Light refreshments upon arrival, bedside snack, soft drinks, coffee. **Dates Open:** All year. **High Season:** Kutztown Folk Festival–July 4th week. **Rates:** $55-$65. **Rsv'tns:** Required. **Reserve Through:** Call direct. **Parking:** Ample free off-street parking. **In-Room:** Color TV, AC, ceiling fans & maid service. **On-Premises:** TV lounge, VCR, laundry facilities, kitchen & indoor spa. **Swimming:** At nearby pool or Dorney Park & Wildwater Kingdom. **Sunbathing:** On the lawn. **Smoking:** Permitted with consideration for others. **Pets:** Not permitted. **Handicap Access:** No. **Children:** Permitted with consideration for others. **Languages:** English.

NEW HOPE

Back Street Inn B&B

Gay-Friendly 50/50 ♀♂

This pastoral section of Pennsylvania is an area of rolling hills, quaint architecture and wonderful restaurants. Here, on an acreage with stately trees, a rippling stream, swimming pool and bountiful flowers, you can unwind at *Back Street Inn*. All of our rooms are air conditioned. Breakfast is gourmet. People come to the New Hope area for craft shops, fine dining, horseback riding, bicycling, antiquing, flea markets, mule barge rides, visiting the park commemorating Washington's crossing of the Delaware, and just to enjoy the wooded scenery and relax.

Address: 144 Old York Rd, New Hope, PA 18938. Tel: (215) 862-9571 or (800) 841-1874.

Type: Bed & breakfast. **Clientele:** 50% gay & lesbian & 50% straight clientele. **Transportation:** Pick up from bus. **To Gay Bars:** 2-minute walk to two gay bars. **Rooms:** 7 rooms with double beds. **Bathrooms:** 2 private bath/toilets & 5 private shower/toilets. **Meals:** Full breakfast. **Vegetarian:** Available with advance notice. **Complimentary:** Mints on pillow. **Dates Open:** All year. **High Season:** May through December. **Rates:** $95-$125 with full breakfast, $78 with continental breakfast, mid-week only. **Discounts:** Call for details. **Credit Cards:** VISA & Amex. **Rsv'tns:** Required two weeks in advance. **Reserve Through:** Call direct. **Minimum Stay:** 3 days on holiday wknds, 2 on wknds in-season. **Parking:** Ample free uncovered lighted off-street parking. **In-Room:** Maid service & AC.

On-Premises: TV lounge, public telephones & refrigerator.
Swimming: Pool on premises.
Sunbathing: At poolside.
Smoking: Permitted with some restrictions.
Pets: Not permitted.
Handicap Access: No.
Children: Permitted if 14 years or older.
Languages: English.

Fox & Hound B & B of New Hope

Gay-Friendly 50/50 ♀♂

On two beautiful acres of park-like grounds stands *Fox & Hound B&B*, a fully-restored historic 1850's stone manor. Full gourmet breakfasts are served on our outside patio or in our spacious dining room. Our ample guest rooms, all with private baths and four-poster canopy beds, are furnished with a fine blend of period antiques and are air-conditioned for your comfort. Guest rooms with 2 beds are available. Within walking distance of the center of New Hope, guests can also enjoy tennis, the swimming pool and carriage rides, upon request.
Address: 246 W Bridge St, New Hope, PA 18938. Tel: (215) 862-5082 or (800) 862-5082 (outside of PA).

Type: Bed & breakfast.
Clientele: 50% gay & lesbian & 50% straight clientele.
Transportation: Car is best. Trans Bridge Bus lines from New Jersey & Port Authority NYC. Pick up from bus.
To Gay Bars: One block walking distance (4 minutes).
Rooms: 5 rooms with twin, double & queen beds.
Bathrooms: All private.
Meals: Continental breakfast Mon-Fri, full breakfast Sun.
Vegetarian: Available upon request.
Dates Open: All year.
High Season: October.
Rates: Summer, spring, fall, Sun-Thurs $55, Fri, Sat, $110-$120, winter specials.
Discounts: Corporate & long term.
Credit Cards: MC, VISA & Amex.
Rsv'tns: Required, especially on weekends. In high season required 2-3 weeks in advance.
Reserve Through: Call direct.
Minimum Stay: Call for details.
Parking: Ample, free off-street parking.
In-Room: Maid service, AC, ceiling fans, TV upon request.
On-Premises: Use of kitchen on limited basis.
Exercise/Health: Tubing & canoeing at nearby river.
Swimming: Pool within walking distance, Delaware river 1/4 mile.
Sunbathing: At poolside.
Smoking: Permitted throughout house.
Pets: Not permitted.
Handicap Access: No.
Children: Permitted if 14 or older.
Languages: English.

Lexington House, The

Gay/Lesbian ♂

The Lexington House dates back to 1749 and offers guests every comfort amidst a charming and gracious old world country setting. It is situated on seven acres of private grounds, complete with a swimming pool built amongst old stone ruins, beautiful landscaping and garden paths. If you wish to explore Bucks County, you will find a wealth of nearby activities, including flea markets, antique shops, art galleries, museums and parks.
Address: 6171 Upper York Rd, New Hope, PA 18938. Tel: (215) 794-0811.

Type: Bed & breakfast.
Clientele: Mostly men with women welcome.
Transportation: Car is best & bus is available.
To Gay Bars: 2 miles.
Rooms: 4 rooms & 2 suites with queen beds.
Bathrooms: All private.
Meals: Continental breakfast.
Complimentary: Coffee, tea, soft drinks & juices.
Wine & cookies in room & mints on pillow.
Dates Open: All year.
High Season: May through Dec.
Rates: $75-$150.
Discounts: Weekly rates available.
Credit Cards: MC, VISA, Amex.
Rsv'tns: Required.
Reserve Through: Call direct.
Minimum Stay: 2 nights on weekends & 3 nights on holidays.
Parking: Ample free parking on property.
In-Room: AC & maid service.
On-Premises: TV lounge & meeting rooms.
Exercise/Health: Health club nearby.
Swimming: Pool on premises.
Sunbathing: At poolside.
Smoking: On the veranda & at poolside. All rooms are non-smoking.
Pets: Not permitted.
Handicap Access: No.
Children: Not permitted.
Languages: English & Spanish.
Your Host: Alex & Bruce.

Pennsylvania

NEW MILFORD

Oneida Campground and Lodge

Gay/Lesbian ♂

Oneida Camp offers 100 wooded and meadowed acres with well-spaced campsites. Cottages and campsites use the bath house, which has hot showers and modern facilities. We are also a spiritual retreat where you can experience comradeship as you commune with new friends. There is a show on Saturday night, volleyball and a nature trail. Our new disco features DJ David Thompson. Beverages are sometimes supplied on weekends at the recreation hall. There is occasional leadership at the meditation center. Nudity is permitted. Call for directions to the campground.

Address: PO Box 537, New Milford, PA 18834. Tel: (717) 465-7011.

Type: Campground and lodge with clubhouse, sauna, disco & rental cottages.
Clientele: Mostly men with women welcome.
Transportation: Small charge for pick up ($10 one way) from Binghamton bus or airport.
To Gay Bars: 20 miles to Binghamton, NY gay bars.
Rooms: 8 rooms & 2 cottages with single & double beds.
Bathrooms: Shared: 4 tubs, 5 showers & 9 bath/shower/toilets.
Campsites: 35 tent sites & 20 sites with electric, sewer & water.
Meals: Coffee hour on Sunday morning, restaurants are 3 miles away.
Complimentary: Beverage at rec hall Saturday night & holiday weekends & Friday night at disco.
Dates Open: May-October.
High Season: May-October.
Rates: Reasonable and vary according to days & number accommodated.
Discounts: 10% for pre-registered groups of 10 or more.
Rsv'tns: Recommended for guesthouse.
Reserve Through: Call direct.
Minimum Stay: No minimum...even day camping ok.
Parking: Ample free parking.
In-Room: Color TV, refrigerator, stove, light housekeeping in general area outside room.
On-Premises: TV lounge, library, meditation center, fitness center, use of kitchen.
Exercise/Health: Sauna & fitness center.
Swimming: Spring-fed lake or swim pond. Planning in-ground pool for 1997.
Sunbathing: On the patio & at poolside.
Nudity: Permitted on the grounds.
Smoking: Permitted in most areas, but request no smoking in rooms.
Pets: Permitted, but must be controlled.
Handicap Access: Not recommended for wheelchairs.
Children: Permitted, parent or guardian required & at discretion of owner.
Languages: English, A.S.L.

PHILADELPHIA

Antique Row Bed & Breakfast

Gay-Friendly 60/40 ♀♂

Perfectly Positioned for the Gay/Lesbian Communities

Antique Row B&B is centrally located for business and tourism, only a few blocks from the convention center. We're a small B&B with mixed clientele. Rooms in this 180-year-old townhouse are attractively furnished with comfortable beds, down comforters, designer linens and sufficient pillows for watching TV and reading in bed. The color cable TV has Bravo, CineMax and Showtime. A more spacious fully-furnished flat for added privacy is also available.

Address: 341 South 12th St, Philadelphia, PA 19107. Tel: (215) 592-7802, Fax: 592-9692.

Type: Bed & breakfast & fully-furnished flat.
Clientele: Mostly straight clientele with a 40% gay & lesbian following.
Transportation: Easy access for all forms of transportation.
To Gay Bars: Within a few blocks of most gay & lesbian bars.
Rooms: 2 rooms & 1 apartment with double or queen beds.
Bathrooms: 1 private shower/toilet & 1 shared bath/shower/toilet.
Meals: Full breakfast.
Vegetarian: Within walking distance to several vegetarian restaurants.
Dates Open: All year.
High Season: Apr-Oct.
Rates: $45-$75.
Discounts: Extended stays.
Rsv'tns: Recommended.
Reserve Through: Call

direct.
Parking: Off-street pay parking ($5.50 for 24 hours). Recommended for safety.

In-Room: Color cable TV & AC. Apartment has telephone, kitchen, refrigerator & coffee & tea-making facilities.

Smoking: Permitted.
Pets: Not permitted.
Handicap Access: No.
Children: Case-by-case depending on child's

age, season & available accommodations.
Languages: English, a little Spanish & a little German.

Glen Isle Farm Country Bed & Breakfast

Gay-Friendly 50/50 ♀♂

Come and experience, as did George Washington on June 3, 1773, the "historic hospitality" of *Glen Isle Farm*. At that time, the farm was known as the Ship Inn. Other guests have included James Buchanan, before he became the fifteenth president of the United States, as well as the United States Continental Congress, while on its way to York. During The Civil War, *Glen Isle Farm* was a stop on the underground railroad, thus it has an important place in civil rights history. Today, the farm is a secluded 8-acre gentleman's estate. The approach is down a long, heavily-wooded drive and across a small stone bridge. The drive circles up to the imposing front entrance, leading you up granite steps and across a broad checkerboard porch of black slate, white marble and red brick, through a glass vestibule and to the wide front door. Once inside, you can feel the wonderful sense of history present in this 264-year-old home.

On your visit, you might enjoy a cool autumn afternoon in the upstairs sunroom, sipping a cappuccino or glass of sherry. Watch the fall colors and the shadows, as they gently cross the walled garden. Play a tune on the grand piano in the music room or just curl up with a good book from the selection in the library. If you are the more active type, you may want to take one of the many day trips available. Visit historic Valley Forge. Take the train to Philadelphia, the nation's first capital. Go antiquing. Or visit beautiful Longwood Gardens and the Brandywine River Museum, the home of the Wyeth school and collection. You may want to take a bike ride or go hiking on the many nearby roads and trails. Maybe you've come in May to attend the Devon Horse Show, or to see some of the nearby Amish country, and enjoy a slice of Shoofly Pie. Come and experience the "historic hospitality" that is *Glen Isle Farm*.

Address: Downingtown, PA 19335-2239. Tel: (610) 269-9100, Reservations/Info: (800) 269-1730, Fax: (610) 269-9191.

Type: Bed & breakfast inn.
Clientele: 50% gay & lesbian & 50% straight clientele.
Transportation: Car or train. Free pick up from train or airport shuttle.
To Gay Bars: 30 miles, or 40 minutes by car, to Norristown or Philadelphia.
Rooms: 4 rooms with queen or king beds.
Bathrooms: All private bath/toilet/showers.

Meals: Full breakfast, other meals by arrangement. Our restaurant is licensed by the county.
Vegetarian: Available with prior arrangement.
Complimentary: Daily wine & hors d'oeuvres hour.
Dates Open: All year.
High Season: April through October.
Rates: $60-$120 + tax.
Discounts: 10% on stays of 7 or more nights. Se-

niors 10%.
Credit Cards: MC & VISA.
Rsv'tns: Required.
Reserve Through: Travel agent or call direct.
Minimum Stay: 2 nights on weekends.
Parking: Ample off-street parking.
On-Premises: Meeting rooms & TV lounge. Weddings, reunions & business meeting space available.
Swimming: Nearby river

& lake.
Sunbathing: On the patio or in the yard.
Smoking: Permitted outdoors only.
Pets: Not permitted. Dogs in residence.
Handicap Access: Limited.
Children: By arrangement.
Languages: English.
Your Host: Glenn & Tim.

IGTA

POCONOS MTN AREA

Blueberry Ridge

For That Romantic Country Feeling

Women ♀

Pat and Greta, of *Blueberry Ridge,* offer you friendship and warmth in the company of women. In a beautiful, secluded cedar house, you'll relax in the hot tub or by the wood-burning stove while enjoying a panoramic view of the Delaware Water Gap. Stroll the woods or go out for a romantic dinner. Winter brings skiing, ice skating, sleigh riding. Summer offers canoeing, whitewater rafting, riding, hiking, golf, tennis. Year-round interests include auctions, antique & candle shopping.

Address: Mail to: McCarrick/Moran, RR 1 Box 67, Scotrun, PA 18355. Tel: (717) 629-5036 or (516) 473-6701.

Type: Bed & breakfast guesthouse.
Clientele: Women only.
Transportation: Car is best.
To Gay Bars: 10 miles or 20 minutes by car to Rainbow Mountain Disco.
Rooms: 4 rooms with double & king beds.
Bathrooms: 1 private, others shared

Meals: Full country breakfast. Holiday weekend specials include all meals.
Complimentary: Baked goods, tea & coffee.
Dates Open: All year.
Rates: Rooms $55-$70.
Rsv'tns: Required.
Reserve Through: Call direct.

Parking: Ample off-street parking.
In-Room: TV, ceiling fan & some rooms have VCRs.
On-Premises: TV lounge, videos, kitchen.
Exercise/Health: Outdoor hot tub.
Swimming: River is 5 miles away.

Sunbathing: On common sun decks.
Nudity: Permitted in the hot tub.
Smoking: Permitted outdoors.
Pets: Not permitted.
Handicap Access: No.
Children: Permitted.
Languages: English, Spanish.

Rainbow Mountain Resort

Gay/Lesbian ♀♂

Our Finest Amenity: "Enjoying The Freedom To Be Yourself"

Rainbow Mountain Resort has a style and setting like no other resort of its kind. You will find us nestled high atop a Pocono mountainside on 85 private, wooded acres with a spectacular view of the surrounding mountains. Welcoming both men and women, we are open year-round, and have a friendly, courteous staff to serve you. Dine on fabulous four-course gourmet

RAINBOW MOUNTAIN RESORT

meals and full American breakfasts, join the crowd in the Dance Club or relax in the Lizard Lounge. Our Olympic-sized outdoor pool is just what the doctor ordered for the summer. Take in a day of antique shopping, or hike the many beautiful trails in the fall. Ski some of the best mountains in Pennsylvania during the winter. Take a romantic horseback ride or canoe down the Delaware River in the spring. Come to *Rainbow*

Mountain Resort to play, to celebrate, to get a good night's sleep. Choose from one of our 46 lovely, antique-filled rooms or cabins. There is always something to do in this four-season resort area. But remember, our finest amenity will always be *"Enjoying The Freedom To Be Yourself."*

Address: RD #8, Box 8174, East Stroudsburg, PA 18301. Tel: (717) 223-8484.

Type: Resort with dance club, piano bar, patio dining, pool bar & restaurant.
Clientele: Good mix of gay men & women.
Transportation: Car is best or bus to Stroudsburg, then taxi.
To Gay Bars: Gay & lesbian bar on premises.
Rooms: 30 rooms & 16 cottages with double & queen beds. Cottages are seasonal, May-October.
Bathrooms: 36 private & 2 shared in lodge.

Meals: Full breakfast & dinner.
Vegetarian: Limited availability on menu.
Dates Open: All year.
High Season: 4-season resort area.
Rates: $55-$95, includes breakfast & dinner.
Discounts: For groups over 25 people, except some holidays.
Credit Cards: MC, VISA, Amex & Discover.
Rsv'tns: Recommended two weeks in advance.
Reserve Through: Travel

agent or call direct.
Minimum Stay: 2 nights on weekends. 3 nights on holidays.
Parking: Ample free off-street parking.
In-Room: Maid service, color TV, ceiling fans & AC.
On-Premises: Meeting room.
Exercise/Health: Tennis, volleyball, badminton, horseshoes, hiking, basketball, paddle & row boats, & skiing.
Swimming: Outdoor

Olympic-sized pool with pool bar.
Sunbathing: At poolside.
Smoking: Permitted. Smoking & non-smoking dining area.
Pets: Not permitted.
Handicap Access: No.
Children: Adult-oriented resort.
Languages: English.
Your Host: Georgeann & Laura.

IGTA

Stoney Ridge

Women ♀

For a respite from the city, stay at *Stoney Ridge,* our charming new cedar log home in the secluded Pocono Mountains of Pennsylvania. The house is beautifully furnished with antiques to give it that warm country feeling, while providing all the modern conveniences. Within 10 miles of here, you can enjoy restaurants, skiing, canoeing, hiking, trout fishing, dancing, antiquing, etc.

Address: mail to: P. McCarrick, RR 1 Box 67 Scotrun, PA 18355. Tel: (717) 629-5036 or (516) 473-6701.

Type: Cedar log home with 2 bedrooms, stone fireplace.
Clientele: Women only.
Transportation: Car is best.
To Gay Bars: 10-minute drive to Rainbow Mountain disco/restaurant.

Rooms: Home with 2 rooms, double beds.
Bathrooms: 2 private shower/toilets.
Dates Open: All year.
Rates: $250/$450/$1250, by weekend, week, month.
Rsv'tns: Required.

Reserve Through: Call direct.
Parking: Ample off-street parking.
In-Room: Telephone.
On-Premises: TV lounge with VCR.
Swimming: River & lake nearby.

Smoking: Permitted without restrictions.
Pets: Permitted.
Children: Permitted.
Languages: English & Spanish.

Don't Forget!

The Women's Index

Our Special Women's Index lists all women-oriented accommodations by page number.

RHODE ISLAND

NEWPORT

Brinley Victorian Inn

Gay-Friendly ♀♂

Romantically decorated with fine antiques, Trompe l'Oeil period wallpapers and satin-and-lace window treatments, *The Brinley* is a haven of peace in this city by the sea. In the heart of Newport's historic district, the *Brinley* is within walking distance of historic sites, including the oldest Episcopal church and America's first synagogue. Close by are the "gilded era" mansions of the 19th century, hundreds of 17th century colonials, the famed America's Cup waterfront, unique shops and restaurants, magnificent beaches and two gay bars.

Address: 23 Brinley St, Newport, RI 02840. Tel: (401) 849-7645.

Type: Bed & breakfast inn.	**Meals:** Continental breakfast.	**Rsv'tns:** Recommended.	courtyard.
Clientele: Mostly straight clientele with a gay/lesbian following.	**Complimentary:** Bottle of champagne for special occasions.	**Reserve Through:** Travel agent or call direct.	**Swimming:** Ocean beach or bay.
Transportation: By car.	**Dates Open:** All year.	**Minimum Stay:** 2 nights on in-season weekends, 3 on holiday weekends.	**Sunbathing:** On beach and in private courtyard.
To Gay Bars: Within walking distance to gay/lesbian bars.	**High Season:** May 23rd-October 1st.	**Parking:** Adequate, free on- and off-street parking.	**Smoking:** Permitted in rooms only.
Rooms: 17 doubles, including 1 suite.	**Rates:** Please call for current rates.	**In-Room:** Maid service, AC, ceiling fans, refrigerators (some rooms).	**Pets:** Not permitted.
Bathrooms: 13 private, others share 2 bathrooms.	**Discounts:** Mid-week & longer stays, multiple reservations (5 rooms).	**On-Premises:** 2 porches, 2 parlors, library & patio	**Handicap Access:** No.
	Credit Cards: MC, VISA.		**Children:** 8 years & older, at owner's discretion.
			Languages: English.

Hydrangea House Inn

Gay-Friendly 50/50 ♀♂

Quiet Sophistication in the "City by the Sea"

During the "gilded" period of Newport, when America's wealthy families were building lavish summer homes and bringing with them every luxury, a little luxury found its way to the natives of Newport, themselves. Gardeners who worked on the mansion grounds, it is said, took home cuttings of the exotic plants they cared for, among them the hydrangea, and grew them in their own gardens. We have taken our name from the hydrangea, which blooms all over Newport, be-cause we, like the gardeners, have brought a little luxury home. And we would love to share that feeling of old, luxurious Newport with you.

Built in 1876, this Victorian townhouse has been carefully transformed, and its 6 guest rooms, each with its own sumptuous personality, are elegantly decorated with antiques. Plush carpeting, thick cozy towels, crystal water glasses, long-stemmed goblets for your wine setups, and afternoon refreshments all help make your stay a real luxury. Your day will start with our gratifying hot buffet breakfast served in the contemporary fine art gallery. For your enjoyment we will serve our special blend of *Hydrangea House* coffee, fresh squeezed juice, home-baked bread and granola, and perhaps raspberry pancakes or seasoned scrambled eggs. The gallery may also serve as a unique setting for small conferences and business meetings. Our location is right on Bellevue Avenue just 1/4 mile from the mansions and in the center of Newport's "Walking District," within steps of antique shops, clothing stores, galleries, ocean beaches and historical points of interest. Your hosts will be happy to recommend restaurants and popular night spots. Buses and the airport shuttle stop outside out door. We know you'll love it here, because we do. In 1989, the **Boston Globe** said of the inn, *"In a city renowned for its lodging, the Hydrangea House is not to be missed!* We're not a mansion, just a special place that's home away from home, with our welcome mat out for new friends.

Address: 16 Bellevue Ave, Newport, RI 02840. Tel: (401) 846-4435, (800) 945-4667, Fax: (401) 846-4435.

Type: Bed & breakfast with contemporary art gallery.
Clientele: 50% gay & lesbian & 50% straight clientele.
Transportation: Car is best. Pick up from airport by shuttle $13 per person. Bus station 5 min walk to inn. Local bus line, taxi.
To Gay Bars: 5-minute walk to gay/lesbian bars.
Rooms: 6 rooms with double or queen beds.

Bathrooms: All private bath/toilets.
Meals: Full breakfast.
Vegetarian: Available upon request.
Complimentary: Homemade chocolate chip cookies, afternoon tea & lemonade.
Dates Open: All year.
High Season: May-October.
Rates: Summer $89-$139. Off season $65-$95, $15 extra person charge.
Discounts: Inquire for

extended stays.
Credit Cards: MC & VISA.
Rsv'tns: Required, but walk-ins based on availability.
Reserve Through: Travel agent or call direct.
Minimum Stay: 2 days June-Sept & weekends all year. 3 days on holidays.
Parking: Ample free off-street parking on site.
In-Room: AC, refrigerator & maid service.
On-Premises: Meeting

rooms.
Exercise/Health: Massage by appt. Gym with weights, exercise room, aerobic class, $8-$12 day 5 min away.
Swimming: 5-minute walk to ocean beach.
Sunbathing: On beach or common sun decks.
Smoking: Permitted outdoors ONLY.
Pets: Not permitted.
Handicap Access: No.
Children: Not permitted.
Languages: English.

Melville House Inn

Where The Past Is Present

Gay-Friendly ♀♂

Staying at the *Melville House* is like a step back into the past. Built c. 1750, the house is located in the heart of the historical Hill section of Newport, where the streets are still lit by gas. The French General, Rochambeau, quartered some of his troops here when they fought in the Revolutionary War under George Washington. The house where Washington and his envoy, Major General Marquis de Lafayette, met Rochambeau is across the street.

Although the *Melville House* is on one of Newport's quietest streets, it is only one block from Thames Street and the harborfront, and many of the city's finest restaurants, antique shops and galleries. We're within walking distance of many places of worship, such as Touro Synagogue (the oldest in the U.S.), Trinity Church (c. 1726) and St. Mary's (where President Kennedy married Jacqueline). The Tennis

continued next page

Rhode Island

Hall of Fame, the famous and lavish mansions of the Vanderbilts, Astors and Belmonts, The Naval War College and Newport's finest ocean beaches are just a very short drive.

The seven rooms, furnished in traditional Colonial style, are available with both private and shared baths. A romantic fireplace suite is available during the cold months. Guests in the suite are greeted with champagne upon arrival, treated to after dinner drinks and served breakfast in bed the next day. Expanded continental breakfast features homemade granola, muffins and various other baked breads, such as buttermilk biscuits, bagels, scones, Yankee cornbread and Rhode Island Johnnycakes. Afternoon tea is served daily. Guests enjoy a cup of tea or our special Melville House Blend coffee, a glass of sherry and biscotti, as we discuss the day's activities and our favorite places for dinner. Your hosts, Vince and David, will share with you their Newport experiences and will do their best to make your visit as pleasant as possible. Stay at the *Melville House*, "Where the Past is Present."
Address: 39 Clarke St, Newport, RI 02840. Tel: (401) 847-0640, Fax: 847-0956.

Type: Bed & breakfast.
Clientele: Mostly straight clientele with a gay & lesbian following.
Transportation: Car is best. Short walk from bus station. Limo from Providence Airport.
To Gay Bars: 2 blocks.
Rooms: 7 rooms with single, double or king beds. 1 fireplace suite available in winter.
Bathrooms: 5 private shower/toilets & 2 shared bath/shower/toilets.

Meals: Full breakfast.
Vegetarian: Served every day.
Complimentary: Tea & sherry at 4pm with refreshments & homemade biscotti.
Dates Open: All year.
High Season: Memorial Day through Columbus Day.
Rates: Summer $95-$125 & winter $50-$85. Fireplace suite $150.
Discounts: For long-term stays.

Credit Cards: MC, VISA & Amex.
Rsv'tns: Suggested for weekends & holidays.
Reserve Through: Travel agent or call direct.
Minimum Stay: 2 nights on weekends & 3 nights on holidays & special events.
Parking: Ample free off-street parking.
In-Room: AC & Maid service.
Exercise/Health: Full-service health club available nearby ($10 day pass).
Swimming: In nearby ocean or at health club.
Sunbathing: At the beach.
Smoking: Not permitted.
Pets: Davey and Spike, the feline innkeepers, do not want to share their affections.
Handicap Access: No.
Languages: English.

WESTERLY

Villa, The

The Romance of Italy Awaits You...

Gay-Friendly ♀♂

in this perfect hideaway of flower gardens, Italian porticos and verandas, where you can swim in a sparkling, sapphire pool surrounded by lush plants and spectacular sunshine. *The Villa* is an ideal setting for weddings, honeymoons and rekindling romances. Summers, here, are warm and golden, with cool ocean breezes and festive evenings of music and Italian cuisine. Or, imagine yourself in winter, gazing into the hypnotic flames of a sensuous, crackling fire. Most units have fireplaces and Jacuzzis, all have cable TV and air conditioning.
Address: 190 Shore Road, Westerly, RI 02891. Tel: (401) 596-1054, (800) 722-9240, Fax: (401) 596-6268.

Type: Bed & breakfast.
Clientele: Mainly straight with gay/lesbian following.
Transportation: Train. Van service from Amtrack (Westerly) Station is free.
To Gay Bars: 1/2 hr drive to New London, CT.
Rooms: 2 rooms & 5 suites with full, queen or king beds.
Bathrooms: All private.
Meals: Expanded continental breakfast.
Vegetarian: Available upon request.
Complimentary: Thursday BBQ.
Dates Open: All year.
High Season: Memorial Day to Labor Day.
Rates: Summer $95-$175, winter $65-$145.
Discounts: Off season, mid-week.
Credit Cards: MC, VISA, Amex.
Reserve Through: Travel agent or call direct.
Minimum Stay: Peak weekends only.
Parking: Ample, free off-street parking.
In-Room: Color cable TV, AC, maid service, telephone, ceiling fans & refrigerator.
Exercise/Health: Jacuzzi.
Swimming: Pool on premises & nearby ocean beach.
Sunbathing: At poolside & beach.
Smoking: Permitted in rooms but not in common areas.
Pets: Please inquire.
Handicap Access: No.
Children: Welcome.
Languages: English & Italian.
Your Host: Jerry.

SOUTH CAROLINA

CHARLESTON

Charleston Beach B & B

Gay/Lesbian ♀♂

Just ten miles from Charleston's historical district, facing the Atlantic Ocean on a picturesque barrier island, *Charleston Beach B&B* is the only exclusively gay/lesbian accommodation at the ocean between Rehoboth Beach, Delaware and Ft. Lauderdale, Florida. Established in 1989, just months before Hurricane Hugo stormed through the neighborhood, our 22-room Dutch Colonial home has been

continued next page

extensively remodeled and imaginatively decorated for the discerning traveler. Four-poster beds and an eclectic mix of antiques and Chinese and Persian rugs grace the Charleston and Keys Rooms on the third floor, while simplicity characterizes the Citadel Bunkroom. All rooms are equipped with refrigerators, fresh flowers and robes and are attractively priced.

On the premises, guests can relax by reading a book from our extensive library, play volleyball in the pool, sunbathe on the many decks surrounded by lush gardens, or simply unwind in the 8-person spa. Full breakfast includes seasonal fruit cup and entrees ranging from Eggs Benedict to French toast and sausage. At our popular social hour with open bar, guests discuss the day's activities and make plans for dinner at Charleston's many fine restaurants. On Sundays, we serve dinners ranging from Teriyaki Chicken to outdoor BBQ.

Nearby attractions include Fort Sumpter, where the Civil War began, Magnolia Plantation, and America's oldest gardens at Middleton Place. Nearby Drayton Hall is the finest example of Georgian-Palladian architecture in the South. Patriot's Point is the world's largest naval and maritime museum. Visitors from around the world are attracted by our mild winter climate, fabulous King Street shopping, excellent Charleston restaurants and special events like the Spoleto Festival or spring and fall house and garden tours. Relax by the ocean, while you enjoy the charm and convenience of one of America's truly unique cities.

Address: PO Box 41, Folly Beach, SC 29439. Tel: (803) 588-9443.

Type: Guest house.
Clientele: Good mix of gay men & women.
Transportation: Complimentary pick up from airport, bus, train.
To Gay Bars: 15 minutes to Charleston's gay bars.
Rooms: 8 rooms & 1 suite with bunk & queen beds.
Bathrooms: 2 private bath/toilets & 3 shared bath/shower/toilets.
Meals: Full breakfast.
Vegetarian: 48-hour notice requested.
Complimentary: Open bar for social hour, BBQ or dinner on Sunday, juices, tea & coffee.
Dates Open: All year.
High Season: Easter-Columbus Day.
Rates: $35-$115.
Discounts: 20% for 7 days.
Credit Cards: MC, VISA & Discover.
Rsv'tns: Recommended.
Reserve Through: Travel agent or call direct.
Minimum Stay: 2 days on the weekends, 3 on holidays.
Parking: Adequate free off-street parking.
In-Room: Maid service, AC, ceiling fans & refrigerator.
On-Premises: TV lounge, laundry facilities & complimentary bicycles.
Exercise/Health: Jacuzzi & seasonal massage.
Swimming: Pool on premises. Beach is 2 blocks away.
Sunbathing: At poolside & on common sun decks.
Nudity: Permitted in Jacuzzi and in deck area.
Smoking: Permitted except in bed.
Pets: Permitted in one room only. Ask for specifics.
Handicap Access: Yes, on first floor only.
Children: Not permitted.
Languages: English.
Your Host: Chuck & Steve.

Charleston Columns Guesthouse (formerly Charleston Charm)

The Charleston Experience: Ultimate Charm and Warm Hospitality

Gay/Lesbian ♀♂

To the residents of Charleston, life in the Historic District is like stepping back into history and sharing timeless charm and majestic beauty on a daily basis. Charleston offers a serene reflection of a lifestyle that has all but vanished. When you come to visit, you will want to stay in accommodations befitting the "Charleston Experience." From the moment you arrive at *Charleston Columns*, you feel the charm and hospitality for which

Charleston is renown. Every effort is made to make your stay memorable.

Begin your day with a healthy continental breakfast, and experience the warm, friendly hospitality that you naturally expect of "The Old South." Information on tours and entertainment, restaurant recommendations, and complimentary maps are cheerfully provided upon request. When you are ready to "do Charleston," they will gladly arrange a tour of ante-bellum homes, a horse-drawn carriage ride around the city, a harbor tour, a guided walking tour or even bicycle rentals.

Like the beautiful city of Charleston, the guesthouse is an elegant survivor of a tempestuous past. Built as a private residence in 1855 for Edward Simonton, a prominent Charleston lawyer, state legislator, Confederate officer and federal judge, it has been the home of a number of notable Charlestonian and South Carolinian public figures. In keeping with its history, the suites, guest rooms and public rooms are graced with 19th-century period-style furnishings and antiques, designer linens, Oriental rugs and ceiling fans. The stately living room, dining room and porches provide a comfortable setting for relaxation and congenial entertainment.

Charleston Columns Guesthouse is located in the Historic District of downtown Charleston, an easy walk to historic sites, great shopping and exciting nightlife. The people of Charleston have been welcoming guests for over 300 years, and they know how to make you feel welcome and right at home. Come see for yourself! **Address: 8 Vanderhorst St, Charleston, SC 29403-6121. Tel: (803) 722-7341.**

Type: Guesthouse.
Clientele: Good mix of gays & lesbians.
Transportation: Car is best. Free pick up from airport or train.
To Gay Bars: 2 blocks or a 5-minute walk, 2 minute drive.
Rooms: 2 rooms & 2 suites with queen or king beds.

Bathrooms: 3 private full bath, 1 shared full bath.
Meals: Continental breakfast. Gourmet coffee, tea, juices, fresh fruit & muffins.
Dates Open: All year.
High Season: Mar-Nov.
Rates: For 2 guests: suites $99-$115, doubles $70-$85. $10 less for singles.

Discounts: One night free for 7 night stay.
Rsv'tns: Recommended.
Reserve Through: Travel agent or call direct.
Parking: Adequate off-street parking.
In-Room: Color cable TV, AC, ceiling fans, maid & laundry service.
On-Premises: TV lounge, laundry facilities for

guests.
Swimming: 7 miles to gay beach.
Smoking: Permitted in kitchen only.
Pets: Not permitted.
Handicap Access: No.
Children: Not especially welcome.
Languages: English.
Your Host: Frank & Jim.

Eighteen Fifty-Four Bed & Breakfast

A Tropical Retreat in the Heart of Charleston

Gay/Lesbian ♀♂

Centrally located in Harleston Village, one of the premier restored areas of Charleston's renowned National Register historical district, *1854* is sited in an unusual antebellum edifice of distinctive Italianate design. Both suites are charmingly decorated with an eclectic mix of antique and modern furnishings, original art and sculpture. They have private entrance and access to a rear garden nestled in a lush grove of banana trees and other tropical plantings. The city's best restaurants, gay bars and shopping are a short walk away.

Address: 34 Montagu Street, Charleston, SC 29401. Tel: (803) 723-4789

Type: Bed & breakfast.
Clientele: Mostly gay & lesbian with some straight clientele.
Transportation: Car is best.
To Gay Bars: Four blocks or ten minutes to all 3 of our local gay bars.
Rooms: 2 full suites with double beds.
Bathrooms: All private

bath/toilets.
Meals: Continental breakfast.
Vegetarian: Available with advance notice.
Complimentary: Wine on arrival.
Dates Open: All year.
Rates: $95-$115. Rates may vary seasonally.
Discounts: 10% discount for stays of 3 or more

nights.
Rsv'tns: Required, but will accept late call-ins.
Reserve Through: Travel agent or call direct.
Parking: Ample free on-street parking.
In-Room: Kitchen, refrigerator, AC, color TV, maid service & private outdoor garden area.
On-Premises: Lush tropi-

cal garden.
Swimming: 10-15 miles from all Charleston beaches, including Folly Beach gay area.
Smoking: Permitted.
Pets: Not permitted.
Handicap Access: No.
Children: Permitted with advance notice only. No infants.
Languages: English.

TENNESSEE

GREENEVILLE

Timberfell Lodge

Men ♂

Impeccable Accommodations, Inspired Cuisine & Courteous Staff

Timberfell is a fully self-contained gay men's resort, including two lodging facilities, *The Lodge* and *The Poolhouse Annex Building*. *The Lodge* is a beautiful three-story stone and log guesthouse nestled in a lush, wooded hollow, with 250 acres of mountain trails and springs and an oak barn, surrounded by grassy meadowland. *The Lodge,* decorated with a lovely, eclectic collection of antiques and Orien-

tal rugs, overlooks a pond and a picturesque willow tree. Guests enjoy a charming living room with a ceiling fan, a large stone fireplace, wide screen TV, VCR, a full video library and a stereo. *The Poolhouse Annex building,* the newest lodging facility at *Timberfell,* is highlighted by the *Corral Room.* This beautiful room is our largest guest room. It comes complete with a large sitting area, a California king-sized waterbed, TV, VCR, stocked bar refrigerator, private sink, private bath and a veranda with a great view. Also, there are the new *Roommate Rooms*, with two double beds in each room. A full gourmet breakfast, hors d'oeuvres, and dinner is included for all guests, for example, French omelets or buckwheat waffles served with blueberries, pure maple syrup and whipped cream. All gourmet dinners are prepared with the highest-quality ingredients, right down to our homemade desserts and fresh-ground café Angelica. Our executive chef studied under French President Mitterrand's former personal chef. The chef and her accomplished sous-chef, are on duty daily to create the finest of gourmet dining experiences. All of the deluxe rooms are furnished with king- or queen-sized beds, TV, VCR, down pillows and handmade quilts. Nearby attractions include Dollywood, Biltmore Estates, the Appalachian Trail, whitewater rafting and historical Jonesborough, Tennessee.

Address: 2240 Van Hill Rd, Greeneville, TN 37745. Tel: (615) 234-0833 or (800) 437-0118.

Type: Resort.
Clientele: Men only, levi/leather & naturists welcome.
Transportation: Pick up from airport & bus.
To Gay Bars: 30 miles or a half-hour drive.
Rooms: 15 rooms with bunk, double, queen or king beds.
Bathrooms: 4 private shower/toilets, 2 private sinks. Others share.
Campsites: 4 RV parking spaces & 50 tent sites. Campers have full bath house clean-up facilities. Electric, sewer & water.

Meals: Modified American Plan: full breakfast, appetizer trays, full dinner with wine.
Vegetarian: Available upon request.
Complimentary: Toiletry baskets & terry cloth robes.
Dates Open: All year.
High Season: April through October.
Rates: $94-$154 single occupancy ($60 for additional person). $94 bunkroom. Campsites $35 with lodge privileges extra.
Discounts: 10% off private rooms if 7 days or

more.
Credit Cards: MC, VISA, Amex & Discover.
Rsv'tns: Required.
Reserve Through: Travel agent or call direct.
Minimum Stay: 2 nights on holidays.
Parking: Free off-street secured parking.
In-Room: Color TV, housekeeping & laundry service. Deluxe rooms have VCR, bar refrigerators & coffee pots.
On-Premises: Central AC, living room with entertainment center & 24-person dining room.

Exercise/Health: 20-person sauna, 8-person Jacuzzi, massages, bikes, bench press, gravity inversion, fishing & hiking trails & canoe.
Swimming: 20 x 40 foot heated pool on premises.
Sunbathing: At poolside, pond, on common sun deck or in backyard.
Nudity: Permitted inside lodge and on all 250 acres.
Smoking: A smoking area is set aside for winter.
Pets: Call ahead.
Handicap Access: No.
Children: Not permitted.
Languages: English.

NEWPORT

Christopher Place

We're Easy to Find, but Hard to Forget

Gay-Friendly 50/50 ♀♂

Surrounded by expansive mountain views, this premiere Southern estate includes over 200 acres to explore, a pool, tennis court and sauna. Relax by the marble fireplace in the library, retreat to the game room, or enjoy a hearty mountain meal in our res-

taurant. Romantic rooms are available with a hot tub or fireplace. Off I-40 at exit 435, *Christopher Place* is just 32 scenic miles from Gatlinburg and Pigeon Forge. Perfect for special occasions and gatherings. **Open Spring 1995.**
Address: 1500 Pinnacles Way, Newport, TN 37821. Tel: (615) 623-6555.

continued next page

Tennessee

Type: Inn with restaurant.
Clientele: 50% gay & lesbian & 50% straight clientele.
Transportation: Car is best. $25 for pick up from airport.
To Gay Bars: 40 miles or an hour drive.
Rooms: 9 rooms & 1 suite with double, queen or king beds.
Bathrooms: Private: 2 bath/toilets, 4 shower/ toilets & 4 bath/shower/

toilets.
Meals: Full breakfast.
Vegetarian: Available with 24-hour notice.
Complimentary: Afternoon tea & lemonade.
Dates Open: All year.
High Season: Jul-Oct.
Rates: $75-$150.
Discounts: Special gift to *Inn Places* readers.
Credit Cards: MC & VISA.
Rsv'tns: Recommended.
Reserve Through: Travel agent or call direct.
Minimum Stay: Some

holidays or special weekends.
Parking: Ample free off-street parking.
In-Room: Color cable TV, VCR, video tape library, AC, ceiling fans & maid service. Some rooms with hot tubs & fireplaces.
On-Premises: TV lounge, meeting rooms, game room, tanning bed, fax, copy, word processing equipment.
Exercise/Health: Sauna

& weights.
Swimming: Pool on premises.
Sunbathing: At poolside.
Nudity: Permitted in sauna.
Smoking: Permitted in game room & on porches.
Pets: Not permitted.
Handicap Access: Yes.
Children: Ages 12 & over welcomed.
Languages: English.
Your Host: Drew & Bill.

ROGERSVILLE

Lee Valley Farm

Gay/Lesbian ♂

The No-Attitude Stress-Free Mountain Retreat

Picture it. Horses grazing on a hillside. A swimming pool sparkling in the middle of a hayfield. Hiking and riding "The Trail of the Lonesome Pine." Steam rising from the hot tub under a starry sky. Campfires. Bass, bluegills, barbeque! Frosty nights, flowers, snowpersons, farm critters, deer, a cozy fire, talking and touching. Romance in a hayloft. Bright, exciting people. A no-glitz real farm. Total escape. Relaxation bordering on coma. *Lee Valley Farm* is as close as you can get to "home, home on the range"...without a mortgage.

Address: 142 Drinnon Lane, Rogersville, TN 37857. Tel: (615) 272-4068, Fax: 272-4068, Email AOL:leesfarm.

Type: Guest farmhouse with cabins & campground.
Clientele: Mostly men with women welcome.
Transportation: Pick up from bus in Morristown or Tri-City Airport in Johnson City possible.
To Gay Bars: 1-1/2 hours by car to Knoxville or Johnson City bars.
Rooms: 1 double in farm house. 2 cabins, 1 with 1 double, & 1 with 3 doubles.
Bathrooms: 1 private & 2 shared plus outdoor hot showers.
Campsites: 6-10 tent

sites. Electric & water hookups. Vans, campers, small RV's. 2 shared baths, 1 outdoor shower at farmhouse & 1 shower in the barn. Outhouse.
Meals: All meals included.
Vegetarian: Available upon request.
Complimentary: Chocolate or lollipops & condoms.
Dates Open: All year.
High Season: June through December.
Rates: $79-$129 single, $139-$179 per couple.
Discounts: Groups, fund

raising orgs., & longer stays.
Credit Cards: MC, VISA & Discover.
Rsv'tns: Required in advance.
Reserve Through: Call direct.
Minimum Stay: 2 days on holidays.
Parking: Ample free parking.
In-Room: Ceiling fans, refrigerator, coffee & tea-making facilities.
On-Premises: Community dining room, pool barn, laundry, TV, VCR, use of kitchen.
Exercise/Health: Pool,

weights, hot tub, massage, horseback riding & fishing. Nearby weights, Jacuzzi & massage.
Swimming: In the pool & spring-fed pond.
Sunbathing: At poolside & on the mountaintop.
Nudity: Permitted.
Smoking: Permitted outdoors and in designated areas.
Pets: Permitted with prior arrangement.
Handicap Access: No.
Children: Not permitted.
Languages: English.

TEXAS

CORPUS CHRISTI & ROCKPORT

Anthony's By The Sea

Gay/Lesbian ♀♂

Just a few minutes from Padre Island National Seashore, *Anthony's By The Sea* is located on a secluded acreage with pool and therapy spa and spacious lawn. *Anthony's* features two master bedrooms, with private baths and seating areas. Two other rooms can be used as separate or connected units by parties traveling together. A separate guest house has one bedroom, private bath, living room and fully-equipped kitchen. We serve gourmet breakfasts, special dinners and optional box lunches. Walk to Rockport's fine restaurants, art galleries, quaint shops, beach and harbor.

Address: 732 S Pearl, Rockport, TX 78382. Tel: (512) 729-6100.

Type: Bed & breakfast.
Clientele: Mostly gay & lesbian with some straight clientele.
Transportation: Car is best.
To Gay Bars: 30 miles to Corpus Christi bars. 10 miles to gay-friendly bar.
Rooms: 4 rooms & 1 cottage.
Bathrooms: 3 private & 1 shared.
Meals: Full gourmet breakfast.
Vegetarian: Available upon request.
Complimentary: Juices, iced tea, coffee, lemonade, & an afternoon snack.
Dates Open: All year.
Rates: $50-$95.
Discounts: 7th day free.
Rsv'tns: Requested.
Reserve Through: Travel agent or call direct.
Parking: Carports.
In-Room: Color TV, VCR, AC, ceiling fans, refrigerator & maid service.
On-Premises: TV lounge, laundry facilities, telephone & full, covered lanai with fans & chandeliers.
Exercise/Health: Weights & Jacuzzi.
Swimming: Pool on premises. 5 blocks to beach.
Sunbathing: On common sun decks & at the beach 5 blocks away.
Nudity: Permitted by the pool.
Smoking: Permitted with restrictions.
Pets: On approval.
Handicap Access: No.
Children: Permitted in the cottage.
Languages: English & Spanish.
Your Host: Tony & Denis

DALLAS

Inn On Fairmount

Gay/Lesbian ♀♂

The Ambiance of an Inn, the Luxury of a Fine Hotel

The *Inn On Fairmount* is located in the heart of the Oak Lawn/Turtle Creek area, minutes from restaurants, clubs and the Dallas Market Center.

There are seven finely-furnished bedrooms and suites with private baths, a beautifully decorated lounge and a Jacuzzi. Coffee and newspaper are placed outside your door each morning. Continental breakfast is served in the lounge as is evening wine and cheese. For the ambiance of an inn and the luxury of a fine hotel, spend a night or two with us and experience the style and good taste which is the *Inn On Fairmount!*

Address: 3701 Fairmount, Dallas, TX 75219. Tel: (214) 522-2800, Fax: (214) 522-2898.

Type: Bed & Breakfast inn.
Clientele: Mostly gay & lesbian with some straight clientele.
Transportation: Car or airport shuttle.
To Gay Bars: 2-1/2 blocks.
Rooms: 7 rooms with twin, queen & king beds.
Bathrooms: All private.
Meals: Buffet-style continental breakfast.
Complimentary: Evening wine & cheese hour.
Dates Open: All year.
Rates: Per night: rooms $80, mini-suites $95, 2-room suite $120.
Discounts: On longer stays.
Credit Cards: MC & VISA.
Rsv'tns: Recommended, especially on weekends.
Reserve Through: Travel agent or call direct.

continued next page

Parking: Ample free off-street parking.
In-Room: Color TV, AC, telephone, video tape library, maid service. Some rooms with ceiling fans. VCR in 2-room suite.
On-Premises: Fax machine.
Exercise/Health: Jacuzzi.
Sunbathing: On common sun decks.
Smoking: Not permitted in lobby.
Pets: Not permitted.
Handicap Access: 1 room with widened doors.
Children: Not especially welcome.
Languages: English, Spanish.
Your Host: Michael.

HOUSTON

Lovett Inn, The

Gay-Friendly 50/50 ♀♂

You'll Love It at the Lovett!

Originally the home of a former mayor, *The Lovett Inn* now offers unique client lodging and distinctive catering accommodations for corporate meetings, seminars, retreats and receptions. Guestrooms and suites, each restored with antiques, have queen-sized beds, adjoining bathrooms, color TV and telephone. Surrounding the inn are landscaped grounds with box hedges and brick paths, a swimming pool and a spa in a magnificent setting.

Address: 501 Lovett Blvd, Houston, TX 77006. Tel: (713) 522-5224, Fax: 528-6708, (800) 779-5224, digital pager: 626-6994.

Type: Inn.
Clientele: 50% gay & lesbian & 50% straight clientele.
Transportation: Airport shuttle to downtown Hyatt, then taxi.
To Gay Bars: 1/2 block to gay/lesbian bars.
Rooms: 3 rooms, 3 suites, 1 apartment & 1 cottage with double, queen or king beds.
Bathrooms: All private. 3 with whirlpool baths.
Meals: Continental breakfast.
Vegetarian: Available.
Complimentary: Tea, coffee, candy in rooms.
Dates Open: All year.
Rates: $55-$150.
Discounts: Group and long-term rates.
Credit Cards: MC, VISA & Amex.
Rsv'tns: Suggested.
Reserve Through: Call direct.
Minimum Stay: Required at peak times.
Parking: Ample, free off-street parking.
In-Room: Color cable TV, VCR, kitchen, coffee & tea-making facilities & laundry service.
On-Premises: Meeting rooms & TV lounge. Laundry available.
Exercise/Health: Jacuzzi. Nearby gym, weights, Jacuzzi, sauna, steam & massage.
Swimming: Pool on premises, 30-60 minutes to ocean beach, lake.
Sunbathing: At poolside or on private sun decks.
Smoking: Permitted in public areas & in some rooms.
Pets: Permitted on approval.
Handicap Access: No.
Children: Permitted on approval.
Languages: English.

IGTA

PORT ARANSAS

Seahorse Inn

Gay-Owned & -Operated Since 1956

Gay/Lesbian ♀♂

Experience the warmth of Port Aransas at the *Seahorse Inn.* We are secluded high atop a sand dune, a short sandy stroll to the beach. In-room antiques and classical decor complete the uncluttered ambience of the inn's ocean view units. In addition to eighteen miles of unobstructed white sandy beaches, we have a very private heated pool surrounded by tropical gardens. *The Seahorse Inn* provides a charming European style tastefully set on the wild dunes of Mustang Island and sun-drenched Port Aransas.

Address: PO Box 426, Port Aransas, TX 78373. Tel: (512) 749-5221.

Type: Self-catering guesthouse with separate entrances. Completely private.
Clientele: Good mix of gay men & lesbians with some straight clientele.
Transportation: Car is best. Free pick up from local airport (for private planes).
To Gay Bars: 28 miles to gay bars in Corpus Christi.
Rooms: 1 room, 1 suite, 1 cottage & 12 efficiencies. All units have cooking facilities.

Bathrooms: All private.
Meals: Self-catering.
Complimentary: Cocktails on various Saturdays, occasional parties.
Dates Open: All year.
High Season: Late May through early September.
Rates: 1 bedroom $45-$75, efficiency suite $75-$120, cottage $65-$105.
Discounts: Seventh night is free.
Credit Cards: MC, VISA,

AMEX, Discover.
Rsv'tns: Recommended.
Reserve Through: Call direct.
Minimum Stay: During certain periods. Please inquire.
Parking: Adequate, free off-street parking.
In-Room: Color cable TV, AC, ceiling fans, kitchen, refrigerator, coffee/tea-making facilities. Optional maid service for extra charge.
On-Premises: Meeting rooms.

Swimming: In heated pool or nearby ocean. 20 miles to gay beach.
Sunbathing: At poolside, beach, patio, common sun decks.
Nudity: At poolside during certain times.
Smoking: Permitted.
Pets: Trained pets welcome.
Handicap Access: No.
Children: Permitted, but not encouraged.
Languages: English.
Your Host: Michael.

SAN ANTONIO

Garden Cottage, The

Gay/Lesbian ♀♂

Come to *The Garden Cottage* in San Antonio. There's no place like it! We offer privacy and a country-style atmosphere, yet we're minutes from downtown, shopping, restaurants, museums, and public gardens. Our cozy cottage, shaded by Texas pecan trees in a quiet residential neighborhood, is conveniently located near San Antonio's historic and cultural attractions. San Antonio is home to the Alamo, River Walk, and its five Spanish missions are part of the National Park System.
Address: San Antonio, TX . Tel: (800) 235-7215.

Type: Cottage adjacent to the San Antonio Botanical Gardens.
Clientele: Mainly gay/lesbian with some straight clientele.
Transportation: Taxi, rental car, or bus.
To Gay Bars: 6 blocks to
gay bar, 15-20 min to lesbian bars.

continued next page

Texas

Rooms: 1 cottage with double beds.
Bathrooms: 1 private shower/toilet.
Complimentary: Drinks, snacks, fruit, popcorn.
Dates Open: All year.
High Season: March-May & Sept-Nov.
Rates: $50-$80.

Discounts: Weekly rate $250-$350.
Rsv'tns: Required.
Reserve Through: Call direct.
Minimum Stay: 2 nights.
Parking: Ample, free off-street parking.
In-Room: Color cable TV, VCR, AC, telephone, ceiling fans, kitchen, refrigerator, coffee & tea-making facilities.
On-Premises: Laundry facilities upon request.
Exercise/Health: Massage $30-$40.
Swimming: 15 min to public pool, 1 hr to river, lake, 2 hrs to ocean beach.

Sunbathing: On patio.
Smoking: Permitted on porch.
Pets: Not permitted.
Handicap Access: Not wheelchair accessible.
Children: Permitted if over age 12.
Languages: English, German.

San Antonio Bed & Breakfast

A Chili Bowl of Culture

Gay/Lesbian ♀♂

Eclectic and stately, with its 32-foot octagonal tower, this 1891 homestead, *San Antonio B&B*, is situated in the King William Historical Neighborhood two blocks from the Riverwalk. Uniquely decorated rooms have private or semi-private entrances. Relax outdoors under the grape arbor, the three arched porticos or on the second-story veranda. We serve continental breakfast in the formal dining room adjacent to the music room, where you'll find a restored 1869 Chickering square grand piano. A touch of the Old West, a trace of the South, a taste of Mexico. That's totally San Antonio!

Address: 510 E Guenther, San Antonio, TX 78210-1133. Tel: (210) 222-1828

Type: Bed & breakfast.
Clientele: Good mix of gays & lesbians.
Transportation: Car is best. Shuttle bus to downtown.
To Gay Bars: 12 blocks or 1/2 mile. 15 min by foot or 3 minutes by car.
Rooms: 3 rooms with full beds.
Bathrooms: 2 private bath/toilets & 1 shared bath/shower/toilet.
Meals: Full breakfast.
Vegetarian: Available upon request.
Complimentary: Fruit & wine.
Dates Open: All year.
High Season: Fiesta, 3rd week in April.
Rates: $75-$100.
Discounts: For more than 3 days.
Credit Cards: MC & VISA.
Rsv'tns: Required.
Reserve Through: Call direct.
Parking: Off-street shaded parking.
In-Room: Color TV, AC, housekeeping & room service.
On-Premises: Meeting rooms & laundry facilities.
Exercise/Health: Jacuzzi & nearby YMCA.
Swimming: Use of nearby condominium pool.
Sunbathing: On common sun decks.
Smoking: Permitted outdoors.
Pets: Not permitted.
Handicap Access: Handicapped welcome. Tell us your needs.
Children: Any age welcomed.
Languages: English & a little Spanish.

Summit Haus & Summit Haus II

Gay/Lesbian ♀♂

Welcome, Wilkommen, Bienvenidos, Bienvenue, Benvenuto, C'mon Over, Stay Awhile...

Summit Haus and *Summit Haus II* are two elegant 1920's bed and breakfast accommodations. Just minutes north of San Antonio's downtown historical, multicultural attractions, they offer luxury, comfort and privacy for less than most hotels.

Furnishings include rare Biedermeier antiques, crystal, porcelain, Persian and Oriental rugs and French and English antiques. The adjacent 2000-square-foot cottage is beautifully-furnished with all the comforts of elegant accommodations in our tradition of Texas hospitality.

Address: 427 W Summit, San Antonio, TX 78212. Tel: (800) 972-7266, (210) 736-6272, (210) 828-3045, Fax: (210) 737-8244.

Type: Bed & breakfast.
Clientele: Gay & lesbian. Good mix of men & women.
Transportation: Car.
To Gay Bars: 1 mile or 5 minutes by car.
Rooms: 2 rooms, 1 suite & 1 cottage with double, queen or king beds.
Bathrooms: 3 private bath/toilets & 1 private

shower/toilet.
Meals: Full breakfast.
Complimentary: Brandy, cognac, soft drinks & beer.
Dates Open: All year.
Rates: $57.50-$150.
Credit Cards: MC, VISA, Amex.
Rsv'tns: Required.
Reserve Through: Call direct.

Minimum Stay: 2 nights on weekends.
Parking: Ample free off-street parking.
In-Room: Color TV, AC, telephone, ceiling fans, refrigerator, coffee & tea-making facilities.
On-Premises: Meeting rooms & laundry facilities.
Sunbathing: In the back-

yard & on common sun decks.
Smoking: Outside on the decks. All other areas non-smoking.
Pets: Not permitted.
Handicap Access: No.
Children: Will accept children over 10 years of age.
Languages: English & German.

SOUTH PADRE ISLAND

Upper Deck, A Guesthouse

Gay/Lesbian ♀♂

Upper Deck is the only openly gay establishment in the vicinity. There is a strong representation of Hispanics in the area, because of our close proximity to Mexico, Matamoros being only 30 minutes away. Convenient air connections are available to Harlingen via Continental, American and Southwest Airlines. Mexican airlines serve other area cities. South Padre Island is world-famous for deep-sea game fishing. Bay fishing, pier fishing and surf fishing are also extremely popular. This area is the home of the area's largest shrimping fleet. Bring your surfboard or wind surfer for some exciting action. Shop or party in Matamoros, Mexico. Enjoy one of the nation's top beaches. Visit the Gladys Porter Zoo in Brownsville, TX, the home of endangered species. Nearby Laguna at Atascosa National Wildlife Preserve is a delight for birders and wildlife enthusiasts. A nude beach, some 15 miles to the north, is a quiet refuge for fun and relaxation.

Our guest house is designed for the gay or lesbian traveler who is interested in meeting new friends, or for lovers who want to enjoy a getaway where they can unwind and be themselves. Now under new ownership, the building is being updated and renewed to provide guests with the most comfortable environment possible. The entire inn can be booked by gay and lesbian groups for conferences, meetings, etc. The area abounds in excellent and moderately-priced restaurants.
Address: 120 E Atol, Box 2309, South Padre Island, TX 78597. Tel: (210) 761-5953.

Type: Guesthouse
Clientele: Good mix of gay men & women.
Transportation: Airport pick up (small charge). Valley bus stop 1 block.
To Gay Bars: Gays discreetly frequent straight bars nearby, 1 hour to Harlingen gay bar.
Rooms: 10 doubles, 2 suites, 1 efficiency & 1 bunk room containing 8 bunks & lockers.
Bathrooms: All private.

Meals: Continental breakfast from 9-12 noon.
Dates Open: All year.
High Season: February 12th-Labor Day.
Rates: $35-$110.
Discounts: Call for special rates.
Credit Cards: Major credit cards welcome.
Rsv'tns: Recommended.
Reserve Through: Travel agent or call direct.
Minimum Stay: High

season weekends 2 nights, holidays 3.
Parking: Parking lot on premises.
In-Room: Color TV, AC & maid service. Kitchen in efficiency.
On-Premises: TV lounge, laundry facilities, game room, kitchen & soda machines.
Exercise/Health: Hot tub on premises. Horseback riding, jet ski nearby.
Swimming: Heated pool

& ocean.
Sunbathing: On beach, common sun deck or at poolside.
Nudity: Nude beach nearby.
Smoking: Non-smoking rooms available.
Pets: Not permitted.
Handicap Access: No.
Children: Not permitted.
Languages: English.

UTAH

SALT LAKE CITY

Anton Boxrud B&B Inn

Salt Lake's Closest B&B to Downtown

Gay-Friendly ♀♂

Your hosts, Mark and Keith, along with two adopted pound pups, invite you to relax in the casual elegance of our historic home. Half a block from the Governor's Mansion, we are the closest B&B to downtown, just a 15-minute walk. In the evenings, enjoy complimentary beverages and snacks. The hot tub can provide liquid refreshment of a different kind. We serve full breakfasts, but don't worry—table manners won't be judged as Liza Doolittle's were when our dining room table served as a prop in *My Fair Lady*.

Address: 57 South 600 East, Salt Lake City, UT 84102. Tel: (801) 363-8035, (800) 524-5511, Fax: (801) 596-1316.

Type: Bed & breakfast.
Clientele: Mostly straight clientele with a gay & lesbian following.
Transportation: Car or taxi.
To Gay Bars: 8 blocks.
Rooms: 6 rooms & 1 suite with single, queen or king beds.
Bathrooms: Private: 1 shower/toilet, 1 full bath. 4 shared full baths.

Meals: Full breakfast.
Complimentary: Evening snacks, beverages, coffee & tea.
Dates Open: All year.
High Season: Jun-Oct (summer) & Jan-Mar (ski season).
Rates: $44-$119.
Credit Cards: MC, VISA & Amex.
Rsv'tns: Recommended.
Reserve Through: Travel

agent or call direct.
Minimum Stay: 2 nights on weekends.
Parking: Ample on-street & off-street covered parking.
In-Room: AC & maid service.
On-Premises: TV lounge, meeting rooms.
Exercise/Health: Jacuzzi on premises. Nearby gym, weights, Jacuzzi,

sauna, steam & massage.
Swimming: Nearby pool & lake.
Sunbathing: At the beach.
Smoking: Permitted outside only.
Pets: Not permitted.
Handicap Access: No.
Children: Welcome.
Languages: English.
Your Host: Mark & Keith.

ZION NATIONAL PARK

Red Rock Inn

Gay-Friendly ♀♂

Experience the spectacular red rock cliffs of Zion National Park in relaxed comfort at *Red Rock Inn*. Each of our six rooms is individually decorated to offer a unique flavor and ambiance. They all have patios with a view and private baths (4 rooms feature jetted tubs). Enjoy your complimentary breakfast (delivered in a basket to your door each morning) in the shade of an old pecan tree as you plan your day in one of the world's most beautiful and inspiring natural wonders.

Address: 998 Zion Park Blvd, PO Box 273, Springdale, UT 84767. Tel: (801) 772-3139.

Type: Intimate bed & breakfast cottages.
Clientele: Mostly straight clientele with a gay & lesbian following.
Transportation: Car is the only way.
To Gay Bars: 150 miles to Las Vegas.

Rooms: 6 rooms with queen beds.
Bathrooms: Private: 4 whirlpool bath/shower/ toilet, 1 full bath, 1 shower/toilet.
Meals: Full breakfast.
Vegetarian: Available with prior arrangements.

Dates Open: All year.
High Season: May to September.
Rates: $65-$85.
Credit Cards: MC, VISA & Amex.
Rsv'tns: Required in high season.
Reserve Through: Call

direct.
Minimum Stay: 2 nights on holidays.
Parking: Adequate free off-street parking.
In-Room: Color cable TV, AC, ceiling fans & maid service.
Exercise/Health:

Massage available by appointment.
Swimming: Nearby pool & river.

Sunbathing: On private sun decks & patios, common patio & lawn.
Smoking: Not permitted.

Pets: Not permitted.
Handicap Access: Yes. One unit & garden area.
Children: Allowed with

special arrangements.
Languages: English.

VERMONT

ANDOVER

Inn at HighView, The

Gay-Friendly ♀♂

Vermont the Way You Always Dreamed it Would Be...

but the way you've never found it, until now. Everyone who arrives at the *Inn at HighView* has the same breathless reaction to the serenity of the surrounding hills. The inn's hilltop location offers incredible peace, tranquility and seclusion, yet is convenient to all the activities that bring you to Vermont, such as skiing, golf, tennis and antiquing. Ski cross-country or hike our 72 acres. Swim in our unique rock garden pool. Enjoy our gourmet dinner, relax by a

blazing fire, snuggle under a down comforter in a canopy bed, or gaze 50 miles over pristine mountains.

Address: RR 1, Box 201A, East Hill Road, Andover, VT. Tel: (802) 875-2724 or Fax: (802) 875-4021.

Type: Inn with restaurant for Inn guests only.
Clientele: Mostly straight with a gay & lesbian following.
Transportation: Car is best. Amtrak to Bellows Falls, VT (19 mi), Albany, NY (83 mi). Taxi from Bellows Falls $20. Limo from Albany $90.
To Gay Bars: 1.5 hours by car. Proximity to a bar is NOT the reason to come here!
Rooms: 6 rooms & 2 suites with single, double, queen or king beds.
Bathrooms: 6 private bath/toilet/showers & 3 private shower/toilets.
Meals: Full breakfast with dinner available on most weekend nights at a prix fixe rate.

Vegetarian: We specialize in Italian cuisine and have many pasta dishes without meat.
Complimentary: Sherry in room & turn-down service. Tea & coffee always. Conferences receive coffee service, snacks.
Dates Open: All year except for 2 weeks in November & 2 weeks in April.
High Season: Sep 15 through Oct 25, Christmas holiday week, & all of February.
Rates: Fall/Winter: $90-$125 double occupancy. $20 per extra person in suite. Summer: $80 double occupancy.
Discounts: For mid-week stays in winter & for longer than 2 days on

weekends when no 3-night minimum is in effect.
Credit Cards: MC & VISA.
Rsv'tns: Required.
Reserve Through: Travel agent or call direct.
Minimum Stay: 3 nights on holiday weekends & week between Christmas & New Years.
Parking: Ample free off-street parking.
In-Room: Maid & laundry service. 1 room with fireplace, 3 with canopy beds, 7 with private balconies & entrances, 2 with AC.
On-Premises: Meeting rooms, TV lounge, laundry facilities, gazebo overlooking view, BBQ picnic area, game room, huge fireplace with comfortable couches in living

room, library & CD player.
Exercise/Health: Sauna.
Swimming: Pool on premises.
Sunbathing: At poolside.
Nudity: Permitted in sauna area, with discretion.
Smoking: Permitted outside only.
Pets: Small pets sometimes permitted depending on how full we are. Please inquire.
Handicap Access: 1 room accessible, but doorway is narrow.
Children: Permitted suites only except during peak season. Please inquire.
Languages: English, Italian & Spanish.

INN Places 1995

ARLINGTON

Candlelight Motel

Gay-Friendly ♀♂

Four Spectacular Seasons to Explore Vermont

In the charming village of Arlington, Vermont, once the home of Norman Rockwell, *Candlelight Motel* is nestled in a valley with magnificent mountain views. Your room has a comfortable bed, private bath, air conditioning and color cable TV. Join us for continental breakfast by the fireplace. Good restaurants are nearby. Vermont has brilliant red and gold foliage in autumn, nearby skiing in winter, and crystal clear days and cool nights in the spring. Four seasons of activities include fishing, hiking, biking, canoeing and skiing. AAA & Mobil rated.

Address: Rt 7A, PO Box 97, Arlington, VT 05250. Tel: (802) 375-6647, (800) 348-5294.

Type: Motel with fireside lounge.
Clientele: Mostly straight clientele with a gay & lesbian following.
Transportation: Car.
To Gay Bars: 1-1/4 hours by car to gay & lesbian bars in Albany, NY.
Rooms: 17 rooms with double or queen beds.
Bathrooms: All private bath/toilets.

Meals: Continental breakfast.
Complimentary: Coffee, tea & juices.
Dates Open: All year.
High Season: Fall foliage.
Rates: $45-$75.
Discounts: Group bookings & ski packages.
Credit Cards: MC, VISA & Amex.
Rsv'tns: Recommended.
Reserve Through: Call

direct.
Minimum Stay: On holiday weekends.
Parking: Ample free off-street parking.
In-Room: Color cable TV, AC, telephone & maid service. Refrigerators in 14 rooms.
On-Premises: Fireside lounge.
Swimming: Pool on premises.

Sunbathing: At poolside.
Smoking: Permitted. Non-smoking rooms available. Fireside lounge is non-smoking.
Pets: Not permitted.
Handicap Access: No.
Children: Permitted.
Languages: English.

IGTA

BRATTLEBORO

Mapleton Farm B & B

Gay/Lesbian ♀♂

Private forests surround our 1803 farmhouse on 25 picturesque rural acres. Guests at *Mapleton Farm* enjoy the traditional appeal of Vermont, its shaded country roads, cross-country skiing, hiking or biking through autumn leaves. A hearty, country-style breakfast is served in our large country kitchen. Nearby Dummerston offers fine dining and a large number of artisans and specialty shops. Downhill skiers find our location convenient to well-known ski areas. Cross-country skiers use charming groomed areas nearby or blaze their own trails on the inn's property.

Address: RD 2, Box 510, Putney, VT 05346. Tel: (802) 257-5252.

Type: Bed & breakfast.
Clientele: Mostly gay & lesbian with some straight clientele.
Transportation: Car is best.
To Gay Bars: 1 hour to Northampton & Springfield, MA bars.
Rooms: 8 rooms with double beds.
Bathrooms: 3 private & 2 shared.

Meals: Full breakfast.
Vegetarian: No meat served.
Complimentary: Drinks.
Dates Open: All year.
High Season: Summer & foliage season.
Rates: Rooms $39-$79.
Discounts: Third night free in winter & spring.
Credit Cards: MC & VISA.
Rsv'tns: Recommended.
Reserve Through: Call

direct.
Minimum Stay: Required on busier weekends.
Parking: Ample off-street parking.
In-Room: Maid service, some rooms with refrigerators, some with color TV.
On-Premises: TV lounge, public telephone.
Swimming: Swimming hole.

Sunbathing: By the river.
Nudity: Permitted at the swimming hole.
Smoking: Permitted outdoors only.
Pets: Permitted with prior notice.
Handicap Access: No.
Children: Under 12 years not permitted.
Languages: English.

BURLINGTON

Howden Cottage

Gay-Friendly ♀♂

Howden Cottage offers cozy lodging and warm hospitality in the atmosphere of an artist's home. We're located in downtown Burlington, convenient to The Marketplace shopping, Lake Champlain, cinemas, night spots, churches, great restaurants, theatre, concerts, the U. of Vermont and the Medical Center Hospital of Vermont. The Shelburne Museum is a short drive, as are several major ski areas and Vermont's spectacular fall foliage.

Address: 32 N Champlain St, Burlington, VT 05401. Tel: (802) 864-7198.

Type: Bed & breakfast.
Clientele: Mostly straight clientele with a gay/lesbian following.
Transportation: Bus stop is one block away.
To Gay Bars: 2-1/2 blocks to gay/lesbian bar.
Rooms: 2 rooms & 1 suite with single, double or queen beds.
Bathrooms: 1 private shower/toilet, 2 sinks & 1 shared bath/shower/toilet.
Meals: Continental breakfast.
Dates Open: All year.
High Season: July-October.
Rates: $35-$75.
Credit Cards: MC & VISA.
Rsv'tns: Suggested.
Reserve Through: Call direct.
Parking: Adequate off- & on-street parking.
In-Room: Sinks in room, AC/heat.
Exercise/Health: Nearby gym, weights, Jacuzzi, sauna, steam, massage.
Swimming: In the Lake or at the YMCA or nearby river.
Sunbathing: Lakeside.
Smoking: Not permitted.
Pets: Not permitted.
Handicap Access: No.
Children: Permitted with prior arrangement.
Languages: English.
Your Host: Bruce.

CENTRAL VERMONT

Autumn Crest Inn

Gay-Friendly ♀♂

Vermont Magazine *Loves Our Romantic Inn!*

"Perched on a knoll overlooking the panoramic Williamstown valley and surrounded by the barns and pastures of a 46-acre work-horse farm, the comfortable, unpretentious inn conveys a refreshing sense of rural authenticity." *Vermont Magazine*

Autumn Crest Inn is a 180-year-old restored farmstead nestled among verdant fields and forest. Enjoy the cozy fireplace in the living room and cross-country skiing in winter, the wraparound porch, clay tennis courts, hiking, biking in summer and world-class dinners and robust breakfasts year-round.

Address: Box 1540 Clark Rd, Williamstown, VT. Tel: (802) 433-6627, (800) 339-6627.

Type: Inn with gourmet restaurant.
Clientele: Mostly straight clientele with a gay & lesbian following.
Transportation: Auto, air to Burlington VT, AMTRAK to Montpelier VT. Pick up from airport, train, bus in Burlington, $20 one way.
To Gay Bars: 1 hr to Burlington.
Rooms: 16 rooms & 2 suites with single, double or queen beds.
Bathrooms: All private.
Meals: Full breakfast, map with dinner on request only.
Vegetarian: Available upon request, other special diets accommodated.
Complimentary: Coffee, tea.
Dates Open: All year.
High Season: Winter, Dec thru Mar, summer, June-Aug, fall, Sept, Oct.
Rates: Summer & winter, $88-$138 per room, fall, $98-$138 per room.
Discounts: Group discounts.
Credit Cards: MC, VISA, Amex, Diners & Carte Blanche.
Rsv'tns: Required.
Reserve Through: Travel agent or call direct.
Minimum Stay: Required during fall foliage season & major holidays.

continued next page

Vermont

Parking: Ample free off-street parking.
In-Room: Color TV, maid service.
On-Premises: Private dining rooms, full liquor license.

Swimming: In pond on premises.
Sunbathing: On grass near pond and on lawn near inn.
Smoking: Non-smoking rooms available, smoking

permitted in living room.
Pets: Permitted with advance notice with $25 deposit. Dogs on leash at all times.
Handicap Access: Yes. One room meets handi-

capped requirements.
Children: Not especially welcome, under 10 years old discouraged.
Languages: English.

MONTGOMERY CENTER

Phineas Swann B&B

A Whimisical, Light-hearted Country Inn

Gay-Friendly 50/50 ♀♂

In the shadows of the rocky summit of Jay Peak Ski Resort lies the little town of Montgomery Center. This warm, friendly New England town is nestled in the northern range of the Green Mountains.

The moment travelers step through *Phineas Swann's* bright raspberry door, they know they have entered a classic, intimate Vermont country inn. French doors, hardwood floors, and woodburning stoves all lend themselves to a relaxed country atmosphere. Trout River is right out back and within walking distance are antique shops, country stores, fine dining and natural waterfalls.

Address: PO Box 43, The Main Street, Montgomery Center, VT 05471. Tel: (802) 326-4306.

Type: Bed & breakfast.
Clientele: 50% gay & lesbian & 50% straight clientele.
Transportation: Car is best. Pick up from airport.
To Gay Bars: 1 hour to gay bars in Burlington, VT & 1-1/2 hours to Montreal.
Rooms: 4 rooms with double & twin beds.
Bathrooms: Private:

1 bath, 1 sink. Shared: 2 full baths.
Meals: Full gourmet breakfast & afternoon tea.
Vegetarian: Available.
Complimentary: 4pm tea with home-baked surprises. Mints & chocolates in room.
Dates Open: All year.
High Season: July, August, February & March.

Rates: $50-$75.
Credit Cards: MC, VISA & Discover.
Rsv'tns: Recommended.
Reserve Through: Call direct.
Parking: Free covered parking.
In-Room: Ceiling fans & maid service.
On-Premises: TV lounge, VCR, game boards & meeting rooms.
Exercise/Health: Snow-

mobile paths, skiing, tennis, hiking, fishing & golf.
Swimming: Swimming hole with mountain water & river.
Smoking: Not permitted.
Pets: Not permitted.
Handicap Access: No.
Children: Not especially welcome.
Languages: English.
Your Host: Michael & Glen.

STOWE

Buccaneer Country Lodge

A Treasure Chest of Vermont Hospitality

Gay/Lesbian ♀♂

Experience Vermont hospitality and discover why our guests return year after year. Stowe is the ski capital of the East and *Buccaneer Country Lodge* is minutes from village, mountain, nightlife, recreational activities and special events. Suites have full kitchens, one queen and two twin beds. One suite has its own fireplace. Motel rooms have two double beds or a queen-size bed, and refrigerator. All have private bath, cable TV, phone and air conditioning. **READER COMMENT:** *"Building in immaculate condition, grounds well landscaped, pool well maintained, pleasant dining room, owners pleasant and helpful."* Peter, Seattle, WA.

Address: 3214 Mountain Rd, Stowe, VT 05672. Tel: (802) 253-4772, (800) 543-1293.

Type: Bed & breakfast motel.

Clientele: Good mix of gay men & women with

some straight clientele.
Transportation: Car.

To Gay Bars: 30-minute drive to Burlington, VT

gay/lesbian bars.
Rooms: 8 rooms & 4 suites with single, double or queen beds.
Bathrooms: All private.
Meals: Full breakfast, except in spring.
Complimentary: Hot soup & hot mulled cider during ski season.
Dates Open: All year.

High Season: Dec 19th-Jan 3rd, fall foliage season.
Rates: Rooms $49-$179.
Discounts: 10% on a non-holiday midweek stay (Sun-Thurs).
Credit Cards: MC, VISA.
Rsv'tns: Recommended.
Reserve Through: Travel agent or call direct.

Minimum Stay: 2 nights (3 nights during holidays).
Parking: Free parking.
In-Room: Cable color TV, telephone, AC, maid service, refrigerator, some kitchens.
On-Premises: TV lounge, hot tub.
Exercise/Health: Hot tub.

Swimming: Pool on premises, lake.
Sunbathing: At poolside.
Smoking: Permitted, except in dining room.
Pets: Not permitted.
Handicap Access: No.
Children: Permitted.
Languages: English, Spanish, French.

Fitch Hill Inn

Elegant, But Not Stuffy

Gay-Friendly ♀♂

Historic *Fitch Hill Inn*, c. 1794, occupies a hill overlooking the magnificent Green Mountains. Its location, central to Vermont's all-season vacation country, offers a special opportunity to enjoy the true Vermont experience. This is the town in which Charles Kuralt said he would like to settle. Antique-decorated guest rooms all have spectacular views. Breakfasts and, by arrangement, gourmet dinners, are prepared by the innkeeper. The library has video tapes, books, and an atmosphere of comfort and ease. The newly-renovated 18th century living room is wonderful for music and reading.

Address: RFD 1 Box 1879, Fitch Hill Rd, Hyde Park, VT 05655. Tel: (802) 888-3834, (800) 639-2903.

Type: Bed & breakfast inn with restaurant for guests only.
Clientele: Mostly straight with a gay & lesbian following.
Transportation: Car is best. We do not pick up from Burlington International Airport except for those on extended stays.
To Gay Bars: 40 miles to Burlington.
Rooms: 4 rooms & 1 suite with single or double beds.
Bathrooms: 1 priv. bath/shower. Shared: 3 bath/shower/toilet, 1 shower, 1 toilet.
Meals: Full breakfast.
Vegetarian: Available with reservation & prior arrangement.
Complimentary: Tea, sherry & snacks. Maple syrup & candy in rooms.
Dates Open: All year.
High Season: Dec 25-Jan 3 & Sept 15-Oct 15.
Rates: $50 to $105 for suite.
Discounts: On stays longer than 2 days except during high season & 10% for AAA.
Credit Cards: MC & VISA.
Rsv'tns: Suggested.
Reserve Through: Travel agent or call direct.
Minimum Stay: 2 nights during high season.
Parking: Ample off-street parking.
In-Room: Maid & laundry service, color TV, telephone, ceiling fans & 300+ video library. Suite has AC & color cable TV.
On-Premises: Meeting rooms, TV lounge, VCR library & cross-country ski trails. Kitchen & refrigerator privileges available.
Exercise/Health: Skiing, hiking, biking, horseback riding, golf & canoeing.
Swimming: Lake & river nearby.
Sunbathing: On the beach.
Smoking: Not permitted inside. Permitted on 3 outdoor porches.
Pets: Not permitted.
Handicap Access: No.
Children: Permitted.
Languages: English, Spanish & some French.
Your Host: Richard & Stanley.

We Appreciate Your Comments!

Positive comments of interest may be included in the next issue, giving future readers the benefit of your experience. And it's a nice way of saying "thank you" to an innkeeper who extended you exceptional hospitality.

See the contents for the Reader Comment Form.

WATERBURY-STOWE AREA

Grünberg Haus Bed & Breakfast

Gay-Friendly ♀♂

Spontaneous Personal Attention in a Handbuilt Austrian Chalet

Our romantic Austrian inn, *Grünberg Haus,* rests on a quiet hillside in Vermont's Green Mountains, perfect for trips to Stowe, Montpelier, Waterbury and Burlington. Choose guest rooms with wonderful views from carved wood balconies, secluded cabins hidden along wooded trails or a spectacular carriage house with skywindows, balconies and modern kitchen. Relax by the fire or warm-weather Jacuzzi, ski expertly-

groomed XC trails, gather fresh eggs or listen to innkeeper Chris playing the grand piano as you savor your imaginative, memorable breakfast. Explore Vermont.

Address: RR2, Box 1595 IP, Route 100 South, Waterbury-Stowe, VT 05676-9621. Tel: (802) 244-7726 or (800) 800-7760.

Type: Bed & breakfast guesthouse & cabins.
Clientele: Mostly straight clientele with a gay & lesbian following.
Transportation: Car is best, pick up from airport $25, bus $5, ferry dock $25, train $5.
To Gay Bars: 25 miles to Pearl's in Burlington, VT.
Rooms: 10 rooms, 1 apartment & 3 cottages with single, double or queen beds.
Bathrooms: 9 private shower/toilets & others share shower/toilets.

Meals: Full, musical breakfast.
Vegetarian: Breakfast always vegetarian.
Complimentary: Set-ups, soft drinks, coffee & tea, cordials & snacks. BYOB OK.
Dates Open: All year.
High Season: Feb & March, July-October & Christmas.
Rates: $27.50-$70 per person.
Discounts: 10% for seniors & stays of 4 or more days.
Credit Cards: MC, VISA,

Amex, En Route & Discover.
Rsv'tns: Suggested.
Reserve Through: Travel agent or call direct.
Parking: Ample free off-street parking.
In-Room: Maid service, fans & balcony. One kitchen unit.
On-Premises: Tennis court, Steinway grand piano, library, fireplace, chickens, BYOB pub. Groomed Xcountry ski center.
Exercise/Health: Jacuzzi, sauna, massage by ap-

pointment, plus 40 acres for hiking.
Swimming: Pool, river or lake nearby.
Sunbathing: At poolside, by river or lake or on common sun decks.
Nudity: Nude swimming areas nearby.
Smoking: Permitted outside.
Pets: Not permitted. Pick up & delivery of pets at registered kennel is available.
Handicap Access: No.
Children: Permitted.
Languages: English.

VIRGINIA

CHARLOTTESVILLE

INTOUCH Women's Camping & Event Center

Home of Virginia's Women's Music Festival

Women ♀

INTOUCH is 100 acres of almost heaven, a plush-rustic resort for women who want to feel welcomed and safe in the outdoors. It offers a women-owned, women-built country club, where you can camp in a soft bed of pine needles or sit on the porch of your private cabin in the woods. Kick off your shoes and nap in the hammock, play beach volleyball, hike 100 acres of trails and streams, or participate in workshops and performances. INTOUCH is home to the Virginia Women's Music Festival (May) and the Wild Western Women's Weekend (September). Take advantage of Virginia's beautiful weather, mountains and history! C'mon home...We'll leave the moon on for ya.

Address: Rt 2, Box 1096, Kent's Store, VA 23084. Tel: (804) 589-6542.

Type: Women's campground & event center with cabins.
Clientele: Women only, with men permitted at specific times.
Transportation: Car is best. Charlottesville airport is 20 minutes away.
To Gay Bars: 20 miles or a 20-minute drive.
Rooms: 5 cabins with double & bunk beds.
Bathrooms: 4 shared showers.
Campsites: 20 RV parking only sites & 50 tent sites. Electricity, water,

outhouses, hot showers, outdoor stage, picnic pavilion & outdoor games & activities.
Vegetarian: Available at festivals.
Dates Open: All year.
High Season: April-September.
Rates: $5 per person for 24 hour period. Members free.
Discounts: Scholarship & work exchange available. Members camp free & receive discounts on events.
Rsv'tns: Required for

non-members.
Reserve Through: Call direct.
Minimum Stay: Maximum stay 2 weeks.
Parking: Ample free parking.
On-Premises: 7-acre lake, stage, pavilion, playing field & hiking trails.
Exercise/Health: 100 acres of hiking trails, playing field & volleyball courts.
Swimming: At lake on premises.
Sunbathing: At the lake

& anywhere they wish on the grounds.
Nudity: Permitted with discretion.
Smoking: Permitted outdoors only.
Pets: Permitted on non-event days.
Handicap Access: Partially accessible.
Children: Welcomed 12 & under.
Languages: English, French & Sign.
Your Host: Janet.

NEW MARKET

A Touch of Country

Daydream on the Porch Swings...

Gay-Friendly 50/50 ♀♂

...or stroll through town, stopping at antique and gift shops, sampling savory fare at local restaurants. There's no need for detailed itineraries, for you've come to relax at *A Touch of Country,* our restored 1870's Shenandoah Valley home in historic New Market. We've gone to lengths to create a warm, friendly atmosphere for your stay, setting the tone with antiques and country collectibles. Come morning, a down home country breakfast fortifies you for visiting the Blue Ridge Mtns., New Market Battlefield, caverns and other points of interest.

Address: 9329 Congress St, New Market, VA . Tel: (703) 740-8030.

Type: Bed & breakfast.
Clientele: 50% gay &

lesbian & 50% straight clientele.

Transportation: Car.
To Gay Bars: 1-1/2 hrs to

gay bar in Charlottesville

continued next page

Virginia

or 2 hours to DC.
Rooms: 6 rooms with double or queen beds.
Bathrooms: All private shower/sink/toilets.
Meals: Full breakfast.
Vegetarian: Available with advance request.
Complimentary: Soda available upon arrival.

Dates Open: All year.
High Season: September-November.
Rates: $60-$75, plus tax.
Discounts: For longer stays.
Credit Cards: MC, VISA, Discover, Amex.
Rsv'tns: Recommended.
Reserve Through: Travel

agent or call direct.
Minimum Stay: 2 days on holiday weekends & October weekends.
Parking: Adequate free off-street parking.
In-Room: Self-controlled AC.
On-Premises: TV lounge.
Swimming: At nearby

pool.
Smoking: Not permitted.
Pets: Not permitted.
Handicap Access: No.
Children: Permitted if well-behaved and over 12 years old.
Languages: English.
Your Host: Jean & Dawn.

VIRGINIA BEACH

Coral Sand Motel

Gay/Lesbian ♀♂

Virginia Beach's Only Gay Resort

We are in the heart of the resort strip and only one block from the ocean. You couldn't ask for a better location! There's free parking, and we're convenient to trolley service. The *Coral Sand Motel* is a Ma and Pa type of operation. The friendly owner at the front desk and understanding employees, make this gay resort a Fun Place In The Sun.

Address: 2307 Pacific Ave, Virginia Beach, VA 23451. Tel: (804) 425-0872 or (800) 828-0872.

Type: Guesthouse & motel.
Clientele: Gay & lesbian. Good mix of men & women.
To Gay Bars: 4 blocks to After Hours.
Rooms: 6 doubles, 4 triples, 9 quads & 1 apartment.

Bathrooms: 15 private & 2 shared.
Meals: Continental breakfast.
Dates Open: All year.
Rates: $45-$125.
Discounts: Military.
Credit Cards: All cards.
Reserve Through: Call the 800 number direct.

Parking: Ample free parking.
In-Room: Color TV, AC, kitchen, refrigerator & maid service.
Swimming: At nearby ocean.
Sunbathing: On ocean beach.
Smoking: Permitted.

Non-smoking rooms available.
Pets: Under 20 lbs permitted.
Handicap Access: No.
Children: Permitted if supervised.
Languages: English & French.
Your Host: Gene.

WASHINGTON

CHELAN

Mary Kay's Romantic Whaley Mansion Inn

Take Someone You Love to Mary Kay's

Gay-Friendly ♀♂

Slip off your shoes, sink into our soft carpets, snuggle into our satin sheets, sip your own champagne and enjoy our superb coffee and our own hand-dipped truffles. *Mary Kay's Romantic Whaley Mansion Inn* is listed by AAA as a 4-diamond B&B. We specialize in romantic rendezvous, birthdays, anniversaries, honeymoons, retreats and marriage encounters. We have six elegant bedrooms with private baths in a historical Victorian mansion. The candlelit breakfast is presented on crystal and sterling silver in the formal dining room. All rooms have VCR, color TV, refrigerators, and free movies.

Address: 415 Third St, Chelan, WA 98816.   Tel: (509) 682-5735, (800) 729-2408 (USA & Canada), Fax: 682-5385.

Type: Bed & breakfast.
Clientele: Mostly straight clientele with a gay/lesbian following.
Transportation: Car is best. Free pick up from bus or airport in Chelan.
To Gay Bars: 175 miles from Seattle gay/lesbian bars.
Rooms: 6 rooms with double, queen or king beds.
Bathrooms: All private.
Meals: 5-course candlelight breakfast.
Vegetarian: Always

available.
Complimentary: Chocolates & truffles.
Dates Open: All year.
High Season: Memorial Day-Labor Day & Christmas-Valentines' Day.
Rates: $105-$125 summer.
Discounts: Off-season specials. 1st night regular price, 2nd night 1/2 price.
Credit Cards: MC, VISA.
Rsv'tns: Required. 72-hour cancellation policy.
Reserve Through: Call direct.

Minimum Stay: 2 days on weekends, 3 days on holidays.
Parking: Ample off-street parking.
In-Room: Color TV, VCR, AC, ceiling fans, refrigerators, maid service & free movies.
On-Premises: Meeting rooms, TV lounge, laundry facilities, & player piano.
Exercise/Health: Cross-country skiing, boating, tennis courts, hiking & walking trails. Nearby fit-

ness center.
Swimming: At Lake Chelan.
Sunbathing: On common sun decks.
Smoking: Permitted outdoors.
Pets: Not permitted.
Handicap Access: No.
Children: Not permitted, unless renting whole house.
Languages: English.
Your Host: Mary Kay & Carol.

LA CONNER

White Swan Guest House

The Best-Kept Secret in La Conner

Gay-Friendly ♀♂

Welcome to the *White Swan Guest House,* an 1890's farmhouse with wicker chairs on the porch, piles of books and a platter of homemade chocolate chip cookies on the sideboard, English-style gardens, fruit trees and acres of farmland. Country breakfast is served in our sunny yellow dining room. The Garden Cottage is a perfect romantic hideaway, with private bath, kitchen and sun deck. Visit nearby La Conner, a charming waterfront village. *White Swan* is ninety miles from Vancouver, BC, one hour north of Seattle and close to the San Juan Islands' and Victoria ferries. **Address: 1388 Moore Rd, Mt Vernon, WA 98273. Tel: (206) 445-6805 until Jan 1, 1995. Then (360) 445-6805.**

Type: Bed & breakfast guesthouse.
Clientele: Mostly straight clientele with a gay/lesbian following.
Rooms: 3 rooms & one large cottage for up to 4 persons. Queen & king beds.
Bathrooms: 2 shared in older home, 1 private in cottage.
Meals: Expanded country continental breakfast, with muffins, fruit, coffee.
Vegetarian: Only vegetarian food is served.
Complimentary: Fresh chocolate chip cookies always available.
Dates Open: All year.
High Season: Months of July & August & Tulip time (April 1st-30th).
Rates: Single $60, double $75, cottage $125-$185.
Credit Cards: MC, VISA.
Rsv'tns: Preferred.
Reserve Through: Call direct.
Parking: Ample off-street parking.
In-Room: Maid & laundry service, kitchen available in cottage.
On-Premises: Kitchen, lounge, gorgeous flower garden, sun deck.
Sunbathing: On lawn or on cottage's private sun deck.
Smoking: Permitted outdoors only.
Pets: Not permitted.
Handicap Access: No.
Children: Welcome in garden cottage.
Languages: English.
Your Host: Peter.

LOPEZ ISLAND

Inn At Swifts Bay

Gay-Friendly ♀♂

An Unpretentious Inn With Celebrated Atmosphere

In the last six years, *The Inn At Swifts Bay* has gained national recognition as one of the finest accommodations in the beautiful San Juan Islands of Washington State. This AAA-approved, elegantly-maintained country home sits on three wooded acres with a private beach nearby. Quiet and romantic, the inn features five guest rooms, three with private bath. Two common areas have fireplaces. The hot tub is at the edge of the woods (robes and slippers provided). Sumptuous breakfasts are the rule. New for 1995 is Hunter Bay House, a luxury waterfront cabin. Read what travel writers say about *Inn At Swifts Bay*. *San Francisco Sun-*

day Chronicle-Examiner: "The most memorable part of the trip...a stay at Inn At Swifts Bay...the setting is beautiful and serene, the accommodations excellent, and the food of gourmet quality!" *Vogue Magazine:* "The Inn At Swifts Bay...stateroom elegant." *Brides Magazine:* "Entrust yourself to the warm hospitality of the Inn At Swifts Bay...in the morning, one of the greatest pleasures of your stay awaits, a breakfast that is famous island-wide!" *West Coast Bed & Breakfast Guide:* "Those who appreciate luxury and superb cuisine will find the Inn At Swifts Bay to their liking. The Tudor-style inn is classy, stylish and oh, so comfortable...a breakfast that is nothing short of sensational!" **Inn Places Reader Commment:** "I am writing to let you know how extraordinarily impressed I was with the Inn At Swifts Bay...the inn is impeccably and tastefully decorated. Everything is done with warmth and quality. All of your needs and desires are met before you know what you want. The inn has a sense of class I have dreamed about, but have never found..."

Address: Lopez Island, WA 98261. Tel: (206) 468-3636 or Fax: 468-3637.

Type: Bed & breakfast inn & cottage.
Clientele: Mostly straight clientele with a gay/lesbian following.
Transportation: By car ferry from Anacortes or daily plane from Seattle, Anacortes. Pick up from airport, ferry dock, or marina.
To Gay Bars: Drive 1 hr to Bellingham or Everett. 1-1/2 hrs to Seattle bars.
Rooms: 2 rooms, 3 suites & 1 cottage with queen beds.
Bathrooms: 4 private

shower/toilets & 1 shared bath/shower/toilet.
Meals: Full breakfast.
Vegetarian: Dietary restrictions considered with advance notice at time of reservation.
Complimentary: Sherry in living room & chocolates on pillows. Fridge with mineral waters, microwave popcorn & tea.
Dates Open: All year.
High Season: May-October.
Rates: $75-$195.
Discounts: For extended

stays in off season.
Credit Cards: MC, VISA, Discover & Amex.
Rsv'tns: Required.
Reserve Through: Call direct.
Minimum Stay: Only on holiday weekends.
Parking: Ample free off-street parking.
In-Room: Maid service.
On-Premises: Telephone, VCR with film library, refrigerator with ice & mineral water.
Exercise/Health: Hot tub & massage (by appointment only).

Swimming: Ocean or lake (very cold!).
Sunbathing: On beach, patio or lawn.
Nudity: Permitted in the hot tub.
Smoking: Not permitted inside.
Pets: Not permitted.
Handicap Access: No.
Children: Not permitted.
Languages: English, limited German & Portuguese.
Your Host: Robert & Christopher.

IGTA

ORCAS ISLAND

Rose Cottage

Orcas Island, Gem of the San Juans

Gay/Lesbian ♀

Rose Cottage is a cozy, private waterfront guesthouse for two on Orcas Island. It has a spectacular sunrise view of Mount Baker, a sunny deck and a long, private pebble beach. Situated above an artist's studio, it nestles among old firs and looks over fragrant vegetable and flower gardens and meandering lawns that end down at the beach. Orcas has excellent kayaking, biking, fishing, hiking and freshwater swimming. Moran State Park is within five miles. The local village, Eastsound, handy for groceries, restaurants and theater, is just under two miles away.

Address: Rt 1, Box 951, Eastsound, WA 98245. Tel: (206) 376-2076

Type: Guesthouse.
Clientele: Mostly women with men welcome.
Transportation: Car is best. Free pick up from airport.
To Gay Bars: 80 miles north to Vancouver, BC or 80 miles south to Seattle, WA.
Rooms: 1 cottage with double bed.
Bathrooms: Private shower/toilet.
Vegetarian: Organic food

store & several restaurants with vegetarian meals 2 miles away.
Complimentary: Tea, coffee, cookies & flowers. (Fresh eggs when the girls are laying!)
Dates Open: All year.
High Season: Jun through Sept.
Rates: Summer $80 per night. Winter $70 per night.
Discounts: Weekly rates 10% discount.

Rsv'tns: Required.
Reserve Through: Call direct.
Minimum Stay: 2 nights weekends & 3 nights holiday weekends.
Parking: Off-street parking for one car.
In-Room: Kitchen, refrigerator & coffee/tea-making facilities.
On-Premises: Deck.
Exercise/Health: Gym, weights, sauna, steam & massage nearby.

Swimming: Ocean beach on premises. Pool & lake nearby.
Sunbathing: At the beach & on private sun deck.
Nudity: Permitted on private deck with discretion.
Smoking: Not permitted.
Pets: Not permitted.
Handicap Access: No.
Children: Not permitted.
Languages: English, French & Italian.

Sweet Cedar Retreat

...an island within an island

Gay/Lesbian ♀♂

Timelessness, peace and solitude distinguish this tasteful one-bedroom cottage in a tranquil cedar grove on Orcas Island's beautiful northern shore. From under plump quilts, you might see deer grazing just outside your window as you lazily awaken to the forest's enchanting music. *Sweet Cedar Retreat* combines the dual advantages of complete privacy and self-sufficiency with easy, walking-distance proximity to spectacular beach sunsets and the unhurried seaside bustle of quaint Eastsound village. Come for sustenance, rejuvenation and sanctuary. Sister accommodation to *Rose Cottage.*

Address: Rt 1, Box 1238, Eastsound, WA 98245. Phone & Fax: (206) 376-5444.

Type: Guesthouse.
Clientele: Good mix of gays & lesbians.
Transportation: Car is best. Free pick up from airport.
Rooms: Fully-furnished 1-bedroom cottage, sleeps 4. Double bed with sofa-bed in living room.
Bathrooms: Private.
Vegetarian: 1 mile to organic food store & several restaurants with

vegetarian meals.
Complimentary: Tea, coffee & little surprises.
Dates Open: All year.
High Season: June through September.
Rates: Summer $85 per night. Winter $75 per night.
Discounts: Weekly rates, 10% off.
Credit Cards: MC & VISA.
Rsv'tns: Required.
Reserve Through: Call direct.
Minimum Stay: 2 nights

weekends, 3 nights holiday weekends.
Parking: Ample off-street parking.
In-Room: Color cable TV, telephone. Full kitchen with coffee/tea-making facilities, refrigerator & other small appliances.
On-Premises: Private deck with BBQ.
Exercise/Health: Nearby gym, weights, Jacuzzi, sauna, steam, massage, tennis courts, hiking

trails & kayaking.
Swimming: Nearby pool, lake & ocean.
Sunbathing: On private deck & grounds.
Nudity: Permitted on private deck, with discretion.
Smoking: Not permitted.
Pets: Not permitted.
Handicap Access: No.
Children: Not especially welcome.
Languages: English & Spanish.

PORT TOWNSEND

Ravenscroft Inn

Take a Short Trip to Far Away...

Gay-Friendly ♀♂

One of the most romantic hideaways in the Pacific Northwest is located high on the bluff overlooking historic Port Townsend, the Olympic Peninsula's Victorian seaport. The *Ravenscroft Inn* is noted for it's colonial style, a replication of a historic Charleston single house.

The Inn offers a unique combination of colonial hospitality, mixed with a casual air that spells comfort to its guests. The hosts take great pleasure in looking after their guests' special requests, whether it's dinner, theatre, concert reservations, or arranging for flowers or champagne, all are carried out with ease and alacrity.

While staying at the *Ravenscroft Inn,* you can explore the Olympic National Park, walk the seven mile sand spit at Dungeness or hike through North America's only rain forest. Port Townsend and its environs meets all your vacation requirements, offering scenic beauty, theatre, unparalleled dining, boating, biking, fishing, kayaking and hiking, to name just a few.

Top this all off with a delectable breakfast and fresh roasted gourmet coffee, served each morning and accompanied by live piano music provided by one of your hosts. **GUEST COMMENT:** "There was never a detail left unattended." **Address: 533 Quincy St, Port Townsend, WA 98368. Tel: (206) 385-2784 or Fax: 385-6724.**

Type: Bed & breakfast.
Clientele: Mainly straight with gay & lesbian following.
Transportation: Car is best. Free pick up from Port Townsend Airport.
To Gay Bars: 2 hrs by car.
Rooms: 8 rooms & 1 suite with single, queen or king beds.
Bathrooms: 3 private bath/shower/toilets & 6 private shower/toilets.
Meals: Full breakfast.

Vegetarian: Available on request. When making reservation, all dietary restrictions addressed.
Complimentary: Sherry, coffee, tea, set-up service, juices.
Dates Open: All year.
High Season: June 20-Oct 15.
Rates: $68-$165 May 15-Oct 15, $65-$135 Oct 16-May 14.
Discounts: Single discount.
Credit Cards: MC, VISA,

Amex & Discover.
Rsv'tns: Required.
Reserve Through: Call direct.
Minimum Stay: Some weekends, special holidays & special events.
Parking: Ample free off-street parking.
In-Room: Color TV on request, maid service.
On-Premises: Meeting room, library, great room.
Exercise/Health: Hot tub in suite. Free use of gym,

weights, Jacuzzi, sauna, steam & massage at nearby Athletic Club.
Swimming: At local school pool.
Sunbathing: On common sun decks & at beach.
Smoking: Permitted on outdoor balconies only.
Pets: Not permitted.
Children: Permitted over 12 years of age.
Languages: English.

Take along the Expert

Ferrari's Places of Interest™ contains articles contributed by gay and lesbian journalists on the scene, giving insight into gay and lesbian communities worldwide. With its accompanying directory, it's the perfect vacation planner.

SEATTLE

Bacon Mansion/Broadway Guest House

Gay-Friendly 50/50 ♀♂

Seattle's Finest B&B for Sun (and Rain!) Lovers!

The Bacon Mansion is an elegant English Tudor house in the Harvard-Belmont Historical District. Here in Capitol Hill, one of Seattle's most exciting neighborhoods, dining, sightseeing, nightlife and boutiques are just a few blocks away. A variety of well-appointed accommodations, from moderate rooms to suites and even a carriage house, warmly welcome every guest. Six rooms have private baths.

We have immense, beautifully decorated day rooms and a large, private, partially-covered patio for sun (and rain!) lovers. Don't miss it!

Address: 959 Broadway East, Seattle, WA 98102. Tel: (206) 329-1864, (800) 240-1864, Fax: (206) 860-9025.

Type: Bed & breakfast guesthouse.
Clientele: 50% gay & lesbian & 50% straight clientele.
Transportation: Shuttle Express from airport, taxi from train.
To Gay Bars: Two blocks to famous Elite Tavern on Broadway.
Rooms: 5 rooms & 2 suites & 1 cottage with double or queen beds.
Bathrooms: Private: 3 shower/toilet, 3 full baths. 2 shared full baths.
Meals: Buffet breakfast.
Vegetarian: Always available.
Complimentary: Tea, coffee, mints on pillow.
Dates Open: All year.
High Season: May through October.
Rates: Summer $65-$160, winter $59-$150.
Discounts: 10% on stays of over 6 nights, winter only.
Credit Cards: MC, VISA & Amex.
Rsv'tns: Required.
Reserve Through: Call direct.
Minimum Stay: Required.
Parking: Ample, off-street parking.
In-Room: Color TV, telephone & maid service.
On-Premises: Meeting rooms, refrigerator & fax.
Exercise/Health: Nearby gym, weights & massage.
Swimming: At nearby pool & lake.
Sunbathing: On patio & common sun deck.
Smoking: Permitted outside only.
Pets: Not permitted.
Handicap Access: No.
Children: Permitted in some rooms only.
Languages: English.
Your Host: Daryl & Tim.

IGTA

Capitol Hill Inn

Gay-Friendly 50/50 ♀♂

Capitol Hill Inn, an elegantly-restored 1903 Queen Anne, delights guests with treasures from a bygone era. Elaborate restoration details include custom-designed wall coverings, period chandeliers, original, intricately-carved wood mouldings. Rooms are lavishly furnished with European antiques, brass beds and down comforters, which are especially cozy on crisp, Seattle nights. A sumptuous breakfast includes such items as blintzes, lox and bagels, quiche and fresh fruit. There are NY Times, books & magazines in the parlour and AAA has given us a 3 diamond rating. We're just seven blocks from the Convention Center.

Address: 1713 Belmont Ave, Seattle, WA 98122. Tel: (206) 323-1955.

Type: Bed & breakfast.
Clientele: 50% gay & lesbian & 50% straight.
Transportation: Airport shuttle $14 per person or taxi approx. $25.
To Gay Bars: 1 block.
Rooms: 5 rooms with single, double, queen or king beds.
Bathrooms: 3 private, others share bathrooms or showers.
Meals: Full breakfast.
Vegetarian: Available upon request.
Dates Open: All year.
Rates: $75-$165.
Discounts: 10% in off-season, winter only.

Credit Cards: MC, VISA & Amex.
Rsv'tns: Recommended.
Reserve Through: Call direct.
Parking: Free parking.

In-Room: Maid service. Suites have fireplaces.
On-Premises: Meeting rooms, living room, public telephone.
Exercise/Health: Jacuzzis

in two suites.
Swimming: At downtown health club.
Smoking: Permitted on the porch or outdoors.
Pets: Not permitted.

Handicap Access: No, stairs.
Children: Not permitted.
Languages: English.
Your Host: Katie & Joanne.

Country Inn

Gay-Friendly 50/50 ♀♂

Enjoy the view from *Country Inn,* our traditional northwest home 15 miles from downtown Seattle. Walk to downtown Issaquah, with its widely acclaimed Village Theatre, assorted restaurants and other cultural attractions, in ten to fifteen minutes, or explore wooded trails, which are even closer. Beautiful Lake Sammamish stretches out to the north of our valley. The area has well-maintained hiking trails, horseback riding, water sports, birdwatching, shopping in quaint Gilman Village, a fish hatchery, a chocolate factory, a zoo, and a winery with a breathtaking view.

Address: 685 NW Juniper St, Issaquah, WA 98027. Phone & Fax: (206) 392-1010.

Type: Guesthouse.
Clientele: 50% gay & lesbian & 50% straight clientele.
Transportation: Car is best. Pick up from airport, bus, train or ferry dock $20.
To Gay Bars: 15 miles or 15 minutes by car.
Rooms: 2 suites with double or king beds.
Bathrooms: 2 private shower/toilets.
Meals: Choice of full

breakfast or continental breakfast.
Vegetarian: Available.
Complimentary: Coffee & tea.
Dates Open: All year.
High Season: May-September.
Rates: Winter $55, summer $75.
Discounts: $10 a day off for 7 or more days.
Credit Cards: MC & VISA.
Rsv'tns: Required.
Reserve Through: Call

direct.
Parking: Ample free off-street parking.
In-Room: Color cable TV, VCR, video tape library, AC, telephone, kitchen, refrigerator, coffee & tea-making facilities, maid, laundry & room service.
On-Premises: Meeting rooms, laundry facilities, private decks & gardens.
Exercise/Health: Weights, hot tub & massage.
Swimming: At nearby

pool or lake.
Sunbathing: On the roof, private sun decks, patio or at the beach.
Nudity: Permitted in the hot tub.
Smoking: Permitted. Non-smoking rooms available.
Pets: Permitted.
Handicap Access: Yes.
Children: Not especially welcome.
Languages: English
Your Host: Mel.

Gaslight Inn

Gay/Lesbian ♀♂

Welcome to *Gaslight Inn,* a Seattle four-square house built in 1906. In restoring the inn, we have brought out the home's original turn-of-the-century ambiance and warmth, while keeping in mind the additional conveniences and contemporary style needed by travelers in the nineties. The interior is appointed in exacting detail, with strikingly rich, dark colors, oak paneling, an enormous entryway and

continued next page

staircase. *Gaslight's* comfortable and unique rooms and suites are furnished with quality double or queen-sized beds, refrigerator and television. Additional features for your special needs, such as private bath and phone service, are available in some rooms. Some rooms also have decks with fabulous views or fireplaces. The living room, with its large oak fireplace, is always an inviting room, as is the library. Through the late spring and summer, we encourage you to relax and unwind at poolside with a glass of wine after a long, busy day. This private, in-ground, heated pool with several decks and interesting plant arrangements, is found at the back of the inn. *Gaslight* is convenient to central Seattle's every attraction, Volunteer Park, City Center, and to a plethora of gay and lesbian bars, restaurants and retail stores in the Broadway district. All of us at *Gaslight Inn* send you a warm advance welcome to Seattle.

Address: 1727 15th Ave, Seattle, WA 98122. Tel: (206) 325-3654.

Type: Guest house.
Clientele: Mostly gay/lesbian with some straight clientele.
Transportation: Shuttle Express from airport $15. (206) 286-4800 to reserve ride.
To Gay Bars: 2 blocks to men's bars, 3 blocks to women's bars.
Rooms: 9 doubles, 5 suites.
Bathrooms: 11 private, others share.

Meals: Expanded continental breakfast.
Complimentary: Coffee, tea & juices, fresh fruit, pastries.
Dates Open: All year.
High Season: Summer.
Rates: $64-$108.
Discounts: 5% for cash payment.
Credit Cards: MC, VISA & Amex.
Rsv'tns: Recommended at least 2 weeks in advance.

Reserve Through: Call direct.
Minimum Stay: 2 days on weekends, 3 days on holidays.
Parking: Ample on-street & off-street parking.
In-Room: Color TV, maid service & refrigerator.
On-Premises: Meeting rooms, living room, library, public telephone.
Swimming: Seasonal heated pool.
Sunbathing: On private

or common sun decks or at poolside.
Smoking: Permitted on decks & porches only.
Pets: Not permitted.
Handicap Access: No.
Children: Not permitted.
Languages: English.
Your Host: Trevor, Stephen & John.

IGTA

Glad Harbor Bed & Breakfast

Breezy Days, Breathtaking Sunsets

Gay/Lesbian ♀♂

Glad Harbor was built out onto the beach in 1950 near the historic Alki Point Lighthouse. The house features a spacious 120-foot waterfront patio with the entire building surrounded on three sides by the Puget Sound!

At low tide, you can watch the seagulls pad among the pools. High tide brings the surf right up to the house, and winter storms are a spectacular treat, with waves crashing against the glass doors!

Daybreak reveals Mt. Rainier to the south, in all its cloud-capped glory. Sunset over the Olympic Mountains to the west is a nightly treat. Breathtaking color and serene seascape combine to create a perfect end to your day. Sailboats of every description pass frequently, racing around Alki Point with colorful spinnakers ballooning.

Pleasure craft, ferries, and many other ships parade daily past *Glad Harbor*. Some are almost close enough to touch, and always near enough to wave to and call out friendly greetings. Enjoy the novelty of fishing from the patio, or relax and enjoy the mild climate as you sunbathe, read, or chat as the quiet surf creates the perfect backdrop.

Wildlife abounds at Alki Point, with an amazing variety of tidal sea creatures to discover during low tide. Gulls, herons, ducks and geese share your tidal strolls, and pods of killer whales or groups of sea lions are not uncommon sights.

Alki Point offers some of the city's best walking, jogging and bicycling paths, with many interesting shops and unique restaurants within easy walking distance. For more excitement, downtown Seattle is just a short distance by car.

Address: 3239 Alki Ave SW, Seattle, WA 98116. Tel: (206) 932-3220

Type: Bed & breakfast. **Clientele:** Mostly gay & lesbian with some straight clientele. **Transportation:** Car is best. Free pick up from airport, train, bus or ferry dock when possible with advance request. **To Gay Bars:** A 15-minute drive. **Rooms:** 3 suites with queen beds. **Bathrooms:** All private.

Meals: Expanded continental breakfast & evening snack. **Vegetarian:** Available upon request. Also available in nearby restaurant. **Complimentary:** Pop, beer, non-beer & evening snack of cheese, crackers, fruit, chocolates & port. **Dates Open:** All year. **High Season:** July & August.

Rates: $75-$95. **Discounts:** On longer stays, negotiable. **Rsv'tns:** Required. **Reserve Through:** Call direct. **Parking:** Ample on-street parking. **In-Room:** Color cable TV, VCR, video tape library, telephone, refrigerator, coffee & tea-making facilities. **Exercise/Health:**

Weights & Jacuzzi on premises. **Swimming:** Puget Sound on premises. **Sunbathing:** On the patio or at the beach. **Smoking:** Permitted on patio only. **Pets:** Not permitted. **Handicap Access:** No. **Children:** Not especially welcome. **Languages:** English. **Your Host:** Mark & Mel.

Hill House Bed & Breakfast

Gay-Friendly 50/50 ♀♂

Wake up to the fragrant smell of fresh brewed coffee, the sweet sound of Baroque music, and the voluptuous pleasure of down comforters. Experience the romance of the *Hill House Bed & Breakfast*, a recently restored 1903 Victorian home located on historic Capitol Hill, just minutes from downtown attractions and the convention center and a short walk to many restaurants, nightclubs and shops. Choose from seven differently-appointed, elegant rooms. Also enjoy a scrumptious full breakfast and plenty of personal attention from your hosts.

Address: 1113 E John St, Seattle, WA 98102. Tel: (206) 720-7161, (800) 720-7161, Fax: (206) 323-0772.

Type: Bed & breakfast. **Clientele:** Gay-owned with 50% gay & lesbian & 50% straight clientele. **Transportation:** Public transportation from the airport: cabs, shuttles, rental cars. **To Gay Bars:** 6 blocks. **Rooms:** 5 rooms & 2 suites with queen beds. **Bathrooms:** 1 shared & 5 private. **Meals:** Full breakfast. **Vegetarian:** Available upon request.

Complimentary: Mints, coffee, tea & cocoa. **Dates Open:** All year. **High Season:** May 15-October 15. **Rates:** Winter $60-$90 & summer $65-$95. **Discounts:** Weekly rates in low season. **Credit Cards:** MC, VISA, Amex & Discover. **Rsv'tns:** Required with 1 week cancellation policy. **Reserve Through:** Call direct. **Minimum Stay:** 3 nights

on holiday weekends & 2 nights on weekends. **Parking:** Ample free off-street & on-street parking. **In-Room:** Variety of facilities. **On-Premises:** Guest refrigerator, CD library, sun deck, sitting & reading room. **Exercise/Health:** Gym, weights, Jacuzzi, sauna & steam at nearby health clubs. **Swimming:** At nearby

gay beach on Lake Washington. **Sunbathing:** On common sun decks. **Smoking:** Smoking allowed outside on porches. **Pets:** Not permitted. **Handicap Access:** No special access. **Children:** Not permitted. **Languages:** English, Filipino. **Your Host:** Ken & Eric.

Inn the Woods

Immerse Yourself in the Tranquility

Women ♀

Inn the Woods is a peaceful, private bed and breakfast for women only. A warm, spacious log home on five acres, Inn the Woods offers two large guest rooms furnished with wicker, antiques, down comforters and original artwork. A hot tub, decks for sunbathing, picnic areas and walking trails complete the setting. A full gourmet breakfast awaits you each morning. One hour from Seattle and ten minutes from picture-postcard Gig Harbor, guests will find exquisite dining, antiques, galleries and shops to suit all tastes. We are one hour from the Olympic Peninsula, Pacific Ocean, San Juan Islands or Victoria, Canada. Guests may enjoy sailing aboard the owners' private sailboat.

Address: 4416 150th St Ct NW, Gig Harbor, WA . Tel: (206) 857-4954.

Type: Bed & breakfast inn 1 hour outside Seattle.
Clientele: Women only.
Transportation: Car is best.
To Gay Bars: 20 minutes to Tacoma, 1 hour to Seattle.
Rooms: 2 rooms with queen or king bed.
Bathrooms: 1 private sink, 1 shared bath/toilet.
Meals: Full breakfast.
Vegetarian: Will accom-

modate any dietary desires or restrictions.
Complimentary: Home baked treats in room, mints at bedside.
Dates Open: Closed mid-December to January 1.
High Season: Summer, May-September.
Rates: $85 per night all year.
Discounts: 10% for weekly stay.
Rsv'tns: Required.
Reserve Through: Call

direct.
Minimum Stay: 2 nights on holiday weekends.
Parking: Ample free off-street parking.
On-Premises: Large stone fireplace in living area, piano, music, parlor games, laundry facilities.
Exercise/Health: Hot tub/spa & private sailing excursions.
Swimming: At nearby ocean, river & lake.
Sunbathing: On common

sun decks.
Nudity: Permitted in hot tub at guests' discretion.
Smoking: Permitted on deck area only.
Pets: Dogs permitted outside only, kennel available with notification. Horse boarding by reservation.
Handicap Access: Wheelchair ramp. Inquire about bath facilities.
Children: Not permitted.
Languages: English.

Scandia House

Gay-Friendly 50/50 ♀♂

Diamond Accommodations in the Emerald City

Enjoy an unobstructed view of Lake Washington, the Bellevue skyline and the Cascade Mountains, as you relax in your king-sized bed, comfortable chairs or private deck. Scandia House, a contemporary B&B in the gay-friendly Mt. Baker neighborhood, is just minutes from Capitol Hill and downtown. It's just a block to Lake Washington's shoreline for scenic running or beach strolling. Your hosts are happy to provide sightseeing ideas, travel directions, restaurant suggestions and information on mainstream or gay/lesbian attractions and events.

Address: 2028 34th Ave S, Seattle, WA 98144. Tel: (206) 725-7825, Fax: (206) 721-3348.

Type: Bed & Breakfast.
Clientele: 50% gay & lesbian & 50% straight clientele.
Transportation: Car is best. 3 blocks from 14 Mt

Baker bus line.
To Gay Bars: 3 miles or a 5-minute drive.
Rooms: 1 room with king bed.
Bathrooms: Private

shower/toilet.
Meals: Expanded continental breakfast.
Vegetarian: Available upon request & nearby.
Dates Open: All year.

High Season: June to September.
Rates: $80-$100 plus state sales tax.
Rsv'tns: Required.
Reserve Through: Travel

agent or call direct.
Parking: Ample on-street parking.
In-Room: Color cable TV, telephone & maid service.

On-Premises: Private deck.
Swimming: Nearby lake.
Sunbathing: On private sun deck or in the yard.
Smoking: Permitted on

decks only. All rooms are non-smoking.
Pets: Not permitted. 2 cats in residence.
Handicap Access: No. Guest room is on 2nd

floor.
Children: Not especially welcome.
Languages: English, Spanish & a little Portuguese, French & German.

Seattle Guest House

Gay-Friendly ♀♂

Seattle Guest House is actually two guest houses situated in quiet residential areas just slightly north and south of downtown Seattle. The houses are very well maintained with plenty of free parking. Rates are reasonable and we make a point of giving personalized service.
Address: 1509 S Winthrop St & 6727 7th NW, Seattle, WA 98144. Tel: (206) 783-5613.

Type: Guesthouse.
Clientele: Mostly straight clientele with a gay & lesbian following.
Transportation: Bus, car, shuttle or taxi.
To Gay Bars: 15 minutes by car to gay/lesbian bars.
Rooms: 4 rooms with single, double or queen beds.

Bathrooms: 2 shared full baths at both locations.
Meals: Continental breakfast.
Vegetarian: Available upon request.
Complimentary: Free drinks upon arrival if requested, coffee, tea, juice at all times.
Dates Open: All year.
Rates: Single $45,

doubles $55.
Discounts: Weekly, monthly discounts.
Rsv'tns: Requested, but walk-ins are welcome.
Reserve Through: Travel agent or call direct.
Parking: Ample, free on-street parking in safe neighborhood.
In-Room: Color TV in double rooms.

On-Premises: TV lounge, laundry facilities, kitchen with microwave, coffeemaker, blender.
Smoking: Permitted outdoors.
Pets: Not permitted.
Handicap Access: No.
Children: Welcome.
Languages: English.
Your Host: Teresa.

Shafer-Baillie Mansion, The

Gay-Friendly ♀♂

Fifteen Thousand Square Feet of Romance, Mystery & Elegance

Antiques of Yesteryear; a quiet and enjoyable atmosphere; formal living room and fireplace with comfortable seating for our guests; full library with TV & VCR; formal dining room seats 50; ballroom with copper fireplace; spacious grounds and garden for summer parties and weddings; port cochere and gazebos on north and south lawns with tables and seating; great food in  your price range; casual buffet or gourmet sumptuous fare. The largest estate on historic *Millionaire's Row* on Seattle's Capitol Hill has undergone a facelift. We're entirely smoke-free. However, smoking is allowed on porches and balconies. At *The Shafer-Baillie Mansion,* you'll enjoy new luxury services and surroundings that are second-to-none. There is a refrigerator and TV in every room and telephones in most rooms; gourmet continental breakfasts between 8:30 and 9:30 am with your morning newspaper. Check-in is 4-6 pm or by appointment. We have eleven suites, most with private baths, and chauffeur's quarters & Carriage House. American Express is accepted with a 5% service fee. With your event in mind, we will help plan your occasion, whether it's a breakfast, luncheon, or meeting all day with both.
Address: 907 14th Ave E, Seattle, WA 98112. Tel: (206) 322-4654, Fax: 329-4654.

continued next page

Washington

Type: Bed & breakfast, meeting rooms, weddings, receptions, conferences, seminars, banquets.
Clientele: 70% straight clientele with a gay & lesbian following.
Transportation: Shuttle Express suggested direct to Mansion. Call Shuttle Express from airport, 5 minutes.
To Gay Bars: 4 blocks to men's, 12 blocks to women's bars.

Rooms: 6 doubles, 1 triple, 6 quads, 2 apartments, carriage house & chauffeur's quarters.
Bathrooms: 10 private, 3 shared.
Meals: Gourmet continental breakfast.
Dates Open: All year.
High Season: May-October.
Rates: Rooms $65-$115, suites $95-$115.
Discounts: Senior citizens, corporate rates, 10% over 7 days.

Credit Cards: Discover & Amex, with 5% service fee.
Rsv'tns: Not required, but usually necessary.
Reserve Through: Travel agent or call direct.
Parking: Ample, free, on-street parking on tree-lined residential street.
In-Room: Maid & room service, color TV, refrigerator. Most rooms with telephone.
On-Premises: Meeting

rooms, TV lounge, private dining room, catering for special events.
Swimming: Pool 10 blocks, lake 1/2 mile.
Sunbathing: On patio, private & common sun decks.
Smoking: Permitted outside on patios, decks, porches.
Pets: Small dogs OK.
Handicap Access: No.
Children: Permitted.
Languages: English.
Your Host: Erv.

WHIDBEY ISLAND (LANGLEY)

Galittoire

ᘐ A L I T T O I ᘉ ᑕ
a contemporary guesthouse

Experience the Aura that Transcends Time

Galittoire exudes the notion of being more than just a guesthouse. It provides an ideal setting for physical, mental and spiritual refreshment and revitalization. It *...is a sleek, contemporary B&B that's almost sensual in its attention to detail.* **1994-95 Northwest Best Places**

Located on Whidbey Island in Puget Sound, *Galittoire* encompasses over ten acres of woodlands and offers luxurious accommodations in a serene setting. The guesthouse, sited in a glade ringed with trees and surrounded by lawn sloping to forest, seems an extension of the natural world with its many windows, glass doors and skylights.

A perfect place from which to explore the unique character of the island, its beaches, farms and small towns, *Galittoire* is a short distance from the seaside village of Langley. Langley strikes a pleasant balance between slow-paced existence and intriguing discovery. The notion of timelessness contributes in giving Langley a way of life that locals fight to preserve and that bustle-weary escapees from the city long to experience.

At *Galittoire,* equal emphasis is placed on "bed" and "breakfast" to realize the best of both. Each of the guest suites is built to enhance maximum privacy. The finest king-sized beds and down bedding assure a good night's sleep. In an elegant sunlit dining room, a gourmet breakfast is served complemented by spiced fruits and homemade freezer jams, honey sweetened mousse, whipped butters or fruit compotes. *Galittoire* combines European graciousness with American spaciousness.

Galittoire pleases and pampers its guests with a variety of diversions. For indoor pleasures, a sauna, hot tub and Jacuzzi are provided, in addition to an exercise room, entertainment room and library. Complimentary transportation to and from the ferry landing, bicycles and island tour information are also available. **Address: 5444 S Coles Rd, Langley, Whidbey Island, WA, 98260-9508. Tel: (206) 221-0548 until January 15, 1995. Then (360) 221-0548.**

Type: Bed & breakfast.
Clientele: Mostly straight clientele with a gay & lesbian following.
Transportation: Car is best. Shuttle Express from Seattle airport to Mukilteo, then ferry to Clinton. Call for free pick up from ferry.
To Gay Bars: 45-minute drive to Everett, 1 hour to Seattle.
Rooms: 2 suites with king beds.
Bathrooms: Private bath/ toilets.
Meals: Full breakfast. Hors d'oeuvres with drinks in the early evening.
Vegetarian: Dietary restrictions considered with advance notice. Vegetarian food also available at local restaurants.
Complimentary: Juices, seltzer, tea & coffee always available. Fresh fruits in suites at turn-down time.
Dates Open: All year.
High Season: May-September.
Rates: $175-$225.
Discounts: For extended stay in off season.
Credit Cards: MC, VISA & Amex.
Rsv'tns: Required.
Reserve Through: Call direct.
Minimum Stay: 2 night minimum on weekends.
Parking: Ample free parking.
In-Room: Room & maid service.
On-Premises: TV lounge, video tape library, telephone, business services & laundry facilities. Ideal setting for executive retreats, weddings & union ceremonies.
Exercise/Health: Gym, weights, Jacuzzi, sauna, hot tub & massage on premises.
Swimming: Nearby ocean & lake.
Sunbathing: On common sun decks, on the lawn or in the woods. At nearby beach.
Smoking: On exterior decks only. Main house & suites are strictly non-smoking.
Pets: Not permitted.
Handicap Access: No. 2 steps into main house & into single level suite.
Children: Unable to accommodate children under the age of 14.
Languages: English, Hindi.
Your Host: Mahésh.

Gallery Suite

Laura Ashley NEVER Slept Here

Gay-Friendly ♀♂

Escape to Langley for a quiet, romantic weekend. Enjoy our regional contemporary art collection and the island's beautiful sunsets. This quaint Victorian town has three fine restaurants, art galleries, shopping, antique shops and many nearby beaches. Come to *Gallery Suite* for a stay in an artfully-appointed waterfront suite with an unobstructed view of Saratoga Passage and Camano Head. Breathe sea air from the spacious deck. Picturesque, seaside Langley is just outside your door. **Address: PO Box 458, Langley, WA 98260. Tel: (206) 221-2978 After Jan 15, 1995: (360) 221-2978.**

Type: Bed & breakfast with art gallery.
Clientele: Mostly straight with a gay & lesbian following.
Transportation: Car, airport shuttle, ferry boat. Pick up from ferry dock.
To Gay Bars: 1 hour to gay/lesbian bars.
Rooms: 1 suite with queen bed.
Bathrooms: 1 private.
Meals: Continental breakfast.
Complimentary: Swiss chocolates, beverages, fruit & cheese.
Dates Open: All year.
High Season: Memorial Day-Labor Day.
Rates: $90 1st night, $80 2nd night & $70 for 3rd & subsequent nights.
Credit Cards: MC, VISA, Amex & Discover.
Rsv'tns: Required, 1 week cancellation policy.
Reserve Through: Travel agent or call direct.
Minimum Stay: 2 nights on holidays, weekends.
Parking: Ample free off-street parking.
In-Room: Maid service, refrigerator, coffee pot, toaster oven.
Exercise/Health: Local gym nearby, massage available.
Swimming: Lake & saltwater passage 1/2 hour drive.
Sunbathing: On private sun decks or patio.
Smoking: Not permitted.
Pets: Not permitted.
Handicap Access: No.
Children: Not permitted.
Languages: English.

WEST VIRGINIA

ELKINS

Retreat At Buffalo Run

Gay-Friendly ♀♂

Situated on five acres, *Retreat at Buffalo Run* is a stately, turn-of-the-century home in West Virginia's Potomac Highland, gateway to the Monongahela National Forest. Wide porches, wrapping nearly all the way around the house, provide many vantage points from which to view the surrounding shade trees, evergreens, rhododendron groves and flower and vegetable gardens that make the *Retreat* a great secluded spot to get away. Marvel at the spectacular fall foliage on the hills surrounding the house. Feed winter birds outside your window. Shopping, golfing, tennis and swimming are nearby.

Address: 214 Harpertown Rd, Elkins, WV 26241. Tel: (304) 636-2960.

Type: Bed & breakfast.
Clientele: Mostly straight clientele with a gay & lesbian following.
Transportation: Car is best.
To Gay Bars: Walking distance to gay/lesbian bar.
Rooms: 6 rooms with double or 7-ft long queen beds.
Bathrooms: 3 shared bath/shower/toilets & 1 shared toilet.
Meals: Full breakfast.
Vegetarian: Available upon request. Meat is served only on special request.
Complimentary: Juice, tea or coffee upon arrival.
Dates Open: All year.
High Season: Fall, spring & summer.
Rates: $46-$57 per day including tax.
Discounts: On long-term stays.
Credit Cards: None.
Rsv'tns: Required.
Reserve Through: Call direct.
Minimum Stay: 2 nights on weekends.
Parking: Ample free off-street parking.
In-Room: Central heat & linen & towel service.
On-Premises: Laundry facilities, living room, dining room, parlor, large porch with swing, portable phone, guest refrigerator, charcoal grill, hammock, 5 acres of meadow, woods, flower, herb & vegetable gardens.
Exercise/Health: Walking distance to Seneca Trail, scenic parks, hiking.
Tubing, skiing, PGA golf course, bowling, pool tables.
Swimming: Mountain streams & lakes nearby & indoor swimming pool on college campus.
Sunbathing: In the backyard or garden area.
Smoking: Permitted outdoors.
Pets: Not permitted.
Handicap Access: No.
Children: Permitted.
Languages: English.
Your Host: Kathleen, Bert & Earl.

HUTTONSVILLE

Mr. Richard's Olde Country Inn

Gay-Friendly ♀♂

Mr. Richard's Olde Country Inn is a pre-Civil-War mansion restored as a bed and breakfast inn with full-service bar and restaurant. We are close to state parks and national forest, and outdoor activities abound, such as mountain bike tours (rentals available), cave exploring, hiking, trout fishing, whitewater rafting, as well as more civilized sports, like golfing. Our guests say they like the clean, cool air. A favorite of tourists is the Cass

restored railroad which regularly toils up and down the mountains. Skiing in these

mountains, by the way, is the best east of the Rockies.
Address: US 219 Route 1 Box 11-A-1, Huttonsville, WV 26273. Tel: (304) 335-6659

Type: Bed & breakfast inn & cottage with restaurant & bar.
Clientele: Mostly straight clientele with a gay & lesbian following.
Transportation: Car is best.
To Gay Bars: 1-3/4 hours to Morgantown, WV.
Rooms: 15 rooms & 1 cottage.

Bathrooms: 10 private, others share.
Meals: Full breakfast.
Vegetarian: Always available.
Dates Open: All year.
Rates: Rooms $50-$65 for 2 including full breakfast. Cottage $85-$150.
Credit Cards: MC, VISA & Amex.
Rsv'tns: Advisable.

Reserve Through: Travel agent or call direct.
Parking: Ample free off-street parking.
In-Room: Maid service. Some rooms have AC, some have ceiling fans.
On-Premises: TV lounge & meeting rooms.
Exercise/Health: Excellent downhill & cross-country skiing.

Swimming: Nearby public pool & river.
Sunbathing: On common sun decks.
Smoking: Non-smoking rooms available.
Pets: Permitted in some rooms.
Handicap Access: No.
Children: Welcome.
Languages: English.
Your Host: Richard.

LOST RIVER
Guest House, The

See our entry under Washington, DC. .

WISCONSIN

DELAVAN
Allyn Mansion Inn, The

Gay-Friendly ♀♂

"Inside...the Year is Always 1885"—Country Living Magazine

Grand Prize winner of the Great American Home Awards presented by the National Trust for Historic Preservation and recipient of the Wisconsin Historical Society's Certificate of Commendation for Historic Preservation because of its "exceptionally thorough and meticulous restoration," the *Allyn Mansion* ranks as one of the finest restoration efforts in the nation. Along with walnut woodwork, frescoed ceilings, ten marble fireplaces and other origi-

nal features, the mansion is completely furnished in authentic Victorian antiques. Guests enjoy the use of three formal parlors and two grand pianos.
Address: 511 E Walworth Ave, Delavan, WI 53115. Tel: (414) 728-9090, Fax: (414) 728-0201.

Type: Bed & breakfast with gift & antique shop.
Clientele: Mostly straight clientele with a gay & lesbian following.
Transportation: Car is best. Airport bus from

continued next page

Chicago or Milwaukee. Pick up from bus.
To Gay Bars: 35 miles.
Rooms: 8 rooms with single, double or queen beds.
Bathrooms: Shared: 7 full baths, 3 bathtubs only & 4 showers only.
Meals: Full breakfast.
Vegetarian: Available upon request.
Complimentary: Wine &

cheese at 6 pm.
Dates Open: All year.
High Season: May-Feb.
Rates: $50 (single, corporate rate). $90 (2nd floor, queen beds, working fireplace).
Credit Cards: MC & VISA.
Rsv'tns: Required.
Reserve Through: Call direct. (Travel agents weekdays only.)
Minimum Stay: No Sat-

night-only stays (Fri-Sat or Sat-Sun minimum).
Parking: Ample free off-street parking.
In-Room: AC. Some rooms with working fireplace.
On-Premises: Fax & meeting space.
Exercise/Health: Nearby gym, weights, Jacuzzi, sauna, steam & massage.

Swimming: Nearby pool & lake.
Smoking: Strictly forbidden anywhere in the house.
Pets: Not permitted.
Handicap Access: No.
Children: Not especially welcome.
Languages: English & French.
Your Host: Ron & Joe.

MADISON

Chase On The Hill Bed & Breakfast

Gay-Friendly 50/50 ♀♂

Escape to the Country!

You are invited to kick off your shoes and enjoy the charm and hospitality of *Chase On The Hill*, a cozy farmhouse built in 1846. Guestrooms are filled with fresh air and sunshine to provide an ideal atmosphere for peace and relaxation. The master bedroom features skylights, queen bed and private bath. Antique furnishings, a woodburning stove and a miniature grand piano add to your enjoyment, along with farm animals and cats in residence. Michael Chase, a professional actor, welcomes you to this retreat which is accessible from Madison, Milwaukee and Chicago.

Address: 11624 State Road 26, Milton, WI 53563. Tel: (608) 868-6646.

Type: Bed & breakfast.
Clientele: 50% gay & lesbian & 50% straight clientele.
Transportation: Car is best. Free pick up from bus.
To Gay Bars: 9 miles to Janesville, 35 miles to Madison.
Rooms: 4 rooms with double, queen or bunk

beds.
Bathrooms: 1 private bath/toilet, 1 shared bath/shower/toilet.
Meals: Full breakfast.
Vegetarian: Vegetarian breakfast served with advance notice.
Complimentary: Afternoon beverages, chocolates on nightstand.
Dates Open: All year.

High Season: Summer.
Rates: $40-$60 all year.
Discounts: For single occupancy.
Credit Cards: MC & VISA.
Rsv'tns: Required.
Reserve Through: Call direct.
Parking: Ample free off-street parking.
On-Premises: Meeting rooms & TV lounge.

Swimming: Lakes nearby.
Sunbathing: On the patio.
Smoking: Permitted outdoors only.
Pets: Not permitted.
Handicap Access: No.
Children: Welcome if over 12 years old.
Languages: English, elementary German.

MAUSTON

CK's Outback

Women ♀

A Womyn's Place to Experience

CK's Outback is a womyn-only retreat located on 77 acres of woods and valleys in south-central Wisconsin. There is an abundance of tent sites, hot showers, a sauna and an activity center. Hiking and bicycling on paths, boating, swimming, fishing, canoeing, golfing and horseback riding are nearby, as are several state parks. In winter, there are limited accommodations for nearby skiing and snowmobiling. Groups are welcome!

Address: W5627 Clark Rd, Mauston, WI 53948. Tel: (608) 847-5247.

Type: Bed & breakfast & campground with

campstore.
Clientele: Women only.

Transportation: Car is best. Charge for pick up

from train or bus.
To Gay Bars: 1 hour 20

minutes to Madison.
Rooms: 3 rooms with double or queen beds.
Bathrooms: 1 shared bath/shower/toilet.
Campsites: 30 camp-sites & 2 RV parking sites. Outhouses by campsites, 4 toilets & 3 showers at activity center.
Meals: Continental breakfast for B&B only.
Complimentary: Coffee

& tea at B&B.
Dates Open: All year.
High Season: July, August.
Rates: Rooms $30-$35 per night, campsites $13 per night.
Discounts: For stays of over 1 week at house.
Rsv'tns: Required.
Reserve Through: Call direct.
Minimum Stay: 2 nights on holiday weekends.
Parking: Adequate free

off-street parking. 2 car maximum for campsites.
Exercise/Health: Sauna, hiking, horseshoe pits, volleyball, cross-country skiing. Numerous out-door activities nearby.
Swimming: At nearby lake.
Sunbathing: On the property.
Nudity: Permitted in "bare hollow".
Smoking: Not permitted

in farmhouse or activity center.
Pets: Maximum of 2 dogs with fee of $2 per dog per night.
Handicap Access: Par-tially. Call for details.
Children: Welcome. Boys up to age 10 only.
Languages: English.
Your Host: Kirie & Connie.

STURGEON BAY/DOOR COUNTY

Chanticleer Guesthouse

A Romantic Country Inn

Gay-Friendly 50/50 ♀♂

Welcome to the *Chanticleer,* situated on 30 private acres in picturesque Door County, WI. With over 250 miles of shoreline, 12 lighthouses, 7 state parks and countless antique and gift shops, you're not far from unlimited fun and adventure. The *Chanticleer's* majestic maples and delicate fields of wild flowers are a grand sight as you stroll on our nature trail. After your walk, tour our beautiful gardens, lounge poolside or relax on your private terrace overlooking the *Chanticleer's* serene countryside. All deluxe suites include double whirlpools, fireplaces and breakfast delivered to your room.

Address: 4072 Cherry Rd, Sturgeon Bay, WI 54235. Tel: (414) 746-0334.

Type: Bed & breakfast.
Clientele: 50% gay & lesbian & 50% straight clientele.
Transportation: Car.
To Gay Bars: 45 miles or a 50-minute drive to 5 bars in Green Bay.
Rooms: 4 suites with queen beds.
Bathrooms: All private bath/toilet/showers.
Meals: Expanded conti-nental breakfast.
Vegetarian: Our break-fast is vegetarian. Vegetarian restaurants nearby.

Complimentary: Tea, coffee, juice, cookies & fresh fruit.
Dates Open: All year.
High Season: Jun-Oct for summer festivals, fall & pumpkin festivals. Feb-Mar for ski season.
Rates: Summer $115-$165, winter $115-$145.
Discounts: 10% summer 5 or more days. 10% winter 3 or more days weekends, 20% Sun-Thurs.
Credit Cards: MC & VISA.
Rsv'tns: Required. Walk-ins welcome if rooms

available.
Reserve Through: Call direct.
Minimum Stay: 2 nights on weekends.
Parking: Ample free off-street parking in paved lot.
In-Room: Color TV, VCR, CD & cassette stereo, AC, coffee/tea-making facili-ties, ceiling fans, refrigerator, fireplace, double whirlpool tub, room & maid service.
On-Premises: Meeting rooms.
Exercise/Health: Sauna

on premises. Nearby gym & weights.
Swimming: Heated pool on premises, nearby lake.
Sunbathing: At poolside, on patio & private & common sun decks.
Smoking: Permitted with restrictions. Non-smoking sleeping rooms available.
Pets: Not permitted.
Handicap Access: No.
Children: Not especially welcome.
Languages: English.
Your Host: Bryon & Darrin.

WASCOTT

Wilderness Way Resort & Campground

Women ♀

Wilderness Way is a women-owned resort and campground on 10 wooded acres with a lake. It's secluded, yet accessible to restaurants and points of interest. Two-bedroom units have kitchen, and linens and towels are furnished. Tent sites and full RV hookups offer maximum privacy and quiet. All sites have tables and fireplaces or grills. Bathrooms include sinks, flush toilets and hot showers. The commons building has a large stone fireplace, offering warmth and cheer on cool, rainy days and nights, and a bug-free refuge from mid-summer's buzzings. **Address: PO Box 176, Wascott, WI 54890. Tel: (715) 466-2635.**

Type: Resort campground.
Clientele: Women only.
Transportation: Car is best.
To Gay Bars: 45 minutes to women's bars.
Rooms: Five 2-bedroom cabins.
Bathrooms: All private.
Campsites: 6 sites with electric hookup & 20 tent sites with showers & rest rooms.

Complimentary: Boat & canoe use with cabin.
Dates Open: All year.
High Season: Memorial Day-Labor Day.
Rates: Cabins (for 2) $44-$64 daily, $250-$350 weekly. Add'l person $8-$10. Camping $10 for two. Electric hookup $4.
Rsv'tns: Required.
Reserve Through: Call direct.
Minimum Stay: 2 nights

for cabins on weekends.
Parking: Free parking.
In-Room: Kitchen, cooking utensils, fans, linens, & towels.
On-Premises: Public telephone.
Exercise/Health: Boats, canoes, hiking & biking.
Swimming: In the lake.
Sunbathing: On the beach by the lake or anywhere on the property.

Nudity: Permitted with restrictions. Talk to manager.
Smoking: Permitted, with restrictions.
Pets: $5 add'l charge in cabins. Owner must keep pet leashed & in view.
Handicap Access: Bathrooms in camping area.
Children: Permitted and welcomed.
Languages: English.
Your Host: Jean.

WYOMING

JACKSON

Bar H Ranch

The Undiscovered Side of the Grand Tetons

Women ♀

In addition to regularly planned trail riding and horsepacking trips, *Bar H Ranch* offers loft accommodation to guests scheduling their own activities. The newly-remodeled barn loft is quite luxurious with lodgepole pine walls and ceilings, wall-to-wall carpet, and oak floors in kitchen and bath. The modern kitchen is fully-equipped with Jenn Aire range and breakfast bar. The bathroom sports a bathtub with claw feet. Sun yourself on the large deck, use the picnic table and chairs, BBQ, or relax and enjoy the fabulous views. Yellowstone and Grand Teton Nat'l Parks and Jackson Hole are all easy drives from the ranch.

Address: Box 297, Driggs, ID 83422. Tel: (208) 354-2906.

Type: Self-contained, private ranch accommodation on a working cattle ranch.
Clientele: Mostly women with men welcome.
Transportation: Car is best. Rental cars available from Jackson Hole Airport.
Rooms: Private loft with double bed.
Bathrooms: Private bath.

Vegetarian: Vegetarian food nearby.
Dates Open: Spring-fall. Closed in winter.
Rates: $400 per week for 2, $75 per day (2 day min) for 2, $10 per extra person.
Rsv'tns: Highly recommended.
Reserve Through: Call direct.
Minimum Stay: 2 nights.

Parking: Ample off-street parking on ranch.
In-Room: Color TV, VCR, telephone, full kitchen, dishwasher, Jenn Aire range with oven, refrigerator & coffee & tea-making facilities.
On-Premises: Deck & BBQ.
Exercise/Health: Horseback riding.
Swimming: Nearby river, lake and public natural hot water pool.
Sunbathing: On private sun deck.
Smoking: Permitted on deck.
Pets: Cat with prior permission, dog may be acceptable.
Handicap Access: No.
Children: Permitted.
Languages: English.

Redmond Guest House

Gay-Friendly 50/50 ♀♂

The Redmond Guest House is situated on a quiet, residential street, five blocks from Jackson's town square. Guests enjoy privacy in the back garden with barbecue and outdoor furniture. The Guest House features lodgepole-pine furniture, a large brick fireplace, color TV and private bath with a queen-sized bed. Guests prepare their own breakfast. The beautiful Jackson valley has long been a premier vacation destination. Even the Northern Plains Indians journeyed here in summer to gather healing herbs and hunt. Horse boarding facilities are available on the property at an additional charge.

Address: Box 616, Jackson, WY 83001. Tel: (307) 733-4003.

Type: Guesthouse.
Clientele: 50% gay & lesbian & 50% straight clientele.
Transportation: Car is best. Free pick up from airport.
Rooms: 1 apartment with single & queen bed.
Bathrooms: Private.
Complimentary: Bottle of wine.

Dates Open: May 1st-September 15th.
High Season: June through September.
Rates: Per night: $95.
Discounts: 10% senior citizen discount.
Rsv'tns: Preferred.
Reserve Through: Call direct.

Minimum Stay: 2 nights on weekends, 3 nights on holidays.
Parking: Ample off-street parking.
In-Room: Color cable TV, kitchen, refrigerator, coffee & tea-making facilities.
On-Premises: BBQ & outdoor furniture.

Sunbathing: On the patio.
Smoking: Permitted outside only.
Pets: May be permitted, please inquire.
Handicap Access: No.
Children: Permitted.
Languages: English.
Your Host: Sue Ann

TRAVEL DIRECTORY

Reservation Services

EUROPE

GI TRAVEL LTD, Unit 2, 124 Rossmore Rd, Parkstone Poole, Dorset, England BH12 2HJ, (0202) 734 100, Fax: (0202) 732 525. Simply, the best worldwide reservation service for gays & lesbians, bonded travel agents. *Member AGLTA, IGTA*

CANADA

ALTERNATIVE TRAVEL, 42 Pine Ave W #2, Montréal, PQ Canada H2W 1R1, (514) 845-7769, Fax: 845-8421. Reservation services, accommodations & local events in Montréal. *Member IGTA*

M.A.N. (MALE ACCOMMODATION NETWORK), 2491 Centre St, Montréal, PQ Canada H3K 1J9, (800) 363-1626.

UNITED STATES

A TROPICAL VACATION RENTAL, PO Box 9108-546, Key West, FL 33041, (800) 939-3415. Vacation rentals in the tropics from 1-BR condos and villas to tropical estates. Great for a few or a large group. Gay-owned and -operated. A variety of properties are available in each area: Florida, Mexico, the Caribbean, Costa Rica and more.

ACCOMMODATIONS KEY WEST, 701 Caroline St, Key West, FL 33040, (305) 294-6637, ext 133, (800) 654-2781, ext 133. Rent a house or condo for the price of a room. We feature from 1-bedroom homes up to 7-bedroom estates with private pools. Meeting all your vacation needs. Ask for Jewel, ext. #133.

ALTERNATIVE ACCOMMODATIONS (NYC), (800) 547-7230. Apartment rentals in New York, NY and Miami, FL.

BED & BREAKFAST INN ARIZONA, Gallery 3 Plaza, 3819 N 3rd St, Phoenix, AZ 85012, (602) 265-9511 (800) 266-STAY (7829). Inns, B&Bs, hotels, resorts, dude ranches, apartments & condos throughout Arizona! Dis-

counts available on self-drive autos.

BENOTT HOSPITALITY GROUP, PO Box 1041, Inglewood Cliff, NJ 07632, (800) 786-6402, (201) 941-2180, Fax: (201) 941-0584.

CARITAS BED & BREAKFAST, 75 E. Wacker Dr. #3600, Chicago, IL 60601. (312) 857-0801, Fax: (312) 857-0805. B&B, home-stay accommodations service.

CITYWIDE RESERVATION SERVICES, 25 Huntington Ave #607, Boston, MA 02116, (800) 468-3593, MA: (617) 267-7424. Reservations at gay and non-gay locations in Boston and New England, 9am-9pm or 10:30am-6pm weekends.

CONCIERGE EXCLUSIF, 75 E Wacker Dr #3600, Chicago, IL 60601, (312) 894-3604, Fax: 857-0805. Personalized assistance with hotel accommodations, theater, sports, sightseeing, limousines, car rentals & nightlife.

FRENCH QUARTER RESERVATION SERVICE, 940 Royal St #263, New Orleans, LA 70116, (504) 523-1246, Fax: 527-6327. Specialize in finding accommodations in small hotels, inns and private guest-homes in the historic French Quarter & famous Garden District of New Orleans. *Member IGTA*

GOOD TIME TOURS, 407 Lincoln Rd #10G, Miami Beach, FL 33139, (305) 864-9431, Fax: 866-6955. Reservation service for South Beach and all of Florida. *Member IGTA*

GREATER BOSTON HOSPITALITY, PO Box 1142, Brookline, MA 02146, (617) 277-5430. B&B reservations throughout the Boston area.

HOMESTAY BY THE BAY, PO Box 2116, Berkeley, CA 94702, (510) 869-4395. Local lesbians and gay men invite you to vacation in their homes. Enjoy breakfasts, gay events, resources, fun. You can network, meet friends in the community and make connections. Accommodations are available throughout San Francisco, Berkeley and Oakland. All host homes are visited and approved, and come with free references.

HOSPITALITY EXCHANGE FOR LEATHER-ORIENTED PEOPLE, 4337 18th St, San Francisco, CA 94114, (415) 864-5239. Complimentary accommodations for the traveling leather men and women worldwide, in exchange for similar accommodations in their homes.

KEY WEST BUSINESS GUILD, Box 1208, Key West, FL 33041, (305) 294-4603, (800) 535-7797. Specializing in gay & lesbian travel in Key West. *Member IGTA*

KEY WEST RESERVATION SERVICE, 628 Fleming St, Key West, FL 33041, (305) 296-7753, (800) 327-4831 (USA & Canada), Fax: (305) 296-6291. Info. on gay & straight Key West accommodations.

MI CASA SU CASA, PO Box 10327, Oakland, CA 94610, (510) 268-8534, (800) 215 CASA (2272), Fax: (510) 265-8534. International and domestic home exchange and hospitaltity network, specializing in short- and long-term exchanges for lesbian and gay and gay-friendly travelers. The Mi Casa Su Casa confidential member catalog connects you with gay and lesbian people around the world. For an agreed time period, you enjoy their home and community while they enjoy yours. Member IGTA.

PALM SPRINGS VISITORS INFO. CENTER, 2781 N Palm Canyon Dr, Mail: 401 S Pavilion Way, Palm Springs, CA 92263, (619) 778-8418, (800)34-SPRINGS. The city's Division of Tourism offers information on all accommodations (gay included). Palm Springs, CA...the destination for everyone.

POSITIVE IDEA MARKETING PLANS (LE SKI LAB), PO Box 712, Winter Park, CO 80482, (303) 726-4562.

Nationwide gay and lesbian information and reservations, accommodations, air, car, activities, entertainment.

PROVINCETOWN BUSINESS GUILD, PO Box 421, 115 Bradford St, Provincetown, MA 02657, (508) 487-2313. Gay & lesbian customers welcome. Provincetown gay visitor information. *Member IGTA*

PROVINCETOWN RESERVATION SYSTEM, 293 Commercial St #5, Provincetown, MA 02657, (508) 487-2021, (800) 648-0364 (US & Canada), Fax: 487-4887. Accommodations, car, local air transport, show & restaurant reservations in Provincetown for gays & lesbians, now also long-distance travel. *Member IGTA*

RESERVATION..CONNECTION, 101 3rd Ave, Pass Christian, MS 39571, (601) 452-3042. Reservation service for gay & gay-friendly accommodations in Mississippi's Gulf Coast.

RESERVATIONS NETWORK, PO Box 680368, Park City, UT 84068, (801) 649-1592, Fax: 649-1593. discount lodging and reservations service for Lake Tahoe, Jackson, Wy and Utah. *Member IGTA*

RIVER SPIRIT RETREAT B&B RESERVATION SERVICE, PO Box 23305, St. Louis, MO 63156, (618) 462-4051, (314) 569-5795. Nationwide reservations for gay women.

ROYAL COMMAND (INC) NETWORK, 108 Mohican Cir, Boca Raton, FL 33487-1520, (407) 994-3558, (800) 71-ROYAL, Fax:(407) 994-3634. Reservations for B&B's throughout the UK and Europe. No Fee.

SOUTH BEACH CENTRAL, (800) 538-3616, (305) 538-3616. Free service, over 200 South Florida hotels to choose from. Airlines, tours, cruises, car rentals.

VACATION DESIGN, PO Box 1261, Plainfield, NJ 07061-1261, (201) 882-1742, Fax: (201) 808-1742. Weekly vacation rentals of European villas, chalets and apartments. *Member IGTA*

WAIKIKI AA STUDIOS, 3242 Kaohinani, Honolulu, HI 96817, (808) 595-7533, (800) 288-4666, Fax:(808) 595-2030. Studios, hosted rentals and B&B reservation service throughout the islands.

WAIKIKI VACATION RENTALS, 1860 Ala Moana Blvd. #108, Honolulu, HI 96815, (808) 946-9371, (800) 543-5663. Fully-furnished condominium rentals in central Waikiki, from budget to deluxe, near to bars and beach.

WESTERN EXPOSURE, PO Box 2116, Berkeley, CA 94702, (510) 869-4395, Fax: 254-0265. We arrange homestays with lesbians, gay men and bisexuals in the San Francisco Bay area. *Member IGTA*

WORLDWIDE ACCOMMODATION REFERRAL, (310) 941-7448, (800) R-GAY-BED (742-9233).

Transportation

PACIFIC (AUSTRALIA)

TURTLE CARS, (61-70) 591 800, Fax: 591 969. New air-conditioned, automatic rental cars. Located at Turtle Cove Resort, Cairns. *Member AGLTA*

UNITED STATES

AUTO EUROPE, (800) 223-5555.

CAPE AIR, Barnstable Municipal Airport, Hyannis, MA 02601, (508) 771-6944, (800) 352-0714. Scheduled air transport between Boston, Provincetown and Martha'sVineyard. *Member IGTA*

MIDWAY RENT-A-CAR, 8420 Sunset Blvd, West Hollywood, CA 90069, (213) 650-5823, Fax: (213) 650-1121.

PARADISE TRANSPORTATION, PO Box 2566, Key West, FL 33045, (305) 296-4800, Fax: 293-8474. *Member IGTA*

THRIFTY CAR RENTAL, 966 Vella Rd, Palm Springs, CA 92264, (619) 323-2212, Fax: (619) 325-3873.

Travel Agents

AFRICA

SOUTH AFRICA

TRAVEL CONSULTANT, THE, 1118 Pretorius St, Hatfield 0083, Pretoria (012) 342-4385/6, Fax: (012) 342-4567. Specializing in gay and lesbian travel, ask for Ken. Mail to: PO Box 6424, Pretoria 0001.

EAST ASIA

JAPAN

EAST WEST TRAVEL, 1082-1 Ochiai, Tama-shi, Tokyo, Japan (0423) 73-6284. Gay-friendly.

EUROPE

DENMARK

INTER-TRAVEL, Frederiksholms Kanal 2, 1220 Kobenhavn K, Denmark (45) 33 15 00 77.

ENGLAND

MAN AROUND LTD, 89 Wembley Park Dr, Wembley Park, MIDDX, England (44-181) 795 1411, Fax: 903 7357. *Member IGTA*

TRAVEL SOLUTIONS II, 7/11 Kensington High St, London GU34 3QT, England (44-171) 938 3390, Fax: 937 4550. *Member IGTA*

FRANCE

ACTITUDE, 33 rue du Petit Musc, Paris 75004, France (33-1) 4887 7744, Fax: 4887 7879. *Member IGTA*

HOLIGAY'S VACANCES ET LIBERTE, 49 Rue Notre Dame de Lorette, 75009 Paris (33-1) 48 74 37 77, Fax: 45 26 09 75. Specializing in gay & lesbian travel. Ask for Basilio. *Member IGTA*

VISTAMAR TRAVEL, 34 Helio Village, 34308 Cap d'Agde, France 33-67 26 0341. *Member IGTA*

GERMANY

AAD WELTWEIT REISEN, Alemannenstr 1-B, D-86199 Augsburg 49-821 906 0011, Fax: 906 0060. *Member IGTA*

NEUE WELT REISEN, Pfalzburger Str 72, 1000 Berlin 15 (30) 883 1946.

REISEBÜRO AM HELLKAMP, Hellkamp 17, 20255 Hamburg, Germany (49-40) 401 92121, Fax: 491 9100. *Member IGTA*

RTS REISE & TOURISTIC SERVICE, Schoenhauser Allee, 130, 10437 Berlin (49-30) 609 7786, Fax: 609 7872. *Member IGTA*

GREECE

WINDMILLS TRAVEL & TOURISM, , Mykonos, Greece Tel/fax (30) (289) 23877 or 22066, telex: 293410 WIND GR. Specializing in accommodations, transportation and excursions in Mykonos & Greece. Ask for Pam. *Member IGTA*

ITALY

VAG VIAGGI, , (39-6) 980 50 20, Fax: (39-6) 980 71 47.

NETHERLANDS

WENS REIZEN, Baronielaan 103, 4818 PD Breda, The Netherlands 76 226340, Fax: 76 221931.

Travel Agents

SPAIN

SKY TOURS, Calle Mayor 8, Madrid 28000, (91) 247-2145.

SWITZERLAND

GO TRAVEL, Limmattalstr. 236, Zürich 8049, Switzerland (41-01) 342 3656, Fax: 342 3651. *Member IGTA*

REISEBÜRO JEKAMI, Münstergasse 48, 3011 Bern (41-031) 312 4040. Specializing in gay and lesbian travel.

UK (ENGLAND)

GI JOHN DARRAH CORP, 53 Manor Park, London SE1 35RA (081) 318 5590. Apts, B&B, holiday pkgs in London.

PRIDE TRAVEL, 47 Preston Rd, Brighton, E Sussex, England BN1 4QE, (01273) 673 818, Fax: 621 082. *Member IGTA*

TRIANGLE TRAVEL, Workshop 4, The Leadmill, 6/7 Lead-mill Road, Sheffield S1 4SF.

PACIFIC (AUSTRALIA)

AUSTRALIAN CAPITAL TERRITORY

JUST TRAVEL, 4/42 Ceils Court, Deakin ACT 2600, Australia (61-6) 285 2644, Fax: 285 2430. *Member AGLTA, IGTA*

NEW SOUTH WALES

ALUMNI TRAVEL, GPO Box 1368, Sydney 2001, NSW Australia (61-2) 290 3856, Fax: 290 3857. *Member IGTA*

ASTRAL TRAVEL & TOURS, #7 Level 3, 250 Pitt St, Sydney 2000 NSW Australia (61-2) 283 2718, FAX: (61-2) 264 1674. *Member AGLTA, IGTA*

F.O.D. TRAVEL, 2nd Fl, 77 Oxford St, Darlinghurst, NSW Australia 2010, (61-2) 360 3616, Fax: (61-2) 332-3326. *Member AGLTA,*

FIORELLA TRAVEL, 92 Pitt St, Sydney 2000 NSW, Australia (61-2) 231 4099, Fax: (61-2) 231 2472. *Member AGLTA,*

H.H.K. TRAVEL, 50 Oxford St, Paddington 2021, NSW Australia (61-2) 332 4099, Fax: 360 2164. *Member AGLTA,*

OXFORD STREET FLIGHT CENTRE, 26 Oxford St, Woollahra 2025 NSW, Australia (61-2) 360 2277, Fax: 360 5665. *Member AGLTA,*

SAMPSONS TRAVEL, PO Box 415, Nowra 2541 NSW, Australia (61-44) 210 522, Fax: (61-44) 213 869. *Member AGLTA,*

SILKE'S TRAVEL, 263 Oxford St, Sydney NSW 2010, Australia (61-02) 380 6244, Fax: 361-3729. *Member IGTA*

STA TRAVEL, 9 Oxford St, Paddington NSW, Australia (61-2) 360 1822. *Member AGLTA,*

TOURS COORDINATION, Suite 1, 2-B Cross St, Double Bay 2028 NSW, Australia (61-2) 327-6600, Fax: (61-2) 362 4989. *Member AGLTA, IGTA*

TRAVEL CALL, 20 Bay St, level 4, Double Bay 2028 NSW, Australia (61-2) 326 1711, Fax: (61-2) 327 5049. *Member AGLTA,*

TRAVEL CONSULTANT, 63 Arthur St, Surry Hills NSW 2010, Australia (61-2) 360 9880. *Member AGLTA,*

TRAVEL OZ (Greyhound/Pioneer Australia), 7/4 Llankelly Place, Potts Point 2011 NSW, Australia (61-2) 368 1284, Fax: (61-2) 357-4639. *Member AGLTA,*

WORLD LINKS EDUCATION, PO Box C235, Clarence St, Sydney 2000 NSW, Australia (61-2) 290 3856, Fax: (61-2) 290 3857. *Member AGLTA,*

NORTHERN TERRITORY

DUCKET TOURS & TRAVEL SHOP, , (61-89) 819 321, Fax: (61-89) 810 777. *Member AGLTA,*

QUEENSLAND

JETSET MAROOCHYDORE, 2/16 Duporth Ave, Maroochydore 4558 QLD, Australia (074) 438 771, Fax: 791 810. *Member AGLTA,*

STA TRAVEL, University of Queensland, Union Bldg, ground floor, St. Lucia QLD, Australia (61-7) 371 2433. *Member AGLTA,*

TRIANGLE VACATIONS, PO Box 186, Alderly 4051 QLD, Australia (61-7) 221 7527, Fax: (61-7) 229 7661. *Member AGLTA, IGTA*

SOUTH AUSTRALIA

PARKSIDE TRAVEL, 70 Glen Osmond Rd, Parkside SA 5063, Australia (61-8) 274 1222, (008) 888 501, Fax: (61-8) 272 7371.

PRIDE TRAVEL, 3A, 28 Hindley St, Adelaide 5000 SA, Austrlia (61-8) 212 3833, Fax: 231 3145. *Member AGLTA,*

STA TRAVEL, 235 Rundle St, Adelaide SA, Australia (61-8) 223 2426. *Member AGLTA,*

VICTORIA

AMERICA YOUR WAY TRAVEL, 93 Jenkins St, Northcote 3070 VIC, Australia (61-3) 481 5218, Fax: (61-3) 482 5158. *Member AGLTA,*

FREEWAY BALACLAVA INT'L (FBI), 204-206 Balaclava Rd, Caulfield 3182 VIC, Australia (61-3) 576 0900, Fax: (61-3) 525 2975. *Member AGLTA, IGTA*

JETSET TRAVEL, Level 9, 5 Queens Rd, Melbourne VIC 3004, Australia (61-3) 828-8904, Fax: (61-3) 828 8998. *Member AGLTA, IGTA*

JETSET TRAVEL BRIGHTON, 254 Bay St, Brighton VIC 3186, Australia (61-3) 596 7100, Fax: (61-3) 596 7761. *Member AGLTA, IGTA*

STA TRAVEL, 222 Faraday St, Carlton VIC 3053, Australia (61-3) 347 6911, Fax: (61-3) 347 0547. *Member AGLTA, IGTA*

STA TRAVEL, 142 Acland St, St. Kilda VIC, Australia (61-3) 525 3188.

THAILAND DO IT RIGHT, PO Box 338, World Trade Centre, Melbourne 3005 VIC, Australia (61-3) 521 2889 tel & fax. *Member AGLTA,*

WESTERN AUSTRALIA

STA TRAVEL, 100 James St, Northbridge WA, Australia (61-9) 227 7569. *Member AGLTA,*

PACIFIC (NEW ZEALAND)

ALTERNATIVE TOURIST CO, THE, PO Box 96 030, Auckland 1030, New Zealand (64-9) 638 8460, Fax: (64-9) 638 8461. *Member AGLTA, IGTA*

GREY LYNN TRAVEL, 555 Great North Rd, Grey Lynn, New Zealand (09) 376 3556.

MILBROOK TRAVEL, 2nd floor, Vulcan Ln, Auckland, New Zealand (9) 358-2220, Fax: (9) 358-2221.

TRAVEL DESK NEW ZEALAND, 2nd floor of the OUT! Centre, 45 Anzac Ave, Auckland, New Zealand (09) 3779 031, Fax: (09) 3777 767.

TRAVEL PLANNERS LTD, 3rd Floor, 20 Fort St, Auckland 1, New Zealand (09) 379 9716.

CANADA

ALBERTA

CMS TRAVEL, 101, 1717 10th St NW, Calgary, AL T2M 4S2, (403) 289-1817, Fax: 289-0162. Ask for Bob. *Member IGTA*

FLETCHER SCOTT TRAVEL LTD, 803 8th Ave SW, Calgary, AL Canada T2P 1H7, (403) 232-1180, Fax: 232-0211. *Member IGTA*

UNIGLOBE SWIFT TRAVEL, #220, 932 17th Ave SW, Calgary, AL Canada T2T 0A2, (403) 244-7887, Fax: 229-2611.

BRITISH COLUMBIA

ENGLISH BAY TRAVEL, 1267 Davie St, Vancouver, BC V6E 1N4, (604) 687-8785, Fax: 682-1027. *Member IGTA*

FUNSATIONAL TRAVEL SERVICES, 2-4529A E Hastings St, Burnaby, BC V5C 2K3, (604) 688-7422, Fax: 291-7529.

HUME HOLIDAYS, 100-1281 W Georgia St, Vancouver, BC V6E 3J7, (604) 682-7581, Fax: 681-2651. Ask for Mike.

MARLIN TRAVEL, 116A 1950 Harvey Ave, Kelowna, BC Canada V1Y 8J8, (604) 860-7887, Fax: 861-3808. *Member IGTA*

PARTNERS TRAVEL INC, 1120 Davie St, Vancouver, BC Canada V6E 1N2, (604) 687-3837, Fax: 687-7937. *Member IGTA*

TEAM TRAVEL, 1140 W Pender St #1800, Vancouver, BC, Canada V6E 4G1, (604) 688-9655, Fax: 688-0902. *Member IGTA*

TRAVEL CLINIC, THE, 1033 Davie St #411, Vancouver, BC V6E 1M7, (604) 669-3321, Fax: 669-3323. *Member IGTA*

UNIGLOBE SPECIALTY TRAVEL, 626 W. Pender St, Vancouver, BC V6B 1V9, (604) 688-8816, Fax: (604) 688-3317.

MANITOBA

GOLIGER'S TRAVEL, 125 Garry St #100, Winnipeg, MAN, Canada R3L 3P2, (204) 943-6224, Fax: 947-0479. *Member IGTA*

OUT 'N ABOUT TRAVEL, 100 Osborne St S #207, Winnipeg, MAN, Canada R3L 1V5, (204) 477-6799, Fax: 475-9493. *Member IGTA*

TPI TRAVEL, 136 Market Ave, 7th fl, Winnipeg, MB R3B 0P4, (204) 942-4565, Fax: 944-8565.

NEW FOUNDLAND

PLANET TRAVEL, PO Box 552, Gander, NF, Canada A1V 2E1, (709) 256-9385, Fax: 256-9375. *Member IGTA*

ONTARIO

ALGONQUIN TRAVEL, 1105 Wellington Rd S, London, Ontario, Canada N6E 1V4, (519) 668-8479, Fax: (519) 668-0700. *Member IGTA*

GETAWAY TRAVEL, 380 Elgin St, Ottawa, ONT K2P 1N1, (613) 230-2250, Fax: 230-3396.

JEEVES TRAVEL, Suite #105, 100 Wellesley St E, Toronto, Ont Canada M4Y 1H5, (416) 962-2422, Fax: 924-5792. *Member IGTA*

LAFABULA TRAVEL & TOURS, 551 Church St, Toronto, ON, Canada M4Y 2E5, (416) 920-3229, Fax: 920-9484.

PANTALONE & BARNETT TRAVEL, 357 Preston St, Ottawa, ON Canada K1S 4M8, (613) 563-3222, Fax: 563-3225. *Member IGTA*

ROBERT Q'S TRAVEL MART, 105 Wharncliffe Rd S, London, Ont Canada N6J 2K2, (519) 672-9020, Fax: 673-1935. *Member IGTA*

TALK OF THE TOWN TRAVEL, 565 Sherbourne St, Toronto, ON M4X 1W7, (416) 960-1393, Fax: 960-6379. Ask for Henry. *Member IGTA*

TCB TRAVEL, 600 Doon Village Rd, Kitchener, ON, Canada N2P 1G6, (519) 748-0850, Fax: (519) 748-0852. Ask for Linda.

TRAVEL CLINIC, THE, 506 Church St #200, Toronto, ON M4Y 2C8, (416) 962-2422, Fax: 924-5792. *Member IGTA*

VINTAGE TRAVEL, 3425 Harvester Rd #106, Burlington, ON L7N 3N1, (905) 348 811, Fax: 639-3315. *Member IGTA*

YOULTEN TRAVEL, Box 2133, Timmins, ON P4N 7X8, (705) 268-6449, Fax: 267-1337. *Member IGTA*

QUÉBEC

CLUB VOYAGES DU PLATEAU, 981 rue Duluth est, Montréal, QC Canada H2L 1B9, (514) 521-3320, Fax: 526-0369. *Member IGTA*

TERRE DES HOMMES, 1122 Boul. de Maisonneuve Est, Montréal, QC, Canada H2L 1Z5, (514) 522-2225, Fax: 522-7987. *Member IGTA*

VOYAGES AQUANAUTES, 1551 Montarville, St. Bruno, QC J3V 3T8, (514) 461-0110, Fax: 461-3199. *Member IGTA*

VOYAGES EXCEPTION-L, 1210 Ste-Catherine est, Montréal, QC Canada H2L 2G9, (514) 521-2155, Fax: 521-9991. *Member IGTA*

VOYAGES LORRAINE, 153 rue Principale, Aylmer, QC Canada J9H 3M9, (819) 684-3536, Fax: 684-0185. *Member IGTA*

VOYAGES OTTAWA, Place du Centre, 200, Prm du Portage, Hull, QC Canada J8X 4B7, (819) 770-4441.

VOYAGES SOLARIS, 215 Boul. Concord, Laval, QC, Canada H7G 2C9, (514) 667-7711, Fax: 667-8670. *Member IGTA*

SASKATCHEWAN

EPIC TRAVEL SERVICES, PO Box 581, Elrose, SK S0L 0Z0, (306) 378-2252.

JUBILEE TRAVEL, Circle 8 Centre, #108-3120 8th St E, Saskatoon, SK, Canada S7H 0W2, (306) 373-9633, Fax: 374-5878. *Member IGTA*

CARIBBEAN

PUERTO RICO

TRAVEL MAKER INTERNATIONAL TOURS, San Claudio Mail Stations, Box 224, Rio Piedras, Puerto Rico 00926, (809) 755-5878, Fax: 755-5850. *Member IGTA*

VIRGIN ISLANDS

CALPARRIO INT'L TRAVELS, W. 67 King St, Frederiksted, St Croix, USVI 00840, (809) 772-9822, Fax: 772-9677. *Member IGTA*

LATIN AMERICA

ARGENTINA

GET-A-WAY TRAVEL, Junin 733, PB, Buenos Aires 1026, Argentina (54-1) 497 828, Fax: 406 650. *Member IGTA*

BRAZIL

GET TOGETHER TRAVEL, R. da Consolaçao 222 cj. 809, 01302-910 Sao Paulo, SP Brazil (55 11) 258 6701, Fax: (55 11) 256 0124. Specializing in gay travel. *Member IGTA*

MEXICO

LAREDO ASESORES, Rio Danubio 63 #5, Col. Cuauhtemoc, DF 06500, (5-525) 8903, Fax: 207 5078. *Member IGTA*

VIAJES HELENA, Blvd. 31 Oriente #1612, 72540 Puebla Pue., Mexico 45 89 79, 33 50 04, Fax: 44 08 65. Ask for Ramón.

VENEZUELA

NEW LIFE TOURS, Apdo Postal 729, 6301 Porlamar, Venezuela (58) (95) 621 137. *Member IGTA*

UNITED STATES

ALABAMA

USTRAVEL STERLING TRAVEL AGENCY, 720 Madison St, Huntsville, AL 35801, (205) 533-1301, Fax: 536-3914. *Member IGTA*

VILLAGE TRAVEL, 1929 Cahaba Rd, Birmingham, AL 35223, (205) 870-4866, Fax: 871-6114. *Member IGTA*

ALASKA

APOLLO TRAVEL SERVICE, 1207 West 47th Ave, Anchorage, AK 99503, (907) 561-0661, Fax: 561-5802. *Member IGTA*

Travel Agents

ARIZONA

ALL POINTS TRAVEL, 3001 Stockton Hill Rd #5, Kingman, AZ 86401, (602) 753-7878, (800) 719-7878. Ask for Brandy.

ARIZONA TRAVEL CENTER, 2502 E Grant Rd, Tucson, AZ 85716, (602) 323-3250, Fax: 325-0560.

CARLSON TRAVEL NETWORK, 13628 N 99th Ave, Sun City, AZ 85351, (602) 974-3668, Fax: 977-9115. *Member IGTA*

CENTURY TRAVEL WEST, 2280 N Oracle Rd, Tuscon, AZ 85705-5431, (602) 624-7458, Fax: 622-1497. *Member IGTA*

DOLPHIN TRAVEL SERVICES, 10632-B N Scottsdale Rd, Scottsdale, AZ 85254, (602) 998-9191, Fax: 998-1110. *Member IGTA*

ECLIPSE TRAVEL, 13850 N 19th Ave, Phoenix, AZ 85023, (602) 789-8454, (800) 842-8921.

FIRSTRAVEL LTD, 5150 N 7th St, Phoenix, AZ 85014, (602) 265-0666, Fax: 265-0135.
Member IGTA

PINNACLE PEAK TRAVELER, 8700 E Pinnacle Peak Rd #106, Scottsdale, AZ 85255, (602) 585-0033.

PRISM WORLD TRAVEL, 5625 E Indian School Rd, Phoenix, AZ 85018, (602) 941-8600, Fax: 994-3650. *Member IGTA*

PSI TRAVEL, 2100 N Wilmot #203, Tuscon, AZ 85712, (602) 296-3788. *Member IGTA*

SUN KACHINA TRAVEL, 1987 McCullich #108, Lake Havasu City, AZ 86403, (602) 855-0066, Fax: 855-7412. *Member IGTA*

TGI TRAVEL AGENCY, 5540 W Glendale Ave #A-102, Glendale, AZ 85301, (602) 939-1445. *Member IGTA*

TRAVEL REGISTRY TOURS & TRAVEL, 3819 N 3rd St, Phoenix, AZ 85012, (602) 263-7761.

VICTORY VACATIONS, PO Box 11429, Tucson, AZ 85734, (602) 295-1173. *Member IGTA*

ARKANSAS

TRAVEL BY PHILLIP, Box 250119, Little Rock, AR 72225-5119, (501) 227-7690, Fax: 224-8638. *Member IGTA*

CALIFORNIA

A & D TRAVEL, 2547 W Shaw #108, Fresno, CA 93711, (209) 224-1200, Fax: 224-1213. Ask for Helen. *Member IGTA*

A TO Z TRAVEL, 17049 Chase St, Northridge, CA 91325, (818) 772-1972, Fax: 772-1863. *Member IGTA*

ABC TRAVEL SERVICES, 6160 Mission Gorge Rd #102, San Diego, CA 92120-3425, (619) 280-9986, Fax: 280-9989. *Member IGTA*

ACADEMY TRAVEL/CARLSON TRAVEL NETWORK, 1948 Armory Dr, Santa Rosa, CA 95401, (707) 526-5961. *Member IGTA*

ACM CORPORATE TRAVEL MANAGEMENT, 11611 Industry Ave, Fontana, CA 92334, (909) 681-5028, (800) 443-4905, Fax: (909) 681-5076.

ADVENTURE TRAVEL, PO Box 669, Aptos, CA 95001, (408) 688-9400. *Member IGTA*

ADVENTURES WITH A RAINBOW, PO Box 293055, Sacramento, CA 95829-3055, (916) 383-0123, Fax: 383-0124. *Member IGTA*

AEREO/BRIDGES TRAVEL, 731 Market St #401, San Francisco, CA 94103, (415) 989-8747.

AFFORDABLE TRAVEL, 8680 Navajo Rd #106, San Diego, CA 92119, (619) 460-6400, Fax: 460-3624. Ask for Ed. *Member IGTA*

ALADDIN TRAVEL, 818 K Street Mall, Sacramento, CA 95814, (916) 446-0633, CA: (800) 433-5386. Ask for Rob Thorbin.

ALL DESTINATIONS TRAVEL, 2810 E Imperial Hwy, Brea, CA 92621, (714) 528-9100, Fax: 528-9243. *Member IGTA*

ALL POINTS TRAVEL, 615A Stockton Ave, San Jose, CA 95126, (408) 288-3280, Fax: 993-8134. *Member IGTA*

ALL TRAVEL, 2001 S Barrington Ave #150, Los Angeles, CA 90025, (213) 312-3368.

ALTERNATIVE VACATIONS TRAVEL, 584 Castro #413, San Francisco, CA 94114, (415) 826-0266, Fax: 445-3519. *Member IGTA*

AMERICAN EXPRESS TRS, 91 Broadway Ln, Walnut Creek, CA 94596, (510) 938-0800, Fax: 938-4362. *Member IGTA*

AMERICAN WAY TOURS, 8110 W Norton Ave #8, West Hollywood, CA 90046, (213) 654-9098. *Member IGTA*

ANCIENT MARINER TRAVEL, 14145 Red Hill Ave, Tustin, CA 92680, (714) 838-9780, Fax: 838-9796. *Member IGTA*

AP TRAVEL SERVICES, 30 Spring St, Salinas, CA 93901, (408) 758-2212.

AQUARIUS TRAVEL & TOURS, 2029 Westwood Blvd, Los Angeles, CA 90025, (310) 475-8851.

AVB TRAVEL, 1548 Palos Verdes Mall, Walnut Creek, CA 94596, (510) 977-4034.

AVENUES OF ADVENTURE TRAVEL, 227 W Las Tunas Dr, San Gabriel, CA 91776, (818) 576-0264.

AZZURRO TRAVEL, 7985 Santa Monica Blvd #206, West Hollywood, CA 90046, (213) 654-3700, Fax: 654-7909. *Member IGTA*

BEHIND THE SCENES TRAVEL, 5200 Lankershim Blvd #240, North Hollywood, CA 91602, (818) 762-5200, Fax: 761-5200. *Member IGTA*

BEYOND THE BAY, 726 Polk St, San Francisco, CA 94109, (415) 441-3440. *Member IGTA*

BOB STEVENS TRAVEL, 270 Arch Street, Laguna Beach, CA 92651, (714) 497-2993.

BON VOYAGE N. TRAVEL & CRUISE CENTER, 4549A 134th St, Hawthorne, CA 90250, (310) 675-6133, Fax: 675-1892.

BOTTOM LINE TRAVEL, 1236 Castro St, San Francisco, CA 94114, (415) 826-8600, Fax: 826-8698. *Member IGTA*

BRYAN INTERNATIONAL TRAVEL, 98 Battery St #302, San Francisco, CA 94111, (415) 731-8411, Fax: 433-5208. *Member IGTA*

CALIFORNIA RIVIERA 800, 1400 S Coast Hwy #104, Laguna Beach, CA 92651, (714) 376-0305, Fax: 497-9077. *Member IGTA*

CALIG WORLD TRAVEL, 358 S Marengo Ave #2, Pasadena, CA 91101, (818) 703-0100.

CASSIS TRAVEL SERVICES, 9200 W Sunset Blvd #320, West Hollywood, CA 90069-3505, (310) 246-5400, Fax: 246-5499. *Member IGTA*

CHASE TRAVEL, 316 E Broadway, Glendale, CA 91209-3060, (818) 246-1661, (213) 245-7611. Ask for Patty.

CLASSIC TRAVEL, 7985 Santa Monica Blvd #103, West Hollywood, CA 90046-5112, (213) 650-8444, Fax: 656-7898. *Member IGTA*

COAST TRAVEL, 1355 N Harbor Dr, San Diego, CA 92101, (619) 239-9973, Fax: 238-4283. *Member IGTA*

COORDINATED TRAVEL MANAGEMENT, 8687 Melrose Ave #M32, West Hollywood, CA 90069-5701, (310) 652-9222, (800) 535-1020. Ask for Richard Ferguson.

COUNCIL TRAVEL, 220 Montgomery St #2630, San Francisco, CA 94104, (415) 863-8553. *Member IGTA*

COUNCIL TRAVEL, 1093 Broxton Ave, #220, Los Angeles, CA 90024, (310) 208-3551, Fax: 208-4407.

COUNCIL TRAVEL LOS ANGELES, 1600 S Bentley Ave #1, Los Angeles, CA 90025, (310) 312-0176, Fax: 208-4407. *Member IGTA*

CRAIG'S TRAVEL SERVICE, 12089 Euclid St, Garden Grove, CA 92640, (714) 638-7381, Fax: 638-3713. *Member IGTA*

CREATIVE JOURNEYS, 5329 Skylane Blvd, Santa Rosa, CA 95403, (707) 526-5444, Fax: 528-3217. *Member IGTA*

CRUISE & TOUR CONSULTANT, 1175 De Meo St, Santa Rosa, CA 95407, (707) 573-1304, Fax: 573-1304.

CRUISE HOLIDAYS, 224 S Robertson Blvd, Beverly Hills, CA 90211, (213) 652-8521, Fax: 652-8524. *Member IGTA*

CRUISE TIME, 1 Hallidie Plaza, #406, San Francisco, CA 94102, (415) 677-0777, (800) 338-0818, Fax: (415) 391-1856.

CUPERTINO TRAVEL, 1211 B Kentwood Ave, San Jose, CA 95129, (408) 255-6900, Fax: 255-7340.

CUSTOM CRUISES INTERNATIONAL, 482 Greathouse Dr, Milpitas, CA 95035, (408) 945-8286.

DAVISVILLE TRAVEL, 420 2nd St, Davis, CA 95616, Ask for Karen.

ELECTRA TRAVEL SERVICES CO, 1258 N Highland Ave #302, Los Angeles, CA 90038, (213) 962-8456.

EMBASSY TRAVEL, 906 N Harper Ave #B, Los Angeles, CA 90046, (213) 656-0743, (800) 227-6669, Fax: (213) 650-6968. *Member IGTA*

ENDLESS TRAVEL, 588 Center Avenue, Martinez, CA 94553, (510) 299-5950, Fax: 299-5954. *Member IGTA*

EUROPEAN TRAVEL, 442 Post St #301, San Francisco, CA 94102, (415) 981-5518, Fax: 986-5166. *Member IGTA*

FESTIVE TOURS, 1220 N Coast Hwy, Laguna Beach, CA 92651, (714) 494-6670.

FIESTA RIVIERA TRAVEL, 230 E 17th St #230, Costa Mesa, CA 92627, (714) 722-8754, Fax: 642-1972. Ask for Terry.

FIESTA TRAVEL, 7185 Navajo Rd, San Diego, CA 92119-1696, (619) 462-1741, (800) 262-1741 (outside CA).

FIRSTWORLD TRAVEL, 7443 Mission Gorge Rd, San Diego, CA 92120, (619) 265-1916, Fax: 265-1930. *Member IGTA*

FIRSTWORLD TRAVEL EXPRESS, 1990 S Bundy Dr #175, West Los Angeles, CA 90025, (310) 820-6868, (800) 366-0815, Fax: 820-2807. *Member IGTA*

FOURWINDS TRAVEL, 3663 The Barnyard, Carmel, CA 93923, (408) 622-0800. *Member IGTA*

FRIENDS TRAVEL, 322 Huntley Dr. #100, West Hollywood, CA 90048, (310) 652-9600, (800) GAY-0069, Fax: (310) 652-5454.

GAY WORLD OF TRAVEL, THE, 15233 NE 90th St, Redmond, CA 98052.,

GO AWEIGH! TRAVEL, 2584 Carbon Ct #2, Colton, CA 92324, (714) 370-4554, Fax: 824-8644. *Member IGTA*

GOLD RIVER TRAVEL & TOURS, 1949 Zinfandel Dr, Rancho Cordova, CA 95670, (916) 638-2749, Fax: 635-9770. *Member IGTA*

GOLDEN EAGLE TRAVEL, 17412 Beach Blvd, Huntington Beach, CA 92647, (714) 848-9090, Fax: 842-6494.

GREGORY HOWELL & ASSOC., 166 South Park #A, San Francisco, CA 94107-1809, (415) 541-5388, Fax: 541-9347. *Member IGTA*

GULLIVER'S WORLD TRAVEL, 2465 S Winchester Blvd, Campbell, CA 95008-4801, (408) 379-0822, (800) 621-2966, Fax: (408) 379-5308. *Member IGTA*

GUNDERSON TRAVEL, 8543 Santa Monica Blvd, West Hollywood, CA 90069, (310) 657-3944, Fax: 652-4301. *Member IGTA*

HILLCREST TRAVEL, 431 Robinson Ave, San Diego, CA 92103, (619) 291-0758, Fax: 291-3151. *Member IGTA*

I.T.S. TRAVEL, 8833 Sunset Blvd #302, Los Angeles, CA 90069, (310) 855-1445, Fax: 855-0840. *Member IGTA*

IMAGES OF TRAVEL, 2141 Brook Hollow Ct, Oxnard, CA 93030, (805) 983-3613.

J & J UNIVERSAL TRAVEL SERVICES, 2348 Walsh Ave, Santa Clara, CA 95051, (408) 987-4030.

JACKSON TRAVEL SERVICE LTD, 1829 Polk St, San Francisco, CA 94109, (415) 928-2500. *Member IGTA*

JACQLEEN'S TRAVEL SERVICE, 6222 Fountain Ave #314, Los Angeles, CA 90028, (213) 463-7404. Ask for Eileen. *Member IGTA*

JERRY & DAVID'S TRAVEL, 1025 W Laurel St, San Diego, CA 92101, (619) 233-5199, Fax: 231-0641. *Member IGTA*

JUST CORPORATE A TRAVEL COMPANY, 510 5th St, Santa Rosa, CA 95401, (707) 525-5105, Fax: 525-5111. *Member IGTA*

KISMET TRAVEL, PO Box 974, Redway, CA 95560, (707) 986-7205, (800) 926-7205.

LAS PALMAS TRAVEL, PO Box 1930, Palm Springs, CA 92263, (619) 325-6311, Fax: 325-3542. *Member IGTA*

LEFT COAST TRAVEL, 1655 Polk St #1, San Francisco, CA 94109, (415) 771-5353, Fax: 771-5354. *Member IGTA*

LEMON GROVE TRAVEL, 7735 Pacific Ave, Lemon Grove, CA 91945-0549, (619) 466-9999, (res.) 295-1984.

LENCI CRUISE & TRAVEL, 1005 Terra Nova Blvd, Pacifica, CA 94044, (415) 355-3919.

LINLI TRAVEL, 19510 Ventura Blvd, #107, Tarzana, CA 91356, (818) 344-3640, Fax: 344-0407.

LOWE'S WORLD TRAVEL,, 322 1/2 W Washington, San Diego, CA 92103, (619) 298-8595, Fax: 294-3359. *Member IGTA*

MAN-2-MAN WOMAN-2-WOMAN VACATIONS, 4535 Noyes St, Pacific Beach, CA 92109, (619) 270-8728.

MISSION CENTER TRAVEL, 3601 Fifth Ave, San Diego, CA 92103-4219, (619) 299-2720. *Member IGTA*

NAVIGATOR TRAVEL, 2047 Market St, San Francisco, CA 94114, (415) 864-0401. Ask for John.

NELSON GOUZE TRAVEL, 34 S 15th St, San Jose, CA 95112, (408) 995-0888, Fax: 995-0889. *Member IGTA*

NEW VENTURE TRAVEL, 404 22nd St, Oakland, CA 94612, (510) 835-3800, Fax: 835-7865. *Member IGTA*

NORWEGIAN CRUISE, 584 Castro St #524, San Francisco, CA 94114, (800) 327-9030. *Member IGTA*

NOW, VOYAGER TRAVEL, 4406 18th St, San Francisco, CA 94114, (415) 626-1169, (800) 255-6951, Fax: 626-8626. *Member IGTA*

ODYSSEY TRAVEL, PO Box 8209, Rancho Santa Fe, CA 92067-8209, (619) 756-0700, Fax: 759-2099. *Member IGTA*

ORCHID TRAVEL SERVICES, 4122 20th St, San Francisco, CA 94114, (415) 552-2468. *Member IGTA*

PASSPORT TICKET TRAVEL, 9048 Brooks Rd South, Windsor, CA 95492, (707) 838-1557, (800) 443-4134.

PASSPORT TO LEISURE, 2265 Market St, San Francisco, CA 94114, (415) 621-8300. Ask for Rob. *Member IGTA*

PERFECT TRAVEL, 7490 La Jolla Blvd, La Jolla, CA 92037, (619) 456-2201, (800) 232-2201.

PIEDMONT TRAVEL SERVICE, 2067 Mountain Blvd, Oakland, CA 94611, (510) 339-8814, (800) 762-5885, Fax: 339-2087. Ask for Jeremy.

PROFESSIONAL TRAVEL SERVICE, 1011 Camino del Mar #116, Del Mar, CA 92014, (619) 481-1264.

RAINBOW TRAVEL, 1055 Monroe St, Santa Clara, CA 95050, (408) 246-1414, Fax: 983-0677. *Member IGTA*

RANCHO MIRAGE TRAVEL, 71-428 Hwy 111, Rancho Mirage, CA 92270, (619) 341-7888, (800) 369-1073, Fax: 568-9202. *Member IGTA*

RED SHOES TRAVEL, 3241 Folsom Blvd, Sacramento, CA 95816, (916) 454-4201, Fax: 456-5331. *Member IGTA*

ROBERTS TRAVEL SERVICE, 260 Stockton St, San Francisco, CA 94108, (415) 433-1991.

SAN VINCENTE TRAVEL, 451 E Tahquitz Canyon Way, Palm Springs, CA 92262, (619) 320-8220.

SANTA ROSA TRAVEL, 542 Farmers Lane, Santa Rosa, CA 95405, (707) 542-0943, Fax: 545-2753. *Member IGTA*

SCANDIA TRAVEL, 76 Gough St, San Francisco, CA 94102, (415) 552-5300, Fax: 552-5076.

SELECT TRAVEL SERVICE, 8380 Santa Monica Blvd #202, West Hollywood, CA 90069, (213) 848-2211, (800) 488-6690. Ask for Rand or Dan.

SF TRAVELERS, 870 Market St #578, San Francisco, Ca 94102, (415) 433-9621, Fax: 433-6018. *Member IGTA*

SLOTSY TOURS & TRAVEL, 1821 W Commonwealth #B, Fullerton, CA 92633, (714) 870-8641, Fax: 870-8241. *Member IGTA*

SPECIAL SERVICE TRAVEL, 1700 N Broadway #310, Walnut Creek, CA 94596-4138, (510) 938-4778, Fax: 938-4779. Ask for Dallas.

SPORTS LEISURE TRAVEL, 9527-A Folsom Blvd, Sacramento, CA 95827, (916) 361-2051, Fax: 361-7995. *Member IGTA*

STA TRAVEL, 7202 Melrose, Los Angeles, CA 90046, (213) 934-8722, Fax: 937-6008. *Member IGTA*

Travel Agents

STERLING TRAVEL, 448-G Costa Mesa Terrace, Sunnyvale, CA 94086, (408) 738-1622, Fax: 828-4394. *Member IGTA*

STEWART-COLE TRAVEL EXPRESS, 6761 Sebastopol Ave, Sebastopol, CA 95472, (707) 823-8402.

SUNDANCE TOURS & TRAVEL, 1040 University Ave B207, San Diego, CA 92103, (619) 497-2100, (800) 472-4070.

SUNRISE TRAVEL, 23891 Via Fabricante #603, Mission Viejo, CA 92691, (714) 837-0620. Ask for Robert.

SUNVENTURE TRAVEL, 1621 Bridgeway, Sausalito, CA 94965, (415) 332-6611, Fax: 332-8098. *Member IGTA*

TIME TO TRAVEL, 582 Market St, #1201, San Francisco, CA 94104, (415) 421-3333, (800) 524-3300, Fax: (415) 421-4857.

TIME TRAVELERS INT'L CONSULTANTS, 3841 4th Ave #287, San Diego, CA 92103, (619) 239-1964, Fax: 298-9150. *Member IGTA*

TOUCHES OF TRAVEL, , (310) 657-7008, (800) 899-1944, Fax: (310) 652-4301. Ask for Chuck or Al.

TRAVEL ADDRESS/GALAXSEA, 6465 N Blackstone Ave, Fresno, CA 93710, (209) 432-9095, Fax: 432-1565. *Member IGTA*

TRAVEL ADVISORS, 650 S Brookhurst St, Anaheim, CA 92804, (714) 535-1174, Fax: 535-3552. *Member IGTA*

TRAVEL BOUND, 16255 Ventura Blvd #500, Encino, CA 91436-2394, (818) 906-2121, Fax: 906-3049. *Member IGTA*

TRAVEL BY GRETA, 17106 Devonshire St, Northridge, CA 91325, (818) 366-9611.

TRAVEL CONNECTION, 5450 Alpine Ct, Paradise, CA 95969, (916) 877-7111. *Member IGTA*

TRAVEL CONSULTANT (CARLSON TRAVEL NETWORK), 1245 Market St, San Francisco, CA 94103, (415) 558-7996, Fax: 558-8960.

TRAVEL ETC., 8764 Holloway Dr, West Hollywood, CA 90069, (310) 652-4430, Fax: 652-1283. *Member IGTA*

TRAVEL EXPERIENCE ON CALL, PO Box 2588, Aptos, CA 95001, (408) 464-8035. *Member IGTA*

TRAVEL LAB, 1943 Hillhurst Ave, Los Angeles, CA 90027, (213) 660-9811, (800) 747-7026, Fax: 660-9814. *Member IGTA*

TRAVEL ONE, One First St #1, Los Altos, CA 94022, (415) 949-5222, Fax: 949-0847. *Member IGTA*

TRAVEL SYNDICATE, 20855 Ventura Blvd #10, Woodland Hills, CA 91364.,

TRAVEL TIME, One Hallidie Plaza #406, San Francisco, CA 94102, (415) 677-0799, Fax: 391-1856. *Member IGTA*

TRAVEL TRENDS, 431 Castro St, San Francisco, CA 94114, (415) 558-6922, (800) 558-6920, Fax: (415) 558-9338. *Member IGTA*

TRAVEL WITH EASE, 1065 W Lomita Blvd #322, Harbor City, CA 90710, (310) 325-8638, Fax: 530-6054. *Member IGTA*

TRAVEL WITH HAL, 2227 Atlanta St, Anaheim, CA 92802, (714) 537-1553. *Member IGTA*

TRAVELERS SERVICES, 21021 Devonshire St #203, Chatsworth, CA 91311-2385, (818) 709-0300, Fax: 882-5738. *Member IGTA*

TRAVELINE, 8721 Santa Monica Blvd #845, Los Angeles, CA 90069, (213) 654-3000.

UNIGLOBE EXPO TRAVEL, 2100 Arden Way #220, Sacramento, CA 95825, (916) 920-1701, (800) 879-8785.

UNIGLOBE PASSPORT TRAVEL, 100 Spear St, San Francisco, CA 94105, (415) 904-6380, Fax: 904-6390. *Member IGTA*

UNIGLOBE RAINBOW TRAVEL, 1624 Franklin St #1102, Oakland, CA 94612, (510) 238-4646, Fax: 238-4656. *Member IGTA*

VIRGIN MADONNA EXPRESS, 7857 Herschel Ave, La Jolla, CA 92037, (619) 459-4897, Fax: 459-4878. *Member IGTA*

WINSHIP TRAVEL, 2321 Market St, San Francisco, CA 94114-1688, (415) 863-2717, Fax: 863-2473. Ask for Raoul. *Member IGTA*

WORLD TRAVEL ARRANGERS, 256 Sutter St 7th fl, San Francisco, CA 94108, (415) 421-4460, Fax: 982-7397. *Member IGTA*

YANKEE CLIPPER TRAVEL, 260 Saratoga Ave, Los Gatos, CA 95030, (408) 354-6400, (800) 624-2664. *Member IGTA*

COLORADO

CARLSON TRAVEL NETWORK, 2032 35th Ave, Greeley, CO 80634, (303) 339-3311, (303) 339-3770. Ask for Kathryn Freese.

COLORADO'S TRAVEL HAVEN, 1905 Yorktown Ave, Ft Collins, CO 80526, (303) 484-2139, Fax: 484-8729. *Member IGTA*

EXECUTIVE TRAVEL SERVICE, 907 17th St, Denver, CO 80202, (303) 292-3600, Fax: 292-4645. *Member IGTA*

GATEWAY TRAVEL & GATEWAY TOURS, 3510 W 10th St, Greeley, CO 80634, (303) 353-2200.

IMPERIAL TRAVEL, 717 17th St, Denver, CO 80202, (303) 292-1334, Fax: 292-5175. *Member IGTA*

LET'S TALK TRAVEL (CARLSON TRAVEL NETWORK), 1485 S Colorado Blvd #260, Denver, CO 80222, (303) 759-1318, Fax: 758-5390. *Member IGTA*

NEW HORIZONS TRAVEL, 3510 W 10th St, Greeley, CO 80634, (303) 353-2200, Fax: 356-8936. *Member IGTA*

PARTNERS TRAVEL SERVICE, 1811 S Quebec Way #63, Denver, CO 80231, (303) 751-2247.

PATH WAYS TRAVEL SERVICE, Crossroads Mall, 1700 28th St #108, Boulder, CO 80301, (303) 449-0099, Fax: 449-4585. *Member IGTA*

TRAVEL BOY COMPANY, 201 Steele St #2-B, Denver, CO 80206, (303) 333-4855, (800) 334-2285, Fax: (303) 333-8559. men-only travel. *Member IGTA*

TRAVEL SOLUTIONS, PO Box 471742, Aurora, CO 80047-1742, (303) 337-3114, Fax: 727-4136. *Member IGTA*

TRAVEL SQUARE ONE, 608 Garrison St #G, Lakewood, CO 80215, (303) 233-8457, Fax: 233-8586. *Member IGTA*

CONNECTICUT

ALDIS THE TRAVEL PLANNER, 46 Mill Plain Rd, Danbury, CT 06811, (203) 778-9399, (800) 369-6528, Fax: 744-1139. Ask for Aldis, Mark or Paul. *Member IGTA*

B.W. TRAVEL, 9 Mott Ave, Norwalk, CT 06850-3339, (203) 852-0200, (800) 288-2589 (outside CT), Fax: 852-8100. Ask for Bernie or Wendy. *Member IGTA*

CONTEMPORARY CRUISE VACATIONS, 444-A Lime Rock Rd, Lakeville, CT 06039, (203) 435-3534.

CORPORATE TRAVEL SERVICES, 412 Cromwell Ave, Rocky Hill, CT 06067, (203) 563-3288.

MCGREGOR TRAVEL, 40 Country Way, Bridgewater, CT 06752, (203) 222-6660, Fax: 222-6536. *Member IGTA*

PLAZA TRAVEL CENTER, 49 College St, New Haven, CT 06510, (203) 777-7334, Fax: 787-9553. *Member IGTA*

REKAP TRAVEL, Crystal Mall, 850 Hartford Tpke, Waterford, CT 06385, (203) 442-7144, Fax: 440-3233.

TOWER TRAVEL, 600 N Colony Rd, Wallingford, CT 06492, (203) 284-8747, (800) 229-TOWER, Fax: (203) 284-3322. Ask for Alan. *Member IGTA*

TRAVEL TRENDS, 45 West Ave, Norwalk, CT 06854, (203) 866-0000, Fax: 838-5719.

TRAVELSTAR INC, 965 Post Rd E, Westport, CT 06880, (203) 227-7233, Fax: 227-3774. *Member IGTA*

WARREN TRAVEL GROUP, 320 Post Rd West, Westport, CT 06880, (203) 454-2034, Fax: 454-8664. *Member IGTA*

WEBER'S TRAVEL SERVICE, 24 Cedar St, New Britain, CT 06052, (203) 229-4846. *Member IGTA*

DISTRICT OF COLUMBIA

ACT TRAVEL, 1722 Eye St NW, Washington, DC 20006, (202) 463-6300, (800) 433-3577, Fax: (202) 452-8597. Ask for Wayne.

AMERICAN EXPRESS TRAVEL RELATED SERVICES, 1150 Connecticut Ave NW, Washington, DC 20036, (202) 457-1325, Fax: 775-0786. *Member IGTA*

ANDEX TRAVEL, 733 15th St NW, Washington, DC 20006, (202) 393-2422, Fax: 393-3296. *Member IGTA*

CENTRAL TRAVEL, INC., 616 17th St NW, Liberty Plaza, Washington, DC 20006-4802, (202) 371-1100, (800) 334-9168, Fax: 898-0935. *Member IGTA*

FORTE INT'L TRAVEL, 1901 Penn Ave NW #406, Washington, DC 20006, (202) 833-4167, Fax: 296-8685. *Member IGTA*

GREAT ESCAPE TRAVEL, 1730 K St NW #910, Washington, DC 20006, (202) 331-3322, (800) 228-0861, Fax: 331-1109. *Member IGTA*

MULLIN TRAVEL, 2424 Pennsylvania Ave NW #118, Washington, DC 20037, (202) 296-5966.

PASSPORT EXECUTIVE TRAVEL, 1025 Thomas Jefferson St NW, Washington, DC 20007, (202) 337-7718, (800) 222-9800, Fax: 342-7475. *Member IGTA*

PERSONALIZED TRAVEL DESIGNERS, 529 14th St NW, Washington, DC 20045, (202) 508-8656, Fax: 508-8668. *Member IGTA*

TRAVEL DESIGNERS, 529 14th St NW #200, Washington, DC 20045, (800) 237-6971, (202) 508-8656, Fax: 508-8668.

TRAVEL ESCAPE, 1725 K St NW, Washington, DC 20006, (202) 223-9354. *Member IGTA*

WORLDWIDE ASSISTANCE SERVICES, 1133 15th St NW #400, Washington, DC 20003, (202) 331-1609, (800) 777-8710, Fax: (202) 828-5886. Ask for George. *Member IGTA*

FLORIDA

A BEELINE TRAVEL CENTER, 6271-6 St Augustine Rd, Jacksonville, FL 32217, (904) 739-3349, Fax: 739-3931. *Member IGTA*

A WORLD OF TRAVEL, 3947 Boulevard Center Dr #101, Jacksonville, FL 32207, (904) 398-6638, Fax: 399-5952. *Member IGTA*

ACBS TRAVEL AGENCY, 628 Decatur Ave, Brooksville, FL 34601, (800) 449-2227, (904) 796-4984, Fax: 799-6049. *Member IGTA*

ADIEUS INT'L TRAVEL, 3170 N Federal Hwy #106, Lighthouse Point, FL 33064, (305) 784-7575.

ALL POINTS TRAVEL, 3324 Edgewater Dr, Orlando, FL 32804, (407) 422-6442, Fax: 423-1725. *Member IGTA*

ALL SEASONS TRAVEL PROFESSIONALS INT'L, 405 Central Ave, St Petersburg, FL 33701, (813) 898-7411, Fax: 894-0030. *Member IGTA*

ALL WORLD TRAVEL, 4014 N 46th Ave, Hollywood, FL 33021, (305) 983-5501.

CONCEPTS OF TRAVEL, 1230 South 3rd St, Jacksonville Beach, FL 32250-6410, (904) 249-9155, Fax: 249-8518.

CRUISE DESTINATIONS, 170 W Spanish River Blvd, Boca Raton, FL 33431, (407) 338-4203, Fax: 394-0319. *Member IGTA*

CURRENT EVENTS TRAVEL, 443 N Lakemont Ave, Winter Park, FL 32792, (800) 569-6753, (407) 628-2228, Fax: 628-5444. *Member IGTA*

DISCOVER TRAVEL, 517 Duval St, Key West, FL 33040, (305) 296-1585, Fax: 296-8747. *Member IGTA*

DONITA'S VACATIONS UNLIMITED, 636 SW 34th St, Ft Lauderdale, FL 33315, (305) 359-2761, (800) 325-2721 (Canada & USA). Ask for Michael.

ELKIN TRAVEL, 885 E Palmetto Park Rd, Boca Raton, FL 33432, (407)368-8788.

EVELINA TRAVEL, 800 West Ave #1-A, Miami Beach, FL 33139, (305) 673-3141, Fax: 673-3313. *Member IGTA*

EXOTIC ADVENTURES, 12769 N Kendall Dr, Miami, FL 33186, (305) 382-7757.

FANTASY ADVENTURES TRAVEL, 138 Beach Dr NE, St Petersburg, FL 33701-3928, (813) 821-0880, Fax: 822-0892. *Member IGTA*

FESTIVE TOURS & TRAVEL, 913 Lake Ave, Lake Worth, FL 33460, (407) 588-6969, (800) 588-4297, Fax: 588-6117. *Member IGTA*

FIRST TRAVEL, 337 South Plant Ave, Tampa, FL 33606-2325, (800) 327-3367, Fax: 254-0889. *Member IGTA*

FLORIDA WORLD TRAVEL, 11228 Park Blvd, Seminole, FL 34642, (305) 392-4111, Fax: 399-8620.

FREDSON TRAVEL & TOURS, 100 N Biscayne Blvd, #701, Miami, FL 33132, (305) 577-8422, (800) 626-8422, Fax: (305) 577-8344.

FUTURE TRAVEL AGENCY, 300 S Luna Ct #4, Hollywood, FL 33021, (305) 964-7950.

GALAXSEA CRUISES, 6584 Superior Ave, Sarasota, FL 34231, (813) 921-3456, Fax: 922-1241. *Member IGTA*

GLOBAL TRAVEL & TOURS, 3018 E Commercial Blvd #103, Ft Lauderdale, FL 33308, (305) 771-0204, Fax: 771-0205. *Member IGTA*

GO KASUAL TOURS, 6935 Ridge Rd, Port Richey, FL 34668, (813) 846-8747.

GOOD BUY TRAVEL SERVICES, PO Box 5700815, Miami, FL 33257, (305) 252-0003.

GREAT ADVENTURE TRAVEL, 2252 Coral Way, Miami, FL 33145, (305) 858-4347, Fax: 858-7485. *Member IGTA*

HAPPY WANDERER, THE, 118 N Ocean Blvd, Pompano Beach, FL 33062, (305) 782-8668, (800) 329-7447.

INTERNATIONAL HOUSE OF TRAVEL, 40966 US Hwy 19 N, Tarpon Springs, FL 34689, (813) 938-1511, Fax: 942-6458. *Member IGTA*

JACQUIN TRAVEL, 2335 NW 107 Ave, Box 40, Miami, FL 33172, (305) 592-5882, Fax: 592-6761. *Member IGTA*

MULTI-TRAVEL & TOURS, 855 Washington Ave, Miami Beach, FL 33139, (305) 672-4600, (800) 762-3688, Fax: 672-4625. Ask for Craig. *Member IGTA*

OASIS TRAVEL, 3152 Northside Dr #100, Key West, FL 33040, (800) 872-8208.

OCEAN TRAVEL SERVICE, 885 E Palmetto Park Rd, Boca Raton, FL 33432, (407) 368-8788, (800) 226-TRIP.

ODYSSEY TRAVEL, 224 E Michigan St, Orlando, FL 32806, (407) 841-8686, Fax: 649-9471. *Member IGTA*

OLWELL TRAVEL SERVICE, 100 NE 3rd Ave #110, Ft. Lauderdale, FL 33301, (305) 764-8510, Fax: 764-7053. *Member IGTA*

PEGASUS TRAVEL MANAGEMENT, 2424 S Dixie Highway #100, Coconut Grove, FL 33133, (305) 859-9955, Fax: 859-8310. *Member IGTA*

PRE-FLIGHT TRAVEL, 9431 Tradeport Dr, Orlando, FL 32827, (407) 851-5635, (800) 929-7387, Fax: (407) 825-2963.

PROFESSIONAL TRAVEL MANAGEMENT, 195 SW 15th Rd #403, Miami, FL 33129, (305) 858-5522. *Member IGTA*

REGENCY TRAVEL, 1075 Duval St C-19, Key West, FL 33040, (305) 294-0175, Fax: 294-3631. *Member IGTA*

ROYAL PALM TRAVEL, 223 Sunset Ave, Palm Beach, FL 33480, (407) 659-6080, Fax: 659-6089. *Member IGTA*

SENATOR TRAVEL, 13899 Biscayne Blvd #143, N Miami Beach, FL 33181, (305) 949-0579, (800) 925-0024.

TAMPA BAY TRAVEL CORP, 4830 W Kennedy #148, Tampa, FL 33609, (813) 286-4202, Fax: 286-4204. *Member IGTA*

TOP FLIGHT TRAVEL, 300 S Luna Ct #4, Hollywood, FL 33021, (305) 966-9111, Fax: 966-9122. *Member IGTA*

TRAVEL ACCESS, 2273 Palm Beach Lakes Blvd, West Palm Beach, FL 33409, (407) 697-2291, Fax: 697-2303. *Member IGTA*

TRAVEL AGENT, THE, 615 N Main St, Chiefland, FL 32626, (904) 493-4826, Fax: 493-2606. *Member IGTA*

TRAVEL AGENTS INT'L, 4507 Gunn Hwy, Tampa, FL 33624, (813) 968-3600, Fax: 968-3713. *Member IGTA*

TRAVEL AGENTS INTERNATIONAL, 3940 N Ocean Blvd, Ft Lauderdale, FL 33308, (305) 565-7104, Fax: 565-7273. *Member IGTA*

TRAVEL BY PEGASUS, 1865 N US #1, Fort Pierce, FL 34946, (407) 464-6330, Fax: 464-6486. Ask for Jody.

TRAVEL EASY INT'L, International Bldg, 2455 E Sunrise Blvd #900, Ft Lauderdale, FL 33304, (305) 564-4561, (800) 542-3279.

TRAVEL GROUP, THE, 1916 14th St #205, Tampa, FL 33605, (813) 248-2634, (800) 365-9474.

TRAVELCRAFTERS, 1941 University Dr, Coral Springs, FL 33071-6032, (305) 753-7540, Fax: 753-6035. *Member IGTA*

Travel Agents

TRAVELMASTERS & TOURS, 4225 W Commercial Blvd, Tamarac, FL 33319, (305) 739-2285. Ask for Frank.

TRIPS ON SHIPS, 3303 Creekridge Rd, Brandon, FL 33511, (813) 684-4383, (800) 521-8473, Fax: 685-5268. *Member IGTA*

TWO GUYS TRAVEL, 525 Margaret St, Key West, FL 33040, (305) 292-9858, Fax: 296-5522. *Member IGTA*

UNIGLOBE ALL SEASONS TRAVEL, 405 Central Ave, St Petersburg, FL 33701, (813) 898-7411.

UNIVERSAL TRAVEL, 215 S Andrews Ave, Ft Lauderdale, FL 33301, (305) 525-5000.

VAGABOND TRAVELS, 601 Northlake Blvd, North Palm Beach, FL 33408, (407) 848-0648.

VENTURE TRAVEL, 1322 NE 105th St #10, Miami Shores, FL 33138, (305) 895-1229, Fax: 892-2881. *Member IGTA*

VIP TOURS & TRAVEL, 4485 N University Dr, Lauderhill, FL 33351, (305) 746-5300, (800) 847-4386, Fax: 746-5309. *Member IGTA*

VISION TRAVEL, 2222 Ponce de Leon Blvd, Coral Gables, FL 33134, (305) 444-8484. Ask for Connie.

WORLDWIDE TRAVEL SERVICES, Tamiami Mall, 8784 SW 8th St, Miami, FL 33174, (305) 223-2323, (800) 441-1954.

GEORGIA

ALL POINTS TRAVEL, 1544 Piedmont Ave, Atlanta, GA 30324, (404) 873-3631, Fax: 873-3633. *Member IGTA*

ANZA WORLD TRAVEL, 3533 Chamblee-Tucker Rd #F, Atlanta, GA 30341, (404) 986-0275.

BUSINESS TRAVEL, 3166 Mathieson Dr, Atlanta, GA 30305, (404) 238-9999.

CARLSON TRAVEL NETWORK/TRIPS UNLIMITED, 1004 Virginia Ave NE, Atlanta, GA 30306, (404) 872-8747, Fax: 873-1267. *Member IGTA*

CONTINENTAL TRAVEL, 1794 Willard Way, Snellville, GA 30278, (404) 972-1187.

CONVENTIONAL TRAVEL, 1658 Lavista Rd NE 6-A, Atlanta, GA 30329, (404) 315-0107, (800) 747-7107, Fax: 315-0206. *Member IGTA*

CROWN TRAVEL, 1000 Piedmont Ave NE, Atlanta, GA 30309, (404) 873-2102.

DIFFERENT DIRECTIONS TRAVEL, 314 Pharr Rd NE, Atlanta, GA 30305, (404) 262-1011.

DISCOUNT TRAVEL, Akers Mill Square, 2971 Cobb Pkwy, #E, Atlanta, GA 30339, (404) 916-0331, (800) 274-6118, Fax: (404) 916-0548. *Member IGTA*

MIDTOWN TRAVEL CONSULTANTS, 931 Monroe Dr #105, Atlanta, GA 30308, (404) 872-8308, Fax: 881-6322. *Member IGTA*

REAL TRAVEL, 2459 Wawona Dr, Atlanta, GA 30319-3713, (404) 636-8500, (800) 551-4202, Fax: 634-3107. *Member IGTA*

TRAVEL AFFAIR, 1205 Johnson Ferry Rd #116, Marietta, GA 30068, (404) 977-6824, (800) 332-3417, Fax: 977-0770. *Member IGTA*

TRAVELERS' CHOICE, 325 Hammond Dr #201, Atlanta, GA 30328, (404) 256-1818.

UNIGLOBE PREMIER TRAVEL, 600 W Peachtree St #1440, Atlanta, GA 30308, (404) 885-1122, Fax: 885-9878. *Member IGTA*

HAWAII

AMERICAN EXPRESS TRAVEL SERVICE, , (808) 947-2607, 926-5441. Ask for Don.

BIRD OF PARADISE TRAVEL, PO Box 4157, Honolulu, HI 96812-4157, (808) 735-9103, Fax (808) 735-1436. *Member IGTA*

CARL ERDMAN TRAVEL, 1001 Bishop St #1010, Pauahi Tower, Bishop Sq, Honolulu, HI 96813, (808) 531-4811.

CLASSIC TRAVEL, 1413 S King St #201, Honolulu, HI 96814, (808) 947-3900, Fax (808) 941-5049.

OUTRIGGER INT'L TRAVEL, 150 Kaiulani Ave, Honolulu, HI 96815, (800) 676-7740. Ask for Mark.

QUEST TRAVEL, The Waialae Bldg, 3660 Waialae Ave

#310, Honolulu, HI 96816, (808) 737-2202. Ask for Verne.

TRAVEL TRAVEL, 320 Ward Ave #204, Honolulu, HI 96814, (808) 596-0336, Fax: (808) 591-6639. Ask for Billy. *Member IGTA*

VACATIONS HAWAII, 1314 S King St #1062, Honolulu, HI 96814, (808) 524-4711, Fax: 524-7947. *Member IGTA*

ILLINOIS

ALL POINTS TRAVEL SERVICE, 3504 N Broadway, Chicago, IL 60657, (312) 525-4700, Fax: 525-7600. *Member IGTA*

AMBASSADOR TRAVEL, 907 E 31st St, La Grange Park, IL 60525, (708) 579-3390.

AMERICAN EXPRESS TRAVEL LINCOLN PARK, 2338 N Clark St, Chicago,IL 60614, (312) 477-4000, Fax: 477-8034. *Member IGTA*

AMERICAN TRAVEL, 2590 E Devon Ave #100, Des Plaines, IL 60018, (708) 803-5400, Fax: 803-5408. *Member IGTA*

CARLSON TRAVEL NETWORK/CRAY'S TRAVEL, 410 S Greenbay Rd, Waukegan, IL 60085, (708) 623-4722.

CLASSIC TRAVEL AGENCY, 138 Ogden Ave, Downers Grove, IL 60515, (708) 963-3030.

CRC TRAVEL, 2121 N. Clybourn, Chicago, IL 60614, (312) 525-3800, Fax: 525-8762. *Member IGTA*

CRYSTAL TOURS & TRAVEL, 5833 N Paulina, Unit B, Chicago, IL 60660-3264, (312) 271-1533. Ask for Norma. *Member IGTA*

EDWARDS TRAVEL ADVISORS, 7301 N Lincoln Ave #215, Lincolnwood, IL 60646, (708) 677-4420, (800) 541-5158, Fax: 677-4434. *Member IGTA*

ENVOY TRAVEL, 740 N Rush St, Chicago, IL 60611, (312) 787-2400, 44-ENVOY, Fax: 787-7109. *Member IGTA*

EXECUTIVE EXPRESS TRAVEL, 2200 W Higgins Rd #255, Hoffman Estates, IL 60195, (708) 519-9710, Fax: 519-9763. *Member IGTA*

HEMINGWAY TRAVEL, 1825 N Clark St, Chicago, IL 60614, (312) 440-9870, Fax: 440-9851. *Member IGTA*

HORIZON EXPERTS IN TRAVEL, 7012 W North Ave, Chicago, IL 60635, (312) 237-1178.

LEADER TRAVEL, One S State St, Corp. Level, Chicago, IL 60603, (312) 346-9707, Fax: 346-9710. *Member IGTA*

RENAISSANCE TRAVEL SERVICES, 4S100 Rt 59L, Naperville, IL 60563, (708) 961-0010, Fax: 961-0018. Ask for Michael.

RIVER NORTH TRAVEL, 432 N Clark St, Chicago, IL 60610, (312) 527-2269. *Member IGTA*

SEVEN SEAS TRAVEL, PO Box 3513, Bloomington, IL 61702-3513, (309) 662-8711, Fax: 663-2948. *Member IGTA*

SHORE TRAVEL, 351 W Hubbard St #105, Chicago, IL 60610, (312) 329-0015, Fax: 329-0752. *Member IGTA*

SPACE TRAVEL, 2052 N Kenmore, Chicago, IL 60613-2002, (312) 944-2304.

TAN TRAVEL, 107 S Marion St, Oak Park, IL 60302, (708) 386-6363, (800) 777-8261, Fax: (708) 386-6471.

THIRTY-FIVE FORTY TRAVEL, 3340 N Clark, #215, Chicago, IL 60657, (312) 477-3540.

TRAVEL N.E.T., 1660 N LaSalle St #606, Chicago, IL 60614, (312) 564-8000. *Member IGTA*

TRAVEL SPIRIT, 2512 N Lincoln Ave, Chicago, IL 60614, (312) 975-0055, Fax: 975-0085.

TRAVEL WITH US, LTD, 919 N Michigan Ave #3102, Chicago, IL 60611, (312) 944-2244, (800) 441-9608, Fax: 944-4370. *Member IGTA*

TRIANGLE TRAVEL, 8501 S 77th Ct, Bridgeview, IL 60455, (708) 599-0411.

TRIANGLE TRAVEL & CRUISE, PO Box 548, Frankfort, IL 60423, (815) 464-6460, (800) 214-5514, Fax: (815) 464-6461. Ask for John. *Member IGTA*

VILLAGE TRAVEL, 3008 N Water, Decatur, IL 62526, (217) 875-5640, Fax: 875-7566. *Member IGTA*

VIVA TRAVEL & TOURS, 2717 W Cermak Rd, Chicago, IL 60623, (312) 254-5900. Ask for Juanita.

YELLOW BRICK ROAD, THE TRAVEL AGENCY, 1500

W Balmoral Ave, Chicago, IL 60640, (312) 561-1800, Fax: (312) 561-4497. *Member IGTA*

YOUR CUSTOM TRAVEL AGENT, 32-W 151 Anderson Lane, Naperville, IL 60563, (708) 851-7888. *Member IGTA*

INDIANA

AMBASSADOR CORPORATE CENTER, 5701 Wesbriar Ln, Evansville, IN 47720, (812) 421-4485, Fax: 421-4493. *Member IGTA*

ATHENA TRAVEL SERVICES, 1099 N Karwick Rd, Michigan City, IN 46360, (219) 879-4461, Fax: 873-9860. *Member IGTA*

FANTASY TRAVEL, 3598 Village Ct, Gary, IN 46408, (219) 887-0553.

TRAVEL AGENTS INT'L, 2648 E 10th St, Bloomington, IN 47408, (812) 333-2262, Fax: 333-7954. Secialize in gay travel, ask for Marilyn.

WORRALL TRAVEL CRUISES & TOURS, 512 E Court Ave, Jeffersonville, IN 47130, (812) 283-5000, Fax: 283-5160. *Member IGTA*

KANSAS

PERSONAL TOUCH TRAVEL, 714 Poyntz Ave #C, Manhattan, KS 66502, (913) 539-6233, Fax: 539-1522. *Member IGTA*

PRESTIGE TRAVEL, PO Box 14985, Lenexa, KS 66285-4985, (913) 599-3700, Fax: 599-3838. *Member IGTA*

KENTUCKY

INTERNATIONAL TOURS & CRUISES, 1235 North Main, Madisonville, KY 42431, (502) 821-0025, Fax: 821-0028. *Member IGTA*

JOURNEYS TRAVEL, , (606) 331-4844, (800) 852-7439. Ask for Vicki.

LOUISIANA

ALTERNATIVE TOURS AND TRAVEL, 3003 Chartres St, New Orleans, LA 70117, (504) 949-5815, Fax: 949-5917. *Member IGTA*

AVALON TRAVEL ADVISORS, PO Box 51979, New Orleans, LA 70151, (504) 561-8400, (800) 783-9977, Fax: 581-3949. *Member IGTA*

GARTRELL TRAVEL SERVICE, 433 Gravier St, New Orleans, LA 70130, (504) 525-4040, Fax: 581-1378. *Member IGTA*

OUT & ABOUT TRAVEL, 11528 Old Hammond Hwy #610, Baton Rouge, LA 70816, (504) 272-7448, Fax: (504) 293-8736. Ask for Lori.

UNIGLOBE AMERICANA TRAVEL, 1440 Canal St, New Orleans, LA 70112, (504) 561-8100, Fax: 525-9020. Ask for Lonnie.

WORLDWIDE TRAVEL & CRUISES, 900 Terry Pkwy #B, Gretna, LA 70056, (504) 394-8834.

MAINE

ADVENTURE TRAVEL INC, PO Box 6610, Scarborough, ME 04070-6610, (207) 885-5060, Fax: 885-5062. *Member IGTA*

MARYLAND

ADVENTURES IN TRAVEL, 3900 N Charles St, Baltimore, MD 21218, (410) 467-1161, Fax: 467-1165. Ask for Ron.

ALL COUNTRIES TRAVEL AGENCY, 8635 Philadelphia Rd, Baltimore, MD 21237, ask for Isabella.

CENTRAL TRAVEL OF SILVER SPRING, 8609 Second Ave, Silver Spring, MD 20910, (301) 589-9440, Fax: 587-3870. *Member IGTA*

FALLS ROAD TRAVEL, 3649 Falls Rd, Baltimore, MD 21211, (410) 467-2600. Ask for Alice.

LAMBDA TRAVEL NETWORK, 8209 Fenton St, Silver Spring, MD 20910, (301) 565-2345.

LEISURE FOX TRAVEL, PO Box 1127, N Beach, MD 20714-1127, (410) 257-0300.

SAFE HARBORS TRAVEL, 25 South St, Baltimore, MD 21202, (301) 547-6565, Fax: 783-1912. *Member IGTA*

TRAVEL CONCEPTS (CARLSON TRAVEL NETWORK), 111 Lexington Rd, Bel Air, MD 21014, (410) 893-6567. *Member IGTA*

YOUR TRAVEL AGENT OF BELTSVILLE, 10440 Baltimore Blvd, Beltsville, MD 20705, (301) 937-0966. *Member IGTA*

MASSACHUSETTS

ADVENTURE TRAVEL, 774 Oak Hill Ave, Attleboro, MA 02703, (508) 222-3416, (800) 241-3540.

ALL PORTS CRUISE CO, 873 Western Ave, Lynn, MA 01905, (617) 581-8887, Fax: 593-0882. *Member IGTA*

ALTERNATIVE TRAVEL, 413 Lowell St, Wakefield, MA 01880, (617) 246-7480, Fax: 246-3646. *Member IGTA*

AROUND THE WORLD TRAVEL, Town House Square, Marblehead, MA 01945, (617) 631-8620, Fax: 639-0775. *Member IGTA*

CLEVELAND CIRCLE TRAVH, 1624 Beacon St, Brookline, MA 02146, (617) 734-2350.

COACH AND FOUR TRAVEL, 454-A Massachusetts Ave, Arlington, MA 02174, (617) 648-7400. Ask for James Ganley.

FIVE STAR TRAVEL SERVICES, 164 Newbury St, Boston, MA 02116, (617) 536-1999, (800) 359-1999, Fax: (617) 236-1999. *Member IGTA*

FRIENDS IN TRAVEL, 5230 Washington St, W Roxbury, MA 02132, (617) 327-8600. *Member IGTA*

GARBER TRAVEL, 20 Gray St, Boston, MA 02116, (617) 472-6203, Fax: 328-8392. Ask for Dana or Jon. *Member IGTA*

GIBB TRAVEL CORP, 673 Boylston St, Boston, MA 02116, (617) 353-0595, Fax: 353-0205. *Member IGTA*

GOING PLACES TRAVEL, 89 Devonshire St, Boston, MA 02109, (617) 720-3660, Fax: 523-7579. *Member IGTA*

IN TOWN RESERVATIONS & TRAVEL, PO Box 1983, 50 Bradford St, Provincetown, MA 02657, (508) 487-1883, (800) 67P-TOWN, Fax: 487-6140. *Member IGTA*

NORFOLK TRAVEL, 158 Main St, Norfolk, MA 02056, (508) 520-1696, (800) 669-0997, Fax: (508) 520-1840. Ask for Cathy.

OMEGA INTERNATIONAL TRAVEL, 99 Summer St (mezzanine), Boston, MA 02110, (617) 737-8511, Fax: 737-8512. *Member IGTA*

OUTER CAPE TRAVEL AGENCY, 30 Briar Lane, Wellfleet, MA 02667-1413, (508) 349-3794, Fax: 349-7207. *Member IGTA*

PRIDE TRAVEL INC, 770 Washington St, Stoughton, MA 02072, (617) 344-2999, Fax: 344-4711. *Member IGTA*

TRAVEL MANAGEMENT, 160 Commonwealth Ave, Boston, MA 02116, (617) 424-1908.

TRAVEL NETWORK, 376 Boylston St, 3rd Fl, Boston, MA 02116, (617) 262-2378, (800) 647-1509, Fax: (617) 859-2929.

TRAVEL PLUS/CRUISE CONNECTION, 1401 Centre St, Boston, MA 02131, (617) 469-5500, Fax: 469-5505.

TRAVEL YOUR WAY, 281 Needham St, Newton, MA 02164, (617) 244-4420.

TROY'S TRAVEL AGENCY, 481 Dalton Ave, Pittsfield, MA 01201, (413) 499-1346, Fax: 499-7396. *Member IGTA*

WITCH CITY TRAVEL, 2 North St, Salem, MA 01970, (508) 744-5777, Fax: 744-6660. *Member IGTA*

WORLD TRAVELERS, 132 Commercial St, Provincetown, MA 02657, (508) 487-6515, (800) 487-8747, Fax: 487-6517. *Member IGTA*

YOUR TRAVEL ARRANGEMENTS, 72 Pearl Ave, Revere, MA 02151, (617) 286-3172.

YOUR WAY TRAVEL, 145 Commercial St, Provincetown, MA 02657, (508) 487-2992.

MICHIGAN

AIR, SHIP & SHORE, 4791 14 Mile Rd, Rockford, MI 49341, (616) 696-3000, Fax: VIP-TKTS. Ask for Anne.

Travel Agents

ALTERNATIVE TRAVEL, , (810) 238-5217.

ANDERSON INTERNATIONAL TRAVEL, 1308 Michigan Ave, East Lansing, MI 48823, (517) 337-1300, Fax: 337-8561. *Member IGTA*

BEE KALT TRAVEL SERVICE, PO Box 721245, Royal Oak, MI 48072, (313) 288-9600, Fax: 435-5370. *Member IGTA*

ELLIOTT TRAVEL & TOURS, 6648 Telegraph Rd, Bloomfield Twp, MI 48301, (313) 287-4222, Fax: 287-9302. *Member IGTA*

ELLIOTT TRAVEL & TOURS, 46000 Geddes Rd #28, Canton, MI 48188, (313) 495-1301, Fax: (810) 851-8825. *Member IGTA*

HORIZONS TRAVEL, 475 Market Pl, Ann Arbor, MI 48108, (313) 663-3434. *Member IGTA*

ROYAL APPLE TRAVEL, 46000 Geddes Rd #28, Canton, MI 48188, (313) 495-1301, Fax: (712) 277-2848. *Member IGTA*

ROYAL INT'L TRAVEL SERVICE, 31455 Southfield Rd, Birmingham, MI 48025, (313) 644-1600, Fax: 644-1510. *Member IGTA*

SAUGATUCK CRUISE & TRAVEL, PO Box 672, Saugatuck, MI 49453, (616) 857-5205. *Member IGTA*

TRAVELWORLD, 29269 Dequindre, Madison Heights, MI 48071, (810) 542-7590, Fax: 399-6753. *Member IGTA*

VACATION DEPOT, 973 Cherry SE, Grand Rapids, MI 49506, (616) 454-4339, Fax: 454-4972. *Member IGTA*

WORLDWISE TRAVEL, 3055 Hayward Dr SE, Grand Rapids, MI 49546, (616) 942-7065, Fax: 956-7790. *Member IGTA*

WRIGHT WAY TRAVEL, THE, 24642 Robin, Taylor, MI 48180, (313) 946-9330. *Member IGTA*

YOUR GUY FOR TRAVEL, 85 Groveland Rd, Ortonville, MI 48462-8815, (810) 627-4393, Fax: 627-6097. *Member IGTA*

MINNESOTA

ALL AIRLINES TRAVEL, 1432 S Lake St, Forest Lake, MN 55025, (612) 464-2920, (800) 832-0304, Fax: 464-2933. *Member IGTA*

ALL AIRLINES TRAVEL, 2610 Garfield Ave S #102, Minneapolis, MN 55408, (612) 872-1706, Fax: 464-2933. *Member IGTA*

KENWOOD TRAVEL, 2101 Hennepin Ave S, Minneapolis, MN 55405-2769, (612) 871-6399, Fax: 871-8502. *Member IGTA*

LNBN PARTNERS IN TRAVEL, 825 On the Mall, Minneapolis, MN 55402-2606, (612) 338-0004, Fax: 338-2396. *Member IGTA*

MAINLINE TRAVEL, 120 S 6th St #202, Minneapolis, MN 55402, (612) 339-8461, Fax: 339-8467.

TIME OUT TRAVEL, 1515 W Lake St, Minneapolis, MN 55408, (612) 823-7244, Fax: 823-7446. *Member IGTA*

TRAVEL ABOUT, 400 S Cedar Lake Rd, Minneapolis, MN 55405, (612) 377-8955, Fax: 377-1670.

TRAVEL COMPANY, THE, 2800 University Ave SE, Minneapolis, MN 55414-3293, (612) 379-9000, Fax: 379-8258. *Member IGTA*

TRAVEL QUEST INTERNATIONAL, 245 Aldrich Ave N #305, Mineapolis, MN 55405-1617, (612) 377-7700, Fax: 374-3888. *Member IGTA*

MISSOURI

A DOOR TO TRAVEL, 410 W 39th St, Kansas City, MO 64111, (816) 561-8486.

BON VOYAGE N. TRAVEL & CRUISE CENTER, 7301 NW Tiffany Spring Rd, Kansas City, MO 64153, (816) 746-5500, Fax: 746-5632. *Member IGTA*

DYNAMIC TRAVEL, 7750 Clayton Rd #105, St Louis, MO 63117, (314) 781-8400, Fax: 781-9339. *Member IGTA*

LAFAYETTE SQUARE TRAVEL, 1801 Lafayette Ave, St. Louis, MO 63104, (314) 776-8747.

PATRIK TRAVEL, 22 N Euclid Ave #101, St. Louis, MO 63108, (314) 367-1468, Fax: 367-3861. *Member IGTA*

NEBRASKA

GOOD LIFE TOUR & TRAVEL, 8200 Fletcher Ave, Lincoln, NE 68507, (800) 233-0404, (402) 467-3900, Fax: 467-5714. Ask for Shasta.

SINN-FULLY FUN TRIPS, 3443 N Street, Lincoln, NE 68510, (402) 474-3048 phone/fax. Ask for Michael. *Member IGTA*

NEVADA

A TO Z BARGAIN TRAVEL, 3133 S Industrial Rd, Las Vegas, NV 89109, (702) 369-8671.

DELUXE TRAVEL LTD., 102 California Ave, Reno, NV 89509, (702) 323-4644, Fax: 323-3561. *Member IGTA*

GOOD TIMES TRAVEL, 624 N Rainbow Blvd, Las Vegas, NV 89107, (702) 878-8900, (800) 638-1066.

TAHOE/RENO EXPERIENCE, PO Box 4878, Incline Village, NV 89450, (702) 831- 2023, Fax: 831-2159. *Member IGTA*

ULTIMATE TRAVEL, 2291 N Green Valley Pkwy, Henderson, NV 89014, (702) 435-4004, Fax: 435-7001. *Member IGTA*

NEW HAMPSHIRE

DIVERSITY TRAVEL, 8 Stiles Rd, Salem, NH 03079, (603) 898-0011, (800) 6390-5018, (603) 898-1841.

WORLDWISE TRAVEL, 477 State St, Portsmouth, NH 03801-4326, (603) 430-9060, Fax: 430-9065. *Member IGTA*

NEW JERSEY

B'LINE TRAVEL, PO Box 222, Haddonfield, NJ 08033, (609) 429-3426. *Member IGTA*

BERKSHIRE TRAVEL, 64 Oak Ridge Rd, New Foundland, NJ 07435, (201) 208-1200, Fax: 208-1204. *Member IGTA*

BUTLER TRAVEL ASSOCIATES, 214 Mayfield Ct, Madison, NJ 07940, (908) 276-8887, Fax: 276-3312. *Member IGTA*

CONLEY'S TRAVEL AGENCY, 309 Gordn Ave, Williamstown, NJ 08094, (609) 262-1111. *Member IGTA*

CTN/TRAVEL TRENDS BY FRAN, 19-03 Maple Ave #1, Fair Lawn, NJ 07410-1553, (201) 794-9170, Fax: 794-9267. *Member IGTA*

EMERALD TRAVEL NETWORK, 36 Evesham Rd, Voorhees, NJ 08043, (609) 424-6677, Fax: 424-0991. *Member IGTA*

EMPRESS TRAVEL, 226 Rt 37 W, Toms River, NJ 08755, (908) 244-7771. Ask for Jazmin.

FLORHAM PARK TRAVEL, 15 James St, Florham Park, NJ 07932, (201) 377-1300, Fax: 377-5635. *Member IGTA*

FRANKEL TRAVEL, 60 E Hanover Ave, Morris Plains, NJ 07950, (201) 455-1111, Fax: 455-0074. *Member IGTA*

FREE SPIRIT CRUISES, 2133 Price St, Rahway, NJ 07065, (908) 388-6729, Fax: 381-5529. *Member IGTA*

FRIENDLY TRAVEL, 309 Gordon Ave, Williamstown, NJ 08094, (609) 262-1111. *Member IGTA*

GALAXSEA CRUISES, 149 Markham Place, Little Silver, NJ 07739, (908) 219-9600, Fax: 219-5191. *Member IGTA*

GOOD COMPANIONS TRAVEL & TOURS, 1105 Cooper Ct #200-A, Voorhees, NJ 08043, (609) 772-9269. *Member IGTA*

GULLIVER'S TRAVEL, 76 Main St, Woodbridge, NJ 07095, (908) 636-1120, (800) 836-8687.

MAIN STREET TRAVEL SERVICE, PO Box 864, Marlton, NJ 08053, (609) 988-0750, Fax: 988-0750. *Member IGTA*

MAPLE SHADE TRAVEL, 4 N Forklanding Rd, Maple Shade, NJ 08052, (609) 779-7277, Fax: 779-8553. *Member IGTA*

MTM TRAVEL GROUP, PO Box 319, Kendall Park, NJ 08824, (908) 940-0912, (800) 647-6730, Fax: 940-0590. *Member IGTA*

PRIDE VACATIONS & CRUISES, 63 N Gaston Ave, Somerville, NJ 08876, (800) 526-PRIDE, (908) 526-6565, Fax: 526-1521. *Member IGTA*

SHREVE LAZAR TRAVEL, 1711 Atlantic Ave, Atlantic City, NJ 08401, (609) 348-1189.

TRAVEL NAC, 317 Williams Ave, Hasbrouck Heights, NJ 07604, (201) 393-0319. Ask for Natalie or Celeste. *Member IGTA*

TRAVEL REGISTRY, PO Box 589, 127 Washington St, Rocky Hill, NJ 08553-0589, (609) 921-6900, (800) 346-6901, Fax: 497-6344.

VAGABOND TRAVEL, 542 Prospect Ave, Little Silver, NJ 07739, (908) 842-5410.

WINGS/DIVISION OF STB TRAVEL, 55 Newark St, Hoboken, NJ 07030, (201)216-1200, Fax: 216-1212. *Member IGTA*

NEW MEXICO

AMF TRAVEL, 10009 Bryan Ct NW, Albuquerque, NM 87114, (505) 898-8389, Fax: 897-8654. *Member IGTA*

ATLAS TRAVEL SERVICE, 1301 Wyoming NE, Albuquerque, NM 87112, (505) 291-6575.

PASSARIELLO TRAVEL, 9320-D Menaul NE, Albuquerque, NM 87112, (505) 296-1584, Fax: 294-5833. *Member IGTA*

THOMAS COOK TRAVEL, 6600 Indian School Rd, Albuquerque, NM 87110, (505) 883-3677, Fax: 884-0008. *Member IGTA*

UNIGLOBE ABOVE & BEYOND TRAVEL, 2225 E Lohman #A, Las Cruces, NM 88001, (505) 527-0200, Fax: 527-0366.

NEW YORK

ACE CRUISE MASTERS, 282 Manhattan Ave #3 South, New York, NY 10026, (212) 749-2626, Fax: 749-5178. *Member IGTA*

ADONIS TRAVEL, DBA DASELI, 300 Vanderbilt Motor parkway #225, Hauppauge, NY 11788, (516) 231-4821, Fax: 231-4825. *Member IGTA*

ALL CONTINENT TRAVEL, 227 E 56th St, New York, NY 10022, (212) 371-7171, Fax: 887-2072. *Member IGTA*

ALLEGRO ENTERPRISES, 900 West End Ave #12C, New York, NY 10025-3525, (212) 666-6700.

AMERICAN EXPRESS TRAVEL, 1185 6th Ave, New York, NY 10036, (212) 398-8585. *Member IGTA*

ATLAS TRAVEL CENTER, 1545 Central Ave, Albany, NY 12205-5044, (518) 464-0271, Fax: 464-0273. *Member IGTA*

AVALON TRAVEL, 9421 3rd Ave, Brooklyn, NY 11209, (718) 833-5500, Fax: 238-3858. *Member IGTA*

BARD GROUP, THE, 239 W 21st St #3B, New York, NY 10011, (212) 242-1165, Fax: 727-9070. *Member IGTA*

BASBRASIL TRAVEL, 551 Fifth Ave #1117, New York, NY 10176, (212) 682-5310, Fax: 953-2398.

BON ADVENTURE, 1173A Second Ave #135, New York, NY 10021, (212) 759-2206, Fax: (212) 593-7612. *Member IGTA*

CATHERINE'S TRAVEL SERVICE, 528 Haley Rd, Ontario, NY 14519, (315) 524-8733.

CHOICE TRAVEL, 130 Garth Rd #448, Scarsdale, NY 10583, (914) 472-5100, Fax: 725-2115. *Member IGTA*

COURTYARD TRAVEL, 50 Brompton Rd Apt 1C, Great Neck, NY 11021, (516) 773-3700, Fax: 829-4931. *Member IGTA*

D.C. WORLD WIDE TRAVEL, 251 W 19th St #4C, New York, NY 10011, (212) 243-7529, Fax: 647-1629. *Member IGTA*

DE PREZ TRAVEL BUREAU, 325 Westminster Rd, Rochester, NY 14607, (716) 234-3615, Fax: 442-8309. *Member IGTA*

DESTINATIONS UNLIMITED, 130 Theater Place, Buffalo, NY 14202, (716) 855-1955, (800) 528-8877, Fax: 855-0016. *Member IGTA*

DEVILLE TRAVEL SERVICE, 7725 3rd Ave, Brooklyn, NY 11209, (718) 680-2700, Fax: 680-2743. *Member IGTA*

EARTH TRAVELERS, 683 Dick Rd, Buffalo, NY 14225, (716) 685-2900. *Member IGTA*

EDLEN TRAVEL, 161 S Middletown Rd, Nanuet, NY 10954, (914) 624-2100, Fax: 624-2315. *Member IGTA*

GATEWAY TRAVEL, 1300 Hylan Blvd, Staten Island, NY 10305, (718) 667-1100.

GINMAR TRAVEL, 392 Central Park W, 8th fl, New York, NY 10025, (212) 866-9452, (800) GIN-MAR1. Ask for Robert.

GREAT EXPECTATIONS, 2345 Highland Ave, Rochester, NY 14610, (716) 244-8430, Fax: 244-8749. *Member IGTA*

HEIDIES TRAVEL & TOUR, 2308 Seneca St, Buffalo, NY 14227, (716) 821-1991, Fax: 826-5658. *Member IGTA*

HISA TRAVEL, 3699 W Henrietta Rd, Rochester, NY 14623, (716) 334-0941, Fax: 334-4212. *Member IGTA*

INDEPENDENT TRAVEL CONSULTANT, 245 8th Ave #233, New York, NY 10011, (212) 229-1801.

ISLANDERS' CLUB/EMPRESS TRAVEL, 224 West 4 St, New York, NY 10014, (212) 206-6900, Fax: 206-6904. *Member IGTA*

J. BETTE TRAVEL, 4712 Ave. N. #279, Brooklyn, NY 11234, (718) 241-3872. Ask for Joan or Toni.

KENNEDY TRAVEL, 267-10 Hillside Ave, Queens, NY 11004, (718) 347-7433, Fax: 347-1291. *Member IGTA*

LE SOLEIL TOURS, 1323 72nd St, Brooklyn, NY 11228, (718) 232-4060. *Member IGTA*

MAINLINE TRAVEL, 680 Pittsford-Victor Rd, Pittsford, NY 14534, (716) 248-2530, Fax: 248-2709. *Member IGTA*

NEW PALTZ TRAVEL CENTER, 7 Cherry Hill Center, New Paltz, NY 12561, (914) 255-7706, Fax: 255-8015. *Member IGTA*

NOAH'S ARK TRAVEL, 33A Roosevelt Dr, W Haverstraw, NY 10993, (914) 429-7556. *Member IGTA*

OPTIMA TRAVEL, 460 State St #202, Rochester, NY 14608, (716) 546-2840, Fax: 458-0620. Ask for Noeme or Ivette.

OUR TIME VOYAGES, 53 Park Place #502, New York, NY 10007, (212) 406-0627, Fax: 406-0631. *Member IGTA*

OUT EVERYWHERE, PO Box 4571, Great Neck, NY 11023, (516) 482-1405, Fax: 466-2847. *Member IGTA*

PARK AVENUE TRAVEL, 25 Buckingham St, Rochester, NY 14607, (716) 256-3080, Fax: 473-7436. *Member IGTA*

PEQUA TRAVEL, 915 N Broadway, N Massapequa, NY 11758, (516) 795-2345.

PIED PIPER TRAVEL, 330 West 42nd St #1601, New York, NY 10036, (212) 239-2412, Fax: 643-1598. *Member IGTA*

PLAZA TRAVEL, 877 Mountain Rd, Owego, NY 13827, (607) 729-2225.

PONDFIELD/QUI TRAVEL, 7 Boyd Place, Bronxville, NY 10708, (914) 779-2757. Ask for Jacqui.

RAINBOW TRAVEL, 1109 1st Ave #4A, New York, NY 10021, (212) 935-7246. *Member IGTA*

ROGERS TRAVEL AGENCY, 140 Medford Ave, Patchogue, NY 11772, (516) 289-5252, (800) 753-2400, Fax: 289-4071. Ask for Marta.

RTA TRAVEL, 93-05 63rd Dr, Rego Park, NY 11374, (718) 275-3144.

SCARSDALE TAN & TRAVEL, 390 Central Park Ave, Greenville Plaza, Scarsdale, NY 10583, (914) 472-2273, Fax: 472-6682. *Member IGTA*

SEALANDAIR TRAVEL, 41 W 72nd St, New York, NY 10023, (212) 697-3447, Fax: 986-2940. *Member IGTA*

STARGAZER TRAVEL & TOURS, 21 W 39th St 5th floor, New York, NY 10018, (212) 840-2900, Fax: 768-8370. *Member IGTA*

STEVENS TRAVEL MGT, 432 Park Ave S, 9th floor, New York, NY 10016, (212) 696-4300, ext 270, Fax: 696-0591. Ask for Fred Shames.
Member IGTA

TRADE WIND, 6 Jay St, Spring Valley, NY 10977, (914) 352-4134. Ask for Greg.
Member IGTA

TRADEWINDS TRAVEL, 9 Hobby St, Pleasantville, NY 10570-0298, (914) 769-6804, Fax: 769-5619. *Member IGTA*

TRAVEL COMPANY OF ALBANY, THE, 41 State St #110, Albany, NY 12207, (518) 434-9900, Fax: 433-9038. Specializing in gay travel.

TRAVEL MASTERS OF N.Y., 20 Lakeview Ave, Rockville Centre, NY 11570, (800) MORE-TVL, (516) 766-0707, Fax:

Travel Agents

766-5126. Ask for Jesse or Sonya. *Member IGTA*

TRAVEL SOURCE NEW YORK, 281 Ave C #8A, New York, NY 10009, (212) 673-6042, Fax: 677-9858. *Member IGTA*

TRAVEL TAMMARO, 139-15 83rd Ave #125, Briarwood, NY 11435, (718) 805-0907.

TRIANGLE TRAVEL, 5 Beekmen St #920, New York, NY 10038, (212) 608-1000, (800) 572-5266.

VIRGA'S TRAVEL SERVICE, Rt. 82, PO Box 460, Hopewell Jct., NY 12533, (914) 221-2455, Fax: 226-6260. *Member IGTA*

WELCOME TRAVEL AGENCY, 340 Portion Rd, Lake Ronkonkoma, NY 11779, (516) 585-7070, Fax: 585-7267. *Member IGTA*

NORTH CAROLINA

CAROLINA TRAVEL, 2054 Carolina Circle Mall, Greensboro, NC 27405, (919) 621-9000. *Member IGTA*

CREATIVE ADVENTURE TRAVEL, 136 Harmon Ave, Winston-Salem, NC 27106, (910) 750-0733, Fax: 724-1272. *Member IGTA*

PINK TRIANGLE TRAVEL, 309 W Martin St, Raleigh, NC 27601, (919) 755-1404, Fax: 829-0830. *Member IGTA*

RAINBOW TRAVEL, PO Box 31288, Raleigh, NC 27622, (919) 571-9054, Fax: (919) 782-1936. Ask for Rolo. *Member IGTA*

TRAVEL ASSOCIATES, 100 W Innes St #102, Salisbury, NC 28144, (704) 637-9000, Fax: 637-9013 *Member IGTA*

TRAVEL CENTER, THE, 905 W Main St, #5, Durham, NC 27701, (919) 682-9378, (800) 334-1085, Fax: (619) 687-0903. Ask for Mària.

TRAVEL QUEST, 3030-A S Main St, High Point, NC 27263, (919) 434-3867, (800) 798-3867, Fax: 454-5329. *Member IGTA*

UNIGLOBE GATEWAY TRAVEL, 1919 South Blvd, Charlotte, NC 28203, (704) 377-1957, Fax: 377-1952. *Member IGTA*

VIDEO BOATIQUE, 5719 Shadow Creek Rd, Charlotte, NC 28226, (704) 544-1727, (800) 685-BOAT (2628). cruise-only travel agency.

OHIO

ACTION TRAVEL - CLEVELAND, 1700 E 13th St #3LE, Cleveland, OH 44114, (216) 575-0823, (800) 854-0601.

AD'E TRAVEL INTERNATIONAL, PO Box 94198, Cleveland, OH 44101, (216) 771-5551, Fax: 771-5552. *Member IGTA*

BROOKSIDE TRAVEL AGENCY, PO Box 89, Brookfield, OH 44403, (216) 448-4232, Fax: 448-5747. *Member IGTA*

CHAPEL HILL TRAVEL CENTER, Chapel Hill Mall #477, Akron, OH 44310, (216) 633-9334, Fax: 633-1697. *Member IGTA*

CINCINNATI CRUISE CONNECTION, 7485 Colerain Ave, Cincinnati, OH 45231-5307, (513) 729-2261, Fax: 729-2264. *Member IGTA*

CORNERS OF THE WORLD INT'L TRAVEL, 1631 Remington Dr #9, Westlake, OH 44145, (216) 892-0022, (800) 368-TRIP. Ask for David.

GREAT WAYS TRAVEL, 4625 W Bancroft St, Toledo, OH 43615, (419) 536-8000, Fax: 536-8005. *Member IGTA*

JUST TRAVEL INC, 82 S High St, Dublin, OH 43017, (614) 791-9500.

L.B. BURGER TRAVEL SERVICE, 517 Bank One Bldg, Youngstown, OH 44503, (216) 744-5035, Fax: 744-4519. *Member IGTA*

PARKSIDE TRAVEL USA, 1431 S Main St #115, Akron, OH 44301, (216) 668-3334, (800) 552-1647, Fax: (216) 724-8014. *Member IGTA*

PIER 'N PORT TRAVEL, 2692 Madison Rd #H1, Cincinnati, OH 45208, (513) 841-9900, Fax: 841-5930.

ROFFLER CRUISE & TRAVEL, 2786 Cleveland Rd, Wooster, OH 44691, (216) 345-7755, Fax: 345-7756. Ask for Neil.

SERENDIB, 14728 Clifton Blvd, Lakewood, OH 44107-2522., *Member IGTA*

SUN LOVERS' CRUISES & TRAVEL, 3860 Rocky River Dr, Cleveland, OH 44111-4111, (216) 252-0900, (800) 323-1362, Fax: 252-0123. *Member IGTA*

TOLEDO TRAVEL CLUB, 4612 Talmadge Rd, Toledo, OH 43623, (419) 471-2820, Fax: 471-2877. *Member IGTA*

TRAVEL AGENTS INT'L, 2855 W Market St #115, Akron, OH 44333, (216) 836-6500, Fax: 836-6506. *Member IGTA*

TRAVEL EXCHANGE GROUP, 1020 Kingston Pl, Cincinnati, OH 45204, (513) 471-5772.

TRAVEL EXCHANGE GROUP, THE, 4600 Montgomery Road #105, Cincinnati, OH 45212, (513) 841-5595. Ask for Melissa. *Member IGTA*

TRAVEL PLACE, THE, 1392 Warren Rd #2, Lakewood, OH 44107, (216) 521-4733, Fax: 521-6986. *Member IGTA*

TRAVELPLEX EAST, PO Box 360956, Columbus, OH 43236-0956, (614) 337-3155, Fax: 337-3165. *Member IGTA*

UNIGLOBE DOWNTOWN TRAVEL, 201 E Broad St, Columbus, OH 43215, (614) 228-8668, (800) 783-8060, Fax: (614) 228-7044.

UNIGLOBE FIVE STAR TRAVEL, 1160 Hanna Bldg, 1422 Euclid Ave, Cleveland, OH 44115, (216) 575-0813, (800) 575-0813, Fax: (216) 575-1614.

VICTORIA TRAVEL, 3330 Erie Ave 1A, Cincinnati, OH 45208, (513) 871-1100, (800) 626-4932, Fax: 871-7344. *Member IGTA*

WEST CHESTER TRAVEL, 7130 Lindley Worley Rd, Pleasant Plain, OH 45162, (513) 877-2762, Fax: 777-4638. *Member IGTA*

OKLAHOMA

INTERNATIONAL TOURS OF CLAREMORE, 5240 SW Brandon Terrace, Claremore, OK 74017, (918) 341-6866. *Member IGTA*

OREGON

ADVANTAGE TRAVEL SERVICE, 812 SW Washington St #200, Portland, OR 97205-3210, (503) 225-0186.

AFFORDABLE VACATIONS, 7435 SW Hermosa Way, Tigard, OR 97223, (503) 684-1236, Fax: 620-5184. *Member IGTA*

BARBUR TRAVEL, 9049 SW Barbur Blvd, Portland, OR 97219, (503) 246-2469 Fax: 246-4689.

CLASSIC WORLD TRAVEL, 656 Charnelton, Eugene, OR 97401, (503) 343-1992, Fax: 343-2489. *Member IGTA*

GLOBAL AFFAIR, 285 E 5th Ave, Eugene, OR 97401, (503) 343-8595, (800) 755-2753, Fax: 687-1558. *Member IGTA*

GULLIVER'S TRAVEL & VOYAGES, 514 NW 9th Ave, Portland, OR 97209, (503) 221-0013, Fax: 230-0355. *Member IGTA*

HAWTHORNE TRAVEL COMPANY, 1939 SE Hawthorne Blvd, Portland, OR 97214, (503) 232-5944, Fax: 232-4662. *Member IGTA*

IN TOUCH TRAVEL, 121 SW Morrison #270, Portland, OR 97204, (503) 223-1062, Fax: 224-4920. *Member IGTA*

J & M TRAVEL, 4415 NE Sandy Blvd #200, Portland, OR 97213, (503) 249-0305, Fax: 280-1717. *Member IGTA*

KAZ TRAVEL SERVICES, 1975 SW First Ave #K, Portland, OR 97201, (503) 223-4585, Fax: 223-2361. *Member IGTA*

MIKUNI TRAVEL SERVICE, 1 SW Columbia St #1010, Portland, OR 97258-2011, (503) 227-3639, Fax: 227-0602. *Member IGTA*

TRAVEL AGENTS INT'L, 917 SW Washington St, Portland, OR 97205-2818, (503) 223-1100, Fax: 497-1015. Ask for Rip. *Member IGTA*

TRAVEL SHOP, THE, PO Box 0987, Beaverton, OR 97075, (503) 684-8533, Fax: 624-1339. Ask for Mark for men's travel. *Member IGTA*

PENNSYLVANIA

BERNIE'S WORLD TRAVEL, 144 E Independence St, Shamokin, PA 17872, (717) 644-0831. *Member IGTA*

BON AMI TRAVEL SERVICE, 309 First St, Apollo, PA 15613, (412) 478-2000, Fax: 478-5226. *Member IGTA*

CAMELOT TRAVEL & TOURS, PO Box 3874, Erie, PA 16508, (814) 835-3434.

CARLSON TRAVEL NETWORK/IOBST TRAVEL SVC, 328 Main St, Emmaus, PA 18049, (610) 965-9025, Fax: 967-4179. *Member IGTA*

FLIGHT OF FANCY, PO Box 234, 408 York Road, New Hope, PA 18938, (215) 862-9665, Fax: 862-9764. *Member IGTA*

HOLIDAY TRAVEL INTERNATIONAL, 5832 Library Rd, Bethel Park, PA 97301, (412) 835-8747, Fax: 835-9149. *Member IGTA*

HORIZON TRAVEL, 4 Market Place, Logan Square, New Hope, PA 18938, (215) 862-3373.

INTERNATIONAL TOURS, 8 Cavender Lane, Landenberg, PA 19350, (215) 255-4862, Fax: 677-1960. *Member IGTA*

LAMBDA TRAVEL, The Bourse #545, Philadelphia, PA 19106, (215) 925-3011. Ask for Scott. *Member IGTA*

LIBERTY TRAVEL, 9376 Fairmont Terrace, Tobyhanna, PA 18466, (717) 894-9076, Fax: 476-9099. *Member IGTA*

MAKEFIELD TRAVEL, 2 Lookout Ln, Washington Crossing, PA 18977, (215) 493-2998, (800) 435-4268.

MORGAN DELFOSSE TRAVEL, 360 Pine Hollow Rd, Level Green, PA 15085, (412) 372-1846.

ODYSSEY TRAVEL, 1501 Wilmington Pike, West Chester, PA 19382, (215) 358-0411, Fax: 358-3752. *Member IGTA*

PITTSBURGH TRAVEL SERVICE, Shops at Station Square, Pittsburgh, PA 15219, (412) 471-7417. *Member IGTA*

SIGMUND TRAVEL BUREAU, 262 S 12th St, Philadelphia, PA 19107, (215) 735-0090.

TURKALY ASSOC./CLASSIC TRAVEL, 1319 Boyle St, Pittsburgh, PA 15212, (412) 322-1696, Fax: 322-0619. *Member IGTA*

WILL TRAVEL, 118 S Bellevue Ave, Langhorne, PA 19047, (215) 741-4492, (800) 443-7460. Ask for Pat.

ZELLER TRAVEL/BROWNSTOWN, 4213 Oregon Pike, Ephrata, PA 17522, (717) 859-4710, (800) 331-4359, Fax: 859-3638. *Member IGTA*

RHODE ISLAND

AIR-SEA TRAVEL, 135 Sandy Bottom Rd, Coventry, RI 02816, (401) 826-2040.

CONTINENTAL TRAVEL AGENCY, 20 Cedar Swamp Rd, Smithfield, RI 02917, (401) 232-0980, (800) 234-5209, Fax: 232-0470. Ask for Jeanne. *Member IGTA*

SOUTH COUNTY TRAVEL, 600 Kingstown Rd, Wakefield, RI 02879, (401) 789-9731, Fax: 792-3647. Ask for Helen.

TRAVEL CONCEPTS, 60 Broadway #906, Providence, RI 02903, (401) 453-6000, (800) 983-6900, Fax: 453-0222. *Member IGTA*

SOUTH CAROLINA

ALL AROUND TRAVEL, Rt 1 Box 502, Eutawville, SC 29408, (803) 854-2475, Fax: 854-2734. *Member IGTA*

B & A TRAVEL SERVICE, 2728 Devine St, Columbia, SC 29205, (803) 256-0547, Fax: 779-4871. *Member IGTA*

PAL TRAVEL, 600 Laurens Rd, Greenville, SC 29607, (803) 235-6885, (800) 776-7257.

RUSSELL TRAVEL SERVICE, 219 Hwy 52 N, #R, Moncks Corner, SC 29461, (803) 761-6888, Fax: 899-7909. *Member IGTA*

TRAVEL MASTERS OF COLUMBIA, PO Box 5916, Columbia, SC 29250, (803) 254-4777.

TRAVEL UNLIMITED, 612 St Andrews Rd #8, Columbia, SC 29210, (803) 798-8122, Fax: 798-9339. *Member IGTA*

TENNESSEE

BRYAN TRAVEL, 5614 Kingston Pike, Knoxville, TN 37919, (615) 588-8166, (800) 234-8166. Ask for Edward or Mike. *Member IGTA*

TEXAS

ADVANCE TRAVEL, 10700 NW Freeway #160, Houston, TX 77092, (713) 682-2002, Fax: 680-3200. *Member IGTA*

AFTER FIVE TRAVEL & CRUISES, 2602 Killdeer Ln, Humble, TX 77396-1826, (713) 441-1369, (800) 335-1369, Fax: (713) 441-1275. *Member IGTA*

B&B TRAVEL CONNECTIONS, 6303 Silver Fox, San Antonio, TX 78247, (210) 979-7811 Fax: 366-9581. *Member IGTA*

BROWN-WILKINS & ASSOC TRAVEL, 3311 Richmond #230, Houston, TX 77098, (713) 942-0664, Fax: 942-0665. *Member IGTA*

BUCKINGHAM TRAVEL, 604 Brazos St #200, Austin, TX 78701, (512) 477-7736, Fax: 477-7739. *Member IGTA*

CREATIVE TRAVEL CENTER, 8670 Spicewood Springs Rd #10, Austin, TX 78759, (512) 331-9560, Fax: 331-6230. *Member IGTA*

CRUISE AGAIN II, 4230 LBJ Freeway #215, Dallas, TX 75244, (214) 392-7086, Fax: 239-9680.

DAVID PEARSON TRAVEL, 2737 Exposition Blvd, Austin, TX 78703-1206, (512) 482-8197. *Member IGTA*

DOUBLE-O-SEVEN TRAVEL, 1120 Nottingham, Cedar Hill, TX 75104, (214) 291-0133. *Member IGTA*

JACKS TRAVEL HOLIDAYS, 1969-C W TC Jester, Houston, TX 77008, (713) 880-3528, Fax: 880-4865. *Member IGTA*

M.S. WORLWIDE TRAVEL SERVICES, 1300 S University Dr #316, Ft Worth, TX 76107, (800) 484-9020 ext 0041, (817) 577-0041, Fax: 577-2945.

ODYSSEY TRAVEL, 11829 Perrin Beitel, San Antonio, TX 78217, (512) 656-0083, Fax: 656-3980. *Member IGTA*

ODYSSEY TRAVEL, PO Box 39776, San Antonio, TX 78219-6776, (210) 655-8722. *Member IGTA*

PLAZA TRAVEL INC, 15851 Dallas Pkwy #190, Dallas, TX 75248, (214) 980-1191, Fax: 980-2877. *Member IGTA*

STRONG TRAVEL SERVICES, 8201 Preston Rd #160, Dallas, TX 75225, (214) 361-0027, Fax: 361-0139. *Member IGTA*

TRAVEL FRIENDS, 8080 N Central #320, Dallas, TX 75206, (214) 891-8833, (800) 862-8833, Fax: 891-8873.

TRAVEL SOURCE, 4131 N Central Expy #450 LB46, Dallas, TX 75204, (214) 520-8844, Fax: 443-9919.

UNIGLOBE FIRST CHOICE TRAVEL, 2236 W Holcombe at Greenbriar, Houston, TX 77030, (713) 667-0580, Fax: 667-0180. *Member IGTA*

UNIGLOBE FOX TRAVEL, 25701 I-45 North #3A, Spring, TX 77380, (713) 363-0808, Fax: 363-0916. *Member IGTA*

WINDSOR TRAVEL, 600 Travis #2075, Houston, TX 77002, (713) 228-1111. Specializing in gay travel. *Member IGTA*

WOODLAKE TRAVEL, 1704 Post Oak Blvd, Houston, TX 77056, (713) 840-8500, Fax: 840-0954. *Member IGTA*

UTAH

CRUISE & TRAVEL MASTERS, 4905 S 900 E #630, Salt Lake City, UT 84117-5703, (801) 268-4470, Fax: 268-5703. *Member IGTA*

JETSTAR TRAVEL, 1740 Meadowmoor Rd, Salt Lake City, UT 84117, (801) 278-1060. *Member IGTA*

VERMONT

AMERICAN-INTERNATIONAL TRAVEL SERVICE, 114 Church St, PO Box 852, Burlington, VT 05402, (802) 864-9827, Fax: 864-0612. *Member IGTA*

CARMEN'S HORIZONS TRAVEL, Broad St, RFD 1, Lyndonville, VT 05851, (802) 626-8176, Fax: 626-8178.

VIRGINIA

CAREFREE CRUISES, Rte 1, Box 24, Midland, VA 22728-9704, (703) 439-2403, Fax: 439-1610. *Member IGTA*

COVINGTON INT'L TRAVEL, 4401 Dominion Blvd, Glen Allen, VA 23060, (804) 747-7077, Fax: 273-0009. Ask for Roy. *Member IGTA*

Travel Agents

CULPEPER TRAVEL, 763 Madison Rd #208-B, Culpeper, VA 22701, (703) 825-1258, Fax: 825-1276. *Member IGTA*

OMEGA WORLD TRAVEL, 5616 Bismach Dr #4, Alexandria, VA 22312, (202) 682-1309.

TRAVEL MERCHANTS, 332 N Great Neck Rd #104, Virginia Beach, VA 23454, (804) 463-0014, Fax: 463-3239. Ask for John. *Member IGTA*

TRAVELINK, 1700-H George Washington Hwy, Yorktown, VA 23693, (804) 599-3000, Fax: 599-6042. *Member IGTA*

UNIGLOBE DIRECT TRAVEL, 1800 Diagonal Rd Plaza-D, Alexandria, VA 22314, (703) 684-8824, Fax: 836-4174. *Member IGTA*

WASHINGTON

A BETTER WAY TO TRAVEL, 10006 NW 4th Ave, Vancouver, WA 98685, (206) 573-4750, Fax: 573-8780. *Member IGTA*

ALL-AROUND TRAVEL, 4701 42 Ave SW, Seattle, WA 98116, (206) 938-3030, Fax: 938-8462. Ask for Davyn. *Member IGTA*

BLACK TIE TRAVEL, 1411 Fourth Ave #920, Seattle, WA 98101, (206) 622-4409, (800) 776-2930.

CAPITOL HILL TRAVEL, 401 Broadway E #204, Seattle, WA 98102, (206) 726-8996, (800) 726-8996, Fax: 726-1004. *Member IGTA*

COUNCIL TRAVEL, 219 Broadway Ave E, #17, Seattle, WA 98102, (206) 329-4567, Fax: 329-1982.

CRUISE WORLD, 901 Fairview Ave N, #A-150, Seattle, WA 98109, (206) 343-0221, (800) 340-0221, Fax: (206) 343-0771.

DONNA'S TRAVEL & CRUISE, PO Box 1529, Stanwood, WA 98292, (206) 629-9751, Fax: 629-9754. *Member IGTA*

ELLENSBURG TRAVEL, 306 N Pine, Ellensburg, WA 98926, (509) 925-6933.

FODOR'S TRAVEL, 1418 E Olive Way, Seattle, WA 98122, (206) 328-5385, Fax: 324-9501. *Member IGTA*

MARY NORTH TRAVEL SERVICE, 3701 SW Alaska St, Seattle, WA 98126, (206) 935-3404, Fax: 938-2107. *Member IGTA*

MUTUAL TRAVEL, 600 108th Ave NE #104, Bellevue, WA 98004, (206) 637-6913, (800) 443-4431, Fax: (206) 637-6999. Ask for Janet. *Member IGTA*

MUTUAL TRAVEL, 1201 3rd Ave, Seattle, WA 98111, (206) 461-2490, (800) 348-8800, Fax: (206) 554-2890. *Member IGTA*

ROYALTY TRAVEL, 1200 5th Ave, IBM Plaza Level West, Seattle, WA 98101, (206) 623-7474, Fax: 623-8283. Ask for Greg or James. *Member IGTA*

SECURITY PACK TRAVEL, 1101 Boylston Ave, Seattle, WA 98101-2818, (206) 322-8305, Fax: 323-5785. *Member IGTA*

SUNSHINE TRAVEL, 519 N 85th St, Seattle, WA 98103, (206) 784-8141. *Member IGTA*

TRAVEL AGENTS INT'L, 513 Olive Way, Seattle, WA 98101-1713, (206) 343-0809, Fax: 343-0810. *Member IGTA*

TRAVEL PLACE, THE, West 505 Parkade Plaza, Spokane, WA 99201, (509) 624-7434. Ask for Myke.

TRAVEL SOLUTIONS, 4009 Gilman Ave W, Seattle, WA 98199, (206) 281-7202, (800) 727-1616, Fax: (206) 281-7139. *Member IGTA*

TROPICAL ADVENTURES TRAVEL, 111 Second North, Seattle, WA 98109, (206) 441-3483, (800) 247-3483 (outside WA), Fax: (206) 441-5431. Ask for Ken.

UNIGLOBE ADVANTAGE TRAVEL, 505 Cedar Ave #C1, Marysville, WA 98270, (206) 659-8054 (ext 6969), (800) 788-3523. Ask for Jared.

VACATION PLACES, PO Box 20457, Seattle, WA 98102, (206) 324-6996. *Member IGTA*

WOODSIDE TRAVEL, 3130 E Madison St, Seattle, WA 98112, (206) 462-1266, (800) 262-1266, Fax: (206) 322-2980.

WEST VIRGINIA

WILD WONDERFUL TRAVEL, 1517 Jackson St, Charleston, WV 25311, (304) 345-0491. *Member IGTA*

WISCONSIN

BOTTOM LINE TRAVEL, 3610 N Oakland Ave, Milwaukee, WI 53211, (414) 964-6199, (800) 933-8330, Fax: 964-6303. *Member IGTA*

FAR HORIZONS TRAVEL, 5902 Hwy 51, McFarland, WI 53558, (608) 258-1600.

HORIZON TRAVEL, N 81 W 15028 Appleton Ave, Menomonee Falls, WI 53051, (414) 255-0704. *Member IGTA*

TRAVEL PLEX, 310 W Wisconsin Ave, Milwaukee, WI 53203, (414) 223-2200, (800) 397-5606, Fax: (414) 223-2211. Ask for David.

TRIO TRAVEL & IMPORTS LTD, 2812 W Forest Home Ave, Milwaukee, WI 53215, (414) 384-8746.

Tour Operators

AFRICA

CROSS TOURS & TRAVEL, Cape Town, South Africa, (27-21) 439 1858, 461 6212, Fax: 434 9999.

NICHE TRAVEL MARKETING, PO Box 64217, Highlands North 2037, South Africa, (27-11) 648 0730, Fax: 648-7140. *Member IGTA*

SOUTHEAST ASIA

COLORS OF ASIA, 16th floor, Jl. Jenderal Sudiramn, Kav. 58, 12190 Jakarta, Indonesia, (62-21) 250 5370, Fax: 250 5371. *Member IGTA*

EUROPE

BAMBOU, 32 rue St. Marc, Paris 75002, France, (33-1) 42 60 460, Fax: 42 60 5617. *Member IGTA*

BEACH BOY HOLIDAYS, W.G.Plein 104, 1054 SC Amsterdam, Holland, (31)(20) 616 47 47, Fax: (31)(20) 12 83 83. *Member IGTA*

DE GRUPSTAL, Wjitteringswei 67, 8495 JM Aldeboarn, The Netherlands, (05663) 1465, (05663) 1230.

DISCUS TRAVEL, Schwetzinger Str 93, 68165 Mannheim, Germany, (49) (621) 40 9627, Fax: 44 1340. *Member IGTA*

FEMINISTISCHER SEGLERINNEN VEREIN, c/o Ute Weidlich, Grüneborgstr 1, 2000 Hamburg 1 Germany, (040) 880 4868.

FINNREISE SPEZIAL, Sächsische Str 38, 1000 Berlin 31, Germany.,

FIRMA HAGI, c/o Floor Hijmans, Huibersstraat 8, 7412JR Deventer, (05700) 41473.

FRAUEN UNTERWEGS, Potsdamerstr 139, 1000 Berlin 30 Germany, (030) 215 1022, Fax: 216 9852.

HANNIBAL, 15 Evelyn Road, Richmond, Surrey TW9 2TF, England, (081) 940 1270 (tel/fax).

HOLIGAYS, Thomas-Mann-Str 56, Bonn 53111, Germany, (49-228) 985 180, 985 18 13, Fax: 985 18 18. *Member IGTA*

KREMLIN TOURS, THE, PO Box 44, Moscow 105318, E-318 Russia, (7-095) 962 91 78, Fax: 962 92 44. *Member IGTA*

MILU TOURS, Motzstrasse 23, 10777 Berlin, Germany, (49-30) 217 6488, Fax: (49-30) 214 3374.

NOUWELLE WASSERSPORT FÜR FRAUEN, c/o Fairlines, Kleiner Schäferkamp 32, 20357 Hamburg 36 Germany, (040) 44 14 56, Fax: 44 05 70.

OZGAY, Leidsestraat 32 or 3L, 1017 PB Amsterdam, The Netherlands, (31-20) 627 3608, Fax: (31-20) 627 4869. *Member AGLTA, IGTA*

PARTNERS IN TRAVEL, Jan Luykenstraat 12, Amsterdam 1071CM, The Netherlands, (31-20) 679 9710, Fax: 676 0463. *Member IGTA*

PORTUGAL TRAVEL, 84 York St, London, W1, England, (44) (071) 723 7774.

REISEBÜRO AM HELLKAMP, Hellkamp 17, 20255 Hamburg, Germany, (49-40) 401 92121, Fax: 491 9100.

SKADI WOMEN'S WALKING HOLIDAYS, Paula Day, High Grassrigg Barn, Killington, Sedbergh, Cumbria LA10 5EW, England, (44-5396) 21188.

STRAND CRUISES, London, England, (171) 836 6363, Fax: (171) 497 0078.

TIMEOUT TOURS & TRAVEL, 68 Wilberforce Rd, London N4 2SR, England, (071) 354 0535, Fax: 354 2606.

TRAVEL MAN, Im Hainchen 18, Königstein 6240, Germany, (6174) 22029, Fax: (6174) 25290.

TREK OUT, 54 Edrich House, Binfield Rd, London SW4 6SS, England, (071) 627 5561, Fax: (44-071) 498 4756.

URANIAN TRAVEL, Infocus House, 111 Kew Rd, Richmond, Surrey, TW9 2PN England, (081) 332 1022, (081) 332 1619.

VAARSCHOOL GRIETJE, c/o Nelly Duijndam, Prinsengracht T/O 187, 1015 AZ Amsterdam, The Netherlands, (31-20) 625 9105.

VROUWEN VAREN, Hoofdstraat 12, 9975 VS Vierhuizen, The Netherlands, (059) 56 27 53, (059) 1474.

WELTWEIT REISEN, Alemannenstr. 1b, 86199 Augsburg, Germany, (0821) 906 0011, Fax: 906 0060.

XENO TOURS, Passauerplatz 6, 1010 Wien, Austria, (0222) 533 0660, Fax: (0222) 533 0650.

MIDDLE EAST

TARGET TOURS, PO Box 29041, Tel Aviv 61290, Israel, (972-3) 517 5149, Fax: 517 5155. *Member IGTA*

PACIFIC (AUSTRALIA)

AUSTRALIA WOMEN OF THE WILDERNESS, PO Box 340, Unley, SA 5061 Australia, tel/fax: (085) 563 586.

BEYOND THE BLUE, 275 Alfred St #205, 2060 North Sydney, NSW, Australia, (61-2) 955 6755, Fax: (61-2) 922 6036. *Member AGLTA, IGTA*

BREAKOUT TOURS, GPO Box 3801, 2001 Sydney, NSW Australia, (61 2) 550 0328, Fax: (61-2) 560 7167. *Member AGLTA, IGTA*

BUTTERFLY HOLIDAY & LEISURE ACTIVITIES, Jan Curtis, 5 Chidlow Ct, Elanora, Qld 4221, Australia, (61) (75) 98 2012, Fax: (61) (75) 34 2709.

CREATIVE TOURS, 3/55 Grafton St, Bondi Junction, Sydney 2022 NSW Australia, (61-2) 386 2111, Fax: (61-2) 386 2199. *Member AGLTA,*

DESTINATION DOWNUNDER, (61-2) 957-3811, FAX: (61-2) 957-1385, toll-free USA only: (800) 397-2681. *Member AGLTA, IGTA*

GRAYLINK TOURS, PO Box 3826, Darwin 0801 NT Australia, (61-89) 480 089 tel & fax. *Member AGLTA, IGTA*

IN ANY EVENT, 2 Isabella St, Balmain 2041 NSW Australia, (61-2) 810 2439, Fax: (61-2) 810 3420. *Member AGLTA,*

INTERNATIONAL TRAVEL NETWORK, 50 Margaret St, level 3, Sydney 2000, NSW Australia, (61-2) 290 2577, Fax: 290 2273. *Member AGLTA,*

NORTH AMERICAN TRAVEL SPECIALISTS, 145 Swan St, 2321 Morpeth NSW, Australia, (61-49) 342 088, Fax: (61-49) 342 008. *Member AGLTA, IGTA*

OFF ROAD AUSTRALIA, 107 Myall St, Oatley, NSW 2223 Australia, (02) 570 5900, Fax: 570 9200.

OTT CRUISES AND VACATIONS, 60-62 Foveaux St, Surry Hills 2010, Australia, (61-2) 281 4166, Fax: 281 7019. *Member AGLTA,*

Q TRAVEL, Shop 33 A Ritz Carlton Hotel, 33 Cross St, Double Bay 2028 NSW Australia, (61-2) 326 1166, Fax: (61-2) 326 2244. *Member AGLTA,*

R & R TOURS, Level 8, 140 William St, Sydney 2000, NSW, Australia, (61-2) 368 0666, Fax: (61-2) 357 4141. *Member IGTA*

RAINBOW CRUISES, 64 Fitzroy St, Surry Hills, NSW 2010, Australia, (61-2) 331 4652, Fax: (61-2) 361 5094.

RICHARD TURNER & ASSOC., PO Box 1332, Potts Point 2011 NSW, Australia, (61-2) 959 3061, Fax: (61-2) 954 4892.

Member AGLTA,

SUNTREK TOURS, 62 Mary St, Surry Hills 2010 NSW, Australia, (61-2) 281 8000, Fax: (61-2) 281 2722. *Member AGLTA,*

SURFERS PARADISE GAY VACATIONS, PO Box 7260, Gold Coast Mail Centre, Bundall, QLD 4217 Australia, (61-75) 922 223, Fax: (61-75) 922 209. *Member AGLTA, IGTA*

WILDWISE, PO Box 299, Darlinghurst, NSW 2010 Australia, (61-2) 360 2099, Fax: (61-2) 380 5699. *Member AGLTA,*

PACIFIC (NEW ZEALAND)

BUSHWISE WOMEN, Box 12054, Christchurch, New Zealand, Tel/fax: (64) (3) 332 4952.

CANADA

FRIENDLY MONTRÉAL AMICAL ENR., CP 451, Suc. C, Montréal, QC H2L 4K4, Canada, (514) 527-1470. *Member IGTA*

FRIENDS OF DOROTHY, 105 Wharncliffe Rd S, London, Ont Canada, N6J 2K2, (519) 672-9020.

JUST LOOKING TOURS, PO Box 24, Stn B, Toronto, Ont, Canada, M5T 2T2, (800) 563-4674, Fax: (416) 324-9298. *Member IGTA*

SUPER NATURAL ADVENTURE TOURS, 626 W. Pender St, Vancouver, BC Canada, V6B 1V9, (604) 688-8816, Fax: (604) 688-3317.

VENUS VENTURES, 40 Riverwood Manor SE, Calgary, AB T2C 4B1, Canada, (403) 279-7924, Fax: 236-8030. *Member IGTA*

WILD WOMEN EXPEDITIONS, PO Box 145, Stn B, Sudbury, Ont, Canada, P3E 4N5, (416) 535-0748, (705) 866-1260.

WILDERNESS OF WOMEN (WOW), write: WOW, Box 548, Tofino, BC V0R 2Z0 Canada, (604) 725-3230.

CARIBBEAN

CATAMARAN NOSY-BE, Societé Régie Armateur, Rte des Salines, 97227 Ste-Anne, Martinique, French West Indies, (596) 76 76 65, Fax: 76 97 43.

JOURNEYS BY SEA YACHT CHARTERS, 6501 Red Hook Plaza #201, St. Thomas, USVI, 00802, (809) 775-3660, (800) TAKE-ME-2 (825-3632), Fax: (809) 775-3070. *Member IGTA*

NEW DAWN ADVENTURES, PO Box 1512, Vieques, Puerto Rico, 00765, (809) 741-0495.

PLANET Q TOURS, W 67 King St, Frederiksted, St. Croix, USVI, 00840, (809) 773-5222, (800) 253-0622. *Member IGTA*

LATIN AMERICA

DAVOS TOURS, Maipo 971 5C, Buenos Aires 1006, Argentina, (54-1) 312 8961, Fax: 313 4432. *Member IGTA*

UNITED STATES

ABOVE & BEYOND TRAVEL, 3568 Sacramento St, San Francisco, CA, 94118, (415) 92-ABOVE (922-2683), fax: 922-1784. *Member AGLTA, IGTA*

ABSOLUTE ASIA, 155 W 68th St #525, New York, NY, 10023, (212) 595-5782, Fax: (212) 627-4690. *Member IGTA*

ACTION ADVENTURE TOURS, 111 Victory Rd, Lynn, MA, 01902, (617) 592-8542.

ADVENTURE ASSOCIATES, PO Box 16304, Seattle, WA, 98116, (206) 932-8352.

ADVENTURE BOUND EXPEDITIONS, 711 Walnut St, Carriage House, Boulder, CO, 80302, (303) 449-0990, (303) 449-9038.

ADVENTURE WOMEN, PO Box 1408, Santa Cruz, CA, 95061, (408) 479-0473.

Tour Operators

ADVENTURES FOR WOMEN, PO Box 515, Montvale, NJ, 07645, (201) 930-0557.

AFRICAN SAFARI TRAILS, 1208 E. Las Olas Blvd, Ft. Lauderdale, FL 33301, (305) 763-4140, (800) AFRICA-5, Fax: (305) 463-6270. *Member IGTA*

AFRICATOURS, 210 Post St #911, San Francisco, CA, 94108, (415) 391-5788, (800) 83-KENYA, fax: (415) 391-3752.

AFTER FIVE TRAVEL & CRUISES, 2602 Killdeer Ln, Humble, TX, 77396-1826, (713) 441-1369, (800) 335-1369, Fax: (713) 441-1275.

AHWAHNEE WHITEWATER EXPEDITIONS, PO Box 1161, Columbia, CA, 95310, (800) 359-9790, (209) 533-1401, Fax: 533-1409.

ALASKA WOMEN OF THE WILDERNESS, PO Box 773556, Eagle River, AK, 99577, (907) 688-2226, (800) 770-2226 in AK.

AMAZANNE ADVENTURES, c/o Five Star Travel, 164 Newbury St, Boston, MA, 02116, (617) 267-2613, ask for Anne.

AMAZON TOURS & CRUISES, 8700 W Flagler St. #190, Miami, FL, 33174, (305) 227-2266, (800) 423-2791, Fax (305) 227-1880. *Member IGTA*

AMPHITRION HOLIDAYS, book through travel agent.

ANOTHER WAY, RFD 5, Box 290-B1, Webster, NH, 03303, (800) 648-2751. *Member IGTA*

AQUATIC ADVENTURES CHARTER SERVICE, PO Box 522540, Marathon, FL, 33052-2540, (305) 743-2421.

ARCADIA ALTERNATIVE ADVENTURES, PO Box 3271, Carmel, CA, 93921, (408) 624-4827.

ARGONAUT TOURS/ODYSSEY TRAVEL, 11829 Perrin Beitel Rd, San Antonio, TX, 78217-2107, (800) 999-4905, (210) 656-0083, Fax: (210) 656-3980.

ARIZONA TRAVEL CENTER, 2502 E Grant Rd, Tucson, AZ, 85716, (602) 323-3250, (800) 553-5471, Fax: (602) 325-5585. *Member IGTA*

ARTEMIS SAILING CHARTERS, PO Box 297, Driggs, ID, 83422, (208) 354-2906.

ARTEMIS WILDERNESS TOURS, PO Box 1574, El Prado, NM, 87529, (505) 758-2203.

AT THE HELM, 1500 Marina Bay Dr #3472, Kemah, TX, 77565, (713) 334-4101, Fax: 538-2016.

ATLANTIS EVENTS, 8335 Sunset Blvd, West Hollywood, CA, 90069, (213) 848-2244, (800) 628-5268, Fax (213) 848-2301. *Member IGTA*

ATLAS SERVICES & TRAVEL, 8923 S Sepulveda Blvd, Los Angeles, CA 90045, (310) 670-3574, Fax: 670-0725. Ask for Rose. *Member IGTA*

BAR H RANCH, Box 297, Driggs, ID, 83422, (208) 354-2906.

BARNACLE BUSTERS, c/o Marina del Rey Divers, 2539 Lincoln Blvd, Marina del Rey, CA, 90291, (310) 827-1131.

BIG FIVE TOURS, 819 S Federal Hwy #103, Stuart, FL, 34994, (407) 287-7995, (800) 345-2445, Fax: (407) 287-5990. *Member IGTA*

BLUE MOON EXPLORATIONS, PO Box 2568, Bellingham, WA, 98227, (206) 966-8805.

CAPE ESCAPE TOURS, 166 Queen Anne Rd, Harwich, Cape Cod, MA, 02645, (508) 430-0666, (800) 540-0808 (MA only), Fax: (508) 430-0843.

CASTRO TRAVEL COMPANY, 435 Brannan St. #214, San Francisco, CA, 94107, (415) 357-0957, (800) 861-0957, Fax:(415) 357-0221. *Member IGTA*

CITY BOUND TRAVEL, 3755 Texas St, San Diego, CA, 92104, (619) 542-1388, (800) 843-8820, Fax: 542-1569. *Member IGTA*

CLASSICAL CRUISES, 132 E 70th St, New York, NY, 10021, (212) 794-3200, Fax: 249-6896. *Member IGTA*

CLOUD CANYON WILDERNESS EXPERIENCE, 411 Lemon Grove Lane, Santa Barbara, CA, 93108, (805) 969-0982.

CLUB LE BON, PO Box 444, Woodbridge, NJ, 07095, (908) 442-1220, (800) 836-8687, Fax (908) 826-1577.

CONFIDENT TRAVEL, 1499 Bayshore Hwy #126, Burlingame, CA, 94010, (415) 697-7274, (800) 872-7252 (outside CA), (415) 697-0499. *Member IGTA*

COPLEY PLACE TRAVEL BUREAU, 4 Copley Place #120, Boston, MA, 02116, (617) 266-8700, Fax: (617) 266-8349.

CRUISE & EXPEDITION PLANNERS, 8323 Southwest Fwy #800, Houston, TX, 77074, (713) 771-1371, Fax: 771-9761. *Member IGTA*

CRUISE FOR FUN, 5871 Bridleway Circle, Boca Raton, FL, 33496, (407) 997-2221, Fax (407) 997-2223. *Member IGTA*

CRUISIN' THE CASTRO, 375 Lexington St, San Francisco, CA, 94110, (415) 550-8110. *Member IGTA*

D&H ASSOCIATES, 252 High St, Lockport, NY, 14094, (716) 433-8782, Fax: 439-1681. *Member IGTA*

DESTINATION MANAGEMENT, 2 Canal St #1415, New Orleans, LA, 70130, (504) 592-0500, Fax: 592-0529. *Member IGTA*

DESTINATION WORLD, (800) 426-3644, Fax: (310) 316-6364.

DESTINATIONS, PO Box 15321, Gainesville, FL, 32601, (904) 378-1821.

DIFFERENT DRUMMER TOURS, PO Box 528, Glen Ellyn, IL, 60137, (708) 993-1716, (800) 645-1275, Fax: (708) 530-0059. *Member IGTA*

DIFFERENT STROKES TOURS, 1841 Broadway #607, New York, NY, 10023, (212) 262-3860, (800) 688-3301, Fax: (212) 262-3865.

DIRECT SAFARIS AFRICA, LTD, 746 Ashland Ave, Santa Monica, CA, 90405, (310) 396-7775. *Member IGTA*

DOIN' IT RIGHT TRAVEL, 2712-B California St., San Francisco, CA, 94115, (415) 931-3526 (phone & fax), (800) 936-3646. *Member IGTA*

DOLPHIN VISION QUEST, PO Box 1408, Santa Cruz, Ca, 95061, (408) 479-0473.

EC TOURS, 265 Southdown Rd, Huntington, NY, 11743, (516) 423-2097. *Member IGTA*

ECO-EXPLORATIONS SCUBA & SEA KAYAKING, PO Box 7944, Santa Cruz, CA, 95061, (408) 335-7199 (tel/fax).

ECOLLAMA, PO Box 8342, Missoula, MT, 59807.,

ECOSCAPES, Kamehameha Square, 75-5626 Kuakini Hwy #1, Kailua-Kona, HI, 96740, (808) 329-7116, Fax: 329-7091. *Member IGTA*

EMBASSY TRAVEL, 906 N Harper Ave #B, Los Angeles, CA, 90046, (213) 656-0743, (800) 227-6668, Fax: (213) 650-6968.

ENVOY TRAVEL, 740 N Rush St, Chicago, IL, 60611, (312) 787-2400, (800) 443-6869, Fax: (312) 787-7109. *Member IGTA*

EQUINOX ALASKAN WILDERNESS JOURNEYS, 618 West 14th Ave, Anchorage, AK, 99501, (907) 274-9087.

EUROPE OUR WAY TOURS, 1308 Michigan Ave, East Lansing, MI, 48823, (517) 337-1300, (800) 723-1233, Fax: (517) 337-8561.

EUROPEAN LUXURY HOTEL BARGE CRUISES, 106 Calvert St, Harrison, NY, 10528, (800) 234-4000, Fax: (914) 835-5449. *Member IGTA*

EURWAY TOUR & CRUISE CLUB, 26 6th St #504, Stamford, CT, 06905, (203) 973-0111, (800) 9-EURWAY (938-7929), Fax: 969-0799. *Member IGTA*

EXECUTIVE TOUR ASSOC., PO Box 42151, Mesa, AZ, 85274-2151, (602) 898-0098, (800) 382-1113, Fax: (602) 898-8853. *Member AGLTA, IGTA*

FAIRY TALE VACATIONS, 250 West 49th St #600, New York, NY, 10019, (212) 315-5221, (800) 97-FAIRY, Fax: (212) 944-5854. *Member IGTA*

FIESTA TOURS, 323 Geary St #619, San Francisco, CA, 94102, (800) 200-0582, (415) 986-1134.

FIVE STAR TRAVEL SERVICES, 164 Newbury St, Boston, MA, 02116, (617) 536-1999, (800) 359-1999, Fax: 236-1999.

FREDSON TRAVEL & TOURS, 100 N Biscayne Blvd, #701, Miami, FL, 33132, (305) 577-8422, (800) 626-8422, Fax: (305) 577-8344.

FRIENDS OF DOROTHY TOURS, PO Box 17296, Beverly Hills, CA, 90209, (310) 652-9600, (800) GAY-0069, Fax: (310) 652-5454.

GATA TOURS, (516) 944-3025, (800) 245-4282, Fax: (516) 944-3137.

GAY 'N GRAY PARTNERS IN TRAVEL, PO Box 726,

Atkinson, NH, 03811, (603) 362-5011. *Member IGTA*

GAY AIRLINE & TRAVEL CLUB, write: PO Box 69A04-FE, West Hollywood, CA, 90069, (213) 650-5112.

GAYVENTURES, 12769 N Kendall Dr, Miami, FL, 33186, (305) 382-7757, (800) 940-7757, Fax 388-5259. *Member IGTA*

GENTRY HOLIDAYS, 2737 E Oakland Park Blvd #E, Ft Lauderdale, FL, 33306, (305) 561-7790, (800) 543-6879, (305) 561-7786.

GREEK ISLAND CONNECTION, 418 E 14th St #3, New York, NY, 10009, (212) 674-4072, Fax: 674-4562. *Member IGTA*

GUNDERSON TRAVEL, 8543 Santa Monica Blvd, West Hollywood, CA, 90069, (310) 657-3944, Fax: (310) 652-4301. *Member IGTA*

HANNS EBENSTEN TRAVEL, 513 Fleming St, Key West, FL, 33040, (305) 294-8174, Fax: 292-9665.

HAWK, I'M YOUR SISTER, PO Box 9109-P, Santa Fe, NM, 87504, (505) 690-4490.

HER WILD SONG, PO Box 515, Brunswick, ME, 04101, (207) 721-9005.

HIMALAYAN HIGH TREKS, 241 Dolores St, San Francisco, CA, 94103, (415) 861-2391.

HOLBROOK TRAVEL, 3540 NW 13th St, Gainesville, FL, 32609, (904) 377-7111, (800) 451-7111, Fax: (904) 371-3710.

HOLIDAYS AT SEA (SUNQUEST TRAVEL CLUB), 1208 Fourth St, Santa Rosa, CA, 95404-4012, (800) 444-8300, Fax: (707) 573-9992.

HOLIDAYS ON SKIS, 810 Belmar Plaza, Belmar, NJ, 07719, (908) 280-1120, (800) 526-2827, Fax: 681-3578. *Member IGTA*

I.M.T.C., 3390 Peachtree Rd NE #538, Atlanta, GA, 30326, (404) 240-0949, Fax: 240-0948. *Member IGTA*

I.T.S CARS & HOTELS, 3332 NE 33rd St, Ft. Lauderdale, FL, 33308, (305) 566-7111, Fax: 566-0036. *Member IGTA*

ITP TRAVEL, 11 East 26th St #1301, New York, NY, 10010-1402, (212) 683-5935, 696-5790, (800) 223-7406, Fax: (212) 725-7776.

JAMES DEAN VACATIONS (a SOPAC travel co.), 7080 Hollywood Blvd #201, Hollywood, CA, 90028, (213) 461-7600, (800) 497-1524, Fax: (310) 724-5363. *Member IGTA*

JERRY DON TRAVEL PRODUCTIONS, 1111 Fort Stockton #E, San Diego, CA, 92103, (619) 298-7211, Fax: 298-8499. *Member IGTA*

JOURNEYS AND JAUNTS, 1216 Holly St NW, Atlanta, GA, 30318, (800) 875-4919.

KENAI PENINSULA GUIDED HIKES, HCR 64 Box 468, Seward, AK, 99664, (907) 288-3141.

KENNY TOURS, 106 Market Ct., Stevensville, MD 21666-2192, (410) 643-9200, (800) 648-1492, Fax: (410) 643-8868. *Member IGTA*

LATITUDES, 2965 Pharr Ct S, #406, Atlanta, GA, 30305, (404) 352-8713. *Member IGTA*

LET'S GO SAILING, 1571 Oliver Ave #8, San Diego, CA, 92109, (619)467-5589. *Member IGTA*

LIFESTYLES T & E, #8 75th St, North Bergen, NJ, 07047, (201) 861-5059. *Member IGTA*

LOIS LANE EXPEDITIONS, 8933 NE Wardell Rd, Bainbridge Island, WA, 98110, (206) 842-9776.

MAN-2-MAN WOMAN-2-WOMAN VACATIONS, 4535 Noyes St, Pacific Beach, CA, 92109, (619) 270-8728.

MANTOURS-USA, 4929 Wilshire Blvd #259, Los Angeles, CA, 90010, (213) 930-1880, (800) 798-4923, Fax: (213) 930-0194. *Member AGLTA, IGTA*

MARIAH WILDERNESS EXPEDITIONS, PO Box 248, Point Richmond, CA, 94807, (510) 233-2303, (800) 4-MARIAH (462-7424), Fax: (510) 233-0956. *Member IGTA*

MAX STUART TOURS, 2511 Ponce de Leon #209, Coral Gables, FL, 33134, (305) 445-6809, (800) 542-2904, Fax: 445-7374. *Member IGTA*

MCNAMARA RANCH, 4620 County Rd 100, PO Box 702, Florissant, CO, 80816, (719) 748-3466.

MEN ON VACATION, 1111 Fort Stockton #E, San Diego, CA, 92103,, (619) 298-2285, Fax: (619) 298-2286. *Member AGLTA, IGTA*

MICATO SAFARIS, 15 W 26th St, 11th fl, New York, NY, 10010, (212) 545-7111, Fax: 545-8297. *Member IGTA*

MOUNT COOK LINE, 1960 Grand Ave #910, El Segundo, CA, 90245, (310) 648-7067, Fax: 640-2823. *Member IGTA*

MOUNTAIN FIT, 633 Battery St 5th floor, San Francisco, CA, 94111, (415) 397-6216, Fax: 397-6217. *Member IGTA*

MTC (MULTINATIONAL TRAVEL CORP), 20 E 53rd St #5E, New York, NY, 10022, (212) 371-8998, Fax: 319-6597. *Member IGTA*

NATRABU INDO-AMERICA TRAVEL, 433 California St #630, San Francisco, CA, 94104, (415) 362-2540, (800) 628-7228, Fax: (415) 362-0531. *Member IGTA*

NEVER SUMMER NORDIC, PO Box 1983, Ft Collins, CO, 80522, (303) 482-9411.

NEW ENGLAND VACATION TOURS, PO Box 560, Mount Snow Village, West Dover, VT, 05356, (802) 464-2076, (800) 742-7669, Fax: (802) 464-2629. *Member IGTA*

OCEANWOMYN KAYAKING, (206) 325-3970.

OLIVIA WOMEN'S CRUISES & RESORTS, 4400 Market St, Oakland, CA, 94608, (510) 655-0364, (800) 631-6277, Fax: (510) 655-4334. *Member IGTA*

ONN THE WATER, PO Box 173, Gig Harbor, WA, 98335, (206) 851-5259.

ORION TRAVEL TOURS, 563 Castro St, San Francisco, CA, 94114, (415) 864-3233, (800) 552-3326, Fax: (415) 864-6527. *Member IGTA*

OTTO TRAVEL HAWAII, PO Box 17733, Honolulu, HI, 96817, (808) 944-8618.

OUR FAMILY ABROAD, 40 W 57th St #430, New York, NY, 10019, (212) 459-1800, Fax: 581-3756. *Member IGTA*

OUT 'N ARIZONA, PO Box 22333, #215, Tempe, AZ, 85285, (602) 897-1276. *Member IGTA*

OUT AND ABROAD, 1459 18th St #178, San Francisco, CA, 94107, (415) 647-4297, Fax: (510) 237-8796. *Member IGTA*

OUT BOUND ADVENTURES, 143 Collingwood St, San Franciso, CA, 94114, (415) 821-9696.

OUTWORLD TRAVEL EXCLUSIVES, 88 Horatio St, New York, NY, 10014, (800) 4-OUTWORLD, (212) 645-9393, Fax: 645-8439. *Member IGTA*

PACIFIC OCEAN HOLIDAYS, 2330 Kuhio Ave #18, Honolulu, HI, 96815-2990, (808) 923-2400, (800) 735-6600 (US only), Fax: (808) 923-2499. *Member IGTA*

PACIFIC WINGS, 2259 Primera Ave, Hollywood, CA, 90068, (213) 876-5931. *Member IGTA*

PADDLING SOUTH & SADDLING SOUTH, 4510 Silverado Tr, Calistoga, CA, 94515, (707) 942-4550.

PALLADIN'S PREFERRED, 2 Berkshire Rd, McKee City, NJ, 08232, (609) 652-7200, Fax: 652-3211. *Member IGTA*

PAPILLON TRAVEL ADVENTURES, 2130 23rd St, Sacramento, CA, 95818, (916) 444-8080, Fax: 444-1010. *Member IGTA*

PASSAGE TO UTAH, PO Box 520883, Salt Lake City, UT, 84152, (801) 582-1896, Fax: 583-8132 (attn: Mike).

PASSPORT TRAVEL & TOURS, 415 E Golf Rd #111, Arlington Heights, IL, 60005, (708) 364-0634, Fax: 364-1813. *Member IGTA*

PASSPORT TRAVEL MGT INC, 1503 W Busch Blvd #A, Tampa, FL, 33612, (813) 931-3166, (800) 950-5864, Fax: 933-1670. *Member IGTA*

PEDAL PUSHER BIKE TOURS, 151 W Main St, PO Box 101, Torrey, UT, 84775, (801) 425-3270.

PINK TRIANGLE ADVENTURES, PO Box 14298, Berkeley, CA, 94710, (510) 452-6114.

PRAIRIE WOMEN ADVENTURES & RETREAT, PO Box 2, Matfield Green, KS, 66862, (316) 753-3465.

PRENDA PRODUCTIONS, 750 NE 62 St #211, Miami, FL, 33138, (305) 751-8385.

PRIDE TOURS, 267-10 Hillside Ave, Floral Park, NY, 11004, (718) 347-1886, Fax: 347-1291. *Member IGTA*

PROGRESSIVE TRAVELS, 224 W Galer #C, Seattle, WA, 98119, (206) 285-1987, Fax: 285-1988. *Member IGTA*

ROBIN TYLER'S WOMEN'S TOURS, CRUISES & EVENTS, 15842 Chase St, North Hills, CA, 91343, (818) 893-4075, Fax: (818) 893-1593. *Member IGTA*

Tour Operators

ROYAL HAWAIIAN WEDDINGS & MAUI SURFING SCHOOL, PO Box 424, Puunene, Maui, HI, 96784, (808) 875-0625, (800) 659-1866, Fax: 875-0623. *Member IGTA*

RSVP TRAVEL PRODUCTIONS/CLUB RSVP, book through travel agent. *Member IGTA*

SAILAWAY CRUISES & TOURS, PO Box 11448, Marina del Rey, CA, 90295, (310) 827-7630, fax: (310) 827-3434. *Member IGTA*

SAILING AFFAIRS, 404 E 11th St, New York, NY, 10009, (212) 228-5755. *Member IGTA*

SANTINI TOURS & TRAVEL, 2108 Ashby Ave, Berkeley, CA, 94705, (510) 843-2363, (800) 769-9669, Fax: (510) 649-0734. *Member IGTA*

SEA SENSE, 25 Thames St, New London, CT, 06320, (203) 444-1404, (800) 332-1404.

SKI CONNECTIONS, 15946 Wellington Way, Truckee, CA, 96161, (916) 582-1889, Fax: 582-4893. *Member IGTA*

SKYLINK WOMEN'S TRAVEL, 746 Ashland Ave, Santa Monica, CA, 90405, (310) 452-0506, Fax: (310) 452-0562. *Member IGTA*

SOMEWHERE OVER THE RAINBOW TOURS & EVENTS, PO Box 76077, Rainbow, TX, 76077, (310) 652-9600, (800) RSVP-GAY, Fax: (310) 652-5454.

SOUTHERN UTAH ADVENTURES, PO Box 21276, Oakland, CA, 94620, (510) 654-5802 (tel/fax), (800) UTAH-ADV.

SPIRIT JOURNEYS, PO Box 5307, Santa FE, NM, 87502, (505) 351-4004, Fax: (505) 351-4999. *Member IGTA*

STAR CLIPPERS, 4101 Salzedo Ave, Coral Gables, FL, 33146, (305) 442-0550, Fax: 442-1611. *Member IGTA*

STEPPINGSTONE ENVIRONMENTAL EDUCATION TOURS, PO Box 373, Narberth, PA, 19072, (800) 874-8784, (215) 493-4802, Fax: (215) 493-8955.

STOCKLER EXPEDITIONS (GRAND TOURS & TRAVEL), 1660 Cliffs Landing #3, Ypsilanti, MI, 48198, (313) 485-4533, Fax: 663-0784.

STONEWALL AIR & SEA, 861 Oak Park, Corpus Christi, TX, 78408, (512) 864-4297. *Member IGTA*

TAL TOURS, 11 Sunrise Plaza # 302, Valley Stream, NY, 11580, (516) 825-0966, Fax: 825-0980. *Member IGTA*

TAOS FITNESS ADVENTURES, 216-N Paseo Pueblo Norte #173, Taos, NM, 87571, (505) 776-1017, Fax: 751-0940. *Member IGTA*

TBI TOURS, 787 7th Ave #1101, New York, NY, 10019, (800) 223-0226, (212) 489-1834, fax: 307-0612. *Member IGTA*

TEN THOUSAND WAVES, 923 Locust, Missoula, MT, 59802, (406) 549-6670.

TIME TRAVELERS, 822 W Roscoe, Chicago, IL, 60657, (312) 248-8173, Fax: 280-9545. *Member IGTA*

TOTO TOURS, 1326 W Albion #3-W, Chicago, IL, 60626, (312) 274-8686, Fax: (312) 274-8695. *Member IGTA*

TOUR WORLD USA, 1130 Connecticut Ave NW #310, Washington, DC, 33308, (202) 293-0517, Fax: 835-1464. *Member IGTA*

TOURS TO PARADISE, PO Box 3656, Los Angeles, CA, 90078-3656, (213) 962-9169, Fax: (213) 962-3236. *Member IGTA*

TRAVEL CLUB, THE, City Centre Box 128, Monroe City, IN, 47557, (812) 743-5137.

TRAVEL KEYS TOURS, PO Box 162266, Sacramento, CA, 95816-2266, (916) 452-5200. *Member IGTA*

TRAVEL NETWORK, 179 High St, Salem, OR, 97301, (503) 399-9947, Fax: 399-4798. *Member IGTA*

TRAVEL SERVICES, PO Box 444, Fulton, CA, 95439, (800) 523-0395, Fax: (707) 545-7678.

TRAVEL WEST, PO Box 1030, Pacific Palisades, CA, 90272, (310) 394-0777. *Member IGTA*

TRIANGLE VACATIONS, 7041 Grand National Dr #236, Orlando, FL, 32819, (407) 345-4996, Fax: 363-7508. *Member IGTA*

UNDERSEA EXPEDITIONS, PO Box 9455, Pacific Beach, CA, 92169, (619) 270-2900, (800) 669-0310, Fax: (619) 490-1002. *Member IGTA*

UNIGLOBE RAINBOW TRAVEL, 1624 Franklin St #1102, Oakland, CA, 94612, (510) 238-4646, Fax: 238-4656.

UP UP AND AWAY TRAVEL, 701 E. Broward Blvd, Fort Lauderdale, FL, 33301, Broward: (305) 523-4944, Dade: (305) 944-4937, (800) 234-0841, Fax: (305) 463-1154.

USA TOURS, 600 W Peachtree St #1440, Atlanta, GA, 30308, (404) 885-1122, (800) 876-0122, Fax: (404) 885-9878. *Member IGTA*

V.I.P. TOURS OF NEW YORK, The Osborne, 205 W 57th St #6AB, New York, NY, 10019, (212) 247-0366, Fax: 397-0815. *Member IGTA*

VEHILANI BEACHCOMBERS, 87-259 Mikana St, Waianae, HI, 96792, (808) 668-7481.

VELOASIA, 1412 Martin Luther King Jr Way, Berkeley, CA, 94709, (510) 524-3873, (800) 884-ASIA, Fax: 524-4382.

VINTAGE AIR TOURS, 310 N Dyer Blvd, Kissimmee, FL, 34741, (407) 932-1400, Fax: 935-0112. *Member IGTA*

VIRGIN VACATIONS, (800) 364-6466, travel agents call (800) 353-6161, Fax: (800) 364-6657.

VIVA TOURS & EVENTS, 150 Nassau St #1416, New York, NY, 10038, (212) 227-1899, Fax: (212) 227-1931. *Member IGTA*

VOLANTE TOURING COMPANY, (617) 424-6855, (800) 487-TRIP.

VOYAGES & EXPEDITIONS, 8323 SW Fwy #800, Houston, TX, 77074, (713) 776-3438, Fax: 771-9761. *Member IGTA*

WARREN COMMUNICATIONS, PO Box 620219, San Diego, CA, 92162, (619) 236-0984, Fax: 239-8700.

WHITNEY YACHT CHARTERS, 648 N Sheridan Rd, Chicago, IL, 60613, (312) 929-8989, (800) 223-1426. *Member IGTA*

WILD HORIZON, 57 Watson St, Portland, ME, 04103, (207) 871-9940.

WILD ROCKIES TOURS, Box 8184, Missoula, MT, 59807, (406) 728-0566.

WINDJAMMER BAREFOOT CRUISES WEST, 7985 Santa Monica Blvd, West Hollywood, CA, 90046, (800) 864-6567, (213) 654-7700, Fax: 654-7909.

WINTERMOON, 3388 Petrell, Brimson, MN, 55602, (218) 848-2442.

WOMEN IN THE WILDERNESS, write: Judith Niemi, 566 Ottawa Ave, St Paul, MN, 55107, (612) 227-2284.

WOMEN IN THE WILDERNESS (CALIF.), 1165 Tunnel Rd, Santa Barbara, CA, 93105, (805) 682-1863 (phone/fax).

WOODSWOMEN, 25 W Diamond Lake Rd, Minneapolis, MN, 55419, (612) 822-3809.

WORLDCRUISE LTD, 16 E 34th St, New York, NY, 10016, (212) 779-7267, Fax: 594-4754. *Member IGTA*

ZIP TOURS, 8806 Clearwater Dr, Dallas, TX, 75243-7106, (214) 342-3280. *Member IGTA*

INN PLACES®

LISTING FORM

PO Box 37887 • Phoenix, AZ 85069 • U.S.A.
Tel: (602) 863-2408

Copyright © 1994 by Ferrari International Publishing, Inc.

IMPORTANT! **Please fill in this space.**	Prepared By: _____ Date Prepared: _____

1. In what country, state or province (if applicable) & city should you be listed? (If your actual city is little-known, is there a better-known city very close by that you should be listed under?)

2. Write the name, address, and telephone(s) and fax of your establishment as you wish them to appear in the listing:

3. *Inn Places® wants to reward you with a free, extra attention-getter.* If you submit an interesting phrase or slogan, our editor will include it FREE at the top of your entry. But, put on your thinking cap: only the phrases judged truly interesting by our editors will be used. Make sure you are one of the inns who will benefit. *(You may submit as many slogans as you like. Use the space below or attach a separate sheet)*

4. *GIVE THEM A REASON TO CHOOSE YOUR INN: TELL THEM ABOUT IT!!*

   Readers say that what most draws them to choose one inn over another is the illustration and the description. Use a separate sheet of paper.

   IMPORTANT NOTE: To go with our new look, our staff will edit *all* descriptions. *All* descriptions are subject to editing for grammar, spelling, punctuation, readability, and appropriate length. Final length will be determined by your advertising order.

5. Are you closed or absent for part of the year? If so, please give us your alternate mailing name, address, telephone and the dates they are in effect. This is only for our private use in locating you for information.

INN Places 1995   **535**

INN Places 1996 Listing Form

6. Which type is your establishment and which facilities do you have?

    Which types apply?

    ❏ B&B   ❏ Guesthouse   ❏ Hotel
    ❏ Motel   ❏ Inn   ❏ Other_____
    ❏ Cottage   ❏ Campground

    Which facilities apply?

    ❏ Restaurant   ❏ Bar   ❏ Other_____
    ❏ Shops (what kind?) ❏ Disco

7. Best description of clientele (Please report what it IS, not what you would like it to be)

    ❏ Men only   ❏ Mostly gay & lesbian with some
    ❏ Women only   hetero clientele
    ❏ Gay/lesbian (good mix of   ❏ 50% hetero and 50% gay/lesbian
      men and women)   ❏ Mostly hetero with:
    ❏ Mostly men (women welcome)   ❏ gay/lesbian following
    ❏ Mostly women (men welcome)   ❏ gay male following
                                          ❏ gay female following

8. (part 1) Best transportation to your location (ex. "Car is best" or "Airport bus to Victoria Station, then taxi")

    (part 2) From which of the following, if any, do you provide pick up service for guests:

    ❏ Airport   ❏ Bus   ❏ Other_____
    ❏ Train   ❏ Ferry Dock

    (part 3) Is there a charge for pick up, if so, how much?

9. How far to the nearest GAY bar? (Answer *ANY* that are appropriate, and please, NO INFO ON HETERO BARS!)
    How many blocks?____ How many miles?____ How many minutes: by foot?____ by car?____

10. (part 1) How many of each of the following accommodations?
    ____Rooms ____Suites ____Apartments ____Cottages ____Other
    (part 2) What kinds of beds are available? (check if yes)
    ❏ Single/Twin   ❏ Double/Matrimonial   ❏ Queen
    ❏ King   ❏ Bunks

11. ***How many rooms have private bath/toilet facilities:***
    private bath & toilet (en suite)____ private shower & toilet (ensuite) ____
    private bath/toilet/shower (en suite)____ private WC/toilet only____
    sink/washbasin only____

    Shared facilities: how many of each do you have?
    bathtub only____   shower only____
    bath/shower/toilet____   WC/toilet only____

12. (part 1) If you have campsites, how many of each type?
    RV parking only____ Tent sites____ Electric only____
    Electric, sewer & water____ Other_____

    (part 2) Please describe the number and kind of shower/toilet facilities &
    recreational facilities

13. Which meals are included in the rate?
    ❏ Continental breakfast   ❏ Lunch
    ❏ Expanded Continental breakfast ❏ Supper
    ❏ Buffet breakfast   ❏ Dinner
    ❏ Full breakfast   ❏ Other_____

14. Under what (if any) conditions is vegetarian food available, and is there
    vegetarian food nearby?

15. What other complimentary food or drink items, if any, are served (ex. cocktails,
    set-up service, sherry in room, tea & coffee, mints on pillow, etc.)

16. Give dates between which you are open each year, or write "all year"

17. Do you have a well-established high season, if so, during which months?

INN Places 1996 Listing Form

18. Rates: Give the **very** lowest and **very** highest possible rates for high and for low season (ex: summer $35-$55, winter $75-$100). If rates are the same all year, just give the one low-to-high range. (Express rates in YOUR OWN CURRENCY and please correctly show how your monetary unit is expressed $ Hfl DM, etc.)

19. What discounts, if any, do you give, and under what conditions? (Be brief)

20. What credit cards do you accept?
     ❏ MC   ❏ Visa   ❏ Amex
     ❏ Diners   ❏ Bancard   ❏ Other
     ❏ Eurocard   ❏ Discover

21. Do you require reservations? ❏ Yes ❏ No

22. Are your rates commissionable to travel agents? WRITE YES OR NO ONLY. (Most agents expect 10-15% commission) When you write "yes" on the form, it will appear in the book as "Reserve through: travel agent or call direct." When you write "no" on the form, book will read "Call direct."

23. Do you require a minimum stay? ❏ Yes ❏ No

24. About parking, is it: (check if yes)
     ❏ Off-street   ❏ On-street   ❏ Covered
     ❏ Free parking   ❏ Pay parking

    Is the amount of parking:
     ❏ Ample   ❏ Adequate   ❏ Limited

    Any other pertinent facts?

25. What is available INSIDE the rooms? (check all that apply)
     ❏ Maid Service   ❏ TV (Black & White)   ❏ Telephone
     ❏ Kitchen   ❏ Color TV   ❏ Refrigerator
     ❏ Air Conditioning   ❏ Color Cable TV   ❏ Ceiling Fans
     ❏ Room Service   ❏ VCR   ❏ Laundry Service
     ❏ Coffee & Tea-making ❏ Video Tape Library
        facilities

26. What is available on the premises?
    ❑ Meeting Rooms   ❑ Laundry Facilities for guests' use
    ❑ TV Lounge   ❑ Other_____

27. Which of the following exercise/health facilities are available on premises or nearby?
    On the premises: ❑ Gym   ❑ Weights
    ❑ Jacuzzi/Spa   ❑ Sauna   ❑ Steam
    ❑ Massage   ❑ Other_____

    Nearby: ❑ Gym   ❑ Weights
    ❑ Jacuzzi/Spa   ❑ Sauna   ❑ Steam
    ❑ Massage   ❑ Other_____

28. Is there swimming? If so, in which of the following places?
    On the premises: ❑ Pool   ❑ Ocean   ❑ River   ❑ Lake
    ❑ Other_____

    Nearby: ❑ Pool   ❑ Ocean   ❑ River   ❑ Lake
    ❑ Other_____

29. Where do guests sunbathe?
    ❑ At Poolside   ❑ Common Sun Decks   ❑ Patio
    ❑ Roof   ❑ Beach   ❑ Other_____
    ❑ Private Sun Decks

30. Is nudity permitted other than in the rooms? ❑ Yes ❑ No   Where?

31. (A) Where is smoking permitted? (B) Are non-smoking sleeping rooms available?

32. Are pets permitted? If so, what are the restrictions, if any?

33. Is your place handicap-accessible? ❑ Yes ❑ No. Describe, if necessary.

34. Are children especially welcomed? ❑ Yes ❑ No. If so, describe.

35. Name ALL languages (including English) spoken by staff. Name the language of YOUR country first.

36. For our information in contacting you, what are the names of the hosts?

37. Check ❑ Yes, if you wish hosts' first names printed in book. If you do NOT check yes, names will NOT appear! Write the first names below, if you wish them to appear differently than in #36.

38. My mailing address is:

PLEASE BE SURE TO ENCLOSE THREE COPIES OF YOUR BROCHURE

PLEASE COMMENT ...

Name of the inn: _____

Location of inn: city _____ country _____

When did you stay there? month _____ year _____

Did you find that the accommodations were as described in the listing?　　　　❑ Yes　　　❑ No

Explain: _____

_____

_____

_____

_____

_____

_____

If you wish, your name can be included after your comments. If you DO want your name used, print your name as you would like it to appear and the city you come from.

Name _____

City _____

If you do NOT wish your name printed, please give it to us below for our private use in verifying your stay at the location.

Name (NOT to be published): _____

If you run out of space, use another sheet of paper.

Mail to:
Ferrari International Publishing, Inc.
PO Box 37887, Phoenix, AZ 85069 USA
(602) 863-2408

BKEI10193

QUESTIONNAIRE

The editors of **INN Places**® *would like to know what you think of this edition. Please use additional paper if necessary.*

Did you find the kind of places you were looking for?

❏ Yes   ❏ No

Did the listings answer all your questions about each place?

❏ Yes   ❏ No

Did the places match the descriptions you read in the book?

❏ Yes   ❏ No

How often do you use *INN Places*® to find accommodations?

_____

Do you use it exclusively?   ❏ Yes   ❏ No

Do you prefer hotels or B&B's?   ❏ Hotels   ❏ B&B's

Have you used this book   ❏ exclusively in your own country?
or   ❏ abroad?

Where?

_____

How often do you buy *INN Places*®?

_____

How long do you use each issue before you buy a new one?

_____

continued next page

QUESTIONNAIRE (CONT'D)

Do you use other Ferrari guides? Which ones?

❑ *Ferrari's Places of Interest*™ ❑ *Ferrari's Places for Women*™
❑ *Ferrari's Places for Men*™

How did you first find *INN Places*®?
❑ Advertisement   ❑ Friend   ❑ Travel agent
❑ Bookstore recommended   ❑ Other (*describe below*)

_____

_____

Do you consider a listing in *INN Places*® to be a recommendation of a place?

❑ Yes   ❑ No

Do you feel that a listing in *INN Places*® implies a certain minimum standard has been met?

❑ Yes   ❑ No

Do you have any comments about the format or content of the listings? Easy to read? Hard to read? Should include? Should exclude?

_____

_____

_____

_____

Was there any confusion about gender designations/clientele? Would you like to see these handled differently?

_____

_____

**Mail To: Ferrari International Publishing, Inc.,
PO Box 37887, Phoenix, AZ 85069 USA
(602) 863-2408**

BKE110193

ORDER FORM FOR ALL FERRARI GUIDES

SHIP TO (NAME) _____ ADDRESS _____

CITY/STATE (PROVINCE) _____ ZIP/POSTAL CODE _____ COUNTRY _____

TITLE	PRICE	QUANTITY	SUBTOTAL
1. FERRARI'S PLACES OF INTEREST™	$16.00/bk		
2. FERRARI'S PLACES FOR MEN™	$15.00/bk		
3. FERRARI'S PLACES FOR WOMEN™	$13.00/bk		
4. INN PLACES®	$16.00/bk		

PLEASE INCLUDE THE SHIPPING/HANDLING:
One book-$3.50　Two books-$4.50　Three books-$5.00　Four books-$5.50
CANADA-$4.00 (single copy) U.S.
OVERSEAS-$9.00 (single copy) U.S. FUNDS

SHIPPING: $ _____

PLEASE ENCLOSE THIS TOTAL: ⇧ $ _____

SEND TO: Ferrari Int'l. Publishing, Inc., PO Box 37887, Phoenix, AZ 85069 USA (602) 863-2408

I02694BK

RV & CAMPING INDEX

This index gives the page numbers of RV and camping facilities worldwide.

WOMEN'S INDEX

This index gives the page numbers of women-oriented accommodations throughout the world.

INN Places 1995

OOPS!

We're supposed to be on page 446.

NEW YORK

New York

Chelsea Pines Inn

Gay/Lesbian ♂

Value, Charm & Convenience in The Village/Chelsea

Our charming establishment is located in an 1850's brownstone that was modernized in the early 1930's and given an art deco look, which has been further enhanced with vintage film posters throughout. *Chelsea Pines Inn* offers clean, comfortable spaces with a firm bed an modest rates. We're conveniently located on the border between Greenwich Village and Chelsea, a short walk from the popular sights, shops, restaurants and nightlife of the famous Sheridan Square/ Christopher St. area. Subway and bus stop at our corner, so getting around is easy and economical.

Address: 317 W. 14th St, New York, NY 10014. Tel: (212) 929-1023, Fax: (212) 645-9497.

Type: Bed & breakfast inn.
Clientele: Mostly men with women welcome.
Transportation: Bus from airport to Manhattan, then taxi or subway.
To Gay Bars: 1 block to men's, 5-minute walk to women's bars.
Rooms: 20 rooms with double or queen beds.
Bathrooms: 3 private & 4 semi-private, others share. All rooms have sinks.
Meals: Expanded continental breakfast with homemade bread.
Vegetarian: Vegetarian restaurant nearby.
Complimentary: Coffee & cookies all day.
Open: All year.
High Season: Spring, summer & fall.
Rates: $55-$89 plus taxes.
Credit Cards: All major cards.
Rsv'tns: Recommended.
Reserve Through: Call/ Fax direct, or travel agent.
Minimum Stay: 2 nights on weekends, 3 nights on holidays.
Parking: Paid parking in lot or garage (1 block).
In Room: Maid service, TV, AC, phone & refrigerator.
On-Premises: Garden.
Smoking: Permitted.
Pets: Not permitted.
Handicap Access: No.
Children: Not permitted.
Languages: English.
Your Host: Jay, Al & Tom.

IGTA

INDEX TO ACCOMMODATIONS

Index to Accommodations

Index to Accommodations

Index to Accommodations

Index to Accommodations